A Companion to Chinese Cinema
features a collection of original
readings that offer a comprehensive
overview of the evolution and
current state of Chinese cinema.
Essays consider Chinese cinema
from a variety of historical and
geo-political centers – Shanghai,
Hong Kong, and Taiwan – and offer
a critical examination of major
accomplishments of Chinese film
studies in various categories: film
history and geography, industry
and institution, media and arts,
genre and representation, and issues
and debates.

This collaborative project brings
together specialists across a range of
disciplines to consider Chinese cinema
from a variety of methodological
approaches and theoretical
frameworks. This interdisciplinary
approach allows for an unprecedented
breadth of innovative ideas that
facilitate a better understanding
of Chinese cinema as it relates to
artistic projects, social practices,
political institutions, and expanding
international markets. *A Companion
to Chinese Cinema* offers an important
analysis of a growing force in
international cinema.

Yingjin Zhang is Professor of Comparative Literature and Cultural Studies at University of California, San Diego, and Visiting Chair Professor at Shanghai Jiaotong University, China. He is the author of *The City in Modern Chinese Literature and Film* (1996), *Screening China* (2002), *Chinese National Cinema* (2004), and *Cinema, Space, and Polylocality in a Globalizing China* (2010); co-author of *Encyclopedia of Chinese Film* (1998); editor of *China in a Polycentric World* (1998) and *Cinema and Urban Culture in Shanghai, 1922-1943* (1999); and co-editor of *From Underground to Independent* (2006) and *Chinese Film Stars* (2010).

A Companion to Chinese Cinema

Wiley-Blackwell Companions to National Cinemas

The Wiley-Blackwell Companions to National Cinemas showcase the rich film heritages of various countries across the globe. Each volume sets the agenda for what is now known as world cinema whilst challenging Hollywood's lock on the popular and scholarly imagination. Whether exploring Spanish, German, or Chinese film, or the broader traditions of Eastern Europe, Scandinavia, Australia, and Latin America, the 20–25 newly commissioned essays comprising each volume include coverage of the dominant themes of canonical, controversial, and contemporary films; stars, directors, and writers; key influences; reception; and historiography and scholarship. Written in a sophisticated and authoritative style by leading experts they will appeal to an international audience of scholars, students, and general readers.

Published:

A Companion to German Cinema, edited by Terri Ginsberg & Andrea Mensch

A Companion to Chinese Cinema, edited by Yingjin Zhang

A Companion to Eastern European Cinema, edited by Aniko Imre

Forthcoming:

A Companion to Spanish Cinema, edited by Jo Labanyi & Tatjana Pavlovic

A Companion to Contemporary French Cinema, edited by Raphaelle Moine, Hilary Radner, Alistair Fox, & Michel Marie

A Companion to Hong Kong Cinema, edited by Gina Marchetti, Esther Yau, and Esther Cheung

A Companion to Italian Cinema, edited by Frank Burke

A Companion to Chinese Cinema

Edited by

Yingjin Zhang

A John Wiley & Sons, Ltd., Publication

Library of Congress Cataloging-in-Publication Data

A companion to Chinese cinema / edited by Yingjin Zhang.
    p. cm. – (Wiley-Blackwell companions to national cinemas)
  Includes bibliographical references and index.
  Includes filmography.
  ISBN 978-1-4443-3029-8 (hardback : alk. paper)
  1. Motion pictures–China–History–20th century. 2. Motion pictures–China–
History–21st century. I. Zhang, Yingjin.
  PN1993.5.C4C66 2012
  791.430951–dc23

                    2011041433

A catalogue record for this book is available from the British Library.

Set in 11/13pt Dante by SPi Publisher Services, Pondicherry, India

1   2012

Contents

Acknowledgments

As this book seeks to provide an overview of Chinese cinema over a hundred years and collectively looks to the future, I would like to express my appreciation of all who have contributed to the development of Chinese cinema and to the field of Chinese film studies around the world. I commend scholars whose collective work has made this project possible, and I acknowledge in particular my 28 contributors for their enthusiasm, cooperation, and patience. A book of this size takes years to complete. As with my previous books, I thank the University of California, San Diego (especially the Academic Senate Committee on Research and the Division of Art and Humanities) for awarding me several research grants, as well as my colleagues and friends in San Diego and elsewhere for sharing my interest in moving the interdisciplinary scholarship forward. I am grateful to the anonymous press reviewers of this book's proposal and manuscript for their endorsements and suggestions; to Jayne Fargnoli and other editors at Wiley-Blackwell for their confidence and guidance along the way; to James Wicks for his meticulous and timely assistance at the initial stage; and to Angie Chau for her diligent work at the production stage. Last but not least, I owe my deepest appreciation to my family – Jean and Alex on the Pacific coast and Mimi on the Atlantic coast – for their unfading love and support in all these years.

Figures

Tables

Contributors

Weihong Bao is Assistant Professor of Chinese Cinema and Media Culture at Columbia University, USA. She is completing a book manuscript entitled *Dances of Fire: Aesthetic Affect and the Intermediation of Chinese Cinema, 1884–1945*. She has started a second book project on the historical interaction between theater and cinema in twentieth-century China, tentatively entitled *The Shadowy Theater of Chinese Cinema*. Her articles have appeared in such journals as *Camera Obscura, Journal of Chinese Cinemas, Journal of Modern Chinese Literature, 19th Century Theatre and Film*, and *Opera Quarterly*.

Chris Berry is Professor of Film and Television Studies at Goldsmiths, University of London, UK. He is the author of *Postsocialist Cinema in Post-Mao China* (2004); co-author of *China on Screen: Cinema and Nation* (2006); editor of *Chinese Films in Focus II* (2008); and co-editor of *Mobile Cultures: New Media and Queer Asia* (2003), *Island on the Edge: Taiwan New Cinema and After* (2005), *TV China* (2008), *Cultural Studies and Cultural Industries in Northeast Asia* (2009), *Electronic Elsewheres: Media, Technology, and Social Space* (2010), and *The New Chinese Documentary Film Movement* (2010).

Michael Berry is Professor of Contemporary Chinese Cultural Studies at the University of California, Santa Barbara, USA. He is the author of *Speaking in Images* (2005), *A History of Pain* (2008), and *Jia Zhangke's The Hometown Trilogy* (2009). He is also the English translator of several Chinese novels, including *Wild Kids* (2000), *Nanjing 1937* (2002), *To Live* (2004), and *The Song of Everlasting Sorrow* (2008).

Yomi Braester is Professor of Comparative Literature and Cinema Studies at the University of Washington, Seattle, USA. He is the author of *Witness against History: Literature, Film, and Public Discourse in Twentieth-Century China* (2003) and *Painting the City Red: Chinese Cinema and the Urban Contract* (2010); and co-editor of *Cinema at the City's Edge: Film and Urban Networks in East Asia* (2010).

Robert Chi teaches in the Department of Asian Languages and Cultures at the University of California, Los Angeles, USA. His research and teaching involves Chinese cinema in the broadest sense. His writings on topics such as memory, documentary, exhibitionism, the Chinese national anthem, and the Nanjing Massacre have appeared in academic journals and critical volumes in Chinese, English, and Italian.

Paul Clark has been Professor of Chinese at University of Auckland, New Zealand since 1993. Earlier he spent ten years as a Research Fellow at the East-West Center in Honolulu, Hawaii, USA, where he helped program the Hawaii International Film Festival. He is the author of *Chinese Cinema: Culture and Politics since 1949* (1987), *Reinventing China: A Generation and Its Films* (2005), and *The Chinese Cultural Revolution: A History* (2008); and co-editor of *China and New Zealand* (2003). His next book is *China Youth Cultures: Red Guards to Netizens, 1968, 1988, 2008* (forthcoming).

Shuqin Cui is Associate Professor of Asian Studies at Bowdoin College, USA. She is the author of *Women Through the Lens: Gender and Nation in a Century of Chinese Cinema* (2003). She has also published many journal articles and book chapters on various topics in Chinese cinema. Her research and teaching interests include cinema, gender, and literature. She is currently working on a manuscript tentatively entitled *The Absence of Presence: An Exploration of Women's Experimental Art in Contemporary China*.

Michael Curtin is Mellichamp Professor of Global Media Studies and Professor of Film and Media Studies at the University of California, Santa Barbara, USA. He is the author of *Redeeming the Wasteland: Television Documentary and Cold War Politics* (1995), *Playing to the World's Biggest Audience: The Globalization of Chinese Film and TV* (2007), and co-author of *The American Television Industry* (2009). He is completing work on *Media Capital: The Cultural Geography of Globalization*. He is co-editor of the "International Screen Industries" book series for the British Film Institute and co-editor of the *Chinese Journal of Communication*.

Darrell William Davis is a Visiting Associate Professor in Visual Studies at Lingnan University, Hong Kong. He is author of *Picturing Japaneseness: Monumental Style, National Identity, Japanese Film* (1996), co-author of *Taiwan Film Directors: A Treasure Island* (2005) and *East Asian Screen Industries* (2008), and co-editor of *Cinema Taiwan: Politics, Popularity and State of the Arts* (2007). He is working on a book about East Asian ethnicity and technology.

Matthew D. Johnson is Assistant Professor of History at Grinnell College, USA. His research interests are cultural institutions, the international history of propaganda, sovereignty and "national image," and twentieth-century state bureaucracies. He is co-editor of a special issue of the *Journal of Chinese Cinemas*,

"Exhibiting Chinese Cinemas," and is working on a manuscript entitled *Before Soft Power: Political Communication and Cultural Diplomacy in China – The Motion Picture, 1927–1972*.

Nikki J. Y. Lee received her PhD in cultural studies at Goldsmiths College, University of London, UK. She has taught at Yonsei University and the Korean National University of Arts. Her research interests cover transnational East Asian cinemas, and South Korean cinema and popular culture. She has published several articles in journals such as *Cinema Journal*. She is co-editor of a forthcoming volume, *The Korean Cinema Book*.

Helen Hok-Sze Leung received her PhD in comparative literature from the University of Wisconsin, Madison, USA and is Associate Professor of Women's Studies at Simon Fraser University, Canada. She is the author of *Undercurrents: Queer Culture and Postcolonial Hong Kong* (2008) and has published widely on queer cinema and cultural politics in anthologies such as *New Queer Cinema* (2004), *Masculinities and Hong Kong Cinema* (2005), and *Chinese Films in Focus II* (2008), as well as in journals such as *Inter-Asia Cultural Studies*, *Journal of Lesbian Studies*, and *Positions*.

Gina Marchetti is Associate Professor in Comparative Literature at the University of Hong Kong. Her first book, *Romance and the "Yellow Peril": Race, Sex and Discursive Strategies in Hollywood Fiction* (1993), won the award for best book in cultural studies from the Association for Asian American Studies. Recently, she has authored *From Tian'anmen to Times Square: Transnational China and the Chinese Diaspora on Global Screens* (2006), *Andrew Lau and Alan Mak's INFERNAL AFFAIRS – The Trilogy* (2007), and co-edited *Hong Kong Film, Hollywood and the New Global Cinema* (2007).

Liyan Qin received her PhD from the University of California, San Diego, USA and currently teaches in the Institute of Comparative Literature and Culture at Peking University (Beijing), China. She specializes in Chinese cinema and literature as well as Chinese–English literary relations. Apart from Chinese translations of English books by J. Hillis Miller and Yingjin Zhang, she has published chapters in English volumes, *The Chinese Cultural Revolution as History* (2006) and *Art, Politics, and Commerce in Chinese Cinema* (2010). She writes a film column for *Writers Magazine*.

Bruce Robinson is a photographer and editor of scholarly works on subjects in Chinese media and society and is based in Austin, Texas, USA.

Stanley Rosen is Director of the East Asian Studies Center and Professor of Political Science at the University of Southern California, USA, specializing in Chinese politics and society. His most recent works include two co-edited volumes,

State and Society in 21st Century China (second edition, 2009) and *Art, Politics, and Commerce in Chinese Cinema* (2010).

Jerome Silbergeld is P. Y. and Kinmay W. Tang Professor of Chinese Art History at Princeton University, USA. He has published more than sixty books, articles, and book chapters on traditional and modern Chinese painting, gardens, and cinema. His books include *Contradictions: Artistic Life, the Socialist State, and the Chinese Painter Li Huasheng* (1993), *China Into Film* (1999), *Hitchcock With a Chinese Face* (2004), *Body in Question: Image and Illusion in Two Chinese Films by Director Jiang Wen* (2008), *Outside In: Contemporary x Chinese x American Art* (2009), and *Humanism in China: A Contemporary Record of Photography* (2009).

Julian Stringer is Associate Professor in Film and Television Studies at the University of Nottingham, UK. He has published widely on East Asian cinema, film festivals, and transnational cinema. His edited or co-edited books include *Movie Blockbusters* (2003), *New Korean Cinema* (2005), *Japanese Cinema* (2007), and *Global Chinese Cinema: The Culture and Politics of "Hero"* (2009). He organized a conference on "Moving Images and the Digital Eco-City" at ZED pavilion, Shanghai Expo, October 2010.

Stephen Teo used to work as a fellow at the Asia Research Institute, National University of Singapore and is now an Associate Professor in the Wee Kim Wee School of Communication and Information, Nanyang Technological University, Singapore. He is the author of *Hong Kong Cinema: The Extra Dimensions* (1997), *Wong Kar-wai* (2005), *King Hu's "A Touch of Zen"* (2007), *Director in Action: Johnnie To and the Hong Kong Action Film* (2007), and *The Chinese Martial Arts Cinema: The Wuxia Tradition* (2010).

James Udden is Associate Professor of Film Studies at Gettysburg College, USA, where he has created a new program in film studies. He is the author of *No Man an Island: Hou Hsiao-hsien and the Aesthetics of Experience* (2009) and has published extensively on Asian cinema in journals such as *Asian Cinema, Modern Chinese Literature and Culture*, and *Post Script*, as well as in two recent anthologies: *The Cinema of Small Nations* (2007) and *Cinema Taiwan* (2007).

Lingzhen Wang is Associate Professor of Chinese at Brown University, USA. Her first book, *Personal Matters: Women's Autobiographical Practice in Twentieth-Century China* (2004), centers on Chinese women's life and writing in relation to dominant discourses of Chinese modernity – nationalism, revolution, socialism, and market commodification. Her second major research project focuses on gender, transnational feminist theory, and Chinese visual modernity, examining particularly the role of female film directors in constructing mainstream Chinese cinema and negotiating gendered and alternative imaginations in the second half of the twentieth century.

Qi Wang is Assistant Professor in Film in the School of Literature, Communication and Culture, Georgia Institute of Technology, USA. She received her MS in comparative media studies from MIT and her PhD in cinema and media studies from UCLA. Her current book project, *Writing Against Oblivion: Personal Filmmaking from the Forsaken Generation in Post-Socialist China*, is on contemporary Chinese independent cinema and its relationship with (post-)socialist historical memory. She has published on Chinese cinema, documentary, and Japanese animation in journals such as *Asian Cinema*, *International Journal of Comic Art*, and *Positions*. She also helps curate the REEL CHINA Documentary Biennial.

Yiman Wang is Assistant Professor of Film and Digital Media at the University of California, Santa Cruz, USA. She has completed a book manuscript on cross-Pacific film remakes. Her work on film remakes and adaptation, border-crossing stars, Chinese cinema, and DV documentaries has appeared in *Camera Obscura*, *Film Quarterly*, *Journal of Chinese Cinemas*, *Journal of Film and Video*, *Literature/Film Quarterly*, *Positions*, and *Quarterly Review of Film and Video*, as well as in volumes such as *Chinese Films in Focus* (2003), *Idols of Modernity* (2010), *Cinema at the City's Edge* (2010), and *The New Chinese Documentary Film Movement* (2010).

James Wicks received his PhD in cultural studies from the University of California, San Diego, USA and is Assistant Professor at Point Loma Nazarenes University in San Diego. His dissertation is entitled "The Antecedents of Taiwan New Cinema: The State of Taiwan Film in the 1960s and 1970s." He has published articles and book reviews in academic journals such as *China Quarterly*, *Film Art* (Beijing), *Journal of Chinese Cinemas*, and *Modern Chinese Literature and Culture*.

Chen Xihe received his MA from the Arts Academy of China and his PhD from Ohio State University, USA. He served as a fellow and deputy director at the Research Department of China Film Research Center (Beijing) in the 1980s and now is a professor in the Film and TV School at Shanghai University, China. His numerous publications include "Industry and Aesthetics of Contemporary Cinema in Mainland China: 1978–2008" (2008) and *Film and TV in Cross-Cultural Context* (2002).

Gary G. Xu is Associate Professor at the University of Illinois, Urbana-Champaign, USA, where he teaches Chinese literature, comparative literature, and cinema studies. He is the author of *Sinascape: Contemporary Chinese Cinema* (2007) and numerous articles and book chapters on Chinese cinema.

Sabrina Qiong Yu teaches Chinese cinema and media at Newcastle University, UK. She received her PhD in film studies from the University of Nottingham. Her research interests include stardom, gender and sexuality, audience/reception studies, transnational Chinese cinema, and Chinese independent documentary films, and her recent articles have appeared in critical volumes such as *Chinese Film Stars* (2010) and *Global Chinese Cinema* (2010). She helped launch a series on star studies with Peking University Press in 2010 and translated Leon Hunt's *Kung Fu Cult Masters* (2003).

Yingjin Zhang is Professor of Chinese Studies, Comparative Literature, and Cultural Studies at the University of California, San Diego, USA and Visiting Chair Professor at Shanghai Jiaotong University, China. He is the author of *The City in Modern Chinese Literature and Film* (1996), *Screening China* (2002), *Chinese National Cinema* (2004), and *Cinema, Space, and Polylocality in a Globalizing China* (2010); co-author of *Encyclopedia of Chinese Film* (1998); editor of *China in a Polycentric World* (1998) and *Cinema and Urban Culture in Shanghai, 1922–1943* (1999); and co-editor of *From Underground to Independent* (2006) and *Chinese Film Stars* (2010). Additionally, he has published six Chinese books and over 130 articles in Chinese, English, German, Korean, Portuguese, and Spanish.

Zhang Zhen is Associate Professor of Cinema Studies at New York University, USA. She is the author of *An Amorous History of the Silver Screen: Shanghai Cinema, 1896–1937* (2005) and the editor of *The Urban Generation: Chinese Cinema and Society at the Turn of the Twenty-first Century* (2007). Her articles have appeared in numerous journals and critical anthologies.

Ying Zhu is Associate Professor of Cinema Studies and Co-coordinator of the Modern China Program at College of Staten Island, City University of New York, USA. Her articles have appeared in leading media journals and numerous edited volumes. She is the author of *Chinese Cinema during the Era of Reform* (2003) and *Television in Post-Reform China* (2008) and co-editor of *Television Drama: A Chinese and US Perspective* (2005, in Chinese), *TV Drama in China* (2009), and *TV China* (2009).

1

General Introduction

Yingjin Zhang

At the time when the world had just entered the new millennium, I ventured to track the exciting development of Chinese cinema through its "box-office boom and academic investment" (Y. Zhang 2002: 16–18). Ten years down the road, Chinese cinema has continued its extraordinary expansion in all aspects, very much like the red-hot Chinese economy, which became the world's second largest when China's GDP (US$1.33 trillion) surpassed Japan's (US$1.28 trillion) in the second quarter of 2010 (*Time* 2010). Yet, even before the awe-inspiring ceremonies at the 2008 Beijing Olympic Games, masterminded by the world-renowned Chinese film director Zhang Yimou (b. 1950), were televised live to captivated audiences globally (Curtin 2010: 118), a series of impressive achievements in Chinese cinema had already occurred. In terms of box office in the United States, two successful Chinese art films from the early 1990s could barely compare to two Chinese blockbusters a decade later: on the one hand, *The Wedding Banquet* (Ang Lee, 1993) was screened in 113 US theaters and grossed US$6.9 million, while *Farewell My Concubine* (Chen Kaige, 1993) opened in three theaters only but grossed $5.2 million; on the other hand, *Crouching Tiger, Hidden Dragon* (Ang Lee, 2000) was screened in 2,027 theaters and grossed $128.1 million, while *Hero* (Zhang Yimou, 2002) was screened in 2,175 theaters and grossed $53.7 million (Rosen 2010: 47). In terms of box office in China, the 2009 top-grossing domestic film, *The Founding of a Republic* (Han Sanping, Huang Jianxin, 2009), reached RMB 415 million (or approximately US$6.1 million) (Yin 2010: 6), representing an increase of 9.9 times over that of the record RMB 42 million set by *Big Shot's Funeral* (Feng Xiaogang, 2001) (Y. Zhang 2010c: 135).[1] Indeed, compared with 88 domestic films and RMB 840 million total box office in 2001 (Y. Zhang 2010a: 172), the 2009 statistics – 456 domestic feature productions and RMB 6,206 million total box office (Yin 2010: 5) – indicate a growth of 5.2 times and 7.4 times, respectively,

A Companion to Chinese Cinema, First Edition. Edited by Yingjin Zhang.
© 2012 Blackwell Publishing Ltd. Published 2012 by Blackwell Publishing Ltd.

thereby consolidating a decade-long unprecedented boom (for the latest statistics, see Rosen's tables in Chapter 11). Equally impressive is the academic investment in Chinese film studies, as colleges in Asia, Australia, Europe, and North America have quickly expanded course offerings in China-related disciplinary and area studies. The *Journal of Chinese Cinemas*, a refereed periodical devoted exclusively to this growing field, was inaugurated in the United Kingdom in 2007, academic publishers have increased the number of new books in Chinese film studies, and innumerable panels, workshops, symposia, and conferences on Chinese cinema are held around the world every year.[2]

Launched at an appropriate time, therefore, *A Companion to Chinese Cinema* seeks to map the expanding field of Chinese cinema in a bold and definitive way. Given its generous length of thirty chapters, the volume offers sufficient depth and breadth to engage a variety of theories, methods, debates, and issues in a fast-developing academic field and to shape the intellectual conversation around key subjects in Chinese cinema and Chinese film studies. To maximize its mapping potential, the volume is designed to be as much prospective in nature (i.e., to start a discussion moving forward) as it is retrospective and reflective (i.e., to trace the history and state of the field). This introduction, as a starter, sets the stage for interactive conversations among chapters included here and publications elsewhere by briefly identifying a few highlights in Chinese film studies in English, delineating the structure of the present volume's coverage, summarizing major contributions from our individual chapters, relating divergent and convergent points among different contributors, and briefly mentioning several areas and topics worthy of additional research.[3]

A quick glance over select English publications from the past three decades helps us outline the contours of the developing field of Chinese film studies, although readers should pursue Chapter 26 for Chris Berry's mapping of the field in terms of language, readership, and discipline. First, at a time when Chinese cinema had just started to attract increasing attention abroad, in the first edition of *Perspectives on Chinese Cinema* Chris Berry (1985: i) rightly emphasized the urgent need for "a multidisciplinary approach" and anticipated that "Chinese cinema can be productively studied from a number of angles."[4] Second, while keeping a similar multidisciplinary emphasis, in *New Chinese Cinemas* (1994) Nick Browne, Paul G. Pickowicz, Vivian Sobchak, and Esther Yau extended the parameters of Chinese cinema to include Hong Kong and Taiwan and justified this extension by pluralizing Chinese cinemas. Third, retaining the plural form of designation, Sheldon Lu in *Transnational Chinese Cinemas* (1997) foregrounded transnationalism as a new framework that goes beyond national cinemas, and the impact of transnationalism is visible in the subsequent scholarship (e.g., Berry and Farquhar 2006). Fourth, in *Chinese-Language Film* (2005) Sheldon Lu and Emilie Yeh have chosen "Chinese-language film" as a more inclusive term that can accommodate films from Chinese territories other than mainland China, Hong Kong, and Taiwan; its equivalent in Chinese, *huayu dianying*, has likewise gained more traction in Chinese scholarship, as Chen Xihe observes in Chapter 25. Finally, with *Chinese Ecocinema* (2009), Sheldon Lu and Jiayan Mi demonstrate that Chinese cinema has a larger role to play in China studies and film studies because cinema is a vital force in renegotiating fractured relationships among nature, history, technology, and culture.

The slight variation in the titles of the above-mentioned anthologies reveals that naming the object of our study has been contentious. In the current English discourse, "Chinese cinema(s)," "Chinese-language cinema," and "Sinophone cinema" are three principal contenders, each carrying its own ideological baggage and each working toward an explicit aim of deterritorialization or reterritorialization. First, the reconceptualization of the national in Chinese cinema as various geographically grounded and "socially, politically, and historically specific projects" (Berry 1998: 132) has undermined the foundational myth of consensus and homogeneity in the national cinema paradigm, and many scholars have accepted that "Chinese cinema" covers Chinese-language films – as well as films with mixed Chinese and other languages – from mainland China, Hong Kong, Taiwan, and other places overseas (Asia, Australia, Europe, and North America). The heterogeneity recognized by this wide coverage has sometimes resulted in a plural designation of "Chinese cinemas," as captured in the two titles mentioned above (Browne et al. 1994; S. Lu 1997) and more recently in the title of the *Journal of Chinese Cinemas*.[5] What is important here is that in reconceptualizing Chinese cinema, the Chineseness is seen as dispersed "historically, politically, territorially, culturally, ethnically, and linguisticially" (Y. Zhang 2004a: 3), thus keeping all kinds of Chineseness open to contention and reconfiguration. Precious due to its open horizons, "Chinese cinema" is preferred in this volume to the other two terms, which seem to be restricted either linguistically or territorially.

Second, in an effort to loosen its grounding in the territorial nation-state, "Chinese-language cinema" highlights the diversity of languages and dialects in Chinese cinema, as already evident in such terms as "Cantonese cinema" (*yueyu pian*), "Mandarin cinema" (*guoyu pian*), and "Taiwanese-dialect cinema" (*taiyu pian*).[6] Perhaps functioning better in Chinese, where *Zhongguo dianying* (Chinese cinema) carries a residual emphasis on the nation-state (*guo*), *huayu dianying* (Chinese-language cinema) extends to include films produced by Chinese diasporas "outside the sovereign Chinese nation-state – for example, Hollywood, Singapore, or elsewhere" (Lu and Yeh 2005: 1). Moreover, "Chinese-language cinema" also foregrounds the heterogeneity internal to a territory by tracking dialects and other accented practices (S. Lu 2007: 150–63). Yet, the fact that Sheldon Lu has switched from "Chinese cinemas" (1997) to "Chinese-language film" (2005) and back to "Chinese ecocinema" (2009) proves that the difference between "Chinese cinema(s)" and "Chinese- language film" is not substantial after all.

Third, albeit equally predicated on the politics of language, Shu-mei Shih (2007: 4) refutes what she perceives as the centripetal force in "Chinese-language cinema" and defines "the Sinophone" as one that refers to "a network of places of cultural production outside China and on the margins of China and Chineseness," the former exemplified by Taiwan and the latter by Hong Kong. While Shih's reterritorialized method of positioning the Sinophone against China in a counter-hegemonic fashion has left many questions unresolved (Y. Zhang 2010a: 20–1), her attempt to map out a vast – albeit scattered and fragmented – space of cultural productions in the Chinese language or by the ethnic Chinese around the world bespeaks the complicated geopolitics of Chinese cinema from its early years to the present day. Indeed, Yiman Wang shows in Chapter 29 precisely such a geographic dispersal in certain phases of Chinese film history, from early cinema to globalization.

My brief discussion above illustrates that critical anthologies have played a crucial role in moving the field of Chinese film studies forward thanks to their productive format of expanded coverage and multi-author collaboration. This volume aims to continue that fine tradition. Apart from this general introduction, 29 originally written chapters collected here are divided into five parts: (1) history and geography, (2) industry and institution, (3) genre and representation, (4) arts and media, and (5) issues and debates. As representative of the interdisciplinary nature of the field, our thirty contributors come from film and media studies, literary and cultural studies, history, political science, and art history, and they have adopted a variety of theoretical frameworks and methodological approaches to given subjects. However, it is crucial to remember from the outset that the volume does not claim to have exhausted every aspect of Chinese cinema, nor does it cover all relevant subjects in its five parts. Each chapter represents its author's take on a particular topic, but taken as a whole the volume promises to provide an inspirational introduction to the rich materials Chinese cinema has offered to the world.

Part I: History and Geography

"Part I: History and Geography" contains seven chapters, three of them focused on the mainland and two others each on Hong Kong and Taiwan. This division of labor highlights the centrality of political geography in Chinese cinema, which is as much a transnational, transregional, and translocal cinema as it is a national cinema (Y. Zhang 2011). Indeed, the cross-border flows of ideas and images were already underway in early Chinese cinema, as Zhang Zhen documents in Chapter 2, "Transplanting Melodrama: Observations on the Emergence of Early Chinese Narrative Film." Using the newly discovered extant fragments of *Poet from the Sea* (Hou Yao, 1927) as a springboard, Zhang acknowledges the multiplicity and mutual imbrication of centers and peripheries as well as modernities and subjectivities in the founding phase of Chinese film history. She deliberately re-anchors the recent scholarly debate on melodrama's global appeal *vis-à-vis* cultural identity in the context of the melodrama film's emergence in China during the 1920s–1930s. Following Cai Guorong's twofold differentiation of the *wenyi* genre, which overlaps in thematic and stylistic parameters with the conventional Western melodrama film, into those concerned with family ethics and those with romances, Zhang argues that Hou Yao (1903–42) best represents the "artistic" wenyi film centered on romantic love, in distinction with early "family ethics" melodrama films geared ostensibly toward kinship, communal sentiments, plebian tastes, and market demands, best exemplified by the works of Zheng Zhengqiu (1889–1935). Furthermore, by situating the wenyi film in the changing Chinese political environment of the 1910s–1920s, Zhang demonstrates that Hou's *Poet from the Sea* stands as a testimony to the cultural and ideological transition that affected both the literary and film scenes, and thus represents a lament for the incomplete project of the May Fourth enlightenment. With references to the D. W. Griffith (1875–1948) fever in 1920s Shanghai as part of the broad transnational "melodramatic imagination," Zhang concludes that Chinese filmmakers succeeded in translating and adapting Euro-American sources, along with Chinese literary and theatrical traditions, in the contradiction-ridden context of China's new culture movement and Shanghai's semicolonial modernity.

Zhang Zhen's deliberation on early Chinese cinema favors a cultural history approach she first adopted in her book on pre-1937 Chinese cinema (Z. Zhang 2005), which is distinguished, among others, by a focused historical perspective (the 1920s in this case), attention to the materiality of cultural production (the archive, print culture), sensitivity to intertextuality and cross-mediality (e.g., film, literature, theater) in a transnational context, and eagerness for theoretical intervention (e.g., melodrama and modernity). Her concentration on melodrama through the case study of Hou Yao's 1920s oeuvres prepares us for Stephen Teo's study of genre and nation in Chapter 15. Regrettably, space limitations have prevented us from including another chapter to deal with the 1930s–1940s, although the interested reader is advised to pursue existing scholarship on these vibrant periods (J. Hu 2000; Pang 2002; Fu 2003; Y. Zhang 2008), from which a large number of films have become available for viewing in video format. In terms of film historiography, however, the postwar period (i.e., 1945–49) still awaits book-length treatment in English.

Instead of concentrating on a particular decade and a key genre as Zhang Zhen does, Paul Clark leads us through important events and representative works during three tremulous decades in the People's Republic of China (PRC) in Chapter 3, "Artists, Cadres and Audiences: Chinese Socialist Cinema, 1949–1978." He starts with the transition years when most filmmakers' careers crossed the 1949 divide. It is through issuing new rules and staging nationwide mass campaigns that the Communist regime experimented, modified, abandoned, or even reversed the new directions it set (e.g., the Hundred Flowers). Nonetheless, the socialist period gradually brought up a new corps of studios and filmmakers, as well as new cadres and audiences, especially those in the vast countryside serviced by mobile projection teams. Mao Zedong's new aesthetic standard of combining revolutionary realism with revolutionary romanticism saw fruition in the revolutionary "model play" (*yangbanxi*) films during the Cultural Revolution (1966–76), and the ensuing period of aftermath and recovery prepared for the emergence of an entirely new generation in the 1980s. Coming from an expert on socialist China, Clark's historical narrative offers a concise overview, but its limited references to English scholarship other than his own (Clark 1987, 2005) points to the paucity of critical attention to socialist cinema, although the situation has changed with a special issue on the 1950s of the *Journal of Chinese Cinemas*, which includes the author's new work on film audiences (Clark 2011).

Compared with the socialist period, the past three decades of Chinese cinema have received much more scholarly attention (X. Zhang 1997; S. Lu 2002; Y. Zhang 2002, 2010a; Y. Zhu 2003; Berry 2004a; Pickowicz and Zhang 2006; Z. Zhang 2007b; McGrath 2008b). In Chapter 4, "Directors, Aesthetics, Genres: Chinese Postsocialist Cinema, 1979–2010," I first delineate the parameters of postsocialism and highlight the concept of simultaneous continuities and discontinuities that mark this period of seismic changes. I can then take time to review three interrelated areas – directors, aesthetics, and genres – and tackle problems engendered by a generational lineup, the significance of avant-garde experiment and international reception, the complication of genre repackaging, and the changing functions of cinema in the age of globalization. I argue that, convenient as it is, dividing directors into generations does little justice to the complexity and heterogeneity of Chinese film history, that several generations share their moments of experimental filmmaking at different historical junctures, and that the principal function of cinema in postsocialist China has switched from aesthetics and education in the late 1970s through 1980s to entertainment in the 2000s. A revisit to two critical debates on Xie Jin's film model and entertainment cinema, respectively, in the second half of the 1980s, together with a comparison of selective market statistics, foregrounds how much Chinese cinema and film criticism have changed in the past three decades.

Leaving mainland China, Robert Chi takes us back in history by resituating Hong Kong cinema in a framework larger than that of mainland-centered Chinese national cinema. In Chapter 5, "Hong Kong Cinema before 1980," Chi pursues a theoretical approach by which one may focus on geography instead of history, on places, regions, and orientations instead of periods. From the geographic perspective, the size and location of Hong Kong are revealed to have exerted a deep impact on its film industry from the very beginning, cultivating a constitutive role of extraterritoriality and a fundamental orientation toward regional networking. History and geography cannot exist without each other, Chi argues; hence particular orientations privilege particular historical narratives for Hong Kong, with nationalism to the north, (de)colonization to the south, modernization to the east, and empire to the west. Seen in this context, Chi suggests, Hong Kong cinema was more a part of Southeast Asia than of China in its early decades. Moreover, just as we may reconceptualize a center as a point through which things pass rather than as a point of origin or arrival, so we can appreciate a place where things like tropes, genres, talent, technology, and capital pass through, recombining and metamorphosing in the process. The outcome of such conceptualization is a decisive shift from the nation to the region, and the meditation on space and cinema enables Chi to map out a whole region with Hong Kong as a new kind of center. To be sure, national factors are still part of the picture, but they manifest themselves differently in various "geo-corporate" models, as those represented by Lai Man-wai (Li Minwei, 1892–1953) and the Shaw Brothers, all locked in the dynamics of border-crossing activities.

In Chapter 6, "The Hong Kong New Wave," Gina Marchetti offers a fresh look at a much-discussed film movement in Hong Kong (E. Yau 2001; Cheuk 2008) by differentiating connotations between "new wave" and "new cinema" in world cinema and connecting the "new" to a new generation who uses new technologies to achieve new effects in largely nontraditional ways. The emphasis on the new leads Marchetti to rediscover King Hu (Hu Jinquan, 1931–97, active in the 1960s) and Tang Shu-shuen (Tang Shuxuan, b. 1941, active in the 1970s) as two notable predecessors to the Hong Kong New Wave, and her profiles of representative directors (e.g., Allen Fong [Fang Yuping, b. 1947], Ann Hui [Xu Anhua, b. 1947]) and their "performing women" on and off screen (e.g., Maggie Cheung [Zhang Manyu, b. 1964], Anita Mui [Mei Yanfang, 1963–2003]) add nuances to shared concerns from two waves of an evolving movement. For Marchetti, the martial arts genre gives the new wave an opportunity to explore complex issues such as androgyny (via Brigitte Lin [Lin Qingxia, b. 1954]) and queer sensibility (via Leslie Cheung [Zhang Guorong, 1956–2003]), and the current return of the real in confronting Hong Kong local conditions has revived a distinguished tradition in Cantonese cinema. Overall, Marchetti demonstrates that Hong Kong cinema is at once local, translocal, and global, as best exemplified by Wong Kar-wai (Wang Jiawei, b. 1958), and her analysis dovetails with some observations from our other contributors on star performance (Sabrina Yu in Chapter 12), women's cinema (Lingzhen Wang in Chapter 17), and queer sexuality (Helen Leung in Chapter 28).

Heading out to Taiwan, James Wicks adopts a different approach than Marchetti's differentiation by categories and, instead, zooms in on a critical text in Taiwan cinema in order to contextualize an often-neglected period – what Guo-Juin Hong (2010) describes as "Taiwan cinema's missing years" – prior to the emergence of Taiwan New Cinema in 1982. In Chapter 7, "Gender Negotiation in Song Cunshou's *Story of Mother* and Taiwan Cinema of the Early 1970s," Wicks analyzes an unusual 1972 film by Song Cunshou (b. 1930), which uses transgressive female sexuality as an entry point to measure the wider political significance of gender identity as represented through passive males yet to earn their authority and active females coming into conformity with patriarchal nationalism, both part of the narrative typical of state-sponsored productions in 1970s Taiwan. Semiotic sequence breakdowns of Song's film reveal its narrative, structural, and aesthetic qualities, while comparisons with other contemporary films demonstrate that gender negotiations were allegorically meaningful in a volatile decade in Taiwan's cold-war history. After all, Wicks argues, the Kuomintang (Nationalist) state in

Taiwan propounded a version of gender inequality in early 1970s cinema that perhaps unintentionally encapsulated its geopolitical quandary, and the fact that subversive work was allowed in official productions indicates that radically challenging films would appear once the political situation changed.

What followed from the 1970s is the by-now familiar story of Taiwan New Cinema (Berry and Lu 2005; Yeh and Davis 2005; Davis and Chen 2007). In Chapter 8, "Second Coming: The Legacy of Taiwan New Cinema," Darrell Davis revisits New Cinema's outstanding auteurist ambitions, its rich formal innovations (e.g., realist, observational styles), and its unique sensitivity to Taiwan history and Taiwanese material that may have made it a "recovery cinema," an act of salvaging repressed unofficial memory. His discussion moves from *xiangtu* (nativism, a counter-hegemonic ideology from the 1980s) to *bentu* (localism, a widespread sentiment from the 1990s onward) and considers controversies surrounding the impact of government subsidies through annual film funds (*fudaojin*). For Davis, New Cinema is Taiwan cinema: a state-supported movement under intense public scrutiny, criticized for its high standards, elitism, and commercial shortcomings. By highlighting *Cape No. 7* (Wei Te-sheng, 2008) as a work of reconciliation and an unusual box-office hit, Davis evaluates Taiwan filmmakers' ability to counter the modernist gloom of post-New Cinema leftovers and the potential of a new *bentu* style to build a hodge-podge of diversity and to bring in rural peripheries, ethnic minorities, and different linguistic and demographic outsiders. True to Davis's evaluation, more recent works from the post-New Cinema have continued to prove that the new bentu is indeed translocal and multilingual in nature, bringing Tagalog and Filipino guest workers into Taipei's cityscape in *Pinoy Sunday* (Wi Ding Ho, 2009) and featuring Hakka dialect prominently alongside Mandarin and Taiwanese in *Cannot Live Without You* (Leon Dai, 2009).

Part II: Industry and Institution

"Part II: Industry and Institution" comprises five chapters on the industrial and institutional aspects of Chinese film. One preoccupation in film scholarship has been with a long tradition of propaganda and censorship in China, but the context of globalization has given rise to new problems (Hollywood dominance, transnational capital flows), new strategies (Chinese blockbusters), new concepts (e.g., media capital, soft power), and new or renewed institutions (the star system, international film festivals). Industrial and institutional concerns provide different lenses through which we can obtain a better understanding of why Chinese cinema has developed in ways specific to its variant contexts of cultural and political economy.

Obviously related to historical and geopolitical developments surveyed in Part I, Chapter 9, "Propaganda and Censorship in Chinese Cinema," places the government control of cinema in a historical and international context and rethinks the intricate relationship between film and politics. For Matthew Johnson, the use of cinema for propaganda purposes is widespread among political and intellectual elites around the globe, and censorship has long been a vital tool of statecraft because political and economic competition always spills over into the realms of mass culture and entertainment. As a powerful medium of new mass media technologies, cinema exerts a tremendous impact on two crucial aspects of state formation – international image and popular mentalities. From war documentaries of the Republican revolution of the 1920s to the educational cinematography movement of the 1930s, Johnson studies cinema's role in times of wars and between the wars, and from there he moves to survey the cold-war era, where two different models of state cinema developed in the PRC and Taiwan. The chapter ends with a brief discussion of "soft power" (a topic also taken up by Ying Zhu and Bruce Robinson in Chapter 23), which the PRC government uses now to justify its new mission to shape global influence, determine patterns of investment, and measure limits of acceptable representation in domestic and foreign productions.

As with soft power, "media capital" is another new critical concept that examines matters beyond nation-state borders. Moving away from the prism of nationalism that used to inform international media studies of how particular states developed their screen industries, Chapter 10, "Chinese Media Capital in Global Context," begins with an explanation of the concept of media capital, which Michael Curtin has developed to assess spatial dynamics of the transnational Chinese cultural economy. For Curtin, the concept of media capital invokes both connotations of the term: capital as a geographic center within a field of interconnected locales and capital as a concentration of resources, reputation, and talent. As such, media capitals are sites of mediation, locations where complex forces and flows interact. Curtin expounds three key principles critical to the structuring role in screen industries around the world: (1) the logic of accumulation, (2) trajectories of creative migration, and (3) contours of sociocultural variation. Media capital, he argues, is a concept that at once acknowledges the spatial logics of capital, creativity, culture, and polity without privileging one among the four. In a succinct account of key industrial and sociocultural trends in Shanghai, Hong Kong, Taipei, Singapore, and Beijing over a century, which he elaborated elsewhere (Curtin 2007), Curtin traces the geographical deployment of resources, talent, and products, and examines recent shifts in activity as media enterprises adapt to the pressures and opportunities posed by the latest wave of globalization.

Similarly focusing on political economy as do Johnson and Curtin, Stanley Rosen examines the role film plays in the evolving relationship between state and society in Chapter 11, "Film and Society in China: The Logic of the Market." As market performance becomes a key factor in political legitimization, governmental strategy has become dependent on making China rich and powerful. This strategy has led to the continuing expansion of a confident and demanding middle class and the coming of age of a new generation of youth who have extensive knowledge of international cultural trends, an individualism that poses a challenge to official voices, and a strong sense of nationalism. Given new changes in Chinese society, Rosen argues, the state now must negotiate with social and cultural forces in trying to balance contradictory values, which are manifested in the tension between producing propaganda films that promote mainstream values and the production of more popular super-commercial blockbusters. Using survey research and public opinion data, box-office statistics, documentary sources, interviews, and case studies, Rosen investigates contradictions and negotiations through government policies toward film, audience exposure and receptivity to films, the influence of film on values, and likely future prospects for film as a factor in the Chinese state's relationship with society.

Rosen's overview of film audience brings us to the appeal of another significant development in the globalizing China, namely celebrity culture, which covers not just screen stars but other performing artists as well as commercial and even political figures (Edwards and Jeffreys 2010). In Chapter 12, "Vulnerable Chinese Stars: From *Xizi* to Film Worker," Sabrina Yu regards screen stardom as part of celebrity culture and proposes her model of star vulnerability in counterposition to the Euro-American model of star power dominant in film studies. With her convictions that stars are culturally made and that a careful examination of national stardom deepens our understanding of national cinema and identity, Yu enumerates examples of cultural specificities in Chinese stardom, such as stars as *xizi* (a derogatory term for actors) or "film workers" (a socialist designation), stars as moral victims (e.g., Ruan Lingyu, 1910–35), and stars as political subordinates (e.g., Jackie Chan [Cheng Long, b. 1954]). As humiliation and tragedy always linger behind glamour, Yu contends that vulnerability defines all aspects of Chinese stars – commercial, political, moral, and cultural. Even the all-star film format and the expectation of all-rounded talent (film, television, music) typical of Hong Kong stars reveals the mechanism of restriction (by way of dispersion) rather than concentration of a star's power. Building on current research on individual Chinese stars (Farquhar and Zhang 2010), Yu's chapter represents a new direction in tackling the phenomenon of Chinese stardom as a whole and in negotiating Hollywood star theories.

In Chapter 13, "Ports of Entry: Mapping Chinese Cinema's Multiple Trajectories at International Film Festivals," Nikki Lee and Julian Stringer conduct a temporal and a spatial analysis of Chinese cinema's representation at leading international film festivals, which has been truly spectacular compared with other national cinemas. They suggest that timing is perfect as globalization initiatives and China's rise as a world economic power since the 1980s have paved the way for the ascendance of Chinese cinema on the world stage. Extending Michael Curtin's concept of media capital (see Chapter 10), which explores the geographic concentration of media industries in large cities, Lee and Stringer investigate what they call "the port city film festival" as another site of media concentration and trace a pattern of such port city festival operations as both repeatable and significant. Their analysis of such A-list film festivals as Cannes, Tokyo, and Venice reveals similar receptiveness to Chinese cinema, but by comparing the selections of and awards to Chinese films over time in different festivals, including the B-list venues such as Rotterdam and Pusan, they also notice different emphases and preferences among these festivals. Some festivals remain loyal to established directors, while others prefer emergent talents; some showcase popular artistic movies, while others support politically provocative and aesthetically experimental films. Berlin is an exception to the port city film festival model, but it has played an important role in promoting Chinese cinema nonetheless. Supported by seven tables of individual festivals' entries and awards, this chapter not only illustrates the crucial importance of international film festivals to the growth of Chinese cinema in the last three decades but also points to a new area of film studies that examines the circulation and reception of films through cultural industries and institutions on the global stage.

Part III: Genre and Representation

"Part III: Genre and Representation" contains five chapters that deal with a select number of key styles, genres, and modes in Chinese cinema, including martial arts film, documentary film, women's film, and urban film. In Chapter14, "In Search of Chinese Film Style(s) and Technique(s)," James Udden mounts a compelling critique of an essentialist brand of "Eastern" aesthetics, which for him is largely based on unsubstantiated and at times contradictory claims of long takes, still camera, flat lighting, empty shots, and the like. Citing concrete examples from a wide array of films, including the classic *Spring in a Small Town* (Fei Mu, 1948), Udden demonstrates that Chinese cinema has produced no monolithic, quintessential Chinese film style, but instead an impressive diversity of cinematic styles and techniques, which displays inventiveness and experimentation due to greatly varying historical contexts. Hong Kong cinema, for instance, translated indigenous acrobatic and generic traditions into distinctively cinematic terms, resulting in the most physical cinema to ever grace this planet. By contrast, Taiwan created a new Asian brand of art cinema that is not simply derivative of either its Japanese or European predecessors. Instead of blindly accepting a distinctive Chinese style, Udden recommends that we come to terms with multifaceted cinematic testaments to an ongoing cultural dynamic. In sum, Udden's recommendation here dovetails with Jerome Silbergeld's (in Chapters 21 and 22), namely that we would do better examining individual works and appreciating their unique contributions to world cinema than searching for some innate, preconceived national characteristics.

The national, nonetheless, remains a fundamental concern in Chinese film history, as evident in Chapter 15, "Film Genre and Chinese Cinema: A Discourse of Film and Nation," where Stephen Teo discusses the symbiotic and at times contradictory relationship between the concept of genre and the rise of the

Chinese cinema as an expression of national cinema. He argues that Chinese filmmakers look upon genre as an indispensable avenue of nationalistic expression in cinema while at the same time seeking to expand this expression as a transnational conceit. In this process, specific Chinese genres are created as amalgamations of indigenous and foreign genres that have nevertheless endured as Chinese cinematic genres, such as martial arts film (*wuxia pian*) and opera film (*xiqu pian*). In particular, Teo explores the somewhat misplaced idealization of *wenyi pian* (literary film) as a "high" genre (see also Zhang Zhen in Chapter 2) and the customary dismissal of *wuxia pian* as a "low" genre. A discussion of Derrida's comment on the genre's law of impurity helps highlight the ambivalence of genre, but Teo believes that this ambivalence can encompass a sense of identity and provide a certain satisfaction in the audience who seeks identification through the indigenous characteristics of given genres. He concludes that genre gives the impression of a national cinema identity but its true purpose may be to mutate that identity as time and circumstance change and as the world draws closer and nations become even more interconnected.

Qi Wang brings us from genre and nation to performance and individuality in Chapter 16, "Performing Documentation: Wu Wenguang and the Performative Turn of New Chinese Documentary." She questions the assumed dominance of an observational aesthetic – construed in opposition to official media practices – in Chinese independent documentary since the late 1980s. With her detailed analysis of the performative motifs in Wu Wenguang (b. 1956), Wang traces a neglected performative turn in the new documentary that proves to have provided a sustaining force for the development and understanding of newer documentaries and mixed-genre experimental videos in China. The performativity in question foregrounds the dynamic between the filmmaker, the camera, and the filmed subjects, as well as the authenticity of documentary information, and our attention to the performative mode, Wang suggests, would help readjust the previous oppositional framework and conceptualize the new documentary as negotiation not only between the official and independent forces but also between the socialist past and the postsocialist present, forgetting and memory, self and other, documentary and other contemporaneous forms of documenting Chinese reality in film and video, as well as in avant-garde art and performance. With her emphasis on performance, Wang adds a fresh insight to a growing body of scholarship in Chinese documentary film studies (Pickowicz and Zhang 2006: 47–122; Berry, Lu, and Rofel 2010; Y. Zhang 2010b).

Rather than focusing on one particular director as Qi Wang does with Wu Wenguang, Lingzhen Wang provides a panoramic view in Chapter17, "Chinese Women's Cinema." With bold strokes, she outlines a critical genealogy of Chinese women's cinema, redefined as cinematic practice by female directors in mainland China, Hong Kong, and Taiwan, and explores three major topics that are critical to feminist film studies – politics of gender and cinema in history, female cinematic subjectivity and spectatorship, and visual pleasures and consumerism. Starting from the early 1920s and going all the way to the 2000s, Wang guides us through the formation and disintegration of commercial, institutional, and personal channels that enable women to enter the filmmaking industry, and she demonstrates that women's participation in filmmaking is geopolitically and historically contingent, and the meaning and significance of their films are diverse and resistant to any uniform interpretations. It is in and through this diverse engagement with historical forces, whether of the market, politics, or patriarchal traditions, as Wang argues, that Chinese women have exhibited their agency, not only in reorienting gender configurations in history, but also in articulating different meanings and aesthetics in their cinematic practices. In current scholarship, rarely has one been provided with a more comprehensive account of Chinese women's cinema in such a concise format, and Lingzhen Wang is commended particularly for bringing to our attention active filmmakers in Hong Kong and Taiwan, a tradition long overlooked in film studies.

In Chapter18, "From Urban Films to Urban Cinema: The Emergence of a Critical Concept," Yomi Braester undertakes a different genealogical work and poses this question: Why should the term "Urban Cinema" be considered a useful category for understanding films focused on the city? Following Rick Altman's argument that generic definitions do not rely on intrinsic categories but rather are invented for the convenience of distributors and critics, Braester launches an inquiry into the motivation for promoting Urban Cinema as a genre in mainland China. Starting with urban films of the late 1980s when the term "urban cinema" (*chengshi dianying*) first appeared, Braester outlines a thematic typology for what appeared then as an emerging genre (e.g., alienated youths, unstable identities) and its distinct visual idiom (e.g., roaming point-of-view shots, widespread urban ruins). Since these films range from official productions (e.g., the Fourth Generation) to independent films (e.g., the Sixth Generation) and new commercial films from the late 1990s onward, Braester reveals overlaps and contradictions between Urban Cinema and New Urban Cinema in creative and critical discourses. A scholar whose recent work has increasingly engaged cinema and the city (Braester 2010; Braester and Tweedie 2010), Braester concludes that filmmakers and critics have deployed Urban Cinema and New Urban Cinema to further their stakes in a charged debate on the meeting point between post-Maoist aesthetics and ideology. This conclusion reminds us of Stephen Teo's meditation on genre in Chapter 15, which likewise argues that genres are vehicles for articulating Chinese filmmakers' visions of nation and identity.

Part IV: Arts and Media

"Part IV: Arts and Media" comprises six chapters and represents the renewed efforts to intervene in continuing deliberations on inter-art and intermedial issues that involve film and literature, film and theater, film and visual arts, and film and television, as well as film and technology. Chapter 19, "The Intertwinement of Chinese Film and Literature: Choices and Strategies in Adaptations," investigates a century of Chinese filmic adaptations of literature. After briefing on scholarship in this area, Liyan Qin locates herself as part of the "sociological turn" in adaptation studies, although her chapter is concerned more with history, politics, and culture than about sociology. A survey of what Chinese filmmakers chose to adapt during different periods prepares for a discussion of different strategies of adaptations, which range from faithful adherence to the original in all possible ways, to subjective attempts to capture the so-called "spirit" of the original as interpreted by the filmmakers, to radical appropriation of the original only as raw material on which to build one's own film. Given this wide spectrum of "fidelity" in adaptations, Qin observes a remarkable reversal of the status of film *vis-à-vis* literature: films once presented themselves as by-products of literature, but starting with Zhang Yimou in the late 1980s (L. Qin 2010), visuality has become foregrounded and the free adaptation style widely adopted, to the extent that nowadays a novel is often released as an add-on to capitalize on the recent success of a film. The respective artistic qualities of film and literature aside, Qin believes that the change in the filmmakers' strategies about what and how to adapt over time sheds light on the dynamic of Chinese history as well as on the mutual influence between culture and history.

Like literature, theater is another art form that was used to elevate the status of film in its formative years, but by the late 1970s Chinese critics began to call for abandoning the "clutch of drama" in filmmaking. Comparing this radical call for abandonment with a subsequent construction of "shadowplay" (*yingxi*) as an indigenous concept of film theory, Weihong Bao revisits the much-debated relationship between film and theater in Chapter 20, "Diary of a Homecoming: (Dis-)Inhabiting the Theatrical in Postwar Shanghai Cinema." She adopts a triple frame – conceptual, historical, and textual – to study the irreducible presence of the theatrical in film from a figural, stylistic, and spectatorial perspective. Conceptually, she traces the distinction between cinema and theater in early Western film theory and draws on recent scholarship on intermediality. Historically, she reviews the symbiosis, cross-fertilization, and mutual distanciation between Chinese cinema and theater in the first half of the twentieth century. Textually, she analyzes a cluster of "homecoming" films that feature the postwar theater workers who returned from the hinterland only to find themselves denied dwelling in Shanghai. For Bao, the displacement of the cinematic and the theatrical effectively evoked asymmetrical binaries of country–city, exteriority–domesticity, and utopic past–dystopic present, and the two media's mutual framing, contiguous aesthetics, and shared exhibition space in the 1940s propelled a transformation in both media on aesthetic as well as political levels. By examining cinematic and dramatic articulations of social space, political message, affective horizon, and modes of spectatorship, Bao ultimately seeks to reconsider cinema and theater as technologies of perception that engage and mediate experiences of social changes in modern China.

As well as being a theatrical, literary, and musical form, film is an intensely visual art – this observation leads Jerome Silbergeld to wonder why art historians have been so slow to take up the subject as part of their studies of Chinese visual history and visual culture. In Chapter 21, "Cinema and the Visual Arts of China," Silbergeld poses challenging questions: What unique insights are offered by film critiques that focus intensely on film's visuality – on body language, the natural setting, visual references to other films and to other visual traditions, literature, and history – especially in a cinematic tradition that has been heavily regulated by script-reading but visually illiterate or irresponsive censors? Starting with previous scattered remarks on the similarity between cinema and Chinese handscroll painting, Silbergeld proceeds to explore whether there is a "Chinese way" of seeing or visual narration, to what degree Chinese film lends itself to Western forms of art analysis, and whether or not Chinese film conforms to Western theories of film and photography. Like James Udden in Chapter 14, Silbergeld is reluctant to attach "national" attributes to cinema or theory without concrete textual evidence. Instead, he proposes that we consider cinema in relation to the visual arts (e.g., shared styles, shared culture), examine the function of the visual arts as they appear in cinema, and treat cinema as a visual art. The result is a fascinating meditation on visual aspects of a composite art that is cinema, including its rendition of temporality, spatiality, symbolism, and imagery, as well as its intricate relationship with painting, photography, and multimedia arts.

A similar interdisciplinary interest informs Jerome Silbergeld's venture into another intermedial area – film and music in Chinese cinema – that has yet to receive a book-length treatment in English. In Chapter 22, "From Mountain Songs to Silvery Moonlight: Some Notes on Music in Chinese Cinema," Silbergeld does not take a conventional approach like that of appreciation of an individual film auteur, as others have done with Wong Kar-wai's globally circulated works (E. Yeh 1999; de Carvalho 2008); instead, he makes a bold statement that the use of lyrics – more than melody – is most distinctive about Chinese cinema and in that sense most serious Chinese films could be loosely considered to be "musicals." This specific type of "musical" quality in Chinese cinema is illustrated through his analysis of various uses of lyrics in such works as *Street Angel* (Yuan Muzhi, 1937), *Third Sister Liu* (Su Li, 1961), and *Yellow Earth* (Chen Kaige, 1984). However, Silbergeld also finds time to reveal the complexity of music and sound – both diegetic and extra-diegetic – in Chinese cinema, which tends to draw on a variety of sources, from Chinese folk songs to classical Western music. For Silbergeld, what is important now is not a rush to construct a theory of Chinese film music but a better understanding of the mutual interaction of Chinese and Western film and music across genres and periods.

Turning attention to a different media platform rather than artistic medium, Ying Zhu and Bruce Robinson evaluate an ongoing effort at integrating film and television in China through the case of CCTV-6 (China Central Television's Movie Channel) in Chapter 23, "Cross-Fertilization in Chinese Cinema and

Television: A Strategic Turn in Cultural Policy." China's film and television industries developed semi-independently up to the mid-1990s (Zhu and Nakajima 2010), and each was unwilling to enter into a serious partnership with the other until the state issued new policies to restructure the entire media sector and to transform it into a commercially competitive, globally influential engine of China's "soft power" (a concept Matthew Johnson also discusses in Chapter 9). Founded in 1996, the Movie Channel soon became CCTV's second most popular channel by promoting cinematic arts and exposing smaller films to a much wider audience, and as such it serves as an example of mutually beneficial collaboration between the two industries. Meanwhile, the China Film Group was formed in 1999 as a film-based multimedia conglomerate (including the Movie Channel), which has been given structural and regulatory advantages and charged with the mission of developing itself into a globally competitive media titan (likewise observed by Michael Curtin in Chapter 10). By tracking developments of the Movie Channel and the China Film Group, Zhu and Robinson highlight a set of issues concerning cross-fertilization between China's film and television industries and its impact on the future direction of Chinese cinema in particular and the Chinese media industry in general. Not surprisingly, institutional analysis such as this chapter presents has raised new questions regarding artistic and ideological qualities in television productions, which are explored in an emergent body of scholarship on China's television (Zhu and Berry 2009) and television drama series (Zhu, Keane, and Bai 2008; X. Zhong 2010).

From the national scale of media restructuring in the current era of globalization, Gary Xu redirects our gaze back to the historical contexts in which Chinese cinema tackles problems of technology. Rather than the institutional analysis offered by Zhu and Robinson (as well as Matthew Johnson and Michael Curtin, respectively in Chapters 9 and 10), Xu experiments with a unique approach in Chapter 24, "Chinese Cinema and Technology." He selects three films from the first half of the twentieth century – *Laborer's Love* (Zhang Shichuan, 1922), *Street Angel* (1937), and *Spring in a Small Town* (1948) – and enumerates key advances in film technology and techniques (e.g., projection, camerawork, editing, lighting, sound) around these representative works. From the period of early cinema, Xu argues, the Chinese fascination with film technology has never abated; better yet, the fascination has been fully embedded in Chinese cinema as an inherent and constant reflection on the effectiveness as well as the limits of imported technologies. Through detailed observations, Xu explores the historical roots of the Chinese fascination with film technology, its relationship with Chinese modernity, and its role in shaping Chinese cinema's unique aesthetics. After a brief overview of the development in the second half of the twentieth century, the chapter ends with a critique of recent Chinese blockbusters as slavish imitations of Hollywood, marked by their shallow plot, porous details, poor performance, and tendency toward cultural homogenization. None of these flaws can be disguised by these films' lavish scenery, glossy picture, rich colors, realistic sounds, rapid editing, and smooth and multi-perspective camerawork. As Xu contends, this is not technological sophistication; rather, Chinese directors, pushed by the demand of global commercial cinema, are getting away from their strength: the keen awareness of and fascination with what film technology really means.

Part V: Issues and Debates

"Part V: Issues and Debates" comprises six chapters. Two of them offer overviews of the evolving scholarship on Chinese film, respectively in Chinese and in English, and the remaining chapters take up a select number of recurring issues in Chinese film studies, such as masculinity and sexuality, homosexuality and queer aesthetics, transnationalism and globalization. In particular, two chapters address two sides of the same transnational practices often neglected by current scholarship: the diasporic formation of Chinese filmmaking (by Yiman Wang) and the trope of the absent American in the transitional period of the Reform-era Chinese cinema (by Michael Berry). Together, the chapters in Part V demonstrate that, just as Chinese cinema has been deeply involved in transnational, translocal practices for over a century, so Chinese film studies must pay attention to fissures and ruptures in filmmaking and film scholarship.

In Chapter 25, "Chinese Film Scholarship in Chinese," Chen Xihe offers a comprehensive survey of film studies in the Chinese language from its early years to the new century. As he explains, Chinese film scholarship in Chinese mostly appears in mainland China, Taiwan, and Hong Kong. Scholarly publications were scattered and fragmentary before the 1980s, but they have entered a booming stage since then, especially in mainland China, where many professional journals are dedicated to publishing articles on Chinese film. For political, historical, and industrial reasons, Chinese film scholarship in the three areas took their corresponding local developments as their main concerns. Given such geocultural grounding, each of them only addressed selective topics of the other areas. The topics that attract common interest in the three areas are groups of directors and films that emerged in the 1980s, such as the mainland's Fifth and Sixth Generations, Taiwan New Cinema, and Hong Kong New Wave. In terms of academic approaches, Chinese film scholarship in mainland China used to take a political and ideological perspective before the 1980s but has turned to an artistic and aesthetic exploration after the 1980s, whereas the scholarship in Hong Kong and Taiwan pays more attention to genre and industry issues. In the 1990s, cultural and industrial approaches became stronger in all three areas. Meanwhile, the development and transformation of Chinese cinema under the impact of globalization also command a strong interest. As a recent trend, Chinese film scholarship in Chinese tends to place Chinese film in all three areas in a dynamic relationship with one another, as well as in relation to Hollywood and world cinema.

Like Chen Xihe, Chris Berry is attentive to academic history, but he restructures his narrative in line with Pierre Bourdieu's institutional perspective on "the field" and offers a compelling account of four stages of the development in Chapter 26, "Chinese Film Scholarship in English." First, Berry traces the field's prehistory in the 1970s to scholars whose primary interests resided in other disciplines (e.g., folklore, sociology) and who did not even command a working knowledge of the Chinese language. Second, as the monolingualism of the 1970s yielded to the prevalent bilingualism of the 1980s as far as scholars are concerned, Berry notices the persistence of monolingual English readership in much of the new scholarship of the 1980s, which was shaped by the politics of international film festivals (the topic Lee and Stringer cover in Chapter 13) and the growth of film studies in Euro-American universities. The availability of English subtitles at the time thus explains the geopolitical imbalance in film scholarship on the PRC, Hong Kong, and Taiwan. Third, as film studies became a new nexus of cutting-edge inter-disciplinary research in the 1990s, Berry argues that Chinese film studies in English followed the dominant trends of text-based analysis and pursued issues of identity, gender, sexuality, aesthetics, and modernity. Fourth, entering the new century, the field is increasingly caught in what Berry calls "the transnational turn" and expends its attention on hitherto neglected areas (e.g., industry, stardom) while continuing to problematize the national cinema paradigm. Berry concludes his account by pointing to areas in need of further research, such as reception studies, experimental cinema, questions of temporality and ethnicity, and the impact of new media technology.

Chris Berry's mapping of the field in terms of issue-oriented methodology is substantiated by chapters that follow. In Chapter 27, "The Return of the Repressed: Masculinity and Sexuality Reconsidered," Shuqin Cui contends that Chinese films after the mid-1980s have consistently staged the return of the repressed, which is masculinity lost or restored, in crisis or in redemption. She selects representative works from three phases to support her argument. The first is the late 1980s to the early 1990s when the Fifth Generation (especially Zhang Yimou's first trilogy) articulated the anxiety of masculinity by projecting ethnographic images of China in an allegorical form, whereby its female spectacle would generate a transnational encounter with Western fantasy and coproduce a cooperative Orientalism. The second is the mid-1990s when the Fifth Generation's collective return to history served the purpose not so much of correcting the historical record as of restoring personal memories of past violence and traumatized youth. Interestingly, Cui contends that Ang Lee (Li An, b. 1954) achieves a similar goal with his controversial return to wartime history in *Lust, Caution* (2007). The third is the late 1990s onward, when a new generation of young directors resorted to family melodrama to emphasize masculinity in retreat and foreground female agency in times of moral crisis. However, Cui notes, as these new films endow their female images with strength and determination, they actually send a (mis)perception of man as victim and woman as aggressor. All in all, Cui's selective reading demonstrates that contemporary Chinese film has exhibited a consistent search for repressed masculinities to withstand hegemonic manipulation, whether it is political, historical, or commercial. In this search the female body always remains gendered – a rhetorical figure for projecting male fears and desires. In the cinematic renditions of masculinity and sexuality, Cui concludes, the majority of Chinese film directors have yet to grant the female image full subjectivity.

In Chapter 28, "Homosexuality and Queer Aesthetics," Helen Leung traces the emergence of "New Queer Chinese Cinema," maps its distinctive articulations across mainland China, Hong Kong, and Taiwan, and locates its significance within Queer Cinema globally. In mainland China, the coexistence of strict censorship measures against homosexual representations on the one hand, and a lively underground film movement on the other, means that queer themes are exclusively found in the works of independent and often underground productions from directors such as Zhang Yuan (b. 1963) and Cui Zi'en (b. 1958). By contrast, queer themes appear mostly in genre films and dramatic vehicles with major stars in Hong Kong, where a handful of queer-identified filmmakers have produced sporadic works and gay directors like Stanley Kwan (Guan Jinpeng, b. 1957) and Yon Fan (Yang Fan, b. 1947) frequently flirt with queer issues. In Taiwan, various factors including a more socially visible *tongzhi* movement, a less intolerant political climate, and a niche market of queer-friendly viewers, result in a more diverse range of queer films, which include big commercial pleasers, smaller festival films, and the works of queer-identified auteurs such as Tsai Ming-liang (Cai Mingliang, b. 1958) and Zero Chou (Zhou Meiling, b. 1969) who have consciously developed complex queer themes and a distinctive queer aesthetic. Through extensive examples, Leung reveals New Queer Chinese Cinema to be vibrant, but she contends that the representation of homosexuality is, ironically, its least interesting aspect. Instead, films that expose the limits of the heterosexual kinship structure, play with the fluidity between gender identity, gender expression, and the sexed body, and chart the unpredictable paths of sexual and emotional bonds are, for Leung, truly worthy of our critical attention.

Moving away from issues of sexuality treated in Cui and Leung, Yiman Wang tackles issues of geocultural production in Chapter 29, "Alter-centering Chinese Cinema: The Diasporic Formation." She examines the diasporic formation of Chinese cinema by tracing its evolving strategies of affectively articulating "home" or "imagined togetherness" (Naficy 2001) at different historical conjunctures. For Wang, Chinese diaspora refers not only to people who migrate out of mainland China, Hong Kong, and Taiwan, but also to internal diaspora between Sinophone regions that have markedly different dialects/languages and cultures. Given this enlarged map, Wang delineates key figures, groups, and practices in four facets of Chinese diaspora filmmaking: (1) pre-World War II diasporic filmmakers inside and outside the Sinophone area, especially those operating in the United States; (2) World War II and civil war migrations, Shanghai to Hong Kong (1937–49) and Hong Kong to California (1941–45); (3) flexible filmmaking: Hong Kong, China, and the global turn; (4) shuttling in-between, going nonmainstream, and creolizing the Sinophone. The diasporic perspective enables Wang to address little-known works from early pioneers (e.g., Marion Wong, Joseph Sunn [a.k.a. Shu-sun Chiu, Zhao Shusen, 1904–90], and Lady Tsen Mei [1888–1985]) as well as contemporary figures (e.g., Shi-zheng Chen [b. 1963], Guo Xiaolu [b. 1973], and Zhang Liling). As the "other" site that traverses the "Chinese" center, Wang argues, diasporic filmmaking constitutes the alter-center where "Chinese" issues are staged and contested in interaction with non-Sinic contexts. Because what diasporic filmmakers have in common is their entangled negotiation with the Sinic languages and affective investment in a sense of "home" or "imagined togetherness," Wang concludes that diasporic Chinese cinema must leave "home" in order to regain it; it must deconstruct the "home" to rebuild it anew in variant images; and it ultimately embodies the accented alter-center of the Sinophone "home."

Continuing with the geopolitics of cultural imagination, Michael Berry directs our attention to a different kind of alterity in Chapter 30, "The Absent American: Figuring the United States in Chinese Cinema of the Reform Era," which explores a recurring trope by which the United States is framed primarily through a strategy of absence in contemporary Chinese cinema. In a section titled "The [Chinese-] American Cometh," Berry sorts through a number of films produced between 1979 and 1982 in order to demonstrate how a new format was developed for imagining America within the parameters of a strict political formula. He then illustrates how a similar theme of absence would also dominate early portrayals of the Chinese immigrant experience almost a decade later under a section titled "Left for Coming to America." Finally, Berry examines how America has been revisited as Chinese cinema shifts away from a politics of absence to a more complex framing. Overall, the series of films examined there helps elucidate larger questions of propaganda, nationalism, and globalism in Reform-Era China. While acknowledging the problematic of "Chinese" and "American" as legitimated national categories, Berry insists that at the core of all of these films – perhaps contrary to the filmmakers' intent – are the celluloid footprints of travelers who freely move from China to America and back again. It is precisely these tales of mobility, border-crossing, and immigration that tell a greater story of identities in flux that challenges the very notion – or myth – of national identity.

Looking Forward: Chinese Cinema in Comparative Film Studies

As explained earlier in this introduction, *A Companion to Chinese Cinema* does not pretend to cover all subjects, and several worthy topics are regrettably not treated at length in this volume. To provide a framework for discussing such missing topics and looking forward to future research, I refer the reader to comparative film studies that goes beyond national cinema and transnationalism and encourages interdisciplinary and cross-media research (Y. Zhang 2010a: 29–41). From that perspective, film music and song certainly call for dialogue between musicologists and film scholars, as in the case of scholarship on leftist cinema (Tuohy 1999; E. Yeh 2002). Often relegated to the margins of film and media studies, animation would benefit from research in interdisciplinarity and cross-mediality. Animation films have a long history in Chinese cinema (Quiquemelle 1991; Yan and Suo 2005), and China's recent investment in this sector – especially in digitization and in higher education – by the government and the industry alike is part of a new synergetic venture in building a regionally or even globally competitive creative industry in China (Lent and Xu 2010: 121–5).

Understandably, there are many other areas of Chinese cinema that are not treated in the current project but deserve further attention. Fortunately, the field is growing fast, and work has been underway to address scholarly lacunae. Under the editorship of Song Hwee Lim and Julian Ward, the *Journal of Chinese Cinemas* has taken an active role in charting new directions through its guest-edited special issues, which include topics like film stars (Farquhar and Zhang 2008), film exhibition (Pickowicz and Johnson 2009), and new media (Yue and Leung 2009). Indeed, compared with television, new media are marked by even smaller screens through wired and wireless communication (e.g., computers, cell phones). New media technologies have revolutionized the production, transmission, reception, and preservation of screen products – fictional, documentary, avant-garde – in contemporary China, and nowadays "smaller screens" regularly intervene in everyday life with its pronounced "lightness of realities" (Voci 2010).

Returning to the framework of comparative film studies, I believe that Chinese cinema would benefit a great deal from a reconsideration of its relationship with Hollywood, not just in the current era of globalization but also in earlier historical periods (Xiao 2010), as well as its relationship with East Asian cinema or Asian cinema in general. Hong Kong cinema has been placed in such a comparative perspective (Marchetti and See-Kam 2007; Tan, Feng, and Marchetti 2009), and similar comparative work has been done on horror films (Choi and Wada-Marciano 2008) and screen industries (Yeh and Davis 2008). Obviously, what we need most at this juncture is not just a mapping of individual national cinemas across Asia (Ciecko 2006; Eleftheriotis and Needham 2006; Vick 2007) – although that kind of project constitutes a necessary first step – but a sustained critical engagement with issues of cross-fertilization, mutual dialogue, and transnational or transregional cooperation among different Asian cinemas (Hunt and Leung 2008).

Finally, the significance of Chinese cinema must be measured by its enduring contribution to world cinema. Merely having its film stills grace the covers of world cinema books in English is by no means sufficient, even though it is apparently a current fashion in academic publication indicative of the increasing visibility of China and Chinese cinema (Nochimson 2010; Ďurovičová and Newman 2010). Likewise, the importance of Chinese film studies must be assessed by its rigorous contribution to international film studies. *A Companion to Chinese Cinema* represents one such effort in critical assessment, as the following 29 chapters promise to open the reader's eyes to a variety of crucial aspects of Chinese cinema informed by the contributors' historical knowledge, theoretical expertise, and analytic rigor.

Notes

1   The currency exchange rate has been limited to a small margin of fluctuations around US$1 to RBM 6.3–6.8 after being pegged at US$1 to RMB 8.1–8.3 for years up to 2005. *The Founding of a Republic* still trailed behind two Hollywood blockbusters in China's 2009 exhibition market: *2012* (Roland Emmerich, 2009), with RBM 460.6 million, and *Transformers II: Revenge of the Fallen* (Michael Bay, 2009), with RBM 455 million (Yin 2010: 11).

2   For instance, Hong Kong University Press has launched two English book series related to Chinese film studies: "The New Hong Kong Cinema" (with fifteen titles by August 2010) and "TransAsia: Screen Cultures" (with six titles).

3   Given its targeted English readership, this introduction will mainly refer to scholarship in English, especially books and anthologies, and the reader is advised to consult Chapter 25 for Chinese-language publications.

4   The multiple roles Chris Berry has played in relation to Chinese cinema are noteworthy. Growing up in the UK, he received his PhD in cinema studies from the University of California, Los Angeles and taught at several universities in Australia, the US, and the UK. He had a stint as a government-appointed foreign film expert in Beijing during the 1980s and has promoted Chinese cinema internationally by helping with English subtitles and writing for film festivals and news media. His interdisciplinary academic work has covered cinema, television, media, queer studies, and psychoanalysis, among others.

5   However, one year after its inception, the editors of a special issue of *Journal of Chinese Cinemas* (Berry and Pang 2008) would question precisely the wisdom of keeping the plural form in an era when mainland China, Hong Kong, and Taiwan are increasingly involved in the transborder coproduction of Chinese blockbuster films.

6   Most notable among other regional dialect films are Amoy (*xiayu*) and Chaozhou: both were produced in Hong Kong mostly for Southeast Asian markets in the 1950s–1960s, and the former's popularity (seventy titles in 1958 and 89 in 1959, compared with nine Chaozhou titles in 1959) actually inspired the production of Taiwanese-dialect film in Taiwan, for *xiayu* (Xiamen dialect) or *minnanyu* (Southern Fujian dialect) are basically the same as Taiwanese dialect (*taiyu*). Other languages, dialects, and accents (e.g., Hakka, Shanghainese, Sichuanese, and ethnic minorities' languages) also appear in Chinese films, but films featuring them in any significant way have never reached a critical mass (Y. Zhang 2004a: 155).

Part I

History and Geography

2

Transplanting Melodrama
Observations on the Emergence of Early Chinese Narrative Film

Zhang Zhen

Critics and historians of moving images have often been blind to the forest of melodrama because of their attention to the trees of genre. (Linda Williams 1998: 61)

Chinese wenyi melodrama generally developed along two lines: those works that deal with family relationships and ethics, and those that depict romances. . . . First, films of this genre use contemporary or recent society as a backdrop; second, they deal with human emotions and are therefore lyrical to an extent. (Cai Guorong, in Law 1997: 15)

Introduction: Retracing Chinese Melodrama

The "rediscovery" of *All that Heaven Allows* (Douglas Sirk, 1955), along with other films in Douglas Sirk's "Universal cycle," galvanized much of the revisionist study of this Hollywood "progressive" auteur (with a Brecht connection) and melodrama film in the 1970s (Klinger 1994). In its opening sequence, Jane Wyman's widow character Carey meets her new gardener (Rock Hudson) and invites him for lunch in her yard full of fall foliage, and thus initiates their fateful romance. The gardener demonstrates his earthy origins and worldly knowledge about trees and flora by pointing to the Golden Rain tree nearby, an "exotic" species from China. He cuts a branch to show her its "rain" splattered leaves. Carey is enthralled. The particular branch introduces a cluster of striking props and colors that make up Sirk's signature "ironic mise-en-scène" eulogized by critics who rediscovered him in the early 1970s (Mercer and Schingler 2004).

 This chapter does not concern Sirk directly, but rather the relationship between Anglo-American melodrama studies spurred by that rediscovery and non-Western

A Companion to Chinese Cinema, First Edition. Edited by Yingjin Zhang.
© 2012 Blackwell Publishing Ltd. Published 2012 by Blackwell Publishing Ltd.

melodramatic traditions (here China, in particular), as obliquely referred to in *All that Heaven Allows*. Indeed, how have cinematic melodramatic tales been staged under "Golden Rain" trees or other native or imported species in China? More specifically, I will anchor the recent debate on melodrama's global appeal *vis-à-vis* cultural identity in the context of melodrama film's emergence in China in the 1920s–1930s, taking advantage of the few extant films from the period, including the recently resurfaced *Poet from the Sea* (1927) by Hou Yao, a pioneering Chinese filmmaker.

Before and beyond the postwar and cold-war moment when *All that Heaven Allows* was made, when mainland China seemed unfathomable behind the iron curtains in Western eyes, is there a history of Chinese melodrama film that can be viewed as parallel to or intersecting with that which has been exhaustively documented and debated in the United States and Europe, and to a lesser extent in other traditions in Asia and Latin America? Despite the proliferation of studies on melodrama in cinema studies since the rediscovery of Sirk and ensuing feminist interventions, followed by the historical turn, the relationship between this body of scholarship and national cinema studies remained a thorny point in "cross-cultural" analysis (Kaplan 1991), further exacerbated by the recent trend of transnational frameworks. While much of the Anglophone scholarship focusing on Euro-American melodrama as genre or a set of subgenres is hardly concerned with the "rest" of the world or simply assumes its universal applicability, studies on national cinema and regional cinema (such as Asia and Latin America) as popular-ized "Third Cinema" tend to gravitate toward a culturalist view that trumpets up native categories if not outright dismisses the term "melodrama" (and other terms with a Western origin) as Eurocentric and irrelevant to particular national and regional cultural–linguistic parlances. In the introduction to *Melodrama and Asian Cinema*, a pioneering project to link or delink melodrama studies East and West, Wimal Dissanayake (1993: 3–4) argues that the term "melodrama" is an inherently Western category and does not have synonyms in Asia or elsewhere and that, if there are vague equivalents of "recent vintage," they mobilize particular "deep-seated cultural psychologies" as though they are timeless properties and thus fundamentally contradistinctive to that of the West. In this generic mapping along the clichéd East–West axis, the intra-Asia cultural variations and historical differ-ences are subsumed under a common Asian culture, as a magnified "national" space *vis-à-vis* the hegemonic West. The articles in that anthology as a whole offer disparate case studies with a mostly textual approach on postwar and contempo-rary films, without systematic historical tracing of the respective melodramatic traditions and their possible interrelations.

At the other end of the spectrum, scholars of revisionist melodrama studies have tried to move beyond generic confines and have ushered in a broader historical and cultural perspective. This scholarship led by Christine Gledhill, Steve Neale, and Linda Williams, just to name a few, has generated inspiring insights and methods for excavating its histories, aesthetics, and ideological and cultural valences. This scholarly trend moves beyond the more psychoanalytically inflected and narrowly periodized "genre" studies centered on the "weepies" or the "woman's film" appealing to female audiences in Hollywood cinema of the 1930s–1940s. Now scholars agree that melodrama's historical formation in theater is far more complex and multifaceted, combining elements of "comedy and tragedy … morality plays, folk-tales and songs … pantomime and vaudeville," and that "the themes and styles of this highly popular theatrical form proved eminently suitable for adaptation to the new cinematic medium" (Mercer and Schingler 2004: 7).

Linda Williams' seminal article "Melodrama Revisited" proposes a radical reorientation in melodrama studies. Boldly moving out of the "basic model" of family melodrama as a classical Hollywood genre marked by excess and ideological contradiction, and "women's film" conceptualized by feminist scholars in the 1970s–1980s (Shartz 1981; Elsaesser 1987; Mercer and Schingler 2004: 12–4), Williams charged the term of the melodramatic mode with new rigor. The article opens with a daring assertion:

> Melodrama is the fundamental mode of popular American motion picture; it is not a specific genre like the western or horror film; it is not a "deviation" of the classical realist narrative … melodrama is a peculiarly democratic and American form that seeks dramatic revelation of moral irrational truths through a dialectic of pathos and action. It is the foundation of the classical Hollywood movie. (L. Williams 1998: 42; see also L. Williams 2001)

In restoring melodrama's centrality in American cinema and the popular democratic imagination of the national culture, Williams not only rectified a traditionally ill-regarded expressive form (or a cluster intermedia form), she also echoed and amplified the key tenets of Christine Gledhill's earlier work on melodrama, in particular the latter's deeply historical and analytical introduction, "The Melodramatic Field: An Investigation," to *Home Is Where the Heart Is*, the pathbreaking anthology she edited and published in 1987. Already there, Gledhill argued that melodrama film is a complex "cultural form" energized by multiple aesthetic resources as well as sociopolitical pressures. Her careful tracing of melodrama's passage from Europe to America, from theater to cinema, intimated a move toward thinking of melodrama not only as trans-generic phenomena but also in translational and transnational terms. In a passage ruminating on melodrama's heterogeneous origins (both classical and popular, in performance and print) and spectatorial appeals founded on aesthetic and institutional intertextuality, Gledhill (1987: 18, 28) reasons: "Based on commerce rather than cultural monopoly, melodrama multiplied through translation, adaptation, and, in the absence of copyright laws, piracy." This insightful observation may be stretched further to account for the transnational or transcultural proliferation and modernization of melodrama, especially in the wake of industrial capitalism and attendant colonial or semicolonial modernity in the era of mechanical reproduction. More than a decade later, Gledhill pushed her original argument beyond the

Euro-American context more explicitly, arguing that "the notion of *modality*, like *register* in socio-linguistics, defines a specific mode of aesthetic articulation adaptable across a range of genres, across decades and *across national cultures*" (Gledhill 2000: 229; added emphasis). This resonates with the analogy drawn by Williams between melodramatic structure and Romantic music (which has been overwhelmingly adapted by the former) (L. Williams 1998: 73). Gledhill's more recent work, in collaboration with Indian scholar Ira Bhaskar, investigates the application of melodrama to Indian cinema, not only in terms of aesthetic practices but also the shifted valence of critical concepts in a cross-cultural context.[1]

These theoretical and methodological developments raise new questions. Williams' project significantly rewrites American film history through an expanded viewfinder, and admirably repositions American cinema as a national cinema tradition produced by the ferment of its struggle for independence from the "Old World," modernity and its continued, tension-ridden quest for national identity based on a highly divisive and multicultural foundation. In declaring that melodrama is the fundamental national form – the expression for democracy and racial equality – however, Williams does not offer further reflections on why and how melodrama has also become a keynote in numerous national or regional cinemas worldwide throughout the twentieth century, especially in the aftermath of momentous historical ruptures such as independence or decolonization movements and revolutions, whose historical geneses, scales, and legacies are often not unrelated or dissimilar to the French Revolution and American Independence. If melodrama is quintessentially "Western" or "American," how might we reconcile the claim that melodrama is fundamentally a cultural form of modernity and different cultures and cinemas may engage in parallel or alternative forms of the melodramatic imagination? The attempts to locate cultural specific-ity of non-Western cinemas have inspired, in the case of Indian cinema, the recuperation of linguistically and religiously heavy-weight categories such as Darsana – a structure of looking or "the power exercised by the authoritative image in Hindu religious culture," whereby "the devotee is permitted to behold the image of the deity" (Rasudevan 2000). Such interventions undermine the overwhelming investment in an Oedipal complex and individualism thought to be at the heart of Euro-American cinema.

A few recent studies concerned with Chinese film melodrama have also directed energy to excavating alternative histories and concepts. Chris Berry and Mary Farquhar draw on its amplified conception and identify a persistent strand of "melodramatic realism" in Chinese-language cinema, in agreement with many Chinese scholars. While a "presentism" is seen pervading most of Chinese melodramatic expressions in cinema, they also note, in light of Jaruslav Prusek's seminal study of the "lyrical and the epic" impulses in modern Chinese literature, that, unlike its Western counterpart, "in China realism and romanticism came hand in hand and were not disassociated until later in the twentieth century" (Berry and Farquhar 2006: 77). This romantic streak, I would add, is distilled from both Chinese traditions of romantic literature and drama (such as *Dream of the Red Chamber* and *Romance of the West Chamber*, favorite subjects of screen adaptation in the late 1920s and onwards) and Western romanticism. Berry and Farquhar single out early films by Fe Mu and the more recent *Yellow Earth* (Chen Kaige, 1984) as pronounced instances of this impulse informed by a reflective and at times nostalgic sentiment. They conclude: "Romanticism and melodrama are intrinsic to realist practices in the broad sweep of the Chinese cinema. Its visual poetry reveals the moral dimensions of the everyday world. The mode favors the dispossessed and was therefore tailor-made for early Chinese reformers who often saw themselves as victims of a modern *and* traditional world order that had to be transformed" (Berry and Farquhar 2006: 82).

Wenyi, a "native" term highlighted by Cai Guorong (quoted in the epigraph above) and indirectly cited by Berry and Farquhar, refers back to the two-pronged Chinese film melodrama tradition – "those works that deal with family relationships and ethics, and those that depict romances" (Law 1997: 15). Two of the earliest feature films, *An Orphan Rescues His Grandpa* (Zheng Zhengqiu, Zhang Shichuan, 1923) and *Sea Oath* (a.k.a. *Swear by God*, Dan Duyu, 1921) are often cited as respective origins of this twin-genealogy. Stephen Teo and Emile Yue-yu Yeh have pursued the wenyi tradition further, arguing for a serious consideration of its historical and analytical salience in Chinese-language cinema. Teo (2006) observes that the wenyi genre – "an enigmatic nomenclature" – encompasses "a broad spectrum of melodrama including the romantic film or love story, the 'woman's picture' or the literary adaptation"; yet he anchors its maturation and proliferation in the postwar period, particularly the suffering heroine-centered and emotion- (or "sentimentality-") infused melodrama made in Hong Kong. Yeh (2009: 443) advocates a more ambitious agenda of uncovering wenyi's conceptual and historiographic distinctiveness, "bypassing translation and making Chinese terms keywords" in order to trace an alternative melodramatic tradition and non-Western theory. She rightly locates the term's provenance in the 1910s–1920s when it was first "translated" from Japanese into modern Chinese vernacular and literary criticism, especially with reference to literature and drama translated or adapted from foreign sources. This trend of the domestication of foreign literature quickly extended to other modern arts including cinema, especially as the Chinese film industry and narrative cinema were fast emerging and thirsty for inspirations in both content and form.

Yeh's revisit to the historical origins of wenyi is highly valuable, but, like Teo and others, she does not pause and go deeper into the cultural ecology of an emergent narrative cinema, melodrama in particular, in the context of a widespread, energetic project of cinematic translation in the 1920s. Yet her observations on the prominence of an ethical humanism and progressive attributes found in Chinese wenyi films in the 1930s and onwards (a film cited by all critics above is Fei Mu's *Spring in a Small Town* of 1947), I think, can benefit from a more sustained "archaeology" of the formative years when the twin-genealogy of wenyi started to take root. In the following I will delve into its rich ferment in that period by way of an intertextual analysis of a few films (or their textual residues if there is no known extant copy) by Hou Yao, a pioneering Chinese filmmaker and critic of the 1920s. His newly resurfaced film, *Poet from the Sea*, along with his other works, sheds important light on the complex origins of the wenyi film or Chinese melodrama, especially with regard to the cultivation of the narrative structure of loss and recovery, and with an orphan character as a point of departure, that has proven to be a protean melodramatic form in Chinese film history. I will then briefly contrast the strand of "artistic" wenyi film centered on romantic love as represented by Hou's work with early "family ethics" melodrama films geared more ostensibly toward kinship and communal sentiments, plebian tastes and market demands.

Lost and Found: Hou Yao and Shanghai Cinema

Hou Yao (1903–42?) is one of the early Chinese filmmakers whose extant work – on film and in print – is of critical importance for reconstructing and rewriting early Chinese cinema centered in Shanghai. Given the extreme paucity of extant films of the formative period of narrative and genre cinema in the 1920s, *A String of Pearls* (Li Zeyuan, 1926) scripted by Hou Yao and *Romance of the West Chamber* (Hou Yao, 1927), both of which resurfaced in the 1990s on the eve of cinema's centenary, have significantly amplified our knowledge of Shanghai cinema and its relation to a broad vernacularizing trend and urban modernity. Hou Yao's book *Techniques of Writing Shadowplay Scripts* (1925) was among the earliest theoretical expositions on the ontology and function of cinema as well as a practical handbook that addressed and impacted on the institutionalization of screenwriting. One of the few writer-directors who first adopted a full-fledged film script at the time, Hou contributed to this new literary practice of scriptwriting by including in the book's appendix his script for *Divorcee* (Li Zeyuan, Hou Yao, 1924) as an "exemplary" screenwriting (Z. Zhang 2005: 151–98). His career in film was cut short when he was killed by the Japanese in Singapore, where he had moved in 1940 to work for the Shaws. Before that, he spent a seven-year sojourn in Hong Kong, during which he also wrote and directed several "national defense" films (Y. Wu et al. 1999: 733).

   Poet from the Sea, which I recently located in a European archive,[2] has affinities with Hou Yao's other films of the same period, yet contains some different orientations and unique clues to his authorship in particular and the formation of a certain strand of romantic melodrama or a proto- "art cinema" in general. Despite their seeming differences in setting, period, and cinematic mode and style, with one morality tale set in an emerging metropolis and the other a costume drama with origins in dynastic China, *A String of Pearls* and *Romance of the Western Chamber* are both literary adaptations from diverse sources (Maupassant and Tang *chuanqi*-Yuan drama, respectively). As such they illustrate the rich reservoir of vernacular modernism mobilized and embodied by early Shanghai cinema (Hansen 2000; Z. Zhang 2005: 1–88, 345–50). Through his innovative "translation" of both Chinese and Western sources in drama and literature, as well as the blending of film genre elements across realism, melodrama, comedy, and the martial arts, Hou Yao experimented with film as a new art form built on other sister arts, with the aspiration to create a socially engaging and formally rigorous cinema, beyond the prevalent commercial model exemplified by major studios such as Tianyi and Mingxing.

Poet from the Sea, which stars none other than Hou Yao himself, is a "pure" film in the sense that it is not an adaptation and showcases an elaborate cinematography and a keen aesthetic investment in film form (including the tinted "color" palette). The central motifs of free love across class barriers and the city–rural contrast were to have lasting repercussions in Chinese melodrama. The hyperbolic poetic gestures, physicality of the rugged seaside setting (or at the "end of the world" [*haijiao*], as the Chinese title suggests), and mostly histrionic rather than realist performance style in *Poet from the Sea* render the film a more salient vehicle for the "melodramatic imagination" geared toward a compounded formalism and emotionalism (Brooks 1976). This sets the film apart from other melodramatic variants in early Shanghai cinema, particularly the popular middlebrow family–ethical melodrama of Zheng Zhengqiu, which is heavily indebted to the "civilized play" (*wenmingxi*) and Mandarin Ducks and Butterflies popular fiction, often involving multiple generations and more extended episodic structure with ample twists and turns. The premise of *Poet from the Sea* is not traditional kinship and family sentiment in upheaval but the viability of a modern (male) individual's burning passion in love and creativity. In that it is quite different from Hou Yao's *A String of Pearls*, which is about an upper-middle-class nuclear family's unraveling and recuperation in the modern city replete with consumer desire and its perils. The two films, however, do share the metanarrative device of "lost and found" – be it a commodity, a love object, or sensory capacity (i.e., eyesight) – and the quest for moral redemption as well as physical and affective restoration.

After writing several "social problem" films including *A String of Pearls* for the Changcheng (Great Wall) Studio – a small company founded by some returning overseas students dedicated to making socially engaged films with high artistic standards – Hou Yao moved to Li Minwei's Minxin (Sun Motion Pictures), lately relocated to Shanghai from Guangzhou.[3] Apparently, Minxin, led by the equally if not more idealistic and artistically inclined Li Minwei (praised as the "father of Hong Kong cinema"), gave Hou Yao much creative freedom, as evidenced in the overflowing romanticism and subjective stylization in *Poet from the Sea*, in contrast to the social realist and didactic tendencies in his earlier films. The film features beautiful location shooting in Hong Kong, where Li Minwei took Hou Yao to direct this film and *A Reviving Rose* (1927) with a similar wenyi bent, complete with star-crossed lovers – who happen to be artists journeying back and forth between

Shanghai and Hong Kong, as well as a suicide attempt at the seaside and scenarios of rescue (Q. Feng 2009: 109–10).[4]

The narrative of *Poet from the Sea* is more skeletal or broad-stroked, punctuated by the poet's (apparently Hou Yao's own) lyrical writing. The original synopsis describes the protagonist (or the filmmaker's alter ego) this way (Zheng and Liu 1996: 1200):

> Young poet Meng Yi-ping, who lost his parents when he was a small child, is eccentric and arrogant. Unable to put up with the corruption- and hypocrisy-infused society, he decided to come to this desolate island where he can, in solitude, appreciate nature's beauty. ... Amidst the thick autumnal foliage, there is a pretty woodcutting girl named Liu Cui-ying. ... (Her father died long ago. Her mother Mrs. Yang is raising her and her brother Liu Yong through farming.) Thus at this serene end of the world, we find this couple of naïve lovers with a pure heart.

While harking back to the theme of free love, as opposed to arranged marriage and filial obligations, which Hou explored as a scriptwriter in *Between Love and Filial Duty* (Li Zeyuan, Mei Xuechou, 1925) and as co-director in *Cupid's Puppets* (Mei Xuechou, Hou Yao, 1925), both made for the Changcheng Studio,[5] *Poet from the Sea* shifts focus from women protagonists seeking socioeconomic independence and emotional fulfillment and a more pronounced female perspective, to the problem of male desire or an intellectual's troubled subjectivity on the margins of society. This shift is also evident in *A Reviving Rose*, which Hou directed and wrote, and *Romance of the West Chamber* made in the same year. More visibly, the male protagonist is an artist (poet, painter, or scholar) who finds himself estranged to varying degrees from the mainstream society but falling for a maiden who rekindles his creative and erotic flames. Predictably, his object of love or source of redemption is often taken away from him only to be restored to him more or less intact. *Romance of the West Chamber* also allowed Hou Yao to experiment with premodern material and genre film that were gaining currency in the second half of the 1920s, thanks in part also to the pressure of a fiercely competitive film industry (Harris 1999).

The predecessor of *Poet from the Sea* and the new string of male artist-centered *wenyi* films is obviously Dan Duyu's (1897–1972) *Sea Oath*. We know very little about this and other films by Dan. The film's brief synopsis suggests a story involving a farmer's girl and an artist whose mutual love is thwarted by the temptation of wealth on the girl's part. Out of guilt and regret, she throws herself into the ocean but is rescued in time by the artist. Though inheriting the setting of a turbulent ocean, *Poet from the Sea* differs from Dan's film by locating the source of corruption elsewhere, in the city and embodied by an upper-class girl's snobbery and greed, though the immediate physical threat to his desire and love interest comes from a local tyrant. More than ever, pristine nature and the country maiden seem to be at stake in the face of the complicit corrosive forces of feudalism and urban modernity.

Figure 2.1   Li Dandan and Lin Chuchu in Minxin's *Mulan Joins the Army* (dir. Hou Yao, Minxin Film, 1928), a popular tale of a cross-dressing female warrior.

The film's feverish romanticism can be glimpsed from the extant footage, which contains the beginning and the ending by the sea, in addition to several crucial scenes in the middle of the film that take place in the island village where Meng Yiping takes up residence in self-exile. None of the scenes set in Shanghai appears in the fragmented print, which was likely brought to Europe by Li Yinsheng, co-owner of Minxin and father of Li Dandan (1912–98) (see Figure 2.1) featured in *Poet from the Sea* (as Cuiying) and other Minxin productions, including *Romance* (as Hongniang the maid) (Q. Feng 2009: 202).[6] The film is replete with point-of-view shots of the poet and his rival (the landlord), coupled and amplified by the consistent use of iris shots of Cuiying. After the poet loses his mind as well as sight in the aftermath of Cuiying's kidnap by the landlord and disappearance (she jumped into the ocean, recalling the heroine's similar act in *Sea Oath*), the point-of-view shots are ingeniously replaced with "point-of-auditing" shots signifying not so much the physical act of listening or hearing as the transcendent force of romantic love projected by the poet's mind. Combinations of a static camera and straight-on positions, extreme long shots of the expansive sea and other nature scenes, and close-ups of faces give the film a highly painterly and contemplative quality. The contrast between an idyllic countryside (under immediate danger of a personified

local evil and more abstract outside forces) and the city of greed and moral
degradation (Shanghai), along with the stark contrast between the purity of a
country girl and a fashionable bad (or enigmatic) modern city girl, were to become
stock melodramatic motifs in Shanghai cinema in the ensuing two decades.[7]

The exaltation of a lyrical modernist subjectivity and art cinema (or wenyi style)
in *Poet from the Sea* echoes other contemporary voices, in particular Tian Han
(1898–1968) and Yu Dafu (both were exposed to aesthetic modernism and the
"pure cinema" movement and joined the Creation Society while studying in Japan).
They were influenced by Freudian psychoanalytic theory, in particular notions of
the neurotic modern subject (or "civilization and its discontents"), sexual repression, and artistic creation as a form of "daydream" – not so much as escape but as
individual and collective therapy. While convinced by the cinema's democratic
appeal to the urban dwellers (including "the proletariat" or *wuchanzhe*), Yu Dafu
cautioned against "the flourishing of the corrupting force of popular taste." He
offers a prescription "for redirecting this taste and gradually raising the level of the
taste of ordinary people in society, we have to resort to wenyi." He concludes,
"cinema and wenyi are like husband and wife, who are very close, always inseparable
and interact often, in order to have a satisfying relationship" (D. Yu 1927).

Tian Han is heavily indebted to Junichiro Tanizaki, a prominent Japanese
modernist novelist and cineaste. He followed Tanizaki's suit and proclaimed
"cinema is the mechanic dream of humanity and, together with wine and music, is
the most outstanding human creation" (Tian 1927). Vehemently opposed to what
he and other writers of the new literary movement saw as the vulgarization of the
medium in the wenmingxi-derived Chinese cinema at the time, Tian Han applied
Tanizaki's cinematic aesthetic to his own screenwriting. *Spring Dream at Lakeside*
(Bu Wancang, 1927) was his renewed effort at filmmaking after previous failures
with *Going to the People* (Tian Han, 1926) and *Lingering Sound of the Broken Flute*
(Tian Han, 1927). As an ostensible art film, *Spring Dream* is quite unique in Chinese
film history. Based on extant written sources, its modernist reverie made up of
dream logic and sadomasochistic pleasure is unlike anything in Shanghai cinema of
the 1920s–1930s. A playwright goes to the West Lake in search of repose and inspiration, but finds himself fatally attracted to an icy beauty with an edgy sex appetite
(Z. Zhang 2005). If Tian Han's "silver dream" about a male intellectual's ambivalent desire for the modern girl is couched in a highly coded modernist language,
Hou Yao's *Poet from the Sea* offers in comparison a much milder formula for a kind
of art-pop melodramatic imagination. On the one hand, it seems to tread in the
footsteps of the "going to the people" folklore movement that also inspired
Tian Han's earlier films (C. Hung 1985). On the other hand, in retooling the
"beauty-meets-scholar" cliché across popular literature and commercial cinema, it
brings the artist's lofty dream down to the earthy environ of an island community.
Yet this is done at the expense of rejecting the city and the modern girl altogether.

The general turning away from a preoccupation with women's social
problems – work, marriage, remarriage, economic independence, and political

representation – is not unrelated to the waning of the May Fourth cultural movement in the mid-1920s. Enlightenment and modernity turned out to be a far more complicated affair than the "liberation of humanity" (*ren de jiefang*) from feudal shackles, and the promise of the New Woman as its symbolic pet project is compromised by the tenaciousness of a deep-seated patriarchal culture on one hand and the grotesque excess of capitalist and semicolonial modernity on the other. Literary historians view this period as a major watershed when the movement fragmented into divergent ideological and aesthetic positions and groups, giving rise to the so-called North–South divide and a *"Haipai* literature" centered in Shanghai (1925–49). The figure of the anguished (*kumeng*), lost (*panghuang*), and lonely (*jimo*) intellectual in search of a way out of the cultural and political impasse was to be found in the works of many writers of the day, including Lu Xun, Mao Dun, and Yu Dafu. Yu left the Creation Society while its other core members Guo Moruo and Cheng Fangwu abandoned its "art for art's sake" pursuit and embraced Marxism (D. Xu 1999: 72–3). Tian Han, also a member since his time in Japan, "converted" shortly after, by famously renouncing his "silver dreams."

Hou Yao was one of the few early cinema personalities who actually had a direct tie to the May Fourth movement proper. A member of the Literary Association (*Wenxue yanjiuhui*), and deeply influenced by Ibsen and his "theater of humanism," Hou perhaps found himself also at a "crossroads" as described by Mao Dun (a founding member of the society), when the "new tides" (the name of the society's journal, *Xinchao*) of the new culture movement "abated" (*luochao*). *Poet from the Sea* and Hou's other films of the second half of the 1920s demonstrate an effort to reconcile "life" and "art" through the unique medium of cinema rather than privileging one category over another, which momentarily aligned his cinematic aesthetic with that of Tian Han and Yu Dafu. In light of this context, *Poet from the Sea* stands as a testimony to the cultural and ideological transition that affected both the literary and film scenes, and a lament for the incomplete project of the May Fourth enlightenment aimed at ushering in "Mr. Science" and "Mr. Democracy" on to the Chinese stage.

Yet, despite the crushing despair shrouding most of the film, *Poet from the Sea* ends with the winning recipe of "lost and found," culminating in reunion and recovery, which was much favored by the cinematic storytellers of the era even when their narrative methods and aesthetic outlooks diverged considerably. Cuiying and Meng Yiping are duly rescued one after another by the lighthouse watchman; and Meng's vision is miraculously restored when the girl softly speaks to him and touches him. The film ends with the couple standing on the balcony of the lighthouse, looking into the horizon in pre-dawn (blue-tinted) light. The lighthouse is obviously the beacon of illumination in darkness, and the little isle on which it stands seems to be the last refuge for the poet. Even the village on the island is hardly a sanctuary and not immune to the encroachment of urban vileness embodied by the modern girl. Yet this further retreat from modern civilization to the isle at the "end of the world" is presented less as a defeat than as an awakening of the true spirit of Enlightenment, however distant it remains on the horizon. While the kind-hearted old man remains the abstracted figure of the nameless "people," it is notable that the trope of "going to the people" is here rewritten as "saved by the people." The old man is the guardian of the lighthouse as well as a surrogate father who safeguards the fragile love of a young couple – one is an orphan and the other fatherless. The social viability of this unconventional family or fledgling community, however, remains to be tested.

In spite of or because of the film's singular "highbrow" tendency, its vernacular grounding and stylistic excess could be instructive to our understanding of the translation of the "melodramatic imagination" stemmed from European drama and literature in the wake of the French Revolution and capitalist modernity, followed by early Hollywood narrative cinema's entry into the Shanghai cinema vernacular, particularly the wenyi film. Elsewhere I discussed Hou Yao's *A String of Pearls* as a domestic melodrama gravitating toward narrative interiority and character psychology in delineating the emerging neurosis of the urban middle class and nuclear family in Shanghai (Z. Zhang 2005: 169–98), in contrast to the "other melodramas" that delighted in adventurous play, action in physical landscape, and a narrative temporality and "view aesthetic" carried over from the "cinema of attractions" (Gunning 1989; Singer 1990; Neale 1993). While consistent with the denunciation of consumerism in the earlier film, Hou's elaborate cinema-tography and continuity editing, theatrical frontality, hyperbolic narrative (chance, last-minute rescue), emotional swings (astonishment), and excessively coded mise-en-scène (e.g., the literally "fledgling" lighthouse) in *Poet from the Sea* offer an intriguing blend of the two kinds of melodrama, a simultaneous probing of interiority and exteriority, psychology and affect. The assessment of Hou's work in that period by Pan Chuitong, a contemporary critic, attests to this mixed mode. Pan commented favorably on a number of Hou's films whether as writer or director, singling out in particular *Poet from the Sea* for its spectacular scenes of the seaside landscape. "The exterior scenes in *Poet from the Sea* include hanging cliffs, beaches, and waves. Only such expansive views can help people forget numerous troubles in life" (C. Pan 1927).[8] At the same time, Pan praised Hou's contribution to a "literary" or "writerly" cinema (*wenxue de tushang*), particularly through his elaborate narrative (*juqing*) and intertitle (*zimu*) compositions.

Griffith Fever and Vernacular Melodrama

Why did the second half of the 1920s provide such fertile ground for Chinese wenyi film to blossom and diversify? The ebb and flow of the late Qing reform, the Republican Revolution, and the May Fourth movement – the social, political, and libidinal energies as well as violence or trauma they produced – provided internal resources and imperatives for multifaceted expressions of passion and regret (X. Tang 2000: 11–48). The formation of a nascent and highly competitive film industry provided necessary infrastructure for the production and distribution of a domestic narrative cinema appealing to a widening audience in China and the diaspora. Another crucial catalyst for the quick growth of Chinese melodrama film was the popularity of a variety of early American melodramas with varying subjects and styles. They often share an aesthetics comprised of action, spectacle, and externalized emotions borrowed from the stage. D. W. Griffith's films are often considered emblematic of this cinematic form in American cinema's transformation toward standardization and institutionalization. It is worth noting that many of his films were exhibited in Shanghai and widely admired by Chinese filmmakers and audiences alike. Zheng Junli (1911–69) reported in *A Brief History of Chinese Cinema* (1936) that in spring 1924 there was a Griffith fever in Shanghai following the success of Griffith's *Way Down East* (1920) and the ensuing re-exhibition of his earlier films including *The Birth of a Nation* (1915), *Intolerance* (1916), *Broken Blossoms* (1919), and *Orphans of the Storm* (1921).[9] Scholar Chen Jianhua (2009: 237–86) recently challenged Zheng's account by consulting print sources such as newspaper advertisements, establishing the first screening of *Way Down East* in Shanghai in May 1922, followed by nearly ten other Griffith films between then and spring 1924. This retracing of Griffith's reception in China is instructive for understanding what Chen describes as the "historical discursive environment" that spurred the emergence of Chinese domestic cinema, in which Griffith, the alleged father of American cinema, especially melodrama, functioned as a "nodal point" in a web of sentiments, debates, and film practices informed by "nationalism and cosmopolitanism, race and gender, visual culture and literature" (J. Chen 2009: 250–1).

This Griffith fever, compounded by the great popularity of the Mandarin Ducks and Butterflies literature and its screen adaptations by writers such as Bao Tianxiao (1876–1973), Zhou Shoujuan (1894–1968), and Zhu Shouju, spurred the proliferation of a variety of "love films" (*aiqing pian*) in Shanghai; by 1926 the number of films in this "genre" took up more than half of the total output, though almost all of these have been lost or are yet to be found (Li and Hu 1997: 148). Leading filmmakers of this "genre" include Bu Wangcang (1903–74), Zhang Shichuan (1889–1953), Hou Yao, Ouyang Yuqian (1889–1962), Hong Shen (1894–1955), Shi Dongshan (1902–55), Ren Pengnian (1894–1968), Xu Hu, Lu Jie (1894–1967), and Chen Tian. If Griffith drew on the ambivalent legacy of the French Revolution and European Enlightenment to address postbellum American society's sociocultural upheavals in nation building and industrialization, the Shanghai filmmakers further translated and adapted these Euro-American sources along with Chinese literary and theatrical traditions in the contradiction-ridden context of the Chinese new culture movement and Shanghai's semicolonial modernity.

This broad transnational "melodramatic imagination" amplified by the Griffith fever thus appealed to writers and filmmakers across a wide political and aesthetic spectrum. While less sympathetic with domestic commercial cinema, Tian Han openly expressed his admiration for Griffith and his "literary" approaches toward developing a cinematic language, such as "close-up," "fade-in," and "fade-out" (J. Chen 2009: 253). Griffith's films raised the bar for filmmaking as a distinctive storytelling form on a par with or even exceeding the older sister arts. The introduction of Griffith and its surrounding media hype also galvanized a budding Chinese narrative cinema that was gaining visibility and positive reception after the success of *An Orphan Rescues His Grandpa*, the first "long serious drama" (*changpian zhengju*), and other ensuing productions from Mingxing, Changcheng, Shenzhou, and Minxin. Comparisons between Griffith and Zheng Zhengqiu, the "father of Chinese cinema," by critics then and now are legion, largely because of their shared interest in social and ethical issues or crises in the advent of modernity, as well as the desire to appeal to a wide audience through elaborate yet intelligible storytelling.

The synergy between the Griffith fever and a nascent domestic film industry, however, produced more varied experiments in melodramatic narration that cannot be subsumed by the "love film" represented by *Way Down West*. Indeed, it was precisely the wide spectrum of Griffith's melodrama that excited the Chinese filmmakers and critics, who in turn found in old and new vernacular resources the inexhaustible possibilities for cinematic storytelling. While some directly transplanted Griffith's signature elements, especially the hero-rescues-beauty sequence and the requisite parallel editing building toward a climax, others filtered the narrative techniques and were more concerned with ethical dimensions of melodrama. The former is evident in *An Orphan* (Zhang Huimin, 1929), which grafts the title of Griffith's *Orphans of the Storm* about a pair of orphan sisters' fates during the French Revolution onto a Sinicized version of *Way Down East*. Interestingly, while the rescue in the snowstorm sequence is strikingly similar to that in *Way Down East*, the rest of the film is preoccupied with enacting the oppression of woman – an orphan too "weak to defend herself" – in a transitional society riddled with contradictory forces. Despite the ultra-modern look of the hero (who rescues Chunmei from a suicide attempt on the rail-tracks, takes her into his home as a maid, and then develops love interest in her), the story, as a Chinese critic aptly observes, is premised on entrenched patriarchal views of women as dependent, passive-aggressive (embodied by the evil concubine of Yang's father and sister), and sources of disharmony or trouble (Z. Xu 2010). However, the last protracted post-snowstorm act involving captivity in the local thugs' den – complete with secret trapdoors and poisonous lizards – resonates with the Huaju Studio's style accentuated by adventure, action, and a narrative temporality of the "other melodrama," while also joining the emerging trend of martial arts–magic spirit film, such as *Red Heroine* (Wen Yimin, 1929), also starring Wu Suxin (1905–?), of the same year.[10]

If the struggle between old (and bad) family values and new romantic love in a "love film" like *An Orphan* seemed contrived, carrying obvious traces of translation, a different strand of melodrama delved into the complex social and affective dynamic of the Chinese family. Spearheaded by *An Orphan Rescues His Grandpa*, a stream of family-melodrama films depicted the deep bonds of extended family broken by modernity and capitalism, often anchoring the locus of innocence-wronged and pathos in either the orphan (*gu'er*) or quasi-orphan and the widowed mother (*guamu*). This narrative template is also evident in *Abandoned One* (Dan Duyu, 1923) (Zheng and Liu 1996: 45), made in the same year as the Mingxing blockbuster, and followed by *The Poor Children* (Zhang Shichuan, 1924), *A Blind Orphan Girl* (Zhang Shichuan, 1925), which foreshadowed the sight-regained theme in *Poet from the Sea*, *A Little Friend* (Zhang Shichuan, 1925), *The Student's Hard Life* (Guan Haifeng, 1925), and *Who's His Mother?* (Gu Wuwei, 1925). This stream thinned considerably in 1926, yet the extant *Mother's Happiness* (Shi Dongshan, 1926) visibly shifted the focus on the orphan child to a widowed mother, whose love and sacrifice go unappreciated by her ungrateful children. The languid narrative rhythm and metaphoric mise-en-scène with vernacularized allusions to classical poetry (e.g., a broken pottery pot, emptied-out home, fallen leaves) yield a maternal drama as an allegory for the birthing pain of a new social order. A decade later, Zhu Shilin (1899–1967) remade the film into a talkie, *Song for a Mother* (1937),[11] starring none other than Lin Chuchu (1904–79), the real-life "good wife and mother," as Li Minwei's domestic and professional partner and the mother of their several children, including the child star Li Keng (1928–65). The same story was given a new interpretation by *A Mother Remembers* (Chun Kim, 1953), a Cantonese melodrama set in postwar Hong Kong, demonstrating the enduring appeal of maternal love as the linchpin of fragmented kinship and community in times of sociopolitical chaos and moral confusion. Films about maternal love thus continued to rival those more ostensibly centered on heterosexual romantic love, creating two parallel and sometimes intertwining strands of melodrama that appealed to generations of Chinese audiences.

Conclusion

While I agree with the general tenor of the observations made in recent studies on Chinese melodrama, I would like to point out that they are largely based on films made after the mid-1930s, when the project of nation building was faced with a more tangible and formidable threat in the wake of the Japanese invasion of Manchuria and the bombing of Shanghai, which inflamed a more concerted nationalist fervor in Chinese film culture. The social, cultural, and moral landscape of the 1920s has in my view a more experimental and plural nature for a society undergoing seismic transitions, and its imprint on the emerging narrative cinema and its diversification is also a less belabored field in large part due to the absence of extant films and related materials. Hou Yao's extant films (and writings), including the fragmented *Poet from the Sea*, provide precious glimpses into this formative period of Chinese cinema and modern visual culture. The narrative elements and cinematic registers in this early example of "love film" in a somewhat high key give important clues to early Chinese filmmakers' exploration of a more expressive – and in some ways more "excessive" – melodramatic form that diverted from other contemporary practices. In addition to the films of the 1930s–1940s, in particular those by Sun Yu (1900–90) and Fei Mu (1906–51) mentioned above that seem to have carried on such wenyi impulses in varying ways, we might also contemplate a longer genealogy of this lyrical art-pop melodrama that would include post-1949 Chinese-language cinema in its new configurations up to the present, including Wong Kai-Wai (Wang Jiawei, b. 1958) and Lou Ye (b. 1965). At the same time, the thicker branch of the family-ethics drama that paralleled and often crisscrossed the love-film branch has demonstrated an equal if not more exuberant vitality, and has found its way into all manner of melodramatic expression – critical realist, socialist realist, healthy realist, and modernist or postmodernist – in Chinese-language cinema, including films by contemporary diasporic filmmakers such as Ang Lee and Tsai Ming-liang, as well as highly popular television drama series. My attempt in this chapter to retrace the convoluted origins and vectors of Chinese melodrama – both as practice and discourse – is hardly for the purpose of constructing a seamless history of genre or subgenres on an evolutionist axis for purely formal reasons, but rather for understanding and conceptualizing anew the unevenness and complexity of Chinese melodrama and, perhaps more importantly, the transformations of "structures of feeling" in modern Chinese culture enabled by cinema and related expressive forms.

Notes

1 Panel presentation, Society for Cinema and Media Studies annual meeting, Chicago, March, 2009; lecture at New York University, March 5, 2010.
2 Unknown to Chinese film scholars and archivists, substantial fragments of a print of the film have been in the collection of the Swiss cinémathèque in Lausanne. The fragments were preserved by Cineteca di Bologna in 1996. With my assistance, the film was shown at the Hong Kong Film Archive in conjunction with the conference "Early Chinese Cinema Revisited" in December 2009, and was again shown at the Orphan Film Symposium in New York, in April 2010.
3 Another part of Minxin headed by Li Beihai (1889–1950) eventually moved back to Hong Kong in 1928 (B. Zhong 2004: 60–3).
4 Li Minwei played the male lead in *A Reviving Rose*, opposite his wife Lin Chuchu, who also played the "bad" city girl in *Poet from the Sea*.
5 The latter was written by Hou Yao's wife, Pu Shunqing, "China's first woman scriptwriter" (Li and Hu 1997: 143). Pu also played an important role (Cailan) in *Divorcee* written by Hou Yao.

6   Li Dandan's real name is Li Xiaqing. She left Shanghai in 1928 to study in England. She returned to Shanghai in 1936 as an accomplished aviator, the first Chinese woman to fly an airplane. According to Feng Qun (2009), Li Yingsheng went to Europe to promote her films, which were well received in London, Paris, Geneva, and Berlin. This may explain why the extant film and two other Minxin films (*A String of Pearls* and *Romance of the West Chamber*) were found in European archives.

7   For example, *Wide Flower* (Sun Yu, 1930), *Two Stars* (Shi Dongshan, 1931), *Wide Rose* (Sun Yu, 1931), *The Blood of Passion on the Volcano* (Sun Yu, 1932), *Pink Dream* (Cai Chusheng, 1932), *Daybreak* (Sun Yu, 1933), and *Boatman's Daughter* (Shen Xiling, 1935).

8   I am grateful to Ain-ling Wong for providing this source.

9   The films were widely known by their Chinese titles and reviewed in film-related publications: *Way Down East* (*Laihun*); *Orphans of the Storm* (*Luanshi guchu*); *Birth of A Nation* (*Chongjian Guangming*), *Broken Blossoms* (*Canhua lei*), and *Intolerance* (*Zhuanzhi du*); see J. Zheng (1936: 38–9).

10 On the kinship between Huaju's modern-style action film and the martial-art film, see Z. Zhang (2005: 199–243). Wu Suxin, Zhang Huimin's partner in love and business, played not only the female lead in Huaju productions, she was also credited as the assistant director for *An Orphan*.

11 The source material is allegedly (A. Wong 2008: 309) an American silent film, *Over the Hill to the Poorhouse* (Harry Millarde, 1920). For a perceptive reading of Zhu's film in particular and the ethic/aesthetics of his work as a whole, see D. Li (2006: 79–90).

3

Artists, Cadres, and Audiences
Chinese Socialist Cinema, 1949–1978

Paul Clark

By the time the last of the privately owned Shanghai studios were nationalized in 1953, films had assumed a prominence in Chinese cultural life and politics that was to continue into the 1980s. The Communist Party saw films as the most effective way to create a new, mass culture and reach the widest possible audience with new messages about socialist construction. The nature of the film medium, however, meant that production of this important art remained in the hands of artists who had emerged in a somewhat different film world, particularly pre-1949 Shanghai. Many of these artists found the adjustments required to serve the new expectations placed in film difficult. A new corps of filmmakers, trained in a new school, would provide more reliable artists for the national film project. Audiences expanded rapidly in the 1950s and 1960s. The films they watched included both Chinese and foreign productions, particularly from the Soviet Union. "Socialist realism" in the latter films was soon replaced in Chinese productions by a somewhat looser rubric, coined by Mao Zedong himself. The "combination of revolutionary realism and revolutionary romanticism" allowed more scope for artists and cadres to draw upon China's historical and aesthetic heritages. By the start of the 1970s, these tendencies reached their apogee in the film versions of the "model performances" at the heart of the Cultural Revolution (1966–76). Audiences continued to find what stimulation they could in these and other films. Out of a combination of pleasure at the images of socialist heroes of this era and pain at the limited choices available, a new view of film emerged in the eyes of a generation forged in the Cultural Revolution, who went on to reinvent postsocialist Chinese cinema in the 1980s.

A Companion to Chinese Cinema, First Edition. Edited by Yingjin Zhang.
© 2012 Blackwell Publishing Ltd. Published 2012 by Blackwell Publishing Ltd.

Continuity and Change: Crossing the 1949 Divide

The establishment of the People's Republic of China on October 1, 1949 marked the most important political shift in China since the fall of the imperial dynasty in 1911 and the setting up of a republic. An ostensibly democratic government was replaced in 1949 by one run by a communist party apparently in close alliance with Moscow. The Cold War became chillier as the world adjusted to the new outpost of the Soviet Union. In China itself, citizens also needed to adjust their behavior to accommodate a new regime with apparently greater ability to influence all segments of society throughout the nation. After years of war against Japan and civil war, 1949 brought the promise of stability and new beginnings.

For the film enterprise the turning point of 1949 meant change as well as continuity. Many artists and others who had been active in the Shanghai film industry in the 1940s had been highly sympathetic to the social reformist policies associated with the Chinese Communist Party (CCP) during the war with Japan (1937–45). When Chinese-controlled production in Shanghai had resumed after 1945, many of the new films expressed progressive political ideas about social equality and the scourge of postwar corruption. Such leftist Shanghai filmmakers fought in the second half of the 1940s a running battle against Nationalist (Guomindang/KMT) government censorship and against less enlightened studio owners. Now in 1949 the triumph of the Communists promised a release from such underground agitation. Now progressive ideas about Chinese society and national unity could be properly aired on screen. Many prominent filmmakers expressed enthusiasm for the new regime and the opportunities it appeared to offer.

The new government in turn approached the film enterprise with some care. Cinema screens did not suddenly go blank as old films were banned and new films were not yet available. New censorship regulations were promulgated calling on filmmakers to avoid pornography, vulgarity, and reactionary political content, among other shortcomings. But many of the privately owned studios in Shanghai were allowed to continue production and distribution within the new guidelines. The Communist Party knew from experience that self-censorship by the filmmakers themselves was a more effective tool than blunt interference. Only in 1953 were all private film production companies taken over by the state-run studio in Shanghai. For the first three years of the Communist regime, therefore, filmgoers could watch both state-made and privately produced works. This ensured that silver screens across the nation continued to offer entertainment or enlightenment to audiences.

For filmmakers 1949 proved also to be less of a break than some had assumed as Communist victory loomed that year. Given the special skills the medium required, the new regime had no choice but to depend on the existing corps of artists and technicians. This was true in Shanghai and also in Changchun in the Northeast.

There the formerly Japanese-run Manchukuo film studio had been taken over in 1946 by the CCP as it consolidated its control over the former Japanese colony. The studio was initially moved to the far northern border of China close to the USSR, but it soon moved back to the old premises in Changchun. As in Shanghai, the studio personnel stayed on. In Changchun the employees included some Japanese technical specialists who wanted to contribute to the new, Communist-run film enterprise. In all Chinese studios the most prominent directors, writers, cinematographers, and other artists in the 1950s through to the 1970s and even later had started their film careers before 1949. These included older-generation filmmakers such as director Wu Yonggang (1907–83), writer-director Cai Chusheng (1906–68), and cinematographer Qian Jiang (b. 1919), and those, like Xie Jin (1923–2008), who had started in the industry in postwar Shanghai and remained active for over half a century after 1949.

New Rules and Directions

The new regime brought new notions of the role of literature and art in society. These views had been set out in 1942, during the war against Japan, in the remote Communist Party headquarters in Yan'an, Northwest China. Speaking at the Yan'an Forum on Literature and Art, party chairman Mao Zedong had announced a reorientation of cultural activity to serve principally a new audience. Mao's audience in Yan'an included well-known writers who had shown their commitment to the Communist cause by undertaking the wartime journey to the remote town. But Mao exhorted them to go further in transforming their attitudes and thence their art. All literature and art, Mao argued, should both entertain and uplift its audience and they should serve the masses. In blunt language and drawing upon a version of his own experience, Mao urged writers to bring their thinking closer to that of ordinary folk, by leaving their ivory towers and artist's garrets to join regular people. But Mao's innovative call to rethink the relationship between writers and their audiences was tempered by an authoritarian thrust that limited potential diversity in cultural production (McDougall and Louie 1997: 194–6).

How Mao's emphasis on a reevaluation of folk traditions would sit with such a modern medium as film was quite unclear in the 1942 Talks and in 1949. Indeed, Mao makes no reference to films in his Yan'an Talks. Despite being a self-conscious attempt to produce new policy for his anticipated national regime, Mao's directives in Yan'an drew heavily on historical notions in China of the proper function of cultural production. Cultivation of higher thoughts and enhancement of social engagement were powerful expectations placed on writing and art since ancient times. Mao himself was an accomplished writer of classical-style poetry who found new-fangled, modern poetry definitely not to his taste (McDougall and Louie 1997: 195). He also liked to watch Chinese opera, encouraging in Yan'an the production of politically corrected traditional drama, as well as the incorporation of local performing arts with modern, political content. Although a Yan'an Film Team had been established in 1938 to record army and Communist Party work in the liberated areas, Mao himself was not a film fan.

Others in the leadership after 1949, however, shared with Lenin the view of film as "the most important art." Films, both feature and documentary, could take a standardized message to audiences across the nation and be subject to less potential interference or change in the process. Moreover, films could be made to be easily followed and could be understood by even the most illiterate viewers. The immediacy of moving images and sound could be irresistible. The propaganda and educational potential of the medium was clear. Film became the central means to create a new, mass culture to serve the needs of the Party government and the supposed needs for education and uplifting of the masses Mao had identified as the main audience for cultural endeavors.

Three studios were identified in Shanghai, Changchun, and Beijing for consolidation and expansion to serve the new expectations placed on the medium. A system of centralized control was also established, building on Nationalist government regulation in the 1930s and 1940s. In the 1950s this proved somewhat more effective. The Ministry of Culture included a Film Bureau that monitored production and distribution according to an agreed annual plan between it and the studios. A feature film project required approval at least in three stages: as an initial idea, as a finished script, and then as a completed film. Built in to the system was a natural caution on the part of studio managers and creative staff: self-censorship was probably the most powerful form of control. To reinforce this, the first major campaign against a work of art after 1949 was directed at a film. *The Life of Wu Xun* (Sun Yu, 1950) was a product of the private Kunlun Studio in Shanghai. Commemorating the life of a nineteenth-century educational philanthropist who had begun life as a beggar, the film had been in production for several years before it was released at the end of 1950. Less than six months later an editorial in *People's Daily* (*Renmin ribao*) denounced the film as negating the importance of class struggle. It was widely known that the author of the editorial was Mao Zedong himself. The campaign against the film proved a useful means to establish the parameters for the new art and literature (X. Yuan 2000). It also provided a useful learning experience to those in the Shanghai film industry who were unfamiliar with the expectations placed on cultural production by the Yan'an Talks. With 1,700 employees at the Shanghai studios, about one thousand in Changchun, and a similar number in Beijing, this was a powerful lesson in the need to adjust thinking and practice (Clark 1987: 45–53).

The next major political campaign that helped shape the growing film industry was the Hundred Flowers movement in 1956. Coining an ancient expression about "a hundred flowers blooming, a hundred schools of thought contending," Mao called on a liberalization in all areas of Chinese life. As was true eleven years later at the start of the Cultural Revolution, Mao was concerned at the routinization of his revolution. To reenergize the revolution, cadres, artists, teachers, and other professionals were encouraged to speak up about abuses of power or bureaucratic excesses. The result in 1956 was an outpouring of criticism and, in film, a widening of styles and subject matter. Satire appeared on China's screens for the first time in a half decade. *Before the New Director Arrives* (Lü Ban, 1956) was typical of the new comedies. A toadying minor official fails to realize that the newcomer to the office is in fact the new director, who sees through the effort to impress and supports the younger staff members who place the interests of the collective above their personal gain. Based on a play, this film was a typical expression of the new openness that the Hundred Flowers campaign encouraged.

One bold voice was that of Zhong Dianfei (1919–87), a relatively young literary editor. In an anonymous article in the *Literary Gazette* (*Wenyi bao*) in December 1956, Zhong argued that the abysmal box-office records of many recent films raised questions about the sacrosanct worker–peasant–soldier (*gong–nong–bing*) orientation of literature and art since Mao's Yan'an Talks. Seventy percent of the films made since 1953 did not recoup their costs, with some earning a mere 10 percent of the money spent on making them. Even a socialist, state-owned economy could not afford such wastage. More important, Zhong argued, these returns indicated that the films were not appealing to audiences and falling short of the potential seen in the medium. Artists and managers, Zhong suggested, needed to apply the worker–peasant–soldier formulas more carefully and with less bureaucratic caution (D. Zhong 1956; see also Zhang and Lu 2007).

By the time Zhong's controversial article appeared, the cultural climate had grown chillier, as Mao drew back from his bold experiment in encouraging greater freedom of expression. By 1957 the backlash had become an Anti-Rightist campaign. Like earlier movements of criticism from the Wu Xun episode onwards, and as a prelude to what was to come in the mid-1960s, the attack on critics of the Party singled out representative figures for denunciation and punishment. One such person in filmmaking ranks was Lü Ban, who was sent into internal exile, unable to complete several more comedy projects. Lü died in 1976 without making another film. The next time a Chinese-made satire appeared on China's screens was in the mid-1980s. The Anti-Rightist campaign forced dozens of prominent film artists to withdraw from work, in some cases for twenty years. Their colleagues learned further lessons on the need for self-censorship.

Expanding Studios and Audiences

The Great Leap Forward, Mao's exhilarating and ultimately disastrous lunge in 1958 toward modernization through mass mobilization, saw an expansion in film production capacity and in the audiences for the new features. New studios were established in interior cities, far from the three bastions of the industry in Shanghai,

Changchun, and Beijing. By taking studio production to these smaller centers, film might connect better with the vast new audiences it was supposed to be serving. Viewers could see themselves reflected on screen, or at least a corrected version of themselves. At this same time, a new artistic concept replaced the lip service that had formerly been paid to socialist realism. The new slogan allowed for a greater incorporation of China's cultural heritage, as film took firmer root in Chinese soil.

Among the more enduring of the new studios were those in Xi'an, Chengdu (Emei Studio), Changsha (Xiaoxiang Studio), and Guangzhou or Canton (Pearl River Studio). These so-called second-tier cities served distinct hinterlands, respectively the Northwest, Sichuan, Hunan, and Guangdong province north of Hong Kong. Film specialists were transferred to the new centers and given a mandate to make some films with a local focus. In smaller centers, such as the northwest Xinjiang Uighur Autonomous Region and Inner Mongolia, the new studios were also tasked to prepare films dubbed in the languages of the region's non-Han Chinese populations. The use of ethnic minority languages on China's screens, however, remained highly limited. Film language was generally standard modern, spoken Chinese: on screen even the least educated peasant was to speak standard, radio-sanctioned Chinese no matter where the film was set. The large, Cantonese-speaking population in the South around Guangzhou was, with a few, rare exceptions, expected to watch and enjoy films in the national language.

The Great Leap Forward enthusiasm for building new studios proved an expensive exercise. Ambitious local cadres in some places insisted that their city deserved a studio. In reality some of the smaller centers were little more than newsreel producers, feeding the Central Newsreel and Documentary Studio in Beijing.[1] Several of the new studios officially established in the late 1950s only produced their first feature films in the 1980s. In the interim some of these studios were virtually closed down. The Nantong studio in Jiangsu province west of Shanghai, for example, consisted in reality of one man, a bicycle, an enamel washbasin, and an antique still camera rescued from a pawnbroker (Clark 1987: 80–1). Meanwhile, in a similar though unexpected decentralization of the film enterprise, the large Shanghai Film Studio was split into three studios: Haiyan, Jiangnan, and Tianma.

By the late 1950s a new corps of filmmakers, trained in the expectations of socialist cinema, was gaining experience. One 1956 estimate put the number of personnel in the film enterprise, including distribution, at around ten thousand, most of whom were newcomers to the industry after 1949. Many film technicians and artists gained their training from work in the studios. But in 1952 a film school had been set up, attached to the Beijing studio. In 1956 the Beijing Film Academy opened, with directing, acting, and cinematography departments. An art department was added in 1959, and engineering and scripting departments in the following year. Between 1952 and 1966 close to two thousand students attended the central film school, for degrees or on short-term courses (Clark 1987: 62–3).

Audiences for films, both foreign and Chinese, expanded rapidly in the 1950s. In 1949 the number of places in China that showed films regularly was estimated at around seven hundred. By 1958 the number of projection units, including cinemas and mobile projection teams in rural areas, had grown to roughly ten thousand. Two years later 14,500 projection teams were showing films throughout the nation, in addition to fixed places for screenings (Clark 1987: 61–2). The range of films that this growing audience was able to watch also expanded. Foreign films have loomed large in popular interest throughout the twelve decades that films have been shown in China. The 1950s through to the 1970s were no different in this regard. What was new was the shift in the origin and kinds of foreign films on China's screens from the 1950s onwards. Movies from the Soviet Union and other socialist countries came to dominate the imported titles. But films also came from a large number of Western nations, sometimes for specialist audiences, as in the case of Shakespeare adaptations from Britain or films left in their original languages, rather than dubbed. Indian films, with their exotic locations, songs, and dances also proved popular (HSDFFG 1978; see also Clark 2011). Moreover, particularly at times of political relaxation, audiences could watch much-loved films from the pre-1949 Shanghai studios. In 1956–7, for example, such titles included the two-part wartime melodrama *The Spring River Flows East* (Cai Chusheng, Zheng Junli, 1947 and 1948), the Chinese version of the "Phantom of the Opera" story *Song at Midnight* (Ma-Xu Weibang, 1937), *Street Angel* (Yuan Muzhi, 1937), and *Plunder of Peach and Plum* (Yuan Muzhi, 1934) (HSDFFG 1978: 53–5).

The Great Leap Forward emphasis on mass mobilization and increased production extended to the film enterprise in 1958 to 1960. Filmmakers seized the opportunity to display their commitment to the Communist revolution by rushing new works on the current campaign to China's cinemas and projection units. In one case, *For Sixty-one Class Brothers* (Xie Tian, Cheng Fangqian, 1960), much was made of the mere sixteen days the film took to complete from script to finish (Clark 1987: 81). Another typical film from this campaign was a biography of a model worker in a cotton spinning factory. *Huang Baomei* (Xie Jin, 1958) climaxed with the eponymous heroine, played by Ms. Huang herself, and her workmates taking flight as fairies over the workshop machinery in a fantasy sequence (Clark 1987: 81). Films like these were a suitable match to the steel produced in so-called back-yard steel furnaces in these years: the quality of both products was equally suspect. The fantasy in *Huang Baomei* was made possible by Mao Zedong's new rubric on art and literature. Instead of trying to emulate the Soviet Union's socialist realism, Chinese artists could "combine revolutionary realism with revolutionary romanticism." This new coinage allowed filmmakers more scope in drawing upon folk, historical, and other legacies (Clark 1987: 63–4). Just as the Great Leap Forward represented a search for a Chinese route to industrialization, so this new artistic slogan allowed for a more Chinese aesthetic approach to filmmaking and cultural production in general. The consequence of the excesses of the Leap was a three-year famine with millions dead. For film artists and managers, valuable lessons were learned that could be applied in the next period of heightened enthusiasm, the Cultural Revolution.

Representative Works of Socialist Cinema

In this context of periodic political campaigns and expanding audiences and industry, the films that have continued to resonate among Chinese viewers covered a range of subject matter and style: reverent literary and opera adaptations, wartime heroics, stories set among ethnic minorities, and dramas of contemporary life.

Adapting the modern classics of twentieth-century Chinese literature proved a challenge for film artists. The context in which the film versions were made and the wider audience for these adaptations meant that considerable changes had to be made to the originals. Lu Xun was the writer most responsible for the creation of a new-style literature in the 1920s and 1930s. When the distinguished scenarist Xia Yan (1900–95) adapted Lu Xun's "New Year's Sacrifice," he needed to strengthen the political message and simplify the narrative complexity of the original story. Lu Xun's typical use of an inadequate narrator, unaware of his own ignorance and prejudices, ensured that the story was as much an attack on the educated, landlord class as an exposé of the suffering of a peasant woman. This woman becomes a servant, is kidnapped and forced into marriage, and, having lost a child and her husband, is treated as unlucky and expelled by her employer, becoming a sacrifice at New Year's time. However, the film *The New Year's Sacrifice* (Sang Hu, 1956) uses an off-screen, voice-of-God narrator at the start and end to assure modern viewers that this was a story of the old society and could not happen again. The only concession to Lu Xun's original narrator occurs when the widow speaks directly to the camera and asks the question that flummoxed the story narrator: "When a person dies, does their soul live on?" Despite this small reference to the original story, the 1956 film version is a plain story of class oppression, acceptable to the censors and accessible to even the uneducated viewer.

This updating of pre-1949 literature for screen can be seen in two other major films from the seventeen years before the Cultural Revolution began. *The Lin Family Shop* (Shui Hua, 1959) also used an off-screen voice to intone a statement on the political message of the film at its start. In adapting a 1932 short story on the trials of a shopkeeper during the onslaught of the Great Depression and start of the war with Japan the scriptwriters needed to avoid too much sympathy for a petty capitalist. Accordingly Mr. Lin is shown exploiting the poor, as well as suffering from the depredations of the powerful in society. The adaptation, however, was one of the more artistically successful of the period. Its opening sequence establishes well its setting in the canal towns of Zhejiang, while underscoring the uncertainty of the times by placing the camera on a rocking boat on a canal. A bucket of dark slops drops into the water as the date 1931 fills the screen. This effort to ensure viewers realized that the setting was pre-1949 was similar to that in the Lu Xun film. The film was one of a number of projects made for the tenth anniversary of the People's Republic.

A more tricky adaptation was *Early Spring in February* (Xie Tieli, 1963), from a 1929 story by the Communist writer Rou Shi who had been executed by the Nationalist regime in 1931. The exemplary origins of the story could not, however, disguise its politics seeming somewhat backward by the mid-1960s. In the early 1960s, a stepping back by more radical elements in the Communist regime, including Mao himself, provided a space for the adaptation. The result was a somewhat indulgent portrait of educated young people in the 1920s. A young teacher arrives in a Zhejiang town and feels sympathy for the uneducated widow of a former classmate. He is also attracted to an educated young woman who likes to play romantic pieces on the piano. The kinds of distancing devices, like an off-screen narrator, used in other adaptations of pre-1949 stories, are not used in *Early Spring*. Despite its careful and fluid direction, obvious from the opening sequence, the film was vulnerable to the shifting political situation when it was released in 1963.

Another kind of adaptation was based on the various strands of Chinese musical theater. The major regional opera forms had strong roots in their areas of origin, but were enjoyed by a wide range of spectators as live performances. In adapting operas to the screen, filmmakers faced the challenge of avoiding a simple, static stage documentary, as well as firm audience opinions on what they liked in the original performances. Making opera films was also a useful way to popularize the reform and modernization of the traditional sung dramas that continued after 1949. Peking opera, Sichuan opera, Cantonese opera, and Shaoxing opera, among other forms, were adapted to the screen with varying degrees of success. These films served as a useful rehearsal for the making of celluloid versions of the model operas, which were at the core of Cultural Revolution cultural production. A partly operatic film released in 1965 combined some opera sequences with elements of film noir. *Stage Sisters* (Xie Jin, 1965) traced the fortunes of two young Shaoxing opera performers before 1949. The young women become enmeshed in the Shanghai underworld until one of them is coached by an underground Communist journalist to resist criminal exploitation. The actors even prepare an opera version of Lu Xun's "New Year's Sacrifice" (Cao and Marchetti 2009).

War stories and other heroic tales set during the Communist rise to power in China and during the Korean War were the mainstay of the Chinese film industry from early in the 1950s. Individual soldier-martyrs, such as *Dong Cunrui* (Guo Wei, 1955), were subject to film commemoration, as were episodes in the war against Japan and the civil war. The August First Film Studio, established in 1952 as a unit in the army, was particularly charged with making war movies that were thought useful to inspire the troops. Set at the end of the 1940s civil war, *Red Crag* (Shui Hua, 1965) told the story of Communist prisoners in a Nationalist prison in Chongqing. Some of China's finest film actors, including the veterans Zhao Dan, Yu Lan, and Xiang Kun, brought a degree of subtlety to their portrayals of martyrs going nobly to execution, or in the case of the latter, as a losing general. Another tale from the revolution had the added attraction of an exotic, subtropical setting. The *Red Detachment of Women* (Xie Jin, 1961) was a band of guerrillas on Hainan island in the far south of China. A former servant escapes her landlord employer and joins the women's militia in the mountains. After the patient coaching from the male Party secretary to the unit, Qionghua learns to direct her anger at her exploitation in productive, revolutionary directions. A catchy musical soundtrack enhanced the film's appeal and allowed for a future development. A portrait of college students' underground efforts during the 1930s, *Song of Youth* (Cui Wei, Chen Huaiai, 1959) was based on a bestselling 1956 novel by Yang Mo, who adapted her book to a film script. Released as a tenth-anniversary work, the film expanded the reach of the popular novel, while preserving the somewhat breathless, melodramatic image of young revolutionaries.

Films set among China's 55 officially recognized ethnic minorities had a particular appeal to China's audiences in the 1950s and 1960s. The exotic settings, either in tropical climes in the Southwest or in the deserts of the Northwest, and unfamiliar customs meant that such films served the kinds of purposes that foreign films continued to have on China's screens. In a nation where tourist travel was highly restricted, these films took viewers on journeys to new worlds. Typical of the genre was *Five Golden Flowers* (Wang Jiayi, 1959), set among the Bai minority in Yunnan. A youth Apeng wants to find a young woman named Jinhua (Golden Flower) whom he had met on his way to a county fair. In his search he comes across four other Jinhuas, each of whom is an exemplary worker in her community. The appeal of minority exoticism is thus combined with mainstream messages about production and the collective. On occasion the minority setting and story could be presented in musical form, perhaps reinforcing a majority Han-Chinese notion of ethnic minorities being more prone to sing and dance. *Ashma* (Liu Qiong, 1964) was based on an ancient Bai legend about the origins of the Stone Forest in Yunnan. On screen it is a rather glamorous modern musical, with songs that propel the story and allow the handsome heroes to outwit the chieftain-landlords. Grittier is the portrayal of Tibetan society in the 1950s in *Serfs* (Li Jun, 1963). The film follows the fortunes of Jampa when the People's Liberation Army (PLA) is establishing its rule in Tibet in the face of resistance from landlords and religious leaders. Jampa is forced to flee the region by his former owner and is wounded in the army's efforts to stop the group. In a noble gesture the young Tibetan soldier who had earlier befriended Jampa at the army base places a *hada* (scarf) around the serf's neck. The film ends with Jampa determined to support Beijing-led reform in Tibet. Most minority films featured the music and dance of the peoples in their exotic locations. Many films set among the Han majority also included two songs, although their mainstream style often could not match the catchy rhythms of the minority cultures. *Visitor on Ice Mountain* (Zhao Xinshui, 1963) combines a story of international spying with the Turkic tunes of the Tajik people of the Northwest. In 1951 Amir, a Tajik recruit in the PLA, thinks that the new bride of a local man is his childhood sweetheart Gulandam. When she fails to respond to a favorite song, Amir begins to suspect that the newcomer may be a spy sent across the border not for marriage but to cause trouble. The hard edge of a well-handled spy story is softened by the memorable music that the film incorporates: after all, songs at weddings are part of local custom.

Patriotism in ethnic minority films was matched by dedication to the revolution and Party in films set in contemporary, mainstream society. *The Young People of Our Village* (Su Li, 1959) was a typical sunny work, about a group of enthusiasts working to bring water to their parched northern village. The cheerful youngsters defy more conservative adults and with Great Leap Forward fervor set about carving a canal through the mountains. But even in this politically orthodox story some concession to real life was possible, seen in a subplot about two of the young men falling in love with a young woman in the group. The film was so successful with audiences that a sequel was made four years later, this time with the group working on the electrification of the community. Contemporary comedy could also carry serious messages about social service and collective responsibility. The three variously sized or aged meat packers in *Big Li, Little Li and Old Li* (Xie Jin, 1962) have different levels of dedication to promoting sports activities in the plant. Eventually Big Li, the most unprepossessing of the three, even takes first prize at the sports meet. Much of the film takes place in the workers' apartment building and relies on several farcical episodes, so there are echoes of several pre-1949 films that used a building's inhabitants as a microcosm of society. Similarly, ordinary people are the central figures in the rural comedy *Li Shuangshuang* (Lu Ren, 1962) (see Figure 3.1). Li Shuangshuang is more active in commune affairs than her husband,

Figure 3.1   The peasant protagonists of the People's Commune comedy *Li Shuangshuang* (dir. Lu Ren, Haiyan Studio, 1962). Courtesy of Paul Clark.

who holds conservative views on the proper role of women. Eventually the husband recognizes his faults and attempts reconciliation. Clever writing and skilled playing by Zhang Ruifang and Zhong Xinghuo made for an appealing presentation, as did the somewhat artificial glossiness given to the picture of rural life in the film. These kinds of so-called middle characters (*zhongjian renwu*), not bad but merely confused, emerged in literature in the early 1960s as part of the shift away from simple socialist realism. These portraits were subject to some discussion about their appropriateness in the Maoist cultural project that emphasized the distinction between enemies and friends. When the cultural climate chilled with the approach of the Cultural Revolution, these discussions turned to denunciation.

The Cultural Revolution: Disruption and Growth

By 1964–5 the first echoes of what would become a large-scale onslaught on the artistic enterprise were first heard in the film industry. This was an indication of the importance of cinema in the minds of the Party leadership. The subject matter of new films began to narrow, characterization shifted away from middling characters, and several films, including *Early Spring in February* and *Stage Sisters*, were the target of lengthy criticism in nationally distributed newspapers. By the late spring of 1966 the Great Proletarian Cultural Revolution was underway. This represented Mao Zedong's latest attack on complacency, driven by his obsession with continuous revolution. In reality it was also a factional contest at the highest levels of the Communist Party. Young Red Guards set out to display their loyalty to Chairman Mao, seizing the opportunity to express resentments toward teachers, parents, and other authority figures and to travel around the nation to establish ties (*chuanlian*) with other youth groups.

With the start of the Cultural Revolution, feature film production stopped. In the first years Mao himself became the most widely watched movie star, in documentaries of him surveying millions of Red Guards in Tiananmen Square, for example. The studios were riven with factional disputes between rival groups, each claiming to be more loyal to Mao's views. By 1968, Mao Zedong Thought Propaganda Teams and the establishment of revolutionary committees were devices to restore a semblance of regular management to Chinese urban workplaces, including the film studios and other film industry units. In the absence of new Chinese-made features and with the official banning of films made in the seventeen years after 1949, China's screens were filled with three kinds of films. Documentaries, including in the early 1970s coverage of Prince Sihanouk of Cambodia's travels in Indochina and China, were one way to fill screens. Foreign films continued to be shown, with the emphasis now on works from Albania, Vietnam, and North Korea, though some Soviet films from Stalinist times continued to circulate. The third kind of films were older Chinese films, including the so-called "three big battles" films, so named because they each had the word "battle" or "fighting" (*zhan*) in their titles. These were *Fighting North and South* (Cheng Yin, Tang Xiaodan, 1952), *Mine Warfare* (Tang Yingqi, Xu Da, and Wu Jianhai, 1962), and *Tunnel Warfare* (Ren Xudong, 1965). Soon Chinese audiences could recite from memory whole scenes of dialogue from these works. In addition, the practice of showing condemned films as "negative teaching materials" allowed access to a range of other pre-1966 films. Attending screenings may have been organized for political instruction, but the pleasures audiences enjoyed in seeing these old titles could be far from sanctioned, even if viewers mouthed appropriate sentiments at study meetings after the screenings.

Adapting to the screen the opera and ballet model performances (*yangbanxi*) offered a way to project perfected versions of the works that were at the core of Cultural Revolution cultural practice. The importance of the adaptation project was reflected in the resources – time, funds, and personnel – lavished on these films. *Taking Tiger Mountain by Strategy* (Xie Tieli, 1970), the first to be released on National Day (October 1) in 1970, had been in production at the Beijing studio for close to three years. Orders came from the central authorities that the production crews for this film and the ballet adaptation, *The Red Detachment of Women* (Pan Wenzhan, Fu Jie, 1971), were not to be disturbed by any factional disputes at the studio when they were set up in the summer of 1968. The results on screen were a step up from the opera and other performance adaptations of the 1950s and 1960s. Given the time and resources to experiment, the crews were able to enhance viewers' enjoyment of the modernized music and twentieth-century settings of these model works. By 1974 all five Peking operas and the two ballets in the Cultural Revolution cannon had been put on screen (Clark 2008: 123–34).[2]

Meanwhile, in 1973, the first new feature films (other than model performance films) emerged from the established studios in Beijing, Shanghai, and Changchun. Some of the first works were color remakes of popular films from the 1950s and 1960s that had been circulating since 1966. Among the fresher works was *Sparkling Red Star* (Li Jun, Li Ang, 1974), the story of the young peasant Winter Boy, his mother's martyrdom and his yearning to join his father in the Red Army in the 1930s. The melodrama, attractive young hero, and two well-written songs that took the film experience into other arenas such as radio, all added up to huge audience appeal. The film continued to evoke fond memories decades after its first release. All the new features from the studios after 1973 were expected to follow Cultural Revolution rubrics, including the "three prominences" (*san tuchu*), a concentric focus on the central hero of the story that was first used in the model operas. In Winter Boy's case, the focus was bearable: in other works it could become silly, adding to the falseness of the film. Audiences grumbled, diverted on occasion by foreign films such as *The Flower Seller* (Choe Ik-kyu, North Korea, 1972), which saw Beijing crowds lining up around the block when it was shown in 1972 and again in 1973, when it broke records for attendance of a foreign film since 1949. Half the seventy full-length features distributed publicly in 1966–76 were foreign films (Clark 2008: 151).

In the last three years of the Cultural Revolution an experiment in documentary filmmaking was driven by a Dutch director and old friend of Communist China, Joris Ivens (1898–1989), in collaboration with the central documentary studio in Beijing. Making the multi-part *How Yukung Moved the Mountains* (1976) helped train Chinese documentarists in cinema verité, which was a far cry from the usual, all-knowing and instructional approach of Chinese documentaries until then.

Just as criticism of films had marked the coming of the Cultural Revolution in the mid-1960s, so the ending of this period also saw films again come under attack. Jiang Qing, the wife of Mao and leader of the radical Cultural Revolution faction in the Party leadership, had assumed a prominent role in cultural production in these years. By 1975 she and her allies (later known as the Gang of Four) felt under threat from more pragmatic leaders. She chose several new feature films as a means to counter-attack. The criticism of *Haixia* (Qian Jiang, Chen Huaiai, Wang Haowei, 1975) (see Figure 3.2), the contemporary story of militia women in a coastal fishing village, and *The Pioneers* (Yu Yanfu, 1974), a fictionalized account of the opening of the Daqing oilfield in the Northeast, soon fizzled once Mao Zedong was known to have dismissed the attacks as nit-picking. Meanwhile, some of Jiang Qing's allies in the studios were working on films that directly supported their factional conflict with the newly disgraced (for the second time) Deng Xiaoping. One of these,

Figure 3.2 The militia heroine of *Haixia* (dir. Qian Jiang et al., Beijing Studio, 1975) confronts her class enemy. Courtesy of Paul Clark.

Counterattack (Li Wenhua, 1976), drew parallels between its story of hidden capitalists among the Communist Party leaders in an unidentified northern province and disputes among the Beijing leadership. The film was never released, though it was shown widely as a "negative teaching example" (Clark 2008: 240–7).

Aftermath and Recovery

The arrest of the Gang of Four in October 1976 one month after the death of Mao saw a great outpouring of public relief that some of the more hysterical rhetoric of the Cultural Revolution decade was over. For filmmakers, the challenge of filling China's screens with works that looked different from those being watched a short time earlier proved a huge task. Film projects take time from initial idea to reaching audiences, many of the provincial studios needed to ramp up production, and the level of experience and skills in all studios had suffered with the closing of the Beijing Film Academy in 1968. In the late 1970s television ownership in China's cities started to take off, presenting a new threat to film's importance in Chinese cultural life. Deng Xiaoping's policy of "reform and opening" (*gaige kaifang*), introduced in late 1978, allowed a real shift in China's economic and social orientation. Cultural globalization characterized the 1980s and subsequent decades.

One response to these changes was to use film to sum up the experience of the Cultural Revolution. A number of films in the late 1970s and first half of the 1980s presented harrowing stories of the persecution of brave individuals in what were now called the "ten years of catastrophe." The best known of these films were directed by the veteran Xie Jin, who had started his film career in the late 1940s. Meanwhile a new generation of filmmakers entered the Beijing Film Academy in 1978 for the newly restored four-year degree program. When they started making their own films in the mid-1980s, it was clear that this Fifth Generation of film artists had been watching closely. Their works reinvented Chinese film, but also shared a deep conviction of the power of film with the works of their older colleagues and their Communist Party managers from the seventeen years covered here.

Notes

1   Television broadcasts began in 1958, but viewership until the 1970s was extremely limited. Even in 1975 there were fewer than half a million television sets in all of China. The numbers grew to five million by 1979 and two hundred million by the end of 1991.
2   In a curious parallel to the model performance filming, in the last year (1975–6) of the Cultural Revolution period, 52 traditional operas were filmed at four studios, mostly on videotape and in the simple style of stage documentaries (*wutai jilupian*). A means of preserving the art of older actors, these were initially intended for an audience of one, Mao himself (Clark 2008: 245–7).

4

Directors, Aesthetics, Genres
Chinese Postsocialist Cinema, 1979–2010

Yingjin Zhang

This chapter delineates the shifting contours of Chinese cinema from 1979 to 2010, an era marked by contending designations – "post-Mao," "postsocialist," "reform and opening," "modernization," "globalization," to name just a few. The "post-Mao" started with the death of Mao Zedong in September 1976, but the term has never gained much currency in Chinese scholarship partly due to the sanctioned status of Mao and his socialist legacy. The official Chinese designation is that of "reform and opening," an unprecedented platform launched by Deng Xiaoping in December 1978 and expanded by his successors in a sustained effort to lead China out of poverty to prosperity by means of modernization and, more recently, globalization.[1] As in other sectors in China, the transformation of the planned economy to the market economy has engendered large-scale "seismic" changes (a metaphor I will return to in the conclusion) in Chinese cinema, which has developed from an exclusive state monopoly to a jumble of official, commercial, and independent operations, and which now revolves around the market more than anything else, although the state has never released its ideological grip through censorship and a separate, marginal field of independent film production has emerged and persisted (Y. Zhang 2010a: 170–86).

Despite the official position on "socialism with Chinese characteristics," many scholars have chosen "postsocialist" to describe Chinese cinema since the late 1970s. The term was used first in Chinese film studies to indicate certain "popular perception" and "an alienated … mode of thought and behavior" (Pickowicz 1994: 61–2) suspicious of or alternative to the socialist norms, as expressed in many popular films Xie Jin directed during the 1980s, but the term's parameters have been gradually extended to encompass cinematic styles (Berry and Farquhar 1994), a political economy (X. Zhang 2000), a periodizing framework (Berry 2004a), a cultural logic (S. Lu 2007: 208), and a global condition (McGrath 2008b: 13–18).

As Sheldon Lu (2007: 210) aptly summarizes: "As a hyphenated construction, post-socialism is by definition the coexistence of multiple temporalities and modes of production, the symbiosis of capitalism and socialism, and the embodiment of continuities as well as discontinuities." As such, postsocialism cannot but be an evolving reality subject to contingency and uncertainty, and it therefore demands our ongoing critical attention.

Given limitations of space, this chapter identifies only a small number of salient discontinuities and continuities in postsocialist cinema. Rather than a chronological narrative of major events, leading artists, and representative films (Y. Zhang 2004a: 225–96), I concentrate on three interrelated areas – directors, aesthetics, and genres – and emphasize the crucial importance of multiplicity and simultaneity by taking up problems engendered by a generational lineup, the significance of avant-garde experiment and international reception, the complication of genre repackaging, and the changing functions of cinema in the age of globalization. I argue that, convenient as it is, dividing directors into generations does little justice to the complexity and heterogeneity of Chinese film history, that several generations share their moments of experimental filmmaking at different historical junctures, and that the principal function of cinema in postsocialist China has switched from aesthetics and education in the late 1970s through 1980s to entertainment in the 2000s. To sustain these arguments, we need to step back from the current exhilarated scene of a whirlwind of record-setting Chinese "mega-films" (*dapian*) or blockbusters (see Table 11.1 in Chapter 11, this volume) and pursue a critical reexamination of recent Chinese film history.

Directors: Problems in a Generational Lineup

In Chinese film studies, a generational lineup of directors constitutes a significant effort at ensuring a sense of continuity in historical narrative. As director-scholar Zheng Dongtian (b. 1944) recalled in 2002 (Y. Yang 2006: 28), by the end of 1984, the emergence of avant-garde films like *Yellow Earth* (Chen Kaige, 1984) had occasioned a retrospective lineup of Chinese directors by grouping major figures who embodied successive mentor–apprentice relationships into various generations. According to this scheme, Zheng Zhengqiu represents the First Generation who worked on early silent cinema during the 1910s–1920s; Cai Chusheng, who served as assistant to Zheng Zhengqiu, belongs to the Second Generation who helped launch the leftist film movement of the 1930s and whose directorial career continued into the 1940s; Chen Huaiai (1920–94), who trained Zheng Dongtian, thus counts in the Third Generation who became active in the socialist period of the 1950s–1960s; Zheng Dongtian, who taught Chen Kaige (b. 1952, Chen Huaiai's son), Tian Zhuangzhuang (b. 1952), and others in the first class admitted to the Beijing Film Academy after the Cultural Revolution (Z. Ni 2002), is included in the rank of the Fourth Generation who emerged in the immediate post-Mao period and whose films dominated in the 1980s; finally, Chen Kaige rounds up in the Fifth Generation who brought Chinese cinema to the international spotlight after the mid-1980s. By 1993, another group of young directors including Zhang Yuan (b. 1963) and Wang Xiaoshuai (b. 1966) appeared with their courageous independent productions and was conveniently named the Sixth Generation, even though many of them, like the Fifth Generation, studied under the Fourth Generation and their international reputation followed the Fifth Generation's only a few years later.

The pedagogical value of this generational lineup is obvious, for common characteristics of each generation are recognized as representative of a given period (usually a decade or two in duration), and continuities and discontinuities are charted out in generational terms. According to this by-now familiar story, the First Generation – including Zhang Shichuan and Hou Yao (see Chapter 2, this volume) – established a viable domestic film industry by adopting an entertainment strategy oftentimes spiced up with modern images and reformist ideas. The Second Generation – including Sun Yu, Fei Mu, and Sang Hu (1916–2004) – brought film into two "golden ages" (S. Huang 1992: 78) by promoting nationalist and leftist ideologies and cultivating realist aesthetics. The Third Generation – including Shui Hua (1916–95) and Xie Jin – adapted to political expectations by developing new historical discourse and revolutionary aesthetics (see Chapter 3, this volume). The Fourth Generation – including Huang Shuqin (b. 1939), Wu Tianming (b. 1939), and Xie Fei (b. 1942) – returned to humanism and articulated popular sentiments closely in line with changing official policies. The Fifth Generation – including Huang Jianxin (b. 1954), Wu Ziniu (b. 1953), and Zhang Yimou (b. 1950) – challenged revolutionary heroism and conventional melodrama by experimenting with new wave cinematic techniques, reaffirming the artist's subjectivity, and inventing a national allegory through meditations on modern Chinese culture and history. The Sixth Generation – including Lou Ye and Jia Zhangke (b. 1970) – identified with the aesthetic and social margins and resisted the political and commercial mainstream by producing outside the state system, showcasing individual perceptions in fragmentary images and narratives, and claiming truth and objectivity as their primary goals (Y. Yang 2005).

As I have already contended (Y. Zhang 2002: 22–6), problems in such a generational lineup abound because sweeping generalizations tend to gloss over the internal contradiction and discontinuity that inevitably mark a generation and its representative directors. With historical hindsight we see clearly that the Fifth Generation directors do not – and cannot possibly – share a homogeneous style over a span of 25 years, nor does any single director in that generation adhere to one exclusive form of filmmaking in his or her career to date. The discontinuity and heterogeneity within a generation are already evident in the multiplicity suggested in the naming of a generation. The emergent Sixth Generation, for instance, were given competing names such as "the new-born generation" (Yin and Ling 2002), "the urban generation" (Z. Zhang 2007b), or simply "new generation"

(Sun and Li 2008). Even though "the post-Sixth Generation" (just like "the post-Fifth Generation") and "the Seventh Generation" have surfaced from time to time, critics and directors seem to have reached a consensus that the generational marker no longer functions adequately in the new century (Y. Yang 2006: 27).[2] Indeed, the sheer number of 526 annual domestic feature productions in 2010 (H. Liu 2011) – compared with twenty in 1977 and 67 in 1979 (Y. Zhang 2004a: 196) – makes it fruitless to sort through differences and decide who belong to which generation and who represent a new generation.

In terms of film criticism, the naming itself matters less than the dynamics between and within the generations, and for such a dynamic of continuity and discontinuity across generations we revisit Dai Jinhua's analysis of the Oedipal rivalry between the son and the father in contemporary Chinese cinema. For Dai, the Fifth Generation (or the "son's generation") managed to break away from the political ideology of their father's generation (i.e., the Third Generation), but only to fall back into the "historical trap." Their "desperate spiritual breakaway" was achieved through acts of symbolic as well as actual "patricide" – paradoxically in the name of the "Father" (i.e., Mao Zedong) – during the Cultural Revolution, an initiation ritual and a "carnival for the sons"; nevertheless, once the fathers' authority was stripped, as "fatherless sons" the Fifth Generation could not but rectify their own name by reestablishing their fathers as legitimate revolutionary heroes.[3] The struggle between the father–son hierarchy and a "fatherless culture" eventually entrapped them in a maze of film language and historical representation, rendering their art like a "wrecked bridge" (*duanqiao*) on a precipitous cliff that would never reach the other side (J. Dai 1999: 35–71). In Dai's judgment, a similar trajectory of an initial breakaway followed by a subsequent entrapment characterizes the Fourth Generation, who successfully escaped the post-Mao political confinement by promoting humanist values and André Bazin's realist theory, but their overwhelming sentimentalism in addressing historical traumas and their newfound fascination with the "backward" rural rituals of an "ancient China" ultimately forced them back into the trap of cinematic convention. True, they tried their best to look out on a changing landscape from a "slanting tower" (*xieta*), but a series of "earthquakes" in the form of social transformations increased the slanting of the tower and finally reduced it to a pile of ruins, entrapping the Fourth Generation in a state of bewilderment and vulnerability (J. Dai 1999: 15–34).

Dai's analysis of the Fourth and Fifth Generations reminds us that continuity and similarity lie just beneath eye-catching discontinuity and rupture, both captured in her vivid images of the slanting tower and the wrecked bridge. Indeed, to trace a later transformation, one striking example of the continuity with the mainstream ideology is the fact that by the turn of the new millennium, some prominent members of the Fourth and Fifth Generations would enthusiastically direct state-funded "main melody" (*zhuxuanlü*) or propaganda features, such as *My 1919* (Huang Jianzhong, 1999) and *The National Anthem* (Wu Ziniu, 1999). This fact is striking because previously both directors had ventured into avant-garde filmmaking, Huang Jianzhong (b. 1943) with *Questions for the Living* (1986), a social intervention more than a ghost story, and Wu Ziniu with *Sparkling Fox* (1993), an existentialist meditation on urban civilization. Even Zhang Yuan, an icon of "underground filmmaking" in much of the 1990s, decided to go through the state system and produce his first "aboveground" feature, *Seventeen Years* (1999), whose Chinese title, *Guonian huijia* (returning home for the spring festival), is read allegorically as a sign of the rebellious Sixth Generation returning home after "wandering" and indulging in emotional irruption and "youthful narcissism" (Yin and Ling 2002: 186–8).

Nonetheless, the force of continuity does not work for the status quo alone. The term "New Chinese Cinema" covers three generations – from the Third to the Fifth – whose works in the 1980s share the same noticeable experimental spirit (to be further illustrated in the next section) and therefore point to a particular kind of continuity in challenging the establishment with innovative practices.[4] The shared interest in avant-garde filmmaking, although taken up at different historical junctures, compels us not to attribute aesthetic innovations exclusively to one generation (i.e., the Fifth) while ignoring similar attempts in other generations. As a matter of fact, what characterizes the thirty years of Chinese postsocialist cinema is that each generation went through the cycle of pursuing aesthetic innovations first and returning to the more or less conventional form of melodrama. The conspicuous discontinuity created by each generation's initial breakthrough is therefore counterbalanced by their subsequent turnaround to the cinematic convention on the one hand and their succeeding generation's initial breakthrough on the other. For instance, *Horse Thief* (Tian Zhuangzhuang, 1986) foregrounds the Fifth Generation's determination to push the minimalist plot and dialogue and to challenge the audience's concept of cinema at a time when the Fourth Generation had become comfortable in restaging traditional culture in rural China, as evident in *A Girl from Hunan* (Xie Fei, 1985) (see Figure 4.1) and *A Good Woman* (Huang Jianzhong, 1985), both following sexual and social tensions resulting from the practice of having a teenage bride marry a toddler husband. Similarly, *Beijing Bastards* (Zhang Yuan, 1993) announced the emergence of a rebellious Sixth Generation at a time when the Fifth Generation was no longer experimental in such heartrending works as *Farewell My Concubine* (Chen Kaige, 1993) and *To Live* (Zhang Yimou, 1994), although both address politically sensitive issues by dramatizing prolonged suffering in a seemingly nonstop succession of political events in twenthieth-century China. More recently, *Red Snow* (Peng Tao, 2006) sets up an existentialist stage for the irrational violence of the Cultural Revolution and demonstrates the extraordinary vitality in China's independent filmmaking at a time when the Sixth Generation were increasingly conventional in their aboveground films, like *Shanghai Dreams* (Wang Xiaoshuai, 2005).

As shown in our brief revisit to the problems in a generational lineup of directors in this section, Chinese postsocialist cinema is indeed an embodiment of continuities as well as discontinuities, and such embodiment occurs at different artistic,

Figure 4.1   A teenage wife (Na Renhua) and her toddler husband in *A Girl from Hunan* (dir. Xie Fei, Youth Studio, 1985).

ideological, and historical registers. Given their prevalence in Chinese film studies, it makes sense that we continue to use the generational markers, but we must keep in mind that the characteristics of each generation refer more often than not to that generation's early phase of experiment. In order to appreciate these experimental phases that, if examined from a higher level, bear resemblances across recent generational divides, we now take a closer look at issues of film aesthetics and international reception.

Aesthetics: Of Avant-Garde Experiment and International Reception

The post-Mao period witnessed an urgent call for changes in Chinese cinema. In 1979, Zhang Nuanxin (1940–95), a female director teaching at the Beijing Film Academy, and Li Tuo, a noted writer and critic, published a long co-authored article, "The Modernization of Film Language," which was immediately celebrated as "the blueprint for experimental film" and "the artistic manifesto of the Fourth Generation" (Y. Ding 2002, II: 10). Writing against what they saw as the "stale" or even "regressive" socialist film language at the time, Zhang and Li selectively reviewed the development of film language in international film history and enumerated new breakthroughs ranging from Italian Neorealism and the French New Wave to other innovative examples from the Soviet Union, Japan, and the United Sates. Their major target was the influence of "theater" (*xiju*) – including theatric conflict, dramatic tension, and narrative plot – on film, which for them had become Chinese cinema's "clutch" that must be thrown away in order to modernize Chinese film language. "Documentary style" (*jilu fengge*) and "long take" (*changjingtou*) aesthetics based on Bazin's realist theory were promoted in lieu of the prevailing reliance on montage and editing. More specifically, mise-en-scène, variation within a single take, color contrast, pace or tempo, split screens, and audiovisual counterpoint were cited as innovative practices that would enrich Chinese film language.

The urge to modernize Chinese film language was shared by many Fourth Generation directors in the early 1980s. *Narrow Street* (Yang Yanjin, 1981) drives home the sense of contingency in life by featuring three alternate endings to a tragic love story in the aftermath of the Cultural Revolution, while *My Memory of Old Beijing* (Wu Yigong, 1982) is permeated with sentimentality through its poetic presentation. However, in terms of artistic impact on Chinese cinema and the international film festival, the Fourth Generation – despite their historical role as the initiators of a modernist film language in postsocialist China – paled in comparison to their students, both the Fifth and Sixth Generations. Zhang and Li's call for nondramatic tempo and audiovisual counterpoint, for instance, is best exemplified in *Yellow Earth*, which reduces its dialogue to a minimum and evokes repressed emotions through the intermittent singing of bitter folk songs and abundant landscape shots of Loess Plateaus. Similarly, rather than characterizing any single Fourth Generation director, the documentary style and long-take aesthetics have become the signature of the Sixth Generation, especially its latecomer Jia Zhangke, as well as an increasing number of young independent directors like Liu Jiayin (b. 1981) and Ying Liang (b. 1977).[5]

Back in the mid-1980s, Chen Kaige was proud of the "concealment" (*hanxu*) style of *Yellow Earth*, which is illustrated by Zhang Yimou's inspirational cinematography. "The boundless magnificence of the heavens; the supporting vastness of the earth," and the "flow of the Yellow River" (Barmé and Minford 1988: 259) – all this takes on more visual and conceptual prominence than do human figures in the film, the latter often dwarfed by a disproportionate composition that emphasizes the volume of the yellow earth and the emptiness of the blue sky. The film's radical visual language puzzled the film establishment of the time. Yu Yanfu (b. 1924), a Third Generation director, complained that the film is by no means faultless (Barmé and Minford 1988: 261): "There are a lot of shots in which the camera simply doesn't move, and the characters remain immobile and silent for long periods. You can't really tell what they're supposed to be thinking." Xia Yan, a Second Generation screenwriter and a ranking film bureaucrat in socialist China, likewise expressed his discomfort with the film's portrayal of "the broad masses" (i.e., local peasants): "I simply fail to understand how people so close to Yan'an could remain completely untouched by the new spirit that came from Yan'an" (Barmé and Minford 1988: 267). Xia and Yu's complaints register the radical potential of the avant-garde film language in challenging, if not subverting, the state-sanctioned aesthetics of revolutionary realism.

In its slow pace and its painterly rendition of natural landscape, *Yellow Earth* is aesthetically linked to contemporary experimental arts in post-Mao China (see Chapter 21, this volume). "Father" (1980), Luo Zhongli's large oil painting of an old peasant, is widely believed to have influenced the artistic design of the taciturn father figure in *Yellow Earth*; likewise, the film's peculiar landscape composition may be traced to a regional painting style from Shaanxi (Wilkerson 1994). An obsession with barren landscapes marks several high-profile Fifth Generation films, from *One and Eight* (Zhang Junzhao, 1984) to *Red Sorghum* (Zhang Yimou, 1987), *Evening Bell* (Wu Ziniu, 1988), and *Life on a String* (Chen Kaige, 1991) (X. Zhang 1997: 282–328). Indeed, the painterly quality of these avant-garde films may have inspired the consistent presentation of wild landscapes in China's West in martial arts films of the 1990s, culminating in the picturesque landscape in *Crouching Tiger, Hidden Dragon* (Ang Lee, 2000), which have spawned countless imitations in recent blockbuster films, including those from Chen Kaige and Zhang Yimou. Even within China's independent productions, *Thomas Mao* (Zhu Wen, 2010) is still located in this painterly tradition, showcasing the Mongolian grassland on the one hand and featuring the real-life painter Mao Yan and his regular model Thomas Rohdewald (a native of Luxemburg) as male leads in a series of existential adventures.

If the Fifth Generation – with its iconic breathtaking rural landscapes – fulfilled Zhang Nuanxin and Li Tuo's "modernist" expectation of innovative color contrast and minimalist plot better than its mentors in the Fourth Generation, the expectation of a sustained documentary style and long-take aesthetics was not met until a decade later when the Sixth Generation pursued its relentless exploration of precarious, anxiety-ridden urban conditions of everyday life in postsocialist China. Instead of painting, a revered form of high art embodied in Western oil painting as well as Chinese ink-wash painting, the Sixth Generation turned to video, an emergent practice associated with amateur art at best. Significantly, it is this "spirit of amateurism" (Z. Jia 2003) that brought a fresh look and a new aesthetics to Chinese cinema in the 1990s. *Mama* (Zhang Yuan, 1991), a prototype of the underground film, contains video interviews with Qin Yan, the film's screenwriter who plays a distressed mother who defies social prejudice to care for her autistic son. Such a relentless documentary method was subsequently adopted in Zhang Yuan's *Beijing Bastards*, which includes the rehearsal footage of Cui Jian, China's first rock star and an icon of subcultural rebellion in the years immediately after the military crackdown on the Tiananmen democratic movement on June 4, 1989. Gradually, the Sixth Generation's typical claim on objectivity and truth was strengthened by real-life actors and locations in films like *Sons* (Zhang Yuan, 1996) and *Quitting* (Zhang Yang, 2001), the former following an alcoholic family and the later a drug addict – Jia Hongsheng (1967–2010), who plays himself before he committed suicide – in their respective struggles for rehab. When Jia Zhangke appeared with *Xiao Wu* (1997), his signature long-take aesthetic (McGrath 2008b: 129–64; Berry 2009) would enhance the appeal of "on-the-spot" (*xianchang*) realism normally attributed to documentary filmmaking (Berry, Lu, and Rofel 2010). To a considerable extent, such documentary realism, replete with shaky camerawork, disheartening subject matter, and existentialist angst, still informs much of current documentary and feature production in China's vibrant independent sector (see Chapter 16, this volume).

Given the Fourth Generation's early commitment to modernizing Chinese film language, it is worth speculating why their works were rarely recognized in international reception. Since the 1980s, major international film festivals in the West have consistently favored the Fifth and Sixth Generations as well as new wave directors from Hong Kong and Taiwan (see tables in Chapter 13, this volume). Even though *Woman from the Lake of Scented Souls* (Xie Fei, 1993) and *The Wedding Banquet* (Ang Lee, 1993) both won the Golden Bear at Berlin in the same year, Lee's film had an impressive subsequent arthouse run in Euro-America, whereas Xie's quickly fell into oblivion, even inside China.

In my view, the international film festivals' lack of interest in the Fourth Generation can be attributed to several factors. First, in terms of cultural content, Fourth Generation films usually demanded a high level of knowledge with regard to Chinese history and culture, and their insistence on capturing Chinese emotional life had made their films rather inaccessible to average international arthouse audiences. In contrast, Zhang Yimou's early films – including *Ju Dou* (1989) and *Raise the Red Lantern* (1991) – resonate with a longstanding Orientalist view of a backward rural China, and those "ethnographic films" (Y. Zhang 2002: 207–39) based on the so-called "Zhang Yimou model" (T. Lu 2002: 157–73) – showcasing aggressive female sexuality, cruel patriarchal repression, traditional architectural confinement, and picturesque wild landscape (Larson 1995) – were fairly successful in international reception during the 1990s.[6] Second, in terms of artistic style, the Fourth Generation was less experimental than the Fifth and Sixth Generations and their films fared poorly with those film festivals that prized innovative styles and auteurist visions. On the other hand, the Fifth Generation had the advantage of a striking visual language that would easily transcend cultural barriers, and the Sixth Generation's initial reliance on rock music secured a certain affinity with the previous Western experience of a youthful counterculture (Donald 1998). Third, in terms of transnational politics, the Fourth Generation was generally perceived as pro-establishment, whereas the Fifth and Sixth Generations, whose early works were often labeled "banned in China" for real or for publicity purposes in the West, attracted attention partly or primarily because of their censorship problems at home. Consciously or not, their sensitive subject matters, along with their experimental styles, have obtained different political ends in the uncharted waters of the post-cold war global cultural arena. To quote a prominent Chinese critic (J. Dai 2002: 90): "Just as the films of Zhang Yimou and his imitators satisfied the West's old Orientalist mirror image, the West again privileged the Sixth Generation as the Other…. Created as a mirror image, it again validated Western intellectuals' mapping of China's democracy, progress, resistance, civil society, and the marginal figure."

As Dai Jinhua (2002: 90–1) observed, the Western reception validated – indeed, appropriated – the Sixth Generation for its own political ends more than innovative aesthetics, and the contrast between the Sixth Generation's international fame and its domestic obscurity thus made it "a scene in the fog" (*wuzhong fengjing*) in the early 1990s. Precisely for such apparently one-sided favoritism from the Western media, since the early 1990s the Fifth and Sixth Generations have frequently been faulted by Chinese critics for catering to Western audiences (Q. Dai 1993). In fact, similar criticism has even come from the West. Here is Shelley Kraicer's (2009) daydream/fantasy:

> There exists, down some dusty grey hutong alleyway of Beijing, a Chinese Indie Director's Discount Emporium. You want to make a film? Step right in and assemble your movie at bargain prices. The shelving on the left is stocked with cast members: long-haired village boys, out of school, drifting aimlessly. At the back is a set of grainy, dusty, brown-grey village-scapes, ready to be populated by said drifters. To the right, useful equipment. Some tripods, but with a restriction: they must be set up at least 50 metres from the subjects being filmed. Right beside is a very long long shelf, holding 3 minute, 10 minute, even 20 minute-long takes, offered for a steal at family-sized package prices. Alternatively, you could go for deep discount on little DV cams, with the proviso that, held close to the subjects, they be shaken as vigorously as possible. The dialogue shelves in the centre are threadbare: screenplays for rent are all dialogue-light. And, off in a corner, is a shelf labelled "Prostitutes." It's over-loaded, with a three-for-the-price-of-one sale.

Kraicer (2009) admit that his imaginary scenario is "a bit mean" but cannot but pose this question: "Who can blame a young director from China, who, with little or no chance of gaining any return on his or her investment within his own country, tries to design a film to suit those foreigners who pay the bills, fund postproduction, and just might offer an overseas distribution deal?"

A young Canadian curator who has recently lived and studied in Beijing for years as an enthusiast more than a skeptic, Kraicer is a new associate in what Dai Jinhua (2002: 89–90) saw as "the refined and arrogant European festival circuit [and the] conceited American film circles," but Kraicer's suspicion of formulaic artistic practices of the Sixth Generation and its followers – elsewhere projected in such iconic objects as "bulldozers, bibles and very sharp knives" (Nornes 2009) – once again raises the question of once-innovative directors falling back into the trap of unimaginative convention. As illustrated in the preceding section, such a cycle of breakthrough followed by entrapment occurred historically to the Fourth and Fifth Generations. Just as the emergent Fifth Generation intended to make their screen images radically different from those of their father's generation, so did the pioneering Sixth Generation rebel against such stock images as yellow earth, sorghum fields, waist drums, red cloth, bandits, and landlords in the Fifth Generation's ethnographic films (Cheng and Huang 2002: 31). The cycle of formulaic stalemate and innovative breakthrough must therefore be understood as part of the very dynamics that generates the simultaneity of aesthetic continuity and discontinuity in Chinese cinema. In this sense, Kraicer's gloomy scenario is only one side of the picture, for the aesthetic dynamic itself ensures that innovative works continue to appear year after year, as the energetic scene of recent Chinese independent filmmaking has proved.

Genres: Between Critical Intervention and Commercial Repackaging

If we leave aside the international reception that consistently prefers avant-garde aesthetics and controversial subjects, we may realize that, rather than the award-winning art films mentioned above, the dominant market force in postsocialist China has always operated in the realm of genre films, in particular melodrama, comedy, and martial arts.[7] In order to delineate the dynamics at work in the domestic film market, we reexamine two critical debates below – the first on "Xie Jin's model" and the second on "entertainment cinema" (*yule pian*) – that capture the anxiety of Chinese film critics and filmmakers in an age of far-reaching transformation.

In 1986, young critic Zhu Dake (b. 1957) published an article criticizing Xie Jin's film model. For Zhu, Xie Jin's films of the 1980s excelled in expanding emotions and making viewers weep so profusely as to be manipulated willingly into accepting the artist's traditional moral values. The way Xie's emotional provocation worked resembled the spread of medieval religions on the one hand and, on the other, the typical Cinderella story of Hollywood commercial films. Like Hollywood, Xie Jin's model had its set procedure of arranging moral–emotional codes: "a good person suffering injustice," "discovery of hidden values," "moral persuasion," and "the triumph of good over evil" – all this aimed to defuse social conflicts and betrays the lingering effects of cultural imperialism. Moreover, Zhu argued, Xie had developed his "cine-Confucianism" (*dianying ruxue*), which was typified by his leading woman character invariably portrayed as gentle, kind-hearted, industrious, resilient, submissive, reserved, and self-sacrificing – an outdated exemplary woman who was nothing but a "deformed product of patriarchal culture," a woman who, in her status as man's accessory, was used to discover and confirm man's values and provide him with happiness. Xie's cine-Confucian woman thus embodied an investment in family and patriotism. As such, Xie Jin's model was regarded as a discordant note in China's cultural change and a retreat from the May Fourth spirit (D. Zhu 1986).

Zhu's article triggered a heated debate in 1986. On the one hand, critics accused Xie of pandering to popular tastes and audiences' desires. Li Jie (1990), for instance, judged Xie Jin's to be "a closed model of stability," a perfect combination of "the three major aspects of Chinese film – politics, entertainment, and art" – that had "brought him a series of successes" as well as "blind cheers and applause"; precisely due to its popularity, "this obsolete film model should be discarded … Xie Jin's era should end." On the other hand, defenders acknowledged Xie's invaluable contribution to Chinese cinema. Zhong Dianfei, a veteran scholar who had suffered political persecution as a "bourgeois Rightist" in 1957 (see Chapter 3, this volume) and who was not rehabilitated until 1978, praised Xie's ability to attract audiences young and old as an unusual accomplishment, for "film cannot live without audiences"; instead of "obsolete," Zhong described Xie as an artist moving "ahead of his time" (D. Zhong 1986).

The debate on Xie Jin's model in 1986 reveals a fundamental dilemma in postsocialist cinema: whereas young critics assumed an avant-garde position and idealistically expected film art to be separated from politics and commercialism, Xie Jin combined art and politics in such a way that resonated with popular sentiments. Xie's commercial success was correctly attributed to the influence of Hollywood melodrama, but this influence alone must not warrant negative judgment. In response to Western melodrama film theory, Nick Browne (1994: 43) proposes a concept of "political melodrama" for Xie Jin's case and defines it as "an expression of a mode of injustice whose mise-en-scène is precisely the nexus between public and private life, a mode in which gender as a mark of difference is a limited, mobile term activated by distinctive social powers and historical circumstances." The popular success of Xie's films like *The Legend of Tianyun Mountain* (1980), the first interrogation of the injustice suffered by bourgeois Rightists on the post-Mao screen, shows that his melodramatic reconfiguration of power, gender, history, and memory, along with his typical concluding catharsis by restoring justice, worked wonders in enabling the audience to articulate pent-up emotions in the aftermath of the Cultural Revolution.

In retrospect, the young critics' premature pronouncements appear rather ironic on several counts. First, except for the socialist period, Chinese cinema always kept its distance from the May Fourth "elitist" enlightenment discourse because the "popular" film melodrama, with its "rhetorical excess, extravagant representation, and intensity of moral claim" (Pickowicz 1993a: 300–1), time and again diluted or even derailed heavy-handed ideological indoctrination. From *Little Toys* (Sun Yu, 1933) and *Dream in Paradise* (Tang Xiaodan, 1947) to *Hibiscus Town* (Xie Jin, 1986), Paul Pickowicz (1993a) locates a long tradition of melodrama in Chinese cinema and contends that the melodramatic imagination is deeply rooted in Chinese life. In fact, melodrama dominated the Chinese silent screen as early as the 1920s (see Chapter 2, this volume). Second, not only has Xie Jin's model of combining politics, entertainment, and art continued in various incarnations since the mid-1980s, but melodrama was actually the foundation in postsocialist cinema involving enthusiastic participation from Fourth, Fifth, and Sixth Generation directors after their respective initial phases of aesthetic experiments. In the new century, former avant-garde directors Chen Kaige (*Together with You*, 2002) and Zhang Yuan (*I Love You*, 2002) turned to melodrama without much hesitation. To a great extent, many films in the "Zhang Yimou model" are melodramatic in nature, except that in this variation the suffering woman may not be rewarded and good may not triumph over evil. Third, in a changed socioeconomic environment from the 1990s onward, box-office successes like Xie Jin's would no longer carry a stigma of commercialism, for a slate of new reform measures – including the financial self-sufficiency required for all state-run film studios (Y. Zhu 2003) – had forced Chinese filmmakers to reevaluate their positions and rethink concepts like art and entertainment.

A revisit to a series of debates on entertainment cinema in the late 1980s helps us better understand the changing dynamics of postsocialism at work on the cultural front. In 1987, the state-funded academic journal *Contemporary Cinema* dedicated its first three bi-monthly issues to a forum, "Dialogues on Entertainment Cinema," and several film directors participated and called for restoring the legitimate status of entertainment in Chinese cinema. Song Cong (b. 1941), for one, raised three theoretical theses: "Entertainment cinema is the mainstay (*zhuti*) of cinema; entertainment mentality is lofty rather than vulgar; entertainment should be treated as an end rather than a means" (D. Li 2002: 599). In December 1988, *Contemporary Cinema* organized a conference on contemporary Chinese entertainment cinema, and many participants subsequently published articles based on their presentations. In his 1989 article, Chen Haosu (then Vice-Minister of Radio, Television, and Film) postulated the ontology (*zhuti*) of entertainment cinema and reversed the previous order of cinematic functions: "the entertainment function is the origin and foundation, whereas the artistic (or aesthetic) function and the educational (or cognitive) function are its extension and development" (D. Li 2002: 587). Chen's radical postulation drew immediate rebuttals. Lu Weiping, for instance, castigated the idea of the ontology of entertainment cinema as "anti-tradition," "anti-culture," "anti-art," and "anti-rationalism" and equated it to a cultural policy of "fooling people" (D. Li 2002: 588–9).

Rather than excessive rhetoric, Jia Leilei struck a balance by bringing the debate to a theoretical level in a 1989 article. First, he defined entertainment cinema as "conventional cinema" (*changgui dianying*) characterized by "its ultimate goal in commercial value, its ontological status in plot-driven narrative, and its primary function in providing pleasure"; second, he pointed to a series of adjustments the artist must make when engaging in entertainment cinema: "merging the principle of individuality into that of collectivity; integrating the subject's unique creativity into the adaptability of the group; transforming breakthrough and transcendence into observance and preservation of rules; shifting from philosophical meditation to emotional persuasion; and molding inspiration into experience" (D. Li 2002: 589–90). Obviously, for Jia and other scholars, the opposite of entertainment cinema was experimental or "exploratory cinema" (*tansuo pian*), which was their familiar territory, endowed with claims to individual creativity and philosophical sophistication but which, unfortunately, started to face serious problems in the domestic market in spite of its growing international reputation.[8]

In fact, the entire film industry was caught in a downward spiral in postsocialist China. Annual movie attendance had declined steadily from 29,310 million in 1979 to 21,900 million in 1986, losing 1,000 million a year on average (D. Li 2002: 580–1), although annual feature productions had more than doubled from 67 in 1979 to 151 in 1986 (Y. Zhang 2002: 196). These two diverging trends meant that film studios were losing huge amounts of money exactly at a time when they were required by the state to be financially self-sufficient and their products were no longer guaranteed automatic distribution that had previously come with a steady stream of flat-fee payments regardless of box office. Under increasing financial pressures, many studios began producing entertainment cinema, and its ratio to the total annual feature production almost tripled from 20 percent in 1987 to 58 percent in 1989. In terms of genre breakdown, martial arts films and cop–gangster thrillers topped the box office; even so, among the top ten, the numbers of copies sold per film still illustrated the market downturn, from the highest 379 copies for the 1988 top-grossing film to 255 copies for the 1991 top film (D. Zhong, Pan, and Zhuang 2002: 249–53). The contraction of the film market accelerated in the 1990s, as annual movie attendance nose-dived further from 14,400 million in 1991 to 3,000 million in 1994, 460 million in 1999, and 220 million in 2001 (Y. Zhang 2002: 192), the last figure a far cry (merely 0.75 percent) from the heyday of 29,310 million in 1979, when audiences flocked to the theaters to watch newly released films produced before the Cultural Revolution.

Interestingly, when the Chinese film market touched bottom around the turn of the new millennium, with the total box office at RMB 850 million in 1999 and RMB 840 million in 2001 (of which a large percentage came from exhibiting Hollywood blockbusters after 1994), it was neither melodrama nor thriller that rushed to the rescue, but comedy. Ever since his *The Dream Factory* (1997) scored RMB 33 million at the box office, Feng Xiaogang's "new year films" (*hesui pian*) – films released during the holiday season from Christmas to Chinese New Year (usually late January to early February), mostly comedies in the late 1990s but increasingly making forays into martial arts and action genres in the 2000s (R. Zhang 2008) – have been all the rage, setting domestic box-office records one after another (see Table 11.2 in Chapter 11, this volume). In a consistent manner, Feng's single yearly release would represent approximately 11–14 percent of the domestic box office (excluding foreign films) in a given year: with RMB 30 million, *A Sigh* (2000), a romantic comedy, accounts for 10.7 percent of the domestic film box office at RMB 280 million in 2000; with RMB 120 million, *A World Without Thieves* (2004), an action thriller, accounts for 13.3 percent of the domestic film box office at RMB 900 million in 2004; and with RMB 260 million, *Assembly* (2007), a war film, accounts for 14.4 percent of the domestic film box office at RMB 1,801 million in 2007 (Y. Zhang 2010a: 172). When Feng's disaster film *Aftershock* (2010) earned RMB 647.8 million, the total box office (combining domestic as well as foreign films) in 2010 would soar to RMB 10,170 million (H. Liu 2011). Although the 2010 total box office is impressive (i.e., twelve times as much as that of 2001), it still represents only 34.7 percent of the record movie attendance in 1979. The percentage is even lower if we factor in the difference in ticket prices over time: a ticket in 1979 cost as little as RMB 0.05 at a student discount, but in 2010 it stood at RMB 80 or more for a blockbuster, and the 3-D IMAX version of *Avatar* (James Cameron, 2009) sold for as much as RMB 150 per ticket.

Set against the current euphoria over the steady double-digit annual growth of China's film market in recent years (Y. Zhang 2010a: 170–86), the two critical debates in 1986–9 summarized above look quite antiquated, even ironic. Not only is box office not a stigma any more, but it has become the primary market force worshipped by most producers and directors, if not yet all critics. Similarly, entertainment is no longer treated with suspicion or trepidation in scholarly and public discourse. After two decades of genre filmmaking, especially when Hollywood blockbusters were allowed to screen in China on a shared-revenue, fixed-quota basis since 1994, entertainment has come back with a vengeance (for it was the driving force in Chinese cinema as early as the 1920s), and no other genre represents this comeback better than martial arts films.

When *The Mysterious Giant Buddha* (Zhang Huaxun, 1980) came out, it was hailed as a breakthrough because the martial arts genre had been banned in socialist cinema regardless of its earlier contribution to the Chinese film industry (see Chapter 15, this volume). Despite its popularity in the late 1980s, the link to entertainment rendered martial arts films a marginal genre unworthy of sustained critical attention. Even though the rush to coproductions with Hong Kong in the early 1990s expanded the genre's appeal, it was not until the unexpected success of *Crouching Tiger, Hidden Dragon* that the genre found its place in China's new initiative in global expansion. With unprecedented support from the state in such areas as guaranteeing the best release windows and cracking down on piracy, Chinese investors quickly teamed up with their Hong Kong partners to produce a slate of high-budget martial arts blockbusters. From *Hero* (2002) to *Curse of the Golden Flower* (2006), Zhang Yimou reinvented himself from an "ethnographer" of Chinese culture to an inventor of fantastic scenes and superhuman actions. The ingredients of magic, romance, sex, violence, and DGI-enhanced special effects are now routinely – and oftentimes mechanically – mixed in the genre, and the casting of top stars from Hong Kong and Taiwan – sometimes also Japan and Korea – has repackaged the genre as a transnational Chinese or even Asian blockbuster brand (Teo 2009).

The current surge of Chinese blockbusters has had a profound impact on postsocialist Chinese cinema. In an age when the entertainment function reigns over the artistic and education functions, the convergence of art, politics, and entertainment – regarded as a "fatal" flaw in Xie Jin's model in 1986 – is now not just expected but celebrated. Not only have the main-melody films moved toward the blockbuster mode of production by recruiting major stars, as in *The Founding of a Republic* (Han Sanping, Huang Jianxin, 2009) – where a veritable hit-parade of Chinese-language film stars is displayed, thinly disguised as historical figures (see

Chapter 12, this volume) – but martial arts films now also directly serve the mainstream ideology of nationalism and patriotism, as in *Bodyguards and Assassins* (Teddy Chan, 2009) and *Ip Man II* (Winston Yip, 2010), where individuals heroically sacrifice their lives to protect the revolutionary cause and national dignity.

Conclusion: After Seismic Changes

I want to conclude my survey of three decades of Chinese postsocialist cinema with the metaphor of seismic changes. The postsocialist period started in 1976, a year marked by a devastating earthquake in Tangshan on July 28 that claimed an estimated 242,769 lives and 435,556 injured (Baidu.com n.d.c). Remarkably, it took 24 years for Chinese filmmakers to confront this disaster in a blockbuster feature, *Aftershock*, which set a box-office record in 2010 and responded, in collective catharsis, to the fresh memories of two recent earthquakes: the Wenchuan earthquake that struck on May 12, 2008 and claimed 69,227 lives and 374,643 injured (Baidu. com n.d.b), and the Yushu earthquake that struck on April 17, 2010 and claimed 2,698 lives (Baidu.com n.d.a). If the Tangshan earthquake had remained a largely repressed traumatic experience in public memory outside Tangshan for decades, the Wenchuan and Yushu earthquakes were quickly turned into a series of nationwide rituals of mourning and fundraising aimed at reaffirming the government's legitimacy at a time when China was preparing, respectively, for two euphoric gala shows of the century – the Beijing Olympic Games in 2008 and the Shanghai International Exposition in 2010.

Beyond the obvious expediency of having three devastating earthquakes bookend the postsocialist period under discussion in this chapter (although the period continues forward), the metaphor of seismic changes vividly captures the grand scale, the profound shock, and the unexpected outcome of the sweeping transformations that have taken place in China over the past three decades. Between these earthquakes were endless pre-shocks and aftershocks, in geological as well as social, cultural, and psychological terms. When Dai Jinhua (1999: 16) described the Fourth Generation as looking out from a "slanting tower" that would eventually collapse amid rumbling earthquakes, she might not be cognizant of the implication that this iconic image of the slanting tower – along with the "wrecked bridge" over a precipitous cliff for the Fifth Generation – also references a landscape of ruins in the aftermath of earthquakes.

Aesthetically and psychologically, then, the images of ruins compel us to look beyond the current euphoria over the box-office booms and examine cracks and fissures glossed over by the illustrious film stars and magic special effects. Historically, as Sheldon Lu (2007: 210) observes, "postsocialism in the era of cautious reform and openness in the 1980s has transformed into postsocialism in the age of grandiose transnational capitalism from the 1990s to the present," but the cultural logic of postsocialism has produced heterogeneity and contingency more than homogeneity and stability. If we turn away from the facade of modernization and globalization, images of ruins of all kinds – natural, cultural, industrial, psychological – abound in the field of independent and semi-independent productions, where young directors have vehemently refused to entertain the audience or please the state. Instead, they stubbornly train their camera on a wide array of gritty, disquieting, and heart-wrenching images of contemporary Chinese life, as in *West of the Tracks* (Wang Bing, 2003), *Still Life* (Jia Zhangke, 2006), and *Little Moth* (Peng Tao, 2007), and these images constitute the hidden side of Chinese postsocialist cinema that deserves critical exploration (Pickowicz and Zhang 2006). After all, postsocialism is nothing but a jumble of contradictions and tensions, an embodiment of continuities and discontinuities, and a coexistence of multiple temporalities, spatialities, localities, mentalities, and subjectivities. Fortunately, cinema has provided us with relentless moving images with which we can track, comprehend, and evaluate the transformation of postsocialism in China amid constant seismic changes.

Notes

1   Three recent English books on Chinese film and television contain "reform" in their titles (X. Zhang 1997; Y. Zhu 2003; X. Zhong 2010).
2   One example is the declaration "There Is No Sixth Generation" from Li Yang (b. 1959), whose independent feature *Blind Shaft* (2003) drew much critical attention (Teo 2003).
3   Acts of patricide are staged twice in *Ju Dou* (Zhang Yimou, 1989), in which the son accidentally kills his nominal father and deliberately murders his biological father. The rectification of the revolutionary hero is exemplified in *One and Eight* (Zhang Junzhao, 1984), in which a wrongly accused Communist cadre leads a group of bandits in fighting against Japanese troops.
4   One additional benefit of the term "New Chinese Cinema" is its implied "new wave" status and its link to similar film movements in Hong Kong (the "Hong Kong New Wave") and Taiwan ("New Taiwan Cinema") in the 1980s (Tam and Dissanayake 1998; Cornelius 2002).
5   Liu Jiayin's *Oxhide* (2005) and *Oxhide II* (2009) consist of extreme long takes of her and her parents in intimate domestic scenes shot with the fixed camera. Long takes also characterize Ying Liang's films, and his 19-minute short *Condolences* (2009) is a one-shot long take on an old woman's inarticulate trauma after a tragic bus accident killed her son.
6   While the majority of such ethnographic films come from the Fifth Generation, *Ballad of the Yellow River* (1989), a Fourth Generation film that fits this model, won the Best Director award for Teng Wenji (b. 1944) at Montreal in 1990.
7   War film was a major genre in the 1980s, but it quickly fell out of favor in the 1990s except for state-funded propaganda mega-series produced to commemorate the anniversaries of the PRC, the Communist Party, the People's Liberation Army, etc. (Y. Zhang 2002: 173–201).

8   *On the Hunting Ground* (Tian Zhuangzhuang, 1985) set the worse record with only one
    copy sold, followed by *King of the Children* (Chen Kaige, 1987) with six copies, *Horse
    Thief* with seven copies, *Evening Bell* with nineteen copies after winning the Silver Bear
    at Berlin in 1989 (initially with zero copy), and *Yellow Earth* with thirty copies (D. Li
    2002: 583). In comparison, *The Great Knight-Errant from the Yellow River* (Zhang Xinyan,
    Zhang Zi'en, 1987), a martial arts film coproduced with Hong Kong, sold 379 copies
    (D. Zhong, Pan, and Zhuang 2002: 351).

5

Hong Kong Cinema Before 1980

Robert Chi

For better or worse, the popular entertainment of one era often becomes the fine art of another. (Alexander Nehamas 2010)

Introduction

Hong Kong cinema has become a favorite example for the field of knowledge production known as cinema studies, and not just because so many of the former's recent films are easily available with subtitles and pleasurable to watch. In the past two or three decades a profusion of scholarship and criticism on Hong Kong and Hong Kong cinema has foregrounded their complexity, their interstitial nature, and their evasion of existing nomenclature. Hence the tendency in that scholarship and criticism to resort to neologisms, catachreses, hyperboles, oxymorons, and other kinds of rhetorical figures, as in disappearance, para-site, postcolonial, translocal, transnational, and one of the most memorable to date, at full speed (E. Yau 2001). To put it another way, Hong Kong cinema is best understood in terms of crossings, intersections, and dialectics. On the one hand, such arguments draw upon the concrete histories of Hong Kong and by extension of Hong Kong cinema. On the other hand, those concrete histories fit perfectly the structure of this contemporary field of knowledge production, which is to say, they fulfill the latter's discursive demands. They exemplify crossings, intersections, and dialectics, along with a host of related items that have grown out of earlier poststructuralist vocabulary such as hybridity, heterogeneity, contestation, marginality, and difference. Finally, the commercial success of Hong Kong cinema makes it – like Bollywood – a recognizable non-Western other for Hollywood oriented cinema

A Companion to Chinese Cinema, First Edition. Edited by Yingjin Zhang.
© 2012 Blackwell Publishing Ltd. Published 2012 by Blackwell Publishing Ltd.

studies, for it too has had studios, stars, fans, moguls, auteurs, genres, vertical integration, global aspirations, institutionalized styles, practical technical innovations, and even media convergence. Thus as an object of study it mediates between the concrete and the conceptual, between the particular and the universal, between the anomaly and the model. In short, Hong Kong cinema is an engine for theorizing.

Most of this theorizing has grown out of cultural studies from the 1980s to the present. In other words, this kind of scholarship and criticism on Hong Kong and Hong Kong cinema has been about the contemporary: it is about things that coexist in its own time. Such scholarship and criticism have shown certain tropes of the collective imagination to be urgent during this time. Those tropes include the sense of a specific Hong Kong identity; the anxiety that commerce and economics overshadow culture and the arts; and the mutual constitution of the metropolis, the movies, and mental life. However, scholars pushing further back in time have necessarily had to take a more historical and therefore somewhat less theory driven approach. As with all cinema, the further back one goes the fewer films are extant. Thus historical research on Hong Kong cinema requires the excavation of archival and paracinematic materials of all kinds, along with their creative interpretation. Still, nothing can or should replace careful and systematic viewing of whatever films are available. One important overall result of such historical research is that tropes such as those just enumerated no longer seem so new. They were already in play during much earlier times.

For example, Poshek Fu (2003) has made the concise but archivally rich argument that "Hong Kong identity" was an urgently felt concern in cinema by the 1930s. More importantly, Fu's argument implies that whatever identity crises existed in the 1980s and 1990s evolved out of earlier configurations rather than arising solely out of contemporary traumatic ruptures like the 1984 Sino-British Joint Declaration, the 1989 Tiananmen Square protests, and the 1997 handover. And finally, it also circles back to the reconceptualization of identity itself in keeping with contemporary discourses on that topic: for what is at issue is not a single, substantive identity but the dynamic process of identification in the face of multiple and possibly conflicting determinations. In other words, it may be the case that identity was felt as an urgent issue in 1980s and 1990s Hong Kong, but it was so as an ideologeme, itself an object of the desire for something solid, an attempt to freeze the process of identification, hence a particular episode in the much longer history of that process. In the best cases, then, it is historical study that can and should lead to new theorizing.

Readers of this chapter are no doubt familiar with the pragmatic editorial and pedagogical reasons for delimiting a topic such as "Hong Kong cinema before 1980." But that gesture brings certain dilemmas as well. For example, the phrase "Hong Kong cinema before 1980" may refer to films made in Hong Kong, films watched or circulated in Hong Kong, or films that are about or set in Hong Kong. Likewise, it may refer to films made before 1980, films watched or circulated before 1980, or films that are about or set in a time before 1980. These variations should remind us that whatever significance a particular film might have is not welded to that film's date and location of production – and that is assuming quaintly that production happens at a single defined date and location in the first place. Instead, films resonate within particular contexts that may be defined more extensively such as a generic tradition, and the meanings of films also change as the latter move through time and space. Moreover, the life of a film is not a linear and one-way trajectory from production to distribution to exhibition to reception. After all, presales to distributors as well as popular reception often shape film production practices, while the form that a film takes during production – its length, its technical format, and so on – may jump ahead to predetermine how it may be exhibited. Finally, not only is there much more to cinema than production, there is also much more to cinema than individual films and their contents. Hence a discussion of "Hong Kong cinema before 1980" may also be organized not around films but around economic, industrial, political, legal, or technological units of analysis.

Since there are already quite a few excellent book-length studies of Hong Kong cinema in English (Teo 1997; Bordwell 2000; Y. Chu 2003; Fu 2003; Law and Bren 2004; Cheuk 2008; K. Yau 2010),[1] I will not present a detailed chronology here. Instead I begin by summarizing the most commonly described history of Hong Kong cinema. I do so in order to reflect upon the historiographical implications of "Hong Kong cinema before 1980." Those implications in turn suggest a reorientation of the basic historical narrative. They also propose a shift in underlying concepts that are significant beyond the domain of cinema studies. Finally, they highlight some concrete possibilities for new research on "Hong Kong cinema before 1980."

Periodization

Existing narratives divide Hong Kong film history into three major periods. The first of these periods lasted from the introduction of the Lumière Cinématographe into Hong Kong in 1897 to the geopolitical division of several competing Chinas in 1949. Hong Kong cinema of this first period is seen as an offshoot of Chinese cinema. The latter is understood in a national sense centered on mainland China, especially Shanghai. From this perspective Hong Kong's position was marginal or secondary at best. Indeed it seemed most important when it served merely as a source of labor and technology, as a branch office for expanding business operations, or as a temporary refuge from political and military crises in the North.

As with most places in the world, cinema in Hong Kong began with importation and exhibition, not with indigenous production. Theaters and other kinds of existing spaces became Hong Kong's initial film exhibition venues, with the first dedicated movie theater being built in 1907. Some of the early film operators also began to make short films locally. Not surprisingly many of those pioneers of cinema in Hong Kong were immigrants or itinerants. For example, the legendary Russian-American entrepreneur Benjamin Brodsky has long been recognized for his pioneering Yaxiya (Asia Film Company) firm based in Shanghai; in fact at least one of the firm's short narrative films, *Stealing a Roast Duck* (Leung Siu-bo / Liang Shaobo, 1909), was made in Hong Kong. The next two decades are sketchy in many existing narratives of Hong Kong film history because few fiction feature films were made in Hong Kong and information about them is scarce. But distribution and exhibition did develop in important ways. For example, in the 1920s Lo Gun (Lu Gen, 1888–1968) built a distribution and exhibition network covering theaters in Hong Kong, Guangzhou, Hankou, and Shanghai (B. Zhong 2007: 50–4). Lo began importing American films before Hollywood studios recuperated distribution rights through their own new Asian branch offices; he later switched to distributing films from Shanghai. Lo briefly attempted film production in the early 1930s but soon went bankrupt. Still, his plan was not unusual because when film production did finally flourish in Hong Kong in others' hands in the 1930s, it came by way of China. In many cases it was a result of mainland capital setting down roots in Hong Kong to make films there using the new sound film technology, hence including Cantonese dialogue. This transplantation happened repeatedly through the later 1930s and the 1940s, though with political motivations under the Japanese invasion and then the civil war appearing to outweigh the economic ones.

The emblematic example of this routing of Hong Kong cinema through Chinese cinema is Lai Man-wai (Li Minwei), who was born in Japan but grew up in Hong Kong (Law and Lai 1999; S. Lai 2003). Lai was committed to two things throughout his adult life: the nation and cinema. He joined Sun Yat-sen's revolutionary United League (Tongmenghui) in 1909 and its successor the Kuomintang (KMT) in 1924. He produced more than thirty documentaries, traveling extensively throughout China to shoot political and military events up through the 1940s. Besides documentary film, Lai was a pioneer in two other fundamental aspects of Chinese film history: fiction filmmaking and industrial organization. In the first fiction film made in Hong Kong by a Hong Kong firm and crew, *Zhuangzi Tests His Wife*, probably made in 1914, Lai plays the wife and may have been both writer and director as well (Law and Bren 2004: 38–40). In the decades to follow, he would produce more than forty fiction feature films. These latter productions resulted from the fact that he also founded or managed a whole array of film companies. The most notable of those firms were Minxin (China Sun) and Lianhua (United Photoplay Service).

The tangled fortunes of these two studios mark out some of the most important parameters of Chinese cinema of the Republican period. Lai Man-wai and his older brother Lai Buk-hoi (Li Beihai, 1889–1959) founded Minxin in Hong Kong in 1923, but the 1925 Hong Kong labor strikes pushed them to relocate the firm to

Shanghai. Then in 1930, Luo Mingyou (1900–67), a Hong Kong native who had built the largest distribution and exhibition network in Northeast China, orchestrated the merger of Minxin with three other existing firms to form Lianhua – a company that was actually founded in Hong Kong but quickly relocated to Shanghai. Luo and Lai Man-wai guided Lianhua until it ceased production in 1937. While its headquarters were in Shanghai, Lianhua did have branch offices in Beijing and Hong Kong. Both the films and the film artists at Lianhua included some of the most famous and influential of the period. Those works and personnel would eventually be canonized as leftist or proto-Communist forerunners of China's proper national cinema.

Throughout his career Lai Man-wai lived in and shuttled regularly among Hong Kong, Shanghai, and Guangzhou. These peregrinations were a product partly of his tireless efforts to develop cinema as a business and as a form of art and propaganda. They were also a product of the extracinematic history of the times in which he lived, especially the status of those three cities as highly developed cultural and commercial centers – itself in part a result of geography and colonialism – as well as the political and military tumult that pervaded China. Thus Lai's landmark achievements, like Sun Yat-sen's revolution itself, would not have been possible without Hong Kong and its special circumstances. Finally, in 1948 Lai went to work for the new Yung Hwa (Yonghua) film studio in Hong Kong. His death there in 1953 came a full four years after the People's Republic of China (PRC) laid powerful claim to the notion of China as a nation. It was also just at the moment when the PRC was consolidating its newly nationalized film industry. Yet commemorative banners at his funeral in Hong Kong celebrated him as "The Father of Chinese Cinema" (*guopian zhi fu*). Here "Chinese cinema" (*guopian*) literally means "national films," films made in or by a nation, that is, in or by China. With the contestations over "China" and its national status stretching throughout the twentieth century and beyond, *guopian* is a keyword in the history of discourses and practices of cinema in Chinese.

The second commonly recognized period of Hong Kong film history stretches from the 1950s to the 1970s. This period is usually described in terms of two seemingly opposite vectors: the emergence of a locally specific Hong Kong cinema and the expansion of Hong Kong cinema into relatively close-range regional networks across East and Southeast Asia. Behind the productive aspect of emergence and expansion is the negative aspect of this period. For, at least on the surface, these new trends were necessitated by the loss of mainland China as both a source of films and an export market during the cold war. All of this corresponded with, on a more concrete level, the maturing of Hong Kong cinema's industrial organization, and on a more general level, the growth of industrial capitalism and its correlates in society and culture.

With the end of World War II and the renewal of civil war within China came massive migration from the North into Hong Kong. From the baseline of about six hundred thousand inhabitants at the end of the war in 1945, the population of Hong

Kong doubled in less than two years, more than tripled in five years, and quintupled in fifteen years. For cinema this meant an immediate influx of talent, labor, and capital; new contestations over nation, identity, and the role of cinema in society; and long-term growth in local audiences as well as shifts in their tastes. Continuing a trend from the war years, filmmakers arriving from the North often brought social and political commitments, both right and left, resulting in the waxing and waning of individual careers like that of the Shanghai mogul Zhang Shankun (1905–57) and of whole firms like Yung Hwa, which Zhang cofounded. One of the most important phenomena of this second period was the maturation of industrial organization, whether in a few prominent examples of major vertically integrated studios like Shaw Brothers or in the symbiotic relations between small producers who relied on presales and exhibitors who relied on fast, cheap, high-volume output. The growth of such commercial mass production of course complemented the growth of a mass market. And by the 1960s and 1970s local moviegoers were younger and far more likely to be both Cantonese speaking and native to Hong Kong. The emblematic figure here is the Cantonese teen idol Connie Chan Po-chu (Chen Baozhu, b. 1949). The 250 films that Chan appeared in from 1958 to 1972 run the gamut from opera films to martial arts adventures to romantic comedies. In one of her most illustrative films, *Movie Fan Princess* (Wong Yiu / Wang Yao, 1966), Chan plays a factory girl who goes from being a movie fan to being a movie star herself, dramatizing all too clearly a fantasy of how cinema works in society.

Much existing scholarship and criticism holds that Hong Kong cinema has had two distinct systems or streams: Cantonese cinema and Mandarin cinema. It is in this second period of Hong Kong film history that the two systems solidified and coexisted, though not always as equals. The systems may be distinguishable in terms of film contents, production values, organizations and personnel, distribution and exhibition practices, and audience demographics and tastes. Moreover, impressionistic descriptions often contrast Cantonese cinema's cheaper and earthier nature with the high production values and cosmopolitan escapism of Mandarin cinema. But concrete investigation reveals both similarities as well as differences, so we should not assume that the two systems, especially their respective markets and viewers, were wholly separate. In fact the ideology of the distinction itself is worth reflecting upon, and there is nothing to stop a single viewer from enjoying films of both types even if s/he is not fluent in both languages.

Cantonese film production did drop sharply during the late 1960s, but there were more concrete reasons for this beyond low aesthetic quality. For example, the smaller Cantonese production studios had financed their operations for years through presales both within Hong Kong and to the wide Southeast Asian market. However, because of local cultural, political, and economic conditions in the emerging nations there, Hong Kong's film exports were increasingly unwelcome. At the same time, vertically integrated organizations like Shaw Brothers and Cathay (Guotai) controlled many exhibition venues. Their theater networks across the whole region naturally favored their own products, which were primarily in Mandarin. Foreign films too, especially those from Hollywood and Japan, commanded an increasing share of the exhibition marketplace. Finally, Television Broadcasts Limited (TVB) went on the air in Hong Kong in 1967, providing free broadcast entertainment rather than subscription cable programming, and it did so primarily in Cantonese.

As a result Cantonese film production stopped completely from early 1971 to late 1973. This crisis was but one symptom of the overall shifting landscape of the 1970s. Indeed, scholars differ somewhat on how to position that decade: its deep transformations belong to either the end of the second period of Hong Kong film history or the beginning of the third. For "independent" production, mostly in Cantonese, soon returned to challenge the vertically integrated studios, especially Shaw Brothers. Ironically enough the challenge originated from within Shaw Brothers itself in three ways. First, in 1970 the longtime Shaw executives Raymond Chow and Leonard Ho left to form Golden Harvest (Jiahe). The latter firm became the most famous challenger to the integrated studios by being more flexible with its contracts and signing stars like Bruce Lee (Li Xiaolong, 1940–73) and Jackie Chan. At the same time, however, Golden Harvest also continued the practice of controlling its own theater chain. Second, the head of Shaw Brothers, Run Run Shaw (Shao Yifu, b. 1907), was in fact the leading shareholder in TVB such that the subsequent decline of his film studio is just the other side of the rise of his television operations. Third, it was the Shaw–TVB coproduction *The House of 72 Tenants* (Chor Yuen/Chu Yuan, 1973) that jump-started Cantonese film production in general. Beyond the orbit of Shaw Brothers, it was during the 1970s that various television stations cultivated fresh talent and rejuvenated genres like slapstick comedy and styles like urban realism, leading eventually to the New Wave cinema of the 1980s. At this time the renewal of commerce with mainland China meant first the recovery of a huge market and second Hong Kong's integration into a larger national system of economic production overall. The return of Hong Kong from Britain to China in July 1997 signaled the completion of these last trends as well as a new phase in this third period that continues to this day, namely the renaissance of Hong Kong cinema as a part of Chinese cinema.

Nationalization

Even from such a brief summary of existing scholarship on Hong Kong film history, we can discern some problematic issues – as well as new avenues for theorizing and historical research. To begin with, the "Hong Kong" of "Hong Kong cinema" functions in a national sense. This is not to say that Hong Kong is a nation but that "Hong Kong cinema" acts as a genre or brand name, an organizing principle that orchestrates diverse phenomena and sets the very terms by which we are to view that cinema. However, the notion of a national cinema as such has attained the dubious honor of being one of the most common objects of critique in cinema studies. One need only do an elementary database search to find a wealth of articles, monographs, anthologies, journals, and whole book series on national cinemas. Drawing upon scholarship across the academy on nations and nationalisms, these critiques in cinema studies apply to all nations. So it is neither surprising nor unique that the notion of Chinese cinema now regularly serves as a negative origin, that which must be invoked at the outset so that we may denaturalize and deconstruct it and therefore move forward precisely in order to study Chinese cinema, constructing and confirming it as an object of knowledge after all (Pang 2007). One way to skirt this new obsession if not with China then with Chineseness is to rewrite the very notion of a national cinema from a substantive thing to the problematic and dynamic interaction between the national and the cinematic (Berry and Farquhar 2006). This strategy helps to illuminate the overlooked interstices of a nation, including its internal minorities, its avant-gardes, and its cheap, lowbrow, or ephemeral bits of popular culture. It is just as fruitful when it looks outside a nation, for example, at diasporic filmmakers, transnational production, or foreign marketing and spectatorship.

As a result of all this, it is now nearly impossible not to assume in advance that the nation is the master signifier of cinema even if it is so only in an absent, deferred, incomplete, negative, paradoxical, or unrepresentable sense. It may even function in a purely discursive way, that is, as no more than a keyword in a common language that allows us to converse about widely disparate cinematic phenomena. This is especially ironic in the case of Hong Kong, which has never been a fully formed nation, probably never will be, and has rarely if ever even been dreamed as such (Abbas 2007). Nevertheless, it is not possible, necessary, or wise simply to discard or ignore the nation, especially because in our world of globalization the nation is not vanishing but evolving into newer and more numerous forms than ever. Instead we can reapproach this complex problematic obliquely by means of the following four ideas.

First, what we should investigate is neither the status of the nation or of any actual nation, nor the phenomenon of nation-faith known as nationalism. Instead we should investigate something more fundamental: "nation-ism" or nationalization, the practice of imagining that the basic unit by which the world is to be mapped in the first place is none other than the nation. Second, as we can see from the huge influence of Benedict Anderson's *Imagined Communities* in the last few decades (perhaps second only to Edward Said's *Orientalism*), the nation is a method of inquiry. Its concepts or features can be partially adapted. For example, the idea of collective imagination without sovereignty has helped to render legible many social phenomena such as minority communities and transnational activist movements. Third, although theorizing ultimately has a speculative orientation toward developing new ways to think, act, and experience, it is history that remains an indispensable, perhaps even the last or most urgent, frontier of the changing nation. This means that the recovery of lost periods of film history is a salutary symptom of the contemporary crisis of national cinema, especially in the wake of new waves, the rhetoric of which always presupposes a difference with older cinematic currents. Hence the ongoing work of writing histories of Chinese cinema before the 1980s triple splash of the Hong Kong New Wave, the New Taiwan Cinema, and the Fifth Generation (see Chapters 4, 6, and 8, this volume).[2] Fourth, and most importantly, such a refiguration of history brings into view other organizing principles, that is, other orderings of time and space and hence of history and narrative. The point then is not simply to prove that Chinese cinema was always already hybrid, heterogeneous, contested, or transnational; nor is it simply to recount the changing relation of Hong Kong to the idea of a nation or to the actual nation of China over time. Still less is it to conclude predictably that Hong Kong is not a nation, that its cinema is not a national cinema, and that it nevertheless can teach us something about nations and their cinemas – especially as a supplement once again to China and Chinese cinema. Those tasks may be important, meaningful, and even necessary, but they are only partial exercises. Instead, the point here is ultimately to position "Hong Kong cinema before 1980" in relation to those various other coexisting and interacting orders, orders without which Hong Kong itself could not exist: not just that of the nation but also of colonialism and modernity.

The notion that history is a frontier of the nation as it heads into the future should remind us that the division of historical time into periods is not merely an academic or epistemological gesture. It is a political one as well. And if such a gesture results in chronological borders, like spatial ones those borders are subject to crossing. The most obvious chronological border in modern China is the year 1949. Thus, for example, it should be noted that prewar cinematic commerce continued between Hong Kong and mainland China well into the cold-war years (A. Wong 2005). One aspect was the movement of talent such as the husband-and-wife team of Cantonese opera performers Ma Si-tsang (Ma Shizeng, 1900–64) and Hung Sin Nui (Hong Xian Nü, b. 1927). Natives of Guangdong, they performed widely in China and Hong Kong during the 1930s and 1940s and then settled in Hong Kong after World War II. Ma Si-tsang appeared in over thirty films there and Hung Sin Nui in nearly a hundred before they moved back to Guangdong in 1955 to continue their careers in China. Another aspect of cinematic border crossing was the circulation of films such as the Shanghainese *yueju* opera film *Liang Shanbo and Zhu Yingtai* (Sang Hu, Huang Sha, 1954). Its impressive 34-day theatrical run in Hong Kong in 1955 was partly due to the efforts of Lai Man-wai's second wife Florence Lim (Lam Chor-chor/Lin Chuchu, 1904–79) (Law and Lai 1999: 190; S. Lai 2003: 32).[3] And yet another important example of film industrial commerce between Hong Kong and China well after 1949 took place on the level of organizations. Founded in 1952, the Sun Luen (Xinlian) group, an alliance of leftist film studios in Hong Kong, was a principal investor in Guangzhou's newly established state-owned Pearl River Studio. The two organizations subsequently coproduced five films from 1961 to 1964.

If the contemporary era of postmodernism and globalization has seen a turn from the problematics of time to those of space, and if much of the productive stress upon the nation nowadays has to do with territory and with sovereignty as the spatial exercise of power, then the foregoing reflections suggest some timely ways to think through "Hong Kong cinema before 1980." To put it simply, instead of history we may focus on geography; and instead of periods we may focus on places, regions, and orientations. The outline of three periods of Hong Kong film history contains the seeds of such a shift already. For upon closer examination, the differentiation of those periods revolves around a number of geocultural orientations, with one or another such orientation dominant in each successive period.

Orientations

Although the work of cataloging may never be final, the China Film Archive's *Encyclopedia of Chinese Films* lists about 2,400 films made in mainland China from 1905 to 1976. In contrast, the ongoing *Hong Kong Filmography* series published by the Hong Kong Film Archive lists well over six thousand films made in Hong Kong during a similar span of years, 1913 to 1974. The Hong Kong figure may yet pale in comparison to, say, Hollywood, but we should remember two things. First, while Hong Kong occupies a land area about 10 percent less than the city of Los Angeles, film production facilities and activities attributed to Hollywood are far more dispersed, stretching across not just the city of Los Angeles but Los Angeles County. Even the range of more distant places where production activities have occurred, such as location shooting, has been far greater for Hollywood than for Hong Kong. Second, while Hong Kong has consistently had a larger population than the city of Los Angeles throughout the history of cinema, even the domestic market (not to mention the international market) for Hollywood films is vast by comparison, encompassing the whole United States. So in order to plot out more fully the geography of Hong Kong cinema, we must start with a simple fact: the size and location of Hong Kong have had a deep impact on its film industry from the very beginning.

First, because Hong Kong is so small in geographic and demographic terms, the market for cinema within its own borders cannot sustain its film industry. To put it another way, Hong Kong's film industry developed such voluminous output relative to that local market, not to mention so many production firms and personnel, because from the beginning many films produced in Hong Kong were made to be shown elsewhere. Of course, given the diversity and competition of its film industry, not all films made in Hong Kong have actually been exported. Nevertheless, the point is that the cinema of Hong Kong is defined by an orientation toward export, that is, by circulation beyond its own borders. This is true even with respect to things that nowadays we might think of as archetypally belonging to Hong Kong cinema, such as Cantonese dialogue and spectacular action choreography. More generally speaking, this thought should also remind us why it is so difficult to think of cinema apart from the nation. For cinema is one of the most powerful and pervasive apparatuses for imagining a community, and as per Anderson's Saussurean account the imagining into being of this community also depends upon and takes place in the imagination of other communities.

Just why so many films have been made in Hong Kong to be viewed elsewhere has to do with the second basic geographical determinant, location. Hong Kong is located between the very large mainland of China to the north and the array of small nations to the south. It is also between Korea, Japan, and Taiwan to the east and northeast; and South Asia – especially India, Pakistan, and Bangladesh – to the west. These coordinates, along with the local topography that is suitable for a marine harbor, were of course crucial to Britain's strategic desire to acquire and develop Hong Kong in the nineteenth century. Thus the subsequent evolution of Hong Kong as a nodal point in international cinematic circulations is a specific extension of the colony's basic character. Still, while Hong Kong cinema has been defined by circulations beyond Hong Kong, those circulations do not extend in any direction whatsoever or to any place whatsoever but to a specific set of actual places with their own historical and geographical peculiarities. For example, the best known of those cinematic circulations from the first few decades of the twentieth century involve mainland China, especially Shanghai. And as noted above, Lai Man-wai's travels took place primarily along the deeply grooved routes connecting Hong Kong, Shanghai, and Guangzhou.

The fact that Hong Kong has now returned to the legal and political jurisdiction of China seems to justify an emphasis from the beginning on that northern orientation in the historiography of Hong Kong cinema. Indeed, that return itself, along with the rediscovery of early cinema in academic and commemorative registers, is one of the main reasons for the recent revival of interest in Lai Man-wai. Textbooks on Chinese film history written in China in the last decade or so have tended to squeeze in a chapter on Hong Kong, and one on Taiwan as well, absorbing them as indivisible parts of Chinese cinema. Other mainstream and official representations like the China National Film Museum in Beijing that opened in 2005 have adopted similar approaches. By defining Hong Kong as an area, region, or zone (*diqu*), such representations do imply a geographical imagination, but it is one that is nevertheless national and centripetal. To be sure, Hong Kong film production did become oriented primarily toward mainland China again in the 1990s as the 1997 handover approached and as Hong Kong cinema itself – as an export production industry and as a local exhibition market – lost significant revenues to competitors like television, home video, personal computing and the Internet, and above all Hollywood. That reorientation was not fully recognized and formalized until the Closer Economic Partnership Arrangement (CEPA) between Hong Kong and the mainland went into effect in 2004. In a sense CEPA completed the "re-turn" of Hong Kong cinema to China, but only in the same ambivalent sense as the overall return of the colony in 1997. For not only was Hong Kong "lost" by a very different homeland to begin with, and not only was it built up to its present advanced state of development under the colonizers, but – most atypically – that advanced state of development actually catapulted it into the national vanguard as the homeland continued its march toward capitalism, modernization, and globalization. More than any other single event, 1997 sums up the intersection of historical and geographical orientations that is Hong Kong.

However, we cannot appreciate the heterogeneity of Hong Kong cinema's orientations and hence the fundamentally constitutive role of extraterritoriality for Hong Kong cinema by focusing only on the one relation between Hong Kong and China. In response Law and Bren (2004) have traced out the movements of people, organizations, capital, technology and technique, films, film styles, and ideologies into and through and out of Hong Kong. What makes their work significant here is that it begins with the 1890s; in other words, Hong Kong cinema was border crossing from the beginning, and in ways that are concretely documentable rather than simply to be glossed or summarized in conceptual terms. Moreover, Law and Bren balance their account between the northern, mainland Chinese orientation and a southern, Southeast Asian one. In a similar example of groundbreaking historical scholarship, Kinnia Yau (2010) has argued that the recent phenomenon of East Asian popular cultures, especially in cinema, television, and music, is founded on historical infrastructure that developed in much earlier decades, including those of the Japanese empire of the first half of the twentieth century. So the contemporary regional media networks that scholars, artists, corporations, states, and of course fans have so eagerly embraced are something like postcolonial literatures: they are as much traces of colonialism as they are new liberatory formations. The general lesson here is that history and geography cannot exist without each other. Hence particular orientations privilege particular historical narratives for Hong Kong, with nationalism to the north, (de) colonization to the south, modernization to the east, and empire to the west.

In fact the crucial southward circuit stretching to other colonial and quasi-colonial territories like Malaya was already under construction during the first golden age of Shanghai film production in the 1920s and 1930s. A combination of economic, demographic, political, technological, and linguistic factors during these years guaranteed the fateful southern face of Hong Kong cinema. With economic competition heating up in the locally saturated market of Shanghai in the second half of the 1920s, and with Southeast Asia's large potential audiences of ethnic or overseas Chinese, films made in Shanghai found a natural outlet beyond China's borders. Then in the first half of the 1930s, competing political imperatives shaping film contents met the newly viable technique of recorded sound on film, especially dialogue. As a result, what dialect could or would be heard in films became a question subject to the laws of both market and politics. It so happened that Southeast Asia was home to many overseas Chinese who spoke some form of Chinese language other than Mandarin, which in state-supported terminology at that time was known as "the national language" (*guoyu*). In terms of sheer numbers, those potential film audiences tended to be of the merchant and working classes rather than, say, intellectuals and literati. And those other forms of Chinese that they spoke included Cantonese; Teochew or Chaozhou dialect; and Amoy or Hokkien, a dominant form of Southern Min within the larger category of Fujian dialects.

Since Hong Kong was both beyond the reach of Chinese state regulation and physically closer to the Southeast Asian market, it became not just a point of transit but a point of production. The result is the emergence of a discernible "Hong Kong" style of cinema in the 1930s, distinguished primarily by its Cantonese dialogue and secondarily by its entertainment and production values, and perhaps even a particular Southern Chinese and modern urban sensibility (Fu 2003: 55–8; Law and Bren 2004: 122). Here too we can see the irony that it was the prospect of extraterritorial markets that motivated the production of a kind of Hong Kong identity. Though this issue deserves further study, such identity production does not mean that the resulting films were simply images of home or purveyors of nostalgia in any simple sense. Shifting our focus somewhat, we could even argue that up through the 1930s, Hong Kong and its cinema were more a part of Southeast Asia than of China. In any event, by the end of the 1930s an important foundation was set: film production in Hong Kong would be shaped for decades to come by distribution and exhibition specifically in Southeast Asia.

Keeping in mind the seminal example of Lai Man-wai, we may debate the relative importance of Hong Kong cinema's northerly orientation toward China as opposed to its southerly orientation toward Southeast Asia during the first half of the twentieth century. Still, if the latter orientation was already in place more than a decade before 1949, the ratio tilted decisively in its favor during the cold war because of two simultaneous developments. As noted above, one development was the restriction of mainland China. On the positive side, the other development was the active investment by Southeast Asian Chinese filmmakers in Hong Kong film production. In general terms such increased activity in producing films in Hong Kong was linked to increased sales in Southeast Asia. In specific terms this meant increased circulation of people, technology, images, and so on. And again, it took place along deeply grooved southern routes, not the northern ones that brought the more famous influx of filmmakers, along with millions of others, from mainland China during and after the war.

The Shaw Brothers, Cathay, and Kong Ngee (Guangyi) organizations exemplified such increased investment during this period, though they were by no means the only ones involved in the Hong Kong–Southeast Asia circuit (Liao et al. 2003; A. Wong 2003, 2006, 2009; Fu 2008). All three organizations were founded by Chinese families, and although not all were founded in Singapore, they did all flourish there before 1949. In Singapore all three had focused primarily on distribution and exhibition, with production a secondary concern. And all three organizations established or enlarged film production divisions in Hong Kong during the 1950s and 1960s such that all three boasted a wide network of divisions and subsidiaries under different names across the region. (For example, most of Cathay's Hong Kong films were products of Motion Picture and General Investment or MP&GI, abbreviated Dianmao in Chinese, and were labeled as such; likewise only some of the Shaw firms were officially called "Shaw Brothers.") Nearly all of the most beloved talents in Hong Kong cinema of the 1950s through 1970s worked on at least one film by these three organizations.

Beyond the similarities that made Shaw Brothers, Cathay, and Kong Ngee the triple axis for this southern orientation, it is worth noting a few differences. The Shaw organization was the oldest and the only one that had direct roots in China, namely Tianyi (Unique Film Productions) that the four famous brothers founded in Shanghai in 1925. With market competition intensifying in Shanghai, the Shaws sought to export their films made there to Southeast Asia as early as 1926. They soon realized that the best way to ensure an outlet in that distant new market was to operate, and eventually to own, theaters themselves. Through this first corporate expansion Singapore became a distribution and exhibition base for the Shaws by the 1930s. They initiated a second expansion when they began making films in Hong Kong in 1934, soon moving their production headquarters from Shanghai to Hong Kong permanently. The organization's third and final geo-corporate expansion came in 1957 when Run Run Shaw moved from Singapore to take over the production operations in Hong Kong, building the legendary Movietown studio.

In contrast, Cathay (1936) and Kong Ngee (1937) were founded in Singapore itself by overseas Chinese – the Loke family and the Ho family, respectively – for the purposes of importing and exhibiting films. Reversing the Shaws' evolution while exemplifying "secondary" migration, Cathay and Kong Ngee expanded from distribution and exhibition in Singapore into film production in Hong Kong only in the 1950s. It should be noted that after the war all three organizations did build additional production operations in Singapore. Nevertheless the three organizations shared a similar division of labor that resulted in an important peculiarity of the Hong Kong–Singapore nexus: where the former became primarily a production center, the latter was a hub for distribution and exhibition.

Some other important differences among Shaw Brothers, Cathay, and Kong Ngee lay in their development and production strategies along with the film styles and contents that those strategies shaped. First and foremost, while in the 1960s Shaw Brothers and Cathay focused their efforts on Mandarin cinema, Kong Ngee made films in Cantonese. This difference is not simply the difference between national and local. While the issue of language in the films of the three organizations deserves much more detailed investigation on its own, suffice to say that both Mandarin and Cantonese could travel across borders to different audiences and markets but no doubt with different itineraries, resonances, and results. To complicate matters further, it should be noted that one of Kong Ngee's subsidiaries in Hong Kong, Chiu Ngee (Chaoyi), specialized in Teochew dialect films to be shipped not to that dialect's hometown in mainland China but back to Southeast Asia. It should also be noted that the intense rivalry between Cathay and Shaw Brothers extended to the Malay language production studios that they owned in Singapore (Millet 2006; Uhde and Uhde 2010). And finally, Shaw Brothers did make at least a dozen parallel films in the late 1960s, that is, they shot those films more than once at the same time with the same story, sets, and crew but different leading actors and actresses. A step beyond dubbing, the result was "the same" film tailored both aurally and visually into Mandarin, Korean, Japanese, Malay, Thai, and even Tagalog versions for the appropriate audiences and geographical markets.

Another difference is that although the Shaw organization has far outlasted the other two, Kong Ngee was perhaps the most prescient in developing a whole family of production firms in the 1960s. Each firm occupied a particular niche; while Chiu Ngee made Teochew films, Sun Ngee (Xinyi) cultivated younger filmmakers, and Yuet Ngee (Yueyi) specialized in martial arts adventures. Other subsidiary units were boutique or personal studios financed by Kong Ngee and operated by some of its own most famous actors and directors. The point was to grant those talents some measure of artistic control while not allowing them to escape to another company entirely. This strategy foreshadowed the rebirth of "independent" productions in the 1970s as described above, and ironically though not surprisingly both Cathay and Kong Ngee ceased film production in the early 1970s.

In a more general sense, Kong Ngee's prescient corporate strategy signals the reconceptualization of a film studio from a massive centralized and self-financed production facility to a physically more modest but financially more flexible investor and manager for other people's projects. It is no accident that this change echoes the economic and industrial history of globalization, for the southern orientation of "Hong Kong cinema before 1980" exemplifies an important conceptual shift that globalization has strongly reinforced. That shift consists simply of redefining what a center is. In industrial capitalism a center is a point of origin, production, emanation, and concentration. But for late or finance capitalism a center is a node, a hub, or a point of transit, translation, transformation, and exchange. Rather than as a point from which things come or a point at which things arrive, we should think of a center as a point through which things pass. In terms of cinema, a center in this revised sense is not a place where films are made, especially in the older sense of a studio lot or sound stage, but a place where things like tropes, genres, talent, technology, capital, production methods, and even management styles themselves pass through, recombining and metamorphosing in the process. This reconceptualization therefore complements recent transnational and comparative studies of, for example, remaking or citing Hollywood films as productive transformation rather than mere copying; or minor transnational connections that are not anchored to the usual centers of political and economic power.

However, beyond this is a deeper confirmation of Hong Kong's significance in a general historical cultural geography. In the imagination of China as nation that is centered on mainland China, Hong Kong is at the southern edge, geographically as well as culturally and politically marginal. And in the imagination of a Chinese national cinema, the leading candidates for a center in the older sense are Shanghai and Beijing. But by revisiting the various orientations of Hong Kong cinema, including others besides the northern and southern ones I have described here, we can map out a whole region with Hong Kong as a new kind of center. Southeast Asia would then serve as a useful contrast to China in part because the former is many nations rather than a single nation. Furthermore, Singapore would be a counterweight to Beijing and perhaps even to Shanghai. This is not an expression of political dissent or resistance to China or to the PRC specifically. It is instead a conceptual shift from the nation and "nation-ism" to a different scale: the region.

Like the local, the notion of the regional has a checkered history but has been rehabilitated in recent years precisely as an answer to globalization, the nation, and even the area of area studies. Yet the regional remains somewhat more amorphous and flexible than the local, the most common revalorization of which locks the local into a dialectical relation with the global. If the regional is neither better nor worse than the local, it is also neither necessarily bigger nor smaller than the national. And if the reconceptualization of a center sounds rather like the moment of the local in that dialectical relation, then the regional functions as the context within which a center operates. With respect to cinema, this scale is useful for its retention of older notions of physical or geographical proximity, material circulations, and state strategies. These notions caution us against what may be overoptimistic imaginings of networks that extend in any direction whatsoever or to any place whatsoever. That is why such a regional orientation is particularly well suited to the study of industrial aspects of "Hong Kong cinema before 1980."

Prospects

The preceding reflections promise many new avenues for research in addition to those alluded to already. For example, as with the theme of time, there are many different kinds of critical approaches to the theme of space and cinema. One may focus on industrial matters of organization and circulation as well as infrastructural sites like studios and theaters. Or one may focus on the representation of space in the form of places, travel stories, exoticism, cities, architecture, sets, and locations. Or one may focus on affective and cognitive phenomenology through questions of style, editing and camera movement, sound, virtuality, the haptic, and so on. Certain approaches may bridge these possibilities. For example, industrial analysis does not preclude politics and ideology. With the intense and protean ideological conflicts from the 1920s through the 1970s throughout East and Southeast Asia and the proliferation of new nations in those regions, for tiny colonial Hong Kong to avoid strong political expressions was a survival tactic. The importance of export markets for Hong Kong cinema further encouraged the making of films whose ability to travel well depended in no small measure on their avoidance of, or at least moderation of, national political messages of all kinds. In their functioning as both fantasy pictures and circulating products, the resulting films mapped out the geopolitical region around Hong Kong. Hence censorship, regulation, and strategies of film development and circulation constitute an important research topic at the crossroads of industry and state (K. Ng 2008). Since it was simultaneously Hong Kong cinema's single biggest offshore market, an indispensable source of talent, and the other major claimant to the nationalistic title of "China," Taiwan – that is, the Republic of China – was especially important in this regard.

In fact all artworks function as double representations – both as pictures and as products, or to put it more generally, both as texts and as objects. Moreover, that doubleness is itself exponentially extended when one considers the interactions of cinema with other arts and media. Throughout the history of Hong Kong cinema, many of its genres have existed in conjunction with other arts and media: musicals alongside pop songs, opera films alongside theater, martial arts adventures alongside novels, slapstick comedy and eventually the New Wave alongside television. Each of these combinations offers rich possibilities for detailed analyses of industrial practices, consumption and fandom, and media aesthetics. Not surprisingly, these interactions often took a reflexive or metafictional turn. For example, *Prince of Broadcasters* (Patrick Lung Kong, 1966) follows the romance between a dashing radio play actor (Patrick Tse Yin, the leading hunk of the Kong Ngee galaxy) and a fresh-faced high school fan girl (Chan Chai-chung/Chen Qisong). At one point the actor's radio play becomes all-too real, while at another it is the impersonal, public medium of broadcasting that serves as the vehicle for heartfelt apologies and personal pleas. Naturally the ending is happy, with the playboy actor finally domesticated, the girl's honor restored, and a beautiful baby girl to complete the new family. The 1960s in fact saw a large handful of films like *Prince of Broadcasters* featuring radio and television backstage dramas about love and fame. As a first step it is easy to imagine that they served as politically conservative fantasies of social mobility for young adult audiences in rapidly industrializing Hong Kong and elsewhere. The next step could be to consider where and how those broadcast media overlapped to produce particular senses of space, place, distance, intimacy, materiality, and so on.

Rethinking "Hong Kong cinema before 1980" can also renew existing areas of historical research and theorizing. Besides their resonance in society at that time, *Prince of Broadcasters* and similar films highlight formal and aesthetic problems of subjectivity and stardom. Long before television and the Internet, cinema led the way in the technological dissection and assemblage that results in the kind of human figure known as the star, as well as in the spectacular display of that very apparatus. Common filmmaking practices like dubbing, playback, stunt and body doubles, and constructive editing constitute the technical repertoire, while popular genres like musicals, opera films, and martial arts adventures each have a specific

Figure 5.1   *"… that's why I'm dressed as a man"*: In *That's for My Love* (dir. Chiang Wai-kwong, Huixia Film, 1953), Yam Kim-fai (left) plays a retired Cantonese opera actress who pretends to be the fiancé of her brother's ex-girlfriend.

set of aesthetic and narrative conventions for such star assembly. A perfect crystallization of these issues is the gender- and genre-bending actress Yam Kim-fai (Ren Jianhui, 1913–89) (see Figure 5.1), one of Hong Kong's biggest stars ever across theater, phonograph, radio, print, and cinema. Although she appeared in 307 films, nearly all made from 1951 to 1964 and dozens of which are easily available today on DVD, she remains almost unknown in English-language scholarship and criticism (for Chinese surveys, see M. Lam 2004; Z. Huang 2009). Indeed the genre that she is most famous for, opera film, is a crucial hybrid that is at the very foundations of Chinese cinema, and it too has attracted little attention in English so far.

In contrast, Bruce Lee remains one of the most recognizable Chinese or Hong Kong stars worldwide, yet by postwar Hong Kong standards he appeared in a tiny number of films. Nevertheless, the score of black and white social realist melodramas in which he appeared in the 1950s may be contrasted fruitfully with the four and a half color kungfu films that made him a legend in the early 1970s. If the latter set of films seems so small in number, it at least serves as a highly concentrated synthesis of, on the one hand, performance and personification, and on the other hand, the multiple orientations of "Hong Kong cinema before 1980." Not coincidentally Lee was the first major star to sign with the newly formed Golden Harvest, and the subsequent kungfu films secured that studio's economic success.

It has been customary to scan those films obsessively for signs of Chineseness or Hong Kongness, especially in Lee's spectacular body exercising "Chinese kungfu" in foreign lands and against foreign bodies. Instead we might ask how Lee's specifically cinematic performance style circulated and reproduced in the form of specular techniques of the body and according to Hong Kong's various but particular orientations. A good reflexive example to consider would be the film *Forever Fever* (Glen Goei, 1998), made in Singapore (Berry and Farquhar 2006: 219–22), while an example of a different orientation would be the fifty-part television series *The Legend of Bruce Lee* (Li Wenqi) first broadcast in China in 2008. In the latter the fictional fates continuously and repeatedly conspire to stir up in the hero vigorous feelings of ethnic national identity and thereby enable the present-day recovery of Lee for a mainland Chinese audience. At the same time, there is virtually no mention of his 1950s acting career. Yet this hero's initial martial arts training is depicted as less a matter of learning from the beginning than of channeling his legendary prowess in the cha-cha, itself a complex border-crossing performance style.

Finally, the kinds of issues and materials of "Hong Kong cinema before 1980" that I have proposed can reshape how we understand Hong Kong cinema even after 1980. For example, *In the Mood for Love* (Wong Kar-wai, 2000) is widely celebrated as a meditation on desire. However, desire is both infectious and misleading. Beguiled by the sensuous cinematic surface, from Maggie Cheung's 21 cheongsams to Nat King Cole's Anglo-Spanish crooning, many readings of the film are framed by what is not there: China, Hong Kong's master other, especially pre-1949 Shanghai. Yet such readings tend to overlook something else that lies in plain sight: Southeast Asia. To be sure, one should not limit the elsewhere of Hong Kong in this film to China and Southeast Asia; the vectors that intersect here point to places like Japan, France, and the Americas as well. But each of the film's four chapters is keyed to particular geographical histories: already overcrowded 1962 Hong Kong with its memorable six-week spike of migration from the North; Singapore on the threshold of independence in 1963; Hong Kong between the Star Ferry riots and the Great Proletarian Cultural Revolution in 1966; and finally the global (read: televisual, newsworthy, Western) ramifications of decolonization refracted through Cambodia in 1966. If the intersection or *tête bêche* of its Chinese and English titles ("the flourishing years" versus "in the mood for love") suggests that what this film imaginatively reconstructs is a feeling of history, it also intimates a history of feelings. Perhaps the ultimate question for "Hong Kong cinema before 1980" would then be: What did it feel like?

Notes

1   In addition to these book-length studies, there are many journal articles, book chapters, and anthologies on Hong Kong cinema. For instance, Yingjin Zhang (2004a) offers one of the most organically integrated accounts of Hong Kong cinema within the general

horizon of Chinese cinema, while the Hong Kong Film Archive has issued groundbreaking anthologies on special topics as well as invaluable reference tools: http://www.lcsd.gov.hk/CE/CulturalService/HKFA/en/4-1.php. The best monograph in Chinese so far is B. Zhong (2007).

2   See the trilogy of special issues of the *Journal of Chinese Cinemas*: 4.1 (March 2010), 4.2 (August 2010), and 4.3 (November 2010).

3   For a survey of other mainland produced films that were distributed to Hong Kong in the second half of the twentieth century, including almost three hundred such films screened in the colony between 1950 and 1980, see H. Zhu (2005).

6

The Hong Kong New Wave

Gina Marchetti

By the time Hong Kong's New Wave filmmakers screened their debut features and Law Wai-ming declared "the beginning of a new era" in *Film Bi-Weekly* in 1979 (Rodriguez 2001: 53), cinematic "new waves" had become old hat.[1] The French New Wave broke away from the domination of Hollywood and European realism and theatrical aestheticism in 1959 and quite a lot had transpired between the breaking of these two cinematic waves. In fact, as *The 400 Blows* (François Truffaut, 1959) and *Breathless* (Jean-Luc Godard, 1960) caused a sensation in Europe, Asia already was incubating its own Japanese New Wave in Tokyo with filmmakers such as Nagisa Ôshima (b. 1932). Italian directors turned away from the "new" perspective of Neo-Realism, and the "new wave" spread rapidly across Europe, giving rise to "new" cinemas in Germany, Czechoslovakia, Yugoslavia, Poland, Hungary, and elsewhere. Not to be outdone by the Europeans, New American Cinema – from the underground to the rise of the Hollywood "brats" – reinvigorated US screens, and the "new" had taken root (Kolker 1980, 1983). By the time the "new" cinema appeared in Hong Kong, Chinese-language film was already on the brink of enormous change: the People's Republic of China (PRC) reopened its film schools to a cohort that would become known as the "Fifth Generation," and Taiwan New Cinema had its debut with two omnibus films, *In Our Time* (Edward Yang et al., 1982) and *The Sandwich Man* (Hou Hsiao-Hsien, Wan Ren, Zeng Zhuangxiang, 1983).

While the "new" of the "new waves" connotes a sea change in the accepted standards of the high-end commercial or art film of a particular national cinema, the "new" of the "new cinemas" often marks the emergence of an internationally recognized art cinema coming from a country that had little or no visibility within top-ranked film festivals previously. The terminology does not follow any hard-and-fast rules, but "new" cinemas of various types do seem to follow particular

A Companion to Chinese Cinema, First Edition. Edited by Yingjin Zhang.
© 2012 Blackwell Publishing Ltd. Published 2012 by Blackwell Publishing Ltd.

patterns. New waves tend to be led by young, highly visible (and vocal) auteurs (typically directors, but also, occasionally, cinematographers, screenwriters, and actors). They make a splash locally (within the domestic press as well as on indigenous screens) and internationally (with entries in major film festivals, journalistic as well as scholarly recognition of their work). The new waves form part of wider political, social, and economic developments, often appearing in conjunction with the recognition of a "new generation" with different attitudes and values, riding on the coattails of a particular avant-garde movement in the other arts, attendant upon a regime change, or the excitement generated by "new" hope within a moribund cultural industry. New waves take advantage of new technologies, which give rise to the "fresh" look or innovative style of the films. They self-consciously break with the old; if the old system tended to be studio bound, they move to the streets, or, if the older generation loves the open air, they take up enclosed spaces and theatrical conceits. Many new wave filmmakers come to the medium through nontraditional means. Rather than apprenticing with the old "masters" of the previous generation, they learn the filmmaking craft as university students, critics, journalists, amateur short filmmakers, or through work in another medium like television.

Most new waves resemble movements in the other arts. The filmmakers share a particular approach, similar backgrounds, and start working around the same time and in the same place. Film festival programmers and journalists group them together; even when individual filmmakers insist the movement does not exist or that they are certainly not part of it if it does exist, their work continues to be linked with films made by their peers. Manifestos and proclamations may or may not appear, but new wave filmmakers tend to be articulate self-promoters who communicate their difference from previous generations of filmmakers quite well. They know each other, sometimes work on films made by their peers, and share facilities and talent – operating in the same studios, with the same producers and distributors, exhibiting in the same festivals, using the same marketing outlets, and often sharing actors, cinematographers, editors, and screenwriters. They are championed by the same curators, journalists, and scholars. Although their styles may vary enormously, they share a common sensibility, returning to key themes, plots, character types, historical incidents, and social or political issues. New waves, in particular, thrive on aesthetic innovation, and they lean toward modernist and/or postmodernist approaches. They do not "revive" a past tradition (e.g., Italian Neo-Realism as an outgrowth of "verismo"), and they do not try to establish something completely "new" and "national" (e.g., New Iranian Cinema). Rather, the "new wave" attempts to wash away the past, break with tradition, and create a new agenda for filmmakers in open conflict with the cinematic status quo.

Although considerable controversy still dogs the Hong Kong New Wave and some filmmakers continue to be uncomfortable with the idea of the "new wave" as a film movement, the facts remain that these Hong Kong filmmakers share the generally recognized characteristics of "new wave" cinemas from the French New Wave up to the present. Educated abroad (primarily in the United States and the United Kingdom), having worked in Hong Kong television (generally under the tutelage of Selina Chow [Zhou Liangyi, b. 1945]), the Hong Kong New Wave – including Ann Hui, Yim Ho (Yan Hao, b. 1952), Tsui Hark (Xu Ke, b. 1951), Patrick Tam (Tan Jiaming, b. 1948), Allen Fong (b. 1947), Alex Cheung (Zhang Guoming, b. 1951) – noticeably rocked the boat of the film industry's status quo. Taking up location filmmaking and local stories, comfortable with new editing techniques and synchronized sound, these filmmakers brought a fresh, more personal approach to the commercial genres popular at the time.

After 1984, a "second wave" appeared, including Wong Kar-wai (b. 1958), Clara Law (Luo Zhuoyao, b. 1957), Stanley Kwan (Guan Jinpeng, b. 1957), Eddie Fong (Fang Lingzheng, b. 1954), Mabel Cheung (Zhang Wanting, b. 1950), Alex Law (Luo Qirui, b. 1953), and others, and Hong Kong cinema began to receive even more international attention at film festivals and from cineastes around the world. As filmmakers in the "first" and "second" waves of the new cinema continue to make films into the twenty-first century, they have been joined by other dedicated filmmakers on the fringes of the movement, including independents like Fruit Chan (Chen Guo, b. 1959), transnational filmmakers like Evans Chan (Chen Yaocheng), documentarists like Tammy Cheung (Zhang Hong, b. 1958), and diasporic figures like Wayne Wang (Wang Ying, b. 1949).[2] As the consequences of Hong Kong's 1997 change in sovereignty from British rule to a Special Administrative Region (SAR) in the PRC continue to be felt, Hong Kong film culture evolves, buffeted by the economic, cultural, and aesthetic changes occasioned by the intensification of the processes of globalization. Filmmakers associated with Hong Kong's "first" and "second" new waves remain active today, and it seems useful to look back on the evolution of the Hong Kong New Wave in light of recent developments in Hong Kong and world cinema.

Was There anything "New" about the Hong Kong New Wave?[3]

In addition to being "old" within the context of the global new waves, Hong Kong, by 1979, had already experienced other "new" developments in its cinema. In the mid-1960s, influenced by the international success of Japanese samurai films by filmmakers such as Akira Kurosawa (1910–98), the "new" *wuxia*/swordplay film emerged, and Hong Kong-based, Chinese émigré filmmakers working in Mandarin, such as King Hu and Chang Cheh (Zhang Che, 1923–2002), became champions of this new approach to martial arts action. Hu's *A Touch of Zen* (1971), for example, won recognition at Cannes in 1975. Although produced in Taiwan after Hu had left Hong Kong, the international accolades for this film brought the "new" cinema of Hong Kong much greater visibility, while providing an art house alternative to the enormous international popularity of Bruce Lee.

Circulating within the art house circuit and at film festivals around the same time, Tang Shu-shuen's *The Arch* (1970) took on the trappings of the international "new" cinemas, and it became "almost certainly the first recognizable new wave work in Hong Kong cinema" (Teo 1997: 139). Tang made the film with Satyajit Ray's (1921–92) cinematographer Subrata Mitra (1930–2001) and with documentarist Les Blank (b. 1935) as co-editor. Like King Hu, she worked within a cosmopolitan atmosphere fully conscious of not only Chinese history and narrative traditions but the latest technological and aesthetic developments in world cinema. *The Arch* stars Lisa Lu (Lu Yan, b. 1927), who had an established career within Hollywood and European cinema as well as within the Chinese-speaking region, adding to its cosmopolitanism (C. Yau 2004).

While *A Touch of Zen* and *The Arch* clearly "belonged" to the new waves that were sweeping world cinema at the time, both Tang and Hu were isolated auteurs rather than the vanguard of any movement. They traveled the world, each settling finally in the United States, and neither found an environment conducive to productive filmmaking. However, Tang did help set the stage for what would become the Hong Kong New Wave. She proved that an outsider, educated abroad and female, could make a Hong Kong film beyond the confines of the studio system. Tang also showed that Hong Kong motion pictures could be linked to the cutting edge of art cinema as well as to the profitable and popular "chop socky" circuit that ran through the Chinese diaspora and into the inner city black, Hispanic, and North African communities of the United States and Europe. Just as the French New Wave self-consciously positioned itself in relation to French art cinema, Hollywood movies, and Italian Neo-Realism, Tang oriented her work in relation to Hong Kong period films, Chinese literary traditions, third world auteurs such as Ray, and American independents such as Les Blank, as well as within an emerging body of work by women filmmakers. As the French New Wave was associated with journals such as *Cahiers du cinema*, many supporters and participants in the Hong Kong New Wave gravitated toward Tang Shu-shuen's publication *Close-Up*. After Tang's departure, the journal evolved into *Hong Kong Film Bi-Weekly* and heralded the beginning of Hong Kong's New Wave (K. Law 1994: 39).

In fact, a lot was happening in Hong Kong in the mid-1970s, which created a fertile environment for the New Wave. Not only did film journals and other cultural publications begin to appear, but the cine-club movement came into full flower with College Cine Club, Phoenix Cine Club, Film Guard, and other small-gauge film groups. In 1977 government funding enabled the Hong Kong Short Film Competition as well as the Hong Kong International Film Festival to take place. Roger Garcia, Jim Shum, Stephen Teo (Zhang Jiande), Comyn Mo, and others associated with the experimental production/distribution entity "Modern Films" began to get recognition and appear in film festivals at around this time (Modern Films).

As a colony somewhere between the "economic miracle" of the emerging Asian "tigers" and the third world, on the border of the PRC in the throws of change after the Cultural Revolution, Hong Kong cinema had a critical consciousness and the cultural capital needed to make an intervention in world cinema. Television, still an emerging medium at the time, ushered in Hong Kong's New Wave by giving young directors the opportunity to be creative. Several made films in support of specific government initiatives (most notably, the Independent Commission Against Corruption). With lighter equipment, synchronized sound, use of available light, the Cantonese vernacular, and quick turnaround, television provided a platform for experimentation as well as training. For many, this experience also established particular aesthetic interests and narrative content. Patrick Tam produced television dramas involving changing attitudes toward women and sexual mores before looking at the same topics in feature films (Pezzotta 2007). Similarly, Ann Hui developed an interest in the plight of the Vietnamese "boat people," refugees from Indochina after 1975, in her television work.

Because of their shared background, common themes, narrative preoccupations, and aesthetic proclivities arise with surprising regularity. The Hong Kong New Wave exemplifies "the way that cinematic representation can keep faith with distinctly Chinese aesthetic traditions within a modernist framework influenced by international art cinema themes" (Rodriguez 2001: 58). Exploring these commonalities provides a good way to appreciate the contributions of the Hong Kong New Wave to Hong Kong as well as world cinema.

The Portrait of the Filmmaker as a Young (Wo)Man

A defining characteristic of all "new wave" cinemas has been an intense interest in the processes of filmmaking, cinema culture and history, and the development of the film artist as "auteur" shown self-reflexively on screen. References to other films, to filmgoing, to making films, to the labor that goes into what appears on screen all become part of the new waves' commitment to explore the medium, uncover its illusions, and celebrate its potential for innovation and personal expression. One of the Hong Kong New Wave's inaugural works, *The Extras* (Yim Ho, 1978), sets its story at the margins of local cinema production – in the world of film extras and bit players.

Closer to the French New Wave, Allen Fong's debut feature *Father and Son* (1981) shares a common sensibility with François Truffaut's (1932–84) *The 400 Blows* (1959) – both autobiographical works about the filmmakers' youth in a changing city. Fong's title calls attention to a 1954 film of the same name by Wu Hui (Ng Wui, 1912–96). However, *Father and Son* cites Hong Kong cinema's past in order to assert its difference. Fong's film, like Truffaut's, favors the perspective of

Figure 6.1 A portrait of the female artist in *Song of the Exile* (dir. Ann Hui, Cos Group, 1990), a semi-autobiographic film.

the son, and the telling narrative device of beginning the film with the death of the father from a heart attack speaks volumes about Fong's insistence that this is a time to let the old (cinematic) fathers die off and provide breathing space for the next generation of filmmakers. The film's protagonist Law plays hooky, sneaks into cinemas, extorts money from the neighborhood kids to watch his shadow plays, and, basically, lives the life of a juvenile delinquent in training to be a filmmaker. However, Law ends up going abroad to attend film school, and his father dies (supposedly happily) with his son's diploma in hand. The film clearly indicates a darker side to Confucian patriarchy, and Law's sister must stay behind in an arranged marriage and remain undereducated in order for her brother to pursue his dream.

Song of the Exile (Ann Hui, 1990) also offers an autobiographical reworking of the story of the development of a young filmmaker, but from the female point of view (Chua 1998; T. Williams 1998; Erens 2000; R. Chow 2007: 85–104) (see Figure 6.1). Hue-yin (Maggie Cheung) goes abroad to film school – like Ann Hui herself (as well as Fong and his fictional stand-in Law). Rather than sacrifice her own ambitions to put a brother through school, the filmmaker, in this case, after leaving behind the inherent limitations of racially and sexually stratified Britain, finds a place back in Hong Kong. However, the context for the artist's development here is not the father–son dyad but a fraught mother–daughter relationship. Rather than the self-sacrificing salary-man on the edges of the middle class as in Fong's film, Hui's mother represents an ethnic "other," for her daughter who has difficulty reconciling her paternal grandparents' Chinese nationalism with the fact that her mother comes from the "enemy" nation of Japan. *Song of the Exile* takes up a nonlinear narrative so that events from various moments of Hue-yin's past offer counterpoint to her coming of age as a woman. In both films, however, what appears on screen parallels the process that went into the education of the filmmaker as a child, adolescent, and young adult. This semi-autobiographical, self-reflexive component adds to an awareness of the narrative techniques employed – particularly the elaborate flashbacks used to structure the film.

Aside from these similarities, *Father and Son* and *Song of the Exile* also draw attention to the position of the Hong Kong New Wave within the region. Financed by Sil-Metropole (Yindu), a PRC-backed enterprise, *Father and Son* represents the continuing importance of mainland China as not only an imaginative space, but also a source of funding, production location, and potential market. *Song of the Exile*, however, has strong Taiwan (Republic of China or ROC) connections. The co-scriptwriter, Wu Nianzhen (Wu Nien-chen, b. 1952), hails from Taiwan and had collaborated with Hou Hsiao-hsien the year before on *City of Sadness* (1989). Switching the tables on Hou's autobiographical *A Time to Live, A Time to Die* (1985), which traces his coming of age in Taiwan (and was co-written with a female scriptwriter, Chu T'ien-wen [Zhu Tianwen, b. 1956]), Hui draws on Wu, a male writer, to tell her story. However, the connections are clear. The Hong Kong New Wave shares resources with the PRC as well as with the ROC, and the political positioning of these fictionalized accounts of the lives of these film artists attests to this. Li Cheuk-to links Fong's reliance on social realism to the film's Sil-Metropole/PRC connections, and the family's struggle to survive in Hong Kong and become upwardly mobile certainly does have an element of class analysis. Ann Hui's film, given its Taiwan connection, has a very different attitude toward questions of national identity, colonialism, class, and life on the mainland.

The fact that *Song of the Exile* appeared after the Tiananmen crackdown of 1989 and uses the 1966–76 period to stand in for more recent political tensions makes considerable sense. Taking a page from the French New Wave's commitment to engaging in politics through cinema, several Hong Kong filmmakers incorporated June Fourth even more directly in their narratives. Clara Law's *Farewell China* (1990), Allen Fong's *Dancing Bull* (1990), Ann Hui's *Ordinary Heroes* (1999), and Shu Kei's (Shu Qi, b. 1956) documentary *Sunless Days* (1990) all include footage of demonstrations in support of the protestors in Tiananmen Square, while Tsui Hark's *A Better Tomorrow III* (1989) allegorizes the Tiananmen protests and their violent suppression in a story set in war-torn Vietnam.

Fong and Hui likely had a basic familiarity with Truffaut and the French New Wave.[4] However, taking *The 400 Blows* as the "father" of the Hong Kong New Wave causes problems. New Wave films function as modernist blends of film references, personal reminiscences, and recreations of the past with nods to the "authenticity" and "authority" of social realist conventions, and, as such, resemble *The 400 Blows* to a large degree. However, *Father and Son* and *Song of the Exile* also deal openly with the refugee status of their protagonists' families as well as Hong Kong cinema itself, and global connections should not obscure the local dimension.

The role of the filmmaker/photographer in chronicling Hong Kong stories plays an important role in New Wave films beyond those films that deal expressly with the development of the filmmaker as an artist. *Boat People* (Ann Hui, 1982), for example, features George Lam as a Japanese photographer in post-1975 Vietnam. Often taken as an allegory for post-1997 Hong Kong, the film highlights the role of the media in creating a global vision of specific political events. Journalists, budding filmmakers, or simply tourists with a camcorder figure prominently in many New Wave films from *Autumn Moon* (Clara Law, 1992) to *Fallen Angels* (Wong Kar-wai, 1995), reiterating the importance of the act of observation, the techniques of the motion picture, and the art of the visual creation of Hong Kong as a screen image (A. Yue 2000a). As such, the Hong Kong New Wave goes far beyond any solipsistic obsession with autobiography and moves from the personal into the wider arena of the political as a range of characters take up the camera for reasons other than self-reflection.

Performing Women

In addition to featuring filmmakers as characters, many new wave cinemas have taken up another type of narrative that works equally well with a self-reflexive approach to screen fiction. These films feature female characters as performers within the fiction (e.g., actresses, models, singers, dancers, prostitutes). Godard's interest in performing women covers most of his career. Inspired by Bertolt Brecht's notion of "alienation" at the heart of epic theater's move to place the audience in a position of critical distance from the drama, Jean-Luc Godard (b. 1930) highlights the fact of performance to keep the constructed nature of the film at the forefront to encourage critical thought. Chinese cinema also has a long tradition of focusing on the performing woman as an allegorical figure of China's need to shake off the old roles assigned by Confucianism and colonialism in order to play a new role within global modernity (Marchetti 1989). The Hong Kong New Wave draws on both traditions. *An Autumn's Tale* (Mabel Cheung, 1987) develops this theme through the education of a young film actress from Hong Kong, who learns about performing in her university classes as well as taking on the social roles needed to be upwardly mobile in New York's Chinese diasporic community (Ford 2008).

Hong Kong's New Wave women represent the changing roles a younger generation of women must adopt in order to survive the economic, political, and social vicissitudes of the postwar world. Engaged in fashioning their own identities while remaining subject to lingering patriarchal privileges, these women represent the emergence of a "new wave" of feminist sentiment, an awaking of female sexual energy, and a very modern sense of femininity divorced from domesticity and subject to the spectacle of the consumer marketplace. As an image on screen, the New Wave woman functions as both a desirable cinematic commodity and as a challenge to traditional notions of womanhood – vacillating between feminist liberation and the constricting roles of sexist tradition and consumerism. As performers, these women represent a sexual battleground between male directors and their own creative integrity as actresses. They function as muses, as empty vessels for the directors' fantasies, as the blank screen on which meaning is projected; however, they also exhibit enormous power in improvised roles that require them to draw on the depths of their own experience.

Maggie Cheung has been particularly visible in this sort of role. In *Song of the Exile* she plays a series of "roles" – from dutiful Chinese granddaughter, rebellious daughter, and naive "outsider" in Japan to the "exotic" exchange student in London. Born in Hong Kong but educated in Britain, Maggie Cheung can draw on her own lived experience in crafting characters compelled to perform in a variety of roles across linguistic and cultural borders in order to survive. As a beauty queen (runner up as Ms. Hong Kong), she also is no stranger to the "feminine masquerade" (Doane 1982) and she brings an awareness of her "performance" as a "woman," as "Chinese," as a "British colonial," as "cosmopolitan," and as an icon of the contemporary "Hong Kong woman" to many of her roles. Cheung began to appear regularly in films in 1984, the same year that Britain and China agreed on the conditions for the change of Hong Kong from British to Chinese sovereignty. As her career developed from 1984 through 1997, she became linked as a performer to many of the anxieties associated with this broader changeover of Hong Kong. Particularly after 1989 and the massive Hong Kong demonstrations in support of the protestors in Tiananmen Square, the roles Cheung performed became darker.

Perhaps Maggie Cheung's most acclaimed foray into playing the performing woman is in "second wave" director Stanley Kwan's *Center Stage*, a.k.a. *The Actress* (1992). Playing Shanghai silent film star Ruan Lingyu, Maggie Cheung begins to plumb the depths of the despair of a society that in many ways mirrors Hong Kong. Trapped within the world of what New German filmmaker Rainer Werner Fassbinder (1945–82) called the "holy whore" of the cinema, Ruan Lingyu shot to stardom in the 1930s, but committed suicide in her mid-twenties after being hounded by the press over the very public dissolution of her troubled marriage.

Kwan comes to Ruan through Maggie Cheung, and the film self-reflexively blends footage of Ruan with reenactments by Cheung, plus extensive interviews with Cheung and others involved with the film as well as Ruan's life. The picture that emerges complicates the historical Ruan and the world of old Shanghai cinema by connecting it with contemporary Hong Kong. Ruan and Cheung symbolize the "modernity" of the city, the contemporary Chinese woman, as well as the medium of the motion picture, and Kwan explores issues of history and film aesthetics, personal and public identity, as well as the relationship between the film star and the press through the Ruan–Cheung dyad (Stringer 1997; S. Cui 2000; Stokes and Hoover 2000; Hjort 2006).

Cheung won "best actress" for her portrayal of Ruan in Hong Kong as well as Berlin, and her acclaim for this particular role likely inspired her future husband Olivier Assayas (b. 1955) to cast her in his film *Irma Vep* (1996), about an aging French New Wave director's attempt to remake the silent serial *Les Vampires* (Louis Feuillade, 1915). Cheung plays a cosmopolitan Hong Kong version of the classic femme fatale as Assayas sends up various figures associated with the European New Wave, including Jean-Pierre Léaud (b. 1944) who plays René Vidal, a version of his mentor Truffaut, conjuring up their collaboration in another film about the making of a film, *Day for Night* (1973). Vidal apparently saw Cheung as the "Cat Woman" in *Heroic Trio* (Johnnie To, 1993) and immediately imagined her as the contemporary globalized embodiment of female modernity. Lou Castel (b. 1943) plays José Mirano, the director who replaces Vidal in the film-within-the-film. Castel also portrayed a director in Rainer Werner Fassbinder's film about filmmaking *Beware of a Holy Whore* (1971), just to even the scales. Léaud and Castel, then, stand in for two of the leading figures of the new cinemas of France and Germany and battle it out over whether a Chinese woman can play an iconic Parisian thief. Although Mirano declares that *Irma Vep* is not "Fu Manchu," Cheung maintains her composure and marketability as an international star playing a version of herself called simply "Maggie" in the film (Khoo 2007).

In the battleground of the international new wave, Maggie Cheung remains neutral and moves on and out of the framing film before its completion. However, before departing from the film (and, later, her marriage to Assayas), Cheung leaves her mark, along with traces of the French New Wave and New German Cinema, linking the two on European turf, placing Hong Kong's new cinema on a par with the European New Wave.

Maggie Cheung has worked with most of the major figures associated with both waves of the Hong Kong new cinema. In 1990 alone, she worked in films directed by Yim Ho (*Red Dust*), Stanley Kwan (*Full Moon in New York*), Ann Hui (*Song of the Exile*), Clara Law (*Farewell China*), and Wong Kar-wai (*Days of Being Wild*). In *Farewell China* she plays a mainland woman who, after immigrating to New York, descends into severe mental illness. Forced to play a variety of "roles" in order to get a visa and survive in a hostile foreign city, she eventually can no longer recognize herself as the wife and mother of the husband and son she left behind in China. In *Full Moon in New York* Cheung also portrays an immigrant in New York City. However, in Kwan's film, she is a successful restaurateur from Hong Kong, who plays it "straight" as a closeted lesbian within her rather closed circle of Chinese-speaking friends in New York. In the same film, Sylvia Chang (Zhang Aijia, b. 1953), associated with Taiwan New Cinema, plays an actress trying to succeed in the city, and, in many respects, the two characters work in tandem as "performers" who construct a mask to survive. They are contrasted with a third character, a naive character from the PRC played by Siqin Gaowa (b. 1949), a mainland actress associated with the Hong Kong New Wave. The women not only represent the meeting of the Chinese-speaking world within the "neutral" territory of New York, they also symbolize three aspects of Chinese New Cinema from Hong Kong, Taiwan, and the PRC.

Maggie Cheung is perhaps best known for her longstanding collaboration with Wong Kar-wai (Brunette 2005; Teo 2005). For Wong, Cheung serves as a site of glamour but also emotional mystery, as a model for elaborate cheongsam that blend into the patterns established within the mise-en-scène as well as the iconic woman of unfathomed depth behind the colorful facade in films such as *In the Mood for Love* (2000). Although she briefly appears as Li-zhen in *2046* (2004), her portrayal of a character by the same name (who may or may not be Li-zhen from *Days of Being Wild*) in *In the Mood for Love* concretizes the themes that characterize Wong's work as an auteur: a preoccupation with time (narrative time, bad timing, missed encounters, memory, historical time), displacement (from Shanghai to Hong Kong, from Hong Kong to Southeast Asia), emotional upheavals (loss, heartache, unrequited love), visual glamour (silken cheongsam, period 1960s hairstyles and furnishings, mirror shots, chiaroscuro lighting), stylish cinematography (use of filters, elaborate moving camera shots) and editing (intricate visual/sound juxtapositions with haunting musical motifs). A Shanghai émigré, Su Li-zhen dresses the "part" of the proper wife to a rising businessman in Hong Kong's narrow exilic community. Displaced by the PRC, alienated from her philandering husband, she develops a relationship (apparently unrequited love affair) with her neighbor, a writer named Chow Mo-wan. The scene in which Li-zhen and Mo-wan role-play confrontations with their respective unfaithful spouses highlights the play between the depth of emotion and the inevitably fleeting and superficial qualities of life as well as cinema. As Cheung plays the role of Li-zhen playing the role of both the wayward wife and the faithful spouse, *In the Mood for Love* reflects back on the performative nature of life as well as art.

Maggie Cheung in *In the Mood for Love* functions as both part of Wong's particular oeuvre as well as an emblem of the Hong Kong New Wave's preoccupation with the performing woman. Hong Kong's New Wave women, however, create very different performances as they take up these roles in films with other directors. *Ah Ying* (Allen Fong, 1983), for example, focuses on the development of the title character (played by "non-actor" Hui So-ying) as she tries to express herself and her ambitions by training to be a film actress under the tutelage of Zhang Song-bai (Peter Wang), a fictional version of Taiwan director Ge Wu (Kowallis 1997). A director in his own right, Peter Wang plays a version of himself as well, and Fong moves between the performances he captures of the acting classes, the staging of a play within the film, and the performances these non-actors put on for the film being made. Like Godard, Fong uses interview techniques in which the actors playing characters playing themselves respond to the queries in ways that inevitably blur the fact and the fiction of the artistic process – a technique Fong uses more fully in *Just Like Weather* (1986). All of Fong's features, in fact, revolve around performance (filmmaking, dance, theater, and opera), and female performers figure prominently in his *Dancing Bull* (1990), set in the world of dance, as well as *A Little Life Opera* (1997), set within a Chinese opera troupe in Fujian, China.

Shu Kei, credited with an appearance in *Ah Ying*, also brought opera women to the screen in *Hu Du Men* (1996).[5] The film's title refers to the threshold between the stage and the wings in Chinese opera, and that liminal space alludes to Hong Kong's identity on the threshold between British and Chinese sovereignty. Tsui Hark's *Peking Opera Blues* (1986), starring Brigitte Lin, looks at the performing woman on the Chinese opera stage (L. Lee 1994; J. Lau 2005), and Ann Hui has returned at several points in her career to the figure of the performing woman, including *The Spooky Bunch (1980)*.

In *The Stuntwoman/Ah Kam* (1996), Ann Hui casts Michelle Yeoh (Yang Ziqiong, b. 1962 in Malaysia), another icon of Hong Kong cinema with a transnational background, as Ah Kam, a woman working in the male-dominated field of film stunt work. Playing a stuntwoman underscores the doubled performance of a woman who stands in for someone else playing a role. (T. Williams 2001). Again, highlighting the idea of performance allegorizes not only the general state of women working in the cinema, but also Hong Kong playing its "role" on the world stage with a "stand-in" identity somewhere between Britain and China, putting its "life" on the line in the service of the fiction of a globalized economy in which Hollywood dominates world screens.

In fact, in many New Wave films about performing women, the actresses symbolize Hong Kong as a city or, more generally, the postmodern dilemma that Hong Kong represents for the world (i.e., the fluidity of identity, the uncertainty of meaning, and the circulation of the image as commodity). *Rouge* (Stanley Kwan, 1987) features one of the more poignant portrayals of this figure in Fleur (Anita Mui), a prostitute/chanteuse in love with an aspiring opera performer (Leslie Cheung) in 1930s Hong Kong (Eng 1993; L. Lee 1994; B. Lim 2001). Fleur first appears in the film singing to her lover while in drag (a veiled reference to the sexual orientations of both Leslie Cheung and Stanley Kwan, who would publicly "come out" a decade after the film's premiere). As a ghost haunting 1980s Hong Kong, Fleur drifts between past and present, life and death, as well as prostitute and loyal lover. As Fleur's ghost searches for her lover who failed to join her in the afterlife as part of a suicide pact, she continues to perform for the media – followed by journalists within the diegesis – and it seems apposite that the dead Fleur and her decrepit lover should reunite on a film set.

This awareness of femininity as a "masquerade" that acts as a homology for what many theorists have called the "schizophrenia" of Hong Kong's postmodern condition can be found in many New Wave films. One of the more striking manifestations of this feminine masquerade occurs in *Chungking Express* (Wong Kar-wai, 1994). Taiwan-born actress Brigitte Lin plays a tough, unnamed drug trafficker who manages to "blend in" with the spectacle of postmodern Hong Kong. She personifies the contradictions that characterize the city – an

Asian woman masquerading as a blonde with a raincoat and sunglasses because she needs to be prepared for anything (rain or shine). Wig, coat, and dark glasses remind us that Brigitte Lin, like Marilyn Monroe (1926–62), is a star – conspicuously playing an "anonymous" character, acting the part of a woman who crosses borders and takes on various roles in order to survive (Marchetti 2000; Tetsuya 2005).

Chungking Express also features Beijing-born pop icon Faye Wong (Wang Fei, b. 1969) who plays Faye, a young woman who drifts in and out of the film, trespassing on the property of others, obsessively reorganizing the commodities that define the contemporary urban environment. Two stars (Lin from Taiwan and Wong from the PRC) cross paths in Hong Kong to perform women adept at switching masks, redefining themselves, working with and against the roles assigned to them by others. They mystify the men around them, hustle to get what they want, and manage to survive. These performing women hold up a mirror to Hong Kong (between Taiwan and the PRC), New Wave Cinema (between the Fifth/Sixth Generation and Taiwan New Cinema), and Chinese women (moving within the diaspora) – mercurial, enigmatic, but enduring survivors.

The Return of the Sword

Wong Kar-wai made *Chungking Express* while taking a break from editing his martial arts film, *Ashes of Time* (1994), and many of the same performers are featured in both. In fact, the same preoccupations that characterize the unnamed woman in *Chungking Express* are taken up by Brigitte Lin as Mu-Rong Yin/Mu-Rong Yang in *Ashes of Time*. Like Maggie Cheung, Brigitte Lin presents a particular face of the Hong Kong New Wave to the world. However, each actress puts on the "feminine masquerade" in a distinct way. Brigitte Lin has been part of the Hong Kong New Wave from the very beginning, featured in Patrick Tam's *Love Massacre* (1981) and working with Yim Ho, Tsui Hark, Wong Kar-wai, and Ann Hui. If Maggie Cheung plays the ultimate diasporic Hong Kong woman wearing her cheongsam like a second skin, then Brigitte Lin performs a new version of the classic Chinese female warrior, often in drag, fighting her way out of the past into the present. She embodies Hong Kong New Wave's reconsideration of outmoded gender as well as genre conventions in the martial arts film.

In this guise, Lin has most often been identified with Tsui Hark. Along with Yim Ho's *The Extras*, Ann Hui's *The Secret* (1979), Peter Yung's (Weng Weiquan, b. 1949) *The System* (1979), and Alex Cheung's *Cops and Robbers* (1979), Tsui's *Butterfly Murders* (1979) is generally cited as one of the inaugural films of the Hong Kong New Wave (Morton 2001; Ho and Ho 2002). Again, just as the French New Wave took up maligned genres and apparently exhausted commercial forms (e.g., the thriller, the B-movie crime story, the science fiction film, the "woman's film") and breathed new life into them, the Hong Kong New Wave not only took up genres conducive to an observational realism associated with location shooting, but also challenged the studios on their own turf with martial arts and historical costume films.[6]

With *Butterfly Murders*, Tsui announces his commitment to rewriting the genre literally by using the perspective of an itinerant man of letters, mirroring the role of the filmmaker, as the frame through which the events of the plot unfold. With attention to the plasticity of nature, manipulation of narrative time with virtuoso editing, and a reworking of the basic values of the genre, including the "heroic" stature of the warrior and the subordination of women within the martial code of *jianghu* (the rivers and lakes of the martial arts world), *Butterfly Murders* stands out, and Tsui continues to work at reworking the genre. Brigitte Lin is featured in his psychedelic extravaganza *Zu: Warriors from the Magic Mountain* (1983), which helped transform the way in which special effects are employed in Hong Kong cinema by including the use of computer-aided optical compositing for fluid camera movement (Teo 2001; Schroeder 2004: 45). Just as King Hu had brought a new understanding of the martial arts genre to Hong Kong in the 1960s, Tsui transformed the genre to conform to the technical and aesthetic standards of global cinema in the 1980s.

Tsui did this, with his wife Nansun Shi, by taking charge of all aspects of production with the establishment of Film Workshop in 1984 (Film Workshop; C. Li 2009). In addition to directing, Tsui worked as producer, screenwriter, and, occasionally, editor on many of the key franchises connected with Hong Kong's New Wave, including *Once Upon a Time in China/Wong Fei-Hung* (started in 1991), *A Chinese Ghost Story* (begun in 1987), *A Better Tomorrow* (inaugurated in 1986),[7] *Swordsman* (begun in 1990), and *Black Mask* (inaugurated in 1996). These lucrative film series put the Hong Kong New Wave in conversation with the "classics" of Chinese film and literature by providing a fresh perspective on the legendary Cantonese martial arts hero Wong Fei-Hung (Huang Feihong), on the romantic ghost stories associated with Liaozhai Zhiyi (*Strange Tales from the Chinese Studio*), on the knight-errant wuxia pian tales popularized in the commercial press by Jin Yong (Louis Cha, b. 1924), as well as on the triad tales of brotherhood in jianghu that had been a staple of Hong Kong cinema for decades.

Drawing on Hong Kong cinema's indebtedness to the new wuxia pian and particularly to King Hu's work in reviving that genre, many of Tsui's films take up Hu's sense of visual design, narrative techniques, and themes. For example, Brigitte Lin stars in Tsui's remake of King Hu's classic *Dragon Gate Inn* (1967) entitled *New Dragon Gate Inn* (1992). One of the most infamous Hong Kong film fiascos, of course, involved the pairing of Tsui Hark with the maestro himself in one of King Hu's last screen efforts, *Swordsman* (1990). Although Hu left the project because of his differences with Tsui, the film inaugurated a series that brought Jin Yong's classic *The Smiling, Proud Warrior* (1967) to the screen at a time when many of the key concerns of the novel – including shifting loyalties and identities – became particularly salient given Hong Kong's scheduled change in sovereignty. Although not in the first installment, Brigitte Lin appears as "Asia the Invincible" in the sequels *Swordsman II* (1992) and *Swordsman III: The East Is Red* (1993). In these two films she plays a martial artist who, following the directives of a secret scroll, castrates himself and metamorphoses into a woman in order to access preternatural martial power. As Esther Yau argues, androgyny here stands in for larger changes facing Hong Kong and its cinema:

> Androgyny, which usually refers to gender ambiguity, names the instability coming from what Judith Butler calls the "citations" of gender norm to mime, exaggerate, and reverse the conventions. By theatricalizing emotion and politics, the performative mode recognizes, denaturalizes, and contests the norm's restrictive boundaries. Androgyny as such can be an analogy for Hong Kong cinema, which uses wit, hyperbole, and sentiment rather than rage to position itself as a (post)colonial cinema that evaluates and counteracts regimes of both the British and the Chinese. Instead of holding on to the norms of a bounded culture, the "culturally androgynous" film cites diverse idioms, repackages codes, and combines g enres that are thought to be culturally, aesthetically, or cinematically incompatible. (Yau 2001: 7)

As the subtitle *The East Is Red* implies, Tsui's film willingly cannibalizes Communist classics such as *The East is Red* (1965) as well as Hollywood-style Hong Kong movies to camp things up by placing "Asia the Invincible" somewhere between imperial eunuchs and the "iron girls" of the Cultural Revolution (Sarkar 2001).

Brigitte Lin plays a similar character on the cusp between the masculine and the feminine in *Ashes of Time* (Dissanayake 2003), based on Jin Yong's *The Eagle Shooting Heroes*, a.k.a *The Legend of the Condor Heroes* (1957). As Mu-Rong Yin / Mu-Rong Yang, Lin embodies a dual sexuality equated with a mercurial identity that confounds any absolute sense of historical continuity, core values, and individual integrity. Instead, New Wave filmmakers like Wong Kar-wai and Tsui Hark recognize the breakdown of not only Hong Kong's historical, colonial identity, but the breakup of any concrete core at the center of the hybridized, transitory present.

Queer Connections

If Maggie Cheung and Brigitte Lin embody the New Wave "woman" on Hong Kong screens, Leslie Cheung represents Hong Kong's New Wave "man" (Marchetti 2003). All three appear in *Ashes of Time*, and it seems apposite that Cheung's character Ou-Yang Feng should be an anti-hero, the go-between for hired killers living in a remote desert area of China. As Ou-Yang, he opposes all the values associated with the wuxia tradition, and he devotes more energy to making a profit than to promoting justice, righteousness, and brotherhood. Dusty, bearded, brooding over a lost love, Ou-Yang anchors the film, but his own unstable identity is mirrored in his encounter with the gender-shifting Mu-Rong Yin/Mu-Rong Yang, who exasperates Ou-Yang by hiring him to kill and protect the same man. As with so many of Leslie Cheung's roles, yin (feminine) and yang (masculine) plague him with contradictory, irresolvable demands, and Cheung remains trapped in the middle.

In his work with other New Wave directors, Cheung remains the same. Just as Jet Li conjures up the Confucian patriarchal martial hero Wong Fei-Hung in order to show him assailed by colonial modernity in Tsui's *Once Upon a Time in China* series, Leslie Cheung reconfigures the scholar-hero in *A Chinese Ghost Story* series. Cheung, in fact, in many New Wave features, such as *Rouge* and *Days of Being Wild* as well as in *Nomad* (Patrick Tam, 1982), incarnates the disintegration of an idealized, traditional Chinese masculinity. In *Days of Being Wild* Cheung plays Yuddy, an "A Fei" character, "flighty," drifting, rootless, shiftless, and shifting (Bettinson 2005). Stephen Teo (1997: 193–4) describes this character as follows: "Leslie Cheung's A Fei (named 'Yuddy') is an abstract everyman, the undefined soul of Hong Kong who seeks to find himself an identity he can respect."

With this role, Cheung defined himself as the "soul of Hong Kong" of the 1990s and as the quintessential Wong Kar-wai protagonist. Positioned between a foster mother from Shanghai and a birth mother in the Philippines, Yuddy drifts between the mainland (PRC) and a past and possible future within the Chinese diaspora. Like Hong Kong, Yuddy's identity remains uncertain, impossible to pin down, and his ability to commit lasts no more than the moment he promises to his girlfriend, whom he inevitably abandons. Cheung plays the young rebel challenging the norms of an outmoded sex–gender system, battling anyone who attempts to make him cling to traditional notions of "love," "family," and "commitment," and floating from one love affair to another without regard for orthodox notions of morality. Troubled, tender, and expressive, Cheung offered up a "new" masculinity outside the constraints of accepted gender norms or sexual divisions.

Cheung also played openly homosexual roles, most notably in *Farewell My Concubine* (Chen Kaige, 1993). It is interesting to note that Stanley Kwan looks closely at Cheung's performance in *Farewell My Concubine* in his documentary *Yin +/− Yang: Gender in Chinese Cinema* (1996) (S. Lim 2006: 153–79). As a New Wave filmmaker, Kwan takes a keen interest in how Hong Kong's approach to gender and sexuality differs from that of his "new cinema" peers across the border in the PRC – a theme he explored obliquely in *Center Stage* as well. As the documentary points out, Leslie Cheung and director Chen Kaige made two different films that came together as a single screen commodity. Whereas Cheung emphasizes the difficulty of being accepted when he cross-dresses on screen and the importance of the "delicacy" that defines his star persona, Chen attempts to rationalize his reorientation of the Lillian Lee source away from the gay bathhouse in Hong Kong where her story concludes.

Leslie Cheung indisputably became the queer face of the Hong Kong New Wave in Wong Kar-wai's *Happy Together* (1997) (Berry 2000; A. Yue 2000b;

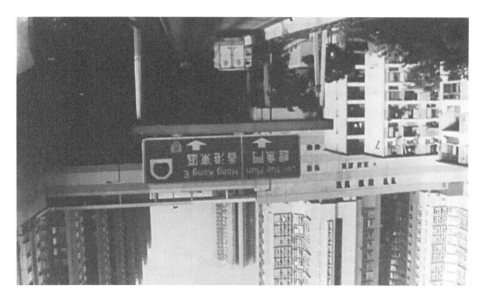

Figure 6.2　Hong Kong's cityscape turned upside down in *Happy Together* (dir. Wong Kar-wai, Jet Tone, 1997).

Tambling 2003; S. Lim 2006: 99–125) (see Figure 6.2). In his final collaboration with Wong, Cheung steps out of the closet on screen. Cheung's Ho Po-Wing personifies a gay diaspora, going to the ends of the earth (humorously rendered with upside-down shots of Hong Kong standing in as the perspective from the other side of the world, Argentina) to "start over" in a relationship that has torn his partner, Lai Yui-Fai, from his family. Far from inconspicuous in his yellow leather jacket, Cheung walks arm in arm with men and publicly embraces them on the streets of Buenos Aires.

The tango defines Ho and Lai's relationship as a struggle for control of two equally powerful forces – passionate, dangerous, tender, violent, elegant, and erotic. Their lovemaking follows the same rhythms. Smoldering and, then, explosive, Ho, the traditional "bottom" in the relationship, overwhelms and devours Lai, a passive "top." Cheung may be "starting over" in the plot, but he is "starting something" on the screen that goes far beyond his other roles in making a statement about being gay, being a "bottom," being Asian, being Hong Kong Chinese in diaspora, and coming out on world screens.

Ho, however, remains elusive, and the character disappears and reappears at several points in the film. In one shot, Ho sits in front of an open window, the breeze blowing, and, in the next instance, he is no longer in the frame, as if the wind had blown him off the screen and out of the narrative. Cheung as Ho crosses a line that remains forever outside traditional definitions of gender, sexuality, Chinese patriarchal identity, and national integrity. As much as China may want to make the gay man/Hong Kong/the divisive effect of the Chinese diaspora disappear into a unified national body, that fantasy cannot be realized by any change of sovereignty that promises "happy" togetherness (S. Lu 2000).

Leslie Cheung's suicide in 2003 came as a tremendous blow. Although queer issues have become an integral part of Hong Kong cinema in films such as Shu Kei's *A Queer Story* (1997), Stanley Kwan's *Lanyu* (2001), and Evans Chan's *Map of Sex and Love* (2001) within as well as beyond the New Wave, no other face has appeared to represent the same constellation of concerns that Cheung embodied on New Wave screens. With Brigitte Lin's retirement, Anita Mui's death from cancer, and Leslie Cheung's passing, part of the visual imagination, performative energy, and physical substance of the New Wave went with them, and the Hong Kong cinema has yet to find actors equal to the challenge.

The Return of the Real

As founding works of the French and Hong Kong New Waves, *The 400 Blows* and *Father and Son* spotlight the growth of a young man in an environment hostile to individual creativity and the pursuit of the arts. However, while *The 400 Blows* proffers no sentimental attachment of Antoine Doinel to his stepfather, *Father and Son* offers an emotional account more in keeping with the Neo-Realist classic *Bicycle Thieves* (Vittorio De Sica, 1948). Just as the father–son relationship between Antonio and Bruno is strained by the chaotic transition from Fascism to postwar modernity in *Bicycle Thieves*, *Father and Son* questions the value of Confucian patriarchy within Hong Kong's global modernity. The bonds of paternal trust and authority are tested in both works, and each film points to a different path to reconciliation and redemption (Berry and Farquhar 2006).

The depiction of the bond between the fathers and sons cannot be divorced from the films' styles. As the sons follow their fathers after arguments, the characters merge into an equally ambivalent urban environment holding the promise of modern prosperity and the weight of poverty and decay. Observational camera techniques, understated "non-acting," use of the vernacular, exploitation of actual locations, episodic narrative structure, liberal use of music, and touches of theatricality provide the proper blend to give an impression of "realism" without negating the emotional impact of the melodrama.

The father–son melodrama has been taken up by other New Wave filmmakers. Given the wide global distribution of *Bicycle Thieves* and its admiration by budding Communist filmmakers in China as well as by conservative film critics such as André Bazin, it comes as no surprise that the film should resonate with filmmakers in Hong Kong as well. *The Orphan* (Li Chenfeng, 1960), featuring the young Bruce Lee, dealt with similar questions of morality, criminality, and redemption. *Gangs* (1988), directed by Lawrence Ah Mon (a.k.a. Lau Kwok-Cheung, Liu Guochang, b. 1949), takes up these issues within the New Wave. More recently, *After This Our*

Exile (Patrick Tam, 2006) returned to the father–son melodrama by focusing on a down-and-out father and son who turn to thievery within Malaysia's diasporic Chinese community.

In addition to the legacy of Italian Neo-Realism, the Hong Kong New Wave also maintains direct links to the Chinese genre of the "tenement film," associated with Shanghai leftwing filmmaking of the 1930s as well as with the social realist tradition in Hong Kong's left-leaning cinema of the 1950s. Although within the New Wave, the tenement has metamorphosed into the public housing complex, the foundation of the genre remains unchanged, focusing on the dialectic between poverty and collectivity, criminal violence and community solidarity, personal loyalties and collective agitation for social change.

This continuing engagement with questions of realism can be seen in three recent films about a troubled local community, Tin Shui Wai: Ann Hui's *The Way We Are* (2008) and *Night and Fog* (2009) and Lawrence Ah Mon's *Besieged City* (2008). All three films look at life in subsidized housing blocks, at the struggle to live in cramped conditions on modest means, at different generations existing in close proximity, and at the failure of key governmental institutions to address the needs of the working poor.

Night and Fog and *Besieged City* root their narratives in stories of domestic violence. Based on an actual case, *Night and Fog* chronicles the spousal abuse that leads to a brutal murder-suicide in Tin Shui Wai. The film takes a critical look at the economics of PRC–Hong Kong marriages, the failure of social workers to adequately intervene in cases of domestic violence, and the promise as well as inadequacy of feminist self-help mechanisms to prevent or remedy abuse within the family. *Besieged City* also plumbs the depths of domestic abuse (including incest), but it examines violence directed primarily at children. Within the confines of the cell-like housing flats, the families disintegrate as older siblings turn a blind eye to severe beatings and rapes in order to maintain their own standing in the household. The cast-off juvenile victims become part of an underground economy of illicit drugs and replicate the cycle of neglect and exploitation that formed them. Because of its focus on the lives of adolescents, *Besieged City* functions as a "youth" film – continuing in a generic tradition that helped to define the New Wave.

While *Night and Fog* and *Besieged City* provide uncompromising examinations of the violence underlying social problems linked to Hong Kong's enormous wealth gap (the widest in the world), *The Way We Are* explores the same place, Tin Shui Wai, from a very different perspective. Observational rather than critical, *The Way We Are* adopts a different sort of cinematic realism to tell its story. The same locations – the housing flats, local schools, playgrounds, hospitals, grocery stores – and the same people appear. The camera does not shy away from exploring the environment as institutionally cold or claustrophobic and inhospitable. However, rather than offering a dramatic encounter with Hong Kong's underclasses, *The Way We Are* celebrates local life. Although set among the working poor, families function, schools meet the needs of students, neighbors look out for each other, and people manage to forge a life for themselves without recourse to criminal gangs or degeneration into domestic violence.

Owing more to the transcendental style characteristic of Yasujirô Ozu (1903–63) or Hou Hsiao-Hsien than to critical or social realism, the film meditates on the core values of family and community by observing the daily rituals that define local lives – from preparing meals to visiting sick relatives to celebrating the Mid-Autumn Festival. Quiet contemplation takes the place of dramatic action, and the film follows many of Bazin's (1971: 58) directives for cinematic realism – "supreme naturalness" and an "invisible system of aesthetics." Using Italian Neo-Realism as his model, Bazin calls for the disappearance of the actor (use of nonprofessionals), the mise-en-scène (locations over sets), the story (no crafted drama), plot (accident over order), action (no spectacle), and montage (nothing added to the meaning of the film through editing). The disappearance of all these elements leads Bazin to the ultimate disappearance of ideology: "Not one gesture, not one incident, not a single object in the film is given a prior significance derived from the ideology of the director" (Bazin 1971: 68).

Of course, it can be argued that this transparent style supports it own ideology. However, Bazin's aesthetics of "disappearance" seems to resonate with Ackbar Abbas's examination of the "politics of disappearance" as Hong Kong transitions from colony to SAR. For Abbas (1997: 24), this "problematic of disappearance" captures "a sense of the elusiveness, the slipperiness, the ambivalences of Hong Kong's cultural space that some Hong Kong filmmakers have caught in their use of the film medium, in their explorations of history and memory, in their excavation of the evocative detail – regardless of subject matter."

With a minimal plot, Ann Hui focuses on the details of quotidian life. She strips away the layers of stylistic flourishes, spectacular compositions, dynamic editing, star performances, and complex, temporally convoluted narratives associated with the Hong Kong New Wave. *The Way We Are* returns Hong Kong cinema to the foundations of the movement and the medium – small-format cinematography (DV), minimal camera movement, use of the vernacular, and attention to the locations that frame the ordinary lives of the city's inhabitants the "way we are."

The Hong Kong New Wave and the World

What may be most "new" about Hong Kong's New Wave may be its postmodern suspicion of the "new." Whereas earlier "new" cinemas operated within realist or modernist conventions, the Hong Kong New Wave adopts a postmodern aesthetic. For example, films such as *The Postmodern Life of My Aunt* (Ann Hui, 2006) self-consciously speak to the postmodern concerns of the New Wave filmmaker (Marchetti 2009). As many scholars (E. Chan 2000; Y. Zhang 2002: 81–8; 2004a: 249–56) have pointed out, Hong Kong's New Wave pastiches older genres without parody; quotations from other films are commonplace, but satire is rare. Filmmakers adapt to the cultural marketplace, and their eclectic, self-reflexive style foregrounds their awareness of their audience's consciousness of images as commodities, political events as spectacles, and the mass media as a frame for the hyperkinetic hyperreality of contemporary existence. The past exists as traces of popular culture invading individual memory – much like Fleur as a stylish icon of the past haunts Hong Kong in the "nostalgia film" *Rouge* (Abbas 1997: 40). Characters mirror spectators who are assumed to be hybrid, divided, mercurial, androgynous, and part of the schizophrenia attendant on the dissolution of the illusion of the subject – performance trumps essence. The Hong Kong New Wave has managed to address global postmodernity through the local idiom, and it speaks eloquently to world cinema as a result.

If the first wave brought the world to Hong Kong as directors came back from studying abroad to reinvigorate Hong Kong television and film, the second wave took Hong Kong to the world with awards showered on filmmakers such as Wong Kar-wai and Stanley Kwan at Cannes and Berlin. The first wave also sent Hong Kong filmmakers "home" to China, after the relaxation of restrictions on cross-border coproductions with the PRC; Ann Hui's *Boat People* used China's Hainan Island to stand in for Vietnam, and Yim Ho's *Homecoming* (1984) and *The Day The Sun Turned Cold* (1994) brought rural China to Hong Kong screens in a way it had not been depicted previously. The second wave took Hong Kong to the other side of the world with Mabel Cheung's *Illegal Immigrant* (1985) and *An Autumn's Tale*, Clara Law's *Farewell China*, and Stanley Kwan's *Full Moon in New York* filmed in New York City, Law's *A Floating Life* (1996) set in Australia, and Wong Kar-wai leading his Hong Kong players to Argentina in *Happy Together*. The presence of Hong Kong émigré Wayne Wang as a founding figure in Asian American film and his continuing interest in maintaining his ties with the Hong Kong New Wave by casting filmmaker Allen Fong, as well as Maggie Cheung and Wang's wife, Hong Kong actress Cora Miao (Miu Jianren, b. 1958), in his films shows that the line between the Hong Kong New Wave and other "new" cinemas continues to be flexible.

As much as the Hong Kong New Wave reinvigorated local production and addressed the political and social consequences of the change of sovereignty in 1997, it has had at least as much to say to world cinema, its shifting standards, its transnational dimensions, and the expectations of the "local" within a global film market. Both "first" and "second" wave directors continue to be active on a global stage long after 1997 has come and gone. Hong Kong filmmakers drift between the domestic market, the twin production/distribution bases of the PRC and Taiwan, and they keep alive connections to Hollywood (e.g., Wong Kar-wai's *My Blueberry Nights*, 2007) and American indies (e.g., Evans Chan's oeuvre). As a "new cinema" emerges in Malaysia and other parts of Southeast Asia, the Hong Kong New Wave connection remains salient. Europe, too, has been not only a platform from which to garner accolades, but a place to do business, as Maggie Cheung's career has shown (e.g., her award at Cannes for "best actress" in Assayas' *Clean*, 2004), and Wong's *Happy Together* proves that even Argentina is on the map. Looking at the Hong Kong New Wave exclusively in terms of its local intervention may be a mistake. However, failing to see the importance of the city of Hong Kong in framing the New Wave's thematic and aesthetic concerns can be equally hazardous. As Hong Kong's New Wave filmmakers continue to mature, they remain in conversation with each other and their city, as well as the world. Moving into the twenty-first century, they lay claim to a vital part of global cinema.

Acknowledgments

Special thanks go to Fanny Chan, Lin Yiping and Natalie Wong for their hard work preparing this manuscript for publication.

Notes

1   I am indebted to the work of many scholars of Hong Kong cinema. For historical overviews, see Teo (1997, 1999) and Cheuk (2008). For the New Wave's encounter with "China," see C. Li (1994) and E. Yau (1994). Stringer (2008) includes extensive material on major figures. For pre-1997 Hong Kong, see Abbas (1997). For a critical anthology, see Cheung and Chu (2004). For the New Wave in relation to Hong Kong popular cinema or transnational Chinese cinema, see Stokes and Hoover (1999), Bordwell (2000), Lo (2005), Marchetti (2006), and Marchetti and Tan (2007).

2   It is interesting to note the importance of women filmmakers (e.g., Ann Hui, Clara Law, and Mabel Cheung) and husband and wife teams (Eddie Fong–Clara Law, Alex Law–Mabel Cheung, Tsui Hark–Nansun Shi [Shi Nansheng], while Wayne Wang–Cora Miao have also been a force on the edges of the New Wave). Women have been essential as arts journalists/activists (e.g., Tang Shu-shuen), television mentors (Selina Chow), screenwriters (Joyce Chan), and actresses within the New Wave orbit.

3   A related question can be asked: How much of the New Cinema of Hong Kong is really part of the "New Wave?" Consider the book series from Hong Kong University Press on Hong Kong's New Cinema. How many of these titles are really part of the New Wave? John Woo (Wu Yusen, b. 1946), Johnnie To (Du Qifeng, b. 1955), King Hu, Peter Chan, Fruit Chan, Yuen Woo-Ping (Yuan Heping, b. 1945) – all featured in the series – may have certain "connections" with the New Wave, but clearly do not share the same history as the directors generally associated with its first and second "waves."

4   Taiwan director Tsai Ming-liang has made a cottage industry out of references to Antoine Doinel/Jean-Pierre Léaud in his films. Tsai has a close working relationship with Ann Hui, who appears in Tsai's film *The River* (1997).

5   Although considered peripheral by some, Shu Kei has been a part of the New Wave as a writer, actor, and director since the early 1980s – including serving as scriptwriter for *The Happenings* (Yim Ho, 1980).

6   Patrick Tam, for example, took up the wuxia genre in his debut feature *The Sword* in 1980.

7   John Woo directed the first two installments in *A Better Tomorrow* and Tsui the third. Although the collaboration with Tsui brings Woo into the New Wave orbit, he remains very much on its periphery. Although educated at foreign-funded Christian schools, Woo did not go abroad or work in television. Rather, he started his career within the Hong Kong studio system, working under the tutelage of Chang Cheh.

7

Gender Negotiation in Song Cunshou's *Story of Mother* and Taiwan Cinema of the Early 1970s

James Wicks

In 1975 the Taiwan government's most prestigious film prize, the Golden Horse for best film, was awarded to director Li Xing (b. 1930) for his film *Land of the Undaunted* (see Figure 7.1), a period piece produced in the "literary art war film" (*zhanzheng wenyi jupian*) tradition. The film, set in China during the Japanese Occupation period, traces both the life and times of inspirational Headmaster Du (Wang Yin, 1900–88) who will not give in to his Japanese oppressors, and his students and teachers, who must make their own difficult choices between preserving the dignity of China or giving in to the aggressors who would tear it down. When imprisoned for his acts of resistance, Headmaster Du informs his Japanese oppressor: "You read our Chinese texts because it is the basis of your culture, your culture is inherited from China.... The Chinese are a strong and resilient people who will never surrender!" Certainly, there would be many profitable ways to analyze *Land of the Undaunted*; however, as the film still in Figure 7.1 makes clear, a focus on the film's gender dynamics is particularly rewarding.

In the film's final sequence, the teachers and students struggle to understand the death of their headmaster, an inspirational figurehead who died while in captivity. The headmaster's passing might have destroyed all hope for the students and instructors he left behind. Yet, in a symbolic act of defiance, an instructor named Mr. Li (Qin Han, b. 1946) reads the headmaster's final letter to an enthusiastic and stirred assembly of students. Since the Japanese military police cannot stand for such behavior, Mr. Li is carted off to prison for his political insubordination. But then, in a final act of civil disobedience, the headmaster's daughter Ms. Du (Lin Fengjiao, b. 1953) picks up the letter and continues reading where Mr. Li had left off.

A Companion to Chinese Cinema, First Edition. Edited by Yingjin Zhang.
© 2012 Blackwell Publishing Ltd. Published 2012 by Blackwell Publishing Ltd.

Figure 7.1 Ms. Du (Lin Fengjiao) reads Headmaster Du's (Wang Yin) letter in *Land of the Undaunted* (dir. Li Xing, CMPC, 1975).

The symbolism is profound on multiple levels. Certainly, the notion that the people of China will never give up despite regional conflict is conveyed clearly. Yet, in terms of gender representation, one observes that the authority of the woman is figuratively granted by the father. Indeed, as the daughter reads her father's words, the scene captures the presence of the daughter in the foreground reading the letter, while the image of the deceased father looms large behind her. His eyes peer over her shoulders as if approving the reading of his words by her tongue. In fairness, when asked about this final image, Li Xing stated that it does not contain any inherent meaning or symbolism (author interview, Taipei, October 2008). However, as far as I may find it possible, I would beg to differ. Seen in the framework of Taiwan's film history in the early 1970s, this imagery conforms to a consistent pattern in which films represent women as adopted into society by way of the approval of strong fathers. These films suggest that to belong to the nation is to have the approval of the patriarchs.

My thesis in this chapter is that the finest film of early 1970s Taiwan cinema, Song Cunshou's remarkable *Story of Mother*, not only demonstrates the ways in which patriarchal figures confer their approval and authority, but also that the representation of gender in the film sheds light on the larger geopolitical predicament of Taiwan's concurrent situation. In order to do so, my analysis of *Story of Mother* follows the constructive theoretical framework presented in Shu-mei Shih's *Visuality and Identity* (2007). My discussion of *Story of Mother*'s representations of women and female sexuality underscores Shih's bold claim that "there is no identity negotiation that is not at the same time a gendered negotiation. In highly volatile situations, the greatest fears and desires as well as the most fantastic projections of confidence are always articulated in gendered terms" (2007: 87).

This assertion is taken from Shih's chapter entitled "The Geopolitics of Desire," which describes how gender and nationalism are oftentimes presented in a binary structure that places the local women in a position verses the patriarchal state system. In this way, women are the "third term" in a binary struggle between a "geopolitical nation-state" and "unwelcome invaders" (Shih 2007: 88). But Shih notes a distinct contrast between this binary system and the phenomenon of gender articulations in Hong Kong and Taiwan at the end of the 1990s, when there was an effort in Taiwan and Hong Kong to "nationalize or territorialize politics and culture" under the threat of transnational migration; namely the influx of incoming *dalumei* in Taiwan and the *biutse* (Cantonese) or *biaojie* (Mandarin) in Hong Kong (Shih 2007: 96). This entailed an effort of women disembedding patriarchy from the nation, so that the nation could be appealed to as an organ unaffiliated with masculinity. Shih writes (2007: 116): "these women deploy their national and transnational allegiances pragmatically and locally to define the meaning of their own politics." In this way, the nation is not an oppressor, but strategically appealed to in order to challenge the idea of "transnational Chinese culture" (alternatively, "pan-Chinese culture" or "global Chinese culture") represented in the mid-1990s media.

What I would like to focus on here is how Shih's gender theorization might also inform our understanding of Taiwan's film representations of the early 1970s. To begin, in terms of "identity negation," it is reasonable to conclude that the Chinese Nationalist (KMT) Party's censorship apparatus approved of films that presented its distinctive characteristics in an ideal manner (R. Huang 1994; Yeh and Davis 2005). Next, an examination of state-approved filmic narratives, themselves structured representations of state-endorsed ideology, reveals that the resolution of conflict entails a "gendered negotiation." In *Story of Mother* specifically, the resolution of the film has everything to do with how men and women were expected to behave in Taiwan society. Additionally, Shih's discussion of "volatile situations" might be evaluated in two ways. First, one could consider that the conflicts within film narratives are presented as "volatile" situations. For example, *Story of Mother* focuses on an estranged relationship that threatens to divide a family in two. Second, the term "volatile" could apply to Taiwan's regional and global identity during what could not be a more turbulent decade for a state that based its legitimacy on international recognition.[1] The KMT government had based its identity as "free China" on the fact that it was recognized as such by the international community – itself a fictional representation that was altered drastically in 1971 with the United Nations' recognition of China. Thus, the tension surrounding these films from the perspective of an audience considering both the fictional narrative and the historical context is the disconnect between the nationalist film project of offering its identity though the filmic medium and a populace that was all too aware of its unpredictable political situation.

Moreover, Shih (2007: 88) describes how a "coherent pan-Chinese" cultural identity might be undermined by "disjunctions and contestations in the cultural and political arenas." While Shih's statement applies to the historical moment of 1990s Taiwan and Hong Kong, the notion that gender negotiation might destabilize a "coherent pan-Chinese" identity is also relevant to the film *Story of Mother*, which similarly "thwarts an easy assertion of the emergence of a pan-Chinese culture" (Shih 2007: 88). The cultural identity that Taiwan propounded in the early 1970s might be termed "pan-Chinese," to use Shih's appellation, because the characters on Taiwan's silver screen, such as those in *Land of the Undaunted*, were expected to be models of a pan-Chinese identity propagated by the "Cultural Renaissance," in contrast to the ideas of the "Cultural Revolution" which was concurrently propagated on the mainland (Tozer 1970). Thus, this chapter describes how the depiction of gender in a captivating filmic text, *Story of Mother*, interconnects with its historical–material context during a time when a series of political setbacks plagued the government.

Taiwan's international prestige was tarnished by its withdrawal from the United Nations in October 1971 when China was given a seat in the United Nations, the signing of the Shanghai Communiqué in February 1972 that paved the way for diplomatic relations between the United States and China, the termination of Taiwan's diplomatic relations with Japan, the death of Chiang Kai-shek in 1975, and the termination of the Mutual Defense Treaty in 1979 as the United States reinstated relations with Beijing. The turmoil and transition that is inherent to assessments of the decade also include the *xiangtu* literature debates waged in literary circles, and on the political front, anti-KMT riots broke out in Southern Taiwan in 1979.

Since this chapter entails a close reading of *Story of Mother*, privileging structural, aesthetic, and narrative analyses in order to inquire into each film's gender dynamics, it is essential to situate this film within this particular historical, social, and material context. Chris Berry provides a model for this type of inquiry in *Postsocialist Cinema in Post-Mao China* (2004a), in which he clarifies that his work is concerned with examining the interrelationship of the history of the Chinese cinematic image and the history of the Chinese cinema as the history of a social institution and thus a site of cultural formation. He states that the two histories entail a process of renegotiation in which society influences the institution of cinema, and cinema influences society. Cinematic discourse and images are the product of social and cultural processes, which as E. Ann Kaplan (2000) writes, is a production that is by no means gender neutral. In turn, the cinematic image affects society – a phenomenon most evident when the discourse of film "precedes or exceeds" political discourse. These "excesses" might be located by noting disjunctions or points of slippage between what is portrayed on the screen and social mandates propagated by state film.

This idea of excess is elucidated by Darrell Davis (1996: 8): film history is usually practiced using a kind of parallelism, establishing connections between the fictional world onscreen (texts) and the actual world contained in primary documents from the same period (context). It is deeply satisfying when we "discover" correspondences between film imagery and documented historical fact – when it looks as if film indeed reflects film history. However, this sells film short. Films are themselves primary documents of history, and can reveal things about their time that other historical records might not. It is in this way that films might accurately depict what is occurring in the social context. Accordingly, the depictions of gender and female sexuality in the following analysis might accurately portray gender roles and the social context of Taiwan in the early 1970s. This is to be expected, and it is a fascinating process in and of itself to observe these connections. But what is at times more captivating, as is the case in this chapter, is the way that *Story of Mother* exposes facets of society that perhaps the KMT government did not intend at the time.

Story of Mother is a rich film that demonstrates, as a kind of social gauge, the possibilities available to directors when they took on projects that explore gender relations. Film critic Cai Guorong recommended this film, along with Bai Jingrui's (b. 1931) *Goodbye Darling* (1970), when I discussed this chapter's topic with him (author interview, Taipei, July 2008; see also Guorong 1982). Both films deal with depictions of gender negotiation and have stood out to scholars of Taiwan cinema and culture. Yeh and Davis (2005: 37) offer a comprehensive analysis of *Goodbye Darling*, stimulating further discussion of the film with insights such as "Bai's *Goodbye Darling* has a number of moments that would have given Taiwan's censors plenty of worry." Similarly, Yingjin Zhang (2004a: 145) states that *Story of Mother* is "a rare study of female sexuality" in Taiwan. At the same time, in many ways these are extremely safe films, films that disclose what the KMT government deemed as acceptable, authorized, and valid representations; certainly, these are images that the state would not release otherwise. *Story of Mother* demonstrates the types of gender identity that are acceptable, and which types of gender characteristics cause trouble in Taiwan's *wenyi* or "literary art" film tradition (Yeh 2007: 203; see also Chapter 2, this volume).

Lu Feiyi (1998) situates *Story of Mother* in the broader scope of Taiwan's film industry, and thus helps clarify the types of films available to audiences during the early to mid-1970s. The number of films submitted for censorship approval from 1970 to 1975 is as follows: 117 (1970), 114 (1971), 81 (1972), 45 (1973), 66 (1974), 49 (1975). By 1975 the number of films submitted for censorship approval was far lower than the highest year of film production in Taiwan, 189 in 1968. This is due to a number of factors. In 1970 Mandarin cinema had effectively pushed Taiwanese cinema totally out of the picture (by 1976 no films in Taiwan were made in Taiwanese or Minnanyu); in addition, Taiwan's so-called "golden age" of cinema, when its films received advance capital from overseas investors in Southeast Asia, was in decline. However, it does not signify the decline of the industry as a whole, for it was to recover from this decrease in production during the late 1970s, and was not to bottom out until the late 1980s and early 1990s. In 1972 when Song released *Story of Mother*, 275 films were screened in Taiwan from abroad, while 135 were from Hong Kong. In 1972 more films were made in the wenyi tradition than any other film category (27), while comedies came in second that year (20), and then martial arts films third (7). During the time in which *Story of Mother* was released, the government enforced a quota on the number of films that could be imported so that the local industry could flourish, which reminds one of the way the national finances were managed in general in Taiwan, film being one aspect of an overall prosperous era of administered economic growth.

Song Cunshou made over 25 films in his career, and certainly a standout film from his oeuvre is *Story of Mother* due to its gender depictions. As a Song Cunshou film retrospective presented by the Chinese Taipei Film Archive and the Taipei Department of Cultural Affairs in Taipei in 2008 attests, Song is one of the major figures of Taiwan cinema in the 1960s and 1970s. He is in the top five directors of this era, along with Li Xing, Bai Jingrui, and Li Hanxiang (1926–96), and Hu Jinquan (King Hu) who "defected" from Hong Kong and made films in Taiwan. Song originally worked in a printing shop and loved to watch films; then, after meeting directors Li Hanxiang and King Hu, he started working as a scriptwriter and log-keeper for the Shaw Brothers (C. Song 1979: 7). Eventually, he worked his way up the production chain until he was an assistant director, and then with Li Hanxiang's assistance at Guolian Studios, Song became a director. In his own words, Song went through stages of being "an audience member, a researcher, and then a creator" of films over a ten year period, and through this process he had the opportunity to perfect his craft (C. Song 1979: 7).

Song's first film was a popular folk melody film (*Minnanyu Huangmeidiao*) in 1966, which was at the height of the subgenre's popularity at the time. He would follow this film with pictures ranging from martial arts epics such as *Iron Petticoat* (1969) to contemporary dramatic family pieces based on Qiong Yao's (b. 1938) novels such as *Outside the Window* (1973). His films are distinguished by his careful use of editing, willingness to work across genre, and his placement of characters into situations where a series of allegiances and binary choices test their psychological limits. His work displays a keen knack for employing understatement wisely and an ability to depict subtle character emotion (Lin and Hui 1979: 29). In addition, Song is the type of consummate director who trusts his audience throughout the film. He withholds key names, dates, and other relevant details until necessary, keeping the audience guessing and entertained, while maintaining that precious balance between revealing too much information like a TV soap opera and not revealing enough information like an intellectualized art house picture.

These generalizations apply to *Story of Mother*, a film that was critically well received but did poorly at the box office. Song stated that film critics might have found the young protagonist in *Story of Mother* too young to experience the events that transpire in the narrative, and it was hard to score a good result at the box office with a film that centers on the life of a middle-aged woman. Instead, Song (1979: 8) argues, audiences preferred romances featuring beautiful clothes and luxurious settings. Regardless, *Story of Mother* includes such aesthetic virtues as well-paced editing, exquisite use of photographed images – such as those otherwise superficial framed family photographs on a domestic wall that in fact provide visual clues foreshadowing future scenes – and a colorful use of thematic images such as oranges prominent in both present-tense and flashback sequences.

Released by the privately run Dazhong Studio, *Story of Mother* is a melodrama that centers on the psyche of a young college student named Qingmao (Qin Han), who must struggle to accept that his mother (Li Xiang, b. 1942) cheated on his father when Qingmao was a young boy. As such, it is the first film to depict a mother's affair in the history of Taiwan cinema (Q. Mao 1980: 70). By the end of the film, Qingmao learns – by way of the advice of the strong female models in his life, namely his girlfriend and his aunt – that he should take a more tolerant view of his mother's former infidelity, and forgive her. Then, in an outrageous final scene, the unfortunate Qingmao is prevented from reconciling with his mother because she is randomly struck by a taxi at a railroad crossing and dies while Qingmao looks on.[2]

Song benefited from the full backing of the Dazhong Studio owners, including both Li Xing and Bai Jingrui, when he directed the film. Since Li and Bai were film directors themselves, they understood that Song needed to retain full freedom to manage everything from actors to financial concerns, and that is what they allowed (C. Song 1979: 8). The film did not pose any problems for Dazhong in terms of censorship, even though it might be considered the *Lust, Caution* of its time due to its representation of sexuality: in the first sequence, and repeated via flashback in sequence 26, the mother expresses deep pleasure while in the arms of her lover. On the one hand, the shot entails the briefest of glances, but on the other hand, it does push the envelope at a time when filming pornography could result in the death penalty (ZDTBW 2006: 467). In any case, the film was made from the start to gain the approval of the censors without causing any problems, and that is indeed what occurred. Li Xing, the producer of the film, stated that he did not want to make films that would be altered later by others (author interview, Taipei, October 2008). In other words, one might say that Dazhong's films were made to be complicit with state policy. In this way, in terms of what Taiwan and Southeast Asia's audiences saw, there was not to be a major difference between the films released by the state and those that would be released by local and transnational private studios for the open market (Rodriguez 1995).

In terms of filmic structure, one notes that in comparison with other Taiwan films early in the decade – for example Li Hanxiang's period film *The Story of Tin-ying* (1970), Li Jia's (b. 1923) comedy *The Fake Tycoon* (1971), Li Xing's *The Autumn Execution* (1972), and Bai Jingrui's romantic film *Love in a Cabin* (1972) – *Story of Mother* displays a complex narrative strategy. One could even argue that its narrative level of sophistication matches the films of the Taiwan New Cinema a decade later. Sequences 7–17 of *Story of Mother* are comprised of an extended flashback, and moreover, an embedded flashback within the flashback. These flashbacks portray events that occur to Qingmao as a young boy (portrayed by a young Tuo Zonghua, who as an adult starred in Ang Lee's *Lust, Caution* in 2007). A sequence breakdown of the film in Table 7.1 enables a more complex understanding of the film's structure and patterns.

Table 7.1 *Story of Mother* sequence breakdown

Story of Mother (Song Cunshou, 1972)

System 1: Filmic apparatus and enunciation
System 2: Principle of spectatorship
System 3: Interactants

> QM = Qingmao (Qin Han); M = his mother (Li Xiang); ML = his mother's
> lover; MZ = his girlfriend, Meizhong; BM = his aunt, Bomu; QB = BM's son;
> F = his father; BF = BM's husband, or Bofu; QMB = his younger brother;
> MH = mother's second husband
>
> Settings
>
> *Primary*: alley (A), university (U), coffee shop(s) (CS), Bomu's home in
> Taipei (BMH), mother and father's home in Jiayi (MFH), mother's house
> after the father dies (MH), Qingmao's dorm room (QMD), Train (T)
> *Secondary*: mother's lover's house (LH), bus stop (BST), city walk (CW),
> hospital (H), funeral site (FS), BM's backyard (BMBY), Meizhong's dorm
> room (MZD), nature walk (NW), hotel (H2)

* Note: shading indicates flashback sequences

Seq.*	Setting	Interactants	Sequence details
1	A, LH	QM, M, ML	Opening credits, spying sequence: QMB sees M making love
2	U, QMD, BST	BM, QM, MZ	Day 1: BM visits QM at the U in order to ask him to reconcile with M
3	CS	QM, MZ, QB	QM is emotionally incapable of hanging out with his friends when thinking about his mother
4	CW	QM	QM goes for a walk through the city to clear his mind
5	T	QM, M, ML	M meets ML on a train, ML offers M and QM oranges, M accepts, QM does not
6	QMD	QM	QM returns to QMD after his walk, he looks at a photograph of his father … fade out to another flashback …
7a	MFH, A, LH	QM, M, F, ML	Sequence 1 is fleshed out with scenes that occur before and immediately following sequence 1
7b	MFH	QM, M	M tries to reconnect with the now distant QM; QM writes a letter to BM
8	T, A	BM, QM	BM takes a train to Jiayi, QM meets her at the station and they go home
9	MFH	QM, F, BM, M	BM encourages F to go to Taipei to seek help for his illness, talks to M
10	H	QM, F, BM, BF	F has his illness diagnosed, then returns home with QM on the train

(Continued)

Table 7.1   (cont'd)

Seq.*	Setting	Interactants	Sequence details
11	MFH	QM, F, M, ML	ML is at home when F returns, F argues with M and then literally falls deathly ill
12	H	F	F dies in the hospital
13	FS	QM, M, BM, BF	BM takes QM, QM's two younger siblings stay with M
14	BMH	QM, BM, QB	QM becomes friends with QB
15	BMBY	QM, QM	QM's younger brother comes to BM for help – his M is not taking good care of him, and in fact, their younger sister dies from neglect
16	MH	QMB	The story of QM's younger siblings is depicted, an embedded flashback
17	BMH	QM, BM, BF	The story of QM's younger brother comes to an end
18	QMD	QM	QM is reflecting (on sequences 7a–17)
19	U	M, MZ	Day 2 of the narrative: M goes to the U to talk to MZ
20	BMH	BM, M	BM and M discuss QM and MZ's relationship
21	MH	QMB, MH, M	M returns home from visiting BM, she is loyal to MH
22	MH	M, QMB	M goes back to Taipei to get in touch with QM
23	QMD, CS	MZ, M	M and MZ discuss how to get QM back into contact with M
24	U, NW	QM, MZ	QM and MZ have a wonderful time together until MZ mentions M
25	BMH	MZ, BM, QM, MZ, BF	Day 3 of the narrative: BM and MZ determine just how they might get QM back together with M; at a nice dinner at BM's home, QM learns that he has been accepted to study abroad in the US, BF encourages him to make peace with his M
26	H2	QM, MZ, M	QM and MZ go to visit M, due to a misunderstanding, it looks like M is sleeping around in the hotel, QM leaves the hotel in anger
	U	QM, MZ	MZ tells QM to get over himself, especially when he says that he thinks all women are like M
28	MZD	MZ, BM	BM visits MZ in her dorm room
29	BMBY, BMH	QM, MZ, BM, BF, QB	BM tells QM that the apparent "lover" in M's hotel was just the owner delivering tea
30	T	QM, MZ	QM and MZ go to visit M in Jiayi
31	MH	QM, MZ, QB	QM and MZ discover their mother is at the hospital

Table 7.1 (cont'd)

Seq.*	Setting	Interactants	Sequence details
32	H	M, MH	M is taking good care of MH (unlike how she treated F)
33	MH, A	M, MH, QB	M returns home to learn that she missed seeing QM
34	BMH	BF, M	M visits BM, but BF says that QM, MZ, and BM are at the train station
35	TX/T	QM, M	M takes a taxi to see QM, meanwhile QM is leaving on a train, M sees QM on the train and runs toward his train, then she is struck by a taxi
36	T	QM, M	QM sees his mother lying on the road as his train takes him further away from her

As an analysis of the sequence breakdown indicates, this is an intricately con-structed film. One of the first important themes that emerges is scopophilia. The idea of looking, seeing, and observing both sexuality and tragedy is projected in the first sequence: the boy follows his mother to her lover's tryst and sees his mother in ecstasy while in bed with her lover (sequence 1), and later in the film Qingmao stays to watch his father confront his mother's infidelity (after which his father dies of health complications), even though his father explicitly tells him to leave the room (sequence 11). Furthermore, the mother is seen from subjective point-of-view shots as she sleuths around Qingmao's university campus to see what he looks like after all of the years she was away from him (sequence 19).[3] The final sequence of the film involves Qingmao witnessing the death of his mother when she is struck by a vehicle at a railroad crossing. Thus, the motif of spying is introduced from the very first sequence of a film that represents multiple sites of tension and dichotomies ranging from distinctions between pre-adolescent naïveté and middle-aged sexuality, public life and the private life, inner circles of friends and outside influences, and the divide between ecstasy and retribution.

A second significant element of this representation of Taiwan culture in the early 1970s is the way the camera tracks and traces the film's dominant female characters as they glide effortlessly through and between the settings represented in the film. This notion is beautifully revealed in the second sequence of the film, in which Aunt Bomu sets the precedent for how female characters traverse the physical spaces of the film. The second sequence is divided into three scenes: first Aunt Bomu enters the university campus and speaks to Qingmao's girlfriend Meizhong, then she proceeds to visit Qingmao in his dorm room, then she exits the scene by taking a city bus to head back home. The three scenes in this sequence are linked by tracing her movement and presence, which also foreshadows the way Aunt Bomu will weave in and out of Qingmao's life later in the film in the flashback sequences; for example, when the young Qingmao writes Aunt Bomu a letter regarding his father's health and his mother's infidelity (sequence 7b), Aunt Bomu in turn comes by train to help Qingmao. And in the final third of the film, she is a key negotiator between Qingmao and his mother. Certainly, Aunt Bomu and Qingmao's girlfriend Meizhong, who separately and independently make peace with the mother before Qingmao attempts such a gesture, move back and forth freely between the spaces the mother occupies and those Qingmao inhabits. In this way, the film is a progressive film of its time; it appears to demonstrate that women's secondary status was slowly changing.

However, two key quotations that at first glance might appear to complement this stature of women in Taiwan society actually function as counterweights to the potential emergence of gender equality.[4] The first quotation comes from Aunt Bomu. In sequence 9 she tells the mother, as they fix dinner together in the kitchen: "As women we marry and have children, and as such we accept our fate." Qingmao is seen in this scene spying on his aunt. He overhears the conversation, and recollects it within a flashback sequence. It is as if he longs for his mother to have taken the advice of his aunt, as if he wishes that his mother would have accepted his aunt's advice and "accept her fate" as a woman who must not commit adultery and thus depart from the path designated by the men in her life.

The second quotation occurs in sequence 11, when Qingmao's father confronts the mother about her secret trysts; she passionately explains: "Although I am a mother, I am a woman too!" This would seem to challenge the father, and introduce to the discussion the suggestion that women should be treated as equal subjects rather than objects; however, it is important to note that this scene as well is presented in the film as a flashback, and as such it is part of the memory that troubles Qingmao. This is the advantage of considering the structure in conjunction with the film's major themes: the mother's statement is framed by her son's psyche and recollection, so she is part of his imagination, part of his worldview. Thus, her assertion "Although I am a mother, I am a woman too!" on the one hand privileges the mother's subjectivity. But, on the other hand, its function in the film is to cause anxiety to the protagonist who, in the present tense of the film, reacts with apprehension because such a statement entails equality with his father. These are statements that weigh on Qingmao's psyche as he negotiates his transition to adulthood. Taken together, these statements suggest that the film does not present a free, uncontrolled, and unmonitored female sexuality as socially acceptable. While the film does push the envelope, and should be applauded for raising uncomfortable societal questions such as how one might accept extramarital affairs, at its most mundane the film maintains the status quo.

Intriguingly, Qingmao does not reconcile with his mother for a majority of the film. Early in the narrative, Qingmao safeguards his father's power by pushing his mother completely out of his life; in this way he blindly holds on to a memory of a perfect father who suffered the ignominy of an unfaithful wife. Throughout this section of the narrative Qingmao's character is depicted as unbearably ignorant and stubborn (see sequence 27). Again, it would seem that this blind acceptance of the father allows a space for the expression of female subjectivity, since clearly Qingmao holds on to notions of patriarchal authority without logic or reason. But it might also be argued that Qingmao's father is cuckolded because his father is too pathetic to prevent it. Indeed, the father is so frail he suffers a fatal heart attack the moment he attempts to confront his wife about her infidelity. After the father passes away, the father's authority is maintained by a son who understands neither his mother nor how to safeguard what is left of his own authority as patriarch. The conflict of the film is that Qingmao is immobilized by his immaturity, and his father was an invalid, terminally ill, and weak patriarch.

So, while women like Aunt Bomu freely maneuver the physical spaces of the film, it is Qingmao's psychological transformation that enables the narrative to progress through its various stages of conflict, climax, and resolution. The world of the film swings according to his whims, whether advertently, when Qingmao intentionally rejects his mother's affection (sequence 7b), or inadvertently, when Qingmao determines to resolve his conflict with his mother (sequence 35). Aunt Bomu and Qingmao's intelligent girlfriend, Meizhong, try to influence Qingmao to change his mind; significantly, it is only after learning that his uncle supports the advice provided to him by Meizhong and Aunt Bomu that Qingmao chooses to reestablish a relationship with his mother (sequence 25).

So, if the central question of the film, a question introduced in the film's second sequence, is should a mother's infidelity and neglect of her children (sequence 15) be held against her indefinitely, then the answer is no, for if one understands the mother's point of view, she deserves compassion. Even her death is cast in a sympathetic light (sequence 36). However, an even more pertinent question remains: Who confers this compassion and sympathy? Considering the way gender is presented in the film, it is down to the up-and-coming member of the patriarchal system, Qingmao, to earn his rightful role as masculine authority by conferring his approval. Due to the fact that the film never actually presents Qingmao when he reestablished a relationship with his mother, but rather the film represents Qingmao's change of heart, it could be said to portray a man in the process of attaining his mantle of patriarchal authority, but one who has not entirely achieved it.

Thus, the viewer's interest derives from watching how the protagonist learns how to solve his problem with his mother. Qingmao preserves his authority by recognizing that his father was weak and that he himself holds the power of integrating his mother back into his life and society. As for the leading women, they are active in so far as they desire to be with men for their sexual pleasure, such as the mother, and in the way they make decisions for themselves, such as Aunt Bomu and Meizhong. The women are considerate, compassionate, and sensitive. Yet one could say that theirs is a subjectivity that poses no threat as long as there are powerful men in charge. And men in the film must be on their guard: at any moment the mother – who is never named, and thus functions as archetype – might have an affair if her husband is a pushover, weak, and ignorant. Such men as Qingmao's father will get the fate they deserve if they are not careful. In the end, these archetypes – the pathetic father and impetuous mother – pass away. What remains is the enlightened son.

If Shuqin Cui (2003) is correct, then ideally gender discussions should arrive via a "self-motivated" movement – rather one than appropriated by a patriarchal nationalism – which would eventually lead to freedom. Or, as Judith Butler once wrote, gender discussions are valuable for they possess the potential of extending the norm of what it means to be human to all participants (Salih and Butler 2004: 3). Yet, I would argue that such perspectives propounded by Cui and Butler are not to be found in the film discussed here. So, rather than a movement from the grass-roots, one might conclude that the structure of *Story of Mother* reveals that this presentation of gender behavior is a creation endorsed by the KMT state. And this was a state in a "volatile" situation, to return to Shih's terminology.

The correlation between the political situation in the early 1970s Taiwan film industry and its representation of gender is surprising. While Taiwan's prestige in international diplomacy decreased as the decade wore on, the state-endorsed *wenyi* film style transitioned to a new era of *kang Ri* (resist-Japanese), films that represented the KMT regime as successful in regional and global conflicts. A key moment in this transition occurred in October 1972, when Central Motion Picture Corporation (CMPC) manager Gong Hong (1915–2004), the father of healthy realism, left his post and Mei Changling (b. 1923) took the helm at the studio. Under Mei's watch, a *kang Ri* film hit the screens entitled *Storm Over the Yang-zi River* (1972). The film was met with popular acclaim alongside the concurrent severance of Japanese–Taiwan relations. This film was soon followed by other films from the early to mid-1970s in the propaganda-dominated, patriotic, nationalist film style. Films of this nature, films that show the defeat of foreign threats whenever and however they arise, include *The Everlasting Glory* (Ding Shanxi, 1974) and *Eight Hundred Heroes* (Ding Shanxi, 1976). Yingjin Zhang (2004a: 143) notes that Taiwan's "policy films" of the mid-1970s "resemble similar genres in the PRC," as they are replete with pride and heroic martyrs.[5] Films were produced in this genre throughout the decade, including *A Teacher of Great Soldiers* (Liu Jiachang, 1978).

Despite these changes, depictions of gender remained in many ways the same. In 1972 *Story of Mother* featured a future patriarch who must forgive the sins of the mother, and learn to emulate his uncle who is a model of strength in contrast to his own sickly, cuckolded father. And in the 1975 film *Land of the Undaunted* gender equality is not fully achieved: speaking is allowed only under the auspices of the father, as discussed at the beginning of this chapter. While the style of films changed dramatically, representations of women's roles in society remained quite similar. So, if one is to look to *Story of Mother* to locate female characters exceeding their cultural norms one might find them to a certain extent, but not to the degree that women earn rights equal to their male counterparts. When I had an opportunity to ask the actress who plays the role of mother in the film, Li Xiang, if she believed that *Story of Mother* helped advance women's rights in Taiwan, bearing in mind that she voices the line "I am a wife, but I am a woman too!" she responded: "No, I do not think that the film had any influence on society. Besides, that was just one line in the film" (author interview, November 2008). But not only this, the organization of the film, as the semiotic sequence breakdowns attest, shows that when female subjectivity is expressed, it is encapsulated or carefully framed within the memory of a future patriarch who might approve or disapprove of female expressions of identity.

So, to return to Davis's point established early in this chapter – "films are themselves primary documents of history, and can reveal things about their time that other historical records might not" – what does a film that represents gender negotiation in the early 1970s reveal about Taiwan's precarious political situation? In the ever-transforming political climate, in the ever-transitioning film market, and in the ever-changing styles of the films, why is it that the portrayal of gender remains constant? Why is it that women require the guidance of a firm father in order to function in society?

One interpretation might be that the fathers, by extension, stand in for the patriarchal KMT authority concurrently in power in Taiwan. If so, a potential reading might be that the consistent representation of the patriarchs throughout the early 1970s correlates with the KMT state's consistent international policy – despite all challenges to their governance and political standing. Politically, the Nationalists constantly propagated their position as the seat of all of China in the early 1970s as both theirs already (since the government was previously recognized as the Republic of China) and something that must be earned and maintained (after they had lost legal representation in the United Nations). The depiction of Qingmao's emotional struggles in *Story of Mother* demonstrates the psychological impasse inherent in this double bind. Qingmao provides a fictional representation of this phenomenon since he is one who is always already the centerpiece of the film, since he is the primary male, and yet at the same time he must both earn and maintain this position by forgiving his mother and recognizing the weakness of his father before him. Shih's statement that "the greatest fears and desires as well as the most fantastic projections of confidence are always articulated in gendered terms" certainly requires qualification. Still, the essence of Shih's sentiment resonates with *Story of Mother* when considering the representation of Qingmao as patriarchal authority. After all, so much is at stake in this national allegory: Will Qingmao maintain his privileged status, or will he, like his father, be cuckolded as well?

Story of Mother could not be produced at any other time or place in history. It is a film specific to the ever-transitional local and contingent context of Taiwan in the early 1970s. And still the influence of the global was always part of the equation, as the local and global interwove in a web of power and history (Abbas 1997: 31; Dissanayake 2006: 25). Ella Shohat writes that in the evaluation of transitional situations, the cultural critic should show the "different levels and valences embedded in it" (quoted in Dissanayake 1994: 40). In this discussion, the valences include the cinematic image and a national film institution set within a volatile social context. Despite all of the variables, one might still locate with a degree of clarity a handful of insights embedded in the gender representations in *Story of Mother*. Naturally, many stones remain unturned, but this case study has attempted to demonstrate that the KMT state propounded a version of gender inequality in early 1970s cinema that perhaps unintentionally encapsulated its geopolitical quandary. As the turbulent 1970s concluded and the transitional 1980s began, new political issues would in turn be captured on celluloid to represent the historical permutations and social instabilities that would follow (see S. Lim 2006).

Acknowledgments

The author would like to thank Taiwan's Ministry of Education for the grant "MOE Talent Cultivation Project of Taiwanese Literature, History and Art" that made the research for this chapter possible.

Notes

1 According to Liao Kuang-Sheng, Taiwan's perennial challenges were three: poverty, authoritarian rule, and the perpetual threat of military action from China (see P. Chow 2002: 285).

2 Viewers have found the abundance of coincidences in the film difficult to accept, especially the conclusion (Jin and Di 1979).

3 Depictions of spying might be found in sequences 1, 11, 19, and 23; other important motifs include flashbacks, representations of death: 12, 16, 30, 35/6; trains: 4, 5, 7b, 8, 10, 15, 26, 35/6; and letter writing: 7b, 10, 23. The soundtrack, which varies between somber and intense, warrants an inquiry in and of itself.

4 Linda Williams considers how women speak to each other within film narratives that privilege patriarchy, and she particularly discusses the way women take up their identities within such systems, either by resistance or struggling within contradictions (see Kaplan 2000: 413).

5 Note that after 1977, when Ming Ji (b. 1939) took over CMPC, the patriotic film tradition was maintained, even as the New Taiwan Cinema movement began.

8

Second Coming

The Legacy of Taiwan New Cinema

Darrell William Davis

Introducing Taiwan New Cinema

Taiwan New Cinema is the most important movement in the country's film history, due to its rich formal innovations and sensitivity to Taiwan history and Taiwanese material. It has had worldwide impact in the form of festival recognition, prizes, and considerable influence (some say undue influence) on successive filmmakers. Though its first phase lasted only about five years, New Cinema launched the careers of directors, writers, and technical talents who remain key figures in current Taiwan moviemaking and film culture. From the early 1980s, New Cinema films tackled contemporary Taiwan subjects, from coming of age in Chen Kunhou's *Growing Up* (1982), Hou Hsiao-hsien's *Boys from Fengkuei* (1983), *A Summer at Grandpa's* (1984) and *A Time to Live, a Time to Die* (1985), to political diagnoses in Wan Ren's *Super Citizen* (1985) and Hou's *City of Sadness* (1989), to keen historical reconstructions in Edward Yang's *A Brighter Summer Day* (1991) and Hou's *The Puppetmaster* (1993). There were also literary adaptations, especially from the Nativist (*xiangtu*) school, such as *Sandwich Man* (Hou Hsiao-hsien et al., 1983) and *A Flower in the Rainy Night* (Wang Tong, 1984), both based on Huang Chunming's stories.

New Cinema is known too for its auteurist ambitions, i.e., employing cinema to express personal reflections on unique experiences, alternative to the prevailing norms. It is not a long list of people, but distinguished: directors Hou Hsiao-hsien (b. 1947), Edward Yang (Yang Dechang, 1947–2007), Wan Ren (b. 1950), Xiao Ye (b. 1951), Ke Yizheng (b. 1946), Wang Tong (b. 1942), Zeng Zhuangxiang (b. 1947), Ang Lee (b. 1954), Chen Guofu (Chen Kuo-fu, b. 1958), Chang Tso-chi (Zhang Zuoji, b. 1961), Tsai Ming-liang (b. 1957), director-cinematographer Chen

A Companion to Chinese Cinema, First Edition. Edited by Yingjin Zhang.
© 2012 Blackwell Publishing Ltd. Published 2012 by Blackwell Publishing Ltd.

Kunhou (b. 1939), writers Zhu Tianwen (b. 1956) and Wu Nianzhen (b. 1952), and critic-producer Peggy Chiao Hsiung-ping (b. 1953). There are others – directors, technicians, writers, critics – who were involved briefly, or who took up filmmaking later in the 1990s, sometimes known as the "post-New Cinema." These people are still working in movies or television, if only as respected faculty at Taiwan's film schools. Though it is valid to discriminate between the New Cinema proper and its later directions as post-New Cinema, it is convenient to let the name cover a longer period until the mid-1990s, and indicate the movement's overall auteurist tendencies and stylistic character. The later works became somewhat mannerist, yet they are more fully realized, and they still cleave to the aesthetic basis of New Cinema. In most respects New Cinema *is* Taiwan cinema: a state-supported movement under intense public scrutiny, criticized for its high standards, elitism, and commercial shortcomings, as well as its discomfort with popular formulae.

In its subjects, New Cinema can be seen as a "recovery cinema," an act of salvage. It used historical material that for a long time was taboo and off limits under a regime that forbade depictions of Taiwan's colonial history and beyond. When New Cinema got under way Taiwan was still under martial law (through 1987), imposed in the late 1940s by the ruling Nationalist Party, the Kuomintang (KMT). This meant anything about the Japanese period, civil war on the mainland, the Communist Party, or postwar KMT rule – all this, plus other sensitive matters, was forbidden. It is not that people risked their lives to approach these taboos in the early 1980s; rather, the rules and regulations were gradually being relaxed, and young filmmakers rushed to take advantage of the thaw (Yeh 2005: 167). And it is notable that the New Cinema films made between 1982 and 1987 were not as openly political as those that came later. By the time Taiwan achieved a pluralistic, multiparty democracy in the early 1990s, some declared New Cinema finished, as for instance indicated by a volume of essays called *Death of the New Cinema* published in 1991, in which young Marxist critics took aim at the movement for its alleged co-optation, projecting a radical ideal from which it had strayed.

Stylistically, New Cinema was realist and observational. Compared to the rousing propaganda backed by the KMT in previous years, New Cinema was exceedingly quiet, cool, sometimes austere. Preferring to stay well back from the action, New Cinema directors employed long shots that both distanced dramatic incident and saved film stock due to production constraints such as meager budgets and casting of nonprofessional, inexperienced actors. This was important, as the early projects were apprentice films made under Central Motion Picture Corporation's (CMPC) policy of "low cost, high production." This shot scale later became a deliberate stylistic choice and hallmark. Stories were often elliptical, with gaps in motivation and causality and abrupt, open endings. They also used long takes, extending the duration of individual shots to decompress time and allow improvisation, chance, and contingency to emerge in such things as the weather, animals, and happenstance. Unlike commercial film reliant on "emoting" as the main principle in staging dramatic events, New Cinema shifts its narrative focus to the spatial setup (often landscape and rural locations), temporal duration, and incidental detours. This is seen as New Cinema's major stylistic contribution as well as a key weakness in advancing Taiwan's commercial cinema during the late 1980s, a time of rampant film imports.

Consider Hou Hsiao-hsien's *A Summer at Grandpa's*. Near the beginning, a panning shot on a car follows it to the driveway of a grand colonial-era building; a family gets out and hesitates, readying themselves. As the long shot is held, the people seem suspended, and we are uncertain where to look. Tilt up at the imposing facade. A shot change to an interior reveals this as a hospital. A patient rouses herself from bed to greet her children. The youngsters rush forward, with their backs to the camera, the husband (Edward Yang) stands on the far side of the bed, and uncle and girlfriend fidget next to him. The camera stays back, immobile, and mother fusses over the kids. Father looks on, while also refusing a cigarette from uncle and other distracting gestures. Different lines of action vie for attention: mother and children; nervous uncle and girlfriend; father caught in between. After over a minute, the shot crosses the bed to show the children's reaction, listening calmly to mother's reproach. Hou pauses before dividing the action into dramatic sections, leaving events whole and letting viewers opt what to watch. When the story shifts to the country, more details emerge, puzzling the kids from Taipei: the old Japanese-style house, country urchins, Taiwanese speech, open fields, trees, animals, and outdoor games. It is fair to say that these New Cinema first flowerings are *bildungsroman*, autobiographical tales about individual life lessons and character formation.

New Cinema's visibility stems not just from directorial talent but from its homeland convictions, approach, and techniques. Taiwan-as-homeland though, is a contested, mutating idea, depending on who mobilizes it and in what context. New Cinema began by exploring the home and family of *bildungsroman* and then expanded toward sociopolitical, historical aspects of Taiwan. Veterans of the movement have distinct recollections. Zeng Zhuangxiang (*Sandwich Man*; *Woman of Wrath*, 1985) felt real excitement in bringing Nativist literature to the screen, and a competitive urge toward famed directors such as King Hu and Li Hanxiang who commanded more attention at the time. There was great satisfaction when these big names came up short in public reception (Z. Zeng 2009). Zeng acknowledged rifts and tensions between those eager to see a new direction, versus those invested in the conservative, Sinocentric status quo.

Xiangtu (Nativist) Style, Beyond Literary Adaptation

Incorporating the materials of native Taiwan life, New Cinema employed different dialects and languages (Minnan, Hakka, and sometimes Japanese), semi-rural settings, and adaptations of Nativist literature. Nativist writing was one artistic manifestation treating the Taiwanese here-and-now, not anti-Communist bathos or idealized Chinese mythology. It was a creative urge "rooted in the land of Taiwan, one that reflects the social reality and the material and psychological aspirations of its people" (Y. Chang 1993: 159). Nativist writers were most influential in the 1970s, a sharp response to Taiwan's diplomatic isolation culminating in US recognition of the People's Republic of China (PRC) in 1979 and a wakeup call to self-discovery. This manifested itself in the "return" to local expressions, music, people, places, and scenes. Huang Chunming, an outspoken Nativist writer, was skillful in handling the reversals and ironic flip-flops that exposed the structural inequities of Taiwan's social system, harmful to the local Taiwanese. This unique feature prompted seven adaptations of Huang's work between 1983 and 1990. That *The Sandwich Man*, a portmanteau film directed by Hou Hsiao-hsien, Zeng Zhuangxiang, and Wan Ren, and produced by KMT-owned CMPC, adapted three Huang stories was provocation in itself. New Cinema films were aimed at a distinct audience of college-educated baby-boomers who were abandoning locally made films in favor of Hong Kong and Hollywood imports (Yeh and Davis 2005: 58, 89).

Taiwanese "real life" subjects were a priority, instead of government-backed stagings of heroism. Directors sought the rhythms and problems of ordinary lives, like laborers, fishermen, miners, and shopkeepers with their families. Believable storytelling was employed about local people and typical, everyday experiences; accordingly the stories outlined power differentials in their marginality and precariousness, versus the status of privileged elites. *A Flower in the Rainy Night* is a good example, about an aging, kindly prostitute intent on starting a new life with a home and a child. It did better at the box office than other New Cinema films such as *Sandwich Man* and *Growing Up*, proving the attraction of Nativist themes and Huang Chunming in particular.

The movement "back to Taiwan" was not limited to cinema or literature; it included music, theater, folk and native cultures, and even modern dance, such as the renowned Cloud Gate Dance Theater founded by choreographer Lin Hwai-min (Lin Huaimin). Lin, a New York-trained native son, is among Taiwan's brightest talents. Originally wanting to be a creative writer, Lin exchanged the Iowa Writer's Workshop for New York to study with Martha Graham and Merce Cunningham in his late twenties, far too late in the physically punishing world of modern dance. Still, Lin learned dance from the basics and returned to his xiangtu Taiwan and formed Cloud Gate in 1973. Right after US termination of formal relations with Taiwan, Lin chose to premiere his new work on seventeenth-century Taiwan in a provincial town, Chiayi, where he grew up. The choice to skip the capital city Taipei and unveil the work – a synthesis of New York-inspired modern dance with local mythology – in the province indicates Lin's conviction of a return to native soil and a reaffirmation of his roots.

Xiangtu transcends literature as an idea running through Taiwan culture and visible already in the Japanese colonial era, long before the arrival of the KMT. It gestures toward ardent belonging and affiliation to Taiwan, in landscape, community, or ethnicity. Though often set in the countryside, this was just an expedient signpost of native belonging. Rural scenes did provide New Cinema with evocative locations, and perhaps made it cheaper to shoot than in studio sets, but this was not a necessity. Unlike xiangtu literature, it need not be committed to anti-Western commentary, like that of Huang Chunming who taunted the mainlander-backed modernists and their European influences: "Why do we need to have foreigners with their noses in the air tell us what is good? Art must grow from the soil itself" (Udden 2009: 51).

New Cinema placed Taiwan and its people firmly in the center as subjects, not as an "island on the edge" or a temporary refuge, nor as postcard images of countryside or coastline. Taiwan is indeed often photogenic, but xiangtu style crucially embeds convictions of Taiwanese home, a dwelling that is rooted and primal. It is not an area of nostalgia, exile, or escape from the claims of modernity. Thus cityscapes are well represented in New Cinema: pockets of tradition, superstition, and community survive, despite cold urban surfaces. Temples, wet markets, betelnut stalls, puppets, festivals, neighborhood rituals – even *juancun,* the decaying compounds of KMT veterans, make appearances. Figured as homeland, Taiwan is a distinct place with personality, varying at different times and regions; sometimes it is an outrageous spot, yet attractive still. Even the vivid, earthy songs in Tsai Mingliang's films, a modernist vision willfully odd, vital, or perverse (Yeh and Davis 2005: 217–48), is a variety of xiangtu.

Censoring/Censuring New Cinema

Wan Ren's "The Taste of Apples" was a controversial part of the portmanteau film *Sandwich Man,* a little too astringent in its adaptation of Huang Chunming's mid-1960s story to a 1983 movie screen. New Cinema's first decisive steps were taken to defy bureaucratic meddling, when journalists exposed to the public attempts to censor Wan Ren's section. Although script censorship at CMPC had just been scrapped, there were misgivings about Wan Ren's satire about a Taiwanese laborer suddenly enriched when he is hit by an American officer's car. Conservatives thought the story insulting – insulting, that is, not to Taiwanese workers but to KMT officials, police, and politicians. The fable revealed the divisions between Mandarin elites and impoverished local Taiwanese, and possibly too the rifts between these same elites and their American overlords. The story takes aim not only at the KMT's "lapdog" role but at the United States as well, especially its icy materialism. Its sympathies are firmly with the grassroots of Taiwan, complete with images of shantytown neglect.

Anonymous complaints about "Apples" made their way to CMPC and a list of offending scenes to cut was prepared and nearly carried out. But new producers

Wu Nianzhen and Xiao Ye discovered the plot and with the help of sympathetic journalists exposed it to ridicule in the local press. The so-called "Apple-peeling incident" brought publicity to struggles over means of expression in movies and highlighted issues of artistic freedom (Yeh and Davis 2005: 60–2). Just a year before, film had been in the grip of government studios and censors, such as the Government Information Office (GIO). Now freedom of expression and opinion was being openly claimed, following the letter of newly circulated production rules within the CMPC. This was uncomfortable to many in the cultural establishment.

Other New Cinema controversy concerned its unprofitable box office versus festival success. From the start, some hated New Cinema for its successes and failures alike. Either it was too "arty," dismissed as the work of foreign film school graduates; or its understated, personal stories implicitly challenged escapist melodrama or martial arts, genres that were once profitable. Usually New Cinema films did poor business, except for surprises like *In Our Time* (Tao Decheng, Ke Yizheng, Zhang Yi, Edward Yang, 1982), *Sandwich Man, Growing Up*, and *Kuei-mei, A Woman* (Zhang Yi, 1985). But they also received acclaim at foreign film festivals, so this was a problem for critics set against them. Until Hou's *City of Sadness* received a Golden Lion at Venice in 1989, the prizes were mostly collected at mid-range events: Nantes, Tokyo, Hawai'i, Locarno, Mannheim, Rotterdam, and London (C. Wu 2007: 80). But this was no consolation; critics accused the filmmakers of pandering to foreign tastes. Edward Yang said he was called names ("Americanized, westernized, traitor, or 'bananas'") and was shocked by the charge that *A Brighter Summer Day* was an anti-local story made by an outsider (Anderson 2005: 113, 100). One writer, Liang Liang, published an article called "Obscure Is Not the Only Way Out" (E. Yeh 2005: 183). He thought New Cinema was ignoring the ticket-buying public in Taiwan, showing little "concern" for either story or audience. This was a classic fallacy of correlation mistaken for causation, supposing festival awards were gained at the expense of local box office, and worse: a few New Cinema films were blamed for the worsening overall slump in local production.

At the time, there were too many interest groups and agendas for New Cinema to fulfill: conservative, liberal-humanist, Marxist (*Death of the New Cinema*), Orientalist (*Cahiers du cinema*), nostalgic (Hasumi Shigehiko), commercial, formalist, radical, and so on (E. Yeh 2005). The fact is that New Cinema was too limited a sample to have any real statistical effect on Taiwan's film industry, yet its fraught reputation carried a long way. New Cinema was less than 10 percent of locally made movies, compared to its wide global impact (see Table 3.1 in Yeh and Davis 2005: 102). It never represented the majority of Taiwan-made films; its artistic ambitions were bold enough to alienate local commercial interests, especially distributors who found the films a hard sell. Foreign festivals and critics took notice of the films' ambition and rewarded some of them, but this counted for little at home, except for Hou's breakthrough film *City of Sadness* in 1989.

Worsening the public reception of New Cinema was the poor box office of Edward Yang's films, seen as a vanguard of formal experimentation. It is true that his films, compared to most others in New Cinema, are convoluted, modernist, even cold. Yang is most interested in networks of urban relations, instead of the Nativist exploration of authentic landscapes and people. He reconfigured typical melodramatic devices such as double crossing, betrayal, infidelity, deceit, and self-delusion to lay out complex social relations motivated by money, sex, and vanity. His debut solo feature *That Day on the Beach* (1983) employs multiple temporalities to depict a tradeoff of wealth with innocence. His subsequent *Taipei Story* (1984) deliberately replaces a sentimental love story with depression, boredom, and loss. The result was rejection from the local audience, even in Taipei (on release for only three days, a record for all New Cinema films). *The Terrorizers* (1986) did better, but retreats further from the Nativist tendency by focusing on an improbable urban network of chance linkages (coincidence, simultaneity) and misconnections (infidelity, betrayal, mistrust). Though Yang's apparent modernist affiliation may not seem compatible with the Nativist sensibilities of others, his films enrich New Cinema, adding an extra key dimension to its repertoire. They certainly prevent any reduction of New Cinema to regionalism or local color. As a whole, New Cinema was thus a synthesis of Nativist and modernist influences. The modernist aspect turned off some viewers and critics – those hostile to festival recognition that signaled auteur consecration. It was a short step to blaming auteur aspirations for the woes of the Taiwan film industry in general.

Indeed, New Cinema was uncommercial and perhaps rightly so, given its government-backed inception, under the CMPC as a KMT subsidiary. Government's input through GIO directives and the CMPC was "positive yet somewhat dubious" (Y. Chang 2005: 20). Traditionally CMPC's major responsibility was to groom a national cinema for propaganda purposes and maintain a guiding presence in the film industry. CMPC's first and most effective attempt was the "healthy realist" pictures in the 1960s. Under managing director Henry Gong Hong, independent filmmakers working in Taiyu (Taiwanese language) production such as Li Xing and Li Jia were recruited, along with young director Bai Jingrui. Under the KMT's tight supervision, these people fashioned a new style of films distinct from the commercial costume dramas and melodramas from the big Hong Kong studios Shaw Brothers and Cathay (Yeh and Davis 2005: 25–7).

New Cinema could be seen as a sequel to the healthy realist pictures of years before, and this pedagogical ancestry may have hindered its long-term profitability. Reliant in large part on government patronage, its maturation and eventual decline transpired in an expanding marketplace, indicating Taiwan's opening to capital intervention and management of culture. Whereas the 1970s to the early 1980s were still years of ideological control, the mid-1980s brought capital accumulation to the cultural sphere, a development that soon became entrenched and irrevocable. New Cinema had to attract capital and compete in the marketplace. But the films continued to receive support from government and outside agencies, as their

Table 8.1 Number of Films Released in Taiwan, 1995–2010

Year	Taiwan film releases	Non-Taiwan film releases (Hollywood, Asian, and European)
1995	18	454
1996	23	230
1997	18	304
1998	15	309
1999	11	306
2000	19	273
2001	10	212
2002	16	250
2003	15	264
2004	23	236
2005	20	260
2006	18	345
2007	22	353
2008	26	376
2009	28	368
2010	38	367

Sources: Data compiled from *Taiwan Cinema* (http://www.taiwancinema.com/lp.asp?ctNode=265& CtUnit=15&BaseDSD=7&mp=1) and *Taiwan Cinema Yearbook* (1996–2010).

natural audience was in festivals, museums, and retrospectives outside commercial venues, and beyond Taiwan. New Cinema's timing also meant it coincided with new waves in both Hong Kong and the PRC, a sea change that raised the tide of East Asian cinema, especially the prizes and networking opportunities at international festivals. Cultural initiatives like New Cinema were extenuating the KMT's relaxation, anticipating by about five years the end of martial law. Some critics such as Huang Jianye believed New Cinema helped hasten the end of martial law, promoted by baby-boomers insistent on personal and social freedoms. It also performed as *de facto* national cinema abroad when Taiwan's entry to major international organizations was blocked by the PRC. Here culture, especially New Cinema, worked as compensatory national representation and cultural diplomacy. This is something the GIO and Taiwan Economic and Cultural Offices abroad still use to portray and promote Taiwan to the world.

The number of Taiwan-made films released locally is pitifully small, not even one tenth of the films on Taiwan's movie screens. They are rare breeds in an overcrowded habitat. Here the government retains a role as patron and partner, particularly through the *fudaojin* subsidy run by the GIO. Despite meager resources, government capital was made available to scripts and projects that fulfilled specific criteria. Every two or three years the criteria, awards, and requirements were changed. In 1992 a cash reward was offered called "Incentives for Domestic Films and Professionals' Participation in International Film Festivals" (C. Wu 2007: 86), rewards pegged to the prestige of the film festival. But in practice it was the big names with track records that consistently accessed the funds.

The fudaojin fund may subsidize up to half the film's budget (maximum US$432,000), along with various tax allowances. At its founding, the subsidy was meant to combat a shrinking domestic output, but the plan was revised after harsh criticism that government funds were wasted on uncommercial art films. A review in 2004 once more changed the priorities, with funding reserved for script development ("guidance funds," for which Leon Dai (Dai Liren, b. 1966) later applied with *Cannot Live Without You*), shorts/documentaries, and cash awards for winners at the box office. The subsidy also attracts some foreign investors, such as Wong Kar-wai's Jet Tone, whose Taipei office has operated since 2005. Linking with cognate enterprises, GIO stands ready to devote NT$20 billion over five years to cultural, creative, and digital-content industries. But it has not been as successful as similar programs like those of South Korea and the UK, which reversed their film industry declines through an aggressive combination of tax credits, quotas, and direct government subsidy to producers (Chan, Fung, and Ng 2010: 39).

Fudaojin, in addition to much internal bickering, cannot escape the consequences of the state being a coproduction partner. This leads to disputes over the films' ownership and nationality. The GIO demanded a return of the NT$4 million grant for *Miao Miao* (Cheng Hsiao-tse, 2007), starring Sandrine Pinna (a.k.a. Yung-yung Chang, Zhang Rongrong, b. 1987), because Hong Kong's Jet Tone suddenly pulled it from the Melbourne International Film Festival in 2009. Though the company blamed this on the festival's politicization in showing a film about Rebiya Kadeer, the Uygur spokesperson, its action echoed that taken by mainland Chinese entries and appeared as a wholesale Chinese boycott. Taiwanese legislators made a loud outcry. Similarly, the GIO wanted to take back the subsidy for *Prince of Tears* (Yon Fan, 2009), another coproduction with Hong Kong, as it was submitted for best foreign film Oscar under the name of Hong Kong. Many critics and commentators are sympathetic but believe the GIO's tactics do not serve Taiwan's film industry.

Maturity and Mannerism in the 1990s

New Cinema represents a range of narrative and stylistic innovations exemplified best by *A City of Sadness* and *A Brighter Summer Day*, though both are technically in the movement's second phase. *City of Sadness* was the first film to tackle the February 28 Incident, a major bloody clash in 1947 between local Taiwan residents and the recently arrived KMT government. The film treated that longstanding taboo in Taiwan society in a detached yet powerful way. Its deliberate formal limitations – multiple protagonists, ellipses, muteness, discursive gendered narration – offered a rich evocation of the incident's brutality, while receiving criticism for avoiding pictures of atrocity (P. Liao 1993). Hou remarked he made the film "not for the sake of opening up old wounds, but because it's vital that we face up to this incident if we are to understand where we come from and who we are as Taiwanese" (*California Chronicle*). Some call it a "subaltern historiology," artfully blending a multiplicity of private and public experiences (Berry and Farquhar 2005: 34). The film was a *cause célèbre* in Taiwan not just for its subject but for its top prize at the world's oldest, most prestigious festival, Venice. The box office was tremendous, silencing charges that New Cinema could not draw audiences. Festival prizes would continue for New Cinema films, but the public would take little heed henceforth. *A Brighter Summer Day* was an even more structured historical sifting, preoccupied with the material culture of the 1960s in a way deciphered elsewhere as "tunnel visions" (Yeh and Davis 2005: 103–18). Both films delineate characters groping for purchase on events and circumstances that are elusive, deeply troubling, and exemplify Taiwan's complex historical experiences. These two films marked a turn toward a more epic scope, away from the personal, individual sketches of early New Cinema. Yang's film was honored at the Tokyo, Nantes, and Asia Pacific festivals, and enjoyed some scholarly attention in Taiwan.

The New Cinema movement gave way to works of individual auteurs such as Hou, Yang, and newcomers like Tsai Ming-liang and Ang Lee. The mutual aid collectively shared among the young directors and technicians in the 1980s yielded to professional specialization, the pursuit of finance, visibility at festivals and festival juries, and media appearances.

A writer of theater and television scripts, Tsai Ming-liang began making films in 1992 (*Rebels of the Neon God*) and pushed the most avant-garde side of New Cinema. Lin Cheng-sheng (Lin Zhengsheng, b. 1959), a documentarist who explored the lives of drifters (*Drifting Life*, 1996), lesbian teenagers (*Murmur of Youth*, 1997), and incest (*Sweet Degeneration*, 1998), later received an award at Berlin for *Betelnut Beauty* (2000), part of Peggy Chiao's "Tale of Three Cities" program. Chang Tso-chi is another New Cinema veteran who continues to make films in a distinctly localist idiom. At the opposite end, Ang Lee used his American training to leverage prize-winning scripts into independent films and sleeper hits (*Pushing Hands*, 1992; *The Wedding Banquet*, 1993). These directors were all funded by the government through the GIO's fudaojin, the scriptwriting and production subsidy set up in 1990, responding to the prize received by *City of Sadness*. Ang Lee was recruited to carry on New Cinema into the 1990s, but *Wedding Banquet*'s global windfall put him out of reach and into the arms of American finance (Davis 2003: 719). Lee's next film, the Taipei-set *Eat Drink Man Woman* (1994), was internationally successful but received criticism at home for its old-fashioned, patriarchal focus that seemed archaic and eroticized. Taipei audiences did not recognize themselves in the film's émigré flavor.

By this time New Cinema's once-tight focus was slackening, in favor of more multiplicity and experimental and even eccentric practice. Hou's *Flowers of Shanghai* (1998) is exemplary in this regard, moving back into nineteenth-century China and a hypnotic, hyperbolic pictorialism. Ang Lee followed Hou's cue a decade later by adapting another Eileen Chang (Zhang Ailing) story, *Lust, Caution* (2007). If Ang Lee took New Cinema's mainstream current, Tsai Ming-liang's films were the most errant, inventive, and mannerist: *Vive L'Amour* (1994, Venice Golden Lion), *The River* (1996, Berlin Silver Bear), *The Hole* (1998, Cannes FIPRESCI), *What Time Is It There?* (2001), *Goodbye Dragon Inn* (2003), and even *The Wayward Cloud* (2005). It is hard to imagine government coffers funding such work – homosexual incest, surrealist fable, a picture palace elegy, porn musical – anywhere but Taiwan.

From Xiangtu to Bentu, Nativism to Localism

We noted the xiangtu as an animating principle of New Cinema, especially in its early phase. Hou Hsiao-hsien and Chen Kunhou made proto-Nativist commercial films well before New Cinema's advent, paving the way to a more coherent movement. Hou's pictures such as *Cute Girl* (1980), *Cheerful Wind* (1981), and *Green, Green Grass of Home* (1982) were light fare that offered stars in countryside melodramas and romantic comedies. Their pictorial strategies anticipate many of the stylistic features of New Cinema in its most canonical aspects.

Chen Kunhou, Hou's partner prior to the late 1980s, maintains that New Cinema should not be seen as mere follower of Nativist literature. With the flourishing of Nativism, a change of style began to take place in photography and its cousin cinematography. This is especially clear in location work where the director of photography (DP) was in control of production, while directors concentrated on the stars and dialogue. For instance, veteran director Li Xing was uninterested in visual style, not even bothering to use the viewfinder in the award-winning *Story of a Small Town* (1979). DP Chen Kunhou was thus left to his own devices. He had the freedom to experiment and explore a photographic style that can be viewed as "nativist," or maybe naturalist, predating the formal adaptation of Nativist literature by New Cinema writers and directors (K. Chen 2009).

According to Chen, a nascent pictorial style closer to the xiangtu had already been devised in the late 1970s, preparing the way for altered subject matter in the early 1980s. Changes in cinematography might have augured shifts in Taiwan film style generally, with Nativist literature reaching cinema later. Films almost forgotten now, such as *Lover on the Wave* (1980), *Spring in Autumn* (1980), and *Six is Company* (1982), were directed by Chen and scripted by "Hou Li," a moniker used by young writer Hou Hsiao-hsien. Produced by Dazhong, the company started by Li Xing and Bai Jingrui in 1970, these films are hearty melodramas that manage to break out of the settings of the contrived romance genre known as *san ting* or "three rooms" (i.e., living room, dining room, coffee shop) and made popular by adapting Qiong Yao's fiction. Chen and Hou made efforts to take the action outside to the beach, riverside, orchards, highways, wet markets, and railroad platforms. In addition, their interest in children as part of daily life gives a fresh look to the mise-en-scène. Sometimes the filmmakers would shoot when performers thought they were just rehearsing (Davis 2003: 726; Udden 2009: 47). Aside from placing their characters in more recognizable daily environments, Chen and Hou were unwittingly outlining the xiangtu style that would eventually typify New Cinema. Gradually Chen and Hou developed the long shot–long take style suited for children, nonprofessionals, and subjects in country settings, a method depicting people as they are, and not twisting them to suit melodramatic purposes. This too is a premise of New Cinema, apart from its more explicit xiangtu themes emphasized by writers and producers.

Xiangtu became distilled, something more like an ideology under New Cinema, not just through ties with xiangtu literature, but its commitment to local characters and predicaments, combined with a detached, often attenuated visual style. The aesthetics of xiangtu became codified with New Cinema, alongside new emphases on auteurism and international profile. These twin pillars would sustain New Cinema, but only for a while.

Localism (*bentu*) expanded in the 1990s, as KMT cultural prescriptions yielded to commercial incentives and imperatives. Bentu is a sensibility that "champions the legitimacy of a distinct Taiwanese identity, the character and content of which should be determined by the Taiwanese people" (Makeham and Hsiau 2005: 1). We could say bentu themes and trends had momentum in the early 1990s by dint of novelty, as the residues of martial law and new liberalization faded. Bentu was circulating and in places adhering well before 2000, when it was instrumental in dislodging the KMT from power. Just as xiangtu ideas were available long before 1987, so *bentuhua* or indigenization was a major part of Taiwan's sociopolitical environment throughout the 1990s under Li Denghui, the KMT's first Taiwanese chairman. The literary reputation of bentu suffered compared to the more elevated *xiangtu wenxue*, sometimes working as "public ritual" at a time when the political stakes were lowering, and gave way to contending forms of cultural legitimation (Y. Chang 2004: 129). Localism became more legitimized in the 1990s as its assumptions and arguments circulated in media, publishing, product marketing, and public discourses. Maukuei Chang (2005: 239–40) writes that "the indigenization of real politics also required the indigenization of the general public's cultural outlook. Here we find a broader indigenization of many areas in the field of culture, including language, literature, arts, movies, popular songs, history, sociology and anthropology in particular." As Taiwan's television and electronic media deregulated, localist sentiment was allowed to amplify, and seemed to strengthen the further south one went from Taipei. Localism was reproduced, multiplied, variegated, and splintered into diverse voices and platforms. On television and radio there was government support for Hakka, aboriginal and other channels that served minority communities. These various bentu platforms differed in their political positions, demographics, and levels of activism. Bentu-led localism was later enshrined as part of cultural and educational policy under Chen Shui-bian's DPP (Democratic Progressive Party) administration in 2000.

As Taiwan's marketplace diversified, New Cinema was thought to be getting stale, according to screenwriter/director Wu Nianzhen (Davis 2005: 252–3). This was because its original immediate background, KMT authority and cultural control, was no longer there. Some New Cinema faces like Wu became media celebrities associated with a burgeoning bentu, and packaged it in commodity forms. Wu had cowritten with Zhu Tianwen several screenplays for Hou Hsiao-hsien, including *Dust in the Wind* (1986), *City of Sadness*, and *The Puppetmaster*. Wu himself directed two films, *Dou-san: A Borrowed Life* (1994) and *Buddha Bless America* (1996), which tried to update New Cinema for a changed context and audience. Then he moved to television, hosting a prime-time travel show of local sites, people, food, history, and memories. Wu Nianzhen's *Taiwan*, broadcast on TVBS (1995–8) and signaling the program's assertive local identity, soon made Wu a famed spokesman for numerous consumer products (e.g., drinks, food, cell phones). These items were able to benefit from a local Taiwanese cachet. Product differentiation was enabled by bentu rhetoric, alongside grassroots declarations of local pedigrees. Bentu then was a focalization of xiangtu ideas, together with a more communicative, populist voice.

Wu Nianzhen, who would star as NJ in *Yi Yi* (Edward Yang, 2000), had assisted on Wang Tong's so-called "native regional trilogy": *Straw Man* (1987), *Banana Paradise* (1989), and *Hill of No Return* (1992). These films mediated Japanese colonial, KMT veteran, and Taiwanese characterizations in a gently mocking comic style. This new localism, a more direct and accessible form of xiangtu, was a valuable asset to the DPP opposition, which eventually took power.

Compared to Nativism, localism seems more of a sentiment than an aesthetic or ideology because of its emotional appeal (something bracketed, if not avoided, in New Cinema) and its straightforward politics of "Taiwan first." If New Cinema rejected KMT propaganda and "three-room" melodrama, its xiangtu was low key and oblique; this made it vulnerable at home as it perpetuated itself on festival circuits. Bentu style addresses Taiwan audiences more than film festival juries (Davis 2003: 730). It does not shy away from commercial entertainment values, and engages audience curiosity with popular formats and narrative momentum. Here we may consider the striking example of *Cape No. 7* (Wei Te-sheng, 2008), long awaited by Taiwan audiences, critics, and film industry figures. This film represents the "second coming" for locally made, audience-friendly, commercially successful cinema.

Cape No. 7: A New Era for Popular Taiwan Movies?

As an unexpected blockbuster, *Cape No. 7* was momentous on at least two counts. It was a giant hit for locally made movies (over NT$350 million in domestic returns alone), and it achieved its success through its shrewd packaging of strong

Taiwanese elements. Further, the film satisfied desires that had been building during the DPP era and before. Companies like Three Dots Entertainment had been intently cultivating niches for popular comedy, horror, and gay films since 2003, though their staff took shots at New Cinema: "Entertainment is seen as a dirty word by many Taiwanese filmmakers," said Chen Yin-jung (a.k.a. D. J. Chen, b. 1980), director of *Formula 17* (2004) (Davis 2007: 155). Audiences and critics alike had for years awaited a movie savior that would address local tastes. *Cape No. 7* took a leaf from Three Dots marketing with brilliant promotion of an online viral outreach while the film was still in production. Distribution was handled by Buena Vista International (Disney), the most powerful movie marketing firm in Taiwan.

The film is an epistolary tale with a Japanese voiceover. Aga, a failed guitarist, returns to Hengchun, in Taiwan's far south, on the coast. He becomes a substitute postman who must deliver parcels but cannot find the addressee for a place called "Cape number 7." The undelivered package contains antiquated love letters written by a recently deceased Japanese man, who had left behind his Taiwanese fiancée right after the war. The package thus links Aga's predicament, as reluctant returnee, with the author's. Both characters and letters are suspended, looking for their rightful place. Musician Aga is shanghaied into leading a local warm-up band. What starts bitterly for Aga becomes unexpected joy, uniting the local community in this remote but beautiful southern village. The letters find their way to the elderly recipient. With coincidence, improvisation, and humor, the unruly villagers eventually join in welcoming a Japanese pop star to their home.

Cape No. 7 was seen as turning the New Cinema page to a new chapter, breaking away from a time when "the island's cinema stuck in a vicious decline that seemed all but irreversible," "an era of high-minded boredom and anti-drama ... an austere, punishing style of filmmaking that plagued Taiwanese cinema like a malaise" (P. Lam 2008: 105). Wei Te-sheng (Wei Desheng, b. 1969), an experienced but struggling filmmaker (four shorts, one feature), felt Taiwan cinema had reached an impasse – this at least was the line taken by many journalists and critics sick of "excesses" of New Cinema and its progeny. Yet Wei had worked in New Cinema, having served as assistant director on *Mahjong* (Edward Yang, 1996) and as associate producer and editor on *Double Vision* (Chen Guofu, 2002), the latter another genre film, a crime thriller that used very effective online marketing.

Cape No. 7 was seen as countering the modernist gloom of post-New Cinema leftovers. Skeptical of metropolitan, elitist film culture, it favored the countryside, seascapes, and popular music. It celebrates minorities – Hakka, aboriginal and even foreigners – and charms with its sunny picture of rural, unspoiled Taiwan. It is inclusive, reaching out to all viewers, not simultaneously, but as a multi-coded entertainment with deft appeals to distinct segments. It was also released throughout East Asia, including mainland China. The film is touching and different, its breath of fresh air providing an excuse for critics and audiences to "vent" about New Cinema's perceived failings.

Cape No. 7 is a bona fide local bentu film – but meticulously calculated. It celebrates local community, homespun ways, village life, and a hodge-podge of diversity. The letter-writer lends lyrical wrapping, in Japanese, around the antics of country Taiwanese. Minnan-nese politicians, aboriginal cops, Hakka salesmen, ornery musicians, grumpy maids, surly kids – all appear as convincing provincials. Like New Cinema, many in the cast were nonprofessionals, including the Japanese folk singer Atari Kousuke (who plays himself as a saint-like figure from afar, as well as the Japanese teacher who writes the love letters "home"). A native of a small Ryukyu island near Taiwan, Atari's appearance in Hengchun lends an air of regional specificity.

Some commented on the film's implicit nationalism, addressing Taiwan audiences as a plural community that treasures its multicultural background (Ying-bei Wang 2009). Indeed a work of reconciliation, it brought into harmony city and country, minorities, languages, and outsiders. What is international was its huge domestic success in Taiwan, an unlikely triumph leading to commercial momentum that reached the whole region. This testifies to New Cinema's representative status, standing for Taiwan cinema, for good or ill. *Cape No. 7*'s victory was longed for by audiences, writers, and businesses whose stock-in-trade was entertainment, not rarefied art cinema. The movie's success was desperately needed, as though Taiwan cinema required a transfusion; but as a referendum on New Cinema, post-*Cape* judgments were often harsh. The ending of *Cape No. 7* shows that not even bentu cinema can stand outside a global community and cultural circulation. Forms of compromise and calculation of diverse interests, markets, and audience segments must be in place from the outset.

Bentuhua took other forms in cinema: popular documentaries such as *Gift of Life* (Wu Yifeng, 2004), *Let It Be: The Last Rice Farmer* (Yan Lanquan and Zhuang Yizeng, 2004), and *Viva Tonal: The Dance Age* (Jian Weisi and Guo Zhendi, 2004), as well as travelogue films like *Island Etude* (Chen Huai'en, 2006) and *The Most Distant Course* (Lin Jingjie, 2007). Thereafter bentu cinema has been redefined and refined as Taiwan engages with global market trajectories.

New Cinema's Afterlife

After the New Cinema, Taiwan films have been searching for purchase, in the sense of paying customers and a solid hold on character. In the 1990s New Cinema became bifurcated because the films produced locally were increasingly art house, while storytelling was left to Hollywood and the Hollywood-financed Ang Lee. Putting it like this is crude, but it also indicates the crucial factor, money. Financing art house specialties for export was something easier, given New Cinema's record, than restarting a commercial cinema that regularly drew domestic audiences. At this time Hollywood, and to some extent Hong Kong and

Japan, was left to supply the entertainment pipeline. One might ask then, does Taiwan need a film industry, rather than a boutique, handmade cinema of exquisite craft and originality? The consensus in Taiwan's cultural bureaucracy is yes, though its actions say otherwise. In what follows, I return to the idea of *bildungsroman*, the process of character formation that New Cinema embarked on in the 1980s and follows still, in fits and starts.

From a Japanese colony, Taiwan eventually developed into a rich, democratic but stateless country, like such places as Xinjiang, Tibet, or Palestine. Due to its economic, technological, and cultural advantages, Taiwan is in a peculiar position. Internally its cultural life is open, active, and diverse. Its filmmakers and artists can tell stories that reconstruct colonial times, the cold-war era, or even martial law. They are free to address niche audiences, by region, topic, class, or sexual orientation. As an irregular nation-state, Taiwan must work vigorously to resist the roles and stereotypes imposed by many global forces, including – but not solely – the PRC. Globally, Taiwan works like a lab experiment in models of national self-definition. Some of these test runs are extreme and given China's priorities, foolhardy. Taiwanese people have nonetheless retained a strong sense of national identity, even as the KMT administration pursues greater integration with the mainland.

Taiwan's film/television professionals have for years practiced their craft for mainland companies. This is no secret, and indicates the flexibility, resourcefulness, and creativity of Taiwan's film and cultural industries in general. Taiwan's overall shift from authoritarianism to an open society, participatory, contested, and dynamic, is remarkable, even as people grow weary of domestic politics. Historically, Taiwan people have borne their fate with resilient aplomb, but striations and scars remain: colonial, military, ethno-linguistic, class, regional, and generational polarization. Now Taiwan is an island of diversity, democratic, peaceful but wary and divided, while remaining the PRC's military and diplomatic foe. Though Taiwan politics and media are a free-for-all, it is still surprisingly free. Whoever is in charge, Taiwan's ruling party remains the butt of intense critical venom – a robust public arena, and often brutal. At present Taiwan's film industry and film policies are again the target of competing visions, especially the perennial dilemma of popular versus elite film styles. This reprises old dichotomies between Nativist and modernist, realist versus experimental versus populist cultural forms, audiences, and markets. Recall too that these divisions mediated ethno-linguistic communities, the mainlander–Taiwanese (*waishengren–benshengren*) cultural formations that persist, with the former usually aligned more with government policy.

When New Cinema was developing thirty years ago, it was both supported and constrained by clear government directives flowing from authoritarian cultural policies. Once these were removed in the late 1980s, New Cinema films and directors were exposed to market conditions, though these were moderated, deflected, and not strictly commercial. The market was unleashed, but also managed by various means, such as subsidies. As it attenuated, New Cinema was not suddenly required to address mass audiences via the box office, but some filmmakers accepted commercial aims more than others. Chen Guofu appeared in *HHH: Portrait of Hou Hsiao-hsien* (Oliver Assayas, 1997) in an emotional scene, saying he would gladly exchange his own films to restore the close camaraderie of New Cinema in the 1980s, when filmmakers and actors gathered at Edward Yang's house, lingering freely to talk shop, life, and movies. Chen's statement was made around 1997, a time when Hou was moving toward pronounced aestheticization (*Goodbye South, Goodbye*, 1996; *Flowers of Shanghai*, 1998) while Chen was going mainstream (*The Personals*, 1998). Chen and Hou were then at opposite ends of a spectrum – entertainment and experimental – that took at least a decade to reconcile. Chen, now executive at Huayi Brothers Media Group in China, is a major player behind Chinese blockbusters while Hou is … Hou Hsiao-hsien.

It is ironic that the heavy, emotionally restrained *City of Sadness* drew so many viewers. *City* was a film that benefited from novelty, though its stylistic qualities probably damaged the prospects of subsequent New Cinema films. It was further assisted by extra-textual factors such as the Venice Golden Lion and its uptake of suppressed historical material, the February 28 Incident. Given New Cinema's uncommercial bent, government and cultural organizations took up the slack, shepherding and sustaining a festival-based cinema of formal rigor, despite box-office weakness. Thus New Cinema became successful enough to become identified with Taiwan film as an emblematic movement, if not quite a brand name. Those who loathed New Cinema still perpetuated it through caricature, attacking its elitism, formalism, and auteurism. Those who appreciated New Cinema perpetuated it by following and elucidating its directors' more recent work, even as the movement itself lost coherence. Some New Cinema auteurs went on to obtain international recognition, and even cultural consecration in Taiwan despite their cinematic work. A filmmaker like Hou Hsiao-hsien is respected and feted at home because of who he is, not because people watch his films. That Hou's movies have not drawn audiences since *City of Sadness* does not diminish his stature; and it is a peculiarity of Taiwan cinema that it enjoys such exceptions and cultural anomalies. The Hollywood adage "You're only as good as your last hit" does not seem to apply in Taiwan.

New Cinema was never popular, never set out to be, nor encouraged by subsidy, policy, or industry incentives to reach ordinary audiences at home. There were ideas in the 1980s of enticing college-age viewers back to Taiwan movies, but this never translated into long-term industrial recovery. In the 1990s New Cinema became mannerist and rarefied, as we have seen. But since 2000, there have been many attempts to revive the film market and cultivate popular audiences, by "tribe," technology, or event-based strategies. Wei Te-sheng's *Seediq Bale* (2011) is an exciting historical epic about an uprising against the Japanese by aborigines, financed by the windfall of *Cape No.7*. To the extent Taiwan film is identified with New Cinema and seen as a genuine art form, box office is a mixed blessing.

Thanks to *Cape No. 7*, Wei finally finished his aboriginal adventure, but this kind of picture (cf. Mel Gibson's *Apocalypto*) has no aesthetic or thematic kinship to New Cinema. Here we notice the ambivalence of popular appeal, when New Cinema is the prevailing model and the category "popular" is usually ceded to Hollywood. New Cinema continued its character formation through the 1990s, all the while solidifying its identification with Taiwan film, and by 2000 the cost was clear: popularity was someone else's turf, almost a liability, and box-office success something foreign to Taiwan cinema. The 1980s dichotomy between artistic and commercial continues to haunt twenty-first-century discourse on Taiwan cinema, even as certain films and trends find success in popular registers. These exceptions represent a kind of revolt against canonical Taiwan cinema. Bentuhua in cultural pursuits overall, not just cinema, is important in its acceptance and harnessing of market forces as a key component of its form. This was something New Cinema never managed, or attempted. While New Cinema's xiangtu pledged allegiance to Nativism, it also used modernist themes and techniques to keep regular audiences at arm's length. Its strategy put New Cinema on the world map, while also gaining a reputation for Taiwan films that may not have been accurate (forbidding) or entirely just (pretentious). Bentu cinema, if there is yet such a thing, is a salutary corrective or at the least a counterweight to its predecessor.

Part II

Industry and Institution

9

Propaganda and Censorship in Chinese Cinema

Matthew D. Johnson

Propaganda and censorship are two sides of the same coin. In common usage, the terms refer to ways in which political organizations such as states, parties, and societies have sought to bend modern communication technologies to their will. While both propaganda and censorship are often represented as antidemocratic in nature, the global reach of war during the early twentieth century resulted in a rapid proliferation of state institutions devoted to public opinion, mass mobilization, military recruitment, and wartime information. Likewise, the history of propaganda and censorship in China is part of a global history of mass politics. Until 1914, "propaganda simply meant the means by which the converted attempted to persuade the unconverted" (Taylor 2003: 4). While propaganda communicates messages, censorship suppresses certain modes of communication, or prevents messages from finding wider audiences. Both are used by those in power to persuade others to behave in specific ways. Propaganda and censorship may be particularly evident during times of war, but they are also enduring features of most societies.

Chinese politics are frequently associated with the use of moral suasion to achieve instrumental ends. On the eve of China's Eight Year War with Japan (1937–45), US social reformer Bruno Lasker (1937: 153) wrote that "in China, the use of psychological conditioning to affect political ends is an old-established art." Chinese history contains numerous examples of dynasties censoring the printed word, or employing it as propaganda (Cheek 1997; MacKinnon 1997). Yet early Chinese revolutionaries, like Liang Qichao, were also vociferous advocates of a free press and free expression; not until the 1920s was "a Bolshevik model for control of the media" reimposed on this "liberal model" of freedom within the cultural sphere (MacKinnon 1997: 4). These developments profoundly shaped domestic filmmaking efforts. In 1919, at the close of the May Fourth movement,

A Companion to Chinese Cinema, First Edition. Edited by Yingjin Zhang.
© 2012 Blackwell Publishing Ltd. Published 2012 by Blackwell Publishing Ltd.

owners of the Commercial Press submitted an official petition to begin producing educational films aimed at promoting popular nationalist sentiment, and countering the effects of negative foreign stereotypes in the mass media. This event symbolizes the first attempt to create a state-sanctioned educational cinema in Chinese history, and as such is roughly contemporaneous with similar efforts taking place around the world.

The history of propaganda and censorship in Chinese film history has been shaped by three broader patterns in the history of the Chinese state: (1) the importance of anti-imperialism in creating common ground between state and nonstate actors, (2) the rise of the Leninist party-state as the dominant form of political organization, and (3) the significance of global transformations, such as world wars and globalization, as key moments of state learning and policy shifts in the cultural realm. Clearly, it is difficult to disassociate this history from broader regional and global contexts. Japanese colonialism, for example, provided much of the capital and institutional infrastructure on which post-1945 Chinese state film production would rest. Propaganda and censorship practices thus represented local examples of an international elite consensus concerning the essential nature of political communication as a tool of mass organization and governance. War, too, was an important matrix for the development of new communications models; in its broadest sense, Chinese film history is part of international communications history. The management of public opinion and promotion of social change have been as important to filmmakers as aesthetic progress. Whether oriented toward the mobilization meeting or the market, cinema has at all times carried with it the traces of state regulation and cultural policy, and as such must be treated as a political artifact.

Anti-Imperialism, Internationalization, and Mass Mobilization: The Rise of the Propaganda State

The early cinema: Responses to imperialism and regulation

Any list of challenges faced by the Qing dynasty (1644–1911) during its later years must include Great Power encroachment in the fields of media and communications. Military and legal assaults on Qing sovereignty were accompanied by unfavorable depictions of China and Chinese subjects in the Western and Japanese popular press. Telegraphs, railways, and postal networks created a global media system in which images of the colonial periphery, which included China's coastal treaty ports, denoted both racial and political inequality. Extant photographs indicate that photographic technology first reached China during the 1850s; the earliest images are of coastal areas around Hong Kong. During the second half of the nineteenth century, "Western and Japanese journals of photographs of starving beggars, public executions, and humiliating punishment of prisoners [were] instrumental in de-romanticizing the image of China" (Wilkinson 2000: 591).

The early cinema soon followed suit. Edison films shot by James H. White and Frederick Blechynden depicted a China of white European privilege and Chinese poverty. This trend became particularly apparent following the Boxer War (1900–1), which resulted in an outpouring of images of conflict and beheadings. Post-Boxer reels – all of them recreations – appeared at almost the same time that panoramic and travelogue "views" of China were also becoming common fixtures of cinematic exhibitions in the West. Of films about China produced in China during the first decade of the twentieth century, most have been attributed to émigré producer–exhibitors A. E. Lauro and Benjamin Brodsky. Yet by roughly 1909, the year in which Brodsky's Asia Film Company filmed *Stealing a Roast Duck* featuring a Chinese cast, verifiable evidence for the emergence of a Sino-foreign film industry begins to emerge. Access to motion picture technology allowed the early Chinese participants in this industry to begin contemplating filmmaking as a political enterprise. Writer-director Gu Kenfu (1921: 11) wrote that realist cinema might be employed as a form of "popular education" (*tongsu jiaoyu*). Other critics followed, many of them referencing the persuasive power that the new medium seemed to possess.

The post-May Fourth, post-Versailles intellectual and political climate also gave rise to a heightened consciousness of the role Western motion pictures played in creating negative images of China abroad. Gu Kenfu (1921: 11) noted that foreign filmmakers arriving in China typically seized upon the country's most "unhealthy" (*buliang*) and "base" (*xialiu*) conditions. Another writer-director, Zheng Zhengqiu, complained of the gradual extension of these foreign images into China, and the "separation" (*gemo*) that existed between foreign prejudices and Chinese reality. The problem, as these filmmakers perceived it, was not only that foreign depictions of China were cruel or insulting, but also that they caused damage to China's international reputation and, potentially, sovereign status. Mingxing Company Founder Zhou Jianyun (1883–?) and cinematographer Wang Xuchang noted that European and US filmmakers, by contrast, had been extremely successful in promoting their own nations' images abroad. The tendency of Chinese people to "fawn on foreign powers," they argued, was a direct result of "the power of [Western] cinematic propaganda" (*yingxi xuanchuan zhi li*) in this regard (Zhou and Wang 1924: 23–4).

Consciousness, in China and elsewhere, that mass media could be used for political purposes existed well before cinema became a popular new media form. However, World War I did create awareness among governments that cinema might be added to the propagandistic powers of the wartime state. In general:

> In "total war," which required civilians to participate in the war effort, morale came to be recognized as a significant military factor, and propaganda began to emerge as

the principal instrument of control over public opinion and an essential weapon in the national arsenal. In both World War I and World War II the democracies and totalitarian regimes imposed constraints on the flow of information and used the media for their own ends. (Welch 2005: x)

The significance of cinema as a tool of shaping mass opinion did not escape Chinese filmmakers in the 1920s. In April 1919 the Shanghai-based Commercial Press petitioned the northern Beiyang government's Board of Agriculture and Commerce suggesting an antidote to the poisonous images. According to its authors, this was justified in light of the fact that most imported foreign films depicted China in ways that

[are] flippant and mendacious, extremely harmful to customs and popular sentiment, and frequently satirize inferior conditions in our society, [thus] providing
material for derision.... So as to [promote] the boycott of imported products that are
harmful to decency, [we] hope to aid popular education, in part by exporting and
selling [our films] overseas, glorifying our national culture, [and] mitigating foreigners' spiteful feelings, while simultaneously mobilizing the affections of overseas
Chinese toward their homeland. (Quoted in Shan 2005: 11–12)

The Commercial Press petition portrayed film as a potentially state-sponsored vehicle of mass enlightenment and informal diplomacy. Moreover, it implied a challenge to foreign-dominated media networks that instilled "spiteful feelings" toward China in audiences worldwide.

Educational filmmaking on behalf of the nation represented an important com-
ponent of Commercial Press Motion Picture Department activities between 1917 and 1922, and was accompanied by the press's plans to create a distribution network reaching every province in China. Like the Commercial Press magazines and textbooks produced in abundance during this same period, it appears that educational films of parades, sporting events, reformist undertakings, and stirring land-
scapes were intended to contribute to the "imagination" of a new community "produced as a cultural enterprise of 'enlightenment'," and through which national citizenship would be shaped and defined (L. Lee 1999: 46–7). Early filmmakers Li Beihai, Li Minwei, Zheng Zhengqiu, and Zhang Shichuan had also sought to trans-
port reform-minded "civilized plays" to the screen, and such agendas became increasingly common worldwide. When racist Hollywood depictions stirred pro-
test among Chinese-American communities in 1920, Los Angeles filmmaker James B. Leong founded his own company devoted to presenting "the real China on the screen, thereby correcting the general impression that Chinese life, as it may be seen through the camera's eye, is chiefly concerned with tong wars, opium smok-
ing, and strange methods of gambling" (*New York Times*, June 6, 1920). Li Zeyuan, a cinematographer living in New York City, produced two titles – *Martial Arts of China* (1922) and *Costumes of China* (1922) – to promote positive views of Chinese

Table 9.1 Individual commercial press titles by year, 1917–27

	1917	1918	1919	1920	1921	1922	1923	1924	1925	1926	1927
Feature films, theatrical adaptations			2	7	4	6	2		2	4	1
Actualités, newsreels, educational titles	2	7	3	5	9		2				

Source: Cheng, Li, and Xing (1980).

culture before relocating his fledgling Great Wall Picture Company to Shanghai in 1924 (W. Gao 2003: 12).

Sustained government involvement was not a feature of China's film industry until the 1930s. However, censorship preceded the establishment of a formal propaganda system by several decades. In 1909, Zhejiang police authorities prohibited Chinese rentals of imported "mechanized films" (*jiqi yingpian*) (Y. Shen 2005: 13). Late Qing efforts focused primarily on ensuring social decorum during screenings, and preventing obscene images from influencing audience morals (Xiao 1994: 86–7). By the 1920s, police and local education departments joined forces to regulate morally suspect mass entertainment, and a more centralized institutional arrangement began to emerge in 1928, with the establishment of the Shanghai Board of Film and Theater Censors. Soon thereafter, the Nationalist Party (KMT) Propaganda Department issued a series of regulations and statutes intended to increase party control over the film industry in its entirety.

Much like filmmakers of the 1920s, cultural officials shared the belief that motion pictures possessed the power to influence audience attitudes. Rather than regulating film production, however, inspections (*shencha, jiancha*) of films and theaters were initially the most common methods of state intervention. By 1928, films shown in Heilongjiang, particularly those imported from the Soviet Union, were required to first be submitted to a permanent committee of educators, police, and government officials, who checked for content that "challenged the dignity of the Chinese people, violated the Three People's Principles, harmed customs of decency or public order, and advocated superstition or falsehoods" (HSDZBW 2003: 631). In 1929 the Jilin provincial education department issued an announcement forbidding from exhibition any film harmful to KMT's reputation (CSDZBW 1992: 181). Similar restrictions would become enshrined in national law later that year with the promulgation of the KMT Central Committee's Film Censorship Law.

The Nationalist Revolution

In China, the propaganda (*xuanchuan*) film emerged at the same moment as Sun Yat-sen's Guangzhou government began to organize its Northern Expedition for national unification (see Figures 9.1, 9.2). The expedition's official filmmaker was Li Minwei, appointed to his position by executive order just prior to Sun's death in 1925. The Northern Expedition marked a new period of KMT rule in which Chinese culture, particularly political culture, was overhauled "according to international categories" (Kirby 2000: 180). Despite the profound anti-imperialist sentiments that lay behind the KMT's revolutionary diplomacy, the party-state it attempted to create was shaped by international institutions like the League of Nations as well as the Comintern. Scholars tend to agree that one of the most important features of twentieth-century globalization was the spread of technical standards and institutional standardization throughout the world (Boli and Thomas 1997: 184–5). State participation in transnational bodies signaled commitment to norms of progress and development. Internationalization also coexisted with the "partyfication" (*danghua*) of political and cultural life during the 1930s; militarization and preparation for war with the Communist Party (CCP), and later Japan, were clearly intertwined with Chiang Kai-shek's New Life movement.

Although KMT filmmaking did not consist solely of forays into nonfiction (newsreel, documentary) film, it is important to note that documentary filmmaking became a named and identifiable practice during the Nanjing Decade (1927–37). Discussing China's film propaganda during this period invokes names like John Grierson (1898–1972), Dziga Vertov (1896–1954), Sergei Eisenstein (1898–1948), Joris Ivens (1898–1989), the US Workers' Film and Photo League, Henry Luce, and William Randolph Hearst. Both the technology and the techniques used in producing propaganda films were made possible by closer contact between filmmaking communities, the development of global cultural networks, and growth of competing internationalist ideologies. State filmmaking became party filmmaking through the efforts of powerful KMT figures like Chen Lifu. In general, the KMT Central Executive Committee came to play an increasingly active role within China's film industry during the early 1930s, at which time it moved to weed out racist foreign media, enforce guidelines for commercial film aesthetics, uproot CCP influence, and engage both state and private studios in the production of films that would complement the KMT's own perspective on national ideology and reconstruction of China.

Once an entrepreneurial partner of Brodsky, by the early 1920s Li Minwei was a catalyst for the cinema's transformation into a political tool. Working with the KMT's Guangzhou-based government, Li promoted the image of Sun Yat-sen as a legitimate national leader through documentary films and newsreels produced by his Minxin (China Sun) Motion Picture Company. Traveling with Sun in Guangzhou, Hong Kong, and Beiping, after Sun's death Li relocated Minxin to Shanghai while solidifying his ties to the Nationalists through a partnership with

Figure 9.1 Memorial and ashes of Sun Yat-sen, erected immediately following the revolutionary leader's death in 1925. From *The National Revolutionary Army's War on Sea, Land, and Air* (dir. Li Minwei, Minxin Film, 1927). Footage appears in *Lai Man-wai: Father of Hong Kong Cinema* (dir. Cai Jiguang, Dragon Ray Pictures, 2002).

Figure 9.2 Chiang Kai-shek takes command of the Northern Expedition. From *The National Revolutionary Army's War on Sea, Land, and Air* (dir. Li Minwei, Minxin Film, 1927). Footage appears in *Lai Man-wa: Father of Hong Kong Cinema* (dir. Cai Jiguang, Dragon Ray Pictures, 2002).

Table 9.2 Individual documentary, newsreel, and actualité titles by year, 1921–9

	1920	1921	1922	1923	1924	1925	1926	1927	1928	1929
Commercial Press	5	9		1						
China Motion Picture		5		1						
Star/Mingxing			5							
Great Wall			2			4	1			
Minghua					1					
China Sun (Li Minwei)				1	8	7	3	1		
Dalu					2					
Zhonghua					1					
British American Tobacco						1				
Baihe						1				
Youlian						1				
Huaju							3			
Great China-Lily								1		1
Minsheng								1		
Xinqi								1		
Sanmin								1		
Fudan								2	3	
Shanghai Photoplay										1
Tianyi								1		

Source: Cheng, Li, and Xing (1980).

Luo Mingyou, a theater magnate with formidable economic and political connections. Li and Luo were not the only producers to organize publicity for important political figures. Warlords Wu Peifu, Feng Yuxiang, and Zhang Zuolin all appeared in films shot by Chinese studios and, in some cases, foreign filmmakers in the employ of British American Tobacco or the Soviet Red Army. In both fiction and nonfiction genres, studios responded to growing popular concern with regard to national and Sino-foreign affairs. The May Thirtieth movement, and 1925 Civil War, both incited a flurry of filmmaking activity. Critics extolled the newsreel as means of inculcating patriotic and antimilitaristic feelings in the populace. One advocate suggested that "current events films" (*shishi pian*), modeled on those produced by Pathé Frères and Hearst-Vitagraph, be used as "methods of political propaganda" for combating foreign slander against China's patriotic movement (Bo 1927).

Although entertainment and educational uses of the cinema were manifold during the 1920s, one of the most significant shifts of the Nanjing Decade was the formulation of a "Military Affairs Propaganda Plan" that brought private filmmakers Li Minwei and Luo Mingyou, and their growing Lianhua (United Photoplay) Film Production and Printing Company, close to the center of KMT power. Economic and political influence within the industry made Lianhua one of the most important Chinese studios of its era. Shortly thereafter, the Nationalists established their own Central Film Cultural Propaganda Committee to serve as a nationwide censor of images, such as racist Hollywood depictions, deemed offensive to public sensibilities (Xiao 2004: 77). Likewise, the party's Propaganda Committee worked closely with Lianhua to produce a monthly news serial, *Lianhua News*, which publicized the achievements of the Nanjing government.

Many scholars have noted that KMT censors also strove to remove CCP influence from the Shanghai film industry, and to prevent pro-war patriots from upsetting the precarious balance of Sino-Japanese relations with cinematic jingoism following the September Eighteenth Incident. Less noted are the efforts the KMT took to create a far-flung state media empire, which included the use of motion pictures. One of the chief architects in this regard was Chen Lifu, who along with elder brother Chen Guofu served as head of the party's Organization Department. Their efforts to party-fy (*danghua*) culture and education within China, though centered on promotion of a "cult of the leader" Chiang Kai-shek, also borrowed heavily from international propaganda–state models then coming into vogue in Japan and Europe. Following a 1931 request put to the League of Nations for assistance in educational reform, a loose coalition of KMT officials, state ministers, and representatives of the film industry formed the National Educational Cinematographic Society of China (*Zhongguo dianying jiaoyu xiehui*) based on the model of the Italian Educational Film Union (*L'Unione cinematografica educativa*), and serving as a national partner of the Italian-sponsored, League of Nations-affiliated International Educational Cinematographic Institute in Rome.

Unifying China through statist cultural projects faced severe obstacles due to ethnolinguistic diversity, poor infrastructure, and insufficient funding. Yet the National Educational Cinematographic Society did send representatives on world tours of film industries in Japan, Europe, and the United States, and Chen Lifu included the Soviet Union alongside Italy as a country to be studied and emulated (ZJDX 1933: 9, 12). Society regional offices in Shanghai staged public screenings in 187 locations during December 1933, attracting 153,862 attendees. As cinematic exchange with other countries intensified, the KMT also vowed to crack down further on proletarian and Hollywood control over China's film industry. Over time, the National Educational Cinematographic Society became a key institution in the promotion of Chiang Kai-shek's cultural influence at the expense of rival Wang Jingwei, whose supporters dominated the Ministry of Education and National Film Censorship Committee. Focusing on Chiang's New Life movement and the militarization of Chinese society, Chen Lifu and other "rightwing" KMT members established their own Central Film Enterprises Guiding Committee both to further bring the private sector into line, and to channel investment toward a Central Film Studio under Central Propaganda Department Film Section head

Zhang Chong. Entering production in 1934, this new studio produced over two hundred unique titles in the form of newsreels, educational films, and specific titles addressing issues of "national turmoil" (*guonan*) and anti-Communist "bandit suppression" between 1934 and 1937. Other institutions participating in party-led filmmaking endeavors included the Nanchang Field Headquarters Political Training Office, Nanking University College of Science, and the National Office for the Promotion of Educational Cinema.

During the Nanjing Decade, the KMT Central Committee and its Propaganda Department appear to have made significant gains in terms of the internationalization of China's film industry according to "developed" (*fada*) standards of central control, and the systematic promotion of national culture and perspectives on world affairs. Thus, as the cinema was becoming increasingly educational in name, it was also becoming a potentially potent tool for mass mobilization on the basis of citizenship. Education in this case referred to the creation of uniform opinion as well as scientific knowledge – or, in the views of National Educational Cinematographic Society members, a kind of "spiritual national defense." Such schemes also carried with them an inherent economic logic, as combating Hollywood hegemony was seen as not only good for audience morality, but also for the financial health of China's own state and private studios. Yet despite their efforts to expand the KMT's mass base of support by claiming larger and larger swaths of the population for domestic films, the party-state model proposed by Chen Lifu and other reformers cohered more in theory than in practice.

Total war and civil war

The outbreak of full military hostilities between China and Japan on July 7, 1937 accelerated and intensified ongoing efforts to party-fy and centralize film production under national control. Nonetheless, one undeniable consequence of the wartime period was the increasing emphasis placed by government officials and filmmakers alike on the necessity of propaganda in cultural production. On both sides of the battle lines separating Free China from the Japan-occupied territories, programs for information, education, enlightenment, and publicity – all euphemisms for propaganda and censorship activities – rapidly expanded. While a homogenous national culture did not necessarily arise in China as a result of Japanese invasion, the institutional and conceptual structures for creating such a structure continued to flourish as total war created pressures for total mobilization. Thus, one of the most important transformations to take place during the wartime period was the gradual erosion of existing commercial, or simply nonstate, modes of cultural production and circulation by large-scale state bureaucracies.

One of the most important of these institutions was the All-China Film Circles Wartime Resistance Association, established in the provisional Free China headquarters of Wuhan on January 29, 1938. In the association's manifesto, spokesman Yang

Hansheng (1938) decried the "numbing" effects of popular entertainment films and called for production of more expedient and direct formats like newsreels and "short features," while advocating construction of a national "projection network." Studio management, in turn, was coordinated by the Military Affairs Commission Political Department Third Office. United front cultural production, which returned CCP artists and intellectuals to the fold of the KMT state, meant that several influential post-1949 filmmakers and screenwriters spent the war years working within the China Motion Picture Corporation under the direction of KMT propagandists like Zheng Yongzhi. Films *Defending Our Soil* (1938) and *Eight Hundred Heroes* (1938) were screened overseas as international propaganda as well as in Wuhan's crowded theaters.

KMT cultural officials also attempted to enlist filmmakers who had remained in Shanghai, or were working in Hong Kong's Cantonese film industry, to support the patriotic cause. During May and June 1938, the Central Film Censorship Committee was reorganized as the Emergency Period Film Censorship Bureau, and opened offices in Hong Kong and Guangzhou to advance the cause of Mandarin "national defense" cinema. Yet their efforts were overshadowed by Japan's military advance, which caused many Hong Kong studios to distance themselves from the emergency government. Instead, the majority of wartime propaganda was produced by three studios located in and around Chongqing – the China Motion Picture Corporation, Central Film Studio, and China Educational Film Studio. Nanking University's Motion Picture Department, relocated to adjacent Beibei, also played a vital role in disseminating educational and informational films under the direction of Sun Mingjing. With the breakdown of CCP–KMT relations by September 1940, however, united front filmmaking virtually ceased and "clean-up and rectification" (*suzheng*) programs shook the Chongqing film world. The Political Department Third Office was closed, and KMT officials like Chen Lifu once again played a central role in orchestrating the shape of propaganda to reflect party sanctioned themes.

The Chongqing film industry was, by 1940, also wholly dependent on import of scarce film stock and equipment from foreign countries, particularly the United States. In order to secure such support institutions like the KMT's International Publicity Bureau not only sought to project a positive image of the war effort under Chiang Kai-shek, but also to restrict or discredit the flow of information concerning CCP achievements coming from Yan'an. From a filmmaking perspective, images of the "Red Capital" were scarce. Antifascist and leftist filmmakers from Europe (Joris Ivens, Roman Karmen) and the United States (Harry Dunham) all arranged visits to Yan'an for documentary purposes, although Ivens was prevented from ever reaching the CCP areas by KMT-employed handlers during filming of *The 400 Million* (1938). Within Yan'an the Eighth Route Army's Film Corps, headed by Yuan Muzhi (1909–78), Wu Yinxian (1900–94), and Xu Xiaobing, engaged in wartime propaganda film production under arduous conditions. Some titles, such as *Yan'an and the Eighth Route Army*, were never completed. Former Shanghai actress Chen Bo'er (1907–51) emerged as a leading CCP filmmaker during this Yan'an period, and during the Civil War would become a key official and creative force in the CCP's first permanent film production facility, the Northeast Film Studio.

Japanese-built studios, and Japanese technicians, represented important flows of capital and knowledge toward China during the 1930s. The Northeast Film Studio, established in 1946, made use of film production equipment removed directly from the Manchuria Motion Pictures Corporation, built in 1939 by the Manchurian government and Manchuria Railway Company. By the time of Japan's 1945 defeat in the Pacific War, two additional, state-of-the-art studios had been completed – one belonging to the North China Film Corporation, in Beiping, and another facility in Shanghai. Japanese and "puppet" government propaganda and censorship organizations were functionally quite similar to those established in Chongqing, and as KMT cultural officials returned to the East they discovered institutions that supported, rather than hindered, reestablishment of state authority in the cultural sphere.

During the Civil War period (1945–9), KMT propagandists, and the Ministry of Defense, relocated their filmmaking operations to Nanjing and other coastal cities,

Table 9.3 Individual film titles released by KMT-Affiliated studios, 1938–45

	1938	1939	1940	1941	1942	1943	1944	1945	Total
China Motion Picture Corporation									
Features	3	2	5			1	2	2	15
Animated films	6	4							10
Newsreels and documentaries	20	6	7					1	34
Central Film Studio									
Features		2	1						3
Newsreels and documentaries	13	6	4	2		1			26
Northwest Film Studio									
Features		1							1
Newsreels and documentaries		2	1						3
China Educational Film Studio									
Newsreels and documentaries									23?
Other organizations									
Huabei News (*Huabei xinwenshe*)	2								2?
Dadi (*Dadi yingyegongsi*)		1	1						2
Jinling University	1	4	4						9?

Sources: D. Li (2000); ZJDX (1940).

while simultaneously taking control of studios and distribution offices confiscated from Japanese owners and investors. In 1947 the returned government moved to reorganize many of these new holdings as a single incorporated body, the Central Film Enterprise Corporation. Principal stockholders and overseers included party stalwarts Chen Lifu, Zhang Daofan, Luo Xuelian, Li Weiguo, Fang Zhi, Pan Gongzhan, and Du Tong. KMT-controlled studios produced newsreels and educational films; the China Motion Picture Corporation, under military control, released recruitment and anti-Communist propaganda shorts. Another common documentary theme was the trial, sentencing, and execution of collaborators. State-owned distribution cartels established large regional operations in East and North China, and largely controlled all import–export trade in film and film equipment. Experimentation with educational cinema also continued in the university sector, with Nanking University filmmaker Sun Mingjing (b. 1911) producing several films devoted to postwar reconstruction, and rural reconstruction groups in Chengdu and Suzhou in cooperation with UNESCO in the field of mass education.

The activities of CCP filmmakers during this period also reveal how party and army had come to embrace film as a crucial tool of mass mobilization during the war years. New organizations like the Northwest Trainee Film Brigade and North China Film Brigade screened a combination of self-produced and Soviet-made newsreels, short documentaries, and features in cities serving as Eighth Route Army field headquarters, or nearby villages. In May 1947 the North China Film Brigade constructed a temporary production facility that released one of the CCP's first newsreels, *The War of Self-Defense, First Report* (Wang Yang, 1947). Former Yan'an filmmakers Yuan Muzhi, Qian Xiaozhang (1918–91), Tian Fang (1911–74), and Chen Bo'er transformed the Northeast Film Studio, located in an abandoned Northeast China mining facility, into a hub of cinematic activity and provided propaganda support for People's Liberation Army campaigns (see Figures 9.3, 9.4, 9.5). Several of the technicians who worked on these early agitprop films were Japanese former employees of the Manchuria Motion Picture Corporation. Distribution, however, was mainly limited to Heilongjiang province and other regions where CCP forces were able to establish military and political control.

From Cold-War Culture Industries
to Commercial "Soft Power"

New China: Refining and expanding the state cinema model

The CCP-created propaganda system of Northeast China served as an important "cradle" for the cohort of studio managers, and creative personnel, who would build the political cinema of the new People's Republic from 1949 onward. Many

Figure 9.3 The People's Liberation Army fights brigandry and oppression, and relies on the masses. From *Coming Back to Their Own Unit* (dir. Cheng Yin, Northeast Studio, 1949).

Figure 9.4 Mao Zedong as master strategist, prior to the fall of Yan'an and relocation of the Central Committee to North China. From *Return Our Yan'an* (dir. Cheng Mo, Qian Xiaozhang, Northeast Film Team, 1948).

Figure 9.5 Tiananmen as an early symbol of CCP political authority: General Ye Jianying addresses a crowd on February 3, 1949, immediately following the surrender of Beiping (Beijing) by the Nationalist army. From *Beiping Entrance Ceremony* (dir. Wu Guoying, Northeast Studio, 1949).

of these individuals were involved in the production of vérité films devoted to capturing CCP pageantry for posterity. With Soviet assistance, they assembled two feature-length documentaries, *China Liberated* (1950) and *Victory of the Chinese People* (1950), distributed both domestically and abroad. Echoing the May Fourth-era concern with national prestige, cultural officials praised these new titles as signifying a successful completion to China's quest for equality with the peoples (*minzu*) of the world (D. Zhong 1950). Here it is important to note that CCP propaganda objectives were not solely limited to establishing a monolithic state-controlled media, or imposing a Yan'an–Soviet cultural hybrid on urban spectators unfamiliar with revolutionary ideology. While these were important goals, it was also a priority that the new government represent itself using the visual language of popular sovereignty – not only for domestic legitimacy's sake, but also as part of a wider diplomatic policy of securing friendly relations with countries beyond the Soviet bloc.

Yan'an cultural officials like Zhou Yang and Lu Dingyi, both members of the Central Committee Propaganda Department, were charged with building and maintaining support for CCP power through cultural means. In the cinematic world, this meant expanding party control beyond the studios Changchun and Beijing, and into Shanghai – the industry's commercial center. While too much may be made of distinctions between Yan'an and Shanghai filmmaking styles, CCP efforts to establish firm central control over the private filmmaking sector were a reality. Two of the most important early institutions in this regard were the Ministry of Cultural Film Bureau and Film Guidance Committee. These were primarily staffed by those with experience in the wartime base areas and Civil

War-era Northeast as propagandists and mobilizers; at one point the committee included Jiang Qing, who may have held a similar position during the Yan'an years. During the early 1950s, state filmmaking became concentrated in three centers – Changchun, Beijing, and Shanghai. Even prior to the Great Leap Forward, however, the State Council was approving plans to establish new regional studios in provincial capitals like Xi'an. Yan'an stalwarts Chen Bo'er and Yuan Muzhi were originally picked as Film Bureau leading cadres, but were gradually replaced by officials with greater industry experience in Shanghai and Hong Kong, veteran film critic and screenwriter Xia Yan being the most notable. This latter group, with its connections to filmmakers loosely affiliated with various leftwing artists' leagues during the 1930s, may be seen as representing a somewhat different "line" within the post-1949 studio establishment. Yet throughout the Mao years (1949–76), cultural production remained firmly under the control of those CCP Propaganda Department figures like Lu Dingyi and Zhou Yang who spoke with the authority of the CCP Central Committee.

In its early years, the foundation of the PRC state studio and propaganda system rested upon facilities confiscated from the KMT government (most of which had earlier been confiscated from Japanese film corporations), and a mixture of human talent from both the state and nonstate sectors. Returnees from Hong Kong's Mandarin-dialect industry also joined the ranks of those selected for work in the newly acquired state studios. "New realism" (*xin xieshi zhuyi*) was the industry's dominant aesthetic (C. Cai 1949; B. Chen 1950). Film censorship committees within the Ministry of Culture and, during the earliest stages of CCP occupation, military control commissions enforced the new strictures with a vengeance, particularly in the wake of the campaign against private studio film *The Life of Wu Xun* (Sun Yu, 1950), which had been censured personally by Mao Zedong on the pages of *The People's Daily*. Eventually, private studios like Kunlun, which had released *Wu Xun*, were squeezed out of the industry by a combination of script reviews, censorship, and buyouts. Thought reform and rectification campaigns among cultural workers followed. The private sector collapsed in 1952, as filmmaking became an unprofitable enterprise for those without political and economic ties to the state. The same period also witnessed successful efforts to remove US and British imports from national distribution chains, solidifying China's cultural ties to allies in the Soviet bloc.

Cinematic production throughout the 1950s and 1960s was thus unambiguously tied to state agendas, although what these agendas should mean in practice remained a subject for debate at the highest levels of cultural policymaking. Audiences, officials realized, needed to be entertained as well as politically educated. Nonfiction films, such as documentaries and newsreels, were valued for their contributions to general scientific knowledge as well as for their ability to spread a positive image of the party-state. Screenwriters were told to emphasize patriotic values alongside those of class struggle. Yet within a Maoist political atmosphere of ideological and administrative homogeneity, arguments for greater topical latitude came most frequently from those close to the party center, rather than filmmakers or critics.

Table 9.4   Beijing-produced films (as numbers of reels), 1949–55

	1949	1950	1951	1952	1953	1954	1955
Documentaries	42	157	82	152	130	156	191
News serials	6	50	83	89	102	111	96
Scientific education			3	17	7	4	4
Foreign language to *Putonghua*		38	18		11	4	11
Putonghua to minority languages				51	101	54	35
Putonghua to local dialects				38	46	8	
Released in foreign languages				67	34	27	27
Total	48	245	186	414	431	364	364

Source: Beijing shi danganguan (n.d.).

A further point concerning the aesthetic homogeneity often associated with China's "mature" propaganda state, and particularly the form that state took during the cold-war period, is that cinematic imports from the Soviet Union, Eastern Europe, and other countries with which the PRC maintained functional trading partnerships also played an important role in shaping the political iconography of the period. Conversely, films which downplayed China's ties to the socialist world, while promoting appreciation of its "ancient" and "Asian" culture, were produced within the PRC for export to other Asian and European regions. Within the context of the 1950s Non-Aligned movement, film was circulated under the rubric of "cultural exchange" between the PRC and other Afro-Asian nations. Soviet guidance was critical at virtually every stage of the filmmaking process, but at the same time CCP cultural officials urged filmmakers to develop a "national style" based on epics and historical events (Y. Shen 2005: 155). Chinese studios also played the role of technical exporters, developing relationships with North Korea and Vietnam during the war-torn 1950s, when both countries relied on outside assistance for production of their own propaganda films. As former Film Bureau advisor V. Zhuravlyoz (1987: 79) observed in 1955, CCP filmmakers sought to enter the "world market" as well as become more effective shapers of mass opinion.

Taiwan: Regimes of colonialism, cold war, and consumption

As in the PRC, state ownership of media institutions, including film studios, was an important feature of Taiwan's postcolonial heritage. Under Japanese colonialism, cinema was used as an "enlightenment machine" as well as for commercial amusement (Davis and Chen 2007: 2). From 1901 onward, film production, dissemination, and exhibition were primarily controlled by Japanese business interests; in 1921 the Governor-General of Taiwan promoted mobile film screenings as a means of encouraging acceptance of Japanese culture among Taiwanese. As the Japanese–Taiwanese motion picture industry expanded during the 1920s, censorship institutions and regulations grew also, with Japanese customs authorities playing an important role in the inspection of important films coming in from Shanghai: "images of China's national flag, Dr. Sun Yat-sen, and Generalissimo Chiang Kai-shek were deleted" (R. Chen 1998: 49). During the Eight Year War, importation of Chinese films was forbidden while films from Tokyo and Manchuria, which tended to promote Japanese imperial rule, were common in Taiwanese theaters. Film companies that had been established in the Japanese colonies, including Taiwan (Formosa) and Korea, held the status of quasi-national institutions. In 1941 the Taiwan Motion Picture Association (Taiwan *Eiga Kyōkai*) was combined with the Taiwan Education Society (*Kyō ikukai*) to further "promote Japanese culture in Taiwan" (Standish 2005: 120–1). Imperialization (*kōminka*) of Taiwanese subjects was, in cinematic terms, further accelerated by Taiwan Motion Picture Association production of features and newsreels encouraging audiences to volunteer for service in the Japanese armed forces.

The end of the Pacific War and arrival of the Republic of China (ROC) government resulted in a division of formerly Japanese-owned film production facilities and theaters between new industry arrivals from Shanghai. Equipment that could be salvaged from Nanjing prior to the CCP takeover was relocated to Taipei. The arrival of the KMT in 1947 created the foundation for a one-party state, whose control over the media was used to promote an ideology based on Sun Yat-sen's teachings – *sanminzhuyi*, or Three Principles of the People. State-sponsored sinicization and anti-Communism were also prominent features of ROC cultural policies. During the cold war, propaganda was an important weapon in Taiwan's diplomatic campaign against the PRC's Beijing-based government, and in the struggle for international support and recognition. In 1949 Wellington Koo, former ROC Ambassador to the United States, "was advised to hire a prominent American public relations specialist whose clients had included an airline and Coca-Cola," and to "sell" Taiwan to the world (Rawnsley 2000).

Within the film industry, propaganda was produced by the KMT (Central Motion Pictures Corporation or CMPC), the Ministry of National Defense (China Motion Picture Studio), and the Taiwan Provincial Government (Taiwan Motion Picture Studio). Japanese films were briefly prohibited, though allowed to return in August 1950. Government-backed films ran the gamut from features to military education to newsreels. The Government Information Office (GIO), as part of the Executive Yuan, included a separate department for oversight of media industry guidance, although between 1949 and 1954 the Executive Yuan's propaganda activities were primarily conducted by the Information Department. Other functions related to the creation of a unified national culture, such as film inspection and censorship, were carried out by the Ministry of the Interior and Ministry of Education. In 1955 a new censorship law was passed, which "decreed that films should be created for the purpose of anti-communism and refrain from questioning the legitimacy of the KMT government, attacking government leaders, harming Taiwan–US relations, or revealing the dark side of Taiwan society" (R. Chen 1998: 51). Instead, rejection of Communism, promotion of government policies, and celebration of the benefits brought to Taiwanese (*benshengren*) by ROC rule were common film themes. The opening of Taiwan's film industry to US and Hong Kong investment resulted in greater diversity of representation and genres; Taiwanese-dialect films flourished briefly after 1955. However, warming relations between the United States and the PRC from the early 1970s onward triggered a return to Mandarin Sinification and patriotism as dominant cultural agendas. "Healthy realism," a genre promoted by the CMPC since 1963, marked an even earlier reemergence of a state culture emphasizing national identity in the singular.

Private studios provided counterbalance to state-owned studios from the 1950s onward, as did imports from Asia, Europe, and the United States. Yet particularly during the period of martial law (1949–87), the ruling KMT used a combination of financial incentives and institutional controls to keep private producers within the bounds of acceptable representation. Guidance and censorship activities ultimately converged within the GIO in 1958, and by 1973 the GIO's Motion Picture Department administered affairs related to the entire industry. Management of international information about the ROC also became an important responsibility of the Council for Cultural Affairs Information Management Unit, established under the Executive Yuan in 1982. As Taiwan was under martial law until 1987, the military has also played a role in the media industry as producer, regulator, and owner (Rawnsley and Rawnsley 2001). To this day, some of the oldest KMT enterprises include press, television, and broadcast companies, as well as the CMPC (D. Xu 1997: 400).

Since the wind-down of the cold war, Taiwan's diverse film industry has been shaped – some might say overrun – by diminishing waves of foreign capital and investment. The 1983 Motion Picture Act marked another watershed by decreeing that Taiwan's film industry follow the policies of the ROC government, rather than the government's ruling party. In more recent years official cultural institutions, including the GIO and Taipei Film Commission, have worked to promote films about Taiwan, and to attract investment to Taiwan that will bolster its local film industry. The ROC government itself is a heavy investor in local film production, announcing a five-year scheme to promote local and coproduced endeavors with financial incentives (Shackleton 2009). The "Regulation Governing the Classification of Motion Pictures" and "Film Inspection Regulations," two supplements to the Motion Pictures Act (a fourth set of measures, "The Enforcement Rules of the Motion Pictures Act," is also frequently cited in discussions of ROC film regulation), have been brought into line with international standards and the ratings systems of foreign countries (Taiwan Cinema 2006). The Golden Horse International Film Festival, active since 1980, has provided another important site of interaction between Taiwan film workers and foreign counterparts, as has the longstanding Asia Pacific Film Festival, another GIO-sponsored event.

During the years of Democratic Progressive Party (DPP) rule between 2000 and 2008, Taiwan's GIO has continued to treat domestic productions as important symbols of local economic and cultural power. Since 2006 the GIO has been supplemented by the National Communications Council (NCC), a new institution intended to regulate Taiwan's information, telecommunications, and broadcasting industries. The NCC also provides enforcement for censorship, although such measures are now vociferously debated at the highest levels of Taiwan's legal system. The Motion Picture Act, first promulgated by Presidential Order on November 18, 1983, remains the most important single set of articles governing motion picture production and exhibition in Taiwan. Its stated goals, to "disseminate Chinese culture, expound national policy, fulfill its social education function, and advocate healthy recreation," indicate that communication through cinema remains an important priority of the ROC's democratic government (GIO 1983). Films shown in Taiwan are also classified according to a multi-tiered ratings system, which limits the types of content that may be legally shown to minors. As propaganda, Taiwan cinema's value in the eyes of the state seems to be that it reminds international audiences of the ROC's role in nurturing a vibrant, culturally attractive society. While state film production for educational purposes continues, the limits placed on cinematic expression are mainly congruent with those imposed by other influential WTO member nations, such as the United States and Japan.

PRC state filmmaking in the reform era

From the beginning of the Reform period (1978 onward), the PRC film industry has undertaken a series of decentralizing and privatizing reforms. This institutional restructuring of the cinematic propaganda system has mirrored earlier ROC reforms dating back to the 1960s in surprising ways, particularly in terms of the opening of markets to nonstate investors, and the promotion of a Chinese national cinema intended to compete with Hollywood at the domestic and regional, if not international, levels. Transitioning from "pedagogy to art to commerce," the cinema of mainland China has given rise to recognizable international brands embodied by Fifth Generation directors like Chen Kaige, Tian Zhuangzhuang, and Zhang Yimou (Y. Zhu 2003: 2). Younger figures Jiang Wen (b. 1963), Jia Zhangke, Lou Ye, and Lu Chuan (b. 1971) have joined the ranks of the commercially successful, often by developing close relationships with overseas investors and distributors. International film festivals play an important role in facilitating these contacts. At the same time, the visibility of festivals from the perspective of media-watchers has overshadowed equally important developments taking place within the state-owned studio system, which remains the primary legacy of the Maoist propaganda state.

Despite the fact that, since the 1980s, the PRC film industry has seemed to be facing successive moments of financial crisis, production of "main melody" (*zhuxuanlü*) films is required of all major studios, which are now essentially production units under the umbrella of state-owned media conglomerates like China Film, Shanghai Film and Television, Shanghai Film, and Western Movie (Schwankert 2005). Since the introduction of reform policies to the PRC's film-making sector, there has been some loosening of the ties binding cultural production and consumption to the state. Not all production and distribution companies are wholly state owned, nor do all filmmakers remain in official *danwei* employ. Access to Sinophone markets such as Hong Kong and Taiwan, overseas capital, and international audiences, along with some autonomy *vis-à-vis* state intervention and control, has created new opportunities for market-savvy firms and directors. Yet it is easy to overestimate the degree to which these reforms represent an actual challenge to the propaganda state model.

The China Film Group Corporation (CFGC) is not the only state institution involved in film production, but it remains one of the most financially powerful in the post-1978 era. This is due in no small part to its previous history as a state-owned distribution and exhibition monopoly during the Mao years – the China Film Corporation. In fact, the CFGC is an amalgam of its predecessor's purchasing, distribution, and exhibition chains (including a television-based movie channel), and nearly the entire central state film production system, including the former Beijing Film Studio and China Children's Film Studio. Established in 1999 with the back catalogs of these two studios at its disposal, the CFGC has produced over two hundred feature films in the past decade. It is one of only two importers of foreign films to the PRC, although controls in this area have been slowly loosening. Like the former Beijing Film Studio, the CFGC appears to work closely with the Film Bureau under the State Administration of Radio, Film, and Television (SARFT) as the primary producer of internationally distributed, state-approved features, which serve as models for the industry as a whole. Its features are regularly selected for domestic awards such as the Golden Rooster, which legitimizes the CFGC's central position in the industry. Not all CFGC features are created according to profit-driven models, and the corporation remains the largest producer of main melody propaganda films in the present day (Yeh and Davis 2008).

In June 2006, SARFT established an incorporated, joint-stock enterprise for the overseas promotion of Chinese cinema and cinema-related cultural exchange. Like uniFrance, or the Motion Picture Association of America (MPAA), China Film Promotion International (CFPI) exists to expand sales of Chinese-language films, and is billed as the "first stop" for interested buyers internationally (Landreth

2006). CFPI not only works to promote titles produced or coproduced by the CFGC, but also those of its seventy member companies. Its primary stockholders are the CFGC and Huaxia Movie Distribution Company, which together comprise the sole companies currently holding official permission to import foreign films into the PRC.

Although institutional connections between SARFT and the CFPI indicate an attempt by the State Council to keep firm control over films exported and marketed as Chinese cinema, this does not mean that no alternatives to state brokerage exist. MPAA Asia Pacific has hosted workshops in Beijing and Hong Kong devoted to disseminating filmmaking models based on "US independent production," and nurturing local talent in the hope of future directorial cooperation between Asia Pacific and US companies (Businessofcinema.com 2007). Other distribution companies, such as Fortissimo (Hong Kong), Wild Bunch (Paris), Arclight (Australia), and the Weinstein Company (United States), have already established positions as purveyors of Chinese films overseas and may continue to pose challenges to the for-profit CFPI in the future. While state-sponsored festivals such as the Shanghai International Film Festival and Beijing Screenings may offer controlled forums within which to showcase the latest approved features, other international festivals provide alternative "scopic regimes" through which alternate visions of regionally specific Chinese cinema are both circulated and defined (C. Wu 2006). Nonetheless, the increase of private capital in China's cultural indus-tries has not occurred without the consent of state institutions. The Ministry of Culture has been one of several bureaucracies involved in reconfiguring markets to create increased opportunities for foreign and domestic capital. One recent result, brokered by the ministry, has been a joint venture between India's Pyramid Saimira Company and the Jiangsu Longzhe Group, which promises Sino-Indian coproduction of films for distribution in China and overseas (Businessofcinema. com 2008). SARFT also continues to frustrate PRC-based filmmakers whose activities run afoul of administration standards for pre-exhibition review, as evidenced by actions against director Lou Ye and actress Tang Wei (b. 1979). Lou failed to clear his *Summer Palace* (2006) for overseas festival exhibition, while Tang Wei's performance of graphic sex scenes in *Lust, Caution* (Ang Lee, 2007) has apparently generated injunctions against future television appearances.

More than anything, World Trade Organization (WTO) membership has profoundly shaped the structure of China's film industry. State controls over how China is to be depicted in films that are shot on Chinese soil or make use of China's considerable filmmaking infrastructure and capital, however, remain fully intact, and the China Film Co-Production Corporation (CFCC) supervises all scripts and films proposed by foreign companies for shooting on location in China. Foreign media executives have fallen over themselves in the rush to enter China's media and entertainment markets. Debates over intellectual copyright protection and piracy aside, this has brought tacit acceptance of a business environment whose state-dominated character clearly strikes some as unfamiliar:

Yes, it's a long timeline. The fact is that China started a lot later than Germany, Japan, Italy or France, but there's no question that it's going to become one of the most important markets in the world. We just have to work with them in the context of China's regulations and customs and practices. Now that we are working on the ground with them in so many of our core businesses, this alone, over time, will create a better environment for change. (Landr1eth 2005)

Spending on media and entertainment has increased from US$18.7 billion in 2000 to $46.4 billion in 2004, according to PricewaterhouseCoopers; box-office totals in China have surged – from $183 million in 2004 to $450 million in 2007 (Coonan 2009). While the 2004 merger between the CFGC, Hengdian Group, and Warner Brothers – resulting in the Warner China Film HG Corporation – represented the first permanent Sino-foreign entertainment joint venture in the history of the PRC, demand from other foreign corporations for investment opportunities on a film-by-film basis also remains high.

Soft Power: Cultural Security and Global Economy

Many mainland-produced tent-pole features (*dapian*) appear to promote a nationalistic sense of Chinese identity, and casts including stars from Hong Kong, Taiwan, and Japan also indicate a push toward a more regionalist imaginary. Indeed, it would be surprising if this were not so. Regional market integration within a context of capitalist globalization defines the contemporary world economy (Ching 2000). Yet "Asianness" is not merely a market commodity. Since 2009, official publications have openly discussed the importance of maintaining a "single system with multiple poles" (*duoyuan yiti*) in the cultural realm (Shi and Li 2009). These same publications stress "cultural security" as an important goal for China as globalization or "opening" advances. The cultural security concept now appears in writings from the members of the CCP Central Committee Politburo, who describe its major challenge as ideological instability and hegemonism within the world system. In insisting on cultural security, and cultural construction as the overarching goals of media policy and reform, these leaders are also arguing that cultural homogeneity is a source of national strength, a defense against US hegemony, and a resource for future state security broadly conceived. From this perspective culture is not simply to be consumed; citizens in the cultural marketplace are not merely consumers. Rather, consumption coexists with a broader mandate to secure the mentalities of citizens against private and foreign interests. Ultimately, this mandate trumps other concerns, such as profitability, which might determine what is and what is not available for consumption.

In his report to the Seventeenth Party Congress, CCP General Secretary Hu Jintao (2007) observed:

Culture has become an increasingly important source of national cohesion and creative power, and has become an increasingly important factor in the competition for comprehensive national power; enriching spiritual and cultural life has become the earnest desire of our country's people. [We] must insist on the progressive orientation of socialist advanced culture, give rise to a new high tide in socialist cultural construction, stimulate the culturally creative vigor of the entire nation [*minzu*], [and] enhance the state's cultural soft power; [we must] make [it possible for] the people's basic cultural rights and interests to obtain safeguards, make socialist cultural life even more rich and varied, and make the people's psychological bearing [*jingshen fengmao*] even more high-spirited and elevated.

Indeed, since 2005, Chinese state rhetoric concerning "peaceful rise," "peaceful development," and a "harmonious world" has been an important component of public diplomacy overseas (S. Ding 2008: 35). How such images can be used to reinforce national power in other areas has been a question that media circles have found themselves urgently pressed to answer. The focus on soft power in Chinese media analysis, in other words, is in no small part a reflection of state-sponsored nationalism and national interest concerns.

China's film industry provides one intriguing case study for examining the implementation of soft-power policy. Since 1998, developing successful culture industries has been a significant objective of the Ministry of Culture (Keane 2004: 269), with China's upcoming accession to the World Trade Organization serving as the catalyst. The value of the cultural sector increased six times since 1990 – from RMB 1.21 billion to RMB 8.37 billion (Keane 2004: 275). Registered enterprises and employment also increased dramatically, with private output surpassing the state cultural sector. Distribution, and overall output compared with that of other nations, remained poor. Privileging value chains over sheer productive capacity, the post-1998 arrangements were intended to correct this imbalance by building greater efficiency and opportunities for outsourcing (Keane 2004: 272–3).

Post-WTO Chinese state policies reveal a more general preoccupation with communications, of which culture constitutes an important component (Schiller 2005: 79). From an enterprise perspective, the rationale appears to be primarily economic. Chinese communications industries possess "strategic" importance only insofar as they serve to coordinate global supply chains while minimizing dependence on US-controlled corporations and infrastructure (Schiller 2005: 85, 88). Insofar as such initiatives have proven successful, particularly in the East Asia region, they have also created conditions of oversupply. Soft power is thus one of several means by which the Chinese state attempts to create new markets for goods and services within a competitive global economy (Schiller 2005: 95).

In the film industry, production is primarily financed by a variety of sources:

government direct support for approved films as well as indirect support for coproductions via tax breaks and reductions of expensive red tape; *foreign investors*, particularly in coproductions and joint venture arrangements; *major business enterprises*, through revenue-sharing arrangements and product endorsements in film; *advertising companies*, often through brokerage of services such as post-production; and *state-owned enterprises*, many of [which], such as the People's Liberation Army, are in fact highly profitable enterprises with interests in communications. (Keane 2006a: 18)

Within this system, domestic studios are still required to produce main melody features – propagandistic works which tend to fare poorly within the commercial distribution system. State-funded studios remain only semi-privatized, although capable of attracting large amounts of private investment and coproduction interest for more market-oriented features. Yet despite low production costs – one reason for Hollywood's continued interest in nurturing connections with Chinese studios and talent – the "international blockbuster" business model remains one of the few successful formulae for attracting overseas interest in lieu of state subsidies. As Hollywood continues to pressure for access to Chinese markets (for imports remain capped), main melody films have also become more market-oriented since 2002 (Wan and Kraus 2002: 429–30). Other East Asian industries, most notably those of Japan and Korea, have further contributed to the sense of a Chinese "cultural trade deficit" despite efforts to revitalize domestic production (Keane 2006b: 289–90). Yet concern for profit and market share has not completely eclipsed politics as an important dimension of cultural reform.

That state emphasis on cultural control, and protection of national industries, has persisted well into China's WTO era has led some scholars to conclude that marketization remains subordinated to political goals (Yeh and Davis 2008: 48–9). If this is true, then it seems that post-2007 soft-power policies will only reinforce a persistent trend. Recently, in an early 2008 issue of *Contemporary Cinema*, several prominent academics and state media consultants addressed the issue of how to incorporate the agenda laid out in Hu Jintao's Seventeenth Party Conference report. According Ni Zhen (b. 1938), one strategy for increasing the power of Chinese cinema at home and abroad is to produce main melody features in the mold of "antifascist" blockbusters such as *Flags of Our Fathers* (Clint Eastwood, 2006). One example of such films is *The Assembly* (Feng Xiaogang, 2007), which deals primarily with the experiences of soldiers during and after the Chinese Civil War. Martial arts films and a handful of other state-funded features have also performed well internationally. Yet according to Ni (2008: 10), the primary reason behind China's inability to boost its image overseas can be traced back to the inability of small or mid-sized private entertainment companies to compete with larger enterprises; another is the persistence of a "habitual" propaganda mentality within state institutions still seeking to make the transition to a free market economy. Of the 400-plus films produced in China in 2007, few were even picked up by commercial distribution chains, or broadcast on CCTV-6, which nonetheless funds production of many of these low-budget titles. Ni (2008: 8) also argues that Chinese films must move from a particularist, national perspective to a more broadly "human" perspective if they are to compete with the diversity of images offered by Hollywood fare.

Quite possibly, the significance of soft-power debate in China stems from WTO accession and confrontation with US-produced commodities in the cultural marketplace. Another important consequence of soft-power policies, however, lies in their depiction of communications as a crucial component in facilitating China's "rise" within a variety of contested arenas. In a world of intense competition for access to developing economies and exclusive bilaterally negotiated trade agreements, soft power might potentially shape outcomes; as in Africa or Southeast Asia, it may at least temporarily make the arrival of foreign economic interests more palatable to local populations, thus allowing leaders to open their markets without sacrificing domestic support. However, it would be inaccurate to say that foreign aid represents soft power within the mainstream of Chinese theoretical debate. Rather, soft power and economic power seem to form part of a tandem by which the Chinese state attempts to gain local trust through inducements such as education, cultural goods, and infrastructure. According to a Chinese Academy of Social Sciences survey, in 2005 China ranked seventh worldwide in soft-power resources, behind the United States, Germany, Britain, France, Italy, and Spain (Lam 2009). Whether the new initiatives will provide additional popularity is still a matter of some debate. But it is important to note that such expenditures, in and of themselves, represent an important consequence of soft power-related debates. While China may be a status quo power (Johnston 2003), it is nonetheless one whose leaders chafe at first-world hegemony, and who seek to shape international norms and structures to their interests while avoiding disastrous military consequences. From this perspective, soft power represents one means of coping with interdependence while attempting to extract relative gains from the system. Finally, regardless of whether soft power works, the fact that policymakers believe that they cannot do without it means that media institutions and context will be shaped accordingly for some time to come.

10

Chinese Media Capital
in Global Context

Michael Curtin

One of the most prominent though often unstated concerns of transnational media studies is the question of location: Where in the world do cultural products come from? Where do they circulate? And what does this tell us about relations of power between various groups and societies? Media industry studies have tended to approach these questions through the prism of nationalism, exploring how particular states developed their screen media and, in the case of those that rose to positions of prominence, how they influenced the citizens of other states with their cultural output (Guback 1969; Schiller 1969; Higson 1989; Crofts 1993; O'Regan 2002). Yet the history of the Chinese film industry complicates this scenario because its infrastructure and aesthetics did not develop within the boundaries of a single state. Rather it operated transnationally for much of its history, gathering financing, talent, and audiences from such diverse locales as Shanghai, Hong Kong, Taipei, and Singapore (S. Lu 1997). As for Chinese television, it began with state-based systems that have, since the 1990s, grown increasingly transnational under the manifold pressures of globalization (Keane, Fung, and Moran 2007). Despite these characteristics, scholars rarely bring a transnational perspective to the study of Chinese screen industries, nor do they tend to analyze film and television through the same lens. Instead, studies of Hong Kong television or Taiwanese cinema or Fifth Generation filmmakers have tended to prevail.[1]

This chapter attempts to overcome these tendencies by providing an analysis of Chinese media industries since the early years of film and television, tracing the geographical deployment of resources, talent, and products, and examining recent shifts in activity as media enterprises adapt to the pressures and opportunities posed by the latest wave of globalization. Employing "media capital" as a heuristic device, it seeks to understand spatial dynamics of the transnational Chinese cultural economy. The chapter begins with a brief explanation of the concept of

A Companion to Chinese Cinema, First Edition. Edited by Yingjin Zhang.
© 2012 Blackwell Publishing Ltd. Published 2012 by Blackwell Publishing Ltd.

media capital, followed by an examination of key industrial and sociocultural trends. It closes by comparing the fortunes of several important centers of Chinese media activity today and discusses the implications of media capital for their futures.[2]

Media Capital

The concept of media capital invokes both connotations of the term: capital as a geographic center within a field of interconnected locales and capital as a concentration of resources, reputation, and talent. Certain locations emerge as centers of creativity by drawing upon cultural influences and resources from near and far. As such, media capitals are sites of mediation, locations where complex forces and flows interact. They are neither bounded nor self-contained entities. Rather we should understand them in the manner that geographers such as Doreen Massey (1992) and Kevin Robins (1991) understand cities, as meeting places where local specificity arises out of migration, interaction, and exchange. Media capitals are places where things come together and consequently where the generation and circulation of new mass cultural forms become possible.

Media capital is therefore a relational concept, not simply an acknowledgment of centrality or dominance. For example, Hong Kong's historical prominence in cinema and television has been crucially dependent on cultural and institutional relations with Guangzhou, Singapore, and Taipei as well as Tokyo, London, and Hollywood. Moreover, the city's status as a media capital is an ongoing matter of negotiation, contention, and competition. During the 1990s Singapore began to tout itself as the "media hub" of Southeast Asia and Taipei eagerly attempted to take advantage of Hong Kong's vulnerability when sovereignty over the territory was transferred to the People's Republic of China (PRC) in 1997. Since that time, the commercial growth of the mainland market has likewise challenged Hong Kong's status with Shanghai and Beijing now competing for cultural prominence. Media capital is therefore a relational, dynamic, and historically contingent phenomenon.

How then should we analyze the histories and fortunes of Chinese media capitals? And what might this analysis tell us about the future of Chinese film and television? Although the forces and factors at play are various and complex, one can nevertheless discern three key principles as playing a structuring role in screen industries around the world since the early twentieth century. Most prominently they include: (1) the logic of accumulation, (2) trajectories of creative migration, and (3) contours of sociocultural variation.

The logic of accumulation is not unique to media industries, since all capitalist enterprises exhibit innately dynamic and expansionist tendencies. As David Harvey (2001: 237–66) points out, most firms seek efficiencies through the concentration of productive resources and through the expansion of markets so as to fully utilize their productive capacity and realize the greatest possible return. These tendencies are most explicitly revealed during periodic downturns in the business cycle when enterprises are compelled to intensify production and / or extensify distribution in order to survive. Such moments of crisis call for a "spatial fix," says Harvey, as capital must on the one hand concentrate and integrate sites of production so as to reduce the amount of time and resources expended in manufacture and on the other hand it must increase the speed of distribution in order to reduce the time it takes to bring distant locales into the orbit of its operations. These centripetal tendencies in the sphere of production and centrifugal tendencies in distribution were observed by Karl Marx (1973: 539) more than a century earlier when he trenchantly explained that capital must "annihilate space with time" if it is to overcome barriers to accumulation. As applied to contemporary media, this insight suggests that even though a film or TV company may be founded with the aim of serving particular national cultures or local markets, it must over time redeploy its creative resources and reshape its terrain of operations if it is to survive competition and enhance profitability.[3] Implicit in this logic of accumulation is the contributing influence of the "managerial revolution" that accompanied the rise of industrial capitalism (Chandler 1977). Indeed, it was the intersection of capitalist accumulation with the reflexive knowledge systems of the Enlightenment that engendered the transition from mercantile to industrial capitalism. Capitalism became more than a mode of accumulation, it also became a disposition toward surveillance and adaptation, as it continually refined and integrated manufacturing and marketing processes, achieving efficiencies through the concentration of productive resources and the extension of delivery systems (Giddens 1990).

The second principle of media capital emphasizes trajectories of creative migration. Audiovisual industries are especially reliant on creative labor as a core resource due to the recurring demand for new prototypes (i.e., feature films or television programs). Yet the marriage of art and commerce is always an uneasy one, especially in large institutional settings, and therefore the media business involves placing substantial wagers on forms of labor that are difficult to manage. As Asu Aksoy and Kevin Robins (1992) observe, "Whether the output will be a hit or a miss cannot be prejudged. However, the golden rule in the film business is that if you do not have creative talent to start with, then there is no business to talk about at all, no hits or misses." In fact, attracting and managing talent is one of the most difficult challenges that screen producers confront. At the level of the firm this involves offering attractive compensation and favorable working conditions, but at a broader level it also requires maintaining access to reservoirs of specialized labor that replenish themselves on a regular basis, which is why media companies tend to cluster in particular cities.[4]

Geographer Allen J. Scott contends that manufacturers of cultural goods tend to locate where subcontractors and skilled laborers form dense transactional networks. Besides apparent cost efficiencies, Scott points to the mutual learning effects that stem from a clustering of interrelated producers. Whether through informal learning – such as sharing ideas and techniques while collaborating on a particular project – or via more formal transfers of knowledge – craft schools, trade associations, and awards ceremonies – clustering enhances product quality and fuels innovation. "Place-based communities such as these are not just foci of cultural labor in the narrow sense," observes Scott (2000: 33), "but also are active hubs of social reproduction in which crucial cultural competencies are maintained and circulated."

This centripetal migration of labor encourages path-dependent evolution, such that chance events or innovations may spark the appearance of a creative cluster, but industrial development depends on spirals of growth fueled by the ongoing migration of talent in pursuit of professional opportunities. Locales that fail to make an early start in such industries are subject to "lock-out," since it is difficult to disrupt the dynamics of agglomeration, even with massive infusions of capital or government subsidies. The only way a new cluster might arise is if a dominant media capital were to falter or if a new cluster were to offer an appreciably distinctive product line.

Despite the productive power and structural advantages of media capitals, the symbolic content of media products attenuates their geographical reach. That is, the cultural distance between say Chinese filmmakers and Turkish or Indian audiences introduces the prospect that the meaningfulness and therefore the value of certain products may be undermined at the moment of consumption or use. Although the centripetal logics of accumulation and of creative migration help us identify concentrations of media capital, the centrifugal patterns of distribution are much more complicated, especially when products rub up against counterparts in distant cultural domains that are often served, even if minimally, by competing media capitals.

Cities such as Cairo, Mumbai, Hollywood, and Hong Kong lie across significant cultural divides from each other, and that explains why producers in these cities have been able to sustain distinctive product lines and survive the onslaught of distant competitors. These media capitals are furthermore supported by intervening factors that modify and complicate the spatial tendencies outlined above. Consequently, the third principle of media capital focuses on contours of sociocultural variation, demonstrating that national and local institutions have been and remain significant actors in the global cultural economy.

During cinema's early years of industrial formation, market forces and talent migrations fostered the growth of powerful producers such as Hollywood, but in reaction governments around the world began to develop policies as early as the 1920s to limit imports and to foster local media production. Attempts to develop local competitors often proved difficult, but many countries were nevertheless successful at promoting radio and later television institutions (most of them public service broadcasters) that produced popular shows and attracted substantial audiences.[5] Broadcasting seemed an especially appropriate medium for intervention, since many of its cultural and technological characteristics helped to insulate national systems from foreign competition. The ensuing parade of broadcast news and entertainment punctuated daily household routines, interlacing public and private spheres, thereby situating national culture in the everyday world of its audiences (Scannell 1991; Silverstone 1994; Morley 2000).

It should also be pointed out that state institutions were not the only actors to organize and exploit the contours of sociocultural variation. Media enterprises have for decades taken advantage of social and cultural differences in their production and distribution practices, especially by employing narratives and creative talent that resonate with the cultural dispositions of their audiences. They furthermore made use of social networks and insider information to secure market advantages, and they invoked ethnic and national pride in their promotional campaigns. Contours of sociocultural variation have provided and continue to provide opportunities to carve out market niches that are beyond the reach of powerful but culturally distant competitors.

Media capital is a concept that at once acknowledges the spatial logics of capital, creativity, culture, and polity without privileging one among the four. Just as the logic of capital provides a fundamental structuring influence, so too do forces of sociocultural variation shape the diverse contexts in which media are made and consumed. The concept of media capital encourages us to provide dynamic and historicized accounts that delineate the operations of capital and the migrations of talent, while at the same time directing our attention to sociocultural forces and contingencies that can engender alternative discourses, practices, and spatialities. Such an approach furthermore aims to address the supposed tension between political economy and cultural studies scholarship by showing how insights from both schools can productively be brought to bear on the study of film and television.

A historical overview of the development of Chinese screen industries helps to suggest the ways in which media capital alters the cultural geography of popular media over time. As we shall see, the early history of Chinese cinema begins in Shanghai and Hong Kong, but then shifts to Southeast Asia and later back to Hong Kong. Most recently, Beijing has become an important center of media activity, but its emerging prominence is fraught with compromise and uncertainty due to obtrusive interventions by the national government. Although it is difficult to predict future developments, one can nevertheless discern key reasons why the fortunes of Chinese media currently seem to be faltering by comparison with screen industries in Hollywood and Mumbai.

Rise and Fall of the Chinese Movie Business

Much like their Hollywood counterparts, Chinese movie companies competed fiercely during the 1920s and 1930s with little government regulation or oversight, allowing the logic of accumulation to play a dominant role during the early development of the industry. In Shanghai, the Shaw brothers experienced notable success, but their Tianyi studio soon found itself competing with companies that commanded more resources, better political connections, and even ties to the underworld, thereby encouraging the Shaws to seek alternative markets in the relatively prosperous and stable territories of Southeast Asia. Like the major American movie companies, the Shaws established an extensive chain of cinemas and fed them feature films produced by their studios in Shanghai, Hong Kong, and Singapore, each of them releasing movies with different emphases and in different varieties of Chinese. Still, audience demand grew faster than supply, encouraging the Shaws to exhibit movies by other producers as well, including major Hollywood studios. Operating as a theater circuit and as a prominent regional distributor helped to insure consistent cash flows for the Shaw studio, giving them an advantage over competitors and fostering a period of robust growth. Meanwhile, in Shanghai and Hong Kong, movie companies experienced numerous difficulties as the mainland underwent a tumultuous period of civil war, world war, and Communist revolution (Fu 2003, 2008; Uhde and Uhde 2000).

Shaw Brothers flourished for more than two decades, benefiting from its expansive operations in Southeast Asia, but that would change in the 1950s, as anticolonial independence movements swept through countries of the region. With nativist political rhetoric intensifying, Shaw executives began to reassess their conception of the market, noting especially the swelling populations of Hong Kong and Taiwan where many mainland refugees settled after the Maoist rise to power. Perhaps taking note of this shift, the competing Cathay theater circuit established a sophisticated studio in Hong Kong and started turning out Mandarin musicals that proved surprisingly popular in diverse markets, suggesting the potential of a pan-Chinese Mandarin cinema (A. Wong 2002).

Shaw Brothers, now under the leadership of Run Run Shaw (Shao Yifu, b. 1907), responded by announcing plans for an even grander production facility, indeed a Movie Town, but such an investment of resources demanded careful consideration as to location. With Shaw's regional cinema circuit and extensive real estate investments headquartered in Singapore, the company was no doubt disposed to expand *in situ*; however, pressures from national independence movements in Southeast Asia created market uncertainties at the very moment when new opportunities seemed to be arising in Hong Kong and Taiwan. Just as importantly, Hong Kong had taken in a substantial number of refugee artists from the mainland studios in Shanghai, Guangzhou, and Chongqing, swelling the size of its creative labor force. Furthermore, the city's relative political stability and the colonial government's benign neglect of Chinese popular culture provided artistic freedom that seemed likely to endure for some time, unlike the prospects for Singapore or Taipei, both of which fell into the hands of authoritarian regimes during the 1950s. Finally, the emergence of Hong Kong as the most important financial center of the Chinese diaspora provided crucial access to capital and other commercial resources. This convergence of "chance occurrences" – most of them engendered by sociocultural forces – made Hong Kong an especially attractive place for Shaw Brothers to relocate its headquarters and to establish an elaborate, fully integrated studio modeled after those from Hollywood's golden age. The establishment of the Cathay and Shaw Brothers studios in Hong Kong initiated a period of tremendous growth and prosperity in Chinese commercial cinema.

Yet only a decade after Run Run Shaw relocated to Hong Kong and asserted his desire to build a pan-Chinese Mandarin cinema, he began to shift his attention to television, declaring cinema a sunset industry. No doubt numerous factors influenced the decision, but perhaps most prominently, Shaw saw television as offering a government-sanctioned domestic media market that was less subject to the vicissitudes of the transnational movie business. Although Shaw Brothers controlled an extensive cinema circuit, a robust distribution business, an elaborate production facility, and deep pools of talent, company executives no doubt continued to worry about political conditions in some of their most important overseas markets, including Singapore, Malaysia, and Taiwan.

By comparison, Hong Kong was politically stable, TV adoption rates were remarkably high, the middle class was expanding, and popular culture was thriving, with television at the very center (E. Ma 1999). So even though Shaw Brothers had established an enduring position of leadership in the transnational Chinese movie business, company executives were quick to recognize the opportunities afforded by a government broadcasting license in a thriving Chinese metropolis. Indeed, Hong Kong was at the time the only Chinese city with a commercial licensing regime that would allow a capitalist enterprise to run a major television station with relatively little political interference. Moreover, it seemed likely that the government would grant few licenses, giving those that secured them oligopoly power in the market.

Shaw turned his production resources to the new medium, thoroughly dominating local advertising, which insured a consistent flow of revenue that allowed TVB to expand its offerings beyond its initial variety and news programs to more expensive genres, such as serial drama. TVB established an early and enduring popularity with audiences, which in turn made it possible for the company to set high advertising rates and demand long-term commitments from sponsors. TVB's leadership resulted both from its aggressive marketing strategies and its ability to recruit, train, and manage creative talent. Within the geographical boundaries set by television licensing authority, Run Run Shaw established a fully integrated broadcasting enterprise that was protected by the British colonial regime.[6]

Interestingly, Shaw's predictions about the impending demise of the Chinese movie business proved to be erroneous. During the 1970s, the industry recovered from its downturn and ultimately flourished alongside TV and an emerging Cantopop music industry. In fact, the three complemented each other with talent migrating back and forth between them, creating a cluster of related firms that fostered experimentation, innovation, and mutual learning effects. Although the film business was no longer anchored by large integrated enterprises, such as Shaw Brothers or Cathay, it nevertheless enjoyed the advantage of being located in a city with a long tradition of film production, substantial pools of talent, and an expansive knowledge base among related media firms. Besides the robust and growing television economy, small independent film production companies flourished and local cinema circuits purchased their output on a consistent basis. Just as significantly, Hong Kong movies continued to enjoy popularity overseas, in territories such as Taiwan and Malaysia, where local distributors acquired the screening rights through presale agreements. These contracts provided crucial support to Hong Kong producers, encouraging a centripetal flow of revenue that helped to finance increasingly elaborate movies that proved popular with transnational audiences throughout the 1980s and much of the 1990s (Teo 1997; Stokes and Hoover 1999; Bordwell 2000; Fu and Desser 2000; E. Yau 2001).

Despite this success, the distribution system never became fully integrated with the production system, which meant that movie producers became increasingly dependent on presale revenues that they only tenuously controlled. Taiwan was one of the most profitable markets for presales and it became even more so with the emergence of new revenue streams from video, cable, and satellite. Competing fiercely for Hong Kong products, Taiwanese distributors engaged in heated and speculative bidding wars that drove up presale prices and encouraged Hong Kong producers to deliver more and more films regardless of quality. Spiraling prices and hyperproduction resulted in scores of shoddy films produced each year. Audiences accordingly became skeptical of the quality of Chinese movies and box-office revenues began to plummet during the early 1990s, around the same time that piracy offered audiences cheaper alternatives to pricey theater tickets.

Consequently, cracks in the distribution infrastructure destabilized the centrifugal distribution of product and the centripetal flow of resources back to moviemakers in Hong Kong. At the same time, hyperproduction undermined the efficiencies and mutual learning effects that had nourished the creative sector. As the quality of films began to decline, the film industry collapsed despite the fact that audiences still expressed a preference for Chinese entertainment and despite the fact that core creative resources were still concentrated in Hong Kong. Hollywood gladly filled the void, coming to dominate Taiwan and other markets not so much because it offered superior products or exercised exceptional clout in these territories, but rather because audiences turned their attention to the only reliable supplier at the time. Consequently, disjunctures in the distribution infrastructure profoundly disrupted patterns of movie circulation that had obtained for decades, causing the Chinese movie business to move into a phase of structural readjustment.

Transformation of the Television Industry

The pangs of transformation did not belong to the film industry alone, for television, too, was destined for change as technological innovation and globalization chafed at broadcasting systems throughout the region. Since their inception, television services in Taiwan, Singapore, and the PRC – as well as Indonesia, Thailand, Vietnam, and Malaysia – were closely controlled by governments that sought to influence information flows, foster native talent, and nurture the distinctive cultural attributes of their respective societies. State-sanctioned broadcasting clustered talent and resources in the political capital of each country creating enclaves of "indigenous" production and topographies of national circulation.

In the PRC, broadcasting was an official propaganda arm of the state, but most countries in East Asia opted for quasi-commercial systems, such as Taiwan, where the government and the ruling political party held sway over a three-station oligopoly, and Singapore, where state-run channels wielded monopoly power, providing commercial as well as ideological leadership. Even under Hong Kong's comparatively liberal regulatory regime, TVB enjoyed an effective monopoly over the colony's airwaves due largely to Shaw's wealth of resources and to the company's privileged status as one of two or three licensees. Relatively immune from local competition, TVB was nevertheless constrained by regulations that discouraged cross-media ownership and by quotas in overseas markets that prevented it from exporting programs abroad. State policies throughout East Asia created islands of media capital within the boundaries of highly regulated national media systems.

During the late 1980s, however, broadcasting changed profoundly, as the end of the cold war altered relations between states and as trade liberalization amplified the influence of transnational market forces. This not only encouraged media flows among Asian countries, it also prodded India and the PRC to develop their television systems and grow their consumer economies. Changes in government policies were furthermore stimulated by expressions of popular will, as citizens sought political and economic reforms. The PRC, Taiwan, and South Korea were only the most visible examples of countries that were swept up in debates over democratization and marketization. Governments that once emphasized trade protection and internal development now began to stress interconnection, communication, and comparative advantage. Policymakers also began to fret about their countries' competitive positions with respect to trade, science, and technology. As these sociocultural forces rippled through the broadcasting systems of Asia, they transformed infrastructures of distribution, trajectories of flow, and patterns of use.

In the midst of these changes, TVB began to experience a decline in profit growth during the late 1980s. The company's opportunities were limited, since televisions were already in every household, the production infrastructure was highly rationalized, and the advertising market was saturated. Consequently, TVB would have a tough time growing its local audience, trimming its production costs, or attracting new advertisers. Moreover, as the population grew wealthier the audience began to fragment due to competition from new technologies and new entertainment options that lured youngsters and wealthier families away from TVB's mass programming. Growth began to stall and executives worried that their future prospects in Hong Kong were grim.

Shaw's company needed what geographer David Harvey (2001) refers to as "a spatial fix." That is, it needed to expand its distribution infrastructure and diversify its services if it was to revive profitability. Restricted from pursuing cross-media enterprises locally, the company looked to overseas markets, first with video rental, then cable, satellite, Internet, and a return to the movie business. Trade liberalization and new technologies were opening media markets around the world and TVB hoped to take advantage of these emerging opportunities. From its previous iteration as a locally licensed broadcaster, it increasingly took on the appearance of a transnational multimedia conglomerate, producing and distributing content for both mass and niche audiences in far-flung locales. This change required a respatialization of media flows, a refiguring of boundaries between media, and a reordering of temporal patterns of media consumption. Local broadcasting could no longer carry the company forward, as indicated by the fact that profit growth was increasingly derived from overseas operations.

Shaw also began to confront fresh competition in its home market, as other Chinese companies turned their attention to television, including Hong Kong's richest tycoon, Li Ka-shing. In the early 1990s, Li began to put together a pan-Asian telecommunications satellite system, but it was the company's fledgling content service, Star TV (under the leadership of Li's son, Richard) that captured the imagination of audiences, investors, critics, and policymakers. Star provided the satellite infrastructure to deliver a platform of services comprised of MTV, BBC, Western sports programming, and Chinese movies. Company executives crowed that pan-Asian satellite TV would have a transformative impact across the region and this proved only too true, as local and national broadcasters soon felt pressured to launch their own satellite and cable services. Moreover, it was not long before global media conglomerates began looking for gateways of opportunity in Asia, hoping to make use of their considerably greater productive resources and programming libraries. In the face of mounting competition, Li's first mover advantage began to shrivel when it became apparent that Star lacked a substantial production capacity, serving largely as a distributor of others' content. Sensing an opening, Rupert Murdoch snapped up Star TV and, after a rocky start, began to expand the number of channels and services, complementing the pan-Asian channels with programming aimed at specific territories in different parts of Asia (A. Chan 1996).

Li's retreat from television exposed one of the central weaknesses of Chinese media. In general, wealthy Chinese entrepreneurs, such as Richard and K. S. Li, have shied away from the media business, seeing it as *déclassé* and speculative. They tend to prefer infrastructural investments in real estate, shipping, utilities, and core commodities. They are more accustomed to wielding political influence, exercising monopoly control over markets, and milking monopoly rents from their customer base. Although media industries can under certain conditions provide such opportunities, they are far more susceptible to shifting patterns of fashion and taste. The Li family was apparently attracted to satellite TV initially as an infrastructural investment, but they soon learned that satellite systems are only as good as the content they deliver, which drew them into the perpetual scramble to anticipate and exploit the quicksilver of popular taste.

In nearby Taiwan, the Wang and Koo families – leading industrialists and financiers – would learn this lesson as well. Using their political connections and vast financial resources, they achieved duopoly control over cable television systems throughout the island during the 1990s. Although cable penetration rose rapidly and the Wangs and the Koos came to dominate, they failed to invest comparable amounts in content creation and soon found themselves competing with dozens of new programming services. The resulting glut of channels put downward pressure on ratings and production budgets. Even the state-owned terrestrial services, now shorn of their oligopoly privileges, began to suffer significant audience erosion. In a market riddled with ferocious competition, the post-martial law government refused to cap the number of cable services and did little to resist the introduction of foreign competitors. It did, however, allow the politically connected Wangs and Koos to consolidate their control of cable infrastructure in exchange for promises that they would upgrade to broadband technology.

By the end of the 1990s, Taiwan had more than one hundred cable channels, with most of them focusing on low-cost genres such as news, talk, game shows, studio dramas, and musical variety. Taiwan furthermore suffers the scourge of imitation that plagues cable television around the globe: whenever a channel successfully targets a new audience niche, it invites look-alike competition that subdivides the niche until profit margins evaporate. These recurring cycles of imitation discourage companies from investing in production resources that might improve the quality of their channels. Instead, most companies grow their audiences by multiplying the number of channels they provide, which further exacerbates competitive pressures. Efforts to improve programming have also been undermined by recurring talent shortages due to the fact that Taipei is not a magnet for the migration of Chinese artistes. Consequently, market fragmentation, talent shortages, limited resources, and political patronage persistently undermine the accumulation of media capital in Taipei. Even those companies that achieve a leadership position must look to overseas markets for future growth. Yet their prospects may remain limited without substantial investments in creative resources.

Singapore experienced similar pressures during the 1990s, as policymakers prodded the industry towards privatization. Anticipating the transition from an industrial to a service economy, government planners invested heavily in satellite, cable, and computer infrastructure, hoping to sustain the country's prominence as a financial center. By emphasizing the development of a globally competitive service economy, the government was forced to take a more open attitude toward transnational communication flows and was therefore pressed to reorganize its media enterprises, encouraging companies to be more creative, to explore new markets, and to imagine themselves as transnational enterprises. Still, many in the media industry and in the population as a whole continue to embrace a conservative perspective on media liberalization, preferring policy leadership and even censorship to a more free-wheeling media economy. Indeed, institutional complacency and social conformity remain two of the key challenges facing media industries in Singapore. As a result, successful artists tend to migrate to Hong Kong or even Taipei in order to improve their professional prospects. As for the leading media companies, they have embraced transnational coproductions as an important vehicle for future growth. Yet few have achieved notable success, largely due to talent deficits and limited distribution capacity in overseas markets. Unlike the early days of Shaw Brothers and Cathay, Singaporean media today are culturally isolated from regional markets and largely dependent on national regulators to protect them from the challenges of globalization.

Western Competitors and Mainland Markets

Of course, Chinese commercial media companies were not the only ones maneuvering to extend their reach in Asia. During the 1990s, Western conglomerates began to position themselves for opportunities engendered by political transitions, market reregulation, and new technologies. Most attractive was the lure of mainland China, often breathlessly referred to as a nation of one billion consumers. Although profoundly impoverished by global standards, China under Deng Xiaoping underwent dramatic transformation, as it sought to modernize in the wake of the Cultural Revolution. By the late 1980s the economy was expanding briskly, as was television ownership. Consequently, Richard Li's inflated promotion of Star TV in the early 1990s resonated with significant changes taking place on the ground. When Murdoch's News Corporation took over Star, he had expansive ambitions for the service and was soon joined by competitors, such as MTV and ESPN. All embraced the early promise of satellite television, aiming to overcome spatial obstacles without needing to staff local stations or construct terrestrial transmitters.

Western satellite executives believed their services, which were seemingly immune from government regulation, could offer programming that would trump the very best of local and national TV. What they did not anticipate was the laborious effort it would require to establish marketing operations on the ground and to secure cable TV clearances from government authorities. Nor did they anticipate that local broadcasters would quickly emulate some of their programming and production strategies. Western conglomerates soon found themselves battling hundreds of competitors in dozens of territories, requiring that they fashion their programs and advertising to meet evolving audience expectations in each particular market. In the end, they came to realize that their Asian satellite services would need to balance global production and distribution efficiencies against distinctive local circumstances, such as audience tastes, market competition, and stylistic variations. Moreover, they came to understand the multiple affinities of viewers, each of them activated by different contexts of media use. Viewing habits and program preferences proved far more diverse than anticipated, with some preferring traditional and mass appeal genres while others sought out edgy and niche products.

Global conglomerates have had a tough time in East Asia, but especially so in the PRC where the government holds tightly to the reins of power. The government owns all television channels, and the State Administration for Radio, Film, and Television (SARFT) provides policy leadership for station executives. SARFT furthermore enforces restrictions on foreign satellite reception and import quotas on foreign programming. China Central Television (CCTV), based in Beijing, is the only official national network and the only television enterprise that is allowed to operate overseas. Originally established to act as a bridge between the Communist Party and the people, CCTV is monitored closely by government officials and treads cautiously with respect to ideology, innovation, and controversy. That said, CCTV is a remarkably commercial institution. Having been shorn of state subsidies, it depends on audience ratings and advertising sales to sustain its expansive operations. The network is an especially popular venue for national advertisers, especially foreign companies seeking broad exposure. Despite this commercial prosperity, CCTV nevertheless exhibits the demeanor of an official media outlet and as such serves the interests of the state before it serves audiences, clients, or commercial partners.

Municipal and provincial television channels sometimes provide lively competition. Hunan TV, a provincial service, has been one of the most innovative, forging coproduction partnerships with Taiwanese and Hong Kong producers in order to craft popular television dramas. Hunan TV also launched the enormously popular Supergirl singing contest, which rocketed to national renown in 2004. Like most provincial telecasters, Hunan TV transmits its signal via satellite, allowing its programs to be picked up throughout much of the PRC, even though it is not officially a national network. Fans around the country followed their favorite Supergirl contestants, avidly debating the merits of performers online and voting for contestants via text message. Concerned about fan enthusiasm and the show's democratic overtones (SMS voting!), Chinese officials reined in the program by instigating format changes that brought an end to the national craze. Meanwhile, CCTV introduced its own tamer version of the show that siphoned off a significant share of viewers and national advertisers. Although broadcasters such as Hunan TV have introduced numerous innovations and successes over the years, they nevertheless operate in the shadow of official institutions that ensure the market power and ideological supremacy of the central government and the Communist Party (Keane, Fung, and Moran 2007; Zhu and Berry 2009; M. Chan forthcoming).

From a policy perspective, the PRC offers one model for those seeking to influence relations between global and local media. Yet government actions in mainland China are less a matter of conscious, proactive policy than a defensive embrace of bureaucratic fiefdoms. Just as CCTV is closely tied to national elites, so too are provincial, county, and municipal television services linked to bureaucrats in their respective domains. Although overall guidance and ideology emanate from the very top, most stations and cable systems are tied to local bureaucracies, each with their own particular interests and objectives. Most troublesome is the fact that television operations are often influenced by the career ambitions of officials that wish to burnish their reputations based on the performance of media enterprises under their control. These structural characteristics tend to marginalize the interests of audiences, to discourage industrial reorganization, to limit capital investment, and to frustrate technological innovation. With respect to media policy, one finds that execution at the local level is open to a range of interpretation further fragmenting the patchwork of interests that sustains the status quo by frustrating innovation, creativity, and entrepreneurial activity.

Awash in a tumultuous sea of conflicting interests, media professionals have a difficult time focusing their attention on cultural products that might suit the diverse and rapidly changing tastes of viewers. Confronted with an oversupply of channels and a paucity of quality programming, station operators find it difficult to improve their prospects or grow their audiences. Even if they had more room to maneuver, programmers would find it difficult to ascertain audience preferences, since the most widely used television ratings are produced by a research service that operates under the wing of CCTV. As for programming, low-cost genres prevail and – as in Taiwan – innovation and success tends to invite rabid and pervasive imitation. These and other obstacles have stunted the development of Chinese television and have helped to insure the ongoing leadership of the national CCTV network. Perhaps the most striking indication of underperformance is that, despite the size and relative wealth of the market, the PRC remains by far a net importer of programming, with much of it coming from Hong Kong, Taiwan, and South Korea (Keane 2001, 2007; Diao 2008; J. Chan forthcoming).

In the movie business, China Film Group – the largest movie distributor and the only authorized distributor of foreign titles – likewise operates as an appendage of the state. It tends to favor directors and productions it considers ideologically safe and widely popular. Like CCTV, it has been shorn of state subsidies and therefore must support itself through commercial ventures. Since 2000, it has focused on blockbuster productions aimed at national mass audiences and increasingly at overseas viewers as well. The operational objectives of China Film stem from a consensus among party leaders that the PRC's cultural status should conform to its global economic and geopolitical status. The state's interest in media enterprises is manifest both in its official policies and its less official acts of explicit favoritism. For example, China Film imposed a "blackout period" on imported movies in December 2002 as it rolled out one of its favored blockbusters, Zhang Yimou's

Hero (2002), a movie that has been widely interpreted as an allegorical justification for authoritarian rule. With little competition, *Hero* scored a major success in mainland theaters that in turn became the springboard for an international run, attracting record box office worldwide. The blackout policy has since been used numerous times to help launch favored productions, such as Zhang's subsequent titles, *House of Flying Daggers* (2004) and *Curse of the Golden Flower* (2006). It is noteworthy that Zhang was then invited to direct the opening ceremonies for the Beijing Olympics, carried throughout the country by CCTV. Its cast of thousands and striking imagery provided a vivid tableau for the program's overriding message of China's harmonious and "peaceful rise," a theme that resonated well with state policy and was reportedly well received by the Communist Party leadership (Y. Zhao 2010). Some critics (e.g., Davis and Yeh 2008) contend that the PRC is pursuing a self-conscious policy of "marketization" that aims to contain, control, and exploit commercial activity in the interests of the Communist Party. Although some see China joining the global economy, forces of sociocultural variation are powerfully shaping the deployment of capital, the creation of content, and the distribution of product. Given the size and influence of government media institutions, private movie companies in Beijing, Hong Kong, Taipei, and Singapore now find themselves contending with the reverberations of official policies and practices of the Chinese government.

Many private companies have nevertheless fared well enough to persist with their endeavors and most seek to hedge their bets by diversifying in markets outside the mainland. Western media conglomerates are not so sanguine about current prospects in Chinese commercial media. Warner Bros. spent years trying to build theaters and satellite services in the mainland before calling it quits in 2007. They were followed shortly thereafter by Murdoch, whose News Corporation invested billions in media ventures and public relations efforts before quietly scaling back its mainland operations and redirecting its resources to other Asian markets. Sony and Disney have likewise trimmed their investments in the PRC. Variety reporter Patrick Frater (2008) summed up the attitude of strategists at these studios by citing one executive who remarked, "China is no longer on top of Hollywood's priority list. It just isn't worth the corporate effort. You get better returns in Russia and better market access in India." Taiwanese and Hong Kong executives tend on the other hand to counsel patience and continue to engage in joint ventures and other opportunities as they arise. And many transnational ventures, especially those that assiduously adapt to local circumstances, do indeed succeed (Fung 2008). Still, the PRC is widely perceived as treacherous terrain for media entrepreneurs, with ambiguous policies, political favoritism, censorship, piracy, and a lack of financial transparency among the most common concerns. On the one hand, this complex operating environment helps to keep foreign capitalists at bay, yet on the other hand it undermines the development of Chinese media capital, both among enterprises based in the mainland as well as those in Hong Kong, Singapore, and Taipei.

Conclusion

As mentioned at the outset, one of the enduring concerns of transnational media studies is the question of location. Where and under what conditions do media enterprises thrive and collaborate such that their products achieve wide circulation and influence, returning regular flows of revenue, talent, and creative inspiration to the geographical center, the media capital? Chinese media today seem gripped by conflicting influences and an uncertain future. Yet, as we have seen, these screen industries have gone through similar periods of structural and geographical transformation. The early movie business in mainland China was superseded by Southeast Asian circuits based in Singapore and later by a pan-Chinese cinema based in Hong Kong. During Hong Kong's golden age, its many film, television, and music enterprises shared resources, personnel, and creative ideas on an ongoing basis, making it an attractive location for talent to develop their skills and advance their careers. It was also the site of lively competition among peers, where status and recognition helped to fuel innovation and risk-taking. And it was a relatively stable and prosperous society that was engaged with the outside world via trade, education, and cultural exchange. Although a colony of Great Britain, it nevertheless benefited from a liberal regulatory regime that kept its distance from the everyday workings of popular culture. In full flower, Hong Kong was unquestionably the media capital of Chinese screen industries.

Today, however, Hong Kong resources have been depleted and its prominence diminished. Its 1997 transfer of sovereignty to the PRC engendered a decade of political uncertainty, market turmoil, and creative self-censorship. Hong Kong media were furthermore victims of their own success, as escalating prices for satellite, cable, and home media rights led to a cycle hyperproduction in the movie business. In an attempt to keep up with demand, companies accelerated their output with little concern for quality. The results were disastrous, as viewers lost faith in talent and producers, which no doubt tempted audiences to turn to pirated products that sold for a fraction of the retail price. The television economy was likewise transformed during the 1990s by the introduction of new satellite, cable, and video competitors with a resulting fragmentation of audiences and a decline in overall quality. What is more, the transfer of sovereignty cast a pall over the city, leading many to wonder about the future of creativity and free expression in Hong Kong, as it became a special administrative region of the PRC. Many thought Hong Kong would lose its cosmopolitan connections and its distinctive status as an entrepôt to Southern China. It would no longer be a magnet for talent or a nexus of transnational commerce and migration. As Hong Kong faltered, Singapore and Taipei aspired to assume the mantle of regional media leadership, but the former suffered from its own culture of self-censorship and the latter was subject to ferocious competition and audience fragmentation in its domestic market.

The growing significance of the PRC in this equation poses significant problems for media companies that hope to serve diverse populations and global markets. In order to succeed in the mainland, they must be sensitive to official policies, which invariably aim to insure state leadership and the supremacy of the Communist Party. Often this undermines the transnational popularity of films and television dramas, since audiences in Hong Kong, Vancouver, Sydney, and Taipei tend to look for edgy, irreverent, or trendy products that compete well with counterparts from media metropolises worldwide. Safe topics and treatments that respect the cultural guidance of the Party leadership have a tough time with global audiences and they likewise find it difficult to compete for the attention of mainland viewers, many of whom have grown accustomed to global media texts courtesy of the black market video trade. Such developments mark a spatial restructuring of Chinese screen industries that have complicated the flows of capital, product, and creative talent, as well as the content of films and television dramas. Today, none of these cities can legitimately claim capital status, although their screen enterprises must nevertheless operate transnationally in East Asia and worldwide.

The Beijing leadership has clearly articulated its aspirations to become the central locus of Chinese media activity, but it suffers from oppressive official oversight and therefore its creative output consistently underperforms. Despite its global aspirations, Beijing is not a media capital but rather a national node of state policy and patronage. Since the early years of screen industries, the most successful transnational media capitals – such as Hollywood, Bombay, and Beirut – have operated at arm's length from the state, catering to popular interests rather than powerful state clienteles. Their resolute focus on commercial imperatives and their attentiveness to mercurial shifts in popular tastes and trends have discouraged producers from aligning themselves too closely to powerful patrons and official culture. Consequently, Beijing will no doubt continue to exercise its commanding influence over state-sanctioned media, but one should look elsewhere for newly emerging centers of Chinese commercial media. Shanghai and Guangzhou – each with a robust ensemble of media enterprises and distinctive regional cultures – seem likely contenders for capital status, but for now their financial resources, institutional structures, and geographical reach are significantly circumscribed by official state policy. Tentative indications of change are nevertheless afoot.

Over the past decade, Beijing leaders have periodically expressed a desire to extend the global influence of Chinese screen media, in part to address the perceived challenge posed by Western media conglomerates and in part because they aspire to cultural prominence that is comparable to the PRC's economic significance. The Beijing Olympics were only the most obvious manifestation of these aspirations and much as they succeeded, the Games nevertheless bore the residual taint of official spectacle. Shortly thereafter the government announced its latest media restructuring plan, aimed at encouraging the formation of mainland-based conglomerates with commercial infrastructures. Should the policy succeed (although in the past, many such reform efforts have not), Shanghai

Media Group is the most likely beneficiary, indicating the Party's willingness to loosen oversight of entertainment media. If that were to occur, one might witness a multipolar dispersion of media resources, with Beijing retaining paramount status in official media (news and information) while Shanghai–Taipei and Hong Kong–Guangzhou carve out distinctive spheres in popular film and television aimed at diverse audiences worldwide. As Yingjin Zhang (2010a) and Laikwan Pang (2010) have pointed out, such translocal connections between key cultural metropolises have a rich and enduring history in Chinese cinema. One would no doubt see a rapid intensification of such connections should the shadow of state policy begin to dissipate even modestly.

Notes

1   Y. Zhang (2004a) and Davis and Yeh (2008) offer recent examples of texts that have begun to integrate the various Chinese cinemas into a single analytical framework. Keane, Fung, and Moran (2007) make a similar effort with television. Although transnational in scope, all three studies restrict their attention to a single medium, film *or* television.

2   This chapter draws upon extensive research conducted for an earlier volume by the author (Curtin 2007), but the argument here distinguishes itself by offering a substantially revised and more concise analysis of the dynamics of Chinese media capital, especially with respect to recent developments in screen industries over the past few years.

3   Monopoly rents are an exception, but as shown in this chapter, monopoly rents have proven less tenable in an era of changing technologies and increasing transborder flows.

4   Although it does not address media industries specifically, an extensive literature discusses the impact of human capital on the clustering of business firms in particular locations (Jacobs 1984; Porter 1998; Florida 2005).

5   The British Broadcasting Corporation, which has served as a model for others, was explicitly charged with responsibility to clear a space for the circulation of British values, culture, and information (Scannell 1991; Hilmes 2003).

6   My discussion of Chinese commercial television in this section is derived from a more extensive treatment (Curtin 2007).

11

Film and Society in China
The Logic of the Market

Stanley Rosen

By 2011, after more than thirty years of reform in China, developments in the film industry reminded observers how far the industry has come, pointed to future directions and still evolving trends, and suggested some of the key issues that are likely to remain contentious for the foreseeable future. Since these developments are closely linked to the interactive role between Chinese film and society, it is useful at the outset to note some of the major recent developments suggested above. First, 2010 continued the familiar annual increase in box-office performance that has been a feature of the Chinese market over the last decade. By 2008 China's box-office revenues had hit RMB 4.3 billion, bringing the country for the first time into the top ten film markets in the world. After climbing to RMB 6.1 billion in 2009, the figure for 2010 reached a remarkable RMB 10.17 billion, a 43 percent increase over the previous year; as recently as 2003 the box-office total had been under RMB 1 billion (H. Liu 2011).[1] While previously lacking an "industry" in any commonly understood sense of that term, Chinese film authorities and filmmakers are now driven more and more by the bottom line, dedicated to making films that will bring audiences into the theaters. The increasing importance of the box office and the implications for the Chinese film industry and Chinese society are a major theme of this chapter.

Second and very much related to the first point, the familiar boundaries – and contradictions – among art, politics, and commerce (Zhu and Rosen 2010) have begun to break down, with films previously designated as "main melody" in China and "propaganda" films abroad successfully finding ways to stimulate audience interest. The best example of this recent phenomenon is *The Founding of a Republic* (Han Sanping, Huang Jianxin, 2009), prepared for the sixtieth anniversary of the founding of the People's Republic of China (PRC), with box-office receipts over RMB 400 million. The age of the "main melody commercial blockbuster" has

A Companion to Chinese Cinema, First Edition. Edited by Yingjin Zhang.
© 2012 Blackwell Publishing Ltd. Published 2012 by Blackwell Publishing Ltd.

arrived. Han Sanping (b. 1953), the CEO of the biggest film group in China, the state-owned China Film Group, openly noted the "need to make mainstream ideology mix well with commercial means" (Danwei.org 2009). Another highly successful main melody blockbuster in late 2009 was "the first commercial spy thriller," *The Message* (Chen Guofu), which subverted many of the conventions of past mainland spy thrillers, and was described in the film's production notes as a "populist film" with "a new look" (Tsui 2009).

There are real questions, however, over the sustainability of this new fusion of politics and commerce. Interviews and survey data suggest that the primary attraction for *Founding*'s audience was the appearance of 177 of China's leading stars and directors, including such Hong Kong legends as Jackie Chan and Jet Li (Li Lianjie, b. 1963), leading to the amusing game of trying to discern which star was hiding under the makeup of a late 1940s historical figure. A number of film industry insiders noted that the willingness of so many stars to donate their time to provide cameos in the film is a testament to the power of Han Sanping, by all accounts the most powerful individual in the film industry, and that it would be difficult to repeat the success of this phenomenon. In addition, the Internet "debate" over *Founding* revealed the increasing importance of the Web, and public opinion more generally, as a factor in the film industry. Well-known blogger Han Han posted a list of the actors in the film who had given up their Chinese nationality, leading to a heated discussion over whether they were still "Chinese," compelling these stars, and the China Film Group on their behalf, to defend their love of China (Chinadaily.com 2009c). While such "ultra-nationalistic" views were clearly in the minority, as we will see below in the case studies of *Lust, Caution* (Ang Lee, 2006) and *Kungfu Panda* (Mark Osborne, John Stevenson, 2008), such online debate now accompanies the release of any prominent film.

A third recent phenomenon is the increasingly complex relationship between Hollywood and China, which now comprises several components. For example, reflecting perhaps his reputation for having a "patriot complex" (*aiguo qingjie*), Han Sanping's interviews are indeed quite openly critical of the Chinese media in fawning over Hollywood films while criticizing the commercial impulses of Chinese filmmakers, and in suggesting his very strong motivation to beat Hollywood in the Chinese market by using Hollywood methods of production and marketing (Danwei.org 2009). But if Han is dedicated to learning about Hollywood, the American industry in turn seems to be refining its knowledge on how to sell tickets in China. In late 2009 the American blockbuster *2012* (Roland Emmerich) became the all-time box-office victor in the Chinese market up to that time, leaving *The Founding of a Republic* in third place, behind *Transformers 2: Revenge of the Fallen* (Michael Bay, 2007). Indeed, for Chinese audiences 2012 had a number of similarities to *Founding*, despite the widely divergent themes of reconciliation in the former and global disaster in the latter. Ironically, *2012* is also a "propaganda" film, one in which only China can save the world. In one theater, the entire audience erupted into applause after a People's Liberation Army (PLA) soldier saluted American refugees arriving in China, and Chinese publications have noted Hollywood's more positive approach to China (BBC Monitoring Asia Pacific-Political 2009; Shanghaiist 2009). Bloggers in China have lost no time in producing lists of "the top ten Hollywood movies that suck up to China" (EastSouthWestNorth 2009); *2012* made it to the top of the list. Both of these films raise important issues about film marketing and audience response, and both films have been extensively discussed in the Chinese media, both positively and negatively.

In late December the World Trade Organization (WTO) rejected China's appeal against a ruling that it must stop forcing content owners from the United States to use state-owned companies to distribute movies and books. While the WTO ruling does not address China's import quota of twenty revenue-sharing foreign films a year and agreed with China that the country has the right to ban foreign films and books that government censors deem objectionable, the ruling appears to break the monopoly that China Film Group and Huaxia Film Distribution – which is partially owned by China Film – currently have on the distribution of foreign films in China (Shackleton 2009). Ironically, one of China's leading producers has accused China Film of favoring Hollywood imports over domestic blockbusters.

The three developments from late December 2009 noted above – the continued rapid growth of the box office in China, the blurring of the lines between political and commercial films, and the evolving relationship between Chinese domestic films and Hollywood productions – are all relevant to the role film plays in the relationship between the Chinese state and the society it governs. With measurable performance replacing ideology as the key factor in political legitimation, governmental strategy has become dependent on making China rich (improving the standard of living and offering more varied lifestyle choices) and powerful (able to take its place among the major powers and demonstrate its ability to be world class in a variety of areas, including film). This strategy has led directly to the continuing expansion of a more confident and demanding middle class and the coming of age of a new generation of youth (the "post-80s generation") who have extensive knowledge of international cultural trends, an individualism that poses a challenge to official and otherwise "authoritative" voices, and a strong sense of "nationalism" (Rosen 2009). Given the changes in Chinese society the state can no longer simply dictate cultural policy, but must "negotiate" with social and cultural forces in trying to balance contradictory values, including the political (e.g., the "propaganda" or socialization function of film) and the commercial (e.g., the need to compete with the ever-present Hollywood product). These contradictions and the negotiations they produce are manifested in a variety of ways, including the tension between producing blockbuster films that promote mainstream values and the production of more popular "super-commercial" blockbusters.

Using survey research and public opinion data, box-office statistics, documentary sources, interviews, and case studies, this chapter will assess government policies toward film, audience exposure and receptivity to film, the winners and losers in China's evolving film industry, and likely future prospects for film as a factor in the Chinese state's relationship with society.

An Overview of the Film Audience

In the United States and many other countries the traditional manner of viewing films – collectively, in a darkened theater populated primarily with strangers – has long been in decline as a revenue stream for the major film studios and production companies. New technologies, including the delivery of films through DVD, the Internet, or television broadcasts, have had a major impact on theater attendance. China has an Internet community that is now the largest in the world, raising questions as to how this revolution in new technology has affected viewing habits. A number of surveys have addressed this question.

For example, the Chinese Film Copyright Protection Association did a sample survey of 1,200 respondents in fourteen large and medium-sized cities, which discovered that, on average, the respondents watched 57 films a year (Wei Zhang 2009). In terms of venue, 47 percent generally watched films on the Internet; 29 percent watched films on television; 17 percent on disks (such as DVD); and 7 percent most often watched films in theaters. Interestingly, those below the age of eighteen were most likely to see a film in a theater (11 percent), while other demographic groups hovered between 6 and 7 percent, a result consistent with other surveys. One survey conducted among university students attending the Fifteenth Beijing College Student Film Festival in 2008, discussed in more detail below, found that over 60 percent of the respondents most often watched films on the Internet, primarily through downloading (Zhou and Song 2008).

The surveyors found a lack of correspondence between film attendance and the importance of the box office in generating revenue for the film industry, contrasting the results with the United States. For example, in 2007 the total revenue for the film industry was RMB 6.7 billion, of which the theatrical box office made up RMB 3.3 billion, or just under 50 percent. Given the importance of theater attendance to the industry, the surveyors were surprised that only 7 percent chose film theaters as their most common means for watching a film. They also noted that in a more mature film market like the United States, the theatrical box office only made up 20 percent of the total film revenue, suggesting both the high ticket prices for theatrical films in China relative to incomes, and the greater development of revenue streams from alternative viewing sources in the United States.

The survey conducted at the Beijing College Student Film Festival included more than eight hundred students from thirty universities in Beijing and ten universities outside the capital, and addressed audience preferences over the entire thirty-year Reform period. First, the surveyors discovered that film directors of the

Fourth and Sixth Generations were not as popular as such well-known Fifth Generation directors as Zhang Yimou and Chen Kaige, and some "films with a special quality" such as *In the Heat of the Sun* (Jiang Wen, 1994) and *Kekexili: Mountain Patrol* (Lu Chuan, 2004). When asked about the benefits the reforms had brought about for the film audience, over 40 percent chose the opportunity to see films from Europe, Japan, and Korea, which was new to them, followed by 29 percent who chose the increasing variety of mainland films; 14 percent chose the ability to see Hollywood films in theaters, and 11 percent chose theatrical showings from Hong Kong, Taiwan, and other coproduced films. This suggested to the surveyors less a lack of interest in Hollywood and Hong Kong films and more a reaction to the high ticket prices needed to see such films in theaters, particularly with the availability of inexpensive alternatives. Offered fifteen names and asked to designate the "real" film stars, it is striking to note that the person who came out on top, scoring even higher than Ge You (b. 1957), Gong Li (b. 1965), and Jiang Wen, was Chen Daoming (b. 1955), who perhaps is best known in films for playing Emperor Qin Shi Huang in *Hero* (Zhang Yimou, 2002), but is even more popular for his leading roles in television dramas, including the Kangxi Emperor in *Kangxi Dynasty* (Chen Jialin, Liu Dayin, 2001), demonstrating, as many surveys have done, the continuing popularity of such TV dramas.

When asked why they would spend money to see films in a theater, of the five choices offered by far the largest number (over 44 percent) chose the opportunity to see special effects and a big spectacle on the big screen; only about 25 percent were attracted by either film stars or a famous director. Given these findings, it is not surprising that in 2010 *Avatar* (James Cameron, 2009) took in around RMB 1.4 billion at the box office, more than double the total of any film ever marketed in China, or that *Inception* was also a major success (see Table 11.1, below). When it came to choosing films to celebrate the New Year, by far the largest number wanted to see comedies (41 percent), explaining the enduring popularity of China's leading director of New Year comedies, Feng Xiaogang, and its leading comedic star, Ge You. When asked which "hot films" they had seen, *Lust, Caution*, to be discussed below, had been seen by the most respondents (72 percent), followed by *Cape No. 7* (Wei Te-sheng, 2008) from Taiwan and *The Warlords* (Peter Chan, Yip Wai Min, 2007) from Hong Kong. It is noteworthy that films that scored highest were either highly controversial films that faced government censorship or films from Taiwan and Hong Kong.[2]

A series of questions was asked about the consumption of low-budget art films. Since one of the main conclusions of this chapter is that art films and independent films more generally have been severely disadvantaged by explicit government strategies and the logic of the market, making it difficult to compete with commercial and main melody films, it is useful to examine some of the results. While students generally see as many art films as commercial films, they also note that they do not spend any money watching the art films (59 percent). Those that do pay to see these films are more likely to watch them on disk (21 percent) than see them in theaters (16 percent). One of the disadvantages such art films face is

Table 11.1   The top box-office hits in China (as of April 17, 2011)

Rank	English title	Chinese title	Year	Box office (RMB 100 million)
1.	*Avatar* (H)	阿凡达	2010	13.78
2.	*Let the Bullets Fly* (M)	让子弹飞	2010	6.64
3.	*Aftershock* (M)	唐山大地震	2010	6.48
4.	*If You Are the One II* (M)	非诚勿扰 II	2010	4.74
5.	*2012* (H)	2012	2009	4.66
6.	*Inception* (H)	盗梦空间	2010	4.57
7.	*Transformers II* (H)	变形金刚II	2009	4.55
8.	*The Founding of a Republic* (M)	建国大业	2009	4.20
9.	*Titanic* (H)	泰坦尼克号	1998	3.60
10.	*If You Are the One* (M)	非诚勿扰	2008	3.25*
11.	*Red Cliff I* (HK)	赤壁上	2008	3.12
12.	*Detective Dee and the Mystery of the Phantom Flame* (HK)	狄仁杰之通天国	2010	2.96
13.	*Bodyguards and Assassins* (HK)	十月围城	2009	2.93
14.	*Curse of the Golden Flower* (M)	满城尽带黄金甲	2006	2.91
15.	*Transformers* (H)	变形金刚	2007	2.82
16.	*A Woman, a Gun and a Noodle Shop* (M)	三枪拍案惊奇	2009	2.61
17.	*Red Cliff II* (HK)	赤壁下	2009	2.6
18.	*Hero* (M)	英雄	2002	2.5
19.	*Assembly* (M)	集结号	2007	2.48*
20.	*Ip Man II* (HK)	叶问II	2010	2.32
21.	*Painted Skin* (HK)	画皮	2008	2.3
22.	*Alice in Wonderland* (H)	爱丽丝梦游仙境	2010	2.26
23.	*Battle: Los Angeles* (H)	洛杉矶之战	2011	2.24
24.	*Harry Potter and the Deathly Hallows I* (H)	哈利·波特与死圣	2010	2.21
25.	*The Message* (M)	风声	2009	2.16
26.	*The Expendables* (H)	敢死队	2010	2.13
27.	*Shaolin (New Shaolin Temple)* (HK)	新少林寺	2011	2.10
28.	*CJ 7* (HK)	长江七号	2008	2.03
29.	*Eternal Moment* (M)	将爱情进行到底	2011	2.028
30.	*The Warlords* (HK)	投名状	2008	2.01
31.	*Sacrifice* (M)	赵氏孤儿	2010	1.96
32.	*The Forbidden Kingdom* (C)	功夫之王	2008	1.88
33.	*Kungfu Panda* (H)	功夫熊猫	2008	1.86
34.	*My Own Swordsman* (M)	武林外传	2011	1.83
35.	*The Promise* (M)	无极	2005	1.795

Table 11.1 *(cont'd)*

Rank	English title	Chinese title	Year	Box office (RMB 100 million)
36.	*Iron Man II* (H)	钢铁侠 II	2010	1.76
37.	*Clash of the Titans* (H)	诸神之战	2010	1.75
38.	*City of Life and Death* (M)	南京南京	2009	1.72

♦ (H) = Hollywood; (M) = primarily mainland; (HK) = primarily Hong Kong; (C) = coproduction, with a major Western as well as a Chinese release. Since almost all of the domestic blockbusters can be considered as coproductions today, I have tried to distinguish those that have primarily mainland components – most often the film's director – from those that have primarily Hong Kong components.

* The figure in this source had a total box office slightly lower than the figure provided in Table 11.2 (260 million). Box-office data are quite often inconsistent between sources, particularly since the use of computerized box-office data is a recent phenomenon in China and most data come from the film companies rather than the theaters, generally leading to inflated results. These problems do not significantly affect the overall results in this table.

Source: Derived from http://mtime.com/my/964883/blog/1255510/ (accessed April 25, 2011).

the lack of an arthouse cinema circuit. China has a relatively small number of screens and the most favorable venues are fully booked for Chinese or foreign blockbusters, leaving little room for everyone else. This situation has led directly to a war of words between commercially successful and arthouse directors over film policy. Art films and independent films more generally are often consumed not in standard theatrical venues, but at film clubs, on university campuses, or in makeshift venues (Nakajima 2006).

Another interesting section of the survey asked the students about their preferences with regard to Hollywood and Chinese domestic films. While 41 percent would see both kinds of films, if they were showing at the same time 33 percent would opt for the Hollywood product over a Chinese film, while 17 percent would choose the Chinese film. This is consistent with other survey data on film preferences of Chinese youth; indeed, in many surveys the Hollywood product scores even higher (Rosen 2008a).

The Increasing Importance of the Box Office in China

During the first decade of China's thirty years of reform, box-office results did not play a major role in the decision-making of China's film authorities. In 1979 film attendance hit 29.3 billion, the highest figure in the Reform era that began at the end of 1978. Since China had a population of around one billion at that time, on average a person would enter a film theater 29 times a year. After 1979 the number of filmgoers steadily declined, but the state took relatively little action to try and ameliorate the decline (F. Xie 2009). Despite the obvious improvement in the diversity of film content in comparison to the Mao years, the primary role of film remained the socialization of the Chinese public, particularly its youth, into a proper system of values.

During periods of greater openness, film authorities did try to encourage filmmakers to produce a more audience-friendly product. For example, pleased when *Red Sorghum* (Zhang Yimou, 1988) won the Golden Bear Award at the Berlin International Film Festival – what became known in China as the *"Red Sorghum* phenomenon"* (Renmin ribao* 1988)[3] – Teng Jinxian, the Director of the Film Bureau of the Ministry of Radio, Film, and Television (now SARFT), told an interviewer in March 1989 that films in the future would be classified into three types. The first type of film would be serious films that would promote the proper ideology for the Reform movement and a correct understanding of past history. He acknowledged that such "important" films, while essential, would be unprofitable. The second type of film would be entertainment and commercial films, which would make up the majority, and "must stand the test of the market and audience judgment." The third type of film would be "artistic and avant-garde films," the purpose of which would not be profits. Although few in number they would be representative of the highest creative level and would be the films that would win awards at international film festivals (Teng 1989).

A month after Teng's appeal for more entertainment-oriented and artistic films, Chinese students were marching to Tiananmen Square, leading to the military crackdown on June 4, 1989. In Teng's summary of the film industry a year later – significantly titled "Harmful Trends in Film Creation" – he enumerated five erroneous trends that needed to be corrected, which, with presumably no irony intended, excoriated filmmakers for doing exactly what he had urged them to do in 1989! The first mistake was "downgrading the ideological and political substance of films, by merely stressing their entertainment and aesthetic value, and neglecting film's social uplift capability" (Teng 1990). Other erroneous trends included "national nihilism," a term also used to criticize the popular 1988 television series *River Elegy (Heshang)*, which offered a critique of China's past and present and urged a closer relationship with the Western world and a greater role for Chinese intellectuals in developing that relationship; the advocacy of abstract human nature, humanitarianism, and the theory of human nature; using the creation of films as a means of personal expression rather than focusing on the economic and social benefits of film; and the increasing importance of money worship in the film industry, in which "everything is subordinated to the box office."

Not surprisingly, the new conservative line coming from film authorities led immediately to an even greater drop in the box office beginning in 1990. By 1992 attendance was down to 1.06 billion, but the lowest point was reached in 1993, with a decline of more than 500 million from the year before. The frequency of film attendance per person was now well below once per year. However, with the political line shifting back toward reform after Deng Xiaoping's southern trip in the winter of 1992, film authorities also got the message and began to draft new regulations that would bring audiences back to the theaters. A variety of solutions were considered and adopted – including limitations on the distribution monopoly held by China Film and introducing flexibility in ticket pricing, both in 1993 – followed by the decision in 1994 to bring in Hollywood films on a revenue-sharing basis, beginning with *The Fugitive* (Andrew Davis, 1993) from Warner Bros., so long as imported films to be shown theatrically would be limited to ten per year (L. Fan 2008; R. Tang 2008; F. Xie 2009; Rosen 2002). After the first Hollywood films began to arrive – and to do very well at the box office – many in the Chinese film industry "demanded protection from the invasion of foreign 'megafilms' that are wiping local movies off cinema screens" (Reuters 1995).

As will be noted below, complaints over access to screen time have continued, but are now far more complicated since most of the combatants come from within the Chinese film industry, and the Hollywood imports are only one part of a larger picture. The overwhelming importance of the bottom line in judging the success of a film has divided the creative community. On one side are the film authorities and those filmmakers who have achieved box-office success, although there is division within this group as well. On the other side are those filmmakers whose films are less commercially viable. Some filmmakers refuse to accept the standard tripartite division that Chinese films must serve a political, commercial, or artistic function, and argue that political or artistic films can also be commercial.

Feng Xiaogang, not surprisingly given his popular success, told the *New York Times* that his films were changing to reflect the times, as we now live in an era where people are looking for more leisure and entertainment. More specifically, as he suggested, "Now China has gradually adopted a market economy.… Movies have changed from a propaganda tool to an art form and now to a commercial product. If someone continues to make movies according to the old rules, he'll have no space to live in today's market" (Barboza 2007). Feng's leading actor, Ge You, has also expressed no interest in making any more arthouse films. As he put it, "if an actor is always acting in movies nobody watches, he's over"; he further noted that Jia Zhangke's films "were not bad, just not popular" (*Straits Times* 2006).

For his part, Han Sanping has shown that it may be possible to combine the political and the commercial in a new hybrid, the "political–commercial blockbuster," as *The Founding of a Republic* and *The Message* have suggested. However, one area that appears to unite both Feng and Han is the limited place for arthouse films in China's developing marketplace. Han has been quite explicit in his critique, bordering on contempt, for China's internationally acclaimed arthouse auteurs:

> Some of our directors, after bringing home an international prize, choose increasingly narrow paths. Even 2 million yuan in box office can't be achieved after an international prize. We allow you to chase it, but you can't complain, and can't complain about how stupid moviegoers are, and how stupid the distribution is,

and how bad the cinemas are; this is a complaining-woman complex and no one will give a damn. (Danwei.org 2009)

For their part, directors known for their art films that do well on the international film festival circuit have been equally open in criticizing the sole emphasis on box-office results. In a panel at the 2009 Shanghai International Film Festival, Wang Xiaoshuai (Chinadaily.com 2009b) castigated those he called "successful members of the 100 million yuan club," but who "fail as directors." Going further in his critique of films that are "too commercial," he concluded that "the biggest problem of Chinese cinema is the over-obsession with money. I strongly believe cinema is art. Films need dignity and confidence. I am happier than these other directors because I can still make films I really like."

Jia Zhangke as well has been critical of Chinese blockbuster successes in part because, with two or three exceptions, the most successful directors are not really mainland directors, but come from Hong Kong and Taiwan. Moreover, using John Woo and Ang Lee as examples, he asserts that they have been so contaminated by their experience in Hollywood that they are no longer making quality films (B. Xu 2008; Z. Jia 2009). He even threatened to sue when *Still Life* (2006), despite winning the top award at the Venice International Film Festival, could not find any theater with digital projection facilities because they were showing Zhang Yimou's *Curse of the Golden Flower* (2006) everywhere. Jia's critique of Zhang Yimou is both artistic and personal. Not only does he think Zhang has lost his artistic integrity, but he also appears to blame members of Zhang's creative team for persuading film authorities that Jia's films gave the world a bad impression of China, leading to a ban on his films at that time (*Straits Times* 2007). Indeed, Jia deliberately chose to open *Still Life* on the same day as *Curse*, to show his contempt for Zhang's work. In turn Zhang's producer Zhang Weiping asserted that Jia was "sick with revenge against the rich" (Osnos 2009). Han Sanping's tirade, quoted above, was clearly intended to respond to directors such as Jia Zhangke and Wang Xiaoshuai, for privileging film as an art without regard to commercial considerations.

There are also some well-known directors who have recognized the importance of the box office, but have argued that art films need not be treated as orphaned children. Lu Chuan, the director of *City of Life and Death* (2009), which made RMB 172 million at the Chinese box office, spoke at the same panel as Wang Xiaoshuai. He suggested that it was "an outdated opinion to divide art and commerce. Film first and foremost is a consumption product. Do not try to guide viewers and look down on them from such a lofty position" (Chinadaily.com 2009b). Ning Hao (b. 1977), the director of the commercial hits *Crazy Stone* (2006) and *Crazy Racer* (2009), likewise sees no contradiction between art and commerce, pointing to the necessity of producing a box-office return commensurate with a film's investment.

Questions of distribution and access to the limited number of digital and other reasonably modern screening facilities have become major issues in the development of the Chinese film industry. Although the number of Chinese cinemas has increased from 900 in 2000 to 1,545 in 2009, and the number of screens has gone from 2,000 to 4,097, the screen-to-audience ratio in China is 1:300,000 compared to 1:7,000 in the United States (Chinadaily.com 2009a; *South China Morning Post* 2009). In a fascinating circle of irony, Jia Zhangke has attacked Zhang Yimou's blockbuster films for dominating all the digital screens, Han Sanping has attacked Jia Zhangke for making films no one wants to see, and now Zhang Weiping has launched a tirade against Han Sanping and China Film for using their monopolistic position in the distribution of imported films to favor Hollywood films such as *2012* and *District 9* (Neill Blomkamp, 2009) over Zhang Yimou's most recent release, *A Woman, A Gun and a Noodle Shop* (2009). In noting the more than four thousand screens available in China and the increasing presence of private capital in the industry, China Film spokesperson Weng Li denied the existence of such a monopoly, suggesting that the audience should decide what to see, while sarcastically adding – in a response that Jia Zhangke would no doubt appreciate – that "just because your new film has arrived, you think nothing else should be screened!" (Ent.163.com 2009a, 2009b; Ent.sina.com 2009).

The war of words between Zhang Weiping and China Film indicates the increasing importance that Chinese producers such as Zhang Weiping and Fang Li – the producer of *Lost in Beijing* (Li Yu, 2007) who laughed off his two-year ban on producing films after *Lost* was removed from theaters because the sex scenes deleted from the mainland theatrical version were posted on the Internet – are playing in the cinema industry. It also reveals that the real battles ahead are between heavyweight producers and directors on one side and film bureaucrats on the other, further marginalizing arthouse directors such as Jia and Wang, no matter how artistically accomplished their films might be. Ironically, Han himself has noted that the dearth of successful producers is one of the major reasons for the continuing obstacles to the Chinese film industry reaching maturity (Danwei.org 2009).

An Overview of Chinese Box-Office Data

Examining the Chinese box office provides a useful guide to how films are consumed in China.[4] First, film revenue is generated primarily at the theater chains in large cities. In 2007, 83.8 percent of all urban box-office revenues came from these theater chains, and the number has been on the increase every year. For example, between 2005 and 2007 ticket sales at these theater chains went from RMB 1.6 billion to RMB 2.8 billion. At the same time, ticket sales at theaters in second-level cities and the rural areas only increased from RMB 446 million to RMB 539 million (Chinese Film Distribution and Screening Association et al. 2008). In 2008 the theater chains dramatically increased their revenue to RMB 4 billion, while the increase in second-tier cities only went from RMB 339 million to RMB 341 million. Even more striking, the "brand name" (*pinpai*) theater chains are increasingly monopolizing the market. For example, in 2008 the five leading theater chains in Guangzhou, Shenzhen, Beijing, Shanghai, and Wuhan took in 58.3 percent of all theatrical revenue in the urban areas (*Research Report on Chinese Film Industry* 2009: 62–71, hereafter *Research Report*), and over 37 percent of all theatrical revenue was generated from just Guangdong, Beijing, and Shanghai (J. Liu 2009). If we add Tianjin to the mix, the top ten theater chains were located in just six cities. Disaggregating the data further, in 2007 rural film markets took in only 6 percent of all revenue; a survey in one Anhui province locality found that around a third of primary and secondary school students in the rural areas had never seen a Chinese or Hollywood blockbuster film (Y. Qiu 2008). Moreover, although as many as 406 films were produced in 2008, very few had rural themes (Q. Zhao 2009).

Second, and clearly related to the first point, much of the box office in China is generated by a relatively small number of films. In 2008 the ten most successful domestic and imported films in China's cities brought in 65.7 percent of the box office. The 146 other new films distributed that year – 85.7 percent of the total number of films distributed – brought in 34.6 percent of the box office, with many films going virtually unseen (*Research Report* 2009). In the first half of 2009 the top nine films brought in 55.9 percent of the total box office, with three films – *Red Cliff II* (John Woo), *Transformers II* (Michael Bay), and *City of Life and Death* – far ahead of all the others (L. Fan 2009).

Looking in more depth at the most successful films of all time in the Chinese market – those which made at least RMB 175 million – offers some additional insights into the film market and audience tastes. Table 11.1 presents the 38 films that have reached the RMB 175 million milestone.

First, leaving aside the most obvious hybrid, the coproduction *The Forbidden Kingdom* (Rob Minkoff, 2008), thirteen of the films (35.1 percent) are Hollywood products, including four of the top seven. This appears to mark a change from earlier years when it appeared to some observers that Chinese film authorities had been reluctant to allow Hollywood films to continue in theaters after they reach the RMB 100 million mark, with the exception of "super-blockbusters" such as the Harry Potter, Spiderman, James Bond, Transformers, and Pirates of the Caribbean franchises (Rosen 2006).

Second, the expansion of the box office in recent years is very clear, with the results no longer as heavily driven by one or two blockbuster releases. Of the thirty films that made RMB 200 million, only two were released before 2006, with ten released in 2010, seven released in 2009, and three released in the first few months of 2011. Moreover, the top four films were released in 2010 and the top eight films were from 2009 or 2010. This trend becomes even clearer when we look at number eighteen on the list – *Hero* (Zhang Yimou, 2002) – in the context of other Chinese films that appeared that year. The RMB 250 million *Hero* generated made up

42.2 percent of all Chinese films at the box office in 2002. The top film in 2003, *Cell Phone* (Feng Xiaogang), brought in 33.9 percent of the total box office. By 2004, *House of Flying Daggers* (Zhang Yimou) only brought in 18.6 percent of the total receipts (*Blue Book of China's Media* 2009: 253). Even *Avatar*, a box office bonanza unlikely to be duplicated, only took in 13.5 percent of the total box office in 2010.

Indeed, the relatively lower percentage for *House of Flying Daggers* can be attributed to a recent phenomenon, the production of multiple blockbusters by the Chinese film industry, driven in part by the Closer Economic Partnership Arrangement (CEPA) signed by the governments of the PRC and Hong Kong on June 29, 2003, and implemented in January 2004 (Davis and Yeh 2008: 102–5). Under this arrangement Hong Kong films have been able to enter the mainland market as coproductions without being subject to the quota restrictions under which foreign films are admitted. Thus, in 2002 and 2003, only three of the top ten domestic box-office successes were coproductions with Hong Kong; by 2004 and 2005 that number had risen to six; and in 2006 and 2007 no fewer than nine of the top ten films were coproductions with Hong Kong (R. Hu 2008a).

While *House of Flying Daggers* brought in less than 20 percent of the 2004 box office, the top five films that year brought in 55.7 percent. As the box office has expanded in recent years, along with an increasing number of quality films, these percentages have dropped, although there has been considerable variation each year. In 2005 the top five films brought in 42.1 percent of the box office, roughly equivalent to the 43 percent of 2006. By 2007 that figure had fallen to 34 percent, although the figure for 2008 was 45.4 percent (*Blue Book of China's Media* 2009: 253); by 2010 the figure was back to 35.6 percent, despite *Avatar*'s success. This provides some background to the complaints of Jia Zhangke and other arthouse directors that there are now a continuing series of blockbuster films, marketed one after the other throughout the year, leaving no space for low- and medium-budget films to make it into theaters. From the perspective of a Jia Zhangke, the "debate" between a powerful producer such as Zhang Weiping and the CEO of China Film, Han Sanping, over whether Chinese or Hollywood blockbusters should be promoted and marketed more heavily, is the equivalent of a fight between two elephants. Jia's films, in this analogy, are simply the grass that is being trampled on by both. Ironically, despite this imbalance in favor of the blockbuster films, the number of films being produced continues to get larger. In 1998 China produced only 82 films, but by 2008 that number had risen to 406! Not surprisingly, only around a hundred films were actually released in theaters (Chinadaily.com 2009a–b). But by 2010 the number of film productions had further increased to 526 (H. Liu 2011).

Third, from Table 11.1 we can see which filmmakers have been most successful in the mainland market. Of the fifteen films on the list with mainland directors, Feng Xiaogang had four entries and Zhang Yimou had three, although Zhang just missed with *House of Flying Daggers* (RMB 154 million). They are followed by Hong Kong's John Woo, who has also been successful in Hong Kong and Hollywood,

Table 11.2 The New Year and Anniversary films of Feng Xiaogang

English title	Chinese title	Year	Box office (RMB million)
The Dream Factory	甲方乙方	1997	33
Be There or Be Square	不见不散	1998	43
Sorry, Baby	没完没了	1999	50
A Sigh	一声叹息	2000	30
Big Shot's Funeral	大腕	2002	42
Cell Phone	手机	2003	56
A World without Thieves	天下无贼	2004	120
The Banquet	夜宴	2005	130
Assembly	集结号	2007	260*
If You Are the One	非诚勿扰	2008	314*
If You Are the One II	非诚勿扰II	2010	473.5
Aftershock	唐山大地震	2010	647.8

* The box office figures for *If You Are the One* and *Assembly* in Table 11.1 are somewhat different; see the explanation for such discrepancies in there.

Source: R. Hu (2008b); Y. Luo (2009); http://mtime.com/my/964883/blog/1255510/.

with two films that made over RMB 200 million. The only other "mainland" films that did as well were the two recent "political" films – *The Founding of a Republic* and *The Message* – made to celebrate the sixtieth anniversary of the founding of the PRC, with almost all the remaining Chinese films coproductions which relied heavily on talent from Hong Kong. Feng and Zhang are clearly the most bankable directors in China. Examining all films that have made at least RMB 20 million at the Chinese box office, we find that twelve were directed by Feng and seven were directed by Zhang (Mtime.com 2009; R. Liu 2008; Y. Luo 2009). As Table 11.2 suggests, Feng has been remarkably consistent with his reliability almost every year with a "New Year film," and his steadily increasing totals mirror closely the upward trajectory of the overall Chinese box office.

Government Strategies in the Development of the Chinese Film Industry: State Initiatives and Societal Responses

The co-optation of the Hong Kong film industry through the CEPA agreement is part of a larger strategy that seeks to incorporate Chinese filmmakers from outside the mainland who have achieved an international reputation into the mainland filmmaking orbit. In terms of directors, the most prominent are Ang Lee and John Woo, both of whom have had successful careers and made high-profile films in Hollywood. The success of John Woo's *Red Cliff I–II* (2008, 2009) has been noted above, but the case of Ang Lee is much more intriguing. In particular, the Chinese government's treatment of Lee's NC-17 film *Lust, Caution* reveals the potential dangers of attempting to co-opt someone as independent as Lee. It also provides a convenient window into the role film plays in the evolving state–society relationship, particularly in terms of the options beyond state control now available to China's rising middle class.

A very persuasive case can be made that Ang Lee is the most successful Asian film director in the world, whether measured in terms of international recognition, artistic achievement, breadth of work, or even box-office results. Not only did Lee win an Academy Award as best director for *Brokeback Mountain* (2005), but his Chinese-language film *Crouching Tiger, Hidden Dragon* (2000) garnered the Academy Award for best foreign-language film for 2000 and is still the top grossing foreign-language film ever marketed in the United States, with its US$128 million more than twice as much as the second place film *Life is Beautiful* (Roberto Benigni, 1997) (Rosen 2010). *Crouching Tiger*, however, won the Academy Award as a Taiwan, not a PRC film, although its qualifications as a mainland Chinese film would appear to be stronger.[5] Film authorities in China were therefore less than pleased that the glory of Lee's victory went to Taiwan. When Lee set out years later to do another Chinese-language film, mainland film authorities were eager to cooperate, despite the controversial nature of the original source, a novella of the same title by Zhang Ailing (Eileen Chang). Indeed, Lee was invited to act as an artistic advisor to the opening ceremony of the Beijing Olympics.

Given the explicit and brutal sexual relationship between the two leading characters, *Lust, Caution* earned an NC-17 rating in the United States, with Lee asserting that the graphic sex was crucial to the story and that he would rather the film lost money than be shown in a "compromised" form (Smith 2008). Although the film was shown unedited in Hong Kong and Taiwan, Lee was permitted to edit out seven minutes for the mainland release. After various delays the film opened on November 1, 2007 with four hundred film prints on two hundred digital screens, grossing more than US$5.36 million in its first four days, making it the most successful opening for a Chinese-language film to that point in 2007 (S. Yu 2007). Film journals for professionals in China detailed the reasons for the film's success, noting how such films made by a world-class director, based on a work by a revered novelist, and cast with attractive and marketable stars could serve as a template in producing and marketing future box-office successes. As these articles noted, an important component in this success would be the advance buzz generated when such films garnered major international awards (Z. Fan 2008).[6] And of course the marketing people were correct. *Lust, Caution* ranked third among domestic films at the 2007 box office, and sixth overall, bringing in RMB 138 million.

As is now well known, that was far from the end of the story. In addition to the excised sex scenes, which were being shown outside China, Zhang Ailing's original story, based in part on her brief, unhappy marriage to Hu Lancheng, an intellectual who collaborated with the Japanese-installed puppet regime in early 1940s

Shanghai, placed a traitor as the leading male character and presented him not only in relatively sympathetic terms given his actions, with the role played by Hong Kong superstar Tony Leung, but in addition allowed him to escape punishment while the student revolutionaries seeking to assassinate him were executed for their efforts. The key female character, played by Tang Wei, chose to save her collaborationist lover, thereby betraying the revolution. In retrospect, the release of such a film – it should be remembered that Lee's *Brokeback Mountain* was denied a release because of its gay-oriented theme – was courting disaster.

The reaction was not long in coming and took several forms. First, in a clear indication of the increasing mobility and sophistication of the Chinese public, those who were able to do so simply traveled to Hong Kong to view the uncut version. As one businessman from Guangxi informed a Western reporter, "I went to Hong Kong with my girlfriend to see *Lust, Caution* because it was heavily censored here. We could have bought a pirated copy of the movie … but we were not happy with the control and wanted to support the legal edition of the film" (French 2007). Indeed, the presence of *Lust, Caution* in Hong Kong provided a boost to the local economy. When the Disney representative based in Shanghai noticed the sudden large spike in attendance at their Hong Kong theme park, she was told that the number of mainland tourists had increased because of Lee's film (Rosen 2008b).

Within the mainland the film was a constant topic on the Internet, where the deleted scenes were of course conveniently posted, particularly on various blogs, with the discussion focusing on the nature of love and the issue of patriotism. Bloggers, newspaper critics, and liberal intellectuals generally supported Lee's vision, and he was widely praised by other film directors for revealing the "complicity and immorality of human nature" (V. Wu 2007). One PhD student from the China University of Political Science and Law in Beijing filed a lawsuit against SARFT, seeking an apology and US$90 in "psychological damages" since the failure to implement a rating system that would allow adults to see the film had infringed upon the public's interest. While it was clear that no court would take the case, it was a further embarrassment to the film authorities and was widely reported in the Western press (*New Zealand Herald* 2007). On the other side were those on the "Left," including such well-known cultural and political critics as Wang Xiaodong, who attacked the film for its ideologically unsound theme, its "insult to the good women of China," and its defamation of patriotic students, among other ills (V. Wu 2007).

Given the controversy it was inevitable that the government would act. Reportedly, as is often the case, the trigger was provided by a veteran Communist Party cadre who, during the annual meeting of the National People's Congress, viewed the film on DVD and was disgusted by what he saw as its "glorification of traitors and insult to patriots," complaining to SARFT that the film should never have been exhibited. As a result, several SARFT staff members lost their jobs (Callick 2008). In addition, SARFT quickly "reiterated" and widely publicized censorship guidelines on its website – while claiming that these were not new and stricter regulations – detailing the various types of content that would not be allowed to be shown in films. The guidelines offered points both specific (e.g., "explicit sex") and general (e.g., "distort the civilization of China or other nations"); however, perhaps just to ensure that nothing was left to chance and that self-censorship would play an important role, the last point (number 10) noted that "any other content banned by relevant state laws and regulations must be banned" (Sina.com 2008).

Ongoing calls for a rating system – and the debate was reignited in the after-math of the *Lust, Caution* controversy – that would restrict the audience for such provocative films were rebuffed. As Liu Binjie, the Director of the General Administration of Press and Publications (GAPP) put it: "Under the current circumstances, a film rating system equals legalizing the mass production of pornographic publications" (Chinaview.cn 2008).

In a further act of retaliation, the widely acclaimed female star of the film, Tang Wei, was banned from Chinese awards shows, advertisements, and Web forums as a result of her role. Her name no longer appeared on a Google search on the Internet in China. Unilever, which had signed a "seven-digit," two-year contract with Tang, and had spent a year to prepare their ad campaign for skin-care cream Pond's, was simply informed not to run the commercial, without being given any official notice. Reportedly, staff members at television stations in Beijing and Shanghai were informed of the ban in meetings, but were not shown any official document. Tang herself would not comment on the ban, hoping the storm would blow over (Callick 2008; Macartney 2008; Zhuang and Lai 2008). By early 2009 the ban had apparently been lifted and Tang was working on a new film in Hong Kong, having joined such other A-list mainland performers as actress Zhang Ziyi (b. 1979) and pianists Lang Lang and Li Yundi in becoming Hong Kong residents under the Quality Migrant Admission Scheme (Mak 2009).

This case has been discussed in considerable detail because it so clearly demonstrates the tensions and contradictions among the various goals the state has envisaged for a revived and rising Chinese film industry, particularly at a time when China is actively pursuing the expansion of its soft power around the world in competition with both the Western powers (the United States and Europe) and the East (Japan and South Korea). It also reveals the limitations on the state's control of society as the middle class now has enough knowledge, disposable income, and mobility to seek advanced culture beyond the circumscribed limits set by the PRC.

This case also raises important questions with regard to censorship. One of the key areas under contention in China is the desirability of a rating system. Liu Binjie's views, cited above, are not necessarily representative of the public at large, and even less so of Chinese netizens. In one Internet poll conducted by *China Youth Daily*, 90 percent of the 2,032 respondents supported such a system, with those opposed making up only 6 percent of the sample (X. Wu 2009). More specifically,

34 percent felt that a rating system could protect adolescents and children from violent and sexual content; another 32 percent felt that such a system would be a stimulus to the creativity of filmmakers; and 25 percent thought that it would give theater attendance an important boost. At the same time, 31 percent worried that the film audience lacked the maturity (*suzhi*) to obey the guidelines from the ratings and 24 percent were concerned that it could lead to the legitimacy of sex and violence in films. The debate over a rating system rises periodically and the various arguments have been spelled out in the Chinese media (Xinhuanet. com 2007; Chai 2009).

If *Lust, Caution* is a useful case study of a commercial art film by a world-renowned director, given space one could devote at least as much time to noncommercial art films that have been released in China, albeit subject to censorship, as I have done elsewhere with *Lost in Beijing* (Rosen 2008b), those that were not released theatrically but allowed a DVD release with a number of scenes excised, such as *Blind Shaft* (Li Yang, 2003), and those that have been denied any Chinese release, as with Lou Ye's recent films *Summer Palace* (2006) and *Spring Fever* (2009). Censorship takes many forms and, of course, is not limited to Chinese films. Some of the most successful Hollywood releases have generated extensive discussion in the Chinese media, and others are shown in truncated form or denied any release, owing to sex, violence, or the presentation of a poor image of China or Chinese people.

Because of the extensive debate it generated in the Chinese media – most films that are banned are discussed very briefly if at all – it is useful to address some of the issues that surrounded *Kungfu Panda*, a film that was released in China to great success (Rosen 2008a). While some self-appointed cultural critics objected to an American film about a Chinese cultural treasure, particularly in the aftermath of the Sichuan earthquake, most commentators praised the film and lamented the fact that martial arts and pandas are both national treasures, but a film with the humor and quality of *Kungfu Panda* could never have been made in China, precisely because they were national treasures. As with the controversies over various political decisions made during the Olympics (e.g., the lip-synching incident in which a more attractive young girl was substituted for the actual singer), decisions on panda films are too important to be left to artists and filmmakers; the political authorities would have to ensure that any Chinese film on this subject was appropriately reverent.

Film director Lu Chuan, in bravely defending the film against its detractors such as performance artist Zhao Bendi, who were calling for a boycott of the film, recalled his own negative experience when he was hired in 2006 to produce an animated film for the Olympic Games. He noted how he kept receiving directions and orders on what the film should include. He and his colleagues were given specific rules on how animated films must promote Chinese culture. For Lu, the joy of filmmaking and creating something interesting had been removed; the film was never made (C. Lu 2009). In the end Zhao Bendi, who had claimed victory when *Kungfu Panda* had its Sichuan debut delayed by one day, was openly ridiculed in the Chinese media (H. Li 2008).

In one online survey about *Kungfu Panda* conducted by *China Youth Daily*, around 70 percent of the 2,865 netizens had already seen the film while less than 8 percent said they were not planning to see it. Further, over 62 percent said they liked American animated films and about 46 percent liked the Japanese variety. Only 14 percent liked Chinese animated films, while as many as 82 percent felt that the biggest weakness of the Chinese films was a lack of creativity (Liu and Han 2008). Other surveys comparing Hollywood and Chinese animation have been equally critical.

Conclusion

This chapter has suggested several key themes that mark the development of the Chinese film industry and the impact of that development on the relationship of the state to Chinese society. First, we have seen the growth of an actual "industry" in the Hollywood sense, with the box office taking on an increasingly important role as the arbiter of the success of a film, representing the victory of economics over art. This process has contributed directly to the rise of the film producer as a major player, and the introduction of private investment capital in the financing of a film. Tensions between producers and film bureaucrats have already erupted into open conflicts of interest, publicized in the increasingly market-driven media and spread widely on Chinese blogs. As producers increase their influence, private money pours into the industry, and public opinion continues to be expressed on the Internet, this contradiction is certain to intensify.

Second, this process of commercialization is still evolving and the intrusion of politics into the market continues, entering at several points and in various ways.[7] For example, Chinese leaders remain concerned about the image of the country that is projected domestically, as they seek to maintain social stability, and abroad, as they seek to enhance China's soft power (*Straits Times* 2010). A major effort has been made and considerable funding has been devoted to developing China's cultural industries, including film, and promoting the products of those industries throughout the world. This desire to present China's best face has had an impact on the kinds of films funded, distributed, and promoted domestically and abroad, leaving the more edgy art films to fend for themselves, often at international film festivals. Thus, the economics of the box office and the political goals of the film bureaucrats equally conspire against those who seek to use the film medium for individual creative expression and as a window on China's current realities.

Third, despite the quite remarkable growth of the Chinese box office in recent years, the numbers are still quite small by Hollywood standards. For example, as a leading industry trade paper noted in detailing the "astonishing climb" of the Chinese box office over the last decade, the US$366 million generated in the first half of 2009 was still less than the global tally of the raunchy Hollywood comedy *The Hangover* (Todd Phillips, 2009). While this astonishing climb has continued unabated – indeed, the box office for the Asia Pacific region increased by 21 percent in 2010, and China now accounts for 40 percent of the total – a recent report issued by the Motion Picture Association of America (MPAA) noted that China remains a "highly restricted market for foreign film distribution" (Verrier 2011). However, as always, the potential riches of the China market still beckon (Coonan 2009).

Notes

1   In the first quarter of 2011, the Chinese box office was down 11 percent from the previous year, reflecting the distortions brought about by the success of the 3-D, IMAX film *Avatar*, which represented 46 percent of the total box office for that quarter. Removing *Avatar* from last year's results would show a 65 percent increase instead of a decline.

2   Despite *Cape No. 7*'s record-breaking box-office success in Taiwan, the version released in mainland China was shortened by more than half an hour by censors, so most viewers simply downloaded or purchased street copies of the unedited version. By contrast, *The Warlords* is number 15 on the all-time box-office list at RMB 201.1 million. Respondents could also choose "None of these films" and could write in the names of other films, but neither of these choices had much support. *Lost in Beijing* (Li Yu, 2007), a film banned after a brief showing, also scored well.

3   As the first Chinese film in the Reform era to win a major Western prize, *Red Sorghum* was endlessly praised and attacked in the Chinese media. What was significant, however, was the fact that such a discussion was allowed to take place. Indeed, *People's Daily* (*Renmin ribao* 1988) encouraged such free discussion at a time when, as the newspaper put it, "'letting leaders make a ruling' will never be successful in dealing with theoretical and academic debates."

4   Box-office returns have long been a controversial and complex issue. The results are published in the media, which get them from the film companies. Many insiders note that the figures are inflated and would be much smaller if they came from the theaters (Chinadaily.com 2009d).

5   Indeed, *Lust, Caution* was also submitted as a Taiwan film for Academy consideration but to Lee's disappointment it was rejected since the selection committee ruled that too few of the film's key crew members came from Taiwan for it to be eligible.

6   Among the major awards noted in this article was the Golden Lion at the 64th Venice International Film Festival, presented on September 8, 2007, prior to the film's November 1 opening in China.

7   One typical example of this intrusion occurred at the Fourteenth Beijing College Student Film Festival in 2007 when *The Knot* (Yin Li, 2006) was announced as the best film. According to interviewees, however, *The Knot* was actually the third choice. The first choice had been *Tuya's Marriage* (Wang Quanan, 2006), a film about a Mongolian

woman seeking a new mate to replace her incapacitated husband. However, complaints about the treatment of Mongolian men – most of whom are presented with various deficiencies in the film – compelled the jurors to make an alternate choice. Since the second choice – *Crazy Stone* – had already received a director's award for Ning Hao, the jurors went to their third choice, *The Knot* (Rosen 2008b).

Vulnerable Chinese Stars
From Xizi to Film Worker

Sabrina Qiong Yu

Introduction

Although the transnational trend in film production and distribution in the past decade has to some extent complicated and challenged the definition of national cinema, national cinema remains a powerful term that has continued to be explored and expanded by the teaching of and research into films within different national contexts. By contrast, while scholars started talking about transnational stardom a while ago (Stringer 2003b; Williams 2003; Park 2009), national stardom appears as a less familiar term that has not yet been adequately defined. This is not to deny those valuable contributions to our understanding of stardom in different national cinemas (Vincendeau 2000; Babington 2001; Austin 2003; Perriam 2003; Hayward 2004; Farquhar and Zhang 2010). While the subjects of these books differ, I notice a common agenda; that is, to identify salient features of film stardom in culturally specific contexts, thus mapping out the differences between the star phenomenon in the particular countries and Hollywood stardom, in a way that could be read as a resistance to Hollywood hegemony in the domain of star studies.

However, in all these efforts to explore stardom in national context, not only does Hollywood still remain "the ultimate reference" (Vincendeau 2000: 2), but the theoretical framework based mainly on Hollywood stars and stardom also dominates the discussion of different national stardoms. In other words, despite obvious dissimilarities in each star culture, none of the above-mentioned work has actually challenged fundamental assumptions in star studies, a field pioneered by Richard Dyer's *Stars* in 1979. These assumptions include stars as a phenomenon of production and consumption, the onscreen and off-screen construction of star persona, and the intertransferability between stars' economic power and cultural power. For example, the recent volume *Chinese Film Stars* pays tribute to Dyer's seminal work given that many of its contributors refer to Dyer's scholarship, although the book also strives to "account for non-Western constructions of stardom" (Farquhar and Zhang 2010: 2). Similarly, despite his dissatisfaction with the undifferentiated application of Hollywood-oriented star theories to other cinemas, Bruce Babington (2001: 4) acknowledges that "the institutions of film stardom exhibit major constants running across different film cultures, but each national cinema produces different inflections of them." These "major constants" are obviously derived from Hollywood stardom, as defined by a roster of film scholars (ironically, most of them British). As a result, the study of film stardom in different national cinemas often looks like a study of variations on the theme of Hollywood stardom rather than an effective effort to define national stardom in a distinctive and definitive way.

In this chapter, I will examine Chinese stars and stardom, an area remaining largely under-discussed. Existing academic writing on Chinese stars is almost exclusively in English. Before Farquhar and Zhang's recent expansion of the coverage,[1] the scholarship was focused on a few internationally well-known Chinese male action stars, in particular, Bruce Lee and Jackie Chan, whose national/transnational identity and masculinity have been discussed at length (Gallagher 1997; Tasker 1997; Hunt 2003; Y. Shu 2003). Moreover, apart from a couple of articles on early Chinese female stardom (M. Chang 1999; Hansen 2000), all research surrounds individual Chinese stars, while the phenomenon of Chinese stardom as a whole has received little attention. While I admit that my research on Chinese stars benefits enormously from dominant star theories (to some extent, stardom is a universal phenomenon and does have some similar manifestations in different cultures), one of my agendas here is to challenge some established perspectives in star studies by foregrounding social, political, and cultural specificities in Chinese stardom. By so doing, I wish to help further define national stardom both as a theoretical concept and a research field, which will in turn provide us with a more solid base for understanding transnational stardom.

The Definition of Chinese Stars

While I am fully aware that I am writing a chapter on Chinese stars, I cannot help wondering if I have undertaken an impossible mission. Even a recent book-length anthology (Farquhar and Zhang 2010) can only go some way to address this extremely wide-ranging topic. We can get some ideas about the difficulty of talking about Chinese stardom by comparing the introduction in this anthology with the introductions in a book on French stars/stardom and another one on British stars/stardom. In the latter two introductions, both authors confidently answer the question about what makes French/British stars different from the dominant star images found in Hollywood films by elaborating the distinctive features of French/British stars/stardom, such as the coexistence of mainstream and auteur cinema in a single star's image and the imbrication of theater and film in the French case (Vincendeau 2000: 2); or less secularization, more restrained publicity, and more emphasis on the onscreen image than off-screen personality in the British case (Babington 2001: 6–7). Farquhar and Zhang, however, did not attempt a similar venture in their introduction to Chinese stars. Instead they chose to highlight the diversity and richness of the discussion in their collection by summarizing each contributor's work. Farquhar and Zhang's choice indicates the difficulty of identifying a series of traits that may be shared by Chinese stars, who emerge from such a broad geographic and social terrain.

A closer examination of the fifteen stars discussed in Farquhar and Zhang's book gives a glimpse into the diversity and complexity of Chinese stardom: one Asian-American star who never made a film inside China (Anna May Wong [Huang Liushuang, 1905–61]); two female stars from early Shanghai cinema (Ruan Lingyu [1910–35] and Li Lili, 1915–2005), two male stars who carried their stardom from the Republican era to the socialist period (Mei Lanfang [1894–1961] and Zhao Dan [1915–80]); two socialist red stars (Zhang Ruifang [b. 1918] and Zhong Xinghuo [b. 1924]) who made their name solely within the People's Republic of China (PRC); three Taiwanese stars coming from totally different eras and genres, two of whom are probably quite unknown to mainland Chinese audiences (Ling Bo [b. 1939], Brigitte Lin, and Lee Kang-sheng [Li Kangsheng, b. 1968]); three internationally famed action/kung fu stars (Bruce Lee, Jackie Chan, and Jet Li) (see Figures 12.1, 12.2), and two influential Hong Kong male stars (Chow Yun-fat [Zhou Runfa, b. 1955] and Leslie Cheung [Zhang Guorong, 1956–2003]). Those listed here offer only a small sample of Chinese stars whose stardom was produced within historically, culturally, and politically diverse film industries. In fact, the only thing they share seems to be their ethnicity. Moreover, the fact that a major star in one context could be largely unknown to audiences in another context within a national cinema challenges the fundamental meaning of national stardom. In this sense, then, the term "Chinese star" is just as tricky and elusive as the concept of Chinese cinema, or Chinese identity.

By disclosing the ambiguity of the terminology I am not suggesting we abandon the term "Chinese star" or replace it with a more fashionable appellation such as "pan-Chinese star/stardom." Quite the opposite, I firmly believe that stars are culturally made and that a careful examination of national stardom will deepen our understanding of national cinema and identity. Fully aware of the complexity of national stardom and without being trapped in essentialism, I wish to investigate unique ways of star-making in the Chinese context, and identify some common features of Chinese stardom resulting from a shared cultural heritage and an increasing interdependence between different Chinese film industries. By Chinese stars I mean those stars who established themselves in one of three Chinese film industries (Taiwan,

Figure 12.1 Bruce Lee, an enduring global martial arts icon, in a triumphant pose in *Fist of Fury* (dir. Lo Wei, Golden Harvest, 1972).

Figure 12.2 Jackie Chan as young Wong Fei-hong, training literally under his *shifu* in *Drunken Master* (dir. Yuen Ho-ping, Seasonal Films, 1978).

Hong Kong, and the PRC) as well as those who made their name in Chinese-language films but crossed over to other cinemas, mostly Hollywood. The latter have been labeled transnational Chinese stars, but the discussion of their transnational stardom has to be based on a proper understanding of Chinese stardom.

Star Power versus Star Vulnerability

The book *Chinese Film Stars* opens with a discussion of *Newsweek*'s employment of Chinese star Zhang Ziyi for its cover image ("the face of a new China") to go with a special report, "China's Century," on its May 9, 2005 issue. Zhang become internationally famous after her role in *Crouching Tiger, Hidden Dragon* (Ang Lee, 2000). An article entitled "Invasion of the hot movie stars" in this special report comments that "Zhang and her fellow Chinese filmmakers have added their own artistic accent to American movies, and have helped turn film into China's most powerful cultural export" (Smith 2005: 37). This commentary, together with the way Zhang is used by *Newsweek*, clearly reveals two fundamental functions of stars: to sell the film and to sell the ideology. In the West, especially in Hollywood, these two functions have led to what is called star power.

Francesco Alberoni (1962: 65) once defined stars as the "powerless elite" because their institutional power is very limited or nonexistent and they do not have access to real political power. But many critics have challenged Alberoni's definition by elaborating stars' economic and ideological significance (Dyer 1979; McDonald 2000). "Star power," a term frequently seen in both journalistic writing and academic discussion, is evidenced by the sky-high salaries stars receive, stars' ability to attract investment and audiences, and their control over scripts, casting, or even direction and production. As some critics note, star power has been enhanced by Hollywood's increasing dependence on block-buster, high-concept, and event films since the 1970s (McDonald 2000). By actively participating in all phases of filmmaking, contemporary stars have changed from employees to entrepreneurs, while their names "function as a kind of social currency that feeds news values and sweeps aside social barriers, providing a passkey to popular culture and to elite social circles" (King 2010: 12). Indeed, stars' economic power results in their social impact, as seen in celebrity endorsements, stars' charity work and other social commitments, and in a few cases, the star-turned-activist (e.g., Jane Fonda [b. 1937], Richard Gere [b. 1949]) or the star-turned-politician (e.g., Arnold Schwarzenegger [b. 1947], Clint Eastwood [b. 1930]). It becomes common that stars use their star power to "raise consciousness, open up public space, generate debates and embody people's ambitions" (Nayar 2008: 101).

On the other hand, star power is often put into doubt by such questions as "have we exaggerated star power?" or "to what extent does a star guarantee the profit?" Martin Barker (2003: 9) even predicts the decline of star power in an era when the increasing emphasis on special effects and the rise of the director–superstar might be "challenging the privileged position of stars." Despite this kind of suspicion, star power has undeniably provided vital momentum to the development of Hollywood cinema. However, one needs to be careful in applying this term to the discussion of Chinese stardom. Zhang Ziyi was used by the American press to represent China's rise as a new superpower in the new century, but her star image in China might not have similar currency. I do not wish to deny the economic and ideological significance of Chinese stars in the Chinese context. What I argue, though, is that stars' economic and ideological importance does not necessarily turn into star power, and in China's case it has in fact largely contributed to what I term star vulnerability. In the following pages, I will discuss Chinese stars' vulnerability across different areas, from the ways they are referred to throughout film history, to their reception *vis-à-vis* traditional morality, and their position within a very particular political environment.

Stars as *Xizi* and Film Workers

It seems appropriate to begin my investigation of Chinese stars by looking at what stars mean in the Chinese context, in contrast to other cultures. As many critics (Morin 1961; Dyer 1979) note, in early Hollywood and European cinemas, film stars achieved godlike status and were "marked with an aura of impenetrable mystery, and endowed with extraordinary gifts and superhuman powers" (Hollinger 2006: 28). This might still be the case in contemporary Indian cinema where stars' "immortality" is circulated in the public sphere (Nayar 2008: 95). In the Italian context, although lacking in power or authority, stars have been perceived as "a true elite which occupies a central place in a community of an industrialized kind" (Alberoni 1962: 69). Modern Hollywood stars are probably more like mortals, but they are still associated with such terms as "talent," "charisma," "extraordinariness," and "heroism," which denote qualities fans admire and wish to identify with.

Chinese stars have never reached such a high social position as their Indian or American counterparts, nor can they be categorized as a cultural elite as in Italy. In China, film stars have long been associated with popular/low culture and their social position has often been poorly regarded throughout the history of Chinese cinema. The low status of Chinese film stars finds its origin in the long-standing contempt for acting/entertainment as a "mean occupation" (*jianye*) in a traditional Confucian society. As Weikun Cheng (1996: 204) reveals, actors occupied the "lowest social position, along with slaves and prostitutes." Until the first half of the twentieth century, actors were mainly referred to as *xizi* in

Chinese (its closest English translation might be "cheap entertainer"), in a clearly derogatory tone. An anecdote told by the first female star from early Chinese cinema, Wang Hanlun (1903–78), provides a bitter testimony of a xizi's humble status. Wang recalled her battle with her family after signing a contract with a film company. Her brother and sister-in-law were indignant with her decision and scolded her: "In the past, xizi were not even allowed to sit on the chair when they came to our house. But now you chose to become a xizi. This is such a disgrace to our ancestors!" Wang had to break with her family and change her surname in order to continue pursuing her acting career (H. Wang 1956: 59). Wang's experience was echoed by other early stars such as Chen Yanyan (1916–99). This deep-rooted cultural bias against actors in Chinese society defined early Chinese stardom in a poignant way.

It was not until the mid-1920s that actors started becoming public figures in Chinese society, when "film magazines and trade publications regularly featured comments on screen acting" (Farquhar and Zhang 2010: 5). The term *mingxing* (bright star) was introduced to the Chinese public as a new appellation for actors, especially for actresses. However, despite this less humiliating, more glorified new title, Chinese actors' social status was not improved much from being a xizi. On the one hand, they were exploited as money-making machines for film companies while they received very little pay and were treated badly (H. Wang 1956; Xuan 1956); on the other hand, they were disdained in public discourse as people without professional skills, who became stars solely because of their sex appeal (X.Dai 1996: 928). As Michael Chang (1999: 129) notes, "during the late 1920s a negative discourse emerged to delegitimize upwardly mobile actresses, and notoriety became the sibling of celebrity." Huang Zongying (b. 1925), an actress from the 1940s, comments on the short and miserable life of Zhou Xuan (1920–57), a famous female star from the same era: "in that era, many actresses had a similar fate to Zhou's; they committed suicide, went mad, died from disease or poverty, died on the street as beggars" (Z. Huang 1957: 79–80). Such a fate befell Ai Xia (1912–34), Ruan Lingyu, Yang Naimei (1904–60), and Zhang Zhiyun (1904–197?), who were all celebrated female stars at that time. Huang's words reveal a collective tragedy for early Chinese female stars, a fate that might be hard to relate to a group of people called stars in other cultures.[2]

It seems clear that Chinese stars were born into misfortune. In fact, from the very beginning, there was a strong bias against the term "star" in Chinese society, a bias that probably originated from its humble association in traditional Chinese culture and its obvious Western origin. The conscious rejection of the concept of star/stardom has become a prominent trait that characterizes socialist stardom in the PRC. Writing on the socialist red star Zhang Ruifang, Xiaoning Lu (2010: 98) rightly points out that "in the Mao era when the socialist ideology prevailed, the very word 'star' fell out of fashion in everyday speech. 'Star' carried a spectrum of negative connotations: corrupted lifestyle, loftiness, individualism and liberalism, all of which originate from the same source, capitalism." Similarly, Krista Hang

(2010: 108) speculates that "the term 'film star' conjures up associations of luxury, fame and leisure that seem to contradict much communist ideology." Since the establishment of the PRC in 1949, Chinese actors, whether known or unknown, have been given a new name – "film worker." This title removed the glamour that was attached to the stars before 1949 and put actors into the same, if not a lower, category as other professions, such as factory, educational, and medical workers. In the Mao era, the peasantry and the working classes were glorified and represented progression and leadership in society while film actors undoubtedly belonged to the backward bourgeoisie, and therefore needed to be helped and transformed. The term "film worker" is an overt rejection of film stars as exceptional, mysterious beings and reflects the party-state's effort to cut off film stars' capitalistic connection and remold them into socialist citizens. Until at least the late 1980s film workers still received salaries similar to those in other professions and their mission was to promote socialist ideology in such a way as to simultaneously entertain and educate audiences. As Xiaoning Lu (2010: 99) observes, "the designation of film workers helped reconceptualize the relation between the star and the spectator: encouraging intimate camaraderie between the star and the spectator rather than spectators' craze for the star." Indeed, given the demystification of film stardom and the identification of acting as part of socialist labor, the star–audience relationship in a socialist society can be very different from the one in capitalist commercial cultures.

Throughout Chinese film history the title of "star" has carried a disparaging implication and even at times become a reason for persecution during political movements such as the Cultural Revolution (1966–76). No wonder many Chinese actors chose to deny this title publicly. For example, in her reply to an audience letter in *Mass Cinema*, Zhang Yu (b. 1957), a famous female star of the 1980s, declared: "I never consider myself as a so-called 'star,' neither in the past, nor in the future. I even hate this term derived from the Western star system as I have never benefited from it; it only brought me misunderstanding and trouble" (Y. Zhang 1984). Zhang would probably be pleased if she was called "film/acting artist" (*dianying/biaoyan yishujia*), a title used by the state to praise excellent film workers, a far more respectful title than "star" within socialist China. For many years, the term "star" actually disappeared from public discourse in the PRC until it came back in the mid-1980s. However, "film worker" as a heavily politicized title for actors has been carried into the new century and remains in official use, whereas "star" is more often used in the popular media.

From this examination of the terms "xizi" and "film worker," two appellations imposed on Chinese film stars during two different eras (the Republican era before 1949 and the socialist era after 1949), we can see how vulnerability is an inherent part of Chinese stardom from its origins and expressed through its designation. We will now turn to another aspect of this vulnerability: stars' paradoxical position as morally suspect, yet publicly expected to conform to rigorous standards of behavior.

Stars as Moral Victims

In many cultures, while on the one hand stars are seen as role models, on the other hand, they have more leeway when it comes to moral evaluation. Based on experimental research, Alberoni (1962: 71) argues that "the moral evaluation of the stars is more 'indulgent' than that reserved by the public for those who are socially nearer to them" due to the fact that "they are not judged institutionally responsible for the results of their actions on the community." While this statement might be true within an Italian or American context, it is certainly not the case for Chinese stars. I will start my discussion of the moral construction of Chinese stars with a well-known star scandal that occurred recently in Hong Kong. In January and February 2008, some sexually explicit photos showing Hong Kong star Edison Chen with a number of women – including two famous female stars, Gillian Chung and Cecilia Cheung – were released online. Millions of Internet users based in Hong Kong and the mainland clicked to view the photos and posted comments. The Hong Kong media were overwhelmed by the phrase *yanzhao men* (sex photo scandal) and the police had to intervene and investigate the source of these photos.

What is relevant here is the impact of the scandal on the three stars involved. Edison Chen (Chen Guanxi, b. 1980) held a press conference to make public apologies to all the women affected and the people of Hong Kong as "this matter has deteriorated to the extent that society as a whole has been affected by this." At the same time, he announced his departure from the Hong Kong entertainment industry indefinitely. Gillian Chung (Zhong Xintong, b. 1981) was attacked by angry fans who felt deceived by her "innocent" star image. Although she also apologized to the public for being "naive and silly," her subsequent television appearance in a disaster relief charity event triggered over 1,400 audience complaints. Consequently, her other promotional activities were cancelled and her scenes in an eagerly anticipated film, *Forever Enthralled* (Chen Kaige, 2008), were deleted. Before her recent attempts to return to the screen, Chung had withdrawn from public life for more than a year and later confessed to having contemplated suicide. Another affected star, Cecilia Cheung (Zhang Baizhi, b. 1980), is also famous for her "innocent" screen image and had just given birth to her first son when the scandal broke. Rumors about her marriage frequently hit the headlines in those months and she has disappeared from the screen since then (only recently returning to public attention because of the birth of her second son).[3] This photo scandal, then, almost ended the careers of three promising young stars, and the public does not seem to have forgotten what happened or forgiven them even after two years.

It is instructive to mention the response of a British/European group to the photo scandal. When I asked my students to discuss it in class, they felt quite puzzled by the damage the scandal caused for the stars involved and said that a similar scandal would have boosted a Hollywood/European star's career.[4] This interesting contrast reveals a defining feature of Chinese stardom, that is, moral construction. Although moral judgment of stars does exist in other film cultures (e.g., Ingrid Bergman [1915–82] was denounced by Hollywood for seven years after the exposure of her affair with Italian director Roberto Rossellini [1906–77] in 1950), it is probably only in Chinese cinema that moral rigor has constantly played such a conspicuous role in star construction. It is rather surprising to see the Hong Kong public's reaction to the photo scandal and the stars involved in what is perceived as a postmodern metropolitan city. However, this public boycott reflects a long-standing moral ambiguity in Chinese society toward movie stars, that is, low moral evaluation and high moral expectation. As a result of this ambiguity, social tolerance of star behavior is extremely low, especially compared with other cultures. This moral ambiguity is so deep rooted that it has crossed historical, geographical, and political boundaries and is manifested in different Chinese contexts from the past to the present.

In Chinese cultural history, actors or entertainers were not only placed at the bottom of society, but have also long been associated with an immoral lifestyle. A famous Chinese saying, "a prostitute is heartless; a xizi is shameless" (*biaozi wuqing, xizi wuyi*), clearly equates actors with prostitutes. In imperial China, stage actors usually served to entertain elite customers such as aristocrats, bureaucrats, and wealthy merchants and were often kept by them. In return for male patronage, actors had to provide companionship or sexual favors.[5] As Weikun Cheng (1996: 205) argues, the popular identification of actors with prostitutes was widely accepted in Chinese society and did not change through the early twentieth century when people believed that women entertainers were essentially sex workers. This impression was presumably reinforced by the fact that many actresses (both stage and screen) were former prostitutes. Stage actresses in early twentieth-century Beijing and Tianjin were reportedly regarded as "rootless drifters – degenerate, undisciplined, and immoral" (W. Cheng 1996: 204). Similarly, in his research on public discourses on female movie stars of the 1920s and 1930s, Michael Chang (1999: 129) notes that the prevalent notion in 1920s Shanghai was "that movie actresses were nothing more than prostitutes in disguise," and therefore were "categorically characterized as degenerate, corrupted, and deceptive 'starlets' – amateurs who, like prostitutes, were morally and sexually suspect." Both Cheng and Chang's research shows that moral stigma has been attached to Chinese film stars from the outset, while at the same time it points to a significant gender shift in this long-standing cultural bias: it is mainly Chinese actresses, rather than actors, whose moral character came to bear the brunt of the attack.

Moral suspicion and concomitant moral surveillance have haunted Chinese stars since the birth of Chinese cinema and are manifested in different forms at different historical moments and social contexts. The disdain for early female stars and the censure of three contemporary Hong Kong stars involved in a photo scandal only provide a glimpse into this moral severity, which can be seen most clearly in the "grand tradition" of Chinese stars – suicide. It is hard to list all the Chinese film stars who have committed suicide, but by discussing the two most famous ones, Ruan Lingyu and Leslie Cheung, I hope to illustrate the way that moral pressure has shaped Chinese stardom.

Ruan and Cheung, respectively from early Shanghai cinema and late twentieth-century Hong Kong cinema, are probably the two stars in Chinese film history who most convincingly attest to Samuel Goldwyn's declaration that "God makes the stars" (Dyer 1979: 16), with their outstanding acting talent and matchless star charisma. Ruan is acknowledged as "the greatest star of the Chinese silent film era" (Hjort 2010: 32) and Cheung is seen as "the most widely adored and admired male diva of the late twentieth century" (Corliss 2003). Moreover, both stars enjoy a posthumous fandom that has been constantly reproduced around the world and has made them into legendary figures. Research on Ruan and Cheung has focused on Ruan's image as a suffering Chinese woman and Cheung's transgressive gender image (M. Chang 1999; Y. Wang 2007; Hjort 2010; Stringer 2010). Critics also identify "vicious gossip" from the tabloids as a major reason behind both stars' suicide (C. Cai 1957; F. Luo 2009). Here, I would like to further suggest that vicious gossip, as a salient variation of moral surveillance, not only contributed to their suicide, but also to the construction of their star image in an incisive way.

Ruan Lingyu's star persona is a mixture of her on-screen tragic image as an injured and oppressed Chinese woman living in semifeudal and semicolonial society and her off-screen personality as a miserable and unfortunate movie actress. Many critics suggest that Ruan's portrayal of those tragic roles and her approach to "living the role" benefited enormously from her own bitter life experience (J. Zheng 1957: 32–3; Hjort 2010: 39). To put it another way, while Ruan seems to play herself (the incarnation of the suffering Chinese woman) again and again, her famous screen roles almost foretell her final self-destruction. Ruan's miserable personal life, resulting from her humble origins and troubles with bad men, was exacerbated by her status as a female star in the 1930s. Although her complicated relationship with two abusive men aroused lots of sympathy after her death, she was ruthlessly attacked by the media at the time and described as an immoral and shameless woman who left her husband to live with another richer man. Ruan certainly put her real-life frustration into her final film role in *New Woman* (Cai Chusheng, 1934), in which she portrayed an actress who committed suicide to escape from social pressure triggered by vicious gossip. Ruan killed herself soon after the release of this film. Like many others, Michael Chang (1999: 156) speculates that "Ruan's reasons for committing suicide were ultimately tied to her fear of being stigmatized as an immoral woman."

Despite being a male star living in modern society, Leslie Cheung similarly suffered from the pressure of media reports and public opinion (see Figure 12.3). On the one hand, Cheung displayed probably the greatest courage of all Chinese stars to overtly challenge society's moral norms by becoming the first major Chinese star to play a gay role on screen, to publicly declare his long-term gay relationship, and to wear red lipstick and red high-heels on stage. On the other

Figure 12.3 Leslie Cheung as a sentimental, moody playboy in *Days of Being Wild* (dir. Wong Kar-wai, In-Gear Film, 1990).

hand, Cheung tried hard to protect himself from moral surveillance by shutting the door of his personal life on the media and outer world. As Julian Stringer (2010: 211) observes, Cheung placed great emphasis on the importance of privacy throughout his career. While this aspect of his off-screen personality retains some narcissistic connotations and corresponds to his onscreen narcissist image, it also shows Cheung's intention to prevent his homosexual orientation from being disclosed by Hong Kong tabloids (a secret he kept until a few years before his death). His relationship with the media reached its nadir when his bold and unorthodox gender performance during his concert series in 1997 provoked the Hong Kong media and resulted in overwhelming criticisms and personal attacks. Whether or not this vicious gossip contributed – as many tend to believe – to his depression and suicide is debatable, but what is certain is that Cheung's lifelong negotiation with the moral pressure he felt from society helps construct an important aspect of his star persona: aloof, mysterious, and narcissistic.

The moral censure imposed on Ruan reflects a deep-rooted moral suspicion of actresses, as well as patriarchal society's fear of moral deviation or degeneracy caused by women's rise to fame via film. As Hjort (2010: 360) argues, "While revolutionary efforts created new opportunities for women, regressive energies easily cast women who pursued the new opportunities as ready targets for social opprobrium." The moral rigor placed on Cheung was triggered by his endeavor to blur gender boundaries through his on-stage and on-screen gender performance, and to legitimate homosexuality by playing a gay role both on-screen and off-screen. Both stars were punished for their perceived gender transgressiveness that went beyond the moral tolerance of their respective times. Interestingly, both

Ruan and Cheung gained understanding and forgiveness from the public after their suicides: while the vicious tabloids and the two abusive partners in her life were identified as the murderers of the innocent Ruan, Cheung's same-sex relationship with Mr. Tang was finally accepted (or at least acknowledged) by his fans and the Hong Kong media. One cannot help wondering, had Ruan and Cheung not committed suicide, would their deviation from patriarchal and heterosexual norms have been forgiven eventually? The answer might be no if we consider how the society in which they lived was marked by moral rigidness and a tabloid press functioning as moral surveillance. In this sense, suicide seems to provide an effective way for those morally suspect Chinese stars to redeem their endangered morality and even to become legends like Ruan and Cheung, if they are lucky enough.

After investigating Chinese stars' moral vulnerability in Republican China and postmodern Hong Kong, it would be remiss of me not to mention the moral construction of stardom in the socialist PRC. Indeed, in the latter, moral scrutiny can only be harsher, as in addition to carrying a moral burden from traditional Confucian society, stars in the PRC are also censored by Communist/socialist moral standards. A recent volume reveals that a notable feature of China's celebrity culture is "the high value placed on attributes such as public propriety, group orientation, academic achievement, resilience and thrift" (Jefferys and Edwards 2010: 17). As the editors state, between 1949 and 1979 "the celebrities in the PRC were heroes and models, promoted by the party-state to propagandize socialist ideology and moral guidance. Films stars, judged by their origin and commercial nature, were not usually perceived to have this function." In fact, as discussed earlier, there were no film stars in the PRC during that period but rather film workers, a group of people whose morality was often perceived as quite problematic, therefore requiring constant surveillance.

After the end of the Mao era, the term "star" gradually came back into public discourse, though with great suspicion. In the 1980s and the first half of the 1990s, when the mass media and Internet were not as dominant and tabloid culture was still in its infancy in the PRC, stars' off-screen lives did not receive as much media attention as nowadays. However, from the limited media exposure of stars' private lives at that time, we can sense a "preoccupation with moral virtue" (Jefferys and Edwards 2010: 17), or more precisely, with *female* stars' moral virtue. The "good woman" image is a guarantee of star appeal while any deviation from moral norms on women's behavior would bring censure. For example, in the 1980s, quite a few female stars – including Shen Danping (b. 1960), Gong Xue (b. 1953), and Joan Chen (Chen Chong, b. 1959) – were criticized or even despised for their personal choice to go overseas to study or get married. In some media reports they were accused of a loss of self-respect and a disregard of their social responsibility for domestic audiences (ZDTBW 2006: 642). Shen Danping, who is married to a German, had to defend herself by emphasizing that "actors are also human and deserve love and marriage" (J. Ye 1985). Female chastity is another persistent moral standard that the Chinese public uses to judge female stars. Unfaithfulness or getting involved in another's marriage is an absolute moral blemish that could damage or even destroy a Chinese female star's career, as we have already seen in the cases of Ruan Lingyu in the 1930s. This situation has changed little, as we see from the cases of mainland star Gong Li in the 1980s, and Taiwan star Yi Nengjing (Annie Shizuka Inoh, b. 1969) in the new century.

However, moral fastidiousness in the PRC toward stars is probably best manifested in the media's constant demonization of Liu Xiaoqing (b. 1951), one of the very first stars of PRC cinema. During the past three decades, Liu has been a controversial figure due to her bold and unconventional behavior: as the first PRC star to publish an autobiography (titled *My Way*), in which she delivers the famous line "to be a famous single woman, the difficulty is beyond our imagination"; as the first star to launch herself into business and to become China's first female billionaire;[6] and as the first movie star to have a much-publicized divorce in the PRC. Liu's blunt honesty, unhidden ambition, narcissistic individualism, open attitude toward love and marriage, and uncompromising personality all conflict with moral definitions of a good woman in Chinese society. Not surprisingly, Liu has been dogged by scandalous media reports throughout her career. Her relationships, her acting, her business, her personality, even her lasting youthful look, have unexceptionally become the targets of media attack. In mainland public discourse, Liu is constructed as a powerful woman who is domineering and overly aggressive. Despite winning more acting awards than any other mainland actor, and despite her achievements in diverse fields (on-screen, on-stage, business), consistent negative media coverage of Liu's off-screen persona has effectively counterbalanced the social impact her subversive star image might have made, and has to a large extent delegitimized her star status. With a totally different star persona, Liu nevertheless seems to be repeating the fate of her predecessors from the early Chinese cinema: her stardom is accompanied by notoriety and she suffers from her success. Bérénice Reynaud (1993: 24) once observed of Gong Li that "the combination of glamour and tragedy is not a new concept for the female star of Chinese cinema." Judging by Liu's situation, we can see that it is not an outdated concept in twenty-first-century China.

Another example – that of Zhang Ziyi, *Newsweek*'s symbol of China's rising power – serves to further demonstrate the continuing role of moral fastidiousness in significantly shaping Chinese stardom. In early 2010 Zhang was embroiled in a so-called *zajuan men* (false donation scandal); she declared she had donated RMB 1 million for Sichuan earthquake relief in May 2008, but it was discovered that the actual donation was RMB 840,000. Although she publicly apologized and made up the shortfall, Zhang received angry criticisms nationwide for her untrustworthiness. Her already much-criticized star image was further damaged by the scandal. Without getting into more details, I suggest that what Zhang and other Chinese stars have experienced, as elaborated above, clearly attests to Chinese stars' vulnerability in face of moral surveillance, no matter how famous they are or how strong their star persona may be.

Stars as Political Subordinates

Let us now turn to the question of stars' vulnerable position within the Chinese political context. In 2009 a film entitled *The Founding of a Republic* (Han Sanping, Huang Jianxin) was released in mainland China and Hong Kong in celebration of the 60th anniversary of the People's Republic of China. Quite unusual for a propagandist leitmotiv film, it achieved box-office success and became the most profitable Chinese film ever. However, what is more intriguing about this film is that it provides an excellent case study of Chinese stardom. The film spectacularly recruited 172 A-list Chinese stars from all over the world (including a few prestigious film directors).[7] Within its 135 minutes of running time, most of these stars make such a brief appearance that they could be easily missed. Despite its all-star cast, the film kept to its modest budget because all the stars offered to waive their fees. Reportedly, many Hong Kong male stars competed for a role in this film, while Chinese netizens were keen to find out which big stars have been missed out from the list. Apparently, taking part in *The Founding of a Republic* was seen as an honor and important acknowledgment for Chinese stars. Even Hong Kong superstar Stephen Chow (Zhou Xingchi, b. 1962), well-known for his unruly and arrogant personality, publicly voiced his concern about not being invited to play a role in this film, which might put his star influence in doubt (Wangyi Entertainment 2009a).

This unprecedentedly heavy employment of stars seemingly confirms a commonplace practice – stars are used to sell a film – which is certainly true. It is likely that many Chinese audiences went to watch the stars more than to see a cliché-ridden propagandist film. Some audiences admitted that they were so busy counting the stars that they missed dialogue and plot (Wangyi Entertainment 2009b). However, taking a closer look at this case, one can ask if it would be possible to find another film in any other national cinema involving 172 stars who were all willing or even competing to play a small supporting part for free. What was their motivation to be involved in this film, if it is not commercial incentive? Existing star theory based on the Hollywood star system would be inadequate to explain such a phenomenon. In a discussion of the socialist red star, Xiaoning Lu (2010: 97–8) questions the assumption that movie stars are by-products of the industrial practices of Hollywood and the like, and emphasizes the importance of studying stardom in historically specific China. Indeed, the process of star-making in a highly politicized, nondemocratic country could be very different from that in a democratic, commercial world such as the United States and Europe.

The relationship between stars and politics is a fascinating but complicated topic and needs to be examined carefully against different social systems. Stars may often reinforce dominant values and reconcile social conflicts (Dyer 1979), but there are also sufficient examples in film history where stars did not advocate or even opposed the dominant ideology. Generally speaking, in a democratic society, stars' economic capital is more easily transformed into social capital. Pramod Nayar (2008: 102) argues that celebrity intervention in the political realm "makes for a degree of democratization when the celebrity opens up the space of the debate precisely by virtue of being a celebrity." Stars can use their star charisma to influence public opinion on certain issues, and thus function as a "crucial component of the practices of democratic representation" (Nayar 2008: 101). However, in a nondemocratic country like the PRC, film stars' economic strength does not usually lead to enhancement of their social and political status, since "the enormous presence of a star indicates a type of social influence that was inconsistent with dominant political interests, and thus the need for its co-option" (Zou 2010: 72). In the PRC, only the party-state enjoys absolute power that is beyond challenge from any other type of power. In such a context, then, it seems more relevant to discuss how Chinese stardom has been shaped and to a large extent produced by the party-state.

As Louise Edwards (2010: 21) points out, "a key aspect of celebrity and fame production in China is the extensive involvement of the Party-state.... In the PRC, the Chinese government is a key player in the cultural industries sector." Some interesting research has been done on socialist stardom between 1949 and 1979: Yingjin Zhang (2010d) suggests Zhao Dan's stardom is integrated with martyrdom in socialist Chinese cinema; Xiaoning Lu (2010: 100) asserts that "red stars" reflect "the relationship between a wider management of propaganda and cultural production in socialist China." Indeed, as Krista Hang (2010: 110) contends, "during the phase of socialist realist cinema, actors were no longer associated with commercial products; their images were fixed solidly on the level of political discourse." It might be safe to suggest that socialist stardom is made by the party-state rather than the commercial machinery of film studio and popular media. A story from 1962 nicely supports this statement. Following instructions from Prime Minister Zhou Enlai and approval by the Ministry of Culture, the portraits of 22 Chinese film actors were hung in all Chinese cinemas as a way of acknowledging "our own stars." Two years later, the pictures were taken down due to a changed political environment, the Rectification Movement of Literature and Art in 1964 (ZDTBW 2006: 384).

The party-state has continued to play a significant role in the construction of Chinese stars during the postsocialist era, an era characterized by its socialist ideology and capitalist economy. A report in 2005 (ZDTBW 2006: 890) is illustrative of this point:

> On 28 December, the commemoration conference for the centenary of Chinese cinema was held in the Great Hall of the People in Beijing. President Hu Jintao met the delegates and gave an important speech. He encouraged film workers around the country to plunge into reality and the masses to experience life ... and to produce more masterpieces that combine ideological content, artistic quality and enjoyability, and make a new contribution to the building of a well-off society and the revitalization of the Chinese nation.... Fifty film workers were rewarded as "distinguished film artists" during the conference.

This short report reveals some crucial features of star construction in the PRC, although we do not see the actual term "star." Firstly, the appellation of "film worker," the venue of the conference (the Great Hall of the People as a symbol of Chinese politics) and a speech given by the President all indicate that stardom in the PRC is a highly politicized phenomenon rather than a mere phenomenon of production and consumption as in a consumer society. Secondly, Hu's speech clearly instructs that the correct way of becoming a star in the PRC is by "plunging into real life" so as to "produce masterpieces," which differs from usual star-making mechanisms in other film cultures. "Experiencing life" is a standard and highly regarded practice in the PRC cinema. In order to faithfully portray a character, actors are often required to live like that character in real life for months. For example, before successfully playing an oculist in *They Are in Love* (Qian Jiang, Zhao Yuan, 1980), famous 1980s male star Da Shichang (b. 1940) went to work with oculists in Beijing Tongren Hospital for a while (Q. Zhang 1980: 29); in order to play the rural women Jiuer in *Red Sorghum* (1987) and Qiu Ju in *The Story of Qiu Ju* (1992), two Zhang Yimou-directed roles that made Gong Li an internationally reputed star, she had to live in the countryside as a way of getting into the role before the filming. A call for "plunging into real life" on the one hand reflects traditional acclaim for naturalistic and realistic acting in Chinese cinema, and on the other hand shows the government's intention to highlight acting as labor rather than a manifestation of talent.[8] After all, outstanding talent and personal charisma implied in the concept of star are highly incompatible with unrivaled party-state power and a socialist ideology that advocates collectivism, thereby creating a need for the stars to be contained and transformed. The emphasis on "producing masterpieces" shows a similar effort to confine star influence to the screen.

President Hu's advice to film workers betrays the nature of PRC stars as propagandistic icons. Since the establishment of the PRC, film has been seen as an important tool of indoctrination and propaganda (ZDTBW 2006: 349) and film stars are part of this ideological mechanism. In the postsocialist period, with the emergence of commercial cinema, film stars' propagandistic function has been toned down but it would be wrong to assume it has completely disappeared. While Chinese people's belief in both the socialist/communist ideal and the party are largely in crisis, the country has seen a nationalist trend with the promotion of loyalty to the nation-state. As Jefferys and Edwards (2010: 16) observe, celebrity culture in the PRC is "embedded within a CCP-led nationalist project that encourages public pronouncements of unabashed patriotism, irrespective of whether such statements are made genuinely, ironically or with a pragmatic eye on sales."

Indeed, "patriotism" (*aiguo*, literally "loving the nation") has become a basic criterion Chinese actors have to meet if they want to establish their stardom in the PRC. It is extremely important for a Chinese star to keep "political correctness" in order to win approval from both the PRC government and audiences. The usual ways of achieving this include starring in a propaganda film, as seen from the case of *The Founding of a Republic*, participating in government-sponsored public events such as the annual Spring Festival evening party, and involvement in charity activities such as making donations in the event of natural disasters. For Hong Kong and Taiwan stars, it is even more important to package themselves as patriotic stars in order to consolidate their star status and expand their fan base in the mainland. Jackie Chan stands as a remarkable example in terms of successfully incorporating patriotism into his star image by overtly promoting Chinese nationalism and supporting official ideology. For a Taiwan star, the best way of doing so is by publicly rejecting the idea of Taiwan's independence and favoring the official advocacy of reunification. On the other hand, any action perceived as not demonstrating loyalty to country would become an ineradicable stigma for a Chinese star, as shown in the recent controversy over some Chinese stars' actual nationality. When transnational Chinese stars Gong Li and Jet Li took on Singapore nationality one after the other, many angry netizens accused them of betraying their country. Consequently, Gong Li's name disappeared from the member list of the National Committee of the Chinese People's Political Consultative Conference (CPPCC), a political honor very few Chinese movie stars had ever enjoyed, while Jet Li had to provide a public explanation of the reasons behind his change of nationality to regain public trust. It thus can be argued that "loving the nation" has become an increasingly visible state strategy of constructing Chinese stars as propagandistic icons, a strategy that is co-implemented by the Chinese public.

Finally, the rewarding of "fifty distinguished film artists" at the commemoration conference for the centenary of Chinese cinema attests once again that political recognition is an effective way to boost stars' social status, and that the party-state continues to play a big role in star-making, as in the socialist era. Even though Chinese film has tried to gear itself to international standards in many respects over the past two decades, its star system is still very different from the one in Hollywood or in other national cinemas, in that stars are not only produced by the film industry, mass media, and audiences, but more conspicuously, by the party-state. The government can arbitrarily use its administrative power to intervene in the economic rules of star production so as to make or eliminate a star, often through the State Administration of Radio, Film, and Television (SARFT), a branch responsible for censoring films, filmmakers, and stars. One recent example of this power is the blacklisting of Tang Wei, a first-time movie actress who rose to stardom overnight due to her excellent performance in the wartime epic *Lust, Caution* (Ang Lee, 2007). The film was a box-office triumph and enjoyed critical acclaim in the mainland, Hong Kong, and Taiwan, while at the same time its sexually explicit scenes (deleted in the mainland-release version) and Tang's character's illicit love for a traitor stirred overwhelming debates in PRC media and on the Internet. While people were expecting Tang to become China's next big star, a sudden and apparently secret order from the authorities, banning the actress from making public appearances and acting in any future mainland-produced films, removed Tang from the screen for two years before she was finally able to return to her acting career in 2010, having adopted Hong Kong citizenship. SARFT did not even bother to provide an official explanation of its decision and left audiences baffled and lamenting Tang's fleeting stardom.

Tang's case acutely reveals that in China box-office success and audience admiration do not always make a star. In the face of a powerful party-state, stars are extremely vulnerable. Political capital might enhance stars' economic power, but the reverse is not true. In fact, Chinese stars have been deprived of the possibility of having any political influence by strictly submitting to state power, since the economic and professional consequences of not doing so are unbearable. The increasing involvement of Chinese stars (including those from Hong Kong and Taiwan) in the promotion of mainstream ideology in recent years demonstrates clearly the vulnerability of Chinese stars in a highly politicized film culture in the PRC.

Chinese Stardom versus Hollywood-Oriented Star Theories

I have discussed Chinese stars' vulnerability in face of both moral and political pressure. But even when it comes to commercial viability, it seems that Chinese stars are not as strong as their counterparts in Hollywood or other national cinemas. Discussing the star system in India, Behroze Gandhy and Rosie Thomas (1990: 107) suggest that compared with Hollywood stars, Indian stars hold more absolute power as they are a "crucial ingredient in the success of any mainstream Indian film." Chinese stars also play an important role in a film's box-office appeal, but I would hesitate to declare that they hold "absolute power" due to the following reasons. Firstly, an all-star cast has almost become a norm in the new century's Chinese commercial film production. So, while it might be unimaginable or at least financially unviable for a Hollywood film to include more than three A-list stars, in contrast, it would be surprising not to see at least three or four big stars in a recent Chinese blockbuster, as in the case of *The Promise* (Chen Kaige, 2005), *Red Cliff* (John Woo, 2008), and *Bodyguards and Assassins* (Teddy Chan, 2009). The all-star cast, a practice starting from Hong Kong film's golden age in the late 1980s and early 1990s (most notable in Wong Kar-wai's films), can certainly enhance a film's commercial competitiveness, but it also means that individual star power is restricted; an A-list star might not get a top salary and often has to play a small supporting role.

Another distinctive feature of Chinese stars is their multimedia and multi-genre existence. While many Chinese stars come from a pop music background (e.g., Leslie Cheung, Anita Mui, Kenny Bee [Zhong Zhengtao, b. 1952]), it has become a trend for movie stars to sing the theme song of the film they star in or to release albums (e.g., Sylvia Chang, Zhao Wei [b. 1976]). It is also quite common for a movie star to put an equal emphasis on television work (e.g., Liu Ruoying [Rene Liu, b. 1969], Zhou Xun [b. 1974]). Unlike their Hollywood counterparts who often make their name in one particular film genre, many Chinese stars excel in different genres (e.g., Brigitte Lin in romantic films and martial arts films; Tony Leung Chiu-Wai [Liang Chaowei, b. 1962] in art films and comedies). The multimedia and multi-genre image of Chinese stars demonstrates their diverse abilities, but also functions as a conscious strategy for survival faced with cut-throat competition. In this sense, Chinese stars' incredible flexibility exactly speaks to their vulnerability within highly competitive film industries.

This vulnerability that defines all aspects of Chinese stars – commercial, political, moral, cultural – can also be seen in transnational Chinese stars. From Bruce Lee to Jackie Chan to Jet Li, transnational Chinese stardom seems to have been exclusively built on Chinese stars' unique physical ability – their martial arts skills. As Leon Hunt (2003) argues, kung fu stardom is Chinese cinema's unique contribution to world cinema. However, while this powerful performance skill made three Chinese male stars internationally famous, it also precisely exposes the vulnerability of these stars. Firstly, the unabashed capitalization on their martial arts skills largely restricts these Chinese stars to the action genre, which helps to perpetuate the Western stereotype of Chinese stars only knowing how to fight. Secondly, the sustainability of the action / kung fu star is put into doubt. Farquhar (2010: 192) is right in asking this of Jackie Chan: "Can a 50-something Hong Kong–Hollywood star, whose image relies on extremes of actual bodily performance, keep going as a star?" Thirdly, the increasing application of digital techniques in contemporary films can make anyone look like a kung fu master onscreen, as in *Matrix* (Andy Wachowski, Lana Wachowski, 1999), thus raising two questions: Do we still need a star with real physical ability? If they lose this global currency, how can transnational Chinese stars survive on the international stage?

As stated earlier, it is very tricky to discuss Chinese stardom due to its great diversity. By examining star vulnerability as a salient trait of stars / stardom in Chinese cinema, I am proposing a new model to tackle the complexity and instability inherent in Chinese stardom. More importantly, my argument aims to show that Hollywood-oriented star theories are insufficient or sometimes inappropriate for the discussion of the Chinese star phenomenon for several reasons. Firstly, in contrast with the common perception that stars are a phenomenon of production and consumption, morality and politics play a more significant role in constructing Chinese stardom than do commercial forces. Secondly, unlike the usual on-screen / off-screen constructions of star personas, Chinese stars can establish their stardom entirely through their professional life, as seen in the example of socialist stardom. Thirdly, compared with ordinary people, Chinese stars are more likely to become moral victims and political subordinates. This observation, together with the state's endeavor to plebeianize stars, indicates a star–audience relationship that cannot be adequately explained by the discourse of fandom. Finally, due to moral constraints and political coercion, Chinese stars' economic power cannot be easily transferred into any form of social capital. For these reasons, I suggest that in the

Chinese context, star vulnerability, rather than star power, is a more useful concept to examine stardom. Due to limitations of space, I have not been able to explore all of the above-mentioned aspects in similar depth, but hopefully future research on Chinese stars/stardom will contribute to our deeper understanding on and beyond these issues, and demonstrate that Chinese stardom, or national stardom in general, is just as rich, instructive, and fascinating as Hollywood stardom.

Acknowledgments

I would like to thank Guy Austin and Sarah Leahy for their valuable comments on the draft of this chapter.

Notes

1   Six chapters of their book were first published as a special issue on Chinese stars in *Journal of Chinese Cinemas* in 2008.
2   Stars in other cultures have experienced similar tragedies, but more as individuals and due to personal reasons rather than the kind of social and cultural oppression seen in Chinese film history.
3   The latest news is that Cheung's marriage to Nicholas Tse finally ended in August 2011. She made a few films in the same year to resume her acting career.
4   For example, Hugh Grant's (b. 1960) prostitute sex scandal in 1995 did not damage his career. By apologizing to the public right away, he was applauded for "his refreshing honesty" (CNN 1995).
5   Opera performers were associated with male prostitution in late nineteenth-century China.
6   Liu Xiaoqing was imprisoned for more than a year in 2002 on a charge of tax evasion.
7   However, the nationalities of the stars stirred a heated discussion on the Internet, in which their Chineseness was questioned. Reportedly, among the 172 famous actors and directors involved in the film, 21 hold foreign nationalities.
8   Paul McDonald (2000) proposes the term "stars as labor" in the context of the Hollywood star system.

13

Ports of Entry

Mapping Chinese Cinema's Multiple Trajectories at International Film Festivals

Nikki J. Y. Lee and Julian Stringer

International film festivals are important to any discussion of the historical significance of Chinese cinema.[1] More specifically, they are of particular consequence in the contemporary era that stretches from the early 1980s to the present.[2] This period of filmmaking activity has witnessed both the development of the globalized festival circuit and Chinese cinema's ascent on the world stage.[3] As scholars (Y. Zhang 2002: 15–41; Davis and Yeh 2008: 140–64) have demonstrated, one benchmark of Chinese cinema's spectacular global success over the past three decades is the glut of prizes it has captured from the small number of prestigious "A-list" international film festivals.[4] These awards constitute a series of achievements that are as impressive as they are impossible to ignore. The relevant milestones are listed in Table 13.1 below.

Such milestones have raised Chinese cinema's international reputation and profit-making potential by attracting the interest and excitement of diverse overseas stakeholders – including producers, distributors, critics, and audiences – whose floppy antennae habitually seek out the global film scene's latest fads and fashions.

However, the success narratives underpinning this series of achievements often prove to be as constricting as they are empowering. Simply put, the acclaim afforded festival prize-winning films and filmmakers inevitably plays a large part in shaping and defining Chinese cinema's global image, fostering in the process expectations and assumptions concerning the kind of cinema represented by the signifier "Chinese." Such narratives contribute to the construction of the phenomenon of Chinese cinema as it is both named by and celebrated at the world's most important film festivals. The results of this circular logic have been explored in the context of the critical reception of historically influential "ethnographic" Fifth Generation titles such as *Red Sorghum*

A Companion to Chinese Cinema, First Edition. Edited by Yingjin Zhang.
© 2012 Blackwell Publishing Ltd. Published 2012 by Blackwell Publishing Ltd.

Table 13.1   Chinese cinema at international film festivals: key milestones

Date	Film	Director	Prize	Country of production
1988	*Red Sorghum*	Zhang Yimou	Golden Bear, Berlin	China
1989	*A City of Sadness*	Hou Hsiao-hsien	Golden Lion, Venice	Taiwan
1989	*Evening Bell*	Wu Ziniu	Silver Bear, Berlin	China
1992	*The Story of Qiu Ju*	Zhang Yimou	Golden Lion, Venice	China
1992	*Centre Stage*	Stanley Kwan	Best Actress (Maggie Cheung), Berlin	Hong Kong, Taiwan
1993	*The Wedding Banquet*	Ang Lee	Golden Bear ex-aequo, Berlin	Taiwan, US
1993	*The Puppetmaster*	Hou Hsiao-hsien	Jury Prize, Cannes	Taiwan
1993	*Farewell My Concubine*	Chen Kaige	Palm d'Or ex-aequo, Cannes	Hong Kong
1993	*The Blue Kite*	Tian Zhuangzhuang	Sakura Grand Prix, Tokyo	China
1994	*Vive L'Amour*	Tsai Ming-liang	Golden Lion, Venice	Taiwan
1997	*Happy Together*	Wong Kar-wai	Best Director, Cannes	Hong Kong
2000	*In the Mood for Love*	Wong Kar-wai	Best Actor (Tony Leung Chiu Wai), Cannes	Hong Kong
2004	*Clean*	Oliver Assayas	Best Actress (Maggie Cheung), Cannes	France

Sources: C. Wong (2007), Y. Zhang (2002: 15–41), Zhang and Farquhar (2010: 13).

(1987), *Ju Dou* (1989), and *Raise the Red Lantern* (1991) (see Figure 13.1), all three directed by Zhang Yimou:

> Such a situation seems to have implicated contemporary Chinese cinema in a prefixed cycle of transnational commodity production and consumption: favorable reviews at international film festivals lead to production of more "ethnographic" films, and the wide distribution of such films is translated into their availability for classroom use and therefore influences the agenda of film studies, which in turn reinforces the status of these films as a dominant genre. (Y. Zhang 2002: 35)

It is important to point out, therefore, that the list of milestones referenced above constitutes a "winners only" view of film history that cannot possibly hope to embrace the entire corpus of Chinese cinema at international festivals. Such success narratives comprise snapshots of a phenomenon extending far beyond the (admittedly gilded) frame provided by the tiny coterie of titles that garner exposure at a limited number of high-profile events.

Figure 13.1   Gong Li as Wife No. 4, faking pregnancy in *Raise the Red Lantern* (dir. Zhang Yimou, Era, 1991).

The comprehensive mapping of every Chinese film ever shown at an international film festival would obviously be an impossible ambition to undertake within the space constraints here.[5] In the context of the present volume, then, the challenge is to identify as a matter of priority the most useful questions. Should historians of Chinese cinema always "remember" the titles and people showered with awards and garlands at global film culture's brightest showcases? Conversely, how much energy should be expended on the "losers," those has-beens and also-rans who failed to set the film festival circuit on fire? Finally, what are scholars to do with the simple fact that there are only so many prizes and flowers to go round? Hierarchical and elitist structures of discrimination – that is to say, the tendency to differentiate between "winners" and "losers" – are built into the very planning and organization of many international film festivals. On these terms, the vast majority of Chinese films and filmmakers never will get the opportunity to capitalize upon the game-changing possibilities opened to those privileged enough to achieve success at an A-list event (Stringer 2003a).

Precisely in order to indicate something of the multidimensional scale of the subject matter under discussion, we aim in what follows to steer a middle ground between analyses of these various and at times dauntingly complicated issues. On the one hand, we wish to acknowledge the imponderable vastness of the history of contemporary Chinese cinema at international film festivals. We therefore emphasize Chinese cinema's multiple points of entry to global film culture by considering data retrieved from a variety of overseas events – our intention is to expand the frame of comprehension so as to "remember" more names and titles than just the famous ones listed in Table 13.1. On the other hand, we wish to explore the ways in which these multiple international events are structured hierarchically in relation to one other. This helps throw into relief the question of why certain Chinese films and filmmakers benefit from participation at particular festivals while others apparently do not.

Underlining our approach are two fundamental theoretical assertions. First, in the period under discussion Chinese cinema established its global brand in a fluid manner. In other words, it is a shape-shifter. Its contours continuously move and blur in tandem with variable and historically contingent factors linked to the ever-changing fads and fashions of international film production, presentation, exhibition, distribution, and consumption.

Second, in order to track Chinese cinema's appearance at overseas festivals since the early 1980s, it is necessary to pay attention to temporal and spatial dimensions of analysis. Chinese cinema has emerged at festivals across both space and time. Double-mapping along these twin vectors recognizes the random (i.e., messy or chaotic) as well as the more patterned (i.e., ordered) aspects of its disparate trajectories. The combination of these twin theoretical assertions around the weight of empirical data accumulated below also illustrates the hitherto neglected relevance of an intriguing historical phenomenon. This is that over the past thirty years Chinese cinema has habitually been presented at one primary overseas location – namely, what we would like to designate as "port city film festivals."

Writing Narratives of Chinese Cinema History

If spatial analysis is concerned with the question of where Chinese cinema has been shown at overseas film festivals, temporal analysis considers the question of when. The latter approach accordingly encompasses a focus on how and at what point in time Chinese cinema has been exhibited at international events, how it accrues cultural and economic meaning and capital as months and years go by, and how accounts of its historically shifting definition get to be written in light of these activities.

In short, the temporal dimension of analysis is inevitably caught up in the practice of constructing narratives of success and failure discussed above in relation to Table 13.1. Consider by way of example struggles over identification of the origins of mainland China's Fifth Generation. A number of competing narratives have been advanced on this issue, linked to yet separate from critical debates concerning the label's validity as a form of classification (see Chapter 4, this volume).[6] According to British critic Tony Rayns, the origins of the Fifth Generation can be traced to April 12, 1985. This is the date when *Yellow Earth* (Chen Kaige, 1984) was screened at the Hong Kong International Film Festival.

There were enough non-Chinese present that evening to ensure that news of this "breakthrough" film quickly reached festival directors and distributors in other countries. The torrid enthusiasm of the Hong Kong audience was repeated when *Yellow Earth* had its western premiere at the Edinburgh and Locarno festivals four months later. (Rayns 1989: 2)

In fact, April 12, 1985 may be thought of as the point in time when the Fifth Generation began to gain recognition outside China: it should more properly be referred to as the beginning of the international discovery of Fifth Generation films.[7] The story of these films and filmmakers' earlier emergence in China is superseded by their recognition by the international film festival circuit's diverse overseas stakeholders. At the same time, however, domestic discourses on such labeling practices, which require timelines as a prerequisite for narration, proved themselves also to be implicated in the festival circuit's influence. Upon its return to China after success at numerous prestigious overseas events, *Yellow Earth* gained enhanced attention from Chinese intellectuals (Rayns 1991; N. Ma 1993).

Similarly, it has been claimed that a comparable scenario was played out in the case of the discovery of the Sixth Generation. As Dai Jinhua (2002: 79) remarks, by this point in history domestic film circles as well as the global film scene were increasingly expecting – nay, yearning for – a new generation of Chinese directors to emerge: "The question constantly popping up at international film conferences that I attended was 'Which generation is it now? The Seventh?' When I responded, 'Still the Fifth Generation', they always greeted the news with disappointed expressions." Directors like Zhang Yuan, Wang Xiaoshuai, Lou Ye, and Jia Zhangke are typically recognized as the Sixth Generation (Cornelius 2002; Said 2002). However, since no conscious and collective movement appears to have emerged, commentators evidently first dreamed up the label "Sixth Generation" and then applied it to individual filmmakers: "the naming of the Sixth Generation precede[d] its praxis" (J. Dai 2002: 74). Furthermore, Dai highlights how young directors at the Beijing Film Academy "obviously internalized this attitude" – that is to say, the notion that a Sixth Generation was now bound to emerge – leading to the formation of a "generational consciousness" (2002: 73–80). In other words, the international film festival circuit's need and desire to discover a new generation of Chinese filmmakers brought the Sixth Generation into being – albeit in conjunction with the participation of Chinese film circles and filmmakers.

The two examples cited above suggest that any narrative of Chinese cinema's historical development is dependent upon the orderly pattern of a clear starting point. In order to gain force and legitimacy, it also needs the reassurance of periodic continuity as well as the accumulation over time of a list of representative directors, films, and movements. Film festivals – and in particular recognition attained through the capture of high-profile international awards – provide undeniable evidence that Chinese cinema's success is not theoretical or illusionary, but rather tangible and empirically verifiable. Put differently, each of Chinese cinema's high overseas achievements functions temporally as an essential institutional platform marking the traces of historical momentum.

By contrast, the spatial dimension of analysis encompasses a focus on how and where Chinese cinema has been exhibited at international film festivals, which events on the global circuit have been of particular importance to its overseas circulation, and where narratives of its interest and importance have been constructed and perpetuated.

Within English-language Chinese cinema studies a particularly influential illustration of the potential benefits of spatial mapping is provided by Michael Curtin (2007). In order to produce his analysis of how and why Chinese film and televison are now so globally successful, Curtin proposes use of the concept of "media capital" to delineate the core location criteria underpinning the growth of specific audiovisual production centers. As Curtin (2007: 23, original emphasis) defines the term:

> Media capital is therefore a concept that at once acknowledges the *spatial* logics of capital, creativity, culture and polity without privileging one among the four. Just as the logic of capital provides a fundamental structuring influence, so too do forces of sociocultural variation shape the diverse contexts in which media are made and consumed. The concept media capital encourages us to provide dynamic and historicized accounts that delineate the operations of capital and the migrations of talent and at the same time directs our attention to forces and contingencies that can engender alternative discourses, practices, and spatialities.

Curtin's study is a singular analysis of the rise of multiple production centers for Chinese film and television. However, he has much less to say about international film festivals and therefore downplays the importance of some of the core travel routes linked to the global distribution and exhibition of contemporary Chinese cinema. The remainder of this chapter seeks to complement Curtin's approach by discussing one hitherto neglected aspect of Chinese cinema's international presentation as we map it temporally as well as spatially.

Constructing a New Narrative: Port City Film Festivals

A closer look at the data contained in Table 13.1 reveals that Chinese cinema's benchmark overseas achievements seemingly revolve around a small number of prestigious A-list international film festivals. First among these is the European triumvirate comprising the annual events in Berlin, Cannes, and Venice, supplemented by Tokyo's status as a high-profile showcase in Asia.

An intriguing observation to make about these festivals is that three out of four of them are located in cities with well-established port infrastructures. Film festivals held in port cities appear to have been historically important to the overseas exhibition and circulation of Chinese cinema. In this sense, Cannes, Tokyo, and Venice are noteworthy not just because they are A-list jamborees but also because they are major port city film festivals – that is to say, primary gateway locations exerting considerable influence on global film culture. The fact that a sizable majority of the leading festivals historically receptive to Chinese cinema are based in port cities constitutes a pattern that is repeated and hence significant.

This hypothesis is supported by information gleaned when looking at other categories of international film festivals. For example, a number of the events designated by the International Federation of Film Producers Association (FIAPF) as Competitive Specialized Feature Film Festivals have also been claimed as important to the building of Chinese cinema's global reputation and profit-making potential, including Hawaii and Pusan (Iordanova and Cheung 2011), as have Non-Competitive Feature Film Festivals such as London and Toronto (C. Wong 2007). To this list of Chinese-friendly port city film festivals may be added the no less compelling examples of New York, Rotterdam, and Vancouver.

Why are port city film festivals so important to the overseas distribution and consumption of Chinese cinema? In considering this vital and hitherto neglected question a number of preliminary answers may be suggested. First, festivals held in port cities are by definition creatures of urban environments, and cities have always been intimately linked to the establishment and maintenance of the international film festival circuit (Stringer 2001). Film festivals provide urban administrators, regional governments, and transnational corporations with a means to compete with rival cities for speculative investments. They accrue economic and cultural capital when able to promote themselves as discoverors, or else facilitators, of the fads and fashions of global film culture.

Second, port cities serve as trade hubs connecting the commercial networks and creative clusters that drive the international film festival economy (Iordanova and Cheung 2010). Situated at the edge of waterways (ocean, sea, river, or lake), they are often located near industrial centers historically attached to manufacturing facilities and well-established trade routes. They are thus places where goods are loaded and unloaded, and cargo transferred, via ships, airports, road links, and high-speed communications technologies. As commercial gateways they are able to swing their doors both ways, allowing transit in and out of the host city with freedom and ease.

Third, port city film festivals are located in urban sites that over the years have strategically invested in tourist and hospitality infrastructures. Such environments are able to cater to large numbers of international visitors seeking cultural distractions. Aside from cinema-related merry-making, they also stage other kinds of festivals, expos, and functions. The ultimate aim of all of this activity is to become a year-round "conference venue" – in other words, the kind of place that can legitimately claim to welcome overseas guests as one aspect of its globally competitive portfolio.

Finally, such locations and events also boast an ability to embody glamour. They trade in their natural assests such as sun and sand; they proudly announce their success in attracting foreign wealth; they make the most of all the tourist attractions and entertainment provisions they can offer. Port cities have frequently nudged themselves into the category of "must-see" tourist destination. Staging an international film festival provides overseas travelers with yet one more reason to visit.

Importantly, all of these elements may be replicated. Because proximity to water and a harbor is a feature of so many of the world's urban conurbations, the port city film festival is a model that can be copied given enough will and resources. (There is little doubt, for example, that Pusan wants to be Cannes.) However, each individual event nevertheless embodies its own particular identity, its own specific take on how the key criteria referred to above may be combined into a unique festival experience. After all, within the terms of economic globalization film festivals market both conceptual similarity and cultural difference (Stringer 2001: 139).

Chinese cinema is not alone in circulating since the early 1980s along the travel routes mapped out by port city film festivals. However, this period has witnessed the maturing of a certain logical synergy between the development of the globalized festival circuit and Chinese cinema's ascent on the world stage. On the one hand, as mainland China's economic power has grown, events such as Cannes, Venice, and Tokyo have needed to engage with Chinese films and filmmakers in order to demonstrate their contemporary relevance as gateways to the world. On the other hand, Chinese cinema has similarly sought to widen its own international reach. It has done this, in part, through gaining priority access to the much-needed infrastructures and publicity opportunities afforded by global film culture's most high-profile festivals.

In light of the above arguments, let us now revisit narratives of Chinese cinema's disparate fortunes at international film festivals. The milestones referred to in Table 13.1 are contextualized below in relation to a series of alternative trajectories to be found among data drawn from the records of five representative port city film festivals: Cannes, Venice, Rotterdam, Tokyo, and Pusan.[8] These events have been singled out both because of their status as important destinations for Chinese cinema's overseas presentation and to highlight the (perhaps surprisingly) large number of accolades Chinese films and filmmakers have earned over the past three decades. In considering the material that follows, we pay particular attention to prizes captured, competition entries (i.e., films that could have won awards but instead lost out), special mentions and citations, and opening and closing screenings (i.e., dedicated events flagging this or that film as noteworthy of attention).

The five port city film festivals analyzed in this manner have refracted Chinese cinema from unique angles. These differences emerge most clearly when each event is considered in relation to all of the others. Contemplating these variable and historically contingent factors helps throw into relief the question of why certain Chinese films and filmmakers benefit from participation at particular festivals while others apparently do not.

As we have already seen, for example, both Cannes and Venice are recognized – as befits their status as two of the world's longest-standing film festivals – as A-list events. They are therefore prime locations where Chinese cinema's achievements are benchmarked and may consequently be mapped.

Table 13.2 reveals that Cannes favors internationally famed filmmakers such as Chen Kaige, Zhang Yimou, Hou Hsiao-hsien, and Wong Kar-wai. These are auteurs with established global brands whose overseas reputations have come to be wrapped up in Cannes' patina of prestige; by the same token, they bring the added values of glamour and relevance to the high-profile event held annually on the Cote d'Azur. Cannes is moreover loyal to such filmmakers because it invites them back to the festival time and again. In turn, French financiers appear to "adopt" these celebrated Chinese filmmakers by investing as coproducers in their future projects – projects which subsequently receive exposure, and sometimes accolades, at Cannes. This particular festival's version of loyalty is therefore double-edged as it implies future collaboration with local European coproducers.

Conversely, Venice evidently presents a greater diversity of Chinese films than Cannes. It too is loyal to its favored Chinese directors, although there are few examples of it investing synergistically, or opportunistically, in coproductions with Italy. Venice has a penchant for provocative and sensational works and it awards prizes in a larger range of categories than just the "Best Film" and "Best Director" sections that largely define Chinese cinema's track record at Cannes. It has thus been a strong supporter of Zhang Yuan and Jia Zhangke: when it rewarded Zhang Yimou with a Golden Lion it was for the contemporary *The Story of Qiu Ju* (1993) rather than the "ethnographic" *Ju Dou* shown in competition at Cannes. In short, Venice is also auteur-centered albeit less conservatively so than Cannes.

In contrast to these two events, Rotterdam, Pusan, and Tokyo are relative new-comers to the international film festival circuit. Rotterdam enjoys a high reputation for discovering new talent with a particular focus on world cinema (especially non-European and non-US cinemas). Pusan belongs to FIAPF's "B-list" of Competitive Specialized Feature Film Festivals; as we have seen, Tokyo is on the A-list. Whereas Cannes and Venice are based in European cities and overwhelmingly promote European filmmakers alongside a limited selection of "adopted" Chinese auteur directors, Pusan and Tokyo are based in East Asian cities geographically and culturally closer to Hong Kong, Taiwan, and mainland China. Both therefore prioritize the presentation of Asian films and pursue programming strategies emphasizing access to regional film markets.

What conclusions may be drawn from Tables 13.4, 13.5, and 13.6? Perhaps because of its niche status as a cutting-edge international event, Rotterdam awards its prizes to less globally famous Chinese directors, allowing it to fulfill its function as a discovery site for new and first-time films and filmmakers. The festival also likes to support politically provocative and aesthetically experimental films. For example, it was an early advocate of the Sixth Generation and it gives more prizes to documentaries and to independent titles.

As a noncompetitive film festival Pusan arguably does not generate the same level of international interest and enthusiasm as the most prestigious A-list

Table 13.2 Chinese cinema at the Cannes International Film Festival

Date	Film	Director	Category/Prize	Country of production
1962	Yang Kwei Fei	Li Han-hsiang	Grand Prix of the CST (Technical Grand Prix)	Hong Kong
1975	A Touch of Zen	King Hu	Grand Prix of the CST	Hong Kong (Taiwan)
1982	The True Story of Ah Q	Cen Fan	In Competition	China
1988	King of the Children	Chen Kaige	In Competition	China
1990	Ju Dou	Zhang Yimou	In Competition	China, Japan
1991	Life on a String	Chen Kaige	In Competition	Germany, UK, Italy, Spain, China
1993	Farewell My Concubine	Chen Kaige	Palme d'Or ex-aequo, International Critics Prize by FIPRESCI	Hong Kong
1993	The Puppetmaster	Hou Hsiao-hsien	Jury Prize	Taiwan
1994	To Live	Zhang Yimou	Jury's Grand Prix ex-aequo	Hong Kong
1994	To Live	Zhang Yimou	Best Actor (Ge You)	Hong Kong
1995	Shanghai Triad	Zhang Yimou	Jury Prize	China
1996	Temptress Moon	Cheng Kaige	In Competition	Hong Kong
1996	Goodbye South, Goodbye	Hou Hsiao-hsien	In Competition	Taiwan
1997	Happy Together	Wong Kar-wai	Best Director	Hong Kong
1997	The Ice Storm	Ang Lee	In Competition	USA
1998	Flowers of Shanghai	Hou Hsiao-hsien	In Competition	Taiwan, Japan
1998	The Hole	Tsai Ming-liang	In Competition	Taiwan, France
2000	Devils on the Doorstep	Jiang Wen	Grand Prix	China
2000	In the Mood for Love	Wong Kar-Wai	Best Actor (Tony Leung Chiu Wai)	Hong Kong

Year	Film	Director	Award	Country
2000	*Yi Yi*	Edward Yang	Best Director	Japan
2001	*What Time Is It There?*	Tsai Ming-liang	In Competition	Taiwan, France
2001	*Millennium Mambo*	Hou Hsiao-hsien	In Competition	Taiwan
2001	*What Time Is It There?/ Millennium Mambo*	Tsai Ming-liang/Hou Hsiao-hsien	Technical Grand Prix (Tu Du-Che)	Taiwan, France/Taiwan
2002	*Unknown Pleasure*	Jia Zhanjke	In Competition	China
2003	*Purple Butterfly*	Lou Ye	In Competition	China
2004	*2046*	Wong Kar-wai	In Competition	China
2004	*Clean*	Oliver Assayas	Best Actress (Maggie Cheung)	France
2005	*Three Times*	Hou Hsiao-hsien	In Competition	Taiwan
2005	*Shanghai Dreams*	Wang Xiaoshuai	Jury Prize	China
2006	*Summer Palace*	Lou Ye	In Competition	China, France
2007	*Luxury Car*	Wang Chao	Un Certain Regard Prize	China, France
2008	*24 City*	Jia Zhangke	In Competition	China
2009	*Spring Fever*	Lou Ye	In Competition	Hong Kong, France
2010	*Chongqing Blues*	Wang Xiaoshuai	In Competition	China

Source: Cannes International Film Festival website (www.festival-cannes.com). Accessed November 17, 2010.

Table 13.3 Chinese cinema at the Venice International Film Festival

Date	Film	Director	Prize	Country of production
1989	City of Sadness	Hou Hsiao-hsien	Golden Lion	Taiwan
1991	Raise the Red Lantern	Zhang Yimou	Silver Lion	China
1992	The Story of Qiu Ju	Zhang Yimou	Golden Lion	China
1993	The Story of Qiu Ju	Zhang Yimou	Best Actress (Gong Li)	China
1993	Chatterbox	Liu Miaomiao	President of the Italian Senate's Gold Medal	China
1994	Vive L'Amour	Tsai Ming-liang	Golden Lion	Taiwan
1994	In the Heat of the Sun	Jiang Wen	Best Actor (Xia Yu)	China
1994	Ashes of Time	Wong Kar-wai	Best Cinematography (Christopher Doyle)	Hong Kong
1996	Buddha Bless America	Wu Nien-chen	In Competition	Taiwan
1997	Keep Cool	Zhang Yimou	In Competition	China
1997	Chinese Box	Wayne Wang	In Competition	France, Japan, USA
1999	Seventeen Years	Zhang Yuan	Special Director's Award, Sergio Trasatti Award – Special Mention	Italy, China
1999	Se-tong	Heng Tang	Best Short Film	Australia, China
1999	Not One Less	Zhang Yimou	Golden Lion	China
2000	Durian Durian	Fruit Chan	In Competition	Hong Kong, France, China
2000	Platform	Jia Zhangke	Netpac Award	Hong Kong, China, Japan, France
2001	Seafood	Zhu Wen	Cinema of the Present – Lion of the Year	China, Hong Kong
2001	Quitting	Zhang Yang	Netpac Award	China
2001	Fish and Elephant	Li Yu	Elvira Notari Prize	China
2001	Hollywood Hong Kong	Fruit Chan	In Competition	Hong Kong, France, UK, Japan
2002	Springtime in a Small Town	Tian Zhuangzhuang	San Marco Prize	China, Hong Kong, France, Netherlands
2002	Public Toilet	Fruit Chan	San Marco Prize – Special Mention	South Korea, Hong Kong, Japan
2002	The Best of Times	Chang Tso-chi	In Competition	Taiwan, Japan

Year	Title	Director	Award/Category	Country
2003	*Goodbye Dragon Inn*	Tsai Ming-liang	FIPRESCI Prize	Taiwan
2003	*The Floating Landscape*	Lai Miu-suet	In Competition	Hong Kong
2004	*The World*	Jia Zhangke	In Competition	China, Japan, France
2004	*Café Lumiere*	Hou Hsiao-hsien	In Competition	Japan, Taiwan
2005	*Brokeback Mountain*	Ang Lee	Golden Lion	USA
2005	*Seven Swords*	Tsui Hark	Opening Film	South Korea, Hong Kong, China
2005	*Perhaps Love*	Peter Ho-sun Chan	Closing Film	China, Malaysia, Hong Kong
2005	*Everlasting Regret*	Stanley Kwan	In Competition	China, Hong Kong
2006	*Still Life*	Jia Zhangke	Golden Lion	China
2006	*Exiled*	Johnnie To	In Competition	Hong Kong, China
2006	*I Don't Want to Sleep Alone*	Tsai Ming-liang	In Competition	Taiwan, France, Australia
2007	*Lust, Caution*	Ang Lee	Golden Lion	USA, China, Taiwan
2007	*Mad Detective*	Johnnie To, Wai Ka-fai	In Competition	Hong Kong
2007	*Help Me Eros*	Lee Kang-sheng	In Competition	Taiwan
2007	*The Sun Also Rises*	Jiang Wen	In Competition	China, Hong Kong
2008	*Plastic City*	Yu Lik-wai	In Competition	Brazil, China, Hong Kong, Japan
2009	*Accident*	Cheang Pou-soi	In Competition	Hong Kong
2009	*Prince of Tears*	Yonfan	In Competition	Taiwan, Hong Kong, China
2009	*Cow*	Guan Hu	Orizzonti Prize for Best Documentary	China
2010	*The Ditch*	Wang Bing	In Competition	Hong Kong, France, Belgium
2010	*Detective Dee and the Mystery of the Phantom Flame*	Tsui Hark	In Competition	Hong Kong
2010	–	John Woo	Golden Lion for Lifetime Achievement	Hong Kong

Source: Internet Movie Database (www.imdb.com). Accessed November 18, 2010.

Table 13.4   Chinese cinema at the International Film Festival Rotterdam

Date	Film	Director	Prize	Country of production
1987	A Time to Live, a Time to Die	Hou Hsiao-hsien	Best Non-American/Non-European Film	Taiwan
1990	Life Is Cheap … But Toilet Paper Is Expensive	Wayne Wang	KNF Award	USA
1992	Five Girls and a Rope	Yeh Hung-wei	FIPRESCI Prize	Taiwan
1994	Red Beads	He Jianjun	FIPRESCI Prize	China
1995	Postman	He Jianjun	Tiger Award, FIPRESCI Prize	China, Hong Kong
1996	Sons	Zhang Yuan	Tiger Award, FIPRESCI Prize	China
1996	Heartbreak Island	Hsu Hsiao-ming	Netpac Award	Taiwan
1997	Frozen	Wang Xiaoshuai	In Competition	China
1997	Ah-chung	Chang Tso-chi	In Competition	Taiwan
2000	Suzhou River	Lou Ye	Tiger Award	China, Germany
2000	Shower	Zhang Yang	Audience Award	China
2001	All the Way	Shi Runjiu	In Competition	China
2002	Weekend Plot	Zhang Ming	In Competition	China
2003	Welcome to Destination Shanghai	Andrew Y. S. Cheng	In Competition, FIPRESCI Prize	China
2004	The Missing	Lee Kang-sheng	Tiger Award, KNF Award, Netpac Award	Taiwan
2004	Uniform	Diao Yi-nan	In Competition, Netpac Award – Special Mention	China, Hong Kong
2006	Walking on the Wild Side	Han Jie	Tiger Award	China, France
2007	How Is Your Fish Today?	Guo Xiaolu	In Competition, Netpac Award – Special Mention	UK
2008	What on Earth Have I Done Wrong?	Doze Niu	Netpac Award	Taiwan
2008	Crude Oil	Wang Bing	Netpac Award – Special Mention	China
2009	The Land	He Jia	Netpac Award	China
2010	Sun Spots	Yang Heng	In Competition	Hong Kong, China

Source: Internet Movie Database (www.imdb.com). Accessed November 24, 2010.

Table 13.5   Chinese cinema at the Pusan International Film Festival

Date	Film	Director	Prize	Country of production
1996	*In Expectation*	Zhang Ming	Closing Film, New Currents Award	China
1997	*Chinese Box*	Wayne Wang	Opening Film	UK, France, USA, Japan
1997	*Eighteen Springs*	Ann Hui	Closing Film	Hong Kong
1998	*Xiao Wu*	Jia Zhangke	New Currents Award	China
1999	*Not One Less*	Zhang Yimou	Closing Film	China
2000	*In the Mood for Love*	Wong Kar-wai	Closing Film	Hong Kong
2003	*The Missing*	Lee Kang-sheng	New Currents Award	Taiwan
2004	*2046*	Wong Kar-wai	Opening Film	Hong Kong
2004	*Soap Opera*	Wu Er-shan	FIPRESCI Award	China
2004	–	Hou Hsiao-hsien	Asian Filmmaker of the Year Award	Taiwan
2005	*Three Times*	Hou Hsiao-hsien	Opening Film	Taiwan
2005	*Grain in Ear*	Zhang Lu	New Currents Award	China
2006	*Crazy Stone*	Ning Hao	Closing Film	China
2006	*Betelut Beauty*	Heng Yang	New Currents Award	China
2006	–	Andy Lau	Asian Filmmaker of the Year Award	Hong Kong
2007	*Life Track*	Guang Hao Jin	New Currents Award	China, South Korea
2007	*The Red Awn*	Cai Shangjun	FIPRESCI Award	China
2007	*Assembly*	Feng Xiaogang	Closing Film	China
2007	–	Edward Yang	Asian Filmmaker of the Year Award	Taiwan
2008	*Jalainur*	Ye Zhao	FIPRESCI Award	China
2009	*The Message*	Chen Kuo-fu	Closing Film	China
2009	*Lan*	Jiang Wenli	KNN Movie Award (Audience Award)	China
2009	*Miss Kicki*	Liu Hakon	Flash Forward Award – Special Mention	Sweden, Taiwan
2010	*Under the Hawthorn Tree*	Zhang Yimou	Opening Film	Hong Kong, China
2010	*New Castle*	Guo Hengqi	Mecenat Award for Best Asian Documentary	China
2010	*My Spectacular Theatre*	Lu Yang	KNN Movie Award (Audience Award)	China

Source: Pusan International Film Festival website (www.piff.org). Accessed November 26, 2010.

Table 13.6   Chinese cinema at the Tokyo International Film Festival

Date	Film	Director	Prize	Country of production
1987	Old Well	Wu Tianming	Sakura Grand Prix, Best Actor (Zhang Yimou), FIPRESCI Prize	China
1991	A Brighter Summer Day	Edward Yang	Special Jury Prize, FIPRESCI Prize	Taiwan
1991	The Spring Festival	Huang Jianzhong	Special Jury Prize, Best Actress (Zhao Lirong)	China
1991	Five Girls and a Rope	Yeh Hung-wei	Silver Award	Taiwan
1992	Secret Love in Peach Blossom Land	Stan Lai	Silver Award	Taiwan
1993	The Blue Kite	Tian Zhuangzhuang	Sakura Grand Prix, Best Actress (Lu Liping)	China
1993	For Fun	Ning Ying	Gold Award	China
1993	Rebels of the Neon God	Tsai Ming-liang	Bronze Award	Taiwan
1993	Moonlight Boy	Wang Qi-zan	Special Mention	Taiwan
1994	The Day the Sun Turned Cold	Yim Ho	Sakura Grand Prix, Best Director	Hong Kong
1994	Back to Back, Face to Face	Huang Jianxin	Best Actor (Zhentou Niu)	China, Hong Kong
1995	The Christ of Nanjing	Tony Au	Best Artistic Contribution	Hong Kong
1995	The Daughter-in-Law	Steve Wang	Bronze Award	Taiwan
1996	The King of Masks	Wu Tianming	Best Director, Best Actor (Zhu Xu)	China, Hong Kong
1996	A Drifting Life	Lin Cheng-sheng	Silver Award	Taiwan
1997	Murmur of Youth	Lin Cheng-sheng	Best Actress (Rene Liu)	Taiwan
1999	Darkness and Light	Chang Tso-chi	Sakura Grand Prix, Gold Award, Asian Film Award	Taiwan
2002	Sky Lovers	Jiang Qinmin	Best Artistic Contribution, Cinematography (Shao Dan)	China

Table 13.6 *(cont'd)*

Date	Film	Director	Prize	Country of production
2003	*Nuan*	Huo Jianqi	Sakura Grand Prix, Best Actor (Teruyuki Kagawa)	China
2004	*Mountain Patrol*	Lu Chuan	In Competition, Special Jury Prize	China, Hong Kong
2004	*The Passage*	Cheng Wen-tang	In Competition	Taiwan
2005	*Loach is a Fish Too*	Yang Yazhou	In Competition, Best Artistic Contribution	China
2005	*You and Me*	Ma Liwen	In Competition, Best Actress (Yaqin Jiin)	China
2005	–	Hou Hsiao-hsien	Kurosawa Akira Award	Taiwan
2006	*Thirteen Princess Trees*	Lu Yue	Special Jury Prize	China
2006	*After This Our Exile*	Patrick Tam	Asian Film Award, Best Artistic Contribution	Hong Kong
2006	*Dog Bite Dog*	Cheang Pou-soi	In Competition	Hong Kong, Japan
2006	*The Exam*	Pu Jian	In Competition	China
2009	*Snowfall in Taipei*	Huo Jianqi	In Competition	Japan, Hong Kong, China, Taiwan
2009	*Heaven Eternal, Earth Everlasting*	Li Fangfang	In Competition	China
2010	*Buddha Mountain*	Li Yu	In Competition	China
2010	*The Piano in a Factory*	Zhang Ming	In Competition	China

Source: Internet Movie Database (www.imdb.com). Accessed November 25, 2010.

events. However, it strives to bask in reflected glory by providing a replica of aspects of the Cannes model: Pusan has therefore also supported established Chinese global auteurs such as Hou and Wong. At the same time, though, the South Korean event balances this conservatism with a more forward-looking stance. It consequently supports young Asian directors and does not hesitate to screen examples of popular genre cinema. Most importantly, Pusan actively seeks to establish networks within Asia by building relationships with regional film industries. This helps explain why the festival has so frequently chosen Chinese (or Japanese) titles as its opening and closing films, and why it instigated the Asian Filmmaker of the Year award to create synergies with both well-established and emerging regional talent.

Like Pusan, Tokyo functions as an alternative exhibition venue to the major European film festivals discussed above. Evidence for this is provided by the fact that over the past twenty years it has offered prizes to some of the less globally acknowledged proponents of Chinese film movements such as the Sixth Generation and New Taiwan Cinema. For example, whereas Tsai Ming-liang is one of Taiwan's darlings of many international film festivals, Tokyo has given more awards to Lin Cheng-sheng, and it was also one of the first events to support Chang Tso-chi. Similarly, in 2004 Cannes belatedly trumpeted the Fifth Generation by acknowledging Zhang Yimou's *To Live*, but Tokyo had already celebrated the movement one year earlier by giving its Sakura Grand Prix to the less famous Tian Zhuangzhuang's *The Blue Kite* (1993). As a general rule of thumb, Tokyo appears to have more affinity with filmmakers from Taiwan, and at times with those from mainland China, than other comparable international film festivals. It thus downplays Hong Kong's popular genres by promoting regional "art cinema." It is also the one festival discussed here that gives as many awards to Chinese actors as it does to Chinese directors.

Finally, a further set of conclusions only comes to light once all the tables above are considered in relation to one another. For example, in comparison with other events Cannes is not only auteur-centered but also willfully behind-the-curve – it reserves its highest accolades for the small number of Chinese auteur directors already garlanded with accolades elsewhere, thus revealing the celebrated French event's scavenger mentality. Cannes neither wants nor needs to be a first-discovery site for Chinese cinema. Venice stays one step ahead of Cannes when it comes to the unearthing and supporting of new talent, but it is Rotterdam and Pusan – albeit in their very different ways – that are in the vanguard of developments in the overseas presentation of Chinese cinema. Both of these festivals regularly award prizes to Chinese filmmakers at early stages of their careers, or before they may or may not get the opportunity to be "adopted" by A-list events such as Cannes and Venice.

So much for orderly patterns. What of the more chaotic aspects of cinema history? For it would be disingenuous of us to neglect to mention the more messy – because inconvenient – truth that not all of the world's most significant film festivals are located in port cities. Certainly, in terms of the argument outlined above, Berlin is the fly in the ointment.

Berlin is an inland film festival that since the early 1980s has energetically promoted Chinese cinema as a matter of course. It has done this, for example, by showcasing the exhibition of popular movies (e.g., Hong Kong genres) as well as the work of established and emerging auteur directors. Berlin has also programmed and awarded prizes to films with a political edge and it has supported politically and aesthetically provocative works; it was hence an early advocate of both the Fifth Generation and the Sixth Generation. Unlike Cannes, but similar to Rotterdam, Berlin prides itself on being a European discovery site for Chinese

Table 13.7 Chinese cinema at the Berlin International Film Festival

Date	Film	Director	Prize	Country of production
1982	*The Three Monks*	A Da (Xu Jingda)	Jury Prize Silver Bear (Short Film, animation)	China
1982	*Crossroads*	Shen Xiling	Competition (Special Screening)	China
1982	*Life After Life*	Peter Wai, Cheun Yung	Competition (Special Screening)	China
1983	*Strange Friends*	Xu Lei	Silver Bear – Honorable Mention	China
1984	*The Struggle Between Snipe and Mussel*	Hu Jinqing	Jury Prize Silver Bear (Short Film, animation)	China
1984	*Ah Ying*	Allen Fong	Competition	Hong Kong
1984	*Blood Is Always Hot*	Wen Yan	Competition	China
1985	*Monkeys Fishing in the Stream*	Shen Zhuwei	Competition (Short Film)	China
1986	*Scarecrow*	Hu Jinqing	Competition (Short Film)	China
1988	*Red Sorghum*	Zhang Yimou	Golden Bear	China
1988	*Beauty Contest*	Wang Shuchen	Competition	China
1989	*Evening Bell*	Wu Ziniu	Silver Bear – Special Jury Prize	China
1989	*Feeling From Mountain*	Wang Shuchen	Competition (Short Film)	China
1989	*The Mantis Stalks the Cicade Grille*	Hu Daoqing	Competition (Short Film)	China
1990	*Black Snow*	Xie Fei	Silver Bear for a Single Outstanding Achievement	China
1991	*Li Lianying, the Imperial Eunuch*	Tian Zhuangzhuang	Competition	Hong Kong
1991	*Drummer From the Huo Yan Mountains*	Guang Chunman	Children's Jury Prize	China
1992	*Center Stage*	Stanley Kwan	Competition, Best Actress (Maggie Cheung)	Hong Kong, Taiwan
1993	*The Woman from the Lake of Scented Souls*	Xie Fei	Golden Bear ex-aequo	China
1993	*The Wedding Banquet*	Ang Lee	Golden Bear ex-aequo	China
1994	*Sparkling Fox*	Wu Ziniu	Honorable Mention	Hong Kong, China

(*Continued*)

Table 13.7 (cont'd)

Date	Film	Director	Prize	Country of production
1995	Summer Snow	Ann Hui	Competition, Silver Bear for Best Actress (Josephine Siao)	Hong Kong
1995	Back to Roots	Ray Leung Pun Hei	Competition	Hong Kong
1995	Red Rose, White Rose	Stanley Kwan	Competition	Hong Kong, Taiwan
1995	Vive L'Amour	Tsai Ming-liang	Panorama (Special Screening)	Taiwan
1996	The Sun Has Ears	Yim Ho	Silver Bear for Best Director – ex-aequo	China
1996	Mahjong	Edward Yang	Honorable Mention	Taiwan
1996	Sun Valley	He Ping	Honorable Mention	Hong Kong, China
1996	Sense and Sensibility	Ang Lee	Competition, Golden Bear	USA
1997	The River	Tsai Ming-liang	Silver Bear – Special Jury Prize	Taiwan
1997	Surveillance	Huang Jianxin, Yang Yazhou	Competition	China
1997	Viva Erotica	Derek Yee, Lo Chi Leung	Competition	Hong Kong
1997	Kitchen	Yim Ho	Competition	Hong Kong
1998	Hold You Tight	Stanley Kwan	Alfred Bauer Prize	Hong Kong
1998	Butterfly Flying	Mu Duo, Wu Yunchu	Competition	China
1998	Sweet Degeneration	Lin Cheng-sheng	Competition	Taiwan, Japan
1998	Xiu Xiu the Sent-Down Girl	Joan Chen	Competition	USA
1999	Ordinary Heroes	Ann Hui	Competition	Hong Kong
2000	The Road Home	Zhang Yimou	Jury Grand Prix – Silver Bear	China
2000	The Island Tales	Stanley Kwan	Competition	Japan, Hong Kong
2000	Breaking the Silence	Sun Zhou	Competition (Special Screening)	China
2001	Beijing Bicycle	Wang Xiaoshuai	Jury Grand Prix – Silver Bear, Piper Heidsieck New Talent Award for Best Young Actor – ex-aequo (Lin Cui and Li Bin)	China, France

Year	Film	Director	Award	Countries
2001	*Betelnut Beauty*	Lin Cheng-sheng	Competition Silver Bear for Best Director, Piper Heidsieck New Talent Award for Best Young Actress (Lee Sinje)	Taiwan, France
2001	*In the Mood for Love*	Wong Kar-wai	Competition	Hong Kong
2001	*A Short Film about Death*	Lin Jun-hong	Competition	Taiwan
2002	*Chen Mo and Meiting*	Liu Hao	PREMIERE First Movie Award – Special Mention	China, Germany
2003	*Blind Shaft*	Li Yang	Silver Bear for an Outstanding Artistic Contribution	Hong Kong, China, Germany
2004	*Hero*	Zhang Yimou	Alfred Bauer Prize	Hong Kong
2004	*20: 30: 40*	Sylvia Chang	Competition	Taiwan, China, Hong Kong
2005	*Peacock*	Gu Changwei	Jury Grand Prix – Silver Bear	China
2005	*The Wayward Cloud*	Tsai Ming-liang	Silver Bear for an Outstanding Single Achievement, Alfred Bauer Prize	Taiwan, France
2006	*Invisible Waves*	Pen-ek Ratanaruang	Competition	Netherlands, Thailand, Hong Kong
2006	*Isabella*	Pang Ho-cheung	Competition	Hong Kong, China
2007	*Tuya's Marriage*	Wang Quan'an	Golden Bear	China
2007	*Mei, 2006*	Arvin Chen	Competition (Short Film)	Taiwan, USA
2007	*Lost in Beijing*	Li Yu	Competition	China, Hong Kong
2008	*In Love We Trust*	Wang Xiaoshuai	Silver Bear for Best Script	China
2008	*Sparrow*	Johnnie To	Competition	Hong Kong
2009	*Forever Enthralled*	Chen Kaige	Competition	China
2009	*Empire of Silver*	Christina Yao	Berlinale Special	Hong Kong, China, Taiwan
2010	*Apart Together*	Wang Quan'an	Silver Bear for Best Script	China
2010	*Little Big Soldier*	Ding Sheng	Berlinale Special	Hong Kong, China

Source: Berlin International Film Festival website (www.berlinale.de). Accessed November 23, 2010.

cinema. Its status as one of the world's longest serving international events may or may not explain its anomolous status here as a nonport city film festival. Either way, Table 13.7 confirms the central position Berlin must occupy in any narrative concerning Chinese cinema's relationship with international film festivals.

The troublesome case of Berlin does not invalidate the argument presented above concerning synergies between port city film festivals and Chinese cinema's ascent on the world stage in the contemporary period. Equally, the fact that there are exceptions highlights how complex a task the mapping of Chinese cinema's multiple trajectories at overseas festivals along both spatial and temporal vectors actually is.

Conclusion

The survey conducted above is necessarily selective and incomplete. However, it is detailed enough to permit the drawing of three initial conclusions. First, during the years of its global ascent Chinese filmmakers have been awarded a very large number of prizes and citations from prestigious festivals. Second, the variety of Chinese films recognized by high-profile overseas events is larger and more varied than previously suspected. Third, the capture of a plethora of awards of all kinds provides the starkest possible evidence of Chinese cinema's growing international reach and influence.

This chapter has hopefully demonstrated that key to the complex and ongoing story of how and why filmmakers from China, Hong Kong, Taiwan, and elsewhere have found gateways to overseas markets is the power and influence wielded by major events such as those held annually at Cannes, Hong Kong, Pusan, and Venice. International showcases like these function on multiple levels simultaneously – connecting spheres of film production, presentation, exhibition, distribution, and consumption – while also molding perceptions of industry leadership and achievement. Festivals flag to the world those titles and people deemed worthy of attention. The single most tangible benefit of recognition by such events may be said to be the confirmation that such and such a film or filmmaker has landed in the right place at the right time.

Notes

1   This chapter makes no attempt to engage with complex, fundamental, and ongoing questions concerning the definition and classification of "Chinese cinema." For major interventions into this debate, see Y. Zhang (2004a), Lu and Yeh (2005), Berry and Farquhar (2006).

2   Little scholarship has been produced to date on Chinese cinema at international film festivals prior to the 1980s. For an exception, see K. Yau (2003) on the Asian Film Festival; see also S. Lee (2011).

3   For the rise of the international film festival circuit, see Stringer (2001) and De Valck (2007). Up-to-date academic debates and bibliographies in film festival studies may be found in Iordanova and Rhyne (2009) and Iordanova and Cheung (2010, 2011). The global ascendancy of Chinese cinema is considered, *inter alia*, by S. Lu (1997) and Curtin (2007).

4   We note in passing here the historical importance of earlier (albeit more isolated) achievements, notably the Grand Prix of the CST (Technical Grand Prix) awarded to *A Touch of Zen* (King Hu, 1971) at the 1975 Cannes International Film Festival. An "A-list" festival is one designated by FIAPF (the International Federation of Film Producers Associations) as a Competitive Feature Films Festival: the thirteen currently accredited in this fashion include Cannes, Berlin, Shanghai, Tokyo, and Venice. For a detailed historical account of how East Asian filmmakers – including China's Zhang Yimou – negotiate the demands of the international film festival circuit, see N. Lee (2005).

5   Studies of domestic Chinese film festivals include Urban Council of Hong Kong (1996), Taipei Golden Horse Film Festival Executive Committee (2003), Nornes (2009), and Rhyne (2011).

6   Yingjin Zhang (2002: 23, 24) identifies three problems with the category "Fifth Generation": the term leads to "the inaccurate assumption that Fifth Generation films share a homogeneous style"; "it tends to gloss over the marked differences in any director's work over time"; and it is all but impossible "to fix precise dates for the Fifth Generation in Chinese film historiography." These problems are particularly evident when Western labeling practices are applied to the films of the Fifth Generation directors. For these reasons, Zhang (2002: 22) asserts that "New Chinese Cinema" is a "more accurate and more manageable term," while Tony Rayns (1989, 1991) prefers the label "Chinese New Wave" as it includes under its rubric films from Taiwan and Hong Kong as well as mainland China. Peter Hitchcock (1992: 118) objects to use of the term "New Wave" because it implies "a European development in Chinese film" and entails "a very 'Western' ideological position *vis-à-vis* Chinese culture."

7   See Bonnie S. McDougall's (1991: 25–167) invaluable archaeology of *Yellow Earth*'s overseas release and reception. For discussions of metaphors of discovery at international film festivals, see Nichols (1994) and Stringer (2005).

8   Because this chapter is concerned with the overseas exhibition of Chinese cinema, consideration of port city Chinese film festivals such as Hong Kong and Shanghai shall unfortunately have to wait for another day.

Part III
Genre and Representation

14

In Search of Chinese Film Style(s) and Technique(s)

James Udden

Recently the literature on Chinese cinema has not emphasized film style and techniques, perhaps because many presume the issue has been resolved. There is, however, a deeper concern as to what is distinctively "Chinese" in the face of transnational and global forces. Unfortunately, writers such as Lin Niantong have taken a narrow, singular path, seemingly searching for *one* definitive Chinese style with *one* viable source. This seems misguided. Chinese-language cinema over the decades has produced no monolithic, quintessential Chinese film style, but instead an impressive diversity of cinematic styles and techniques. Moreover, these are not the mere result of a singular cultural font or aping foreign models; rather, they also display inventiveness and experimentation due to greatly varying historical contexts.

What is most surprising is where and when the most distinctive styles and techniques have emerged. A closer analysis of the films from before 1949 does not reveal a "traditional" Chinese style for the most part, but a mostly conventional commercial cinema conducted according to the norms of the time, including Hollywood's. *Spring in a Small Town* (Fei Mu, 1948), on the other hand, is truly distinctive on many levels, yet it does not confirm the attempted definitions of a traditional Chinese style. The Fifth Generation in China has been very concerned with Chinese tradition, but how much they developed a distinctive Chinese style is not as clear. Rather, it is the Sixth Generation, along with filmmakers in Hong Kong and Taiwan, who have done the most to distinguish Chinese-language cinema as a whole. By looking at all these distinct shades of Chinese-language filmmaking in greater detail, we will find a multifaceted cinematic tradition whose overall strength lies in how it defies any singular definition.

Let us begin with summarizing briefly the most systematic definitions of what a Chinese style *should* be: Lin Niantong's *Chinese Film Aesthetics* (1991) and the

A Companion to Chinese Cinema, First Edition. Edited by Yingjin Zhang.
© 2012 Blackwell Publishing Ltd. Published 2012 by Blackwell Publishing Ltd.

English-language anthology edited by Linda Ehrlich and David Desser, *Cinematic Landscapes* (1994). Both share common themes. For example, there is a shared assumption that a Chinese cinema relies more on long takes than editing. Lin Niantong (1991: 7–35) calls this "montage within the long take," which is a marriage of Eisenstein and Bazin that predates such "marriages" found in later European cinema. Another common assumption is that camera mobility reigns supreme. Lin Niantong (1991: 41–9) attributes this to a tendency in Chinese painting dubbed *you*, which literally means "to float" or "to drift." The writers in *Cinematic Landscapes* echo this with notions of "multiple perspectives" and "elastic framing" with the general goal of combining "monocular perspective of the camera with the multiple perspectives of Chinese painting" (Wilkerson 1994: 39–41). Thus, the claim is made that lateral tracking shots are often found in Chinese films because this resembles unveiling a Chinese handscroll (Hao 1994: 52). This relates to a third common idea: Chinese cinema emphasizes flatness over depth, a tendency also supposedly derived from traditional culture. In addition to mostly lateral tracks and pans, Chinese films also apparently lack chiaroscuro since avoiding this adds to the flatness (Hao 1994: 54). Two writers specifically cite *Twin Sisters* (Zheng Zhengqiu, 1933) as a prime example of "flatness of composition, horizontal extension, and even lighting" (Z. Ni 1994a: 69), so as to "obscure the vanishing point and weaken the sense of depth" (Hao 1994: 47). Finally, there are some common assumptions about a properly Chinese shot scale. Lin in particular finds "a medium-shot system" to be predominant in classical Chinese cinema, based on the core idea that the camera should be neither too far away nor too close, which apparently comes from traditional aesthetics. Yet he states that overall a more distanced framing is more traditional, even when wider than a medium shot (N. Lin 1991: 75–8). The writers in *Cinematic Landscapes* espouse similar notions, relating this to such ideas as "distanced framing" and "the lyrical over the narrative" (Berry and Farquhar 1994: 100; An 1994: 120). Others assert a pervasive traditional sense of "boundlessness," "emptiness," and "vast horizontal extension" (Z. Ni 1994a: 67–9) where human figures in Chinese painting are dwarfed by their surroundings, resulting in a large number of "empty shots" that convey the oneness of humanity and nature (Hao 1994: 50). The result is a more poetic and less anthropomorphic cinema, since the Chinese tradition of painting and poetry, and the films that draw from this, "stress lyrical evocation over narrative development" (Wilkerson 1994: 42).

But how much do films from the Golden Age of Chinese cinema actually conform to these generalizations? A careful analysis of a sample of fourteen films from 1933 to 1948 consistently reveal particular works conforming to one trait, only to violate another, since various traits are at cross-purposes with each other. At best, there does appear to be a medium-shot system of sorts, yet even this claim is subject to qualifications. Even the most highly touted Chinese film from this era, *Spring in a Small Town*, does not fit several of the techniques discussed above, most of all when it comes to lighting and staging in depth. Moreover, it appears that

Table 14.1   A sample of fourteen Chinese films from 1933 to 1948

Title	Average shot length	% of shots with motivated camera movements	% of shots with unmotivated camera movements	% of total that are medium shots	% medium close-up or close-up
Little Toys (1933)	8.8*	11%	5%	35%	29%
Spring Silkworms (1933)	17.6*	19%	16%	31%	24%
Twin Sisters (1934)	21.2	11%	1%	38%	25%
The Goddess (1934)	8.6*	16%	3%	31%	33%
New Woman (1934)	9.4*	16%	4%	41%	30%
Song of China (1935)	7.1*	20%	8%	42%	24%
Big Road (1935)	8.2*	18%	3%	41%	18%
Street Angel (1937)	8.9	30%	8%	52%	33%
Crossroads (1937)	12.4	42%	4%	39%	29%
Dream of the Red Chamber (1944)	15.9	40%	9%	33%	24%
8000 Li of Cloud and Moon (1947)	16.5	39%	4%	40%	10%
The Spring River Flows East (1947)	11.2	15%	12%	40%	16%
Long Live the Mistress (1947)	17.0	34%	3%	50%	26%
Spring in a Small Town (1948)	24.5	52%	10%	50%	9%

* These six titles are all silent films with dialogue and expository titles. These titles have not been included in the shot counts. Otherwise, the cutting rates for these six films would have been even faster than they are, which firmly echoes the norms of 1920s silent cinema elsewhere.

these writers overlook other techniques that make this a remarkable film, and yet which no extant definition of a Chinese style can account for.

For now, let us begin with the long take. Is Chinese cinema from this era a long-take cinema? When compared to how most films are edited today, certainly, but when compared to the norms of the 1930s and 1940s, not really. The sample of fourteen films (see Table 14.1) reveals a wide variation of average shot lengths (ASL) that generally conforms to patterns others have found elsewhere. It is true that six of the fourteen films exceed 15 seconds per shot on average, yet note that four of these six are from 1944 onwards. Only two – *Spring Silkworms* (Cheng Bugao, 1933) and *Twin Sisters* – of nine films from 1933 to 1937 have average shot lengths of over 15 seconds per shot, whereas six of those same nine all fall under 10 seconds per shot. The fact that we see longer takes in the 1940s over the 1930s is fascinating, because this also occurred in Hollywood. Based on an exhaustive analysis done by Barry Salt, starting in 1939 there was a move toward longer takes by Hollywood directors. Thus, *His Girl Friday* (Howard Hawks, 1940) averages 13 seconds per shot, while *The Letter* (William Wyler, 1940) averages 18 seconds. Salt's overall sampling of Hollywood films from the late 1930s to the later 1940s reveals that Hollywood films on average lengthened their ASLs from 8.5 seconds to 10.5 seconds (Salt 1992: 231). Moreover, his charts reveal that in the 1940s he found a few Hollywood films that averaged over 20 seconds per shot. This is a trend that peaks in the early 1950s, after which the editing begins to accelerate again (Salt 1992: 239–40). It has never ceased to the present day, where it is now quite common for even nonaction films to average less than 5 seconds per shot.

Even if one argues that the shot durations of Chinese films from this time period (at least based on this sample) are still slightly longer on average than Hollywood, then we should remember that this apparently was also true of European films of this era with the exception of Great Britain (Salt 1992: 232). It should also be noted that none of these figures, not even Fei Mu's classic, come anywhere near the longest average shot lengths for this era. Both Jean Renoir (1894–1979) in France and Kenji Mizoguchi (1898–1956) in Japan have multiple films that average more than 30 seconds per shot by this point, and even Hollywood did as well, such as *Fallen Angel* (Otto Preminger, 1945) that averages 33 seconds per shot (Bordwell 2006: 121). Most shocking are two films in the late 1940s from none other than Alfred Hitchcock (1899–1980), who otherwise was the master of precise yet rapid editing: *Rope* (1948) is 7.3 *minutes* per shot (almost one shot per actual film reel), while *Under Capricorn* (1949) is around 44 seconds per shot (Bordwell 2008: 32–42).

It matters little here why this trend occurred when it did, especially since there is no single cause; what matters is that it occurred both in China *and* elsewhere during this same era. It is possible that people have assumed Chinese cinema is a long-take cinema because they only compared these films to more contemporary examples. That, however, is dubious since to compare any film from the 1930s and 1940s to any today will yield skewed results and unwarranted generalizations.

Equally questionable is Lin Niantong's notion that somehow Chinese cinema combined long takes with montage residing within it. Eisenstein's conception of montage went well beyond conflict between shots to showing conflict *within* shots, even if he never required that this be done in long takes *per se* (Eisenstein 1988: 183). So both in numbers and in more elusive qualities, it is hard to find anything that distinguishes Chinese cinema from this time in terms of shot duration.

The same can be said for camera mobility. The implication by Lin and others is that somehow camera mobility will preserve the multiple perspectives of Chinese painting within the monocular perspective of the camera lens. Furthermore, the almost floating or drifting quality (*you*) would therefore help mitigate any single fixed point of reference. It is further suggested that these are primarily horizontal movements, not ones in depth. The numbers indicate otherwise. First, in every film sampled except one (*Spring in a Small Town*), more than half the shots are completely static for the duration of the shot. *Twin Sisters* is of particular interest here because it directly contradicts the above definitions of a Chinese style: it is a long-take film, relatively speaking, and yet only 12 percent of the shots contain any camera movement. More common are the figures from the 1940s, where increased average shot lengths results in greater camera mobility, once again an international norm even in postwar art cinema. More importantly, when the camera does move in Chinese films from the 1930s and 1940s, in nearly every instance it is for the same reasons they move in non-Chinese films: a huge percentage of these contain pans, tilts, or tracks to follow characters as they walk, run, stand up, sit down, etc. Thus, they are "motivated" camera movements. Even the "unmotivated" shots can often be qualified: in almost every case the camera moves away from one person or group of people to another person or group of people doing something else nearby, allowing the camera to reveal new narrative information. Another repeated movement is a track that is simply done for punctuation, a common reason to move a camera in any national cinema.

Strongly related to ideas about camera mobility is the notion of flatness, another putatively predominant and defining feature of Chinese films from the Golden Age. The first qualification is that lateral tracks and pans do not mitigate depth, but accentuate our sense of depth since they trigger certain depth cues due to shifting relations between objects and people on various planes of depth. Second, films also display a fair number of track-ins as well, which clearly violates the "rules" of the Chinese style. In *Dream of the Red Chamber* (Bu Wancang, 1944), for example, track-ins are a stylistic norm throughout the film, and often they are done to bring the camera into a medium close-up for dramatic emphasis. There are noticeable track-ins elsewhere: a track-in over a table in both *New Woman* (Cai Chusheng, 1934) and *Street Angel* (Yuan Muzhi, 1937); a track-in to a medium close-up of a father when he realizes his daughter is about to elope in *Song of China* (Luo Mingyou, Fei Mu, 1935); the last shot of *Little Toys* (Sun Yu, 1933) tracks in to a medium close-up of Ruan Lingyu as she implores the people of Shanghai to stand up and fight foreign aggression; the multiple track-ins early on to emphasize different characters in *The Spring River Flows East* (Cai Chusheng, Zheng Junli, 1947–8). These are not lone examples in these films, only some of the more salient ones.

It is true that a more flat lighting scheme would lessen the sense of depth, but it is not true that Chinese films from this period tend to do only that. Instead, we find a mixture of lighting schemes often employed according to the dramatic needs of the moment. In *The Spring River Flows East*, for example, one shot tracks in on the married couple at night as they contemplate an impending separation. The lighting is strongly directional with ample shadows motivated by a window seen on screen left. The opening scene in the apartment of *Goddess* (Wu Yonggang, 1934) (see Figures 14.1, 14.2) features a definite gradation of light and dark, including some spots seen on the background. An intense 3-shot late in *New Women* is replete with dark shadows resulting from very pronounced underlighting. Even *Twin Sisters*, the supposed exemplar of flatness and even lighting, has pronounced shadows in certain shots: a medium shot indoors at night with only a candle on the left leaving deep shadows behind, or later that same evening the father returns injured, and the concern of both the mother and the daughter is shown in close-ups with pronounced low-key sidelighting. Like elsewhere, charged narrative moments such as these often receive the most dramatic lighting. How deep or shallow the image is does not seem to be of primary concern.

If it seems doubtful that the long take, camera mobility, or flatness are distinguishing traits of classical Chinese cinema, the notion of a medium-shot system is more complicated. For example, if one compares the figures in the sample this study is based on with Barry Salt's (1992: 219–22) figures for his sample, one will note that there indeed does seem to be a much higher percentage of medium shots in China compared to the West. However, there are some important qualifications to be made. For starters, it is very difficult to measure shot scales with even a modicum of precision. One reason is that shot scales are on a continuum: where exactly does a medium shot become a medium long shot or a medium close-up? The answer varies from person to person, and it is not clear whether Salt's standards and those of Lin Niantong's are even the same. In doing this study I chose to take a very liberal interpretation of the medium shot. Therefore, if a shot's frameline was cut off at the thighs, in most cases I called it a medium shot, since I consider a medium long shot to be much closer to the ankles. However, I also called a framing that cuts off halfway up someone's chest a medium shot, since medium close-ups in my book should only include the head and shoulders. However, I noticed that at times one shot would be the first shot scale, while the second shot would be the second shot scale, or vice versa: either way, this is a clear change in shot scale, yet I counted both as medium shots in order to mitigate my own biases. Other problems also emerge. In many shots there are multiple characters and not all have the same shot scale. In many shots characters move not just laterally, but in depth, and thus their shot scales change in the middle of the shot. In other cases the camera moved in depth and that changed the shot scale, as noted above. Once again,

Figure 14.1 A defiant look from the tragic silent movie star Ruan Lingyu in *The Goddess* (dir. Wu Yonggang, Lianghua Film, 1934).

Figure 14.2 Ruan Lingyu as the caring mother prostitute watching her son doing homework in *The Goddess* (dir. Wu Yonggang, Lianghua Film, 1934).

just to play it safe I called many shots a medium shot even though it was not always an open and shut case; I suspect now my figures are very inflated as a result.

Even if my figures are indeed accurate and comparable with Salt's, this does not seal the deal for the medium shot and Chinese cinema. What is striking about this sample is an almost ubiquitous norm for strategically employing different shot scales. Normally one keeps the camera at medium shot or wider, thus reserving bona fide medium close-ups (head and shoulders only) for *dramatic emphasis*. True close-ups are almost singularly reserved for key *narrative* details, usually an object of sorts. In *Long Live the Mistress!* (Sang Hu, 1947), for example, a wife notices a brooch on another woman as having been previously in her husband's possession. Her reaction is emphasized in a medium close-up, while the brooch is isolated in a close-up, a conventional yet effective eyeline match. In *New Woman* such medium close-ups are common for several dramatic moments, but one true close-up of a face occurs when a mother is looking at a mirror to prepare to become a prostitute – the only way she can save her sick daughter. In *Street Angel* several medium close-ups are used when Xiaohong is forced to sing a song to her boyfriend who is upset with her profession. When he storms out in anger, there are three medium close-ups of her reaction, her boss's reaction, and his friend's reaction, all in succession. We should remember what was hinted at above: even shots that do not begin as a medium close-up (and were not counted as such) may end up that way as the result of a track-in, another technique for dramatic emphasis. For a cinema that as a whole is supposed to emphasize the lyrical over the narrative, and supposed to decenter the human focus to a larger world of nature, it is striking how much these films are anthropomorphic and narrative based, to the point where they are barely distinguishable from Hollywood films from the same period. Certainly there are poetic touches, but that is all they are. They hardly drown out the narratives.

Conspicuously absent from the above discussion is the last title listed in the sample: *Spring in a Small Town*. First, it is an exceptional film, and arguably the greatest Chinese film of its time; second, this is also the most cited film when discussing issues regarding Chinese film aesthetics. However, it is quite remarkable what people have taken away from this, and what they have missed. For example, Lin Niantong (1991: 75, 86) cites this film as an example of "the medium-shot system" and a "flat and expansive" sense of space at the expense of depth. Closer examination makes one wonder if he saw a different version, or a different film altogether.

This film does have the longest average shot length of any pre-1949 film discussed here. Still, it is not quite what the ASL found in non-Chinese directors from this time such as Mizoguchi, Renoir, Otto Preminger (1905–86) or late-1940s Hitchcock. Certainly it has the highest percentage of shots with camera movement, but 84 percent of those camera movements are primarily motivated by figure movements inside the frame. Moreover, almost none of these camera movements are lateral tracks. Even those few that are usually have a narrative motivation behind them. The most notable example is late in the last evening when Zhang

Zhichen and the younger sister are outside: the camera tracks down along the wall of the house to show Zhou Yuwen pensively sitting alone in her room. Even this is not a flat, lateral track, since the camera is angled as such that we get strong recessional depth. Other camera movements are actually designed to pick up subtle shifts in character interactions in a remarkably understated and sophisticated fashion. Particularly noteworthy is the first shot of the first evening of Zhichen's visit. The shot begins with Yuwen in the foreground in a medium shot, while in the background the young sister is singing to Zhichen. Depth is emphasized by this staging alone. The camera then pans left to show Yuwen administering medicine to her sick husband, Dai Liyan, only to pan back to the right to reveal that Zhang is looking longingly at her. The camera then pans left back to Liyan, then pans right yet once again, when Liyan joins his sister and his friend. The camera then pans back to the left to show Yuwen alone on the bed, with her back to the camera. Finally, this same long take ends with a pan back right to show the other three finishing the song. In one prolonged yet bold stroke, Fei Mu beautifully and subtly sets up an entire web of relationships upon which this film will build.

Many of the other camera movements in the film are track-ins, and often they are employed to greatly exaggerate depth, not mitigate it. Early on in the film Old Huang goes looking for Liyan outdoors: in the first shot of this major character, the camera tracks in through a hole in the wall to see him sitting among the ruins, while the next shot tracks in to Old Huang in a medium close-up at the end. Later when Old Huang announces to Yuwen that the new guest's surname is Zhang (Zhichen), the camera tracks to emphasize that this surname has some significance. Yet, she remains in profile, so it is not too forced or obvious.

However, camera movements alone are not what emphasize depth in this film; so do staging in depth and most of all chiaroscuro lighting. Indeed, the chiaroscuro in some scenes is so pronounced, and so unforgettable, that it is surprising that none of the writers discussed here ever brings it up. This is especially true of the guest room where Zhichen stays, which in many ways is the geographical fulcrum upon which this whole narrative is balanced. Note in particular that moment when the electricity is cut off at midnight, and note how dark and deep those shadows are. Such images recur with subtle variations on each narrative night in this film (see Figure 14.3).

To be fair, there is clearly a preponderance of medium shots in this film, and there are at least a dozen shots that can be considered true "empty shots," something not easily found in any of the other films we are discussing. But many of these are poetic touches that enrich a simple narrative being told in a complex and delicate manner. They are not necessarily the lyrical *over* the narrative. The shots of the moon at night are more obvious perhaps, but the empty shots of the water during the rowing scene deftly punctuate everything that is not being spoken, but is being captured by furtive glances and subtle pans and tilts between Zhichen and Yuwen. This notwithstanding, there are still more medium close-ups than empty shots in the film as a whole, and once again these are reserved for calculated effect.

Figure 14.3 A scene of strong chiaroscuro with power outage in *Spring in a Small Town* (dir. Fei Mu, Wehnhua Film, 1947).

When Yuwen first goes outside to meet their new guest, a medium close-up of him, followed by a medium close-up of her, make manifest to us that they know each other, and once loved each other. Even more subtle are two inserted medium close-ups of Liyan lying in bed, which are cross-cut in a very precise rhythm with the guest room on the first night. Despite being shrouded in shadows, in the first medium close-up we can see his eyes open, in the second they are closed. Does he suspect something or not? Yet nothing stands out more than a key cut-in during the drinking game, the very night when passions will nearly get the best of every one of these characters. When Yuwen begins to engage in this game with Zhichen, the next shot is a significant reaction shot of Liyan as he realizes there is something more going on (see Figure 14.4). The camera then pans slowly to the right to catch her in a medium close-up after he sits down out of the frame. Then it pans further to the right when he walks behind her. One might think this is very forceful and direct in the Hollywood manner from this description, yet it is anything but, since his expressions indicate more shock than rage. Liyan's discovery of their love for each other carries its own surprises – he does not really blame either one of them and judges only himself.

No other Chinese film of this time that we know of has quite these qualities, and neither do most films outside of China. What we see thus far suggests a touch of Renoir and a smidgen of Mizoguchi. As remarkable as all this is, most of all the complex staging in depth and the use of highly gradated lighting, none are what

Figure 14.4 Emphatic cut-in to a medium close-up of the husband in *Spring in a Small Town* (dir. Fei Mu, Wehnhua Film, 1947).

most distinguishes this film. There is something else here – hitherto overlooked – that stands virtually alone: the voice-over.

Voice-overs had become commonplace since *Citizen Kane* (Orson Welles, 1941), but the voice-over in *Spring in a Small Town* is strikingly original; it serves a radically different purpose than the film noir norm, a purpose not found in either traditional or modernist norms of the time. This voice-over is deeply psychological in nature, something that traditional Chinese aesthetics has little to say about. It suggests all the tensions, contradictions, and shades of a frustrated Chinese housewife after the war. Significantly, the voice-over makes an ambiguous and subtle shift from the third to second person at the moment she first sees Zhichen: "He certainly did not know that I had married Liyan. Why did you come? What did you need to come for? How can I even face you?" Most remarkable is how this Chinese housewife bares the deepest longings and frustrations of her soul *only early on*. After Zhichen's arrival, however, her voice-over becomes mostly descriptive and perfunctory. In short, after having penetrated the psychological depths of a Chinese woman caught in quiet desperation, thereafter we can only guess at her true thoughts, being forced to rely instead on oblique, ambiguous cues found in her cryptic expressions and minutest actions.

Timing here is quite significant. Postwar cinematic modernism was taking baby steps in 1948. Italian Neo-Realism was at its peak with a new sense of realism coupled with a more episodic sense of narrative, which later filmmakers will pursue further. But who anywhere was doing a voice-over in as fresh a new way as this? Only two examples come to mind, and both come just *after* this film: *Silence of the Sea* (Jean-Pierre Melville, 1949) and *Diary of a Country Priest* (Robert Bresson, 1950). This is not to suggest that either one of these filmmakers got this idea by somehow seeing Fei Mu's film – it is highly unlikely they ever even heard of it, let alone saw it. Perhaps this new sort of voice-over was the best way to express a postwar angst that no existing cinematic norm of the time could quite muster, but this could only be theorized, not proven. What is undeniable is that Fei Mu did this with no real model or precedence, nor even real outlet. After all, this film did not make it to Venice or any major film festival, and it is unlikely Fei Mu was even thinking in those terms. Had it been shown at a major film festival back then, who knows what would have happened? Instead, it would be *Rashomon* (Akira Kurosawa, 1950) two years later that first opened the doors of Asian cinema to the international film festival world. China as a whole went another path with Mao's takeover, and Fei Mu's masterpiece became not just the lost opportunity – it literally became the lost film, only to be unearthed in the 1980s. That it even got made in the first place in the throes of a civil war, and was made so well, is miracle enough. It is also the first clear sign that Chinese cinema in time would no longer be content to be a derivative cinema; cinematic inventiveness was indeed in the Chinese blood so long as conditions allowed it. The question now is when and where.

In China proper this would take some time, largely due to politics. After the Communist takeover in 1949 there would be no room for Fei Mu, who would be banished to Hong Kong as a "rightist." He never made another film, and soon died in 1951. Ignoring completely the experimentation of *Spring in a Small Town*, the existing conventions of Chinese cinema were deployed for overtly political ends in the new PRC. In effect this meant a Hollywood-like style but with a socialist face; in other words it was a self-effacing style, only now the central focus was not psychological or individual character conflicts, but class conflicts represented by individual characters. The actual films of the Maoist era confirm that this was modeled after Soviet socialist realism, no matter what actual political break occurred in 1960. What is notable here is that in many ways the Maoist films did not differ much from the typical pre-1949 film; they only differ radically from Fei Mu's one-off experiment. Take *New Year Sacrifice* (Sang Hu, 1956), for example: the average shot length is somewhat long at 13.7 seconds per shot, but with camera movements in less than 20 percent of the shots, and with three-quarters of those being motivated by figure movements. Once again, there is a predominance of the medium shot, yet both medium close-ups and track-ins are reserved for dramatic emphasis, often in conjunction with each other. Early in the film, a track-in occurs to a medium close-up of the protagonist who realizes she is being sold off after becoming a widow. A later close-up of her hairpiece is conjoined in an eyeline match with her new master (who is concerned at this symbol of widowhood), a convention almost as old as Hollywood itself. This will persist in other films made during this time. Gina Marchetti (1997: 70–1) has analyzed Xie Jin's *Two Stage*

Sisters, noting how traditional elements of Chinese opera are combined with the "transparency and clarity so prized by both Hollywood and socialist realism." Once again, the style is invisible, forcing us to focus on a linear narrative that is easy to follow, including the political messages behind it.

The Cultural Revolution became the great cinematic interregnum, strangling filmmaking in China for a decade-long standstill where one feature-length narrative film per annum was made for what was now becoming close to a billion people. Film schools closed down and only reopened in the late 1970s after Mao's death. This fact arguably explains two phenomena: why it is that so much attention is paid to the graduates of the first post-Mao class from the Beijing Film Academy, the so-called Fifth Generation, and why it is that there was no apparent direction for this new generation when it comes to style and technique.

Clearly, traditional Chinese culture is the thematic undercurrent of these early Fifth Generation films, but stylistically speaking, it is hard to see what is either traditional or experimental about them. Films such as Chen Kaige's *Yellow Earth* (1984) and *King of the Children* (1987), or Zhang Yimou's *Red Sorghum* (1987), made a bold use of color and landscapes, but they did not do so in a discernible pattern that can then distinguish this movement from others in the world. This did not prevent writers from *Cinematic Landscapes* from trying to impose a traditional origin to these aesthetic features, especially when dealing with *Yellow Earth* and *King of the Children*. Chen Kaige admitted he was consciously drawing from Chinese traditions, including those from painting, when making these two works. Interestingly, however, in both cases the camera does not move much at all. *Yellow Earth* only has camera movement in about 22 percent of its shots, while in *King of the Children* the figure is only around 13 percent.[1] Chris Berry and Mary Ann Farquhar (1994: 85–6) claim that this reflects the traditional idea in Chinese painting about brushwork: the goal is not realistic rendering, but the delineation of an idea (*yi*) that comes before the brush. Thus, the often static camera and unchanging focus in *Yellow Earth* is because the idea being conveyed in this case is "stillness." Similarly, An Jingfu (1994: 122) finds a traditional pedigree for the hundred or so "empty" and "vast" landscape shots in *King of the Children* as follows: "Like Chinese landscape paintings, most of these shots are still." Perhaps this is the idea Chen Kaige is consciously drawing from, but this conclusion about "stillness" is the exact opposite of Lin and others who say the "mobile camera" is quintessentially Chinese. If indeed both stillness and movement are Chinese, then every shot of every film ever made on this planet is Chinese. Undoubtedly we have reached a theoretical dead end in trying to impose a traditional origin to certain cinematic techniques.

Either way, as Chen Kaige's and Zhang Yimou's careers progress, they seem to drift further and further away from the striking possibilities their earliest films suggest, and more toward a conventional style of international mainstream filmmaking done with exotic touches. It is often argued that they do this for easy Western consumption given the difficulties faced at showing their films in China.

The Fifth Generation themselves almost admit as much. In 1996 Zhang Yimou (2001: 88) made this telling remark in an interview: "No one can come up with styles that shock everyone any more; it isn't possible.... You can only use the techniques already available to film, so in this respect you don't go and look for any new devices because there aren't any." However, it is not clear what status Zhang Yimou would grant what had already occurred in nearby Hong Kong and Taiwan. By stark contrast, the films in both territories reflect a very different attitude: perhaps familiar techniques can be used in a strikingly new and perhaps "shocking" way. No longer are we talking about a lonely individual such as Fei Mu striking out on a new distinctive path, but an entire industry in one case (Hong Kong), and an entire film movement in the other (Taiwan).

If there is one place where one aspect of Chinese tradition has been transformed into a fresh and unprecedented array of cinematic styles and techniques, it would have to be Hong Kong. This is somewhat surprising, since Hong Kong was a British colony and thus supposedly the most Westernized of the three Chinese territories. Certainly Chinese films had always had Beijing opera and the martial arts as part of their content; yet it was only in the freedom offered in Hong Kong that they managed to dovetail these traditions with purely cinematic techniques that enhanced the physicality of these two traditions beyond the normal limits of time and space, creating what arguably can be called the most physical cinema to ever emerge anywhere. The details of this have already been well documented and well explained elsewhere, and there is no need to reiterate what requires a book-length explanation (Bordwell 2000). For our purposes here we need only look at a couple of examples of how much Hong Kong cinematically enhanced these traditions.

The first example is just one brief part of a scene from King Hu's swordplay (*wuxia*) classic, *Dragon Gate Inn* (1967). At one point in the film there is a long take – 29 seconds long – with a lateral track that frames a female character mostly in a medium shot as she has to fend off no less than ten assailants all by herself. Taken in isolation, one could argue that this is a quintessentially "Chinese" shot; looking close at this long take and placing it in the context of the shots before it, however, belies a brilliantly conceived cinematic rendition of traditional Chinese acrobatics. First, in roughly 20 or so seconds before this long take, King Hu uses nearly *thirty* shots, which average less than a second each! Moreover, these quick shots are edited together in a distinctively precise and rhythmic fashion: standing in place, quick medium shots (to medium close-ups) of her looking and ducking are interspersed with several quick shots of different assailants shooting arrows at her. In each case, right at the cut we see the arrows just leaving the bow. Yet when we see her reaction, the arrows are already flying by her as she evades them. This was a peculiar King Hu trademark: eliding some of the action through editing (in this case the flight path of the arrows) to compress the time while enhancing and accentuating the action in a rhythmic fashion. This face-paced prelude is what makes the long take stand out. The medium-shot scale is chosen not to be true to tradition, but because it provides the perfect balance of revealing and concealing: it reveals all of her spins and turns as she handles no less than ten assailants in 30 seconds of time, yet it conceals the actual location of most of these assailants until the moment they enter the frame almost at the same time she discovers them as well. Each time she is able to adapt in an instant and parry yet another blow. Most remarkable is the end of the long take. The camera stops its track right just in front of a wall that she is now standing behind. Deep in the shot (depth yet again!) two more assailants emerge. With her back to the camera she edges toward the wall, seemingly unaware of what the viewer suddenly sees: the arm and sword of yet a tenth assailant that suddenly appears in front of the wall, ready to take a swipe at her. Yet before he gets his chance, she evasively flips backwards. A straight cut shows her already in mid-air in this back flip, while the next shot a second later shows her already landing upright. One cannot paint a scene like this, nor can one even stage it on a live stage. Yet for King Hu, such ingenuity, such a precise orchestration of cinematic techniques in a way that no Hollywood director has ever done, was pretty much a day's work.

The other example is from a kung fu classic by Lau Kar-leung (Liu Jialiang, b. 1935). Lau may have begun as a martial arts coordinator, but when he directs his own films, he does not rely on precise rhythmic choreography alone, but uses every possible stylistic device to enhance – even stylize – the acrobatics in a purely cinematic fashion. Take, for example, his *Dirty Ho* (1979). As is typical of Hong Kong films of this genre, the plot is exceedingly simple and character psychology is an afterthought at best: a Chinese prince merely wants to collect art and drink a lot of wine, but his older brother wants him killed anyway before the emperor picks a successor. In one scene, the protagonist is invited to a wine-tasting session, but in reality it is a trap set by his older brother's henchmen. The beauty (and humor) of the scene is that both the protagonist and his potential assailant maintain throughout a surface decorum of a friendly table gathering, yet underneath it all they are actually engaged in a pitched martial arts battle of wits where even the servant gets involved. The main part of the action is continuous over 7.5 minutes handled in ninety shots, which average out to about 5 seconds per shot – no long takes here. Yet, amazingly, there are almost no repeated camera set-ups, the norm in Hong Kong, unlike Hollywood. As precisely rhythmic and overtly performative as the action is, Lau uses a plethora of cinematic techniques to make this even more dazzlingly precise, rhythmic, and forceful. The first "blow" comes from a servant serving wine, yet a quick zoom out and pan left reveals that the prince is deflecting this attack by pretending to talk to his "host" seated on the other side. Later the host/assailant flashes a fan in an exaggerated fashion: at the end of one shot the fan fills the screen; and the next shot the fan is moved away from the screen to reveal an entirely new camera set-up from a low angle, which then pedestals up to a straight-on angle. Later this same fan is flipped open, and this moment is captured by a quick zoom out to a medium shot. No less than three times the servant is flipping backwards, and the middle of the flights is captured in a quick, slow-motion shot. If you want every conceivable camera movement, you can find it here. If you want every conceivable camera angle, you can find it here. If you want variable camera speeds, you will find it here. Yet such polystylistic tendencies are not random or haphazard, they are all as carefully orchestrated as – and as carefully synchronized with – the equally impressive physical antics by the actors. In terms of drama and characterization, there is not much here. But Lau did not intend this to be taken seriously; he intended to dazzle, and dazzle he does. Rarely have humans and machines danced in this way, but in Hong Kong one can find hundreds of scenes such as this. Nobody else could really keep up, including Taiwan.

After being intertwined in an exceedingly complex fashion for several decades, in the 1980s the film industries in Hong Kong and Taiwan clearly parted ways. If Hong Kong was excelling at an imaginative cinematic appropriation of an acrobatic tradition for a popular cinema, Taiwan was soon doing something radically different: a new art cinema tradition that would eventually find adherents throughout East Asia. There are two mistakes people have made when it comes to Taiwanese cinema from the 1980s onwards. One is that it draws heavily from Chinese tradition. The other is that it is mostly derivative of an international art cinema tradition. The argument for tradition is hard to sustain when one looks carefully at the defining features of Taiwanese cinema from the 1980s onwards. The long take does indeed become an almost ubiquitous feature of this cinema, but what also distinguished Taiwanese cinema was a very odd tendency toward long takes *with a mostly static camera*, once again in direct contradistinction to the mobility so cherished by those searching for a Chinese aesthetic. Those who argue that Taiwanese cinema made these films according to art cinema/festival norms are in a stronger position. Yet, once again, nobody since filmmakers from the 1910s in Europe had consistently pursued this stylistic tendency. The Taiwanese New Cinema and after is certainly more diverse than this description suggests. Still, it was the obsessively consistent pursuit of static long takes that became Taiwan's clear mark of distinction, not only from the other two Chinas, but even from European art cinema, where only isolated examples of this tendency occur at best.

This is largely because of the efforts of one director in particular. Like Fei Mu before him, Hou Hsiao-hsien slowly developed an aesthetic without any real models to follow, including the directors from the 1910s, of whom he was unaware (Bordwell 2005a: 253). Yet unlike Fei Mu, Hou had many others who followed some of his cues throughout Asia. Hou now has on record one of the most static and yet poetic long-take films in history, *The Puppetmaster* (1993), which averages 83 seconds per shot and yet less than a third of those shots have even a modicum of camera movement. He also has one of the longest-take narrative films on record with *Flowers of Shanghai* (1998), which averages nearly three minutes per shot. As it turns out, however, Hou mastered so much more than the long take and the static camera (and the latter he eventually abandons.) He combined this dual tendency up to 1993 with an increasingly profound distancing, yet unlike any European contemporaries who would do this on Brechtian grounds, Hou did this to accomplish a different sort of feeling (Bordwell 2005a: 206). He also engaged in some of the densest staging strategies ever attempted in lieu of ample camera movements, most of all in his monumental *City of Sadness* (1989) and *Flowers of Shanghai*. Over time he relentlessly pursued challenging images sitting on the margins of visibility; he also developed equally daring lighting schemes culminating in the breathtaking *Flowers of Shanghai*. Yet perhaps these techniques are too elusive and too challenging to imitate: the static long take is another matter entirely.

By comparison, Zhang Yimou and Chen Kaige are quite conventional, editing-based directors. David Bordwell (2005a: 186–7) has illustrated this clearly with an eating scene from Zhang's *Raise the Red Lantern* (1990). This scene is the meal where the first three wives eat for the first time with the new fourth wife, played by Gong Li. After a clear establishing shot showing the space and where everyone is seated, Zhang then edits to closer views in a clear and conventional fashion to show how the three wives are each reacting to the newcomer. Particularly noteworthy are three successive shots where we see the first and second wife provide some food for the new wife, while the third wife coldly does nothing. For the entire scene the third wife says not a word, and yet she is given several reaction shots showing her evident displeasure. It is impossible to miss what this scene is about: the third wife is most displeased about the new arrival, and the editing makes this palpably clear much like in any Hollywood film. The scene as a whole is 1 minute 50 seconds in length, and is covered in 21 shots. The longest take lasts only 18 seconds (when the servant reads the menu); the shortest takes here are around 2 seconds. The ASL for this scene is thus a 5.2 seconds per shot, a very typical figure for a Hollywood film today.

One would be hard pressed to find a Hollywood director who would have handled this scene any differently. But no Hollywood director would handle this scene the way Hou undoubtedly would have. If you look at Hou's eating scenes, you will find a style unlike anybody else's today. Instead of editing around the table, Hou is likely to hold the camera at a distance from one side only, in perhaps one long take, or two or three shots at best. Instead of placing everyone on one side of the table and facing the camera, Hou would instead risk foreground heads occluding those in the background, since he prefers not using a high angle in most cases. The examples are too numerous to count, and have been documented elsewhere (Bordwell 2005a: 186–237; Udden 2009). Like Wong Kar-wai (b. 1958) (and Abbas Kiarostami [b. 1940] in Iran), Hou is arguably the most original director in the world over the last quarter century. He owes this not to following any tradition, Chinese or otherwise. He innovated in daring ways according to what the conditions he operated under allowed him.

It should be noted that one of the reasons that innovative developments in cinematic style and techniques occurred in Hong Kong and Taiwan, and not in the PRC, is largely due to a complex assortment of historical factors, and not a radical displacement of talent. Caught in the throes of perpetual war and revolution, mainland directors have suffered many added handicaps and political pressures that Hong Kong directors never faced, and which Taiwanese directors no longer faced starting in the 1980s. So traumatic was the Cultural Revolution for cinema as much as anything else that one suspects that the Fifth Generation found it sufficient to make films again, and did not require to be the cutting edge. In recent years, directors like Zhang Yimou seem to be following other models. Films such as *Hero* (2002) and *House of Flying Daggers* (2004) are almost hyperbolic derivations of the Hong Kong action cinema – they are not Hong Kong films with a socialist face; they are more like Hong Kong cinema with a Hollywood blockbuster budget, CGI included. Coupled with this is a surprising nationalistic bombast, something confirmed by Zhang's unforgettable orchestration of the opening ceremonies of the 2008 Beijing Olympics.

The same cannot be said for the Sixth Generation, led most of all by Jia Zhangke. The younger generation clearly is willing to venture on new paths that the older directors abandoned relatively early on. Initially, many of these directors did these films in an underground mode, finding funding and distribution strictly through foreign sources, while their films could only be seen in China in pirated form. Recently, however, even these filmmakers are receiving official sanction from the government, most notably starting with *The World* (Jia Zhangke, 2004), coproduced by the Shanghai Film Group. This may indicate some larger changes afoot, much as the Taiwanese New Cinema began before the lifting of martial law in 1987. Then again, it may not, for China is radically different in so many ways from either Hong Kong or Taiwan. Still, the issue at hand here is style and techniques, and in this regards the Sixth Generation signals a group of filmmakers, not a lone filmmaker, beginning to fulfill the aesthetic promise once shown by Fei Mu, and more recently by Hong Kong and Taiwan. Jia Zhangke certainly stands at the forefront of all this, especially after winning the top prize at the Venice Film Festival for *Still Life* (2006). It has been suggested that Jia's films, with their pronounced proclivity toward long takes, represent a "transnational aesthetic" that largely follows art cinema norms established by European and other Asian directors such as Hou (McGrath 2007). However, once again there is something quite different in Jia's case. Certainly he is part of a long-take tradition, and certainly he owes something to Hou, whom he openly admits is his chief inspiration. Yet he hardly follows Hou in exacting detail, including not being as beholden to the static long take as other directors in Asia have been in recent years. Moreover, it may be that Jia is in the process of blurring the lines between documentary and fiction in ways that have never been attempted before.

In short, this story is not over, and now it appears that attention is finally shifting back to China. If anything should result from this chapter, it is a hesitancy to declare once and for all what is a Chinese style and what is a purely Chinese cinematic technique. History suggests that there is no *essential* Chinese style, only multiple Chinese styles and techniques. We find that does not happen in an orderly fashion, but can appear in the most unlikely of places at the most unlikely of times, such as what occurred in both Hong Kong and Taiwan. It also suggests that these styles and techniques are not purely of traditional origin, nor of foreign origin; sometimes these are new modern traditions grown purely in native soil. This means that whatever happens next in Chinese-language cinema may come as a surprise, even if by now it should not surprise us in the least.

Note

1   It is important to realize that Chen Kaige is *not* a long-take director like Kenji Mizoguchi or Hou Hsiao-hsien. The average length of a shot in *Yellow Earth* is under 10 seconds, an unexceptional figure. Even in *King of the Children* the average shot length is just under 17 seconds, which nowhere near matches the figures of his Japanese and Taiwanese counterparts. Thus, while Chen uses little camera movement, he does rely on editing more than has been acknowledged.

15

Film Genre and Chinese Cinema
A Discourse of Film and Nation

Stephen Teo

Under what conditions do culturally specific genres arise? How do imported (usually Hollywood) genres affect the generic range of a given national production sector? Does Chinese production even have genres? (Stephen Crofts 2006: 56)

Introduction: "Does Chinese production even have genres?"

Though it seems self-evident that the Chinese cinema is a cinema of genres, it is pertinent to start off this chapter by posing Stephen Crofts' question "Does Chinese production even have genres?" as an interrogation into the nature of Chinese genres and its correlation with the concept of nation. Crofts' question was put in an essay arguing for the reconceptualization of national cinema in the face of global interconnectedness and the tendency of co-financing and coproduction. I will respond to the question by investigating what genres exist in Chinese cinema, inevitably to consider their ambiguous nature if also at the same time to reaffirm them as an integral component of the development of the Chinese national cinema. Does genre contain a recurrence of common traits by which one recognizes a national cinema? The premise of Crofts' question is that the Chinese cinema developed under conditions that he describes as "the intersections between given genres and the national" (Crofts 2006: 56). By "intersections" we can infer a transnational zone, essentially dominated by Hollywood, infringing into both the perimeters of genre and the borders of a national cinema. Here, "national cinema" is a concept that is "usually defined against Hollywood" and Hollywood "is hardly ever spoken of as a national cinema" (Crofts 2006: 44). The assumption that Crofts puts to us is that Hollywood genres must have affected

A Companion to Chinese Cinema, First Edition. Edited by Yingjin Zhang.
© 2012 Blackwell Publishing Ltd. Published 2012 by Blackwell Publishing Ltd.

the generic range of Chinese production to a lesser or greater extent, from its nascent period right up to its current phase of development, and would therefore have infected so-called national traits within genres. Crofts is certainly right in this assumption – and Chinese scholars have pointed out the same thing (Bao 2005; Z. Zhang 2005; X. Qin 2008).

Yet there is still an imperative to consider whether national traits exist in given genres in Chinese cinema with a view toward answering Crofts' question, which might be seen as a rhetorical device challenging the proposition that Chinese production has genres. The implications are twofold: the first is that Chinese production does not have genres that are indigenous to Chinese cinema, and the second is that Chinese production does have these genres but they are so alienating to foreigners as to make them completely irrelevant in the context of world cinema. Both implications are, needless to say, wrong. However, in addressing genre and its association with the concept of national cinema, we are probably faced with two kinds of tendencies in Chinese cinema discourse. One tendency is to talk about the development of Chinese cinema without any reference to genre. Chinese cinema can have production, obviously, without the need to think in terms of genre. One can basically ignore genre and think of Chinese cinema in other stipulations, for example, aesthetics and narrative, history and space.[1] However, though these approaches may yield productive results, it is the contention of this chapter that genre is integral to the cinema in its capability to convey prototypical narratives that have universal reach. Indeed, prototypical narratives are basically genre narratives, and it would be impossible to ignore genre from the standpoint of universality. The problem is the identification of prototypical narratives – genre narratives in essence – with the narratives of the nation or those of a culturally and ethnically specific group. Under what circumstances do universal stories become vehicles that carry culturally and nationally particularistic consequences? In *Understanding Indian Movies*, Patrick Hogan (2008: 17) has offered an answer by pointing to paradigmatic works "that define literary excellence, whether narrative, emotional, or moral/thematic."[2] Paradigmatic works present fundamental principles about "spiritual and social authority," which are, in nature, often "religious or political – in a broad sense, one may say 'national' – stories" (Hogan 2008: 17). These stories generate cognitive understanding in a universal fashion, but there are "differences in the precise stories that achieve this status in different traditions" (Hogan 2008: 17).

This brings us to the other tendency, which is to question the adequacy of the national cinema model as a means of defining Chinese cinema and its association with genre. Politics and ideology have certainly created the conditions for such a tendency – and one is not merely referring to the politics of the China–Taiwan divide but to the politics of the nationalism discourse itself. There are those who are predisposed against nationalisms of all sorts and those who think nationalism can be progressive and indeed abstract. I have at various times referred to "abstract nationalism," and at the risk of repeating myself, I deem it necessary to briefly refer to it once again by way of explicating and defining the relationship between genre and nation. To the critics of nationalism, the concept can simply be reduced into its most essentialist, exclusive, conservative, monolithic, and self-aggrandizing formulation. Some will no doubt say that there is no such thing as abstract nationalism because nationalism is, more often than not, oppressive. However, following Elías José Palti (2001: 329), nationalism is not necessarily conservative or reactionary as an idea. As an objective phenomenon, it can be both abstract, on one level, and essentialist, on another; it can be shaded and nuanced by different levels of perception and cognition. It seems to me that any society can develop some kind of buffer zone of nationalism to prevent the collapse of nationalism into complete essentialism, and it is on this abstract level that one can present progressive ideas.

A national cinema is arguably predisposed toward nationalism of the abstract kind inasmuch as it must take into account the national as well as the global patterns of production and distribution. In the case of the Chinese cinema, this transnational pattern is true not just in the current age of globalization but back in the stage of history when Chinese filmmakers were grappling with the creation of a national cinema in the 1920s and making films not merely for a domestic audience but also for a diasporic audience. "The special local, critical, cultural, historical and industrial milieu of each cinema needs to be 'translated' into a form available for various kinds of local and international circulation," writes Tom O'Regan (1996: 4). The idea of translation is implicit in a national cinema, and translation must perforce render nationalism abstract. O'Regan also states that those who write about national cinemas "have no choice [but to] deploy hybrid forms of analysis" (O'Regan 1996: 4). In the context of the Chinese cinema discourse, one way of defining "Chinese" cinema without putting it within the confines of the national is to view it in purely linguistic terms – as a "Sinophone" identity (Shih 2007), or in separate compartments of Mandarin, Cantonese, or Taiwanese dialect film.[3] Yingjin Zhang (2004a: 1) has pointed out the inadequacy of the national cinema model inasmuch as "China" is made up of three territories (the mainland, Hong Kong, and Taiwan) and not one. Here we have three components of an object that we might call Chinese cinema.

Historical circumstances have brought about the dispersal of filmmaking talent into three separate territories. Yet, the notion of a national cinema is one of the driving forces that compel Chinese filmmakers to make films in whatever diverse and disparate circumstances they find themselves. This is true of Hong Kong cinema, which is the most commercial and free-wheeling of the three. Despite (or perhaps because of) its private nature, the Hong Kong film industry has actually sought to identify itself as a Chinese national cinema. The Shaw Brothers Studio was representative of this tendency, its products being regarded as conclusively "national" in character by the Nationalist (KMT) government-in-exile in Taiwan, though I argue that the nationalism of Shaws' films and most Hong Kong films is abstract in heart and spirit.

The national cinema model is useful in practice as demonstrated by Hong Kong studios' adoption of it, and it can also be useful to study not just Chinese films in general, but Chinese genre film. This is not to accept uncritically the assertion of Chinese cinema and genre as a representation of "'China' as singular, essential, and naturalized" (Berry 1998: 131). Any investigation of genre in the Chinese cinema will naturally raise a question of the connection between genre and nation. In this instance, I view the concept of the national accordingly as a positive and productive space to think about micro and macro questions on film genre and Chinese cinema. To go beyond the national, or the nation-state, may not be as productive, in my view, simply because it appears to deny reality.

In discussing Chinese cinema, Chris Berry (1998: 149) has proposed a "performative model of collective agency" that can exceed the model of "the modern, unified nation-state." He refers to a tendency of individual agency that may broadly be defined as humanistic on a collective, universal plane and that is "resistant to state projects and politics" (Berry 1998: 149). Taking *City of Sadness* (Hou Hsiao-hsien, 1989) as the example to illustrate his performative model, Berry does not refer to genre as such, though it is my view that genre can better play a role as as a "performative model of collective agency" in the cinema wherein the permutations of individual agency resistant to the state can be achieved – and I will go on below to elaborate on this. Performative agency, as Berry has proposed it, is ultimately ambiguous perhaps because its idealism is predisposed against the nation-state in all its realistic, and oppressive, manifestations. Berry's proposal is well taken, I think, inasmuch as anyone of a vaguely liberal disposition can sympathize with its aims, though it strikes me that any performative model of collective agency would turn out in practice to be a rehearsal for none other than that which Berry decries – the nation-state.

If performative agency is seen in more revolutionary terms, or within the conditions of third world developing communities struggling against colonialism or neocolonialism, the concept of national cinema may be used as a tool of performative agency in the sense of nation-building or in the critical sense of Third Cinema ideology,[4] and if we consider genre as an embedded part of national cinema, its properties are imaginary and essentialist, which can certainly function as a "putative collective consciousness" (Berry 1998: 130). Lest such association might be thought of as the kind of absolutist national collective agency that smacks of fascist organization and mobilization, there is always an element of hope and democracy at play in such mass movements, as Arjun Appadurai (2007: 29) has intimated, though as he has also observed, "it is not clear whether there is any deep or inherent affinity between the politics of democracy and the politics of hope." The cinema, it seems to me, is the very kind of space where the politics of hope can be given expression as a vague notion of democracy, and as I have brought up genre in connection with collective agency, genre itself contains this very element of wish-fulfillment.

It has to be stressed, however, that genre's function in the cinema is dialectical in nature. This is in contrast to the idea of film as reflective of reality. The one genre in the Chinese cinema that best exemplifies the concerns stated here is the *wuxia* genre, which is fantastic and idealistic in essence but often regarded at the same time as nationalistic. It is a paradigmatic source of tales of chivalry and adventure, with a certain historicist–political slant stressing the need to rebel against despots or the oppressor whenever the circumstances present themselves. Its dialectical counter-pointing of the nation-state is historicist and nationalistic, as well as allegorical and transnationalistic. This is perhaps best illustrated by the examples of two films, *Crouching Tiger, Hidden Dragon* (Ang Lee, 2000) and *Hero* (Zhang Yimou, 2002).

In the context of wuxia, the notion of chivalry is all-inclusive of attitudes derived from Confucian ethics governing relationships between father and son, master and disciple, and brothers and friends, as well as husband and wife. *Crouching Tiger* stands as a film that examines this ethical worldview of wuxia. However, the spirit of chivalry (or wuxia) is taken to its height when it is applied to society at large rather than just within the narrow confines of the family. It extends indeed to the nation and governs the highest relationship between the ruler and his subject, as in *Hero*. This wuxia spirit is behind the genre's historicism. Effectively, chivalry translates as history in action or history come to life, brought into being by knights-errant or *xia* who are executors of history in their own right rather than historians who observe events and write about history. The knight-errant is conscious of his or her role in shaping events and the destiny of the nation, and within the bounds of the genre, it is probably more important to refer to the nation-state as an abstract entity that is somehow bonded with the central figure of the xia or because the latter is compelled to take up arms against the former whenever justice and righteousness are at stake. The "nation" is in this way crucial to the genre, since its leading protagonist, the xia, needs a cause to justify his or her act of violence, and no cause is greater than that of the nation. At the same time, the dialectical agency of wuxia opposes the confines of the nation by its fantastic visions that are universal. Ideals such as loyalty, fidelity, charity, trust, and peace are above all the universal values of the wuxia spirit that the genre would strive to define (Du 1968: 63). Among Chinese indigenous genres, wuxia today is perhaps the best known throughout the world. It has become a representative genre of the Chinese national cinema because of its stronger propensity to convey a certain sense of nationalism and values of justice, duty, and honor. Genre in this sense defines the collective values, ideals, and traditions of the nation. The characteristics of the genre are then the characteristics of the nation, defining both the nation and its cinema.[5]

Inasmuch as genre can be borrowed and applied to the specifics of a particular nation, as part of the nation's cinema, genre is an unstable concept, like the nation itself. My view of Chinese genres is to conceive of Chinese cinema as a rich and diverse source of national narratives as well as different types of stories, not so much to critique the concept of the nation-state but to examine how genre and the nation-state can coexist and complement each other. The richness and diversity of Chinese cinema is not wholly compelled by culture but by political circumstance of division; for instance, the wuxia and horror genres, banned in China over a long period,[6] could only develop in Hong Kong, thus adding to the richness of Chinese cinematic culture in general. This is the uniqueness of Chinese cinema. A national cinema can be divided into separate film industries of different political jurisdictions and yet be a national cinema. Clearly, this is the stance of Taiwan's Golden Horse Awards and the Hong Kong Film Awards in their annual deliberations of Chinese films.

Indeed the idea of national cinema is not incompatible with diversity or dispersal if we go by O'Regan's view of Australian national cinema. O'Regan (1996: 2) has come up with the innovative idea that national cinema studies is an examination of "films and their diverse conditions of production" and that such studies "routinely survey the connections between text and local and international production, reception and distribution, and between these and the local and international, among society, cultures and peoples." O'Regan (1996: 2–3) states: "'National cinemas' present themselves to audiences, film workers and critics alike as so many contingent links among disparate elements, disparate telling, varied film-making projects. National cinemas are, in this sense, not so much coherent as dispersed."

Still, while the concept of the national remains a problematic one in addressing the territorial inconsistencies of the Chinese cinema, it is fair to say that all three Chinese cinemas are essentially genre cinemas. Genre, in this case, becomes a unifying force that entwines three cinematic entities – separate film industries, divided by politics and ideology. Genre is generic to Chinese cinema of all political shades and territories; it provides cohesiveness to the various Chinese cinemas. But having said that, it is still imperative to consider the nature of genre in Chinese cinema and how it shapes and defines the national. What genres may in fact be called national given the inadequacy of the national as a paradigm and the fact that a national cinema exists as an appropriation of many forms and styles that can be both indigenous and foreign? Here we may be getting to the root of Crofts' question, which is an attempt to redefine the concept of national cinema, albeit in doing so, we are addressing the nature of genre – its exaggerated, fantastic, and wish-fulfilling premises *vis-à-vis* the idea of nation – rather than by addressing the strengths and weaknesses of the political and economic foundations of the nation-state. In yet another sense, genre as a device muddies the concept of national cinema through its abstraction of narratives and characters. Above all, genre is driven by the diluting tendencies of the political economy of film production.

Of Names and National Identity

If we acknowledge that there is a definite correlation between genre and the national, it would be necessary to examine how the creation of a Chinese national cinema in Shanghai during the 1920s was marked by the adaptation of traditional, indigenous genres from literature and the stage as a countermovement against the domineering presence of European and American film products. The first film made in China, *Dingjun Mountain* (Ren Jingfeng, 1905), consisted of extracted scenes from a Peking opera performed by Tan Xinpei. The genre of *Dingjun Mountain* is ambivalent. It can either be an opera film, a historical costume film, or a martial arts film, as the Chinese critic Chen Mo (1996: 78–9) has pointed out. All these genres are indigenous, but had no precedents in terms of a cinematic presence, and it was the task of Chinese filmmakers to establish them in Chinese cinema. Chinese filmmakers adapted genres from Western cinema, such as the slapstick comedy, the detective film, the swashbuckler, the historical epic, and the melodrama weepie. While retaining the surface features of foreign genres, Chinese filmmakers implanted indigenous organs and infused their own arteries and vessels into the bodies of these genres. Melodramas became *wenyi* films – the term *wenyi* being an amalgam of literature and art – that emphasized the more feminine tendency of the genre as well as the more civil virtues of literature and art that somehow graced the genre as the Chinese saw it. Wenyi was used to differentiate the melodrama or love story from more martial or warlike genres such as the swashbuckler, the action-adventure, the detective film, the epic, and the historical film. The Chinese went on to introduce their own martial genre into the genre pool – the wuxia film, which, as I argued above, is best able to emit the sense and sensibility of a national cinema identity. The path toward wuxia's rise as a national genre cut through other indigenous genres (about which I will have more to say shortly). It also had the ability to imitate the swashbuckling quality of Western adventure heroes and their chivalrous values in such genres like the western and the action-adventure film. Thus, the identity of wuxia itself grew out of other genres, both indigenous and foreign.

Wuxia was a tradition passed on through historiography, the novel, folklore, and popular performing traditions such as *tanci* (oral storytelling accompanied by music) as well as opera. As a tradition, it is over two thousand years old, but as a genre in the cinema it is only eighty years old if we date it back to the first installment of *The Burning of the Red Lotus Temple* (Zhang Shichuan, 1928; altogether, eighteen installments were produced and released from 1928 to 1931). The genre's entry into cinema halls was preceded by such traditional forms as the opera film (*xiqu pian*), the period film (*guzhuang pian*), and the fantastic (*shenguai pian*, indicating spirits and monsters). All these genres exuded cultural qualities that were immediately recognizable to a Chinese audience even when they were indebted to or influenced by Hollywood genres such as the western, the epic, the swashbuckler, and even the detective film, all of which were popular in Shanghai in the 1920s. Qin Xiqing (2008: 8) tells us that two currents swept through the film industry, one belonging to the Chinese stream and the other to the "European" stream (the term "European" also included American tendencies and influences).

A trend of "Europeanization" (*ouhua*) was evident in the Chinese cinema from its inception, and this elicited a counterresponse wherein Chinese filmmakers adopted the "Chinese style," which often worked out as injecting Chinese cultural features into foreign elements, or adopting Chinese genres on top of foreign ones. In this sense, the Chinese cinema is a classic case of a national cinema in which the thrust toward the national remained uncompromised by the presence and influence of Hollywood. Indeed, the presence of Hollywood and other foreign cinemas, mostly European, provided an impetus toward the creation of the national as a means eventually of supplanting the foreign. Chinese filmmakers were seeking to execute a "breakthrough" by "selecting national historical subjects" as film materials (X. Qin 2008: 146), in order to overcome their own production deficiencies in comparison with the standards of foreign films. The instrument of their "breakthrough" was genre, or rather, indigenous genres that could reflect nationalist characteristics and stories, with which Chinese audiences could identify.

In selecting genre as their instrument, Chinese filmmakers were, on the one hand, also trying to follow the standards and genre practices of Hollywood production, particularly the period epic films of Cecil B. DeMille (1881–1959) and D. W. Griffith (1875–1948) (X. Qin 2008: 146). The Hollywood influence on Chinese production practices serves to remind us once again of Crofts' question: "Does Chinese production even have genres?" Under the circumstances, the question thus seems less polemical and more insightful of the way a national cinema is formed. On the other hand, Chinese production has certainly given us genres, and it is these genres that give a certain tinge of national characteristics by which one can identify Chinese cinema as national. Chinese filmmakers chose Chinese genres as a response to the foreign – and I would say that they were driven more by professional and commercial motivations than by a political agenda of nationalism.

The major studio at the time specializing in "Chinese" genres was the Unique Studio (Tianyi), which had no interest in political or social themes whatsoever. Its founding principles were to espouse "old moral values, old family ethics, with the aim of carrying on Chinese civilization and strongly rebuff Westernization" (M. Yu 1980). Unique's modern successor, the Shaw Brothers Studio in Hong Kong, carried on these principles in its reliance on old-world genres such as the *huangmei diao* ("Yellow Plum Melody") opera films and *guzhuang* epics. In melodramas, there was an emphasis on traditional values of family ethics. Its so-called "new school" wuxia films somehow also fitted in with the old-world values of ancient China, though, it has to be said, the Shaws also adopted a modern outlook and incorporated Western-style genres such as the musical and, later, the James Bond-type action picture. The modern Shaw Brothers Studio of the 1960s and 1970s replicated the patterns of Chinese production in the Shanghai period of the 1920s and 1930s, but developed more freely along Western lines while it also engaged with the opposing yet complementary line of Chinese genres.

Adopting indigenous genres for the cinema in the Shanghai period was not a straightforward process. Corresponding with the move toward the indigenization of genres was an implicit recognition that Chinese cinema was still in its infancy compared with the American and European cinemas. In the 1920s the Chinese film industry was not technologically advanced, and it had essentially to start from ground zero as far as genre film was concerned. The early genre films in the Chinese cinema started out with a certain confusion in their names and in their actual content. For example, the period costume film (guzhuang pian) was not always in period costume. Actors were actually dressed in modern clothes, in Western-style lounge suits, though in other scenes there would be a sudden switch to period costumes; and nor were period costume films authentically historical films. This suggests a lingering sense that the turn toward "Chineseness" could not be completely executed, perhaps for commercial reasons in that the domestic audience was still used to the foreign blockbusters, and that a completely Chinese genre film would be regarded as too abrupt a transition for the audience to accept.

The progress of the genres was also somewhat haphazard and ultimately subjected to the whims of censorship, as happened with the wuxia genre which was banned on grounds of superstition in 1931 (Teo 2009: 38–57). At the time, the wuxia film was generally derided by intellectuals and the literati for its fantastic visions of flying swordsmen and swordswomen who could project forces of energy from the palms of their hands. It was a low genre inasmuch as it was popular among the illiterate masses. The wuxia film in fact grew out of the shenguai pian, which in turn was an offshoot of the guzhuang pian. The major attribute of shenguai was its supernaturalism and this became merged with the revolutionary and chivalric action principles of wuxia pian. This proved to be particularly problematic for intellectuals and the country's censors. Intellectuals, driven by the May Fourth cultural movement toward scientific and rational thinking, saw the genre as a low form that only had appeal to the uneducated, illiterate masses. Governing circles were on the other hand driven by educational and didactic imperatives. Cinema came under the purview of the Education Ministry, which was also responsible for censorship. One of the first duties of the Film Censorship Committee, when it was formed in 1931, was to look into the question of wuxia shenguai pictures, as the genre came to be known. As early as 1929, the Education Ministry had noted in a circular:

> Recent Chinese films were inclined toward historical shenguai subjects, some films advocating superstition and rule of divinity, others prating about Confucian ethical codes and ancient ways. The practice has become a fashion, violating principles of [scientific] progress in literary art. Would this not have an adverse impact on education? This ministry will [consequently] draw up a comprehensive plan to reach conclusive standards for the production of Chinese films.[7]

The Education Ministry's "comprehensive plan" involved a proscription of wuxia shenguai pictures. By this time, the outcry against the genre had reached a crescendo following the suicide of a mother whose two young children had left home for Mount Emei, the spiritual home of mythical xia, in search of immortals to teach them martial arts skills. The newspapers feasted on the story, and the government felt the pressure of public opinion to ban the genre (Gong 1968: 165; see also Henriot 1993: 65–102; Pan 1984: 61–5). The banning of the genre had adverse effects on the Shanghai film industry, which immediately felt the effects of a recession. The wuxia shenguai film was a money-spinning genre in the best of times, but it could still be counted on to pull in the masses during hard times. In 1932 the film industry was facing bankruptcy. The economy of Shanghai's hinterland, based on the silk-manufacturing textile business, had collapsed, while the film industry itself was threatened by the massive influx of foreign films and the power of foreign companies that held trusts in theaters in Shanghai and other treaty ports. Censorship affected the productivity cycle as it led to the stoppage of the production of a profitable genre.

The banning of the wuxia genre in the Chinese cinema stunted the genre's development in the Chinese film industry in Shanghai but its subsequent growth outside the mainland has tremendously benefited Chinese cinema in general, in terms of transnational outreach and making Chinese film better known internationally. The popularity and longevity of wuxia appear to have outlasted the guzhuang and shenguai genres, which were its antecedents, but wuxia remains something of an enigma because of the embedded characteristics of these other genres. Yet these characteristics appear to distinguish wuxia from other genres, in particular kung fu, which is deemed to be "realistic" and "modern" (in the sense that its characters are not dressed in ancient costumes). They also delineate the cultural facets that establish nuances and traces of identity to a lesser or greater degree, that eventually make up the formulation of a national cinema identity. Despite the opprobrium and condemnation that it suffered from intellectuals and the Education Ministry, wuxia and its root genres, shenguai and guzhuang, paved the way toward a national cinema. This is now recognized in retrospect by film scholars today. Qin Xiqing (2008: 8) wrote that wuxia and guzhuang touched "a highly sensitive and fragile nerve" that was Chinese national identity and that their "traditional stories" adapted from historical sources fostered the sense of national identity in the audience, and the method and style of combat that differed so strikingly from Western techniques brought about a satisfaction of the identity need.

Be that as it may, the development of wuxia and its root genres was never a smooth process. All these names – guzhuang, shenguai, wuxia – tend to confuse the characteristics of any one particular genre. The early wuxia films were not always guzhuang pian, for example – and in the end, they all seem to join together, so that today, a wuxia pian is really a historical costume movie and a fantastic shenguai movie at the same time. There is a further complication when the name is associated with kung fu, as both wuxia and kung fu became staple genres in the Hong Kong film industry. Kung fu, it could be said, was a specific product of the Hong Kong Cantonese cinema and was never as popularized in the Shanghai industry. Certainly the Hong Kong antecedence of kung fu is now widely recognized if we count only the postwar period from 1949 onwards, beginning

Figure 15.1   Opera film *Dream of the Red Chamber* (dir. Cen Fan, Shanghai Studio, 1962), featuring an all-female cast vocalized in Shanghainese, coproduced by Shanghai and Hong Kong, with Zhu Shilin as artistic advisor.

with the "Wong Fei-hong" series and on to the films of Bruce Lee, Liu Jialiang, Jackie Chan, Sammo Hung (Hong Jinbao, b. 1950), and others. Even in the present, there are some critics who cannot distinguish between wuxia and kung fu. In the mainland there are critics who regard wuxia as interchangeable with the form known as the *baishi* guzhuang pian – classical-costumed tales of anecdotal history that took their ancient stories from popular tradition (e.g., J. Dai 2005). The term *baishi guzhuang pian* is evidently still current, used to refer to a generic series of period-costume, historical films, and it may be used in preference over wuxia. The reason may be that critics growing up in China in the 1960s and 1970s would have no recognition of wuxia as a separate genre, since they would have no means at the time to see wuxia films as they would have been banned in the mainland. In contrast, over the same decades, a wuxia renaissance was taking place in Hong Kong, in both the Mandarin and Cantonese industries. The specific characteristics of wuxia film would have been entirely missed by a generation growing up in the mainland, though they would be familiar with the period-costume features and the historical settings from other genres in the mainland cinema, such as the opera film and the historical epic (see Figure 15.1).

The profusion of names in Chinese pointing to generic classifications as well as specific genres has no doubt confused the issue of identifying genres and their characteristics. For instance, the martial arts genre contains wuxia, kung fu, guzhuang, and shenguai. The baishi guzhuang pian can incorporate wuxia, shenguai, and xiqu pian (the opera film). If studying Chinese cinema is to study genres, it may be a fruitless exercise to consider just what genre is more or less typical of its type. Under the circumstances, Crofts' question may more be a cry of frustration. Derrida (1980: 61) tells us that in nature and art,

> genre, a concept that is essentially classificatory and genealogico-taxonomic, itself engenders so many classificatory vertigines when it goes about classifying itself and situating the classificatory principle or instrument within a set. As with the class itself, the principle of genre is unclassifiable.

Genre study in itself may be a process of coming to grips with the various "classificatory vertigines." In the Chinese cinema it tends to breed confusion and though the process of genre study might entail clearing the decks in an effort to reduce complexity to simplicity, in the end, one must come to a realization that the development of Chinese genres is often arbitrary and contingent on public tastes that can result in mixtures of styles and typologies over time. Yet, the movement toward the incorporation of indigenous genres in Chinese cinema is beset with a form of naturalization, a kind of internal law that deems natural "structures or typical forms whose history is hardly natural but, rather, quite to the contrary, complex and heterogeneous" (Derrida 1980: 60). If we seek to understand genre, on the one hand, there is the injunction: "As soon as the word 'genre' is sounded, as soon as it is heard, as soon as one attempts to conceive it, a limit is drawn. And when a limit is established, norms and interdictions are not far behind" (Derrida 1980: 56).

This law of genre immediately comes up against a counter-law, "an axiom of impossibility that would confound its sense, order, and reason," and would result in "impurity, corruption, contamination, decomposition, perversion, deformation, even cancerization, generous proliferation, or degenerescence" (Derrida 1980: 57). The law of genre is "precisely a principle of contamination, a law of impurity, a parasitical economy" (Derrida 1980: 59). In applying this law to Chinese genre film, we may get at the gist of Crofts' question. Chinese production does not have pure genres, and while early Chinese filmmakers may have appropriated indigenous genres into cinematic practice, they have subjected them to contamination and impurity through absorbing the influences of world cinema and the need to serve a wider diasporic audience. But what are the "norms and interdictions" of the indigenous genres in the first place? For detractors of the wuxia genre, for example, they may well be its historicist trappings, its propensity for heroic myth and fantastic violence that can serve the purposes of the state and propagate authoritarianism or fascism. On the other hand, if such norms and interdictions were seen more positively, wuxia functions as the arch-genre of the Chinese national cinema simply because it defines China as a nation in some way. Indeed Chinese film historians such as Du Yunzhi (1968: 62) have tended to raise the genre to "a special status" in Chinese film history for providing a production tendency "possessing national characteristics." Along this line, the idea of genre as a natural form of the nation-state appears to complicate the issue of genre's heterogeneity and impurity. Zhang Yimou's *Hero* serves as a prime example of the natural convergence between genre and nation, whether seen in terms of the limitations of the nation-state (its despotic authoritarianism) or exuding the nation's characteristics. It is evidence of how genre and nation can indeed work in agreement, serving each other's purposes for good or for bad. Detractors have called the film fascistic (e.g., E. Chan 2009), in their own way implicitly recognizing the association of genre and nation.

While the claim of fascism leveled at *Hero* needs to be weighed against the state of impurity of the genre itself (its premise as fantasy or wish-fulfillment), and the truth-is-relative complexity of the film's own narrative, its association of genre and nation seems quite normal and undisputed. Despite the attempt to "naturalize" wuxia as history, *Hero* is at the end of the day a romantic fantasy strewn with flying knights-errant who spew forth metaphors about the sword and the nation (and, as such, it is only one of many such films over the expanse of the genre's development, though it is probably the most outstanding of its kind). Its militaristic trimmings are in keeping with the essentialist nature of the genre as a whole and the mythical concept of the struggle of good and evil – in short, no better or worse than some-thing like *Lord of the Rings* (Peter Jackson, 2001), for example. Critics rail against the cultural and nationalist essentialism of the wuxia genre in general but fail to realize that a genre is nothing if it is not essentialist. This may be the ultimate law of genre.

Perhaps critics may really be attacking *Hero* for its low-culture vulgarity, for its "impurity" as high-culture representation of China (or its pretension to be such). Yet a film like *Hero* actively counterpoints vulgar essentialism through its narrative complexity and aestheticization. It actively seeks to inflect violence through an inquiry about the nature of the sword and its aesthetics, and its bias toward the state is counterbalanced by the focus on individuals as determining agents of history rather than the state. The film's abiding image to my mind is that of the empty space left behind by Jet Li's assassin – that space in which he as an individual has stopped the arrows from filling in, and which, as a symbol, is as important if not more so than the image of the Great Wall that closes the film. The knights-errant-cum-assassins of *Hero* are the kind of individuals who achieve "performative agency" in resistance of the state, and it is they who ultimately remain unsung and underes-timated probably because the element of wish-fulfillment in the genre, ironically, is not exactly realized (the tyrant is not killed, and the state is not overthrown).

In trying to explicate what wuxia is, we might need to transcend genre by defining what is infinite about wuxia. This essentially relates to the inherent universality of paradigmatic works that allow us to recognize the mass appeal of these models from the perspective of the cognitive capabilities of human emotion. Genre in this sense transcends the confines and limitations of national cinema. The space in *Hero* that I have cited above as a space of individual resistance against the nation-state repre-sents the universal aspiration of humanity. This seems innate and unequivocal, but the space is infinite and so is its meaning. It signals that there is no end of history in the genre. The historicism of wuxia is in this sense beyond measure, and the heroes of the genre are forever on the quest for justice and historical relevance. This is not to say that *Hero* is a great film but rather that it is a fine example of its genre. The truth about a film like *Hero* is of course that it may contain a multiplicity of meanings from its other images, and that the total cognitive significance of the work is that human emotions are never fixed and meanings will fluctuate.

Paradigmatic works generate understanding through the senses and the intellectual resources of the audience to identify with universal meanings and characters in the narratives. In another sense, within the context of Chinese cinema, we might need to consider history alongside the political and spiritual dimensions of the genre. Wuxia has a long tradition that well antedates the cinema. It is intertwined with history and literature. Its foundations and antecedence are masked or even suppressed by the industrial tendencies of filmmaking and distribution determining tastes and the classifications of films in Chinese-language cinema (which explains its various nomenclatures in different periods of time). However, genre study is perhaps only a window of opportunity that should be seized as a means toward the greater end of cultural exchange and understanding. The objective of this chapter is to demonstrate that the wuxia film, or any other genre film in the Chinese cinema, is a subject that can stand as a cultural product as well as a national one, or indeed, that there is a convergence of cultural and national identities between genre and nation. Despite all its norms and interdictions or even its corruption through the heterogeneous forces of global and Hollywood cinemas – the implications, after all, of Crofts' question – genre film in the Chinese cinema is a vehicle of national cinema driving through the tunnel of transculturalism and transnationalism. Chinese filmmakers inevitably want their genres to cross borders and influence other cinemas just as they have been influenced by the genres of Hollywood and the cinemas of the world.

Conclusion

This chapter had set out to reply to Crofts' question "Does Chinese production even have genres?" and the answer at this conclusion is largely in the affirmative, though the investigation of genres has also led to more questions about the suitability of the national cinema model as a receptacle of genres, and vice versa, to the suitability of genre as a container of traits and characteristics that may be defined as national. The nature of genre itself is inevitably ambivalent and the cinema that is defined through genre is an abstract model of production distinguished by the dynamics of ambivalence. Yet the ambivalence of genre can encompass a sense of identity and provide a certain satisfaction in the audience seeking identification through the local indigenous characteristics of given genres. Names and characteristics of genres may overlap but a collective sense of values and ideals permeates through to the spectators who find a common identity in the abstract. Perhaps the one final conclusion that may be drawn is that genre gives the impression of a national cinema identity but that its true purpose may be to mutate that identity as time and circumstance change and as the world draws closer and nations become even more interconnected.

Notes

1   For the development of early Chinese cinema as performance of space, see C. Li (2008).
2   In his interview with Barnouw (2000: 28), Run Run Shaw referred to taking stories from "volumes and volumes" of Chinese books familiar to Chinese everywhere; as the "last of the great movie moguls," Shaw knew how to draw on universality based on paradigmatic works.
3   See, for example, the Hong Kong International Film Festival retrospective catalogs of past years featuring specific studies of Mandarin and Cantonese cinemas. Sheldon Lu and Emilie Yeh (2005: 1) argue that Chinese-language film can be synonymous with the nation-state if taken as "a Mandarin-language film made and released in the People's Republic of China (PRC)," but language can "spill over" the "territorial fixity of the nation-state" if the Chinese-language film "is made outside the sovereign Chinese nation-state."
4   The concept of national cinema can fit into the parameters of Third Cinema as a cinema of identity in postcolonial development, functioning as a voice of the marginalized, in the first instance, and as a critique of Western approaches to popular culture, in the second instance. Third Cinema's linkage with the question of the national seems quite natural, as Paul Willemen (1994: 191) emphasizes: "if any cinema is determinedly national, even regional, in its address and aspirations, it is Third Cinema." Given that he has elsewhere voiced a fundamental objection to the question of the national – basically that it is a construct of the political ideology of the ruling coalition constituting the national bourgeoisie, which will cynically invoke the "'national culture' in order to get the state to help them to monopolize the domestic market" (Willemen 1994: 191) – it is important to note that, for Willemen, the national can assume a certain progressive nature only when it is mediated by the radicalism of Third Cinema.
5   Darrell Davis and Emilie Yeh (2008: 117) have put forward the notion of "genre/ nation" as a marketing tool in the recent practice of Hollywood remakes of Asian films: "Genres provide a brand of taste distinction, a safety net and a representative agent for national film industries"; and genre functions "as the leading edge in global circulation of East Asian cinema."
6   The wuxia genre has since made a comeback in China – in fact since the late 1970s – but the horror genre remains proscribed.
7   *Shen bao*, October 29, 1929, cited in X. Dai (1996: 1422). The mention about "Confucian ethical codes" reflected the anti-Confucian movement that went parallel with the anti-superstition movement at the time. In 1934, the KMT did an about-turn when it launched the New Life movement, advocating Confucianism as an antidote to the scourge of Western liberalism.

16

Performing Documentation
Wu Wenguang and the Performative Turn of New Chinese Documentary

Qi Wang

[Documentary] is first and foremost a discovery of the self. (Wu Wenguang, in X. Lü 2003: 21)

I was following their lives, but at the same time I am layered within the film. So, the people who view the film are trying their hardest to feel their lives as they watch, and are also seeing me there, or perhaps that triggers them to think of something else. I feel like that connects with an emotional exchange between myself and the viewers. (B. Wang [2003] on *West of the Tracks*)

In May 1988, Wu Wenguang (b. 1956), a 32-year-old unemployed man who had a BA in Chinese literature and who had taught in high school and worked as a television journalist before leaving it all, turned a borrowed video camera onto his freelance artist friends in Beijing. Like his filmed subjects, the filmmaker himself was far away from home (Kunming, Yunnan province), belonged to no "work unit," had little money, and basically scraped temporary living spaces from friends or in cheap rented homes. At that moment, Wu was unaware that he was making the first independent documentary in contemporary China: *Bumming in Beijing: The Last Dreamers* (1990). As a matter of fact, the concept of documentary (*jilupian*) did not dawn upon him until a few years later, after *Bumming in Beijing* entered the 1991 Yamagata International Documentary Film Festival (YIDFF) and other international film festivals in Hong Kong, Canada, the United States, and Britain (X. Lü 2003: 6).

Three months after Wu started filming *Bumming in Beijing*, in August 1988, China Central Television (CCTV) producers Shi Jian and Chen Jue began shooting *Tiananmen*, an eight-episode documentary about Beijing. They were determined to go against the officially ordained "special-topic program" (*zhuantipian*) produced

A Companion to Chinese Cinema, First Edition. Edited by Yingjin Zhang.
© 2012 Blackwell Publishing Ltd. Published 2012 by Blackwell Publishing Ltd.

at state-owned television stations in the 1980s. Exemplified by *River Elegy* (first broadcast in June 1988, CCTV), such television documentaries are characterized by prewritten narratives, impersonal voice-over delivered in immaculate Mandarin, beautiful images for illustrative purposes, and an empathetic but subtly condescending attitude of intellectuals contemplating Chinese society and history. In contrast, experimenters such as Shi and Chen started adopting a more bottom-up perspective on reality and history through interviews or first-person accounts of ordinary people, synchronized sound recording, lower camera angles, mobile long takes, and other strategies (Reynaud 2003; Voci 2004: 80–90). Continuing with their search for a less mediated and more authentic representation of reality, Shi, Chen, and their "Structure, Wave, Youth, Cinema" Experimental Group also organized discussions at the Beijing Broadcasting Institute, the top training ground of China's television and media personnel.

The coincidence of these two attempts at an alternative presentation of Chinese reality, coming respectively from outside and inside the official system and joined by other like-minded figures, forms the backbone of Lü Xinyu's momentous writing (2003: 13–22) on the rise and significance of the New Documentary movement. Since the late 1980s, the search for a more "spontaneous" style of realism – called *jishizhuyi* and often quoting the observational practices of Frederick Wiseman (b. 1930) and Ogawa Shinsuke (1935–92) as inspiring models – has become the most widely acknowledged commitment as well as accomplishment of new Chinese documentaries (Berry 2006b: 134). After *Bumming in Beijing* and *Tiananmen*, Chinese documentary has seen a prominent and steady crop of observational pieces.[1]

Academic discussions of the new documentaries have been both enthusiastic and wary. On the one hand, partly due to the significant parallelism manifest in the contemporaneous independent feature films by Zhang Yuan, Wang Chao (b. 1964), Jia Zhangke, and others that feature a comparable thematic interest in the disfranchised social strata and an aesthetic commitment to grainy realism, critical attention to these documentaries has been justifiably focused on their subversive indexical value. As early as 1991, at her initial encounter with the new Chinese documentary when *Bumming in Beijing* was shown at the Vancouver Film Festival, Bérénice Reynaud (1996: 235–6) immediately felt the pulse of "a new kind of filmic history" being written by "a new generation of film and video artists" who were struggling to achieve a grainier form of realism. Similarly, Lü Xinyu (2003: 23) recognizes their value and power of enabling "each individual [to] enter history" and "receive the spotlight." As aptly summarized by Lin Xudong (2005: 26–7), the new documentaries dissolve the official, absolutist dogmas and present "a concrete, confrontational, open and individualistic 'reality'," thus helping to move "the structural epicenter of Chinese documentary film … away from off-screen narration and toward the events actually taking place on screen." On the other hand, while cognizant of these valences of the new documentary, scholars have started to introduce greater nuances in understanding the complexities in regard to the "relational," compromised status of their independence in negotiation with "a three-legged system, composed of the party-state apparatus, the marketized economy, and the foreign media and art organizations" (Berry 2006a: 109). The authenticity of their verité information also becomes debatable because of their erasure of the filmmaker's presence, blind belief in objectivity, and exploitation of the filmed subjects (Y. Zhang 2004b). The indexical value of these alternative realities is revealed to be necessarily contingent upon specific factors in the cultural market such as official demands for change and recutting and the international politicization of the independent works as underground and counter-authoritative. Such complications might have the new practice "co-opted, canonized, replaced, or forgotten" because it seems to become increasingly institutionalized by official media such as television; they also tend to purposefully incorporate multiple levels of representation and mediation such as blending performative mechanisms under the surface of an observational mode (Johnson 2006; Y. Zhang 2007b). Despite their attractive and meaningful propensity for alternative information on under-represented Chinese realities, the truth value of new documentaries as professed in the observational mode cannot be taken for granted. Filmmakers may succeed in criticizing official representations by way of prying open a surface reality, yet at times the deceptiveness of the cinematic apparatus tends to suture them into the apparatus itself so that they become oblivious of the innate danger of narrativization that happens in all modern history writing (Rosen 1993). Such tension between intent and representation, content and form, the irreducible subjectivity of the filmmaker and the evasive objectivity of documentary truth, seems to lie behind the contradiction between the practitioner's early enthusiasm with an observational vision and later emphasis on the individual or personal status (*geren hua*) of their practice, which has prompted these nagging questions: "Why did we start? Who are we? How do we narrate? And why?" (X. Lü 2003: 14–15, 152–6, 236–42; 2006b: 15; n.d.).[2]

The key to these interrelated questions and challenges could be found in what I see as the neglected performative turn of the new documentary, and more specifically in the notion of the documentary filmmaker as a performer of documentation. While having been occasionally noted such as in Wu Wenguang's bringing forth his own body and voice (Reynaud 2003), this complex performative tendency is sometimes blended in the observational mode as a persistent temperament, sometimes (and increasingly so) fully blown up as commanding the overall structure of a documentary. It deserves a more systematic assessment because of its considerable size, its promise of reflexive solutions to existing problems in the observational practice, and its potential of further expanding the discussion of documentary in interdisciplinary dialogues with other comparable expressions and documentations of Chinese reality.

The performative turn is not only already manifest in earlier monumental works such as *Bumming in Beijing* and *I Have Graduated* (dir. Wang Guangli, prod. Shi Jian, 1994) but also sustained in later phenomenal pieces such as *West of the Tracks*

(Wang Bing, 2003) and a number of other newer works (Q. Wang 2008, forthcoming). Often exceeding the discursive framework of an oppositional political stand and observational realism, the performative works go beyond being a "fly on the wall" and feature a much more personal, physical, and direct interaction with (or even intervention in) the sociohistorical field. The resulting dynamic between the filmmaker, the camera, and the filmed subjects, together with the authenticity of the information thus captured and documented, presents a much more complicated problematic than could be addressed by the observational practice (S. Chao 2006; Y. Zhang 2007b). Apart from offering solutions to existing problems inherent in the observational practice, such a shift of attention to the performative mode would also help stretch and readjust the previous oppositional framework within which we discuss the New Documentary movement and understand it as a negotiation not only between the official and independent forces but also between the socialist past and the postsocialist present, forgetting and memory, self and other, documentary and other contemporaneous forms of documenting Chinese reality that are being explored not only in film and video but also in avant-garde art and performance (X. Lü 2006a; W. Cui 2008; Q. Wang 2008; X. Lin 2009).

Standing at the crux is the subject of the documentary filmmaker as a performer of the documentation process. The performative documentary presents a different set of ideological and aesthetic commitments such as highlighting the filmmaker's subjectivity, rather than objectivity, in relation to his or her documented materials. This is often accomplished through an embodied camera and deliberately unsmooth editing strategies that foreground the process of filmmaking rather than just offer a smudge-free finished product. With the steady growth of newer documentaries and mixed-genre experimental videos, this performative mode is turning out to provide a crucial and sustaining force for the development and understanding of nonfiction film/video in China; therefore an up-to-date reassessment of its beginnings is much needed.

In the following discussion, I will first go back to the beginning of the New Documentary movement and examine how this performative turn has been embedded there but got immersed and neglected in the more dominant discourse on unofficial, alternative visions and grassroots information achieved by observational noninterference. I contend that Wu Wenguang, while acknowledged as one of the most important filmmakers of the movement, has failed to be understood accurately for his works have always tended to be performative rather than observational. For that reason the rest of the article will conduct a close examination of the trajectory of his work in documentary and in dance theater (with Living Dance Studio, founded by Wu and choreographer Wen Hui, his wife). The former demonstrates an increasing degree of performance in terms of content and the filmmaker's position; the latter consistently integrates documentary and video as a crucial component. I will save for elsewhere the task of conducting in-depth analysis of later works by others that fall into the category of the performative documentary because examples are ample and many of them deserve to be studied from different angles with regard to their specific agendas.[3] All those other strands evoke performance and highlight the subject of the documentary for various purposes, effects, and provocations that would, when juxtaposed with practices in the observational mode, introduce greater nuances in our reception and understanding of documentaries or any reality-based accounts as narratives constructed by specifically positioned subjects. As illustrated by Wu's creative repertoire, the relationship between performance and documentary is intricately connected rather than oppositional. My discussion hopes to provide a consistent reference point for existing and future discussions of new Chinese documentary and its close relationship with other artistic forms of relating to Chinese reality in general.

Let us go back to the beginning of our story. YIDFF played a crucial role in connecting the new Chinese documentarians with their international predecessors and comrades, especially Wiseman and Ogawa. After Wu's first exposure at YIDFF in 1991, a total of six filmmakers joined the ride in 1993.[4] Wu's *1966, My Time in the Red Guards* (1993) became the first winner of the Ogawa Shinsuke Prize, which was inaugurated that year to honor start-up Asian documentary filmmakers. That same year, Wiseman's *Zoo* (1993) won the Mayor's Prize (Award of Excellence) at YIDFF and, to commemorate Ogawa's death in 1992, the festival also organized a retrospective of eleven documentaries by Ogawa Productions. Duan Jinchuan (b.1962), arguably the most important practitioner of observational direct cinema in China, acknowledges the direct influence of Wiseman's *Central Park* (1989) on his *The Square* (1994, co-directed with Zhang Yuan). (Zhu and Mei 2004: 107). Duan felt that he could also use the Wisemanian "dispersed focus structure" (*sandian jiegou*) – what Bill Nichols (1981: 208–36) calls a "mosaic structure" – which features no "concrete characters, individual destinies, or heightened conflicts." For him, Wiseman's methodology appears very effective in the search for the symbolic order implied in a chosen subject (Zhu and Mei 2004: 107–8). With the camera as a fly on the wall, *The Square* and *No. 16 South Bakhor Street* (Duan Jichuan, 1995) choose a space whose workings are symbolic of the inner mechanisms of socialist Chinese society: Tiananmen Square in Beijing and a residence community committee office in Lhasa, Tibet.

Over the years the observational practice has seen many followers, the most famous of which include *Before the Flood* (Li Yifan, Yan Yu, 2003) and *Houjie Township* (Zhou Hao, Ji Jianghong, 2003). Wu Wenguang also acknowledges Wiseman's impact on his work, but that seems manifest more in a poetically inspiring manner than through a methodological commitment to noninterference. As critics suggest, while the mosaic structure in Wiseman is open, his editing is not; and its apparent noncomplicity risks covering up its maintenance of the viewer's "imaginary" relationship to the images (Nichols 1981: 235; Grant 1998). In an article written in May 2000, Wu reflects on Wiseman and Ogawa's influences on him. With Wiseman he discovers that the so-called independent film or video making "is a way of life, something that runs in your veins"; from Ogawa, he sees that documentary "should have a direct relationship with the reality we live in every day, a relationship with social work" (W. Wu 2006a: 138). Assisted immensely by the digital video camera, Wu was soon drawn to cultivating a more personal and fluid partnership with the technology: "I have abandoned the notions of themes and plotlines, abandoned the idea of pursuing a single aim like a hunter; instead, I ramble around by myself, a minicam in hand, distancing myself ever more from the professional filmmaker" (W. Wu 2006a: 138).

In retrospect, it seems that the early enthusiasm for observational verité was a historical coincidence between, on the one hand, an urgent Chinese need for an effective yet low-profile approach to reality different from those available in the official trope, and on the other hand, the perhaps chance (and lucky) discovery of Wiseman's practice and Ogawa's focus on the collective social phenomenon. The fact that Jean Rouch (1917–2004), whose catalytic approach to documentary is drastically different from direct cinema, actually had visited China right after 1988 but apparently made no splash on the Chinese documentary scene at that particular moment, provokes us to rethink how different the New Documentary movement might have looked had they followed Rouch instead[5] Would Rouch's interventionist style have been welcomed or would it have been regarded as too overtly expressive of the filmmaker's intentions, something that was loathed in the official productions and that would risk arousing the unwanted attention of the censors? By asking this hypothetical question I want to point to the dilemma in the early practitioners' search for a strategy to "legitimize" an alternative mode of representation – observational in this case – within the official media system and the historical contingency of their insufficient reflexivity in adopting that strategy (X. Lü 2003: 14, 229–42).

As a matter of fact, a more personal and involved practice of documentary was already manifest at the beginning of the New Documentary movement. It failed to receive enough attention due to the more urgent pursuit of alternative content through a less intrusive observational strategy and the timely availability of theoretical support from Wiseman and Ogawa. By that I mean that the performative turn was already present – and certainly in no small measure informed by the repercussions of 1989 on these filmmakers – not only in Wu's *Bumming in Beijing*, which needs to be reassessed more accurately, but also in other works such as *The Holy Land for Ascetics* (dir. Wen Pulin, ed. Duan Jinchuan, 1992). It is important to note that all of these subtly personal and performative works were made before the Chinese filmmaker's exposure to Wiseman and Ogawa at YIDFF. In other words, the new documentaries already harbored a performative tendency at its origin, whose shape and impact only became more distinct later on (Leary 2003; Reynaud 2003; Jaffee 2006).

In *Bumming in Beijing* Wu documents struggling artists like himself, whose independence from state-run "work units" was an increasingly visible new social phenomenon in the late 1980s (X. Zhu 1987; Berry 2006b). Wu presents interviews whose honest and comfortable tone often renders them into confessions. Wu at times includes his own questioning voice from off screen and his camera often communicates familiarity and empathy such as when it contemplatively observes the artists' living spaces through panning or static long takes. In this first piece, Wu already demonstrates an interest in documenting performative situations by bracketing its main body with theatrical performances of *The Great God Brown*, Eugene O'Neill's 1926 play directed by avant-garde theater director Mou Sen who is one of the five artists featured in the documentary. Another subject, painter Zhang Xiaping, produces a parallel performance in which she evokes God in delirium. During her solo exhibition at the Central Academy of Art, Zhang breaks down in a frenzy, claiming that "this is God speaking." Later, she is seen lying on the floor, questioning repeatedly "Who the fuck am I?!" Mou and Zhang's staging of emotional or spiritual anguish, both evoking the name of a god, is not accidental. Such performed angst bespeaks an intense spiritual condition suffered by these young artists from a "structuring absence": the Tiananmen Incident on June 4, 1989 (Berry 2007b: 118–20). As Wu remarks in the bonus section of the *Bumming in Beijing* DVD, "something was about to end ... I needed to film it and document it." The making of *Bumming in Beijing* is an act of participation on Wu's part to join his friends' narration of the late 1980s.

Something similar takes place in Wang Guangli's (b. 1966) more actively embodied camera. While *I Have Graduated* certainly exhibits traits of observational documentary such as suppressing the voice of the filmmaker during interviews, it contains a few remarkable traveling shots, especially at the beginning and the end as structuring brackets, which give away the filmmaker's presence not only as an observer but more importantly as a conscious participant in what turns out to be an elegiac gesture in memory of the Tiananmen Incident of 1989. For example, the end traveling shot in nighttime Beijing is actually a performance and the documentation of that performance: Wang deliberately planned and timed this take, retrieving the route along which the army trucks had driven on the early morning of June 4, 1989 on their way to the massacre (Q. Wang 2008: 229–38).

Joining Wu and Wang is Wen Pulin (b. 1957), a renowned avant-garde artist and art critic. While we are still in need of a thorough research on Wen's video documentations of Chinese avant-garde art and performance since 1985, which no doubt would further complicate and enrich our understanding of the origins of the new documentaries, I want to quickly point out here that in *The Holy Land for Ascetics*, Wen himself appears regularly and provides a personal account – with an accented Mandarin, imperfect sentences, and throat-clearing from time to time – of his and his brother Wen Puqing's encounter with and understanding of the pilgrims at Qingpu, Tibet, both of them "clearly ... as outsiders" (Reynaud 2003).[6] Such features of personal intervention and investment in the documentary's subject (matter) would be rare in a strictly observational piece.

With his second documentary, *1966, My Time in the Red Guards* (1993), Wu's performative streak becomes more prominent: he mobilizes another performance – its preparation as well as staging – as a central structuring device and explicitly includes his own participation in the documentary. Continuing the early new documentary filmmakers' obsession with China's recent past, of which they themselves are an organic outgrowth, *1966* is a documentary about personal experiences of the Cultural Revolution presented through first-person memoirs of five former Red Guards, including Fifth Generation director Tian Zhuangzhuang. Rather than being invisibly observational on the side, Wu reveals the seams of his documentation by starting the main body of the piece with a scene of setting up for an interview with Tian. Both Tian and Wu appear in front of the camera: Tian is arranging the lighting device and turns it on; the light falls on none other than Wu. The filmmaker himself is at the receiving end of the technology of filmic documentation. Throughout the documentary, Wu does not shy away from being on camera and at times functions as what Jean Rouch calls a "catalyst" through not only the camera but also on-screen directing. Apart from giving on-camera instructions to his cameraman about what to film and highlight (e.g., Tian's certificate of merit from 1965), at times Wu prompts (re)actions from the interviewees in such a deliberate manner that it renders his own action into a performance. For example, when Liu Longjiang, a businessman from Beijing, exhibits some old photographs, Wu asks him where they were taken and who are the people in them. Wu is faking ignorance here in order to elicit Liu's personal delivery of testimony, and Liu's answers, as obvious as the pictures, turn out to be "on the rostrum of Tiananmen ... [where] Jiang Qing (Madame Mao), Premier Zhou Enlai" and other state leaders received Red Guards like Liu himself. Iconic images such as Tiananmen, Madame Mao, and Premier Zhou cannot go unrecognized by someone like Wu whose generation grew up with such images. His on-screen demand for their identification not only accentuates the iconicity of such historical information but also highlights a juxtaposition of powerful figures with ordinary subjects of history such as the former Red Guard Liu.

Wu punctuates the memoirs with scenes of the all-women Cobra rock band working on the title song, "My 1966," which is performed at the end of the documentary. Wu himself frequently appears in discussions with the band members, questioning them as well as himself about the authenticity of hearsay accounts of the Cultural Revolution (such as from those interviewed): "We only heard but didn't see with our own eyes. You can only imagine [what it was like to be a Red Guard]." The parallel structure of remembering and questioning renders *1966* more than a passive documentation of former Red Guards' memories. The film constantly folds and ripples under the demand of being recognized as personal, subjective, and experiential, and it is necessarily subject to other positions of reception and even suspicion (as by Wu and the Cobra musicians). Wu provides these other positions – particularly his own – an opportunity of full display at the end of the documentary. Meant for no other audience but Wu's camera, the Cobra performance of "My 1966" takes place in an obviously abandoned building emptied of the past. Accompanying the musicians up the stairs, along the corridors, through the doors and across the debris, Wu's camera, like a fellow-traveler, strides with choreographed energy and becomes visually the most active performer in this scene. As the band starts playing and sings lyrics written, curiously, from the position of an onlooker commenting on the bygone youthful experience of socialist idealism – "1966, a red train/crowded with happy lambs" – the camera moves between and around the musicians, inspects them, dollies in from a higher angle, and even reveals a prearranged track on which it moves up to the central player.[7] Contrasting with the earlier interview sequences that largely present former Red Guards seated in private interior spaces, the musical finale sums up the mobile and (self-) inquisitive energy that marks the sequences of the Cobra band (and Wu himself) in a fully embodied style, concluding the documentary with a performance riddled with visible subjective stances and movements rather than comfortably falling on an objective closure as observed by a fly on the wall. As we shall see, in lieu of the pure observational mode, Wu's propensity for embodied and performative engagement would only see greater and more conscious development in his later works: he would finally restore the unrepresented part – his own account of the Cultural Revolution experience as a non-Red-Guard, which he admittedly excluded from *1966* with much regret and dissatisfaction – in *Memory* (Wu Wenguang, Wen Hui, 2008), a multimedia theatrical piece mixing footage from *1966* and live performances, including Wu's own.[8]

In fact, Wu's first physical performance – acting on a theatrical stage – is already featured in his third documentary, *At Home in the World* (1995), a sequel to *Bumming in Beijing* in which he presents updated accounts of the five artists, four of whom now live abroad. Wu continues to show a propensity for performed situations by including *The Dossier of 0*, an avant-garde theatrical piece based on Yu Jian's poem of the same title. Also directed by Mou Sen, it features the performance of not only Wu but also the documentary filmmaker Jiang Yue (b. 1962) whose *The Other Bank* (1995) is another interesting example of the performative mode (J. Wang 1999; Leary 2003).[9] During a rehearsal, as if warming up for his later full-scale performance of personal memory in *Memory*, Wu narrates on stage a typical experience of socialist youth: how he envied schoolmates for their more desirable working-class or peasant family background because his father was merely a clerk. Accompanied by Yu Jian's provocative verses – "A high noon in April/An erotic temperature/A temperature for adultery/A temperature for erection" – and against an abstract design of an orchard with erect iron poles, each capped with an apple, the filmmakers-turned-actors perform as human-shaped vehicles of sexual (and certainly not apolitical) energy, their acting filled with bodily gestures, movements, strides, but no words whatsoever.[10] They turn around, grab apples off the poles, go to the work table, vehemently shove them into a presser, and repeat this mechanical round with increasing speed. Wen Hui, dressed like a typical female sent-down educated youth, appears on stage holding a board of apples and starts screaming at the men's craziness. The scene becomes hysterical when Wu and Jiang begin throwing one apple after another at a huge fan that is now turned on. At the line "masturbation is the initial verb," Wu brings an apple close to the fan, slips in front of it in a deliberately dance-like move, stands up, and repeats the cycle before finally freezing in the middle of the throwing when the fan is turned off. On top of an already much freer interaction between him and his subjects in front of the camera, Wu's unconcealed identity and theatrically highlighted physicality in such performance sequences burns through the barrier between the camera and the documented field, leaving an indelible body-print on the documentary as a gigantic flourishing signature.

Joining Wu's performance are those of photographer Gao Bo and painter Zhang Dali, making *At Home in the World* constantly tilt toward the past that continues to exist in these artists' bodies, memories, and art. Similar to his deliberate prompting for performances of remembrance in *1966*, Wu elicits a singing moment from Gao, asking him what music he listens to now that he lives in Paris with a French wife. Gao responds with "Cui Jian" – reputedly the father of Chinese rock whose songs are crucial to the memory of 1989 – and immediately starts humming Cui's "Start Over": "My feet on the ground, my head against the sun." As if aware of a comparable private, amateur performance of the same song in *Bumming in Beijing*, then under a much less cozy light in his shabby room, Gao comments that "now it's only for fun. Back then it was a shared language." The shared experience of the past – of not only the earlier years of high socialism and revolutionary youth but also of 1989 – remains a structuring absence that is only fit to be performed rather than spoken of. Zhang Dali in turn does what he calls "action art" – *Dialogue* – a sprayed painting series that he produces, through a deliberate engagement of his body in action, on walls around the Italian town where he lives. Zhang performs such a painting in front of the camera: as he walks along a wall, he swiftly sprays a single-line human profile without stopping at all as if it were part of his navigation through his foreign home.[11] Inside or next to such abstract profile sketches are marked words from their collective memory: *geming* (revolution), *wo de dashen* ("my Great God," referring to Mou's *The Great God Brown* for which Zhang had worked as art director), and even *sb* (jerk). Rather than clinical observational documentaries, these early works of Wu are more like portraits and even self-portraits, as their emotive undercurrents are deeply rooted in the shared historical experience of China's recent past. This personal embeddedness in the experience of his subjects seems to be a crucial force informing Wu's discomfort with and resistance to strict observational noninvolvement.

Following *At Home in the World*, Wu had a three-year break during which he was active in the dance theater of Living Dance Studio before beginning the filming of *Jiang Hu: Life on the Road* (1999) in 1998. Featuring "Yuan Da" (Far and Wide), an amateur entertainment troupe that roams the countryside around Beijing and neighboring provinces and provides corny programs to local people, *Jiang Hu* is full of socio-ethnographic information as the camera witnesses the routine operations of the troupe and its members' interactions. Sometimes tension is revealed when members confess to Wu their worries and complaints in a hushed voice. The documentary is so far the most observational piece from Wu, as he remains silent and invisible behind the camera. However, Wu expressed dissatisfaction with this erasure of his actual interaction and participation. Reflecting on the making of *Jiang Hu* about six years later (see Figures 16.1 and 16.2), Wu (2006a: 138–9) mentions a scene he has excluded with regret:

> That day, in order to celebrate and because the troupe members hadn't seen a piece of meat in days (the wok had gone all rusty), I went to the butcher's shop in town and bought ten catties of pork, came back, picked up a ladle, and cooked up a big wokfull of my specialty, hongshao braised pork. The cook stove was right next to the stage where a performance was in full swing, so the aroma of braised pork wafted out into an atmosphere already full of song and dance. Everyone backstage crowded around the stove; as the actors finished their parts and came off stage they made straight for the wok, and when it was their turn to go back on stage they went directly from stove-side to center stage; the songs being sung on stage were echoed back off stage. It really felt like a festival; everyone was in high spirits. In my right hand I held the ladle and in my left the DV camera, kidding around and randomly recording stuff; after a while someone else took the camera, and then countless hands snatched it back and forth, everyone filming each other.

Someone loyal to observational noninterference would indeed find it hard to excuse the last two cut-off images of camera-holding: the camera is held in one hand by the filmmaker and juxtaposed with a cooking ladle in his other hand, rendering it hard for the filmmaker to extricate himself objectively from his subjects as he is cooking and serving them. More threateningly, the camera is then used by numerous subjects, who have now usurped the tool of documentation, not only filming themselves but also returning the gaze to the "original" film-maker, Wu. However, while Wu at that moment was not confident about the pro-vocative power of such out-of-control moments of "losing" his camera to his subjects, he already seemed to be exploring similar subversive acts in dance theater. The latter has virtually become his experimental lab within which he tests and bends the fickle dividing line between filmmaker and subject, documentary and performance, documentation and reality.

Between 1995 and 1998, a few years before the production of *Jiang Hu*, Wu and Wen created *Living Together/Toilet* (1995), *Dining Alone with 1997* (1996), and *Dress/ Video* (1997) (see Figure 16.3). The first two incorporate documentary data in a more or less crude form, presenting as titular backgrounds the couple's pictures from real-life situations and documentary footage – filmed on July 16, 1996 – of Beijing residents speaking of their reactions to Hong Kong's imminent handover in 1997. However, *Dress/Video* starts to mobilize documentary video in a more sophisticated manner as it becomes an integral part of the performance's narrative. Starting with a projected video of the dancer (Wen) putting on makeup – captured in close-up and medium shots – and getting ready in the dressing room, *Dress/ Video* juxtaposes the dancer's performance on and off video as well as on and off stage. To add to the mise-en-abyme effect of Wen's simultaneous performance

Figure 16.1 A close interaction kept invisible: Wu cooking for and being filmed by his subjects in *Jiang Hu* (dir. Wu Wenguang, 1999). Courtesy of Wu Wenguang.

Figure 16.2 A close interaction kept invisible: Wu playing with and being filmed by his subjects in *Jiang Hu* (dir. Wu Wenguang, 1999). Courtesy of Wu Wenguang.

Figure 16.3 Wu Wenguang, camera in hand, flashlight in mouth, with Wen Hui in *Dress/Video* (1997). Courtesy of Wu Wenguang.

across two media, Wu himself as the creator of the video appears in an extraordinary power shot captured from a lower angle, somewhat overshadowing the performance as a menacing face of surveillance. Furthermore, the video makes visible the audience in the theater (according to the version presented in October 1998), hence not only foregrounding the immediacy of the performance, its intimate relationship to off-stage reality and the filmmaker's ironic authority over the image, but also revealing the three sides surrounding the production and reception of a documentary – the subject, the filmmaker, and the audience – as integral components of one media construct.

After the tug with noninterfering observation and objectivity in *Jiang Hu* and before his emergence with a more freewheeling diary film *Diary: Snow, Nov. 21, 1998* (2000), which he cuts out of footage from "unpremeditated" shooting and foregrounds his own voice through first-person subtitles (H. Wu 2000: 60), Wu steadily experimented with performative documentation in dance theater and incorporated a more conscious and critical stance toward the role of the documentary camera. Works such as *Report on Birth* (1999), *Dance with Farm Workers* (2001),

Report on Body (2002), and *Report on 37°8* (2005) all have their creative origins in documentary (W. Wu 2001a: 94–5).[12] It is interesting to note that *Report on Birth*, created simultaneously with *Jiang Hu* between 1998 and 1999, contains what was at the time Wu's most (self-)critical performance – as a video-camera-holding film-maker. Overall, Wu's employment of documentary video in dance theater demonstrates three essential features. First, first-person narrations or oral histories form the narrative core of the performances. For example, *Report on Birth* features stories told by the mothers of the dancers, including Wu's own; *Memory* reuses interviews from *1966*. Second, documentary footage captured outside the theatrical space forms a reality parallel with which dancers perform a bodily dialogue. For example, *Dining Alone with 1997* contains footage of people randomly selected in the streets of Beijing to talk about their reactions to Hong Kong's handover; *Report on 37°8* includes footage of the SARS epidemic in 2003. Third, video footage simultaneously captured within the theatrical space forms another live parallel to the performance on stage. While the first two aspects tend to anchor the performances in reality, it is in the third mode of live video where Wu mobilizes his own physicality and presence as a camera-holding filmmaker and performs a critique of the documentary camera as a questionable means of extracting information and truth.

All three *Report* performances contain footage of dancers' faces and bodies immediately captured by Wu, who moves on stage with a video camera in hand. Interestingly, Wu, according to co-director and choreographer Wen Hui, often designs his own moves despite the fact that he has never trained in dance. In *Report on Birth*, appearing as a filmmaker and the only male among four female dancers, Wu assumes a deliberately aggressive posture, stretching his arm forward stiffly with the camera. Wu's style of handling the camera, both on stage and in actual documentary filmmaking, is to place it at waist level instead of raising it to his eyes. When rendered on stage with an exaggerated stiffness, this style produces the visual effect of a phallic prosthesis. His face, highly attentive, is nevertheless expressionless. His walk is slow, steady, and unstoppable, always moving toward the female dancers, forcing them to recoil, bend, or dance around the camera as if trying to avoid its aggressive force. The women are still in the middle of narrating or performing their respective experiences of giving birth or being born when Wu appears on stage. As he moves from one woman to the next, whomever his camera approaches, that woman will immediately stop her narration or movement, as if yanked out of her own world by the protruding camera. The camera – simultaneously running as the footage captured by it is being projected onto a big screen at the back of the stage – functions like a magic silencer of the women's stories. Wu seems determined to expose the menacing force of his camera. He follows the women around and eventually forces one of them to the backstage. Both Wu and the dancer disappear from the stage at this point, but the simultaneous video projection shows what is going on backstage: obviously cornered by Wu's relentless camera pressing for a close-up, the dancer looks poignantly puzzled and helpless. The exploitative and violent nature of the camera becomes highlighted in this performative documentary interplay.

Simultaneous with these onstage experiments of the problematic role of the documentary camera, Wu followed up his interrupted filmmaking first with the highly personal and informal *Diary: Snow, Nov. 21, 1998* and then with *Dance with Farm Workers* (2001), the latter borne out of the production of the dance theater performance of the same title. Capturing each stage of the creation process complete with the recruiting of farm workers, their training, rehearsals, and the final performance, *Dance with Farm Workers* hides nothing about Wu and Wen's direct involvement. Wu appears in front of the camera, communicating and rehearsing with everybody else as well as recording the performance. This ease with traveling beyond the camera – virtually redeeming the regrettably excised moment of cooking and filming in *Jiang Hu* – becomes all the more heightened when the documentary ends with a video within a video, a performance within a performance: the farmer dancers gather in front of a projected video and replace the screen with their bare bodies on which a man is seen hammering at a mirror reflection of onlookers, one of them holding a camera. The mirrored image breaks in the video, only to reveal another set of onlookers standing behind it, serving as a perfect comment nodding at Wu's own self-conscious filmmaking. The farmer dancers and their bodies have been at the disposal of his camera. In the end, the flickering image breaks under the audience's gaze while the strong bodies remain.

Wu's (self-)critique of the documentary camera's exploitative status continued in the *Report* series and would culminate in by far the most direct indictment in *Fuck Cinema* (2005), his last documentary to date. Filmed between 1999 and 2001, *Fuck Cinema* had an earlier version in 2002, bearing an ironically antonymic title, *I Love Cinema*, which was "professionally done, cleanly cut, very objective like many documentaries with a standard length of 90 minutes fit for broadcasting on television and screening in theaters or for sales" (R. Ma 2009). However, Wu remained unsatisfied with that version and in his final cut decided to restore the voice of Wang Zhutian, his chief subject, who provides a scathing on-camera criticism of Wu's exploitative camera and noninvolving stance. Organized over three parallel narrative threads – the vainly ambitious freelance screenwriter Wang, the pirate DVD vender Xiao Wu, and a series of auditions of aspiring young actresses for an alleged prostitute role – *Fuck Cinema* presents the various facets of filmmaking: preproduction, production, and distribution. As unflattering as the documentary's title, Wu's camera is ironically critical of all the players in the chain: Wang's opportunistic obsession and unrealistic ambition, the insincere encouragement from producers and directors (including Sixth Generation director Zhang Yuan), the exploitation of young women at the auditions, as well as Wu's own abuse of his subjects (especially Wang). In the audition scenes, the camera becomes dangerously exploitative as each aspiring actress, after a brief interview on their thoughts about prostitution, is asked to stand against the wall in the hotel room where the auditions take place. In the narrow space between a chair and a bed, the young women are told to face the camera and then turn to one side to show their profile and figure. They are often asked to take off an outer jacket or waistcoat so that their figures can be seen more fully. At moments the camera becomes clearly voyeuristic as it moves to gaze at the women's faces, eyes, breasts, and legs. On several occasions it dwells upon their curvy chests for an extended length of time. By contrast, the male director or producer remains invisible, and his low and emotionless voice always comes from off screen. It is hard to imagine that Wu is unaware of such obvious objectification and exploitation of women as filmed subjects.

I suggest that these audition scenes might best be understood as another form of Wu's performance to expose and critique the camera as well as the filmmaker. For that same reason he includes the most direct indictment of documentary filmmaking even at his own cost. Toward the end of *Fuck Cinema*, Wang reads out loud his written reflections on Wu's role as a documentarian of his recent life. The speech openly questions Wu's camera:

> I took my script and went to find Wu Wenguang. I don't know why, but whenever Wu meets me he is always armed with his DV camera, and while talking to him I am always fearfully dodging the lens, which points at me like a gun.... While running about pitching my script, I was constantly facing Wu Wenguang's video camera, and as I grew used to it the feeling of unease disappeared. Some people asked: Wu Wenguang is making a documentary about you, you are working as an extra for him, how much does he pay you per day? I pondered this for a moment, then tactfully said that the relationship between Wu and me was one of mutual assistance, both of us were benefiting from it ... . But once, after I had been racing around all day, I felt more than ever that my situation was hopeless, and I asked Wu to help me find a job, which would solve the basic problems of food and accommodation. He thought this over in silence for quite a long time, then pointed to a roadside stall and said: "Go ask him how he managed it." My face twisted into a desolate pathetic smile when I heard these words. When in my despair I continued to implore him, Wu's face suddenly hardened: "I've been running around with you all day, but it's all just for fun." I was on the verge of tears, then all of a sudden I toughened up. I stared angrily at Wu and said rudely: "It may be fun for you, but it's suffering for me." Wu didn't know what to say, and for the first time he put away that gun-like camera of his.

As Wang reads on, the camera stays steadily on him, and Wu remains silent behind the camera, very likely not without embarrassment.

In consideration of the facts that the filming of *Fuck Cinema* finished before 2001, during and after which came the *Report* series and *Dance with Farm Workers*, and that Wu spent five years in editing before finally deciding to retain and highlight the tense interaction between his camera and subjects, *Fuck Cinema* could be regarded as a deliberate and reflexive criticism of observational documentary. Not surprisingly, Wu ends *Fuck Cinema* with a sequence that might be cut out of an observational piece as it reveals the "staging" of a scene with spoken contributions and collaborations of the filmmaker and the filmed subject. The DVD vender Xiao Wu suggests that Wu should stop following him and instead film him as he disappears into the traffic, and after that he can bike back to join Wu. But Wu insists, "I'll follow you." After several rounds of communication, Xiao Wu starts biking in the busy nighttime street, and Wu follows. As Xiao Wu picks up speed and draws away, we see the camera looking for him amid the night traffic and we hear Wu's breathing become heavier because of running – an important index of the filmmaker's physical enactment of documentation which is also curiously present in Wang Bing's *West of the Tracks* (Q. Wang 2006). Xiao Wu disappears into the traffic. We hear Wu running and panting and notice his camera shaking. "Xiao Wu!" Wu calls out to no avail. The screen blacks out. The life of the subject symbolically becomes an unreachable world beyond the reach of the camera. The filmmaker documents others, but what he documents is above all the process of documentation, a process full of unpredictable interactions marked by the participation of not only the filmmaker but also the filmed subjects. Such documentation is always open to question and therefore deserves attention as to who owns, rightfully so or not, the information captured as such. A year after the release of *Fuck Cinema*, Wu devoted himself to the "Village Film Project" (2006), in which one of the new documentaries' favorite subjects – villagers – started filming their own life and voiced their own opinions from inside the filmed field.[13]

Let me end this discussion with one final scene of performative documentation. As if making up for his early inadvertent absence from *1966* and finally restoring his own status as a concretely positioned historical subject as his former interviewees, Wu reuses the documentary images sixteen years later in *Memory*, a performance featuring three actors (Wu, Wen, and Feng Dehua) and combining dance, narration, physical acts and multimedia elements. Completely forgoing the observational disguise of his early practice, Wu performs on stage a first-person documentation of memory: while at times he is seated in a lit back corner of the stage visibly working at a workstation from where he controls and manipulates the projected images, he also appears at center stage and performs a solo narration of his childhood memory of how he had envied his older sister for being able to go to Beijing as a Red Guard and see Chairman Mao, how he hated the fact of being born too late – by three years – to become a Red Guard, and how he then secretly enjoyed the unexpected aborting of his sister's pilgrimage plan. His belated personal account of the Cultural Revolution, not as an objective observer but as an active and subjective participant operating on a level comparable to his former interviewees, completes the documentary *1966* with a physical performance of unscripted narrating, spontaneous remembering, and live gestures. What counts is no longer the professed authenticity of "objectively" acquired information but a kind of truth that, while always evasive, is nevertheless palpable on the edge of the camera frame, on both sides of which are the performances of documentation and the documentation of performances.

Notes

1   Representative Chinese documentaries in the observational mode include: *Before the Flood* (2003), *Crazy English* (Zhang Yuan, 2000), *Dream Walking* (Huang Wenhai, 2006), *Extras* (Zhu Chuanming, 2002), *Floating* (Huang Weikai, 2005), *Floating Dust* (Huang Wenhai, 2004), *Houjie Township* (2003), *Hurricane* (Duan Jinchuan, 2005), *Pediatric Department* (Wang Hao, 2006), *In Public* (Jia Zhangke, 2003), *Senior Year* (Zhou Hao, 2005), *No. 16 South Bakhor Street* (1995), *The Secret of My Success* (Duan Jinchuan, 2002), *The Square* (1994), and *Yin Yang* (Kang Jianning, 1997).

2   Apart from Wu Wenguang's more consistent claim for the individual or personal status of his documentary vision, CCTV's Shi Jian also discusses something similar. The first to raise the question "Why did we start?" was Chen Meng, another producer at CCTV as well as a major proponent of the new documentary within the system (X. Lü 2003: 236–42).

3   These performative works include family related personal documentaries *Family Video* (Yang Tianyi, 2001), *Losing* (Zuo Yixiao, 2004), *Unhappiness Does Not Stop At One* (Wang Fen, 2000); authorial and essayistic titles *Jade Green Station* (Yu Jian, 2003) and *Crow in Winter* (Zhang Dali, 2004); artist documentaries *Nightingale, Not the Only Voice* (Tang Danhong, 2000) and *Dream Walking* (Huang Wenhai, 2006); and LGBT pieces *Night Scene* (Cui Zi'en, 2003) and *50 Minutes of Women* (Shi Tou, 2005). For the last subgroup, see Q. Wang (forthcoming).

4   These six are: Jiang Yue with *Catholicism in Tibet* (1992); Hao Zhiqiang with *Big Tree County* (1993); Wang Guangli with *I Have Graduated* (1992); Wu Wenguang with *1966, My Time in the Red Guards* (1993); Wen Pulin and Duan Jinchuan with *The Holy Land for Ascetics* (1992); Fu Hongxing with *Tibetan Opera Troupe in the Khams* (1993). See http://www.yidff.jp/93/93list-e.html (accessed October 2, 2009).

5   Lü Xinyu (2003: 326) mentions Rouch's visit as an invited juror for the Magnolia Award International TV Program Competition, a new event since 1988 at the Shanghai International TV Festival, which was first established in 1986. Also see http://www.imdb.com/Sections/Awards/Shanghai_International_TV_Festival/ (accessed November 4, 2009). In both cases the exact year in which Rouch visited Shanghai is not specified.

6   The Wen Pulin Archive of Chinese Avant-Garde Art at Cornell University contains some 360 hours of digital video documenting the history of contemporary Chinese art, installation, and performance since 1985. See http://wason.library.cornell.edu/Wen/index.php.

7   The lyrics are by poet Yu Jian, a friend of Wu's. Yu's works are featured in Mou's experimental theater, Wu's *At Home in the World*, and Jiang Yue's *The Other Bank*.

8   Wu revealed such regret in a conversation with the author on August 11, 2009.

9   Special thanks to Bérénice Reynaud for bringing to my attention this illustrative performative moment in *At Home in the World* at Visible Evidence XVI, 2009.

10 Apart from the biblical reference to temptation, it would be interesting to note *The Season of Picking Apples* (1971), a North Korean film featuring a beautiful young woman devoted to the teachings of the Great Leader Kim Il-Sung. The film gained great popularity in China in the early 1970s when the generation of Wu, Jiang, Mou, and Yu, all teenagers at the time, might be experiencing sexual awakening like the fictional character Monkey Ma in *In the Heat of the Sun* (Jiang Wen, 1994).

11 Later Zhang Dali reinvents the same profile sketches in his photography series (*Demolition Forbidden City*, 1998; *Demolition Ping'An Avenue*, 1999), in which important Beijing sites such as the Forbidden City and Ping'an Avenue are captured through the empty frame in the shape of an abstract human profile created on a wall in a demolished site.

12 Before Wu started on *Jiang Hu*, Wen Hui interviewed various women on tape recorder, including some dancers and their mothers on their experiences and thoughts on giving birth or being born. These documents eventually appeared in *Report on Birth*.

13 For the Village Film Project (2006) Wu ran a workshop for a group of villagers selected from around China and assisted them in filming their village lives (W. Wu 2005, 2006b). Among the project's short episodes, *A Nullified Election* (Zhang Huancai), *I Film My Village* (Shao Yuzhen), *Allocation of Land* (Wang Wei), and *Returning Home for the Election* (Ni Nianghui) are a few fresh works that bear traces of documentation, display first-person narration on camera, and feature lively interaction of the filmmaker with the filmed subjects, all offering new examples of performative documentary.

17

Chinese Women's Cinema

Lingzhen Wang

Women's cinema has been defined in a variety of ways. It could suggest films that are made by, addressed to, or concerned with women, or all three (Butler 2002: 1). In this chapter, Chinese women's cinema refers to Chinese-language (dialects included) films that are directed (and occasionally written) by Chinese women in Greater China, including mainland China, Hong Kong, Taiwan, and the Chinese diaspora. Chinese women have made many types of films: mainstream, commercial, experimental, and those targeting a female audience and focused on women's issues. Rather than perceiving women's cinema as containing intrinsic and generic values, whether aesthetic, sexual, or political, this chapter intends to historicize the concept, examining diverse meanings produced by Chinese women in their cinematic negotiations with various historical forces in different geopolitical contexts.

First, the chapter is engaged with a critical genealogy of women's cinema in Greater China. Although there are more than a hundred Chinese woman directors, and their films number in the hundreds, Chinese women's cinematic practice has still been largely ignored both in academia and by the public. A critical history of women's films has yet to be constructed. Second, the chapter will examine the dynamic relationship among female authorship, cinema, and history. The linkage between women and cinema is highly historical, contingent, and diverse. Women have come to the directing profession by a variety of routes. It is thus important to pinpoint the historical moments when women become filmmakers, to observe the formation and disintegration of commercial, institutional, and personal channels that enable women to enter the filmmaking industry, and to understand both the potential and limitations of women's cinema in history. Given the large number of Chinese woman directors and their films, the fundamental goal of this chapter is to trace out general trajectories of women's cinema in different geopolitical

A Companion to Chinese Cinema, First Edition. Edited by Yingjin Zhang.
© 2012 Blackwell Publishing Ltd. Published 2012 by Blackwell Publishing Ltd.

locations and critically analyze the character and significance of female cinematic authorship in history and in relation to other women's cinematic practice.

Initial Stage: Chinese Women's Engagement with Filmmaking, 1920s–1940s

Chinese women began participating in filmmaking as directors and screenwriters in 1920s Shanghai, when the film industry functioned essentially as a profit-driven business. Xie Caizhen is recognized as the first woman director in Chinese history, whose film *An Orphan's Cry* (1925), a family melodrama, was well received at the time. Like many other early women filmmakers, Xie was originally an actress and performed in her own film. Unfortunately, not much is known about Xie's life and career. The year 1925 also saw the appearance of the first Chinese woman screenwriter, Pu Shunqing, whose screenplay *Cupid's Puppets* was made into a film in 1925 (P. Shu 1994). Pu was influenced by the May Fourth antitraditional movement, and she was also known as a May Fourth playwright, promoting women's independence in the 1920s. Yang Naimei, a top silent film star in the 1920s, also wrote a screenplay, *A Wondrous Woman*. Yang established the Naimei Film Company in 1928, and in the same year produced its first and only film, *A Wondrous Woman*, in which Yang starred. Although Yang was first inspired by a contemporary news story about a young Chinese woman's suicide as a way to escape an arranged marriage, she transformed the story in her screenwriting and turned it into a figuratively autobiographical story. The title *A Wondrous Woman* itself captures the image and ideal of the radically unconventional woman that Yang embodied both on and off screen. Similar to Yang Naimei, Wang Hanlun was another star-turned-filmmaker who set up a film company, the Hanlun Film Company, in 1929. She helped direct, edited, and also starred in *Revenge of an Actress* (1929), a love story that ends with the heroine killing herself in front of her real lover after many years of separation.

The relationship between women and filmmaking at this initial stage appeared to be accidental. This first small group of female filmmakers for the most part made only one film each. Their status as actresses, especially as female stars, played a significant role in their involvement in film directing and screenwriting. Because they often played lead roles in their own films, their authorial ambitions and creativity were often compromised by the types of roles they had been famous for. Both Yang Naimei and Wang Hanlun, for example, continued their previous signature images and performances in films they made themselves: Yang the sexually unconventional and Wang the tragic and virtuous, whose life was often ended either by her own hand or by others at the end of the film. The relationships with men of this first group of female filmmakers also help us understand both the male-centered character of (early) filmmaking and reasons for women's success in the 1920s Shanghai film industry. Pu Shunqing collaborated with her well-known director husband, Hou Yao, who made her screenplays into films. Yang Naimei, on the other hand, was said to rely on a warlord general in the North to back her film company financially. In other words, general institutional or social support was lacking for women at the time to pursue filmmaking.

Despite the highly contingent character of their participation in early filmmaking in China, the first group of Chinese women filmmakers produced various types of films, illustrating early on the diverse nature of women's cinema and the complex negotiations women had to make with mainstream ideologies, the film industry, and commercial as well as popular culture. While *An Orphan's Cry* followed a popular genre of the time, the family melodrama, which stages polarized moral forces and stresses traditional family lineage and conservative values in a rapidly changing environment, *Revenge of an Actress* continues the late Qing Mandarin ducks-and-butterflies tradition, a popular urban literary genre that dwells on sentimental love and forbidden romance and promotes the function of literature as primarily entertainment. *Cupid's Puppets*, on the other hand, turned to a different source of inspiration. The film criticizes the traditional family institution, especially its practice of arranged marriage, by advocating freedom in love and marriage, a major theme of the May Fourth cultural movement. *A Wondrous Woman* further distinguishes itself with its autobiographical nature (Yiman Wang 2009). Although the film conforms to one of the existing female cinematic character types – the sexually promiscuous and morally suspect woman – Yang unabashedly promoted in this film her own unconventional sense of female self and her wish for self-creation, providing thereby a complicated negotiation among the self, the commercial film industry, and cinematic representation. These diverse approaches to filmmaking by the earliest group of Chinese woman directors would continue in modern Chinese history.

The leftwing cultural movement that promoted the representation of oppressed classes and gender and advocated anti-imperialist nationalism began to affect Chinese filmmaking in the early 1930s. Ai Xia and Chen Boer emerged as two leftwing writers–stars, but their lives and careers marked two different trajectories in women's pursuit of self and filmmaking at the time. Originally a stage actress affiliated with the leftwing dramatic movement and then a member of the Leftist Dramatists League, Ai Xia joined Star Motion Pictures Company in 1932. Her film script *A Woman of Today*, which was made into a film in 1933, demonstrates Chinese women's continued effort to negotiate with historical demands and social confinement. The heroine is shown as able to transform herself at the end of the film from a love-driven, love-confined young lady to a socially awakened and self-conscious woman. The film, as the author herself admitted, contains a distinctive autobiographical trajectory (Pang 2002: 122), representing the author's sense of self and her strong desire for self-creation. Ironically, while the heroine played by Ai Xia herself successfully adopts a new role on the screen, Ai Xia, the author and star of the film, failed in her own life to make the transformation. She committed suicide in 1934 after struggling with social confinement and emotional stress. Her death raised many questions about being a woman in a highly commercialized industry in early twentieth-century China; it also revealed gaps among leftwing ideology, cinematic representation, and individual embodiment of the New Woman in the early 1930s.

Chen Boer, also a leftwing writer–star in the 1930s, successfully transformed herself into a revolutionary filmmaker. Famous for her lead roles in several leftwing stage dramas and films, especially *Plunder of Peach and Plum* (Ying Yunwei, 1934), Chen was active in social activities and anti-Japanese movements. She joined the Communist Party in 1937, left Shanghai for Yan'an in 1938, and became an important cultural figure in Yan'an in the 1940s (G. Shao 1999: 54). She produced several influential plays and stage dramas during the Sino-Japanese War. In 1946 she persuaded the Communist government to establish a Yan'an film studio. In the same year, she wrote and directed the first feature film ever produced in Yan'an, *Working Hero in the Communist Base*, a story centered on a real-life local hero in Yan'an, referencing at the same time many important movements in Yan'an: land reform, the rectification movement, the self-reliance movement, and the military defense of Yan'an (S. Liu 2006: 66). Chen was not able to finish this ambitious film due to the outbreak of the Civil War, but she had proved herself as the first screenwriter and feature film director in the history of the Chinese Communist Revolution. Later on, Chen helped transform the former Manchuria Film into the Northeast Film Studio and supervised production of the first group of PRC films, including *Bridge* (Wang Bin, 1949), *The White-Haired Girl* (Wang Bin, Shui Hua, 1950), and *Steeled Fighters* (Cheng Yin, 1950). Chen Boer's story reveals the significance of institutional support for women's filmmaking. As the first woman screenwriter and director fully supported and endorsed by the Communist government, Chen foreshadowed the emergence of the first group of socialist woman directors in the 1950s.

In the 1930s and 1940s the world also saw the rise of the first professional and the first Chinese-American woman director: Esther Eng (b. 1914), a second-generation Chinese-American who developed her early filmmaking career in Hong Kong and who successfully made more than ten Cantonese films (see Figure 17.1). Born into a Chinese-American business family, Eng cultivated her lifelong passion for the Cantonese theater and performing arts in San Francisco beginning at a young age. Japan's invasion of China in the early 1930s seemed to expedite Eng's decision to make films to support her motherland (Law and Bren 2004: 91–7). She set up a film company with support from her father in 1935 and produced *Heartaches*, a patriotic film that depicts the loyalty to their country of young Chinese and Chinese-Americans as well as their sacrifices during the war. This was the first Cantonese sound film made in Hollywood. Although Eng did not direct the film, it bore the stamp of her later films with its twin focus on patriotism and women. Eng began her directing career in Hong Kong in 1936, and her first feature debut, *National Heroine* (1937), foregrounds women's military

Figure 17.1 A photograph of the early Chinese-American woman director Esther Eng, dated October 1928.

roles in the war of resistance against Japan. Eng made four more films in Hong Kong, and these films cover a variety of genres, combining political, popular, and commercial elements. In 1939 she made an all-female film, *Women's World* (also known as *The Thirty-Six Amazons*). It was a broad critique of contemporary Hong Kong, and the 36 women represent different professions and different levels of society. Eng returned to the United States in 1939, and her next five films were made there mostly in the 1940s, focusing primarily on love stories. Her last film, *Murder in New York Chinatown*, which she codirected, was made in 1961.

The role of Esther Eng as a pioneer woman filmmaker with a long and active career demands more in-depth research and evaluation. She established a quite different model for female directors in Chinese-language filmmaking. Growing up in San Francisco in the 1920s and 1930s as a Chinese-American with a business family background and a lesbian identity, Eng exhibited extraordinary independence in her choices and in the development of her own career. She brought a pro-feminist and Chinese-American consciousness to her films. Her cross-dressing practice and transnational/transcultural filmmaking granted her some unusual opportunities to obtain media visibility and eventually success in a male-dominated industry. At the same time, however, her status as an American Chinese or overseas woman director also significantly marginalized her films' influence in the filmmaking history of both Hong Kong and the United States. Her strong political loyalty to China revealed the sense of identity of the second generation of overseas Chinese during the war period in the 1930s and 1940s, and her films are the first to represent lives and concerns of Chinese-Americans.

A New Beginning: Chinese Woman Directors in the 1950s

The end of the Chinese Civil War (1946–9) marked the formation of three distinctive Chinese systems and geographical areas: socialist mainland China, Taiwan under the Nationalist Party's rule, and colonial Hong Kong under British governance. With relatively stable political situations in the three geopolitical locations, film production across the divides increased in the 1950s. The policy and development of the film industry and culture in the three areas, however, also began to diverge, forming different cinematic trajectories and traditions. The rise of the first generation of professional woman directors across the three Chinese communities was closely tied to their own historical situations, geopolitical contexts, and personal backgrounds. It is important to note that although their cinematic practices exhibited different social, cultural, and market influences and demands, the first group of professional woman directors all actively participated in mainstream film production in their own communities.

After 1949, many Shanghai filmmakers moved to Hong Kong and continued their Mandarin film production until the 1970s. Two women who became film directors in the 1950s and 1960s in Hong Kong were among these migrants: Chen Juanjuan (1928–76), "China's Shirley Temple," and Ren Yizhi (Yam Yi-Ji, 1925–78), the daughter of the famous film director Ren Pengnian (1894–1968) (S. Wei 2010). The Hong Kong film industry grew significantly in the 1950s, and the influence of Shanghai film culture continued, especially in the early postwar period, despite the competitive, local, Cantonese film tradition. Much like the first group of women filmmakers in Shanghai, both Chen and Ren were actresses-turned-directors. Chen was a famous film star, and Ren, like the leftwing writer–stars in 1930s Shanghai, was also a prolific screenwriter. Ren studied as well as codirected many films with Zhu Shilin, a famous Shanghai director who moved to Hong Kong in 1946 and headed production of the leftwing film company Phoenix (Y. Zhang 2004a: 158). Both Chen and Ren directed and codirected a number of films, especially Ren, who was quite active in the 1960s, independently directing seven films with her own screenplays, including *Ah, It's Spring!* (1961), *The Four Daughters* (1963), and *The Fair Ladies* (1967). Centering on love, marriage, and women's roles in a modern, urban society, these films belong to a well-received tradition of Mandarin films at the time and contain an upbeat tone and a happy ending. Chen and Ren's experiences as actresses, and their family backgrounds in the film industry, helped advance their filmmaking careers in the 1950s and 1960s in Hong Kong, but their productivity was mostly sustained by the more stable social, economic, and political conditions.

The Taiwan film industry in the 1950s and 1960s was quite different from that of Hong Kong. With no heritage of its own, Taiwan film production began to develop in the 1950s only after the Nationalist government moved there (Y. Zhang 2004a: 113). Due to Nationalist political censorship, its inconsistent cultural policy, and the development of the local and rural economy, the 1950s saw the rise of popular Taiwanese-dialect films produced by private companies. Chen Wen-min, a woman of peasant origin, accidentally became the first woman screenwriter and director in Taiwan. Chen was already a savvy small-business owner and a mother of seven children when her husband talked her into the business of theater management (Y. Chen 2003: 202–46). She built the Ta-ming Theater and established the Ta-ming Film Company in San Chong in Taipei County in 1954 and soon began investing in Taiwanese-dialect romance films due to the disappointing performance of her theater business. She wrote her first screenplay, *The Enemy of Women*, in 1957, and it was immediately made into a film with the same title. Her second screenplay, *Xue Rengui and Liu Jinhua*, inspired by the success of a Taiwanese-dialect film, *Xue Rengui and Wang Baochuan* (He Jipeng, 1955), was finished in 1957. She invited Shao Luohui, a famous Taiwanese-dialect film director at the time, to direct the film. During their second collaboration on filming Chen's third screenplay, *Xue Rengui's Eastern Campaign* (1957), however, Shao dropped out of the project due to an irresolvable dispute. Chen was forced to finish the project on her own. This unpleasant incident created the first woman director in Taiwan history. Talented and hardworking, Chen took only sixteen days to shoot her next film project, *Lost Bird* (1957). From 1958 to 1959, Chen directed seven more Taiwanese-dialect films,[1] focusing on stories of underprivileged women and their troubled family relationships. Her films attracted a large female audience and received considerable media publicity (Y. Chen 2003: 220, 249).

Chen Wen-min's story as the pioneer woman director in Taiwan reflects first and foremost the success of the local, private business model that granted people like her, inexperienced but talented, certain access to filmmaking resources and competition. Chen entered the film industry primarily as an independent business woman. Although she became a successful film director and producer, her entire involvement in filmmaking should be understood first from the business perspective. The popularity of Taiwanese-dialect films that rely on folk history and local culture, with which Chen herself was familiar, proved another factor for understanding Chen's "accidental" success. Finally, Chen was an extraordinarily gifted and independent woman. She demonstrated how much a woman could achieve in a socioeconomic environment largely inhospitable to women, especially to those with working-class origins.

Mainland China in the 1950s was undergoing unprecedented political, social, and economic transformation. Chinese women's emancipation reached its highest level in world history, and the Chinese film industry repositioned itself in relation to the socialist economy and party-state leadership. As a result, the first generation of woman directors emerged under state sponsorship and institutional support. The implementation of socialist state feminism, which claimed absolute equality between men and women, played a significant role in Chinese women's engagement with filmmaking. The lack of adequate professional filmmakers at the founding moment of the PRC was another reason for incorporating female former leftwing cultural workers into the film industry. Wang Ping (1916–90), Wang Shaoyan (b. 1924), and Dong Kena (b. 1930), the three best-known woman directors of the 1950s and 1960s, all received great institutional endorsement from state film studios when they began their filmmaking careers. Like Chen Boer, these three women all participated in leftwing or Communist-led stage and film productions in the 1930s and 1940s.

The trajectory of Wang Ping offers a representative picture for the first group of women filmmakers in socialist China (Z. Song 2007). Born into a well-to-do but conservative Muslim family in Nanjing, Wang was influenced by the May Fourth cultural movement and leftwing drama activities during her school years. She joined the leftist Mofeng Art Troupe in 1933 and rose to fame in 1935 by playing Nora in Ibsen's *A Doll's House* at the Taotao Grand Theater in Nanjing. The play was such a success that Wang could no longer hide her true identity. She was soon fired by the principal of the elementary school where she taught, and then the Nanjing government prevented all schools in Nanjing from recruiting her. The aftershock of this nationally known "Nora incident" led to the arrest of several leftwing and underground Communist drama activists in Nanjing. Wang was forced to leave Nanjing for Beijing at the age of eighteen, and there she met her future husband, Song Zhidi, a talented leftwing playwright. They got married in 1936 and she became a mother of two by 1948. Wang's extensive involvement with leftist drama and cinema and her pro-Communist credentials made her a most desirable candidate for the first generation of filmmakers in socialist China. Although she had no film-directing experience, she was appointed as a film director at August First Film Studio in 1951, where she directed its first feature, *Darkness before Dawn* (1956), which was also the first feature by a woman director in socialist China. Wang Ping joined the Communist Party in 1953, and four of her seven features are regarded as models of socialist film: *The Story of Liubao Village* (1957), *The Everlasting Radio Signals* (1958), *Locust Tree Village* (1961), and *Sentinels under the Neon Lights* (1964).

Wang Ping's story was shaped mostly by the major political and cultural forces of twentieth-century China. Her trajectory from a Chinese "Nora" to a leftwing activist, and then to a Communist film director, corresponded to the struggle, development, and triumph of Communist China. Wang's experience provided a strong personal anchor, enabling her to articulate revolutionary ideals and aesthetics in socialist cinema. Fundamentally, however, Wang's extraordinary accomplishment as a major film director in pre-Cultural Revolution socialist China illustrates, in addition to her own talents and experience, the significance of state feminism that institutionally supported women in all working professions. Wang's success is thus also marked by historical limitations that confined her within mainstream cinema.

Development of Women's Cinema in the 1960s and 1970s

Women's cinema in the three geopolitical locations continued its distinctive orientations with different stylistic and thematic changes in the 1960s and 1970s. In mainland China, Wang Ping's contemporaries made their most representative works in the 1960s by venturing into various cinematic narrative styles and film genres. Dong Kena's *Grass Grows on the Kunlun Mountain* (1962) initiated a (female) subjective mode of representation. Her use of female first-person voice-over, subjective camera, and personal flashbacks exposes in an unexpected way discrepancies between the dominant revolutionary ideology and individual identification on issues regarding gender, revolutionary ethics, and personal sacrifice. This subjective mode of representation would be emphasized and combined with personal expression in women's cinema in the 1980s. Wang Shaoyan directed one of the most popular revolutionary opera films of the time, *Red Coral* (1961), and Yan Bili made a children's film, *Little Football Players* (1965). Dong and Wang were both productive in the 1960s: Dong directed and codirected six films and Wang four films. The Cultural Revolution (1966–76) disrupted regular film production in China, especially during the period from 1966 to 1972. Both Dong and Wang, however, resumed film directing around 1974, and Dong continued her filmmaking until the 1990s, becoming the most prolific woman director in mainland China.

In the 1960s a younger generation of woman directors began receiving professional training in Beijing and Shanghai film schools as well as from veteran film directors such as Xie Jin, Sang Hu, Cheng Yin (1917–84), Xie Tieli (b. 1925), and Ling Zifeng (1917–99). In the early 1980s, immediately after the Cultural Revolution, this group of woman directors helped reorient Chinese mainstream cinema.

Meanwhile, *The Arch* (Tang Shu-shuen, 1970), a Hong Kong film directed by an independent woman filmmaker, gained international recognition. Tang was one of only two woman directors active in 1970s Hong Kong, the other being Kao Pao-shu (Gao Baoshu, 1939–2000), an actress-turned-director who made her directorial debut, *Lady with a Sword* (1971), with Shaw Brothers and then established the Pao-shu Company in 1971, producing and directing six other films in the 1970s. Tang Shu-shuen's trajectory was different from Kao's. Tang was born and grew up in Hong Kong. At the age of sixteen she moved to Taiwan after her father was recruited by the Nationalist government (C. Yau 2004: 10). She went on to study film at the University of Southern California in 1960 and returned to Hong Kong after graduation. She made four films in the 1960s and 1970s, experimenting with different genres and styles. Her first film, *The Arch*, revises an existing folktale about female chastity in traditional China into a story that foregrounds female desire and its complicated psychological negotiations with patriarchal codes. The film distinguishes itself by its use of the female gaze and subjective camera that heightens female subjectivity and desire, and of frozen shots that create a different understanding of the female sense of time and space (C. Yau 2004: 29–66). The film was invited to the Cannes Film Festival's Directors' Fortnight, and later it was awarded Best Actress, Best Cinematography, and Best Art Direction at Taiwan's Golden Horse Film Awards. Tang's second film, *China Behind* (1975), was set in the Cultural Revolution but was shot in Taiwan. Although the film was banned from release in Hong Kong due to its focus on a sensitive topic of the time, it shows Yang's continued effort to explore different cinematic styles, such as handheld camera, documentary-like photographic images, and the use of a largely nonprofessional cast. Tang's first two films offered rare and new possibilities for Hong Kong cinema in the 1970s, a period of rapid economic growth, mass industrialization, and extensive commercialization of culture. The documentary and realistic style of *China Behind* as well as the film's primary concern about the fate of ordinary individuals amid political or economic adversity, are said to have heralded the New Wave in Hong Kong cinema (C. Yau 2004: 11). Tang's last two genre films, *Sup Sap Bup Dap* (1975), a social satire/comedy, and *The Hong Kong Tycoon* (1979), a melodrama, are set in contemporary Hong Kong, exposing common social problems in the increasingly capitalist metropolis.

Tang Shu-shuen was the first Chinese woman director who formally studied film in the West and returned to Hong Kong to make films. Her own family background and the geopolitical and cultural contexts of colonial Hong Kong in the 1960s and 1970s made possible such a transnational career trajectory. This transnational trajectory has evolved into a trend continued by most of the best-known Hong Kong woman directors, such as Ann Hui, Mabel Cheung, Clara Law, and Barbara Wong (Huang Zhenzhen). Tang's status as a hybrid in the 1970s, a Chinese woman with a Western higher education, and as both an insider and outsider of Hong Kong culture, provides a pertinent point for understanding her films, which are innovative and diverse in both content and style, implicitly yet persistently posing challenges to existing cultural, social, and cinematic codes. Such a dual status did not seem, however, to have saved her and her films from being lost or forgotten in Hong Kong film history. Like other early Hong Kong woman directors, Tang was rediscovered only at the turn of the new century.

In the 1960s and 1970s in Taiwan, film production as an industry and culture underwent drastic changes. Taiwanese-dialect films were still popular in the early 1960s, but Mandarin films gradually came to dominate the Taiwan market in the late 1960s. Influences from different sources, such as Taiwanese folktales and theater, Taiwan government, modern Taiwan literature, and Hong Kong film culture, were all evident in the development of Taiwan cinema during those decades. More woman directors appeared in Taiwan, and they produced a diverse body of films. In 1958 actress-turned-director Chang Fang-shia codirected with Li Xing *Brother Wang's and Brother Li's Tour of Taiwan*, an instant hit that pushed forward the wave of comedy in Taiwanese-dialect film production. From 1961 to 1979, Chang independently directed about twenty films, becoming the most prolific Taiwan woman director to date. Based on the titles, most of her films belong to popular genres with a flavor of Taiwanese local tradition and theater. In 1967 Wang Man-jiao, another actress-turned-screenwriter in Taiwan, directed a comedy titled *Adventure of a Cloth Seller*. Wang directed only one film, and she was better known as a scriptwriter (S. Wei 2010).

In the mid-1960s, with the government's promotion, "Healthy Realism" became the new trend. But soon it was replaced by a wave of romantic melodrama, in which Chiung Yao (Qiong Yao), the popular romance writer, created her own romance film genre. Liu Li-li emerged as the best known and most prolific woman director of Chiung Yao's films. She began directing Chiung Yao's film *Wild Goose on the Wing* in 1979, and by 1983 she had ten of Chiung Yao's films to her credit. She continued her passion for Chiung Yao's stories and directed similar television dramas in the late 1980s and early 1990s. Yang Chia-yun was another woman director who began her career by directing a Chiung Yao romance, *Love Comes from the Sea* (1980). She made other types of films, including *Crazy She Devil* (1981) and *Cold Killing* (1982), two films that center on women, revenge, and organized crime. In the mid-to-late 1970s, due to Taiwan's declining political status in international affairs, the government film studios encouraged and supported patriotic propaganda films. Wang Ying, who returned to Taiwan with a master's degree in filmmaking from Boston University in 1968, directed *Diaries of a Female Soldier*, based on Xie Bingying's well-known diaries written during the Northern Expedition and published in 1928 (X. Lin 1998). The film won an Excellence in Drama award at the Golden Horse Awards. Wang made two other features in 1979 and 1985, in addition to several well-received documentaries.

Transformation and Reshaping of Chinese Women's Cinema since the 1980s

The late 1970s and early 1980s witnessed innovations in all three Chinese cinemas. The new wave movements in mainland China, Hong Kong, and Taiwan not only redefined regional/national cinema, but also heralded significant changes in women's cinema. As a matter of fact, in both Hong Kong and mainland China, woman directors actively participated in the new waves, although in Taiwan the situation varied to a certain extent. The historical contexts and significance of the three new wave cinemas are different, but they all broke from their immediate film and cultural traditions, ushering in unprecedented opportunities for different kinds of cinematic practices. The number of woman directors in all three places rose and stayed high from the mid-1980s to the mid-1990s, totaling around one hundred; the number of their films created a record among all the countries in the world. For the first time, Chinese women's cinema across the divides began to manifest a strong sense of self-consciousness; a persistent validation of alternative or marginalized intersubjective relationships; an active attitude toward engaging social and cultural issues; and a creative reimagination of self, nation, and life in a transnational and cross-cultural background. Aesthetically, woman directors have demonstrated enormous diversity and creativity, transforming mainstream cinematic language, narrative structure, and visual style.

Given the large number of woman directors and their films since the 1980s, this section consists of a general historical introduction to woman directors in each of the three places, and a focused discussion of one major critical topic most characteristic of women's cinema in each location.

Mainland China

In mainland China the open-door economic reform initiated in 1978 as a response to the economic and political disaster brought on by the Cultural Revolution heralded a new era not only for economic change but also for social and cultural transformation. The emergent new wave cinema in mainland China drew its first inspiration from French New Wave, Italian Neo-Realism, and André Bazin's theory of the long take, and then climaxed in the practice of male, Fifth Generation filmmakers. Although woman directors like Zhang Nuanxin pioneered in the introduction of new wave cinema, her own film practice was significantly different from those works by the Fifth Generation in her attention to a gendered consciousness in women's cinema. Understandably, women's cinema of the 1980s and 1990s as a whole was diverse and plural, covering all types and genres, from the mainstream to the experimental, and from the personal to the commercial.

There are several historical reasons for the rise of woman directors in the 1980s. In addition to the new cultural policy implemented in the Reform era, also key were the effects generated by the practice of socialist state feminism prior to the Cultural Revolution, which had offered women relatively equal access to professional film schools and to directing positions in state film studios. At Beijing Film Academy (BFA) and the Central Academy of Drama in Beijing (CADB) from the 1950s to the 1960s, about 20 percent of the students admitted to every directing class were female. As a result, by 1979 more than fifty female directors were graduates of the two academies, about half of whom were major directors in their assigned studios (S. Wei 2010). This institutional support contributed significantly to the productivity of woman directors in the 1980s and 1990s.

Historically, the end of the Cultural Revolution brought several generations of woman directors into an active mode of production. Veteran woman directors from the 1950s to the 1970s, such as Wang Ping, Dong Kena, Wang Shaoyan, Yan Bili, and Jiang Shusen (b. 1930), immediately returned to filmmaking after the Cultural Revolution. Dong Kena stood out for both her productivity and her persistent focus on women. Among her many award-winning films, *The Girl Ming* (1984), *Xiangsi Women's Hotel* (1985), and *The Women of Yellow Earth Hill* (1988) create vivid depictions of a wide range of female subjects in 1980s China. Woman directors from a younger generation, who graduated in the 1960s but stayed mostly inactive due to the Cultural Revolution, emerged in the early 1980s as the most important group. Among them are Zhang Nuanxin, Huang Shuqin (b. 1940), Wang Haowei (b. 1940), Shi Shujun (b. 1939), Shi Xiaohua, Ji Wenyan, Guang Chunlan (b. 1940), Xiao Guiyun (b. 1941), Ling Zi (b. 1941), Wang Junzheng (b. 1945), and Qiqin Gaowa (b. 1941). Many directors in this group helped diversify mainstream films, and several of them also pioneered new cinematic practices. Wang Haowei's award-winning comedy *What a Family!* (1979) and the acclaimed *Sunset Street* (1983) reoriented public attention toward social rather than political aspects of everyday life among common people in urban settings. Shi Shujun began her directing career by filming female adolescents in *Girl Students' Dormitory* (1983) and *The Vanished High School Girl* (1986), exploring gender and youth culture in the postsocialist era. Xiao Guiyun directed and codirected many monumental films on major historical events in modern China, among which *Founding Ceremony of the People's Republic* (codirector, Li Qiankuan, 1990) won numerous film awards. Huang Shuqin, after several films made in the mainstream style, rose to fame with *Woman Demon Human* (1987) (see Figure 17.2), a film based on the real-life story of Peking opera singer Pei Yanling that explores the predicament of a woman who embraces different visions and desires in modern Chinese society. The film is praised as the first feminist film in China (J. Dai 2002: 153). Other women from the same generation, such as Bao Zhifang, Wu Zhennian, and Zhao Yuan, who studied with famous male directors in the mid-1970s as assistant directors, were also ready to make films in the early 1980s. Zhang Yuan (b. 1926), Qin Zhiyu, Liu Guoquan (b. 1945), and Lu Xiaoya (b. 1941) are representatives of yet another group who were originally actresses in the 1960s and 1970s and who became directors in the 1980s. Lu Xiaoya's *Girl in Red* (1984), a coming-of-age story based on Tie Ning's autobiographical fiction, touched its contemporary audience by its fresh portrait of an independent girl growing up in a complex society. Several individual woman directors, such as Mai Lisi (b. 1956) and Chen Li, do not belong to any of the aforementioned groups but have made many films since the 1980s. Mai Lisi codirected many films with her husband Sai Fu (1953–2005) in the 1980s and 1990s. Her independently directed film *Taekwondo* (2003) reveals the difficult growth of female consciousness in contemporary China (D. Li 2006: 178–81).

Figure 17.2   An actress (Pei Yanling) performing Zhongkui the male demon, encounters her stage counterpart in *Woman Demon Human* (dir. Huang Shuqin, Shanghai Studio, 1987).

In 1982 the first group of film students after the Cultural Revolution graduated from Beijing Film Academy. Female directors of this so-called Fifth Generation proved to be quite innovative in the 1980s and 1990s. Hu Mei (b. 1956), Li Shaohong (b. 1955), Ning Ying (b. 1959), Peng Xiaolian (b. 1953), and Liu Miaomiao (b. 1962) have all exhibited in their films different aesthetic styles and thematic concerns. For example, Li Shaohong made a name for herself by first directing two psychological thrillers, *The Case of Silver Snake* (1988) and *Bloody Morning* (1990); Ning Ying became famous for her Beijing trilogy, *For Fun* (1993), *On the Beat* (1995), and *I Love Beijing* (2001), depicting different generations of Beijing dwellers with a unique documentary and experimental style; and Peng Xiaolian is known for her social and critical approach to women's stories in *Women's Story* (1987) and *Shanghai Women* (2001).

With the penetration of China's market economy, which rapidly gained momentum starting in the early 1990s, the state-owned film industry and studio system in China were undergoing great changes during the mid-to-late 1990s. The state retreated both from its previous full sponsorship of film production and from its full support of women. The late 1990s saw a significant reduction in films made by women, and many woman directors of previous generations began fading out of filmmaking circles. The most stable source for younger woman directors since the late 1990s has been professional film and drama schools. The best-known directors from this group include Ma Liwen (b. 1971), Li Hong

Figure 17.3 A scene of female intimacy in *Fish and Elephant* (dir. Li Yu, 2001), reputedly the first lesbian film in mainland China.

(b. 1967), and Xiao Jiang. Li Hong, after Li Shaohong, became known for her psychological thrillers such as *Curse of Lola* (2005); and Xiao Jiang's *Electric Shadows* (2005), a nostalgic film about a girl's experience of growing-up that was intimately tied to mass films made in the 1970s and the early 1980s, probes the role of cinema in the formation of people's emotional identities. Actresses-turned-directors have also persisted in the younger generation: Xu Jinglei (b. 1974) and Yu Feihong (b. 1971) are two of them. Xu's transcultural adaptation of Max Ophuls' *Letter from an Unknown Woman* (1948) in her commercially oriented *A Letter from an Unknown Woman* (2004) has led to some interesting comparative studies by film scholars (Kaplan forthcoming; E. K. Tan forthcoming). Another group of women, such as Li Yu (b. 1973), Liu Jiayin, and Yin Lichuan (b. 1973), turned to directing from their previous professions as television anchor, screen or literary writer, and artist. Li Yu worked at a local television station and made several documentary films before she directed her first independent experimental feature, *Fish and Elephant* (2001) (see Figure 17.3), claimed to be the first lesbian film in mainland China. She ventured into mainstream film with her well-made second feature, *Dam Street* (2005), and in 2007 her *Lost in Beijing*, a film that foregrounds sexuality and social commodification, became a box-office hit, transforming her into a successful commercial film director. Liu Jiayin received her MA degree in screenwriting from the BFA, and her two critically acclaimed digital features, *Oxhide* (2004) and *Oxhide II* (2009), center on autobiographical and personal materials with a distinctive documentary style. Since the late 1990s, some over-seas Chinese, including well-known Chinese actresses, filmmakers, and students who studied abroad, have returned and made films in China, constituting another cohort of woman directors. Joan Chen, Hu An, Wu Junmei (Vivian Wu, b. 1966), Chen Miao (Michelle Chen), and Jin Yimeng are representatives of this group.

One of the most remarkable achievements of mainland woman directors since the early 1980s is the practice of a subjective and personal mode of cinema. The subjective mode, although rare, was not completely absent in pre-1980s women's cinema. Dong Kena in the 1960s used subjective camera, first-person voice-over, and subjective flashbacks in *Grass Grows on the Kunlun Mountain*. But the subjective mode was not linked to the personal narrative until the early 1980s, when Zhang Nuanxin made her first film, *Drive to Win* (1981). The personal narrative here refers to the construction of emotional as well as historical experiences directly or indirectly related to the filmmaker. In other words, women's cinema turned self-expressive and self-conscious in mainland China when a small group of woman directors began practicing a subjective and personal mode of cinema in the early 1980s.

Zhang Nuanxin was a pioneer of both mainland new cinema and women's personal cinema in the late 1970s and early 1980s. Born in Inner Mongolia, Zhang moved to Beijing when she was three years old. She graduated from the BFA in 1962, and in 1979, immediately after the Cultural Revolution, she cowrote with her husband Li Tuo "The Modernization of Film Language," an essay that was hailed as "the artistic manifesto of the fourth generation" and "the outlines of experimental film" (Y. Zhang 2004a: 231). The essay not only calls for a documen-tary style of filmmaking in reaction to the previous socialist realism and traditional dramatization, but also stresses the importance of cinema as subjective expressions of the filmmaker's emotions and styles. In other words, Zhang does not call for an objective mirroring of reality; rather she advocates a representation of reality through a particular subjective perspective. She once claimed, "none of my films are objective … . My films always contain my subjective views and express my own feelings" (Y. Yang 1996: 91–2).

It was this highly personal documentary mode of filmmaking that functioned significantly in the early 1980s, not only to decentralize the previous collective socialist realism, but also to separate Zhang as a woman director from her male contemporaries in Chinese new cinema, who adhered more to a distanced and nonpersonal (social or cultural) documentary style. Zhang's *Drive to Win*, for which she also wrote the screenplay, was not only among the first efforts to modernize Chinese film language in the early post-Mao era, but also the first film to express a woman director's emotional reflections on self and history. The plot of the film, which centers on a woman volleyball player's drive to win an international championship immediately after the Cultural Revolution, seems not too different from the mainstream ideology of the time, but the way the story is told and the attitude the heroine exhibits toward her career and life depart significantly from

Figure 17.4 Repressed love: an emotional moment when the female protagonist treats her male patient/love interest in *Army Nurse* (dir. Hu Mei, August First Studio, 1985).

the then-conventional mode of filmmaking. By experimenting with female first-person voice-over, subjective camera and sound, long takes, location shooting, and nonprofessional actors, Zhang transformed the potentially melodramatic, linear, and nationalistic plot into a historical woman's (the heroine's and the director's) subjective negotiation of and personal reflections on the meaning of self, nation, and life.

This personal mode of cinema was further developed by Hu Mei, a Fifth Generation director, in her film debut, *Army Nurse* (1985) (see Figure 17.4), and by Zhang herself in *Sacrifice of Youth* (1985). Both films are based on women's autobiographical novels, but at the same time they both reveal deeply Hu and Zhang's sense of youth, love, and history. Historical women's personal experiences and points of view are thus validated and represented in public theater; equally significantly, an important intersubjective relationship has also been established between women writers and women film directors in expressing their shared views of self in history. Ma Liwen, a graduate of CADB in 1996, continued this subjective and personal mode of filmmaking in her first feature, *Gone is the Person Who Held Me Dearest in the World* (2002), which is based on woman writer Zhang Jie's autobiographical essay published in 1994. Ma's film, which centers on the mother–daughter relationship, goes further in foregrounding the female voice, subjective perspective, and emotional experience. This personal mode of cinema has recently contributed to the practice of autobiographical films and films centering on mother–daughter intersubjective relationships by younger generations of mainland woman directors.

Hong Kong

The year 1979 marked the beginning of Hong Kong New Wave cinema. Hong Kong's cinema is essentially commercial, and the new wave did not necessarily challenge that. To many critics and filmmakers, Hong Kong New Wave is a historical "coincidence," the significance of which lies more in its setting in motion a diverse new trend of transformation of Hong Kong cinema. There was no coherent philosophy or unified style to characterize Hong Kong New Wave, but its experimental spirit ushered in a golden age of Hong Kong cinema in the 1980s and 1990s, generating a group of world-famous auteurs like Tsui Hark, John Woo, Stanley Kwan, and Wang Kar-wai.

Woman directors played a significant role in the development of Hong Kong New Wave. According to some recent scholarship, it was Tang Shu-shuen and her films that provided the most critical transition to new wave in Hong Kong film history (C. Yau 2004: 11). Beginning in 1979, another woman director, Ann Hui, became part of the impetus behind new wave. *Her Secret* (1979), a mystery thriller based on a real-life murder case, together with Tsui Hark's *The Butterfly Murders* (1979), was regarded as the sprouting of Hong Kong New Wave. Hui proved to be the most versatile and diverse new wave film director in Hong Kong, making both arthouse and commercial films. The new wave also introduced a group of women into filmmaking. Rachel Zen, also known for her television dramas, made three fresh and realistic films on family and love from 1981 to 1989; Angela Mak Leng Chi, wife of Yim Ho, a well-known new wave director, made five films from 1983 to 1986 in a variety of genres; Angela Chan directed three films in the 1980s, including *My Name Ain't Suzie* (1985). The second half of the 1980s saw the emergence of a "second wave." Among the well-known second-wave filmmakers are two woman directors, Mabel Cheung and Clara Law, both of whom were graduates of overseas film schools and local television apprentice-ships, and both of whom have continuously made critically acclaimed films since 1985. More Hong Kong women directed films in the 1980s and 1990s, but most of them did not continue after making their first films.

Since the mid-to-late 1990s, due to financial, political, and commercial uncertainties, the Hong Kong film industry has been in decline. Despite this distressing situation, a group of young independent women filmmakers emerged in Hong Kong and have produced some impressive works. Barbara Wong, a 1993 graduate of New York University, was first known for her documentary *Women's Private Parts* (2001). By 2009 she had made six films, most of them combining commercial elements with gendered consciousness. Carol Lai (Miu-suet Lai, Li Miaoxue, b. 1965) turned her career from marketing to filmmaking in 2001 and has made four films, including two thrillers, *The Third Eye* (2006), and *Naraka 19* (2007). Yau Ching (You Jing), a filmmaker, cultural and feminist critic, and media artist, received her MA in film art from New York University and her PhD in media arts from Royal Holloway College, University of London. After winning several awards for her short films, she made her first feature, *Let's Love Hong Kong* (2002), an alternative film that explores lesbian sexuality, identity uncertainty, and the urban environment. Yan Yan Mak (Mai Wanxin), a 1998 graduate of the Hong Kong Academy for Performing Arts, had made three films by 2005. Her first low-budget, experimental feature, *Gege* (2001), and *Butterfly* (2004), her second, well-made indie film on lesbian love and politics have attracted critical attention and have won several film awards. Susie Au (Ou Xeuer) studied film in New York and returned to Hong Kong in 1992. She first became a well-known music video director. In 2006 her debut feature *Nana on the Run* received mixed reviews.

Women's cinema in Hong Kong has distinguished itself with its transnational, transcultural, and border-crossing characteristics. Hong Kong's historical situation as a British colony up to 1997, and as a cosmopolitan and financial center of the capitalist world, accounts to a large extent for the various kinds of transnational and cross-cultural movements between Hong Kong and other Asian and Western countries. The majority of Hong Kong woman directors since the 1980s have studied or lived abroad. Different from mainland Chinese woman directors, whose rise in the directing profession had relied on institutional support within the nation-state boundary until the late 1990s, Hong Kong woman directors have long negotiated with Hong Kong's intensely commercial market in a highly transnational context. Compared with their male counterparts, Hong Kong woman directors have demonstrated a much more pronounced preoccupation with transnational and transcultural issues, such as migration, diaspora, and reflections on Chinese identity in a global setting. As early as the mid-1930s, Esther Eng had already pioneered as a transnational and cross-cultural woman filmmaker in the Hong Kong and Hollywood film industries, bringing Chinese-Americans into cinematic representation. Tang Shu-sheun set another example in the 1960s and 1970s for a transcultural and transregional cinematic approach to filmmaking. What these two woman directors brought to Hong Kong cinema was not just different cinematic styles, but also transnational consciousness and concerns over gender, nation, and social problems. Since the new wave in the late 1970s, transcultural hybridity has become the trademark of Hong Kong cinema.

Ann Hui's personal experience and cinematic practice have embodied the transnational/transregional trajectory. Born in Anshan, Manchuria to a Chinese father and Japanese mother, she moved to Macau and then to Hong Kong at the age of five. She studied English and comparative literature at the University of Hong Kong and filmmaking at the London International Film School. She entered Television Broadcasts Limited (TVB) as a director after returning to Hong Kong in 1975, making many social awareness serials and documentaries. She won public recognition in 1979 with *Secret*, a film known for its narrative innovations, but during her early filmmaking she was also known for her Vietnamese trilogy – *The Boy from Vietnam* (1978), *The Story of Woo Viet* (1981), and *Boat People* (1982) – a group of films that center on the trials and tribulations of Vietnamese refugees

Figure 17.5   Mother and daughter caught in a series of conflicts in *Song of the Exile* (dir. Ann Hui, 1990).

and examine social and political issues on a transnational level. Hui made *Song of the Exile* (1990) (see Figure 17.5), a semi-autobiographical film that interweaves subjective memory, political history, and the mother–daughter relationship, highlighting the significance of transnational landscapes and cultures (mainland China, Macau, Hong Kong, Britain, and Japan) in constituting personal identities and intersubjective relationships. Whereas mainland women's subjective cinema practiced by Zhang Nuanxin and Hu Mei in the 1980s showed an indispensable political dimension of the personal within national boundaries, Hui's *Song of the Exile* illustrates a compelling aspect of the transnational in the negotiation of the personal from in-between situations. In addition to reflecting on her own cross-cultural upbringing and experience, Hui has also brought border-crossing practice into her own filmmaking career, successfully making films in different types and genres, including the above-mentioned socially conscious, experimental, and personal films. With 25 films to her credit by 2009, she has also become the most prolific Chinese woman director in the world.

Mabel Cheung and Clara Law have furthered the transnational trend and deepened cross-cultural imagination in their most representative works. Cheung and Law share a lot in their career paths: both studied English literature at the University of Hong Kong; both went to work at Radio / Television Hong Kong from 1978 to the early 1980s; both went abroad, Britain and / or the United States, to study drama and film; and both returned to Hong Kong in the mid-1980s to make films. Historically, in the 1980s and 1990s, due to anxieties about Hong Kong's return to the PRC in 1997, migration from Hong Kong to Canada and the United States

Figure 17.6   Two Hong Kong sojourners struggle to make a living in *An Autumn's Tale* (dir. Mabel Cheung, Cos Group, 1987).

surged; likewise in mainland China, as the open-door economic reform continued, migration to Western countries also increased. These personal and historical backgrounds provide a pertinent focus for understanding the cinematic practice of Cheung and Law, especially their persistent attention to the changing state of and issues related to migration and to the question of being Chinese and Hong Kong Chinese in a political and transnational context. Cheung's first three films, *The Illegal Immigrant* (her graduate work, 1985), *An Autumn's Tale* (1987) (see Figure 17.6), and *Eight Taels of Gold* (1989), known as the Migration trilogy, focus exclusively on Chinese immigrants (mostly from Hong Kong and mainland China) and their struggles in the United States. Law also has several early films focusing on similar topics: *They Say the Moon is Fuller Here* (her graduate work, 1985), *The Other Half and the Other Half* (1988), and *Farewell China* (1990). In their cinematic representations of Chinese immigrants in the United States or their relatives back home, Cheung and Law have captured the diverse historical significations of the massive migration movement in Chinese history. Identity reimagination and recreation are juxtaposed in their films with identity loss and alienation, and the globalized American Dream is accompanied by racism, Orientalism, and the difficulty of cultural assimilation. Since the early 1990s, both Cheung and Law have ventured into other types of films, but their concerns over transnational migration and diaspora have continued, although the direction of migrations represented in their films may be reversed or become multidirectional, as in Cheung's *Beijing Rocks* (2001), which portrays young overseas Chinese migrating back to China. In the mid-1990s Law herself immigrated to Australia. Her personal uncertainty about the handover was one factor, but more importantly Law had found herself and her experimental style increasingly at odds with the demands of the Hong Kong film industry for generic repetition and quick profit (D. Li 2003). As a Chinese-Australian, she has continued to probe issues and questions about global migration, as well as racial and gender confrontations in her award-winning film, *The Goddess of 1967* (2000). Although the number of women's films on the topic of migration *per se* has decreased in Hong Kong cinema in the new century, the transcultural character of Hong Kong women's cinema continues in the aesthetic style, critical value, and cultural references manifested in the younger generation's cinematic works.

Taiwan

The development of Taiwan women's cinema in the 1980s and 1990s was linked to several important historical and cultural movements, particularly the New Taiwan Cinema movement in the early 1980s, the women's visual arts movement in the early 1990s, and the wave of women's documentary filmmaking that has emerged since the mid-1990s. After Chiang Kai-shek's death in 1975, Taiwan began a series of economic, cultural, and political reforms under the leadership of Chiang Ching-kuo. More liberalized cultural expression was allowed in the late 1970s and early 1980s, and New Taiwan Cinema was born during this transformational period (Kellner 1998). Led by male directors such as Edward Yang, Hou Hsiao-hsien, and Chang Yi, and supported by the government's Central Motion Picture Corporation (CMPC), New Taiwan Cinema promotes social realism, local/native culture, and cinematic innovation (semi-documentary) as a critical response to political melodramas and commercial genre films (romance and martial arts) of the 1970s. Although women did not directly participate in the New Taiwan Cinema movement as a leading force, women writers, however, made significant contributions to the new cinema. New Taiwan Cinema itself was much influenced by Taiwan native-soil literature and women's literature; many influential films in the 1980s were direct adaptations from women's literature: *Ah-Fei* (Wan Jen, 1983, originally by Liao Hui-ying), *The Boys from Fengkuei* (Hou Hsiao-hsien, 1983, originally by Chu Tien-wen), *Kui-Mei, A Woman* (Chang Yi, 1985, originally by Hsiao Sa), *Women of Wrath* (Zeng Zhuang Xiang, 1985, originally by Li Ang), and *Osmanthus Alley* (Chen Kunhou, 1988, originally by Hsiao Li-hung). With their shared social concerns over ordinary and marginalized people in Taiwan, New Taiwan Cinema directors successfully depicted in their films a group of suffering but strong women figures. Although not directly related to new Taiwan cinema, Li Mei-mi, a woman director, also began exploring women's issues in the early 1980s. Her *Unmarried Mother* (1980) analyzes the challenge unmarried mothers confront in Taiwan society, and her *Girl's School* (1982) looks into issues related to homosexuality on campus, provoking many debates and discussions (S. Wei 2010).

Due to the persistent masculine character of filmmaking in Taiwan, only a few individual women with special resources and connections could direct in the early 1980s. In content and form, women's cinema took a historical turn in the mid-to-late 1980s as a result of the combined influences from New Taiwan Cinema and women's practice of literature. Still limited in number, woman directors began examining a variety of social issues, particularly those concerning the self, gender, and sexuality. Sylvia Chang, a well-known actress in Taiwan and Hong Kong who had played several lead roles in both New Taiwan Cinema and Hong Kong New Wave, turned to directing in 1986. Her feature debut, *Passion* (1986), explores female bonding, heterosexual love and marriage, and extramarital affairs, topics she would return to more than once in her later films. Shau-Di Wang (Wang Xiaodi, b. 1953), another important film director at the time, studied both drama and film in the United States and received an MA in theater from Trinity University before she returned to Taiwan in 1979. In 1987 she independently designed and codirected a three-part anthology film, *The Game They Call Sex*, with Sylvia Chang and Jin Kuo-zhao, focusing on the awakening of women's consciousness about their sexuality and constructed gendered roles. Both Chang and Wang continued their directing careers. Chang's *Siao Yu* (1995), a film that explores an ordinary Chinese woman's experience of self-awakening in the wave of emigration to the United States, has remained her most critically acclaimed film. Her later films edged more toward mainstream melodrama, centering on social issues concerning gender and family but with distinctive commercial appeal. Wang, on the other hand, continued to explore different types of films, including children's films, martial arts films, and cartoon drama films.

In 1993 the first Taiwan women's film festival was launched in Taipei through the concerted efforts of Women Awakening members Li Yuan-chen, Wang-P'ing, Chang Hsiao-hung, Ting Nai-fei, and Black and White Film Studio managed by Huang Yu-shan. Five years later the Taipei Women's Film Association (precursor to the Taiwan Women's Film Association) was established. Since then, an international women's film festival has been held annually in Taiwan (Y. Huang 2006: 242–3). Many international feminist films were introduced to Taiwan via the film festival, greatly stimulating the development of women's cinema and women's independent filmmaking in Taiwan. In 1995 the Graduate Institute of Sound and Image Studies in Documentary was established at Tainan National College of the Arts. Some of the graduates from the institute, such as Tseng Wen-chen (Zeng Wenzhen), have made not only award-winning documentaries but also well-received films like *Fishing Luck* (2005). Around 1995 the biannual international documentary film festival and documentary channels on public television were also formed, contributing to the arrival of a Taiwan documentary filmmaking movement. This documentary movement, together with the Taiwan women's international film festival, has helped produce generations of women filmmakers who have become persistently concerned with feminist issues, Taiwan local cultures and customs, and the representation of history.

Figure 17.7 Searching for lost memories and romance in *The Strait Story* (dir. Huang Yu-shan, B & W Film, 2005).

Huang Yu-shan has been an important figure in Taiwan women's cinema as she has worked as a critical link among different filmmaking movements since the 1980s. After graduating from the Department of Western Languages and Literatures of Chengchi University in 1976, Huang worked as assistant director for Li Xing between 1977 and 1979. She went to the United States to study film and returned to Taiwan in 1982 with an MA from New York University. She had made several documentaries before she began her first feature, *Autumn Tempest* (1988), under the influence of the new cinema and with support from CMPC. Huang's first three films focus on exploring the female body, sexual desire, and patriarchal exploitation of women in Chinese society. Her two recent features, *The Strait Story* (2005) (see Figure 17.7) and *The Song of Chatien Mountain* (2007), combine historical materials, including those censored in the past, personal memories, and a distinctive documentary style, providing a revised perspective on Taiwan's history, culture, and people.

For over two decades Taiwan feature film production has relied heavily on the grants provided by the Government Information Office (GIO), which is still the major source of official and public support for filmmaking today. Since Taiwan joined the World Trade Organization in 2000, filmmakers have confronted more intensified competition and faced further challenges of the market. Independent filmmaking has become the dominant mode of film production. Thanks to the conscious effort made by woman directors to promote women's films, the widespread impact of the documentary filmmaking movement, and the development of digital filmmaking and Internet technology, women's cinema in Taiwan has been able to survive and continuously attract both audiences and critical attention. Younger generations of filmmakers appearing at the turn of the new century have also begun to address directly the market demand. Alice Wang (Wang Yuya), who received her MA in film from Nihon University in Japan and made TV advertisements for a Japanese television station before she turned to filmmaking, has aimed to bring commercial forces into Taiwan mainstream films by focusing on youth, love, sexuality, and Taiwan local cultures. Her *Love Me, If You Can* (2003), a youth idol drama with a lesbian love plot, was well received by audiences and critics. D. J. Chen is another woman director whose primary interest lays in comic and commercial films. She studied media in college and made several short films before directing her first feature, *Formula 17* (2004), a surprise box-office hit and the highest-grossing fiction film (NT$6 million) in Taiwan in 2004 (B. Hu 2004). Young and dynamic, Chen, in this youth-idol queer film, combines Taiwan urban queer culture with various commercial elements, including comic effects, and has successfully renewed the mainstream film formula. Other mainstream and commercially oriented woman directors include veteran filmmaker Sylvia Chang and Emily Liu (Yi-Ming); the latter's *Woman Soup* (2001) focuses on four adult women's search for love and sexual fulfillment.

Another group of woman directors has pursued art and experimental films with pronounced social and feminist concerns. Some of them have also alternated between art and commercial films. Singing Chen's (Chen Xinyi) feature debut *Bundled* (2000) centers on various types of drifting and homeless populations on the margins of Taiwan society. Chen graduated with a degree in public media from Fu Ren University and had extensive documentary filmmaking experience before she shot *Bundled*. Her second feature, *God Man Dog* (2008), probes various social issues in different realms of Taiwan society. Although these social problems contain undisputed universal characteristics, Chen demonstrates her special talents in signifying these problems with particular Taiwan local flavor and meaning. Lisa Chen (Chen Xiuyu) had worked in advertising for many years before she decided to study film in New York in 1999. She has produced two well-received films centering on women from two age groups: *Voice of Waves* (2002) explores a young woman's memory about the emergence and loss of a love relationship between herself and a female classmate in their high school years, and *Autumn of Blue* (2003) examines the internal crisis of a woman during menopause. Zero Chou (Zhou Meiling, b. 1969) is another indie woman filmmaker whose feature films are also tied closely to her documentary works. Chou studied philosophy at Chengchi University and worked as a journalist after graduation in 1992. She has made several influential and award-winning documentaries, such as *Corner's* (2001) and *Poles Extremity* (2002). Among her features, she is best known for her three queer films: *Splendid Float* (2004) (see Figure 17.8), *Spider Lilies* (2007), and *Drifting Flowers* (2008). *Splendid Float* won several prizes at the Golden Horse Awards, including the best Taiwanese film of the year (2004).

Figure 17.8   Showcasing female solidarity in *Splendid Float* (dir. Zero Chou, Zeho Illusion, 2004), from an active queer female director.

The most salient characteristic of Taiwan women's cinema since the 1980s is its persistent exploration of the body and sexuality in all types of film: arthouse, mainstream, commercial, and documentary. The attention to women's bodies and their sexual desires was first registered in New Taiwan Cinema as part of the movement's general concern over marginalized groups in a politically oppressive regime. When woman directors like Shau-Di Wang and Huang Yu-shan re-presented these themes in their films in the late 1980s, they shifted the focus to women's awakening consciousness of their own bodies and sexualities. This cinematic expression of women coming to terms with their own bodies and sexual desires has helped mark gender and sexuality as distinctive categories that require critical examination of patriarchal repression and the compulsive heterosexual paradigm in modern society. Taiwan women's cinema became self-conscious when it revised the previous general exploration of the female body and sexuality into specific gender examination and self-expression. Striking images of a woman gazing at the reflection of her own nude body in front of a mirror, for example, appeared in several films by directors like Huang Yu-shan (*Autumn Tempest and Twin Bracelets*, 1989), causing quite a stir among audiences at the time. These scenes and images do not just interrogate the patriarchal ownership of women's bodies; more importantly, they reveal women's (characters' and filmmakers') awakening consciousness about their own bodies and self-identities.

While such feminist representations of the female body have continued in women's films, new significations of the female body also appeared in the 1990s, especially after several international Taiwan women's film festivals centering on the body and sexuality (Y. Huang 2006: 245). In some documentary and experimental films, the female body becomes the means for exploring different sexual desires and identities. Chien Wei-ssu's (Jian Weisi, b. 1962) short experimental film *A Woman Waiting for Her Period* (1993) probes into a woman's experience of her own body and the relationship of such experience to her ambiguous desire and social relationships. Zero Chou's docudrama *A Film about the Body* (1996), and especially her award-winning documentary *Corner's*, also turns to the body to reexamine and reimagine marginalized or repressed desires, identities, and homosexual, intersubjective relationships. Cinematic representation of homosexuality by Taiwan woman directors can be traced to 1982, if not earlier, when Li Mei-mi's (b. 1946) *Girl's School* came out. Huang Yu-shan's *Twin Bracelets*, which focuses on a Fujian local tradition of female sisterhood, also explores the political and sexual implications of such female bonding. It was not until the late 1990s that cinematic representations of (homo)sexual relationships became conventionalized. Mainstream and commercial filmmakers such as Sylvia Chang (*Tempting Hearts* [1999], *20, 30, 40* [2004]), Alice Wang, and D. J. Chen have all drawn on the cultural as well as commercial values of homosexual representations. A critical breakthrough in the representation of the body and homosexual intersubjective relationships was made recently by several independent directors, especially the lesbian filmmaker Zero Chou. Although her second queer film, *Spider Lilies*, incorporated a mainstream formula and became a commercial success, her first and third films, *Splendid Float* and *Drifting Flowers*, significantly go beyond conventional portraits of homosexual relationships, tying the representation of sexuality to the exploration of life and death and to local customs and folk cultures. Compared with other homosexual/lesbian films made in mainland China, Hong Kong, and Taiwan, which are mostly set in an urban, cosmopolitan landscape with a transnational appeal, Zero Chou's films have most successfully reconfigured the body and homosexual relationships into local Taiwan history and cultures, articulating an embedded and concrete aesthetic of Taiwan queer cinema.

Conclusion

As the history and practice of Chinese women's cinema illustrate, women's participation in filmmaking is geopolitically and historically contingent, and the meaning and significance of their films are diverse and resistant to any uniform interpretations. Gender matters critically in understanding Chinese women's cinema, but gender itself is a historically and geopolitically specific concept and practice that always requires close examination and study. Although since the 1990s Chinese women directors across geopolitical divides have confronted increasingly similar issues generated primarily by the demands of the market and cultural commercialization, women directors have responded differently. It is in and through this diverse engagement with historical forces – whether of the market, politics, or patriarchal traditions – that Chinese women have exhibited their agency, not only in reorienting gender configurations in history, but also in articulating different meanings and aesthetics in their cinematic practices.

Note

1   For a list of Chen Wen-min's films, see http://www.dianying.com/ft/person/ChenWenmin (accessed February 28, 2010).

18

From Urban Films to Urban Cinema
The Emergence of a Critical Concept

Yomi Braester

In surveying urban films in China since the early 1980s, we must first ask: What distinguishes urban films? Why should the term "Urban Cinema" be considered a useful category for understanding these films? What makes this category important enough for Chinese film that entire books (and this chapter) are dedicated to Urban Cinema? Although Urban Cinema may first seem to include any film shot in a densely built environment, the term has in fact appeared in specific historical contexts and under circumstances that have never been critically explored. In fact, the emergence of Urban Cinema as a concept is interlinked with other major developments in film, including the rise of commercial movies in China and the cinematic response to China's entry to the World Trade Organization.

The term "Urban Cinema" (*chengshi dianying*) first appeared around 1986 and suggested a new trend. Insofar as it suggests common thematic concerns, the term resonates with the long-standing ideological tension between city and countryside, as well as with China's recent urbanization on an unprecedented scale. Yet Urban Cinema is not only determined by economic data; nor is it simply reflective of the new social conditions. It also aspires to genre-like distinction, assuming typical plot conventions and consistent formal iconology. From its inception, Urban Cinema has been implicated in critical debates over the relation between avant-garde film and genre movies, as well as discussions on the role of these forms in the Chinese film industry. In short, the history of Urban Cinema is key to understanding the politics of Chinese film production, reception, and scholarship. The first half of this chapter presents an outline of the post-Maoist Urban Cinema (also see Z. Zhang 2007b; Braester 2010) and the second half turns to the critical discourse that gave rise to Urban Cinema as a concept.

A Companion to Chinese Cinema, First Edition. Edited by Yingjin Zhang.
© 2012 Blackwell Publishing Ltd. Published 2012 by Blackwell Publishing Ltd.

Urban Films: Major Themes and Concerns

A survey of Chinese cinema shows the prominence of urban themes and an umbilical relation to urban culture. The pre-World War II center for film industry was Shanghai, and Chinese film was associated with Shanghai's cityscape, studios, and theaters (Y. Zhang 1999). Films continued to explore city-related topics after 1949, yet true to Mao's guerrilla-war principle that "the countryside surrounds the cities" urban life did not figure prominently. In fact, films such as *A Married Couple* (Zheng Junli, 1951) and *Sentinels under the Neon Lights* (Wang Ping, 1964) focused on condemning the city, and Shanghai in particular, as a haven for reactionaries and spies intent on corrupting the Communist forces (Braester 2010). In the mid-1980s the early films of Fifth Generation directors continued to portray the countryside, although through the critical eyes of city dwellers who had been sent down during the Cultural Revolution.

In the mid-1980s, however, a number of films on city life drew critical attention. The new environment of the post-Maoist economic growth was portrayed in *Yamaha Fish Stall* (Zhang Liang, 1984), *Juvenile Delinquents* (Zhang Liang, 1985), *Sunshine and Rain* (Zhang Zeming, 1987), and *With Sugar* (Sun Zhou, 1987). These films were produced and set in Guangzhou, which Deng's economic reforms targeted for modernization. These films stood out for common themes – youth coming to grips with a budding consumerist society, running unattached and often alienated lives, exploring sexual freedom and dabbling in avant-garde art. *With Sugar* initiated a slew of films depicting the budding rock music and experimental art scenes. Youthful rebellion was subsequently presented in *Rock Kids* (Tian Zhuangzhuang, 1987), *Obsession* (Zhou Xiaowen, 1988), *Beijing Bastards* (Zhang Yuan, 1993), *Weekend Lover* (Lou Ye, shot in 1993, released in 1996), *The Days* (1993) and *Frozen* (1995) by Wang Xiaoshuai, *Dirt* (Guan Hu, 1994), *The Making of Steel* (Lu Xuechang, 1998), and *Quitting* (Zhang Yang, 2001). Rock music in the films of the 1990s functioned as an "articulation of dissent and resistance" (Y. Zhang 2007a: 61). More broadly, these films represent a variety of the young rebel genre (X. Zhou 2007).

A related theme is the lionizing of hoodlums (*liumang*), smooth operators (*wanzhu*), and hooligans (*pizi*) as heroic rebels. In accordance with the "the apotheosis of the liumang" (Barmé 1999: 62–98), many urban films were based on the "hooligan literature" (*pizi wenxue*) of Wang Shuo (b. 1958), including *Samsara* (Huang Jianxin, 1988) and *The Troubleshooters* (Mi Jiashan, 1988). By 1997, Zhang Yimou – the leading director of the Fifth Generation – ventured into city comedy with the aptly titled *Keep Cool*, which follows a hotheaded young liumang through landmarks of recent urban development. This and Zhang's subsequent *Happy Times* (2000) showcased the director's ability to add a twist to trendy genres – in this case, urban comedy, followed by martial arts films. The hooligan cool indicates how thematic concerns soon spilled into box-office considerations.

The focus on the alienated and marginalized also coincided with the portrayal of unstable identities. The protagonists of urban films may be amnesiac, delirious, or clinically schizophrenic, as in *Red Beads* (He Jianjun, 1993), *Sons* (Zhang Yuan, 1996), or *Quitting*. These films often also blur the line between real and performed identity. Female characters in particular appear as doubles, easily taken for each other, in three films that came out in quick succession: *A Lingering Face* (Lu Xuechang, 1999), *Lunar Eclipse* (Wang Quan'an, 1999), and *Suzhou River* (Lou Ye, 2000). The urban setting of these films is seemingly tangential, but it underlines the connection between the harsh built environment and individual psychological crisis. As these examples show, from its inception and into the twenty-first century urban films have portrayed social conditions previously deemed inappropriate for the screen, and at the same time turned them into parables of modern existence.

Some films, however, attempt to present an objective record. Many urban films exhibit what may be called a documentary impulse, an urge to preserve the disappearing cityscape on celluloid (Braester 2010: 226–8). A prominent exponent is Ning Ying's Beijing trilogy – *For Fun* (1992), *On the Beat* (1995), and *I Love Beijing* (2000), which trains the lens on sites and entire districts about to be demolished and gentrified. Chinese urban films owe much of their reputation as biting and cutting-edge to documenting, against the official line, the shady fringes of the unregulated market economy, including the sex industry, drug abuse, and pirated merchandise (Pickowicz 2006: 7). The insistence on recording the unadorned reality, together with the adoption of production models unfettered by the state-owned production and distribution system, won directors the distinction of dissidents. Their films were lionized as transgressive and "underground," gaining a small cult following and international prestige (Pickowicz 2006: 10). Urban films went beyond specific themes: they became associated with a young and rebellious crowd, acquired political connotations, and provided social commentary.

Toward a Distinct Visual Idiom

Common visual tropes and formal approaches further distinguish urban films. Whereas critics have noted distinct themes, the visual idiom has drawn little attention. Considering the many directors and settings involved, it is impossible to find imagery, not to mention a cinematic language, common to all. Yet certain forms of camerawork recur frequently, complementing and supporting the themes mentioned above.

As may be expected, in urban films the lens often targets the built environment. Extreme long shots of large expanses alternate with eye-level, point-of-view (POV) shots that replicate what city dwellers see and experience. *Sunset Street* (Wang Haowei, 1983) takes place in a district of single-story buildings (shot near Qianhai) and ends with a shot that surveys large modern buildings (the new development at Tuanjiehu). Ning Ying's trilogy follows its protagonists as they move around the city – first by foot (*For Fun*), then by bicycle (*On the Beat*), and finally by taxi (*I Love Beijing*), but the camera also tilts up to show high-rises encroaching on the old communities. In most urban films the focus is on vernacular architecture rather than iconic monuments. Movies portraying Shanghai, for instance, often depict colonial-era residences, and especially the *longtang* – a unique hybrid architectural form, of townhouses that open up to a common lane. These can be observed in *A Beautiful New World* (Shi Runjiu, 1999), *Shanghai Women* (2002) and *Kids from Shanghai* (2009) by Peng Xiaolian, and the documentary *Nostalgia* (Shu Haolun, 2006). Monuments of commercial and political significance make rare appearances. *38 Degrees* (Liu Xin, 2003) situates the plot in an apartment overlooking the Shanghai Oriental Pearl TV Tower, but this rare, slick gesture may be attributed to the movie's combination of blatant commercialism and propaganda. By contrast, when the same TV tower is briefly caught in the lens in *Suzhou River*, it is in a jittery shot that does little to aggrandize the landmark. In general, urban films shun postcard images and emphasize the everyday.

Another recurring trope is that of urban ruins, or more precisely images resulting from the demolition-and-relocation projects that were tearing up China's cityscape in the 1990s and 2000s. Given the fast pace in which cities have been rebuilt – leading to a rapid visual transformation, disappearance of cultural heritage, and destruction of communities – destroyed structures and dislocated citizens have become emblematic of the cities' looks and social reality. Such images are found in increasing numbers, in parallel with the introduction of policies for urban restructuring. Probably the earliest shot of demolition in progress is included in *Sunset Street*; the massive projects in preparation for the Asian Games of 1991 are obliquely portrayed in *No Regret about Youth* (Zhou Xiaowen, 1992); the drive for gentrification toward the PRC's fiftieth anniversary is reflected in *A Tree in House* (Yang Yazhou, 1999), *Shower* (Zhang Yang, 1999), *Seventeen Years* (Zhang Yuan, 1999), and *Life Show* (Huo Jianqi, 2000). The director most closely associated with images of demolition-and-relocation is Jia Zhangke, who features the topic prominently in *Xiao Wu* (1997), *Still Life* (2006), and *24 City* (2008). These films capture the transformation of urban centers around China, including not only in Beijing but also in Chengdu, Tianjin, Wuhan, and smaller towns in Shanxi and Sichuan. These fictional refractions of urban reality were accompanied by highly critical (and often banned) documentaries, such as *Demolition and Relocation* (Zhang Yuan, 1998) and *Meishi Street* (Ou Ning, 2006). The images of demolition have become a symbol of the fragility of urban aspirations.

The pervasive shots of protagonists roaming around the city – in POV, over-the-shoulder, and tracking shots – have arguably become one of the recognizable characteristics of urban films. *I Love Beijing* may be described as a road movie, albeit one that never leaves the capital. The protagonist is a taxi driver, and the camera keeps taking in views of the city, seen through the car windows. *Stolen Life*

(Li Shaohong, 2005) tells of a young woman forced to give up her baby for adoption. The camera follows the woman into her basement room, in tracking shots that not so much juxtapose the underground dwelling with the open streets as put the two on a par, mazes that entrap her. *Keep Cool's* opening sequence, of a young man pursuing his former girlfriend, consists of tracking shots edited through rapid jump-cuts. The sequence starts in a quick-pace chase across town by bus and bicycle and ends in trailing the protagonists running through a modern high-rise compound. The frenzied scene introduces the viewer to the cityscape in which the plot is about to take place and at the same time reflects the mindset of the drifting man.

The function of tracking shots, often using handheld cameras, to enhance the experience of the city and allude to the themes introduced above – mental alienation, youthful experimentation, liumang cool, and living on the fringe of accepted and legal norms – may be traced back to *Black Snow* (Xie Fei, 1990). The movie emphasizes the material and social transformation of the post-Maoist city as reflected in the protagonist's inner psyche. Notably, the film's opening credits sequence features a 71-second long take that tracks Quanzi, a young man just released from prison, as he winds his way back home through a rundown Beijing neighborhood. This was the first steadycam shot in Chinese cinema, and it drew critical attention and sparked widespread use of the technique. The shot disturbs the "coherent perception of the environs" (X. Tang 2000: 258). It follows closely behind Quanzi and presents his subjective view; it also shows the city closing upon the man and watching over him. This shot may be contrasted with a later one, when an escaped prisoner comes to see Quanzi. Fearing police surveillance, he enters through the roof rather than through Quanzi's initial path. The opening sequence is mirrored in the film's last scene, in which the critically stabbed Quanzi staggers until he collapses in a public square, again tracked by the camera. The tension between Quanzi's subjective point of view and the public space in which he dies anonymously shows the individual as shaped and obliterated by the urban environment.

Younger directors took up the cinematic idiom established by *Black Snow*. Lou Ye's directorial debut *Weekend Lover* features many steadycam tracking shots. The film's opening shot follows the juvenile delinquent Axi going up and down a maze of stairwells, sometimes turning around to check that no one is pursuing him, looking directly at the camera. Toward the end, a similar shot tracks along Axi's rival, Lala, who stumbles away from Axi's murder scene. The shots that bracket the film may be read as a tribute to *Black Snow*, but the pace and sound are much more dynamic. Lou Ye continued to develop the trope in his following feature, *Suzhou River*. Like Lou's previous film, *Suzhou River* is also located in the rundown outskirts of old Shanghai. It begins with a haunting collage of unsteady pans taken from a boat moving down Suzhou Creek. The sequence is mirrored by the ending sequence, a series of point-of-view shots down the same stream, which resemble the increasingly erratic gaze of a drunkard.

The visual trope established in the opening and concluding sequences of *Black Snow* appears also in modified forms, as in *Good Morning, Beijing* (Pan Jianlin, 2003). The plot takes place during a single night and cuts back and forth between a man trying to ransom his kidnapped girlfriend and a woman locked in an apartment, where she is forced into prostitution. The man spends the entire night following the kidnappers' directions and driving from one Beijing landmark to another. The woman endures her fate in an indistinct, bare, and windowless apartment. Insofar as the two stories are interlinked – presumably, the young woman is the man's kidnapped girlfriend – they present two complementary aspects of the disorienting and entrapping city. Whereas the man's path introduces the larger urban context, the woman's point of view is confined to the claustrophobic space where she withdraws into herself. The oppressive atmosphere persists through the movie's last shot, in which the woman tears away the black cardboard that covers a full-wall window, through which the woman watches, from atop a high rise, an urban scene at dawn. The titular morning greeting to Beijing acquires a sarcastic tone. A slow zoom-in – equivalent in function to a tracking shot – frames the woman within the city, against the pane that serves as an invisible barrier from the urban surroundings. The zoom-in ends in overlapping the frame with the window, conflating the cinematographic frame with the woman's field of vision and constrained gaze.

In identifying with the protagonists' point of view – whether by POV shots simulating the ambulatory city dweller or superimposing the frame on her field of vision – urban films stress the individual's physical and mental position within the city. Moreover, the visual tropes underline that the main element binding together urban films are not thematic but rather ideological.

For an emblematic example, we may turn again to *Weekend Lover*. The film follows juvenile delinquents through Shanghai with dynamic tracking shots. Counterbalancing these explorations, the film is interspersed with immobile shots – rooftop vistas of the large city, eye-level views of recognizable locations, and street signs. These shots place the film in concrete settings, signaling specific districts and locales. Yet the last street sign seen in the film is blank; the young protagonists' mental confusion is mirrored in geographical disorientation. The empty street sign points at the same time to the built environment and to the inhabitants' inner psyche. It is an index of the instability if not vacuity of the youngsters' lifestyle. The themes to which the sign alludes and that are prominently featured in the film – the rapidly developing city, the sex-drugs-and-rock 'n' roll counterculture, the alienated individual – are strongly associated with what was, by then, called Urban Cinema. Yet the empty sign may also remind us that "Urban Cinema" itself is a vague if not empty idea that can be filled in to fit viewers' preconceptions. Any neat laundry list of thematic and formal characteristics by which to identify Urban Cinema belies the complex reasons for putting together the film and the city. Urban Cinema as a critical concept was invented as part of the discourse on the desired path for Chinese film.

The Emergence of Urban Cinema as a Subject of Discourse

The historical and formal outline just provided may be useful as a survey of what has become known as Urban Cinema, but it does not amount to a coherent roadmap. Even this concise typology demonstrates that thematic and visual analysis cannot provide an exhaustive description and may run into inconsistencies. Insofar as all these films belong together under the panoply of Urban Cinema, it is due to their critical reception since the mid-1980s.

The first discussions of Urban Cinema evidence a rigid and confused approach. The term seems to have appeared first in 1986, and one of the earliest attempts to define it took place in a symposium convened in 1988 by the journal *New Film*, titled "Urban Cinema Has Great Prospects" (Bian et al. 1988). The speakers – Shanghai-based critics and filmmakers – made unstructured remarks. They compiled lists of films that may count as Urban Cinema, citing Shanghai oldies as well as revolutionary films such as *Sentinels under the Neon Lights* (Wang Ping, 1964) and *Song of Youth* (Chen Huaiai, Cui Wei, 1959). The motivation for the symposium, however, was the recent Cantonese movies mentioned above as well as *Swan Song* (Zhang Zeming, 1985), *Black Cannon Incident* (Huang Jianxin, 1986), *Hey, Pals!* (Wang Fengkui, 1987), and *Young Couples* (Zheng Dongtian, 1987). Following Maoist standards of evaluating art by its ability to "reflect real life," the symposium participants praised Urban Cinema for allowing filmmakers to portray their familiar surroundings and characters of every walk of life, in accordance with recent social changes.

The slogans aired by the participants evidence the tenacity, as late as 1988, of a centralistic, prescriptive approach to the film industry. The host, *New Film's* editor Bian Shanji, set the tone by asking how Urban Cinema would help the future growth of Chinese film. Bian argued that Urban Cinema must describe urban existence, grasp urban consciousness, promote the national characteristics of Chinese film, and avoid localism. For Bian, it seems, film is primarily a tool for social engineering. Others took the opportunity to call for a rejuvenation of Chinese cinema. The scholar Zhou Bin pointed out that after the success of *Yellow Earth* (Chen Kaige, 1984) and *Red Sorghum* (Zhang Yimou, 1987), Fifth Generation landmarks that focus on the countryside, Urban Cinema is poised to leave a significant mark. As the director and scriptwriter Bian Zhenxia put it, "one day, the breakthrough for [Chinese] film may come through Urban Cinema" (Bian et al. 1988: 58).

The pigeonholing approach, identifying films as Urban Cinema according to preconceived themes, went hand in hand with such prescriptive demands. This approach continued the Maoist practice of classifying films according to preset "subject matter" (*ticai*). This system, modeled on the Soviet Union's film industry and adopted in the early 1950s, was used to oversee production and ensure that films represented one of three major categories, namely the lives of workers, peasants, and soldiers. The number of films in each category was kept roughly equal, both at the national level and in each film studio (H. Chen 1989: 38). At first Urban Cinema expanded the known categories but did not challenge the existing classification.

Urban Cinema, however, could potentially destabilize the categorization according to subject matter. At the "Great Prospects" symposium, Qian Xiaoru noted that *Sunshine and Rain* and *With Sugar* differed from earlier works in that they did not simply take the city as their subject matter, but rather addressed urban culture, in response to the contemporary reforms policy. The film scholar Chen Xiaoyun published a two-part essay in 1990–1, analyzing urban cinema along new critical trends. Chen quotes Fredric Jameson (in Chinese translation): "modernism is art about anxiety, including all sorts of intense emotions and inexpressible desperation" (X. Chen 1990: 85). Chen, and others writing in the same vein, ushered in a symbolic understanding of Urban Cinema, based not on the concrete references to the city but rather on the portrayed economic conditions and mental states and on ideological implications.

As with other critical fields, film studies were quickly transformed by neo-Marxist terminology. Urban Cinema rose to prominence as a showcase for the new approach. It is in this context that we should understand Wei Xiaolin's statement that Urban Cinema conveys "the experience of anomie and disorientation in … the age of market economy" (qtd. in X. Tang 2000: 251). Xiaobing Tang, who introduced Jameson's criticism to Chinese readers, cites Wei and places *Good Morning Beijing* (Zhang Nuanxin, 1990) and *Black Snow* in a Jamesonian context. Tang explains that in these films "the urban landscape recedes, as it were, into the distance and turns simultaneously into an untranscendable historical condition and an experiential immediacy that together smother any coherent reception" (2000: 249). In other words, the materiality of the city remains a determining factor, but it is perceived only through individual experience, and a disorienting one at that. Through his reading of early exponents of Urban Cinema, Tang observes the formation of "modernist subjectivity" in Beijing in the late 1980s. Urban Cinema, by this account, does not simply offer a phenomenological description of the new cities; rather, it signals an ideological transformation and can be taken for a manifestation of the political unconscious of the PRC in the late 1980s and 1990s.

Other observations also looked beyond subject matter to understand the distinguishing features of Urban Cinema. Chris Berry (1988), writing with foresight, noted that in urban films "cities are not just something to be represented" and drew attention to the new trend's distinct "slice-of-life realism" and "absurdism." In other words, urban cinema reacts against the mannered and self-important films of the Maoist period. A similar point is made by Chen Xiaoyun (1991: 88), comparing *The Troubleshooters* to *Catch 22* (Mike Nichols, 1970). These characterizations note the attitude, both of dramatic characters and of the filmmakers, rather than the films' physical urban setting.

More recently, Zhang Zhen combined the concepts of Urban Cinema and the "Newborn Generation" (*xin shengdai*) of filmmakers to coin the "urban generation." The term represents the results of Deng's economic reforms, and in this capacity reacts to large-scale urbanization and globalization; it is an alternative cinema that goes beyond the mythmaking of the Fifth Generation directors, as well as beyond the "underground" stage of the Sixth Generation; it goes beyond state propaganda and beyond the commercial mainstream and serves as a tool of social criticism (Z. Zhang 2007a). Zhang's definition, which synthesizes earlier ones, further underlines the need to understand the stakes in Chinese film classification practices.

Genre Trouble

The various attempts to define Urban Cinema not only indicate the outline of the trend and its importance in turning post-Maoist film into a form of social criticism; they are also highly informative of the critical discourse on Chinese film in the PRC and abroad. The approaches to Urban Cinema have ranged from accepting existing classifications at face value, to fine-tuning them, and to searching for new ones. Yet under what kind of category should Urban Cinema be subsumed?

A recent essay is typical of the scholarly conundrum. Wu Xiaoli (2009: 111) describes "Urban Cinema" as a "collective concept." For Wu, Urban Cinema joins "rural subject matter, industrial subject matter, war subject matter, historical subject matter, main melody [propaganda] subject matter, and the New Year's movie subject matter." Wu's use of "subject matter" as the guiding principle is questionable on two accounts. First, Wu expands subject matter far beyond the Maoist division of films as dedicated to workers, peasants, and soldiers. Second, as Wu expands the definition of subject matter, she refers to what most scholars would associate with genre – war films, costume drama, patriotic melodrama, and popular comedy. Yet Wu carefully avoids calling Urban Cinema a genre, coining an alternative term, namely "collective concept." Such maneuvering may be observed also in earlier discussions of Urban Cinema. For example, Chen Xiaoyun (1990: 87) juxtaposed martial arts films, which are restricted to "famous mountains and temples," with the modern content of Urban Cinema. Considering that martial arts films are regularly discussed under the rubric of genre film (*leixing pian*), the contorted phrasing to avoid calling Urban Cinema a genre calls for explanation.

Herein lies an unspoken yet central reason for the emergence of Urban Cinema as a concept: it offered a form of classification that went against the logic of commercial genre film. At the same time that urban films suggested an alternative to Maoist aesthetics, the market was being exposed, for the first time, to Hollywood blockbusters and Chinese imitations. Urban Cinema showed another path. Benefiting from the relaxation of preproduction censorship and increased control given to individual filmmakers, Urban Cinema could focus on marginalized subcultures and self-marginalizing countercultures. The critical embrace of Urban

Cinema was permeated with the exuberance of the 1980s "culture fever," a somewhat anti-establishment trend. Those lionizing Urban Cinema for its experimentalism and social criticism differentiated it between an indigenous form of art film and the newly introduced popular genres.

An explicit attempt to place Urban Cinema and genre film on separate grounding is found in an essay by the director, critic, and Beijing Film Academy professor Zheng Dongtian. This seminal essay, published in 1997 in response to Zhang Yimou's *Keep Cool*, solidified the use of Urban Cinema as a critical term by placing it within a sociohistorical context. In Zheng's view, Urban Cinema is a rejection of the Maoist vilification of cities as commercial centers (one may recall *A Married Couple* and *Sentinels under the Neon Lights*). Urban Cinema is also a corrective to Fifth Generation directors' initial exoticist focus on rural subject matter (*Yellow Earth* and *Red Sorghum* spring to mind). At its core, Urban Cinema is an alternative to Maoist cinematic practices; it is motivated by the attempt to foil the state-sponsored discourse based on socialist and nationalist ideals. Zheng also links Urban Cinema to the new economic conditions. He identifies the urban films with Sixth Generation directors, who "grew up together with the cities." Zheng quotes the director Huang Jianxin, who notes that Deng's reforms and the subsequent collapse of the social safety net have brought about a new, individual consciousness. To the observations provided in the late 1980s, Zheng adds both institutional factors (a generation shift) and ideological concerns (reading the films as existential parables).

Implicit in Zheng's argument, however, is a challenge not only to Maoist aesthetics and ideology but also to Maoist film classification. The main classification, as I have mentioned, distinguished among industrial, rural, and military subject matters. Other classifications were just as crass. The inventory of the Shanghai Municipal Film Bureau (Shanghaishi dianyingju 1963), issued for internal use and comprising films from 1950 to 1962, differentiates among fiction films (*yishu pian*, literally "art films"), animated films (*meishu pian*), feature-length documentaries (*chang jilu pian*), short documentaries (*duan jilu pian*), educational films (*kejiao pian*), and 3-D films (*liti dianying*). Most film posters of the Maoist and early post-Maoist period distinguished only between "fiction film" and "documentary film," and at times drew attention to technological advances ("in color" or "wide screen"). Nevertheless, posters occasionally included Hollywood-style generic descriptions, namely "art film" (yishu pian), "opera film" (*xiqu pian*), "comedy" (*xiju pian*), "thriller" (*jingxian pian*), or "counterespionage" (*fante pian*). For example, *A Light Gunboat in the Raging Sea* (Wang Bin, Tang Xiaodan, 1955) was billed as a "war fiction film" (*zhandou gushi pian*), and *At Ten O'clock on National Day* (Wu Tian, 1956) as a "counterespionage thriller."

By contrast, Zheng Dongtian skirts existing genre classifications and distinctions based on subject matter. Rather than linking Urban Cinema to certain themes, he emphasizes the viewpoint of the urban generation. Zheng reiterates the essence of Urban Cinema criticism, suggesting a cinematic category, and promoting a body of cinematic works, based not on visible attributes but on inner subjectivity. The introduction of Urban Cinema as a concept that straddles thematic and ideological concerns demonstrated the inadequacy of subject matter and genre as critical tools.

By the late 1990s, when Zheng wrote his essay, the threat to critical filmmaking came not only from the state's ideological control but rather, perhaps more acutely, from the market's exposure to commercial films. In 1994 China Film was licensed to import and distribute ten foreign films every year. Intended to bolster dwindling box-office revenues, the system created an unbalanced competition between Hollywood blockbusters and domestic films. In the aftermath of the invasion of foreign blockbusters, when only state-sponsored propaganda seemed profitable (due to generous subsidies), critics pinned their hopes on Urban Cinema. It presented an indigenous approach to film, with the potential of drawing urban audiences interested in truthful portrayal of their condition rather than imported fluff or phony idealization.

The unabashedly elitist approach of Urban Cinema proponents rejected the path taken at the same time by filmmakers and critics who saw the solution to the film industry's sustainability in reorganization according to genre. Since the late 1990s, genre films grew in number and in popularity. Productions became identifiable as comedy, martial arts, action, romance, detective, historic epic, and horror films, to the point where "genre films" became synonymous with commercial cinema. Critics were also paying attention to genre, in interpreting contemporary films as well as reading the history of Chinese cinema retrospectively in terms of genre. Jia Leilei (2005a) dedicates a chapter to film genres, discussing foreign and Chinese films of all periods. Jia devotes space to comedies, romances, musicals, westerns, sci-fi, gangster, erotic, martial arts, war, and horror films. Yin Hong and Ling Yan (2002: 58) note the formation of proto-generic films in 1956–66, even though these works "cannot be discussed in the full sense of genre films."

The emergence of genre criticism in China has succeeded, in ways other than those envisioned by Urban Cinema proponents, in distancing film discourse from the Maoist assumption of direct correspondence of themes and form to the state production system and state ideology. Chen Xiaoyun, Zheng Dongtian, and others promoted Urban Cinema as a genre-like concept that would serve as an antidote to genre film. Ironically, filmmakers of a younger generation aimed at turning Urban Cinema itself into a commercial genre.

The New Urban Cinema

Whereas the emergence of Urban Cinema reflected the concerns of the 1980s and 1990s – a burgeoning urban culture, disenchantment with Maoist aesthetics, and anxiety about the commercialization of the film industry – the turn of the twenty-first century was characterized by a willingness to accommodate market forces. Early Urban Cinema filmmakers were often content with carving out a cult niche. In many cases, being labeled rebels and having their films banned boosted their popularity and revenues outside China (Barmé 1999: 188–98). By contrast, the late 1990s saw the rise of films on urban themes and with urban attitudes that aimed straight for the box office.

In 1997, just as Zheng Dongtian was looking for a viable Chinese response to Hollywood blockbusters, Feng Xiaogang started churning out commercial hits, beginning with *The Dream Factory* (1997). Feng's lighthearted style may partly be attributed to his background as a TV industry veteran, unlike most directors who graduated from the Beijing Film Academy. Feng paid special attention to marketing and billed his productions as New Year's movies – a promotional device borrowed from the Hong Kong film industry. It was also in 1997 that Zhang Yang (b. 1967) directed the highly profitable *Spicy Love Soup*, set in Shanghai, followed by *Shower* (1999), depicting change in Beijing's old city. Zhang, too, came from outside the film industry, having graduated from the Central Academy of Drama. His films, which broke domestic box-office records, were produced by Imar, the first Sino-foreign joint-venture film company, and were fully funded by foreign investors. The trend also encompassed former Urban Cinema rebels such as Wang Xiaoshuai, who directed *Beijing Bicycle* in 2001. *Beijing Bicycle*, a transnational production with the Taiwanese Peggy Chiao Hsiung-ping as Wang's involved producer, follows mainstream thematic and visual formulas. Ling Yan (1999) commended *Spicy Love Soup*, *Beautiful New World* (another Imar production), and *Love in the Internet Age* (Jin Chen, 1999) for providing "myths for the new urban citizens." These films contributed to blurring the boundaries between highbrow avant-garde and market-oriented commercial films. They succeeded not only in revitalizing the PRC film industry but also in gaining popularity abroad, to the extent that audiences outside China may identify Urban Cinema with these later productions.

These films, however, were labeled as "New Urban Cinema" (*xin chengshi dianying*) as part of a new marketing strategy. The term was probably first used in 2000 in publicity materials by Beijing Forbidden City &Trinity Pictures Company. Soon after, essays in the news media followed suit. Sun Chen (2000), writing for the *People's Daily* overseas edition, quoted uncritically the publicity material and mentioned New Urban Cinema as a contribution to boosting box-office revenues, noting the popularity of *Poetic Times* (Lü Yue, 1999), *Seventeen Years*, and *I Love Beijing*, all of which had just been released. Directors too started to refer to themselves as belonging to a generation of urban sensibilities. Notably, Zhang Yibai (b. 1963), the director of *Spring Subway* (2002), claimed that his film was an exponent of New Urban Cinema and as such aimed at "reflecting and discovering the beauty of modern city life" (Qian 2002). For Zhang, New Urban Cinema was the new mainstream.

Spring Subway is indicative of New Urban Cinema – a feel-good, unchallenging flick. There is even a "main melody," state propaganda New Urban Cinema production – *Bright Heart* (Hao Ran, 2002). Yet to cash in on the avant-garde aura of Urban Cinema, the later trend keeps the boundaries with the earlier trend blurred. Unlike the Urban Cinema of the late 1980s and early 1990s, New Urban Cinema is a commercial genre whose promotion and reception follow the same pattern as genres such as martial arts films. The methodological problems into which critics such as Zhang Zhen and Chen Xiaoyun run in trying to reconcile critical and commercial forces in urban films may be attributed at least in part to the prism through which these movies have been viewed after the emergence of New Urban Cinema. The issue becomes even thornier given that the two trends share much in common and that some films dating to the turn of the century straddle the trends (*Suzhou River* and *I Love Beijing* may serve as good examples).

In examining Urban Cinema and New Urban Cinema, their place in the development of the Chinese film industry, and their role in Chinese film criticism, it may be useful to keep in mind studies in film genre and especially the observations of Rick Altman. Genre theory often focuses on repetition and difference, reaffirmation and novelty, as the way in which genre develops and keeps its relevance (e.g., Neale 1980: 48). Yet this approach assumes that genres are preexisting and self-contained categories. Altman (1989: 15–29), by contrast, contends that genres are invented and modified to serve the *ad hoc* marketing needs of the film industry. Rather than being made according to a recognizable blueprint, genre films are identified pragmatically as part of an ever-changing negotiation between producers and audiences. Genres are, so to speak, back-engineered to fit spectators' expectations. Urban Cinema was invoked as a concept to fit the critical discourse of the 1980s; New Urban Cinema emerged as a genre in the context of the new marketing practices at the turn of the twenty-first century. Neither term has a clear and stable relation to themes, images, or ideological concerns associated with the city.

The claim that Urban Cinema as a concept is not directly related to urban concerns does not void the interaction between film and the city. It should be acknowledged, however, that the rise of a distinct urban consciousness since the late 1980s (Visser 2010) is refracted through movies made by directors and promoted by critics aware of the emerging discourse and eager to participate in it. Insofar as Urban Cinema and New Urban Cinema represent an urban consciousness – both portraying it and claiming to be representative of it – they often do so independently, or even against the grain, of discourses on urban development and governance. Filmmakers and critics have deployed Urban Cinema and New Urban Cinema to further their stakes in a charged debate on the meeting point between post-Maoist aesthetics and ideology. And yet urban films, and Urban Cinema in particular, remain powerful expressions of contemporary Chinese society.

Part IV
Arts and Media

19

The Intertwinement of Chinese Film and Literature

Choices and Strategies in Adaptations

Liyan Qin

Adaptation of literature has been very important for Chinese film from the 1920s till now. Chinese filmmakers have used a wide range of literary sources, both Chinese and foreign, ancient and contemporary. This chapter seeks to trace the general history of Chinese filmic adaptations of literature and identify strategies of filmmakers working within different cultural, political, and commercial contexts in different periods. With traceable textual sources, adaptations offer us a convenient venue to address broader questions about culture, history, and politics. Deletions, additions, and other changes that filmmakers make highlight their strategies in ways that may not be so obvious in films made from original scripts. Change in filmmakers' adaptation strategies about what and how to adapt sheds light on the dynamic of Chinese history in the last century as well as on the mutual influence between culture and history.

Scholarship on Adaptation Studies

I will first outline relevant scholarship in this field to situate my position. Western scholars have been exploring American and European adaptations since the 1950s. Traditional scholarship in the field largely addresses several interrelated questions: Should literature be adapted into films? What is adaptation? What is the nature of film *vis-à-vis* literature? In the early days of Western filmmaking, adaptations were sometimes viewed with suspicion, and much early scholarship was aimed at defending adaptation. André Bazin (2000: 25) argues that what film takes from novels is "only the main characters and situations," and cinema is a kind of digest for literature (see Bluestone 1957). In all, scholarship in this vein often takes a

A Companion to Chinese Cinema, First Edition. Edited by Yingjin Zhang.
© 2012 Blackwell Publishing Ltd. Published 2012 by Blackwell Publishing Ltd.

formalist approach, with the explicit purpose to evaluate the aesthetic excellence of an adaptation film, measured either by its faithfulness to the original or by its innate values.

Informed by recent theoretical developments on semiology, intertextuality, and reception, some scholars have worked out new approaches to address adaptation, with the emphasis shifted to the flow and negotiations between texts. On the one hand, for many scholars, adaptations are full of quotations and references and always in dialogue with their literary sources and other texts, and as such they are by definition intertextual. On the other hand, Shenghui Lu (2004) approaches adaptation from the perspective of reception, since film adaptation is one way of reading the literary source, and the film in turn needs the reading of its own audiences. These studies therefore discredit the traditional notion of "fidelity" and break the hierarchy between literature (as high art, source, and original) and the adapted film (as low art, derivative, and imitation).

Even more groundbreaking is the "sociological turn" that some scholars have called for and practiced recently, oftentimes informed by newly emergent theories. As early as 1984, Dudley Andrew (2000: 35) made such a call:

> It is time for adaptation studies to take a sociological turn. How does adaptation serve the cinema? What conditions exist in film style and film culture to warrant or demand the use of literary prototypes? Although the volume of adaptation may be calculated as relatively constant in the history of cinema, its particular function at any moment is far from constant. The choices of the mode of adaptation and of prototypes suggest a great deal about the cinema's sense of its role and aspirations from decade to decade. Moreover, the stylistic strategies developed to achieve the proportional equivalences necessary to construct matching stories not only are symptomatic of a period's style, but may crucially alter that style.

With the release of two recent books in this field (Naremore 2000; Stam and Raengo 2004), we have evidence that the sociological turn for adaptation studies has gained momentum. Both books show dissatisfaction with traditional scholarship on adaptation. Thus, in selecting articles for his book, Naremore (2000: 10) tries to move "away from the Great-Novels-into-Great-Films theme," and prefers "writings that give somewhat less attention to formal than to economic, cultural, and political issues."

Another field that is useful for adaptation studies in terms of methodology is translation studies, since adaptation has often been seen as a kind of translation, with both often accused of "violating" the original. The limit of traditional translation theories is that they cannot entirely avoid the notion of fidelity. However, recent scholarship on translation proves inspiring. Especially useful is the poststructuralist deconstruction of the original–translation binary with their concept of textuality. As Lawrence Venuti (1992: 7) summarizes, the poststructuralists "question the concepts of originality and authorship that subordinate the translation to the foreign text." On translation studies specific to the Chinese context, Lydia Liu has done pioneering theoretical work. Adopting a "China-centered approach," Liu (1995: 26, 28) believes that "meanings … are not so much 'transformed' when concepts pass from the guest language to the host language as invented within the local environment of the latter." If we change Liu's "translingual" to "transmedia" and view film as "the host language" and literature as the "guest language," her observations are very useful for adaptation studies.[1]

Building on existing scholarship, I situate my research in the context of the recent sociological turn in adaptation studies, although my study is more about history, politics, and culture than about pure sociology. I try to combine atomic and global perspectives, and take the films as given cultural products, without arguing about their aesthetic value or whether they have degraded or improved their literary sources. Particular attention is paid to analyzing those changes made by filmmakers that are historically or culturally significant and to uncovering underlying patterns across films and periods to show the filmmakers' strategies.

In the following two sections, to present a general picture of the choices and strategies in a century of Chinese adaptations, I will discuss two interrelated issues: what Chinese filmmakers choose to adapt during different periods, and how they adapt different kinds of literary sources.

What Literary Sources have been Preferred and Why

The list of Chinese film adaptations of literature may seem chaotic and random at first glance. Yet, after reading the adaptations against one another, against other films and the history of literature, patterns gradually take shape. What do Chinese filmmakers in different periods tend to adapt? What literary sources are taken up in one period and dropped in another? These are some of the questions to be addressed in this section (see also L. Qin 2010: 158–9).

Dingjun Mountain (Ren Qingtai, 1905), known as the first Chinese film, was born in a hybrid form, showing that the birth of Chinese cinema was deeply embedded in the popular culture at that time. With a fixed camera faithfully recording a fully costumed Peking opera actor, in a role based on the popular classic novel *Romance of the Three Kingdoms*, the film had a close link with the stage and literature. Indeed, opera films (*xiqu pian*), featuring Chinese operas in many local forms, constitute an important genre, which had dominated the Chinese screen for decades and only suffered a decline in recent years. Another stage origin of Chinese film was Western-style drama. Unlike classical operas that tell stories about the ancient past, the so-called civilized drama (*wenming xi*), an early form of modern Chinese drama, often addressed contemporary issues and supplied many materials for early Chinese films. Zheng Zhengqiu, the main director of Asia Studio, was also a dramatist. He and Zhang Shichuan directed *The Difficult Couple* (1913), the first Chinese short feature, and the whole cast was from their all-male civilized drama troupe. Thus, the earliest Chinese films were already closely linked to stage performance. The early decades of the twentieth century were also a time of massive translation of Western literature into Chinese. These avidly read translations soon became part of Chinese popular literature and inspired early filmmakers to make use of Western stories. Thus, one of the earliest long features in China, *Ten Sisters* (Guan Haifeng, 1921), based on a French detective story and mingling a Western plot with martial arts and the modern urban crime of insurance fraud, was a real hybrid.

At the same time as Chinese filmmakers looked to foreign literature for sources, they also took advantage of the rich ore of Chinese literature. In the early 1920s the Commercial Press, which had a special department for filmmaking, began to adapt a series of traditional Chinese stories into films. Stories in *Strange Stories Narrated by Liaozhai* by Qing writer Pu Songling (1640–1715) seemed to offer favorite subjects. Pu's short stories are perfect for short features. Moreover, it is easy for filmmakers to find entertaining elements in Pu. The Taoist practitioner in the film *An Empty Dream* (Ren Pengnian, 1922), who believes he can go through a wall, provided the filmmakers with an opportunity to use special effects. Filmmakers can also extract moral messages from these stories. Thus *The Pious Daughter-in-Law's Soup* (Ren Pengnian, 1923) extols the virtues of a daughter-in-law who, true to traditional Chinese moral requirements, remains loyal to her mother-in-law no matter how evil the latter is.

In 1927–8 many films were made based on traditional Chinese stories, and scholars describe the trend as a "traditional film movement" (*guzhuangpian yundong*) (Li and Hu 1997: 22). The movement was initiated by Tianyi Studio, which, after its establishment in 1925, focused on making such films to attract audiences in China and the Chinese diasporas in Southeast Asia. According to Shao Zuiweng (1898–1979), one of the four brothers who founded Tianyi, the strategy was more than a mere business decision: "At that time, Chinese new literature was advocating folk literature, and Mr. Shao also believed that folk literature was the only real Chinese mass literature" (Li and Hu 1997: 89). Either a business or cultural choice or a combination of the two, Tianyi's strategy was very successful. Because these films promoted such traditional values as filial piety, and because other companies rushed after Tianyi to make similar but mostly bad-quality films, Tianyi was condemned by official film history as "stealing from classical fiction" (Cheng, Li, and Xing 1980, I: 86). However, by making films based on popular literature in traditional China, which was then still very much alive among audiences, Tianyi carved out a cinematic space of its own in differentiation from May Fourth new literature at home and the powerful Hollywood films from abroad.

From 1928 to the onset of the leftist film movement in the early 1930s, Shanghai studios again rushed to one genre, this time martial arts films. This rush took advantage of the martial arts novels popular during the 1920s. The immensely successful series *Burning the Red Lotus Temple* (Zhang Shichuan, 1928–32), based on an already well-received martial arts novel, continued for eighteen episodes, saved the almost bankrupt Mingxing studios, and generated a series of films about "burning" something.

Although literati have always participated in filmmaking, no group of writers was as concerted in their efforts and as clear in their goals as the leftists in the 1930s. They were determined to use film as a means to educate the masses, inculcate into them an awareness of social ills in China, and interpret and resolve those ills in Marxist terms. It is noteworthy that leftists such as Xia Yan, Ah Ying (1900–77), Zheng Boqi (1895–1979), and Tian Han carried out their political plans by entering studios as scriptwriters. This underlines the importance of scriptwriters in the early decades of Chinese cinema. The scriptwriter, instead of the director, seemed to be the hub of the filmmaking process. The partnership in the leftist movement often came in the form of a leftist scriptwriter with an already established director, with the former influencing and bringing the latter into the leftist agenda. Since the political message was what most concerned the leftist writers, they preferred writing original scripts to adaptations, with only a few exceptions.

During the Second Sino-Japanese War (1937–45), while films in the hinterlands were mainly propaganda to boost national resistance, in the isolated foreign settlements in Shanghai films enjoyed a surprising prosperity. Zhang Shankun, owner of Xinhua, the biggest studio in the foreign settlements, returned to traditional Chinese themes popular before the leftist movement. However, in this time of national crisis, even such seemingly apolitical films incorporated propaganda into entertainment and conveyed the message of national resistance in a circuitous but unmistakable way. This might not only be due to the intentions of the filmmakers (for Zhang Shankun would later collaborate with the Japanese), but to an effort to appeal to patriotic sentiments in a period when patriotism could mean profits at the box office. *Mulan Joins the Army* (Bu Wancang, 1939) was a case in point. Based on a traditional poem about a girl who, disguised as a young man, joined the army and fought for her country on her father's behalf, the film was very popular.[2]

The year 1945 saw the defeat of the Japanese. Yet, to the public's disappointment, China did not enjoy the victory for long, as it plunged into civil war between Nationalists and Communists. From 1945 to 1949, adaptations from classical Chinese literature declined sharply. Also gone were martial arts. However, many foreign literary works were translated into Chinese and later appeared on the screen. Significantly, during this period, Chinese filmmakers chose to adapt some Russian literary works. Wenhua Studio was a successful player in this area. Its adaptations include *Mother and Son* (Li Pingqian, 1947) from a play by Aleksandr Ostrovsksy (1823–86), *Night Inn* (Huang Zuolin, 1947) from a play by Maxim Gorky (1868–1936), and *The Watch* (Huang Zuolin, 1949) from a novel by Leonid Panteleev (1908–87). The preference for Russian literature in this period might be evidence that the public and the filmmakers were discontented with the political situation and were harboring sentiments favoring the Communists.

After the establishment of the People's Republic of China (PRC) in 1949, adaptation of literature continued to be extremely important for Chinese films.

However, in the years 1949–66, Chinese cinema was drastically changed in terms of the dominant ideology, film language, and methods of production and distribution. Cinema became an enterprise owned by the government with the mission of propaganda and education. Films based on foreign literature, which used to be common before 1949, totally disappeared. No foreign literature, not even Soviet literature, was believed to be adequate to capture China's socialist reality and glorious revolutionary past. Adaptations of classical Chinese literature suffered a similar fate. With an often destructive ideological reinterpretation of Chinese tradition, history, and literature, classical literature was found to be far too flawed. Traditional themes could only be expressed in the least politicized genres such as opera films. One exception to this rule was *The Old Man and the Fairy* (1956), based on a Ming dynasty short story and directed by Wu Yonggang, an established director since the 1930s. The film depicts the conflicts between a righteous poor man and an evil rich man, in a binary similar to the then-prominent class demarcation, with the final victory of the former, of course. Yet, situated in ancient China, it can only resort to fairies and fantasies to facilitate the poor man's triumph. No wonder that in 1957 the director was labeled a Rightist in the Anti-Rightist campaign against intellectuals the Communist Party distrusted, illustrating the huge political risks for traditional Chinese themes in the socialist era. Most film adaptations of this period deal with the immediate past and the present, recounting the history of the rise of the Party and its leadership in the people's struggles against evil enemies. Leftist literature was another major type permitted on the screen. Works by established leftist writers, such as Lu Xun, Mao Dun, Ba Jin, and Rou Shi, were turned into films (the adaptation strategies of films based on leftist literature will be discussed in the next section).

Even when filmmakers chose to adapt themes that might entertain audiences, such as love and marriage, they would make sure to divide the films into two temporal dimensions: the past (before 1949) when everything goes wrong, and the present (after 1949) when all wrongs are put right. Two films on love and marriage, *A Changed World* (Wu Tian, 1959) and *Spring Comes to the Withered Tree* (Zheng Junli, 1961), both adapted from plays, suggest this drastic change of the order of things in their titles. Both tell a story about frustrated love and separated lovers in the old society, who enjoy a happy reunion after 1949. By removing obstacles in the way of the lovers, the new regime is depicted as having removed at the same time some social evil: in the former, gas explosions in coal mines and in the latter, a plague.

There was a particular genre that fitted well with political requirements yet could at the same time provide the entertainment the audience so hungered for. This was the counterespionage film *(fante pian)*. Featuring Communist police tracking down Nationalist or American secret agents, these films mingle elements of suspense, horror, and even sex. The genre was intimately connected to popular anti-spy novels. On the one hand, the film–literature genre was a continuation, although in another guise, of detective stories and films made before 1949. On the other hand, heavily influenced by Soviet novels, the genre was rooted in the socialist reality of campaigns against alleged secret agents. The anti-spy genre provides an interesting case of popular and entertaining elements ensconced in political correctness.

Films and literary works produced during the Cultural Revolution (1966–76) were few in number, aptly summarized by a common saying as "eight model plays and one writer." Almost all previous films or literature were denounced as "poisonous weeds," and Hao Ran was the most frequently adapted writer in the latter part of the Cultural Revolution. What is noteworthy is that all eight model films can be categorized as adaptations, based on Peking operas or ballet, which were in turn adaptations of local operas or literary works. These opera films about revolutionaries faithfully stick to the original actions and singing sessions, and at the same time employ such filmic techniques as composition and lighting to sharpen the contrast between the good and the evil. It was the first time that opera films were given so much political significance and took up so many propaganda functions.

In 1979, after a short period of recovery and with the official launching of "reform and open door" policies, film adaptations entered a new era. An important genre in both film and literature at this time aimed at exposing the wounds caused by the Cultural Revolution and other radical campaigns. For example, different from his works before and during the Cultural Revolution, Xie Jin's films on former-Rightists made in the new era are faithful renditions of contemporary literary works. The original novels he based his films on belong to the genre called "reflection literature" (*fansi wenxue*), which are about the life of former-Rightists and written by the so-called "returners" (*guilai zhe*) – former Rightist writers who now returned to writing. These literary works and the films adapted from them share a narrative pattern of the upright Rightist suffering at the hands of evil guys; in the end, justice is restored and the Rightist is rehabilitated. Such literary works and their film versions were both extremely influential among the public and officially acknowledged, which suggests a rare consensus among film and literature, the public and the government.

In the early 1980s, leftist literature, which vanished in the Cultural Revolution, reappeared on screen. Yet, this was not a return to the pre-Cultural Revolution style and scope of adaptations. We still see those established leftist writers or playwrights: Lu Xun, Lao She, and Cao Yu. Lu Xun remained a favorite for filmmakers, yet their selection of his works changed. While the film *The New Year's Sacrifice* (Sang Hu, 1956) still emphasized the misery and oppression of the old society, filmmakers in the new era selected those stories of Lu Xun with no apparent political implications. One such adapted film was *Regret for the Past* (Shui Hua, 1981), a despondent story about a young couple's love and then estrangement. The other was *The Story of Ah Q* (Cen Fan, 1981), revisiting the May Fourth tradition of exposing the ugliness of the Chinese national character. Meanwhile, in response to literary historians' efforts to rewrite literary history before 1949, filmmakers also looked at non-leftist modern Chinese literature. Shen Congwen, for example, was resurrected in literary history, and two films, *Border Town* (Ling Zifeng, 1984) and *A Girl from Hunan* (Xie Fei, 1986), were based on his stories, depicting love and life in a pristine rural area not touched by revolution.

Communist history was still tapped. However, now the focus was no longer the inevitable military victories, the perfect heroes and heroines, or the class clashes, but often private experiences. One way for films to re-narrate Communist history is to make use of marginalized literary sources. For example, *The Lily* (Qian Xuege, 1981) came from a short story written by female writer Ru Zhijuan in 1958. Unlike the mainstream masculine narratives of wars and struggles, the story explores the delicate and intricate line between comradely love and sexual attraction. Overall, in films made at this time, revolution took on a humanist color.

Indeed, the Fifth Generation filmmakers began their career by using such marginalized revolutionary literature. They first made themselves known with *One and Eight* (Zhang Junzhao, 1983) and *Yellow Earth* (Chen Kaige, 1984), both inspired by literary works. *One and Eight* was based on a narrative poem by Guo Xiaochuan written in 1959, while the basic plot of *Yellow Earth* was taken from a lyrical essay. Both sources are far from optimistic in tone. In *One and Eight* a staunch revolutionary is wrongly condemned as an enemy by his comrades and has to spend his days with eight bandits. In *Yellow Earth* the Communist soldier fails to bring enlightenment and happiness to local people. It might not be coincidence that the Fifth Generation, when they first emerged, made use of a poem and a lyrical essay. Poetry and essays do not emphasize plot even if they have narrative elements, and thus fit well with the Fifth Generation's artistic pursuit to downplay the plot. Furthermore, poems and essays, shorter than novels, leave much room for filmmakers to assert their freedom. The literary work and even the script provided not so much a restricting framework but a enabling vehicle for the film-makers to construct what they believed to be the most important thing for film: visual images.

When the Fifth Generation ended their experimental phase and entered the mainstream, they began to pay attention to novels, especially those by contemporary writers on the Republican period. Zhang Yimou and Chen Kaige showed surpris-ingly similar tastes in this respect. Zhang's *Red Sorghum* (1987), *Ju Dou* (1990), and *Raise the Red Lantern* (1991) and Chen's *Temptress Moon* (1995) were all based on contemporary novels and depict a phantasmagoric Republican world full of sexual oppression, murder, and incest. Both Zhang's *To Live* (1994) (see Figure 19.1) and Chen's *Farewell My Concubine* (1993), again based on contemporary literature, narrate twentieth-century Chinese history through the rise and fall of traditional Chinese artists. Similar life experiences, mutual influences, and the same national and international contexts combined to produce a narrative pattern in the two otherwise different directors.

It seems that in recent decades, when a new generation of Chinese filmmakers emerge on the scene and wants to assert themselves, they tend to downplay the literary qualities of their films. The same thing has been happening to the Sixth

Figure 19.1 Mourning an untimely death in *To Live* (dir. Zhang Yimou, Era, 1994). The caption reads: "Chairman Mao, I have taken away Comrade Xu Fengxia."

Generation. To emphasize their uniqueness and creativity, they often began with writing scripts themselves or cooperating with avant-garde scriptwriters. Take Zhang Yuan, for example. His early experimental films were from original scripts, but he began to adapt literature after he was established. His recent film *Little Red Flowers* (2005) was based on a novel by Wang Shuo, a rebellious writer closely involved in Chinese filmmaking since the late 1980s. It may be expected that, as the Sixth Generation become more and more integrated into the mainstream, their attention to literature and the proportion of their films adapted from literature will only increase.

The "Fidelity" Issue and the Status of Film *vis-à-vis* Literature

Although it is common for moviegoers, critics, and even filmmakers themselves to judge the success of an adaptation by its approximation to the literary source, total fidelity is impossible and a contradiction, as has been amply discussed by scholars of adaptation and translation. As Walter Benjamin (1968: 71) theorizes on translation, "a translation issues from the original – not so much from its life as from its afterlife," which necessarily involves changes. In the case of film adaptation, the changes arise from the interrelationships not so much of two languages but of two media. Still, we can distinguish between relatively faithful adaptations and freer ones. I will take fidelity itself as an issue in Chinese film history. Like films elsewhere, the strategies of Chinese adaptations range from faithful adherence to the original in all possible ways, to subjective attempts to capture the so-called "spirit" of the original as interpreted by the filmmakers, to radical appropriation of the original only as a raw material on which to build one's own film. Where each adapted film finds itself in this spectrum of fidelity is the result of a combination of factors, especially what the literary source is and when the film is made.

In 1957 Xia Yan (1992: 498), then a high-ranking official in charge of cultural productions, argued that different literary works should be dealt with differently:

> I believe that [adaptations] should vary according to the nature of the originals. If the originals to be adapted are classics, works by such masters as Tolstoy, Gorky, and Lu Xun, then I think the adaptors should by all means be faithful to the original. The deletions, additions, and changes of even details should not go beyond or damage the overall message of the original and its unique style. However, if the original to be adapted is myth, folk legend, or the so-called "folk history," then I believe adaptors can have more freedom to add, delete, or change.

Xia Yan's rule foregrounds a key point, which is what can be counted as classics, and his passage draws our attention to the canonization process of literature. Tolstoy and Gorky, whose works Xia Yan mentioned as classics, only became canonized in China after 1949. Some of their works were adapted before 1949, and filmmakers did not have qualms in making them "Chinese," along with other drastic changes. It is only after 1949 and through officially distributed literary histories that Lu Xun, Gorky, and to a lesser degree, Tolstoy, became enshrined. In this canonization process, aesthetic values were less important than political messages. It is not a coincidence that both foreign writers Xia Yan mentioned came from Russia.

Interestingly, Xia Yan did not include traditional Chinese literature in his list of classics. Indeed, his observation about the free adaptation of traditional Chinese literature is a valid summary of Chinese films up till then. The first century of Chinese cinema coincided with a wholesale revamping and critiquing of the Chinese tradition, first against such Western values as democracy and science, then against the Communist values of class struggles. With this generally critical attitude, even filmmakers who harbored some respect for Chinese literary classics deemed it necessary to inject some "new" messages into their films.

Many early film critics voiced such sentiments. In the late 1920s when films on classical topics reached a climax, scriptwriter and director Chen Zhiqing (1897–?) argued that filmmakers must reevaluate traditional materials and choose materials that "represent strenuous struggles and poverty," while those about a peaceful life were ineligible (X. Dai 1996: 639–42, 659). Another contemporary critic concluded that only those traditional literary sources with "motion and energy" were suitable for the screen, while the romantic hero and heroine of _Dream of the Red Chamber_ were too sentimental and unwholesome (X. Dai 1996: 514). These values dovetailed with the May Fourth ideology and, in the face of Western challenges, played up the strong and energetic aspect of Chinese culture. Other important May

Fourth new concepts, including individualism, freedom, and human rights, also found their way into films based on classical Chinese literature. *The Romance of the West Chamber*, when adapted into a film in 1927, was rewritten along the lines of such Western values. The director and scriptwriter Hou Yao believed that the original author of the play, Wang Shifu, who lived in the late thirteenth and early fourteenth centuries, "was a person imprisoned in the Confucian system [*lijiao*], yet he was brave enough and passionate enough to write the play to promote sacred love, divinely endowed human rights and to fight against the Confucian system" (X. Dai 1996: 326). Hou Yao's method of adaptation was to keep what he believed was the modern "spirit" of the play and to add plots that he believed did not contradict that spirit, without caring much about faithfulness in details.[3]

The practice of injecting "correct" messages into the materials in the Republican period continued in the adaptation of the leftist canon, which reached its climax in the 1950s and 1960s, although this time around the messages are Communist in nature. It is interesting to note a striking contradiction in such films: they present themselves as very faithful to their leftist literary sources, and yet at the same time important changes were made. Generally, the filmmakers made the gesture to be faithful to the original, partly because the so-called canonical works had become familiar to the general public and deviations could be eye-catching and controversial. However, in the socialist era, leftist literary works could not be left just as they were to cause confusion or pessimism in the audiences. Messages of resistance and solidarity among the poor were thus added into the films, making them closer to the socialist "Red Canon," which depicts class struggles under direct Communist leadership.

Since visual images are often ambiguous, a way to make the message clear in these adaptations of leftist literature is to articulate it verbally. *The New Year's Sacrifice*, based on a story by Lu Xun of the same title and written into a script by Xia Yan, is typical in this respect. The film is framed by two lengthy passages printed on the screen. At the beginning, we read a passage from Lu Xun, though not from the same short story itself:

> We lament those people of the bygone age, and we promise: we ourselves and others will be pure, bright, brave and upbeat, and we will get rid of the mental confusion and the forces in this world that harm oneself and others … . We also vow to make humankind enjoy its rightful happiness.

This passage, taken from an article written by Lu Xun in 1918 (1981: 125), now resembles the Communist message of class struggle and optimism. At the very end of the film, after the protagonist Xianglin Sao dies of misery, a male voice-over reads out the verdict, summarizes the story, and points out its moral: "Xianglin Sao, this hard-working, thrifty, and kind woman, after innumerable miseries and humiliations, dropped dead. That happened forty years ago, yes, that happened in a bygone age. Fortunately, that age is gone, never to return." The two passages enclose the

Figure 19.2 An old policeman witnessing Beijing's deterioration in *This Life of Mine* (dir. Shi Hui, Wenhua Film, 1950).

story, condemn the old society, and at the same time distance audiences from what happens on the screen and make them feel good about living in a new age.

Based on Lao She's story, *This Life of Mine* (Shi Hui, 1950) (see Figure 19.2) can illustrate in another way the narrative pattern imposed on such adaptations. Films based on leftist literature must both expose the evils of the old society and look forward to a bright Communist future, which was usually added by the filmmakers. The protagonist of *This Life of Mine*, a low-level policeman and reluctant participant in the oppression process, has to die before the birth of the new nation because he is not conscious of class ideology and thus does not know the answer to his sufferings. Different from Lao She's story, the film ends on a triumphant note with the liberation of the whole country by the Communist army. Such practices of imposing political correctness were as much a habit as a way of self-protection and perhaps a reluctant bow to the dominant political discourse.

Different from the case of classical Chinese literature, in spite of these sometimes drastic changes made to leftist literary works, the films imply no resentment or discontent. They still present themselves as paying homage to the writers and base their legitimacy on being filmic translations of the originals. Even the credits at the beginning of these films suggest an obvious hierarchy. In both *The Lin Family Shop* (Shui Hua, 1959) and *The New Year's Sacrifice*, the first credit, occupying the whole screen, is given to the original author, Mao Dun and Lu Xun, respectively. The second credit, again occupying the whole screen, is the scriptwriter Xia Yan. The director only comes as third on the credit list. Also, both *This Life of Mine* and *The Lin Family Shop* begin with an image of a book. *This Life of Mine* even has a disclaimer, not for the filmmakers, but for Lao She the literary author: "This film is adapted from Mr. Lao She's novel. The adaptors are responsible for whatever deviates from the original novel." In this film the episodes are presented as chapters of the book, and we often hear the protagonist reading from the book itself. All these gestures of paying respect to the literary source and the original writer were intended to make people believe that the film is an exact representation of the book, foregrounding the elevated status of the canonical writers and canonical literature. The filmmakers were willing to make these resources "perfect" by tinkering with the message without endangering the writer's authority.

These gestures also show the relative status of film *vis-à-vis* literature. Film until then had not enjoyed a high status as a form of art. One way to promote the respectability of film was to relate it to already established art forms, first drama and then fiction. In his 1926 handbook on scriptwriting, Hou Yao (1992: 49) wrote that film (*yingxi* or shadowplay) "is a kind of drama, and whatever drama has, film has too." In another 1926 article, Hou argued that "film is literature, it is living literature," because it has the essential elements of literature (X. Dai 1996: 501). The emphasis on the literary qualities of a film led to an emphasis on the script, the linguistic base of the film. This tendency to privilege plot and narrative is very strong in Chinese film tradition. Hence a unique branch of film studies in China, "film literature" (*dianying wenxue*), which is a vague label referring to the scriptwriting alone, or narration and characterization, or all filmmaking aspects except for the technical ones.

This secondary and even dependent status of film more or less continued after 1949, and could be seen in a 1956 critical piece written by Yuan Wenshu (1911–93), then head of Shanghai Film Studio, on what constitutes the unique qualities of film. Yuan argued that "the novel is the richest art among all literature and art." However, literature cannot reach the uneducated masses, and here is when film steps in, to popularize and make literature accessible to a larger audience (W. Yuan 1992: 378–9). The filmmakers' strategies of adapting leftist literature, making changes yet trying to appear faithful to the literary works, revealed the lower status of film *vis-à-vis* literature.

However, in the late 1970s and early 1980s, even before the typically free adaptations of the Fifth Generation, filmmakers, especially when dealing with contemporary literary materials, became more confident. Wu Yigong, the director of *My Memory of Old Beijing* (1982), traces some problems of the film not to the script but to the flaws in the novel itself, perhaps partly because the novel was written by a Taiwanese author (Y. Wu 1992: 528). Huang Jianzhong, the assistant director of *Little Flower* (Zhang Zheng, 1979), refuses to categorize the film as an adaptation, since the film only uses some material from the novel. To support his notion of adaptation, Huang quotes Béla Balázs to the effect that adaptors should only deem the original novel as material to be worked on. Believing that this approach stems from the uniqueness of film art, Huang (2002: 51–2) argues that "we must acknowledge the director's camera and the writer's pen are two different tools of art." Huang here links the change in adaptation styles with an awareness of film as a unique art form. Indeed, both theorists and younger filmmakers felt a newly found confidence in film art. While in the early decades of its development Chinese film was flattered if it was allied with other already established art forms, now, to promote the ontological status of film, theorists tried to separate film from drama and later on from literature. Arguments in this vein had popped up in the past, but had never been so systematic and so in line with contemporary filmmaking practices.

It was with the launching of the Fifth Generation that visuality became foregrounded and the free adaptation style widely adopted. Directors still constantly look to literature for material and inspiration, yet what they seek is often a plot or a clue upon which to build their film. In adapting their sources they not only have no qualms in making changes; in resorting to a stylized use of elements unique to the film, they make the final product fully their own. Take *Black Cannon Incident* (Huang Jianxin, 1986), for example. Drastically different from the original novel, Huang adopted the style of "black humor," which he got from reading such Western novels as *Catch 22*. By drawing the audience's attention more to color, composition, and sound than to the progress of the plot, Huang tried to give the audience something they could never have experienced through other art forms.

In the twenty-first century, the ascendancy of film *vis-à-vis* literature is even more pronounced. Films once presented themselves as by-products of literature, but now the situation is reversed, and a novel is often released as an add-on to capitalize on the recent success of a film. Thus, famous writer Liu Zhenyun published his book *Cell Phone* at the end of 2003, almost at the same time as the film with the same title, directed by Feng Xiaogang, premiered nationwide. Obviously, the film and the novel were meant to be sold in a package together, with the novel as a secondary item. Similarly, after the high-profile release of *The Promise* (Chen Kaige, 2005), the prestigious People's Literature Press published a novel based on the film. Clearly, being related to a film has become the selling point for a literary work.

In the new millennium filmmakers' respect for their sources has further declined. Free adaptation is the norm now. There are no literary works so authoritative that they cannot be freely changed. Few films are made with the purpose to promote or distribute canonical literary works. In the 1950s, 1960s, and even the 1980s, film directors usually retained the titles of the literary works they adapted, hoping to remind the audience of their sources. Since then it has become common practice for a film adaptation to adopt a different title and acknowledge the literary source only inconspicuously, demonstrating the filmmaker's wish to claim the film as their own and pass off an adaptation as an original written work. Take *The Assembly* (Feng Xiaogang, 2007), for example. The initial plot of the film is based on Yang Jinyuan's short story "The Lawsuit" (*Guansi*), but the script written by famous writer Liu Heng is a big change from Yang's story. In the credits of the film, what appears first is "A film by Feng Xiaogang," and its Chinese wording – "Feng Xiaogang *zuopin*" instead of the conventional "Directed by Feng Xiaogang" – has the connotation of giving credit for the film to Feng. The names of the producers then appear; then the scriptwriter's name, Liu Heng, with a tiny line underneath acknowledging the film's link with Yang Jinyuan's short story. Thus, adaptation is no longer a way to secure authority for a film. Instead, adapted films often seek to hide or deny their adapted nature. These tendencies, already begun in the 1980s, have greatly increased since 2000.

Concluding Remarks: Writers' Films?

Testifying to the higher status of film in relation to other art forms in China in the new millennium, it is common for those successful in the areas related to entertainment to try their hand at filmmaking. Meng Jinghui, a theater director, directed a film in 2002. Cui Jian, the godfather of Chinese rock music, also directed a film in 2009. The enthusiastic participation of writers in filmmaking is even more common. Even though there might be some who consider writers involved in films as "losing their chastity" (H. Liu 2007: ii), for many writers, getting involved in filmmaking is certainly a step up. So now we have a popular Chinese word for people from other fields who participate in filmmaking: *chudian* (electrify), which carries the connotation of promise, opportunity, and excitement.

Writers now are usually happy to adapt their own works for directors and make the changes directors want them to make. However, the predominance of directors and producers in the industry also brings with it certain problems. Han Sanping, head of China Film Group Corporation and one of the biggest tycoons in the Chinese film industry, was dissatisfied with the current situation of Chinese films with their pompous packages but thin content – although he himself produced many such films. To remedy this, in 2007 he proposed the concept of "writers' film" (*zuojia dianying*). This is not meant to be a Chinese version of the auteur film, but a kind of film centered on the writer instead of the director or the producer. The first of such films to be launched was *Lost and Found* (Ma Liwen, 2008), written by Liu Zhenyun, who was also responsible for finding a director. It is not surprising that, instead of a famous director against which the writer could have little leverage, Liu chose Ma Liwen, an emerging young director, who said that "I respect the script and its independence, and I just do my job as a director" (G. Wu 2008: 77–9). The film was a modest success commercially. We can only wait and see what the next writers' films will be and how they will fare in the long run. Yet it is certain that with the booming film industry in China, film will strengthen its dominant position *vis-à-vis* literature, and writers will be more and more willing to take part in filmmaking, although the forms of that participation may vary considerably.

Notes

1   Compared with the ample scholarship on Western adaptations, scholarship on Chinese adaptation, in Chinese or in Western languages, is meager in number and mostly confined to case studies on individual films, but it points in important and interesting directions. See Robinson (1984), Pickowicz (1993b), and Z. Zhang (2004).

2   Important changes were made to the original story to fit it for the new historical and political contexts. Thus, the minority girl in the folk poem is transformed into a Chinese girl in the Tang dynasty, when Chinese culture reached its peak of achievement, and the girl was fighting against non-Han invading armies.

3   After 1949, films on such traditional subjects suffered a sharp decline, only to be revived in recent decades. The genre assumed a new form in the twenty-first century. Ancient China became a convenient backdrop to fashion a new type of Chinese blockbuster with huge investments, pompous sets and costumes, superhuman martial arts skills, full-scale battle scenes, court intrigues, and sexual desires. Even if some of these blockbusters are inspired by literary works, the link is so tenuous that the original narratives have changed beyond recognition, as in the case of *The Banquet* (Feng Xiaogang, 2006), a reputed adaptation of Shakespeare's *Hamlet*.

20

Diary of a Homecoming
(Dis-)Inhabiting the Theatrical in Postwar Shanghai Cinema

Weihong Bao

In 1979, just as China was entering a "New Era" of socioeconomic reform, Chinese filmmakers and critics declared their departure from years of marriage with modern spoken drama in an effort to "modernize the film language" (Zhang and Li 1979). Initiated by an article from the *Film Art* editor Bai Jingsheng, entitled "Throwing Away the Crutch of Drama," the ensuing debate concerned cinema's aesthetic status in relation to other media, with the radicals blaming Chinese cinema in the past, especially during the socialist era, for being too entrenched in the tradition of theater. For advocates of film reform, Chinese cinema was seriously encumbered by Chinese theater, particularly by spoken drama's spatial and temporal confinement, embellished performance style, and narrative structure privileging dramatic conflict. The call for the "divorce of film from drama" issued by Zhong Dianfei became structurally necessary for a "modernized" cinema, with an emphasis on the ontology of film based on its medium-specificity, which was believed to condition cinema's distinct aesthetic expressivity.

This call to restore cinematic autonomy, which provoked heated debates among Chinese filmmakers, dramatists, and film critics, was paralleled by historiographic attempts to locate and critique the theatrical roots of Chinese cinema through the discourse of *yingxi* or shadowplay. Film theorists such as Zhong Dafeng and Chen Xihe put forth the notion of yingxi as constituting a resilient indigenous film theory and film aesthetic, tracing its genealogy from early Chinese conceptions of cinema. While yingxi was one of the earliest primary Chinese terms for cinema, its connotations did not solidify until the early 1920s, when yingxi became directly associated with drama and exerted an enduring influence.[1] For both Zhong Dafeng and Chen Xihe, this association between cinema and drama was entrenched in a pragmatic functionalist (*gongneng mudi lun*) literary tradition, rendering literature and art as vehicles of moral edification and spiritual enlightenment. By making an

A Companion to Chinese Cinema, First Edition. Edited by Yingjin Zhang.
© 2012 Blackwell Publishing Ltd. Published 2012 by Blackwell Publishing Ltd.

analogy to the more edified art of drama, as Zhong and Chen argue, the yingxi discourse served to elevate film from its earlier association with lower forms of entertainment; more importantly, this dramatic analogy provided an indigenous ontology (*bentilun*) of cinema based on its social functions, which set it apart from a Western ontology of cinema built on film technology and its medium-specific aesthetics, particularly by privileging image and shot (X. Chen 1986: 85–6; D. Zhong 1986: 76). Hence the term yingxi/shadowplay was treated as an "endocentric compound," with ying/shadow functioning as a secondary modifier (X. Chen 1986: 82–3), a cinematic means serving the theatrical end of *xi*/play. Furthermore, as Chen summarizes, this theatrical association had developed into a dominant, tightly interwoven system encompassing a social functionalist film ontology and theater-based film form and film style with impact on film production, popular film reception, and film criticism. Despite historical ruptures in the mid-1930s and the late 1970s with the respective introduction of montage and Bazinian film aesthetics, yingxi persisted as the "super stable structure" (X. Chen 1986: 90; D. Zhong 1986: 80) for over eight decades after the inception of Chinese cinema.

Such historical narratives, while highlighting the overshadowing presence of theater in Chinese cinema, nevertheless contribute more to mythologizing quintessential "Chinese" film aesthetics than to addressing the changing dynamics between cinema and theater in modern China on concrete terms. Three sets of misconceptions are in operation. First, theater is reduced to dramatic narratives and conflict, rather than a synthetic or intermedial art encompassing plural aspects of performance, mise-en-scène (costuming, lighting, sound effects, choreography, set design), temporal and spatial construct, and spectatorial address.[2] Second, both the "modernization of film language" debate and the yingxi historiography treat theater in modern China as fixed forms and practices. Two dominant dramatic forms, spoken drama and "Civilized Play," are treated as variations of Western realist theater without addressing their historical complexity and specificity. Despite such conceptions, modern Chinese theater has evolved and permutated just as Chinese cinema has, not only as aesthetic mode and entertainment form but importantly as technologies of perception. Third, the relationship between Chinese cinema and theater has been depicted as one-way traffic from theater to cinema, with an implicit narrative of cinema as foreign technology "Sinicized" through indigenous entertainment forms and cultural conceptions. What gets occluded through such a narrative is not only the complex two-way traffic and mutual imbrication between cinema and theater in modern China but also the changing status of dominant local entertainment forms, as well as the plurality and instability of "cultural" conceptions of cinema and theater, art and entertainment. As a result of these three sets of misconceptions, the historical relationship between cinema and theater remains to be thoroughly explored and given due attention, despite repeated claims for Chinese theater's stranglehold on cinema, either in one's search for an "indigenous" film theory or in a reformist effort to enable the modernization of film aesthetics.

To be sure, the filmmakers' and film critics' call to restore cinematic autonomy, paralleled by historiographic attempts to dissociate the "shadow" from the "play" by film scholars, was itself a deeply committed political gesture in the New Era when Chinese filmmakers, dramatists, and critics convened to reflect upon the socialist past and the social role of cinema and drama, two of the most important forms of public art. Their desire to break away from the confines of theater, as repeatedly put forth by various participants in the debate, was intended to do away with the ideological function of film associated with the tableau-like acting style, static camera framing, overdramatized lighting schemes, and verbose didactic dialogue that were treated as staples of spoken drama. To do away with this ideological instrumentalization of art, then, the Chinese filmmakers/dramatists/ critics made a perverse political move to reject the political function of art by insisting on the "purity" and "internal principles" of the artistic medium.

What remains significant in the yingxi historiography and the debate on modernizing film language, however, is the assumption of political associations with an individual medium. How do we read political resistance to politics in terms of medium-specificity? Why was theater singled out as the target of symbolic rebellion among the various media (e.g., music, painting, photography, poetry) that were recognized as integral components of cinema? What had constituted this tension between cinema and theater; and what was at stake when cinematic autonomy was called forth as the new condition of possibility? While these questions can be approached from a variety of angles and temporal frames, this chapter takes a slice of the history of Chinese cinema and theater to illustrate the historical entwinement of the two media and the intricate politics of intermediality. More specifically, I examine postwar Shanghai films and their complex negotiation with the legacy of spoken drama against the landscape of drastic social changes from wartime Chongqing to postwar Shanghai. This inquiry will allow me to address the three sets of misconceptions regarding cinema and theater I outlined above that not only plagued the yingxi historiography and the debate on modernizing film language in the Chinese context but also the history of film theory and recent trends in new media studies. I shall highlight the rich dimensions of this historical phenomenon by means of three distinct steps. First, I examine the distinction between cinema and theater in early film theory in Western contexts to provide a conceptual framework that throws into historical relief the discourse of medium-specificity that still haunts film theory in China and the West. Second, I conduct a historical inquiry that explores the practices of cinema and spoken drama in China by briefly outlining their early interactions that intensified during wartime Chongqing. Third, I turn to postwar Shanghai cinema, where I focus on the subgenre of "homecoming" films to tease out through film aesthetics how the politicization of cinema and theater took place through a problematic distinction of the two media. This triple frame – conceptual, historical, and textual – mobilizes the central concern for my inquiry: to consider cinema and theater as technologies of perception that engage and mediate experiences of social change in modern

China. Political concerns with the relationship between cinema and drama in wartime and postwar China greatly resonated with the 1980s debate. In the end, I hope my inquiry will bear upon the debate on cinema and theater in international film studies and contemporary new media studies, which tend to reproduce similar media distinctions along a teleological trajectory.

Cinema's Undesirable Other: Theater, Medium-Specificity, and Intermediality

Before I move into the historical specificity of postwar Shanghai cinema, it would be helpful to frame this history from a different perspective by thinking about the status of medium-specificity in the history of film theory and the challenge posed by recent studies on intermediality. By bringing in this international context and the new direction in film and media studies, I would like to examine what specific purchase we can gain for the larger field of media studies from an inquiry into the historical relationship between cinema and theater in modern China.

The teleological narrative of cinema as a modern, technologically based medium breaking free from the shackles of theater is not unique to the history of modern Chinese film and media. It would not be an exaggeration to say that the discourse of film had been constituted by a self-conscious differentiation from theater more than from any other forms of art, considering that theater had been a rival to which cinema was most akin. Classical film theorists in the West, including Vachel Lindsay (1915), Hugo Münsterberg (1916), Vsevolod Pudovkin (1929, 1933), Béla Balázs (1952), Rudolf Arnheim (1957), and Siegfried Kracauer (1960) had labored at length to highlight the distinct features of cinema in contrast to theater. The discourse of cinema as an emergent distinct medium evolved around the celebration of cinema as "the seventh art," most famously put forth by Italian writer Ricciotto Canudo (1911), who hailed cinema as a new synthetic art reconciling spatial art (the plastic arts including architecture, sculpture, painting) and temporal art (music, poetry, and dance) built on Hegel's *Lectures on Aesthetics* and Lessing's *Laokoön* (1766). Whereas theater remained akin to cinema in Canudo's early discussion, which referred to cinema as the new theater and evoked Greek tragedy and farce for comparison, his later discussion (1923) consciously distanced film from theater in foregrounding cinema's distinct and "essential" qualities. Similarly, Vachel Lindsay, in allegedly the earliest work of film theory, outlined "Thirty Differences Between the Photoplays and the Stage" (Lindsay 1915: 105–15) while comparing film to sculpture, painting, and architecture in motion, following Canudo's similar analogies. In another early example of film theory, Hugo Münsterberg (1916) systematically contrasted cinema with theater. In these and later discussions, film theorists continued to differentiate the two media in organizations of space and time, acting style, and modes of spectatorship.

Cinema was identified with mobile framing, velocity, movement, visual and later acoustic expressivity, and realism and genuineness, whereas theater was antithetically associated with frontal framing (the proscenium stage), stasis, immobility, verbal expressivity, artificiality, and inauthenticity.

Among these differences, the spatial and temporal construct in the two media has been repeatedly singled out as the key distinction. Cinema was celebrated for its explosion of "the space-time continuum" (Arnheim 1957: 20–7) that provided new means of expressivity, whereas space and time on the stage were conceived as static and fixed. In the same vein, film spectators were described as enjoying utter mobility on the screen whereas the theater audience was immobilized in their seat with a fixed point of view. Erwin Panofsky (1934: 71), in defining the film's unique possibilities as "dynamization of space" and "spatialization of time," summed up these differences in spatial and temporal operations:

> In a theater, space is static, that is, the space represented on the stage, as well as the spatial relation of the beholder to the spectacle, is unalterably fixed. The spectator cannot leave his seat, and the setting for the stage cannot change during one act (except for such incidentals as rising moons or gathering clouds and such illegitimate reborrowings from the film as turning wings or gliding backdrops). ...
>
> With the movies the situation is reversed. Here, too, the spectator occupies a fixed seat, but only physically, not as the subject of an aesthetic experience. Aesthetically, he is in permanent motion as his eye identifies itself with the lens of the camera, which permanently shifts in distance and direction. And as movable as the spectator is, as movable is, for the same reason, the space presented to him. Not only bodies move in space, but space itself does, approaching, receding, turning, dissolving, and recrystallizing as it appears through the controlled locomotion and focusing of the camera and through the cutting and editing of the various shots .... This opens up a world of possibilities of which the stage can never dream. (Panofsky 1934: 72)

Panofsky's spatial conception of cinema and theater, both in representational and spectatorial spatial construction, typifies existing attitudes toward the two media. Even Susan Sontag (1966: 30), in a nuanced early attempt to complicate the relationship between cinema and theater three decades later, eventually drew the divide between the two media around the axis of spatial continuity (theater) versus discontinuity (cinema).

Panofsky's crucial distinction between "physical" and "aesthetic" mobility, which he deployed to underscore the mobility in film viewing, was nevertheless not without presuppositions. In describing the spectatorial immobility in theater, Panofsky excluded "such illegitimate reborrowings from the film as turning wings or gliding backdrops" (1934: 72), which enabled spatial movement on stage and correspondingly, the spectators' "aesthetic" experience of mobility. Similarly, Münsterberg (2002: 133–4) commented on how "playwrights nowadays try to steal the thunder of the photoplay and experiment with time reversals on the legitimate stage," which he considered "an aesthetic barbarism" and "intolerable in ambitious dramatic art." These experiments on stage have been repeatedly dismissed as exceptions that prove the rule. Thus, Münsterberg (2002: 59) acknowledged Reinhardt's revolving stage only to show how it was surpassed by film in the latter's sheer speed of scene changes. Lindsay (1915: 113–15), after observing that "men like Gordon Craig and Granville Baker are almost wasting their genius on the theater," suggested that these experimenters on stage should turn to photoplay (film) to channel their creative energies.

These repeated attempts to demarcate a clean-cut boundary between the two media demonstrate that it was less the "impurity" of these "exceptions" that posed particular problems. Instead, the celebration of cinema as a distinct new medium propelled a logic of reduction that reified theater at the expense of its complexity and historical changes. As Münsterberg (2002: 129) flatly put it: "We shall not enter into a discussion of the character of the regular theater and its drama. We take this for granted." This reductive rhetoric bears an uncanny resemblance to tendencies in contemporary new media studies which, as Tom Gunning forcefully argues, displace the promises and disappointments of older media into a forward-looking digital utopia. Ironically, more than any other media today, it is cinema that occupies the same epistemological position as theater used to do, now treated as "the bad object" (Gunning 2004: 39).

Yet, beyond this teleological tendency, the crux of the issue also lies in the political associations of respective media. As Sontag (1966: 26) points out, the privileging of "realism" of the cinematic medium is "a covert political–moral position" in insisting on the democratic appeal of cinema for the mass society. Theater, by contrast, "means dressing up, pretense, lies. It smacks of aristocratic taste and the class society." This politics of the media resonates with the Chinese film debate in the 1980s, which, in parallel with the promotion of Bazinian film theory, extolled the democratic promise of cinema as a realist medium resisting the political instrumentalization long identified as the overshadowing of theater in film aesthetics. Nevertheless, the political association of cinema and theater in modern China took a different trajectory, just as its European and American counterparts deserve equal attention so as to arrive at a more complex history than Sontag's generalizations. Importantly, however, the historical and political associations with the two media were intimately entwined with key concerns about the spatial and temporal construct of cinema and theater.

This emphasis on the medium-specific politics of space and time was underwritten by discussions on cinema's radical impact on perceptual changes, which set cinema apart from the temporal and spatial confines of theater both in terms of representation and spectatorship. Modernist discourses on the medium-specificity of cinema – Epstein (1921) and Balázs on the close-up, Benjamin on the optical unconscious, Kracauer (1960) on cinema as the photographic medium, to name a few – reinstated cinema as a unique medium whose power to alter our perceptions is contingent upon its technologically enabled aesthetic strategies. Notably, Bazin challenged this critical tradition by questioning the hypothetical purity and autonomy of cinema. Reflecting upon the history of cinema, Bazin (1967: 55) acknowledged its indebtedness to "the twin crutches of literature and theater" since its very inception. Using comedy as an example, Bazin points out the irony of medium-specificity when traits of theater were "very marked on that class of film considered purely and specifically cinematic" (1967: 81).

Bazin's insight is furthered by recent discussions on intermediality, which urge us to examine the relationship between cinema and theater in a new light. Although still an ill-defined, general term subsuming diverse critical approaches, intermediality, as Irina Rajewsky observes, has emerged as a key concept, heralding a new field of research on medial border-crossings and hybridization, bringing attention to the materiality and mediality of artistic and cultural practices. On a general level, the scope of intermediality pertains to border-crossing phenomena occurring between media, rather than within (intramedia) or across media (transmedia, defined as "the appearance of a certain motif, aesthetic, or discourse across a variety of different media") (Rajewsky 2005: 46). On a more specific level, while studies on intermediality have varied by discipline (e.g., media studies, art history, theater studies, new media, film studies) and objects of research, I find it useful to follow Rajewsky's three subcategories of intermediality: media transposition, media combination, and intermedial reference. Media transposition refers to how a given media product transforms into another medium (e.g., film adaptation, novelization). Media combination comes closest to notions of multimedia and mixed media, a combination of at least two distinct media, ranging from mere juxtaposition to "genuine" integration of the distinct media but without privileging any individual medium.

The key notion, however, is intermedial reference. According to Rajewsky, intermediality describes how the media product, by resorting to its own media-specific means, constitutes itself by referring to "either a specific, individual work produced in another medium … or to a specific medial subsystem (such as a certain film genre), or to another medium *qua* system" (2005: 53). Importantly, in contrast to "media combination," only one medium (the referencing instead of the referenced medium) is present, which "thematizes, evokes, or imitates elements or structures of another, conventionally distinct medium through the use of its own media-specific means" (Rajewsky 2005: 53). For Rajewsky, it is necessary to differentiate between intermedial reference and intramedial reference. In contrast to intramedial and intertextual reference, a media product does not "use" or "reproduce" elements of another media system but "evokes" or "imitates" them. In this sense, intermedial reference asserts media border-crossing and consequently media difference by bringing forth an "as if" character and "a specific, illusion-forming quality" that evokes the presence of another medium in audience reception as well as media representation (Rajewsky 2005: 54). This notion of intermedial reference introduces a significant reflective quality of the media product, not so much in terms of self-referentiality, but more precisely a conscious reflection upon the relationship between itself and another medium so as to constitute itself. A media product with intermedial reference in this sense is a meta-media.

Rajewsky's subcategories of intermediality, particularly intermedial reference, will be instrumental for my discussion on Chinese film and theater. More important, Rajewsky's conception suggest that we treat intermediality not only as a "critical category for the concrete analysis of specific individual media products or configurations" but also as a "fundamental condition" (2005: 47). As André Gaudreault and Philippe Marion (2002: 13) point out, cinema's singularity as a medium is the result of a comprehensive process of institutionalization, therefore it is erroneous to treat "the birth of a medium as synonymous with the invention of a technique." For them, cinema could be understood as "born twice," first as an extension of earlier practices, second as institutional legitimacy that recognizes a medium's specificity. In this process, the media practitioners' "reflexive understanding of the medium" (Gaudreault and Marion 2002: 14) is intimately entwined with the medium's institutionalization. In this sense, what we understand as intermedial reference could be seen as an act of medium reflection, which remains indispensable for the constitution of a medium.

What remains occluded, however, is how the constitution of a medium in terms of both medium-specificity and intermediality is entwined with larger social, political, and economic conditions. Current studies in intermediality tend to treat the subject as a purely formal, technical, and genealogical issue (the latter risks reproducing another evolutionary model), which, despite the effort to address the interactions among media, could ultimately participate in the medium's institutionalization. In this sense, an inquiry into the relationship between cinema and theater in modern China helps us address the limit of current studies by precisely exploring how the "internal" politics of medium-specificity and intermediality are inseparable from broader social and political practices. Furthermore, it is important to note that these aesthetic as well as political practices play a significant role in reshaping and politicizing public perceptions. In the following discussion, I will examine more specifically how the intermedial dynamic between cinema and theater in modern China has transformed the spatial and temporal construct of the two media with heightened political significance.

Under the Eaves of Chongqing: The Politics of Intermedial Reference

Chinese cinema has enjoyed a rather complex and entwined history with theater ever since its inception. Between 1896 and the mid-1920s, while Chinese cinema developed in tandem with a variety of modern dramatic forms, early Chinese cinema benefited most significantly from its affinity with *Wenmingxi*, a modern popular drama based on Japanese *Shimpa* and *Shingeki*, Western realist theater, and Peking opera. Between 1913 and 1922, Wenmingxi's multiple genres, stage sets, dramatic plots, and acting styles provided the material resources and human talents for the earliest Chinese cinema, especially when two of the most significant figures in Chinese silent cinema, Zhang Shichuan and Zheng Zhengqiu, alternatively worked for cinema and Wenmingxi, enabling a mutual borrowing of techniques and narratives between the two media (C. Tan 1992; Zhong, Zhang, and Zhang 1997; Z. Zhang 2005: 89–117). This interaction enabled new spatial and temporal practices on the Wenmingxi stage. Sharing exhibition venue and format with cinema, Wenmingxi alternated with cinema to be shown in serial format in the same theater space and even deployed film projections on stage to extend the fictional construct of space (W. Bao 2005).

Between the mid-1920s and mid-1930s, theater and cinema enjoyed a parallel development. While cinema acquired greater popularity, with more than 170 film companies in China by 1926, the audience for spoken drama, previously limited to urban educated youth, grew significantly after the 1930s, with the professional and semiprofessional drama troupes providing traveling performances across the nation.[3] The emergence of sound cinema also spurred the popularity of spoken drama, with the film industry borrowing not only performance techniques and vocal and language (Mandarin) training but also actors and playwrights from the spoken drama circle. In 1937 the Carleton was converted from a movie palace to accommodate drama performances, indicating considerable public recognition of spoken drama.

This interaction arrived at a significant juncture during the Second Sino-Japanese War when the Japanese bombing of Shanghai sent a significant number of established stars, young talents, and industrial profiteers on the road to the vast hinterland. With the establishment of Chongqing as the wartime capital, many of these people joined Zhongzhi (China Film Studio) and Zhongdian (Central Film Studio), owned partly by the state.[4] The haphazard economic conditions, lack of film stock and facilities, and heavy censorship from the Nationalist government, made the theater a necessary conduit for the surplus supply of film talent and political energy. Both Zhongdian and Zhongzhi ran their own drama troupes, performing regularly in the Chongqing region (sometimes as far as Chengdu and Kunming) for financial self-support and to popular acclaim. In addition, independent amateur and professional drama companies flourished and competed with the film studios and their drama troupes for actors, technicians, programs, and theaters.[5] The theatricalization of public life was even further intensified with frequent mobilization events such as street plays, parades, and the annual "Drama Art Festival" (1937–41) and "Fog Season Art Festival" (1941–5) when Chongqing was immersed in theater performances in creatively formed public spaces.

In the same theater, films and spoken drama shared a mutual space, scripts, stars, and audiences. Alternation between film exhibition and drama performance heightened the public's consciousness of the continuity between the cinematic and theatrical space. In a 1941 newspaper publicity piece, the film *Baptism by Fire* (Sun Yu, 1941) and the spoken-drama play *Nation Stands Above All* (*Guojia zhishang*) are introduced side by side:

> If you have seen *Nation Stands Above All*, you cannot skip *Baptism by Fire*
> From stage to screen!
> The same crew for *Nation Stands Above All* works together to make *Baptism by Fire*
> From screen to stage!
> The same crew for *Baptism by Fire* works together to make *Nation Stands Above All*
> If you have seen *Baptism by Fire* you cannot skip *Nation Stands Above All* (*Saodang bao*,
> May 3, 1941)

If publicity pieces like this exploited the stage–screen continuity for commercial interest, the fluid boundary between stage and screen in Chongqing theater was often highly politicized.[6] An extreme example is the scandalous burning of the film *Mulan Joins the Army* (Bu Wancang, 1939) in Chongqing's Weiyi Theater on January 27, 1940. During the opening of the film, a young man went on stage and condemned the film, associating its Shanghai origin and its director Bu Wancang with pro-Japanese collaboration. With another man planted in the audience calling for action, the audience followed the two men to the projection room, took away the film print, and burnt it outside the movie theater. This event, involving a ploy devised by renowned dramatists Hong Shen (1894–1955) and Ma Yanxiang and filmmaker He Feiguang (1913–97), evoked great controversy in journalism across Chongqing, Shanghai, and Hong Kong and has been cited as evidence of the hyperbolic anti-Japanese fervor in the hinterland that turned into geopolitical prejudice (P. Fu 2003: 40–8). What interests me here, however, is how the event pivoted a film screening into a theatrical act that effectively invoked the mass audience's mimetic response. By reversing the external framing from that of the camera to that of the theater, this event brings out the social space of the spectators and the political potential of the movie theater beyond the hermeneutic circle within the screen image.

The interplay between film and theater in Chongqing led to mutual aesthetic transformations. What Rajewsky outlined as the range of intermedial practices was frequently seen in wartime Chongqing. Examples of medial transposition abound: film adaptations of successful plays, most notably *Storm at the Frontier* (Ying Yunwei, 1942), and theater adaptations of popular films such as *Crossroads* (Shen Xiling, 1937) were common practices. Media combination, in terms of mixed-media presentations, also occurred frequently on stage and screen. Just as films would feature theater performance, as in *The Light of East Asia* (He Feiguang, 1940), so in theater film projection was deployed to create a strong impression of film/stage superimposition. Moreover, examples of intermedial reference proliferated. A handful of feature films evoked a range of theater practices, particularly theatrical direct address of the audience, as seen in *Youth China* (Su Yi, 1941), and film narration mimicking storytelling performance, which framed the story of *Eight Hundred Heroes* (Ying Yunwei, 1938). Meanwhile, stage plays made conscious use of cinematic technologies and techniques. Lighting control was used to create a sense of film framing or to facilitate scene changes in the effect of cinematic fade-in and fade-out. A most systematic use of intermedial reference is seen in *Under the Eaves of Chongqing*, a 1944 stage play written by Xu Changlin (1916–2001) and directed by veteran filmmaker Shi Dongshan. The play, originally titled *The Wall* (Qiang), portrayed the dual faces of wartime Chongqing by staging two families living next door to each other in sharp contrast. Set on the second floor of an ordinary apartment building in Chongqing, the two rooms on stage are alternately occupied by a leftist literary writer with his wife and child, and a wealthy merchant with his mistress. Two parallel dramas evolve around the two households, which attract human traffic in their social circles: one centering on the sickness of the child, the other the business intrigue that eventually bamboozles the merchant himself. As the play contrasts the immigrant intellectual circle's material hardship and camaraderie with the profiteers' decadence and backstabbing, controlled lighting, sound, and grouped performance within the architectural divide alternate the audience's attention between the two rooms by the effect of crosscutting. The merchant's well-lit room uses so much electricity that every time it lights up, the other room dims down. While actions and dialogue in one room proceed, the other room remains silent. Near the end, the alternation between the two rooms accelerates to a heightened simultaneity, with parallel actions in the two rooms creating linguistic and visual rhyming, achieving the effect of the split screen, or montage within a single shot.

Such contrasts between two social spheres by means of systematic crosscutting and montage are familiar aesthetic strategies for Shanghai leftwing films in the 1930s. Films such as *Dawn of the Metropolis* (Cai Chusheng, 1933) and *New Woman* (Cai Chusheng, 1935) had deployed montage as a politically charged editing principle to display the social landscape of Shanghai in systematic contrasts between societies high and low, rich and poor, labor struggle and decadent leisure. Not surprisingly, these leftwing cinematic techniques were adopted by the Chongqing stage, given the fact that the stage director Shi Dongshan, who had no prior stage experience before his migration to Chongqing, had been an active filmmaker in Shanghai since the 1920s. *Under the Eaves of Chongqing* evoked a deliberate resonance with Xia Yan's celebrated stage play *Under the Eaves of Shanghai*, with a changed title and modified stage directions. Xia Yan's play, written in 1937 on the eve of the Second Sino-Japanese War, was not staged until 1939 when it was performed in Chongqing and acclaimed for its ingenious use of cinematic techniques.[7] By staging five families in the cross-section of a Shanghai *shikumen* housing complex – a common vernacular building for middle- and lower-class people – the play showcased the parallel lives of the families and their social interactions in an architectural montage orchestrated by controlled lighting, performance, and contrast between silence and dialogue. Similar to Shi Dongshan, the playwright Xia Yan had participated in Shanghai filmmaking in the early 1930s before he started his theater career in 1936. As the co-translator of Pudovkin's montage film theory, Xia Yan put the montage theory into practice in his writing of film scripts and stage plays, most famously in the screenplays for *Torrents* (Cheng

Bugao, 1933) and *Twenty-Four Hours in Shanghai* (Shen Xiling, 1933), as well as the staging of his play *Sai Jinhua* (1936), which deployed film projection at the beginning (Anhui daxue 1980).

Through its deliberate effort to imitate, evoke, and thematize the medial susbsystem of montage and the medium of cinema, *Under the Eaves of Chongqing* is a provocative example of how the practice of intermedial reference, crucial to the constitution of theater, is highly politicized. The play does not merely evoke in the audience the illusory presence of cinema by its systematic mapping of montage. By referencing its film precedents, the play reflects upon its relationship to cinema in general but more specifically to the leftwing film tradition. In allying with the leftwing social critique through its radical use of montage, the play wedges itself in the mediasphere of Chongqing where theater competed with a variety of film productions: Chongqing cinema versus productions from Shanghai and Hong Kong films, Hollywood cinema versus films from the Soviet Union, Britain, and India (W. Bao 2009). Among these films, Hollywood films remained a key point of anxiety and competition, as is enacted in another intermedial reference within the play, when the wealthy couple's indulgence in Hollywood movies is characterized as a sign of decadence. By providing itself as the outer frame to reflect upon competing film traditions, the play crosses the media boundary between cinema and theater in search of an incisive social mapping.

Significantly, the intermedial reference to montage is realized by staging (bad) housing, an enduring theme encompassed by Shanghai leftwing cinema as well as other film traditions. Kracauer (1960: 64) identified housing as a key trope that, through an emphasis on coexistence, evidences cinema's "inherent affinities" with the continuum of physical reality and contains the power to reveal the "reality of another dimension." Using the Soviet film *Bed and Sofa* (Abram Room, 1926) as an example, Kracauer (1960: 65) observed how, by allowing the spectators' intimate viewing of the overcrowded lodging, the film confronts the audience with the "unaccountable togetherness" of physical existence. Bazin, citing Jean Cocteau's *Les Parents terribles* (1948), also commented on how the room on the stage, when transposed onto the screen into the apartment, became more cramped and intensified the sense of "delicately balanced and inescapable coexistence" (1967: 90). This affinity with reality might explain why the shikumen housing complex has been a favorite subject for a number of Shanghai films, such as *Shanghai Old and New* (Cheng Bugao, 1936), *Children of the Troubled Times* (Xu Xingzhi, 1935), *Street Angel* (Yuan Muzhi, 1937), and most notably *Crossroads*.

While the room has been a spatial prototype for realist theater, by transposing its filmic version – the apartment – back onto the stage, *Under the Eaves of Chongqing* juxtaposes two domestic interiors in close proximity to evoke the cinematic rendition of reality in relation to its theatrical counterpart. In this gesture of intermedial reference, the play contrasts the intimate physical reality (the cinematic crampness) with a sense of staging, a theatrical display of not only cinematic reality but also techniques of montage, which weaves distinct spaces into a "dense fabric" (Kracauer 1960: 65).[8] At the same time, the play also contrasts the spatial totality of theater with the montage dissection of cinematic space. The protocinematic division of stage spaces is traversed by a total sound space and the movement of the human body. When the characters knock on the flimsy wall, eavesdrop, or even enter each other's room, the spaces are made more palpable and porous than a cinematic frame. The wall eventually breaks down, providing a spatial allegory of not only desired social changes in Chongqing but also the theatrical intervention of the cinematic alienation of spaces. By reflecting upon the medial relationship between cinema and theater, *Under the Eaves of Chongqing* eventually positions the audience within a double spectatorship, which I am tempted to characterize as "intermedial." This intermedial spectatorship enables a critical social perception precisely by complicating the spatial and temporal constructions of the two media.

Although by now an obscure play, *Under the Eaves of Chongqing* was tremendously popular in its time, credited with more than a hundred performances between August 1944 and February 1945, and starring major actors such as Xiang Kun, Tao Jin, Wei Heling, and Zhao Yunru (C. Xu 1945). Created on the eve of Japan's defeat, the play ends with the intellectuals' departure and promised reunion beyond the hinterland, articulating the mass anticipation of the end of war and an overdue homecoming.

Disenchanted Homecoming: Homelessness, Entrapment, and Provincializing Shanghai

Wartime Chongqing theater sheds light on the pronounced theatrical presence in postwar Shanghai cinema, which manifests itself in acting style, spatial organization, and spectatorial address as well as narrative reference and rhetorical configuration. A prime example can be found in a number of celebrated "homecoming" films. Produced by the major studios including Kunlun, Wenhua, and Zhongdian, these films repeatedly featured the returning intellectuals and cultural workers denied physical and symbolic dwelling in the estranging city of Shanghai. The failure of homecoming experienced in the returnees' social and spatial dislocation – captured acutely in a medley of genres ranging from melodrama and comedy to gothic horror – is invariably marked by the presence of the theatrical in a figural, stylistic, and spectatorial sense. More important, these films not only negotiated a prior aesthetic legacy but also framed it in a larger problematic of the postwar remapping of social and media order that orchestrates geopolitics with an ideology of medium-specificity. It is in this sense that postwar homecoming films provide a rich site for us to examine the media interplay between the theatrical and cinematic as entwined with articulations of social spaces and cultural memory, refigured in the housing problem prevalent in these films, evoking asymmetrical binaries of country–city, exteriority–domesticity, and utopic past–dystopic present. In this section, I explore the significance of this theatrical visibility in the homecoming films and investigate the aesthetic as well as social–spatial implications of the cinematic–theatrical nexus that had such a lasting impact.

To a large extent, postwar Shanghai cinema was revitalized by a "homecoming" cinema. The home return of previously Shanghai-based film workers from hinterland China brought a rich influx of talent, experience, and techniques that contributed significantly to the postwar flourishing of the Shanghai film industry. At the same time, this home return was never a comfortable fit. As regards medium, many of the returned film workers were "amphibious" (*liangqi*) between stage and screen, both of which underwent significant transformation, as discussed in the previous section. On the social level, the returnees were caught up in the shock at the unaffected glamour of cosmopolitan Shanghai – a glamour that barely concealed a socioeconomic crisis. As breadwinners retired from semi-state-sponsored wartime mobilization, the returned film workers encountered everyday problems of housing, unemployment, high inflation, and the invasion of American dollars, goods, and films, the latter of which posed the most direct threat to their profession.

Homecoming dramatizes a "postnostalgic condition" (Chaudhuri 1997: 92). A doomed homecoming frustrates the desire for recuperating a prior identity and often signifies the end of a homogeneous idea of place with a changed cultural outlook and expectations. For returning film workers, restoring their prewar film practices was impossible because film practice had changed both in the hinterland and in Shanghai. In addition to their imbrication with theatrical practice, wartime Chongqing films also frequently relied on location shooting and natural light – largely due to budget constraints and shortage of sound stages (Ying 1946: 9). Wartime Shanghai films, in contrast, were largely produced in sound studios and rarely included any exterior shots. Produced in politically precarious conditions under partial and then total Japanese occupation, wartime Shanghai films had a claustrophobic look, augmented by the confines of limited genre and thematic choices that included romance, domestic comedy, and costume drama. This contrast in the look of wartime Shanghai and Chongqing films was quickly reflected in postwar film production through the spatial binary between exterior and interior.

The double displacement in the returnees' media practices and social experiences was most effectively reimagined in the recurring motif of housing problems in the homecoming films. In these films the house was treated alternatively to connote shelter and (female) imprisonment, family reunion and isolation, and security and menace. The positive terms, however, were only accessed negatively for the returnees as exclusion and rejection. In *Dream in Paradise* (Tang Xiaodan, 1947), written by Xu Changlin, the homecoming avidly anticipated in *Under the Eaves of Chongqing* turns into the most desolate homelessness. In the film, architect Ding Jianhua and his wife return from the hinterland only to find their Shanghai home occupied by a former friend-turned-collaborator. As they seek shelter under

Figure 20.1   Shadows in the domestic interior in *The Spring Cannot Be Shut In* (dir. Wang Weiyi, Kunlun Film, 1948).

their own roof, the friend also deprives them of their newborn child and Ding's architectural design for their dream house. The film ends with the Ding family sent out on the road, passing through a Corbusier-style glass house based on Ding's design. While the wife looks through the glass walls into their ideal home, the discrepancy between the location shot of the house exterior and the studio shot of its interior provides an acute moment of medium self-reflexivity: the transparency of the glass house encourages the fantasy of a bourgeois home but denies the onlooker its physical access, just as the Shanghai studio interior remains closed to the returnees who are kept on the road and the exterior.

In *The Spring Cannot Be Shut In* (Wang Weiyi, 1948), however, the bourgeois home is a site of menace and incarceration. Starting with the gothic horror staple of female confinement, the film, via the heroine's voice-over, initiates a flashback to her wartime participation in resistance mobilization, ended by her marriage when her husband locks her up away from her comrades. In a counterintuitive spatial mapping, the theatrical and the cinematic are figured as the binary opposition between the exterior and the interior. The heroine's theatrical space remains outside in the countryside and bathed in cheerful natural light, whereas the cinematic is located in the domestic interior, a gothic studio haunted by the ontological shadows of cinema (see Figure 20.1). This spatial arrangement is consistent with *Dream in Paradise*, where the Shanghai film studio remains configured in the domestic interior while the returnees are kept in the exterior. The exterior, though, is identified differently in the two films: one with the cinematic wandering on the road (*Dream in Paradise*) and the other with the outdoor theatrical performance (*The Spring Cannot Be Shut In*). In the latter's pairing of the theatrical with the utopian exterior and the countryside, and the cinematic with the dystopic interior and the city, the film reverses the tragic longing for a bourgeois home in *Dream in Paradise* and provides a double commentary on the media and social reality. By ending with an emphatic "homelessness" outside the bourgeois home where the young people find their utopian community at an experimental farm on the outskirts of Shanghai, the hinterland returnees inverse the urban prejudice against their provincial identity: the provincial carves out an outer frame that ends up provincializing Shanghai; and the theatrical destabilizes the self-sufficient space of a cinematic interior trapped in its claustrophobic narcissism.

Diary of a Homecoming: The Ecstasy of Flying Vegetables

To describe postwar Shanghai cinema as a purely "homecoming" cinema, however, obfuscates a fully fledged film industry during wartime Shanghai (P. Fu 2003). After eight years of struggling for a third space between entertainment and politics, many Shanghai film workers were put out of business with the shift of political regime by the end of the war. With decreasing employment opportunities and income, some film stars themselves encountered housing problems. In an article entitled "The Tarnished Stars," female star Chen Yanyan was reported to have lost her job and planned on renting out part of her luxurious mansion for US$1,500. Male star Liu Qiong (1913–2002) was retained at a police station on the second-day opening of his stage play. The police custody concerned a housing dispute in which Liu Qiong was asked to move out of a second-floor apartment he rented because the previous tenant – a possible Japanese collaborator who had been imprisoned – was quickly released and claimed the place back (F. Ye 1946: 20–1). This dispute resulted in the loss of a full-house performance, when the audience demanded their money back.

These housing disputes connect real-life housing problems with the professional dislocation of the wartime Shanghai stars, when they were exorcised from the stage and the screen. There was a more delicate rapport between returned film workers and those who had stayed on in wartime Shanghai. Moreover, wartime Shanghai hosted an equally active modern theater that had absorbed a considerable number of film professionals.[9] This complexity points to the conceptual limit presented in *The Spring Cannot Be Shut In*, which propels the media binary between theater and cinema in line with the geopolitical dichotomy between Chongqing and Shanghai, figured in the spatial division between exterior versus interior, country versus city, the street versus the house. That the exterior is identified with the theatrical should not be a surprise considering the frequent practice of

Figure 20.2 A heavy-handed montage sequence in *Dream in Paradise* (dir. Tang Xiaodan, Zhongdian Studio 2, 1947).

environmental theater beyond the realist stage in the wartime hinterland. Creative use of local public spaces such as streets, temples, courtyards, and school playgrounds had been a staple of wartime hinterland theater performance, which continued the avant-garde theater tradition from the 1920s. Yet this postwar recollection of a radical theater displaces not only the regular professional stage but also film practices in the hinterland to realize the symbolic power of a place and a theater. In this context, *Diary of a Homecoming* (Zhang Junxiang, 1947) provides a provocative reflection that seeks for an alternative treatment of homecoming that accommodates the complexity of history beyond geopolitical and media binaries.

The film has a similar plotline to other homecoming films and begins with the hinterland celebration of the end of the war and a young couple's departure for Shanghai. Upon their arrival in the metropolis, they immediately encounter a housing problem. Even though they are provided with free temporary lodging at the top of an Art Deco building – a nonspace above the ceiling – the woman (Bai Yang, 1920–96) is determined to find their dream home. Their search sends them on the road in endless frustration. Executed in a montage sequence of two pairs of feet superimposed on the landscape of the city, such wandering became a recurrent figure of the cinematic, similar to *Dream in Paradise* when the husband's job search in the city is shown in heavy-handed superimposition, diagonal framing, and sound and image montage (see Figure 20.2). The couple finally end up in a luxurious mansion, but soon find out that their hostess's husband is imprisoned as a Japanese collaborator. And now a Chongqing "takeover" official (*jieshou dayuan*) has claimed the house as well as the woman, as part of the real estate.

From this point on, the domestic interior becomes the locus where geopolitical divisions and media distinctions are renegotiated in a shared space. The imprisoned husband is released and repossesses the house while the takeover official returns with his hooligan friends for revenge; in the meantime, the young couple's friends – the Shanghai theater workers – also arrive at the house with beers and firecrackers to celebrate the couple's success in house hunting. In an elaborate fight sequence that lasts twelve minutes, social and media conflicts are worked out physically through the body. Everyone does his or her fair share of fighting in a cacophony of domestic strife, self-defense, and gangster brawl.

This battle for disowned and repossessed homes, however, does not remain on the allegorical level; rather, it executes aesthetically an intense interplay between the theatrical and cinematic while problematizing their distinctions. This interplay does not commence with this sequence but starts from the very beginning of the film. Shortly after the film opens, a long shot of a courtyard shows a farmer and his wife arguing with their landlord about the land levy. The camera recedes and pans left, revealing a stage director in the foreground interrupting the play. As the stage director critiques the actor's lack of identification with the landlord, the actor blames the inadequacy of his costumes and the camera cuts to a close-up of his worn-out shoes and exposed toes. The stage director asks for the costume department, and the camera pans gradually to the right to reveal the staff in charge of the costumes. In this short sequence, theatrical and cinematic conventions interact with each other in negotiating articulations of space and levels of realism. While the camera manipulates the multiple framing and demonstrates its epistemological power in revealing our perceived reality as a play in rehearsal, it also shows a conscious effort to maintain a certain totality of space in using the panning in preference to cutting to introduce the spatial continuity of the site.

This beginning simultaneously elicits two spectatorial positionings: that of the theater audience with restricted vision and knowledge, and that of cinema which enjoys the revelation of hidden spaces and the continuum of physical reality. Bazin outlined three types of cinematic analysis of reality corresponding to three points of view and classic patterns of cutting: (1) "a purely logical and descriptive analysis" (a weapon lying beside the dead body), (2) "a psychological analysis" that fits the point of view of a character, (3) "a psychological analysis from the point of view of spectator interest" (1967: 91–2). According to Bazin, the spectator interest in this third type of analysis could either be highly directed by the film or be more spontaneous. The moving handle of a door – with cutting rendering it visible to the audience but not to a character – for instance, would be a directed interest, whereas films by Orson Welles (1915–85) and William Wyler (1902–81) hesitate to fragment space at will and allow spectators to make their own choices.

For Bazin, this third type of point of view, that of the spectator, is the common denominator between stage and screen. In this third type of cinematic analysis of reality, the camera is reduced to the role of the spectator, which performs "the pitiless gaze of an invisible witness" (Bazin 1967: 92). In this sense, the cinema as an event seen through a keyhole is not so much the privilege of voyeuristic viewing but a helpless gaze that remains outside – in Bazin's words, the position of "exteriority" (1967: 93).

In this early sequence of *Diary of a Homecoming*, cinema and theater converge at the spectator's viewpoint. When the camera reveals the "reality of another dimension" both through close-up and camera movement, the point of view is evidently not that of the stage director but the view seen from behind or beside him. More interestingly, our visual attention is not directed by the camera *per se* but conjointly by the theater actor who tells us where and what to see. In this "tell and show," conventions of cinematic analysis of reality are put on display and rendered with a degree of theatricality. A reflection upon two modes of spectatorship is thus initiated at the very beginning of the film. Later, when news of the end of war reaches the theater troupe, the actors burst out joyously and break various architectural framings of the site. This scene of celebration simultaneously asserts the actor's body and the versatility of the camera, seeking a delicate balance between stage and cinematic realism while enriching modes of spatial articulation through the convergence of theatrical and cinematic spectatorship.

The fight sequence toward the end of the film echoes the opening sequence discussed above in its kinesthetic energy and the infringement of multiple frames within the space, but it becomes emphatically cinematic in its interaction with the theatrical. In the midst of flying crockery and vegetables, the camera suddenly tilts to the left and right, giving the impression of a shaking house. More surprisingly, a carrot flies across the dining room to the window, soaring in slow motion. This ecstasy of the flying vegetable, indeed a celebration of cinematic special effect, is repeated in the next shot when a carrot flies in slow motion and hits the gang leader (see Figure 20.3). This transformation of inanimate objects into animate weapons and of real space/motion into a virtual space/motion is also preceded by a self-reflexive mimetic event that contradicts the diegetic logic. Bombarded by vegetables and wine bottles, a lesser gangster played by the playwright Li Tianji ducks behind his inanimate double, a clay sculpture of the folk-religious legend Crazy Monk Ji (Ji Gong). This diegetically contradicts a scene that happens five minutes earlier at the opening of the fight sequence, when Li Tianji, in a frenzy of self-realizing destruction, first hesitates then smashes his sculpture double after mimicking its expression. The shattered sculpture now miraculously resurrects (with only a broken arm). With a lettuce thrown on its head forming a lock of mock hair, the shadow behind turns the hair into a hat while transforming itself into a monk turning in the opposite direction (see Figure 20.4). This is immediately followed by cinematic manipulation of frame and motion in the tilting-camera and

Weihong Bao

Figure 20.3   A flying carrot caught in slow motion in *Diary of a Homecoming* (dir. Zhang Junxiang, Zhongdian Studio 1, 1947).

Figure 20.4   Shadow play with a resurrected sculpture in *Diary of a Homecoming* (dir. Zhang Junxiang, Zhongdian Studio 1, 1947).

flying-apple scene. The sculpture and its shadow hence make a powerful reflection upon the making of their own representation in the media interaction between the cinematic and the theatrical. If the sculpture stands in for Li Tianji as the mimetic but real object, much like the three-dimensional theatrical in real space, its shadow comments on the ontological nature of the making of the ensuing images. At the same time, the theatrical is no more real than the sculpture itself, which is the result of the cinematic editing and reordering of temporality.

In this battle between the cinematic and the theatrical, the three onlookers – the young couple and the hostess – raise the issue to the level of spectatorship. At two moments during the fight sequence the three are literally spectators of the scene. The hostess, at first exhilarated by the kinesthetic movement, waves her fists and moves her body, exhibiting a mimetic kinesthetic response to the scene. Later, the three of them become bored, and only when the woman's birdcage is attacked does she become agitated and join in the fighting. In this moment the live act conflates with the cinematic/virtual reality, and the onlookers are simultaneously theater and film spectators, watching the flying carrot in slow motion and the resurrected sculpture while allowing themselves to throw objects across the space and join in the fight. Such contiguity between an image and real space, or the cinematic and theatrical, indeed maintains the legacy of wartime Chongqing while exerting a new cinematic order beyond the studio interior.

Out of the total destruction of the fight sequence emerges the new subject that anticipates a changed social and media order. After the annihilation of the bourgeois constituents of the private individual, the radicalized subjects seek a communal living space and a new cinematicity no longer inhabitable in the bourgeois house and the studio interior. The hostess also leaves home with the young couple and their friends but identifies herself as an avid spectator of wartime Shanghai theater. With Shanghai meeting Chongqing, theater meeting theater, the cinematic asserts itself only when it is disguised as – and politically identified – with theater. That theater is only inhabitable at the top of the Art Deco building, a utopian nonspace as a refuge for the failed modernist project, and the hostess does not forget to bring her own birdcage.

Conclusion

This chapter examines the historical interaction between Chinese cinema and theater to explore the intricate politics of intermediality that challenges essentialized notions of medium-specificity and the implied teleology of media technology that overshadow our understanding of Chinese film history. Just as theater has long been disavowed in the West as cinema's undesirable other – integral to the discourse of medium-specificity in the constitution of cinema as a social institution – this argument returned to haunt the 1980s film and theater debate in China, along the very logic of media teleology to "modernize" Chinese cinema. The "shadowplay" historiography served as the mirror image of the "modernization" discourse, in its "ontology" of Chinese cinema as one deeply indebted to theater while simultaneously reducing that theater to a culturally

essentialized one without qualifying its historical heterogeneity and permutations. Whether the "shadowplay" historiography could be appropriated for the
"modernization" discourse or an "indigenization" discourse, one would need to
critique both discourses to take into serious consideration the historical interaction
between cinema and theater in modern China. As a case study, I have tried to
illustrate the complexity of such interaction by locating the theatrical presence in
postwar Shanghai cinema as historically constituted by the wartime imbrications
between cinema and modern spoken drama in the hinterland. This interaction,
however, is never an internal and innocent relationship between media. The
postwar negotiation of a new cinematic order, caught in the intense interplay
with the legacy of the theatrical, was significantly framed in a larger problematic,
that is, the postwar reconstruction of social space and cultural memory.
Homecoming films provided a rich case study for examining the interdependence
between the ideology of medium-specificity and geopolitics that has had such a
lasting impact. This historical detour helps us reflect upon the 1980s debate on
"throwing away the crutch of drama" that led to a paradigmatic shift in Chinese
film history. Ironically, Zhang Junxiang (1910–96), the director of *Diary of a
Homecoming*, who transformed himself into a film director from a prominent
playwright and stage director in wartime Chongqing, became a token for "the
crutch of theater" to be thrown away by the new generation.

Notes

1   It is important to recognize the split positioning in Zhong Dafeng's treatment of
    yingxi. Despite his early attempt to account for yingxi as a historically specific practice
    in China from the 1920s (D. Zhong 1986), Zhong's later writings (1994) resonated with
    Chen Xihe in situating yingxi as an enduring indigenous film theory and practice that
    persists until today.
2   D. Zhong (1986: 79; 1994: 31) discusses yingxi as a dual-layered theoretical framework,
    the external layer seeking cinema's similitude to theater in techniques and aesthetics,
    and the inner core striving for a social functionalist theory of cinematic narrativity. For
    Zhong, this inner core has far more importance and a stronger hold in Chinese film
    history. The dramatic narrative of conflict, as Zhong astutely acknowledges, is a result
    of local spectatorial habit as well as the global impact of the Hollywood narrative
    mode, part and parcel of China's semicolonial condition.
3   For a survey of the Chinese film industry before 1927, see S. Cheng (1927). One of the
    most prominent spoken-drama troupes was China Drama Traveling Troupe 中国旅
    行剧团, established in Shanghai in 1933 and active until 1947 (Chen and Liu 2000).
4   In 1941 the third studio, China Educational Film Studio, was established in Chongqing.
5   The most popular amateur and professional drama companies include Roar Drama
    Society (*Nuhou jushe*), Shanghai Amateur Dramatist Society (*Shanghai yeyu juren
    xiehui*), and the National Drama School (*Guoli juxiao*) (M. Shi 1995; X. Sun 1989).
6   Meeting a real-life character after the film was a feature of the exhibition of *Eight
    Hundred Heroes* (Ying Yunwei, 1938) in Chongqing, 1941 (*Xinshu bao*, May 3, 1941).

7   Interview with Wan Sheng, Chongqing, June 15, 2008. Also see S. Wan (1991).

8   Likewise, Bazin discusses how theater practices approximating the realistic effect of cinema (André Antoine's "Théâtre Libre" or "free theater" is an example) differ from the latter in their viewing conditions: "The mere fact that it is exposed to view on the stage removes it from everyday existence and turns it into something seen as it were in a shop window. It is in a measure part of the natural order but it is *profoundly modified by the conditions under which we observe it*" (1967: 89, emphasis added).

9   A prime example is Fei Mu, who left his film studio to join a theater troupe in 1941 on the eve of the Japanese takeover of the Shanghai film industry. An active theater producer and director, Fei Mu worked with veteran film actors, set designers, and other film professionals in collaboration with celebrated dramatists such as Huang Zuolin (1906–94), Wu Renzhi, and Gu Zhongyi. The vibrant professional theater scene in Shanghai fostered interactions between cinema and theater, stimulating stage innovations that made creative use of film aesthetics. See A. Wong (1998) and L. Ding (2008).

21

Cinema and the Visual Arts
of China

Jerome Silbergeld

It was a scene right out of a painting – it was so gorgeous. I remember thinking to myself, This is what film is all about. (Tian Zhuangzhuang, in M. Berry 2005: 62)

Where is the depth? The depth is hidden. Hidden where? Hidden in the surface. (Chu T'ien-wen, in M. Berry 2005: 248)

Observed relationships between different artistic media have a long and respected history in China. The ninth-century art historian Zhang Yanyuan noted that Zhang Xu (a century earlier) was inspired in his calligraphy by the sword dance of Lady Gongsun and that the poet Du Fu, in turn, was inspired to commemorate this in verse; similarly, Zhang claimed that the painter Wu Daozi's "wielding of the brush was more advanced" after watching General Pei Min's swordsmanship (Acker 1974: 233).[1] In our own time, movement through a painted Chinese handscroll has been compared many times over to motion pictures, in passing if not in detail. In his introduction to the Chinese art of landscape painting, Michael Sullivan likened the unfolding events in Zhang Zeduan's famous twelfth-century handscroll, the *Qingming shang he tu*, to the time-sequencing of cinema: "The painter takes us on a leisurely walk by the riverside, over the bridge, through the city gate, and into the busy streets, as though he were tracking with a movie camera" (Sullivan 1979: 70). There may have been a few earlier such references, but not until filmmaking had gained sufficient cultural status and crossed a threshold of artistic recognition would comparison of the elite art of Chinese painting to the popular medium of cinema be deemed a suitable means for encouraging readers' appreciation of Chinese painting and not embarrassingly *déclassé*.[2] We should not be surprised, however, that more detailed analyses of Western art developments in a cinematic

A Companion to Chinese Cinema, First Edition. Edited by Yingjin Zhang.
© 2012 Blackwell Publishing Ltd. Published 2012 by Blackwell Publishing Ltd.

framework had already occurred by this time. "The camera," wrote Wylie Sypher (1960: 266–7), "used with artistic consciousness, became the cinema and revised the stylizations of the daguerrotype into the multidimensional art that is deeply congenial to cubist painting.... By its revolution in thought and method of representing the world, cubism created a cinematic style." Sypher's formulation (1960: 266) implicitly recognized "motion" pictures as a series of rapidly projected still photographs – "not Hollywood, which ordinarily uses the camera merely to record a nineteenth-century plot, [but] an artistic technique of presenting things as they exist in time by means of a composite perspective."[3]

Given Sypher's careful qualification of "cinema," and put on guard by the specificity of his comparison, one might wonder about the aptness and perhaps worry about the ease of characterizing a thousand-year-old Chinese painting like Zhang Zeduan's and its nearly two-millennia-old format, the Chinese handscroll, as "cinematic." True enough, the Chinese handscroll's lack of singular viewpoint facilitates a continuously expanding compositional structure, and like commercial films it typically begins and ends with text – including a painting title and concluding colophons that parallel somewhat a movie's title and concluding credits; some scrolls even feature text interspersed with the images, like film intertitles (Murray 1988). But while the Qingming Scroll visualizes many intriguing vignettes, it includes no narrative by which to clearly identify its time, place, or purpose. Before the advent of modern museum display, the longer Chinese handscroll was not fully stretched out for viewing but unrolled a bit at a time, serially rather than continuously, and read more like a page-book than a movie: the viewer, traditionally, was active and controlled the viewing, with abundant opportunity to examine carefully, contemplate slowly, and scroll back and forth; whereas with film the audience views at the mercy of the medium's own (increasingly energized) rate of movement.[4] Thus the two media have certain similarities, but comparing them invites the question of why one should consider such a comparison at all and what assumptions underlie the task. The vast majority of extant Chinese scrolls, for example, are landscapes with minimal narrative development, from a period after which figure painting had gone into decline and emotional drama was disfavored by Chinese patrons of "high" art.[5] What can such paintings possibly tell us about the aesthetic origins of Chinese cinema or about how to view Chinese cinema in a distinctively Chinese manner?

Why, indeed, should we expect that the modern mass medium of Chinese cinema would owe anything to the elite medium, whether courtly or scholarly, of traditional Chinese painting? After all, even if we focus here on "art" films or "arthouse" cinema, just how do we define that in a Chinese context, where "art theaters" have ever existed scarcely and the intellectual elite has never controlled the patronage of cinema as they once did the patronage of painting? Does comparison to a more popular medium, like Buddhist painting, printmaking, shadow puppets, or stage theater, make better sense?[6] Or perhaps a comparison of cinema to modern and contemporary Chinese painting? Or comparison to a more closely related medium, like Chinese photography? Or should we be dissuaded from comparing media by John Szarkowski's (1966: 6) caveat regarding photography, that "an answer" to the development of that medium "would not be found by those who loved too much the old forms" (i.e., the imitation of painting) and that "the photographer must find new ways to make his meaning clear?"[7] Should we focus, if not on format, then on more subtle aspects of style? If so, given the considerable influence of Western film on Chinese-language film, must we also evaluate the possibility that Western art (via its influence on Western film) has made a deeper impact on Chinese cinema than has Chinese art? And what should we make of those intentional stylistic markers by which certain Chinese filmmakers have determined to assure that an international audience recognizes and appreciates the "Chineseness" of their films (e.g., at the crudest level, the Chinese lanterns, exotic footrubs, and weird "theatrical" masks in Zhang Yimou's *Raise the Red Lantern*, 1991; or the tropes on calligraphy in his *Hero*, 2002)? Conversely, what remains of any "Chineseness" when ethnic Chinese filmmakers produce films intended to be, more or less, "Western" – like Ang Lee's *The Ice Storm* (1997), *Ride with the Devil* (1999), and others, with American subjects serving as analogues to modernization in Taiwan family life and to China's civil war?

We are told, by one who should know, that "Audiences know what to expect, and that is all they are prepared to believe in" (Stoppard 1967: 84). When David Bordwell (2005b: 144) writes of film as a language to be learned, referencing the "classical continuity system" that was "associated with Hollywood since the 1910s … a lingua franca of film style for all the world's mass-market cinemas," so that the film-literate audience does not duck at the sight of an oncoming train and recognizes the dialogical intent of shot/reverse shot editing, does that mean that for the Chinese audience the new language of cinema, in succeeding the classical language of traditional painting, is really a "discontinuity system?" Or are there significant continuities between these two systems, with an infusion of Chinese visual traditions into Chinese cinema, and if so, then what should we make of those writings which, in the extreme, have treated the cinematic medium as profoundly "alien" to China and its culture, and which would render this entire comparative exercise futile (e.g., R. Chow 1995: 94)?

Without setting such complex questions aside – and recognizing still other uncertainties: What arts of which periods form the basis for a meaningful consideration of this topic? Compared to what movies, from what periods? Is this a search for coincident parallels and cultural affinities or for direct artistic/historical influence? Can the critical standards that have been applied, historically, to one medium be brought to bear upon another? – this topic can be examined (and the unexpressive vagueness of the "and" in this chapter's assigned title, "Cinema and the Visual Arts," avoided) by considering cinema in relation to the visual arts (shared styles, shared culture, and so forth), by looking at the function of the visual arts as they appear in cinema, and by treating cinema as a visual art.

Whether one welcomes the cultural diversification it has accompanied or laments the "loss of national essence" it has contributed to, cinema has been a part of Chinese culture much too long to be regarded as inherently and forever foreign. Chinese filmmakers bring their own culture to the medium, but just what culture is that? As an agent of globalization, film participates in the mythology of binaries – of an originary, intact native "Han" culture not greatly subject to diversifying external stimuli before the arrival of "modernity" – whereas the reality of Chinese art is that it exposes a cultural history of great variety and maturity and many "early modernities."[8] To return to handscrolls, an example by Ni Zan, in both brushwork and composition, may be a study in calm stability; by Wu Zhen, a harmonic rhythm; while ones by Muqi or Yujian are explosive; and yet another by Xia Gui has all the changes of pace found in good filmmaking, moving laterally, then pausing to recede into depth and detail, again rushing laterally before being suddenly halted, and so forth (Silbergeld 1982: 58–60). The medium and format are Chinese, but what do these examples tell us about the style, temperament, and personality of Chinese painting (in the singular), to which one might compare Chinese film (also posed in the singular)? The answer has to come as a warning against generalizations and as an appreciation of types as stereotypes: traditional Chinese texts on painting were inordinately given to categorization, labeling the six aesthetic criteria – no more, no fewer, no other; identifying painters who "took Ni Zan as their model" or "followed Xia Gui" as a sole means of describing their styles; classifying the various types of brushstrokes, acceptable or not, used for rocks or drapery or specific plants. And yet these categories differentiate as well as conglomerate, and asserting a commonality of Chinese painting shaped by its distinctive use of the Chinese brush and water-based pigments is as informative as asserting that all movies are alike for being made with a camera and projected on a flat rectilinear screen (Chinese splashed-ink and finger-painting and Western Cinerama excepted). To an argument that the Chinese language itself (assuming that its various dialects truly constitute one language) might somehow shape the distinctive cultural basis for a coherent Chinese mode of painting or cinema – "linguistic relativity" (cf. Whorf 1956; Wan and Chong 2004) – the actual "Chinese"-speaking audience offers resistance: the largest grossing Chinese-language film of all time, *Crouching Tiger, Hidden Dragon* (Ang Lee, 2000) was often ridiculed "at home" for the admixture of dialect accents spoken by its leading actors.[9]

Disregarding the variation found in traditional Chinese painting, and overlooking the fact that by the time film production began in China much of the Chinese art world had already risen in rebellion against tradition, there are a number of features that might be said to embody a "Chinese" visuality: flatness (lack of plasticity and parallelism to the picture surface – although by the Song period, organic form and spatial depth were handled with considerable subtlety and accorded great importance [Silbergeld 1982: 31–9]); arbitrary use of color, in low-saturated hues; resistance to "natural" lighting; suppression of dramatic impulse; incompletely defined settings; appreciation of emptiness and stillness; minimal camera movement; slowness: long takes, long cuts, "real-time" action and dialogue. These are the characteristics that may appear, especially to a Western audience, to be particularly "Chinese" about Chinese-language films. And so, when Edward Yang in *A Brighter Summer Day* (1991) trains his camera on an open doorway for 30–40 seconds at a time and lets the characters in the room beyond move back and forth laterally, in and out of view, sometimes speaking, sometimes silent, the flatness, the stillness, the diminution (through distance and invisibility) of emotional tension seem to convey an aura of authentic "Chineseness." So, too, do similar scenes by Hou Hsiao-hsien, Tsai Ming-liang, and Ang Lee, all from Taiwan, which by this standard produces the most "Chinese" of all films. By contrast, when John Woo, Tsui Hark, Jackie Chan, and other Hong Kong filmmakers dating back to the "flying" martial arts scenes of King Hu draw on the acrobatic traditions of Chinese theater, blend this with the dynamic choreography of "Hollywood style," exaggerate it (into what David Bordwell [2005b] calls "intensified continuity"), and hand it back so as to change the fundamentals of action and fighting in American film (only the guys in black hats fought with their feet in the era of John Wayne [1907–79] and Gary Cooper [1901–61]), this represents either the least Chinese of Chinese-language films in style or at least a different kind of "Chinese cinema" (colonial, perhaps), with a "distinctive staccato rhythm … amplified by color, music, editing, framing, and other film techniques" (Bordwell 2005b: 147).

Leo Lee (1991: 13–14) once proclaimed a link between the early establishment of a certain kind Chinese camerawork and Chinese life itself:

> The general visual style of most 40s films I have seen is subdued: instead of trick camerawork and flashy editing, they tend to rely on static long and medium shots. The close-ups are used relatively sparingly … and mostly to accentuate a high point in the characters' interaction and an emotional peak. Rapid zooms and pans are seldom used. Dissolves, wipes, fade-ins and fade-outs are generally employed to conform to the changes of time and scene (dissolves for brief time changes and fades for longer lapses).… The rhythm of this type of film is slow, rather than frenzied, and perhaps parallels the rhythm of ordinary life – Chinese style.

Hao Dazheng (1994: 52) references Zhang Zeduan's Qingming Scroll in writing, "To enjoy a long tableau with small figures, one must shift one's line of sight left and right, or up and down, a necessary condition for the appreciation of Chinese visual representation. This reminds one of the tracking technique used in films.… Chinese moviegoers evidently take great pleasure in reenacting their experience with paintings.… Depth of space was a problem in Chinese visual representation." This "moving focus," as George Rowley (1947: 61–3) and subsequent writers on Chinese painting have called it, which has its counterpart in the cinematographer's tracking shot, might be regarded as essentially Chinese, as is the static long take used to attain a sense of stillness; and yet as James Udden (2002: 59) has observed, "If finding an essential 'Chineseness' is based on both a moving camera and a static camera, then this is the classic scenario of something explaining everything in reality explaining nothing." Udden (2002: 69n21) goes on to note that "one will be hard pressed to find lateral tracks in any greater number in Chinese films than anywhere else."

It is probably the long take, together with the medium-to-long range shot and lengthy pauses between conversation – all designed to establish a sense of "real-time" cinematic activity – that have been most widely regarded as essential Chinese characteristics in filmmaking. A recent study of Hollywood film structure confirms the reduction in average length of cuts over the decades, from about 13 seconds between cuts in 1945 to less than 7 seconds in 1965 to about 4 seconds in 1985 and 2005 (Nothelfer, DeLong, and Cutting 2009). Comparable figures for Taiwan filmmakers indicate increasing times between cuts, including 18 seconds per cut for Hou Hsiao-hsien's *A Summer at Grandpa's* (1984), 24–25 seconds for Hou's *A Time to Live, A Time to Die* (1985), 32–35 for his *Dust in the Wind* (1986), 42–44 seconds for his *A City of Sadness* (1989), 83–84 seconds for his *The Puppetmaster* (1993), 114 seconds for his *Good Men, Good Women* (1995) (S. Shen 1995: 211–12; Udden 2002: 62; Silbergeld 2004: 108), and 200 seconds for Hou's *Flowers of Shanghai* (1998), which used only one take per scene (M. Berry 2005: 250); Edward Yang's *Confucian Confusion* (1994), 48 seconds; Tsai Ming-liang's *Vive l'Amour* (1994), 36 seconds, and his *The Hole* (1998), 53 seconds (Bordwell 2005b: 156). The evidence is striking, but so is the attendant mythology, as Bordwell (2005b: 156) writes:

> Some researchers have claimed that the long take is a distinctive long-standing tradition of Chinese cinema, but I cannot find the evidence for this; the 1930s and 1940s films I have checked yield a range of shot lengths about equal to that we find in other national cinemas of the sound era, including that of the United States.

Moreover, Jiang Wen's *In the Heat of the Sun* (1994), which averages 6.28 seconds per cut, and his *Devils on the Doorstep* (2000), which averages only 4.22 seconds per cut (my count), are probably typical of recent PRC cinema. Reflecting on such data while writing of Hou Hsiao-hsien and about (or against) "the question of a Chinese style," Udden (2002: 54) concludes similarly: "Unfortunately, neither Hou Hsiao-hsien, nor the culture from which he arose, are that simple."

The brush-and-ink linearity of Chinese painting, drawing subjects with incomplete form rather than with filled surfaces as in oil painting, and producing more of an "idea" than an illusion of material reality, has also been referenced in relation to the physical "emptiness" and spiritual richness ("inner truth") of *Yellow Earth* (Chen Kaige, 1984), as has the "swift execution" and roughness of Chinese brushwork (Berry and Farquhar 1994: 85ff.). The Chinese penchant for writing about and painting with colors more "suitable" to typological or to "decorative and expressive purposes" than to realistic ends provides the basis for an examination of Chen Kaige's and Zhang Yimou's use of color in *Yellow Earth* and *Ju Dou* (1990) by Jenny Lau; the former film is said to have drawn its "contemplative effect" and "discursive strength" from the coloration of Chinese landscape painting, while in the latter the bold "'splashes' of red, yellow, or green that occupy major parts of shot compositions" are likened to the spontaneity and accidentalism of Chinese "splashed ink" painting (*pomo*; never mind that historically pomo eschewed the use of color) that "generates a spirit of freedom or rebelliousness in the film" (Lau 1994: 133, 140, 143). Once again, Udden (2002: 61) is the skeptic:

> It is one thing to say that Chinese film artists past or present have consciously tried to find ways of expressing indigenous art forms within the medium of film, which they clearly did with opera and later on with martial arts; it is a very different thing to argue that indigenous culture permeated the very fabric of these films' style as if by a process of unseen osmosis. Once this is assumed, these writers can easily make anything seem Chinese (i.e., both a static and a moving camera), all the while quarantining these arguments from careful comparisons with non-Chinese examples.

This is a subtle problem. Culture is, in part, osmotic; cultural "knowledge" may well be acquired in a less than fully conscious manner. More important than what a filmmaker knows is what his film says. But Berry and Farquhar (1994: 85) bolster their assertions with evidence of authorial intentionality, quoting Chen Kaige's assertion that in *Yellow Earth* he was pursuing "an inner truth based on outer reality," and Zhang Yimou's statement – "In traditional Chinese aesthetics, a painting's value lies in its idea (*hua gui zai liyi*) and this idea precedes the brush (*yi zai bi xian*). I think cinematography is just the same."

It is perhaps not an uncommon career-pattern that led many filmmakers from studio arts to film: Zhang Yimou studied painting and was a serious photographer before going into cinema; Tian Zhuangzhuang was a photographer; Lou Ye studied animation arts; Jia Zhangke studied art (next door to a film theater); Edward Yang designed comic books. Tian Zhuangzhuang, today, can still describe the Mongolian sunrise when making his early film, *On the Hunting Ground* (1985), and remember how its beauty made his hair stand on end, exclaiming: "It was a scene right out of a painting – it was so gorgeous. I remember thinking to myself, *This is what film is all about*" (M. Berry 2005: 62). Again, the real issue here is perceptions: the filmmakers' own perceptions – accurate, credible, or otherwise – of tradition and Chineseness. "I personally feel that *Yellow Earth* is a very 'Chinese' film," says Chen Kaige, lest there be any doubt about this; on the other hand, he can also particularize "China": "I still don't understand Shanghai" (M. Berry 2005: 90, 98).

What seems most clear in the case of the "Fifth Generation" movement in its prime is its intention to draw on Chinese tradition in its most characteristic forms, setting many of its narratives in the past as a secure means of commenting on the politically insecure present, and in doing so to engage popular perceptions of China's traditional arts and culture.[10] In this way, its filmmakers (given their greater popularity abroad than at home) partake in the cultural education (accurately or not) of more than one public, for their own cinematic ends. But that generation held no monopoly on the long take. Jia Zhangke, an arch-representative of post-Fifth Generation film and (until recently) of independent filmmaking, rejects costume drama and historical allegory in favor of China's here-and-now, and yet he remains intensely interested in the loss of identity and the undermining of basic social values by China's headlong plunge into market capitalism and cultural assimilation.

The minimalist settings, long takes, and long silences in his films, from *Xiao Wu* (1997) to *Still Life* (2006), are nostalgic devices – reminiscent of the *Yellow Earth* film era, just as *Yellow Earth* was reminiscent of Republican era films like *Goddess* (Wu Yonggang, 1934) and *Street Angel* (Yuan Muzhi, 1937) – and even more pronounced, perhaps, than in those earlier films. One will not be surprised by Jia recalling that watching *Yellow Earth*, when it first came out, "changed my life. It was at that moment … that I decided I wanted to become a director and my passion for film was born" (M. Berry 2005: 185; see also McGrath 2007). It is as director Li Yang has put it: "Generations are not divided by ages, they are divided by ideas and orientations" (M. Berry 2005: 231).

When is tradition not just about the past, and when is landscape more than a landscape? *Yellow Earth* begins with a lateral scan of the barren loessic landscape of the film's title (conspicuously handscroll-like) and ends with a vertical scan of the same, top to bottom three times over (as with a hanging scroll). It raises the question (as does the barren tree at the very outset of the Qingming Scroll, set in that same yellow earth some nine centuries earlier): After all the travelers have come and gone, and after all the governments and their ideological schemes are forgotten, will the landscape and the lives of those people it nourishes remain the same – essentially Chinese? When asked about "the people … both literally and figuratively, drowned by the massive landscape" of this dry and barren yellow earth, Chen responded, "This is all connected to the Cultural Revolution. We all know that the Cultural Revolution was a fascist collective movement…. I wanted to pose the question: Can the individual survive amid the rushing floodlike power of the collective, or will he be swept away and destroyed?" (M. Berry 2005: 91).

In *Ju Dou* and *Raise the Red Lantern*, historical architecture plays a major role in portraying traditionalism – the rigid tradition of patriarchal authoritarianism, set in the past but representing the years surrounding the Tiananmen disaster (Silbergeld 1999: 287–92). "That was right after June Fourth," said Zhang Yimou of *Red Lantern*, "and I don't know why, but against that particular historical backdrop I suddenly found myself having all kinds of ideas about the inherent nature of the Chinese people. I shot the film very quickly, immediately after June Fourth, so it is inundated with symbolism" (M. Berry 2005: 130). Typically, just as these filmmakers intentionally take liberties with their temporal settings, so do their presentations of art intentionally or otherwise take considerable liberty with art-historical chronology. Chen Kaige's response to Tiananmen, *Farewell My Concubine* (1993), is a lament for the brutalization of culture by politics; in it, the theatrical arts may be taken as a trope for the art of cinema or any artistic medium manipulated by militarists and politicians. The critical scene in which the central figure, young actor Zheng Dieyi, is ceremonially confirmed in his dedication to the theater and as a female impersonator is accompanied by the handscroll-like horizontal panning of his fellow students, lined up side by side, alternating with the panning of an actual handscroll illustrating the concubine's role he plays. Ironically, in this salute to tradition, the exegetic handling of the handscroll and accompanying off-stage sounds related to the scroll is distinctively modern, the most up-to-date borrowing yet, at that time, in terms of Chinese filmmaking style (Silbergeld 1999: 100–3).

Yellow Earth begins with a historical introduction, a textual preamble presented in late-clerical script orthography of about the fourth century and seal-script brushwork of a still earlier era, wholly anachronistic by the period, the 1930s, in which the film is set and yet intent on visualizing its theme of an unchanging China (Silbergeld 1999: 43–4 and fig. 25). Nearly two decades later, Zhang Yimou's *Hero* (2002) employs calligraphy as a major didactic vehicle, beginning with the film's title, boldly executed in blood-red characters (but anachronistic given the film's Qin dynasty setting, in orthography and brush manner no older than the Tang dynasty, some eight hundred years later). Throughout the film, brushwork is equated with swordsmanship (as it has been since ancient times,[11] although one might argue that the martial arts style of the film has little to do with early China) in phrases ("Both calligraphy and swordplay rely on one's strength and spirit"; "Legend said his skill as a swordsman was rooted in his calligraphy") that seem intended to civilize and help justify the militant pursuit of national unity and social stability by the First Emperor – and by China's present-day rulers. "How odd" that the character for sword could be written in so many different ways, the First Emperor-to-be remarks, with a very old Chinese trope for social chaos. "It makes the written language impossible to comprehend. Once I've conquered the six Kingdoms and all the northern tribes, I will eradicate this problem by mandating one style of writing." In this highly derivative film, stylistically no more indebted to Ang Lee's *Crouching Tiger, Hidden Dragon* than to Leni Riefenstahl's (1902–2003) cinematically brilliant, morally toxic *Triumph of the Will* (1935), Zhang's cinematic reconstruction of Qin architecture is dazzling and based on professional models of imperial halls (cf. Steinhardt 2002: 39–41); but these, in turn, are based merely on foundation remains whose sufficiency for such detailed three-dimensional reconstructions an architectural historian will necessarily treat with some skepticism. Can Zhang distinguish Qin architecture from Tang? The architecture and costuming are steeped in the iconic black color of the Qin dynasty, and Zhang claims that in both *Hero* and his *House of Flying Daggers* (2004) his own strong interest in color shaped the choice of historical setting, not the other way around: "The story [*Hero*] really could have been set in any dynasty … but I knew that I wanted to shoot a black imperial palace"; the setting of *Flying Daggers* was supposedly shaped by Zhang's interest in Tang mural paintings at Dunhuang (M. Berry 2005: 116–17). One might think that cinema, as the art of our time, would direct some of its attention beyond the handscroll or traditional architecture to the other arts of our own time, but there is less of this than one might expect. Only in a few films is it modern art that provides the visual cues, and even this is usually a vehicle for some other complaint (not about art itself) with an eye to the past – a lament for the disappearance of traditional values or a complaint about the persistence of past vices.[12]

In the color-film era not many resist the use of color, but *Devils on the Doorstep*, set in the last months of the war against Japan, does this in pursuing the illusion of "realism," a documentary-like visual authenticity (Silbergeld 2008). It may seem ironic that eliminating much of the information normally brought to our eyes would seem more realistic, but many painters from the late Tang, Song, and afterwards once felt that way (Munakata 1965), eliminating the "distraction" of color in order to peer into a deeper, inner reality. Modern black-and-white photographers have often felt that way as well, but for a contemporary Chinese filmmaker like Jiang Wen and his distinguished cinematographer, Gu Changwei (b. 1957), their visual reference was most likely directed straight to the early technology of film. However, to obtain the "look" of documentary camerawork, *Devils* had to do more than eliminate color; achieving photographic intimacy, naturalistic lighting, handheld camera movement, accuracy in costuming, and spontaneity in acting were all essential to the effect. Put simply, however, "Chinese cinematic realism is as diverse as elsewhere" (Berry and Farquhar 2006: 75).

The postmodern rise of multimedia arts has been matched in the camera arts by a breach between the genres of staged and documented subjects, between fiction and fact, between professional and amateur styles, between cinematography, videography, and photography (Silbergeld 2011). To the spectacle of China's Three Gorges Dam project, for example, have come artists of many different media, to witness, document, and express their artistic responses to the shared tragedy of environmental destruction and human displacement. Art historian Wu Hung created an exhibition featuring four of these artists in different media: performance and video (Chen Chiulin), oil painting (Liu Xiaodong), ink painting (Ji Yunfei), and photographic installation (Zhuang Hui). For the exhibition catalogue, an essay on Jia Zhangke's semifictional film *Still Life*, about the pre-deluge demolition at Fengjie, and Jia's simultaneously made documentary *Dong* (2006), about painter Liu Xiaodong's depiction of the migratory workmen at Fengjie, observed the almost invisible intersection between fiction and documentation wherein an accidental work-related death captured in the filming of *Dong* also appears in *Still Life*, while one of Liu's painted subjects turns out to be one of Jia's actors (McGrath 2008a: 45).[13] What features do these works share, despite their different media and obviously different appearances? Above all, perhaps, a stillness that speaks of a boundless patience and emotional resignation, despite the intent to protest an environmental destruction born of political impatience; a gritty naturalism, tinged with (modernist? antimodernist?) elements of irony and disbelief, like the space vehicles that appear out of nowhere and with no explanation in *Still Life*; and a sad dislocation between social life and the natural environment, so contrary both to the idealism of traditional Chinese painting and to the conquest of nature noisily celebrated in Maoist art.

Riding the rising tide in China of documentary photography (Wang and Hu 2003; Silbergeld 2009a) and documentary film,[14] director Li Yang made three documentary films before turning to documentary-like fiction. To convey a sense of authenticity in his film *Blind Shaft* (2003), about corruption in China's mining industry – much of it filmed 700 feet underground in the narrow confines of a coal mine and intentionally "forcing" the audience "to see the film as if watching a documentary" – Li established the following principles:

> The shooting camera was always shoulder mounted so we could shoot at eye level, which provides a very objective perspective. I had already determined this stylistic approach before we even started shooting; it was to be (1) no long shots; (2) constantly moving cameras; and (3) no shots higher than eye level.... By doing away with all high and low shots, I wanted to strip the film down to the simplest possible cinematic language .... I tried to carry this same approach through with the color employed in the film. I stayed with simple, pale colors in the coal mine areas whereas in the city, there are many colors, which seem to be in disarray. (M. Berry 2005: 226, 228)

It may seem peculiar that "realism" is effected in Jia Zhangke's *Still Life* by a motionless camera taking distant shots and in Li Yang's *Blind Shaft* by a constantly moving camera, often in close-up range with a fast editing rhythm, but theirs are different realities. As Li Yang himself has said, "Realism does not necessarily mean shooting reality as it is.... What is the point of 'art' if all you want to do is capture pure reality?" (M. Berry 2005: 226–7).

The strategies of a filmmaker and those of a photographer are as different as their media. Geng Yunsheng spent seven seasons shooting in the remote coal-mining district where Yunnan, Sichuan, and Guizhou provinces conjoin. Li became similarly aware of the "unimaginable surprises" in China's ecologically rapacious mining industries ("almost 100 percent illegal operations," he claims of its coal mines):

> They don't live in buildings, they just dig holes in the ground, build a makeshift shack on top, and install a door, which is the type of dwelling you see in the first scene in the film. They are like rat holes .... The bedding that most of the coal miners sleep on is actually as dirty and black as the coal itself.... And usually there is a shortage of water – at least, clean water – in mining areas. The water there has very high levels of coal and sulfur contamination. So the coal miners do not wash themselves very often. (M. Berry 2005: 218–19)

Jonathan Noble (2008: 33) equates coal with exploitation, writing that "The sordidness of the mineshaft is ... highlighted in [the scene] in which the miners take a bath to clean the black coal dust from their weary bodies."

The coal miners' bathing scene in *Blind Shaft* is not all that different from Geng Yunsheng's photograph, "Miners at Wusheng Mountain," both works from 2003: surplus labor stripped down to bare bodies (see Figures 21.1 and 21.2). Both Li and Geng are alert to the need to present a convincing product to their audience in order to deliver an effective reformist message. Geng emphasizes the virtues of "stylistic beauty," noting "how greatly images used to present such [horrible]

Figure 21.1 Miners in *Blind Shaft* (Tang Splendor, 2003): director Li Yang, cinematographer Liu Yonghong.

things are … able to take on a formal, painterly aesthetic appearance."[15] But Geng could hardly document high-level corruption and the lack of effective government regulation with single-frame photographs. Instead, he focused on the miners themselves and their hardships, "hoping to impress on his viewers the incomprehensibility of such conditions today." Li, however, felt obliged to develop an engaging narrative in order to develop a broader base of interest, introducing an elaborate crime plot with a Hitchcock-like twist at the end, via a pair of low-level grifters engaging with their bosses in the corruption of the industry, implying that a failure to maintain high moral standards at the top – above ground, in mining terms – has lowered the standards at the bottom of the shaft. Li says:

> Many arthouse films are very slow, trying to fit a lot of ideas into their structure…. I do not think that arthouse films have to be slow, because what happens is that they are often so slow that ordinary audiences lose their patience…. I kept thinking about what it is about Hollywood movies that allows them to conquer audiences around the world. Although you can say that a lot of Hollywood movies are shallow, it is undeniable that they also excel in several areas and are often incredible on the technical side… . I decided that the film I was going to make had to have a fast rhythm, and I did not want to tell the audience too much. (M. Berry 2005: 220, 230)

What they share by way of purpose, Li's film and Geng's photographs did not share by way of reception. Geng says his photographs "had an impact on the audience wherever they were shown and were praised unanimously for the good photography." But Li's film was subject to industrial and government reprisal, both

Figure 21.2 Geng Yunsheng's "Miners at Wusheng Mountain" (2003). Gelatin silver print. P. Y. and Kinmay W. Tang Center for East Asian Art, Princeton University, on loan to the Princeton University Art Museum. © 2003 Geng Yunsheng.

threatened and actual. What one might expect as the reason for this difference – that a film is considered by government censors to be a more dangerous medium than a photograph – is not the reason offered by Li. As related by Li about his arrival at one coal mine to shoot, "because of my camera, people there took me for a journalist." He recalls:

> They all had guns drawn. I was very scared.... Pretty soon people from the Public Security Bureau showed up as well, and they were ready to arrest me. They could have made up some excuse to arrest me, or even kill me – they had thought I was a journalist.... Later on I heard that less than an hour after they had been notified of my presence, all the small coal mines in that county were shut down. Word had spread that a journalist – supposedly me – was sent by the central government to secretly investigate the mines. (M. Berry 2005: 219)

Li concludes that "It would have been impossible, and even dangerous, to have [the film's postproduction] done in China" (M. Berry 2005: 224). Jonathan Noble analogizes the "narrative, figurative, literal and social aspects of the 'underground'" in *Blind Shaft*'s mining to Li's "underground" filmmaking (Noble 2008: 33–4). Unlike such well-received industrial exposés out of mainstream Hollywood studios as *The China Syndrome* (1979, IPC / Columbia Pictures) or *The Insider* (1999, Touchstone / Disney), Li's "illegal film" was and still remains banned from commercial screening in China.[16]

Beyond the troubled question of a "national style," then, what Chinese film shares with the other Chinese visual arts is a body of cultural reference, of content and context, both historical and contemporary. Such references, which often explain the filmmakers' stylistic and thematic choices, work best when specific and take us beyond homogenizing generalizations about style. Frequently, these references are most powerful when left unspoken, as purely visual moments – "iconography" for the art historian. Sometimes that silence is meant to provide a modicum of maneuverability in the face of censorship by text-savvy, image-challenged censors.[17] I have written about a number of iconographies in relation to particular films, drawing on traditional Chinese painting, prints, and architecture for comparison and direction: the investment of mirrors with moral implication in *Good Men, Good Women* (Silbergeld 2004: 88–93); the long and significant history of the broom as a symbol of spiritual or political purification in *Hibiscus Town* (Xie Jin, 1986) (Silbergeld 1999: 221–5); obscurely but significantly, the anthropological authenticity of a jar-sinking rain-making ritual in *Yellow Earth* (Silbergeld 1999: 14–15, 38–43); not at all obscurely, the political implications of a solar eclipse in *Red Sorghum* (Zhang Yimou, 1987) (Silbergeld 1999: 76–9); coded landscape images of the trysting female and the historical link between female subordination and drowning (Silbergeld 1999: 32–43, 175–7, 180–5; Silbergeld 2004: 25–8); the demonization of women as in *Woman from the Lake of the Scented Souls* (Xie Fei, 1993) and others (Silbergeld 1999: 214–16); the demonization of minorities and foreigners in *Devils on the Doorstep* (Silbergeld 2008: 117–27); how, in traditional terms, to read figural placement in relation to influence and authority, as in *Yellow Earth* and *Farewell My Concubine* (Silbergeld 1999: 44–9, 100, 103–5); distinctive concepts of anthropomorphism and zoomorphism in relation to justice and punishment in *Devils on the Doorstep* (Silbergeld 2008: 105–27); the madman or fool as a visible symbol of enlightenment in *Hibiscus Town* (Silbergeld 1999: 219–23); the persistence of the pagoda's death-imagery in contemporary Chinese architecture in *Suzhou River* (Lou Ye, 2000) (Silbergeld 2004: 28–31); the long-standing tradition of the image-within-an-image, as related to double-personality in *Good Men, Good Women* (Silbergeld 2004: 83–8, 90–2); the moral significance of tree tops in *Good Men, Good Women* (Silbergeld 2004: 109–15); the multivalent symbolism of ox-herding in *King of the Children* (Chen Kaige, 1987) (Silbergeld 1999: 264–76); and, especially, the grand tradition of allegory itself, as in *Farewell My Concubine* and others (Silbergeld 1999: 108–11 and widely throughout). These examples can easily be located and need not be elaborated on here.

Cinema is the visual art of our time and thus the visual language of cinematic style needs to be considered in its own right. Immediately the question arises as to what that language is and whether Chinese-language film has its own language, stylistic or iconographic, different from other film traditions. There are as yet no publications attempting to systematize Chinese cinema as a visual subject, like Rudolf Arnheim's *Film as Art* (1957), David Bordwell and Kristin Thompson's *Film Art* (1986), and Bruce Kawin's *How Movies Work* (1992). But more important than the comparativist issue of Chinese film's ethnic identity are the quality and particular visual qualities unique to each individual film as a creative work of art. As a Chinese art historian, my writings on cinema have primarily emphasized the visuality of the subject and the rewards of intense visual scrutiny. I have recently composed an essay on first and last Chinese film scenes, working on the assumption "that a writer would pay no more attention to anything than to the impression made by the first and final moments of his or her work, and that any film director would do so, too." My choice of examples there "was not based simply on the opening or concluding moments themselves but rather on the ways in which such moments introduced, intensified, and summarized the qualities of what followed or preceded them" (Silbergeld forthcoming-a). The subject of Chinese film as a visual art is vast and largely unexplored, but one can turn to other chapters in this volume for studies of period style, regional style, film techniques, genres, and other important approaches to the construction of cinematic art.

Notes

1 Writing at virtually the same time, Zhu Jingxuan recorded Wu Daozi as saying of General Pei's swordsmanship that "the sight of such vigor ought to help me wield my brush" (Acker 1974: 234).

2 In the fourth edition of his popular textbook on the Chinese arts, Sullivan (1996: 172) writes that Zhang Zeduan's "vision is almost cinematic," a trope not present in the first two editions. In the earliest editions of this text, Sullivan (1960: 144–5), like other writers of his time, drew a different metaphor for "what we might call the 'shifting perspective' of Chinese painting," namely that its "nearest parallel is to be found not in European art, but in music." See also Rowley (1947: 60–1, 63, 69) and Sickman and Soper (1956: 108).

3 Western cinema had been heralded much earlier as a visual art, by Rudolph Arnheim (1957) and by the eminent art historian Erwin Panofsky (1934: 234–5), who wrote: "Today there is no denying that narrative films are not only 'art' – not often good art to be sure, but this applies to other media as well – but also, besides architecture, cartooning, and 'commercial design,' the only visual art entirely alive." Panofsky went on to specify that cinema appealed "directly and intensely to a folk art mentality."

4 I do not agree with Bordwell's (1985: 29) statement that "A film … does not 'position' anybody," but I do agree with his very next sentence, "A film cues the spectator to execute a definable variety of *operations*." Still, cinema reception theory remains quite poorly informed by controlled study of the viewing audience.

5 Regarding the gradual disappearance of dramatic subject matter from Chinese painting after the Tang period, and even more strikingly after the Song, see Ledderose (1973). For a study of what might be called a "theory of emotions" underlying the calm demeanor of Chinese literati painting, see Cahill (1960). For a fine but unusual example to the contrary, see Shang Xi's fifteenth-century painting *Guan Yu Capturing his Enemy Pang De*, discussed in the context of *Red Sorghum* (Silbergeld 1999: 58–9, fig. 43). After reading this chapter in manuscript, James Cahill suggested that if we

had access to more of the "non-elite kinds" of Chinese painting "that originally made up the larger bulk of Chinese painting as it was produced, and what was acquired and enjoyed by the much larger audience," but which unfortunately today is "so badly preserved, so neglected, so misrepresented … so misunderstood … isn't known, or accessible," then a different comparison of film with painting, more useful and relevant, might have been drawn (personal correspondence, August 28, 2009).

6   Panofsky (1934: 70) wrote of Western cinema, "Instead of imitating a theatrical performance already endowed with a certain amount of motion, the earliest films added movement to works of art originally stationary, so that the dazzling technical invention might achieve a triumph of its own without intruding upon the sphere of higher culture. The language, which is always right, has endorsed this sensible choice when it still speaks of a 'moving picture' or, simply, a 'picture,' instead of accepting the pretentious and fundamentally erroneous 'screenplay.'" However, in China, exactly the opposite was true: the first films were of staged operas (whose players moved, not the camera), and the medium was long known as *yingxi*, literally "reflection theater." Still, while puppetry plays a significant role in *The Puppetmaster* and *To Live* (Zhang Yimou, 1994), it does not significantly shape their style, nor did traditional theater more greatly help to shape the style of *Farewell My Concubine* (Chen Kaige, 1993).

7   Szarkowski (1966: 9), too, had Chinese handscroll painting in mind: "The [nineteenth-century] photographer looked at the world as though it was a scroll painting, unrolled from hand to hand, exhibiting an infinite number of croppings – of compositions – as the frame moved onwards."

8   An early artistic avant-garde, in the form of a fad for cursive calligraphy in the late second–early third century, and a diatribe against it by Zhao Yi, *Fei cao shu* (Polemic against cursive writing) suggests just how far back in time one can push the concept of "early modernity" and its discontents (Acker 1954: liv–lviii).

9   "Only Zhang Ziyi spoke with a standard Beijing accent; Chang Chen spoke with a Taiwanese accent; Chow Yun-fat, a Cantonese accent, and Michelle Yeoh, a Malaysian–English accent" (Dilley 2007: 133–4). Perhaps this accounts for the lopsided success of the film, strong in the United States ($128 million) but weak in China and elsewhere abroad ($85 million), as compared to Zhang Yimou's *Hero* ($53 million in the United States and $123 million abroad). See http://www.boxofficemojo.com/ (accessed August 3, 2009).

10   In discussing the banning of *Farewell My Concubine*, for example, Chen Kaige says, "There are those who say the suicide was a crucial factor because the government couldn't accept a suicide in 1977 – it would have been okay had it been in 1975" (i.e., acceptable if set during Mao's reign but not during Deng's) (M. Berry 2005: 96).

11   For the oldest surviving text on calligraphic technique, known as "The Battle-Array of the Brush," from the fourth century, see Barnhart (1964).

12   An example of the former is *Black Cannon Incident* (Huang Jianxin, 1985), and of the latter, *The Story of Qiu Ju*; see Silbergeld (1999: 239–54, figs. 222, 227; 120–31, figs. 121, 122).

13   *Still Life* complements Jia's immediately preceding film, *The World* (2004), about migratory labor and the workplace ecology of Beijing's largest theme park. My essay on *The World* (Silbergeld 2009b) locates it within the long history of Chinese architectural theme parks.

14 In China, photography has earned (in the 1930s and 1940s), lost (after 1949), and regained (in the 1990s) the status of an art medium, and the artistic status of documentary photography has proved even more elusive. On conceptual photography, see Wu and Phillips (2004).

15 This and other comments by Geng Yunsheng are from personal correspondence, January 2009.

16 Noble (2008: 35–7) writes that this was the result of Li's choice not to apply to the State Administration of Radio, Film, and Television for permission to film, and he points out the strategic advantages of this.

17 Art historians will probably understand if I claim that my treatment of this "Chineseness" question is Panofskian rather than Wölfflinian.

22

From Mountain Songs to Silvery Moonlight

Some Notes on Music in Chinese Cinema

Jerome Silbergeld

Writing about cinema for those who may not have seen the films is difficult; writing about film music for an audience without the music or the films at hand is even more so. Still, as most filmgoers are quite aware, the subject is a critical one, for music often plays such a crucial role in the cinematic experience. Few filmgoers fail to recognize the tug that movie music has on them, setting the mood, warning or surprising them, cueing them as to how they might interpret a scene or a character. Much has been written about Western film music by those who turn images and music into words.[1] And yet, I should like to adopt the position taken by Hsiu-Chuang Deppman in her study on the adaptations of literature to the screen, to the effect that any overarching theory is perhaps impossible and at any rate less useful than the unique detailed analyses that each artistic case affords:

> Since different combinations of factors can become decisive in almost every individual case of adaptation, I think it is a mistake to try to decide the matter in advance. I believe, *a fortiori*, that because one cannot fix criteria in a general hierarchy, no abstract science for the study of Chinese adaptation is ever likely to form, and so I have adopted in this book an approach that is responsive, descriptive, and *ex post facto* rather than predictive, prescriptive, or *a priori*. (Deppman 2010: 3)

Still, there is one overarching judgment that I would like to make at the outset on Chinese film music, namely that while "music" refers both to melody and to lyrics and while both have considerable importance, it is the use of lyrics that I believe is most distinctive about Chinese cinema, and this to such a degree that I might say most serious Chinese films before the current decade could loosely be considered to be "musicals." Generalizations other than this, and especially generalization intended to characterize any single, distinctive application of melody as "Chinese"

A Companion to Chinese Cinema, First Edition. Edited by Yingjin Zhang.
© 2012 Blackwell Publishing Ltd. Published 2012 by Blackwell Publishing Ltd.

(stereotypically: slow-paced and contemplative themes for solo instruments), deteriorate before the endless diversity generated, over a century of Chinese film production, by drawing upon Chinese "operatic," folk, and classical music sources;[2] by the various sources of traditional and modern Chinese and Western styles, sometimes mixed beyond recognition; and by complex interactions between diegetic (heard by those within the film) and non-diegetic (in the "background," heard only by the audience) uses of sound and music.[3]

Made when sound was still new to Chinese film and "genrefication" had not yet set in, *Street Angel* (Yuan Muzhi, 1937) easily blended vaudeville and music, romance and politics, slapstick comedy and high tragedy. A variety show bursts upon the opening scene with a battle of bands, with Western and Daoist musicians performing at the same time on the streets of Shanghai, in a cacophony representing the chaos of China in the midst of changing times. The Daoist musicians are part of a wedding march for a cross-eyed bride, and who wouldn't become cross-eyed trying to focus on this musical intersection? The male protagonist of the film, a trumpet player in the Western marching band, catches a glimpse of the bride and goes cross-eyed himself on the spot. His girlfriend, who is all smiles at first, is a musician as well, but the audience is soon shown, beneath that smile, a stepdaughter purchased by her parents as a virtual slave for what she can bring in as a cabaret singer, while her older sister is sent out to perform tricks as a street prostitute. Actress Zhou Xuan who performed this famed role rose from it to become the most famous Chinese singer of her generation, much like Edith Piaf (1915–63) and equally tragic at the end.

The thrust of the film's narrative was for the boyfriend to come to grips with the older sister's prostitution, for which he despises her throughout most of the film; but when she sacrifices her life to help the young couple flee the grip of the heartless parents, he recognizes at last that the sin of prostitution was not that of the sister but of the corrupt society which thrust this fate upon her. *Street Angel* also clarified and conjoined the professions of musical performance, prostitution, and acting, as they really were conjoined throughout most of Chinese history (and much of European history), well into the twentieth century, both in the public imagination and in fact. Later films featuring music and prostitution, like *The Street Players* (Tian Zhuangzhuang, 1991) and *Farewell My Concubine* (Chen Kaige, 1993), continued to explore this conjunction. *Lust, Caution* (Ang Lee, 2007), which reconstructs the time and place of *Street Angel* from a different social and narrative vantage point, makes direct contact with the earlier film in a critical scene in Shanghai's wartime red-light district, where the female protagonist sings Zhou Xuan's signature song from *Street Angel*, "The Wandering Songstress" (symbolically introduced in *Street Angel* by the younger sister's caged songbird), which has a lingering fame in China much like that of the song "As Time Goes By" from *Casablanca* (Michael Curtiz, 1942). In *Lust, Caution* the singer is a seductress and would-be assassin, targeting a collaborationist master-spy for the Japanese, and her song occurs at the very point at which the two adversaries acknowledge the prostitute-like roles that each of them have adopted, she in bed with him, he in bed with the Japanese. "The girl is like a thread," Zhou Xuan sings in the original, to her boyfriend's accompaniment on the *erhu*, "the boy is a needle. Strung together, they never will part." In *Lust, Caution* the two are strung together by their enmity, two spies each trying to penetrate the other until one or the other is crushed; and for the young singer-actress-spy in *Lust, Caution* who, significantly, sings unaccompanied, this is a moment where lowering her guard to feel genuine affection for her rival helps to seal her fate.

Typically, song appears as an occasional interlude in Chinese film, as the expression of emotion that "erupts" when necessary and, like the Greek chorus or the spoken Shakespearean aside, serves to guide the audience toward the meaning of the narrative in progress. This is an age-old tradition in Chinese culture, emotionally direct yet allegorical in form and rhetorically indirect, going back to the combination of folk songs and court paeans anthologized in the *Shijing* (translated as the *Book of Songs, Classic of Poetry,* or *Book of Odes,* dating back to the ninth or eighth centuries BCE and reputedly edited by Confucius himself).[4] All that remain today are the lyrics of these songs, China's oldest, and not the original melodies. In the film *Third Sister Liu* (Su Li, 1961), the authentic songstress of that name (born 705) takes on a proto-Communist identity for the occasion, and in her initial appearance she voices the rationale for "the people's" music (trans. Loh 1984: 165–76) (see Figure 22.1).

> Whatever sentiment is in the mind suppressed
> Erupts like fire in songs from the breast.
> Mountain songs are like springs so clear,
> Sung in vales and jungles everywhere.
> They rush and roar like floods unfurled
> Breaking all dikes, inundating the world....
> If songs are not sung, sorrow will spread.
> If roads are not walked upon, weeds will grow.
> If steel knives are not sharpened, rust will erode them.
> If heads are not held high, backs will bend....

The beauty of this opening scene lies in the film's matching of these lyrics ("floral fragrance at the foot of the mountains" and so forth) with cinematic imagery, as well as in the fine musical performance. The persecuted songstress makes it clear that when the people are oppressed, the music of the people will erupt in revolutionary song, and in the course of her music she reveals the risks of singing too openly. What we learn from films like *Yellow Earth* (Chen Kaige, 1984), discussed below, is how the government (today, as long ago) will monitor popular songs to see how well it is faring among the people, as a kind of polling process, and then will manipulate the results to convince the public that it is doing well, like rigging the poll numbers. It takes the words right out of their mouths and gives them back new ones. Haun Saussy (1993: 107) has written of the conversion of folk song to Confucian "allegory": "Poetry tattles on society – a society formed (in part) by the

Figure 22.1   Folk wisdom triumphs in a mountain song competition in *Third Sister Liu* (dir. Su Li, Changchun Studio, 1960).

canons of its poetry. The work of art, it seems, gets lost and found between its two functions of documenting mores and changing them."

Many of the earliest Chinese-made films were staged performances, beginning with *Dingjun Mountain* (Ren Jingfeng, 1905), from a section of a Peking opera, and the model (*yangban*) films of the Cultural Revolution revived that tradition. Unlike most of later Chinese films, then, The *White-Haired Girl* (Sang Hu, 1972) is a full-fledged musical – Jiang Qing's (Madame Mao's) "revolutionary" balletic version of the traditional opera, staged during her reign as China's cultural czar in the Cultural Revolution (see Figure 22.2). In it, the dancers do not speak or sing but perform to the accompaniment of background music, as in a silent film. At this peak of China's determination to chart its own course, to go "modern" at a revolutionary pace and overtake both the Soviet Union and America on its own terms, one might have expected something particularly nationalistic from a model film like this, something closely derived from Chinese opera and distinctively "Chinese." But the music and dance were a mixture of East and West, which proved particularly challenging in the isolationist phase of the Maoist era. This story of persecution and class conflict, of a peasant girl sold to her impoverished father's landlord as a slave and assaulted by him, then escaping to the mountains, reaches its pitch when she returns home – with her hair turned prematurely white – to gain her revenge in a peasant uprising. The landlord and his accountant are hauled off stage to be executed by the white-haired girl's boyfriend (it's a man's job, after all) and two shots ring out – beats of an orchestral drum – to announce completion of the deed.

Figure 22.2　Lovers reunited to fight against evil in a model ballet film, *The White-Haired Girl* (dir. Sang Hu, Shanghai Studio, 1973).

This leads to a Communist-style celebration, a hallelujah chorus danced by a Doris Day-like heroine to the tune of Prokofiev-style Russian motherland music, followed by a Tchaikovskyesque waltz of the flowers, and concluded by Mao Zedong coming up over the hills in the form of a red rising sun.

Of this high-Maoist style, Harold Schonberg, the *New York Times* music critic, wrote in October 1973:

> To Western eyes the ballet is anything but revolutionary. It is a naive, innocent propaganda fairy tale, primarily stemming from Russian ballet, saturated with the dance vocabulary of the West. Once in a while, Chinese elements are introduced – native instruments, the pentatonic scale, and even a few microtones. But … most Western listeners would classify the score of *The White-Haired Girl* as movie music. Certainly all the clichés are there.

Schonberg, actually, was writing from Shanghai about the live theatrical version famously attended by President Richard Nixon and the First Lady in the company of Jiang Qing (for context, see Witke 1977: 432), but what he heard nonetheless was "movie music" – undistinguished, clichéd, tawdry stuff. As for the *White-Haired Girl* dance troupe, which Schonberg (1973) wrote of as "rehearsed to a point where they could bear comparison with the Rockettes," and he described it as "highly provincial … [and] apparently unaware of the amount of meaning that can be packed into conventional ballet movement." It's like ketchup on scrambled eggs: of course Nixon liked it!

Despite Jiang Qing's pretentions, the real revolution in Chinese cinema still lay ahead. *Yellow Earth*, which is often considered a turning point in Chinese film history, was conceived by its original author, Ke Lan, as a musical paean to the government and the people, set in a well-watered and flowery valley with no reference to North China's parched and unyielding yellow earth. But the filmmakers, including the musical composer Zhao Jiping, overhauled Ke Lan's work, step by step, and the songs became fewer and more sober each step of the way, like the film itself. The film's title followed a similar progress, evolving from Ke Lan's romantic *Echo in the Deep Valley* (*Shen gu hui sheng*) to *Silent Is the Ancient Plain* (*Gu yuan wu sheng*) and finally to its present title *Huang tudi* (McDougall 1991: 27, 32, 34). Set in 1938, the story features an Eighth Route soldier who gathers peasant tunes and rewrites them to have them sung as Communist propaganda, a gentle form of ideological reeducation. Yet the bitterness of the peasants' tunes seems gradually to penetrate his naive self-assurance. At a wedding where the couple are too poor to afford auspicious servings of fish for the guests, in order to avoid its absence they serve up reusable wooden fish laden with sauce, as the hired wedding singer chants:

> Pairs of ivory chopsticks // are set out on the table [though of course they are not],
> The sieved wine from the silver pot // is poured with a golden ladle … [which of course, it is not]. (Trans. McDougall 1991: 187)

This is sung as if lyric fantasy could somehow replace reality, but one of the unconvinced guests informs the song gatherer, "He just sings bitter songs."

In the rude home where the song gatherer is housed, the downtrodden, emotionless peasant father at first refuses to sing for him, since he is "not happy and not sad." It is the young daughter, Cuiqiao, about to be married off at age fourteen, who sings (in a local style known as *xintianyou*),[5] but only when she thinks the gatherer is not there to hear and record her music:

> Of all the five grains // the green pea is the roundest,
> Of all us poor folk // daughters are the saddest. (McDougall 1991: 192)

When the father at last sings, it's the daughter's fate he has in mind:

> Betrothed at thirteen // at fourteen a wife,
> At fifteen a widow // for the rest of her life.
> Three loud cries // on all ears fell.
> Three low cries // she jumps into the well. (McDougall 1991: 233)

Eventually, the song gatherer teaches the daughter and her younger brother to sing something like a politically reconstructed ode from the Classics:

> The hammer, the sickle // and the scythe,
> For workers and peasants // shall build a new life.

The piebald cock // flies over the wall,
The Communist Party will save us all. (McDougall 1991: 255)

It is this song the daughter has on her lips, the last line of it cut off in the middle, before "save," when she drowns. The song comes back ironically, last line and all, in the final moment of the film, after it has been made clear that the Party, as yet, has saved no one (McDougall 1991: 262). In many films like *Yellow Earth*, it is not the frequency of music nor of their non-diegetic background music but rather the strategic placement of songs and their exegesis of the films' thematic intent that justifies regarding them as significantly "musical."

Although *Yellow Earth*, looking back in time and to the impoverished rural landscape in place, leaned heavily upon folk traditions for its music, it helped to open the door to a new and more liberated era in filmmaking, especially in what are regarded as "art" films. *Army Nurse* (Hu Mei, 1985) defined itself by focusing on a single pivotal scene, and that scene was defined musically by a creative interplay between diegetic sound and non-diegetic music. The narrative features a young woman packed off as a youth during the Cultural Revolution to serve at a remote military hospital. As the years go by, she grows up there deprived of a normal child-hood, of a private or romantic life, and wedded instead to her work. At one point, however, she is attracted to a handsome young soldier, a relationship forbidden to her, which leads her to refuse him medical attention when his bandages need chang-ing, but she then relents, and for one brief moment – ten seconds only – she expresses her need and longing by resting her head on his shoulder. It is the only love-moment in the film and the only one in her life, and for all her years of pent-up and suppressed desire these few seconds must suffice. One can hardly imagine that film director Hu Mei would not have given particular attention to the film music accompanying this brief instant, just as she has to the striking medium and tight close-up shots of the couple, and the musical solution was innovative for its time. In this scene, a nearby repairman, seen earlier, hammers away at a broken window; outside, an army bugle blows. Both of these diegetic sounds become part of the non-diegetic music as the young nurse yields to her personal longings and then reverts quickly to the military discipline expected of her. The hammering, com-bined with and then transferred to percussive cellos, becomes the dramatic but threatening heartbeat of her desire; the call of a bugle, now internalized, draws her to her soldier but also to the duty that disrupts her desire from becoming fulfilled. Massed, rising strings express her romantic longing, then dissolve in quavering notes and a rising arpeggio of plucked harp strings as if awakening from a dream. The audience is left uncertain when these diegetic sounds cease to be "real" and instead become part of her developing but ultimately undeveloped fantasy, in her own brief period of disrepair. I previously historicized this scene (Silbergeld 1999: 158):

Their physical encounter is brief and so chaste it would scarcely qualify as a sexual encounter in America; but initiated by a girl, narrated by a woman, and representing a whole culture so starved for personal affection after ten paranoid years of destroying all internal enemies, the brief ten seconds when army nurse touches military patient became one of the most emotionally charged moments in modern Chinese cinema.

A similar transformation of sound into music occurs during the opening credits of *Old Well* (Wu Tianming, 1986), a film about a group of youths' efforts to find a source of water sufficient to permit the survival of their native village, located in the rocky Taishan Mountains in a landscape strikingly like that in Fan Kuan's famous early Song dynasty painting. As the opening credits begin to roll, the opening shot is a tight close-up inside a well shaft, filling the screen with the muscular arms and back of a village youth (*Old Well*'s lead actor and cinematographer Zhang Yimou), shown deep in shadow, hammering away at hard rock. As the pounding continues, the film's background music gradually joins in: two notes at first, a wailing sound, repeated high and higher on the scale, and on the fifth repetition further joined by percussion that picks up on the sound and rhythm of the hammer. At this musical cue, the camera begins a slow, symbolic journey up the shaft toward the round circle of light far above, and as it rises the music becomes syncopated, increasingly animated, and finally accelerates to double-time on traditional Chinese instruments as the camera approaches the subterranean entrance, like a birthing process through which hard labor and sheer determination give new life and bring new hope to the community (E. Wang 1988; Silbergeld 1999: 92–4; Silbergeld forthcoming-a).

Occasionally, the understanding of a film, or part of it, turns on an understanding of music, and in the West our understanding of Chinese folk music often falls short. *The Day the Sun Turned Cold* (Yim Ho, 1994), for example, involves a family father who is being cuckolded by his wife and who may – perhaps – later be murdered by her and her lover. The son claims to have been a circumstantial witness to this, but is he to be believed or is he acting out a childhood fantasy? (Silbergeld 2004: 48–72). The melodic accompaniment for this film is appropriately tragic, bitter-sweet Schubertian chamber music by Otomo Yoshihide that reflects the son's love–hate relationship with his parents: slow, dolorous, modulating between major and minor in mode. This classicizing music, kept to the background, serves its purpose well – even in this rural setting, where the villagers would never have heard such music – and the composer modulates it well: sweeter for nostalgic moments; galloping along with the jingle of horse bells while sleighing through the snow; low, slow, and grim at the worst of times. Yet no less interesting is a wordless folk tune that leaps into the foreground, diegetic, but only briefly and perhaps all but unnoticed by many viewer-listeners. As the father is first coming to realize his predicament, he finds himself in public practicing music with villagers who are rehearsing for a village celebration – fellow townsmen who have come to recognize the father's problem before he did and who are now gossiping behind his back. At this moment, the wife and her lover are secretly trysting at the family home, under the scrutinizing eye of the son, and the father has his suspicions. Surrounded by his fellow musicians, the father plays a brief tune of his own – a folk tune of some kind – on the wailing double-reed *suona* while the camera zooms slowly into a tight close-up of his sadly frowning face. The others listen, and one of them asks, "Mr. Guan, what was that tune?" The father replies, "What was that tune, indeed?" Immediately afterward, the father takes a performance break, dashing home purportedly to get new reeds for his instrument but mostly to surprise his wife there and confirm his suspicions. He fails to arrive in time to succeed. Still, the villagers' question remains unanswered: they don't know the tune and neither do we. This could go unnoticed, or it could raise a lingering curiosity: What does it tell us about what the father knows, or thinks he knows? Is it a tune of cuckoldry? Of revenge or submission? Is it a clue to the father's recognizing his fate? What opera or folk tune does it come from? Or did the filmmakers just make it up? I have yet to meet an ethnomusicologist or anyone who can identify this tune.

Increasingly in recent decades, as Chinese film music becomes ever more Westernized, Western classical music has been used not only to establish mood melodically but also to reference lyrical content and context that enrich the films in which they appear. *In the Heat of the Sun* (Jiang Wen, 1994) uses Mascagni's romantic "Prelude" to *Cavalleria Rusticana* (Rustic Chivalry) widely throughout the film, from the moment the film's misguided lead character first sees a photo of his romantic heroine, then sets the climactic moment of his humiliation to the broken-hearted pulsation of the opera's "Intermezzo Sinfonico." In doing so, it relies not only on Mascagni's haunting melodies but also invokes parallels, for those who know Western opera, between the cinematic narrative and the opera's tale of disillusionment, betrayal, and crushed romance (Silbergeld 2008: 55–60).

The Western classics also play an understated but telling role in *Yi Yi* (Edward Yang, 2000), a study of generational patterns and the predictable phases of life. A particularly poignant moment in the film occurs at a concert performance of Beethoven's First Sonata for Piano and Cello, attended by the adolescent daughter Ting-Ting of the film's protagonist family, during her first experiment in dating. As the two musical instruments first join in sonority, in the languid, romantic opening measures of Beethoven's second movement, the music raises the question of whether the young, awkward couple will join hands, or even become a real couple. What the audience will perhaps recognize is how the young man is simply dating Ting-Ting in order to arouse the jealousy of his long-time girlfriend, Lili, Ting-Ting's next-door neighbor and a cellist herself, the filmmaker cueing the audience by this substitution of the cellist on stage for the cellist it already knows. Ting-Ting is stealing glances at him, while he is watching one cello player and thinking about the other. Ting-Ting can hardly be oblivious to this but cannot resist being drawn in deeper and deeper to the boy's own troubles. (He will, ultimately, murder Lili's lecherous teacher, who has been sleeping with Lili's mother and perhaps with Lili as well.) The structure of the duet on stage mirrors that of the scene and of the film as a whole, beginning tentatively, followed by gentle pairings, then becoming less lyrical and ever more complicated. What the film audience most likely does *not* recognize is that the musicians on stage are played by director Edward Yang at the piano and his wife, Peng Kaili, an accomplished professional musician who recorded the piano music that Yang is "performing," accompanying him on the cello (or accompanying herself, actually). For a film about role exchange, these transferred identities constitute a kind of filmmakers' inside joke, a play within their own play, entirely consistent with the nature of the film (Silbergeld forthcoming-b).

Yang's own family was very much a part of this film about families, lodged there especially in his wife's music. Peng composed and performed much of the film's background music including its opening theme, drawn from Beethoven's "Ode to Joy" chorus and converted to a tender ode to the unchangeable past, *andante cantabile*. The title itself, *Yi Yi* or "One-One," is the Chinese equivalent of the "one-and-a-two" with which the Western band leader begins a performance; it also stands for the way in which the film's family of four each go off in their own way, one by one, to grasp the deeper meaning of their lives, only to return at the end (like Dorothy back to Kansas) with the realization that the meaning was there all along, lodged within the family. While music appears infrequently in *Yi Yi*, as often diegetic as not, nearly every presentation of it in the film merits deeper inspection. Early in the film, Ting-Ting's father runs into his childhood sweetheart after thirty years apart, and when he departs from the family to reexamine things, he reunites with her in Japan to relive his past and ponder how his life might have been had he not broken off their engagement. Soon after first meeting her again, there is a moment when he climbs into his car with a prospective Japanese business partner, Mr. Ota, whom he has also just met and who will become something of a muse to him throughout the later course of the film. As the father turns on the engine, the music system offers up Bellini's song "Vaga luna, che inargenti" ("Wandering moon, which dapples with silver") and Ota surprises him by whistling the melody, which initiates a nostalgic conversation in broken English about music, with a prefiguration of the reunion that will take place between father and ex-lover in Japan just when the daughter is at the concert on her first date:

> OTA: "When I was a little boy, my family was very poor. Music make me believe life
> is beautiful."
> FATHER: "My father listen to music every day, but I hate his music.... When I was
> fifteen, I fell in love. Suddenly, all of his music means something. Then she left;
> the music stays with me."
> "She didn't like music?"
> "Many people think music is useless. You cannot get any money from listening to
> music. She also think this way."
> "So she left you?"
> "No. I decide to leave her. But you know, I just met her a few days ago, after thirty
> years."
> "This must be *her* music. I can almost see her face now."

Music, here, has become mood, characters, present situation, and future plot – all in one. And while the film's characters can hear the music, it has become much more than that which can be heard. How well can the audience hear and understand this heightened level of musical engagement?

It is worth saying, in conclusion and in place of any summary or theorization, that what matters most is that music has now entered Chinese-language film at this level – where it can work in great sophistication at all levels, where it can express at least as much and perhaps even more than most in the audience can grasp. China's film music no longer springs from revolutionary necessity but arises from global exchange. On the map, Beijing, Shanghai, and Taipei are closer to Mascagni's and Bellini's Italy than they are to Hollywood, although today such distances hardly matter. The influences of Western music, Western film, Chinese music, and Chinese film now flow rapidly in all directions and their mutual inter-action offers ever more sophistication for the years to come in film production and audience education the whole world over.

Notes

1 Gorbman (1987), while not new, provides a good introduction to the subject with an annotated bibliography. Next to nothing has been written about Chinese film music.

2 Classical Chinese music has played little role in film music, perhaps because it all sounds rather alike to today's audience and gives filmmakers few recognized specifics to draw upon. I once asked Princeton Professor Gao Yugong why China had no great music tradition compared to that of Europe. I assumed he would agree to the premise and anticipated that he would say something about the lack of a Chinese equivalent to Christian church music, out of which Europe's secular classical music traditions arose. What he said, instead, with *qin* music (the Chinese classical zither) in mind, was that China's classical music repertory was "like having five great works by Bach and all the rest by Mendelssohn." (I repeat this with apologies to Mendelssohn lovers.)

3 There is virtually no published writing on this subject, and this chapter does not offer a history of the subject but a consideration of some of its major issues, presented more or less in chronological order. I am focusing here only on what has been referred to as "art" or "arthouse" films. A consideration of martial arts and other entertainment film genres would yield a very different essay, and to include them all together would considerably dilute this or any but a much longer account. I confess to knowing too little about Chinese music *per se*; I play piano, not the *qin, suona,* or *erhu.*

4 The classic expression of this idea is given in the "Great Preface" to the *Book of Odes* (for original text and an alternate translation, see Legge 1960: 34): "When emotions are stirred within, they are given form as speech. When speaking about them is inadequate, then they are sighed as laments. When sighing them as laments is inadequate, then they are chanted as songs.… Emotions are given sound, and when sounds are combined into compositions these are called musical modes. The musical mode when the world is well ordered is tranquil, expressing pleasure, for the government is harmonious. The musical mode when the world is chaotic is resentful,

expressing anger, for the government is wicked. The musical mode when the state is in ruins is mournful, expressing contemplation, for the people are in distress."

5　McDougall (1991: 173) has identified this style and translated it "roughly" as "following the natural flow." Director Chen Kaige later stated his remorse for having a professional singer perform these songs to a romanticized Westernized orchestral accompaniment (McDougall 1991: 46).

23

Cross-Fertilization in Chinese Cinema and Television

A Strategic Turn in Cultural Policy

Ying Zhu and Bruce Robinson

Introduction

China's film and television industries developed semi-independently until the state stepped in with measures aimed first at reinvigorating film and then at restructuring the entire media sector. Film disdained early opportunities to grab a stake in television. Vested interests, institutional inertia, and other barriers also discouraged film studios from breaking into television and related markets, but events, regulatory changes, and most recently a geostrategic decision to enhance China's "soft power" have all worked to bring the kindred creators forcefully together. In the "events" category, the booming popularity of television dramas and other entertainment programs from the 1990s on, coupled with film industry woes, caused a steady drain of film industry talent and money toward television. Yet it was not until the state stepped in with a striking series of measures aimed initially at encouraging horizontal integration and later at simply creating media conglomerates that the film industry was finally able to capitalize on new outlets for its pictures. Chinese film has done much better as a consequence, though still not as well as it might. Likewise, by now cross-fertilization is structurally embedded in China's media industries – as a matter of policy, and responding both to new economic imperatives and to an even newer strategic imperative – and Chinese popular culture in general is gaining ground, but still against self-imposed limits in a global arena that will test its persistent pairing of market and propaganda functions, and the imagined strategic value of its film and television industries.

A Companion to Chinese Cinema, First Edition. Edited by Yingjin Zhang.
© 2012 Blackwell Publishing Ltd. Published 2012 by Blackwell Publishing Ltd.

Leading the way, China Central Television (CCTV) launched its Movie Channel (CCTV-6) in 1996 as a joint venture with China Film Corporation, then China's exclusive film distribution and sales agent, and soon to become the anchor of the China Film Group, a cinema-based multimedia conglomerate formed in 1999 as part of a state-directed reorganization designed to protect and expand China's media industries after its accession to the World Trade Organization (WTO), and for additional economic and strategic purposes. In 2004, CCTV-6's advertising revenue reached RMB 700,000 million, a windfall for China Film Corporation (S. Shi 2005). Consistently ranked among the most popular channels, CCTV-6 has also helped to expose small films to a much wider audience. Using CCTV-6 as a case study of collaboration between film and television in China, this chapter tracks the path and current state of cross-fertilization between the two creative industries and considers its implications for the future of Chinese cinema in particular and Chinese media in general as the state uses its regulatory baton to orchestrate a purposeful, profitable, global-scale media sector. As we believe that these developments are part of a geostrategic turn in Chinese cultural policy, the chapter ends with some preliminary thoughts about Chinese film and television as strategic assets on the world stage.

Chinese Cinema and Television

Chinese television began in the late 1950s. The Soviet Union supplied equipment and technical assistance. Development was interrupted first in the winter of 1960 when China broke relations with the Soviet Union, which caused the latter to withdraw economic and technological aid. A second setback came during the Cultural Revolution when television broadcasting was partially suspended from 1966 to 1976. Full-scale operation resumed in the late 1970s, and television's popularity began to take off in the mid-1980s.

The early relationship between China's film and television industries was antagonistic, similar to relations between Hollywood's major studios and the US television networks in the 1950s (Y. Zhu 2003). This antagonism was one reason behind the film studios' early reluctance to pursue the television and home video markets. The studios' lack of control over the distribution and exhibition of their own films – which was the job of the state's distributor, not the studios – was another reason for this failure of imagination and planning for the new distribution channels that television might afford. Ignoring and even looking down upon television in its infancy, Chinese film paid a hefty price, missing any early opportunity it might have had of gaining a stake in television and home video's huge potential market. Acting in kind, television took a protective stance on its developing markets, initially fending off film's belated interest in television production and exhibition when it did come.

A dual system of state-subsidized and advertiser-sponsored Chinese television put the growing television industry in an advantageous position relative to the financially self-reliant film industry. Television was also able to purchase the broadcast rights to motion pictures at low prices. As the commercialization of China's cultural industries was accelerated in the mid-1990s and beyond, CCTV was forced to increase the price it paid for motion picture broadcast rights, yet the increase was too small to put a dent in the studios' production costs. Meanwhile, local stations were allowed to broadcast films purchased by other nearby local stations without paying royalties to the studios. The lack of horizontal integration between film and television hurt film more than television, but it also resulted in a waste of existing studio production facilities and human resources, forcing television to build its own production lots and cultivate its own talent pools (Z. Deng 1996).

Policymakers were keenly aware that home video and television had invigorated film in Hollywood by multiplying its distribution channels. Understanding this, the then Ministry of Radio, Film, and Television (MRFT) began in the early 1990s to encourage horizontal integration (Y. Zhu 2003: 85). In October 1993, CCTV took over the shrinking News Studio, a state-controlled film studio specializing in newsreels and documentaries. News Studio began to produce news programs for television and its much larger audience. With financial backing from CCTV, News Studio also produced feature-length documentaries for theatrical distribution. In April 1995, Science Studio, a studio specializing in films on new developments in science and technology, also merged with CCTV. In January 1996, Shanghai Animation Studio merged with Shanghai Television. As a result, the demand for animation from the animation studio increased drastically. The same year CCTV launched its Movie Channel as CCTV-6 and broadcast films provided by various studios. In addition to bringing extra revenue to the film studios, the Movie Channel promotes cinema and exposes small-budget films to a much wider audience.

Following this lead, beginning in the summer of 1996, many provincial studios began to merge with local television stations to form integrated film and television production centers. The mergers allowed film studios to take in as much as a hundred million RMB (US$14.6 million) from television commercials in 1996 (Y. Zhu 2003). In January 1997, to tap into the newly available financial resources from local television and film companies, MRFT relaxed its film licensing rules, granting provincial television stations and film distribution and exhibition companies the right to produce feature films, which had previously been reserved only for state-run film studios. In December 1997 the state permitted the establishment of three Video CD production lines, effectively linking film with the television, video, and music industries. The same year China Film Company (the state distributor) and China Music Video Corp. launched a joint venture, Huayun Laser Disc Ltd., to put feature films on laser discs for home viewing (S. Zhao 1999). Reform initiatives on horizontal integration worked to the film industry's benefit, expanding its financial resources and acquiring new outlets for feature films.

Industrial integration continued in the late 1990s, following Hollywood into the age of conglomeration. Studios and other production companies either partnered with distributors and theater chains, or were absorbed into burgeoning entertainment conglomerates, or became conglomerates through diversification. Among other benefits, mergers and conglomeration created alternative "profit centers" to protect against business downturns in any particular area. Studios and newly established production companies in major production centers such as Beijing as well as Sichuan and Jiangsu provinces initiated collaboration with local theater chains. In April 1997 the Beijing Municipal Distribution Company, Beijing TV, the Cultural and Art Publishing Company, and the Center for Television Art created a joint venture, the now-formidable Forbidden City Ltd. In early 1998, Jiangsu Yangtze Film Co., one of the largest regional film companies, wooed first-tier theaters and county-level film distribution companies to form a partnership. In addition, the company acquired a new film and television production company, the Yangtze Film and TV Production Center. The China Midwest Film and TV Shareholding Co. Ltd. was set up to pool the resources of Xi'an Film Studio and other film studios and companies in neighboring provinces, including Emei Film Studio. In a similar move, the Pearl River Film Studio in Southern China set up its second theater chain to cover the Pearl River Delta and the rest of Guangdong province. The Liaoning Northern Film Shareholding Co. Ltd. (LNF) was formed in early 1998 to consolidate film companies from eleven cities in Northeastern China. Its film distribution revenue has grown 16 percent since its establishment in 1997 (Y. Zhu 2002). The company is also investing in feature film production. In addition, it has created the Northern Theater chain by bringing together the province's top sixty cinemas. By the end of 1998 many provincial distribution and exhibition companies had consolidated with local studios to form regional film groups.

The consolidation of the audiovisual industry, particularly the collaboration between film and television, has been especially important to the film industry. Only about a third of domestic movies are screened in cinemas across China each year. In 2005, for instance, 260 films were produced in China but only sixty of them made it to the big screen (Uktradeinvest 2007). Many others were sold to film channels on television stations such as CCTV-6 and the Eastern Movie Channel of Shanghai Media Group. The Movie Channel, in particular, provided a platform and a source of revenue for films that did not get theatrical distribution. Carried by cable to an estimated 30 million households at the time, CCTV-6 also aired 389 foreign films (including films from Taiwan and Hong Kong) in 1998 and began to directly invest in the production of made-for-television films (or telefilm) in 1999 (L. Zhu 2005). About a hundred films were produced annually between 1995 and 2003. Only twenty were released to theaters each year, leaving somewhere in the neighborhood of a thousand movies that fell into distribution limbo, including some that won prizes in overseas competitions (Martinsen 2006). Among the films that failed to make it to the big screen, 75 percent were bought by the Movie Channel, which on average broadcasts seven to eight domestic films every day.[1]

Administrative jurisdiction over film was handed over from the Ministry of Culture to the MRFT in July 1996, the same time that film studios gained the right to share the income from television commercials. More institutional restructurings followed. In March 1998 China's parliament restructured its twelve ministries and put the former MRFT under a new Ministry of Information Industry (MII), which oversees the electronics industry, posts, and telecommunications. China's administrative merger of these three industries under a single ministry followed the general trend of trans-industrial activities in the West, attempting to create synergy among the three sectors.

Film reform in the late 1990s focused on more consolidation and reorganization, including, in a new departure, the state-directed creation of multimedia conglomerates. The result was the emergence of a few mega-media conglomerates that exercise monopolistic control over regional markets. Among them, China Film Group (CFG) emerged as the most formidable single player, consolidating production, distribution, and exhibition of film, television, and home video. Leading the charge at CFG is the China Film Company (CFC), the state-sponsored company established in 1951 to handle film distribution nationwide (Yeh and Davis 2008). Prior to 1988, CFC functioned as a wholesale agent, acquiring films produced by the studios and covering the cost of making prints available for nationwide circulation. CFC then distributed the films through its multilayered system based on the state's hierarchical administrative ladder, with the capital city and other major metropolises at the top, then the provinces and finally municipal seats and counties. CFC also handled film promotion, providing guidance to its branch distribution units and exhibition circuits. In addition, CFC imported international films and functioned as exporter and promoter of Chinese films abroad to festivals, arthouses, and educational programs. The export and import business was handled by CFC's subsidiary, China Film Import & Export Company (CFIEC). Thus, CFC was the agency responsible for the most crucial piece of the film industry, sales and distribution, before becoming the foundation of the now all-encompassing China Film Group (Yeh and Davis 2008).

China Film Group

China Film Group (CFG) was established in February 1999, consolidating eight formerly separate entities into China's foremost media conglomerate: the original China Film Company, plus Beijing Film Studio, China Children's Film Studio, China Film Coproduction Corporation, China Film Equipment Corporation, China Movie Channel (CCTV-6), Beijing Film Developing and Printing & Video Laboratory, and Huayun Film & TV Compact Discs Company. With this, CFG officially became

Table 23.1 China Film Group corporate structure

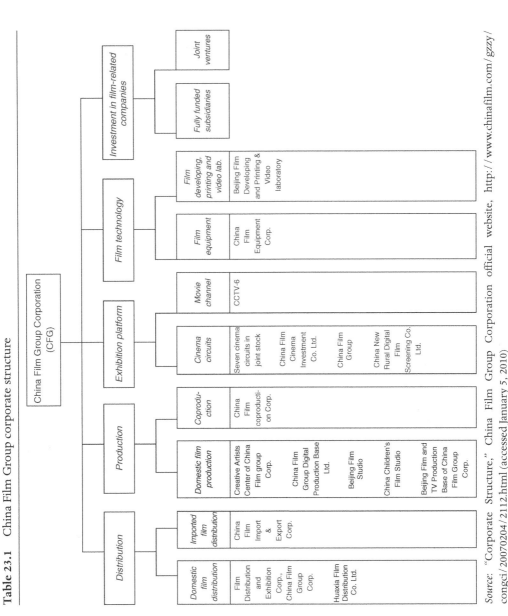

Source: "Corporate Structure," China Film Group Corporation official website, http://www.chinafilm.com/gzzy/congci/20070204/2112.html (accessed January 5, 2010)

"the most comprehensive and extensive state-owned film enterprise in China with the most complete industry chain that facilitates film production, distribution and exhibition as a coordinated process and integrates film, TV, and video into one single entity" (PR Newswire Asia 2007). According to Yeh and Davis (2008: 44), in 2004 CFG produced 35 features and 110 telefilms, and invested in 52 additional films, thus becoming the country's dominant film producer.

The corporate structure of CFG shows "a streamlined operation; secure access and shareholding in film/television assets, and alignment of various sectors to build a mega-media entity" (Yeh & Davis 2008: 40).

CFG has managed to establish a dominant position in the audiovisual marketplace. In its mission statement, the group lists five cornerstone industries as foci of development: film and television production, film distribution and exhibition, digital cinema, film import/export, and investment in cinema construction. These cornerstone industries include postproduction, equipment leasing, marketing and merchandising, optical disc manufacture, advertising, property management, and real estate development. The group also takes the lead in financing, coproduction, joint ventures, and cinema circuits. It owns fourteen fully funded subsidiaries, 34 major holding companies and joint stock companies, and the Movie Channel, with total assets of RMB 2.8 billion (US$410 million). CFG is the dominant force in domestic production and exhibition, and in film import and export.

In the late 2000s an increasing focus on domestic pictures, sharply rising box-office receipts in China, and continued state endorsement mean that CFG is poised to become even stronger. China's box office surged 27 percent to US$450 million in 2007. Two of 2007's top-grossing films, *The Warlords* (Yim Ho) and *The Assembly* (Feng Xiaogang), were Chinese coproductions, and the same year Chinese domestic films brought in US$273 million from overseas sales according to data from the State Administration of Radio, Film, and Television (SARFT) (Coonan 2009). Meanwhile, foreign, mostly US pictures constituted 46 percent of China's box office in 2007. Hollywood movies made US$158 million in China, up 38 percent from 2006. The Chinese box office for *Transformers* was US$38 million, making China the fourth-largest market in the world for *Transformers* after the United States, South Korea, and the United Kingdom. Clifford Coonan (2009) reports that CFG President Han Sanping is confident that the Chinese market will see annual growth of 30 percent over the next five to eight years, which indicates a market worth US$1.3 billion by the end of 2011. An avowed nationalist, Han urged local filmmakers to make more patriotic and "ethically inspiring" movies. As Coonan (2009) notes, CFG's tentacles extend into every area of the business: it has the money, it owns the facilities, it represents most of the talent, and it has a big say in deciding what movies get made, either as stand-alone pictures or as coproductions. CFG also benefits from rules favoring domestic movies over foreign pictures for exhibition during blackout periods at various times of the year, including Chinese New Year and the National Day holiday. During blackout periods Chinese films do not have to compete with Hollywood blockbusters.

Currently, CFG operates seven cinema circuits with four hundred theaters, which together account for about half of the country's total box office. Because many cinemas are in dire need of refurbishing and upgraded technology, US$98 million will have been used for renovation of facilities, an ongoing process that ran until 2010.[2] China Film's digital exhibition unit, Digital Cinema Line, which already boasted 184 screens, planned to increase the number to a thousand by the end of 2008. The digital movie project will have accounted for US$56 million of the funds raised. China Film's main revenue streams are advertising and distribution, which account for one-half and one-quarter of its income, respectively. More comes from equipment sales, processing and printing film, agency services, and production.

When Han revealed in August 2007 that CFG was planning a public offering, ten investment banks bid to act as underwriters for the initial public offering (IPO), despite a failed 2005 plan for a partial listing in Hong Kong. The stage seemed finally set for CFG to become China's first listed film company. In January 2008, SARFT gave its blessing to the IPO plan, and the IPO was expected to proceed once the go-ahead from the China Securities Regulatory Commission was in place in early 2010. The amount CFG would seek to raise was not clear. However, step one would be a seven-year secured bond as the foundation of a fund worth RMB 500 million (US$68 million) (*China News Network* 2009). CFG, however, would face restrictions on which parts of its business it could include in the IPO. The government will not want any broadcasting assets to fall into foreign hands, so the television business, including the Movie Channel, was unlikely to be part of the package. This would provide a challenge for CFG at IPO time: how to convince foreign investors that they will be able to get more than a symbolic stake in the Chinese film business. For the time being, CFG's television subsidiary, CCTV-6, plays no small role, substantially benefiting from and contributing to the larger enterprise.

CCTV-6

The China Movie Channel Program Center (CMPC) officially launched CCTV-6, or China Movie Channel (CMC), the first and only nationwide movie channel in China, in 1996. CMPC currently holds the largest library of Mandarin movies, owning the domestic broadcast rights to more than 95 percent of Chinese films, with 85 percent of the rights extending fifty years, and international rights to most of those same films (Television Asia Online Guide). Since 1999, CMPC has produced more than a hundred television movies per year. A domestic pay television channel, China Home Cinema (CHC), and the North America China Movie Channel were launched in 2004. In 2005, CMC started airing in Hong Kong, and in 2006, two more channels, the CHC-HD Movie Channel and the CHC

Action Movie Channel, were added to the program list. CMC was also recently added to Pacific Century Cyberworks' (PCCW) Now Broadband offerings in Hong Kong, joining a portfolio that includes films from Star Movies, Star Chinese Movies, Mei Ah Movie Channel, Turner Classic Movies, and MGM. Finally, CMC is available via satellite and the Internet in the United States, and via cable in Canada, in both places as part of a suite of channels offered by CCTV's international subsidiary, China International TV Corp. Meanwhile, CMPC has also started to provide video-on-demand service in China and has transformed itself into a multi-channel platform of high standard programming (ChinaFilm.com).

CCTV-6 now airs daily ten Chinese and imported feature films and a variety of animated movies, documentaries, and special-topic programs with a nationwide viewership of 852 million, ranking it as one of the top satellite TV channels in China in terms of ratings and market share, and the second most viewed channel nationwide, leading the way among specialty channels. Recent data suggest 60 percent urban coverage (CSM Media Research).[3] The same source reveals that only 20 percent of the population attended a theater screening in 2008. Yet 87 percent of the people surveyed have CCTV-6 and 9 percent of them watch the channel every day. Of those surveyed, 66 percent rate the films shown on CCTV-6 as very good or comparatively good. Most people would select the Movie Channel first when selecting pay television channels. The most popular movies for the channel are classics and comedies from the mainland and Hong Kong.

CMC has exclusive rights to broadcast major film festivals in China and around the globe and has hosted and broadcasted many national and international award ceremonies, concerts, and variety performances. In 2003 it signed a multi-year licensing deal with Walt Disney's Buena Vista Intl. Television-Asia Pacific (BVITV-AP) to broadcast the Academy Awards live (Rothroc 2003). The deal includes the 30-minute Red Carpet pre-show and thus continues the Oscars' exclusive run on CCTV-6 in China.

The CCTV-6 broadcast of the 75th Academy Awards in 2003 marked the first time that Chinese television carried the Academy Awards live. As it happened, Zhang Yimou's *Hero* was nominated for Best Foreign Language Film that year. CMC capitalized on the opportunity with a television special about Zhang and his colleagues at the Oscars, stirring broad public excitement. The special became a national event (Rothroc 2003). The deal was renewed in 2007, with CCTV also contracting to air the Disney Channel's High School Musical as part of a separate, multi-movie package.

In 2004 CMC signed a multi-year television deal with Warner Bros. International Television Distribution (WBITD), which allows CCTV-6 to broadcast selected current and older feature films as well as made-for-television movies (Kay 2004). More recently, CMC entered into a multi-year licensing deal with the US Academy of Television Arts and Sciences to broadcast the annual prime-time Emmy Awards, beginning with the 56th Emmy Awards live from Los Angeles in September 2009. For Jia Qi, Vice President of CCTV-6, "The broadcast of the

Emmy Awards by China Movie Channel is a latest move in terms of introducing well-known film and TV activities and programs to our audience" (Academy of Television Arts and Sciences 2004).

The main functions of CMC, according to its Director Yuan Xiaoming, are to promote domestic films and to provide additional windows for film exhibition (*Shichang guancha* 2002). As such, a television program aimed at promoting "classic" feature films was launched in September 1998, with the television premier of a Sixth Generation film, *The Making of Steel* (Lu Xuechang, 1995). The program "A Date with Film Classics" showcases well-known foreign and Chinese films every Saturday at 8:00 p.m. It has featured award-winning hits such as *The Fugitive* (Andrew Davis, 1993) and *Close Encounters of the Third Kind* (Steven Spielberg, 1977). Another program, "China Film Report," was added to promote films in movie theaters. The channel occasionally puts together promotional events for major blockbuster films, such as the premier of *House of Flying Daggers* (Zhang Yimou, 2004) on July 10, 2004 and the promotional screenings of *A World Without Thieves* (Feng Xiaogang, 2004) and *Kungfu Hustle* (Stephen Chow, 2004) (S. Shi 2005). It also exposes Chinese films and related entertainment news and variety shows to the rest of the world, with separate feeds to Asia, Europe, and America.

The staples of CMC have been old classics, low-budget pictures and, since 1998, telefilms treating contemporary topics. CMPC initiated the telefilms idea and screened its first title, *Peace All Year Round* (Qi Jian, 1998), at 5 p.m. on March 2, 1999. "Telefilm" (*dianshi dianying*) received its official name in January 2000 at a symposium jointly convened by CMPC, the China Film Art Research Center, and the film journal *Contemporary Cinema*. The next year saw CMPC's establishment of the Telefilm Lily Awards (*Zhongshi dianying baihejiang*) to encourage the production of quality television movies. The same year the venerable Golden Rooster Awards established the Best Telefilm award category. The same category was established at the Beijing College Student Film Festival in 2002. Telefilm production took off rapidly: 5,203 such titles had been screened by March 2, 2009, with an average output of a hundred telefilms per year. During prime time in 2008, 51.5 percent of domestic films screened on CCTV-6 were telefilms. Telefilms are also screened on the CMPC's three pay channels – CHC Home Theater, CHC Action Movies, and CHC Digital Movies – and on its two overseas channels, CMC North America and Europe and CMC Hong Kong, as well as in digital and mobile theaters. As a result, over a hundred telefilms have been picked up by television stations across East and Southeast Asia.

Characteristically, telefilms are low budget, averaging RMB 900,000 (US$132,000) per film, and churned out in short production cycles. With decent production values and a range of sturdy formats, they strive for popular, critical, and political approval. Telefilms tackle mostly contemporary topics that promote mainstream or "main melody" values. Among them, contemporary dramas account for 81 percent, revolutionary histories 4.5 percent, costume and martial arts dramas 12 percent, and others 2.5 percent. A critic suggests that with this focus on contemporary, topical dramas, telefilms fill a void left by Chinese feature films, which have aggressively moved toward Hollywood-style big-budget and high-tech historical epics (L. Lin 2007). *Sing Whenever I Want To* (Fang Junliang, 2006), for instance, draws on a pop phenomenon, the Pop Idol/American Idol-style Super Girl contest, which appeared on Hunan Satellite Television in 2004, while *Showdown* (Wang Jiabin<chinese/>, 2004) captures the headline issue of unfair tax practices in rural villages.

While the relationship between CMC and the film industry has for the most part been mutually beneficial, competition between the two inevitably arises over audience share. CMC must compete with cinemas for viewing experience and with the Internet and the home video market for flexibility of viewing. To this end, CMC has tried to add value and lure audiences in two ways: first by grouping films thematically for concentrated screening during special events, which has been an effective way of promoting old films; and second by creating programs that discuss films and film practices as a way of promoting its telefilms.

A look at the programming pattern in 2007 provides a glimpse of CMC's strategy. Early in the year, to celebrate the Chinese New Year, domestic comedy classics such as *Twin Business* (Wang Binglin, 1987), *The Cleverest Escape* (Sun Min, 1995), *Flirting Scholar* (Lik-Chi Lee, 1993), and *Fong Sai Yuk* (Corey Yuen, 1993) were screened daily at noon in January and February. During the long Labor Day weekend in May, the channel scheduled over ten newly released big-budget domestic and foreign films. A cluster of children's films were screened for the June First Children's Day. Throughout the month of June, to celebrate the 10th anniversary of Hong Kong's return, the channel scheduled renowned Hong Kong–mainland coproductions daily; June also saw over twenty popular films geared toward the summer market. On August First, Army Day, a slew of military-related features was shown. In 2009, main melody films were screened during prime time to commemorate the 30th anniversary of the Party's open door and economic reform policies, as well as the 60th anniversary of the founding of the People's Republic.

Grouping or clustering of films is one movie programming tactic. Another way CMC has added value to film viewing on television is through companion programs that highlight the featured screening. The program "Golden Years: Reunion," for instance, comes on immediately following the broadcast of a domestic classic film with prerecorded interviews with major stars and key production members who share anecdotes and reminisce. An unscientific sampling based on conversations with regular viewers suggests that these gossipy follow-up programs are a major attraction for CCTV-6 viewers. Another program, "A Date with a Quality Film," features classic imports. In this case the featured film is preceded by a short program of film highlights and potential talking points, and followed by expert discussions and analysis. "World Film Report" discusses the history, current state, and future direction of world cinema while highlighting the achievement of filmmakers of Chinese cultural heritage. "The Sound of Music" provides a glimpse into the world of film soundtracks via interviews with directors, composers, and critics. Even celebrity gossip programs such as "Star Podcast," with popular stars making brief appearances to promote their favorite film of the week, manage to inject a little pedagogical value into their otherwise promotional skits.

In fact, the variety of programs on the history and the art of film on CCTV-6 has helped to raise film literacy among the domestic audience. The channel broadcasts 350–400 foreign titles each year, a volume unmatched by mainstream media in any other country in the world (*Leaders Magazine* 2008). Indeed, after chats with some of the channel's loyal followers, it is astonishing to discover how sophisticated and knowledgeable some of these viewers are about the world of cinema. It is as if they had attended an introduction to a cinema studies course in the United States. It comes as no surprise that CCTV-6 audience demographics reflect higher than average educational levels and incomes, with white-collar professionals predominant.

Over the years CMC has managed to reduce the time gap between a film's theatrical release and its television screening for both domestic and imported titles. It is not a particularly pressing issue, as theater attendance in China, especially in rural areas, remains vastly under-cultivated. On average, urban Chinese attend a movie theater only once every five years, and the average is significantly lower in rural areas. High ticket prices are a persistent problem, but a boon to CMC. The current financial crisis also benefits the channel, as cinema lovers increasingly resort to watching films at home. The financial crisis also reduces the production output of costly and time-consuming serial television dramas, giving another push to CMC's films.

As Internet use drastically expanded in China (*Renmin wang* 2006), the program "Love Cinema" debuted in August 2006, offering Internet users the chance to vote on a topic of the week for the televised in-depth discussion about filmmaking. Amateur online reviews and film clips, flash animation shorts, and Internet pop quizzes are all incorporated into the television program. CMC has also increased the budgets of a few high-quality productions such as the martial arts serial telefilm *Lu Xiaofeng*. From September 2009, it allowed Internet users to access selected telefilms on its website. CCTV-6 began encouraging digital filmmaking in the early 2000s and switched the majority of its productions to the high-definition format in 2004. It produced 106 digital films in 2006 alone. A companion television program, "Cinema Dream Factory," debuted the same year, encouraging new talents to turn to making digital films (Y. Yue 2007). Currently, digital, 16 mm, and 35 mm films coexist.

As of early 2010, the major program lineup on CMC reflected a mixture of feature films, star gossip shorts, and in-depth film reports, with programs such as "World Film Report," "Global Film Information Express," and "Love Film: Grassroots Film Feast" dominating the channel's prime-time programming. Special programs on Fridays included "Film Personalities" at 12:22 p.m. and "Weekly Film Guide" at 9:53 p.m. The channel's insatiable appetite for programming to fill its time slots has led it to actively cultivate creative talents from the film industry.

Over the years, young and old filmmakers alike have made inroads into producing telefilms and serial dramas. The downturn in Chinese cinema in the mid-1990s steered many private investors away from film production and into the more profitable sector of television drama production. Yet until the late 1990s, big-name film directors still mostly disdained television production. At the time, Fourth Generation director Teng Wenji even lamented his own participation in popular television dramas. When interviewed in Beijing in the summer of 1997, Teng commented that only a handful of directors were able to resist the financial temptation of making profitable television dramas. As late as 2000, in a speech to a group of film school students, the late director Xie Jin praised Zhang Yimou for his refusal to venture into television drama (*World Journal* 2000). Yet the number of creative talents absorbed into the television industry has increased dramatically since the early 2000s. Filmmakers turned television producers/directors have been rewarded handsomely for such migrations. Guo Baochang, one of the founding members of Chinese new wave film, became a household name not for his films but for a serial television drama he directed, *Grand Mansion Gate* (2000). The series debuted on CCTV in 2001 to top ratings and has been rerun on CCTV and other stations a number of times. Its success led to a 32-episode sequel in 2003. Famous Fourth Generation filmmaker Xie Fei ventured into television by adapting the stage play *Sunrise* for a television drama in 2002. The shrinking film market has also pushed renowned Fifth Generation filmmakers such as Wu Ziniu, Li Shaohong, Hu Mei, and Chen Kaige into making television dramas. Their participation has raised the standard for television dramas, bringing the seriousness and aesthetic vision of Fourth and Fifth Generation filmmaking to the smaller screen.

Younger directors, on the other hand, are bringing the MTV aesthetic to television dramas, as many of them have made a living shooting television commercials and music videos. Television dramas and telefilms have been the bread and butter of less established young filmmakers. Guan Hu (b. 1967), the director of *Dirt* (1994), earned back his investment in feature films only after selling his film rights to CMC. To earn a living, he spent five years making television dramas and telefilms exclusively and only recently returned to the big screen to make *Cow* (2009). Besides Guan Hu, the production of telefilms has provided the training ground for other young talents, such as Yang Yazhou (b. 1956), the director of *Empty Mirror* (2002). CMC's discovery and cultivation of new talents is perceived as an important contribution to the film industry.

CMC's dominance in film on television is not without controversy. Changchun Film Studio, Xi'an Film Studio, and Shanghai Film Studio all applied and received permission to launch film channels, only to realize that the television rights to a large number of their own productions had been preempted by CMC's film licensing. CMC has licensed exclusive long-term television broadcasting rights to over 95 percent of all Chinese movies. In 2003 a number of film studios with permission to launch movie channels complained to SARFT about CMC's lock on the country's film output. In an effort to solve the problem, SARFT issued policy guidelines on November 25, 2003, allowing newly established movie channels to broadcast television dramas. To encourage the screening of feature films, the previous policy for airing television dramas on a movie channel (at that time CCTV-6 was the only domestic film channel in China) limited the practice to eight episodes per week, and no more than two episodes per day. In addition, though CCTV-6 has acquired more than three thousand titles from abroad, only 25 percent of prime-time programming can be imported, a rule that applies to all Chinese channels.[4] The new exception for start-up movie channels stipulates that television dramas must not exceed 45 percent of the air time given to movies and must not be aired in prime time. New movie channels are also allowed to carry foreign movies for up to one third of their airtime. Meanwhile, the old limits on television dramas and imports remain unchanged for CCTV-6 (*CMM Intelligence* 2003).[5]

The domestic film market has stabilized since the mid-2000s, with box-office receipts reaching RMB 4.34 billion (US$636 million) in 2008. Also in 2008, together with more imports, there were over four hundred domestic films produced, thus expanding CMC's selection pool (Ni and Tan 2009). CMC continues to grow and invest heavily in acquiring movie rights; in 2008 it installed a new color image restoration system to restore and preserve some of the station's older films and television shows (*Broadcast Engineering* 2006).

The case of CMC suggests that cross-fertilization between Chinese film and television industries has for the most part spurred Chinese cinema by bringing significant new sources of revenue to the film industry. CCTV-6 has a revenue-sharing relationship with the Film Bureau and has invested a portion of its profits back into film production, and has in recent years coproduced one out of every two Chinese movies. CCTV-6 further promotes the culture of film viewing and appreciation, though not in movie theaters. CMC actively promotes film awareness and consumption as the primary organizer and sponsor of almost all of China's major domestic film awards and ceremonies. To celebrate the centenary of Chinese cinema, in 2005 CMC organized a large-scale, multimedia, musical and theatrical stage production of *The Song of Movies*, engaging top artists of Chinese heritage from around the globe. In addition, it has secured the exclusive rights to telecast top international film-award ceremonies, including the Oscars, Cannes, and the Golden Globes. Finally, it promotes film in programs such as "China Film Report" and "World Film Report," which accompany movies with related information. By recruiting heavyweight filmmakers to make drama programs for television, it has also enhanced the quality of dramatic productions on television. And by opening the door to the little-known filmmakers, it also provides a training ground for new film talents to grow and mature. CCTV-6 has been a windfall to many small-scale feature films that would otherwise have a difficult time finding any exhibition avenue. It has thus played the paradoxical role of promoting cinema and generating extra revenue for the film industry while deterring patrons from theater attendance. Given the high ticket prices and comparative inconvenience of going to the movies, many cinema lovers prefer to watch their favorite films at home.

Finally, we should note that for all that CCTV-6 in particular and industrial integration and conglomeration in general have done for expanding the market for Chinese films, and improving the quality of (mainly) narrative television programming and discovering and developing ever-increasing pools of new creative talent, beyond the first and very important concession that shifting the economic foundation of China's cultural industries to a commercial basis entailed, creative autonomy and range continue to be limited by a state determined to mind popular culture as its ideological ward.

Additionally, although China Media Group has been our example of conglomeration, and CCTV-6 our case study under the CMG umbrella, CMG is not the only media titan that China has created. For instance, another noteworthy conglomerate, Shanghai Media Group (SMG) was created in 2001. With "close to $1 billion in revenue" in 2008, and "a profitable array of television units, including a home shopping network, an animation channel, fashion and lifestyle programming, as well as radio, newspaper, magazine and film production units" (Barboza 2009), SMG looks a lot like CMG, and is cast in the same strategic mold (more discussion below).

From Cross-Fertilization to Consolidation: Media Policy as Geostrategy

Vastly commercialized, consolidated, and expanded over three decades of reform, China's film and television industries are no longer exclusively controlled "mouth-pieces." They are instead purveyors of ideologically inoffensive, profitable entertainment, treating audiences to a more loosely guided "main melody" rather than blunt-force propaganda. This could and often has been described as an organic process, an unavoidable concession to the broader reform process that has powered rapid economic development, an increasingly complex society, and China's rising prominence in the world. At the same time, though, the party-state is, if anything, more earnest than ever about managing culture. It has continued to maintain its primacy as supreme cultural curator even as it overhauls the cultural economy and the mechanism of its management. In this context, the most frequently asked question about contemporary Chinese popular culture, especially in combination with the rise of the Internet and social media, is whether it is, on balance, more a progressive force for enhancing civic activity and advancing political reform, or a hegemonic force for inculcating market logic and reinforcing the Party's authority. That is an important question, but because this chapter is primarily a record of recent policy moves designed to create synergistic, globally competitive media conglomerates, we want to speak briefly here to a subject that has not yet achieved "FAQ" (frequently asked question) status: the growing geostrategic or international public relations aspect of China's evolving cultural policy.

The party-state in China has been at least as concerned as other nation-states with defending and developing domestic cultural production, with media industries being the leading producers of the mainstream culture. The decision to commercialize and expand its media industries, to rethink and reregulate them precisely as cultural industries, was partly the evolutionary adaptation suggested above and partly a defensive move:

> The term "cultural industries" (*wenhua chanye*) was first used in national cultural policy debates during the 1990s but it was not formally used until 2001, whereupon it gained impetus due to intellectual paranoia about cultural globalization. "National cultural security" (*wenhua anquan*) was code for a fear that WTO accession would lead to a crisis in Chinese culture, and that allowing economic control of sensitive media would constitute a Trojan horse. (Keane 2009)

The Trojan horse metaphor was used for all the threats that Western culture and cultural industries might possibly pose, but within that cautionary metaphor was the glint of a revelation. By the early 2000s China's leaders were at least beginning to think not just about how to defend and maintain control over their own media, but also about building China's own "horse," namely, cultivating its cultural industries to enhance its international stature via popular culture.

This is partly a matter of pride. In the late 1990s the Chinese film industry was in the doldrums, when several Hollywood blockbusters screened in the country each year dominated the domestic box office. In 1998, when James Cameron's *Titanic* crashed onto the scene with new box-office records nearly everywhere in the world, including China, then President and Party leader Jiang Zemin was so impressed with both the film's narrative content (in which he discovered a positive socialist message) and its paradigmatic Hollywood blockbuster production pedigree, that he advised Politburo members to see the film in order "to better understand our opposition, the better to enable us to succeed" (Eckholm 1998). Jiang's extended comments enjoined the Chinese film industry to develop comparable special effects technologies and produce its own big-budget, high-tech films to compete with Hollywood on its own terms. From the defensive posture that China had shared with countries around the world in response to the threat of US-led cultural homogenization, China's leaders were shifting to a more assertive tack.

At the same time, intellectuals and party leaders were thinking intensely about how to put a diplomatic face on China's rise in the world, a discussion that would eventually extend even to agonizing over which term to use before the international community: "peaceful rise" or "peaceful development" (Lampton 2008: 32–3; Leonard 2008: 88–93). This thinking about China's rise and how to represent it was part of a broader strategic discussion about the sources of nations' power in the globalized, post-cold war era, about China's own strengths and weaknesses, and about best strategies for managing China's ascent to Great Power status. The consensus was that "soft power," or "the attractiveness of your culture and ideas, your legitimacy in the eyes of others, and your ability to set the rules in international organizations," is a critical component of "comprehensive national power" in the contemporary era (Leonard 2008: 94).

The term "soft power" is from American political scientist Joseph Nye, who used it first in the early 1990s. The concept is not especially new or unique, deriving more or less from the same notion that earlier ideas about "cultural imperialism" referred to, and the same understanding of the popular mind as a critical staging ground of contemporary power struggles. In this version, though, it is a positive strategic element of national "ideational power" (Lampton 2008), and popular culture led by the screen media is just one aspect of it.

In the first decade of the new century, China has come to regard soft power as key to its national ambitions, and begun cultivating it in a number ways. Examples include the following:

> [The] Education Ministry will set up 100 "Confucius Institutes" to teach Chinese and promote Chinese culture.... China's international TV station [CCTV-9] ... is designed to grow into a global news station to rival CNN. Beijing has expanded and professionalized the party-controlled news wire Xinhua in the hope that it will be taken as seriously as Reuters or AP. It plans to quadruple the number of foreigners learning Chinese ... by 2010. It has opened its universities to foreign students. (Leonard 2008: 94)

While popular culture *per se* is only one element of China's soft-power strategy, it is one that President Hu Jintao confirmed as critical in a 2007 report to the Seventeenth National Congress of the Communist Party of China: "Culture has become a more and more important source of inspiration for national cohesion and creativity and a more and more significant factor in the competition of national comprehensive power (*zonghe guoli*)" (quoted in Zhang Weihong 2009). "The adoption of the term 'soft power' in Hu's report," Zhang (2009) argues, "reflected a broader and deeper trend in placing increasing strategic importance on culture in China."

"Strategic importance" seems exactly right. From Jiang Zemin's *Titanic*-inspired admonitions forward, the party-state appears to have realized that popular culture can be a positive strategic resource for China, reimagining the force of ideas behind "cultural imperialism" as something that China can use itself, and thinking about culture not as just an internal concern but also as a tool that might be useful overseas. As China emerges as a Great Power it is thinking less in terms of defending culture but more in terms of competing with Hollywood and Western media conglomerates on their terms, and for broader purposes than winning at the box office.

In this context, it is evident that all the recent state-directed consolidation and conglomeration of China's media industries is in some degree a new departure. If the commercialization of culture was primarily an evolutionary accommodation and the deployment of a new, subtler regime of cultural control, the latest moves are an extension of that process with an added, outward-looking element. No longer concerned just about managing culture at home, China is pursuing national strategic opportunities afforded by large-scale, commercial cultural industries, lately drafting popular culture into the service of a wider effort to develop and utilize soft power as an element, alongside military and economic power, of "comprehensive national power" (Lampton 2008).

At this point it is fair to say that China's Reform era has enjoyed an exceptional run of success, good fortune, and domestic and international good will along the way to the country's spectacular emergence as a new (or renewed) Great Power. It has, moreover, impressed some parts of the world, and caused the rest mainly to give it a pass, with its hybrid development strategy pairing liberal markets with authoritarian governance. Success and acceptance have come in such measure that the current administration has begun to actively cultivate and sell its development model as, in effect, a Brand China alternative to the classical Western model of liberal democracy, and the undeniable appeal of this formula is the most convincing demonstration of Chinese ideational or soft power to date.

At the same time, and in the same way, the state has commercialized China's media without freeing them from the party's strict ideological oversight, and embarked on a campaign to create a handful of Brand China global media titans to compete with the likes of Hollywood and CNN, to prove that, in effect, "anything you can do I can do better." And again, Chinese film and television have enjoyed some global success, though the extent of that success may be mostly invisible to non-Chinese-speaking audiences. The largest part of China's outward media strategy so far has been concerned with "interpellating" or promoting positive association with the PRC among Chinese audiences overseas, and as Lampton (2008: 162) points out, "in the satellite, cable television, and the Internet era," non-Chinese-speaking "populations can be unaware of developments in the parallel universe of Chinese language diffusing all around them." The current centerpiece of the outreach effort is The Great Wall Satellite TV Platform launched in 2005 by the China International TV Corporation (CITVC), a subsidiary of CCTV. Great Wall delivers a suite of nineteen Mandarin language channels, including to CCTV-6 via satellite to Vietnam, Thailand, South Korea, Hong Kong, Macau, and Taiwan, as well to the Dish Network and via the Internet in the United States, and to Canada's leading cable provider (Rogers Cable). Meanwhile, in a development that global audiences do recognize, Chinese film has parried the martial arts genre into prominence and generated a handful of bright avatars of Chinese popular culture like director Zhang Yimou and actors Gong Li and Zhang Ziyi.

Certainly, it makes sense for China to cultivate soft power, perhaps particularly the variety that it might be afforded if it could produce genuinely competitive popular culture on the scale that it has in mind with the creation of media titans like the China Film Group. And perhaps particularly now, because there are signs that China's honeymoon as an emergent Great Power, and especially as a foil to American hubris under the Bush administration, may be coming to an end. Expectations of Chinese leadership at the Copenhagen Climate Change Conference in December 2009 were disappointed as China took a good deal of the blame for the failure to produce a solid agreement. This and other recent demonstrations of Chinese insensitivity to global popular opinion reveal a party-state still prone to missteps that cause the Western press to raise "the question of whether China's political system is compatible with the international respect it craves" (Dyer 2010).

Chinese popular culture is surely the avatar of a different, softer China, but can it be made popular enough to "improve the nation's image overseas" (Barboza 2009)? Quoted in the *New York Times* after talking with "state broadcasting executives," Jim Laurie noted that "there appears to be a feeling at the highest levels of government that they need a media machine commensurate to the rising status and power of China" (Barboza 2009). Creative cross-fertilization notwithstanding, the film and television industry reforms described here have focused just on the machinery of cultural production, on economies of efficiency and scale, without changing the basic terms of the creative process. Joining forces has been a boon to film and television alike, and a whole new category of productions, telefilm, seems to have discovered a niche treating topical subjects of local immediacy, but all must still hew to the main melody. It remains to be seen whether cultural industries as ideologically fettered as China's will be able to rise to a level of global prominence anywhere near the country's economic and political prominence. Meanwhile, *Titanic* director James Cameron's film *Avatar* opened on January 4, 2010 in China, ready to set a new box-office record.

Acknowledgments

The authors thank Pei Yali of Shanxi Normal University for her insights on how Chinese filmmakers crossed over to making television programs and Yuqian Yan of the University of Chicago for research assistance in this project.

Notes

1   According to Zhao Pei (1996), of the annual production not purchased by the Movie Channel, 25 percent were sold to the army, as the army maintains its own film distribution network, so that soldiers end up watching movies on the big screen that are unavailable to civilian audiences; 65 percent were sold as audiovisual media because rights for DVDs and other media can be sold to domestic and foreign distributors; 5 percent were shown in second-tier theaters; and 15 percent were shelved until further notice as producers unwilling to throw away their chances at the big screen may opt to

forgo other distribution avenues and sit on their films until another opportunity arises. For example, *Jasmine Women* (Hou Yong, 2004), which stars Zhang Ziyi, waited for release after its completion in 2003. See http://fzwb.ynet.com/article.jsp?oid=8610694.

2   As Coonan (2009) elaborates, many companies are now busy building multiplexes in China, including US niche player Imax, which expects to have forty screens in China by 2012. The first three screens used Imax's lower-cost MPX theater technology, with the remaining seven employing its new digital projection technology, while all screens rolled out after 2009 used digital tech. Big cities such as Shanghai, Beijing, Chongqing, and Guangzhou have already seen the arrival of plush multiplexes, but the second-tier market is still largely untapped. Warner Bros. dipped its toe in this market but withdrew after legislative changes made it impossible for them to operate in China. Those same rule changes benefited local companies, and China Film Group is keen to exploit the possibilities that an expansion of the exhibition network has to offer.

3   Around 92 percent of metropolitan areas have access to CCTV-6.

4   Due to these restrictions, over the years CCTV-6 has rarely broadcast television dramas.

5   This article suggests that a better solution would have simply been to allow the new movie channels to buy, swap, and/or deal among themselves or other film producers and to leave it to the market to decide winners and losers.

24

Chinese Cinema and Technology

Gary G. Xu

This chapter discusses film technology in the context of Chinese cinema, a topic rarely studied by Chinese film scholars in a systematic fashion. By film technology, I refer to the various technological apparatuses – machines, equipment, and ways of utilizing these machines and equipment – involved in the processes of filmmaking and film exhibition. Different technologies existed in different stages of cinema's development: the early cinema, the sound film, the color film, the 3-D film, and so on. In order to make this enormous topic manageable, I categorize film technology in these rather large, sometimes overlapping, and potentially unstable categories: studios, cameras, camera supports and camera movements, lenses, lighting, editing, trick effects, film stock and processing, sound (or the lack thereof), color, and projectors.

There are several potential pitfalls in discussing the relationship between technology and Chinese cinema. First, since cinema was exported to China and China never occupied a central position in the technological advancement of cinema, there seems to be an inevitable time lag between Western – French, British, American, Italian, and, to a certain extent, Russian – cinema and Chinese cinema. Technologically, China always seems to play catch-up, in cinema and in all the other science-related areas of modern life. Although there is no solid or direct evidence suggesting a link between the technological lag and the lack of interest in studying technology in Chinese cinema, it is not hard to imagine that this is indeed the case. What is there to study if the foundation of Chinese cinema is built on technological imitation? This attitude needs to be revised if we do not hold an evolutionary view regarding cinema. We must understand that silent films are not necessarily inferior to sound films, or black-and-white films to color films. One of the consequences of Hollywoodization is the indoctrination of the belief in parallel development between cinema and technology: the more sophisticated the

A Companion to Chinese Cinema, First Edition. Edited by Yingjin Zhang.
© 2012 Blackwell Publishing Ltd. Published 2012 by Blackwell Publishing Ltd.

technology, the better the film. Due to this belief, there has been an incessant pursuit of technological improvement for bigger, wider, faster, clearer, and glossier pictures while sacrificing characterization, narrative development, and true cinematic innovation in challenging conventional visual expressions (Kehr 2009). The most recent example is *Avatar* (James Cameron, 2009), which, despite its weak and porous plot, has been hailed as a "game changer" because of the technological advancement it made (Acland 2010). Due to global Hollywoodization and China's quest for a Westernized technological modernity, Chinese cinematic technology has never garnered serious attention from film scholars. Film professionals and trade publications are exceptions.

Second, while inherent evolutionism is at work in much of the discussion about Chinese cinematic technology, an evolutionism that reduces film scholarship to apologies for cinematic primitivism, there is also a reverse mentality that attributes Chinese cinematic innovations to technological deficiencies. The logic goes like this: certain technological disadvantages have given Chinese cinema – and, by extension, other "technologically backward" national cinemas – an interesting appeal and can even be responsible for certain cinematic innovations. Hou Hsiao-hsien's trademark long-take technique, for instance, has been explained as an inadvertent result of the crudeness of the early Taiwan film industry: "the most important factor was film stock, which became a sort of celluloid gold, something so precious that every effort was made to use as little of it as possible.... Any stylistic flourish was more or less a desperate attempt to hide the lack of production values and, most of all, the lack of film stock. Hou himself would be steeped in these practices for many years" (Udden 2003: 127). There is no denying that the make-do spirit could be responsible for many of the unique features of less developed film industries and for Hou Hsiao-hsien's art in particular. But an obvious question should be addressed: Why Hou? Many Taiwan directors worked under the same technological constraints, but only Hou stood out. In fact, many factors besides the lack of film stock also contributed to Hou's long-take aesthetics: Ozu's influence, the French connection, the historical development of the long-take technique in Chinese cinema, Zhu Tianwen's contribution as his primary screenwriter. One can even argue that, among all these factors, the film stock issue is only a minor one.

Both attitudes – criticizing Chinese cinema for its technological backwardness and praising it for its working around the technological constraints – are suspiciously like technological determinism. While film technology is fundamental to filmmaking, it is by no means the deciding factor. Expanding issues of technology to the material condition of human society, for instance, Gilles Deleuze (1989: 77) points to the real cinematic constraint – money:

> [W]hat defines industrial art is not mechanical reproduction but the internalized relation with money. The only rejoinder to the harsh law of cinema – a minute of image which costs a day of collective work – is Fellini's: "When there is no more money left, the film will be finished."... This is the old curse which undermines the

cinema: time is money.... In short, the cinema confronts its most internal presupposition, money, and the movement-image makes way for the time-image in one and the same operation. What the film within the film expresses is this infernal circuit between the image and money, this inflation which time puts into the exchange, this "overwhelming rise." The film is movement, but the film within the film is money, is time.

Elsewhere, I have built on Deleuze's observations and argued that Hou Hsiao-hsien's films contain a profound self-reflection upon cinema's internalized relation with money (G. Xu 2007: 111–32). The technological aspects of his films, such as camera movement and the long take, are manifestations of this self-reflection, not the other way around.

Using Hou Hsiao-hsien as a brief example, I want to hammer home this point: technology indeed shapes cinema, but it does not fully control cinema, nor does it determine cinematic innovations based on its own advancement or constraints. In discussing the relationship between Chinese cinema and technology, we must keep in mind that the awareness of the technological lag – not the lag itself – just might be one of the most important factors contributing to the uniqueness of Chinese cinema. Chinese filmmakers have never stopped being fascinated with cinematic apparatuses; it is their constant awareness of film technology that made Chinese cinema a continuing "cinema of attraction" – to paraphrase Tom Gunning (1986), who argues that the early cinema's technological appeal to spectators had long given way to the dominance of Hollywood's narrative cinema.

In what follows, I delineate important milestones of film technology in each phase of Chinese cinema. In order not to repeat the historical development of technology, I also provide brief technological readings of representative films of each period. These readings support my argument about Chinese cinema as a continuous cinema of attraction in terms of Chinese filmmakers' internationalization of their awareness of technological challenges.

Early Cinema and *Laborer's Love*

By "early Chinese cinema" I refer to the period between 1896 and 1931, corresponding to Cheng Jihua's periodization in his history of Chinese cinema (Cheng, Li, and Xing 1963). This period saw cinema's introduction into China and the development of a Chinese film industry before the full bloom of talkies.

Projection

China had film exhibitions several years before the first Chinese film was made. In 1896, less than a year after the birth of cinema in Paris, *Western Moving Tricks* (*xiyang yingxi*) was screened in Shanghai's Xu Garden by Western businessmen. No details were recorded about the kind of machine used for the projection (Cheng, Li, and Xing 1963: 8). The projectors must have been the same earliest prototypes used in Europe and America: converted cameras, mostly descending from the Edison Kinetograph, with added lamp-house and condenser lens.

The initial film exhibitions, first in Shanghai and then in Beijing, all in makeshift theaters, were apparently made possible by traveling Western merchants and some Chinese returning from overseas. China had its first permanent movie theater, Shanghai Hongkou Theater, with 250 seats, in 1908, established by a Spanish merchant. In 1914, Shanghai Victorian Theater was the first to use Edison Kinetophone disc recordings to time sound with projected images. In 1929, Shanghai Olympic Theater installed China's first sound-on-film projector, the RCA Photophone system (SDW 1999). In 1930, Shanghai Huawei Trading Company manufactured China's first film sound playback system, named Si Da Tong (Far-reaching sounds). Because it was far cheaper than the imported systems, it was widely adopted in Chinese movie theaters.

Camera

The early cinematography in Chinese cinema was not much different from still photography. The imported camera was always set at the frontal position and the actors performed as if they were on a theater stage. The immobile camera kept rolling until the 200-feet film reel came to the end. The camera had only one 50 mm lens and could only be slightly tilted up or down; it could not ascend or descend, nor could it move from side to side. Most interestingly, it did not have a motor: reeling was achieved entirely through the cameramen's arm movement. For shooting the 16-frame-per-second early films, the Shanghai cameramen had to undertake rigorous training before they could actually begin to film. The several months of training entailed holding a camera and cranking at a steady speed. Shanghai film industry veterans used the term "whipping up ice-cream" to joke about the technique (SDW 1999: 126). Still, no matter how steady the cameraman, hand-reeling could never achieve perfect mechanical precision. This is why all the extant early films – Chinese or Western – suffer from flickering pictures partly due to the uneven camera speed.

Lighting

In 1913 the first Chinese fiction short, *The Difficult Couple* (Zhang Shichuan, Zheng Zhengqiu), was shot in the open-air studio of Asian Cinema Company on Hong Kong Road in Shanghai. The lighting source was natural sunlight. Tianyi Film Studio, founded in 1925, did not have a studio space of its own. It would shoot films on a piece of lawn, on which a temporary wooden floor was installed. To avoid the shadows cast by sunlight, a piece of white cloth was placed at the top of the three space-enclosing wooden boards, so the light was diffused and soft. This was similar to what Georges Méliès (1861–1938) had begun to use from 1899: he suspended thin cotton sheets over the stage, as can be seen in his *L'Affaire Dreyfus* (1899) (Salt 1992: 40).

Chinese filmmakers quickly realized the limits of natural lighting. In 1921, when Shanghai Yingxi Company began to shoot *Sea Oath*, the director and cinematographer Dan Duyu (1897–1972) was not happy with the lack of image crispness due to the direct sunlight. One day, at a screening of a Western film, he noticed there were flickering stars in the characters' eyes. It took him a while to realize that the stars were the result of light reflection. This inspired him to paste tinfoil on a piece of wooden board to reflect sunlight; as a result, his images became much better defined than those by directors of the same period.

China's first indoor studio was set up in Shanghai in 1918. Located on the top flour – the fourth flour – of the Commercial Press's headquarters on Baoshan Road, the studio was China's first to use an all-glass roof. Mercury vapor lamps began to be adopted so that shooting could take place during nighttime. In 1921 China's first feature-length fiction film, *Yan Ruisheng* (Liao Enshou), which was ten reels long, was shot in this glass-top studio, and so was another early feature, *The Vampires* (Liao Enshou, 1921), which was fourteen reels long.

Cinematography and editing

Although limited by early cameras' immobility, Chinese filmmakers began to experiment with camera movement, varied length of shots, trick effects, and special effects editing at a very early time. In 1913 the fifth short film produced by Asia Film Company, *An Anxious Night* (Zhang Shichuan), had already made use of close-ups. A comedy, the film focuses on the funny facial expressions caused by a small insect as it crawls on the heads and faces of a sleeping couple. According to one source (X. Qin 2009: 68–70), close-ups were widely used in early Chinese films, especially on four particular objects: clocks, characters writing, sound sources, and photographs. These close-ups function to make up for the lack of sound and to move the narrative forward.

The increasingly sophisticated cinematography and the audiences' amazement with special effects spurred the boom of martial arts films between 1925 and 1931. *Romance of the Western Chamber* (Hou Yao, 1927) shows how mixed-length shots make martial arts fighting scenes exciting: in medium shots, two warriors fight first on horseback and then on foot; their fighting scenes are intercut with overhead shots of two groups battling each other; double exposures are used to increase the number of combatants; close-ups of weapons and facial expressions are intercut with the fighting. Impressive cinematographic maneuvers were reportedly what made *The Burning of Red Lotus Temple* (Zhang Shichuan, 1928) a great sensation.

Although the film is no longer extant, records show that it contained numerous special effects: light emitting from the tips of swords, people flying in the sky and spitting out swords, lightning coming out of palms, and so on. In addition, a monk would shrink a group of fighters, catch them, and put them in his sleeves before releasing them one by one. The highest-grossing film of this period, *The Burning of Red Lotus Temple* inspired numerous imitations. By 1931, 227 martial arts films had been produced (L. Jia 2005b: 8).

The editing techniques in this period were quite simple. Since the films were mostly shot by immobile cameras and on entire reels, the early editing only needed to connect the reels together or to insert dialogue stills into the reel wherever the characters open their mouths and get ready to speak. Pioneers such as Zhang Shichuan and Zheng Zhengqiu edited their own films. Zhang also hired his sister Zhang Ying to help him edit *The Difficult Couple* and thus made her China's first professional film editor. They used the crudest editing machines: a ruler and a 32-cog gear, operated entirely by the editor's hands.

Laborer's Love: Fascination with Early Film Technology

As the earliest extant Chinese film, *Laborer's Love* (1922) has been studied extensively by film scholars. Zhang Zhen (1999: 38) argues that the film's "stylistic features tend to oscillate between those of a 'cinema of attractions' and a 'cinema of narrative integration'." All the details in the film indeed contribute to the dramatic tension, hence the "narrative integration." The 22-minute short's rather crude narrative, however, is not what makes it a successful comedy. The slapstick physical comedy elements, which would rarely occur again in Chinese cinema, came from the film's utilization of existing technologies (Rao 2006: 33–4).

At first glance, there seems to be nothing special in the film's cinematography. The camera was obviously set at the frontal position, and the shots are mostly medium ones. There are, however, interesting close-ups at crucial moments: nine out of the film's 130 shots are close-ups. Some are on the old doctor's reading glasses in order to generate comical confusion over the field of vision; some are on the clock, to tell time and to separate night from day. The film's reliance on natural sunlight makes it impossible to tell night from day if not for these clock close-ups. Superimpositions are used when the carpenter-turned-fruit-seller yearns for the doctor's lovely daughter: her face appears at the top of the screen, superimposed with the scene of his thinking of her. The most important technological aspect is the editing that allows a character to throw a piece of fruit in one shot and another character to catch the fruit in the next shot. The trajectories of the flying object are not always well calibrated: in one shot a character throws the object toward the ground, but it is caught high in the air in the following shot. Still, the throw-and-catch was the main draw of the film. This is why the film was originally titled

Zhiguo yuan (Marriage made possible through throwing and catching fruit). The film relies on editing and variable speed to satisfy the audience's curiosity about the new medium.

Many factors have contributed to China's lack of physical comedy after the initial success of *Laborer's Love*. Ideologically, Zheng Zhengqiu and Zhang Shichuan were quickly placed in the same category with the Mandarin Ducks and Butterflies Saturday School of urban entertainment that includes popular fiction, newspapers, and cinema. "Entertainment for entertainment's or profitability's sake" was dismissed by left-leaning cultural critics (Cheng, Li, and Xing 1963: 54–9). But perhaps more importantly, the fascination with movements in cinema and the technology that made those movements possible was what accounted for the boom in physical comedy in early world cinema. Chaplin and early Mickey Mouse cartoons were all products of this type of fascination. Raw, sudden, and jerky physical movements, unexpected obstacles in the process of those movements, movement transitions impossible in real life made possible by film editing – these were what made Chaplin, Mickey Mouse, and *Laborer's Love*'s fruit-seller funny. With the audience's increasing familiarity with film technologies, the unexpectedness of such movements diminished, and the enthusiasm for such comedy naturally abated.

The Sound Film and *Street Angel*

This period runs between 1931 and 1937, a period that saw silent films replaced by talkies. Film historians tend to term this period Chinese cinema's first golden age, mainly based on the social advocacy themes fully developed by left-leaning film-makers. While social realism was indeed important to the draw of the cinema, we cannot overlook the importance of sound technologies for the boom in cinema during this period. In fact, I would argue that attention to film technologies during this period prevented the films from becoming overtly didactic. What makes this period "golden" is not so much the dominance of leftist ideology as the exploration of visual/audio technologies.

The milestones of technological developments during this period include the following:

1   In 1931 the first disc-recorded sound film, *Sing-Song Girl Red Peony* (Zhang Shichuan), became China's first sound film. This was the result of a collaboration between Mingxing Studio's image production and the sound technology of French company Pathé Frères. For this sound-film experiment, Mingxing threw in substantial investment: 120,000 Chinese dollars and a six-month-long production. The result did not live up to Mingxing's expectations, but the studio was even more determined to complete the switch from silent films to talkies (M. Lü 2009: 42).

2   In 1931, seven months after the premiere of *Sing-Song Girl Red Peony*, Tianyi
     Studio screened its film *Spring on Stage* (Li Pingqian). For some, this was China's
     first sound-on-film talkie, but others argue that the first talkie was *Clear Sky
     After Storm*, a film made by Guangzhou's Great China Studio and Jinan Studio,
     which rented Japanese equipment and completed postproduction in Japan.
     The film was premiered in Shanghai's Hongkou Theater in June 1931, earlier
     than the screening of *Spring on Stage* (M. Lü 2009: 42).

3   Also in 1931, Mingxing Studio sent its star screenwriter Hong Shen to the
     United States to purchase an entire set of equipment, including cameras and
     machines for recording, lighting, editing, projecting, and film printing. Hong
     Shen came back with not only the machines but also four American techni-
     cians, who trained almost an entire generation of technical support personnel
     in Shanghai.

4   In 1932 China-West Film Equipment Company was founded in Shanghai. This
     was China's first enterprise specializing in film technology. This company
     could not only take care of regular maintenance of imported film equipment,
     but also made cameras and printing and recording machines.

5   In 1933 Situ Yimin, Gong Ruike, and Ma Dejian invented Sanyou (Three
     Friends), China's first film recorder using photoelectric cells to record and
     reproduce sound directly on film. Cai Chusheng's classic *Song of the Fishermen*
     (1934) was among the earliest films to use this invention: the eponymous
     theme song was recorded on the film by the new machine. *Plunder of Peach
     and Plum* (Yuan Muzhi, 1934) was entirely recorded by the Sanyou machine.
     The three inventors had their names prominently displayed in the film's open-
     ing credit. Because of the seamless integration of image with sound, *Plunder
     of Peach and Plum* has been generally considered China's first complete
     talkie.

6   In 1935 Cheng Chonglan founded Venus Film Equipment Company, specializ-
     ing in lighting equipment. Later, Cheng created China's first 35 mm movie
     camera, which was widely used by Chinese studios well into the 1950s.

7   In 1937 Zengtai Film Equipment Factory was founded in Shanghai. It special-
     ized in projector manufacturing (Hua et al. 2005).

From these milestones we can tell that Chinese filmmakers in this period were no
longer satisfied with using imported technology. Nationalism was probably not
the reason for their discontent; cost was the main factor. By using Chinese
equipment, costs were significantly reduced and profit margins increased. Despite
the cost reduction, however, the transition to sound required much greater capital
than before. As a result, Chinese film studios were quickly consolidating: there
were more than a hundred studios in 1926; the number was reduced to twenty in
1931; the "big three" – Mingxing, Tianyi, and Lianhua – dominated film production
(G. Xia 2007: 35). Shanghai further solidified its position as the center of Chinese
cinema by not only boasting almost all of China's important film studios but also

Figure 24.1 Two sisters alarmed by a sound in *Street Angel* (dir. Yuan Muzhi, Mingxing Film, 1937), with Zhou Xuan on the right.

monopolizing the production of China's film equipment. Chinese films in this period reached a peak in *Street Angel* (Yuan Muzhi, 1937) (see Figure 24.1).

Street Angel: Allegory of sound film technology

Prior to *Street Angel*, Yuan Muzhi had already achieved notable success in sound film technology with *Plunder of Peach and Plum*. His fascination with the new technology found the perfect outlet in Mingxing's ambitious production of *Street Angel*. No other film studios were more active in pursuing sound film technology than Mingxing, which purchased an entire set of equipment from the United States in 1931 and had its own technicians well trained in operating these machines. Using this equipment and a highly skilled crew, Yuan Muzhi was able to make one of the best films not only in China but also in the world. The reason that *Street Angel* became a timeless masterpiece has to do with Yuan's use of all available film technologies at hand; more importantly, the film comprises a self-reflection rarely seen in early world cinema. The film reflects upon its own use of sound film technology and at the same time pays tribute to the disappearing age of silent films.

Yuan's skillful integration of sound in *Street Angel* is first of all manifested in the film's cinematography: almost every cut, or every shot transition, is sound-triggered.

To use a Chinese phrase, the cinematography in this film can be best described as *wensheng er dong* – to move only upon hearing a sound. *Street Angel* can thus be very well described as sound-oriented: every sound in the film has a purpose, and attention is drawn as much to the narrative development as to the sounds.

The film begins with Xiao Chen playing trumpet in a wedding procession. This is followed by whistling, drumming, quarreling, laughing, singing, a baby crying, and glass breaking, among many other sounds of everyday life. These sounds do not simply increase the sense of verity in showing everyday life; they have structural or cinematographic functions. Take, for instance, a bird's chirping. Xiao Hong hangs out the bird cage as a way to communicate with her lover Xiao Chen, who lives across a narrow alley from her. The bird chirps, and the medium shot switches to a close-up in which Xiao Chen's head turns toward her. The same goes for the trumpet playing. The trumpet is being blown by Xiao Chen in a close-up, and the shot switches to several consecutive medium shots featuring Xiao Chen's friends, who line up behind him in a fake yet happy marching band. The smooth transition enabled by the sounds is impressive. And the sounds help make vivid the lives in the *nongtang* (alleys), which are known for their cramped conditions, the difficulty of their residents in making a living, the camaraderie among the poorest, and the conflicts between landlords and tenants. The same set of motifs associated with *nongtang* was reenacted over and over again in the ensuing films, especially those made in Hong Kong, such as the "72 tenants" film series (G. Xu 2007: 91–2).

The most impressive sound arrangement in relation to the cinematography is the singing of the theme songs: "Four Seasons" (*Siji ge*) and "At the Edge of the World" (*Tianya ge*). Both songs are rewritten folk songs from Southern China (C. Li 2006). The scene of Xiao Hong singing the first song is juxtaposed with newsreels about Japan's invasion of Northeast China and Chinese refugees' evacuation from their hometown, hinting that the suffering of Xiao Hong and her sister Xiao Yun is rooted in the nation's war trauma. The message of the leftists' resistance mobilization is unmistakable. However, in an uncanny way, this technique of sound–picture juxtaposition and contrast foretells what was to come in modern visual/audio technology: MTV technique. What is interesting about MTV technique is that what is being sung does not need to be closely related to what is being shown; the references of the song and of the background film montage can be entirely different. There is arbitrariness in combining the picture with the sound, but the arbitrariness fits with how the human sensory system functions as a whole: what you see and what you hear make combined sense; what you see is often tricked by what you hear and vice versa. The MTV arbitrariness thus appears natural, so much so that all kinds of consumerist/political messages can be placed in the visual without being noticed by those who enjoy the song. Xiao Hong's singing of "Four Seasons," at the beginning stage of sound/visual manipulations, draws attention to the sheer novelty of such practice.

As if the singing of the first song is not enough for showing the potential of combined manipulation of sound and visuals, the second song, "At the Edge of the World," is sung twice on different occasions in the film. The background montages differ on each occasion and the mood shifts accordingly. It is truly impressive how skillful the director was in controlling the dialogue between sound and film.

Even more impressive is Yuan Muzhi's vivid awareness of the fading away of the silent film, so much so that he deliberately created scenes to bid farewell to the silent era. In these scenes we see Xiao Chen and his friends perform through the window for Xiao Hong across the alley. The window, of course, serves as the movie screen: the window curtains need to be drawn in order for the "projection" to start. The performance is undertaken in silence, which makes it a silent film sequence. Nostalgia for the disappearing silent film is palpable.

1940s Cinema, Fei Mu, and *Spring in a Small Town*

The rise of talkies in China coincided with Shanghai's "orphan island" period when it developed a spectacular metropolitan culture full of contradictions and ideological struggles (L. Lee 1999). Ideologically, Chinese cinema centered in Shanghai was the site for battles between the leftists, the Nationalist Party's (KMT) New Life propaganda, and the urban entertainers preoccupied with film's commercial and artistic values. Technologically, the film industry became more mature and better organized than before; almost all technological advances in world cinema had found their way into Shanghai, while Chinese filmmakers made their own contributions to film technology. The milestones during this period (1937–49) include the following:

1 In 1938 Yuan Muzhi and his colleague Wu Yinxian (1900–94) went to Yan'an to join the Communist army, bringing filmmaking equipment with them. This marked the beginning of Communist filmmaking, although it was limited to documentaries.
2 In 1942 China-West Film Equipment Company manufactured China's first standard 35 mm film projector.
3 In 1945 the Chinese Communist Party founded the Northeast Film Studio, which took over part of the filmmaking equipment from Manchuria Film Studio (Man'e), Japan's colonial propaganda machine in Manchuria. Man'e's filmmakers who were Chinese mostly went to Shanghai and Hong Kong, becoming instrumental to the postwar expansion of the Shanghai film industry and helping build the foundations of Hong Kong's film industry. Some equipment, however, was seized by the Communists and enabled them to found Xingshan Film Production Base, which was soon reorganized as Northeast Film Studio.

4   In 1947 Shanghai's Venus Film Equipment Company manufactured China's first 35 mm film camera, which was an imitation of the Mitchell NC ("newsreel") camera. Just as the Mitchell NC was the industry standard for Hollywood during much of the twentieth century, the Venus camera was the Chinese film industry's workhorse for the majority of the twentieth century. The first film shot by the Venus camera was *The Spring River Flows East* (Cai Chusheng, Zheng Junli, 1947), one of the best Chinese films of all time.

5   In 1947 Shanghai Wenhua Film Studio produced *Phony Phoenix* (Huang Zuolin, 1947). Huang, a graduate of Cambridge University, translated the dialogue into English so that the film could be dubbed into English and distributed in the United States. This was the first time a Chinese film was dubbed into English.

6   In 1948 Fei Mu directed China's first color film, *Remorse of Death*. Like China's very first film, *Dingjun Mountain* (1905), this first color film was the result of joining cinema with Peking opera. It was made in an attempt to reproduce the splendor of the performance of Mei Lanfang, who was at the peak of his acting career and his fame as a patriotic artist. Wu Xingzai (1904–79), the founder of Huayi Film Studio, reasoned that the color film would be the ideal medium for reproducing Mei's colorful dresses, stage lights, and face painting. He hired Fei Mu to direct the film. The camera was a 1930 Cine Ansco 16 mm. The film was sent to the United States to be printed into 35 mm color. However, the box office in Shanghai was disappointing, mainly because the blue hue was too strong and the film did not come close to reproducing Mei Lanfang's stage performance (Di and Liu 2007: 56).

7   In 1949 the chemistry lab at Northeast Film Studio successfully produced its own emulsion coating, making it possible for China to produce film stock and reduce its reliance on expensive imported film stock (Hua et al. 2005: 39).

There were many famous filmmakers during this period, but Fei Mu emerged as China's finest director. Between 1933, when he made his first feature film *Night in the City*, and 1948, when he made his seventeenth and last, *Spring in a Small Town* (see Figure 24.2), Fei Mu gave a distinctive identity to the Chinese cinema in the 1930s and 1940s in terms of film language, film style, cinematography, and technological innovation. What sets him apart from the majority of the Chinese directors of his time is his clear awareness of the constraints and potential of film technology and his attempt to work this awareness into his unique cinematic aesthetics.

Fei Mu's technological awareness is evident in his writings and speeches about filmmaking. In one of his early essays, Fei talks about his attention to film narrative in contrast to theatrical narrative: in his third feature film, *A Sea of Fragrant Snow* (1934), which stars Ruan Lingyu, he deliberately omits theatrical suspense at the beginning of the film so that the images can flow in a nondramatic way (Fei 1934a). He soon makes it clear that this attention to the uniqueness of film narrative is not so much about film style as about film technology. In another 1934 essay, he

Figure 24.2 Under the candlelight in *Spring in a Small Town* (dir. Fei Mu, Wenhua Film, 1947), tormented love continues.

discusses "film aura" (or "air," *kongqi*), which to him is equivalent to film narrative. There are four ways to acquire "aura" in filmmaking, he contends: through the unique features of the camera; through the properties of the object being filmed by the camera; through a roundabout way; through sound. What are the unique features of the camera? He refers to different camera angles and light exposure:

> The eye of the camera is often more perceptive than the human eye, therefore we can achieve different effects through the use of the camera. The camera angle can be adjusted in accordance with the film's style, and the light exposure can vary depending on the mood changes in the film. (Fei 1934b: 216)

Further variations can be created by combining such mechanical features with the objects being filmed. Fei discusses how to immerse objects in the beauty of their surroundings by means of camera angles, timing, lighting, composition, and so on. As for the roundabout way, he refers to the utilization of extra details not necessarily related to the main story or characters.

Fei had been consistent in prioritizing the technological aspects of filmmaking. Later in his career, he expanded his technological vision to reflect on the entire Chinese film industry. In a 1948 essay entitled "Finding a Way Out for China-Made Films," he touches upon everything from the lack of investment in cinema to the dilemmas of filmmakers preoccupied with realism for social intervention. He makes two important points: (1) Chinese films tend to pay attention to content while neglecting form; (2) technically and technologically, Chinese filmmakers have made fundamental mistakes in four aspects: trying to build big stage setups in small studios; trying to compose complex lighting schemes with limited lighting sources and technology; using amateur actors for sophisticated performances; being too ambitious with stylistic maneuvers without the support of or investment in highly skillful cinematography, sound recording, or printing (Fei 1948: 336).

These candid words were actually revolutionary in Fei Mu's time. They outraged an entire generation of filmmakers who wanted cinema to undertake multiple social, political, and ideological functions and who believed that films needed to be sympathetic to social underdogs, to mobilize the resistance war against the Japanese, or to propagate Marxism. The result of the dominance of the left-leaning ideologues in filmmaking was the popularization of the make-do spirit while sacrificing exploration of the technological potential of film. Fei Mu resisted this trend as best as could, and his resistance paid off in producing Chinese cinema's all-time classic, *Spring in a Small Town* (1948).

Spring in a Small Town as an allegory of lighting

Much has been discussed about *Spring in a Small Town*, especially after it was remade into *Springtime in a Small Town* (Tian Zhuangzhuang, 2002) and voted in 2005 by the Hong Kong Film Critics Association as the greatest Chinese film ever made. The discussions cover many aspects of the film: the voice-over and the first-person narrative (L. Yu 2006), the elements of Chinese aesthetics, Fei Mu's pioneering and provocative use of the long take (Fitzgerald 2008), his lyricism (A. Wong 1998), and the film's reflection of the traumatic memory related to World War II (Fitzgerald 2008). Most of these aspects overlap: for Fitzgerald, Fei Mu's long takes draw attention to the ruins and thus allegorize the traumatic memory. And all these discussions touch upon Fei Mu's technological sophistication and consciousness. One technological aspect of the film, however, has been more or less overlooked: the film's focus on lighting.

As much as *Laborer's Love* reflects upon the early cinema's obsession with physical movement, and as much as *Street Angel* bids farewell to the age of silent film, *Spring in a Small Town* also has a tale to tell about film technology. We must remember that Fei Mu made China's first color film. This means that he was particularly sensitive to colors and lighting. Made in the same year as *Remorse of Death*, *Spring in a Small Town* could and should be read as a dialogue between the black-and-white film and the color film. In this film, Fei Mu explores fully the color nuances of the black-and-white by manipulating lighting in such a way as to allow space expansion and depth extension, with plenty of hues and shades waiting to be filled by the full explosion of colors. I thus read this film as an allegory of lighting in terms of its internalization of the awareness of lighting's potentials for color film.

When Zhichen, a medical doctor, intrudes into the peaceful but melancholy ruins in which Liyan and Yuwen reside, the world is suddenly filled with bright spring sunlight, which is also supposed to be good for the health of Liyan, who suffers from tuberculosis and a heart ailment. But soon night falls. And, we are told, the electricity is cut every night. Candles are brought to light up the darkness in Zhichen's guest room; Yuwen follows the candlelight to his room. These two individuals equally tormented by sexual desire begin to struggle in darkness and in light: the door is closed and the light goes out, but soon the candle is lit and the door is forced open. Every act of closing and opening the door is a lengthy struggle, psychologically and cinematically: it was technically difficult to find a light source so precise as to reveal the room's darkness without making the characters invisible. The characters are not only visible in the dark, we can even make out their shifting, emotion-filled facial expressions through the shade cast by the faint light on the sides of their noses and around their eyes. What makes the story of the light even more interesting is Fei Mu's ingenious use of the slow dissolve: the light gradually dissolves away, with the images still lingering in the viewer's sensory system.

The use of lighting in *Spring in a Small Town* reminds us of Fei Mu's remarks quoted above: "the light exposure can vary depending up the mood changes in the film." If, as he acknowledged himself, he had failed to create a narrative unique to film in his earlier work *A Sea of Fragrant Snow* due to the pull of conventional theatrical tension, Fei Mu succeeded in creating this narrative in *Spring in a Small Town* by allowing the lighting to take the lead. The lighting – between light and darkness, between the desire to be free and the obligation to stay within the ruins – leads a moody narrative determined by spacing, camerawork, and light sources, not the characters' relationships.

1949 and Beyond

That *Spring in a Small Town* has been recognized as the finest achievement in Chinese film history is testimony to China's rekindled interest in film technology after more than thirty years of neglect. Between 1949 and 1984, Chinese films were one of the major sites for ideological control and political struggle. Content dominated form, and the film industry got by with using imported Soviet technology. China was still developing its own film technology, but was doing so at a slow pace and for practical purposes only.

While mainland China went through more than thirty years of neglect of film technology, Hong Kong and Taiwan were actively seeking technological advancement in filmmaking from the 1950s to the 1980s. These activities, independent of the film industry in mainland China, are too numerous and too multifaceted to be touched upon in the limited space of this chapter.

Some of the most notable technological achievements of this period in mainland China include the consolidation of film studios. Filmmaking resources were reorganized into five major studios: Beijing Studio, Shanghai Studio, Changchun

Studio, August First Studio (controlled by the military), and Central Newsreel and Documentary Studio. Although all the studios were state controlled and did not allow individual creative freedom, their sheer size made it possible to plan technological innovations based on identified needs.

In 1953 Shanghai Studio produced China's first animated color film, *The Little Heroes* (Jin Xi). In a production style true to Soviet collectivism, Shanghai Studio first set the goals and then put together a project team under the rubric of "color film experiments." The team included Wan Chaochen (1906–92) – he and his three brothers are considered the fathers of Chinese animation; Wan Guoqiang, a chemist, who was able to synthesize the color-developing agent TSS in the studio's lab; and Li Jingwen, a Soviet Russian Chinese who had experience in film developing. Only upon the successful completion of the team's experiment did the head of the studio give the go-ahead for the actual shooting of the film (Q. Xu 2005: 40).

In 1959 another major project was started: China's own 3-D film. August First Studio was chiefly responsible for this project. The project came to fruition in June, when the first 3-D film, titled *Lijiang Impression* and made to promote tourism, was screened. A series of 3-D films followed: short features, documentaries, and animations. The first full-length feature, *A Magician's Adventure* (Sang Hu, 1962), was produced. To facilitate the audience's enjoyment of 3-D films, fifteen major cities built 3-D cinemas between 1960 and 1964 (Q. Xu 2005: 76–7).

After filmmaking almost entirely stalled between 1966 and 1976, development of film technology once again became a priority for the Chinese film industry. The focus was on independent development with increasing communication with world film industries.

In terms of internalizing awareness of film technology, the first major challenge to the lack of attention to such technology was the production of *Yellow Earth* (Chen Kaige, 1984). The film was revolutionary in multiple ways: picture composition, sound effects, cinematography, nonlinear and nondramatic narrative, and so on. What the film truly did at the time was call attention once again to the importance of technology to filmmaking. This burst of creative energy – stimulated by the desire to depart from content-dominated mainstream film – continued after *Yellow Earth* and made the period between the mid-1980s and the present another golden age of Chinese cinema. It saw the production of such excellent films as *Farewell My Concubine* (Chen Kaige, 1993), *Not One Less* (Zhang Yimou, 1998), *Beijing Bicycle* (Wang Xiaoshuai, 2000), *Suzhou River* (Lou Ye, 2000), and *Devils on the Doorstep* (Jiang Wen, 2000). Each of these films has its own unique reflection on film technology (G. Xu 2007).

While Chinese films have made notable progress in combining available film technology and visual/narrative creations, another trend began to appear from the mid-1990s and has gradually been squeezing the space available for the development of China's native film. This trend is the increasing obsession with Hollywood productions, concurring with China's opening of its cinema market to

Hollywood imports since 1994. The first import was *The Fugitive* (Andrew Davis, 1993). This was a sensational hit in China mainly because of the appeal of the high production values typical of contemporary Hollywood: big investment, mega star, rapid action, fast pace, and pure entertainment. Such high-production value films have since been termed *dapian* – literally, "big films." Between 1993 and 2007 China imported ten Hollywood *dapian* each year, and at least twenty annually after 2007, as per China's World Trade Organization agreement. The numbers of imported *dapian* may appear insignificant, but these films lived up to the hype by taking a majority share of China's cinema box office.

What is worse is Chinese films' increasing imitation of the *dapian* style and fetishization of Hollywood-style film technology. Zhang Yimou, Chen Kaige, and Feng Xiaogang – the "big three" of contemporary Chinese film directors – have all been focusing on films with high production values. Zhang's *Hero* (2002), Chen's *The Promise* (2005), and Feng's "New Year's films" have all displayed the symptoms of Hollywood blockbusters: shallow plots, porous details, poor performances, and cultural homogenization. None of these flaws can be disguised by the films' lavish scenery, glossy picture, rich colors and realistic sounds, rapid editing, or smooth and multi-perspective camera work. This is not technological sophistication. On the contrary, Chinese directors, pushed by the demands of global commercial cinema, are getting away from their strengths: keen awareness of and fascination with what film technology really means.

Part V
Issues and Debates

25

Chinese Film Scholarship in Chinese

Chen Xihe

Chinese film scholarship in Chinese has a history as long as that of Chinese film industries. The earliest works on Chinese film appeared in Shanghai in the 1920s, published mostly in Shanghai until 1949, after which film criticism developed independently in the mainland, Taiwan, and Hong Kong. Chinese film studies were conducted within a limited professional circle, with limited output, until around 1980, and afterward film research entered a stage of rapid development in all three Chinese regions. This development was not only a result of industrial developments but also that of film education and studies, which were gradually established as an academic discipline in various universities. Along with the lifting of the ban for the cross-strait exchanges between the mainland and Taiwan and the return of Hong Kong to China's sovereignty in the 1990s, there have been more academic exchanges between the three regions, and more cooperative works in Chinese film scholarship than ever before. The concept of "Chinese-language film" (*huayu dianying*), which transcends geopolitical boundaries and covers Chinese films in all regions, has been accepted and provides a new horizon for film studies. Today, Chinese film scholarship in Chinese is in a prosperous phase and covers a variety of foci, perspectives, and methodologies.

The selected texts of Chinese film scholarship discussed in this chapter are divided into three categories. The first category includes analyses conducted in historical research. These works are often considered the most conventional type of film scholarship and consist of various general and specialized historical as well as thematic studies. The second category is film criticism, which differs from general newspaper film reviews and involves not only strong value judgments but also considerable theoretical and academic issues. In addition, Chinese film criticism has a profound sociopolitical impact on academic research, as evident in the 1950s criticism of *The Life of Wu Xun* (Sun Yu, 1950), the 1980s attack on "Xie Jin's film model," and the 1990s postcolonial criticism of the Fifth Generation. The third

A Companion to Chinese Cinema, First Edition. Edited by Yingjin Zhang.

category is theoretical. The theories of Chinese film differ from general film theories because they are theories about Chinese film or theoretical understandings of the nature of Chinese film. For example, there was a theory of "shadowplay" (*yingxi*) in the 1920s, a debate on the ontology of film intent on "divorcing film from drama" in the late 1970s, and the discussion of "mainstream film" in the new century. Compared to Chinese film scholarship overseas, published in English or other languages, the latter two categories of Chinese scholarship are peculiar to film studies in China. They do not distance themselves from their subjects under the pretext of objectivity, but rather are directly involved in the practice and development of Chinese film with certain political positions at stake.

Pre-1949 Scholarship

Works on Chinese film studies published in Chinese can be traced to the 1920s when the center of the Chinese film industry began to take shape in Shanghai. In February 1921 the earliest film newspaper in China, *Yingxi congbao*, began circulation in Shanghai. In December 1921, *Yingxi zazhi*, a monthly edited by Gu Kenfu (?–1932), appeared in Shanghai. In 1925, *Chinese Film Yearbook*, edited by Zhou Jianyun, was published in Shanghai and became the first one of its kind (B. Wen). The preliminary works on Chinese film history also emerged. Xu Chihen's 138-page book, *A Grand View of Chinese Shadow Play* (1927), begins with a chapter entitled "The Origin of Chinese Film" and covers film production companies, producers, directors, actors and actresses, movie theaters, publications, and other related information. Although primarily information based, the book presents an overview of the early Chinese film industry and serves as a valuable first-hand observation.

In the mid-1920s, Chinese intellectuals explored the film ontology in a "Chinese style." The traditional Chinese concept of film as "drama" (*xi*) yielded the peculiar term "shadowplay" (*yingxi*). As Bao Tianxiao (1876–1973) recalled (1973:93), "when the film first came to China … we just said 'go watch the shadowplay.' We can see the film's origin was coming from the theater." Shortly after Xu Zhuodai (1881–1958) wrote the first book on film studies in China (1924), Hou Yao, a famous director and screenwriter, systematically explored the structure, function, narrative, and images of shadowplay; as he asserts (1925: 5): "Shadowplay is a kind of drama, so every rule for drama is proper for shadowplay." Although Xu's and Hou's books were not concentrated on film ontology, they theoretically elaborated a special Chinese understanding of film.

Discussions of Chinese film and film studies continued through the 1930s and 1940s. Given the long turbulent years of the anti-Japanese war and the Civil War, this period saw very few mature, systematic, or complete works in Chinese film scholarship. Before 1949, film remained an emerging art and the Chinese film industry was at an early stage of development.

Scholarship from 1949 to the Late 1970s

After the People's Republic of China (PRC) was established in 1949, Chinese film industries were divided into three relatively independent regions: the mainland, Taiwan, and Hong Kong. Accordingly, Chinese film studies in the three regions were fairly independent. Overall, the scholarship of Chinese film on the mainland was the most fully developed. This is because the mainland was the most important base for a Chinese film industry and culture for a long time and film was entrusted with an urgent ideological mission by the state. Consequently, film production and research received a great deal of attention on all fronts. During this period, Beijing replaced Shanghai as the most significant center for Chinese film on the mainland, where Chinese film studies experienced great political turmoil while producing important academic works.

The mainland

Among works on Chinese film studies in this period, one crucial text is the political criticism by Mao Zedong (1951), which exerted a profound impact on the direction of Chinese film studies in the mainland for three decades. Mao severely criticized *The Life of Wu Xun*, which had been widely praised by audiences, critics, and even officials. For him, film should serve the cause of constructing a new China, celebrating "new social-economic patterns, the new class power, new characters and new ideas," and opposing "the enemies who oppressed Chinese people" as well as "the old social-economic patterns and superstructure." Thus, Mao established a new national politics as the core value for a new Chinese film industry as well as of new Chinese film criticism and research. In the ensuing years, Chinese film scholarship developed a new tradition called "socialist realism," which upheld the political interest of the new regime.

A major representative of this new tradition is *A History of the Development of Chinese Film*, cowritten by Cheng Jihua and his colleagues (1963). It took many years and much work collecting source materials to finish the book, which became an influential work in the field. The two-volume book is divided into three parts: Part I, "The Origin and Development of Chinese Film" (1896–1931), Part II, "The Party Led the Chinese Film Culture Movement" (1931–7), and Part III, "A New Phase of the Progressive Film Movement and Rising of People's Film" (1937–49). This work provides a detailed description of the history of Chinese film before 1949, including film industries in Shanghai, Hong Kong, Yan'an, Chongqing, and Japanese-controlled Manchuria. The book's framework and periodization affected the great number of subsequent Chinese film histories. The writing of the book received government support and guidance, and the branch divisions of the China Film Artists Association helped collect source materials. The result was an "official history" marked by its orthodox viewpoints, represented by its dichotomized description and analysis of proletariat versus bourgeoisie, progressive versus reactionary, revolutionary versus counterrevolutionary in a history of Chinese film before 1949.

During this period some intellectuals expressed ideas unaligned with the political interests of the new regime. Zhong Dianfei (1956) criticized the policy that had resulted in many domestic films losing audiences and money at the box office. He caused a big controversy and became the target of a political backlash, with himself classified as a bourgeois rightist in 1957. Similarly, even though Qu Baiyin's (1962) proposal that film should "get rid of old words" and go for "new thinking, new image, and new styles" received a positive response in film circles, he was severely denounced when the political climate subsequently changed.

Nonetheless, the Chinese government set up several key institutions in this period. On October 28, 1956, *Chinese Film*, a monthly magazine sponsored by the Film Bureau in the Ministry of Culture, was established in Beijing, and Chen Huangmei (1913–96) was put in charge. For a long time, the magazine was the primary platform for academic research in the mainland. *Chinese Film* later merged with *International Film* and was renamed *Film Art* (*Dianying yishu*). In the early 1960s, *Film Art* launched a debate about the "nationality" (*minzuxing*) of Chinese film and published articles on rural films and traditional arts (Ke 1960; C. Xu 1962). Nationality remained a key topic for Chinese film scholarship during this time.

Taiwan

Taiwan's film industry started slowly in the 1950s and moved toward prosperity in the 1960s and 1970s. Among significant film publications, Lü Sushang's (1961) history covers the early twentieth century till the 1960s and was an early informative study with historical value. Du Yunzhi's (1972) three-volume book provides a detailed study on film history in mainland China before 1949, which remained one of a few studies on early mainland Chinese films conducted by Taiwanese scholars before the 1980s. In addition, the book covers the film history of Taiwan and Hong Kong up to 1970 and promotes those films of the 1960s produced with quality and in the realist style. Understandably, Du's history and Cheng Jihua's are often at odds with each other with respect to their ideological positions on the same historical events, characters, and films. The emergence of Taiwan's film history studies can be said to echo the needs of the local society to view Taiwan as the "orthodox" perspective, and to reconstruct a history and identity of Chinese culture different from the mainland's version.

As for film journals, *Impact* (*Yingxiang*), founded by Wang Xiaoxiang on December 10, 1971, was most influential among Taiwan film critics in the 1970s. The magazine was suspended twice in the 1980s and 1990s, and ceased publication in 1998. However, it covered the most prosperous time of Taiwan film in the 1970s and was once regarded as a symbol of film criticism in Taiwan.

Hong Kong

The film industry in Hong Kong flourished greatly during this period, although its ideological stance was caught in the conflict between the mainland and Taiwan. In general, political issues were largely avoided in film content and serious film research was limited. With the distinctive commercial characteristics of Hong Kong film, the studies of film were mostly reviews and comments published in local newspapers and magazines, such as *Southern Film* (*Nanguo dianying*), *Hong Kong Movie News* (*Xianggang yinghua*), *City Entertainment* (*Dianying shuangzhou kan*), *Cine-Art House* (*Yingyi*), and *Ming Pao Daily News* (*Mingbao*). More serious academic film studies emerged only after Hong Kong's economy had taken off and confidence in the local culture established itself in the following decades.

Scholarship from the Late 1970s through the 1990s

Significant changes in the sociopolitical and economic situations of the mainland, Taiwan, and Hong Kong occurred from the end of the 1970s to the early 1980s. The decade-long Cultural Revolution was over by the late 1970s on the mainland, and the economies of Hong Kong and Taiwan received a big lift in the 1970s. In this context there were significant developments in the film industries of the three regions: the Hong Kong New Wave began in the late 1970s, the New Cinema movement appeared in Taiwan in the early 1980s, and the Fifth Generation was on the rise in the mainland by the mid-1980s. Meanwhile, Chinese film scholarship in the three regions also entered a new stage, not only in terms of the greater quantity of publications but also in remarkably modern, academic quality. Generally speaking, Chinese film scholarship in the mainland had a stronger "revolutionary" spirit *vis-à-vis* traditional concepts and academic positions, as it directly promoted the new film movement in the mainland. Taiwan's film studies were filled with an urgent concern for the local experience and considered the cultural and historical experience in Taiwan film to be its focus. Chinese film studies in Hong Kong established a distinct academic awareness, taking studies of film genre and history as its starting point.

The mainland

The most important academic development in this period was the introspective look at traditional Chinese film ontology. As mentioned above, the traditional Chinese concept of film as drama had yielded the term *yingxi* (shadowplay), and this drama-film concept found its furthest extreme in the practice of filming "model plays" (*yangbangxi*) during the Cultural Revolution. This concept of film-as-drama was seriously challenged when Bai Jingcheng (1979) urged filmmakers to throw away the crutches of drama, and a heated debate on the relationship between theater and film ensued. For Bai, compared to drama, film has a freer time-space form with a unique montage technique; therefore, "after the first step has been taken with help from drama, film today can become a new art different from any art, and now is the time for film to throw away the crutches of drama." Similarly, Zhang Nuanxin and Li Tuo (1979) called for "the modernization of film language" and Zhong Dianfei (1987) proposed a "divorce of film and drama." While debating film language, many people became involved in rethinking the nature of film and its relationship with theater and literature. After the debate, the once-dominant idea of the drama-film was completely shaken. The debate encouraged a new generation of Chinese filmmakers to pay attention to the visual aspect of film and modern narrative methods and to get rid of conventional aesthetics and political doctrines. This debate directly contributed to the emergence of a new film movement represented by the Fifth Generation.

This ontological reflection also added a historical dimension to film studies. In the early 1980s, under the strong influence of Western film theory, Chinese film academics generally agreed that China had long replaced film theory with political theory; consequently, China probably had no true film theory. Has China ever had any film theory? In the new historical conditions, how should Chinese film practice be evaluated theoretically? These were the important questions addressed by Chinese scholars at the time. Proceeding from the recovery of Hou Yao's 1926 book, Chen Xihe (1986) constructs shadowplay as a traditional Chinese film theory and aesthetic. For him, Chinese cinema should not be judged by Western theories and models, but rather be based on China's own cultural logic in order to measure whether China has a film theory, and to review China's tradition of film theory. In comparison with Western theories, Chen claims that shadowplay is the core concept of traditional Chinese film theory and aesthetics, a view shared by Zhong Dafeng (1986).

Under the influence of modern thinking, another important development in Chinese film studies in the mainland was the debate on "Xie Jin's film model," initiated by *Wenhui bao*, a Shanghai newspaper. On the one hand, Zhu Dake (1986) attacked Xie Jin's films, then at their peak of popularity. Zhu claimed that Xie's films were conservative in terms of aesthetics and ideology, for Xie's aesthetic mode resembled Hollywood melodrama and commercial films, and his ideology followed China's Confucian values. Zhu called for an end to Xie Jin's film model. On the other hand, Jiang Junzhu diametrically opposed Zhu's view and fully endorsed Xie Jin's values. The *Wenhui bao* debate concluded with an article by Zhong Dianfei (1986), who praised Zhu's theoretical courage but reaffirmed Xie Jin's significance. The discussion of Xie Jin continued in the late 1990s, as in Wang Hui (1998) and Li Yiming (1999), both following Zhu Dake's criticism but providing thorough analyses of the close relationship between Xie Jin's film and dominant Chinese political discourse (see Chapter 4, this volume).

One of the major works on Chinese film history published in the 1980s was *Contemporary Chinese Film* (1989) edited by Chen Huangmei, which covers 35 years

(1949–84) in the new China, thus exactly complementing Cheng Jihua's history. There are eight sections in the book: Section I, "Feature Films in the Rising Period (1949–59)"; Section II, "Feature Films in the Winding Period (1960–65)"; Section III, "Feature Films in the Cultural Revolution (1966–76)"; Section IV, "Feature Films in the New Era (1977–84)"; Section V, "Documentary Films and Science-Education Films"; Section VI, "Animation and Dubbed Foreign Films"; Section VII, "Film Theory and Film Education"; Section VIII, "Film Distribution and Exhibition, International Exchange, and Film Technology." The book was considered a respectable academic achievement of the time. Many mainland textbooks in Chinese film history published in the next decade were based on the framework and source materials both of Chen's book and Cheng's book, often without achieving major breakthroughs.

Chinese film scholarship in the mainland entered a prosperous age in the 1980s. In addition to a variety of academic publications, film education and research institutes also developed considerably. In 1982, Beijing Film Academy had its first class of graduates (known as the Fifth Generation) after the Cultural Revolution, and China Art Academy enrolled the first class of graduate students in film studies in the mainland. In 1984, China Film Art Research Center was established in Beijing and became an important academic film institute. Back in 1979, *Film Art*, which had been suspended during the Cultural Revolution, resumed publication. In 1984, *Contemporary Cinema* (*Dangdai dianying*) was founded, followed by the publication of *Journal of Beijing Film Academy* in 1985. These three journals have become the flagship academic venues in Chinese film studies in the mainland. In addition, *Chinese Film Yearbook*, edited by the China Film Association, began publication in 1981, and it has become a standard reference source for data, documents, theories, and commentaries.

In the 1990s, Chinese film scholarship entered a stable period of development. Issues of "main melody films" (*zhuxuanlü dianying*) and film industry reform attracted more attention. Yin Hong absorbed Western film theory and analyzed new narrative strategies and functions of major main melody films, such as *Founding Ceremony of the People's Republic* (Li Qiankuan, Xiao Guiyun, 1990). By no means contentious, his works (Yin and Chen 1993; Yin 1995) marked a breakthrough from previous studies on main melody films. As for film industry reform, Ni Zhen (1994b) was a pioneer in dealing with the commercialization of Chinese film. His exploration of the market environment, various film genres (e.g., commercial film, art film), the impact of television on film, and the convergence and conflicts among the mainland, Hong Kong, and Taiwan film industries, laid a foundation for subsequent research. In terms of art film, Dai Jinhua's (1993) intervention constituted an important achievement during this period. She stood on a critical position of modernity and absorbed auteurist, ideological, and feminist criticism from Western film theories to evaluate the cultural significance of the Fourth and Fifth Generation directors within a broad sociohistorical context.

In the mid-1990s, the postcolonial criticism of the Fifth Generation became radical and attracted much attention. Zhang Yiwu (1993, 1994) denounced the films of Zhang Yimou and other Fifth Generation directors from the late 1980s and early 1990s, which were popular in many major Western film festivals. He argued that those so-called "auteur films" or "art films" offered cultural consumption for Western audiences and positioned China as a "cultural other" in the postcolonial, globalized context, thereby signifying a surrender to the taste of Western film festivals and to the demand of foreign investors. Similarly critical, Wang Yichuan (1998) announced the end of Zhang Yimou's national myth. For Chinese postcolonial criticism, the centrality of Western theory placed Zhang Yimou's films in the framework of East–West power relations, while the domestic context of these films remained secondary.

In addition to contemporary issues, the collecting and editing of China's academic works were significant achievements in the 1990s. *China Encyclopedia: Film Volume* (1991) reached the highest standards at the time in terms of systemization, integrity, rigor, and accuracy of information, and its editorial board included Xia Yan, Zhang Junxiang, and Cheng Jihua. Luo Yijun edited the first comprehensive anthology of Chinese film theory (1992), which collects numerous archival materials and keeps track of the evolution of Chinese film criticism through much of the twentieth century.

A new development in film historiography was Li Suyuan and Hu Jubin's (1997) book, which provides an overview of the development of the Chinese silent film industry. The authors divide this silent period into six stages: prehistory (1896–1904), germination (1905–21), exploration (1922–6), developmental (1927–31), maturation (1932–4), and decline (1935–6). Although smaller in scale than Cheng Jihua's history, this new history contains more details about early Chinese film and incorporates new research from the 1980s (as in its specific sections for early Chinese film theory), and it offers a new assessment of early martial arts films. Other film histories (Zhong and Shu 1995; Y. Ding 1998; H. Lu 1998) were also outstanding achievements of this period. Among them, Hu Xingliang and Zhang Ruilin (1995) incorporated the mainland, Taiwan, and Hong Kong into Chinese film history in a complete framework.

Before the 1980s, the mainland's academic research rarely specialized in Taiwan and Hong Kong films. The first in-depth study of Taiwan film came from Chen Feibao (1988), a foundational work covering 1895–1985, while an early academic interest in Hong Kong came from Li Yizhuang (1994). Anticipating the return of Hong Kong in 1997, mainland attention to Hong Kong film strengthened. China Film Archive issued the first comprehensive reference on Hong Kong film (ZDZ 1998), which was followed by a collection of research articles on Hong Kong cinema (Cai, Song, and Liu 2000).

Taiwan

Since the 1980s, Taiwan's film studies have yielded significant change and critics have become younger and more professional, familiar with Western film theory and trends of world film, thus marking a qualitative difference from previous generations. They take film directors as the central figures of filmmaking, interpret their intended meanings, and analyze their styles and techniques. This new trend began in 1980 with the *Min Sheng Daily News* column dispatched by Ke Li from New York, and it continued in 1981 with the *United Daily News* column written by Peggy Chiao (Jiao Xiongping), who pursued her studies in the United States. From 1982 to 1987, various articles about the development of Taiwan's film industry and New Cinema appeared in film magazines such as *World Film*, *Film Appreciation (Dianying xinxiang)*, *400 Blows (sibai ji)*, and *Long Take (Chang jingtou)*. Chiao edited a collection of representative film commentaries from newspapers and magazines and provided a comprehensive view of Taiwan New Cinema of the 1980s (Jiao 1988).

By the late 1990s, Taiwan film scholars had made significant headway with film history, image data collection, and film preservation. Chen Ru-shou began his study of Taiwan New Cinema with an overview of Taiwan's film history in the Japanese colonial period and connected the history of the film industry and film style with the contemporary social and historical background. Chen Ru-shou (1993: 7) intended this book to "focus on presenting the history and culture experience of Taiwan's film, especially on the expression of several concepts, such as language, history, culture, and identification, and to outline a clear and complete changing process of Taiwan film history." Using a research method different from textual analysis, Li Tianduo (1997) attempted to reexamine the development of Taiwan's film history and locate its historical impact in different times and societies. Following historical changes chronologically – from the colonial and postcolonial periods through liberation, the authoritarian system, the retreating situation, the frustrated nation, the collapse of the authoritarian regime, the mass consumption culture, to the post-authoritarian system and onward – Li measures Taiwan film against its historical background. Lu Feiyi (1998) approached the fifty years of Taiwan film history in greater detail by combining political, economic, and aesthetic perspectives. In a unique way, he structured his book with a chapter covering every five years, and the book discusses the history of Taiwan's film production alongside political backgrounds, historical movements, industrial structures, and social and cultural fields. It is a must-read for Taiwan film studies.

In the 1990s, after the lifting of the ban on cross-strait exchanges, Taiwan scholars paid more attention to Chinese-language films made in mainland China and Hong Kong. Li Tianduo (1996) edited a selection of academic articles from the three Chinese regions, many written by mainland scholars. The cross-strait perspective was likewise instituted in another Taiwan volume edited by Zheng Shusen (1995), which gathered contributions from mainland China, Hong Kong, and Taiwan, as well as from overseas Chinese scholars and American scholars (e.g., Fredric Jameson and Paul G. Pickowicz). The cross-strait perspective became so prominent that Liang Liang (1998) urged that "Chinese film" should be seen as constituted by films from all regions of Taiwan, Hong Kong, and mainland China, so that the lack of any one of these would make the picture incomplete.

Hong Kong

If the rise of the Hong Kong New Wave from 1979 onward is a sign of cultural self-consciousness in Hong Kong, then a parallel development was the awakening of academic awareness in film during the same period. Lin Niantong (1984, 1985, 1991) was a pioneer in film theory, who studied the psychology of film audiences and explored Chinese film from the perspective of traditional Chinese aesthetics. The Hong Kong government also played a vital role in promoting research in film history. The Hong Kong International Film Festival (HKIFF) published a special bilingual catalogue – *Hong Kong Cinema Retrospective* – each year addressing a differ-ent genre, period, or auteur, starting with "James Wong Howe Recalled" in 1978.[1] Hong Kong's return in 1997 was undoubtedly a major historical event, which had a tremendous impact on Hong Kong film studies. The repositioning of Hong Kong identity, the cultural ties between Hong Kong and mainland China, the tradi-tions and contexts of Hong Kong and mainland films all became hot topics throughout the 1990s. As a result, HKIFF changed its 1980s focus on retrospectives and published a series exploring border-crossing issues.[2]

After the mid-1990s, research on Hong Kong film history became more productive. Known as "the number-one Hong Kong film historian," Yu Muyun completed the first three volumes of his Hong Kong film history (1996, 1997b, 1998), with volumes four and five coming shortly afterwards (2000, 2001). He also edited an illustrated history (1997a). Hong Kong Film Archive was active in producing research materials, such as filmographies (Hong Kong Film Archive 1995, 1997, 1998). Other academic publications quickly followed, addressing issues of genre, auteur, and folk culture (H. Wu 1993; Law, Zhuo, and Wu 1997; A. Wong 1998).

Hong Kong's academic research from this period paid more attention to exchanges between the mainland and Taiwan. In 1996 Hong Kong Baptist University organized the First International Chinese-Language Films Conference (1980–96), and scholars came from the mainland, Hong Kong, Taiwan, North America, and Australia to reassess the development of Chinese film in the three regions in the preceding two decades (Ye, Zhuo, and Wu 1999). Many more such collaborative publications would follow in the new century, in all three regions.

The New Century

After entering the new century, film academics continued to flourish in the three regions. On the one hand, film criticism was concerned about the development of local film industries and culture in each region; on the other hand, scholars had more mutual concerns, exchange, and even cooperation, as film industries became more intertwined in the age of globalization. Chinese-language film has become a fundamental perspective in Chinese film studies in all three regions.

The mainland's film research has grown the most because of sustained economic development, the inherent advantages of the mainland market and industry, and the rapid expansion of film education in universities and graduate schools. Research undertaken in Hong Kong and Taiwan pays more attention to film development on the mainland and to relationships with the mainland.

The mainland

The prosperous development of the mainland since the early 1980s has enabled film scholarship there to flourish. Compared with previous periods, there were more comprehensive studies in this period. Around 2005, in celebrating the centennial of Chinese cinema, a series of film history monographs was published. Among them, an important trend was to reexamine film history from all three regions. Li Daoxin (2005) examined the cultural implications of Chinese cinema in a framework that integrates the mainland, Taiwan, and Hong Kong; Zhang Baiqing and Jia Leilei (2006) used various film subjects and genres rather than a chronological outline as their distinctive framework; Zhou Xing (2005) placed emphasis on key artistic trends in Chinese film history. During this period, *Film Art* and *Contemporary Cinema* featured special columns such as "Rewriting Film History" and "Cover Figures" and published important works of film history, such as those re-verifying China's reputed first film, *Dingjun Mountain* (Ren Jingfeng, 1905).

China Film Art Research Center launched two impressive book series, "Centennial Book Series of Film Studies" and "Chinese Film Compendium." The first series includes twelve specialized histories: film theory (Hu Ke), film industry (Shen Yun), film technology (Xu Qianlin), film culture (Yang Yuanying), film acting (Liu Shibing), animated films (Yan Hui and Suo Yabin), children's films (Zhang Zhilu), comedy films (Rao Shuguang), martial arts films (Chen Mo), war films (Huangfu Yichuan), documentary films (Shan Wanli), and science and education films (Zhao Huikang and Jia Leilei). The second series consists of four volumes of primary materials related to all aspects of Chinese cinema after 1905. Apart from these publications, opera films also received attention (X. Gao 2005).

In the new century, there have been more comprehensive works on Chinese film theory and criticism than ever before. Li Daoxin (2002) produced an in-depth analysis of the development of Chinese film criticism from 1897 to 2000, which caused quite a stir among academics because Li contended that film criticism in China was strong in ideological intervention but weak on aesthetic analysis. Li Suyuan (2005) provided a comprehensive survey of Chinese film theories before 1949, dividing them into three phases: growing up (1921–30), transition (1931–7), and expansion (1938–49). By discussing representative texts of high quality from the early periods, Li Suyuan demonstrates his admirable knowledge. Different from Li Suyuan's historical focus, Hu Ke (2005) followed the various trends of Chinese film theories from early cinema to the contemporary world and distinguished himself with a strong capacity for critical thought. Apart from historical studies, anthologies of film criticism also became more comprehensive. Ding Yaping (2002) expanded on Luo Yijun's (1992) work by including more selections and writing a longer general introduction and short commentaries preceding each selection. Luo Yijun himself updated his earlier work in an expanded anthology of Chinese film theory (2003).

Among contemporary issues, industry research came to the forefront as the market reform in Chinese film production, distribution, and exhibition intensified. Terms such as market, audience, attendance, and investment became keywords for film studies. This industry research reached its peak around China's entry into the World Trade Organization in 1999. Major academic journals such as *Contemporary Cinema* and *Film Art* were rightly concerned with these issues and published many valuable studies. Zhong Dafeng (2005) expanded the horizons of Chinese-language film by situating cultural and industrial matters within the framework of Asian cinema. Among other important works (M. Jia 2002; Zhang and Yang 2002; L. Ye 2008, 2009), the annual memoranda for the Chinese film industry that Yin Hong contributed to *Contemporary Cinema* and *Film Art* deserve special mention, as do several annual film industry reports published by China Film Press in 2007–9. Serial reports like these (e.g., Zhang and Yu 2006) are officially sponsored and generally considered systematic and authoritative.

Another trend in contemporary film studies is the theoretical construction of national cinema and mainstream culture, which have shifted from an ontological, aesthetic perspective in the 1980s to an ideological, political perspective. Hu Ke (2008) proposed that China's mainstream films are a product combining socialist value with market ideology and are bound to move toward popularization. Jia Leilei (2008) suggested that there should be a China-oriented mainstream film model compatible with socialist cultural values and a classical narrative pattern. The focus of these studies overlaps with the Western model of national cinema, but its theoretical resources have absorbed the theory of socialism with Chinese characteristics and a more strategic perspective on China's global repositioning.

In the new century, studies on Hong Kong and Taiwan films had more fruitful results in the mainland. On the tenth anniversary of Hong Kong handover, China Film Archive published a collection of articles by scholars from Hong Kong, the mainland, and overseas (ZDZ 2007). While Zhao Weifang (2007) chronicled Hong Kong film achievements in a history spanning a hundred years, Zhou Chengren and Li Yizhuang (2009) drew on their years of research to focus on the period from 1897 to 1945. In the meantime, books on Taiwan film have also appeared in the mainland (Z. Song 2006; W. Sun 2008).

Taiwan

Auteur studies on Taiwan New Cinema have been conducted more in-depth than previously (Lin, Shen, and Li 2000; J. Huang 2001), while Li Xing, a key director of the 1960s and after, also received substantial attention (R. Huang 1999; Jiao and

Qu 2008). Outstanding historical research was presented by Huang Ren (2004), who surveyed Taiwan film criticism from the colonial period to the present, as well as one hundred years of Taiwan film (Huang and Wang 2004). Huang also edited the "Taiwan Film Studies Series," which published works by Li Tian-Duo, Liu Xiancheng, and others. In addition, important articles can be found in *Film Appreciation*, a quarterly founded in 1983 and published by Taiwan's National Film Archive.

The framework of Chinese-language film extended the focus beyond Taiwan. Liu Xiancheng (2001) gathered articles by Taiwan, Hong Kong, mainland China, and international scholars to explore the deep structure in film language, cultural reproduction, film auteurs, and film history. Peggy Chiao (X. Jiao 2005) introduced the history and current state of films in Taiwan, Hong Kong, and the mainland and evaluated Chinese-language film as a whole, emphasizing the integration and interaction among the three regions. Compared with previous works by Taiwan scholars, Chiao represents a more intensive and comprehensive understanding of mainland cinema and Chinese-language film as a whole.

Hong Kong

Since the 1997 return of Hong Kong, Hong Kong film has repositioned its cultural identity and directly confronted the mainland film market in a new period of globalization. Not surprisingly, the 2000 HKIFF catalogue is entitled *Hong Kong Cinema Retrospective: Border Crossings in Hong Kong Cinema*. The reflection on Hong Kong film's cross-border practice has extended to historical research. Zhong Baoxian (2007) offered an encyclopedic centennial history of the Hong Kong film and television industry, culture, and aesthetics. Two other venues are likewise noteworthy: Hong Kong Film Critics Society has continued the annual publication of *Hong Kong Cinema Retrospective*, while Hong Kong Film Archive successfully completed *Hong Kong Filmography, VI* (Hong Kong Film Archive 2007).

Important new studies of the Hong Kong New Wave include Zhuo Botang (2003), whose comprehensive analysis of Hong Kong filmmaking in the 1980s measures the impact of the television industry on new wave directors and their films' historical significance. New books on Hong Kong auteur and genre research have also emerged, respectively dealing with Tsui Hark / martial arts film (He and He 2002) and John Woo / action films (Zhuo 2006), among others.

Conclusion

Since the beginning of Chinese cinema, Chinese film scholarship in Chinese has primarily appeared in mainland China, Taiwan, and Hong Kong. The body of this scholarship came to fruition during the 1980s and has continued to flourish up to now. For different political, historical, and industrial reasons, Chinese film scholarship in the three regions treated their corresponding regional developments as their respective main focus for a long time. Each of them studied only selective and limited topics from developments in the other regions. The topics that attracted common interest in the three regions included the emergence of new movements such as mainland China's Fifth and Sixth Generations, Taiwan New Cinema, and the Hong Kong New Wave, all from around the 1980s. In terms of academic approach, Chinese film scholarship in the mainland primarily adopted a political and ideological perspective before the 1980s and has subsequently turned to artistic, aesthetic, and cultural aspects, while scholarship in Hong Kong and Taiwan concentrated on industrial, historical, and genre approaches. Starting in the 1990s, industrial concerns have increased in mainland China, while issues involving the development of and changes in Chinese film under the impact of globalization also commanded a strong following.

As a recent trend, Chinese film scholarship in Chinese has tended toward putting Chinese film in perspective with regard to the three dynamically related regions as well as to the world. Chinese-language film has been accepted by a growing number of scholars in the three regions as a basic framework for Chinese film studies. With this background, many academic activities in the three regions have been integrated into the overall context of Chinese-language film and have become a kind of collective endeavor. For example, since the 1990s, many Chinese film symposia and anthologies have been the collective work of film scholars in all three regions. A new development in this period was the publication of a large-scale history project, *An Illustrated History of Chinese Film, 1905–2005* (ZDTBW 2006), to commemorate the centenary of Chinese cinema. The editorial board for the book consisted of prominent scholars such as Cheng Jihua from the mainland, Li Xing from Taiwan, and Wu Siyuan from Hong Kong. In order to complete this vast undertaking, selected experts from the three regions spent four years putting together nearly a thousand pages, 1.3 million words, and 2,700 pictures. This milestone achievement has symbolic significance for the development of Chinese film scholarship.

Notes

1   The HKIFF issues cover the following topics: "Cantonese Cinema Retrospective, 1950–1959" (1978), "Hong Kong Cinema Survey, 1946–1968" (1979), "A Study of the Hong Kong Martial Arts Film" (1980), "A Study of the Hong Kong Swordplay Film 1945–1980" (1981), "Cantonese Cinema Retrospective, 1960–69" (1982), "A Comparative Study of Postwar Mandarin and Cantonese Cinema: The Films of Zhu Shilin, Qin Jian and Other Directors" (1983), "A Study of Hong Kong Cinema in the Seventies" (1984), "The Traditions of Hong Kong Comedy" (1985), "Cantonese Melodrama,1950–1969" (1986), "Cantonese Opera Film Retrospective" (1987), "Changes in Hong Kong Society through Cinema" (1988), and "Phantoms of the Hong Kong Cinema" (1989).

2   These HKIFF border-crossing issues include "The China Factor in Hong Kong Cinema" (1990), "Overseas Chinese Figures in Cinema" (1992), "Mandarin Films and Popular Songs (the 40s–60s)" (1993), "Cinema of Two Cities: Hong Kong–Shanghai" (1994), "Early Images of Hong Kong and China" (1995), and "Transcending the Times: King Hu and Eileen Chang" (1998).

26

Chinese Film Scholarship in English

Chris Berry

What are the fundamental features of Chinese film studies in English today, and how can we account for them? To answer this question, we need to understand Chinese film studies in English as an academic field. Pierre Bourdieu (1993) defines a social field as a set of relationships between agents who take up social positions, using their cultural and in this case intellectual capital to advance their interests according to the rules and values that govern the field. Such an approach can describe the field, but how did it come into being? How and why has it changed? As a structuralist, Bourdieu's model did not prioritize accounting for change, beyond accommodating the ideas of power and struggle among the existing agents (Bourdieu 1998). However, new forces intervene in fields, bringing different values, and the field can be and is often unexpectedly reconfigured. Its history is disjunctive, contested, contingent, and unpredictable, in the sense invoked by Foucault's (1977) idea of genealogy, rather than a smooth or organic evolutionary development according to a single set of values.

One way of seeing what is taken for granted or fundamental today is to put the current situation up against the backdrop of the past. This chapter focuses on the emergence of four general characteristics of the field today. In all four cases it may come as a surprise to learn that the situation was ever different. Although this chapter discusses the main trends in scholarship, it does not go into detail on the debates among scholars working on these various topics. These can be easily accessed from reading the works themselves and other lengthier and more detailed published reviews of the field (Y. Zhang 2002: 43–114). Rather, the aim is to understand the less immediately visible characteristics of the field that are simply assumed but also provide its fundamental – and ever changing – topography.

First, serious scholars working on Chinese film in English are assumed to be bilingual, or at least reasonably proficient in both languages. This is the earliest

A Companion to Chinese Cinema, First Edition. Edited by Yingjin Zhang.
© 2012 Blackwell Publishing Ltd. Published 2012 by Blackwell Publishing Ltd.

fundamental feature of the field's topography and was in place by the 1980s. Second, we assume that our primary readership is monolingual (although some may be bilingual). Since the mid-1980s, this has consisted primarily of students. Therefore, the changing availability of films with subtitles plays a heavy role in determining trends in scholarship and research, and so far it has guaranteed that scholarship is not representative of Chinese film production as a whole.

Third, the primacy of textual exegesis in shaping our field of English-language film studies and related disciplines is taken for granted today. Film studies issues, theories, trends, and methods have become ours since the 1990s, even though we also draw on other disciplines and foreign-language academia (including Chinese-language academia). Fourth, today we talk about "transnational Chinese cinemas" or "Chinese-language cinemas." This stands in contrast to the assumption of "national cinema" that shaped Chinese film studies in English in the 1980s and into the 1990s. In the conclusion, the chapter notes the consequences of this "transnational turn" and places the field itself in its transnational context.

Prehistory: Bilingual Scholars

Today, it is taken for granted that any serious scholar of Chinese film studies in English must be proficient in both languages, or must have made very careful arrangements to overcome any problems in either language. Precisely what bilingual proficiency means is complicated by the high level of variation in China's spoken languages, making it unreasonable to expect even Chinese-born scholars to have a command of all the different spoken Chinese heard in Chinese cinema. But it is difficult to imagine any foreigner embarking on a serious Chinese film research project without learning Chinese.

However, linguistic proficiency was not always assumed. The first monograph in English on Chinese cinema is Jay Leyda's *Dianying–Electric Shadows* (1972). Leyda was already known for having studied in Russia with Eisenstein and translated his work (Eisenstein 1942, 1949) and as a scholar of Soviet cinema (Leyda 1960). Having also worked in the Chinese film industry between 1959 and 1964, Leyda was in a unique position to publish on what was then a little-known and inaccessible object of study. However, although he had a command of Russian, Leyda did not know Chinese. His book was a breakthrough, but sadly it was littered with language errors, such as the same person appearing to be a number of different people because of different roman letter spellings of the same Chinese character name. This chapter focuses on works in English, but, as Paul Clark (1986) pointed out, Régis Bergeron's multi-volume French-language history of Chinese cinema (1977, 1983–4) is bedeviled by similar issues.

Problems resulting from lack of Chinese and/or poor command of English (in the case of some translations from Chinese) continue to occur in later work, at least well into the 1980s. But the criticism expressed in Clark's 1986 review of Bergeron indicates that this was no longer considered acceptable. Trying to understand why it was once acceptable enables us to interrogate some of the founding conditions of the field. Is Leyda's book the founding moment – the origin – of the field? Is it even useful to think of the foundation of the field as a moment? Or is it more appropriate to think of it as a coming into configuration of conditions that enabled the field?

Pinpointing origins always presents problems for historians. Discussing the vicissitudes of deciding when the first Bangladeshi film was made, Zakir Raju (2000) offers useful insights into this problem. What is Bangladesh? The modern-day nation-state did not exist when films were invented. By extension, what is Chinese for the purposes of Chinese film studies in English? Only films from the People's Republic of China (PRC)? Or any kind of Chinese-language cinema? Leyda's book is about the PRC. But the folklorist Wolfram Eberhard's (1972) narrative analysis of Hong Kong and Taiwan cinema appeared at more or less the same time as Leyda's *Dianying*. (There is some question about the date of publication, as the title page states 1972, whereas the opposing page states "First published ... in 1974.") A wider geographical understanding of what "Chinese" means would make it a contender for the foundational text.

Raju also asks what counts as a film. Does it have to be a certain length, or a dramatic feature? In addition to asking the same questions about what counts as a film, we might ask what counts as scholarship. Does it have to be a full monograph to be a foundational text? Does it have to be published by a university press? Or can it appear in other forms? A narrow definition might cut out Eberhard's monograph because it was published by the Orient Cultural Service. Given space limitations, this chapter focuses mostly on monographs, with apologies to those who, like me, prefer to publish mostly in the essay form. (It also necessarily means omitting a number of significant anthologies that have contributed to the development of the field.) Then there is the question of who counts as a Bangladeshi filmmaker. Can a citizen of another country working in Bangladesh be accepted as having made the first Bangladeshi film? Similarly, does one have to be a film studies scholar? Leyda was, but Eberhard was a folklorist. Five years later, Ian Jarvie (1977) published a book on Hong Kong film audiences, but he was a sociologist rather than a film studies scholar. Although various disciplinary backgrounds are possible, the hegemony of film studies and related fields means that it is difficult to be accepted today without at least a working knowledge of the theories and procedures of that field.

Another important characteristic of Bourdieu's understanding of the field is that there has to be a relationship between the agents in it. Leyda, Jarvie, and Eberhard all had different disciplinary backgrounds, and could be said to be in dialogue with others in their own disciplinary fields rather than any emergent Chinese film studies field. Because there were no other film studies scholars working on Chinese film in English, even Leyda was engaged with film studies in general. (Otherwise, the language problems in his book might have been discovered prior to publication.)

In this sense, these 1970s monographs can be considered as part of the prehistory of the field. They were isolated events. There was no other significant monograph in English until Paul Clark's history, *Chinese Cinema* (1987), which appeared fifteen years after Leyda's book. By the time Clark's history appeared, a growing number of conference papers and journal articles had already been published, along with one edited collection (Berry 1985). If there is a real need to find a monograph to mark the origin of the field, Clark's has the strongest claim, because it was in conversation with other scholarship on Chinese film. But rather than overinvesting in firsts, it is more illuminating for our understanding of the contemporary field to note why Leyda's work was an almost isolated event, and why the conditions that made it acceptable in 1972 no longer prevailed fifteen years later and have not prevailed since.

First, why were other authors not writing on Chinese film? Bruce Lee's kung fu films may have been packing them in at inner-city American movie theaters (Desser 2000), but that did not seem to motivate sustained scholarship in either film studies or Chinese studies in the 1970s. Here, the crucial role of international film festivals in drawing attention to and making films available needs to be highlighted. Although festivals continue to play a gatekeeper role (Lewin 1947: 145), this was especially true before the development of the videotape, never mind the DVD. When audiences see films from places they may be unfamiliar with, this can stimulate demand for writing. After the 1950s successes of Japanese films at the leading international festivals, Joseph Anderson and Donald Richie published *The Japanese Film: Art and Industry* in 1959, initiating Japanese film studies in English. No Chinese films – including films from Hong Kong and Taiwan – had won comparable awards then. Without such exposure, there was not much demand from within the emergent discipline of film studies in English or mainstream publishing on cinema. In the case of Chinese studies scholars, cultural elitism often combined with a purist notion of the premodern and especially pre-Communist as the only true China to maintain the focus of scholars on the highbrow and the ancient.

Finally, writing on Chinese cinema was impeded by issues of access. In Hong Kong and Taiwan, there were no film archives enabling research in this period. Either, like Eberhard and Jarvie, the researcher was on the spot, or research was almost impossible. The PRC had an archive. But access was difficult for most foreign scholars after 1949, and impossible once the Cultural Revolution had started in 1966. This is certainly a reason why readers were prepared to tolerate the shortcomings of Leyda's volume. He presumably had no way to go back to double-check his material, and other scholars could not enter China at the time, either. Furthermore, it offered unique insights no one else could provide then. However, although China's "opening up" (*kaifang*) from 1979 on did not make it easy for foreign scholars to work there immediately, it did make lack of basic language competence increasingly unacceptable.

1980s: Monolingual Readers

A second assumption shaping the field to this day is that, while the scholars should be bilingual, the readership is mainly monolingual. For authors like Leyda, Eberhard, and Jarvie, writing in various other fields with no particular connections to China, this was self-evident. Authors introducing Chinese films to cinémathèque and film festival viewers in the West had to make the same assumption. Of course, if all our readers were bilingual, then there would be no need for a field of Chinese film studies in English at all! What was once a highly specialized interest among researchers is now taught to undergraduates on a regular basis. As a result, the primary readership is generated by enrolment in these courses. This in turn shapes Chinese film scholarship in English powerfully through the availability (or unavailability) of films with reasonably good English subtitles in formats that can be screened in the classroom. Publishers therefore favor work on films that students and general readers can see.

The rapid increase in university level teaching helped transform the study of Chinese cinema from something located in other academic fields into a field in its own right. Why did teaching on Chinese film pick up so quickly in the late 1980s? First, Chinese films started to win awards at major film festivals. This not only brought them to the attention of cinephiles as *Rashomon* (Akira Kurosawa, 1950) had done for Japanese films in the postwar era. It also gave what had hitherto been seen as mere entertainment (or propaganda) artistic status, making it suitable for university according to the standards that prevailed then (and persist now). The oft-cited breakthrough moment was the sensational screening of *Yellow Earth* (Chen Kaige, 1984) (see Figure 26.1) at the 1985 Hong Kong International Film Festival (Rayns 1989:1), heralding the arrival of the mainland art filmmakers known as the "Fifth Generation."

Second, financial pressures and enrolment became increasingly important in universities, and especially in areas unlikely to be prioritized by government or supported by commercial research such as the humanities. Film departments were established widely during the 1980s, and film courses were offered more and more widely in a range of other humanities departments, including East Asian or Chinese studies. Combined with the new prestige of Chinese cinema, it is not surprising that they took off, stimulating demand for films and classes.

What kind of Chinese films received the most attention? As Yingjin Zhang (2002) has argued persuasively, festival preferences for arthouse were also inflected by the Orientalism that was (and may still be) deeply and widely ingrained in Western culture. Reflecting on the field after a decade or so of growth, Yeh Yueh-yu and Abe Mark Nornes (1998) further complained that it was dominated by work on the PRC, and they attributed this to the leftist prejudices of Western critics and academics. That may be part of the picture. But limited access to films from outside the PRC with reliable English subtitles was

Figure 26.1 Lunch break from field work in *Yellow Earth* (dir. Chen Kaige, Guangxi Studio, 1984); the low-angle shot reveals an empty sky.

also part of the picture. All too often, the "Chinglish" subtitles on Hong Kong films turned even action films into comedies.

Ironically, today, the picture is reversed, with the Maoist heyday of 1949–79 being one of the more neglected periods in Chinese film studies in English. With the turn to "marketization" (*shichanghua*), the Maoist era has become an embarrassment or an irrelevance for many people. Lack of availability of DVDs with reliable subtitles is also a reason. Of course, these elements are connected, because political trends and other factors help to create the demand that leads to the availability. Therefore, tracing determinations on availability of films with English subtitles is important to understand the development of the field. In other words, why were PRC films from the 1949–79 era much easier to find with subtitles in the 1980s than they are today?

Circumstances that emerged after the Cultural Revolution ended in 1976 and before the breakthrough of *Yellow Earth* not only led to the resumption and growth of film production in the PRC itself. The "opening up" that followed Deng Xiaoping's ascent to power in 1978 also led to improved access. Initially, this took the form of government-to-government cultural exchanges with countries used to conducting cultural relations on such terms, especially those of Western Europe. Major retrospectives from the prerevolutionary era and from the PRC after 1949 were held in Paris, Turin, and London at the beginning of the early 1980s. Each was accompanied by catalogs, including essays that went beyond documentation into critical scholarship (Rayns and Meek 1980; Müller 1982a, 1982b; Quiquemelle and Passek 1985).

Similar exhibitions of Hong Kong and Taiwan film were more difficult because the same exchange mechanisms did not exist. At this time, both the PRC and the Republic of China (ROC based in Taiwan) claimed to be the sole legitimate government of the entire territory of China. Forced to choose, most foreign governments had recognized the PRC after US President Nixon's visit to China in 1972. Hong Kong was a British colony, without a separate sovereign government of its own. As already mentioned, neither Taiwan nor Hong Kong had an active and well-resourced film archive at this time, either. At a deeper level, these difficulties can be traced to the dominance of the nation-state system and its institutions in international circulation before the fuller impact of neoliberalism and globalization.

The major retrospectives of pre- and postrevolutionary cinema from the PRC connected to film-as-art taste cultures, leading to Chinese films appearing on the film festival circuit under the rubric of the search to "discover" new auteurs, new cinemas, new classics, and so forth. In the early 1980s, colleges, festivals, and other specialist exhibitors were heavily dependent on embassy collections of 16mm prints. Without embassies, Hong Kong and Taiwan were again at a disadvantage. Videotape changed the way of accessing the films, but the arrival of China's own "new wave" of Fifth Generation directors in the mid-1980s only entrenched the emphasis on the PRC as their films went from festivals into video release.

Film-as-art tastes extended to academia. In the mid-1980s this continued to exclude the Hong Kong popular films circulating in Chinatown cinemas from much serious attention, as they were considered lowbrow. However, the founding and development of the Hong Kong International Film Festival from the late 1970s did provide an important site for the production of scholarship in English on Hong Kong cinema at this time. Young cinephiles in Hong Kong had set up film clubs, festivals, and other activities during this period (Jimmy Choi 2008). Among the Hong Kong International Film Festival's various events was an annual retrospective section, focused on a different theme, genre, historical period, or other aspect of Hong Kong cinema each year. The bilingual catalog published to accompany the retrospective has been a crucial source of both information and critical perspectives ever since. However, you had to be at the festival to get these materials, severely limiting their circulation and making it impossible to set them as class texts.

The film festival circuit has continued to be the primary gatekeeper determining the availability of films with English subtitles to the present day. Initially, this privileged arthouse cinema. Only when Hou Hsiao-hsien, Edward Yang, and then Tsai Ming-Liang won awards at international film festivals from the late 1980s on did Taiwan cinema begin to circulate and get written about more regularly (C. Wu, 2007). Even though the unavailability of some classic Taiwan auteur works has impeded teaching and research, the prominence generated by film festival awards means there are now books devoted to all three aforementioned directors (Udden 2009; J. Anderson 2005; Rehm, Joyard, and Rivière 1999), and a number of monographs and collections devoted to recent Taiwan cinema has appeared (Yip 2004; Berry and Lu 2005; Yeh and Davis 2005; Davis and Chen 2007).

Similarly, academic work has been generated on the recent waves of mainland Chinese cinema that have followed the festival-to-DVD path, including various monographs (R. Chow 1995; Pickowicz and Zhang, 2006; Z. Zhang 2007b).

In contrast, many popular and famous films have been relatively neglected because they are not highlighted by film festival awards or available on well-subtitled DVDs. Similarly, unavailability of historical cinema outside the archive has discouraged scholarship. An extreme example would be the Taiwanese-language cinema of the 1950s and early 1960s. Although produced in large numbers and very popular, it was never a festival cinema. Not only are these films unavailable on DVD, but most of the original prints do not even have Chinese subtitles, and relatively few people can understand Taiwanese. Shaw Brothers are another example. Of course, the Shaw Brothers brand is globally famous. But until this century, they refused to release their back catalog on video or DVD, thus limiting scholarship. When they changed their policy and released subtitled DVDs by the hundred, the first monograph in English followed (Fu 2008). Similarly, prerevolutionary cinema became available initially on VCD without subtitles (and more recently with reliable subtitles on DVD in a few cases), aiding research and making publication possible (Y. Zhang 1999; J. Hu 2000; Pang 2002; Fu 2003).

One important exception to the difficulty of accessing popular and/or historical cinema is Hong Kong action cinema. The global popularity of this cult genre, including such influential figures as Quentin Tarantino (b. 1963) and the transfer of directors like John Woo and Ringo Lam (Lin Lingdong, b. 1955) to Hollywood, has spearheaded the release of many Hong Kong films made since 1980 on DVD. This has supported a wide range of books on recent Hong Kong action cinema in particular and Hong Kong cinema in general (Teo 1997; Stokes and Hoover 1999; Bordwell 2000; Fu and Desser 2000; E. Yau 2001; Morris et al. 2006; Teo, 2009), as well as the ongoing series of small monographs on single films from Hong Kong University Press.

1990s: The Hegemony of Film Studies

Today, teaching on Chinese cinema is found in a variety of departments, but most commonly in Chinese or East Asian studies departments and in film or cinema studies departments. Of the two, the theories, methods, and trends found in film studies and related disciplines based on varieties of textual exegesis, such as comparative literature or visual culture, are dominant. While a "language department" might provide a base, a scholar is expected to work with the approaches of the discipline relevant to their interests. This has not always been the case. But since this pattern consolidated around the early 1990s, most of the major trends in Chinese film studies have followed those of film studies in general.

If we look at the first books on Chinese cinema again, we can see that only Leyda's was produced from within film studies. Eberhard was a folklorist, Jarvie a sociologist, and Clark's training was in history and East Asian languages. Each of these disciplinary backgrounds is clearly reflected in their books. As mentioned before, until the 1980s, cinema studies departments were few. They were usually found in universities that offered training in film production, such as New York University, where Jay Leyda taught. But by the early 1990s a number of anthologies and monographs had appeared mostly written and edited by scholars within film studies or related text-based disciplines (e.g., Berry 1985, 1991; Browne et al. 1994; Ehrlich and Desser 1994, although the latter also covers Japanese film). This manifested the new centrality of textual analysis as the field of Chinese cinema studies in English consolidated itself. Why did this shift occur?

First, there was the rapid development of film studies itself in the 1980s, resulting in its emergence as a discipline with its own theories and methods. This is not the place to offer a detailed account of the history of film studies in general, but suffice to say that in the 1980s, what is sometimes known as "screen theory" (after the British journal *Screen*) took hold. Earlier efforts had tried to get film taken seriously by trying to position it as art rather than entertainment. For example, auteur theory claimed films were not collective and artisanal or industrial products but the expressions of their directors (Caughie 1981). Instead, a semiotic approach combined with Marxism and psychoanalysis to understand cinema as a language system that worked to position its viewers as subjects who took up certain positions in the discourse (and therefore certain beliefs) (Metz 1974, 1982). The emphasis here is that any language (including the language of film or literature or painting) is not a transparent "medium" but has its own power. This placed a focus on the formal structures of film as forms of language. For example, in what continues to be the most frequently cited film studies essay, Laura Mulvey (1975) argued over thirty years ago that mainstream Hollywood cinema used shot and reverse-shot structures to position viewers to identify with male characters who were the subjects of a gaze on female characters that was either sadistic or fetishistic in its operations.

The advent of screen theory meant that film scholars developed a highly specific set of concepts and terms to address the particularities of their medium. Any scholar who wanted their work to be taken seriously within the field as up to date had to take this on board. The base in semiotics, psychoanalysis, Marxism, and the text gave film studies a lot in common with sister disciplines such as comparative literature, and a variety of theoretical paradigms have been adopted one after the other ever since. With the notable exception of scholars like Perry Link, Leo Ou-fan Lee, and Paul G. Pickowicz, East Asian and Chinese studies departments were also still more interested in high-culture classics from the era before contact with the West, or at least prior to the 1949 Liberation. Furthermore, they were both resistant to contemporary critical theory, which they saw as "Western" and of little relevance to China, or at least the kind of premodern China they were most interested in. In these circumstances, many young scholars interested in Chinese film migrated toward film studies and related disciplines.

Perhaps the most prominent example of a new scholar of Chinese literature and culture emerging from outside East Asian and Chinese studies in the early 1990s was Rey Chow. Chow received her PhD in Modern Thought and Literature at Stanford University and went on to create a huge splash with her first book, *Woman and Chinese Modernity* (1991). An examination of gender in early twentieth-century Chinese literature, the contents page is preceded by citations from Nietszche, Benjamin, and Spivak. This implicitly repudiates the idea of "Western" theory as irrelevant to understanding Chinese culture. The book was vehemently rejected by many established figures in the mainstream of East Asian and Chinese studies, and Chow remains a highly controversial scholar to this day. But the book's engagement with gender, modernity, and many of the theories and debates in text-based disciplines made it possibly the first contemporary text on Chinese literature to have a wide appeal outside Chinese studies. Chow repeated this success with *Primitive Passions* (1995). Analyzing China's Fifth Generation cinema through the lenses of postcolonial theories of self-ethnography, as well as visuality and sexuality, her work spoke to the cutting edge of cinema studies as surely as *Woman and Chinese Modernity* engaged with scholars of literature.

Ever since the consolidation around contemporary critical theory in the early 1990s that Chow and various other scholars helped to promote, Chinese film studies in English has found its primary base in film studies and related text-based disciplines. Therefore, it has followed many of the primary trends in that field. In the 1990s, films were approached as representational or as discourses engaged in the construction of concepts, understandings of the world, and values. In Chinese film studies in English, by far the most dominant trend has been the "national cinemas" assumption that films can tell us something about the territory they come from. In one way or another, films are read as ways of understanding one or other aspect of life and culture in Taiwan, Hong Kong, the PRC, or the Chinese diasporic populations. This "methodological nationalism," as its critics understandably dub it, underpins much if not a majority of work in the field. Today, the national is no longer assumed as universal in a wide range of scholarship including film studies, where national cinema is no longer taken for granted. Therefore, books and articles have appeared that self-reflexively examine the national dimensions of Chinese cinema (J. Hu 2000; Pang 2002; Y. Zhang 2004a; Berry and Farquhar 2006).

As in film studies itself, another major area of work has centered on gender and sexuality. Following the argument that gender is a fundamental element of almost all aspects of culture, it comes up in most writing in the field, and has led to books on feminism and women in Chinese cinema (J. Dai 2002; S. Cui 2003), masculinity in Hong Kong cinema (Pang and Wong 2005), and queer studies and homosexuality in the Chinese cinemas (S. Lim 2006). Scholarship centered on North American cinema has become as interested in race and ethnicity as gender. So far, although there are articles, there have not been any books on these issues in Chinese cinemas, perhaps because it is not such a self-evidently all-pervasive issue.

Identity (individual or national) is not the only cultural phenomenon that is read through film texts. In mainstream film studies the connections between cinema and the city have become of increasing interest (Clarke 1997; Shiel and Fitzmaurice 2001) as questions of urban change and the shift from modern to postmodern and global cultures have come into general view with ideas like the "global city" (Sassen 1991). In few societies has urban life been transformed as quickly as in Hong Kong, Taiwan, and the PRC, so it makes sense that work on the city and cinema is emerging as a trend in the field (Abbas 1997; Braester 2010; Braester and Tweedie 2010).

As a result of the emphasis on film and representation derived from film studies, various potential areas of work have not been undertaken. Since Leyda and Jarvie's pioneering work, Chinese film audiences have been largely neglected. Little attention has been paid to policy, economics, or technology. There have only been three significant variations to this pattern of focus on the text as representation or constructor of understandings, values, and concepts. All three also follow trends within mainstream film studies.

First, one of the most prominent scholars within film studies has carved out a different approach. David Bordwell and his adherents also put films at the center of film studies, and do not generally pay much attention to audiences. However, their effort is on detailing the characteristics of the films and in particular their formal features, and then accounting for them in terms of the conventions and practices of the industry and the individual filmmaker working within that industry, rather than relating them to larger cultural patterns. This approach is not only manifested in his own book on Hong Kong cinema (Bordwell 2000), but also other works that learn from his approach (e.g., Yeh and Davis 2005; Curtin 2007; Udden 2009).

Second, in film studies as a whole, there has been a renewed interest in early cinema and pre-cinema. Reasons include interest in cinema as technology provoked by digitalization and the eclipse of celluloid as the defining characteristic of film. In the case of Chinese film studies in English, as already noted, the release of prerevolutionary films in the 1990s aided scholarship. However, very few Chinese films before the late 1920s have survived. From within a text-centered approach, this foreclosed upon research. Yet if film is understood as a culture rather than a set of texts or an industry (Harbord 2002), then the survival of stills, reviews, information about movie theaters, scripts, and so on makes research into early film culture possible. In Chinese film studies in English, the application of such an approach has appeared in Zhang Zhen's breakthrough analysis, *An Amorous History of the Silver Screen* (2005), and is shaping a wide range of cutting-edge work on other topics (McGrath 2008b; Braester 2010).

Finally, the long-standing emphasis on film texts to the neglect of all other aspects of cinema has begun to wane in mainstream film studies in recent years. Various aspects of the industry from production (Caldwell 2008) to distribution

(Acland 2003) have received greater attention. This may be a knock-on effect of the emergence of creative industries as both a field of study and an object of government policy, although most scholarship within film studies does not assume measuring the success of an art form in economic terms as much as the more mainstream and policy-oriented discourse does. In Chinese film studies in English, landmark works have appeared with similar approaches (Curtin 2007; Davis and Yeh 2008, although the latter covers a wider territory than only Chinese-language film). In addition to individual star studies, just as the phenomenon of stardom and celebrity are well-established topics in film and media studies as a whole (Gledhill 1991; Stacey 1993), so too they are becoming more established in Chinese film studies in English (Farquhar and Zhang 2010; Edwards and Jeffreys 2010).

Since 2000: The Transnational Turn and More

The more recent trends observed in the section above have taken us up to the present day of writing this essay. Each of the taken-for-granted characteristics that shape Chinese film studies in English in fundamental ways continues to operate. In other words, although the assumption of bilingualism among scholars goes back to the very beginnings of the field, it was not eclipsed by monolingualism among readers. The fundamental characteristics have come into place next to each other, reconfiguring the field in each case. The hegemony of film studies and related disciplines also continues to operate, with Chinese film studies in English following most of the major trends in the main discipline.

By way of conclusion, this section considers the distinctiveness of the field in three regards. First, how has Chinese film studies in English not followed the mainstream of film studies, and why? Second, what are some of the ways Chinese film studies in English are similar to or different from Chinese film studies in Chinese? And third, how is the most fundamental new trend drawn from the hegemony of film studies, which could be called the "transnational turn," being manifested within Chinese film studies in English?

Chinese film studies in English has diverged from the mainstream of film studies in certain ways. Availability on DVD with subtitles can explain the relative absence of work on short films, experimental cinema, home movies, and so forth. Documentary cinema has also made little headway so far, and for much the same reason, although the powerful impact of Chinese independent documentary is changing that situation (Berry, Lu, and Rofel 2010). Already noted is a relative paucity of work on ethnicity and race in Chinese cinemas. Reception studies are also very rare indeed. There continues to be a chilling effect of the mainland Chinese political and social environment where, despite many changes and the rollback of the government in many areas of life, people are often reluctant to go on the record about their frank opinions. If this changes, audience research will be facilitated.

Next, the impact of Deleuzian theory and its concern with temporality has been widely felt through mainstream cinema studies (for an early and influential example, see Rodowick 1997). But it has made little impact on Chinese film studies in English so far. Deleuze is a philosopher, and philosophy positions itself not as a particular Western mode of analysis and knowledge production differentiated according to historical periods, but instead as the pursuit of absolute truth. (This is, of course, the hubris of much Western modern thought.) This implies that work on the topic outside the West is at best a mere extension or afterthought, and not of fundamental value. To be fair to Deleuze, his work in *Cinema I* on the "movement-image" (1986) assigns that way of knowing time (as a succession of metrically divided presents) to modernity and mainstream Hollywood studio cinema in particular. But when he turns to neorealism and the other cinemas of what he calls the "time-image" in *Cinema II* (1989), it is all too easy to (mis)read this work as implying access to some transcendent true time obscured or withheld from us by modernity. As a result, temporality in the cinema has been written about as a general topic, when in fact most of the authors have been dealing with time in reference to particular cinemas of particular periods. Bliss Cua Lim has recently shown the way out of this impasse with her work on temporality in Asian films in the fantastic mode. She insists on historical and cultural specificity (B. Lim, 2009), and hopefully this will open the door to more studies of this kind, including in Chinese cinema studies in English. Also drawing heavily on Deleuze is the recent interest in affect in cinema, complemented by a broader interest in emotion and feeling. Rey Chow has opened up the latter area of work in Chinese film studies in English with *Sentimenal Fabulations* (2007).

Finally, in regard to aspects of mainstream film studies not taken up into Chinese film studies in English, there is the impact of the digital. Because the digital has swept away the ontological ground of celluloid that had distinguished film from other media, it has provoked outpourings of research in mainstream film studies. In Chinese film studies in English, there has been very little written on the topic. Paola Voci's (2010) book examines the new-media moving-image texts that we have all been neglecting to our peril, and therefore opens important new doors. Yet, much as with work on temporality, most work on the digital has been written with the Western hubris that assumes it is writing about universal truth when it is only writing about the West. As in Lev Manovich's (2002) hugely influential work, most of the writing to date is fascinated with the capacity of the digital to erase the indexical truth value attached to cinema and photography. Certainly, Hollywood investment in computer-generated images (CGI) and effects has underlined this. While mainstream Chinese cinema is going down the same route with its own big-budget blockbuster culture (Rawnsley and Rawnsley 2010), the appeal of the mini-DV camera for independent filmmakers and particularly documentarians has been its ability to supposedly capture the contingent on camera and at the same time enable single-person filmmaking

(Berry, Lu, and Rofel 2010), indicating that there are contested ideas about the digital and cinema to be explored through Chinese film.

If there are ways in which Chinese film studies in English does not follow mainstream film studies, then there are also many divergences between Chinese film studies in English and Chinese film studies in Chinese. Or, at least there are many such divergences in the case of the PRC. Scholars working in Hong Kong and in Taiwan often operate with theories and methods that are very similar to those used in the West, and indeed many if not most of the leading scholars there have had experience of either studying or working in the West. Furthermore, in many cases their own bilingual capacities mean that they often publish in both English and Chinese. The nuanced differences between them would be worthy of further investigation.

However, although many scholars currently working in English began their careers in the PRC and increasing amounts of scholarship are translated from English into Chinese (and occasionally the other way around, e.g., J. Dai 2002), film studies in the PRC pursues its own distinctive path. This is clearly worth a full-length study in its own right and the remarks here are necessarily brief and somewhat speculative. But, overall, film studies scholars in the PRC are more concerned with the well-being of the industry, its structural reforms, technological change, new genres, and so on, and less invested in ideological critique based on textual analysis. Prior to the 1980s moment of close contact between Chinese and Western film studies (Y. Zhang 2002: 44), film studies in China was primarily seen as a research arm of the cinema enterprise. Therefore, the current tendency may be a continuation of that earlier pattern, albeit with an emphasis on market more than the pedagogical mission of the cinema during the Mao era (1949–76). Furthermore, in a society that does not permit political opposition, ideological critique is too sensitive and risky to be widely attempted.

A final way in which Chinese film studies in English is beginning to carve out its own distinct character concerns what could be called the "transnational turn." In mainstream film studies, globalization has been felt in the interest in diasporic cinema (Naficy 2001) as well as the global ambition of Hollywood (Miller et al. 2001). But in Chinese film studies in English, the impact has, if anything, been even greater, and it has gone beyond the type of topic studied.

The national and national cinemas were always an awkward fit in the Chinese case, where a number of different cinema industries and cultures could be called "Chinese" as well as a number of territories, and where at different times there were very active flows between them. As a result, when Sheldon Lu published his anthology *Transnational Chinese Cinemas* (1997), it had a watershed effect. Since that date, it has been impossible to engage in work on "national cinema" without defining and justifying the term and what it means in the Chinese case or cases. Furthermore, a lot of recent publishing in Chinese film studies in English uses the term "transnational" or "global" in its title to mark its engagement with these issues, which are now as fundamental to the field as any of the other features discussed in this chapter (S. Lu 2002; Y. Zhang 2002, 2010a; K. Lo 2005; Marchetti 2006; Morris, Li, and Chan 2006; Curtin 2007; S. Lu 2007; Hunt and Leung 2008; K. Chan 2009; Rawnsley and Rawnsley 2010). The adoption of the term "Chinese-language cinemas" (for example, Lu and Yeh 2005) is a further indicator of this transnational turn away from the national cinemas paradigm, and this particular term is even more prominent in Chinese-language scholarship (as *huayu dianying*).

At the same time as the Chinese in Chinese film studies in English has been reconfigured from national to transnational, the field has also been transnationalized in terms of the scholars themselves. The presence of large numbers of scholars and students born in Chinese-speaking territories has changed the original situation back when Leyda, Jarvie, and Eberhard were writing. Then, scholars publishing about Chinese film in English often functioned as a "bridge" to or "window" on what was presumed to be a distant place few of our readers would be familiar with. Yet today we take it for granted that both the scholars involved and our readers either have now or are likely to have in the future direct experience of China. This final shift is certainly a change as fundamental, permanent, and taken for granted as any of the other ones discussed here. It contests and helps to remove the Orientalism identified as a structural and discursive commonplace in earlier scholarship (Y. Zhang 2002: 43–114). But it also adds a new level of complexity and unpredictability. With the possibility of ever greater contestations of values, expectations, and methods working across borders and through the field itself, the future of the field is becoming even harder to predict at the same time as it continues to grow exponentially, and this can surely only make it a more exciting field of research and publication in the future.

27

The Return of the Repressed
Masculinity and Sexuality Reconsidered

Shuqin Cui

This chapter examines how gender and sexuality – as a category of analysis and reflection of historical conditions – participate in the formation of Chinese-language cinemas and their spectatorship. Seen in critical retrospection, an important signature of Chinese film production has been the search for and construction of repressed masculinity and sexuality. In the 1980s and early 1990s, when the lost generation of the Cultural Revolution returned to cultural production, their sense of a stifled masculinity led to an effort to restore the male body and identity in the making of new wave cinema. Yet the return of the repressed is most evident in how the female image appears as a discursive emblem and visual trope. Taking Zhang Yimou's "allegorical red trilogy" – *Red Sorghum* (1987), *Ju Dou* (1989), and *Raise the Red Lantern* (1991) – as examples,[1] I argue that the new wave filmmakers look to the female body as a site for the projection of oppressed national experiences and as a sign for castrated male sexuality. It is through the spectacle of woman that the films generate national allegories and initiate a transnational encounter, where international fantasy and Chinese iconography coproduce a cooperative Orientalism.

While new wave cinema employs allegorical forms to recover a repressed masculinity, other films examine lost masculinity and subdued sexuality by returning to history through memory. In *Farewell My Concubine* (Chen Kaige, 1993), the unfolding of history coincides with the revelation of an alternative masculinity articulated through female impersonation. The opera role *dan* and its embodiment of transgendered identity achieve an idealized femininity on the opera stage while preserving male privilege in gender relations. Behind the operatic mask and costume, however, lies a reshaped male body and repressed homosexuality. Similar to what *Farewell* does, *Lust, Caution* (Ang Lee, 2007) returns to China's national history to recall a lost memory. Lee's adaptation of Chang's

A Companion to Chinese Cinema, First Edition. Edited by Yingjin Zhang.
© 2012 Blackwell Publishing Ltd. Published 2012 by Blackwell Publishing Ltd.

story, nonetheless, rewrites a female narrative to advance a piece of history ignored by mainstream historiography and to assert a male subjectivity shadowed by national–political conflicts.

Unlike the new wave directors who won international renown, the younger generation of film directors gained attention by choosing to represent outsiders: rebellious urban youth, social misfits, and others on the economic margins. In shifting from personal film practice to mainstream productions, these directors refused to abandon art films and committed themselves to depicting contemporary social realities. Often they relied on the screen persona of a strong female figure to drive the film narrative and compel a negotiation of power. Foregrounding heroines as social and visual centers of attention, the films cast concern over troubled masculinity and repressed sexuality in the context of an emerging commercial society. *Tuya's Marriage* (Wang Quan'an, 2008) and *In Love We Trust* (Wang Xiaoshui, 2008), for instance, place a female figure at the heart of a social predicament to instigate negotiations that men find difficult to handle. The filmic configuration of leading women created by male directors can be read as an expression of male anxiety about how to secure identity and status in a fast-changing society.

The Anxiety of Masculinity

The emergence of new wave cinema in the 1980s reflected a cultural interest in revisiting China's history and examining its problems. Prominent members of the first graduating class of the Beijing Film Academy after the Cultural Revolution participated in the cultural awakening of the 1980s through their early films. Reviewing these films today, one realizes that the new wave expressed a deep concern for the nation and for a people oppressed by tradition or politics. Directors pursued a cinematic language that would enable them to rewrite the national experience. Along with the broad historical themes and visual modes of expression came an anxiety over repressed masculinity. In their early films the new wave directors employed particular visual systems within a framework of national history to search for a male subjectivity made marginal and a masculinity restrained from action by political forces.

Masculinity and the assertion of the male body preoccupy the screen space. In *One and Eight* (Zhang Junzhao, 1984), set during the resistance war against the Japanese, black-and-white footage of combat and a mise-en-scène of eight captured bandits chained together, standing against the northern desert, announced the emergence of the Fifth Generation cinematic aesthetics. The images of eight violent men, wretched in appearance, subvert the conventional boundaries between heroes and villains by presenting the outlaws as masculine heroes. In *Yellow Earth* (Chen Kaige, 1984), the efforts of an army officer to save the poor and enlighten a peasant woman are rebuffed; the film does not allow the male hero to either free his female heroine or alleviate poverty. Patriarchal tradition and revolutionary ideology leave scant freedom for individual action. The effort to question history is often stymied, illustrating the difficulty the male hero faces when trying to elude the phallic symbol of collective conventions, traditional or revolutionary. In *Horse Thief* (Tian Zhuangzhuang, 1986), a Tibetan horseman living on the social margins moves to the religious center of Tibetan Buddhism. The Tibetan landscape and dutch-angle shot distort the potential engagement between God and disciple. Multiple superimpositions of prostration reinforce the power of religious strictures over vulnerable individuals.

The early new wave films show a strong tendency toward recovering repressed masculinity through the guise of national allegory and historical reflection. Fredric Jameson's concept of third-world literature and intellectuals holds that the obsession with the return of the personal to the national bespeaks a desire to move from the margins to the center: it is precisely the anxiety over marginality that drives personal writing toward "national allegories" and a "political dimension" (Jameson 1986: 100). Similarly, in her book *Masculinity Besieged*, Xueping Zhong (2000: 11) sees "Chinese male gender anxiety over masculinity as a preoccupation with the lack of a male power position"; she defines this preoccupation as a male "marginality complex … filled with the desire to overcome the marginalized position by moving toward the center." The intention of the individual is not to allegorize but rather to use the national as a legitimate framework and a discursive strategy for returning from the periphery and asserting the personal. Moreover, the return occurs in multiple dimensions. Screen masculinity therefore marks a subversive tendency toward the norms of both traditional and socialist cinema. The bandits, the ethnic minority, and the vulnerable Communist officer in the films mentioned above, for instance, defy the conventions of the heroic male figure. Gone from the screen is the prominent revolutionary hero of socialist cinema or the modern man of early films, replaced by the primitive and the masculine.

In addition, the mise-en-scène of barren landscape and the predominance of cinematography challenge the traditions of cinema narrative and melodrama. Early new wave directors pursued the visual and the unconventional as they worked to introduce themselves into a mainstream film industry constrained by political ideology and burdened by film tradition. While directors inscribed their signature on film history with their maverick works, the attempt to move from margin to center had serious drawbacks. The innovative films could hardly be appreciated by a mass audience, and the unusual masculine images remained problematic. The new wave experiment did not last long, but the anxiety over masculinity lingered. Zhang Yimou's first trilogy continued the search for masculinity and treated sexuality as a central theme. The symbolic power of the phallus and the defining importance of gender inform the narratives and visual aesthetics that mark Zhang's directorial signature and visual style. More important, in his construction of masculinity and sexuality, it is the female image and female body that serve as a point of departure and a site of projection. Thus one cannot discuss issues of gender and sexuality in Chinese cinema without engaging Zhang Yimou's early films and evaluating their contribution to the aesthetics of Chinese cinema: the female spectacle and the drama of repressed desire.

Eugene Wang (1991: 85–6) refers to *Red Sorghum* as "a cinematic milestone that proposes a powerful Chinese version of masculinity as a means of cultural critique" and locates the notion of Chinese masculinity in the "return of the collectively repressed – the exiled outlaws, drunkards, rebels who were historically marginalized and expelled from official historical documents and survived only in folktales, romances, myths, and historicized fictional narratives." This return of the repressed and the marginalized occurs through the female image as a visual trope and the female body as the sexual other. As the film uses a first-person narrator to recall a heroic legend of "my grandpa and grandma" in the past, the voice-over of a male heir establishes a gendered discourse: the male voice enunciates history as the female body signifies desire. Indeed, the "ideology of the body and aesthetics of masculinity" has been described as the central concern of Zhang's filmic articulation (S. Lu 1997: 108).

The return of the repressed begins with the screen image of a male body framed from a woman's point of view. A group of sedan carriers ridicule the bride with their lewd songs and jostling movements. The camera leads us first to the heroine confined inside the sedan chair, then to her view of the body of a sedan bearer. The point-of-view shot frames a half-naked, muscular male body, highlighting its vital force and sexual attraction. The positioning of the woman as the voyeur does not imply that she possesses the male body; rather, it leads vision toward an "aesthetics of masculinity," a body infused with primitive vigor and sexual energy. In a celebration of masculinity, the film situates the female body against the mise-en-scène of the sorghum field, where the hero rescues the bride from an arranged marriage, and they engage in sexual intercourse. To legitimate the discourse of masculinity as national heroism, the film later returns the female body to the same mise-en-scène, where war violence traumatizes the nation and terminates the woman's life. Penetrated first by sexual intrusion, then by Japanese bullets, the female body (falling down in slow motion) simultaneously signifies national history and masculine energy.

The bloody conclusion to the 1989 student protest at Tiananmen Square erased the carnival atmosphere and signaled the end to a period of cultural reflection. In the abrupt transformation from the cultural fever of the 1980s to the commercial impetus of the 1990s, the cinematic new wave fragmented, with some directors turning to history, some moving on to commercial pursuits. *Ju Dou* continues the aesthetic articulation of masculinity and sexuality. But rather than advance the primal power of the masculine body, this film examines how male identity is repressed by tradition and history. Whereas *Red Sorghum* releases pent-up sexual desires and celebrates "primitive passions" (R. Chow 1995), *Ju Dou* features an enclosed dye mill and an excessive drama of oedipal triangles.

Ju Dou examines the complex of repressed sexuality and distorted masculinity through character configurations – a socially empowered yet sexually impotent patriarchal figure and a sexually lustful yet socially constrained "nephew." The release of repression again finds in the female body a site for projecting either punishment or fulfillment. Off-screen sounds indicate how the owner of the dye mill violently abuses the female body to compensate for his impotence. The mise-en-scène of "horse riding" with the master on top of the female body forcefully defines gender relations in the patriarchal structure. Although the film situates the man in an authoritative social position that allows him to possess the woman, his sexual impotence haunts him, tormenting him with anxiety and provoking his rage. Sexual violence enables the husband figure to assert his patriarchal power and transform his sexual impotence through punishment of the female other, as his "sexual perversion" may be "a necessary means to achieve the narcissistic goal of becoming a paternal producer" (M. Yue 1996: 61). Projecting social power as well as sexual lack through the female body is Zhang's narrative innovation, a cinematic articulation of the male psyche.

How is the subject to recover male sexuality and masculine identity if he is confined to the margins of society? *Ju Dou* introduces a nephew of low social status and uses point-of-view shots to direct the male gaze toward the female body he desires but cannot legally possess. The gaze through a peephole leads the vision of the protagonist and the audience toward the female body. The act of peeping does not generate much pleasure in looking, however, as the film positions Ju Dou and Tianqing in the relationship of aunt and nephew. The desire to love one's "aunt" is fraught with guilt. In addition, the film challenges the male gaze when the woman returns the gaze and exposes her bruised body. The point-of-view structure and the returned gaze shift the socially defined "aunt–nephew relationship" to that of a mutually desiring couple. The film assigns woman the role of transgressor of social and ethical boundaries; she initiates the sexual affair with her "nephew." Foregrounding the woman as sexually assertive allows the male protagonist to play the moral guardian when ethical values are challenged and to act as a rebel when an affirmation of masculine identity is needed. The trademark image of Zhang Yimou's films is a woman, burdened and surrounded by conflicts, signifying a need to reassert masculine power and recover male sexuality.

When the cinematic image of China assumes an allegorical form, its female spectacle may generate a transnational encounter where Western fantasy and Chinese spectacle coproduce a cooperative Orientalism: "the production side 'orientalizes' to satisfy the international gaze, while the reception side embraces such self-exhibition with fascination" (S. Cui 2005: 838–9). In the 1990s, when Chinese cinema finally joined the international circle through arthouse distributions and film festivals, the screen image of oppressed Chinese and exotic ethnography corresponded to the China of Western fantasy. From the mise-en-scène of the confined dye mill in *Ju Dou* to that of the iron-house mansion in *Raise the Red Lantern*, Zhang's "allegorical red trilogy" has contributed to the appeal of a visually intriguing China. To a Western viewer, the story of one master and his four wives–concubines conjures up the old stereotype of an exotic/erotic Orient. Visual icons of red lanterns and sounds of foot massage add to the viewer's sensual pleasure. While the film is visually stunning and satisfying to the spectator's imagination, in terms of gender discourse the self-Orientalizing is oppressive.

Raise the Red Lantern transforms the stage of masculinity into a theater of punishment where wives and concubines win and lose favor with the master, as indicated by whom he chooses to sleep with on a given night. In this film the patriarchal figure does not need to physically possess the female body to project power or desire; he simply manages the drama of competition from off-screen. The largely absent male figure wields an omnipresent authority to establish order and mete out punishment through modes of ethnography. The lantern ritual, for instance, signifies the present status of the wife–concubine. Whereas the lantern's lighting identifies the woman chosen to spend the night with the master, its veiling marks one who has violated the master's rules. The positioning of wives–concubines on the stage of sexual competition for the master's favor occurs in the absence of a masculine figure, and "the invisibility of the male figure leaves a space that invites international spectatorship to project its gaze directly and exclusively on the female image" (S. Cui 2005: 844).

This vision of masculinity is also evident in the relationship between fantasy and spectatorship. Linda Williams (1994–5: 57) explains fantasy as the staging of desire in the form of mise-en-scène: "The fantasist, like the spectator, does not necessarily identify in any fixed way with a character, a gaze, or a particular position, but rather with a series of oscillating positions which fantasy's mise-en-scène of desire facilitates." Because the mise-en-scène of an Oriental setting in the absence of a patriarchal figure creates a void that invites the projection of fantasy, the international spectator can become the desiring subject of Chinese film and assume a masculine position. As the wives and concubines plot to win a night with the master, the spectator can participate in the drama and imagine taking the master's position of power. Interactions between the fantasist, the spectator, and the fantasized female image thus generate a transnational negotiation where international masculinity meets Oriental femininity through ethnographic and cinematic mise-en-scène.

Returning to History, Revising Historiography

Although the return to history in search of neglected masculinity and sexuality constitutes a central theme in Chinese-language films, the history uncovered and the historiography reconsidered may serve different purposes. After making their initial allegorical films, new wave directors turned to the past century of turbulent Chinese history. *Farewell My Concubine* (Chen Kaige, 1993), *Blue Kite* (Tian Zhuangzhuang, 1993), and *To Live* (Zhang Yimou, 1994) offer epic narratives of social unrest and individual suffering. The collective return to history for these new wave directors was not so much a matter of correcting the historical record as a quest to restore personal memories of past violence and traumatized youth.

Film directors of the younger generation also turned to history to recover personal memory. Their history, however, recalls not a time of war or the Cultural Revolution, but a time of rupture, as China began to undergo rapid economic development in the 1990s. A sense of anxiety and uncertainty characterizes their filmic practices. *Platform* (Jia Zhangke, 2000), *Peacock* (Gu Changwei, 2005), *Shanghai Dreams* (Wang Xiaoshuai, 2005), and *Sunflower* (Zhang Yang, 2005) all center on the coming-of-age experience. These directors situate their generation in the historical moment of the 1970s, when they coped with China's social and economic transitions like the protagonists of their films.

The role of personal memory in visual historiography involves not only local experience and film directors in China but also leads to a transnational engagement. *Lust, Caution* also exemplifies the return to marginalized national history, in this case the Wang Jingwei puppet regime during the Second Sino-Japanese War.[2] The primary focus of Ang Lee's film, however, is masculinity and sexuality under the shadow of historical conflict. In this section, I will focus on *Farewell My Concubine* and *Lust, Caution* to illustrate how the films' uses of historical drama act to reclaim lost masculinity and repressed sexuality. *Farewell* poses the issue of homosexuality as an alternative masculinity, whereas *Lust, Caution* concerns the denial of male subjectivity.

In *Farewell My Concubine*, political history and personal memory unfold with Peking opera as the central stage and a male actor who specializes in *dan* roles as the central figure.[3] With operatic female impersonation as a form of gendered construction, the film narrative enacts a tension between hegemonic and alternative masculinities. On the one hand, hegemonic masculinity, in R. W. Connell's words, refers to the "male role" as a "variety of masculinity to which others – among them young and effeminate as well as homosexual men – are subordinated" (Adams and Savran 2002: 110). In this film, hegemonic masculinity is expressed through the role of the king and in the heterosexual norms governing gender relations. On the other hand, alternative masculinity is evident in the role of the concubine via female impersonation and in the play of ambiguous homosexuality. Both modes of masculinity, however, are subordinated to the collective hegemony of historical forces, from traditional power to revolutionary movements.

The film pointedly addresses the question of how the corporeal discipline and rhetorical practice of opera tradition can transform a man from a biological male into a cultural female. The relation between hegemonic and alternative masculinities thus appears to be a matter of power negotiation. Three metaphors – symbolic castration, corporal punishment, and costuming – mark the historical and visual construction of the alternative gender and sexual transformation (S. Cui 2003: 151). Consider how a hegemonic masculinity (social norms and opera tradition) shapes the male body and imposes an ideology. In terms of operatic female impersonation, the practitioner of an alternative masculinity resists as well as pursues a gendered identity that differs from conventionally defined masculinity and femininity. Thus the man who plays the female role maintains the privilege of a cultured femininity on stage while still able to call on his embodied masculinity when in confrontation with women. Incorporating both masculine and feminine elements, the female impersonator presents a striking example of multifaceted masculinity.

The filmic articulation of gender identity transformation begins with the loss of maleness through symbolic castration: a mother amputates her son's extra finger in hopes of gaining him admission to an opera troupe, a man's world. The castration scene shows one's biological being yielding to social construction as the desire for cultural or institutional acceptance motivates self-denial. But the act of castration that legitimates the boy's position in the opera school also assigns him to a female role. Once symbolic castration gains the desiring subject admittance to opera training, corporal punishment further shapes the body and imposes the language that a female impersonator must speak and perform. The operatic and symbolic language system forces the speaking subject to sing, "I'm by nature a maiden, not a boy." Any resistance to this gesture of submission elicits further physical and psychological punishment. Thus, opera training under the discipline of the lash forges an identity via corporal punishment; it not only physically imprints theatrical skills into the body but also psychologically convinces the subject that he is by nature a girl, not a boy.

The new gender identity is signified by the facial mask and theatrical costume that confer on the female impersonator a stage persona with feminine beauty. The highly stylized *dan* role, played by a male actor perceived as a female beauty on stage, blends masculinity and femininity. The male body in female disguise challenges traditional gender norms and poses the issue of power negotiation when "the woman in mask" confronts a woman in nature. As Dieyi immerses himself completely in the female role he plays on and off stage, the androgynous persona occupies the screen as both visual spectacle and intergendered identity. With the opera role of the king symbolizing masculinity and the female impersonator femininity, the film leaves little space for woman. The confrontation between the *dan* Yuji and the prostitute Juxian thus constitutes a competition between a woman in disguise and a woman by nature.

By situating Juxian in a heterosexual and Dieyi in a homosexual relationship with Xiaolou, the king figure, the film intensifies the dramatic triangle with sexual and political conflict. Juxian's domestic position as Xiaolou's wife and a potential mother – she has a miscarriage – keeps her within gendered restraints as man's other. In contrast, the dual identity of a man playing a woman's role enables Dieyi to disclose his homosexual longing for Xiaolou, but his psyche is traumatized by the loss of masculinity. Neither the real nor the masked woman, however, is able to escape political abuse. The film reaches a climax at the height of the Cultural Revolution, where the king betrays his stage concubine and the concubine betrays the woman. Juxian's suicide expresses her despair over her betrayal by the man she loves. Dieyi's on-stage suicide, masked as Yuji the concubine, affirms once more the importance of the male bond to his sense of self as well as how deeply his cultural identity has melded with the persona of the female impersonator.

Lust, Caution presents another drama of impossible love. The film returns to the historical memory of the Japanese occupation of Shanghai under the collaborationist regime of Wang Jingwei in the early 1940s. The spatial and temporal setting opens a chapter of history either absent from or marginalized by the master narratives. Indeed, *Lust, Caution* may be seen as "attempting nothing less than a personal confrontation with this repressed chapter of modern Chinese history" (L. Lee 2008: 238). The director's turn to history romanticizes a sensitive historical subject through sexual politics, as the drama of a female spy and the target of her assassination take center stage. An adaptation of Eileen Chang's short story of the same title, the film intends to re-present a particular history and its literature through a fictional, cinematic reconstruction of a time and space previously suppressed.

The film begins with flashbacks to a series of episodes purposely fragmented in the original story but reimagined through cinema. The first inserted flashback depicts the performance of a patriotic stage drama that inspires nationalist sentiments in the protagonist and awakens her to the allure of theater. Audiences' roar of "China will not fail" encourages the student players to extend the stage performance into the realm of action, and they plot a political assassination. Chia-chih is assigned the role of seducer to entice a chief collaborator. The sequence gives the film a reference to national history and supplies a sense of nostalgia to the director. Moreover, the flashbacks fill a void and clarify the ambiguity that the original story sustains, thereby establishing a linear narrative structure that meets cinematic conventions and audience expectations. More important, the inserted flashbacks transform a woman's writing, narrated from a female perspective and punctuated with fragments to create a sense of paradox, into a cause-and-effect mainstream melodrama.

In addition, the film constructs a gendered narrative with performance as its central trope. Chia-chih plays her roles simultaneously as a spy–agent in the disguise of Mrs. Mai and as a lover to Mr. Yee, the collaborator. Such positioning lands the protagonist in a performative entrapment between the discourse of national salvation and the desire of female sexuality. Judith Butler sees gender as an act constantly rehearsed through script and directed by cultural conventions: "The distinction between the personal and the political or between private and public is itself a fiction designed to support an oppressive status quo: our most personal acts are, in fact, continually being scripted by hegemonic social conventions and ideologies" (Felluga 2003). The script that directs the protagonist's performance is through symbolic "hailing" or "interpellating" of the woman into patriotic commitment. After the successful show, Chia-chih returns to the stage. "Come up here, Chia-chih," a voice off screen "hails" the subject. In a "one-hundred-and-eighty-degree physical conversion" (Althusser 1971: 174–5) through a reversed shot, Chia-chih and the audience realize that the patriotic theater group is recruiting her for the role of assassin. The symbolic address of "hey, come up here" also conveys the director's call to the woman to assist his reconstruction of memory. With the female character on stage and her image within the screen, the film

Figure 27.1   A flashback in *Lust, Caution* (dir. Ang Lee, Focus Features, 2007): Tang Wei as an innocent, manipulated agent.

constitutes a dialectical relation between gender and nation where the female body performs for the national interest while the male voice leads the drama on stage and directs the film from behind the camera.

Ang Lee's fascination with stage drama has its roots in personal experience: his youthful passion for theater and performance (Mo and Fu 2008: 2). In identifying with the screen persona of the young hero and in his position as director, Lee returns to a past lost in history but persistent in memory. Whereas his pursuit of theater gave him a freedom from social norms and familial constraints, his rescreening of a stage drama returns him to a personal history shadowed by nationalist discourse and the effects of diaspora on identity. Formerly a nonnative in Taiwan and later an Asian-American in the United States, Lee incorporates in the film elements of his personal history. However, his superimposition of theater-within-film rewrites Chang's fiction and changes the gender perspective. The added historical reference locates sexual politics within the legitimacy of national resistance and normalizes literary fragments in cinematic melodrama. Chang's unapologetic story and her subjective perspective lose their force in the adapted film (see Figure 27.1).

Both Ang Lee and Eileen Chang express sentiments from the past previously lost or repressed, but their means of doing so differ profoundly. Whereas the film inserts the personal into the national, Chang's story distances the national and complicates the personal. An audience acquainted with the impassioned patriotic drama staged in cinematic flashbacks will find it absent from Chang's story, as she presents the reader with a self-parody through memory, related in stream of consciousness and third-person commentary. Chang's fictional narrative juxtaposes or oscillates between distinct images and moments of disclosure:

First, in a present location, Chia-chih was anxiously waiting for the arrival of Mr. Yee. A third-person narration, then, explains: "She had, in a past life, been an actress; and here she was, still playing a part, but in a drama too secret to make her famous." Afterward follows a flashback to the past where the theater troupe staged one last public performance after the university relocated to Hong Kong .... The crowded lecture auditoriums and Hong Kong people's apathy towards China's national emergency always reminded them of their refugee status and sense of exile. (Chang, Wang, and Schamus 2007: 17–18)

In this short passage, Chang's story reveals the female protagonist in different times and spaces, between memory and events. The nonlinear narrative and fragmented structure may defy the reader's expectations, but the method enables female experience and expression to unfold in an unconventional way. The third-person narrator and the fiction writer are most concerned with the protagonist's outsider status. For Chang, the experience of leaving Shanghai for Hong Kong created a sense of displacement, as her own education and personal life became unmoored.[4] Setting her fictional protagonist against the spatial dislocation, Chang's story highlights personal disillusionment more than national crisis in wartime China. Her heroine's action becomes, on the one hand, a "form of feminine rejection" (Chang, Wang, and Schamus 2007: 65) turning away from the national and the political, and, on the other hand, a literary enactment of how man betrays woman.

On the surface, the film *Lust, Caution* resembles a conventional wartime spy thriller, but it is not. Lee's return to history also means a return to repressed male sexuality. Beyond the staged drama spectacle, the film adds three explicitly sexual scenes, which have provoked intense, contentious reactions.[5] These controversial scenes provide the central channel through which Lee explores the theme of repressed male subjectivity and sexuality. The film takes Chang's sharp claim that "The way to a woman's heart is through her vagina" as a point of departure to a visual and psychological construction of sex and sexual politics. Screened first is a sadomasochistic love scene in which the male protagonist binds, whips, and abuses the female body to demonstrate his authority and release his repressed sexual desire. The psychological anxiety evident in sexual violence stems from the pressure of surviving under a repressive regime, and the sadistic penetration of the female body asserts a sense of compensatory power. As the film visualizes the way to a woman's heart through her vagina, Lee has turned Chang's words into "a flesh that literally bares the devices of seduction and conquest," devices that "tangibalized Chang but also cannibalized her, exposing to all a ruthless incorporation of Chang's allusions" (Davis 2008).

The explicit sex scenes do not simply reflect male sexual anxiety and social authority. Lee also attempts to look deeply into human psychology through sexuality and to subvert the stereotyped characterization that labels one as either a revolutionary martyr or a war collaborator. In the second sexual encounter, two protagonists search for each other through the most explicit lovemaking positions. The sex act draws two opponents deep into an emotional world where the spy and her target experience illicit sentiments of love. The film allows sex and the body to transgress political as well as moral boundaries. In addition, sex and its visual representation continue to function as performance. Both desiring and suspecting each other, the two protagonists use sex to go beyond their political roles to search for authentic feelings. The two words, "lust" and "caution," as James Schamus explains, "are functions of each other, not because we desire what is dangerous, but because our love is, no matter how earnest, an act, and therefore always an object of suspicion" (Chang, Wang, and Schamus 2007: xii).

The connotations may be different if we view sex and sexuality from the perspective of gender. The female body and sexuality become political when the underground resistance recruits and exploits a female agent. In the film, only once is the female protagonist allowed to give voice to the pain that penetrates her body and soul. In one sequence, the camera shifts among three characters as Chia-chih reveals how painfully the man violates her body: "Every time he hurts me until I bleed and scream before he comes, before he feels alive.… Every time when he finally collapses on me, I think, maybe this is the moment you'll come" (Chang, Wang, and Schamus 2007: 195–6). Her angry voice embarrasses the men who have assigned her body to serve political ends, but they are quick to silence her: "The most important quality to an agent is loyalty – loyalty to the party, to the leader, and to your country." Exploited by the nationalists and finally executed by the collaborator, the female body is first betrayed and then persecuted.

Lee works to reestablish repressed male sexuality and identity, but the skeptical description of sex in Chang's story addresses not sexual desire but rather submission and humiliation. To play the role of seducer Chia-chih is persuaded to lose her virginity to one of her comrades. After the assassination plan fails, the protagonist regrets that "she was an idiot," and, "for a long time, she agonized over whether she had caught something from Liang Jun-sheng" (Chang, Wang, and Schamus 2007: 22–3). When the plan resumes, Chia-chih continues to act as Mr. Yee's mistress. Sex for the protagonist, echoed in Chang's comment, becomes a principled act: "In truth, every time she was with Yee she felt cleansed, as if by a scalding hot bath; for now everything she did was for the cause" (Chang, Wang, and Schamus 2007: 23). Belief in nationalism yokes the sex act to the purifying power of ideology. Chia-chih yields to complete self-sacrifice: "He possessed her utterly, primitively – as a hunter does his quarry, a tiger his kill. Alive, her body belonged to him; dead, she was his ghost" (Chang, Wang, and Schamus 2007: 46).

The film *Lust, Caution* conjures up not only 1940s Shanghai but also 1940s Hollywood film noirs and wartime romantic melodramas (D. Lim 2007). The storyline of female seduction and political intrigue, revealed in multiple flashbacks, sets the film within the genre of noir narrative. The metropolitan setting of wartime Shanghai and Hong Kong makes the space nostalgically glamorous yet dangerous. Moreover, the special effects of extreme low-key lighting and black–white contrast shadow the characters in the entrapment of lust and caution. The most reflexive signature of film noir is the *femme fatale* with her excessive sexual and destructive power. The deadly woman uses her sex and charm to lure her prey into a trap. But in Lee's *Lust, Caution* the *femme fatale* is romanticized rather than made rapacious. She is at once seductive and innocent. She allures and sacrifices. The film presents her beauty and femininity as a fulfilling resource rather than a destructive force. Here the *femme fatale* is a much needed female other in whom repressed male masculinity and sexuality could find refuge.

The significance of the *femme fatale* is suggested by Kate Stabels (1998: 166): "Today's deep crisis of masculinity is eminently visible in popular culture and is nowhere more marked than around the *femme fatale*. Mass market cinema has a unique ability to reflect insecurities in the male image, and the *fatale* figure which combines sadistic and masochistic male fantasies is a potent lightning rod for male anxieties." The fantasies projected onto Lee's *femme fatale*, however, are transgressive in multiple ways. In the eyes of the underground resistance, she is a spy–agent acting in a role. For the antagonist, she is the idealized object who fulfills male sexual desires and averts a crisis of masculinity. As for the film director, he seeks to find himself through the female image he creates: "She's like the female version of me – I identify with her so closely that, by pretending, I found my true self" (James 2008). Lee's identification with his female image helps us understand how man finds himself in a configuration of the female other: through her body to release repressed sexual desires, through her heart to awaken a latent empathetic humanity, and through her mind to mirror the oppressive conditions.

One further sequence absent in the literary source is a folk tune Chia-chih performs for Mr. Yee, "Wondering Singing Girl" (see Figure 27.2). The mise-en-scène is a Japanese tavern where geishas entertain soldiers. Although Lee situates his two protagonists in a Japanese-occupied enclave, the song transports them to a national imaginary. The folk tune softens Mr. Yee's caution and sweetens the mood. For that moment, the melody and lyrics enable the two to go beyond their opposing political identities. The music originates from the classic film, *Street Angel* (Yuan Muzhi, 1937), where two musical pieces, "Four Seasons" and "Wondering Singing Girl," bridge a romantic relationship between a singsong girl and a poor trumpet player when China was threatened with full-scale Japanese invasion. Its performance in *Lust, Caution* suggests the feasibility of a seemingly impossible love in defiance of political imperatives. For the female protagonist, the song speaks to her dilemma of falling in love with a man she means to kill. For the male protagonist, the music and its feminine quality return him to an experience of simple human feelings. Lee identifies the image of woman with the nostalgia aroused by the music: "A Chinese man or literati, when fallen to a hopeless condition, would view himself as a woman. Nostalgic desire towards one's youth and nation would locate a woman as a site for projection" (*Kan Dianying* 2007).

The original story and the film also contradict each other due to differences in perspective. Near the end of the story, Chang lets her heroine experience a moment of love but at the cost of her life. Thus, "if Chia-chih's act at the end of the story is indeed an expression of love, it paradoxically destroys the very theatrical contract

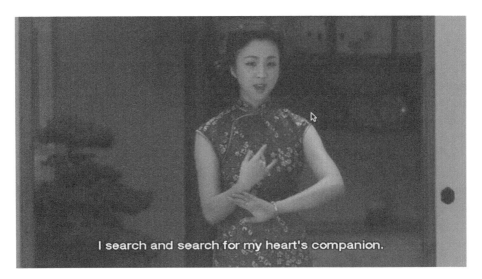

I search and search for my heart's companion.

Figure 27.2   Singing a folk song in *Lust, Caution* (dir. Ang Lee, Focus Features, 2007): "I search and search for my heart's companion."

that made the performance of that lover possible – in killing off her fictional character, she effectively kills herself" (Chang, Wang, and Schamus 2007: xii). After Mr. Yee executes Chia-chih and her fellow students, Chang explains Yee's thinking: "She must have hated him at the end. But real men have to be ruthless. She wouldn't have loved him if he'd been the sentimental type" (Chang, Wang, and Schamus 2007: 44). The self-serving Yee imagines a happier fate for himself: "He had enjoyed the love of a beautiful woman, he could die happy – without regret" (Chang, Wang, and Schamus 2007: 46). In contrast, Lee refuses to dishonor his male protagonist but softens and frames him under noir shadows. In a high-angle shot and extreme black–white lighting contrast, Mr. Yee, after giving the order for execution, retires to Chia-chih's room and sits on her bed. With his image reflected in the mirror, his shadow projected on the wall, he appears mournful. Ang Lee preserves his male protagonist and reestablishes the male screen persona as legitimate and sensible.

Family Melodrama and the Search for Masculinity

As the market economy blossomed in China, the formally innovative new wave yielded to commercial allure and foreign imports entered the domestic market after the mid-1990s, but a younger generation of film directors deserves critical attention. Beginning with a form of urban cinema before moving to films addressing social concerns, these directors pursued an artistic, personal approach. Nevertheless, commercial pressures and official censorship created the dilemma of

Figure 27.3 The titular bride in *Tuya's Marriage* (dir. Wang Quan'an, Huaxia Film, 2006): a Mongolian woman struggling to support her crippled husband.

how to maintain an independent status while adjusting to mainstream norms. The filmmakers' disillusionment often finds expression in their images of women. Their film narrative frequently centers on a female protagonist, unfolds from a female perspective, and narrates to a female consciousness. Her male counterpart, on the contrary, often appears on the margins of both social and cinematic mise-en-scènes. The woman-centered films are made through the lens of male directorship, however, and male directors honestly consider gender issues and respect their female heroines. But what is concealed behind the screen image of a strong or ideal woman? What accounts for the strategy of making a woman-centered film? And can the family melodrama cure the crisis of masculinity while furthering one's film career?

Tuya's Marriage and *In Love We Trust* both anxiously explore midlife crises and waning masculinity through a woman as central image. Although they differ in subject and approach, both films enact the drama within a family beset by a moral dilemma. This structure may lead us to respond to the films as family melodrama or woman's cinema. Close examination, however, demonstrates that male-directed films about women encompass established film genres. The female image in *Tuya's Marriage* serves as the primary resource for familial survival and moral salvation (see Figure 27.3). The film reveals how the heroine Tuya struggles to survive with her disabled husband and two young children in the harsh grasslands of Inner Mongolia. The setting of the grasslands places the family melodrama in a specific social and ethnographic locality. The mise-en-scène of herding sheep against the storm and walking with a camel for thirty miles to fetch drinking water casts a virtuous Mongolian woman for the audience to respect and for the characters to depend on. The screen persona confronts both an ever-changing reality difficult for male characters to handle and the sociocultural norms they wish to preserve.

Tuya's Marriage is a family drama involving a woman and three men. The husband of the female protagonist is disabled as a result of an accident when drilling a well for the family. The coding of male disability signifies the marginal status of the ethnic minority as well as the deterioration of masculinity and male sexuality. The sign of disability calls for the construction of a strong and ideal woman to face hardship and revive the lost masculinity. In seeking a means to restore the familial norm, the film has the couple agree on a legal divorce in order for Tuya to marry another man to support the family. Tuya accepts the suggestion but stipulates that any suitor who intends to marry her must take her husband as well. Thus the film puts its female protagonist in a moral bind, as she seeks remarriage for family survival yet refuses to abandon her disabled husband. The decision is announced in the woman's voice, and the film uses its female image to simultaneously sustain heterosexual convention and moral regulation. The sacrifice of the female and the personal to the familial reflects the director's expectation of women in society and in film: a nexus to hold the family together, a labor resource to feed the hungry, a virtuous mother/wife sacrificing herself for others. This idealization of the female image, I argue, conceals a desire for as well as frustration with lost male masculinity and sexuality.

Among many suitors comes a man of wealth and resources. The entry of an oil businessman into the film narrative opens a new contrast between the primitive and the modern, the rural and the urban. Owning money and an automobile, the man can easily take Tuya's whole family out of poverty and into an urban area. Nonetheless, Tuya rejects the offer of wealth and refuses urban modernity. With such a plot twist, the film tries to preserve an untamed space via female virtue where man can leave economic pressures and competition behind. In one sequence, the businessman drives Tuya and her two children "out of poverty and into urbanity" but leaves her disabled husband in a nursing home. A cross-cut shifts between two locations as the businessman requests sex while the husband attempts suicide. Trapped in between, Tuya rejects affluence and returns to her old life. Her choice is an indication of the ideology of traditional against modern, of rural against urban.

As the family crisis continues, the film has its independent and virtuous woman protect the disabled husband and accept another local man. The potential yet paradoxical solution to the family crisis is to connect the heroine to a local herdsman who owns a truck and helps Tuya to drill the well. This local entrepreneur is the man who embodies technological masculinity and conventional heterosexuality. Here, *Tuya's Marriage* recalls *Ermo* (Zhou Xiaowen, 1994), where a rural woman's pursuit of a television set, a symbol of modernity, is dramatically located against a triangular relationship. Whereas the sexually impotent husband, a deposed village chief, signifies the bygone era of Mao's China, a male neighbor who owns a truck and does business in town stands for success in the new market economy. The filmic positioning of a female heroine against urban temptation and beyond heterosexual norms reflects a desire to

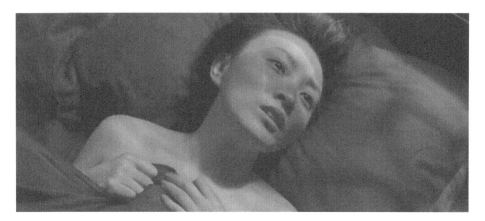

Figure 27.4 A red bed in *In Love We Trust* (dir. Wang Xiaoshuai, Debo Film, 2008): a divorced husband and wife try to save their dying child.

restore masculinity and sexuality in different terms. *Ermo* ends with the woman returning to her husband and rural life, as traditional gender discourse cannot fully endorse the threat of female sexuality and female transgression. *Ermo* and *Tuya's Marriage* both rely on a strong woman to capture the deteriorating tradition and emergent technological masculinity. *Tuya's Marriage* remains ambiguous on the question of whether Tuya can save her family and maintain her good name. The film ends with the wedding procession, where Tuya's former husband and her new groom have a violent confrontation. Tuya can do nothing but cry alone in front of the camera.

In Love We Trust also presents a family drama as moral dilemma, where a couple faces the crisis of finding a bone marrow donor to save the life of their daughter suffering from leukemia (see Figure 27.4). The film challenges the limits of morality because the only solution is to have the couple, both divorced and remarried, produce another baby behind the backs of their spouses after *in vitro* insemination has failed. Like *Tuya's Marriage*, *In Love We Trust* configures a similarly strong and persistent female figure to challenge the impossible and drive the narrative. The single-minded female protagonist, Mei Zhu, determines to have another baby with her divorced husband. By initiating first *in vitro* insemination, then real intercourse, the female character is the agent of power negotiation.

The woman's decision to have sex with her former husband in order to save their daughter disputes the norms of marriage. The nonnegotiable female decision places two male protagonists, her former and current husbands, in a moral quandary. It is precisely through this male dilemma that the narrative unfolds. Mei Zhu's former husband, a housing project manager remarried to a flight attendant, suffers from business pressure and a midlife crisis. Both his former and current wives want to have a child, and this demand reinforces his crisis of masculinity and sexuality. Mei Zhu's current husband can act only as a kind-hearted supporter.

His characteristic act is to excuse himself from embarrassment and leave to buy a pack of cigarettes.

By locating its two male subjects in subordinated positions, the film reveals how economic conditions in contemporary China challenge family relationships and gender roles. As male subjects are driven into narrative corners and find their dominance challenged, the film casts the aggressive female character as the source of pressure on her men. Her insistence on pursuing a pregnancy with her divorced husband allows the men no choice but cooperation. As the film endows its female image with strength and determination, it actually sends a (mis)perception of man as victim and woman as aggressor. The emphasis on masculinity in retreat thus foregrounds female agency in times of moral crisis.

The driving force of female persistence also challenges power relations between women themselves. Both women advance legitimate reasons to possess the male body: Mei Zhu (former wife) for saving her sick child, Dong Fan (current wife) in the name of her wifely right. The director turns the life-and-death issue into the single force driving both the narrative and power negotiation. As the film cross-cuts between the two family spaces linked by the dying child, female competition is not framed as confrontational. Dong Fan visits Mei Zhu's family when Mei Zhu is not home, as the film wants her to see the lovely girl suffering from leukemia and the kind stepfather caring for the girl as his own. Ethical sympathy trumps heterosexual regulation, and Dong Fan resolves to change her mind and support her husband in having another child with his former wife. The film attempts to depict a utopian world beyond cultural conventions and heterosexual constraints.

The idea of saving the child through female determination mocks China's one-child policy and breaches an ethical boundary. Beyond the powerful screen image and narrative force, however, the possibility of saving a life depends on the viability of male sperm: the two families compete for the male body and sexual reproductive power. The female protagonist, no matter how determined, must rely on a man's potency to ensure her daughter's survival. Both *Tuya's Marriage* and *In Love We Trust* are based on real-life stories. Both directors choose realistic cinematography to frame a social world where characters are trapped in moral, ethical, and gendered dilemmas.

Conclusion

In retrospect, Chinese films after the mid-1980s have consistently demonstrated the return of the repressed, which is masculinity lost or restored, in crisis or in redemption. The repressed appears in different forms and encompasses several dimensions. New wave films offer bodily images absent from socialist cinema. Historical films search for lost male identity by returning to stories forgotten or marginalized. The films of young directors project the anxiety of masculinity in crisis through ordinary characters and everyday life. Despite various forms of the repressed, the representation of masculinity always operates in relation to femininity and female sexuality. The central female image and her visual persona in new wave films bear the burden of male desires as well as frustrations. The explicit sexual encounters in Ang Lee's film allow man to release through the female body a repressed sadomasochistic power and perhaps even a troubled diasporic identity. The strong woman figure in family melodrama mirrors diminished masculinity in a market economy and the recuperative powers of female sexuality. Moreover, female impersonation works to accommodate homosexual anxiety and project an alternative masculinity.

Masculinity and femininity are articulated as gendered discourse, categories of analysis, and visual iconography, and they have helped secure an international reputation for Chinese-language cinema. As this chapter demonstrates, one finds in Chinese film production an ongoing search for and restoration of repressed masculinities to withstand hegemonic manipulation, whether political, historical, or commercial. In this search the female body always remains the gendered other and the rhetorical figure for projected male fears and desires. In the cinematic renditions of masculinity and sexuality, the majority of Chinese film directors have yet to grant the female image full subjectivity.

Notes

1   "Allegorical red trilogy" refers to Zhang Yimou's early films, noted for their allegorical narratives and thematic use of the color red.
2   Official history treats the regime as collaborationist and Wang Jingwei as a national traitor.
3   In its traditional form, Peking opera is an all-male world, and *dan* refers to a female impersonator who embodies ideal femininity.
4   Eileen Chang lost the opportunity to attend the University of London and was one semester short of earning her degree from the University of Hong Kong due to the fall of the city to Japan. A sense of loss and exile remains a shadow throughout her literary career.
5   Reactions to the film's sex scenes were varied and dramatic. Mainland viewers reportedly traveled to Hong Kong to see the uncut version of the film. While Taiwan cultural critic Long Yingtai enthused, "Bravo, as sex can entail such depth of aesthetics in Ang Lee's film," mainland writer Yan Yanwen demanded an apology from Ang Lee because the film "raped China's national history and culture" (X. Feng 2008).

28

Homosexuality and Queer Aesthetics

Helen Hok-Sze Leung

Introduction: The New Queer Chinese Cinema

The designation "New Queer Chinese Cinema" has entered the lexicon of film festival programming as well as film scholarship since the late 1990s. I first noticed it in a festival catalogue in which Tony Rayns (2002) claims that *Enter the Clowns* (Cui Zi'en, 2002) "inaugurates a new Queer Chinese Cinema." Not only have many Chinese-language films been labeled "of queer interest" in major international film festivals, many are also directly programmed, and some have won major awards, in queer film festivals worldwide. Increasing scholarship on the subject, including the recent publication of several book-length studies (S. Lim 2006; Leung 2008; Martin 2010), has also reinforced the notion that there is a newly emergent "queer cinema" in the Chinese language. It is likely that the average filmgoer understands "queer cinema" to mean, simply, films with gay characters. Yet, if presented with a list of Chinese-language films that have been programmed or studied as "queer cinema," many would surely be stunned by their diversity. These films span every genre and style: from gritty, low-budget underground films, to highly commercialized genre films, to esoteric arthouse fare. Some may also be puzzled by the fact that many of these films – such as *Hold You Tight* (Stanley Kwan, 1998) and *I Don't Want To Sleep Alone* (Tsai Ming-liang, 2006) – do not appear to have readily recognizable gay characters at all. What draws all these different films together under the rubric of "queer cinema" is much more – and much more interesting – than the mere fact of gay representation. As I will show in this chapter, this body of films is considered a "queer cinema" not only, or even primarily, because they portray lesbian, gay, bisexual, and/or transgender characters, but

A Companion to Chinese Cinema, First Edition. Edited by Yingjin Zhang.
© 2012 Blackwell Publishing Ltd. Published 2012 by Blackwell Publishing Ltd.

more often because they unsettle the parameters of heterosexuality and its kinship structure; confound expectations of coherence between gender identity, gender expression, and the sexed body; expand the possible configurations of sexual and emotional bonds; and subvert the aesthetic conventions and heterocentric presuppositions of mainstream cinema. Ironically, while it is debatable whether a "gay cinema" actually exists in the Chinese language, there should be much less doubt that a "queer cinema" clearly does.

The putative "newness" of this queer cinema can be a somewhat misleading description. Cui Zi'en's (b. 1958) films did not "inaugurate" a queer Chinese cinema so much as they represent an important, recent strand of it. As shown in *Yang ± Yin: Gender in Chinese Cinema* (Stanley Kwan, 1996), a cinematic essay that is at once an example of the queer Chinese cinema and one of the most important commentaries on it, covert undercurrents of homoeroticism as well as overt play of cross-gender expressions have appeared frequently in Chinese-language films since the early beginning of cinema itself. One may even say that queerness has always existed in Chinese cinema. What is "new" is our understanding of them as a body of work, as a "queer cinema."

Wittingly or unwittingly, the term "New Queer Chinese Cinema" also invokes the legacy of "New Queer Cinema," the name given to a wave of queer independent American films that emerged in the early 1990s. What characterizes this cinematic movement is not only the films' bold and unapologetic portrayal of gay characters, but more importantly their radical oppositional queer politics. Michele Aaron (2004: 3) sums up the spirit of New Queer Cinema with one word: defiance. Aaron (2004: 7) further explains that this defiance is "leveled at mainstream homophobic society but also at the 'tasteful and tolerated' gay culture that cohabits with it." The queerness of New Queer Cinema thus lies with its resistance to not only normative gender and sexual expressions, but also any tendency within gay culture to assimilate. It is a cinema that shows indifference to positive image, fixed identity, and mainstream acceptance. It thrives on provocation, ambiguity, and strangeness. Historically, New Queer Cinema was intimately rooted in the direct action politics of AIDS activism (Pearl 2004). It was also the beneficiary of the independent tradition that emerged from the New American Cinema of the 1960s (Pramaggiore 1997). As those historical moments passed with the waning of AIDS activism in the United States and Hollywood's effective co-optation of independent filmmaking, this cinematic wave also seems to have run its course. B. Ruby Rich, who coined the name "New Queer Cinema" (Rich 1992), documented its development, and later sounded its death knell (Rich 2000), has remarked that Asian cinema – along with transgender cinema, documentaries, and the visual arts – represents the most exciting current developments in queer cinema (Rich 2007). As one of the most diverse and thriving among the various Asian cinemas, Chinese cinema seems poised to receive such a mantle. However, the contexts of production and reception, thematic concerns, and aesthetic directions of Chinese films are remarkably different from that of New

Queer Cinema. At the same time, not unlike New Queer Cinema, these films pose challenges not only to the supposed "normality" of heterosexuality but also to conventional understanding of gay sexuality and identity.

Speaking of a New Queer Chinese Cinema in the singular runs the risk of obscuring the regional differences as well as overlaps and crossovers between cinematic practices in mainland China, Hong Kong, and Taiwan. How queerness appears on screen is influenced and constrained by each region's different social, political, and cultural climate. In mainland China the coexistence of strict censorship measures against homosexual representations on the one hand and a vibrant underground cinema movement on the other means that queer themes are mostly found in the works of independent filmmakers like Zhang Yuan, Li Yu, and Cui Zi'en who work primarily outside the studio system. In Hong Kong, by contrast, queer themes appear predominantly in genre films such as romantic comedies, melodrama, and martial arts or gangster action films. There are also a handful of queer-identified independent filmmakers like Yau Ching Scud (Yun Xiang, b. 1966), Kit Hung (Hong Rongjie), and Simon Chung (Zhong Desheng), while experimentation with queer aesthetics can be found in the works of mainstream directors such as Stanley Kwan and Yonfan (Yang Fan, b. 1947). In Taiwan, a more socially visible lesbian and gay movement, a less intolerant political climate, and a niche market of queer-friendly viewers have resulted in a more diverse range of queer films, including commercial pleasers like *Formula 17* (Chen Yin-jung, 2004), smaller festival films like *Blue Gate Crossings* (Chih-Yen Yee, 2002), and the works of auteurs Tsai Ming-liang and Zero Chou, who have consciously developed complex queer themes and a distinctive queer aesthetic over a substantial body of works.

Despite these differences, however, there are frequent coproductions and wide dissemination of films across the three regions, leading to interesting and unpredictable results. Exemplifying this phenomenon is *Lanyu* (Stanley Kwan, 2001), a film based on an anonymously published Internet novel, *Beijing Story*, that has enjoyed a large cult following in mainland China. The novel, known for its melodramatic plotlines and explicit gay sexual content, caught the attention of producer Zhang Yongning, who convinced Stanley Kwan and screenwriter Jimmy Ngai, both from Hong Kong, to adapt it for the screen. Yet, unlike many of the star-studded productions Kwan was known for in the past, *Lanyu* was shot underground on a very modest budget in Beijing without official permission or a big-name cast. It was banned in mainland China (although still readily available through pirated DVDs and on peer-to-peer networks online) but achieved critical acclaim as well as commercial success in Hong Kong and especially in Taiwan, where it swept the Golden Horse Awards and spawned a big fan following. It also propelled its relatively unknown mainland actors Hu Jun and Liu Ye into major stardom. The film can be partly credited for starting a subsequent wave of Taiwanese films that feature beautiful young stars in queer plots. As a queer film *Lanyu* reaps from a confluence of specific influences from all three regions: queer Internet subculture and underground production methods in mainland China, commercial filmmaking talents from Hong Kong, and a popular market for queer drama in Taiwan. The film reminds us that even as we conceive of a singular Queer Chinese Cinema, we can only understand its dynamics by paying attention to the distinctiveness and mutual influences across various Chinese cinemas.

Queer Mainstreaming

Critical writings on queer cinema rarely refer to the "mainstream" without derogative connotations. Mainstream cinema's treatment of queer characters and plots tends to be viewed negatively by critics, as homophobic stereotyping (Russo 1987), the co-optation of queer sexuality by capitalism (Hennessy 2000), or the recuperation of a heteronormative gaze (Halberstam 2005). Scholars on Chinese cinema have also launched similar lines of critique (Chou 1995; A. Yue 2000b; C. Yau 2005). Such criticism is important and necessary as it exposes the ideological workings of normative culture, particularly its capacity to tame and recuperate potentially subversive images and narratives. It cautions queer communities against any simplistic celebration of inclusion while also calling for an uncompromising queer cinema that is independent in spirit and radical in its politics. However, this suspicion of mainstream representations can sometimes lead to reluctance to account for, and even less to honor, the affection queer audiences feel for many mainstream films despite their supposed political failings. Considering the fact that the majority of queer Chinese-language films, particularly those produced in Hong Kong and Taiwan, are "mainstream" whether in terms of their production method and personnel, target audience, or thematic and aesthetic conventions, it becomes all the more important not to approach these films only as examples of an "insufficiently" queer cinema. Rather, we can seek to understand how they instigate a specific kind of queer pleasure. While most of these films are clearly not characterized by a spirit of defiance, they also offer much more than mere ideological capitulation.

In contrast to the reception of *Brokeback Mountain* (Ang Lee, 2005) in the United States, which, despite the film's immense popularity, was characterized by a great deal of uneasiness around the "queering" of a genre known for its stalwart heterosexuality, few in the world of Chinese-language cinema seem to have been scandalized by queer treatments of genre films. It may be that the "mainstream" quality of these films – i.e., the adherence to, rather than departure from, genre conventions – gives audiences a sense of familiarity despite the decidedly unfamiliar presence of queerness. At the same time, it is precisely this sense of familiarity that exposes the latent queer potential of the particular genre itself. Several examples can be gleaned from Hong Kong cinema during the 1990s. This period saw the recent decriminalization of male homosexuality and the emergence of a fledgling gay rights movement. Under this generally more receptive cultural climate for exploring issues of gender and sexuality, queer themes periodically appeared, without much fanfare, in many popular genres films. One common characteristic shared by these films is the absence of gay identity narratives. *A Queer Story* (Shu Kei, 1998), which dramatizes the negative consequences of a gay man's closeted life through a romantic comedy, is the exception that proves the rule. In contrast to *A Queer Story*, none of the other queer-themed films of this period are concerned with the reality of gay lives or with homophobic oppression. Instead, they take familiar generic motifs – such as the ambition of martial arts practitioners, the masculine bond of loyalty between triad gangsters, the comedic effects of situational misunderstanding, or the nostalgic longing for the past in melodrama – and recalibrate the ways in which these themes are gendered and sexualized. Let me illustrate with several examples.

Swordsman 2 (Ching Siu-tung, Stanley Tong, 1992) crafts a story around Dongfang Bubai, a villain from a popular novel who undergoes castration in order to practice a powerful form of martial arts. While the character is portrayed in a monstrous light in the novel, the film's unexpected casting of Brigitte Lin, an actress known for her great beauty, transforms the fictional depiction of monstrosity into enigmatic femininity on screen. In effect, *Swordsman 2* has "queered" three familiar themes in martial arts film. First, it approaches the transformative effect of martial arts on the gendered body as a form of transsexuality. Yet, unlike in the novel, the result from this practice is not portrayed as mutilated monstrosity but instead a perfectly crafted body that is both beautiful and unassailable. Second, the film superimposes two stock relationship types onto its two main characters: the attraction between Dongfang Bubai and the hero Linghu Chong, played by Jet Li, resembles both the free-spirited camaraderie and mutual admiration between men and the heterosexually coded eroticism between the hero and his love interest. Third, when faced with scenes of coy flirtation between the two, the audience is made to see double: their nondiegetic recognition of the stars leads to a sighting of familiar heterosexuality which, within the diegesis, actually signifies the attraction a man feels for a transsexual woman. The film does not allow the audience to "tell the difference" between the two, thus disturbing the boundaries that are supposed to demarcate heterosexuality categorically from queer attraction.

A similar manipulation of gendered relations is carried out in *Portland Street Blues* (Yip Wai-Man, 1998). A spin-off from the Young and Dangerous series, the film is a stylish and clever reworking of the triad gangster genre known for its flaunting of heroic masculinity and intense bonds between men. The film introduces a twist to this formula by replacing the conventional hero with Sister Thirteen, a lesbian character played to great effect by a dashing Sandra Ng who embodies every aspect of conventional heroic masculinity, including not only dressing style and mannerisms but also sexist attitudes toward women and unflinching loyalty to other men. Through the development of Sister Thirteen as a generic masculine hero, the film manages to queer two genre conventions. First, its visual presentation of Sandra Ng as Sister Thirteen shows that heroic masculinity can be successfully and attractively embodied by a woman. Second, its placement of a female character into intense masculine friendships with other men has a startling effect: it shows that the emotional attachment between a masculine woman and other men does not resemble heterosexuality so much as it reenacts the homosocial bonding between men that is so commonplace in the genre.

The ways in which genre conventions are queered in *Swordsman 2* and *Portland Street Blues* reveal that a character's sexed body and his/her gender presentation may not always align as expected. As this alignment shifts in unexpected directions, so too does the emotional and erotic relation between characters. In fact, this insight has long been exploited on screen, particularly through cross-dressing, to achieve comedic effects. Chris Straayer (1996) has analyzed the many uses of the "transvestite disguise" in American cinema. During the 1990s, Hong Kong comedies took this generic convention further to explore explicitly and, some-times self-reflexively, the relation between gender presentation and sexual attraction. In the popular comedy *He's a Woman She's a Man* (Peter Chan, 1992), actor Leslie Cheung plays a homophobic straight man, Sam, who starts to question his own sexuality when he becomes attracted to Wing, a young man whom he plans to nurture as the next big recording star. As is predictable in the genre, Wing turns out to be a cross-dressing woman, thus resolving Sam's sexual identity crisis. What makes this film more interesting than its contemporary Hollywood counterparts that deploy such "functional" transvestite disguises – i.e., characters cross-dressing in order to achieve a purpose, like in *Tootsie* (Sydney Pollack, 1982) or *Mrs. Doubtfire* (Chris Columbus, 1993), rather than as a form of personal gender expression – is the film's various subtexts. The intense off-screen speculation at that time around Leslie Cheung's homosexuality, which local audiences at the time would have been aware of, adds a layer of irony to the film's heteronorma-tive resolution. In the famous last scene which takes place in an elevator where Sam confusedly confronts Wing, dressed now in feminine clothing, with the bisexual declaration: "I don't care if you're a man or a woman, I love you!" Within the film's diegesis, the ending's heterosexual coupling tames and eclipses the state-ment's bisexual connotations. Yet, through the audience's awareness of the gossip surrounding Cheung's homosexuality, the film also hints at the other possibility of Sam's declaration, thereby restoring the bisexual implications of the statement. Furthermore, the film acknowledges its own influence from a long tradition of cross-dressing both on the theatrical stage and on the cinematic screen by pointing the audience toward a long queer heritage. In a further twist that is developed in the film's sequel, *Who's the Woman Who's the Man* (Peter Chan, 1994), Wing, still presenting herself as a young man, becomes attracted to, and subsequently seduces, an actress named Fong who is known for impersonating male roles on screen. Through this latter character, the film pays homage to the stardom of Chinese actresses like Yam Kim-fai and Chan Po-chu, whose cross-dressing roles on screen and rumored bisexuality off screen are iconic and legendary.

While many conventions in these popular genres – bodily transformation, masculine bonding, and cross-dressing – seem particularly amenable to queering, the thematic elements as well as affective structure of melodrama have in turn wielded considerable influence on how contemporary queer subjects represent themselves. Fran Martin's (2010) meticulous study of female same-sex attraction in Chinese culture during the twentieth and early twenty-first centuries shows that such desire has primarily been articulated in a "memorial mode": a "backward glance" that grieves the impossibility of queer female relationships in the hetero-marital present. This perpetual longing for the past, and the emotional intensity it entails, perfectly fit the narrative and emotional arc of melodrama (Teo 2006). In fact, films like *Twin Bracelets* (Huang Yu-shan, 1991), *The Intimates* (Jacob Cheung, 1998), and *Butterfly* (Yan Yan Mak, 2004) barely register as unconventional even when they portray attraction between women. Thematic elements such as the suffering of women, intimate female bonds, and intense nostalgic sentiments so closely follow generic conventions that when the films add an erotic dimension to the emotional intimacy between women, it appears like a logical development, rather than a rupture, of the genre. What is intriguing about these narratives of female same-sex intimacy, so well articulated within melodramatic conventions, is their difference from the temporal and the spatial narratives of lesbian identity in the West. In contrast to what Biddy Martin (1998: 387) has characterized as the lesbian "coming out narrative," which moves from adolescent repression to adult liberation, usually accompanied by the movement from small town or countryside to the city (Halberstam 2005: 35), the story of queer female desire found in these films locates erotic intensity between women both in the past and in rural or small-town settings. *The Intimates*, cross-cutting between two temporalities, actually contrasts the idealized love between two women that is located in the past and in a rural context with the faithlessness and fickleness of heterosexual relations in the urban present. In this way, the melodramatic mode of expressing female same-sex desire also presents a historically and culturally specific alternative to the globalized narrative of lesbian identity.

Besides the queering of various genres, an equally interesting phenomenon is the recent development, predominantly in Taiwan, of a subgenre of youth films (*qingchun pian*) that is premised on ambivalent queer sexual entanglements among young people. Critics (B. Hu 2004) have noticed this trend since the release of the surprise hit *Formula 17*. However, not everyone views the development in a positive light. Hong Kong critic Tong Ching-Siu names this subgenre the "gay mystique film" (*tongxinglian yiyun pian*), citing *Blue Gate Crossing*, *Eternal Summer* (Lester Chen, 2006) and *Miao Miao* (Cheng Hsiao-tse, 2008) as examples. In Tong's (2008) view, these films provide a "pretentious distortion" of youth by emphasizing erotic intrigue over the "innocence" of friendship. Criticism like Tong's betrays unease not only with the films' queer erotics, but even more so with their ambivalent resolutions. In these films, the erotic tension is not resolved, as is conventionally the case, with either the restoration of heteronormativity or the development of gay identity. Instead, the surprise "twists" of these films' romance narrative complicate matters further. *Blue Gate Crossing*, at first sight, seems to be telling a conventional story of a heteronormative love triangle: a young girl has a crush on her best female friend who only has eyes for another boy. Yet, at the very end, the film reveals that the boy is in fact in love with the young lesbian and hopes that in the future she may find attraction for boys like him. *Eternal Summer* essentially tells the same story while reversing the gender roles and placing a girl in the middle of two boys, one of whom secretly harbors sexual attraction toward his best friend. The film ends with the exposure of the secret but not each character's reactions to the exposure. By deliberately withholding these reactions, the film leaves the possibilities of how the relations will develop to the audience's imagination. *Miao Miao* also appears to duplicate the triangular plot of *Blue Gate Crossing* but with two additional twists. First, we are shown in flashbacks that the boy – and the object of one of the girls' crush – has a queer past in which he has been emotionally and, perhaps, also sexually intimate with a young gay man. Second, the film's ending makes clear that the girl knows that her best female friend is in love with her, but leaves it ambivalent how she actually feels about it.

In their refusal to reduce adolescent sexuality into narratives of sexual identity, these films blur the boundary between not only heterosexuality and homosexuality, but also between friendship and sexual attraction. They do not resolve these youthful desires either with the heteronormative dismissal of them as "mere phases" or with the "coming out" certainty of gay identity. These films present a universe in which there are multiple ways in which desire can be configured among gendered bodies, while erotic energy flows fluidly without the constraints of sexual identity. In this regard, the queer intrigue in these films accentuates the themes of growing pains, adolescent uncertainty, and young romance, all of which are commonplace in youth films. And despite the hostility of critics like Tong, this subgenre has proven to be both critically and commercially successful, especially in Taiwan. There are several possible reasons for this receptive climate. First, compared to other Chinese-speaking regions, the development of the gay and lesbian civil rights movement – organized under the banner of *tongzhi* – in Taiwan has been much more visible. It has at times even been exploited by mainstream politicians who support some of the movement's initiatives in order to appear more "progressive" than their opponents (W. Chu 2003). Furthermore, from the time of the movement's inception, there has been a concurrent effort among a group of theorists and creative writers to experiment with queer aesthetics (Chih and Hung 1997; H. Chang 2000). Working with the notions of *ku'er* and *guaitai* as local articulations of "queer," these writers deconstruct boundaries of normality while exploring the polymorphous nature of both gender and sexual expressions. Both of these factors – the mainstream presence of the lesbian and gay civil rights movement and the ongoing intellectual and artistic experimentations with queer aesthetics – likely contribute to a degree of acceptance for the kind of "pomosexual" sentiments that fuel this subgenre of youth films.

Another factor that has likely contributed to the favorable reception of these youth films is the popularity of the Boys' Love (BL) – also known as *danmei* in Chinese – subculture. Originating from Japanese girls' comics (*shojo manga*) and popularized throughout various parts of Asia, BL denotes a subculture of stories, images, and music about male–male erotic relationships that are created and consumed by young heterosexual women. In Chinese-speaking regions, the phenomenon has developed and flourished in Taiwan (Y. Chen 2008) as well as Hong Kong and Mainland China (T. Liu 2009) during the 1990s. While this particular subcultural representation of male homosexuality has invited criticism from some feminists and gay men for its lack of realism or supposed (hetero)sexism and homophobia (Lunsing 2006), its influence on youth films in Chinese-language cinema has borne more complex results. In an article analyzing the Asian influences in *Brokeback Mountain*, Chris Berry argues that the deployment of BL aesthetics can be considered the film's "Chinese characteristic." Berry also notes the commercial success of Chinese-language films that present homosexuality in a similar style and the significant participation of women in the production and consumption of these films (Berry 2007a: 35–6). It is worth noting that all of Berry's examples of BL-influenced films indicate significant gay male involvement as well. For instance, even though Berry doubts that *Lanyu* was made primarily for a gay audience and points out that the original Internet novel was written by a woman, it is also true that the film's director and screenwriter are both out gay men, while the sexual explicitness of the Internet novel has long enjoyed a large gay male following in China. The 2003 hit TV series *Crystal Boys*, adapted from one of the earliest and most influential novels by a gay writer in the Chinese language, is also cited by Berry as an example of BL aesthetics and a precursor to the subsequent queer youth films, many of which star actors from the series. Although there are marked generational differences between the original novel and the TV adaptation in their respective understandings of gay identity, community, shame, and pride, the series' relevance to gay male culture is undeniable, no matter how much crossover appeal it has to mainstream female viewers (H. Huang 2006). In other words, unlike the primarily heterosexual female focus of BL subculture, films that have been associated with its aesthetics are, by contrast, far more entangled with gay culture, whether in their production or consumption. In that sense, these films cannot be thought of, as BL subculture often is, as a strictly heterosexual female phenomenon. Furthermore, even though the first wave of youth films following in the footsteps of *Lanyu* and *Crystal Boys* are centered on beautiful young men, later films in the subgenre like *Miao Miao* and *Candy Rain* change their focus to erotic entanglements among girls and young women. Thus, while the enthusiastic reception of queer youth films is likely made possible in part by the already existent subcultural appreciation of BL, the films themselves are developing in other, indeed queerer, directions.

Queer Auteurs

While most of the mainstream films discussed in the last section were made by heterosexual directors, there are also a number of openly gay and lesbian filmmakers active in the various Chinese film industries who are known for the queer contents of their works. What, however, is the relation between a film-maker's sexual identity and their authorship in queer cinema? This is by no means a simple or self-evident question. Song Hwee Lim (2006:153–79) approaches Stanley Kwan as a "gay director" and analyzes the "queer poetics" of Tsai Ming-liang's films (2006: 126–52). At the same time, Lim takes issue with Richard Dyer's claim that lesbian and gay directors have exclusive access to sign-systems that best represent lesbian and gay lives. Such a claim, Lim argues, constructs lesbian and gay discourse to be insular and exclusive while ruling out any possi-bilities for cross-cultural exchanges. Furthermore, Lim (2006: 126, 178) notes the ambivalence of both Stanley Kwan and Tsai Ming-liang, who strongly resist assuming the burden of representation and the categorization of their works as "gay films." In a subsequent discussion on the relevance of auteur theory in the study of Chinese cinemas, Lim cautions against approaching "auteur" as a self-evident category of analysis. Instead, Lim analyzes how an "author function" is produced, for whom, and to what effect. Using Tsai Ming-liang as an example, he shows how Tsai's filmmaking practices enable a specific kind of spectatorial pleasure that derives from, and in turn concretizes, a recognition of Tsai as an auteur (S. Lim 2007). My own approach to "queer auteurs" in this section is indebted to Lim's formulations. My emphasis is not so much on identifying openly lesbian or gay filmmakers but rather on the various and particular ways in which certain filmmakers produce an "author function" through a discursive construction of queerness. And since inspired and detailed studies of established filmmakers like Tsai and Kwan already exist in abundance, I will keep my focus on younger filmmakers whose works have received less attention.

Although Stanley Kwan is the most famous Chinese-speaking filmmaker to have publicly declared his gay identity, when examples of "gay directors" are brought up in more recent publications on Hong Kong's film industry, the much less well-known names of three young independent directors – Scud, Kit Hung, and Simon Chung – are more frequently mentioned (Pong 2009). Compared to an established and prolific filmmaker like Kwan, these younger directors appear less resistant to the label and more forthcoming about their sexual identity, politics, and relation to queer cinema. Their relatively young résumés, each consisting of less than a handful of features to date, all deal with gay themes that coincide with the directors' publicly available biographical narratives. Scud's upbringing in main-land China, ambition as a filmmaker of "art films," and dramatic erotic encounters are all recounted, literally by himself on the voice-over, in *Permanent Residence* (Scud, 2009). Simon Chung sets his first feature *Innocent* (2005) in Toronto where a young man from Hong Kong struggles with immigrant life and the racialized dynamics of his relationship with an older white man, a narrative that echoes his own family's history of migration to Canada (Collett 2009a). The portrayal in *Soundless Wind Chime* (Kit Hung, 2009) of an interracial relationship and a young Chinese man's diasporic experience in Europe parallels Hung's own account of his relationship with a Swiss boyfriend and experience of studying in Europe and North America (Collett 2009b).

The coincidences between the filmmakers' self-representation and the thematics of their works certainly contribute to their reception as "gay directors," but there are also other elements at work that shed a more complex light on the relation between authorship, gay lives, and queer cinema. Scud has invited controversy not only in the mainstream reception of his films but also among gay audiences. Most obviously provocative is the display of male frontal nudity and intense homoerotic desire between men that is present in all three of his feature films. Moreover, this homoerotic explicitness is not kept contained within the filmic diegesis. Instead, as a signature move, Scud continually plays with the boundaries between on-screen fiction and off-screen reality. He casts nonprofessional actors who are actual baseball players to play themselves (and pose nude in certain scenes) in *City Without Baseball* (Lawrence Lau, Scud, 2008). The release of *Permanent Residence* was accompanied by a photo book in which the director inserted himself in the shoot to "exchange roles" with the actors so they could "turn the camera back on him posing nude." These tactics tease audiences into blurring the line between the sensationalist fictional representations on screen and the context of everyday life. Despite this commitment to increasing the visibility of gay erotics, however, Scud's personae as a "gay director" sometimes goes against the expectations of activist discourse in Hong Kong. *City Without Baseball* has surprisingly invited more vocal criticism from gay activist organizations than even antigay religious groups (Editorial 2008). This fall out, which included a threat from several prominent gay activists to boycott the film, was in part caused by Scud's perceived reluctance to condemn one of his actors, baseball player Leung Yu-Chung who, despite his willingness to participate in the film, expressed hostility to homosexuality during his appearance with Scud on gay DJ Brian Leung's radio show "We Are Family," which has a large gay following. The aftermath of the incident prompted a heated but ultimately useful discussion among gay and lesbian activists on the nature of freedom of speech and tactics toward homophobic expressions (C. Yau 2008). Scud's subsequent films *Permanent Residence* and *Amphetamine* (2010) (see Figure 28.1) deal with difficult subject matters – gay men's obsessive desire for straight men, drug use, the cult of masculinity – that do not readily endear the director to gay audiences. Scud's self-construction as a "gay director" is thus premised not only on his openly gay identity or play with homoerotic explicitness on and off screen, but paradoxically also on his penchant for pushing against the acceptable boundaries of gay self-representation in Hong Kong.

Figure 28.1 A tangled love relationship in *Amphetamine* (dir. Scud, Artwalker, 2010), a queer exploration of sexuality and addiction.

Outside of Hong Kong, the most notable young filmmakers of queer cinema are undoubtedly Beijing-based author, film studies professor, and director Cui Zi'en and Taiwanese filmmaker Zero Chou. In contrast to the young filmmakers from Hong Kong, the queer authorship of Cui and Chou is not primarily constructed on autobiographical interpretations of their films. Instead, their prolific output articulates a coherent aesthetic and political vision that contributes to their profiles as queer auteurs. Their films also offer a specific form of spectatorial pleasure that derives from what Song Hwee Lim (2007: 226–9) has theorized as "intratextual" practices. Lim develops this notion to explain the "serial" (although nonlinear) character of Tsai Ming-liang's films and the pleasure afforded by a recognition of the intricate referentiality that links elements of one film to another. While the intratextuality of Cui's and Chou's films does not approach the complexity and nuance of Tsai's, the notion is useful to illustrate how Cui's and Chou's films invite audiences to read them as a body of work rather than as single films in isolation and, in so doing, consolidate the queer authorship of the filmmakers.

In an introduction to Cui Zi'en's early works, Chris Berry (2004b: 196) suggests that Cui's films are animated by "an unholy trinity of themes: the sacred, the profane, and the domestic." As it turns out, Berry's pithy characterization quite accurately describes Cui's subsequent output, all of which tackle the triangulated themes of religion, sexuality, and kinship relations. While same-sex relations between men are present in all of his films, Cui's interest in sexuality goes far beyond homosexuality. His films are inhabited by queer characters who are bisexual and polyamorous (*Old Testament*, 2002), transgender (*Enter the Clowns*, 2002), sex workers (*Ayaya Feeding Boys*, 2003), or simply sexually curious (*Star Appeal*, 2004). Queer sexuality is never an identity issue but more symbolically a vehicle for Cui to deconstruct the twin pillars that underpin social "normality": the respective discourse of morality (*daode*) and of kinship (*lunli*). Cui's Catholic upbringing, which he mentions frequently in interviews, likely influences him to express "morality" in religious language, such as the use of biblical allusions in *Old Testament* and the exploration of "redemption" in *Ayaya Feeding Boys*. Kinship structure and familial dynamics are also a dominant preoccupation: parental or sibling relations are daringly explored as incestuous entanglements in Cui's *Enter the Clowns*, *Night Scene* (2004), *Withered in a Blossoming Season* (2005), and *My Fair Son* (2007). Rather than disavowing religious morality and kinship relations as oppressive normalizing structures, queer sexuality is articulated through religious language and kinship relations. Such a scandalous tactic arguably provides a more radical critique than what is possible in simpler portrayals of oppression.

Cui's films also display a deliberate indifference to representational realism and aesthetic conventions. Until his most recent documentary *Queer China, "Comrade" China* (2009), which represents a break from this stylistic commitment and the first of Cui's films that is clearly intended for mainstream audiences, all of Cui's previous films have adhered to his principal concern with "deconstructing all the traditions in filmmaking" (Q. Wang 2004: 193) or, as the director puts it more starkly in Chinese, "raping cinema" with a "rigid, rough, sharp, tedious cinematic language" (Z. Cui 2003). This aesthetically violent language is evident in Cui's fondness for long shots with little depth of field, abrupt and rapid panning shots in place of cuts, and muted and claustrophobic lighting, as well as episodic and disjointed narrative structure. This visually demanding and, indeed, displeasing aesthetic has become Cui's authorial signature. He further accentuates his authorship with the recurrent character Xiao Bo, which Cui plants in virtually all of his films as the one stable element in his (literally and metaphorically) destabilizing style. Not unlike Tsai Ming-liang's famously recurrent character Xiao Kang, Xiao Bo is not a coherent character but a marker used to highlight the intratextual connections within a body of films. In addition, Cui's starring and producing credits in other films, a substantial output of fiction and theoretical writings, and an active history of organizing underground queer film and cultural events in Beijing have established him to be more than a queer auteur, but a queer public intellectual with considerable visibility and social impact.

Contemporaneous to Cui and similarly prolific, Taiwanese director Zero Chou establishes herself as a queer auteur in a far less self-conscious, yet equally significant, way. In a scene halfway through the film *Drifting Flowers* (Zero Chou, 2008) (see Figure 28.2), an aging gay man walks despondently down a street when he notices a row of movie posters on the wall. He caresses the poster, lingering on the image of two men about to kiss. The title of the movie on the poster is *Spider Lilies* and the small imprint of the Teddy Award (the award for best queer film at the Berlin International Film Festival) is visible on the corner. This scene would

Figure 28.2 Sitting at the railway station in *Drifting Flowers* (dir. Zero Chou, The Third Vision Films, 2008), a film exploring the dynamics of queer friendship.

have been unremarkable for any audience unless they are familiar with the director's career, in which case it would likely elicit laughter and delight. *Spider Lilies* (Zero Chou, 2007), which indeed won the Teddy Award and gave Chou her first international recognition as a queer director, is a film about an erotic involvement between two young women. The fake poster in *Drifting Flowers*, which replaces the women in the original poster with two men, is a sly intratextual joke that also, more seriously, captures the inclusive spirit of Chou's queer vision. In numerous interviews Chou has described her ambition to produce a "six-color rainbow cinema," matching each of her first three features to a color on the rainbow which she sees as a symbol of LGBT communities (Diwu Tiefeng 2008; M. Lo 2008: 1).

More than just a symbolic exposition, Chou's films can be likened to the rainbow also because they explore gay men and lesbians of all stripes, as well as the interactions and friendship between them. Already in an early documentary, *Corner's* (2001), Chou interweaves reportage about the closing of a gay male bar in Taipei with lyrical depictions of lesbian eroticism. Working against autobiographical expectations for a lesbian director, Chou made *Splendid Float* (2004), which is about a gay male Daoist priest who holds funeral rites by day and performs as a drag queen in a dance troupe at night. Chou has mentioned that she subsequently made *Spider Lilies* partly to satisfy lesbian viewers who lamented that she had not yet made a film about her own community (M. Lo 2008: 2). The fake poster in *Drifting Flowers*, which switches the images of lesbians with gay men, is especially appropriate as the film itself explores, with great originality and nuance, friendship between queer men and women. Divided into three distinct time periods, the film shows vignettes from the lives of two lesbian women, Diego and Lily, and a gay man named Yan. Diego and Yan were best friends in their youth, while Yan and Lily had married for appearance's sake during their twenties, but did not see each other again until old age. The film pays close attention to the role gender plays in the dynamics of queer friendship.

Two scenes, one at the end of the second section and the other at the beginning of the third, illustrate this rarely explored theme. The first scene is set in the twilight years of the character when an aging Lily is suffering from Alzheimer's and Yan is being treated for HIV. In her illness, Lily has misrecognized Yan to be her late lover and insists on dressing him like a woman, for fear that "a woman looking too butch would invite trouble." After initial resistance, Yan eventually complies with the request, as he has decided to take care of Lily like a life partner would. This section of the film closes with a shot of a rainbow in the sky, followed by a long shot of the couple, both dressed in women's clothing, sitting contentedly together, framed by the stone pillars on the station platform and the shoreline behind them. This beautiful portrait of the "couple" illustrates a friendship that is based not on sexual attraction but on compassion, mutual dependence, and a shared experience of living queer lives. The film jumps back in time after this scene to begin the last section, which is set in the characters' youth, when a teenage Yan and Diego, a young butch, are horsing around by the shore. The scene starts with Yan leaning toward Diego, feigning a kiss. The two then discuss why they are such good friends, with Diego claiming it is because Yan "is so much like a girl," while Yan looks at Diego wistfully and wonders how good it would be if Diego "really was a boy." This scene provides a nuanced and finely tuned portrayal of the complex dynamics between two queer friends. While Yan is attracted to Diego's boyishness, Diego is in turn drawn to Yan's femininity. In other words, they each appreciate the other's queer gender presentation – precisely what would have been considered inappropriate or transgressive in the heteronormative world. This appreciation does not, however, lead to sexual involvement, remaining only as sparks of attraction in what is primarily a friendship bond. Such pitch-perfect evocation of the everyday context of queer lives is in fact very rare in any queer cinema, which tends to be focused on the sexual lives of a single group of queer people, such as gay men only.

The far more complex, interactive, and inclusive queer universe depicted in Chou's films does not only serve as her authorial signature but also signals a highly original direction in queer cinema globally. At the same time, Chou's films are also unmistakably local in their strong evocation of geographical and cultural specificity. Her interest in Taiwan's different locales is evident in her documentary *Poles Extremity* (2001), which takes the camera to four extreme "points" on the island of Taiwan in search of a specific cinematic language for each. This interest in local contexts continues in her queer films, which construct locale-specific details such as the Daoist funeral rites in *Splendid Float*, the traumatic memory of Taiwan's "912 earthquake" in *Spider Lilies*, and the waning tradition of the street puppet theater in the port city of Kaohsiung during the 1960s in *Drifting Flowers*.

The mixed Taiwanese and Mandarin dialogue in all the films is also carefully calibrated to reflect the linguistic specificity of a character according to his or her background and the time period of the actions. In other words, not only is Chou establishing herself as a queer auteur, she is more emphatically presenting herself as a Taiwanese queer auteur.

Queer Docs

I would like to conclude this chapter with a brief discussion of the documentary genre, which may appear to be a rather peripheral part of queer Chinese cinemas. Compared to the sheer quantity of dramatic features, the number of queer documentary films is slim indeed. There are however at least two reasons that warrant more critical attention to the genre in the future. First, as DV technology becomes widely available at very low cost and as instant dissemination is made possible by peer-to-peer network and social media sites, it is very likely that we can look forward to a proliferation of "micro-cinemas" that capture and archive queer phenomena while bypassing censors and marketing considerations. The short film, in this respect, has long served the important function of highlighting local sites of queer community-building and ephemeral moments of queer activism. For instance, the importance of Taipei's Gin Gin Bookstore – one of the very few bookstores in Asia devoted to the dissemination of LGBT books and media – as a collective queer space is the subject in *Welcome to My Queer Bookstore* (Larry Tung, 2009). The "public action" of several lesbian and gay activists to perform same-sex "weddings" on Valentine's Day on the streets of Beijing is captured in *New Beijing, New Marriage* (Fan Po Po, David Cheng, 2009). These short films may appear to be of relevance only to a small local audience but, when viewed as parts of a larger repository of queer shorts, their "snap shots" contribute to a valuable archive of queer lives that rarely find representation in official or mainstream discourse.

Second, the documentary form provides many queer auteurs with an alternative outlet to explore political and aesthetic concerns that may not fit into the purview of their fiction films. When asked about the stylistic departure he made in his documentary feature *Queer China, "Comrade" China*, Cui Zi'en mentions that he has often "wavered between a gay rights perspective and a queer perspective" (K. Zhao 2009). Indeed, while the deconstructive stance of Cui's experimental films is in perfect accord with queer theory, its role in the gay rights movement is much more ambivalent. By contrast, the near-encyclopedic reach of *Queer China, "Comrade" China* gives a comprehensive portrait of LGBT activism in mainland China today. While its linear narrative and conventional "talking heads" format clearly contradict the aesthetic vision Cui so persistently pursues in his fiction films, the film is also far less demanding and intimidating for casual viewers, thus increasing the exposure of its subject matter. In this way, the documentary form gives Cui a vehicle to balance out his political commitments without having to compromise his aesthetic commitment in his fiction films.

We find a similar balancing act, but going in the opposition direction, in Stanley Kwan's intensely personal documentaries *Yang ± Yin: Gender in Chinese Cinema* and *Still Love You After All These* (1997). While Kwan's dramatic features never stray, whether in theme or style, too far outside the parameters of the commercial film industry, his documentaries allow him to experiment with intimate sexual expression and artistic self-reflection. Both documentaries, one on the history of Chinese cinema and the other on the transfer of Hong Kong's sovereignty, interweave Kwan's autobiographical explorations of his sexual and gender history with reflections on history, politics, and his own cinematic practice. Likewise, while Zero Chou has filmed all of her dramatic features around queer themes, her documentaries have focused on other social justice issues, such as the trauma of the 912 earthquake on children's memory in *912 Rumors* (2005), and the plight of blind children in *Vision of Darkness* (2005). Paying attention to these oft-neglected documentary works can show us alternative insights into their filmmakers' queer vision, while expanding our understanding of queer cinema in general.

Conclusion

In examining various examples of the New Queer Chinese Cinema, it becomes clear that the representation of homosexuality is, ironically, the least interesting aspect of this cinema. Instead, we find films that expose the limits of the heterosexual kinship structure, play with the fluidity between gender identity, gender expression, and the sexed body, and chart the unpredictable paths of sexual and emotional bonds. We also see filmmakers developing queer styles by deploying generic conventions in novel ways, making creative use of autobiographical narratives, and writing authorial signature over a coherent body of works. It is indisputable that there is a vibrant queer cinema in the Chinese language. Its future development and potential impact on queer cinema globally deserves our continual critical attention.

29

Alter-centering Chinese Cinema
The Diasporic Formation

Yiman Wang

What is home? Who gets to define home for whom? How is home related to "Chineseness" in the context of diasporic Chinese cinema? These questions have stimulated much discussion and accrued intense political valences due to China's vast regional, linguistic, cultural, economic, and political differences, compounded by the checkered history of internal and external migration, displacement, rupture, and reconstruction. Scholars of Chinese studies, media studies, cultural studies, and ethnic studies have been searching for a rubric that can adequately describe the untotalizable "Chineseness" and (internal and external) Chinese diaspora. Such rubrics, relating to Chinese "mediascape" (Appadurai 1990), include "transnational" (S. Lu 1997; Marchetti 2006; Berry and Pang 2008), "Chinese language" or *huayu* (S. Zheng 1995; Lu and Yeh 2005), "diasporic" (R. Chow 1995; Ang 1998; M. Yue 2000, 2003; W. Sun 2006), "Sinophone" or *huawen* (Shih 2007), and "global" (Ong and Nonini 1997). Deployed to interrogate the intention and extension of the notion of "Chineseness," these rubrics combine to make three interventions: problematizing the homogenous understanding of Chinese identity by critiquing its (violent) disavowal of differences (S. Lu 1997; C. Berry 1998; Y. Zhang 2004a), refocusing upon the Sinophone identity that contests the Han-ethnicity–mandarin-Chinese centrism (Shih 2007), and valorizing "open-ended and plural 'post-Chinese' identities" enacted by diasporic Chinese (Ang 1998).

Despite their ideological differences, these critics share a central concern with the definition of "home" and the seat of belonging. This concern carries an affective appeal to "home" as the site of emotional investment even if the very definition of "home" is called into question. Such affective politics of belonging and identity/identification fuels diasporic Chinese cinema as well as other media texts since the early twentieth century.

A Companion to Chinese Cinema, First Edition. Edited by Yingjin Zhang.
© 2012 Blackwell Publishing Ltd. Published 2012 by Blackwell Publishing Ltd.

Let us start with a recent diasporic documentary, *Persisting with Tears in Eyes*, made by Zhang Liling in Japan. Tale-tellingly retitled *Home Is in My Heart* (*Jia zai wo xin zhong*) in China, this documentary sets the tone of home-oriented pathos with an opening suggestion, "Viewers, please have your handkerchiefs ready," and a closing question, "My Chinese compatriots, what are your thoughts after watching this documentary?" In between the opening and the ending unfolds a 108-minute documentation of a Shanghai low-class family's Sisyphean labor and hope from 1989 to 2004, a drama that, indeed, constantly melts Chinese and Japanese viewers (as well as the documented family members) into tears. During the fifteen-year period, the husband, Mr. Ding, laboring in Tokyo as an illegal worker (*heihu*, literally "a black person"), sees his daughter only once in 1997 when she makes a flight connection via Tokyo to New York to pursue college education with Ding's hard-earned money. And he sees his wife only once in 2002 when she is finally granted her US visitor visa (at the twelfth application) and embarks on a flight to New York via Tokyo. Mr. Ding eventually returns to China in 2004, putting an end to his fifteen-year "black person" life in Tokyo.

Zhang Liling, who came to Japan as a student in 1989, started the documentary in 1996, tracking Ding's family in Tokyo, Shanghai, and New York for ten years. Upon airing at prime time by Fuji TV, a mainstream TV channel, it was enthusiastically received by Japanese and Chinese audiences alike, and applauded for depicting perseverant love that transcends space, time, and generational differences. Starting from November 28, 2009, the documentary was rescreened, this time in Japan's movie theaters, to crowds of tearful viewers. Battling current financial crisis and collective despair, the audience found solace and inspiration in the family's perseverant love that enabled it to get through difficult times while empowering the younger generation.

This apparent time- and nation-transcending sentimentalism imbues not only the family drama and its reception, but also Zhang's documentary drive. This is manifested in the frequent camera zooms onto family members' faces from different angles, capturing every muscle movement as they try to fight back the tears, only to be reduced to inconsolable weeping at home, in the subway, and at the airport. Meanwhile, the Japanese male voice-over narrates, explains, and comments like an olden-time *benshi*, soliciting the audience's emotional resonance and sympathy. The intense pathos, the idealization of "home," and the consoling reaffirmation of collective efforts in hard times make Zhang's documentary palatable and desirable for the official ideology and mainstream audience.

For scholars of diasporic studies who privilege the interstitial existence, the fragmentary style, and the subversive or resistant standpoint, which irrevocably throw "home" and "nation" into question, the documentary's stylistic and ideological conformism is problematic. On closer analysis, however, the seemingly conservative and pathos-laden reification of "home" actually registers the family members' "diasporic consciousness" (*à la* Clifford 1997), which Ming-bao Yue (2003: 212) interprets as "a general condition that mediates, in a lived tension, the experiences of separation and entanglement: living here while remembering/desiring another place." For Yue as for Clifford, the schizophrenic diasporic consciousness challenges essential categories and necessitates a switch to "acts of relationships (i.e., networks and routes)" (M. Yue 2003: 213). The necessity of de-essentializing and redefining "home," however, does not negate, but rather reinforces its symbolic and affective significance, especially when the diasporic movement is pressured and rifted with economic and geopolitical difficulties.

The power of pathos in *Persisting with Tears in Eyes* derives precisely from the Shanghai family's subordinated status. As an illegal worker in Tokyo, Mr. Ding stays "underground" as an "inflexible noncitizen" (as opposed to the "flexible citizenship" fostered by global capitalism). He cannot visit his family in Shanghai for fifteen years because his documents have expired, and he has literally lost his "identity," and yet is determined to over-stay in Japan as a cheap laborer. His wife cannot go visit their daughter in the United States for five years because she is denied an entry visa eleven times consecutively. For these unsuccessful migrants, national borders remain intractable and forbidding. To become diasporic is, literally and painfully, to become scattered beyond retrieval, as indicated by the etymological meaning of diaspora. Indeed, this diasporic family represents "people caught in the cracks of globalization" (Ezra and Rowden 2005: 7).

Whereas the family members' pathos seemingly reifies the concept of home, their long-term dispersion means that their "home" has necessarily become an idea or "imagined togetherness" – to appropriate Benedict Anderson's (2006) theorization of the modern nation-state as "imagined community." The constant reimagination of the "home" is all the more important precisely because of the fragility of the actual home. Home-as-construct for "inflexible noncitizens" thus signals an existential situation, rather than playful, postmodern mental gymnastics. Such affective attachment to "home" as "imagined togetherness" underpins Hamid Naficy's study of exilic and diasporic filmmaking. As he contends, diasporic identity is constituted by "the nurturing of a collective memory, often of an idealized homeland," which may be state-based or stateless, yet is inevitably "based on a desire for a homeland yet to come" (Naficy 2001: 14). He distinguishes diasporic cinema from exilic and postcolonial cinemas in these terms: "exilic cinema is dominated by its focus on there and then in the homeland, diasporic cinema by its vertical relationship to the homeland and by its lateral relationship to the diaspora communities and experiences, and postcolonial ethnic and identity cinema by the exigencies of life here and now in the country in which the filmmakers reside" (Naficy 2001: 15).

One may question the extent to which diasporic memory is "vertically" oriented toward the "homeland" on the "collective level." If diasporic experiences vary with each individual (even though certain patterns do emerge), then diasporic identity/identification and filmmaking can hardly be generalized as a predetermined collective act. Accordingly, the diasporic filmmakers' emotional investment no longer needs to be channeled toward the "homeland" alone, but to "home" as well. Furthermore, the "vertical" connection with the "home" and "homeland" implies that the latter are relegated to "there and then," which denies their coevalness or simultaneous change. To acknowledge their coevalness, it is important to see the diasporic filmmakers relating to their "home" and "homeland" laterally – as much as they relate to the diaspora communities.

In the context of Chinese diaspora and diasporic filmmaking, the affective investment in "home" as "imagined togetherness" unfolds on two levels: first, internal as well as external diaspora; second, negotiation with and creolization of Sinic languages. Chinese diaspora refers to not only people who migrate out of mainland China, Hong Kong, and Taiwan, but also entails what I am calling internal diaspora between Sinophone regions that have markedly different dialects / languages and cultures. This broadened notion of "Chinese diaspora" acknowledges multiple modes of intersecting with "Chinese" while imploding any prescribed "Chineseness." Second, Sinic languages in diasporic filmmaking may become foregrounded (as in Shih's theorization), backgrounded (as in Ang's case), or jumbled, as I shall argue. By separating Chinese diasporic identification(s) from Sinic languages, we may begin to fathom the linguistic performance in the diasporic filmmakers' construction of their subject positions *vis-à-vis* the Sinophone "home."

Guided by these concerns, I map out the diasporic formation of Chinese cinema by tracing its evolving strategies of affectively articulating "home" or "imagined togetherness" at different historical conjunctures. I use the term "diasporic formation of Chinese cinema" to stress the co-implication (instead of segregation) between diasporic filmmaking and Chinese cinema. My "map" of the diasporic formation encompasses four facets, which do not pretend to be exhaustive, but rather heuristically highlight some key developments and figures that emerge from specific historical and political exigencies. These facets challenge us to redefine and reinvent the concept of "diasporic Chinese cinema," especially in relation to the affective understanding of "home." These four facets are as follows:

- Pre-World War II diasporic filmmakers inside and outside the Sinophone area
- World War II and civil war migration: Shanghai to Hong Kong (1937–49) and Hong Kong to California (1941–5)
- Flexible filmmaking: Hong Kong, China, and the global turn
- Shuttling in-between, going nonmainstream, and creolizing the Sinophone

Pre-World War II Diasporic Filmmakers Inside and Outside the Sinophone Area

If Chinese cinema has been transnational from the beginning (S. Lu 1997: 4), it has also always been diasporic. Since the early twentieth century, Chinese filmmakers have been constantly shuttling between disparate Sinophone regions, especially

Shanghai and Southern China (Huanan, including Hong Kong, according to the parlance at the time), and in a few cases, Taiwan (oftentimes via Japan). One most conspicuous example is Lai Man-wai (Li Mingwei). Known as the "Father of Hong Kong Cinema," Lai founded Hong Kong's first movie studio, Minxin (China Sun) in 1923, which he later moved to Shanghai. In October 1930 Lai cofounded Lianhua (United Photoplay and Publishing Service), registered in both Shanghai and Hong Kong, initially headquartered in Hong Kong, yet mostly operating from Shanghai. It developed into a major film company in Shanghai, with Lai's Minxin incorporated as Studio One. It remained important until Japan's second bombing in Shanghai in August 1937 (Law and Bren 2004).

Many of the pre-1937 internal diasporic film activities were intertwined with external diasporic film activities. The US examples included Joseph Sunn (a.k.a. Joseph Chiu, Joseph Sunn Jue, Chiu Shu-sun, Zhao Shushen, 1904–90), Moon Kwan (Kwan Man-ching, Guan Wenqing, 1894–1995), and Li Zeyuan. A Cantonese native who moved to San Francisco at an early age, Sunn studied cinematography and setting while working on *The Silk Bouquet* (Harry Revier, 1926), starring Anna May Wong. He shot some mud animations for Ralph Wolfe's Mud Stuff series.[1] Like Sunn, Moon Kwan was also a Cantonese native, but he had formal film education in Los Angeles while working as an extra in Hollywood in 1915. He worked as the technical advisor for D. W. Griffith's *Broken Blossoms*, a.k.a. *The Yellow Man and the Girl* (1919), in which he also played a monk (uncredited). Upon returning to China in 1920, Kwan immediately applied his American film training to the emerging Chinese film industry. He advised Minxin and worked for Lianhua as consultant, scriptwriter, and director (Law and Bren 2004; Zhou and Li 2009). During the 1920s and 1930s, he represented Lianhua, traveling to the United States several times to raise funds and purchase filming equipment.

In 1933 Kwan traveled to various American and Canadian-Chinese communities and showed three Lianhua productions: a documentary, *Army Route 19's Glorious Battle against the Japanese Enemy* (1932), and two feature films. The trip facilitated the nationalist campaign among Chinese immigrants whose Chinese identification had been more defined by their home region (rather than national) affiliations. Kwan's tour "prepared the ground for the first large network of 'Chinatowns' that would comprise an important market for Hong Kong cinema" (Law and Bren 2004: 79). Indeed, this Chinatown network was to sustain Cantonese cinema during Hong Kong's occupation by Japan from 1941 to 1945 (to be elaborated later).

Kwan's 1933 tour also led to his meeting with Joseph Sunn, resulting in the latter's founding of Grandview Talking Pictures Company (Daguan). Casting two Cantonese opera actors, Kwan Tak-hsing (Guan Dexing, 1906–96) and Wu Dip-ying (Hu Dieying, b. 1911), who were sojourning and performing in San Francisco, Sunn directed one of the earliest Cantonese talkies, *Romance of the Songsters* (1933). Kwan's connection with Sunn eventually led Luo Mingyou, head of Lianhua, to consider incorporating Grandview as the "overseas Lianhua," which would increase the production of Cantonese films geared to North American Chinese immigrants. Whereas the plan fell through due to financial reasons, Sunn relocated Grandview to Hong Kong in 1934 to make Cantonese films, some of them directed by Kwan.

Another film company launched by Chinese in the United States and later relocated to the Sinophone area was Great Wall Film Company (Changcheng), registered in New York in April 1921. The company's birth was directly related to overseas Chinese students' indignation with two China-bashing American films, *The Red Lantern* (Albert Capellani, 1919) and *The First Born* (Colin Campbell, 1921). In an attempt to remedy the image of China in the West, the overseas Chinese went to film schools, formed the film group "Zhenzhen Society," and eventually launched Great Wall in Brooklyn. Run by journalists Mei Xuechou and Liu Zhaoming, and students Li Zeyuan and Cheng Peilin, Great Wall collectively made two short films, *Chinese Costumes* (1922) and *Chinese Martial Arts* (1922), distributed by Urban Motion Picture Industries Incorporation. In 1924 they moved the company to Shanghai, producing socially oriented "problem films" and genre films until 1930.

Film historians have attributed the short life of the ambitious Great Wall to the founding members' "maladjustment" to the "Chinese environment of film production" (Xiao and Chen 2004: 44). In comparison with Joseph Sunn, this group did not rely upon family business (i.e., overseas Chinese capital) or a Chinatown audience (i.e., compatriots who presumably shared the same culture and language/dialect). The distribution of their debut short films through an American company indicates their intention to reach an American audience with the hope of changing Western perceptions of China. The China they tried to convey, through professionalism and the English language,[2] was an imagined, idealized, modern China posited as their "homeland" and cultural origin. Yet, their lack of in-depth experience with China led to their disconnection from the Chinese audience.

Grandview and Great Wall therefore represented two distinct understandings of "home" or cultural origin. For Sunn, "home" was never entirely imagined, but existed in the microcosm of the Cantonese community in San Francisco where he was an everyday participant; in other words, Sunn's "home" was a mobile lingua-cultural matrix that maintained a certain stability across the geopolitical border. The relatively stable and specific lingua-ethnic identity ensured the sustainability of Grandview. For the founding members of Great Wall, however, "home" started as a rhetorical counterpoint to the derogatory Western perception of China. It was an abstract idea distanced from everyday experiences and was therefore unsustainable. Sadly, when an abstract conception of "China" did become important after 1932, both as a nation-state besieged by imperialist powers (especially Japan) and as a "homeland" in need of rescue, Great Wall had already folded and its Chinese-American founding members dispersed.

World War II and Civil War Migration

If pre-1937 internal and external diasporic filmmaking was more contingent upon an individual person's or group's decisions that were not always directly affected by the sociopolitical situation, the shuttling between 1937 and 1949 (extending into the 1950s) was more closely tied up with macro-scale political emergencies. With the eruption of the Second Sino-Japanese War in July 1937, followed by Shanghai's bombing in August 1937, the three major Shanghai studios (Lianhua, Mingxing, and Tianyi) suffered fatal damage. Lianhua and Mingxing folded, while Tianyi moved to Hong Kong, where it had already set up distribution branches since the late 1920s and launched a production branch in 1934 to cater to Southern Chinese and Southeast Asian Chinese communities. Tianyi's southward relocation eventually produced the empire of the Shaw Brothers, which reigned in Hong Kong and Southeast Asia from the late 1950s to the 1970s, rivaled only by Cathay (formerly MP&GI or Motion Pictures & General Investments Ltd.) founded by Loke Wan Tho (Lu Yuntao, 1915–64), the European-educated son of a wealthy Chinese family in Malaysia.

Among the southward migration following the fall of Shanghai, there were also progressive filmmakers and dramatists, including Cai Chusheng, Situ Huimin, Ouyang Yuqian (1889–1962), and Xia Yan, who relocated strategically with the hope of politicizing Hong Kong cinema so as to build a "national defense cinema" that would glorify China's military, civilian, and underground resistance against Japanese aggression (Law and Bren 2004: 130–5). For most of these new arrivals, the reality of late 1930s Hong Kong was invisible and invisibilized due to the privileging of "national defense films." When Tianyi's boss, Shao Zuiweng, renamed the South China Film Society (*Huanan dianying xiehui*) the Overseas Chinese Film Union (*Huaqiao dianying gonghui*) in 1937, he sent a clear message: ethnic Chinese in Hong Kong were interpellated as Chinese subjects sojourning in an area ruled by a non-Chinese government; and the southern Chinese regional identity had to be subsumed to the Chinese national polity (Zhou and Li 2009: 222).

The invisibilizaton of Hong Kong is manifested in national defense films made in Hong Kong, yet set in Shanghai, such as *Baoshan City Bathed in Blood* (Situ Huimin, 1938), the first Shanghai–Hong Kong coproduction, and *Orphan Island Paradise* (Cai Chusheng, 1939) (see Figure 29.1). In *Orphan Island Paradise*, the setting of Shanghai is evoked through the back projection of sketches and quasi-documentary footage that display Shanghai's trademark Bund scenery. Such a visual idiom privileges Shanghai as the site of resistance and the seat of hope, while obscuring Hong Kong, despite its supply of material and sometimes human resources. Such diasporic consciousness (living/sojourning in one place while desiring the other) was to be rehearsed from the Civil War (1945–9) through the 1960s among previously Shanghai-based film workers who then sojourned in Hong Kong.

Figure 29.1   *Orphan Island Paradise* (dir. Cai Chusheng, Dadi Film, 1939): the protagonists performing a duet in front of a back-projected Shanghai Bund landscape.

As the war spread to Hong Kong after the Pearl Harbor attack, Hong Kong's filmmakers refused to collaborate with Japanese aggressors, precipitating the complete suspension of film production in occupied Hong Kong. Under such circumstances, Joseph Sunn moved Grandview back to San Francisco, where he started filming with 16 mm color stock. Once again, the Chinese-American communities sustained his film career, although some of these films were released in Hong Kong after the war. The synopses and a couple of surviving film prints suggest that Sunn's American-made films focus on dramas of young Chinese-Americans swamped by modern urban entertainment. Their ethnic and cultural "origin," taking the form of Cantonese operatic performance, figures as just another entertainment. Commenting on *The Gold Braided Dress* (Wong Hok-sing, 1947), lavishly shot on 16 mm color film, a reviewer writes: "The film has both Westerners and Chinese characters. It is both nostalgic and modern. There are dances and opera shows, as well as panoramic shots of San Francisco and its parks. For those who haven't been to San Francisco, this is truly eye-opening" (*Jianguo Daily*, July 21, 1947). What was proudly touted as a "new phase of Chinese cinema" (*Huaqiao wanbao*, February 1946) was received by a Western viewer as a bemusing mixture of incongruous elements. Writing about Sunn's *Pear Blossoms in the Storm*, another 1947 color talkie,[3] James Hudson (1947) stressed the film's "entirely Occidental," "local 'modern' background," as he was amused by the "casual mixing of Oriental and Western music."

Grandview's interest in Chinese-Americans' settlement in a modern American urban setting was already manifest in a film shot in San Francisco in 1940. The film title, *The Light of the Overseas Chinese* (Joseph Sunn), suggestively emphasizes the "light" that overseas Chinese reflect on their "motherland" by leading a successful life in America. In this film, an old Chinese couple reflects upon their struggle to build a home in the adoptive land of America. The Grandview films thus consistently valorize the emotional investment in "home," wherever it is located. Flexible in terms of location, all characters (including the younger generation), nonetheless, largely stick to the Cantonese language. The linguistic continuity between American Chinese communities and Hong Kong suggests that these films do not just showcase exotic American scenery and modernity, but also envision sustainable, albeit image-made, togetherness across the geopolitical border.

An interesting parallel with Sunn's hopeful diasporic picture in California during and after the war would be the films made by previously Shanghai-based filmmakers who migrated to Hong Kong during and after the Civil War between the Communists and the Nationalists (1945–9). Some important figures include Zhu Shilin, Fei Mu, Fang Peilin (1908–49), and Zhang Shankun. Like Sunn's films that clinged to his native Cantonese language and catered to overseas Chinese as well as Hong Kong audiences, these internal diasporic directors also fostered a mainland exclave in Hong Kong. They shot films in Mandarin Chinese, oftentimes cast migrant actors from Shanghai (e.g., Cheng Juanjuan, Wei Wei, and Zhou Xuan), and targeted mainland audiences who had fled to Hong Kong in the 1940s.

As the most prolific diasporic director, Zhu Shilin made drama films centering upon the misunderstandings and disagreements in everyday life among the lower middle class, and their ultimate reconciliation and mutual support. Zhu's emphasis on difficult life circumstances dovetails with the poor living conditions in postwar Hong Kong. In *Housewarming* (1954) and *Between Fire and Water* (1955), for instance, he uses realistic details of the crowded living space and water shortage to dramatize neighborhood conflicts – to be resolved only through collaboration. Unlike the straightforward success stories offered by Sunn's American productions, Zhu's films demonstrate that "homing" consists in the difficult process of dwelling – finding the right place to live, meeting everyday needs, managing the messy neighborhood. Thus, whereas Zhu's diasporic characters do not actively interact with local Cantonese characters, they share the same space and shoulder the same responsibility of making a home and a community (temporary or permanent) out of the harsh postwar reality.

Flexible Filmmaking: Hong Kong, China, and the Global Turn

Making a home while sojourning or settling down involves what Naficy calls the vertical attachment to the "homeland" and lateral networking in the adoptive land. Yet, for those who re-home in the adoptive land of Hong Kong (the British "crown colony" until 1997), the "homeland" (China) is never the static "past" to be related to vertically (in a nostalgic or recuperative manner), but rather the ever-present that is constantly changing, thereby necessitating lateral interactions with diasporic communities. Responding to China's transmogrifications since the 1990s, including its 1997 reclaiming of sovereignty over Hong Kong and its globalizing turn, Hong Kong residents find it increasingly necessary to rebuild, reconfigure, and sometimes even relocate their "home." Much has been written about Hong Kong residents' fear of the impending deadline (July 1, 1997) and losing their home and identity. What has been understudied are the ways in which "home" is reimagined in the space of Hong Kong in concatenation with other spaces. Such concatenation is produced by what I call flexible filmmaking that takes advantage of multilocation shooting, with the result of foregrounding Hong Kong as a serialized space, a space whose meaning and identity depend on other interconnected locations. This is illustrated in *Mary from Beijing* (Sylvia Chang, 1992), *Durian Durian* (Fruit Chan, 2000), and Wong Kar-wai's *Happy Together* (1997) and *In the Mood for Love* (2000). The diasporic dimension of these films demonstrates that Hong Kong's location-specific identity is an imaginary that constantly shifts with its historically volatile landscape, ethnoscape, and financescape.

Mary from Beijing revolves around a Beijing woman's successful attempt to obtain Hong Kong residency shortly before Hong Kong's handover to China. This narrative intertwines with a subplot depicting a British-educated Hong Kong businessman deciding to move his business back to Hong Kong, starting factories in Beijing, while studying Mandarin Chinese. Toward the end of the film, she finds work as a tour guide, introducing Hong Kong to wealthy Taiwan housewives in her flawless Mandarin Chinese. To consummate her successful relocation to Hong Kong, the film ends with her romantic union with the Hong Kong businessman, which unambiguously celebrates their future home in Hong Kong as the base for strengthening their business relationship with other places, including Beijing and Taiwan. In this light, the closing shot of her Hong Kong residence card portends that post-1997 Hong Kong will become a new and more prosperous "home" for those who know how to take advantage of its mediatory geopolitical position.

Contrary to this vision, *Durian Durian*, Fruit Chan's first film partially shot and set in mainland China, foregrounds the perils of low-class migration laborers. Xiao Yan, a stage actress, leaves her Chinese home to work in Hong Kong as a prostitute. When her short-term residency permit expires, she returns to her hometown in Northeast China, only to find herself unable to resume her previous life with her husband. Her migratory experience as a subaltern sex worker destroys the possibility of homing in her sojourning location (Hong Kong) and her hometown in China. Her "inflexible noncitizen" status originates from the global capitalism that envelops China and Hong Kong alike. Within this system, the China–Hong Kong relationship is not so much Hong Kong's subjection to China's dictatorship as Chinese women's subjection to the capitalist logic. Contemporary Hong Kong's geopolitical status therefore is revealed as interconnected with China's capitalist turn, which facilitates the meeting of Chinese cheap labor with Hong Kong's capital.

Hong Kong's imbrications with other spaces through political interactions, population migration, and capital flow are also manifest in *In the Mood for Love*. Originating from a Shanghai émigré family in Hong Kong, Wong seeks to evoke and preserve his memory of the Shanghai exclave in 1960s Hong Kong by deploying mnemonic details (some relayed through his mother), including the Shanghai dialect, Zhou Xuan's Mandarin pop songs, women's graceful cheongsams, housewives' mahjong games, Peking opera, and Nat "King" Cole's American rendition of "Quizás, Quizás, Quizás." Interestingly, Wong's 1960s Hong Kong was filmed in Bangkok. Wong's justification is that Bangkok (especially its Chinatown area) was more evocative of Hong Kong in the 1960s than was hyper-developed Hong Kong itself. This seemingly expedient decision, evocative of the Hollywood practice of space swapping (Elmer and Gasher 2005), inadvertently touches upon the colonial and Chinese diasporic histories in Southeast Asia. The interchangeability of the Chinatown of Bangkok and 1960s Hong Kong stems precisely from their shared history of European colonization and Chinese migration. *In the Mood for Love* thus inscribes two layers of diaspora – from mid-twentieth-century Shanghai to Hong Kong, and from China to Southeast Asia – which renders the Hong Kong space serial and dependent upon other spaces. Within this serialized space, homing in Hong Kong becomes necessarily a transitory act.

Such spatial swapping, linked with flexible filmmaking, also underpins *Happy Together*, which was mostly shot in Argentina, with only one intriguing shot of Hong Kong upside down, from the perspective of Argentina – on the obverse side of the globe. Hong Kong and Argentina's mirroring relationship once again hints at their shared colonial history. Furthermore, it reinforces Hong Kong's transit status as the disappearing space/home from which to flee due to the anxiety surrounding the 1997 handover. It was in response to this anxiety and the media's curiosity about whether he was going to make a handover film that Wong initially decided to shoot the film in far-flung Argentina. His attempt to escape, however, reconfirmed the inescapability of the issue of diaspora that beset Hong Kong. During shooting, Wong's feeling of dislocation in Argentina started to echo his childhood experience of living in Hong Kong as a new immigrant. In both cases, "TV, radio, and newspapers stop[ped] existing for you because of the language barrier."[4] Thus, to shoot the film in another (irrelevant) place ends up reinforcing the feeling of diaspora, inside and outside the diegesis, which ultimately correlates with a new round of diaspora, this time from Hong Kong to Euro-America and Australia.

In *Happy Together* and *In the Mood for Love*, Wong's flexible filmmaking enables spatial swapping that makes Hong Kong a serialized space that is both fragmented by diasporic movements and concatenated, even interchangeable, with other spaces across the border. The serialized space means that identity and "homing" in Hong Kong are always correlated with other spaces, especially the constantly "updated" mainland China. As China gets sutured into global capitalism, its wide variety of landscapes, its cheap labor force, and its expansive market become increasingly valuable to Hong Kong filmmakers, including those who left Hong

Kong for America in the late twentieth century. Jackie Chan, Chow Yun-fat, Jet Li, and John Woo have all started collaborating with the Chinese media industry and making films in Mandarin Chinese.[5] Likewise, Wong Kar-wai is now embarking on a most unlikely collaboration with Zhao Benshan (b. 1957), a popular mainland lowbrow comedian, in a putative martial arts film, *The Grand Master*. This unusual collaboration signals Wong's exploration of new strategies for broadening his market share in mainland China. As parts of China (especially Beijing and Shanghai) emerge into a world-class "media capital" (Curtin 2007: 285–6), it is not surprising that a number of Hong Kong/Hollywood celebrities have purchased (one of their) homes in large Chinese cities. If this does not really constitute "re-homing" (for it by no means signals a return flow), it does suggest that China's marketization has significantly reconfigured its geopolitical border, putting a new spin on questions of what is Hong Kong identity and what is Chinese identity.

Shuttling In-Between, Going Nonmainstream, and Creolizing the Sinophone

There is a huge gap between the "home" that multiplies across the border for new-age flexible citizens and the "home" that figures as "imagined togetherness" in *Persisting with Tears in Eyes*. In between these two extremes is a wide spectrum of "homing" tactics and negotiations that unfold diegetically in the characters' world and extra-diegetically in the diasporic filmmakers' world. In this section, I use three case studies to discuss how "home" continues to galvanize affective and critical investment in contemporary noncommercial, external diasporic Chinese filmmaking.

Shi-zheng Chen, Clara Law, and Xiaolu Guo (b. 1973) relocated, respectively and for different reasons, to the United States, Australia, and England. Chen, an established experimental dramatist who had studied regional opera and experienced the Cultural Revolution in China, moved to the United States in the late 1980s. His debut film was the award-winning *Dark Matter* (2007). Clara Law is a veteran director from Hong Kong who immigrated to Australia in anticipation of Hong Kong's handover. Xiaolu Guo, who grew up in post-Cultural Revolution rural China, graduated from Beijing Film Academy and became a novelist and filmmaker currently dwelling in England. Since 2003, Guo has written and directed nine documentaries, shorts, and feature films in Mandarin Chinese and English. All three artists work across media or genres (between opera, theater and film, or between documentary and feature film). They also tap into personal immigration experiences as part of the conditions of production. Key to their immigration experiences is the encounter with non-Sinic languages and mixed perspectives that significantly reconfigure the "home" in a world that is increasingly contracted, yet intractably territorialized.

Clara Law's pre-immigration films, *Farewell China* (1990) and *Autumn Moon* (1992), already deal with the pressure to leave and the schizophrenic fragmentation of home. Her films in Australia, such as *Floating Life* (1996) and *The Goddess of 1967* (2000), have continued these concerns in different contexts. Her first foray into documentary, *Letters to Ali* (2004), critiques Australian immigration policy regarding political refugees. Focusing on an Afghan refugee boy named Ali, who is segregated until the settlement of his case, and his relationship with his potential foster family, the documentary poignantly comments on the state-sponsored divestment of an inflexible noncitizen of his "home."

Negotiation with the perils of displacement from the standpoint of an inflexible noncitizen similarly underpins Shi-zheng Chen's *Dark Matter*. Loosely based on a real-life incident in 1991 involving a frustrated Chinese student's shooting spree at the University of Iowa, the film hopes to "explore the mysterious and powerful forces unleashed when a young Chinese immigrant strives to make his mark in a culture that is at once seductive and impenetrable" (S. Chen 2007: 13). From the outset, the film interweaves the Chinese student's home-bound nostalgia with excitement and befuddlement in a new world. It opens with the student writing a letter to his parents in China, his voice-over exuding excitement at being accepted into the elite lab headed by his most admired professor. Meanwhile, a nondiegetic female choir is heard in the background, performing "Missing My Hometown" (*Nian guxiang*), adapted from the English song "Goin' Home," which is in turn arranged from the second movement of Antonín Dvořák's Symphony No. 9, "From the New World," composed during his visit to the United States in the late nineteenth century. The slow, soothing tempo and the lyrics of "Missing My Hometown" express the inconsolable nostalgia of a "lonely guest" (*guke*) wandering in a "strange land" (*taxiang*), longing to return to his hometown (*guxiang*). As his "new world" becomes increasingly hostile and intolerable, the student keeps on writing letters home and reporting fabricated successes. His schizophrenic existence ultimately leads him to a shooting spree.

Importantly, the student refuses to go home when he suffers frustration in America. In other words, "home" is desirable and nostalgia is possible only if he is able to take root in the "new world," which, ironically, means staying away from home. Herein lies the diasporic paradox: for a home to remain a home, it must exist elsewhere as an idea evoked and desired through letters, phone calls, and imagination. A diasporic figure, therefore, is always longing to return home, yet simultaneously keeping it unreachable. This paradox stems from the student's diasporic encounter with foreign perspectives and languages, which simultaneously hinders assimilation and problematizes the reified "home." The deliberately jumbled dialogue mixing English and Chinese, along with the heavy accent of the mainland actor, Liu Ye, foregrounds precisely the improvisational, performative, and tension-ridden nature of the diasporic identity.

The struggle with a foreign language in a foreign land also structures Xiaolu Guo's artistic work in England. Speaking in the voice of Z, a character in her 2007

English novel, *A Concise Chinese–English Dictionary for Lovers*, Guo muses, "When a body floating in air, which country she belonging to?" This deterritorializing idea potentially invalidates the nagging issue of national identity. Yet, the incorrect grammar immediately undermines its validity by instantly labeling the character as an imperfect foreigner. The inexorable foreignness mirrors Guo's own struggle for a legal identity as a recent immigrant living in "a permanent state of impermanence" in the UK. Responding to a British police letter that states "you cannot be granted leave to remain," she questions, "Must I leave, or could I remain?" (X. Guo 2008). She ultimately learns to mobilize the "leave to remain" status for her artistic creation from a foreign perspective. The decision to write *A Concise Chinese–English Dictionary for Lovers* in grammatically incorrect English mimics precisely a foreigner's speech, which shows how the foreign status puts one in a childlike state of mind.

The foreign perspective is redoubled in her "fictional documentary" *We Went to Wonderland* (2008), detailing her Communist parents' visit to London. Here, the foreign perspective of the two old Chinese Communist Party members who are also peasants is not just national, cultural, and linguistic, but also ideological and class based. Their foreign perspective that is simultaneously "childlike," Communist, and rural embodies "the individual voice" that Guo tries to reclaim. Insisting upon the individuality of her and her character/subject's perspectives, she states, "I refuse to represent China because China has many faces. I refuse to represent culture" (X. Guo n.d.).

Despite her rejection of the burden of representation, Guo's inquiry into issues of noncitizenship and degrees of mobility (or an outsider's lack of legal rights in general) pertains to the prevalent displacement and de-homing resulting from China's internal as well as external diaspora. Her documentary *The Concrete Revolution* (2004; its Chinese title *Qian ru routi de chengshi* literally means "The city that cuts into flesh"), shot back "home" (in Beijing and her hometown in Southern China), is a case in point. Observing Beijing's construction craze in ramping up for the 2008 Olympic Games, the documentary shows that the wholesale makeover not only destroys home for Beijingers, but also erects a generic cosmopolitan super-space that is alienated from its builders, who, as migrant workers, have to leave their home behind in order to build homes in the city.

These three nonmainstream filmmakers/artists use their artistic creation to negotiate the interstices between unprecedented globalization and spatial contraction on the one hand, and reinforced national border surveillance on the other. Their works stress the affective investment in "home" while interrogating the meanings of "home" for those who travel under variant circumstances. They value traveling without romanticizing it, engage with border-crossing communication without presuming its success, and embark on the "journey to the West" without aiming at assimilation. Theirs is an "accented cinema," a cinema that not only deploys "accented speech of the diegetic characters or the directors," but also foregrounds "the displacement of the filmmakers and their artisanal production modes" (Naficy 2001: 4). As "empirical subjects, situated in the interstices of

Figure 29.2   Against London's picture-perfect cityscape of Big Ben and the House of Commons in *She, A Chinese* (dir. Xiaolu Guo, UK Film Council, 2009).

cultures and film practices" (Naficy 2001: 4), they create films as well as operas and novels that deal with the osmosis between here and there, present and past. By so doing, they simultaneously engage with the updated "home" (then and there) and reinvent it in imagination (here and now).

"Home," in diasporic movements, can exist only in what Guo describes as "leaving and longing" (Rose 2009) with regard to her feature film, *She, A Chinese* (2009) (see Figure 29.2). Such individual and collective emotional investment in the idea of a "home" as imagined togetherness underpins all the internal and external diasporic axes I have explored in this chapter, ranging from underground "inflexible noncitizen/resident" to the cosmopolitan globetrotter. The degree of mobility varies tremendously in each case. However, they combine to manifest the variegated endeavors to cross the border in order to rebuild a "home," despite the loss of the actual home. In this floating process of "leaving to remain," what is redefined is not just the idea of "home," but also, increasingly, the Sinic languages *per se*. Lai Man-wai, the father of Hong Kong cinema who shuttled between different dialects of Shanghai and Southern China; Li Zeyuan, the non-Mandarin speaking director of the Great Wall Company; Joseph Sunn, whose American productions depended on Cantonese audiences; Wong Kar-wai, whose mental exile resulted from his inability to understand local TV, radio, and newspapers while making *Happy Together* in Argentina; the Chinese father who eventually adopted Japanese in Zhang Liling's *Persisting with Tears in Eyes*; the "childlike" English in *A Concise Chinese–English Dictionary for Lovers*; the jumbled and accented English in Shi-zheng Chen's *Dark Matter* – all of these examples demonstrate the long-standing creolization of diasporic Sinophone cinema.[6]

Conclusion

The diasporic formation of Chinese cinema that I have sketched in this chapter demonstrates that diasporic filmmaking has historically been imbricated with and inherent to the construction of Chinese cinema. As the "other" site that traverses the "Chinese" center, diasporic filmmaking constitutes the alter-center where "Chinese" issues are staged and contested by being placed in interaction with non-Sinic contexts. Most importantly, this alter-center fosters variant articulations of "home" as an affective and political symbol. These diasporic "homing" strategies become more important now than ever as China emerges as a global power, striving to become one of many "homes" for flexible citizens while ceasing to be the only home for inflexible noncitizens.

For some contemporary diasporic filmmakers, the affective investment in the idea of "home" and "imagined togetherness" draws upon their childhood moviegoing experiences. Ang Lee, for instance, was inspired to make *Crouching Tiger, Hidden Dragon* (2000) by King Hu's *Dragon Gate Inn* (1967). To Lee, "China" is an idea or an image as depicted in martial arts films that acquired a large audience following in his childhood Taiwan. Similarly, Tsai Ming-liang, an ethnic Chinese raised in Malaysia and distinguished by an internationally renowned film career in Taiwan, also pays homage to *Dragon Gate Inn* in his *Goodbye Dragon Inn* (2003). As the title suggests, Tsai's film casts a lingering farewell look at a movie culture that is disappearing along with a to-be-demolished theater, under the very eyes of two old men who starred in Hu's 1967 film. Additionally, Tsai's films are punctuated by frequent references to pop songs performed by Grace Chang (Ge Lan, b. 1934) in the 1960s Mandarin classics produced by Cathay. Tsai's affective evocation of these songs and films not only testifies to the prevalence of diasporic Chinese film culture in mid-twentieth-century Southeast Asia. More importantly, it illustrates the cultivation of a "home" image in a distant place (Malaysia), an image of the 1960s effervescence that contrasts sharply with present-day aphasic, unhomely Taiwan.

Lee and Tsai's investment in China imaginaries manufactured by the mid-twentieth-century Taiwan and Hong Kong film industries seems to suggest a "vertical" relationship with the "there and then," as Naficy argues. Yet, the fact that this "past" is movie-made and is revived by peripatetic filmmakers suggests that it is never sealed elsewhere, but always relived now and here as alternative Sinophone "home" imaginaries that actively interact with international audiences. As a result, the Sinic languages that apparently buttress the "home" imaginaries are creolized, rather than reified or completely jettisoned. It is precisely by deploying multifaceted linguistic practices and "homing" imaginaries that internal and external diasporic directors (including Lee and Tsai) can hope to effectively address different regional and national audiences. In other words, what all the diasporic filmmakers have in common is their entangled negotiation with the Sinic languages and affective investment in a sense of "home" or "imagined togetherness." It is by claiming and performing while interrogating the linguistic and affective lineage that diasporic identifications become possible. In the final analysis, diasporic Chinese cinema must leave "home" in order to regain it; it must deconstruct the "home" to rebuild it anew in variant images; and it ultimately embodies the accented alter-center of the Sinophone "home."

Notes

1 Three of the 1926 animations, *Green Pastures*, *The Penwiper*, and *Long Live the Bull*, are available for viewing at http://www.open-video.org/results.php?keyword_search=true&terms=Animation (accessed June 10, 2009).

2 According to Wang Hanlun (Great Wall's main actress who starred in its first three films in Shanghai), Li Zeyuan, the director of *The Abandoned Wife* (1924), did not speak Mandarin Chinese or Shanghai dialect, but only English (Xiao and Chen 2004: 37).

3 The copy in the Hong Kong Film Archive is in black and white.

4 In the documentary *Buenos Aires Affair Zero Degree: The Making of Happy Together* (Pung-Leung Kwan, 1999), Wong says, "I felt ostracized by the world … . Day after day, I came to understand the feeling of exile."

5 Jackie Chan recently played a journalist in China's propaganda blockbuster, *The Founding of a Republic* (Han Sanping, Huang Jianxin, 2009), as well as playing himself in a Chinese action comedy, *Looking For Jackie* (Zhang Liangfang, 2009). John Woo also made his first Mandarin film, *Red Cliff I–II* (2008, 2009), adapted from a well-known classic Chinese novel.

6 Gaik Cheng Khoo (2009) further problematizes the "diasporic Chinese cinema" in her study of Southeast Asian independent filmmakers of Chinese ancestry who choose to make films not in Sinic languages. Their filmmaking challenges the status of the Sinic languages in diasporic Chinese cinema.

30

The Absent American

Figuring the United States in Chinese Cinema of the Reform Era

Michael Berry

From classic productions as diverse as *The Good Earth* (Sidney Franklin, 1937) and *55 Days in Peking* (Nicholas Ray, 1963) to more recent action-adventure films such as *The Mummy: Tomb of the Dragon Emperor* (Rob Cohen, 2008) and *The Forbidden Kingdom* (Rob Minkoff, 2008), Hollywood has built up its own vernacular shorthand on how to frame China through film. This framing process includes a series of long-entrenched tropes, stereotypes, and orientalist fantasies, from Charlie Chans and Fu Manchus to Dragon Ladies and martial arts heroes. In recent years, Hollywood's Chinese canvas has expanded into new arenas with studios using China as the primary backdrop for wartime period dramas like *The Children of Huangshi* (Roger Spottiswoode, 2008) and *The Painted Veil* (John Curran, 2006) and utilizing the skyscrapers and modern exteriors of Shanghai and Hong Kong as large-scale action set pieces for *Mission: Impossible III* (J. J. Abrams, 2006) and *The Dark Knight* (Christopher Nolan, 2008). Collectively, these popular images have had a profound effect on how China is perceived and imagined in the United States and beyond. But how has the Chinese film industry positioned America within its own dream factory of celluloid images? What are the key tropes and vernacular shorthand that China has used to frame America? And how have the United States and the figure of the American been transformed and retranslated over the course of the past several decades?

The Korean War (1950–3), which broke out shortly after the 1949 founding of the People's Republic of China and pitted the young PRC against the United States, cast a long shadow over Sino-US relations. During the ensuing cold-war period, the United States was positioned as an evil capitalist empire and Americans were framed largely as imperialist spies or faceless soldiers in a myriad of classic Chinese war films such as *Shanggan Ridge* (Sha Meng, Lin Shan, 1956), *Heroic Sons*

A Companion to Chinese Cinema, First Edition. Edited by Yingjin Zhang.
© 2012 Blackwell Publishing Ltd. Published 2012 by Blackwell Publishing Ltd.

and Daughters (Wu Zhaoti, 1964), and *Flying Tigers* (Zheng Zhiguo, Yu Chunmian, 1978). In the majority of these films the "American" remains a shadowy figure who appears fleetingly on the battlefield but is rarely much more than a symbolic embodiment of imperialist evil. With American soldiers portrayed by Chinese actors in face paint and wearing prosthetic noses, it is rare for Korean War films to allow any dialogue for American characters. In the few cases where there are visible American characters, such as the model opera film *Raid on the White Tiger Regiment* (Su Li, Wang Yan, 1972), their characterization is predictably flat and one-dimensional in keeping with the aesthetic principles of socialist realism and the anti-American political line. A widespread embargo on everything American during this period (1949–78) also meant that virtually no direct unmediated American films or cultural products were allowed entry into China, thus giving these negative representations all the more propagandistic power to shape public perceptions. It was not until 1978 and Deng Xiaoping's Reform era that new spaces for cultural engagement with America began to open up. This chapter explores the shifting place of the United States and, alternately, the figure of the American, in contemporary Chinese cinema during the crucial transition period of the early Reform era.

By isolating two modes of cinematic representation I hope to elucidate a series of distinct phases that cultural negotiation and representation of the United States has gone through in China. The majority of works considered fall into two categories, which can be generally termed "The [Chinese-]American Cometh," portraying direct encounters with Americans who come to China in a variety of capacities, and "Left for America," which depict the experience of Chinese who come to America for work, study, tourism, or immigration. Within the confines of these two general categories, however, I argue that Chinese cultural discourse on America has undergone a dramatic transformation over the course of the past three decades since the Reform era. These transformative shifts have been inextricably linked to larger sociohistorical changes in China from a socialist to market economy and a major overhaul of the film industry itself, which has moved from the age of state-sponsored film studios to a series of privately owned film companies that now freely enter into coproductions with both state-run studios and Hollywood as well as other foreign film studios and production companies. As the industry evolves and diversifies, one of the most significant aspects of this transformation in terms of the topic at hand has been a shift from "America" signified, in large part, by tropes of absence, distance, and invisibility to later conceptions that reframe America more directly. These direct representations have come with a greater degree of complexity and subtlety; however, they are by no means immune from the nationalistic undertones which so greatly dictated early post-Cultural Revolution films about America.

The primary emphasis of this chapter will be placed on this first phase during which the United States was framed primarily through a strategy of absence. Beginning with "The [Chinese-]American Cometh," I will offer readings of a series of films produced between 1979 and 1982 in order to demonstrate how a new format for imagining America within the parameters of a strict political formula was developed. This carefully rendered formula was at once an all-inclusive "carrot and stick" method: specifically designed to reintroduce America to China (in the wake of the reestablishment on January 1, 1979 of official diplomatic relations) and satisfy public curiosity about the United States while, at the same, carefully offsetting the allure with an even more potent patriotic discourse. I will then extend my argument by demonstrating how a similar theme of absence would also dominate early portrayals of the Chinese immigrant experience almost a decade later under the title "Left for America." Finally, the chapter will offer a preliminary discussion on how America has been revisited as Chinese-language cinema has shifted away from a politics of absence to a more complex framing. The series of filmic texts examined will help elucidate larger questions of propaganda, nationalism, and globalism in Reform-era China. From the starting point of the absent American and the unique cinematic formula developed in the late 1970s and early 1980s to reconcile a burgeoning new global curiosity with the nationalist imperatives of patriotism, I will go on to demonstrate how this politics of absence not only framed early representations of Americans into China but became the *modus operandi* for several key films presenting the global flows of Chinese into America as well. But what were the formal conditions that made this strategy of absence possible? How would these same global flows be rendered once a shift in perspective rendered the absent visible? And how can the human flows that are at the core of each film define, or perhaps undermine, the larger national project that so many of these films attempt to undertake?

The [Chinese-]American Cometh:
From *Love on Lushan* to *The Herdsman*

With the cultural fever of the late 1970s and early 1980s came a massive influx of Western literature, philosophy, pop music, film, and television into China. It was undoubtedly these direct American cultural imports that carried great weight in shaping the Chinese public's perceptions as they were introduced to a new incarnation of America. Television miniseries like *The Man from Atlantis* (Lee S. Katzin, 1977–8) had an enormous impact on this process of cultural renegotiation with America. And while these direct imports naturally went through their own process of selection and censorship, early attempts to portray Americans in China through local Chinese film productions during the transition period of 1979–82 were another matter altogether. It is here that early tensions between new market demands for knowledge and engagement with the fascinating world of the West and old state policies that cling to national and cultural legitimacy begin to become visible.

Figure 30.1 Transnational romance: Geng Hua (Guo Kaimin) and Zhou Yun (Zhang Yu) in *Love on Lushan* (dir. Huang Zumo, Shanghai Studio, 1980).

One of the earliest films in this tradition is *Love on Lushan* (Huang Zumo, 1980), which has since become an iconic example of Chinese cinema from the Reform era. The film has also garnered notoriety for holding the Guinness World Record for having the single longest theatrical run at the same theater, being shown daily at the Lushan Theater since its premiere in 1980.[1] At the time of its release, the film was popular for other reasons: sweeping cinematic vistas of the beautiful mountain resort of Lushan, the "American factor" that highlighted a "forbidden love" with an overseas Chinese protagonist, and of course that risqué on-screen kiss – one of the very first for post-Cultural Revolution Chinese cinema – that, though modest by today's standards, tested the mores of 1980 audiences. The film traces the love story of Zhou Yun (Zhang Yu), an overseas Chinese from America who meets local Chinese Geng Hua (Guo Kaimin [b. 1958]) while visiting Lushan (see Figure 30.1). Their courtship is carried out against the scenic backdrop of Lushan. After suffering a five-year separation (when Zhou Yun returns to America) and near-rejection by Geng Hua's family, the couple are united and the film ends with the two families happily together at the mountain resort where the lovers first met.

Another important character in the film is Lushan itself. Throughout the film as the lovers grow closer, their relationship is punctuated by countless shots of Lushan's idyllic trickling streams and mountain backdrop, which functions almost as a cinematic version of a traditional Chinese landscape painting. Lushan's variety of historical identities is highlighted throughout the film, from Buddhist retreat to political meeting place in modern China. Huang Zumo takes great pleasure in displaying the bold calligraphy carved into majestic mountainside rocks and embellishing poetic lines from Tang masters Li Bai and Bai Juyi commemorating their own visits to Lushan. Collectively these elements help establish Lushan as a site firmly branded with a quintessentially Chinese local identity. The degree to which the film so powerfully encapsulates all of the historical, material, and geographic coordinates of Lushan can also be seen in the aforementioned record-breaking local theatrical run of the film, which also doubles as a kind of tourist film. The quintessentially "Chinese" aspects of Lushan can also be seen reflected in the male protagonist, Geng Hua. As a local resident with a father who was a revolutionary hero, Geng further cements the film's allegiance to a nationalist symmetry, neatly aligning the protagonist with the setting.

However, we are still left with the question as to why *Love on Lushan* resorts to such an elaborate multileveled construction of Chinese nationalism. As one of the very first PRC films that attempts to renegotiate the placement of America in the sphere of popular culture – and, on one level, articulate a new political line for post-1979 Sino-US relations – the film only seems able to approach America through a thick buffer of nationalist insulation. It is in this sense that I argue the primary function of Lushan's historic, cultural, and nationalistic objectification is not so much to serve as a handy tourist film, but to consciously neutralize or nullify the impact of America. The film then performs an intricate diplomatic dance, recognizing America (as the PRC did on January 1, 1979 when relations were normalized), while conservatively embedding that recognition within a plethora of pro-Chinese cultural codes.

Although the American returnee (Zhou Yun) is central to the construction of the film, she is actually portrayed by a PRC actress and the United States is never directly displayed on screen. (During the sequences in which the couple are seperated, the film only follows the male protagonist Geng Hua, sealing the narrative within the idealized world of Lushan). Instead, the US subtext is hinted at through details like Zhou Yun's outgoing personality, fashion sense, and utilization of English dialogue. And while English is only used with great reserve in the film, it plays an important role in two central courtship sequences between Zhou and Geng. In one sequence Geng is alone in the woods reciting English from a textbook when a voice (Zhou hiding behind a tree) corrects him. The lines are thus repeated in English: "I love my motherland. I love the morning of my motherland" (see Figure 30.2). However, before Zhou has the chance to reveal herself, their recitation practice is interrupted by Geng's mother, a foreshadowing of the later threat his family poses to their relationship, and also a form of negation against this English discourse. The content of the English, however, is important in that it emphasizes the same nationalist worldview that Lushan's scenery and so many other central details of the film endorse. It is as if every element of foreign influence must be drowned out by much bolder strokes of patriotic pro-China sentiment. This same ode to the motherland is later repeated in the film, this time at sunset with Zhou Yun and Geng Hua face to face as their love grows. By now Geng Hua's English is fluent and we are presented with a curious interplay of romance plus nationalism, in the heart of Lushan but facilitated by the foreign tongue of

Figure 30.2 Geng Hua ("China") reciting in English "I love the morning of my motherland" in *Love on Lushan* (dir. Huang Zumo, Shanghai Studio, 1980).

English. On another level this example of the English lesson can be seen as a metaphor for the film's larger ideological drive, recognizing – even fetishizing – the foreign language but using it to articulate a uniquely Chinese nationalistic vision. In this sense, the sequence can also be seen as a metaphor for Zhou Yun herself, the exotic foreign element who, eventually, will go on to embody the epitome of Chinese patriotism.

When it comes to English and romance, Zhou Yun serves as Geng Hua's "instructor." Geng Hua, on the other hand, is rendered passive. When they first meet, it is Geng Hua who is objectified and has "his picture taken," and later it is Zhou Yun who follows him into the forest and teases him with her English game. And much later, when Zhou Yun lies seductively on a rock, her body language brimming with sexuality and suggestion, Geng Hua remains awkwardly ill-prepared as to how he should respond. Ultimately it is Zhou Yun who takes the initiative and kisses Geng Hua on the cheek – Geng's biggest concern being that someone might see them. It is partly due to this type of conservatism that Zhou gives her love the pet name "Confucius" – a moniker that also hints at his affinity for classical poetry but most importantly identifies Zhou as an authentic avatar for China itself, a fact further embellished by his given name Hua, or "China." While Zhou Yun's bold pursuit of Geng Hua and rather strong displays of sexuality would seem out of place according to the gender norms of the time, it is precisely her identity as an overseas Chinese that works to explain and rationalize her bold actions. With her as the pursuer, Geng Hua – or China – is able to preserve his moral propriety and proper conduct.

As their courtship continues, the challenges presented to traditional gender roles unfold in new ways: in countless traditional Chinese narratives of marriage it is the boy's family that must win the approval of the girl's family. In this case, however, it is Geng Hua's father, who has deep reservations about his son marrying the daughter of his old friend turned Nationalist traitor. It is revealed that the fathers of the two lovers have a strained history. Once comrades-in-arms in the Nationalist army, their friendship was shattered when Geng's father deserted in order to join up with the Communist army. The one-time friends become bitter enemies facing each other on the battlefield. Superficially, in terms of the plot structure the hidden back-story of familial strife works as a tool to add cinematic tension, creating a hurdle for the lovers to overcome that proves even more trying than the physical distance between their two nations. On another level, however, this subplot also serves as a means through which to revisit and renegotiate patriarchal family history and also a crucial page in modern Chinese history. The Zhou family is stained by the multiple sins of personal betrayal (destroying old friendships), political betrayal (remaining loyal to the Nationalists), and national betrayal (immigrating to America).

A prolonged sequence follows in which Geng and Zhou must painstakingly wait while Geng's father makes the difficult decision whether or not to endorse their relationship. After a string of emasculating details over the course of their early romance, this reversal resituates the Geng family in the position of power. As Zhou Yun waits anxiously by the phone, the question is not whether Zhou Yun will accept Geng Hua, but whether the Gengs (China) will accept Zhou (America). The tone of the ultimate approval comes over as a benevolent acceptance of atonement for all the past sins committed by the Nationalists – as well as those committed in the name of American imperialism. When the two fathers finally meet in Lushan during the film's climax, Zhou, head lowered, comes with an air of repentance, while Geng stands tall, magnanimously forgiving his old friend. Another key element of the film's ending is the fact that Geng Hua doesn't leave for America as we might expect; instead, Zhou Yun and her entire family return to Lushan, site of Zhou and Geng's romance and their parents' early friendship.

Looked at from the perspective of Sino-US relations of the era, *Love on Lushan* must be read as much more than a cute love story or an attempt to eroticize the figure of a spunky (Chinese-)American. The film is a very carefully engineered attempt to reintroduce "America" into the fabric of modern China – but of course this introduction would only be carried out according to China's own terms. After being labeled for decades with monikers such as "paper tiger" and "American imperialists," the sudden establishment of official diplomatic relations with the United States presented a challenge on how to readjust China's formally pejorative view of the United States in the cultural sphere. America is aligned with naïveté, openness, and a tainted past (connections with the Nationalist regime), but the country is never directly portrayed and all of the Americans are ethnic Chinese. This final point is especially important in helping to establish the primacy of Chinese cultural nationalism, in which ethnicity supersedes citizenship as a marker of identity.[2]

Adapted from a popular work of fiction by Zhang Xianliang, *The Herdsman* (Xie Jin, 1982) on many levels extends the formula of *Love on Lushan* in its continued cinematic negotiation with Sino-US relations. Released just a year before China's Anti-Spiritual Pollution campaign of 1983–4, which was aimed at curbing the spread of liberal Western ideas, fashions, cultural products, and ideas, *The Herdsman* goes further in acknowledging the materialistic temptations of America, but once again offsets these forces with an even bolder display of nationalistic commitment. Directed by veteran filmmaker Xie Jin, *The Herdsman* would go on to win great critical acclaim and numerous film awards in China. The plot centers on Xu Lingjun, a humble 41-year-old schoolteacher from the Chilechuan Ranch in Northwest China. Abandoned by his father at the age of 11, Xu leads a difficult life in China where he is eventually labeled a Rightist and forced to answer for his father's crimes. It is only with the coming of the Reform era that Xu seems to turn himself around, start a family, and become a schoolteacher. However, as the film opens in 1980, Xu Jingshan (Liu Qiong), the long-lost father, suddenly returns to China in hopes of bringing his son back with him to America.

From the opening sequence of *The Herdsman*, Xie Jin already establishes a powerful visual contrast between life in the countryside and the big city. Intercutting shots of the Inner Mongolian grasslands (herdsmen on horseback, flocks of sheep, and sweeping postcard landscapes) with images of life in the capital of Beijing (the Forbidden City, the Temple of Heaven, modern hotels, and the international airport), the film immediately sets up a powerful spatial contrast. This contrast establishes the internal plot of the film, a negotiation between the tranquil countryside and the urban, modernized side of Beijing frequented by "international guests" and "overseas compatriots." As the plot progresses, it also becomes clear that this process of radical juxtapositioning also transpires on the temporal level. It is not just the country verses the city that is subject for renegotiation, but also the past versus the present; while viewed from the present event of the returning father Xu Jingshan, the film continuously jumps back in time to portray key events that have occurred in his son's life over the previous three decades. This series of extensive flashbacks encapsulates everything from Xu Jingshan's traumatic departure to Lingjun's difficult childhood as an orphan, his struggle to find a place in the world, and his eventual romance and happy marriage. Significantly absent from this flashback chronology are any direct representations of Xu Jingshan's life in America, which is suppressed as in *Love on Lushan*. Naturally, one rationale for this absence is simply the lack of funding for even a short on-location shoot in America; however, the larger reason lies with an ideological stance that becomes clear when looked at within the larger framework of the film itself.

Although the film does not feature any direct representations of America, like *Love on Lushan*, it employs a "dual exoticism" – on the one hand romanticizing a fantasy-like vision of an ontological homeland embodied in the pure images of

Figure 30.3   Forsaking the Father for the Motherland: Xu Lingjun (Zhu Shimao) seeing off his father Xu Jingshan (Liu Qiong) in *The Herdsman* (dir. Xie Jin, Shanghai Studio, 1982).

wild horses, rolling hills, and open grassy fields while, at the same time, a second vision of the exotic is revealed through Xu Jingshan, a powerful Chinese-American industrialist who has succeeded abroad. While this second view of exoticism is largely veiled in mystery, *The Herdsman* does offer viewers voyeuristic glimpses into the world of luxury Xu Jingshan represents: five-star hotels, banquet dinners, a beautiful private secretary, transnational travel, and expensive Western suits. It is through these sequences, which also to some extent equate a global vision with the modern urban center of Beijing, that we actually get the first glimpse of Caucasians and other Westerners as part of the luxury hotel lobby mise-en-scène and a level of five-star service and courtesy unheard of for average Chinese citizens in 1980. In almost every case, however, materialist luxury is offset by a higher moral criticism: Xu Lingjun is shocked by the wastefulness of his father spending eighty yuan – several times the average Chinese monthly income in 1980 – on a single meal at a luxury hotel, not to mention the film's allusions to an affair between Xu Jingshan and his private secretary.

By the time the film moves toward its conclusion, the roads laid out before Xu Lingjun are clearly delineated: return to his family and quiet life as a teacher in Inner Mongolia, or go to San Francisco where he will be positioned to take over his father's successful business. While the reality of early 1980s China and the intense interest in nearly all things American might indicate a clear answer for Xu Lingjun, the generic compulsion of this cinematic form necessitates another choice: Xu and his family stay behind and return to their idyllic life on the grasslands (see Figure 30.3). The similarities in structure, ideology, and form between *Love on Lushan* and *The Herdsman* hint at a concerted effort to accept this "America Other" back into the fold of contemporary Chinese culture and society, but only within the framework of a much larger and more powerful conception of Chinese nationalism.

When writing about this film in 1982, director Xie Jin attempted to further downplay the overseas component of his film:

> There was also an issue that viewers were quite concerned about … whether or not the main protagonist should go abroad or not. But for us it rested on Xu Lingjun facing the question of his own fate (including the past and future fate, and not the simple question of whether or not to go abroad). From this angle we can approach the film from a broader perspective. As far as patriotism is concerned, we didn't set out to stress or exaggerate those themes, it was simply the objective outcome of the story's natural development. (J. Xie 2007: 164)

Xie's comments on *The Herdsman* seem to ignore the elephant in the room – for most Chinese audiences in 1982 the defining question the film posed was inextricably tied to Xu Lingjun's predicament: China versus America, nationalism versus immigration, or as Zhang Xianliang's original novel posited the problem, the spirit versus the flesh.

Xie Jin's comments aside, the following description of a series of lectures surrounding the release of the film proves quite telling when it comes to the film's nationalistic intentions and the true significance of Xu's decision to remain in China. "After the film's premiere in 1982, Zhu Shimao (b. 1954), the actor who portrayed Xu Lingjun, was invited to go on a university speaking tour where he gave a series of presentations on patriotism. After his lectures, which often lasted nearly two hours, the auditoriums would fill with thunderous applause and the audiences often got quite animated, some university students even spontaneously proclaimed their intent to go to those backwater places to improve themselves" (Chen and Zou 2005: 255–6). We should not forget that the establishment of this new nationalistic sense of self is very much predicated on a conscious denial – or at least neutralization – of the America other.

Prescription for Absence: Defining the Tropes

Looked at collectively, films like *The Herdsman* satisfy a series of tropes, which help establish this mini-genre of American-themed films during the Reform era. Taken as a whole these tropes can be seen as a cinematic formula, with a series of formal and ideological elements obligatory for the genre to function. In defining this small but important mini-genre, the following tropes can be isolated:

1   A multigenerational plot that juxtaposes two generations of experience, using the younger generation's story to resolve leftover regrets from a previous generation. This allows films in the genre to simultaneously address deep historical fissures in modern Chinese history, including the 1945–9 Civil War (*Love on Lushan* and *The Herdsman*) and the 1966–76 Cultural Revolution (*The Herdsman*).

2 Older generation returnee characters often portrayed as decadent, repentant, and standing on the wrong side of history. Examples include Zhou Yun's father, the former Nationalist soldier/American capitalist in *Love on Lushan* and Xu Jingshan in *The Herdsman*.

3 The temptation of America revealed through opportunities for money, work, study, materialist enjoyment, or a more comfortable lifestyle, which are ultimately renounced for larger nationalist goals in China.

4 Direct representation of "America" is eschewed for a strategy of concealment. This concealment is carried out on several levels: America is itself kept off screen (not even revealed through flashbacks) and the figure of the "American" is concealed under the ethnic veil of the "Chinese-American" where ethnic identification with China trumps citizenship or national identification with America.

5 "America" or the "foreign" is further displaced with an embellishment of iconic Chinese sites and other examples of the *guocui* or quintessential aspects of Chinese culture, which can include mountain scenery (*Love on Lushan*), picturesque grasslands (*The Herdsman*), and cultural identifiers such as Confucian values and classical poetry.

The internal coherence of these themes, persuasive as they may seem, still begs the question of just how pervasive these themes were in other films and whether or not it is sufficiently significant to constitute a mini-genre, or even a trend in contemporary Chinese cinema. Although *Love on Lushan* and *The Herdsman* are perhaps the best-known examples of films produced within this mold, I would argue that by pinpointing the above generic tropes we are able to identify this as a much larger subgenre in Chinese film history. One earlier example that is interesting to consider is *Loyal Overseas Chinese Family* (Ou Fan, Xing Jitian, 1979). Produced just a year prior to *Love on Lushan*, *Loyal Overseas Chinese Family* can be seen as playing a key role in establishing the mold followed by later films. Although the United States is not featured in the film, the ideological skeleton that would be revisited later on was already in place and would be quickly adapted for American-themed films after the 1979 establishment of diplomatic relations between the United States and China. The film is also instructive in identifying certain tropes seen later in Chinese-language cinema about America as being part of a larger early Reform-era ideological continuum that attempted to use mass culture to renegotiate China's relationship with the West.

One of the film's key plotlines involves the returnee Siguo ("longing for the nation") giving his little sister Sihua ("longing for China") an opportunity to join him in England as a foreign student – another central trope of almost all the *huaqiao* films of this period (e.g., the father Xu Jingshan offering to take Xu Lingjun to San Francisco in *The Herdsman* or the threat of Zhou Yun taking Geng Hua to the United States in *Love on Lushan*). It is precisely this international temptation luring Sihua away from China that also provides a crucial juxtaposition to the national temptation that lured the sibling's parents back to China in 1949, as portrayed through flashback. The film's key structural elements all fall in line with the previously outlined generic tropes, culminating with the obligatory renunciation of the foreign for a pro-Chinese return. In the end, the siblings live up to their collective names: not only does Sihua join the People's Liberation Army and remain in China but even her wayward brother Siguo renounces his life abroad to return to China, rejoining his family and the nation he longs for.

Looking back on the film today, one cannot help but see the casting choice of Joan Chen as Sihua with a certain degree of irony. We can read the daughter of the loyal overseas Chinese family who returns to help rebuild the nation against the real-life actress who, born in China, immigrates to America where she achieves fame through films like *The Last Emperor* (Bernardo Bertolucci, 1987) and mainstream American television serials such as *Miami Vice* (David Anspaugh, 1985) and *Tai-Pan* (Daryl Duke, 1986). This would also be the fate of Zhang Yu – while she played the role of patriotic overseas returnee Zhou Yun in *Love on Lushan*, the actress would eventually move to the United States in 1985.[3] This would even be the fate of Zhu Shimao: while the character of Xu Lingjun who he portrayed in *The Herdsman* chose his Chinese motherland over his American father, the actor would also immigrate to America in the early 1990s. It is precisely through this juxtaposition of real-life American immigration stories against the fictional lives of their characters that the ideological imperative of the original films is most powerfully illustrated. After three decades cut off from mainstream cultural developments in the West, the Open Door policy brought with it an intense interest in America and the West. A combination of cultural curiosity about the "Western Other" coupled with a more pragmatic desire for a better standard of living helped fuel a large-scale wave of foreign study in the 1980s. This *liuxue chao* ("overseas-study tide") and *chuguo re* ("going-abroad fever") would become central cultural keywords of 1980s China, and films like *Love on Lushan* and *The Herdsman* (as well as their antecedent *Loyal Overseas Chinese Family*) speak to an attempt by state-run film studios to navigate through this new era. On the one hand, these films attempt to satisfy a genuine public interest in "the foreign," providing a voyeuristic look into the lives of these Chinese-American figures while, at the same time, countering the temptation of immigration with a new nationalist discourse. It is through the process of this cultural negotiation that America is viewed through a lens of absence (of physical representation) and assimilation (of Chinese-Americans into a quintessential conception of cultural China). And although this trend seems to begin with the early Reform era, identical themes and tropes concerning America can actually be located in Chinese-language cinema from Taiwan a generation earlier. Works like *Home Sweet Home* (Bai Jingrui, 1970) feature an almost identical structure and propagandistic bent, fulfilling virtually all of the defining tropes of the subgenre of Chinese films about America outlined here. This representational congruence seen between "America" in Taiwan cinema of the 1970s and PRC cinema of the early 1980s attests to the startlingly similar ways in which these two regimes attempted to frame Sino-US relations and walk a tightrope between global desires and larger nationalist imperatives.

When examining this phase of Chinese films about America produced during the early Reform era, it is instructive to consider the concept of Occidentalism. Xiaomei Chen has identified two distinct forms of Occidentalism, the first of which, "official Occidentalism," effectively describes the dynamic at play in the films discussed above. Chen describes official Occidentalism as a process through which the Chinese state uses "the essentialization of the West as a means for supporting a nationalism that suppresses its own people. In this process, the Western Other is construed by a Chinese imagination, not for the purpose of dominating the West, but in order to discipline, and ultimately to dominate, the Chinese Self at home" (X. Chen 2002: 3). In the early 1980s when this initial series of cinematic negotiations with America was taking place, the Chinese film industry, for all intents and purposes, was essentially a state-run cultural enterprise. Films like *Love on Lushan* and *The Herdsman* were official studio productions and thus fall neatly into Chen's conception of official Occidentalism, in the sense that they seem to use the West to endorse state ideology and control citizens (i.e., discourage them from going abroad and giving in to other Western temptations). At the same time, these texts tread a political and ideological terrain that is often more nuanced and can benefit from a further elaboration of Occidentalism. For Claire Conceison, the first and seemingly most important trait of Occidentalism in cultural representations is the quality of being "paradoxical (or contradictory / dialectical) in character and function" (Conceison 2004: 55). And while the films examined seem to superficially present a unified top-down ideological stance, there is also a more complex dance being played out as China attempts to give a certain degree of recognition and legitimacy to the United States while, at the same time, ultimately criticizing Western materialism and selfishness in favor of a more robust nationalistic vision. The myriad paradoxes that arise amid this process of cultural and political negotiation can indeed be read as a central trait of this phase of Occidentalism in Chinese cinema of the era. The larger contradiction of course is the simple fact that, collectively, these films all represent China's most important examples of cinematic recognition and interaction with the United States; however, the underlying strategy used to engage with it is one of displacement, invisibility, and absence.

Left for America: Invisible Immigration in *After Separation*, *Those Left Behind*, and *The Days*

The previously discussed films all use absence as a strategy to render the trope of "The American Cometh." However, a similar strategy of absence was curiously also employed just a few years later in the early 1990s to explore the inverse movement from China to America. Typically, this movement would be rendered via tales of the new immigrant experience or the theme of "coming to America," but – extending the trope of absence – we are instead presented with a series of films exploring the experience of being "left for America." It is here that direct portrayal of immigration is suppressed in favor of a perspective that privileges those left behind and abandoned. These include Feng Xiaogang's very first effort as a film screenwriter, *After Separation* (Xia Gang, 1992), which depicts the uncanny relationship between a man and woman in Beijing who meet after their respective spouses go abroad for study, and *Those Left Behind* (Hu Xueyang, 1993), which has a similar structure.

Like earlier films that attempted to figure America, neither *After Separation* nor *Those Left Behind* featured any direct portrayals of the United States or any of the other locations the characters' spouses leave for (including Canada and Japan). Instead the focus is the emptiness and desperation of those left in China. The English word "Hi!" is the first utterance in *After Separation*, but it is actually a goodbye, heard at Beijing Airport just before the protagonist Gu Yan (Ge You, who would win a Best Actor award for his role) sees his wife off to Canada for study. She smiles excitedly as she goes through security and, as her husband sadly gazes at her across the gate, she doesn't even bother to look back at him, but struts out of sight into a new international space. Gu Yan barely has time to reflect before a complete stranger begs him to take care of a woman who has apparently fainted, so that the stranger can catch his plane. Thus begins an unorthodox friendship between Gu Yan and Lin Zhouyun (Xu Fan), who bond through their mutual abandonment.[4] For Zhouyun, the departure comes with a particularly high price – abandonment, physical collapse, and a miscarriage. Thus, from the opening scene, the film is already aligning the coveted experience of "going abroad" with a set of devastating consequences – even death. And while the film certainly contains numerous comic elements, *After Seperation* exchanges the trademark humor of many of Ge You and screenwriter Feng Xiaogang's collaborations for a markedly darker and more somber tone.

Although the destination for the spouses of both Lin Zhouyun and Gu Yan is Canada, the United States also plays a central role in the later development of the plot. From costume design (one character wears an American-flag sweatshirt) and music (the prominent use of the American country song "The Yellow Rose of Texas") to plot (Zhouyun's attempt to "buy" citizenship for US-administered Palau as a stepping stone to US citizenship), the United States and its myriad symbols become a central focus for the characters left behind. And like the earlier films examined here, once characters leave China they are rendered invisible in the filmic narrative – even phone calls to the spouses go unanswered. Instead, the film highlights the plight and eventual bonding of Gu Yan and Zhouyun in Beijing.

One of the more curious elements of *After Separation* are the numerous sequences highlighting various forms of performance, imitation, and deception that punctuate almost the entire body of the film. Minor examples range from Gu

Yan's ubiquitous HIGHLIGHT AIRMAIL baseball hat – a representative of the large number of nonsensical English phrases and lettering appearing in Chinese fashion in the 1980s and 1990s that here speaks to a misguided adoration of the West – to the ridiculous sequence where Gu Yan has his newlywed friends pose for a series of wedding photos like those "Westerners hang over their fireplaces." Gu proceeds to orchestrate his friends as they strike poses beside an American-style fireplace adorned with a portrait of Sophia Loren, pace up and down a gaudy prop staircase, and mount a prop motorcycle before a painted beach backdrop full of balloons. Here the production of an imagined romantic internationalism stands in conflict with pragmatic abandonment of marriage for international dreams experienced firsthand by Gu and Lin – even one of the newlyweds fantasizes about immigrating to Australia. But the real charade comes from more elaborate plays of deception – Gu Yan impersonating famous Chinese writer Wang Yue (a stand-in for Wang Shuo, thus a copy of a copy), or his later elaborate scheme to encourage Lin to pay US$2,000 for a Palau passport.

During one key sequence, Gu Yan offers to take a series of photos of Zhouyun and the pair embark on a whirlwind tour of the historic sites of the ancient capital, alternately visiting the Great Wall, the Thirteen Ming Tombs, and Yuanmingyuan. Their symbolic tour of the capital culminates at the center – the Forbidden City. However, when Zhouyun and Gu Yan arrive at the entrance it is symbolically closed and Gu's offer to go to Tiananmen Square is also rejected, breaking the grand illusion at play. In *After Separation* the "tour of Beijing" seems to play a similar role to the "national tours" that appear in the other films examined; however, unlike the "pure" nationalistic framing of the grasslands of Inner Mongolia and the scenic sites of Lushan, here the placement of Beijing's historic sites is markedly self-conscious about the performative staging at work. The protagonists travel to these sights not for experience, but rather to stage a series of photographic images – not at all unlike the comic wedding photo sequence earlier in the film, which serves as a foreshadowing of this scene. Instead, the tour serves as a desperate compensation, an attempt to recreate a record or semblance of that which most represents "China" in the midst of a crisis of identity.

The dimension of performance reaches its culmination during Spring Festival – a traditional holiday of family union – when the absence of the protagonists' spouses is particularly palpable and pronounced. Gu and Lin decide to "play house" and pretend to have a "family" together for five days. Like the tour of Beijing, the Spring Festival charade serves as yet another means through which the film constructs a performance of cultural identity – together, Gu and Lin perform quintessential Spring Festival rituals such as making dumplings and lighting firecrackers. The levels of performance, deception, and elaborate charade that run throughout the film are all part of a larger cultural critique – and intricately tied to the immigration craze, a movement that points at the ultimate performance, a metamorphosis of national identity. It should then come as no surprise when Gu Yan's wife ultimately divorces him (taking literally his tongue-in-cheek recommendation to find a new foreign husband),[5] or when Zhouyun abandons him a second time with her own voyage abroad. As she prepares to go through airport security, Zhouyun's departure is momentarily delayed when she cannot find her passport. It is soon revealed that she secretly placed her passport in Gu Yan's jacket pocket, relinquishing her ability to travel to Gu, submitting both her freedom of immigration – and identity – to him. However, by this point in the film, immigration has taken on the role of an almost unstoppable flow, a deluge of human movement blindly raging away from China's borders … and ultimately leaving Gu Yan behind.

In *Those Left Behind* the protagonist Naiqing was abandoned four years earlier by her musician husband for San Francisco. As the story progresses, we see the ways in which America has corrupted him as he takes a mistress and gives up his dreams of a career in music for the more practical pursuit of a degree in business administration. Naiqing, in turn, seeks comfort in the arms of another abandonee, Jiadong, a cab driver whose wife has gone to Japan (where her material comforts are apparently provided by side work as a sex worker). While America-proper remains off screen, Naiqing and her other "left behind" friends – who form something of a social club, frequently meeting at a bar run by Wenwen, yet another abandonee – live in a world inundated by omnipresent symbols of the land they long for: an oversized map of the United States, commercials for American coffee, or a cigarette lighter imprinted with the image of the American flag. While these symbols represent their American dreams, they are cinematically positioned as tools of oppression.

Both films feature sparse musical soundtracks, dark lighting, and an overuse of nighttime interior shots, all highlighting the dark, moody, noir-like tone. More often than not, the narratives are punctuated not by action, but by waiting – for an overseas phone call from a lost spouse or a visa to be approved. As *Those Left Behind* continues, the negative vision of the West is further embellished, with peripheral characters like Wenwen and Ah Xiu both prostituting themselves to foreigners – a powerful metaphor that depicts not only power relationships but also a broader moral judgment on the act of going abroad. And in the end, when Naiqing finally does decide to go to San Francisco, she writes to her lover back home:

> Jiadong, I was so happy to receive your letter and the photos you sent. When I saw the pictures of your pet pigeons, the General Post Office building on the Bund, the Suzhou River Hospital, and our old longtang neighborhood, I was struck by a deep nostalgia; it is the kind of feeling that I only found after I discovered myself here in this foreign land.

Once she leaves China, Naiqing disappears from the film, but even her letter home is punctuated not by wondrous tales of America (*meiguo* or "beautiful country"), but descriptions and images of her lost homeland. This notable absence serves as the final denial of the West's temptations. For Naiqing, who while in China longed only for America, it is only through the torturous trip abroad that she finally discovers her own latent patriotic love for China. The fact that her journey abroad is immediately preceded by her somewhat reluctant abortion of her child simultaneously serves as yet another way in which the film associates leaving China behind with a form of death.

It is certainly tempting to read the unified ideological message in *After Separation* and *Those Left Behind* – produced by two of the larger state-run studios, Beijing Film Studio and Shanghai Film Studio, respectively – as a top-down political discourse. That is why briefly considering *The Days* (Wang Xiaoshuai, 1993), one of the seminal works of the Sixth Generation, can be instructive. Though heralded as among the first truly independent Chinese films produced entirely outside the official studio system, *The Days* presents a view of America and an ideological stance remarkably close to that of *After Separation* and *Those Left Behind*. Tracing the final dissolution of the relationship between two artists, Dong (Liu Xiaodong) and Chun (Yu Hong), the central power driving the lovers away from one another is Chun's hypnotic attraction to the United States, to where she eventually "disappears" at the film's climax.

The most gripping and understated film (shot in black and white on a shoestring budget) of those examined here, *The Days* extends multiple tropes introduced in earlier films, including a gendered vision of immigration (as Gu Yan jokes in *After Seperation*, "Chinese husbands are like a training course for women to practice on before they go abroad") and, for the third time, a juxtaposition of abortion with immigration. And just before Chun's departure, the film again features a highly symbolic journey to the Chinese heartland – this time to Dong's hometown in the Northeast. The trip, which can be read against the fetishization of the ontological motherland in films like *The Herdsman*, is here given a treatment similarly disappointing as the Beijing tour in *After Separation*. The family home has been relocated and the couple can barely find it; when they do, Chun not only feels out of place (it is after all Dong's hometown, not her own) but even the beautiful sites Dong described to her are gone, replaced by gray high-rise buildings and factories. Chun leaves early, departing alone to find her "spring" elsewhere – in New York. And like earlier films, with her departure comes absence, the narrative instead quietly following Dong as he completes a final painting of his lost lover – Chun standing at the Great Wall gazing out toward Russia through a set of binoculars – a final artistic rendering of her renouncement of China for her new international future. Meanwhile, Dong descends to the brink of madness and is admitted to a psychiatric ward, a final footnote to the devastating forces of the American Dream. As an independent film, *The Days* also helps substantiate that the critical stance *vis-à-vis* Chinese immigration to America articulated in so many state-sponsored films of this era can be read as more indicative of a much broader set of social concerns.[6]

If the obligatory happy reunion of lovers and families that concludes films like *Love on Lushan* and *The Herdsman* is a result of their respective protagonists' "correct" decision to renounce the decadent West for their motherland, films like *After Separation*, *Those Left Behind*, and *The Days* can certainly be read as the counterexample – the anguish, waiting, infidelities, and betrayals all consequences of giving in to the Western temptation. Though markedly different in form and tone, these later films can be seen as part of an ideological continuum alongside previous films about America from the early Reform era. While superficially focusing on America, the real subject of all these films is firmly rooted in an indigenous Chinese political interest to offset the allure of the West. Collectively, all of these films have an overarching strategy of invisibility and distance when it comes to direct representation of a markedly absent promised land.

When discussing the absence of direct representations of America in many of these titles, some attention should be paid to the more practical considerations that certainly played an important role in this phenomenon. Having only recently emerged from the economic devastation of the Cultural Revolution, Chinese film studios would have found it impossible in the late 1970s or early 1980s to fund location shooting in the United States or employ professional American actors. At the same time, while these economic and practical factors (e.g., the extreme difficulty for Chinese crew members to obtain US visas) certainly contributed to the decision to relegate America to the shadows in these "US"-themed films, I maintain the overwhelming reason for this strategy of absence was ideological.

Departures and Returns

In the previous sections I examined how strategies of absence and assimilation helped frame America and the figure of the (Chinese-)American, in part to help offset an impending "overseas study tide" and "going abroad fever" that swept up countless Chinese in a sea of international fantasies during the 1980s and 1990s. After this initial wave of films, the United States and the figure of the American entered a gradual process whereby what was formally absent became visible. It was actually Xie Jin, director of *The Herdsman*, who is often credited with having directed the first PRC feature-length film shot almost entirely in the United States – *The Last of the Aristocrats* (1989). Adopted from a short story by veteran writer and longtime US resident Bai Xianyong, the film traces the lives of four Chinese women in America who immigrated during the Chinese Civil War. Although using actual locations in the United States, the story Xie chose to adapt is actually one that had been singled out by literary critic C. T. Hsia as exhibiting an "obsession with China" – an "obsessive concern with China as a nation afflicted with a spiritual disease and therefore unable to strengthen itself or change its set ways of inhumanity" (Hsia 1999: 533–4), a trait that in this case further hints at the ideological linkage between this visible manifestation of America and its absent predecessors.

In the wake of *The Last of the Aristocrats* Chinese cinema began to produce more and more films that actively sought to satisfy local audiences' growing curiosity about a country that was playing an increasingly visible role in China's cultural and economic life – a fact received in China with a mix of intense curiosity and trepidation over the imperialist implications of such a presence. Feng Xiaogang, another filmmaker who initially framed America through a trope of absence (serving as screenwriter for *After Separation*), would go on to make more American-themed films than perhaps any other contemporary PRC director. These include Feng's hit comedy about Chinese in Los Angeles, *Be There or Be Square* (1998), and a satire chronicling a troubled American film director (Donald Sutherland) trying to shoot a bio-pic about the last emperor in China's Forbidden City, *Big Shot's Funeral* (2001). Respectively tracing the dual cross-cultural interactions of Chinese in America and Americans in China, these two films – both marketed as *hesui* New Year film events – were perhaps the two most commercially successful examples in this category. Thinking back to the *Patton* (Franklin Schaffner, 1970) fantasy that opens *The Dream Factory* (Feng Xiaogang, 1997) and, of course, the blockbuster 1993 television series *A Beijinger in New York* (Zheng Xiaolong, 1993), for which Feng served as cowriter, the looming presence of the United States in Feng's body of work becomes even clearer. Adapted from a bestselling novel by Glen Cao (Cao Guilin), *A Beijinger in New York* went further than any previous work of film or television in its reimagination of the immigration experience in America for countless Chinese viewers. The curious blend of voyeuristic objectification concerning American materialism – beautiful houses, luxury automobiles, mistresses, and money – and scathing moral critique of the pitfalls of capitalism – divorce, infidelity, drug use, juvenile delinquency, loss of ideals, greed, and corruption – would provide a vision of the United States that, while certainly propagandistic at times, ultimately proved to be more ideologically complex that earlier portrayals.

This more recent series of films and television series directly depicting the United States can be seen as straddling the earlier discourse of official Occidentalism alongside its counterpart, which Xiaomei Chen defines as anti-official Occidentalism. This second form speaks to an alternate use of the West in order to challenge government perspectives and state ideologies and "can be understood as a powerful anti-official discourse using the Western Other as a metaphor for a political liberation against ideological oppression within a totalitarian society" (X. Chen 2002: 5). As the Chinese film industry became increasingly privatized and global, the overwhelming power of the political agendas displayed in films like *Love on Lushan* and *The Herdsman* gradually lost ground to more market-driven agendas. Over the course of this privatization, Sino-US relations have also experienced a series of complex challenges, ranging from the 1999 US bombing of the Chinese embassy in Kosovo to the 2001 spy plane crisis, and the rise of Chinese neonationalism represented by such popular publications as the 1996 bestseller *The China that Can Say No* and 2009's *Unhappy China*, all of which has greatly affected not only the way in which America has been portrayed by the Chinese film industry but also the frequency with which it can be portrayed.

While the mid-1990s seemed to represent a peak in terms of cinematic and television portrayals of America – roughly beginning with *A Beijinger in New York* and culminating with *Be There or Be Square* – portrayals that navigate between the official and anti-official Occidentalism continue to find wide audiences in China. These include "coming to America" stories like the popular drama *The Guasha Treatment* (Zheng Xiaolong, 2001), by the director of *A Beijinger in New York*. The film explores the darker side of cultural misunderstanding when a small Chinese-American boy is taken away from his family by Child Services after bruises caused by a traditional Chinese medicinal treatment – *guasha* – performed by the boy's grandfather visiting from Beijing are taken as evidence of child abuse. Other "coming to America" films include *Hi, Frank* (Huang Shuqin, 2002), a melodrama about an elderly Chinese woman's romance with an old American veteran during her visit to the United States, marketed in China as the "Chinese version of *Bridges of Madison County*." In the 2009 critical flop *Gasp* (Zheng Zhong, 2009), it is another Frank (John Savage) who, struggling with a near-bankrupt company and a drug-addict daughter, comes to China hoping to sell his failing company to a Chinese businessman played by Ge You. The dual movements of "the American cometh" and "coming to America" appear to have greatly diversified, exploring new themes and approaches, while shifting to a more straightforward representational approach, seemingly leaving behind the tropes of absence and invisibility.[7]

Conclusion

In this age of the global heteroglossia where, given the proliferation of direct representations of America in recent Chinese-language cinema, the ever-growing presence of foreigners on Chinese talk shows, variety shows, and television miniseries, and the increasing visibility of America's own cultural products via Hollywood and other corporate giants, it may come as a surprise that the specter of the absent American continues to linger. To demonstrate the continued presence of this trope in the Chinese cinematic imagination of America, I will end with two examples that respectively demonstrate official and anti-official Occidentalism. Released in celebration of the centenary of the birth of Chinese cinema and produced a full quarter of a century after *Love on Lushan*, *The Song of Yimeng* (Zhang Xin, 2005) nonetheless features all of the central tropes of the genre outlined earlier. These tropes include a "Chinese-American protagonist" (this time updated for a new generation, the protagonist actually goes abroad during the early 1980s, returning in the 2000s to meet the daughter he never knew he had), the absence of direct portrayals of America, a multi-generational plotline used to resolve past historical traumas, the temptation of immigration, and of course the idyllic setting of the film, Yimeng Mountain, which like Lushan or Chilechuan in Inner Mongolia, serves as a distinctly Chinese natural setting to offset the allure of America. *The Song of Yimeng* offers a seemingly belated response to the political call of the early 1980s, regurgitating the textbook formula of those films produced from 1979 to 1982. The film demonstrates that even in this age of diversification, elements of official Occidentalism not only linger, but continue to articulate a political line that shows surprisingly little development from its inception twenty-five years earlier.

At the same time, the figure of the absent American can also be seen in what Xiaomei Chen would call anti-official Occidentalism, as demonstrated by *Drifters* (Wang Xiaoshuai, 2003), a powerful film by a Sixth Generation director. Exactly one decade after exploring a traumatic departure in *The Days*, Wang Xiaoshuai presented an equally devastating vision of return. Here a highly self-conscious absence is used as potent metaphor that can be read, on the one hand, as a critique of the America Dream, but also as a more scathing self-criticism of those in China who are dazzled, blinded, and in some cases destroyed by that dream. The film tells the story of Wang Yunsheng, a drifter from Fujian who has returned home after being deported from the United States. The director observes his subject from an emotional distance as the latter numbly floats around his home-town, starting a relationship with a young opera performer and attempting to reconnect with his lost son – fathered while he was in America – taken away from him by his in-laws. While the film is set entirely in Fujian, America remains the unseen core of the work. Even in promotional materials for the film, Wang Xiaoshuai speaks extensively about the role the United States had on the film's conception and design:

> The idea for this story came from a friend who went to the US and came back after getting married and having a child there. Family problems began to occur and even-tually he couldn't even see his own son.... In the 1980s and 1990s, the trend of going overseas was also like that. Going to the other end of the world – a big deal! The entire country would change. What I wanted to say is, when something like this hap-pens to a family that is unable to fight against societal forces in terms of both social status and consequence, it's a tragedy of the entire people. This is the case with the son's family, which appears to have the ability to control its life because it has estab-lished roots in the US. (X. Wang 2005)

Ultimately, *Drifters* is an important film in the genre for borrowing the strategy of absence employed by earlier Chinese films about America, but resituating it in a fresh new light that exposes the inner brutality of what happens when failed American dreams collide with an unforgiving Chinese reality. Part of the film's ability to present its subject matter in such a bold and uncompromising manner is no doubt indebted to yet another global flow – the film's Hong Kong production companies, Purple Light Films and People Productions. Unlike early films like *Love on Lushan* and *The Herdsman* where America is at once objectified and highlighted but then negated for loftier nationalistic ideals, *Drifters* opens with the American fantasy already in shambles – Wang Yunsheng is already back in Fujian struggling to put his life together – and the Chinese reality he must face is not one of reunion, national pride, and celebration, but a more Lu Xun-esque vision of oppression and desolation. After all his time in America, the experience seems to have left almost no trace on Wang Yunsheng – his speech, clothes, economic status, and worldview appear untouched. Instead, it has stripped him of his son and his dignity.

The Song of Yimeng and *Drifters* serve as two examples of how strategies of absence and invisibility continue to be used by both official and non-official filmic discourse on America. We also see an evolution from powerful wealthy foreigners returning to China to "help" less fortunate Chinese – such as the industrialist father in *The Herdsman* – to Americans coming to China in a state of weakness and vulnerability – the bankrupt Frank looking to save his career in *Gasp*, the creatively bankrupt film director in *Big Shot's Funeral*, or Wang Yunsheng, the desperate "failed American" in *Drifters* who returns to China without even US citizenship. Through this process one can trace a shift that mirrors the transformation of China's own self-image over the past three decades, from the political and economic turmoil of the late 1970s to the Olympic metropolis of 2008. Curiously, although America is the subject of the films featured in this chapter, few have had US distribution and none have had any significant impact on the American market. In fact, *Big Shot's Funeral*, Feng Xiaogang's comedy intended as a Sino-US crossover, earned a paltry $820 at the US box office.[8] The relative commercial invisibility of these films in America further reinforces what we have known all along – these are films that tell us more about China than they do about the United States. While these films depict the United States with varying degrees of visibility and absence, China is always in the foreground. And as much as these works attempt to endorse, neutralize, or critique the shifting figure of America, on a much deeper level they serve as self-narratives about China's own predicament and place in the world.

Finally, all of the films featured here – and even the framework of this very chapter – seem to superficially subscribe to fixed notions of "China" and "America," national categories that define identity. Indeed, many of these films self-consciously employ a process of objectification and "Othering" when it comes to the foreign in order to further define notions of Chineseness and national identity. At the same time, the emphasis on iconic natural sites – Chilechuan, Lushan, Yimeng Mountain, etc. – is used to simultaneously build up a tangible, physical "China" that can be mapped and upon which that identity can be projected. However, returning to these sites, we find that at the core of all of these films – perhaps contrary to the filmmakers' intentions – are the celluloid footprints of travelers who freely move from China to America and back again. It is precisely these tales of mobility, border-crossing, and immigration that tell a greater story of identities in flux that challenges the very notion – or myth – of national identity.

Notes

1   News of *Love on Lushan*'s remarkable theatrical run being included in the *Guinness Book of World Records* has garnered extensive media coverage within China, featured on CCTV and in numerous newspapers and websites, including this announcement from the Lushan Department of Tourism: http://www.china-lushan.com/lshl/lshl.html.

2   I am not attempting to claim that the figure of the Chinese-American is somehow less a legitimate representation of "America" than Caucasian Americans, African-Americans, or other ethnic groups, but the key here is rather the means through which the identity of the Chinese-American opens a window through which the figure can be ambiguously both American while culturally, ethnically, and ethically Chinese.

3   After an extended stay in America, Zhang Yu would eventually return to mainland China in 1993 to continue her acting career.

4   Like Joan Chen and Zhang Yu, lead actress Xu Fan (b. 1967) also took foreign citizenship (Canada), a detail that serves as yet another real-life commentary on the theme of the film and was heatedly debated within China.

5   When his wife's lawyer comes to deliver the divorce papers, he offers the awkward words of consolation, "Don't be too upset, my wife is in Hungary. I'm sure she'll do the same to me before too long," thus alluding to the ubiquitous nature of this phenomenon.

6   An alternate reading to the immigration wave portrayed in *After Separation*, *Those Left Behind*, and especially *The Days* would be to connect the desperate desire to leave China (and layers of heavy symbolism such as abortion and the negation of Chinese national cultural symbols) with the traumatic aftermath of the Tiananmen Square Massacre. This phenomenon can be characterized as a form of "centrifugal trauma" (M. Berry 2008: 6–7, 298–364), whereby state violence triggers an "un-imagining" of the home nation and the formation of new global movements.

7   The films briefly covered in this section are far from an exhaustive list of Chinese productions set in or depicting America or Americans released in recent years. I have also not discussed films directed by Western directors like *Restless* (Jule Gilfillan, 1998), a film about an American woman in Beijing, or *Dark Matter* (2007), an American independent film by US-based Chinese director Chen Shi-zheng depicting the tragic real-life story of a Chinese physics student in America.

8   Box office figures for *Big Shot's Funeral* provided by Box Office Mojo: http://boxofficemojo.com/movies/?id=bigshotsfuneral.htm (accessed April 28, 2010).

Bibliography

A San 阿三 (2008), "Nande chunzhen – dianying *Wuye zhi cheng* ji jiezhong erlai de ping yu ji" 难得纯真–电影《无野之城》及接踵而来的评与击 (Rare innocence: *City Without Baseball* and its criticism and attacks, *Inmedia* (June 25), http://www.inmediahk.net/. Accessed March 30, 2010.

Aaron, Michelle (ed.) (2004), *New Queer Cinema: A Critical Reader*, Edinburgh: Edinburgh University Press.

Abbas, Ackbar (1997), *Hong Kong: Culture and the Politics of Disappearance*, Minneapolis: University of Minnesota Press.

Abbas, Ackbar (2007), "Hong Kong," in *The Cinema of Small Nations* (eds Mette Hjort and Duncan Petrie), Edinburgh: Edinburgh University Press, 113–26.

Abel, Richard (ed.) (1988), *French Film Theory and Criticism: A History/Anthology 1907–1939*, 2 vols., Princeton: Princeton University Press.

Academy of Television Arts and Sciences (2004), "Emmys in China: Broadcast Deal Signed" (June 9), http://cdn.emmys.tv/news/2004/june/china.php. Accessed December 7, 2009.

Acker, William (ed. and trans.) (1954 and 1974), *Some T'ang and Pre-T'ang Texts on Chinese Painting*, Leiden: E. J. Brill.

Acland, Charles R. (2003), *Screen Traffic: Movies, Multiplexes and Global Culture*, Durham, NC: Duke University Press.

Acland, Charles R. (2010), "*Avatar* as Technological Tentpole," *Flow* 11: 1.

Adams, Rachel and David Savran (eds) (2002), *The Masculinity Studies Reader*, Oxford: Blackwell.

Aksoy, Asu and Kevin Robins (1992), "Hollywood for the 21st Century: Global Competition for Critical Mass in Image Markets," *Cambridge Journal of Economics* 16: 12.

Alberoni, Francesco (1962), "The Powerless 'Elite': Theory and Sociological Research on the Phenomenon of the Stars," in *Stardom and Celebrity: A Reader* (eds Sean Redmond and Su Holmes), Los Angeles: Sage, 2007, 65–77.

Althusser, Louis (1971), *Lenin and Philosophy and Other Essays*, London: New Left Books.

A Companion to Chinese Cinema, First Edition. Edited by Yingjin Zhang.
© 2012 Blackwell Publishing Ltd. Published 2012 by Blackwell Publishing Ltd.

Altman, Rick (1989), *Film/Genre*, London: British Film Institute.

An, Jingfu (1994), "The Pain of a Half Taoist: Taoist Principles, Chinese Landscape Painting, and *King of the Children*," in *Cinematic Landscapes: Observations on the Visual Arts and Cinema of China and Japan* (eds Linda Ehrlich and David Desser), Austin: University of Texas Press, 117–26.

Anderson, Benedict (2006), *Imagined Communities: Reflections on the Origin and Spread of Nationalism*, London: Verso.

Anderson, John (2005), *Edward Yang*, Urbana: University of Illinois Press.

Anderson, Joseph L. and Donald Richie (1959), *The Japanese Film: Art and Industry*, Tokyo: Tuttle.

Andrew, Dudley (2000), "Adaptation," in *Film Adaptation* (ed. James Naremore), New Brunswick, NJ: Rutgers University Press, 28–37.

Ang, Ien (1998), "Can One Say No to Chineseness? Pushing the Limits of the Diasporic Paradigm," *Boundary 2* 25.3: 223–42.

Ang, Ien (2001), *On Not Speaking Chinese: Living between Asia and the West*, London: Routledge.

Anhui daxue zhongwenxi 安徽大学中文系 (Anhui University Chinese Department) (ed.) (1980), *Xia Yan Sai Jinhua ziliao xuanbian* 夏衍《赛金花》资料选编 (Selected material on Xia Yan's *Sai Jinhua*), Hefei: Anhui daxue.

Appadurai, Arjun (1990), "Disjuncture and Difference in the Global Cultural Economy," *Public Culture* 2.2: 1–24.

Appadurai, Arjun (2007), "Hope and Democracy," *Public Culture* 19.1: 29–34.

Arnheim, Rudolf (1957), *Film as Art*, Berkeley: University of California Press.

Austin, Guy (2003), *Stars in Modern French Films*, London: Arnold.

Babington, Bruce (ed.) (2001), *British Stars and Stardom*, Manchester: Manchester University Press.

Bai Jingcheng 白景晟 (1979), "Diudiao xiju guaizhang" 丢掉戏剧拐杖 (Throw away the crutches of drama), in *Dianying yishu yanjiu ziliao* 电影艺术研究资料 (Reference material on film art), Beijing: Zhongguo dianyingjia xiehui, vol. 1, n.p.

Baidu.com 百度 (n.d.a), "4.14 Yushu dizhen" 4.14 玉树地震 (April 14 Yushu earthquake), http://baike.baidu.com/view/3481647.htm. Accessed May 10, 2011.

Baidu.com 百度 (n.d.b), "5.12 Wenchuan dizhen" 5.12 汶川地震 (May 12 Wenchuan earthquake), http://baike.baidu.com/view/1587399.htm. Accessed May 10, 2011.

Baidu.com 百度 (n.d.c), "Tangshan da dizhen" 唐山大地震 (Tangshan earthquake), http://baike.baidu.com/view/3267.htm. Accessed May 10, 2011.

Balázs, Béla (1952), *Theory of the Film: Character and Growth of a New Art*, London: D. Dobson.

Bao, Tianxiao 包天笑 (1973), *Zhuanyinglou huiyi lu xuji* 釧影楼回忆录（续集）(Memoirs from Zhuanyinglou, sequel), Hong Kong: Da Zhonghua.

Bao, Weihong (2005), "From Pearl White to White Rose Woo: Tracing the Vernacular Body of Nüxia in Chinese Silent Cinema, 1927–1931," *Camera Obscura* 20.3: 193–231.

Bao, Weihong (2009), "In Search of a 'Cinematic Esperanto': Exhibiting Wartime Chongqing Cinema in the Global Context," *Journal of Chinese Cinemas* 3.2: 135–47.

Barboza, David (2007), "A Leap Forward, or a Great Sellout?" *New York Times* (July 1): 7.

Barboza, David (2009), "China Yearns to Form Its Own Media Empires," *New York Times* (October 5), http://www.nytimes.com/2009/10/05/business/global/05yuan.html. Accessed December 26, 2009.

Barker, Martin (2003), "Introduction," in *Contemporary Hollywood Stardom* (eds Thomas Austin and Martin Barker), London: Arnold, 1–24.

Barmé, Geremie (1999), *In the Red: On Contemporary Chinese Culture*, New York: Columbia University Press.

Barmé, Geremie and John Minford (eds) (1988), *Seeds of Fire: Chinese Voices of Conscience*, New York: Hill and Wang.

Barnhart, Richard (1964), "Wei Fu-jen's *Pi Chen T'u* and the Early Texts on Calligraphy," *Archives of the Chinese Art Society of America* 18: 13–25.

Barnouw, Erik (2000), "Last of the Great Movie Moguls," *Asian Cinema* 11.2: 24–9.

Bazin, André (1967), *What Is Cinema?* vol. 1, trans. Hugh Gray, Berkeley: University of California Press.

Bazin, André (1971), *What Is Cinema?* vol. 2, trans. Hugh Gray, Berkeley: University of California Press.

Bazin, André (2000), "Adaptation, or the Cinema as Digest," in *Film Adaptation* (ed. James Naremore), New Brunswick, NJ: Rutgers University Press, 19–27.

BBC Monitoring Asia Pacific–Political (2009), "Analysts Say Hollywood Portraying China in More Friendly Way" (November 21). Original source Xinhua News Agency (November 21).

Beijing shi danganguan 北京市档案馆 (Beijing Municipal Archive) (n.d.), *Statistical Materials on Beijing Cultural Industries, 1949–1958*, 北京市文化事业统计资料 1949–1958, Beijing, 10–11.

Benjamin, Walter (1968), "The Task of the Translator," in *Illuminations* (ed. Hannah Arendt, trans. Harry Zohn), New York: Schocken Books, 69–82.

Bergeron, Régis (1977), *Le Cinéma Chinois, 1905–1949*, Lausanne: Eibel.

Bergeron, Régis (1983–4), *Le Cinéma Chinois, 1949–1983*, 3 vols., Paris: L'Harmattan.

Berry, Chris (ed.) (1985), *Perspectives on Chinese Cinema*, Ithaca: Cornell University East Asia Paper No. 39.

Berry, Chris (1988), "Chinese Urban Cinema: Hyper-realism Versus Absurdism," *East-West Film Journal* 3.1: 76–87.

Berry, Chris (ed.) (1991), *Perspectives on Chinese Cinema*, London: British Film Institute.

Berry, Chris (1998), "If China Can Say No, Can China Make Movies? Or, Do Movies Make China? Rethinking National Cinema and National Agency," *Boundary 2* 25.3: 129–50.

Berry, Chris (2000), "Happy Alone? Sad Young Men in East Asian Gay Cinema," *Journal of Homosexuality* 39.3 / 4: 187–200.

Berry, Chris (2004a), *Postsocialist Cinema in Post-Mao China: The Cultural Revolution after the Cultural Revolution*, London: Routledge.

Berry, Chris (2004b), "The Sacred, the Profane, and the Domestic in Cui Zi'en's Cinema," *Positions* 12.1: 195–201.

Berry, Chris (2006a), "Independently Chinese: Duan Jinchuan, Jiang Yue, and Chinese Documentary," in *From Underground to Independent: Alternative Film Culture in Contemporary China* (eds Paul Pickowicz and Yingjin Zhang), Lanham, MD: Rowman and Littlefield, 109–22.

Berry, Chris (2006b), "Wu Wenguang: An Introduction," *Cinema Journal* 46.1: 133–6.

Berry, Chris (2007a), "The Chinese Side of the Mountain," *Film Quarterly* 60.3: 32–7.

Berry, Chris (2007b), "Getting Real: Chinese Documentary, Chinese Postsocialism," in *The Urban Generation: Chinese Cinema and Society at the Turn of the Twenty-First Century* (ed. Zhang Zhen), Durham, NC: Duke University Press, 115–34.

Berry, Chris (ed.) (2008), *Chinese Films in Focus II*, London: British Film Institute.

Berry, Chris and Mary Ann Farquhar (1994), "Post-Socialist Strategies: An Analysis of *Yellow Earth* and *Black Cannon Incident*," in *Cinematic Landscapes: Observations on the Visual Arts and Cinema of China and Japan* (eds Linda Ehrlich and David Desser), Austin: University of Texas Press, 81–116.

Berry, Chris and Mary Ann Farquhar (2006), *China on Screen: Cinema and Nation*, New York: Columbia University Press.

Berry, Chris and Lu Feii (eds) (2005), *Island on the Edge: Taiwan New Cinema and After*, Hong Kong: Hong Kong University Press.

Berry, Chris and Laikwan Pang (2008), "Introduction, or, What's in an 's'?" *Journal of Chinese Cinemas* 2.1: 3–8.

Berry, Chris, Xinyu Lu, and Lisa Rofel (eds) (2010), *The New Chinese Documentary Film Movement: For the Public Record*, Hong Kong: Hong Kong University Press.

Berry, Michael (2005), *Speaking in Images: Interviews with Contemporary Chinese Filmmakers*, New York: Columbia University Press.

Berry, Michael (2008), *A History of Pain: Trauma in Modern Chinese Literature and Film*, New York: Columbia University Press.

Berry, Michael (2009), *Xiao Wu, Platform, Unknown Pleasures: Jia Zhangke's 'Hometown Trilogy'*, London: British Film Institute.

Bettinson, Gary (2005), "Reflections on a Screen Narcissist: Leslie Cheung's Star Persona in the Films of Wong Kar-wai," *Asian Cinema* 16.1: 220–38.

Bian, Shanji 边善基 et al. (1988), "'Chengshi dianying' dayou kewei" "城市电影"大有可为 ("Urban Cinema" has great prospects), *Dianying xinzuo* 电影新作 (New films) 6: 54–63.

Blue Book of China's Media (2009), *2009 nian: Zhongguo chuanmei chanye fazhan baogao* 中国传媒产业发展报告 (Report on the development of China's media industry 2009), Beijing: Shehui kexue wenxian chubanshe.

Bluestone, George (1957), *Novels into Film*, Baltimore: Johns Hopkins University Press.

Bo Jin 柏晋 (1927), "Shishi yingpian tan" 时事影片谈 (A discussion of newsreels), *Yinxing* 银星 (Silver stars) 7; reprinted in *Zhongguo wusheng dianying* 中国无声电影 (Chinese silent film) (ed. Dai Xiaolan), Beijing: Zhongguo dianying chubanshe, 1996, 618–20.

Boli, John and George M. Thomas (1997), "World Culture in the World Polity: A Century of International Non-Governmental Organizations," *American Sociological Review* 62.2: 171–90.

Bordwell, David (1985), *Narration in the Fiction Film*, Madison: University of Wisconsin Press.

Bordwell, David (2000), *Planet Hong Kong: Popular Cinema and the Art of Entertainment*, Cambridge, MA: Harvard University Press.

Bordwell, David (2005a), *Figures Traced in Light: On Cinematic Staging*, Berkeley: University of California Press.

Bordwell, David (2005b), "Transcultural Spaces: Toward a Poetics of Chinese Film," in *Chinese-Language Film: Historiography, Poetics, Politics* (eds Sheldon Hsiao-Peng Lu and Emilie Yueh-Yu Yeh), Honolulu: University of Hawaii Press, 141–62.

Bordwell, David (2006), *The Way Hollywood Tells It: Story and Style in Modern Movies*, Berkeley: University of California Press.

Bordwell, David (2008), *Poetics of Cinema*, London: Routledge.

Bordwell, David and Kristin Thompson (1986), *Film Art: An Introduction*, 2nd edn, New York: Alfred Knopf.

Bourdieu, Pierre (1993), *The Field of Cultural Production: Essays on Art and Literature* (trans. Randal Johnson), New York: Columbia University Press.

Bourdieu, Pierre (1998), "Social Space and Field of Power," in *Practical Reason: On the Theory of Action*, Cambridge: Polity Press, 31–4.

Braester, Yomi (2010), *Painting the City Red: Chinese Cinema and the Urban Contract*, Durham, NC: Duke University Press.

Braester, Yomi and James Tweedie (eds) (2010), *Cinema at the City's Edge: Film and Urban Networks in East Asia*, Hong Kong: Hong Kong University Press.

Broadcast Engineering (2006), "China Movie Channel Restores Old Films and TV Shows," *Broadcast Engineering* (October 6), http://broadcastengineering.com/news/china_old_films_tv/. Accessed December 7, 2009.

Brooks, Peter (1976), *The Melodramatic Imagination: Balzac, Henry James, Melodrama, and the Mode of Excess*, New Haven, CT: Yale University Press.

Browne, Nick (1994), "Society and Subjectivity: On the Political Economy of Chinese Melodrama," in *New Chinese Cinemas: Forms, Identities, Politics* (eds Nick Browne et al.), New York: Cambridge University Press, 40–56.

Browne, Nick, Paul G. Pickowicz, Vivian Sobchak, and Esther Yau (eds) (1994), *New Chinese Cinemas: Forms, Identities, Politics*, New York: Cambridge University Press.

Brunette, Peter (2005), *Wong Kar-wai*, Urbana: University of Illinois Press.

Businessofcinema.com (2007), "MPAA extends China Film Production Workshop" (July 12), http://www.businessofcinema.com/news.php?newsid=3883. Accessed July 12, 2007.

Businessofcinema.com (2008), "Pyramid Saimira to Invest Rs 4 Billion in China" (April 19), http://www.businessofcinema.com/news.php?newsid=7945&page=1. Accessed June 21, 2007.

Butler, Alison (2002), *Women's Cinema: The Contested Screen*, London: Wallflower Press.

Cahill, James (1960), "Confucian Elements in the Theory of Painting," in *The Confucian Persuasion* (ed. Arthur F. Wright), Stanford: Stanford University Press, 115–40.

Cai, Chusheng 蔡楚生 (1949), "Zai Wenhua bu dianying ju yishu weiyuanhui kuoda zuotanhui de fayan" 在文化部电影局艺术委员会扩大座谈会的发言 (Speech at the Ministry of Culture Film Bureau Artistic Committee Expanded Conference), October 31; reprinted in *Zhongguo dianying yanjiu ziliao* 中国电影研究资料 (Chinese cinema research materials) (ed. Wu Di 吴迪), Beijing: Wenhua yishu chubanshe, 2006, vol. 1: 45–51.

Cai, Chusheng 蔡楚生 (1957), "Zhuiyi Ruan Lingyu" 追忆阮玲玉 (In memory of Ruan Lingyu), *Zhongguo dianying* 中国电影 (China cinema) 2: 27–9.

Cai, Guorong 蔡国荣 (ed.) (1982), *Liushi niandai guopian mingdao mingzuo xuan* 六十年代国片名导名作选 (Mandarin cinema in the 1960s: Famous directors and notable films), Taibei: Zhonghua minguo dianying shiye fazhan jijinhui.

Cai, Guorong 蔡国荣 (1985), *Zhonguo jindai wenyi dianying yanjiu* 中国近代文艺电影研究 (Studies on modern Chinese wenyi cinema), Taipei: Dianying tushuguan.

Cai, Hongsheng 蔡洪声, Song Jialing 宋家玲, and Liu Guiqing 刘桂清 (eds) (2000), *Xianggang dianying 80 nian* 香港电影 80 年 (Eighty years of Hong Kong film), Beijing: Beijing guangbo xueyuan chubanshe.

Caldwell, John (2008), *Production Culture: Industrial Reflexivity and Critical Practice in Film and Television*, Durham, NC: Duke University Press.

California Chronicle (n.d.), online daily, Los Angeles, "City of Sadness," http://www.californiachronicle.com/articles/yb/139386965. Accessed January 7, 2010.

Callick, Rowan (2008), "China's Censorship Syndrome," *The Australian* (May 14): 29.

Canudo, Ricciotto (1911), "The Birth of a Sixth Art," trans. Ben Gibson, Don Ranvaud, Sergio Sokota, and Deborah Young from "Naissance d'un sixieme art," *Les Entretiens idealistes* (October 25); reprinted in *French Film Theory and Criticism: A History/Anthology 1907–1939* (ed. Richard Abel), Princeton: Princeton University Press, 1988, vol. 1: 58–66.

Canudo, Ricciotto (1923), "Reflections on the Seventh Art," in *French Film Theory and Criticism: A History/Anthology 1907–1939* (ed. Richard Abel), Princeton: Princeton University Press, 1988, vol. 1: 291–303.

Cao, Dongqing and Gina Marchetti (trans.) (2009), "*Stage Sisters*: Excerpts from Reels Nine and Ten," *Renditions: A Chinese–English Translation Magazine* 71: 30–46.

Caughie, John (ed.) (1981), *Theories of Authorship*, London: Routledge and Kegan Paul.

CCTV (China Central Television) (2009), "Box Office Takings to Hit 6 Billion Yuan in China" (December 2), http://english.cctv.com/20091202/102295.shtml. Accessed December 23, 2009.

Chai, Aixin 柴爱新 (2009), "Xianzai shi dianying shencha zui kuansong de shihou" 现在是电影审查最宽松的时候 (Now is the most tolerant period of film censorship), *Liaowang dongfang zhoukan* 瞭望东方周刊 (*Liaowang* oriental weekly) 9 (February 28): 25.

Chan, Anthony B. (1996), *Li Ka-Shing: Hong Kong's Elusive Billionaire*, Hong Kong: Oxford University Press.

Chan, Evans (2000), "Postmodernism and Hong Kong Cinema," *Postmodern Culture* 10.3, http://muse.jhu.edu/journals/pmc/v010/10.3chan.html. Accessed March 10, 2010.

Chan, Evans (2009), "Zhang Yimou's Hero: The Temptations of Fascism," in *Chinese Connections: Critical Perspectives on Film, Identity, and Diaspora* (eds Tan See-kam, Peter X. Feng, and Gina Marchetti), Philadelphia: Temple University Press, 263–77.

Chan, Joseph M. (forthcoming), *Chinese Television Industry*, London: British Film Institute.

Chan, Joseph M., Anthony Fung, and Chung Hung Ng (2010), *Policies for the Sustainable Development of the Hong Kong Film Industry*, Hong Kong: Hong Kong Institute of Asia-Pacific Studies.

Chan, Kenneth (2009), *Re-Made in Hollywood: The Global Chinese Presence in post-1997 Transnational Cinemas*, Hong Kong: Hong Kong University Press.

Chandler, Alfred (1977), *The Visible Hand: The Managerial Revolution in American Business*, Cambridge, MA: Belknap Press.

Chang, Eileen, Wang Hui Ling, and James Schamus (2007), *Lust, Caution: The Story, the Screenplay, and the Making of the Film*, New York: Pantheon.

Chang, Hsiao-hung 张小虹 (2000), *Guaitai jiating luoman shi* 怪胎家庭罗曼史 (Queer family romance), Taipei: Shibao.

Chang, Maukuei (2005), "The Movement to Indigenize the Social Sciences in Taiwan: Origin and Predicaments," in *Cultural, Ethnic and Political Nationalism in Contemporary Taiwan* (eds John Makeham and A-chin Hsiau), New York: Palgrave Macmillan, 221–60.

Chang, Michael G. (1999), "The Good, the Bad, and the Beautiful: Movie Actresses and Public Discourse in Shanghai, 1920s–1930s," in *Cinema and Urban Culture in Shanghai, 1922–1943* (ed. Yingjin Zhang), Stanford, CA: Stanford University Press, 128–59.

Chang, Yvonne Sung-sheng (1993), *Modernism and the Nativist Resistance*, Durham, NC: Duke University Press.

Chang, Yvonne Sung-sheng (2004), *Literary Culture in Taiwan: Martial Law to Market Law*, New York: Columbia University Press.

Chang, Yvonne Sung-sheng (2005), "*The Terrorizer* and the Great Divide in Contemporary Taiwan's Cultural Development," in *Island on the Edge: Taiwan New Cinema and After* (eds Chris Berry and Feiyi Lu), Hong Kong: Hong Kong University Press, 13–25.

Chao, Shiyan 赵锡彦 (2006), "*Hezi* neiwai de qingyu zhengzhi – jianlun *Nü tongzhi youxing ri*" 《盒子》内外的情欲政治——兼论《女同志游行日》 (The erotic politics inside and outside *The Box* – and a discussion on *Dyke March*), in *Ling yan xiang kan: haiwai xuezhe ping dangdai zhongguo jilupian* 另眼相看——海外学者评当代中国纪录片 (Reel China: A new look at contemporary Chinese documentary) (ed. Ping Jie), Shanghai: Wenhui chubanshe, 143–51.

Chaudhuri, Una (1997), *Staging Place: The Geography of Modern Drama*, Ann Arbor: University of Michigan Press.

Cheek, Timothy (1997), *Propaganda and Culture in Mao's China: Deng Tuo and the Intelligentsia*, Oxford: Clarendon Press.

Chen, Boer 陈波儿 (1950), "*Gushi pian cong wu dao you de biandao gongzuo*" 故事片从无到有的编导工作 (Directing feature films from the very beginning); reprinted in *Zhongguo dianying yanjiu ziliao* 中国电影研究资料 (Chinese cinema research materials) (ed. Wu Di 吴迪), Beijing: Wenhua yishu chubanshe, 2006, vol. 1: 58–66.

Chen, Feibao 陈飞宝 (1988), *Taiwan dianying shihua* 台湾电影史话 (History of Taiwan film), Beijing: Zhongguo dianying chubanshe.

Chen, Huangmei 陈荒煤 (ed.) (1989), *Dangdai Zhongguo diangying* 当代中国电影 (Contemporary Chinese film), Beijing: Zhongguo shehui kexue chubanshe.

Chen, Jianhua 陈建华 (2009), *Cong geming dao gonghe: Qingmo zhi minguo shiqi wenxue, dianying yu wenhua de zhuangxing* 从革命到共和: 清末至民国时期文学, 电影与文化的转型 (From revolution to republicanism: Transformations in literature, cinema and culture from late Qing to the Republican period), Nanning: Guangxi shifan daxue chubanshe.

Chen, Jingliang 陈景亮 and Zou Jianwen 邹建文 (eds) (2005), *Bainian Zhongguo dianying jingxuan: disan juan xin shiqi Zhongguo dianying* 百年中国电影精选: 第三卷, 新时期中国电影 (Selection from a hundred years of Chinese Cinema, volume 3: Chinese cinema of the new era), Beijing: Zhongguo shehui kexue chubanshe.

Chen, Kunhou (2009), Conversation with Darrell W. Davis, Taipei (December 3).

Chen, Mo 陈墨 (1996), *Daoguang xiaying mengtaiqi: Zhongguo wuxia dianying lun* 刀光侠影蒙太奇: 中国武侠电影论 (Montage of swordplay and swordfighters: A treatise on Chinese wuxia cinema), Beijing: Zhongguo dianying chubanshe.

Chen, Ru-shou Robert (1998), "Taiwan Cinema," in *Encyclopedia of Chinese Film* (eds Yingjin Zhang and Zhiwei Xiao), London: Routledge, 47–62.

Chen, Ru-shou 陈儒修 (1993), *Taiwan dianying de lishi wenhua jingyan* 台湾新电影的历史文化经验 (The history and culture experiences of Taiwan's new cinema), Taipei: Maitian.

Chen, Shi-zheng (2007), "Director's Statement," in *Dark Matter* Press Kit, http://www.dark-matterthefilm.com/. Accessed November 12, 2009.

Chen, Xiaomei (2002), *Occidentalism: A Theory of Counter-Discourse in Post-Mao China*, Oxford: Rowman and Littlefield.

Chen, Xiaoyun 陈晓云 (1990), "Gudu de chengshi – chengshi dianying yanjiu zhi yi" 孤独的都市—城市电影研究之一 (The lonesome city: Studies in urban cinema, 1), *Wenyi pinglun* 文艺评论 (Literature and art criticism) 4: 84–9, continued on 67.

Chen, Xiaoyun 陈晓云 (1991), "Huangdan de dushi – chengshi dianying yanjiu zhi er 荒诞的都市—城市电影研究之二 (The absurd city: Studies in urban cinema, 2), *Wenyi pinglun* 2: 87–93.

Chen, Xihe 陈犀禾 (1986), "Zhongguo dianying meixue de zai renxi: Tan *Yingxi juben zuofa*" 中国电影美学的再认识—谈《影戏剧本作法》 (Rethinking Chinese film aesthetics: On *Filmscript Writing*), *Dangdai dianying* 当代电影 (Contemporary cinema) 1: 82–90.

Chen, Yan-ru (2008), *Subculture Studies: Boys' Love in Taiwan*, PhD thesis, National Tsing Hua University, Taiwan.

Chen, Yansheng 陈炎生 (2003), *Taiwan de nüer: Taiwan diyiwei nüdaoyan Chen Wenmin de jiazu yiken fendou shi* 台湾的女儿: 台湾第一位女导演陈文敏的家族移垦奋斗史 (The daughter of Taiwan: The rural migration and struggles of the family of Chen Wenmin, the first Taiwan female film director), Taipei: Yushanshe.

Chen, Yueshan 陈樾山 and Liu Ping 刘平 (eds) (2000), *Tang Huaiqiu yu Zhongguo lüxing jutuan* 唐槐秋与中国旅行剧团 (Tang Huaiqiu and the Chinese drama traveling troupe), Beijing: Zhonguo xiju chubanshe.

Cheng, Jihua 程季华, Li Shaobai 李少白, and Xing Zuwen 邢祖文 (1963, 1980, 1998), *Zhongguo dianying fazhan shi* 中国电影发展史 (A history of the development of Chinese film), 2 vols., Beijing: Zhongguo dianying chubanshe.

Cheng, Qingsong 程青松 and Huang Ou 黄鸥 (eds) (2002), *Wode sheyingji bu sahuang: xianfeng dianying ren dang'an – shengyu 1961–1970* 我的摄影机不撒谎: 先锋电影人档案—生于 1961–1970 (My camera doesn't lie: Documents on avant-garde filmmakers born between 1961 and 1970). Beijing: Zhongguo youyi chuban gongsi.

Cheng, Shuren 程树仁 (ed.) (1927), *Zhonghua yingye nianjian* 中华影业年鉴 (Chinese cinema year book), Shanghai: Zhonghua yingye nianjian.

Cheng, Weikun (1996), "The Challenge of the Actresses: Female Performers and Cultural Alternatives in Early Twentieth-Century Beijing and Tianjin," *Modern China* 22.2: 197–233.

Cheuk, Pak Tong (2008), *Hong Kong New Wave Cinema (1978–2000)*, Bristol: Intellect Books.

Cheung, Esther M. K. and Chu Yiu-wai (eds) (2004), *Between Home and World: A Reader in Hong Kong Cinema*, Hong Kong: Oxford University Press.

Chih, Ta-wei 纪大伟 and Lucifer Hung 洪凌 (eds) (1997), *Ku'er jishi lu* 酷儿启示录 (Queer achipelago: A reader of the queer discourse in Taiwan), Taipei: Yuanzun wenhua.

China News Network (2009), "Huang Xiaoming shengjia baozeng wuqianwan, Huayi xiongdi dansheng jiu yiwan fuwen" 黄晓明身价爆增五千万, 华谊兄弟诞生九亿万富翁 (Huang Xiaoming is worth 50 million; Huayi Brothers reborn with nine billion in wealth), http://www.chinanews.com.cn/cj/cj-cfgs/news/2009/10–16/1913702.shtml. Accessed December 7, 2009.

China Post (2009), English-language daily, Taipei, "Without Government Help, Taiwan Film Industry Will Fail: Director" (February 19), http://www.chinapost.com.tw/taiwan/arts-&-leisure/2009/12/18/237109/Without-govt.htm. Accessed January 22, 2010.

Chinadaily.com (2009a), "Silver Screen Salvo Lights Way" (February 10), http://www.lexisnexis.com. Accessed May 7, 2010.

Chinadaily.com (2009b), "Director in Despair" (June 18), http://www.lexisnexis.com. Accessed November 27, 2009.

Chinadaily.com (2009c), "'Foreign' Presence Stirs Up Controversy" (September 2), http://www.lexisnexis.com. Accessed December 24, 2009.

Chinadaily.com (2009d), "Welcome to Make-Believe World of Box-Office Returns" (November 21), http://www.lexisnexis.com. Accessed December 11, 2009.

ChinaFilm.com. (n.d.) "China Movie Channel Program Center," http://exp.chinafilm.com/About/200806/745.html. Accessed December 7, 2009.

Chinaview.cn (2008), "China Not to Implement Film Rating for the Moment" (March 4); original source Xinhua News Agency (March 4), http://news.xinhuanet.com/english/2008–03/04/content-7717024.htm. Accessed May 15, 2011.

Chinese Film Distribution and Screening Association 中国电影发行放映协会 (2008), "2007 Zhongguo dianying shichang baogao (jiexuan)" 2007 中国电影市场报告（节选） (2007 report on the Chinese film market [selection]), *Zhongguo dianying shichang* 中国电影市场 (Chinese film market) (July): 10–3.

Ching, Leo (2000), "Globalizing the Regional, Regionalizing the Global: Mass Culture and Asianism in the Age of Late Capital," *Public Culture* 12.1: 233–57.

Choi, Jimmy (2008), Interview with Chris Berry, Hong Kong, March 30.

Choi, Jinhee and Mitsuyo Wada-Marciano (2008), *Horror to the Extreme: Changing Boundaries in Asian Cinema*, Hong Kong: Hong Kong University Press.

Chou, Wah-shan 周华山 (1995), *Tongzhi lun* 同志论 (On *Tongzhi*), Hong Kong: Tongzhi yanjiushe.

Chow, Peter C. Y. (ed.) (2002), *Taiwan's Modernization in Global Perspective*, Westport, CT: Praeger.

Chow, Rey (1991), *Woman and Chinese Modernity: The Politics of Reading between East and West*, Minneapolis: University of Minnesota Press.

Chow, Rey (1993), *Primitive Passions: Visuality, Sexuality, Ethnography, and Contemporary Chinese Cinema*, New York: Columbia University Press.

Chow, Rey (1995), *Writing Diaspora: Tactics of Intervention in Contemporary Cultural Studies*, Bloomington: Indiana University Press.

Chow, Rey (2007), *Sentimental Fabulations, Contemporary Chinese Films: Attachment in the Age of Global Visibility*, New York: Columbia University Press.

Chu, Wei-cheng 朱伟诚 (2003), "Tongzhi · Taiwan: xing gongmin, guozu jiangou huo gongmin shehui 同志·台湾: 性公民、国族建构或公民社会 (Queering Taiwan: Sexual citizenship, nation-building or civil society), *Nüxue xuezhi: funü yu xingbei yanjiu* 女学学志: 妇女与性别研究 (Journal of women's and gender studies) 15: 115–51.

Chu, Yingchi (2003), *Hong Kong Cinema: Colonizer, Motherland and Self*, London: Routledge.

Chua, Siew Keng (1998), "The Politics of 'Home': *Song of Exile*," *Jump Cut* 42: 90–3.

Ciecko, Anne Tereska (ed.) (2006), *Contemporary Asian Cinema: Popular Culture in a Global Frame*, New York: Berg.

Clark, Paul (1986), "Review of Regis Bergeron, *Le Cinéma Chinois*," *China Quarterly* 108: 730–1.

Clark, Paul (1987), *Chinese Cinema: Culture and Politics since 1949*, New York: Cambridge University Press.

Clark, Paul (2005), *Reinventing China: A Generation and Its Films*, Hong Kong: Chinese University Press.

Clark, Paul (2008), *The Chinese Cultural Revolution: A History*, New York: Cambridge University Press.

Clark, Paul (2011), "Closely Watched Viewers: A Taxonomy of Chinese Film Audiences from 1949 to the Cultural Revolution Seen from Hunan," *Journal of Chinese Cinemas* 5.1: 73–89.

Clarke, David J. (ed.) (1997), *The Cinematic City*, New York: Routledge.

Clifford, James (1997), *Routes: Travel and Translation in the Late Twentieth Century*, Cambridge, MA: Harvard University Press.

CMM Intelligence (2003), "Movie Channels Planned, But Will SARFT Let Them Compete?" *CMM Intelligence* 7.9 (December 17), http://www.cmmintelligence.com/?q=node/4925. Accessed December 7, 2009.

CNN (1995), "Spin Cycle: Hugh Grant Finds 'Honesty' Best Policy" (July 17), http://edition.cnn.com/SHOWBIZ/HughGrant/. Accessed November 12, 2010.

Codell, Julie F. (2007), *Genre, Gender, Race, and World Cinema*, Oxford: Blackwell.

Collett, Nigel (2009a), "Coffee with Simon Chung Tak-sing," *Fridae* (March 20), http://www.fridae.com/newsfeatures/2009/03/20/2242.coffee-with-simon-chung-tak-sing. Accessed January 13, 2010.

Collett, Nigel (2009b), "In Chime with Our Time: Kit Hung," *Fridae* (June 3), http://www.fridae.com/newsfeatures/2009/06/03/8394.in-chime-with-our-times-kit-hung. Accessed March 30, 2010.

Conceison, Claire (2004), *Significant Other: Staging the American in China*, Honolulu: University of Hawaii Press.

Coonan, Clifford (2009), "Booming B.O. Changes China's Market View," *Variety* (November 1): 8.

Corliss, Richard (2000), "Too Much for Star Power," *Time* (September 4).

Corliss, Richard (2003), "That Old Feeling: Days of Being Leslie," *Time* (April 3).

Cornelius, Sheila (2002), *New Chinese Cinema: Challenging Representations,* London: Wallflower Press.

Cremin, Stephen (2011), "China Box Office Down 11% in Q1," filmbiz.asia (April 8), http://www.filmbiz.asia.news/china-box-office-down-11–in-q1?utm. Accessed May 8, 2011.

Crofts, Stephen (1993), "Reconceptualizing National Cinema/s," *Quarterly Review of Film and Video* 14.3: 49–67.

Crofts, Stephen (2006), "Reconceptualizing National Cinema/s," in *Theorizing National Cinema* (eds Paul Willemen and Valentina Vitali), London: British Film Institute, 44–58.

CSDZBW (Changchun shi difang zhi bianzuan weiyuanhui) 长春市地方志编纂委员会 (Gazetteer editorial committee of Changchun municipality) (ed.) (1992), *Changchun shi zhi: dianying zhi* 长春市志: 电影志 (Gazetteer of Changchun municipality: Cinema), Changchun: Dongbei shifan daxue chubanshe.

CSM Media Research (n.d.), "30 City Movie Research (Door to Door Interviews) Beijing, Shanghai, Guangzhou Movie Theater Study," http://www.csm.com.cn/en/business/b41.html. Accessed December 7, 2009.:

Cui, Baoguo 崔保国 (ed.) (2009), *2009 nian: Zhongguo chuanmei chanye fazhan baogao 2009* 年: 中国传媒产业发展报告 (Report on the development of China's media industry in 2009), Beijing: Shehui kexue wenxian chubanshe.

Cui, Shuqin (2000), "Stanley Kwan's *Center Stage*: The (Im)possible Engagement Between Feminism and Postmodernism," *Cinema Journal* 39.4: 60–80.

Cui, Shuqin (2003), *Women Through the Lens: Gender and Nation in a Century of Chinese Cinema*, Honolulu: University of Hawaii Press.

Cui, Shuqin (2005), "Raise the Red Lantern," in *Film Analysis: A Norton Reader* (eds Jeffrey Geiger and R. L. Rutsky), New York: W. W. Norton, 830–49.

Cui, Weiping 崔卫平 (2008), "Bashi niandai de jingshen loudong huo yi 'yishu' de mingyi" 八十年代的精神漏洞或以"艺术"的名义 (The spiritual leak of the eighties, or in the name of 'art'), *Women shidai de xushi* 我们时代的叙事 (Narrative of our times), Guangzhou: Huacheng chubanshe, 8–13.

Cui, Zi'en 崔子恩 (2003), *Choujiao dengchang* ba dianying qiangbao de yiwu shichu 《丑角登场》把电影强暴得一无是处 (*Enter the Clowns* rapes cinema into uselessness), *Diyi guanzhong* 第一观众, http://fanhall.com/news/entry/7168.html. Accessed February 10, 2010.

Curtin, Michael (2007), *Playing to the World's Biggest Audience: The Globalization of Chinese Film and TV*, Berkeley: University of California Press.

Curtin, Michael (2010), "Introduction to 'In Focus: China's Rise'," *Cinema Journal* 49.3: 117–20.

Dai, Jinhua 戴锦华 (1993), *Dianying lilun yu piping shouce* 电影理论与批评手册 (A handbook of film theory and criticism), Beijing: Keji wenxian chubanshe.

Dai, Jinhua 戴锦华 (1999), *Xieta liaowang: Zhongguo dianying wenhua, 1978–1998* 斜塔瞭望：中国电影文化 1978–1998 (Looking out from the slanting tower: Chinese film culture, 1978–1998), Taipei: Yuanliu.

Dai, Jinhua 戴锦华 (2002), *Cinema and Desire: Feminist Marxism and Cultural Studies in the Work of Dai Jinhua* (eds Jing Wang and Tani E. Barlow), London: Verso.

Dai, Jinhua 戴锦华 (2005), "Order/Anti-Order: Representation of Identity in Hong Kong Action Movies," in *Hong Kong Connections: Transnational Imagination in Action Cinema* (eds Meaghan Morris, Siu-Leung Li, and Stephen Ching-Kiu Chan), Hong Kong: Hong Kong University Press, 81–94.

Dai, Qing (1993), "Raised Eyebrows for *Raise the Red Lantern*," *Public Culture* 5: 333–7.

Dai, Xiaolan 戴晓兰 (ed.) (1996), *Zhongguo wusheng dianying* 中国无声电影 (Chinese silent film), Beijing: Zhongguo dianying chubanshe.

Danwei.org (2009), "What Makes the Most Profit? Risk Does; China Film Group CEO Interview with *Southern Weekly*" (posted by Alice Xin Liu, September 28), http://www.danwei.org/film/what_makes_the_most_profit_ris.php. Accessed December 23, 2009.

Davis, Darrell William (1996), *Picturing Japaneseness: Monumental Style, National Identity, Japanese Film*, New York: Columbia University Press.

Davis, Darrell William (2003), "A New Taiwan Person? Conversation with Wu Nien-chen," *Positions: East Asia Cultures Critique* 11.3: 717–34.

Davis, Darrell William (2005), "Borrowing Postcolonial: Wu Nianzhen's *Dou-san* and the Memory Mine," in *Chinese-Language Film: Historiography, Poetics, Politics* (eds Sheldon Hsiao-Peng Lu and Emilie Yueh-Yu Yeh), Honolulu: University of Hawaii Press, 237–66.

Davis, Darrell William (2007) "Trendy in Taiwan: Problems of Popularity in the Island's Cinema," in *Cinema Taiwan: Politics, Popularity and State of the Arts* (eds Darrell William Davis and Ru-Shou Robert Chen), London: Routledge, 146–58.

Davis, Darrell William (2008), *"Lust, Caution* and Eileen Chang: A Posting" (March 13), http://www.cupblog.org/?p=126. Accesssed November 12, 2010.

Davis, Darrell William and Emilie Yueh-yu Yeh (2008), *East Asian Screen Industries*, London: British Film Institute.

Davis, Darrell William and Ru-Shou Robert Chen (eds) (2007), *Cinema Taiwan: Politics, Popularity and State of the Arts*, London: Routledge.

de Carvalho, Ludmila Moreira Macedo (2008), "Memories of Sound and Light: Musical Discourse in the Films of Wong Kar-wai," *Journal of Chinese Cinemas* 2.3: 197–210.

De Valck, Marijke (2007), *Film Festivals: From European Geopolitics to Global Cinephilia*, Amsterdam: Amsterdam University Press.

Deleuze, Gilles (1986), *Cinema I: The Movement-Image* (trans. Hugh Tomlinson and Barbara Habberjam), Minneapolis: University of Minnesota Press.

Deleuze, Gilles (1989), *Cinema II: The Time-Image* (trans. Hugh Tomlinson and Robert Galeta), Minneapolis: University of Minnesota Press.

Deng, Zhufei 邓烛非 (1996), "Yingshi wenhua chuzai dabiange qianye" 影视文化处在大变革前夜 (The dawn of film and television industries' big reform), *Dianying yishu* 电影艺术 (Film art) 1: 85.

Deppman, Hsiu-Chuang (2010), *Adapted for the Screen: The Cultural Politics of Modern Chinese Fiction and Film*, Honolulu: University of Hawaii Press.

Derrida, Jacques (1980), "The Law of Genre," *Critical Inquiry* 7.1: 55–81.

Desser, David (2000), "The Kung Fu Craze: Hong Kong Cinema's First American Reception," in *The Cinema of Hong Kong: History, Arts, Identity* (eds Poshek Fu and David Desser), New York: Cambridge University Press, 19–43.

Di, Shijie 邸世杰 and Liu Hongcai 刘洪才 (2007), *Guangbo dianying dianshi jishu fazhan jianshi* 广播电影电视技术发展简史 (A brief history of the technological development of radio, television, and film), Beijing: Zhongguo guangbo dianshi chubanshe, vol. 2.

Diao, Ming Ming (2008), *Research into Chinese Television Development: Television Industrialization in China*, PhD thesis, Macquarie University.

Dilley, Whitney Crothers (2007), *The Cinema of Ang Lee: The Other Side of the Screen*, London: Wallflower Press.

Ding, Luonan 丁罗南 (2008) *Shanghai huaju bainian shishu* 上海话剧百年史述 (Historical accounts of Shanghai's one hundred years of drama), Guilin: Guangxi shifan daxue chubanshe.

Ding, Sheng (2008), *The Dragon's Hidden Wings: How China Rises with Its Soft Power*, Lanham, MD: Lexington Books.

Ding, Yaping 丁亚平 (1998), *Yingxiang Zhongguo: Zhongguo dianying yishu 1945–1949* 影像中国——中国电影艺术：1945–1949 (Image China – Chinese film art: 1945–1949), Beijing: Wenhua yishu chubanshe.

Ding, Yaping 丁亚平 (ed.) (2002), *1897–2001 Bainian Zhongguo dianying lilun wenxuan 1897–2001* 百年中国电影理论文选 (Selected works from a hundred years of Chinese film theory 1897–2001), 2 vols., Beijing: Wenhua yishu chubanshe.

Dissanayake, Wimal (ed.) (1993), *Melodrama and Asian Cinema*, Cambridge: Cambridge University Press.

Dissanayake, Wimal (ed.) (1994), *Colonialism and Nationalism in Asian Cinema*, Bloomington: University of Indiana Press.

Dissanayake, Wimal (2003), *Wong Kar-wai's Ashes of Time*, Hong Kong: Hong Kong University Press.

Dissanayake, Wimal (2006), "Globalization and the Experience of Culture: The Resilience of Nationhood," in *Globalization, Cultural Identities, and Media Representations* (eds Natascha Gentz and Stefan Kramer), Albany: State University of New York Press, 25–44.

Diwu Tiefeng 第五铁峰 (2008) "Wangyi dujia duihua Zhou Meiling: Wo xiang pai liuse xingbie yiti yingpian" 网易独家对话周美玲：我想拍六色性别议题影片 (Exclusive conversation with Zero Chou: I want to make a six-colored gender issue cinema), Ent.163.com (February 1), http://ent.163.com/08/0201/17/43KPUUJ1000300B1.html. Accessed April 19, 2010.

Doane, Mary Ann (1982), "Film and the Masquerade: Theorizing the Female Spectator," *Screen* 23.3–4: 74–86.

Donald, Stephanie Hemelryk (1998), "Symptoms of Alienation: The Female Body in Recent Chinese Film," *Continuum* 12.1: 91–103.

Du, Yunzhi 杜云之 (1968), "Wuxia pian yu xiayi jingshen" 武侠片与侠义精神 (Wuxia film and the spirit of chivalry), *Xianggang yinghua* 香港影画 (Hong Kong movie news) (February): 62–3.

Du, Yunzhi 杜云之 (1972), *Zhongguo dianying shi* 中国电影史 (Chinese film history), 3 vols., Taipei: Taiwan shangwu shudian.

Ďurovičová, Nataša and Kathleen Newman (eds) (2010), *World Cinemas, Transnational Perspectives*, London: Routledge.

Dyer, Geoff (2010), "China Needs Admirers to Match Its Ambitions," *Financial Times* (January 3), http://www.ft.com/cms/s/0/662c409a-f878–11de-beb8–00144fcab49a.html. Accessed January 4, 2010.

Dyer, Richard (1979), *Stars*, London: British Film Institute.

EastSouthWestNorth (2009), "The Top Ten Movies that Suck Up to China" (from 放牧都市 blog), http://www.zonaeuropa.com/20091122_1.htm. Accessed December 23, 2009.

Eberhard, Wolfram (1972), *The Chinese Silver Screen: Hong Kong and Taiwanese Motion Pictures in the 1960s*, Taipei: Orient Cultural Service.

Eckholm, Erik (1998), "Why 'Titanic' Conquered the World; Beijing," *New York Times* (April 26), http://www.nytimes.com/1998/04/26/movies/why-titanic-conquered-the-world-beijing.html. Accessed January 2, 2010.

Editorial (2008), "Dianying *Wuye zhicheng* yanyuan yanzhong shiyan daozhi dianying zao beige 电影《无野之城》演员严重失言导致电影遭杯葛 (Actor of *City Without Baseball* seriously misspoke, leading to boycott of film), *Fridae* (June 12), http://www.fridae.com/newsfeatures/2008/06/12/6072. Accessed January 13, 1010.

Edwards, Louise (2010), "Military Celebrity in China: The Evolution of 'Heroic and Model Servicemen'," in *Celebrity in China* (eds Louise Edwards and Elaine Jeffreys), Hong Kong: Hong Kong University Press, 21–44.

Edwards, Louise and Elaine Jeffreys (eds) (2010), *Celebrity in China*, Hong Kong: Hong Kong University Press.

Ehrlich, Linda and David Desser (eds) (1994), *Cinematic Landscapes: Observations on the Visual Arts and Cinema of China and Japan*, Austin: University of Texas Press.

Eisenstein, Sergei M. (1942), *The Film Sense* (trans. Jay Leyda), New York: Harcourt Brace Jovanovich.

Eisenstein, Sergei M. (1949), *The Film Form* (trans. Jay Leyda), New York: Harcourt Brace Jovanovich.

Eisenstein, Sergei M. (1988), "The Fourth Dimension in Cinema," in *Eisenstein: Writings 1922–1934* (ed. Richard Taylor), Bloomington: Indiana University Press, 181–94.

Eleftheriotis, Dimitris and Gary Needham (eds) (2006), *Asian Cinemas: A Reader and Guide*, Honolulu: University of Hawaii Press.

Elmer, Greg and Mike Gasher (eds) (2005), *Contracting Out Hollywood: Runaway Productions and Foreign Location Shooting*, Lanham, MD: Rowman and Littlefield.

Elsaesser, Thomas (1987), "Tales of Sound and Fury: Observations on the Family Melodrama," in *Home Is Where the Heart Is: Studies in Melodrama and the Woman's Film* (ed. Christine Gledhill), London: British Film Institute, 43–69.

Eng, David L. (1993), "Love at Last Site: Waiting for Oedipus in Stanley Kwan's *Rouge*," *Camera Obscura* 32: 75–101.

Ent.163.com (Netease entertainment 网易娱乐) (2009a), "Zhang Weiping paohong Han Sanping gao longduan: dajia gan nu bu gan yan" 张伟平炮轰韩三平搞垄断：大家敢怒不敢言 (Zhang Weiping bombards Han Sanping for running a monopoly: Everyone dares to be angry, but no one dares to speak) (December 17, from *Yangcheng wanbao* 羊城晚报), http://ent.163.com/09/1217/11/5QNVF15300033O66.html. Accessed December 28, 2009.

Ent.163.com (Netease entertainment 网易娱乐) (2009b), "Zhongying huiying Zhang Weiping paohong: meiyong jinkoupian daya guochan pian" 中影回应张伟平炮轰：没用进口片打压国产片 (China Film responds to Zhang Weiping's bombardment: We haven't used imported films to suppress Chinese films) (December 18, from *Guangzhou ribao* 广州日报), http://ent.163.com/09/1218/04/5QPR1830000300B1.html. Accessed December 19, 2009.

Ent.sina.com (Sina Entertainment 新浪网影音娱乐) (2009), "Zhongying fayanren fanbo Zhang Weiping paohong yanlun: bu cunzai longduan" 中影发言人反驳张伟平炮轰言论：不存在垄断 (China Film spokesperson refutes Zhang Weiping's attack: No such monopoly exists), http://ent.sina.com.cn/m/c2009–12–18/03032814392.shtml. Accessed December 28, 2009.

Epstein, Jean (1921), "Magnification" (trans. Stuart Liebman), in *French Film Theory and Criticism: A History/Anthology 1907–1939* (ed. Richard Abel), Princeton: Princeton University Press, 1988, vol. 1: 235–41; originally published as "Grossissement," in *Bonjour Cinema*, Paris: Editions de la sirène.

Erens, Patricia Brett (2000), "Crossing Borders: Time, Memory, and the Construction of Identity in *Song of the Exile*," *Cinema Journal* 39.4: 43–59.

Ezra, E. and T. Rowden (2005), "What is Transnational Cinema?" in *Transnational Cinema: The Film Reader* (eds E. Ezra and T. Rowden), London: Routledge 2005, 1–12.

Fan, Lizhen 范丽珍 (2008), "30 nian: cong 'lutian qiuchang' dao wuxingji yingyuan" 30 年：从露天球场到五星级影院 (Thirty years: From open air showings on athletic fields to five star theaters), *Zhongguo dianying bao* 中国电影报 (Chinese film news) (December 4): 16–17.

Fan, Lizhen 范丽珍 (2009), "Piaofang shouru nishi zengcheng guochanpian zai chao jinkou pian" 票房收入逆势增长国产片再超进口片 (Box office income for domestic films again counters and surpasses imported films), *Zhongguo dianying shichang* (August): 9–13.

Fan, Zheng 钒铮 (2008), "*Se · jie*, chuixiang suimo guochan yingshi: zong dongyuan hao-jiao 色·戒, 吹响岁末国产影视：总动员号角 (*Lust, Caution*, sounding the bugle to mobilize filmgoers for domestic films at the end of the year), *Zhongguo dianying shichang* (January): 18–20.

Farquhar, Mary (2010), "Jackie Chan: Star Work as Pain and Triumph," in *Chinese Film Stars* (eds Mary Farquhar and Yingjin Zhang), London: Routledge, 180–95.

Farquhar, Mary and Yingjin Zhang (eds) (2008), Special issue on "Chinese Stars," *Journal of Chinese Cinemas* 2.2.

Farquhar, Mary and Yingjin Zhang (eds) (2010), *Chinese Film Stars*, London: Routledge.

Fei, Mu 费穆 (1934a), "'Daoxu fa' yu 'xuanxiang' zuoyong" "倒叙"法与""悬想"作用 (The functions of "backtrack" narrative and "theatrical suspense"), in *1897–2001 Bainian Zhongguo dianying lilun wenxuan 1897–2001* 百年中国电影理论文选 (Selected works from a hundred years of Chinese film theory 1897–2001) (ed. Ding Yaping), Beijing: Wenhua yishu chubanshe, vol. 1: 214–15.

Fei, Mu 费穆 (1934b), "Lüe tan 'kongqi'" 略谈"空气" (On "aura"), in *1897–2001 Bainian Zhongguo dianying lilun wenxuan 1897–2001* 百年中国电影理论文选 (Selected works from a hundred years of Chinese film theory 1897–2001) (ed. Ding Yaping), Beijing: Wenhua yishu chubanshe, vol. 1: 216–17.

Fei, Mu 费穆 (1948), "Guochanpian de chulu wenti" 国产片的出路问题 (Finding a way out for China-made films), in *1897–2001 Bainian Zhongguo dianying lilun wenxuan 1897–2001* 百年中国电影理论文选 (Selected works from a hundred years of Chinese film theory 1897–2001) (ed. Ding Yaping), Beijing: Wenhua yishu chubanshe, vol. 1: 331–40.

Felluga, Dino (2003), "Modules on Butler: On Performativity," *Introductory Guide to Critical Theory*, http://www.cla.purdue.edu/academic/engl/theory/genderandsex/modules/butlergendersex.html. Accessed November 12, 2010.

Feng, Qun 风群 (2009), *Li Minwei pingzhuan* 黎民伟评传 (A biography of Li Minwei), Beijing: Wenhua yishu chubanshe.

Feng, Xin 冯欣 (2008), "*Se · jie* pinglun ziliao zhailu" 《色·戒》评论资料摘录 (Extracts of criticism on *Lust, Caution*), *Dianying yishu* 1: 38–9.

Film Workshop (n.d.), http://www.filmworkshop.net/english/index.htm. Accessed March 10, 2010.

Fitzgerald, Carolyn (2008), "*Spring in a Small Town*: Gazing at Ruins," in *Chinese Films in Focus II* (ed. Chris Berry), London: British Film Institute, 205–11.

Florida, Richard (2005), *Cities and the Creative Class*, London: Routledge.

Ford, Stacilee (2008), *Mabel Cheung Yuen-ting's An Autumn's Tale*, Hong Kong: Hong Kong University Press.

Foucault, Michel (1977), "Nietzsche, Genealogy, History," in *Language, Counter-Memory-Practice: Selected Essays and Interviews by Michel Foucault* (ed. Donald F. Bouchard), Ithaca: Cornell University Press, 139–64.

Frater, Patrick (2008), "Hollywood Weighs Ying and Yang Of China," *Variety* (August 4), http://www.variety.com/article/VR1117989939?refCatId=2520&query=yin+yang. Accessed November 18, 2010.

French, Howard W. (2007), "Cinephiles, Pack Your Bags, an Uncut Version Awaits," *New York Times* (December 19): A4.

Fu, Poshek (2003), *Between Shanghai and Hong Kong: The Politics of Chinese Cinemas*, Stanford, CA: Stanford University Press.

Fu, Poshek (ed.) (2008), *China Forever: The Shaw Brothers and Diasporic Cinema*, Urbana: University of Illinois Press.

Fu, Poshek and David Desser (eds) (2000), *The Cinema of Hong Kong: History, Arts, Identity*, New York: Cambridge University Press.

Fung, Anthony Y. H. (2008), *Global Capital, Local Culture: Transnational Media Corporations in China*, New York: Peter Lang.

Gallagher, Mark (1997), "Masculinity in Translation: Jackie Chan's Transcultural Star Text," *Velvet Light Trap* 39: 23–41.

Gandhy, Behroze and Rosie Thomas (1990), "Three Indian Film Stars," in *Stardom: Industry of Desire* (ed. Christine Gledhill), London: Routledge, 107–31.

Gao, Weijin 高维进 (2003), *Zhongguo xinwen jilu dianying shi* 中国新闻纪录电影史 (A history of Chinese news and documentary films), Beijing: Zhongyang wenxian chubanshe.

Gao, Xiaojian 高小健 (2005), *Zhongguo xiqu dianying shi* 中国戏曲电影史 (A history of Chinese opera film), Beijing: Wenhua yishu chubanshe.

Gaudreault, André and Philippe Marion (2002), "The Cinema as a Model for the Genealogy of Media," *Convergence* 8.4: 12–18.

Giddens, Anthony (1990), *The Consequences of Modernity*, Stanford, CA: Stanford University Press.

GIO (Government Information Office, Republic of China) (1983), "The Motion Picture Act," http://www.gio.gov.tw/ct.asp?xItem=31551&ctNode=4041. Accessed December 7, 2009.

GIO (Government Information Office, Republic of China) (2009), "Taiwan Cinema," http://www.taiwancinema.com/mp.asp?mp=2. Accessed December 1, 2010.

Gledhill, Christine (1987), "The Melodramatic Field: An Investigation," in *Home Is Where the Heart Is* (ed. Christine Gledhill), London: British Film Institute, 5–39.

Gledhill, Christine (ed.) (1991), *Stardom: Industry of Desire*, London: Routledge.

Gledhill, Christine (2000), "Rethinking Genre," in *Reinventing Film Studies* (eds Christine Gledhill and Linda Williams), New York: Oxford University Press.

Gong, Jianong (Robert Kung) 龚稼农 (1968), *Gong Jianong congying huiyi lu* 龚稼农从影回忆录 (Gong Jianong's memoirs of his screen life), Hong Kong: Culture Books.

Gorbman, Claudia (1987), *Unheard Melodies: Narrative Film Music,* Bloomington: Indiana University Press.

Grant, Barry Keith (1998), "Ethnography in the First Person: Frederick Wiseman's *Titicut Follies*," in *Documenting the Documentary: Close Readings of Documentary Film and Video* (eds Barry Keith Grant and Jeannette Sloniowski), Detroit: Wayne State University Press, 238–53.

Gu, Kenfu 顾肯夫 (1921), "'Yingxi zazhi' fakan ci" 《影戏杂志》发刊词 (Introduction to the inaugural issue of *Shadowplay miscellany*), *Yingxi zazhi* 影戏杂志 (Shadowplay miscellany) 1.1, in *1897–2001 Bainian Zhongguo dianying lilun wenxuan 1897–2001* 百年中国电影理论文选 (Selected works from a hundred years of Chinese film theory 1897–2001) (ed. Ding Yaping), Beijing: Wenhua yishu chubanshe, vol. 1: 5–12.

Guback, Thomas H. (1969), *The International Film Industry: Western Europe and America since 1945*, Bloomington: Indiana University Press.

Gunning, Tom (1986), "The Cinema of Attraction: Early Film, Its Spectator and the Avant-Garde," *Wide Angle* 8.3–4: 1–14.

Gunning, Tom (1989), "An Aesthetic of Astonishment: Early Cinema and the (In)credulous Spectator," *Art and Text* 34: 31–45.

Gunning, Tom (2004), "What's the Point of an Index? or, Faking Photographs," *Nordicom Review* 25.1–2: 39–49.

Guo, Xiaohan 郭小寒 and Rong Chenpu 容晨朴 (2005), "Wu Wenguang, yong shenti jilu" 吴文光，用身体记录 (Wu Wenguang: Documenting with the body") (April 29), http://www.cheagle.com/fArticleView.exml?ArticleID=6320. Accessed November 9, 2009.

Guo, Xiaolu (2008), "Do I Stay or Do I Go," *Guardian* (April 28), http://www.guardian.co.uk/commentisfree/2008/apr/28/immigration.china. Accessed May 5, 2009.

Guo, Xiaolu (n.d.), "Interview with Flymedia," http://www.flypmedia.com/issues/07/#12/5. Accessed November 11, 2009.

Guojia dianying ziliaoguan 国家电影资料馆 (Chinese Taipei Film Archive) (ed.) (1966–2008), *Cinema in the Republic of China Yearbook*, Taipei: Guojia dianying ziliaoguan.

Halberstam, Judith (2005), *Transgender Bodies, Subcultural Lives*, New York: New York University Press.

Hang, Krista Van Fleit (2010), "Zhong Xinghuo: Communist Film Worker," in *Chinese Film Stars* (eds Mary Farquhar and Yingjin Zhang), London: Routledge, 109–18.

Hansen, Miriam Bratu (2000), "Fallen Women, Rising Stars, New Horizons: Shanghai Silent Film as Vernacular Modernism," *Film Quarterly* 54.1: 10–22.

Hao, Dazheng (1994), "Chinese Visual Representation: Painting and Cinema," in *Cinematic Landscapes: Observations on the Visual Arts and Cinema of China and Japan* (eds Linda Ehrlich and David Desser), Austin: University of Texas Press, 45–62.

Harbord, Janet (2002), *Film Cultures: Production, Distribution, Consumption*, Los Angeles: Sage.

Harris, Kristine (1999), "*The Romance of the Western Chamber* and the Classical Subject Film in 1920s Shanghai," in *Cinema and Urban Culture in Shanghai, 1922–1943* (ed. Yingjin Zhang), Stanford, CA: Stanford University Press, 51–73.

Harvey, David (2001), *Spaces of Capital: Towards a Critical Geography*, London: Routledge.

Hayward, Susan (2004), *Simone Signoret: The Star as Cultural Sign*, New York: Continuum.

He, Siying 何思颖 and He Huiling 何慧玲 (eds) (2002), *Jianxiao jianghu: Xu Ke yu Xianggang dianying* 剑啸江湖——徐克与香港电影 (Tsui Hark and Hong Kong film), Hong Kong: Hong Kong Film Archive.

Hennessy, Rosemary (2000), *Profit and Pleasure: Sexual Identities in Late Capitalism*, London: Routledge.

Henriot, Christian (1993), *Shanghai 1927–1937: Municipal Power, Locality and Modernization*, Berkeley: University of California Press.

Higgins, Dick (1984), *The Poetics and Theory of the Intermedia*, Carbondale: Southern Illinois University Press.

Higson, Andrew (1989), "The Concept of National Cinema," *Screen* 30.4: 36–46.

Hilmes, Michele (1997), *Radio Voices: American Broadcasting, 1922–1952*, Minneapolis: University of Minnesota Press.

Hilmes, Michele (2003), "Who We Are, Who We Are Not: The Battle of Global Paradigms," in *Planet TV: A Global Television Reader* (eds Lisa Parks and Shanti Kumar), New York: New York University Press, 53–73.

Hitchcock, Peter (1992), "The Aesthetics of Alienation, or China's 'Fifth Generation'," *Cultural Studies* 6.1: 116–41.

Hjort, Mette (2006), *Stanley Kwan's Center Stage*, Hong Kong: Hong Kong University Press.

Hjort, Mette (2010), "Ruan Lingyu: Reflections on an Individual Performance Style," in *Chinese Film Stars* (eds Mary Farquhar and Yingjin Zhang), London: Routledge, 32–49.

Ho, Sam and Wai-leng Ho (eds) (2002), *The Swordsman and His Jianghu: Tsui Hark and Hong Kong Film*, Hong Kong: Hong Kong Film Archive.

Hogan, Patrick Colm (2008), *Understanding Indian Movies: Culture, Cognition, and Cinematic Imagination*, Austin: University of Texas Press.

Hollinger, Karen (2006), *The Actress: Hollywood Acting and the Female Star*, London: Routledge.

Hong, Guo-Juin (2010), "Historiography of Absence: Taiwan Cinema before New Cinema," *Journal of Chinese Cinemas* 4.1: 5–14.

Hong Kong Film Archive (ed.) (1995), *Xianggang zaoqi dianying guiji 1896–1950* 香港早期电影轨迹 1896–1950 (Trajectory of Hong Kong Early Films 1896–1950), Hong Kong: Hong Kong Film Archive.

Hong Kong Film Archive (ed.) (1997), *Xianggang yingpian daquan* 香港影片大全 (Hong Kong Filmography, Vol. 1 [1913–1941]), Hong Kong: Hong Kong Film Archive.

Hong Kong Film Archive (ed.) (1998), *Xianggang yingpian daquan* 香港影片大全 (Hong Kong Filmography, Vol. 2 [1942–1949]), Hong Kong: Hong Kong Film Archive.

Hong Kong Film Archive (ed.) (2007), *Xianggang yingpian daquan* 香港影片大全 (Hong Kong Filmography, Vol. 6 [1965–1969]), Hong Kong: Hong Kong Film Archive.

Hou, Yao 侯曜 (1925, 1992), *Yingxi juben zuofa* 影戏剧本作法 (Techniques of writing shadowplay scripts), Shanghai: Taidong tushuju; reprinted in *Zhongguo dianying lilun wenxuan: 1920–1989* 中国电影理论文选 1920–1989 (Selected works of Chinese film theory, 1920–1989) (ed. Luo Yijun), Beijing: Wenhua yishu chubanshe, 1992, vol. 1: 47–65.

HSDFFG (Hunan sheng dianying faxing fangying gongsi) 湖南省电影发行放映公司 (Hunan provincial film distribution and exhibition company) (1978), *Yingpian (changpian jiemu) pianming paicibiao* 影片（长片节目）片名排次表 (Film [feature length] title list), Changsha: no publisher, 148.

HSDZBW (Heilongjiang sheng difang zhi bianzuan weiyuanhui) 黑龙江省地方志编纂委员会 (Gazetteer editorial committee of Heilongjiang province) (ed.) (2003), *Heilongjiang sheng zhi: di sishiliu juan, wenxue yishu zhi* 黑龙江省志: 第四十六卷, 文学艺术志 (Gazetteer of Heilongjiang province: Volume 46, culture and literature), Ha'erbin: Heilongjiang renmin chubanshe.

Hsia, C. T. (1999), *A History of Modern Chinese Fiction*, 3rd edn, Bloomington: Indiana University Press.

Hu, Brian (2004), "*Formula 17*: Testing a Formula for Mainstream Cinema in Taiwan," *Senses of Cinema* (December), http://archive.sensesofcinema.com/contents/05/34/formula_17.html. Accessed February 3, 2010.

Hu, Jintao 胡锦涛 (2007), *Zai Zhongguo gongchan dang di shiqi ci quanguo daibiao dahui shang de baogao* 在中国共产党第十七次全国代表大会上的报告 (Report at the seventeenth national congress of the Chinese Communist Party), http://news.xinhuanet.com/newscenter/2007–10/24/content_6938568.htm. Accessed March 14, 2010.

Hu, Jubin (2000), *Projecting a Nation: Chinese Cinema before 1949*, Hong Kong: Hong Kong University Press.

Hu, Ke 胡克 (2005), *Zhongguo dianying lilun shiping* 中国电影理论史评 (A critical history of Chinese film theory), Beijing: Zhongguo dianying chubanshe.

Hu, Ke 胡克 (2008), "Zouxiang dazhonghua de zhuliu dianying" 走向大众化的主流电影 (Toward the popularized mainstream film), *Dangdai dianying* 1: 10–4.

Hu, Rong 胡嵘 (2008a), "Hepaipian: jijie ziben boji yingshi" 合拍片: 集结资本搏击影视 (Coproductions: Concentrate capital, fight for movies and television), *Zhongguo dianying bao* 中国电影报 (January 10): 8.

Hu, Rong 胡嵘 (2008b), "Toushi Zhongguo dianying hesui shinian" 透视中国电影贺岁十年 (A perspective on ten years of Chinese New Year films), *Dianying yishu* 2: 56–60.

Hu, Xingliang 胡星亮 and Zhang Ruilin 张瑞麟 (eds) (1995), *Zhongguo dianying shi* 中国电影史 (Chinese film history), Beijing: Zhongyang guangbo dianshi daxue chubanshe.

Hua, Ximei 华锡梅, Ma Shouqing 马守清, Li Nianlu 李念芦, and Tian Junren 田俊人 (2005), Zhongguo dianying jishu bainian jishi 中国电影技术百年纪事 (Chronicle of the hundred years of Chinese film technology), *Yingshi jishu* (Film and television technology) 12.

Huang, Hans Tao-Ming (2006), "Cong boliquan dao tongzhi guo: rentong xing su yu xiuchi de xing/bie zhengzhi – yige *Niezi* de lianjie" 从玻璃圈到同志国：认同型塑与羞耻的性/别政治——一个《孽子》的连结 (From gay circle to homosexual nation: *Crystal Boys*, identity formation and politics of sexual shame), *Taiwan shehui yanjiu jikan* 台湾社会研究季刊 (Taiwan: A radical quarterly in social studies) 62.6: 1–36.

Huang, Jianye 黄建业 (2001), *Yang Dechang dianying yanjiu* 杨德昌电影研究 (Studies of Edward Yang's films), Taipei: Yuanliu.

Huang, Jianzhong 黄健中 (2002), "Xiao hua" 小花 (Little Flower), in *Bainian Zhongguo dianying lilun wenxuan* (ed. Ding Yaping), vol. 2: 49–64.

Huang, Ren 黄仁 (1994), *Dianying yu zhengzhi xuanchuan* 电影与政治宣传 (Film and government propaganda), Taipei: Wanxiang.

Huang, Ren 黄仁 (1999), *Xingzhe yingji: Li Xing, dianying, wushi nian* 行者影跡：李行，電影，五十年 (The passerby's trace: Li Xing, cinema, fifty years), Taipei: Shibao wenhua.

Huang, Ren 黄仁 (2004), *Taiwan yingping liushinian: Taiwan yingping shihua* 台湾影评六十年：台湾影评史话 (Sixty years of Taiwan film criticism: A history of film criticism in Taiwan), Taipei: Yatai.

Huang, Ren 黄仁 and Wang Wei 王唯 (eds) (2004), *Taiwan dianying bainian shihua* 台湾电影百年史话 (One hundred years of Taiwanese film), Taipei: Xuesheng.

Huang, Shixian 黄式宪 (1992). "Zhongguo dianying daoyan 'xingzuo' jiqi yishu puxi" 中国电影导演"星座"及其艺术谱系 (Chinese film directors' star galaxies and their artistic features), *Dangdai dianying* 6: 77–85.

Huang, Yu-Shan 黄玉珊 (2006), "Nüxing yingxiang zai Taiwan – Taiwan nüxingdianying fazhanjianshi" 女性影像在台湾——台湾女性电影发展简史 (Cinematic images of women in Taiwan – a brief history of the development of women's cinema in Taiwan), in *Nüxing, yingxiang, shu: congnüxingyingzhan kan nüxingyingxiang zhi zaixian* 女性，影像，书：从女性影展看女性影像之再现 (Women, cinematic images, and books: On representation of women's image from women's film festivals), Taipei: Shulin.

Huang, Zhaohan 黄兆汉 (ed.) (2009), *Changtian luo caixia: Ren Jianhui de juyi shijie* 长天落彩霞：任剑辉的剧艺世界 (Yam Kim-fai: Portrait of a Chinese opera performance prodigy), Hong Kong: Sanlian.

Huang, Zongying 黄宗英 (1957), "Jiu shehui de xisheng ping: daonian Zhou Xuan" 旧社会的牺牲品 ——悼念周璇 (Victim of the old China – in memory of Zhou Xuan), *Zhongguo dianying* 中国电影 (Chinese cinema) 10.

Hudson, James (1947), "喜相逢In Other Words: Boy Meets Girl," *San Francisco Chronicle* (September 21), http://softfilm.blogspot.com/2009/03/joseph-sunn-jue-darryl-zanuck-of.html. Accessed July 8, 2009.

Hung, Chang-tai (1985), *Going to the People: Chinese Intellectuals and Folk Literature, 1918–1937*, Cambridge, MA: Council on East Asian Studies, Harvard University.

Hunt, Leon (2003), *Kung Fu Cult Masters: From Bruce Lee to Crouching Tiger*, London: Wallflower Press.

Hunt, Leon and Leung Wing-fai (eds) (2008), *East Asian Cinemas: Exploring Transnational Connections on Film*, London: I. B. Tauris.

Iordanova, Dina and Ruby Cheung (eds) (2010), *Film Festival Yearbook 2: Film Festivals and Imagined Communities*, St. Andrews, UK: St. Andrews Film Studies.

Iordanova, Dina and Ruby Cheung (eds) (2011), *Film Festival Yearbook 3: Film Festivals and East Asia*, St. Andrews, UK: St. Andrews Film Studies.

Iordanova, Dina with Ragan Rhyne (2009), *Film Festival Yearbook 1: The Festival Circuit*, St. Andrews, UK: St. Andrews Film Studies.

Jacobs, Jane (1984), *Cities and the Wealth of Nations*, New York: Random House.

Jaffee, Valerie (2006), "'Every Man a Star': The Ambivalent Cult of Amateur Art in New Chinese Documentaries," in *From Underground to Independent: Alternative Film Culture in Contemporary China* (eds Paul Pickowicz and Yingjin Zhang), Lanham, MD: Rowman and Littlefield, 77–108.

James, Nick (2008), "Cruel Intentions: Ang Lee," *Sight and Sound* (January), http://www.bfi.org.uk/sightandsound/feature/49419. Accessed November 12, 2010.

Jameson, Fredric (1986), "Third-World Literature in the Era of Multinational Capitalism," *Social Text* 15: 82–104.

Jarvie, Ian C. (1977) *Window on Hong Kong: A Sociology Study of the Hong Kong Film Industry and Its Audience*, Hong Kong: University of Hong Kong Press.

Jefferys, Elaine and Louise Edwards (2010), "Celebrity/China," in *Celebrity in China* (eds Louise Edwards and Elaine Jefferys), 1–20.

Jia, Leilei 贾磊磊 (2005a), *Yingxiang de chuanbo* 影像的传播 (Disseminating images), Guilin: Guangxi shifan daxue chubanshe.

Jia, Leilei 贾磊磊 (2005b), *Zhongguo wuxia dianying shi* 中国武侠电影史 (A history of Chinese martial arts films), Beijing: Wenhua yishu chubanshe.

Jia, Leilei 贾磊磊 (2008), "Chonggou Zhongguo zhuliu dianying de jingdian moshi yu jiazhi tixi" 重构中国主流电影的经典模式与价值体系 (Reconstructing the classic mode and value system of Chinese mainstream film), *Dangdai Dianying* 1: 21–5.

Jia, Ming 佳明 (ed.) (2002), *Zhongguo dianying: chuangzuo yu shichang* 中国电影: 创作与市场 (Chinese film: Production and market), Beijing: Zhongguo dianying chubanshe.

Jia, Zhangke 贾樟柯 (2003), "Yeyu dianying shidai jijiang zaici daolai" 业余电影时代即将再次到来 (The age of amateur cinema will return), in *Yigeren de yingxiang: DV wanquan shouce* 一个人的影像: DV完全手册 (*All about DV: Works, making, creation, comments*) (eds Zhang Xianmin 张献民 and Zhang Yaxuan 张亚璇), Beijing: Zhongguo qingnian chubanshe, 306–8.

Jia, Zhangke 贾樟柯 (2009), *Jia xiang 1996–2008: Jia Zhangke dianying shouji* 贾想 *1996–2008*: 贾樟柯电影手记 (Jia's thoughts, 1996–2008: Jia Zhangke's notes on film), Beijing: Beijing daxue chubanshe.

Jiang, Junxu 江俊绪 (1986), "Xie Jin dianying shuyu shidai he guanzhong" 谢晋电影属于时代和观众 (Xie Jin's film belongs to the times and audience), *Wenhui bao* 文汇报 (July 8).

Jiao, Xiongping (Peggy Chiao) 焦雄屏 (ed.) (1988), *Taiwan xindianying* 台湾新电影 (Taiwan New Cinema), Taipei: Shibao.

Jiao, Xiongping (Peggy Chiao) 焦雄屏 (2005), *Ying xiang Zhongguo* 映像中国 (Imaging China), Shanghai: Fudan daxue chubanshe.

Jiao, Xiongping 焦雄屏 and Qu Guizhi 区桂芝 (eds) (2008), *Li Xing: yijiazi de huihuang* 李行：一甲子的辉煌 (Li Xing: Glorious for sixty years), Taipei: Yuesheng.

Jin, Shihui 金士会 and Di Zhonghai 狄仲海 (1979), "Yunmenwu jitan *Chuangwai yu Muqin Sanshisui*" 云门舞集谈《窗外》与《母亲三十岁》 (Cloud Gate Dance Troupe discusses *Outside the Window* and *Story of Mother*), *Yingxiang zazhi* 影响杂志 (Influence) 24: 20–3.

Johnson, Matthew David (2006), "'A Scene Beyond Our Line of Sight': Wu Wenguang and New Documentary Cinema's Politics of Independence," in *From Underground to Independent: Alternative Film Culture in Contemporary China* (eds Paul Pickowicz and Yingjin Zhang), Lanham, MD: Rowman and Littlefield, 47–76.

Johnston, Alastair Iain (2003), "Is China a Status Quo Power?" *International Security* 27.4: 5–56.

Kan dianying (2007), "*Se · Jie* shi yizhong rensheng" 《色戒》是一种人生 (*Lust, Caution* is way of life), *Kan dianying* 看电影 (Watching film) 18: 27–30.

Kaplan, E. Ann (1991), "Problematizing Cross-Cultural Analysis: The Case of Women in the Recent Chinese Cinema," in *Perspectives on Chinese Cinema* (ed. Chris Berry), London: British Film Institute, 141–55.

Kaplan, E. Ann (ed.) (2000), *Feminism and Film*, New York: Oxford University Press.

Kaplan, E. Ann (forthcoming), "Affect, Meaning, and Trauma Past Tense: Hu Mei's *Army Nurse (Nuer lou)* (1985) and *Letter from an Unknown Woman (Yige moshen nüren de laixin)* (2004)," in *Engendering Cinema: Chinese Women Filmmakers Inside and Outside China* (ed. Lingzhen Wang), New York: Columbia University Press.

Kawin, Bruce F. (1992), *How Movies Work*, Berkeley: University of California Press.

Kay, Jeremy (2004), "Warner Bros Signs First Volume TV Deal in China," *Screen Daily* (March 31), http://www.screendaily.com/warner-bros-signs-first-volume-tv-deal-in-china/4018002.article. Accessed December 7, 2009.

Ke, Ling 柯灵 (1960), "Shilun nongcunpian – jiantan dianying de minzuhua, qunzhonghua" 试论农村片——兼谈电影的民族化、群众化 (On rural films: Some thoughts on nationalization and popularization of film), *Dianying yishu* 电影艺术 9: 57–63.

Keane, Michael (2001), "Broadcasting Policy, Creative Compliance and the Myth of Civil Society in China," *Media, Culture and Society* 23.6: 783–98.

Keane, Michael (2004), "Brave New World: Understanding China's Creative Vision," *International Journal of Cultural Policy* 10.3: 265–79.

Keane, Michael (2006a), "Exporting Chinese Culture: Industry Financing Models in Film and Television," *Westminster Papers in Communications and Culture* 3.1: 11–27.

Keane, Michael (2006b), "From Made in China to Created in China," *International Journal of Cultural Studies* 9.3: 285–96.

Keane, Michael (2007), *Created in China: The Great New Leap Forward*, London: Routledge.

Keane, Michael (2009), "Design for a Post-Economic Crisis China," paper presented at the 2009 Chinese Studies of Australia Conference, University of Sydney, July 8–11, https://wiki.cci.edu.au/display/CIA/Rethinking+China's+emergence. Accessed December 27, 2009.

Keane, Michael, Anthony Y. H. Fung, and Albert Moran (2007), *New Television, Globalization, and East Asian Cultural Imagination*, Hong Kong: Hong Kong University Press.

Kehr, Dave (2009), "The Next Big (Well, Wide) Thing," *New York Times* (March 29).

Kellner, Douglas (1998), "New Taiwan Cinema in the 80s," *Jump Cut* 42: 101–15.

Khoo, Gaik Cheng (2009), "What is Diasporic Chinese Cinema in Southeast Asia," *Journal of Chinese Cinemas* 3.1: 69–71.

Khoo, Olivia (2007), *The Chinese Exotic: Modern Diasporic Femininity*, Hong Kong: Hong Kong University Press.

King, Barry (2010), "Stardom, Celebrity, and the Money Form," *Velvet Light Trap* 65: 7–19.

Kirby, William C. (2000), "Engineering China: Birth of the Developmental State, 1928–1937," in *Becoming Chinese: Passages to Modernity and Beyond* (ed. Wen-hsin Yeh), Berkeley: University of California Press, 137–60.

Klinger, Barbara (1994), *Melodrama and Meaning: History, Meaning, and the Films of Douglas Sirk*, Bloomington: Indiana University Press.

Kolker, Robert Phillip (1980), *A Cinema of Loneliness*, New York: Oxford University Press.

Kolker, Robert Phillip (1983), *The Altering Eye: Contemporary International Cinema*, New York: Oxford University Press.

Kowallis, Jon von (1997), "The Diaspora in Postmodern Taiwan and Hong Kong Film: Framing Stan Lai's *The Peach Blossom Land* with Allen Fong's *Ah Ying*," in *Transnational Chinese Cinemas: Identity, Nationhood, Gender* (ed. Sheldon Hsiao-Peng Lu), Honolulu: University of Hawaii Press, 169–77.

Kracauer, Siegfried (1960), *Theory of Film: The Redemption of Physical Reality*, Oxford: Oxford University Press.

Kraicer, Shelly (2009), "Pushing Beyond Indie Conventions," dGenerate Films, http://dgeneratefilms.com/critical-essays/shelly-kraicer-pushing-beyond-indie-conventions/. Accessed May 15, 2011.

Kuo, Jason C. (2000), *Art and Cultural Politics in Postwar Taiwan*, Seattle: University of Washington Press.

Lai, Shek (ed.) (2003), *The Diary of Lai Man-wai*, Hong Kong: Hong Kong Film Archive.

Lam, Michael 迈克 (ed.) (2004), *Ren Jianhui duben* 任剑辉读本 (A Yam Kim-fai reader), Hong Kong: Hong Kong Film Archive.

Lam, Perry (2008), "Cape of Good Hope," *Muse* 22: 105–7.

Lam, Willy (2009), "Chinese Media State Goes Global," *Asia Times Online* (January 30), http://www.atimes.com/atimes/China/KA30Ad01.html. Accessed March 14, 2010.

Lampton, David M. (2008), *The Three Faces of Chinese Power*, Berkeley: University of California Press.

Landreth, Jonathan (2005), "Perspectives: China – Taking the Long View," *Hollywood Reporter* (July 28), http://www.hollywoodreporter.com/hr/search/article_display.jsp?vnu_content_id=1001014299. Accessed June 23, 2008.

Landreth, Jonathan (2006), "China Launches Film Sales Unit," *Hollywood Reporter* (September 20), http://www.allbusiness.com/services/motion-pictures/4918586-1.html. Accessed June 21, 2008.

Larson, Wendy (1995), "Zhang Yimou: Inter/National Aesthetics and Erotics," in *Cultural Encounters – China, Japan, and the West: Essays Commemorating 25 Years of East Asian Studies at the University of Aarhus* (eds Soren Clausen, Roy Starrs, and Anne Wedell-Wedellsborg), Aarhus, Denmark: Aarhus University Press, 215–26.

Lasker, Bruno (1937), "Propaganda as an Instrument of National Policy," *Pacific Affairs* 10.2: 152–60.

Lau, Jenny Kwok Wah (1994), "*Judou*: An Experiment in Color and Portraiture in Chinese Cinema," in *Cinematic Landscapes: Observations on the Visual Arts and Cinema of China and Japan* (eds Linda Ehrlich and David Desser), Austin: University of Texas Press, 127–45.

Lau, Jenny Kwok Wah (2005), "*Peking Opera Blues*: Exploding Genre, Gender and History," in *Film Analysis: A Norton Reader* (eds Jeffrey Geiger and R. L. Rutsky), New York: W. W. Norton, 738–54.

Law, Kar (1994), "An Overview of Hong Kong's New Wave Cinema," in *At Full Speed: Hong Kong Cinema in a Borderless World* (ed. Esther C. M. Yau), Minneapolis: University of Minnesota Press, 31–52.

Law, Kar (1997), "Archetypes and Variations: Observations on Six Cantonese Films," in *Cantonese Melodrama, 1950–1969*, The Tenth Hong Kong International Film Festival, Hong Kong: Urban Council.

Law, Kar and Frank Bren (2004), *Hong Kong Cinema: A Cross-Cultural View*, Lanham, MD: Scarecrow.

Law, Kar 罗卡 and Lai Shek 黎锡 (eds) (1999), *Li Minwei: ren, shidai, dianying* 黎民伟: 人, 时代, 电影 (Lai Man-wai: The man, the time, and cinema), Hong Kong: Mingchuang.

Law, Kar 罗卡, Zhuo Botang 卓伯棠, and Wu Hao 吴昊 (eds) (1997), *Xianggang dianying leixing lun* 香港电影类型论 (Genre theory of Hong Kong film), Hong Kong: Oxford University Press.

Leaders Magazine (2008), "A Global Ambassador for Chinese Movies: An Interview with Yan Xiaoming, President, Movie Channel Program Center of China, Beijing," *Leaders Magazine* 28.4: 60.

Leary, Charles (2003), "Performing the Documentary, or Making It to the Other Bank," http://archive.sensesofcinema.com/contents/03/27/performing_documentary.html. Accessed November 9, 2009.

Ledderose, Lothar (1973), "Subject Matter in Early Chinese Painting Criticism," *Oriental Art* N.S. 19.1: 69–83.

Lee, Daw-ming (2009), "A Preliminary Study of the Market for Documentaries in Taiwan," *Asian Cinema* 20.2: 68–82.

Lee, Leo Ou-fan (1991), "The Tradition of Modern Chinese Cinema: Some Preliminary Explorations and Hypotheses," in *Perspectives on Chinese Cinema* (ed. Chris Berry), London: British Film Institute, 6–20.

Lee, Leo Ou-fan (1994), "Two Films from Hong Kong: Parody and Allegory," in *New Chinese Cinemas: Forms, Identities, Politics* (eds Nick Browne et al.), New York: Cambridge University Press, 202–15.

Lee, Leo Ou-fan (1999), *Shanghai Modern: The Flowering of a New Urban Culture in China, 1930–1945*, Cambridge, MA: Harvard University Press.

Lee, Leo Ou-fan (2008), "Ang Lee's *Lust, Caution* and Its Reception," *Boundary 2* 35.3: 223–38.

Lee, Nikki J. Y. (2005), *Travelling Films: Western Criticism, Labelling Practice and Self-Orientalized East Asian Films*, PhD dissertation, Goldsmiths College, University of London.

Lee, Sangjoon (2011), "Table 1: The Asia-Pacific Film Festival (from 1954)," in *Film Festival Yearbook 3: Film Festivals and East Asia* (eds Dina Iordanova and Ruby Cheung), St. Andrews, UK: St. Andrews Film Studies, 242–6.

Legge, James (1960), *The Chinese Classics, IV: The She King or The Book of Poetry*, Hong Kong: Hong Kong University Press.

Lent, John A. and Ying Xu (2010), "Chinese Animation Film: From Experimentation to Digitalization," in *Art, Politics, and Commerce in Chinese Cinema* (eds Ying Zhu and Stanley Rosen), Hong Kong: Hong Kong University Press, 111–25.

Leonard, Mark (2008), *What Does China Think?* New York: Public Affairs.

Lessing, Gotthold Ephraim (1766), *Laokoön: An Essay on the Limits of Painting and Poetry* (trans. Ellen Frothingham), Boston: Little, Brown, 1910.

Leung, Helen Hok-sze (2008), *Undercurrents: Queer Culture and Postcolonial Hong Kong*, Vancouver: University of British Columbia Press.

Lewin, Kurt (1947), "Frontiers in Group Dynamics II: Channels of Group Life; Social Planning and Action Research," *Human Relations* 1.2: 143–53.

Leyda, Jay (1960), *Kino: A History of the Russian and Soviet Film*, London: Allen and Unwin.

Leyda, Jay (1972), *Dianying – Electric Shadows: An Account of Films and the Film Audience in China*, Cambridge, MA: MIT Press.

Li, Caixia 李彩霞 (2006), "Lun dianying *Malu tianshi* zhong yinyue suo chengzai de xushi gongneng" 论电影《马路天使》中音乐所承载的叙事功能 (On the narrative functions carried by the music in the film *Street Angel*), *Zaozhuang xueyuan xuebao* (Journal of Zaozhuang College) 6: 99–102.

Li, Chao 李超 (2008), *1905–1949 Zhongguo dianying: kongjian chengxian 1905–1949* 中国电影空间呈现 (1905–1949 Chinese cinema: The representation of space), Beijing: Zhongguo dianying chubanshe.

Li, Cheuk-to (1994), "The Return of the Father: Hong Kong New Wave and Its Chinese Context in the 1980s," in *New Chinese Cinemas: Forms, Identities, Politics* (eds Nick Browne et al.), New York: Cambridge University Press, 160–79.

Li, Cheuk-to (ed.) (2009), *A Tribute to Romantic Visions: 25th Anniversary of Film Workshop*, Hong Kong: Hong Kong International Film Festival.

Li, Daoxin 李道新 (2000), *Zhongguo dianying shi, 1937–1945* 中国电影史 1937–1945 (A history of Chinese film, 1937–1945), Beijing: Shoudu shida chubanshe.

Li, Daoxin 李道新 (2002), *Zhongguo dianying piping shi* 中国电影批评史 (A history of Chinese film criticism), Beijing: Beijing daxue chubanshe.

Li, Daoxin 李道新 (2005), *Zhongguo dianying wenhua shi* 中国电影文化史 (A history of Chinese film culture), Beijing: Beijing daxue chubanshe.

Li, Daoxin 李道新 (2006), *Zhongguo dianyingshi yanjiu zhuanti* 中国电影史研究专题 (Monographic study of the history of Chinese film), Beijing: Beijing daxue chubanshe.

Li, Dian (2003), "Clara Law," *Senses of Cinema* (August), http://archive.sensesofcinema. com/contents/directors/03/law.html. Accessed January 20, 2010.

Li, Hongyu 李宏宇 (2008), "'Gongfu xiongmao' gunchuqu?" 功夫熊猫滚出去? (Should "Kungfu Panda" get the hell out of here?), *Nanfang zhoumo* 南方周末 (Southern weekend) (June 26): D21, 27.

Li, Jie (1990), "Xie Jin's Era Should End" (trans. Hou Jianping), in *Chinese Film Theory: A Guide to the New Era* (eds George Semsel et al.), New York: Praeger, 147–8.

Li, Suyuan 郦苏元 (2005), *Zhongguo xiandai dianying lilun shi* 中国现代电影理论史 (A history of modern Chinese film theory), Beijing: Wenhua yishu chubanshe.

Li, Suyuan 郦苏元 and Hu Jubin 胡菊彬 (1997), *Zhongguo wusheng dianying shi* 中国无声电影史 (History of Chinese silent film), Beijing: Zhongguo dianying chubanshe.

Li, Tao 李涛 (1996), "Ting Tian Han jun yanjiang hou" 听田汉君演讲后 (After listening to Mr. Tian Han's speech *Zhongguo wusheng dianying* 中国无声电影 (Chinese silent film) (ed. Dai Xiaolan), Beijing: Zhongguo dianying chubanshe, 498–99.

Li, Tianduo 李天铎 (ed.) (1996) *Dangdai huayu dianying lunshu* 当代华语电影论述 (Contemporary Chinese film discourse), Taipei: Shidai wenhua.

Li, Tianduo 李天铎 (1997), *Taiwan dianying, shehui yu lishi* 台湾电影、社会与历史 (Taiwan film, society and history), Taipei: Yatai.

Li, Yiming 李奕明 (1999), "Xie Jin dianying zai Zhongguo dianyingshi shang de diwei" 谢晋电影在中国电影史上的地位 (The position of Xie Jin's film in Chinese film history), *Dianying yishu* 2: 4–22.

Li, Yizhuang 李以庄 (1994), "Xianggang dianying yu Xianggang shehui bianqian" 香港电影与香港社会变迁 (Hong Kong film and social changes in Hong Kong), *Dianying yishu* 2: 15–23.

Liang, Liang 梁良 (1998), *Lun liang'an sandi dianying* 论两岸三地电影 (On films of the mainland, Taiwan and Hong Kong), Taiwan: Maolin.

Liang, Xinhua 梁新华 and Mi Zou 谜舟 (eds) (1987), *Xin dianying zhi si* 新电影之死 (Death of the new cinema), Taipei: Tangshan.

Liao, Gene-fon 廖金凤, Cheuk Pak Tong 卓伯棠, Poshek Fu 傅葆石, and Yung Sai-shing 容世诚 (eds) (2003), *Shao shi yingshi diguo* 邵氏影视帝国 (The Shaw film and television empire), Taibei: Maitian.

Liao, Kuang-Sheng (2002), "Experiences and Major Policies in Taiwan's Development," in *Taiwan's Modernization in Global Perspective* (ed. Peter Chow), Westport, CT: Praeger, 285–93.

Liao, Ping-hui (1993), "Rewriting Taiwanese National History: The February 28 Incident as Historical Spectacle," *Public Culture* 5.2: 281–96.

Lim, Bliss Cua (2001), "Spectral Times: The Ghost Film as Historical Allegory," *Positions* 9.2: 287–329.

Lim, Bliss Cua (2009), *Translating Time: Cinema, the Fantastic, and Temporal Critique*, Durham, NC: Duke University Press.

Lim, Dennis (2007), "In Ang Lee's 'Lust, Caution,' Love is Beautiful to See, Impossible to Hold," *New York Times* (August 27).

Lim, Song Hwee (2006), *Celluloid Comrades: Representations of Male Homosexuality in Contemporary Chinese Cinemas*, Honolulu: University of Hawaii Press.

Lim, Song Hwee (2007), "Positioning Auteur Theory in Chinese Cinema Studies: Intratextuality, Intertextuality and Paratextuality in the Films of Tsai Ming-liang," *Journal of Chinese Cinemas* 1.3: 223–45.

Lin, Lining 林俐凝 (2007), "2007 nian Dianying pingdao dianshi dianying yantaohui zhongshu" 2007年电影频道电视电影研讨会综述 (A summary of the Movie Channel conference on Chinese telefilm study), *Dangdai Dianying* 2: 72–7.

Lin, Niantong 林年同 (1984), "Zhongguo dianying lilun yanjiu zhong youguan gudian meixue wenti de tantao" 中国电影理论研究中有关古典美学问题的探讨 (The question of the classical aesthetics in Chinese film theory studies), *Dangdai Dianying* 2: 100–7.

Lin, Niantong 林年同 (1985), *Jing you* 镜游 (Roaming images), Hong Kong: Shuye.

Lin, Niantong 林年同 (1991), *Zhongguo dianying meixue* 中国电影美学 (Chinese film aesthetics), rev. edn, Taipei: Yunchen.

Lin, Qixing 林启星 and Hui Jingchao 会敬超 (eds) (1979), "Renshi Song Cunshou – Song Cunshou fangwen lu" 认识宋存寿——宋存寿访问录 (Understanding Song Cunshou – a Song Cunshou interview), *Yingxiang zazhi* 24: 26–31.

Lin, Wenqi 林文淇, Shen Xiaoyin 沈晓茵, and Li Zhenya 李振亚 (eds) (2000), *Xilian rensheng: Hou Xiaoxian dianying yanjiu* 戏恋人生——侯孝贤电影研究 (Theater lover's life: Studies of Hou Hsiao-hsien films), Taipei: Maitian.

Lin, Xiaoping (2009), *Children of Marx and Coca-Cola: Chinese Avant-Garde Art and Independent Cinema*, Honolulu: University of Hawaii Press.

Lin, Xinhong 林杏鸿 (1998), "Lunwen zhaiyao" 论文摘要：《台湾女导演创作影像探讨——权力与环境下的风格再现》 (Thesis abstract: "Exploration of cinematic images by Taiwan woman directors"), *Guoli Chenggongdaxue funü yu liangxing yanjiu jianbao* 国立成功大学妇女与两性研究室简报 (Newsletter of women's and gender studies, National Chenggong University) 7: 13.

Lin, Xudong (2005), "Documentary in Mainland China," *Documentary Box* 26 (October), 24–36.

Lindsay, Vachel (1915), *The Art of the Moving Picture*, New York: Macmillan; reprinted New York: Modern Library, 2000.

Ling, Yan 凌燕 (1999), "Xin dushi shimin shenhua" 新都市市民神话 (The myths of the new urban citizens), *Dianying wenxue* 电影文学 (Film literature) 11: 11–4.

Liu, Hanwen 刘汉文 (2011), "2010 niandu Zhongguo dianying chanye fazhan fenxi baogao" 2010 年度中国电影产业发展分析报告 (An analysis of the development of the Chinese film industry in 2010), *Dangdai dianying* 3: 17.

Liu, Heng 刘恒 (2007), *Jijiehao* 集结号 (Assembly), Beijing: Renmin wenxue chubanshe.

Liu, Jia 刘嘉 (2009), "Cong yinmu shu de bianhua kaoliang Zhongguo dianying shichanghua jincheng" 从银幕数的变化考量中国电影市场化进程 (Judging the development of the film marketization of Chinese films from the change in the number of screens), *Dianying yishu* 5: 91–100.

Liu, Lydia H. (1995), *Translingual Practice: Literature, National Culture, and Translated Modernity – China, 1900–1937*, Stanford, CA: Stanford University Press.

Liu, Rui 刘锐 (2008), "Lishi piaofang paihangbang xianshi wo guo da dianying chanye yi chuju guimo" 历史票房排行榜显示我国大电影产业已初具规模 (Historical box office rankings for China's blockbuster films reveal that a film industry has begun to take shape), *Zhongguo dianying bao* (July 18): 2.

Liu, Rui 刘锐 and Han Mei 韩妹 (2008), "Mindiao xianshi jin 14.2% de ren ai kan guochan donghuapian" 民调显示仅 14.2% 的人爱看国产动画片 (Poll reveals only 14.2% of the public likes to watch Chinese animated films), *Zhongguo qingnian bao* 中国青年报 (China youth daily) (June 27): 2.

Liu, Shouhua 刘守华 (2006), "Zhanhuo fengyan zhong de Yan'an dianying ye" 战火烽烟中的延安电影业 (Yan'an film industry during the war), *Bainian chao* 百年潮 (Hundred year tide) 1: 63–7.

Liu, Ting (2009), "Conflicting Discourses on Boys' Love and Subcultural Tactics in Mainland China and Hong Kong," *Intersections* 20 (April), http://intersections.anu.edu.au/issue20/liu.htm. Accessed February 23, 2010.

Liu, Xiancheng 刘现成 (ed.) (2001), *Shiduo sanluo de guangying: Huayu dianying de lishi, zuozhe yu wenhua zaixian* 拾掇散落的光影：华语电影的历史、作者与文化再现 (Collecting scattered lights and shadows: History, auteur and cultural representation of Chinese-language cinema), Taipei: Yatai.

Lo, Kwai-cheung (2005), *Chinese Face/Off: The Transnational Popular Culture of Hong Kong*, Urbana: University of Illinois Press.

Lo, Malinda (2008), "Interview with Zero Chou," *AfterEllen* (May 4), http://www.afterellen.com/people/2008/5/zerochou?page=0%2C1. Accessed April 4, 2010.

Loh, Wai-fong (1984), "From Romantic Love to Class Struggle: Reflections on the Film *Liu Sanjie*," in *Popular Chinese Literature and Performing Arts in the People's Republic of China, 1949–1979* (ed. Bonnie McDougall), Berkeley: University of California Press, 165–76.

Lu, Chuan (2009), *"Kungfu Panda* Gives Food for Thought," *China Daily* (July 5): 4.

Lü, Feiyi 卢非易 (1998), *Taiwan dianying: zhengzhi, jingji, meixue 1949–1994* 台湾电影：政治、经济、美学 *1949–1994* (Taiwan film: Politics, economics, aesthetics 1949–1994), Taipei: Yuanliu.

Lu, Hongshi 陆弘石 (1998), *Zhongguo dianying shi* 中国电影史 (Chinese film history), Beijing: Wenhua yishu chubanshe.

Lü, Meng 吕蒙 (2009), "Zhongguo zaoqi dianying tongqi luyin siwei de yunniang yu tixian" 中国早期电影同期录音思维的酝酿与体现 (Plans and fruition of sound recordings on film in early Chinese cinema), *Beijing dianying xueyuan xuebao* 北京电影学院学报 (Journal of Beijing Film Academy) 1: 39–44.

Lu, Sheldon Hsiao-Peng (ed.) (1997), *Transnational Chinese Cinemas: Identity, Nationhood, Gender*, Honolulu: University of Hawaii Press.

Lu, Sheldon Hsiao-Peng (2000), "Filming Diaspora and Identity: Hong Kong and 1997," in *The Cinema of Hong Kong: History, Arts, Identity* (eds Poshek Fu and David Desser), New York: Cambridge University Press, 273–88.

Lu, Sheldon Hsiao-Peng (2002), *China: Transnational Visuality, Global Modernity*, Stanford, CA: Stanford University Press.

Lu, Sheldon Hsiao-Peng (2007), *Chinese Modernity and Global Bio-Politics: Studies in Literature and Visual Culture*, Honolulu: University of Hawaii Press.

Lu, Sheldon Hsiao-Peng and Emilie Yueh-Yu Yeh (eds) (2005), *Chinese-Language Film: Historiography, Poetics, Politics*, Honolulu: University of Hawaii Press.

Lu, Sheldon Hsiao-Peng and Jiayan Mi (eds) (2009), *Chinese Ecocinema: Nature, Humanity, Modernity*, Hong Kong: Hong Kong University Press.

Lu, Shenghui (2004), "What Is Film Adaptation," *IRIS* 30: 113–27.

Lü, Sushang 吕诉上 (1961), *Taiwan dianying xiju shi* 台湾电影戏剧史 (A history of film and theater in Taiwan), Taipei: Yinhua.

Lu, Tonglin (2002), *Confronting Modernity in the Cinemas of Taiwan and Mainland China*, New York: Cambridge University Press.

Lu, Xiaoning (2010), "Zhang Ruifang: Modelling the Socialist Red Star," in *Chinese Film Stars* (eds Mary Farquhar and Yingjin Zhang), London: Routledge, 97–107.

Lü, Xinyu 吕新雨 (2003), *Jilu zhongguo: dangdai Zhongguo xin jilu yundong* 纪录中国：当代中国新纪录运动 (Documenting China: The new documentary movement in contemporary China), Beijing: Sanlian.

Lü, Xinyu 吕新雨 (2006a) "Xinjilu yundong de li yu tong" 新纪录运动的力与痛 (The power and pain of the new documentary movement), http://www.xschina.org/show.php?id=6840. Accessed December 12, 2009.

Lü, Xinyu 吕新雨 (2006b) "Jintian, 'renwen' jilu yiyuhewei?" 今天，"人文"纪录意欲何为？ (What does "humanistic" documentary intend to do now?), *Dushu* (Reading) 10, http://www.xschina.org/show.php?id=7716. Accessed February 8, 2010.

Lü, Xinyu 吕新雨 (n.d.) "Jilupian: women weishenme yao chufa" 纪录片：我们为什么要出发 (Documentary: Why did we start), http://www.gdtv.com.cn/southtv/articleaaX.htm. Accessed November 9, 2009.

Lu, Xun 鲁迅 (1981), "Wo zhi jielie guan" 我之节烈观 (My concept of loyalty and chastity), in *Lu Xun quanji* 鲁迅全集 (Complete works of Lu Xun), Beijing: Renmin wenxue chubanshe, vol. 1: 121–33.

Lunsing, Wim (2006), *"Yaoi Ronso:* Discussing Depictions of Male Homosexuality in Japanese Girls' Comics, Gay Comics and Gay Pornography," *Intersections* 12 (January), http://intersections.anu.edu.au/issue12/lunsing.html. Accessed February 23, 2010.

Luo, Feng 洛枫 (2009), *Zhang Guorong: jinshe de hudie* 张国荣：禁色的蝴蝶 (Leslie Cheung: Butterfly of forbidden colors), Guilin: Guangxi shifan daxue chubanshe.

Luo, Yijun 罗艺军 (ed.) (1992), *Zhongguo dianying lilun wenxuan: 1920–1989* 中国电影理论文选 *1920–1989* (Selected works of Chinese film theory, 1920–1989), 2 vols., Beijing: Wenhua yishu chubanshe.

Luo, Yijun 罗艺军 (ed.) (2000), *Zhonguo dianying lilun wenxuan: 1920–1989* 中国电影理论文选 *1920–1989* (Selected works on Chinese film theory, 1920–1989), 2 vols., Beijing: Shoudu shifan daxue chubanshe.

Luo, Yijun 罗艺军 (ed.) (2003), *20 shiji Zhongguo dianying lilun wenxuan* 20 世纪中国电影理论文选 (Selected works of twentieth-century Chinese film theory), 2 vols., Beijing: Zhongguo dianying chubanshe.

Luo, Yuhong 骆育红 (2009), "Shiguang zuobiao shang de Feng Xiaogang dianying" 时光坐标上的冯小刚电影 (The relationship between Feng Xiaogang's films and changing times), *Dangdai dianying* 10: 109–12.

Ma, Eric Kit-wai (1999), *Culture, Politics, and Television in Hong Kong*, London: Routledge.

Ma, Ning (1993), "New Chinese Cinema: A Critical Account of the Fifth Generation," *Cineaste* 17.3: 32–5.

Ma, Ran 马然 (2009), "Ni yao cao dianying ma? *Cao tamade dianying* zai Shanxing" 你要操电影吗？ (Do you want to fuck cinema? *Fuck Cinema* at Yamagata) (October 31), http://fanhall.com/group/thread/15517.html. Accessed November 9, 2009.

Macartney, Jane (2008), "Star Blacklisted for 'Glorifying Traitors'," *The Times* (London) (March 11): 44.

MacKinnon, Stephen R. (1997), "Toward a History of the Chinese Press in the Republican Period," *Modern China* 23.1: 3–32.

Mak, Clara (2009), "Tang Returns … Cautiously," *South China Morning Post* (February 9): 6.

Makeham, John and A-chin Hsiau (eds) (2005), *Cultural, Ethnic and Political Nationalism in Contemporary Taiwan*, New York: Palgrave Macmillan.

Manovich, Lev (2002), *The Language of New Media*, Cambridge, MA: MIT Press.

Mao, Qiongying 毛琼英 (1980), "Song Cunshou hui gaixian yizhe ma?" 宋存寿会改弦易辙吗？ (Can Song Cunshou change his course?), *Shijie dianying* 世界电影 (World cinema) 149: 70–1.

Mao, Zedong 毛泽东 (1951), "Yingdang zhongshi dianying *Wu Xun zhuan* de taolun" 应当重视电影《武训传》的讨论 (Pay attention to the discussion about film *The Life of Wu Xun*) *Renmin ribao* 人民日报 (People's daily) (May 20).

Marchetti, Gina (1989), "The Blossoming of a Revolutionary Aesthetic: Xie Jin's *Two Stage Sisters*," *Jump Cut* 34: 95–106.

Marchetti, Gina (1997), "*Two Stage Sisters*: The Blossoming of a Revolutionary Aesthetic," in *Transnational Chinese Cinemas: Identity, Nationhood, Gender* (ed. Sheldon Hsiao-Peng Lu), Honolulu: University of Hawaii Press, 59–80.

Marchetti, Gina (2000), "Buying American, Consuming Hong Kong: Cultural Commerce, Fantasies of Identity, and the Cinema," in *The Cinema of Hong Kong: History, Arts, Identity* (eds Poshek Fu and David Desser), New York: Cambridge University Press, 289–313.

Marchetti, Gina (2003), "Farewell, Leslie Cheung," *Film Appreciation Journal* 116: 14–21.

Marchetti, Gina (2006), *From Tian'anmen to Times Square: Transnational China and the Chinese Diaspora on Global Screens, 1989–1997*, Philadelphia: Temple University Press.

Marchetti, Gina (2009), "Gender Politics and Neoliberalism in China: Ann Hui's *The Postmodern Life of My Aunt*," *Visual Anthropology* 22.2–3: 123–40.

Marchetti, Gina and Tan See-kam (eds) (2007), *Hong Kong Film, Hollywood and the New Global Cinema: No Film is an Island*, London: Routledge.

Martin, Biddy (1988), "Lesbian Identity and Autobiographical Differences," in *Women, Autobiography, Theory* (eds Sidonie Smith and Julia Watson), Madison: University of Wisconsin Press, 387.

Martin, Fran (2003), *Situating Sexualities: Queer Representation in Taiwanese Fiction, Film and Public Culture*, Hong Kong: Hong Kong University Press.

Martin, Fran (2010), *Backward Glances: Contemporary Chinese Cultures and the Female Homoerotic Imaginary*, Durham, NC: Duke University Press.

Martin, Fran and Larissa Heinrich (eds) (2006), *Embodied Modernities: Corporeality, Representation, and Chinese Cultures*, Honolulu: University of Hawaii Press.

Martinsen, Joel (2006), "Missing Chinese Movies," *Danwei: Chinese Media, Advertising, and Urban Life* (April 22), http://www.danwei.org/media_and_advertising/missing_chinese_movies_1.php. Accessed December 7, 2009.

Marx, Karl (1973), *Grundrisse: Foundations of the Critique of Political Economy*, New York: Vintage.

Massey, Doreen (1992), "A Place Called Home?" *New Formations* 17: 3–15.

McDonald, Paul (2000), *The Star System: Hollywood's Production of Popular Identities*, London: Wallflower Press.

McDougall, Bonnie S. (1991), *The Yellow Earth: A Film by Chen Kaige, with a Complete Translation of the Filmscript*, Hong Kong: Chinese University Press.

McDougall, Bonnie S. and Kam Louie (eds) (1997), *The Literature of China in the Twentieth Century*, New York: Columbia University Press.

McGrath, Jason (2007), "The Independent Cinema of Jia Zhangke: From Postsocialist Realism to a Transnational Aesthetic," in *The Urban Generation: Chinese Cinema and Society at the Turn of the Twenty-First Century* (ed. Zhang Zhen), Durham, NC: Duke University Press, 81–114.

McGrath, Jason (2008a), "The Cinema of Displacement: The Three Gorges Dam in Feature Film and Video," in *Displacement: The Three Gorges Dam and Contemporary Chinese Art* (ed. Wu Hung), Chicago: Smart Museum of Art, University of Chicago, 33–46.

McGrath, Jason (2008b), *Postsocialist Modernity: Chinese Cinema, Literature, and Criticism in the Market Age*, Stanford, CA: Stanford University Press.

Mercer, John and Martin Schingler (2004), *Melodrama: Genre, Style and Sensibility*, New York: Wallflower Press.

Metz, Christian (1974), *Film Language: A Semiotics of the Cinema*, trans. Michael Taylor, New York: Oxford University Press.

Metz, Christian (1982), *The Imaginary Signifier: Psychoanalysis and the Cinema* (trans. Celia Britton, Annwyl Williams, Ben Brewster, and Alfred Guzzetti), Bloomington: Indiana University Press.

Miller, Toby, Nitin Govil, John McMurria, and Richard Maxwell (2001), *Global Hollywood*, London: British Film Institute.

Millet, Raphaël (2006), *Singapore Cinema*, Singapore: Editions Didier Millet.

Mo, Wa 墨娃 and Fu Huimin 傅会敏 (2008), *Yuedu Li An* 阅读李安 (Reading Ang Lee), Beijing: Beijing daxue chubanshe.

Modern Films (n.d.), http://citypod.net/index.html. Accessed March 10, 2010.

Morin, Edgar (1961), *The Stars* (trans. Richard Howard), New York: Grove.

Morley, David (2000) *Home Territories: Media, Mobility, and Identity*, London: Routledge.

Morris, Meaghan, Siu-Leung Li, and Stephen Ching-Kiu Chan (eds) (2006), *Hong Kong Connections: Transnational Imagination in Action Cinema*, Hong Kong: Hong Kong University Press.

Morton, Lisa (2001), *The Cinema of Tsui Hark*, Jefferson City, MO: McFarland.

Mtime.com (2009), "Zhongguo neidi dianying piaofang lishi paihang 中国内地电影票房历史排行 (Box-office rankings of films exhibited in mainland China all-times), http://www.cinema.com.cn and http://www.entgroup.cn.http://www.mtime.com/my/964883/blog/1255510/. Accessed 23 December 23, 2009.

Müller, Marco (ed.) (1982a), *Ombre Elettriche: Saggi e Ricerche sul Cinema Cinese*, Milan: Electa.

Müller, Marco (ed.) (1982b), *Ombres Électriques: Panorama du Cinéma Chinois 1925–1982*, Paris: Centre de Documentation sur le Cinéma Chinois.

Mulvey, Laura (1975), "Visual Pleasure and Narrative Cinema," *Screen* 16.3: 6–18.

Munakata, Kiyohiko (1965), *The Rise of Ink-Wash Landscape Painting in the T'ang Dynasty*, PhD dissertation, Princeton University.

Münsterberg, Hugo (1916), *The Photoplay: A Psychological Study*, New York: D. Appleton.

Münsterberg, Hugo (2002), *Hugo Münsterberg on Film: The Photoplay – A Psychological Study and Other Writings* (ed. Allan Langdale), London: Routledge.

Murray, Julia K. (1988), "What is 'Chinese Narrative Illustration'?" *Artibus Asiae* 80.4: 602–15.

Naficy, Hamid (2001), *An Accented Cinema: Exilic and Diasporic Filmmaking*, Princeton: Princeton University Press.

Nakajima, Seio (2006), "Film Clubs in Beijing: The Cultural Consumption of Chinese Independent Films," in *From Underground to Independent: Alternative Film Culture in Contemporary China* (eds Paul Pickowicz and Yingjin Zhang), Lanham, MD: Rowman and Littlefield, 161–87.

Naremore, James (ed.) (2000), *Film Adaptation*, New Brunswick, NJ: Rutgers University Press.

Nayar, Pramod (2008), *Seeing Stars: Spectacle, Society and Celebrity Culture*, New Delhi: Sage India.

Neale, Stephen (1980), *Genre*, London: British Film Institute.

Neale, Steve (1993), "Melo Talk: On the Meaning and Use of the Term 'Melodrama' in the American Trade Press," *Velvet Light Trap* 32: 66–89.

Nehamas, Alexander (2010), "Plato's Pop Culture Problem, and Ours," *New York Times* (August 29), http://opinionator.blogs.nytimes.com/2010/08/29/platos-pop-culture-problem-and-ours/. Accessed August 29, 2010.

New York Times (1920), "Screen: People and Plays" (June 6): 65.

New Zealand Herald (2007), "Censored Version of Ang Lee Film Brings Lawsuit from Fan," *New Zealand Herald* (November 17).

Ng, Kenny K. K. (2008), "Inhibition vs. Exhibition: Political Censorship of Chinese and Foreign Cinemas in Postwar Hong Kong," *Journal of Chinese Cinemas* 2.1: 23–35.

Ni, Ning 倪宁 and Tan Yufei 潭宇菲 (2009), "Bawo jiyu, nishiershang – dianying pingdao de 'zhuanyehua' zhi lu" 把握机遇, 逆势而上——电影频道的"专业化"之路 (The road towards specialty channel), *Chuanmei baodao* 传媒报道 (Media report) (April): 94–6.

Ni, Zhen (1994a), "Classical Chinese Painting and Cinematographic Signification," in *Cinematic Landscapes: Observations on the Visual Arts and Cinema of China and Japan* (eds Linda Ehrlich and David Desser), Austin: University of Texas Press, 63–80.

Ni, Zhen 倪震 (1994b), *Gaige yu Zhongguo dianying* 改革与中国电影 (Reform and Chinese film), Beijing: Zhongguo dianying chubanshe.

Ni, Zhen (2002), *Memoirs from the Beijing Film Academy: The Genesis of China's Fifth Film Generation* (trans. Chris Berry), Durham, NC: Duke University Press.

Ni, Zhen 倪震 (2008), "Ruan shili he Zhongguo dianying" 软实力和中国电影 (The soft power and Chinese film), *Dangdai dianying* 2: 4–10.

Nichols, Bill (1981), *Ideology and the Image: Social Representation in the Cinema and Other Media*, Bloomington: Indiana University Press.

Nichols, Bill (1994), "Discovering Form, Inferring Meaning: New Cinemas and the Film Festival Circuit," *Film Quarterly* 47.3: 16–30.

Noble, Jonathan (2008), "*Blind Shaft*: Performing the 'Underground' On and Beyond the Screen," in *Chinese Films in Focus II* (ed. Chris Berry), London: British Film Institute, 32–9.

Nochimson, Martha P. (2010), *World on Film: An Introduction*, Oxford: Wiley-Blackwell.

Nornes, Abé Mark (2009), "Bulldozers, Bibles and Very Sharp Knives: The Chinese Independent Documentary Scene," *Film Quarterly* 63.1: 50–5.

Nothelfer, Christine E., Jordan E. DeLong, and James E. Cutting (2009), "Shot Structure in Hollywood Film," *Indiana Undergraduate Journal of Cognitive Science*, 4: 103–13.

Ong, Aihwa and Donald M. Nonini (eds) (1997), *Ungrounded Empires: The Cultural Politics of Modern Chinese Transnationalism*, London: Routledge.

O'Regan, Tom (1996), *Australian National Cinema*, London: Routledge.

O'Regan, Tom (2002), "A National Cinema," in *The Film Cultures Reader* (ed. Graeme Turner), London: Routledge, 139–64.

Osnos, Evan (2009), "The Long Shot; Can China's Archly Political Auteur Please the Censors and Himself and Still Find a Mass Audience?" *The New Yorker* 85.13 (May 11): 88ff, http://www.lexisnexis.com. Accessed December 28, 2009.

Palti, Elías José (2001), "The Nation as a Problem: Historians and the 'National Question'," *History and Theory* 40.3: 324–46.

Pan, Chuitong 潘垂统 (1927), "Dianying yu wenxue" 电影与文学 (Film and literature), Minxin special issue for *Xixiangji*, no. 7.

Pan, Ling (1984), *Old Shanghai: Gangsters in Paradise*, Singapore: Heinemann.

Pang, Laikwan (2002), *Building a New China in Cinema: The Chinese Left-Wing Cinema Movement, 1932–1937*, Lanham, MD: Rowman and Littlefield.

Pang, Laikwan (2007), "The Institutionalization of 'Chinese' Cinema as an Academic Discipline," *Journal of Chinese Cinemas* 1.1: 55–61.

Pang, Laikwan (2010), "Hong Kong Cinema as a Dialect Cinema?" *Cinema Journal* 49.3: 140–3.

Pang, Laikwan and Day Wong (eds) (2005), *Masculinities and Hong Kong Cinema*, Hong Kong: Hong Kong University Press.

Panofsky, Erwin (1934), "Style and Medium in the Motion Pictures," originally published in *Bulletin of the Department of Art and Archaeology*, Princeton University; reprinted in *The Visual Turn: Classical Film Theory and Art History* (ed. Angela Dalle Vacche), New Brunswick, NJ: Rutgers University Press, 2002, 69–84.

Park, Jae Yoon (2009), "Asian's Beloved Sassy Girl: Jun Ji-Hyun's Star Image and Her Transnational Stardom," *Jump Cut* 51, http://www.ejumpcut.org/archive/jc51.2009/SassyGirl/index.html. Accessed November 15, 2011.

Pearl, Monica (2004), "New Queer Cinema: An Introduction," in *New Queer Cinema: A Critical Reader* (ed. Michelle Aaron), Edinburgh: Edinburgh University Press, 23–35.

Perriam, Christopher (2003), *Stars and Masculinities in Spanish Cinema*, New York: Oxford University Press.

Pezzotta, Alberto (ed.) (2007), *Patrick Tam: From the Heart of the New Wave*, Udine: Centro Espressioni Cinematografiche.

Pickowicz, Paul G. (1993a), "Melodramatic Representation and the 'May Fourth' Tradition of Chinese Cinema," in *From May Fourth to June Fourth: Fiction and Film in Twentieth-Century China* (eds Ellen Widmer and David Der-wei Wang), Cambridge, MA: Harvard University Press, 295–326.

Pickowicz, Paul G. (1993b), "Sinifying and Popularizing Foreign Culture: From Maxim Gorky's *The Lower Depths* to Huang Zuolin's *Ye dian*," *Modern Chinese Literature* 7.2: 7–31.

Pickowicz, Paul G. (1994), "Huang Jianxin and the Notion of Postsocialism," in *New Chinese Cinems* (eds Nick Browne et al.), 57–87.

Pickowicz, Paul G. (2006), "Social and Political Dynamics of Underground Filmmaking in China," in *From Underground to Independent: Alternative Film Culture in Contemporary China* (eds Paul Pickowicz and Yingjin Zhang), Lanham, MD: Rowman and Littlefield, 1–21.

Pickowicz, Paul G. and Matthew D. Johnson (eds) (2009), special issue on "Exhibiting Chinese Cinemas," *Journal of Chinese Cinemas* 3.2.

Pickowicz, Paul G. and Yingjin Zhang (eds) (2006), *From Underground to Independent: Alternative Film Culture in Contemporary China*, Lanham, MD: Rowman and Littlefield.

Ping, Jie 平杰 (ed.) (2006), *Ling yan xiang kan: haiwai xuezhe ping dangdai Zhongguo jilupian* 另眼相看——海外学者评当代中国纪录片 (Reel China: A new look at contemporary Chinese documentary), Shanghai: Wenhui chubanshe.

Pong, Johannes (2009), "Boys on Film," *Hong Kong Magazine* (April 24), http://hk-magazine.com/feature/boys-film. Accessed January 13, 2010.

Porter, Michael (1998), "Clusters and the New Economics of Competition," *Harvard Business Review* (November): 77–90.

PR Newswire Asia (2007), "Perfect World Expects to Launch Closed Beta Testing for 'Chi Bi' in Dec. 2007" (November 19), http://www.prnasia.com/pr/07/11/07525811–1.html. Accessed December 31, 2009.

Pramaggiore, Maria (1997), "Fishing for Girls: Romancing Lesbians in New Queer Cinema," *College Literature* 24.1: 59–75.

Pudovkin, Vsevolod (1929), *On Film Technique* (trans. Ivor Montagu), London: Victor Gollancz.

Pudovkin, Vsevolod (1933), *Film Technique: Five Essays and Two Addresses* (trans. Ivor Montagu), London: G. Newnes.

Qian, Chengcan 钱程灿 (2002), "Zhongguo xinshengdai dianying daoyan: biaoshu de yuwang 中国新生代电影导演：表述的欲望 (The Chinese newborn generation film directors: The desire of expression), *Qingnian bao* 青年报 (April 18), http://news.eastday.com/epublish/gb/paper148/20020418/class014800007/hwz648692.htm. Accessed December 8, 2009.

Qin, Liyan (2010), "Transmedia Strategies of Appropriation and Visualization: The Case of Zhang Yimou's Adaptation of Novels in His Early Films," in *Art, Politics and Commerce in Chinese Cinema* (eds Ying Zhu and Stanley Rosen), 163–74.

Qin, Xiaolin 秦晓琳 (2009), "Zhongguo wusheng dianying zhong de wuti texie yanjiu" 中国无声电影中的物体特写研究 (Studies of close-ups of inanimate objects in China's silent films), *Beijing Dianying xueyuan xuebao* 3: 68–73.

Qin, Xiqing 秦喜清 (2008), *Oumei dianying yu Zhongguo zaoqi dianying 1920–1930* 欧美电影与中国早期电影 *1920–1930* (Early Chinese cinema and the films of Europe and America 1920–1930), Beijing: Zhongguo dianying chubanshe.

Qiu, Yuefei 邱越飞 (2008), "Xin xingshi xia jiejue zhongxiao xuesheng kan dianying nan de sikao yu changshi" 新形势下解决中小学生看电影难的思考与尝试 (Thoughts on how to solve the difficulties primary and middle school students have in watching films), *Zhongguo dianying shichang* (June): 20–1.

Qu, Baiyin 瞿白音 (1962), "Guanyu dianying chuangxin wenti de dubai" 关于电影创新问题的独白 (A monologue on film innovation), *Dianying yishu* 3: 50–7.

Quiquemelle, Marie-Claire (1991), "The Wan Brothers and Sixty Years of Animated Film in China," in *Perspectives on Chinese Cinema* (ed. Chris Berry), London: British Film Institute, 175–86.

Quiquemelle, Marie-Claire and Jean-Loup Passek (eds) (1985), *Le Cinema Chinois*, Paris: Centre Georges Pompidou.

Rajewsky, Irina O. (2005), "Intermediality, Intertextuality, and Remediation: A Literary Perspective on Intermediality," *Intermédialités* 6: 43–64.

Raju, Zakir (2000), "National Cinema and the Beginning of Film History in/of Bangladesh," *Senses of Cinema* (November), http://www.latrobe.edu.au/screeningthepast/firstrelease/fr1100/rzfr11d.htm. Accessed December 28, 2009.

Rao, Shuguang 饶曙光 (2006), "Zhongguo xiju dianying dianji zhi zuo: Laogong zhi Aiqing" 中国喜剧电影奠基之作：《劳工之爱情》 (The founding work of China's comedy films: *Laborer's Love*), *Dianying xinzuo* 3: 31–5.

Rasudevan, Ravi (2000), "The Politics of Cultural Address in a Transitional Cinema: A Case Study of Indian Popular Cinema," in *Reinventing Film Studies* (eds Christine Gledhill and Linda Williams), New York: Oxford University Press, 130–64.

Rawnsley, Gary D. (2000), "Selling Taiwan: Diplomacy and Propaganda," *Issues and Studies* 36.3: 1–25.

Rawnsley, Gary D. and Ming-Yeh T. Rawnsley (2001), *Critical Security, Democratization, and Television in Taiwan*, Aldershot: Ashgate.

Rawnsley, Gary D. and Ming-Yeh T. Rawnsley (eds) (2010), *Global Chinese Cinema: The Culture and Politics of Hero*, London: Routledge.

Rayns, Tony (1989), "Chinese Vocabulary: An Introduction to *King of the Children* and the New Chinese Cinema," in Chen Kaige and Tony Rayns, *King of the Children and the New Chinese Cinema*, London: Faber and Faber, 1–58.

Rayns, Tony (1991), "Breakthroughs and Setbacks: The Origins of the New Chinese Cinema," in *Perspectives on Chinese Cinema* (ed. Chris Berry), London: British Film Institute, 104–13.

Rayns, Tony (2002), "*Enter The Clowns*," program notes for the 2002 Vancouver International Film Festival (September), http://www.viff.org/viff02/filmguide/filmnote.php?FCode=ENTER. Accessed December 1, 2009.

Rayns, Tony and Scott Meek (1980), *Electric Shadows: 45 Years of Chinese Cinema*, London: British Film Institute.

Rehm, Jean-Pierre, Olivier Joyard, and Danièle Rivière (1999), *Tsai Ming-liang*, Paris: Editions DisVoir.

Renmin ribao 人民日报 (People's Daily) (1988), "Commentator Views Freedom in Art Creation" (September 14), translated in Foreign Broadcast Information Service (FBIS), FBIS-CHI-88–183 (September 21): 34.

Renmin wang (2006), "CNN IC fabu dishibaci Zhongguo hulianwang fazhan zhuangkuang tongji baogao" CNN IC 发布第十八次中国互联网络发展状况统计报告 (CNN IC Broadcasts the 18th China Internet Development Statistic Report), *Renmin wang* 人民网 (People's net) (July 19), http://it.people.com.cn/GB/42891/42894/4608289.html. Accessed December 7, 2009.

Research Report on Chinese Film Industry 2009 中国电影产业研究报告 (2009), Beijing: Zhongguo dianying chubanshe.

Reuters (1995), "China Film Industry Protests Foreign Megafilms" (April 9), from ClariNet Electronic News Service. Accessed April 11, 1995; webpage unavailable now.

Reynaud, Bérénice (1993), "Glamour and Suffering: Gong Li and the History of Chinese Stars," in *Women and Film: A Sight and Sound Reader* (eds Pam Cook and Philop Dood), London: Scarlet, 21–9.

Reynaud, Bérénice (1996), "New Visions/New Chinas: Video-Art, Documentation, and the Chinese Modernity in Question," in *Resolutions: Contemporary Video Practices* (ed. Michael Renov), Minneapolis: University of Minnesota Press, 229–57.

Reynaud, Bérénice (2003), "Dancing with Myself, Drifting with My Camera: The Emotional Vagabonds of China's New Documentary," *Sense of Cinema*, http://archive.sensesofcinema.com/ contents/03/28/chinas_new_documentary.html. Accessed November 10, 2009.

Rhyne, Ragan (2011), "Comrades and Citizens: Gay and Lesbian Film Festivals in China," in *Film Festival Yearbook 3: Film Festivals and East Asia* (eds Dina Iordanova and Ruby Cheung), St. Andrews, UK: St. Andrews Film Studies, 110–24.

Rich, B. Ruby (1992), "New Queer Cinema," *Sight and Sound* 2.5: 31–4.

Rich, B. Ruby (2000), "Queer and Present Danger," *Sight and Sound* 10.3: 22–5.

Rich, B. Ruby (2007), "From ID to IQ: New Queer Cinema Then and Now," closing keynote address, *Image et Nation 20!*, Montreal: Concordia University, November 17.

Robins, Kevin (1991) "Prisoners of the City: Whatever Could a Postmodern City Be?" *New Formations* 15: 1–22.

Robinson, Lewis (1984), "Family: A Study in Genre Adaptation," *Australian Journal of Chinese Affairs* 12: 35–57.

Rodowick, David N. (1997), *Gilles Deleuze's Time-Machine*, Durham, NC: Duke University Press.

Rodriguez, Hector (1995), *The Cinema of Taiwan: National Identity and Political Legitimacy*, PhD dissertation, New York University.

Rodriguez, Hector (2001), "The Emergence of the Hong Kong New Wave," in *At Full Speed: Hong Kong Cinema in a Borderless World* (ed. Esther C. M. Yau), Minneapolis: University of Minnesota Press, 53–69.

Rose, Steve (2009), "Xiaolu Guo: I Wrote the Film with P. J. Harvey in Mind," *Guardian* (March 30), http://www.guardian.co.uk/music/2009/mar/30/pj-harvey-xiaolu-guo. Accessed November 15, 2009.

Rosen, Philip (1993), "Document and Documentary: On the Persistence of Historical Concepts," in *Theorizing Documentary* (ed. Michael Renov), London: Routledge, 58–89.

Rosen, Stanley (2002), "The Wolf at the Door: Hollywood and the Film Market in China," in *Southern California and the World* (eds Eric J. Heikkila and Rafael Pizarro), Westport, CT: Praeger, 49–77.

Rosen, Stanley (2006), "Hollywood and the Great Wall," *Los Angeles Times* (June 18): M7.

Rosen, Stanley (2008a), "Film and China's Youth Culture," *Education About Asia* 13.3: 38–43.

Rosen, Stanley (2008b), "Priorities in the Development of the Chinese Film Industry: The Interplay and Contradictions among Art, Politics and Commerce," paper presented at the conference on "Locality, Translocality, and De-Locality: Cultural, Aesthetic, and Political Dynamics of Chinese-Language Cinema," Shanghai University, July 12–13.

Rosen, Stanley (2009), "Contemporary Chinese Youth and the State," *Journal of Asian Studies* 68.2: 359–69.

Rosen, Stanley (2010), "Chinese Cinema's International Market," in *Art, Politics and Commerce in Chinese Cinema* (eds Ying Zhu and Stanley Rosen), 35–54.

Rothroc, Vicki (2003), "CCTV-6 Renews Oscar Broadcast Chinese Channel to Air Awards Show," *China Film News* (March 13): 1, http://www.variety.com/article/VR1117959717.html?categoryid=1982&cs=1. Accessed December 7, 2009.

Rowley, George (1947), *Painting: Principles of Chinese Painting*, Princeton: Princeton University Press.

Rubinstein, Murray A. (2007), *Taiwan: A New History*. Armonk, NY: M. E. Sharpe.

Russo, Vito (1987), *The Celluloid Closet: Homosexuality in the Movies*, New York: Harper.

Said, S. F. (2002), "In the Realm of the Censors," *Daily Telegraph* (June 28).

Salih, Sarah and Judith Butler (eds) (2004), *The Judith Butler Reader*, Oxford: Blackwell.

Salt, Barry (1992), *Film Style and Technology: History and Analysis*, 2nd edn, London: Starword.

Sarkar, Bhaskar (2001), "Hong Kong Hysteria: Martial Arts Tales from a Mutating World," in *At Full Speed: Hong Kong Cinema in a Borderless World* (ed. Esther C. M. Yau), Minneapolis: University of Minnesota Press, 159–76.

Sassen, Saskia (1991), *The Global City: New York, London, Tokyo*, Princeton: Princeton University Press.

Saussy, Haun (1993), *The Problem of a Chinese Aesthetic*, Stanford, CA: Stanford University Press.

Scannell, Paddy (1991), *A Social History of British Broadcasting*, Oxford: Blackwell.

Schiller, Dan (2005), "Poles of Market Growth? Open Questions about China, Information, and the World Economy," *Global Media and Communication* 1.1: 79–103.

Schiller, Herbert I. (1969, 1992), *Mass Communication and American Empire*, 2nd edn, Boulder: Westview.

Schonberg, Harold (1973), "Must Ideology Command a Culture?" *New York Times* (October 7), http://query.nytimes.com/mem/archive/pdf?res=F20B17FE3D5D127A93C5 A9178-BD95F478785F9. Accessed April 20, 2011.

Schroeder, Andrew (2004), *Tsui Hark's Zu: Warrior from the Magic Mountain*, Hong Kong: Hong Kong University Press.

Schwankert, Steve (2005), "Team Effort Yields Pix: Gov't Taps Shingles as Official Production Partners," *Variety* (May 17), http://www.variety.com/article/VR1117923034.html?categoryid=1907&cs=1&query=. Accessed December 26, 2009.

Scott, Allen J. (2000), *The Cultural Economy of Cities*, Los Angeles: Sage.

SDW (Shanghai difangzhi weiyuanhui) 上海地方志委员会 (Shanghai gazeteer committee) (ed.) (1999), *Shanghai dianying zhi* 上海电影志 (The history of Shanghai cinema), Shanghai: Shanghai shehui kexue chubanshe.

Semsel, George S., Xia Hong, and Hou Jiaping (eds) (1990), *Chinese Film Theory: A Guide to the New Era*, New York: Praeger.

Shackleton, Liz (2009), "First Steps of a Box-Office Giant," ScreenDaily.com (July 30), http://www.screendaily.com/news/opinion/first-steps-of-a-box-office. Accessed October 18, 2009.

Shan, Wanli 单万里 (2005), *Zhongguo jilu dianying shi* 中国纪录电影史 (A history of Chinese documentary cinema), Beijing: Zhongguo dianying chubanshe.

Shanghaiist (2009), "2012: Lessons on How to Be a Chinese Box-Office Hit" (November 17), http://shanghaiist.com/2009/11/17/2012_lessons_on_how_to_be_a_chinese.php. Accessed November 15, 2010.

Shanghaishi dianyingju 上海市电影局 (Shanghai Municipal Film Bureau) (ed.) (1963), *Yingpian mulu, 1950–1962* 影片目录, 1950–1962 (Film catalog, 1950–1962), internal document, Shanghai.

Shao, Gongyou 邵功游 (1999), "Jianxin de licheng, zhongda de gongxian – huiyi Yuan Muzhi yu Chen Boer" 艰辛的历程，重大的贡献——回忆袁牧之与陈波儿 (Difficult journey, important contributions: In memory of Yuan Muzhi and Chen Boer), *Dangdai dianying* 3: 53–5.

Shartz, Thomas (1981), *Hollywood Genres: Formulas, Filmmaking and the Studio System*, Philadelphia: Temple University Press.

Shen, Shiao-ying (1995), *Permutations of the Foreigner: A Study of the Works of Edward Yang, Stan Lai, Chang Yi, and Hou Hsiao-hsien*, PhD dissertation, Cornell University.

Shen, Yun 沈芸 (2005), *Zhongguo dianying chanye shi* 中国电影产业史 (A history of the Chinese film industry), Beijing: Zhongguo dianying chubanshe.

Shi, Man 石曼 (1995), *Chongqing kangzhan jutan jishi* 重庆抗战剧坛纪事 (Chronicles on Chongqing wartime theater), Beijing: Zhongguo xiju chubanshe.

Shi, Sheng 时声 (2005), "Dianying pingdao jingyibu dazhao wenhua xiaofei qiangshi chanyelian" 电影频道进一步打造文化消费强势产业链 (The Movie Channel continues to cultivate cultural production chains), *Shichang guancha* 市场观察 (Market observer), 12: 5–6.

Shi, Weida 施惟达 and Li Yan 李炎 (2009), "Lüelun xin shiqi de wenhua jianshe" 略论新时期的文化建设 (Overview of cultural construction of the new era), *Sixiang zhanxian* 思想战线 (Ideological frontlines), 35.2: 79–83.

Shichang guancha (2002), "Shixian zhiwo chaoyue, zhuzhao qiangshi pingpai" 实现自我超越，铸造强势品牌 (Transforming and building strong brand name), *Shichang guancha* 12: 104–5.

Shiel, Mark and Tony Fitzmaurice (eds) (2001), *Cinema and the City: Film and Urban Societies in a Global Context*, Oxford: Blackwell.

Shih, Shu-mei (2007), *Visuality and Identity: Sinophone Articulations Across the Pacific*, Berkeley: University of California Press.

Shu, Ping 舒平 (1994), "Diyige dianying nübianju: Pu Shunqing" 第一个电影女编剧: 濮舜卿 (The first female film scriptwriter: Pu Shunqing), *Dianying xinzuo* 5: 62.

Shu, Yuan (2003), "Reading the Kung Fu Film in an American Context: From Bruce Lee to Jackie Chan," *Journal of Popular Film and Television* 31.2: 50–9.

Sickman, Laurence and Alexander Soper (1956), *The Art and Architecture of China*, Baltimore: Penguin Books.

Silbergeld, Jerome (1982), *Chinese Painting Style: Media, Methods, and Principles of Form*, Seattle: University of Washington Press.

Silbergeld, Jerome (1999), *China Into Film: Frames of Reference in Contemporary Chinese Cinema*, London: Reaktion Books.

Silbergeld, Jerome (2004), *Hitchcock with a Chinese Face: Cinematic Doubles, Oedipal Triangles, and China's Moral Voice*, Seattle: University of Washington Press.

Silbergeld, Jerome (2005), "Mountains and Water, *Shan Shui*: What Do We Mean by 'Landscape' in Chinese Landscape Painting?" *Journal of the International Snuff Bottle Society* 37.1: 4–20.

Silbergeld, Jerome (2008), *Body in Question: Image and Illusion in Two Films by Chinese Director Jiang Wen*, Princeton: P. Y. and Kinmay W. Tang Center for East Asian Art and Princeton University Press.

Silbergeld, Jerome (2009a), "Chinese Seen by the Chinese: Documentary Photography, 1991–2003," in *Humanism in China: A Contemporary Record of Photography* (ed. Jerome Silbergeld), New York: China Institute in America, 1–18.

Silbergeld, Jerome (2009b), "Façades: The New Beijing and the Celluloid Ecology of Jia Zhangke's *The World*," in *Chinese Ecocinema: Nature, Humanity, Modernity* (eds Sheldon Lu and Jiayan Mi), Hong Kong: Hong Kong University Press, 113–27.

Silbergeld, Jerome (2011), "The Photograph in the Movie: On the Boundaries of Cinematography, Photography, and Videography," in *Bridges to Heaven: Essay on East Asian Art History in Honor of Wen C. Fong* (eds Jerome Silbergeld, Dora Ching, Alfreda Murck, and Judith Smith), Princeton: Princeton University Press, 875–96.

Silbergeld, Jerome (forthcoming-a), "First Lines, Final Scenes in Text, Handscroll, and Chinese Cinema," in *Looking at Asian Art: Perspectives in Memory of Father Harrie Vanderstappen* (eds Martin Powers and Katherine Tsiang), Chicago: University of Chicago Art Media Resources.

Silbergeld, Jerome (forthcoming-b), "The Ghosts of Patriarchy Past: Family Dynamics and Psycho-Politics in Recent Chinese-Language Cinema," in *The Family Model in Chinese Art and Culture* (eds Jerome Silbergeld and Dora Ching), Princeton: Princeton University Press.

Silverstone, Roger (1994), *Television and Everyday Life*, London: Routledge.

Sina.com (2008), "Guangdian zongju chongshen dianying shencha biaozhun, jiulei neirong xu shanjian xiugai 广电总局重申电影审查标准，九类内容须删剪修改" (SARFT reaffirms the standards for film censorship, revisions are made in nine categories) (March 7), www.sina.com.cn. Accessed July 3, 2008.

Singer, Ben (1990), "Female Power in the Serial Queen Melodrama," *Camera Obscura* 22: 90–129.

Smith, Neil (2008), "Sex 'Pivotal' to Lust, Says Lee," BBC News (January 2), http://news-vote.bbc.co.uk/mpapps/pagetools/print/news.bbc.co.uk/2/hi/entertainment/7096083.stm. Accesed November 15, 2010.

Smith, Sean (2005), "Invasion of the Hot Movie Stars," *Newsweek* (May 9): 36–7.

Song, Cunshou 宋存寿 (1979), "Wo de wushi huigu" 我的五十回顾 (My retrospective at fifty years of age), *Yingxiang zazhi* 24: 7–9.

Song, Zhao 宋昭 (2007), *Mama de yisheng: Wang Ping zhuan* 妈妈的一生: 王苹传 (The life of my mother: Biography of Wang Ping), Beijing: Zhongguo dianying chubanshe.

Song, Zhiwen 宋子文 (ed.) (2006), *Taiwan dianying sanshinian* 台湾电影三十年 (Thirty years of Taiwan film), Shanghai: Fudan daxue chubanshe.

Sontag, Susan (1966), "Film and Theater," *Tulane Drama Review* 11.1: 24–37.

South China Morning Post (2009), "HK Films Shine at the Mainland Box Office" (September 4), http://www.lexisnexis.com. Accessed May 7, 2010.

Stabels, Kate (1998), "The Postmodern Always Rings Twice: Constructing the Femme Fatale in 90s Cinema," in *Women in Film Noir* (ed. E. Ann Kaplan), London: British Film Institute, 164–82.

Stacey, Jackie (1993), *Star Gazing: Hollywood Cinema and Female Spectatorship*, London: Routledge.

Stam, Robert and Alessandra Raengo (eds) (2004), *A Companion to Literature and Film*, Oxford: Blackwell.

Standish, Isolde (2005), *A New History of Japanese Cinema: A Century of Film*, New York: Continuum.

Steinhardt, Nancy (ed.) (2002), *Chinese Architecture*, New Haven, CT: Yale University Press.

Stokes, Lisa Odham and Michael Hoover (1999), *City on Fire: Hong Kong Cinema*, London: Verso.

Stokes, Lisa Odham and Michael Hoover (2000), "Resisting the Stage: Imaging/Imagining Ruan Lingyu in Stanley Kwan's *Actress*," *Asian Cinema* 11.2: 92–8.

Stoppard, Tom (1967), *Rosenkrantz and Guildenstern Are Dead*, New York: Grove.

Straayer, Chris (1996), *Deviant Eyes, Deviant Bodies: Sexual Re-Orientation in Film and Video*, New York: Columbia University Press.

Straits Times (2006), "No More Art Films for Him; Despite Being Acclaimed for His Role in *The Banquet*, Ge You Would Rather Stick to Doing Commercially Successful Movies" (September 20), http://www.lexisnexis.com. Accessed December 28, 2009.

Straits Times (2007), "Capturing the True China; Unlike Zhang Yimou, Up-and-Coming Director Jia Zhangke's Films Focus on Ordinary Folk" (June 7), http://www.lexisnexis.com. Accessed December 28, 2009.

Straits Times (2010), "China Banks on Films to Project Power; Govt Throwing Weight Behind Local Films with Eye on Soft Power Gains" (January 30), http://www.lexisnexis.com. Accessed February 17, 2010.

Stringer, Julian (1997), "*Centre Stage*: Reconstructing the Bio-Pic," *Cineaction* 42: 28–39.

Stringer, Julian (2001), "Global Cities and the International Film Festival Economy," in *Cinema and the City: Film and Urban Societies in a Global Context* (eds Mark Shiel and Tony Fitzmaurice), Oxford: Blackwell, 134–44.

Stringer, Julian (2003a), "*Boat People*: Second Thoughts on Text and Context," in *Chinese Films in Focus: 25 New Takes* (ed. Chris Berry), London: British Film Institute, 15–22.

Stringer, Julian (2003b), "Talking About Jet Li: Transnational Chinese Movie Stardom and Asian American Internet Reception," in *Political Communications in Greater China: The Construction and Reflection of Identity* (eds Gary D. Rawnsley and Ming-Yeh T. Rawnsley), London: Routledge Curzon, 275–90.

Stringer, Julian (2005), "Putting Korean Cinema in Its Place: Genre Classifications and the Contexts of Reception," in *New Korean Cinema* (eds Chi-Yun Shin and Julian Stringer), Edinburgh: Edinburgh University Press, 95–105.

Stringer, Julian (2008), *Blazing Passions: Contemporary Hong Kong Cinema*, London: Wallflower Press.

Stringer, Julian (2010), "Leslie Cheung: Star as Autosexual," in *Chinese Film Stars* (eds Mary Farquhar and Yingjin Zhang), London: Routledge, 207–24.

Sullivan, Michael (1960), *An Introduction to Chinese Art*, London: Faber and Faber.

Sullivan, Michael (1979), *Symbols of Eternity: The Art of Landscape Painting in China*, Stanford, CA: Stanford University Press.

Sullivan, Michael (1996), *The Arts in China*, Berkeley: University of California Press.

Sun, Chen 孙晨 (2000), "'Xin chengshi dianying' miaozhun dushi qingnianren" "新城市电影"瞄准都市青年人 ("New Urban Cinema" aims at urban youth), *Renmin ribao hai-wai ban* 人民日报海外版 (People's daily overseas edition) (March 9).

Sun, Shaoyi and Li Xun (eds) (2008), *Lights! Camera! Kai Shi! In Depth Interviews with China's New Generation of Movie Directors*, Norwalk, CT: Eastbridge.

Sun, Wanning (ed.) (2006), *Media and the Chinese Diaspora: Community, Communications and Commerce*, London: Routledge.

Sun, Weichuan 孙慰川 (2008), *Dangdai Taiwan dianying 1949–2007* 当代台湾电影 (Contemporary Taiwanese film 1949–2007), Beijing: Zhongguo guangbo dianshi chubanshe.

Sun, Xiaofen 孙晓芬 (1989), *Kangri zhanzheng shiqi de Sichuan huaju yundong* 抗日战争时期的四川话剧运动 (Spoken drama movement in Sichuan during the anti-Japanese war), Chengdu: Sichuan daxue chubanshe.

Sypher, Wylie (1960), *Rococo to Cubism in Literature and Art*, New York: Vintage.

Szarkowski, John (1966), *The Photographer's Eye*, New York: Museum of Modern Art.

Taipei Golden Horse Film Festival Executive Committee (ed.) (2003), *40th Anniversary of Golden Horse Awards*, Taipei: Golden Horse Awards.

Taiwan Cinema (2006) "Censorship, Rating System and Law Enforcement on Illegal Screenings," http://www.taiwancinema.com/fp.asp?xItem=53044&ctNode=124&mp=4. Accessed December 7, 2009.

Tam, Kwock-kan and Wimal Dissanayake (1998), *New Chinese Cinema*, Hong Kong: Oxford University Press.

Tambling, Jeremy (2003), *Wong Kar-wai's Happy Together*, Hong Kong: Hong Kong University Press.

Tan, Chunfa 谭春发 (1992), *Kai yidai xianhe – Zhongguo dianying zhifu Zheng Zhengqiu* 开一代先河——中国电影之父郑正秋 (The pioneer – Zheng Zhengqiu, father of Chinese cinema), Beijing: Guoji wenhua chuban gongsi.

Tan, E. K. (forthcoming), "Transcultural Adaptation of the *Unknown Woman*: Chronotope and Transtextuality in the Repositioning of the Female Subject in Xu Jinglei's *A Letter from an Unknown Woman*," in *Gender and Chinese Cinema: New Interventions* (eds Lingzhen Wang and Mary Ann Doane), New York: Columbia University Press.

Tan, See-Kam, Peter X. Feng, and Gina Marchetti (eds) (2009), *Chinese Connections: Critical Perspectives on Film, Identity and Diaspora*, Philadelphia: Temple University Press.

Tang, Rong 唐榕 (2008), "Sanshinian Zhongguo dianying tizhi gaige licheng huigu (shang)" 三十年中国电影体制改革历程回顾（上）(The process of structural reform of Chinese film over the last thirty years, part 1), *Zhongguo dianying bao* (October 9): 16–7.

Tang, Shukun 唐书琨, Jian Erqing 简而清, and Ya Fo 亚佛 (1970), "Daoyan zuotanhui: Tang Shuxuan, Hu Jinquan, Song Cunshou" 导演座谈会：唐书琨，胡金铨，宋存寿 (A directors symposium: Tang Shuxuan, Hu Jinquan, Song Cunshou), *Yinse shijie* 银色世界 (Cinemart), 12: 63–5.

Tang, Xiaobing (2000), *Chinese Modern: The Heroic and the Quotidian*, Durham, NC: Duke University Press.

Tasker, Yvonne (1997), "Fists of Fury: Discourses of Race and Masculinity in the Martial Arts Cinema," in *Race and the Subject of Masculinities* (eds Harry Stecopoulos and Michael Uebel), Durham, NC: Duke University Press, 315–36.

Taylor, Philip M. (2003), *Munitions of the Mind: A History of Propaganda from the Ancient World to the Present Day*, 3rd edn, Manchester: Manchester University Press.

Television Asia Online Guide, "China Movie Channel," http://www.onscreenasia.com/annualguide/Channels/detail-37–CHINA%20MOVIE%20CHANNEL. Accessed December 11, 2009.

Teng, Jiaxian (1989), "Teng Jinxian Expounds China's Film Policy," *China Screen* 3: 10.

Teng, Jiaxian (1990), "Harmful Trends in Film Creation," *China Screen* 3: 10.

Teo, Stephen (1997), *Hong Kong Cinema: The Extra Dimensions*, London: British Film Institute.

Teo, Stephen (ed.) (1999), *Hong Kong New Wave: Twenty Years After*, Hong Kong: Provisional Urban Council.

Teo, Stephen (2001), "Tsui Hark: National Style and Polemic," in *At Full Speed: Hong Kong Cinema in a Borderless World* (ed. Esther C. M. Yau), Minneapolis: University of Minnesota Press, 143–58.

Teo, Stephen (2003), "'There Is No Sixth Generation!': Director Li Yang on *Blind Shaft* and His Place in Chinese Cinema," *Senses of Cinema* 27, http://www.sensesofcinema.com/contents/03/27/li_yang.html. Accessed May 12, 2011.

Teo, Stephen (2005), *Wong Kar-wai*, London: British Film Institute.

Teo, Stephen (2006), "Chinese Melodrama," in *Traditions in World Cinema* (eds Linda Badley, R. Barton Palmer, and Steven Jay Schneider), Edinburgh: Edinburgh University Press, 203–13.

Teo, Stephen (2009), *Chinese Martial Arts Cinema: The Wuxia Tradition*, Edinburgh: Edinburgh University Press.

Tetsuya, Akiko (2005), *The Last Star of the East: Brigitte Lin Ching Hsia and Her Films*, Los Angeles: self-published by Tetsuya.

Tian, Han 田汉 (1927), "Yinse de meng" 银色的梦 (Silver dream), *Yinxing* (Silver star) 5: n.p.

Time (2010), "China: The New No. 2" (August 30): 12.

Tong, Ching-siu 汤祯兆 (2008), "Ling yitao Taiwan tongxinglian yiyun dianying" 另一套台湾同性恋疑云电影 (Yet another gay mystique film from Taiwan), *Asian Times Online* 亚洲时报在线 (November), http://www.atchinese.com/index.php?option=com_content&view=article&id=54694:2009–03–23–10–23–45&catid=184:2009–01–12–15–00–04&Itemid=105. Accessed February 10, 2010.

Tozer, Warren (1970), "Taiwan's 'Cultural Renaissance': A Preliminary View," *China Quarterly* 43: 81–99.

Tsui, Clarence (2009), "In From the Cold: Chen Kuo-fu Revisits and Updates the Dormant Mainland Spy Genre with his Latest Espionage Epic," *South China Morning Post* (October 8): 8.

Tuohy, Sue (1999), "Metropolitan Sounds: Music in Chinese Films of the 1930s," in *Cinema and Urban Culture in Shanghai, 1922–1943* (ed. Yingjin Zhang), Stanford, CA: Stanford University Press, 200–21.

Udden, James (2002), "Hou Hsiao-hsien and the Question of a Chinese Style," *Asian Cinema* 13.2: 54–75.

Udden, James (2003), "Taiwanese Popular Cinema and the Strange Apprenticeship of Hou Hsiao-hsien," *Modern Chinese Literature and Culture* 15.1: 120–45.

Udden, James (2009), *No Man an Island: The Cinema of Hou Hsiao-hsien*, Hong Kong: Hong Kong University Press.

Uhde, Jan and Yvonne Ng Uhde (2000), *Latent Images: Film in Singapore*, Singapore: Oxford University Press.

Uhde, Jan and Yvonne Ng Uhde (2010), *Latent Images: Film in Singapore*, 2nd edn, Singapore: National University of Singapore Press.

Uktradeinvest (2007), "The Film and Television Industry China Opportunities for the UK Producer: An Overview 2007," https://www.uktradeinvest.gov.uk/ukti/ShowDoc/BEA.../345/40815. Accessed December 5, 2009.

Urban Council of Hong Kong (ed.) (1996), *20th Anniversary of the Hong Kong International Film Festival*, Hong Kong: Urban Council of Hong Kong.

Venuti, Lawrence (ed.) (1992), *Rethinking Translation: Discourse, Subjectivity, Ideology*, London: Routledge.

Verrier, Richard (2011), "Global Movie Ticket Receipts Rise in 2010," *Los Angeles Times* (February 24): B3.

Vick, Tom (2007), *Asian Cinema: A Field Guide*, New York: Haper Collins.

Vincendeau, Ginette (2000), *Stars and Stardom in French Cinema,* London: Continuum.

Visser, Robin (2010), *Cities Surround the Countryside: Urban Aesthetics in Post-Socialist China*, Durham, NC: Duke University Press.

Voci, Paola (2004), "From the Center to the Periphery: Chinese Documentary's Visual Conjectures," *Modern Chinese Literature and Culture* 16.1: 65–113.

Voci, Paola (2010), *China on Video: Smaller-Screen Realities*, London: Routledge.

Wan, Jihong and Richard Kraus (2002), "Hollywood and China as Adversaries and Allies," *Pacific Affairs* 75.3: 419–34.

Wan, Minggang 万明纲 and Chong Yuan 种媛 (2004), "Yuyan yu siwei guanxi de wenhua yanjiu zongshu" 语言与思维关系的文化研究综述 (A review of cross-cultural research on the relationship of thinking and language), *Xinli kexue* 心理科学 (Psychological science) 27.2: 431–3.

Wan, Sheng 万声 (1991), "Huigu *Shanghai wuyanxi* de shouci yanchu" 回顾《上海屋檐下》的首次演出 (Recollections on the first performance of *Under the Eaves of Shanghai*), *Chongqing wenhua shiliao* 重庆文化史料 (Historical documents on Chongqing) 1: 7–9.

Wang, Bing 王兵 (2003), "*Tie Xi Qu: West of Tracks*, An Interview with Wang Bing," http://www.yidff.jp/2003/interviews/03i030–e.html. Accessed October 22, 2009.

Wang, Eugene (1988), "The *Old Well*: A Womb or a Tomb?" *Framework*, 35: 73–82

Wang, Eugene (1991), "*Red Sorghum*: Mixing Memory and Desire," in *Perspectives on Chinese Cinema* (ed. Chris Berry), London: British Film Institute, 80–103.

Wang, Hanlun 王汉伦 (1956), "Wo de congying jingguo" 我的从影经过 (My acting career), *Zhongguo dianying* 中国电影 (Chinese cinema), 2: 59–63.

Wang, Huangsheng 王璜生 and Hu Wugong 胡武功 (eds) (2003), *Zhongguo renben: Jishi zai dangdai* 中国人本：纪实在当代 (Humanism in China: A contemporary record of photography), Guangzhou: Lingnan meishu chubanshe.

Wang, Hui 汪晖 (1998), "Zhengzhi yu daode jiqi zhihuan de mimi" 政治与道德及其置换的秘密 (Politics, morality, and the secret of their displacement), *Dianying yishu* 2: 23–45.

Wang, Jifang 汪继芳 (1999), *Ershi shiji zuihou de langman: Beijing ziyou yishujia shenghuo shilu* 二十世纪最后的浪漫：北京自由艺术家生活实录 (The twentieth century's last romance: Documents of freelance artists in Beijing), Beijing: Beifang wenyi chubanshe; part of chapter 4 available at http://www.bioon.com/BOOK/yishu/artist-gb/23.htm. Accessed November 9, 2009.

Wang, Qi (2004), "The Ruin is Already a New Outcome: An Interview with Cui Zi'en," *Positions* 12.1: 181–94.

Wang, Qi (2006a), "Navigating on the Ruins: Space, Power and History in Contemporary Chinese Independent Documentaries," *Asian Cinema* 17.1: 246–55.

Wang, Qi (2006b), "Chi sheyingji de ren – shi shui?" 持摄影机的人——是谁？ (Who is the man with a movie camera?), in *Ling yan xiang kan: haiwai xuezhe ping dangdai Zhongguo jilupian* 另眼相看——海外学者评当代中国纪录片 (Reel China: A new look at contemporary Chinese documentary) (ed. Ping Jie), Shanghai: Wenhui chubanshe, 155–62.

Wang, Qi (2008), *Writing Against Oblivion: Personal Filmmaking from the Forsaken Generation in Post-Socialist China*, PhD dissertation, University of California, Los Angeles.

Wang, Qi (forthcoming), "Embodied Visions: Chinese Queer Experimental Documentaries by Shi Tou and Cui Zi'en," *Positions*.

Wang, Sharon Chialan (2009), "*Cape No. 7* and Taiwan's National Consciousness," *Asian Cinema* 20.2: 244–59.

Wang, Xiaoshuai (2005), "Notes from the Director Wang Xiaoshuai," in DVD notes for *Drifters*, Film Movement.

Wang, Yichuan 王一川 (1998), *Zhang Yimou shenhua de zhongjie: shenmei yu wenhua shiye zhongde Zhang Yimou dianying* 张艺谋神话的终结——审美与文化视野中的张艺谋电影 (End of Zhang Yimou's myth: Zhang Yimou's films in the perspective of aesthetics and culture), Zhengzhou: Henan renmin chubanshe.

Wang, Yiman (2005), "From the Indexical to the Spectacle: On Zhang Yimou's Postmodern Turn in *Not One Less*," *Journal of Film and Video* 57.3: 3–13.

Wang, Yiman (2007), "A Star is Dead, a Legend is Born: Practicing Leslie Cheung's Posthumous Fandom," in *Stardom and Celebrity: A Reader* (eds Sean Redmond and Su Holmes), Los Angeles: Sage, 326–40.

Wang, Yiman 王亦蛮 (2009), "Xiezuo haishi biaoyan: zheshigewenti—20 shiji 20, 30 niandai Shanghai nüyanyuan, zuojia ji 'xinnüxing' zhi si" 写作还是表演：这是个问题——20 世纪 20、30 年代上海女演员、作家及"新女性"之死 (To write or to act: that is the question – 1920s to 30s Shanghai actress-writers, and the death of the "new woman"), *Wenyi yanjiu* 文艺研究 (Research on art and literature) 4: 98.

Wang, Ying-bei (2009), "Love Letters from the Colonizer: The Cultural Identity Issue in *Cape No. 7*," *Asian Cinema* 20.2: 260–71.

Wangyi Entertainment (2009a), "172 ge mingxing doumei ta/ta? Jiemi *Jianguo daye* shao le shei" 172 个明星都没他/她？ 揭秘《建国大业》少了谁 (Not found among 172 stars? Who is missing in *The Founding of a Republic*?) (July 9), http://ent.163.com/09/0709/16/5DPUPIRS000300B1.html. Accessed July 6, 2010.

Wangyi Entertainment (2009b), "*Jianguo daye* shangzuo chao 7 cheng, mingxing taiduo qiang fengtou"《建国大业》上座超7成，明星太多抢风头" (70% theater attendance for *The Founding of a Republic*, but too many stars compete for attention) (September 16), http://ent.163.com/09/0916/19/5JBV2Q39000300B1.html. Accessed July 6, 2010.

Wei, S. Louisa (2010), "Women's Trajectories in Chinese and Japanese Cinemas: A Chronological Overview," in *Dekalog 4: On East Asian Filmmakers* (ed. Kate E. Taylor), London: Wallflower Press.

Welch, David (2005), "Introduction: 'Winning Hearts and Minds': The Changing Context of Reportage and Propaganda, 1900–2003," in *War and the Media: Reportage and Propaganda, 1900–2003* (eds Mark Connelly and David Welch), London: I.B. Tauris, ix–xxii.

Wen, Biezhuang 温别庄, "Bainian Shanghai dianying dashiji" 百年上海电影大事记 (A centennial review of major film events in Shanghai), Oriental publicity and education information network, http://www.dfxj.gov.cn/dfxjw/dfxj/node2831/node2863/node2881/userobject1ai46132.html. Accessed November 12, 2010.

Whorf, B. L. (1956), *Language, Thought, and Reality*, Cambridge, MA: MIT Press.

Wilkerson, Douglas (1994), "Film and the Visual Arts in China: An Introduction," in *Cinematic Landscapes: Observations on the Visual Arts and Cinema of China and Japan* (eds Linda Ehrlich and David Desser), Austin: University of Texas Press, 39–44.

Wilkinson, Endymion (2000), *Chinese History: A Manual*, Cambridge, MA: Harvard–Yenching Institute.

Willemen, Paul (1994), *Looks and Frictions: Essays in Cultural Studies and Film Theory*, London: British Film Institute.

Willemen, Paul and Valentina Vitali (eds) (2006), *Theorizing National Cinema*, London: British Film Institute.

Williams, Linda (1994–5), "Reviewed Work(s): *Cinema and Spectatorship* by Judith Mayne," *Film Quarterly* 48.2: 56–7.

Williams, Linda (1998), "Melodrama Revisited," in *Refiguring American Film Genres: History and Theory* (ed. Nick Browne), Berkeley: University of California Press, 42–88.

Williams, Linda (2001), *Playing the Race Card: American Melodrama from Griffith to P. J. Simpson*, Princeton: Princeton University Press.

Williams, Tony (1998), "Border-Crossing Melodrama: *Song of the Exile* (Ann Hui, 1990)," *Jump Cut* 42: 94–100.

Williams, Tony (2001), "Michelle Yeoh: Under Eastern Eyes," *Asian Cinema* 12.2: 119–31.

Williams, Tony (2003), "Transnational Stardom: The Case of Maggie Cheung Man-yuk," *Asian Cinema* 14.2: 180–96.

Witke, Roxane (1977), *Comrade Chiang Ch'ing*, Boston: Little, Brown.

Wong, Ain-ling 黄爱玲 (ed.) (1998), *Shiren daoyan – Fei Mu* 诗人导演——费穆 (The poet director – Fei Mu), Hong Kong: Hong Kong Film Critics Society.

Wong, Ain-ling 黄爱玲 (ed.) (2002), *The Cathay Story*, Hong Kong: Hong Kong Film Archive.

Wong, Ain-ling 黄爱玲 (ed.) (2003), *The Shaw Screen: A Preliminary Study*, Hong Kong: Hong Kong Film Archive.

Wong, Ain-ling 黄爱玲 (ed.) (2005), *The Hong Kong–Guangdong Film Connection*, Hong Kong: Hong Kong Film Archive.

Wong, Ain-ling 黄爱玲 (ed.) (2006), *The Glorious Modernity of Kong Ngee*, Hong Kong: Hong Kong Film Archive.

Wong, Ain-ling 黄爱玲 (ed.) (2008), *Guyuan chunmeng: Zhu Shilin de dianying rensheng* 故园春梦：朱石麟的电影人生 (Spring dream of the hometown: The cinema and life of Zhu Shilin), Hong Kong: Hong Kong Film Archive.

Wong, Ain-ling 黄爱玲 (ed.) (2009), *The Cathay Story*, rev. edn, Hong Kong: Hong Kong Film Archive.

Wong, Cindy Hing-Yuk (2007), "Distant Screens: Film Festivals and the Global Projection of Hong Kong Cinema," in *Hong Kong Film, Hollywood and New Global Cinema: No Film is an Island* (eds Gina Marchetti and Tan See Kam), London: Routledge, 177–92.

World Journal (2000), "Xie Jin on Contemporary Chinese Film," *World Journal* (January 21): E7.

Wu, Chia-chi (2006), *Chinese Language Cinemas in Transnational Flux*, PhD dissertation, Los Angeles: University of Southern California.

Wu, Chia-chi (2007), "Festivals, Criticism and the International Reputation of Taiwan New Cinema," in in *Cinema Taiwan: Politics, Popularity and State of the Arts* (eds Darrell William Davis and Ru-Shou Robert Chen), London: Routledge, 75–91.

Wu, Guanping 吴冠平 (2008), "Ta jiao Liu Yuejin——Ma Liwen fangtan" 他叫刘跃进——马俪文访谈 (His name is Liu Yuejin: Interview with Ma Liwen), *Dianying yishu* 2: 76–9.

Wu, Hao 吴昊 (1993), *Xianggang dianying minsuxue* 香港电影民俗学 (Hong Kong film folklore), Hong Kong: Ciwenhua.

Wu, Hung (ed.) (2000), *Exhibiting Experimental Art in China*, Chicago: Smart Museum of Art, University of Chicago.

Wu, Hung and Christopher Phillips (eds) (2004), *Between Past and Future: New Photography and Video from China*, Chicago: Smart Museum of Art, University of Chicago, and New York: International Center for Photography and Asia Society.

Wu, Vivian (2007), "Film a Vehicle for Political Sensibilities; Critics, Supporters Use Movie to Put their Case," *South China Morning Post* (December 9): 6.

Wu, Wenguang 吴文光 (ed.) (2000), *Xianchang* 现场 (On the scene), vol. 1, Tianjin: Tianjin shehui kexue chubanshe.

Wu, Wenguang 吴文光 (ed.) (2001a), *Xianchang* 现场 (On the scene), vol. 2, Tianjin: Tianjin shehui kexue chubanshe.

Wu, Wenguang 吴文光 (2001b), *Jianghu baogao* 江湖报告 (Reports of Jianghu), Beijing: Zhongguo qingnian chubanshe.

Wu, Wenguang 吴文光 (ed.) (2005), *Xianchang* 现场 (On the scene), vol. 3, Nanning: Guangxi shifan daxue chubanshe.

Wu, Wenguang 吴文光 (2006a), "DV: Individual Filmmaking" (trans. Cathryn Clayton), *Cinema Journal* 46.1: 136–40.

Wu, Wenguang 吴文光 (2006b), *Document: Chinese Contemporary Art*, vol. 1, Beijing: Beijing Storm Culture and Media.

Wu, Wenguang 吴文光 (n.d.), Caochangdi Workstation website 草场地工作站, http://www.ccdworkstation.com/. Accessed August 1, 2009.

Wu, Xiaodong 吴晓东 (2009), "Zhongguo dianying fenji 89.9% wangyou shuohao" 中国电影分级 89.9% 网友说好 (89.9% support a film rating system in Internet survey), *Zhongguo qingnian bao* (February 26): 7.

Wu, Xiaoli 吴小丽 (2009), "Zhongguo dangdai chengshi dianying: lishi de xingge jueding mingyun 中国当代城市电影: 历史的性格决定命运 (Contemporary Chinese urban cinema: Its fate determined by historical character), *Shanghai daxue xuebao* 上海大学学报 (Journal of Shanghai University) 16.1: 101–12.

Wu, Yigong 吴贻弓 et al. (eds) (1999), *Shanghai dianying zhi* 上海电影志 (Shanghai film gazetteer), Shanghai: Shanghai kexue chubanshe.

Wu, Yigong 吴贻弓 et al. (eds) (1992), "Dui sanwenshi dianying de zhuiqiu" 对散文式电影的探求 (Pursuit of essay-like films), in in *Zhongguo dianying lilun wenxuan: 1920–1989* 中国电影理论文选 *1920–1989* (Selected works of Chinese film theory, 1920–1989) (ed. Luo Yijun), Beijing: Wenhua yishu chubanshe, 1992, vol. 2: 521–34.

Xia, Guangfu 夏光富 (2007), "Mo zhuan sheng shiqi de Zhongguo yingye jingying" 默转声时期的中国影业经营 (Chinese film industry management during the silence-to-sound period), *Sichuan xiju* (Sichuan theater) 4: 35–7.

Xia, Yan 夏衍 (1992), "Zatan gaibian" 杂谈改编 (Miscellaneous words on adaptation), in *Zhongguo dianying lilun wenxuan: 1920–1989* 中国电影理论文选 *1920–1989* (Selected works of Chinese film theory, 1920–1989) (ed. Luo Yijun), Beijing: Wenhua yishu chubanshe, 1992, vol. 1: 494–503.

Xiao, Zhiwei (1994), *Film Censorship in China, 1927–1937*, PhD dissertation, San Diego: University of California.

Xiao, Zhiwei (2004), "The Expulsion of Hollywood from China, 1949–1951," *Twentieth Century China* 30.1: 64–81.

Xiao, Zhiwei (2010), "American Films in China Prior to 1950," in *Art, Politics, and Commerce in Chinese Cinema* (eds Ying Zhu and Stanley Rosen), Hong Kong: Hong Kong University Press, 55–69.

Xiao, Zhiwei 肖志伟 and Chen Mo 陈墨 (2004), "Kuahai de "Changcheng": cong jianli dao tanta – Changcheng huapian gongsi lishi cutan" 跨海的"长城"：从建立到坍塌——长城画片公司历史粗探 (The "Great Wall" that crossed the ocean: Its rise and fall – a preliminary study of the history of Great Wall Film Co.), *Dangdai dianying* 3: 36–44.

Xie, Fei 谢飞 (2009), "Zhongguo dianying zhuanxing 30 nian" 中国电影转型 30 年 (The transformation of Chinese film over thirty years), *Liaowang xinwen zhoukan* 瞭望新闻周刊 (Outlook weekly) 1 (January 5): 60–3.

Xie, Jin 谢晋 (2007), *Xie Jin dianying xuanji: fansi juan* 谢晋电影选集：反思卷 (The films of Xie Jin: Reflections), Shanghai: Shanghai daxue chubanshe.

Xinhuanet.com (2007), "Cutting of *Lust, Caution* Renews Calling for Film Rating System in China" (September 10), http://news.xinhuanet.com/english/2007–09/10/content_6700355_3.htm. Accessed July 5, 2008.

Xu, Baike 徐百柯 (2008), "Zhongguo dianying maobing zai na? Jia Zhangke fangtan" 中国电影毛病在那：贾樟柯访谈 (Where are problems in Chinese films? An interview with Jia Zhangke), *Zhongguo qingnian bao* (November 26): 9.

Xu, Changlin 徐昌霖 (1944), *Chongqing wuyanxia* 重庆屋檐下 (Under the eaves of Chongqing), Chongqing: Shuowenshe.

Xu, Changlin 徐昌霖 (1945), *Chongqing wuyanxia* 重庆屋檐下 (Under the eaves of Chongqing), Shanghai: Dalu tushu zazhi.

Xu, Changlin 徐昌霖 (1962), "Xiang chuantong yishu tansheng qiu bao" 向传统艺术探胜求宝 (Learning from traditional arts), *Dianying yishu* nos. 1, 2, 4.

Xu, Chihen 徐耻痕 (1927), *Zhongguo yingxi daguan* 中国影戏大观 (An overview of Chinese shadowplay), Shanghai: Dadong.

Xu, Daoming 许道明 (1999), *Haipai wenxue lun* 海派文学论 (Studies on haipai literature), Shanghai: Fudan daxue chubanshe.

Xu, Dianqing (1997), "The KMT Party's Enterprises in Taiwan," *Modern Asian Studies* 31.2: 399–413.

Xu, Gary G. (2007), *Sinascape: Contemporary Chinese Cinema*, Lanham, MD: Rowman and Littlefield.

Xu, Qianlin 许浅林 (2005), *Zhongguo dianying jishu fazhan jianshi* 中国电影技术发展简史 (A brief history of China's film technology), Beijing: Zhongguo dianying chubanshe.

Xu, Zhuodai 徐卓呆 (1924), *Yingxi xue* 影戏学 (The study of shadowplay), Shanghai: Huadong.

Xu, Ziwei 徐子澂 (2010), "Mingyuo dianying zhaji zhi *Xuezhong guchu*" 民国电影札记之《雪中孤雏》 (Notes on films of the republican period: *An Orphan in the Storm*), http://blog.sina.com.cn/s/blog_5d7251ff0100hpas.html. Accessed August 7, 2010.

Xuan, Jinglin 宣景琳 (1956), "Wo de yinbu shenghuo" 我的银幕生活 (My screen life), *Zhongguo dianying* 3: 72–5.

Yan, Hui 颜慧 and Suo Yabin 索亚斌 (2005), *Zhongguo donghua dianying shi* 中国动画电影史 (History of Chinese animation films), Beijing: Zhongguo dianying chubanshe.

Yang, Hansheng 阳翰笙 (1938), "Guanyu guofang dianying zhi jianli" 关于国防电影之建立 (On establishing national defense films), *Kangzhan dianying* 抗战电影 1 (March 31),

Hangkou; quoted in Jihua Cheng et al., *Zhongguo dianying fazhan shi* 中国电影发展史 (A history of the development of Chinese film), Beijing: Zhongguo dianying chubanshe, 1998, vol. 2: 18–19.

Yang, Yuanying 杨远婴 (1996), *Taimen de shengyin: Zhongguo nüdaoyan zishu* 她们的声音：中国女电影导演自述 (Their voices: Chinese women film directors' self-narration), Beijing: Zhongguo shehui chubanshe.

Yang, Yuanying 杨远婴 (2005), *Dianying zuozhe yu wenhua zaixian: Zhongguo dianying daoyan puxi yanxun* 电影作者与文化再现：中国电影导演谱系研寻 (Film auteurs and cultural representation: Studies in the genealogy of Chinese film directors), Beijing: Zhongguo dianying chubanshe.

Yang, Yuanying 杨远婴 (2006), "Zhongguo dianying daoyan de daiqun jiegou" 中国电影导演的代群结构 (A structure of generations and groups of Chinese film directors), in *Zhongguo dianying zhuanye shi yanjiu: dianying wenhua juan* 中国电影专业史研究：电影文化卷 (ed. Yang Yuanying 杨远婴), Beijing: Zhongguo dianying chubanshe, 3–28.

Yau, Ching (2004), *Filming Margins: Tang Shu Shuen – A Forgotten Hong Kong Woman Director.* Hong Kong: Hong Kong University Press.

Yau, Ching 游静 (2005), *Xingbie guangying: Xianggang dianying zhong de xing yu xingbie wenhua* 性别光影：香港电影中的性与性别文化研究 (Sexing shadows: Genders and sexualities in Hong Kong cinema), Hong Kong: Hong Kong Film Critics Society.

Yau, Ching (2008), "Anti-gay Speech: A Necessary Evil?" *Fridae* (June 12), http://www.fridae.com/newsfeatures/2008/06/12/2072.anti-gay-speech-a-necessary-evil. Accessed March 30, 2010.

Yau, Esther C. M. (1994), "Border Crossing: Mainland China's Presence in Hong Kong Cinema," in *New Chinese Cinemas: Forms, Identities, Politics* (eds Nick Browne et al.), New York: Cambridge University Press, 180–201.

Yau, Esther C. M. (ed.) (2001), *At Full Speed: Hong Kong Cinema in a Borderless World*, Minneapolis: University of Minnesota Press.

Yau, Kinnia Shuk-ting (2003), "Shaws' Japanese Collaboration and Competition as Seen Through the Asian Film Festival Evolution," in *The Shaw Screen: A Preliminary Study* (ed. Wong Ain-ling), Hong Kong: Hong Kong Film Archive, 279–91.

Yau, Kinnia Shuk-ting (2010), *Japanese and Hong Kong Film Industries: Understanding the Origins of East Asian Film Networks*, London: Routledge.

Ye, Feng 叶枫 (1946), "Andan wuguang de mingxing" 黯淡无光的明星 (The tarnished stars), in *Zhongguo yingtan* 中国影坛 (China screen) 1.1.

Ye, Juelin 叶觉林 (1985), "Weishenmo yao dangzuo 'quwen' zhuanbo ne?" 为什么要当作"趣闻"传播呢？ (Why was it circulated as an "anecdote"?), *Dianying pingjie* 电影评介 (Film criticism) 7: 45.

Ye, Lang 叶朗 (ed.) (2008, 2009) *Wenhu chanye lanpishu* 文化产业蓝皮书 (Blue book of culture industry), Beijing: Jincheng.

Ye, Yueyu 叶月瑜, Zhuo Botang 卓伯棠, and Wu Hao 吴昊 (eds) (1999), *Sandi chuanqi: huayu dianying ershinian* 三地传奇：华语电影二十年 (A legend from the three regions: Twenty years of Chinese-language films), Taipei: Guojia dianying ziliao guan.

Yeh, Emilie Yueh-yu (1999), "A Life of Its Own: Musical Discourses in Wong Kar-wai's Films," *Post Script* 19.1: 120–36.

Yeh, Emilie Yueh-yu (2002), "Historiography and Sinification: Music in Chinese Cinema of the 1930s," *Cinema Journal* 41.3: 78–97.

Yeh, Emilie Yueh-yu (2005), "Poetics and Politics of Hou Hsiao-hsien's Films," in *Chinese-Language Film: Historiography, Poetics, Politics* (eds Sheldon Hsiao-Peng Lu and Emilie Yueh-Yu Yeh), Honolulu: University of Hawaii Press, 163–87.

Yeh, Emilie Yueh-yu (2007), "The Road Home: Stylistic Renovations of Chinese Mandarin Classics," in *Cinema Taiwan: Politics, Popularity and State of the Arts* (eds Darrell William Davis and Ru-Shou Robert Chen), London: Routledge, 203–16.

Yeh, Emilie Yueh-yu (2009), "Pitfalls of Cross-Cultural Analysis: Chinese *Wenyi* Film and Melodrama," *Asian Journal of Communication* 19.4: 438–52.

Yeh, Emilie Yueh-yu and Abe Mark Nornes (1998), "Introduction," *Narrating National Sadness: Cinematic Mapping and Hypertextual Dispersion*, University of California, Berkeley, Film Studies Program, http://cinemaspace.berkeley.edu/Papers/CityOfSadness/intro.html. Accessed February 19, 2010.

Yeh, Emilie Yueh-Yu and Darrell William Davis (2005), *Taiwan Film Directors: A Treasure Island*, New York: Columbia University Press.

Yeh, Emilie Yueh-yu and Darrell William Davis (2008), "Re-nationalizing China's Film Industry: Case Study on the China Film Group and Film Marketization," *Journal of Chinese Cinemas* 2.1: 37–51.

Yin, Hong 尹鸿 (1995), "Zai xuanhua he saodong zhong zouxiang duoyuan: 90 niandai Zhongguo dianying celüe fenxi" 在喧哗和骚动中走向多元化：90 年代中国电影策略分析 (Analysis of Chinese film strategy in the nineties), *Tianjin shehui kexue* 天津社会科学 (Tianjin social sciences) 3: 69–75.

Yin, Hong 尹鸿 (2010), "2009: Zhongguo dianying chanye beiwang" 2009: 中国电影产业备忘 (Memorandum on 2009 Chinese cinema), *Dianying yishu* 2: 5–14.

Yin, Hong 尹鸿 and Chen Han 陈航 (1993), "Jinru 90 niandai de Zhongguo dianying" 进入 90 年代的中国电影 (Chinese films in the nineties), *Dangdai dianying* 1: 6–12.

Yin, Hong 尹鸿 and Ling Yan 凌燕 (2002), *Xin Zhongguo dianying shi, 1949–2000* 新中国电影史, 1949–2000 (A history of film in new China, 1949–2000), Changsha: Hunan meishu chubanshe.

Ying, Jun 应钧 (1946), "Fang Shi Dongshan: Changtan 'cong Shanghai dao houfang'" 访史东山：畅谈"从上海到后方" (An interview with Shi Dongshan: Vivid recollections "from Shanghai to the hinterland"), *Zhongguo yingtan* 1.1: 9.

Yip, June (2004), *Envisioning Taiwan: Fiction, Cinema, and the Nation in the Cultural Imaginary*, Durham, NC: Duke University Press.

Yu, Dafu 郁达夫 (1927), "Dianying yu wenyi" 电影与文艺 (Film and the arts), *Yinxing* (Silver stars), no. 12; reprinted in *Zhongguo dianying lilun wenxuan: 1920–1989* 中国电影理论文选 *1920–1989* (Selected works of Chinese film theory, 1920–1989) (ed. Luo Yijun), Beijing: Wenhua yishu chubanshe, 1992, vol. 1: 84–9.

Yu, Lina 于丽娜 (2006), "*Xiaocheng zhi chun* yu Zhongguo dianying zhong de diyi rencheng xushi" 《小城之春》与中国电影中的第一人称叙事 (*Spring in a Small Town* and the first-person narrative in Chinese cinema), *Neimenggu daxue yishu xueyuan xuebao* (Journal of Inner Mongolia University College of Arts) 4: 3–9.

Yu, Muyun (Yu Mo-wan) 余慕云 (1980), "Xianggang dianying shihua" 香港电影史话 (A historical narrative of Hong Kong cinema), *Dianying shuangzhou kan* 电影双周刊 (City entertainment) 50: 30.

Yu, Muyun (1996), *Xianggang dianying shihua* 香港电影史话 (History of Hong Kong film), vol. 1, Hong Kong: Ciwenhua.

Yu, Muyun (ed.) (1997a), *Xianggang dianying bashinian* 香港电影八十年 (Eighty years of Hong Kong film), Hong Kong: Urban Council of Hong Kong.

Yu, Muyun (1997b), *Xianggang dianying shihua* 香港电影史话 (History of Hong Kong Film), vol. 2, Hong Kong: Ciwenhua.

Yu, Muyun (1998), *Xianggang dianying shihua* 香港电影史话 (History of Hong Kong Film), vol. 3, Hong Kong: Ciwenhua.

Yu, Muyun (2000), *Xianggang dianying shihua* 香港电影史话 (History of Hong Kong Film), vol. 4, Hong Kong: Ciwenhua.

Yu, Muyun (2001), *Xianggang dianying shihua* 香港电影史话 (History of Hong Kong Film), vol. 5, Hong Kong: Ciwenhua.

Yu, Sen-lun (2007), "*Lust, Caution* Has Record-Breaking Opening in China," Screendaily. com (November 7), http://www.screendaily.com/lust-caution-has-record-breaking-opening-in-china/4035772.article. Accessed November 15, 2010.

Yuan, Wenshu 袁文殊 (1992), "Dianying zhong de renwu, xingge he qingjie" 电影中的人物、性格和情节 (Characters, personalities and plots in film), in in *Zhongguo dianying lilun wenxuan: 1920–1989* 中国电影理论文选 *1920–1989* (Selected works of Chinese film theory, 1920–1989) (ed. Luo Yijun), Beijing: Wenhua yishu chubanshe, 1992, vol. 1: 378–9.

Yuan, Xi 袁晞 (2000), *Wu Xun zhuan pipan jishi* 吴训传批判纪事 (Record of the criticism on *Life of Wu Xun*), Wuhan: Changjiang wenyi chubanshe.

Yue, Audrey (2000a), "Migration-as-Transition: Pre-Post-1997 Hong Kong Culture in Clara Law's *Autumn Moon*," *Intersections* 4, http://intersections.anu.edu.au/issue4/yue.html. Accessed March 10, 2010.

Yue, Audrey (2000b), "What's So Queer About *Happy Together*? a.k.a. Queer (N)Asian: Interface, Community, Belonging," *Inter-Asia Cultural Studies* 1.2: 251–64.

Yue, Audrey and Helen Hok-sze Leung (eds) (2009), special issue on "Chinese Cinemas as New Media," *Journal of Chinese Cinemas* 3.1.

Yue, Ming-bao (1996), "Visual Agency and Ideological Fantasy in Three Films by Zhang Yimou," in *Narratives Agency: Self-Making in China, India, and Japan* (ed. Wimal Dissanayake), Minneapolis: University of Minnesota Press, 56–73.

Yue, Ming-bao (2000), "On Not Looking German: Ethnicity, Diaspora and the Politics of Vision," *European Journal of Cultural Studies* 3.2: 173–94.

Yue, Ming-bao (2003), "'There Is No Place Like Home': Diasporic Identifications and Taiwan Cinema of the 1960s and 1970s," *Postcolonial Studies* 6.2: 207–21.

Yue, Yang 岳扬 (2007), "2006 nian dianying pingdao shuzhi dianying chuangzhuo de jiben qingkuang" 2006 年电影频道数字电影创作的基本情况 (Basic assessment of digital film production of the Movie Channel in 2006), *Dangdai dianying* 2: 78–80.

ZDTBW (Zhongguo dianying tushi bianji weiyuanhui) 中国电影图史编辑委员会) (ed.) (2006), *Zhongguo dianying tushi: 1905–2005* 中国电影图史 *1900–2005* (An illustrated history of Chinese film, 1900–2005), Beijing: Zhongguo chuanmei daxue chubanshe.

ZDZ (Zhongguo dianying ziliaoguan) 中国电影资料馆 (China Film Archive) (ed.) (1998), *Xianggang dianying tuzhi 1913–1997* 香港电影图志 *1913–1997* (An illustrated history of Hong Kong film 1913–1997), Hangzhou: Zhejiang shying chubanshe.

ZDZ (Zhongguo dianying ziliaoguan) 中国电影资料馆 (China Film Archive) (ed.) (2007), *Xianggang dianying 10 nian* 香港电影 *10* 年 (10 years of Hong Kong film), Beijing: Zhongguo dianying chubanshe.

Zeng, Zhuangxuang (2009), personal conversation with Darrell W. Davis, Taipei, December 10.

Zhang, Baiqing 章柏青 and Jia Leilei 贾磊磊 (eds) (2006), *Zhongguo dangdai dianying fazhan shi* 中国当代电影发展史 (A history of contemporary Chinese film), Beijing: Wenhua yishu chubanshe.

Zhang, Boqing 章柏青 and Lu Hongshi 陆弘石 (eds) (2007), *Dianying de luogu zhi shiji huisheng* 电影的锣鼓之世纪回声 (Echoes of a century of gongs and drums at the movies), Beijing: Zhongguo dianying chubanshe.

Zhang, Huijun 张会军 and Yu Jianhong 俞剑红 (eds) (2006), *Zhongguo dianying chanye nianbao: 2005–2006* 中国电影产业年报: *2005–2006* (The annual report on China's film industry: 2005–2006), Beijing: Zhongguo dianying chubanshe.

Zhang, Junxiang 张骏祥 (1982), "Dianying wenxue yu dianying texing de wenti" 电影文学与电影特性的问题, *Dianying xinzuo* no. 5.

Zhang, Nuanxin 张暖忻 and Li Tuo 李陀 (1979), "Tan dianying yuyan de xiandaihua" 谈电影语言的现代化 (The modernization of film language), *Dianying yishu* 3: 40–52; trans. by Hou Jiaping, in *Chinese Film Theory: A Guide to the New Era* (eds George Semsel et al.), New York: Praeger, 10–20.

Zhang, Qiu 章秋 (1980), "Yan shenmo, yao xiang shenmo" 演什么，要象什么——上影演员达式常谈角色创造 (Acting realistically: Da Shichang talks about the portrayal of character), *Dianying huabao* 电影画报 (Screen pictorial) 3: 29.

Zhang, Rui (2008), *The Cinema of Feng Xiaogang: Commercialization and Censorship in Chinese Cinema after 1989*, Hong Kong: Hong Kong University Press.

Zhang, Wei 张巍 (2009), "Dazhong guankan dianying qingkuang wenjuan diaocha baogao" 大众观看电影情况问卷调查报告 (Report of a survey on film viewing by the populace), *Zhongguo dianying bao* (April 30): 21.

Zhang, Weihong (2009), "Soft Power in the Chinese Context," paper posted on the ARC Centre of Excellence for Creative Industries and Innovation website, https://wiki.cci.edu.au/display/CIA/Rethinking+China's+emergence. Accessed December 27, 2009.

Zhang, Xudong (1997), *Chinese Modernism in the Era of Reforms: Cultural Fever, Avant-garde Fiction, and the New Chinese Cinema*, Durham, NC: Duke University Press.

Zhang, Xudong (2000), "Epilogue: Postmodernism and Post-socialist Society – Historicizing the Present," in *Postmodernism and China* (eds Arif Dirlik and Xudong Zhang), Durham, NC: Duke University Press, 437–8.

Zhang, Yimou (2001), "Paving Chinese Film's Road to the World: Interview with Li Erwei," in *Zhang Yimou Interviews* (ed. Frances Gateward), Jackson: Mississippi University Press, 74–98.

Zhang, Yingjin (1999) (ed.), *Cinema and Urban Culture in Shanghai, 1922–1943*. Stanford, CA: Stanford University Press.

Zhang, Yingjin (2002), *Screening China: Critical Interventions, Cinematic Reconfigurations, and the Transnational Imaginary in Contemporary Chinese Cinema*, Ann Arbor: Center for Chinese Studies, University of Michigan.

Zhang, Yingjin (2004a), *Chinese National Cinema*, London: Routledge.

Zhang, Yingjin (2004b), "Styles, Subjects and Special Points of View: A Study of Contemporary Chinese Independent Documentary," *New Cinemas: Journal of Contemporary Film* 2.2: 119–35.

Zhang, Yingjin (2007a), "Rebel without a Cause? China's New Urban Generation and Postsocialist Filmmaking," in *The Urban Generation: Chinese Cinema and Society at the Turn of the Twenty-First Century* (ed. Zhang Zhen), Durham, NC: Duke University Press, 49–80.

Zhang, Yingjin (2007b), "Thinking Outside the Box: Mediation of Imaging and Information in Contemporary Chinese Independent Documentary," *Screen* 48.2: 179–92.

Zhang, Yingjin (2008), "Beyond Binary Imagination: Progress and Problems in Chinese Film Historiography," *Chinese Historical Review* 15.1: 65–87.

Zhang, Yingjin (2010a), *Cinema, Space, and Polylocality in a Globalizing China*, Honolulu: University of Hawaii Press.

Zhang, Yingjin (2010b), "Of Institutional Supervision and Individual Subjectivity: The History and Current State of Chinese Documentary," in *Art, Politics, and Commerce in Chinese Cinema* (eds Ying Zhu and Stanley Rosen), Hong Kong: Hong Kong University Press, 127–41.

Zhang, Yingjin (2010c), "Transnationalism and Translocality in Chinese Cinema," *Cinema Journal* 49.3: 135–3.

Zhang, Yingjin (2010d), "Zhao Dan: Spectrality of Martyrdom and Stardom," in *Chinese Film Stars* (eds Mary Farquhar and Yingjin Zhang), London: Routledge, 86–96.

Zhang, Yingjin (2011), "National Cinema as Translocal Practice: Reflections on Chinese Film Historiography," in *The Chinese Cinema Book* (eds Song Hwee Lim and Julian Ward), London: British Film Institute / Palgrave.

Zhang, Yingjin and Mary Farquhar (2010), "Introduction: Chinese Film Stars," in *Chinese Films Stars* (eds Mary Farquhar and Yingjin Zhang), London: Routledge, 1–16.

Zhang, Yiwu 张颐武 (1993), "Quanqiuxing houzhimin yujing zhong de Zhang Yimou" 全球性后殖民语境中的张艺谋 (Zhang Yimou in the global postcolonialist context), *Dangdai dianying* 3: 18–25.

Zhang, Yiwu 张颐武 (1994), "Hou xinshidqi Zhongguo dianying: fenlie de tiaozhan" 后新时期中国电影：分裂的挑战 (Chinese film in the post-new era: Challenges of divergence," *Dangdai dianying* 5: 4–11.

Zhang, Yu 张瑜 (1984), "Zhang Yu he yiwei guanzong de tongxin" 张瑜和一位观众的通信 (Zhang Yu's letter to an audience), *Dazhong dianying* 大众电影 (Popular cinema) 9: 16.

Zhang, Zhen (1999), "Teahouse, Shadowplay, Bricolage: *Laborer's Love* and the Question of Early Chinese Cinema," in *Cinema and Urban Culture in Shanghai, 1922–1943* (ed. Yingjin Zhang), Stanford, CA: Stanford University Press, 27–50.

Zhang, Zhen (2004), "Cosmopolitan Projections: World Literature on Chinese Screens," in *A Companion to Literature and Film* (eds Robert Stam and Alessandra Raengo), Oxford: Blackwell, 144–63.

Zhang, Zhen (2005), *An Amorous History of the Silver Screen: Shanghai Cinema 1896–1937*, Chicago: University of Chicago Press.

Zhang, Zhen (2007a), "Bearing Witness: Chinese Urban Cinema in the Era of 'Transformation' (*Zhuanxing*)," in *The Urban Generation: Chinese Cinema and Society at the Turn of the Twenty-First Century* (ed. Zhang Zhen), Durham, NC: Duke University Press, 1–45.

Zhang, Zhen (2007b) (ed.), *The Urban Generation: Chinese Cinema and Society at the Turn of the Twenty-First Century*, Durham, NC: Duke University Press.

Zhang, Zhenqin 张震钦and Yang Yuanying 杨远婴 (eds) (2002), *WTO yu Zhonguo dianying* WTO 与中国电影 (WTO and Chinese film), Beijing: Zhongguo dianying chubanshe.

Zhao, Ke 赵珂 (2009), "Cui Zi'en: Zhongguo de tongxinglian dianying hai chuyu zifa qi" 崔子恩: 中国同性恋电影还处于自发期 (Cui Zi'en: Chinese gay film is still in the self-motivating phase), *Kuake dianying* 夸克电影 (Quacor) (December 31), http://www.quacor.com/show.php?contentid=49238. Accessed April 3, 2010.

Zhao, Pei 赵培 (2006), "Yingmu feidian: qianbu guochanpian youyingwuzhong" 银幕 "废"电: 千部国产片有影无踪 (Wasted screen space: A thousand domestic pictures disappeared), *Fazhi wanbao* 法制晚报 (Evening legal news) (April 21), http://fzwb.ynet.com/article.jsp?oid=8610694. Accessed December 7, 2009.

Zhao, Qianhai 赵乾海 (2009), "Dianying qie bu yao paoqi nongmin xiongdi 电影切不要抛弃农民兄弟 (Our rural brothers definitely must not be ignored by our films), *Zhongguo wenhua bao* 中国文化报 (Chinese cultural news) (March 6): 6.

Zhao, Shi 赵实 (1999), "Chuangzao huihuang, pandeng gaofeng" 创造辉煌，攀登高峰——改革开放二十年的中国电影回顾 (Two decades of film reform), *Dianying yishu* 1: 4–12.

Zhao, Weifang 赵卫防 (2007), *Xianggang dianying shi 1897–2006* 香港电影史 *1897–2006* (A history of Hong Kong film 1897–2006), Beijing: Zhongguo guangbo dianshi chubanshe.

Zhao, Yuezhi (2010), "Whose Hero? The 'Spirit' and 'Structure' of a Made-in-China Global Blockbuster," in *Reorienting Global Communication: Indian and Chinese Media Beyond Borders* (eds Michael Curtin and Hemant Shah), Urbana: University of Illinois Press, 161–82.

Zheng, Dongtian 郑洞天 (1997), "Chengzhang de fannao: Chengshi dianying xinlu saomiao" 成长的烦恼——城市电影心路扫描 (The sorrows of growing up: A survey of approaches in urban cinema), *Dangdai dianying* 4: 67–9.

Zheng, Junli 郑君里 (1936), *Xiandai Zhongguo dianying shilüe* 现代中国电影史略 (A brief history of Chinese cinema), Shanghai: Liangyou tushuguan.

Zheng, Junli 郑君里 (1957), "Ruan Liyu he ta de biaoyan yishu" 阮玲玉和她的表演艺术 (Ruan Liyu and her acting art), *Zhongguo dianying* 2: 31–3.

Zheng, Peiwei 郑培伟 and Liu Guiqing 刘桂清 (eds) (1996), *Zhongguo wusheng dianying juben* 中国无声电影剧本 (Chinese silent film scripts), vol. 2, Beijing: Zhongguo dianying chubanshe.

Zheng, Shusen 郑树森 (ed.) (1995), *Wenhua piping yu Huayu dianying* 文化批评与华语电影 (Cultural criticism and Chinese-language film), Taipei: Maitian.

Zhong, Baoxian 钟宝贤 (2004, 2007), *Xianggang yingshiye bainian* 香港影视业百年 (A hundred years of Hong Kong film and television), Hong Kong: Sanlian.

Zhong, Dafeng 钟大丰 (1986), "'Yingxi' lilun lishi suoyuan" "影戏"理论历史溯源 (Tracing the history of "shadowplay" theory), *Dangdai dianying* 3: 75–80.

Zhong, Dafeng 钟大丰 (1994), "Zhongguo dianying de lishi jiqi genyuan: zailun 'yingxi'" 中国电影的历史及其根源: 再论'影戏' (History and origins of Chinese cinema: Another discussion of "shadowplay"), *Dianying yishu* 1: 29–35; 2: 9–14.

Zhong, Dafeng 钟大丰 (ed.) (2005), *Wenhua Yazhou: Yazhou dianying yu wenhua hezuo* 文化亚洲: 亚洲电影与文化合作 (Cultural Asia: Asian film and cultural cooperation), Beijing: Renmin ribao chubanshe.

Zhong, Dafeng 钟大丰, Pan Ruojian 潘若简, and Zhuang Yuxin 庄宇新 (eds) (2002), *Dianying lilun: xinde quanshi yu huayu* 电影理论: 新的诠释与话语 (Film theory: New interpretations and discourses), Beijing: Zhongguo dianying chubanshe.

Zhong, Dafeng 钟大丰 and Shu Xiaoming 舒晓鸣 (1995), *Zhongguo dianying shi* 中国电影史 (A history of Chinese Film), Beijing: Zhongguo guangbo dianshi chubanshe.

Zhong, Dafeng, Zhen Zhang, and Yingjin Zhang (1997), "From *Wenmingxi* (Civilized Play) to *Yingxi* (Shadowplay): The Foundation of Shanghai Film Industry in the 1920s," *Asian Cinema* 9.1: 46–64.

Zhong, Dianfei 钟惦棐 (1950), "Tan 'Zhongguo renmin de shengli' de sixiang xing" 谈《中国人民的胜利》的思想性 (On the ideological content of *Victory of the Chinese People*), *Renmin ribao* (September 24): 9.

Zhong, Dianfei 钟惦棐 (1956), "Dianying de luogu" 电影的锣鼓 (Film gongs and drums), *Wenyi bao* 文艺报 (Literary gazette) 23: 3–4.

Zhong, Dianfei 钟惦棐 (1986), "Xie Jin dianying shi si" 谢晋电影十思 (Ten thoughts on Xie Jin's films), *Wenhui bao* 文汇报 (Wenhui daily) (September 13).

Zhong, Dianfei 钟惦棐 (1987), "Yizhang bingjia tiaoer" 一张病假条儿 (A sick leave note), in *Dianying ce* 电影策 (Movie policy), Shanghai: Shanghai wenyi chubanshe, 108–11.

Zhong, Xueping (2000), *Masculinity Besieged? Issues of Modernity and Subjectivity in Chinese Literature of the Late Twentieth Century*, Durham, NC: Duke University Press.

Zhong, Xueping (2010), *Mainstream Culture Refocused: Television Drama, Society, and the Production of Meaning in Reform-Era China*, Honolulu: University of Hawaii Press.

Zhongguo baike quanshu (ed.) (1991) *Zhongguo baike quanshu: dianying juan* 中国百科全书: 电影卷 (China encyclopedia: Film volume), Beijing: Zhongguo baike quanshu chubanshe.

Zhou, Chengren 周承人 and Li Yizhuang 李以庄 (2009), *Zaoqi Xianggang dianying shi 1897–1945* 早期香港电影史 1897–1945 (A history of early Hong Kong film 1897–1945), Shanghai: Shanghai renmin chubanshe.

Zhou, Jianyun 周剑云 (ed.) (1925), *Zhongguo dianying nianjian* 中国电影年鉴 (Chinese film yearbook), Shanghai: Press unknown.

Zhou, Jianyun 周剑云 and Wang Xuchang 汪煦昌 (1924), "Yingxi gailun" 影戏概论 (Introduction to the photoplay), *Changming dianying hanshou xuexiao jiangyi* 昌明电影函授学校讲义 (Lectures of the Mingchang motion picture correspondence school); reprinted in *1897–2001 Bainian Zhongguo dianying lilun wenxuan 1897–2001* 百年中国电影理论文选 (Selected works from a hundred years of Chinese film theory 1897–2001) (ed. Ding Yaping), Beijing: Wenhua yishu chubanshe, 2002, vol. 1: 22–8.

Zhou, Xing 周星 (2005), *Zhongguo dianying yishu shi* 中国电影艺术史 (A history of Chinese film art), Beijing: Beijing daxue chubanshe.

Zhou, Xing 周星 and Song Weicai 宋维才 (2008), "Gaige kaifang 30 zhounian Zhongguo yingshi yu daxuesheng de hudong diaocha wenjuan fenxi baogao" 改革开放 30 周年中国影视与大学生的互动调查问卷分析报告 (Analysis of a survey of university students with regard to Chinese film on the 30th anniversary of reform and opening), *Dangdai dianying* 7: 120–5.

Zhou, Xuelin (2007), *Young Rebels in Contemporary Chinese Cinema*, Hong Kong: Hong Kong University Press.

Zhu, Dake 朱大可 (1986), "Xie Jin dianying moshi de quexian" 谢晋电影模式的缺陷 (Faults in Xie Jin's film model), *Wenhui bao* (July 18); trans. Hou Jianping as "The Drawback of Xie Jin's Model," in *Chinese Film Theory: A Guide to the New Era* (eds George Semsel et al.), New York: Praeger, 144–6.

Zhu, Hong 朱虹 (ed.) (2005), *Shanyao zai tongyi xingkong: Zhongguo neidi dianying zai Xianggang* 闪耀在同一星空: 中国内地电影在香港 (Sparkling in the same starry sky: Mainland Chinese cinema in Hong Kong), Hong Kong: Sanlian.

Zhu, Jingjiang 朱靖江 and Mei Bing 梅冰 (eds) (2004), *Zhongguo duli jilupian dangan* 中国独立纪录片档案 (Dossiers of Chinese independent documentary), Xi'an: Shaanxi shifan daxue chubanshe.

Zhu, Linyong (2005), "Film industry reshuffle slated for June," *China Daily* (January 6), http://www.chinainvest.com.cn/E/invest/spotlight/S20050106–07.html. Accessed December 7, 2009.

Zhu, Xiaoyang 朱晓阳 (1987), "Mangliu Zhongguo" 盲流中国 (Vagabond China), *Zhongguo zuojia* 中国作家 (Chinese writers) 4.17: 153–67.

Zhu, Ying (2002), "Commercialization and Chinese Cinema's Post-Wave," *Consumption, Markets and Culture* 5.3: 187–209.

Zhu, Ying (2003), *Chinese Cinema during the Era of Reform: The Ingenuity of the System*, Westport, CT: Praeger.

Zhu, Ying and Chris Berry (eds) (2009), *TV China*, Bloomington: Indiana University Press.

Zhu, Ying, Michael Keane, and Ruoyun Bai (eds) (2008), *TV Drama in China*, Hong Kong: Hong Kong University Press.

Zhu, Ying and Stanley Rosen (eds) (2010), *Art, Politics and Commerce in Chinese Cinema*, Hong Kong: Hong Kong University Press.

Zhu, Ying and Seio Nakajima (2010), "The Evolution of Chinese Film as an Industry," in *Art, Politics, and Commerce in Chinese Cinema* (eds Ying Zhu and Stanley Rosen), Hong Kong: Hong Kong University Press, 17–33.

Zhuang, Pinghui and Chloe Lai (2008), "Firm in the Dark Over Order to Pull Ad with Tang Wei," *South China Morning Post* (March 13): 4.

Zhuo, Botang 卓伯棠 (2003), *Xianggang xinlangchao dianying* 香港新浪潮电影 (Hong Kong New Wave cinema), Hong Kong: Cosmos.

Zhuo, Botang 卓伯棠 (2006), *Wu Yusun dianying jiangzuo* 吴宇森电影讲座 (Seminar on John Woo Films), Hong Kong: Cosmos.

Zhuravlyoz, V. (1987), "Mission in China (Memoirs of a Movie Director)," *Far Eastern Affairs* 2: 77–90, 107.

ZJDX (Zhongguo jiaoyu dianying xiehui 中国教育电影协会) (ed.) (1933), *Zhongguo jiaoyu dianying xiehui huiwu baogao, ershiyi niandu* 中国教育电影协会会务报告，二十一年度 (1932 report of the National Educational Cinematographic Society of China general affairs group), Nanjing: Zhongguo jiaoyu dianying xiehui.

ZJDX (Zhongguo jiaoyu dianying xiehui 中国教育电影协会) (ed.) (1940), *Guochan yingpian kaocha, di san ji* 国产影片考察，第三集 (Examination of domestic film production, vol. 3), Nanjing: Zhongguo jiaoyu dianying xiehui.

Zou, John Y. (2010), "Mei Lanfang: Facial Signature and Political Performance in Opera Film," in *Chinese Film Stars* (eds Mary Farquhar and Yingjin Zhang), London: Routledge, 69–85.

Filmography

CCTV = China Central Television (Beijing); CMPC = Central Motion Pictures Corporation (Taiwan)

1905

Dingjun Mountain (Dingjun shan 定军山), d. Ren Jingfeng 任景丰, Beijing: Fengtai Photography.

1909

Stealing a Roast Duck (Tou kaoya 偷烤鸭), d. Leung Siu-bo 梁少坡, Hong Kong: Asia Film and Theater.

1913

An Anxious Night (Yiye bu'an 一夜不安), d. Zhang Shichuan 张石川, Shanghai: Yaxiya.

The Difficult Couple (Nanfu nanqi 难夫难妻), d. Zhang Shichuan 张石川, Zheng Zhengqiu 郑正秋, Shanghai: Yaxiya.

1914

Zhuangzi Tests His Wife (Zhuangzi shi qi 庄子试妻), d. Lai Man-wai 黎民伟 or Lai Buk-hoi 黎北海, Hong Kong: Huamei.

1915

The Birth of a Nation (Chongjian Guangming 重见光明), d. D. W. Griffith, US: D. W. Griffith Productions, Paramount.

1916

Intolerance (Zhuanzhi du 专制毒), d. D. W. Griffith, US: Triangle Film.

1919

Broken Blossoms (Canhua lei 残花泪), d. D. W. Griffith, US: D. W. Griffith Productions.

The Red Lantern, d. Albert Capellani, US: Metro Pictures.

1920

Over the Hill to the Poorhouse, d. Harry Millarde, US: Fox.

Way Down East (Laihun 赖婚), d. D. W. Griffith, US: D. W. Griffith Productions.

A Companion to Chinese Cinema, First Edition. Edited by Yingjin Zhang.
© 2012 Blackwell Publishing Ltd. Published 2012 by Blackwell Publishing Ltd.

1921

The First Born, d. Colin Campbell, US: Hayakawa Feature Play.

Orphans of the Storm (Luanshi guchu 乱世孤雏), d. D. W. Griffith, US: D. W. Griffith
 Productions.

Sea Oath, a.k.a. *Swear by God* (Haishi 海誓), d. Dan Duyu 但杜宇, Shanghai: Shanghai
 yingxi.

The Vampires, a.k.a. *Ten Sisters* (Hongfen kulou 红粉骷髅), d. Liao Enshou 廖恩寿,
 Shanghai: Xinya.

Yan Ruisheng (Yan Rusheng 阎瑞生), d. Liao Enshou 廖恩寿, Shanghai: Zhongguo yingxi
 yanjiu she.

1922

Costumes of China (Zhongguo de fuzhuang 中国的服装), d. Li Zeyan 李泽源, New York:
 Great Wall Picture.

An Empty Dream (Qingxu meng 清虚梦), d. Ren Pengnian 任彭年, Shanghai: Commercial
 Press.

Laborer's Love (Laogong zhi aiqing 劳工之爱情), d. Zhang Shichuan 张石川, Shanghai:
 Mingxing.

Martial Arts of China (Zhongguo de guoshu 中国的国术), d. Li Zeyan 李泽源, New York:
 Great Wall Picture.

1923

Abandoned One (Qi'er 弃儿), d. Dan Duyu 但杜宇, Shanghai: Shanghai yingxi.

An Orphan Rescues His Grandpa (Gu'er jiuzu ji 孤儿救祖记), d. Zheng Zhengqiu 郑正秋,
 Shanghai: Mingxing.

The Pious Daughter-in-Law's Soup (Xiaofu geng 孝妇羹), d. Ren Pengnian 任彭年, Shanghai:
 Commercial Press.

1924

The Abandoned Wife (Qifu 弃妇), d. Li Zeyuan 李泽源, Shanghai: Changcheng.

The Poor Children (Ku'er ruonü 苦儿弱女), d. Zhang Shichuan 张石川, Shanghai: Mingxing.

1925

Between Love and Filial Duty (Zhaixing zhi nü 摘星之女), d. Li Zeyuan 李泽源, Mei
 Xuechou 梅雪俦, Shanghai: Changcheng.

A Blind Orphan Girl (Mang gunü 盲孤女), d. Zhang Shichuan 张石川, Shanghai: Mingxing.

Cupid's Puppets (Aishen de wan'ou 爱神的玩偶), d. Mei Xuechou 梅雪俦, Hou Yao 侯曜,
 Shanghai: Changcheng.

A Little Friend (Xiao pengyou 小朋友), d. Zhang Shichuan 张石川, Shanghai: Mingxing.

An Orphan's Cry (Guchu beisheng 孤雏悲声), d. Xie Caizhen 谢采贞, Shanghai: Southern Star.

A String of Pearls (Yichuan zhenzhu 一串珍珠), d. Li Zeyuan 李泽源, Shanghai: Changcheng.

The Student's Hard Life (Ku xuesheng 苦学生), d. Guan Haifeng 管海峰, Shanghai: Baihe.

Who's His Mother? (Shui shi muqin 谁是母亲), d. Gu Wuwei 顾无为, Shanghai: Da
 Zhongguo.

1926

Going to the People (Dao minjian qu 到民间去), d. Tian Han 田汉, Shanghai: Nanguo
 dianying she.

Mother's Happiness (Ersun fu 儿孙福), d. Shi Dongshan 史东山, Shanghai: Da Zhonghua.

The Silk Bouquet, d. Harry Revier, US: Fairmont Productions.

Tretya meshchanskaya (Bed and Sofa), d. Abram Room, Moscow: Sovkino.

1927

Lingering Sound of the Broken Flute (Duandi yuyin 断笛余音), d. Tian Han 田汉, Shanghai: Shanghai College of Arts.

Mr. Wu, d. William Nigh, US: MGM.

The National Revolutionary Army's War on Sea, Land, and Air (Guomin geming jun hai lu kong dazhan ji 国民革命军海陆空大战), d. Li Minwei 黎民伟, Shanghai: Minxin.

Poet from the Sea (Haijiao shiren 海角诗人), d. Hou Yao 侯曜, Shanghai: Minxin.

A Reviving Rose (Fuhuo de meigui 复活的玫瑰), d. Hou Yao 侯曜, Shanghai: Minxin.

Romance of the West Chamber (Xixiang ji 西厢记), d. Hou Yao 侯曜, Shanghai: Minxin.

Spring Dream at Lakeside (Hubian chunmeng 湖边春梦), d. Bu Wancang 卜万苍, Shanghai: Mingxing.

1928

Burning of the Red Lotus Temple (Huoshao honglian si 火烧红莲寺), d. Zhang Shichuan 张石川, Shanghai: Mingxing, 18 episodes, 1928–31.

A Wondrous Woman (Qi nüzi 奇女子), d. Shi Dongshan 史东山, Shanghai: Naimei Film.

1929

An Orphan (Xuezhong guchu 雪中孤雏), d. Zhang Huimin 张惠民, Shanghai: Huaju.

Red Heroine (Hongxia 红侠), d. Wen Yimin 文逸民 (in official sources) or Yao Shiquan 姚士泉 (on print), Shanghai: Youlian.

Revenge of an Actress (Nüling fuchouji 女伶复仇记), d. Bu wancang 卜万苍, Shanghai: Hanlun Film.

1930

Wide Flower (Yecao xianhua 野草闲花), d. Sun Yu 孙瑜，Shanghai: Lainhua.

1931

Clear Sky after Storm (Yuguo tianqing 雨过天晴), d. unknown, Guangzhou: Great China and Ji'nan.

Sing-Song Girl Red Peony (Genü Hongmudan 歌女红牡丹), d. Zhang Shichuan 张石川, Shanghai: Mingxing.

Spring on Stage (Gechang chunse 歌场春色), d. Li Pingqian 李萍倩, Shanghai: Tianyi.

Two Stars (Yinhan shuangxing 银汉双星), d. Shi Dongshan 史东山, Shanghai: Lianhua.

Wide Rose (Ye meigui 野玫瑰), d. Sun Yu 孙瑜, Shanghai: Lianhua.

1932

Army Route 19's Glorious Battle against the Japanese Enemy (Shijiulu jun kangri zhanshi 十九路军抗日战史), Shanghai: Lianhua.

The Blood of Passion on the Volcano (Huoshan qingxue 火山情血), d. Sun Yu 孙瑜, Shanghai: Lianhua.

Pink Dream (Fenhongse de meng 粉红色的梦), d. Cai Chusheng 蔡楚生, Shanghai: Lianhua.

1933

Dawn over the Metropolis (Duhui de zaochen 都会的早晨), d. Cai Chusheng 蔡楚生, Shanghai: Lianhua.

Daybreak (Tianming 天明), d. Sun Yu 孙瑜, Shanghai: Lianhua.

Little Toys (Xiao wanyi 小玩意), d. Sun Yu 孙瑜, Shanghai: Lianhua.

Night in the City (Chengshi zhi ye 城市之夜), d. Fei Mu 费穆, Shanghai: Lianhua.

Romance of the Songsters (Gelü qingchao 歌侣情潮), d. Joseph Sunn 赵树燊, San Francisco: Grandview.

Spring Silkworms (Chuncan 春蚕), d. Cheng Bugao 程步高, Shanghai: Mingxing.

Torrent (Kuangliu 狂流), d. Cheng Bugao 程步高, Shanghai: Mingxing.

Twenty-Four Hours in Shanghai (Shanghai ershisi xiaoshi 上海二十四小时), d. Shen Xiling 沈西苓, Shanghai: Mingxing.

Twin Sisters (Zimei hua 姊妹花), d. Zheng Zhengqiu 郑正秋, Shanghai: Mingxing.

A Woman of Today (Xiandai yi nüxing 现代一女性), d. Li Pingqian 李萍倩, Shanghai: Mingxing.

1934

Goddess (Shennü 神女), d. Wu Yonggang 吴永刚, Shanghai: Lianhua.

New Woman (Xin nüxing 新女性), d. Cai Chusheng 蔡楚生, Shanghai: Lianhua.

Plunder of Peach and Plum (Taoli jie 桃李劫), d. Ying Yunwei 应云卫, Shanghai: Diantong.

A Sea of Fragrant Snow (Xiangxuehai 香雪海), d. Fei Mu 费穆, Shanghai: Lianhua.

1935

Children of Troubled Times (Fengyun ernü 风云儿女), d. Xu Xingzhi 许幸之, Shanghai: Diantong.

Boatman's Daughter (Chuanjia nü 船家女), d. Shen Xiling 沈西苓, Shanghai: Mingxing.

Song of China (Tianlun 天伦), d. Luo Mingyou 罗明佑, Fei Mu 费穆, Shanghai: Lianhua.

The Road (Dalu 大路), d. Sun Yu 孙瑜, Shanghai: Lianhua.

Triumph of the Will (Triumph des Willens), d. Leni Riefenstahl, Germany: Leni Riefenstahl-Produktion.

1936

Shanghai Old and New (Xinjiu Shanghai 新旧上海), d. Cheng Bugao 程步高, Shanghai: Mingxing.

1937

Crossroads (Shizi jietou 十字街头), d. Shen Xiling 沈西苓, Shanghai: Mingxing.

The Good Earth, d. Sidney Franklin, US: Metro-Goldwyn-Mayer.

National Heroine (Minzu nüyingxiong 民族女英雄), d. Esther Eng 伍锦霞, Hong Kong: Guangyi.

Song at Midnight (Yeban gesheng 夜半歌声), d. Ma-Xu Weibang 马徐维邦, Shanghai: Xinhua.

Song for a Mother (Cimu qu 慈母曲), d. Zhu Shulin 朱石麟, Shanghai: Lianhua.

Street Angel (Malu tianshi 马路天使), d. Yuan Muzhi 袁牧之, Shanghai: Mingxing.

1938

Baoshan City Bathed in Blood (Xuejian baoshancheng 血溅宝山城), d. Situ Huimin 司徒慧敏, Hong Kong: Xinshidai.

Defending Our Soil (Baowei women de tudi 保卫我们的土地), d. Shi Dongshan 史东山, Wuhan: Zhongzhi.

Eight Hundred Heroes (Babai zhuangshi 八百壮士) d. Ying Yunwei 应云卫, Wuhan: Zhongzhi.

Yan'an and the Eighth Route Army (Yan'an yu balujun 延安与八路军), d. Yuan Muzhi 袁牧之, Yan'an: Eight Route Army Film Corp., production 1938–40.

1939

The 400 Million, d. Joris Ivens, New York: History Today.

Mulan Joins the Army (Mulan congjun 木兰从军), d. Bu Wancang 卜万仓, Shanghai: Xinhua.

Orphan Island Paradise (Gudao tiantang 孤岛天堂), d. Cai Chusheng 蔡楚生, Hong Kong: Dadi.

Women's World (Nüren shijie 女人世界), d. Esther Eng 伍锦霞, Hong Kong: Wode Film.

1940

Light in East Asia (Dongya zhiguang 东亚之光), d. He Feiguang 何非光, Chongqing, Zhongzhi.

The Light of the Overseas Chinese (Huaqiao zhi guang 华侨之光), d. Joseph Sunn 赵树燊, Hong Kong: Grandview.

1941

Baptism By Fire (Huo de xili 火的洗礼), d. Sun Yu 孙瑜, Chongqing: Zhongdian.

Youth China (Qingnian Zhongguo 青年中国), d. Su Yi 苏怡, Chongqing: Zhongdian.

1942

Casablanca, d. Michael Curtiz, US: Warner Brothers.

Storm at the Frontier (Saishang Fengyun 塞上风云), d. Ying Yunwei 应云卫, Chongqing: Zhongzhi.

1944

Dream of the Red Chamber (Honglou meng 红楼梦), d. Bu Wansang 卜万苍, Shanghai: Huaying.

1946

Working Hero in the Communist Base (Bianqu laodong yingxiong 边区劳动英雄), d. Chen Boer 陈波儿, Yan'an: Eight Route Army Film Corp.

1947

Diary of a Homecoming (Huangxiang riji 还乡日记), d. Zhang Junxiang 张骏祥, Shanghai: Zhongdian Studio 1.

Dream in Paradise (Tiantang chunmeng 天堂春梦), d. Tang Xiaodan 汤晓丹, Shanghai: Zhongdian Studio 2.

Eight Thousand Li of Cloud and Moon (Baqianlilu yunyuyue 八千里路云与月), d. Shi Dongshan 史东山 Shanghai: Kunlun.

The Gold Braided Dress (Jinfen nishang 金粉霓裳), d. Huang Hesheng 黄鹤声, San Francisco: Grandview.

Long Live the Mistress! (Taitai wansui 太太万岁), d. Sang Hu 桑弧, Shanghai: Wehnhua.

Mother and Son (Mu yu zi 母与子), d. Li Pingqian 李萍倩, Shanghai: Wehnhua.

Night Inn (Ye dian 夜店), d. Huang Zuolin 黄佐临, Shanghai: Wehnhua.

Pear Blossoms in the Storm (Baoyu lihua 暴雨梨花), d. Joseph Sunn 赵树燊, San Francisco: Grandview.

Phony Phoenix (Jiafeng xuhuang 假凤虚凰), d. Huang Zuolin 黄佐临, Shanghai: Wehnhua.

Spring in a Small Town (Xiaocheng zhi chun 小城之春), d. Fei Mu 费穆, Shanghai: Wehnhua.

The Spring River Flows East (Yijiang chunshui xiang dong liu 一江春水向东流), d. Cai Chusheng 蔡楚生, Zheng Junli 郑君里, Shanghai: Lianhua, Kunlun, two parts 1947, 1948.

War of Self-Defense, First Report (Ziwei zhanzheng xinwen, di yi hao 自卫战争新闻，第一号), d. Wang Yang 汪洋, Su Heqing 苏河清, Zhangjiakou: Jin-Cha-Ji Military Group Film Team.

1948

Les Parents terribles (The storm within), d. Jean Cocteau, Paris: Les Films Ariane.

Return Our Yan'an (Huan wo Yan'an 还我延安), d. Cheng Mo 程默, Qian Xiaozhang 钱筱璋, Northeast Film Team, documentary.

Remorse of Death (Shengsi hen 生死恨), d. Fei Mu 费穆, Shanghai: Huayi.

Spring Cannot Be Shut In (Guanbuzhu de chunguang 关不住的春光), d. Wang Weiyi 王为一, Shanghai: Kunlun.

1949

Beiping Entrance Ceremony (The Democratic Northeast No. 10) (Beiping ru cheng shi [Minzhu Dongbei di shi hao] 北平入城式 [民主东北第10号]), d. Wu Guoying 吴国英, Changchun: Northeast Studio, newsreel.

Bridge (Qiao 桥), d. Wang Bin 王滨, Changchun: Northeast Studio.

Coming Back to Their Own Unit (Huidao ziji budui lai 回到自己部队来), d. Cheng Yin 成荫, Changchun: Northeast Studio, documentary.

The Watch (Biao 表), d. Huang Zuolin 黄佐临, Shanghai: Wehnhua.

1950

Liberated China (Jiefangle de Zhongguo 解放了的中国), d. Sergei Gerasimov, Beijing: Beijing Studio / Moscow: Gorky Studio.

The Life of Wu Xun (Wu Xun zhuan 武训传), d. Sun Yu 孙瑜, Shanghai: Kunlun.

Rashomon, d. Akira Kurosawa, Japan: Daiei.

This Life of Mine (Wo zhe yibeizi 我这一辈子), d. Shi Hui 石挥, Shanghai: Wehnhua.

Victory of the Chinese People (Zhongguo renmin de shengli 中国人民的胜利), d. Leonid Varlamov, Beijing: Beijing Studio / Moscow: Central Studio for Documentary Film.

The White-Haired Girl (Baimao nü 白毛女), d. Wang Bin 王滨, Shui Hua 水华, Changchun: Northeast.

1951

A Married Couple (Women fufu zhi jian 我们夫妇之间), d. Zheng Junli 郑君里, Shanghai: Kunlun.

1952

Fighting North and South (Nanzhengbeizhan 南征北战), d. Cheng Yin 成荫, Tang Xiaodan 汤晓丹, Shanghai: Shanghai Studio.

1953

The Little Heroes (Xiaoxiao yingxiong 小小英雄), d. Jin Xi 靳夕, Shanghai: Shanghai Animation Studio.

A Mother Remembers (Cimu lei 慈母泪), d. Chun Kim 秦剑, Hong Kong: Hongmian.

That's for My Love (Wo wei qing 我为情), d. Chiang Wai-kwong 蒋伟光, Hong Kong: Huixia.

1954

Father and Son (Fu yu zi 父与子), d. Wu Hui 吴回, Hong Kong: Union Film.

Housewarming (Qiaoqian zhi xi 乔迁之喜), d. Zhu Shilin 朱石麟, Hong Kong: Longma.

Liang Shanbo and Zhu Yingtai (Liang Shanbo yu Zhu Yingtai 梁山伯与祝英台), d. Sang Hu 桑弧, Huang Sha 黄沙, Shanghai: Shanghai Studio.

1955

All That Heaven Allows, d. Douglas Sirk, US: Universal.

Between Fire and Water (Shuihuo zhijian 水火之间), d. Zhu Shilin 朱石麟, Hong Kong: Longma.

Dong Cunrui (Dong Cunrui 董存瑞), d. Guo Wei 郭维, Changchun: Changchun Studio.

Light Gunboat in the Raging Sea (Nuhai qingqi 怒海轻骑), d. Wang Bin 王滨, Tang Xiaodan 汤晓丹, Changchun: Changchun Studio.

Xue Rengui and Wang Baochuan (Xue Rengui yu Wang Baochuan 薛仁贵与王宝钏), d. He Jipeng 何基朋, Taiwan: Huaxing.

1956

At Ten o'clock on National Day (Guoqing shidian zhong 国庆十点钟), d. Wu Tian 吴天, Changchun: Changchun Studio.

Before the New Director Arrived (Xin juzhang dao lai zhi qian 新局长到来之前), d. Lü Ban 吕班, Changchun: Changchun Studio.

Darkness before Dawn (Chongpo limingqian de heian 冲破黎明前的黑暗), d. Wang Ping 王苹, Beijing: August First Studio.

The New Year's Sacrifice (Zhufu 祝福), d. Sang Hu 桑弧, Beijing: Beijing Studio.

The Old Man and the Fairy (Qiuweng yüxian ji 秋翁遇仙记), d. Wu Yonggang 吴永刚, Shanghai: Shanghai Studio.

Shanggan Ridge (Shanggan ling 上甘岭), d. Sha Meng 沙蒙, Lin Shan 林杉, Changchun: Changchun Studio.

1957

The Enemy of Women (Nüxing de chouren 女性的仇人), d. Gao Laifu 高来福, Taipei: Gaohe.

Lost Bird (Mangmang niao 茫茫鸟), d. Chen Wen-min 陈文敏, Taipei: Daming Film; Gaohe.

Mambo Girl (Manbo nülang 曼波女郎), d. Yi Wen 易文, Hong Kong: MP&GI.

The Story of Liubao Village (Liubao de gushi 柳堡的故事), d. Wang Ping 王苹, Beijing: August First Studio.

Xue Rengui and Liu Jinhua (Xue Rengui yu Liu Jinhua 薛仁贵与柳金花), d. Shao Luohui 绍罗辉, Taiwan: Gaohe.

Xue Rengui's Eastern Campaign (Xue Rengui zhengdong 薛仁贵征东), d. Luo Shaohui 绍罗辉, Chen Wen-min 陈文敏, Taiwan: Gaohe, Damin Film.

1958

Brother Wang's and Brother Li's Tour of Taiwan (Wangge Liuge you Taiwan 王哥柳哥游台湾), d. Chang Fang-shia 张方霞, Li Xing 李行, Taiwan: Tailian Film.

The Everlasting Radio Signals (Yongbu xiaoshi de dianbo 永不消逝的电波), d. Wang Ping 王苹, Beijing: August First Studio.

Huang Baomei (Huang Baomei 黄宝妹), d. Xie Jin 谢晋, Shanghai: Tianma.

1959

A Changed World (Huan le renjian 换了人间), d. Wu Tian 吴天, Changchun: Changchun Stuido.

Five Golden Flowers (Wu duo jinhua 五朵金花), d. Wang Jiayi 王家乙, Changchun: Changchun Studio.

The 400 Blows, d. François Truffaut, France: Les Films du Carrosse, Sédif Productions.

The Lin Family Shop (Linjia puzi 林家铺子), d. Shui Hua 水华, Beijing: Beijing Studio.

Song of Youth (Qingchun zhi ge 青春之歌), d. Cui Wei 崔嵬, Chen Huaikai 陈怀皑, Beijing: Beijing Studio.

Young People of Our Village, The (Women cun li de nianqingren 我们村里的年轻人), d. Su Li 苏里, Changchun: Changchun Studio.

1960

For Sixty-One Class Brothers (Weile liushiyi ge jieji xiongdi 为了六十一个阶级兄弟), d. Xie Tian 谢添, Chen Fangqian 陈方千, Beijing: Beijing Studio.

The Orphan (Renhai guhong 人海孤鸿), d. Li Chenfeng 李晨风, Hong Kong: Huanlian.

Third Sister Liu (Liu Sanjie 刘三姐), d. Su Li 苏里, Changchun: Changchun Studio.

1961

Ah, It's Spring! (Manyuan chunse 满园春色), d. Ren Yizhi (Yam Yi-ji) 任意之, Hong Kong: Yihua Film.

Locust Tree Village (Huaishu zhuang 槐树庄), d. Wang Ping 王苹, Beijing: August First Studio.

Murder in New York Chinatown (纽约唐人街碎尸案), d. Esther Eng 伍锦霞, New York: studio unknown.

Red Coral (Hong shanhu 红珊瑚), d. Wang Shaoyan 王少岩, Beijing: August First Studio.

The Red Detachment of Women (Hongse niangzijun 红色娘子军), d. Xie Jin 谢晋, Shanghai: Tianma.

Spring Comes to the Withered Tree (Kumu feng chun 枯木逢春), d. Zheng Junli 郑君里, Shanghai: Haiyan.

1962

Big Li, Little Li and Old Li (Da Li, xiao Li he lao Li 大李，小李和老李), d. Xie Jin 谢晋, Shanghai: Tianma.

Grass Grows on the Kunlun Mountain (Kunlunshan shang yike cao 昆仑山上一棵草), d. Dong Kena 董克娜, Beijing: Beijing Studio.

Li Shuangshuang (Li Shuangshuang 李双双), d. Lu Ren 鲁韧, Shanghai: Haiyan.

A Magician's Adventure (Moshushi de qiyu 魔术师的奇遇), d. Sang Hu 桑弧, Shanghai: Tianma.

Mine Warfare (Dilei zhan 地雷战), d. Tang Yingqi 唐英奇, Xu Da 徐达, Wu Jianhai 吴健海, Beijing: August First Studio.

1963

Early Spring in February (Zaochun eryue 早春二月), d. Xie Tieli 谢铁骊, Beijing: Beijing Studio.

55 Days in Peking d. Nicholas Ray, US: Allied Artists.

The Four Daughters (Simei tu 四美图), d. Ren Yizhi (Yam Yi-ji) 任意之, Hong Kong: Phoenix.

Serfs (Nongnu 农奴), d. Li Jun 李俊, Beijing: August First Studio.

Visitor on Ice Mountain (Bingshan shang de laike 冰山上的来客) d. Zhao Xinshui 赵心水, Changchun: Changchun Studio.

Young People of Our Village, Part Two (Women cun li de nianqingren, xuji 我们村里的年轻人，续集), d. Su Li 苏里, Yin Yiqing 尹一青, Changchun: Changchun Studio.

1964

Ashma (Ashima 阿诗玛), d. Liu Qiong 刘琼, Shanghai: Haiyan.

Heroic Sons and Daughters (Yingxiong ernü 英雄儿女) d. Wu Zhaodi 武兆堤, Changchun: Changchun Studio.

Sentinels under the Neon Lights (Nihongdeng xia de shaobing 霓虹灯下的哨兵), d. Wang Ping 王苹, Shanghai: Tianma Studio.

1965

The East is Red (Dongfang hong 东方红), song and dance essemble, Beijing: August First Studio.

Little Football Players (Xiao zuqiudui yuan 小足球队员), d. Yan Bili 颜碧丽, Shanghai: Shanghai Studio.

Red Crag (Liehuo zhong yongsheng 烈火中永生), d. Shui Hua 水华, Beijing: Beijing Studio.

Tunnel Warfare (Didao zhan 地道战), d. Ren Xudong 任旭东, Beijing: August First Studio.

Two Stage Sisters (Wutai jiemei 舞台姐妹), d. Xie Jin 谢晋, Shanghai: Shanghai Studio.

1966

Movie Fan Princess (Yingmi gongzhu 影迷公主), d. Wong Yiu 王尧, Hong Kong: Chi Luen.

Prince of Broadcasters (Boyin wangzi 播音王子), d. Patrick Lung Kong 龙刚, Hong Kong: Sun Ngee.

1967

Adventure of a Cloth Seller (Maibu xiongge danao taohuagong 卖布兄哥大闹桃花宫), d. Wang Man-jiao 王满娇, Taiwan: Wanjin.

Dragon Gate Inn (Longmen kezhan 龙门客栈), d. King Hu 胡金铨, Taipei: Union Film.

The Fair Ladies (Bailing liren 白领丽人), d. Ren Yizhi (Yam Yi-ji) 任意之, Hong Kong: Phoenix.

1969

Iron Petticoat (Tie niangzi 铁娘子), d. Song Cunshou 宋存寿, Taipei: Lianbang.

1970

The Arch (Dong furen 董夫人), d. Tang Shu-shuen 唐书璇, Hong Kong: Film Dynasty.

Home Sweet Home (Jia zai Taipei 家在台北), d. Bai Jingrui 白景瑞, Taipei: CMPC.

Patton, d. Franklin Schaffner, US: Twentieth Century Fox.

The Story of Ti-ying (Tiying 缇萦), d. Li Hanxiang 李翰祥, Taipei: CMPC.

Taking Tiger Moutnain by Strategy (Zhiqu Weihushan 智取威虎山), d. Xie Tieli 谢铁骊, Beijing: Beijing Studio.

1971

The Fake Tycoon (Miao jile 妙极了), d. Li Jia 李嘉, Taipei: Dazhong.

Lady With A Sword (Feng feifei 凤飞飞), d. Kao Pao-shu 高宝树, Hong Kong: Shaw Brothers.

The Red Detachment of Women (Hongse niangzijun 红色娘子军), ballet version, d. Pan Wenzhan 潘文展, Fu Jie 傅杰, Beijing: Beijing Studio.

A Touch of Zen (Xianü 侠女), d. King Hu 胡金铨, Taipei: International Film.

1972

The Autumn Execution (Qiujue 秋决), d. Li Xing 李行, Taipei: Dazhong.

The Flower Seller (Mai hua guniang 卖花姑娘), d. Choe Ik-kyu, Pyongyang: Korea Art Film Studio.

Love in a Cabin (Baiwu zhilian 白屋之恋), d. Bai Jingrui 白景瑞, Taipei: CMPC.

Raid on the White Tiger Regiment (Qixi baihu tuan 奇袭白虎团), d. Su Li 苏里, Wang Yan 王炎, Changchun: Changchun Studio.

Storm Over the Yang-zi River (Yangzijiang fengyun 扬子江风云), d. Li Hanxiang 李翰祥, Taipei: CMPC.

Story of Mother (Muqin sanshi sui, 母亲三十岁), d. Song Cunshou 宋存寿, Taipei: Dazhong.

The White-Haired Girl (Baimao nü 白毛女), d. Sang Hu 桑弧, Shanghai: Shanghai Studio.

1973

The House of 72 Tenants (Qishi'er jia fangke 七十二家房客), d. Chor Yuen 楚原, Hong Kong: Shaw Brothers, TVB.

Outside the Window (Chuangwai 窗外), d. Song Cunshou 宋存寿, Taipei: Bashi niandai.

1974

China Behind (Zaijian Zhongguo 再见中国), d. Tang Shu-shuen 唐书璇, Hong Kong: Film Dynasty, completed in 1974, released in 1987.

The Everlasting Glory (Yinglie qianqiu 英烈千秋), d Ding Shanxi 丁善玺, Taipei: CMPC.

The Pioneers (Chuangye 创业), d. Yu Yanfu 于彦夫, Changchun: Changchun Studio.

Sparkling Red Star (Shanshan de hongxing 闪闪的红星), d. Li Jun 李俊, Li Ang 李昂, Beijing: August First Studio.

1975

Diaries of a Female Soldier (Nübing riji 女兵日记), d. Wang Ying 汪莹, Taipei: China Film Studio.

Haixia (Haixia 海霞), d. Qian Jiang 钱江, Chen Huaikai 陈怀皑, Wang Haowei 王好为, Beijing: Beijing Studio.

Land of the Undaunted (Wu tu wu ming 吾土吾民), d. Li Xing 李行, Taipei: CMPC.

Sup Sap Bup Dap (Shisan buda 十三不搭), d. Tang Shu-shuen 唐书璇, Hong Kong: Zhenna Film.

1976

Counterattack (Fanji 反击), d. Li Wenhua 李文化, Beijing: Beijing Studio.

Eight Hundred Heroes (Babai zhuangshi 八百壮士), d. Ding Shanxi 丁善玺, Taipei: CMPC.

How Yukung Moved the Mountains, d. Joris Ivens, Marceline Loridan, France: Capi Films.

1977

Close Encounters of the Third Kind, Steven Spielberg, US: Columbia.

The Man from Atlantis, d. Lee S. Katzin, US: Solow Production, 1977–8.

1978

The Boy from Vietnam (Laike 来客), d. Ann Hui 许鞍华, Hong Kong: TVB.

The Extras (Qieli fei 茄哩啡), d. Yim Ho 严浩, Hong Kong: Film Force.

Flying Tigers (Feihu 飞虎), d. Zheng Zhiguo 郑治国, Yu Chunmian 于纯绵, Beijing: August First Studio.

A Teacher of Great Soldiers (Huangpu jun hun 黄埔军魂), d. Liu Jiachang 刘家昌, Taipei: CMPC.

1979

The Butterfly Murders (Diebian 蝶变), d. Tsui Hark 徐克, Hong Kong: Seasonal Film.

The China Syndrome, d. James Bridges, US: Columbia.

Cops and Robbers (Dianzhi bingbing 点指兵兵), d. Alex Cheung 章国明, Hong Kong: Bang Bang Films.

Dirty Ho (Lantou he 镧头何), d. Lau Kar-leung 刘家良, Hong Kong: Shaw Brothers.

The Hong Kong Tycoon (Baofa hu 暴发户), d. Tang Shu-shuen 唐书璇, Hong Kong: Longyi Film.

Little Flower (Xiaohua 小花)，d. Zhang Zheng 张铮, Beijing: Beijing Studio.

Loyal Overseas Chinese Family (Haiwai chizi 海外赤子), d. Ou Fan 欧凡, Xing Jitian 邢吉田, Guangzhou: Pearl River Studio.

The Secret (Fengjie 疯劫), d. Ann Hui 许鞍华, Hong Kong: Unique.

Story of a Small Town (Xiaocheng gushi 小城故事), d. Li Xing 李行, Taipei: Dazhong.

The System (Hanggui 行规), d. Peter Yung 翁维铨, Hong Kong: Bang Bang Films.

What a Family! (Qiao zhe yijiazi 瞧这一家子), d. Wang Haowei 王好为, Beijing: Beijing Studio.

Wild Goose on the Wing (Yaner zai linshao 雁儿在林梢), d. Liu Li-li 刘立立, Taipei: Superstar.

1980

Cute Girl (Jiushi liuliu de ta 就是溜溜的她), d. Hou Hsiao-hsien 候孝贤, Taipei: Dazhong.

The Happenings (Yeche 夜车), d. Yim Ho 严浩, Hong Kong: Golden Harvest.

The Legend of Tianyun Mountain (Tianyunshan quanqi 天云山传奇), d. Xie Jin 谢晋, Shanghai: Shanghai Studio.

Love Comes from the Sea (Meili yu aichou 美丽与哀愁), d. Yang Chia-yun 杨家云, Taipei: Yangguang Film.

Love on Lushan (Lushan lian 庐山恋), d. Huang Zumo 黄祖模, Shanghai: Shanghai Studio.

Lover on the Wave (Wo talang er lai 我踏浪而来), d. Chen Kunhou 陈坤厚, Taipei: Dazhong.

The Mysterious Giant Buhhda (Shenmi de dafo 神秘的大佛), d. Zhang Huaxun 张华勋, Beijing: Beijing Studio.

Spring in Autumn (Tianliang haoge qiu 天凉好个秋), d. Chen Kunhou 陈坤厚, Taipei: Dazhong.

The Spooky Bunch (Zhuangdao zheng 撞到正), d. Ann Hui 许鞍华, Hong Kong: Hi-Pitch Productions.

The Sword (Mingjian 名剑), d. Patrick Tam 谭家明, Hong Kong: Golden Harvest.

They Are in Love (Tamen zai xiangai 他们在相爱), d. Qian Jiang 钱江, Zhao Yuan 赵元, Beijing: Beijing Studio.

Unmarried Mother (Weihun mama 未婚妈妈), d. Li Mei-mi 李美弥, Taiwan: Qianji.

1981

Cheerful Wind (Feng'er tita cai 风儿踢踏踩), d. Hou Hsiao-hsien 候孝贤, Hong Kong: Golden Century.

Crazy She Devil (Fengkuang nüshaxing 沙疯狂女煞星), d. Yang Chia-yun 杨家云, Taiwan: studio unknown.

Drive to Win (Sha ou 沙鸥), d. Zhang Nuanxin 张暖忻, Beijing: Youth Studio.

Father and Son (Fuzi qing 父子情), d. Allen Fong 方育平, Hong Kong: Phoenix.

Love Massacre (Aisha 爱杀), d. Patrick Tam 谭家明, Hong Kong: David & David Investment.

The Lily (Baihe hua 百合花), d. Qian Xuege 钱学恪, Beijing: Youth Studio.

Narrow Street (Xiaojie 小街), d. Yang Yanjin 杨延晋, Shanghai: Shanghai Studio.

Regret for the Past (Shangshi 伤逝), d. Shui Hua 水华, Beijing: Beijing Studio.

The Story of Ah Q (A Q zhengzhuan 阿Q正传), d. Cen Fan 岑范, Shanghai: Shanghai Studio.

The Story of Woo Viet (Hu Yue de gushi 胡越的故事), d. Ann Hui 许鞍华, Hong Kong: Pearl City Films.

1982

Boat People (Touben nuhai 投奔怒海), d. Ann Hui 许鞍华, Hong Kong: Bluebird.

Cold Killing (Lengyan shaji 冷眼杀机), d. Yang Chia-yun 杨家云, Taipei: Yongsheng.

Girl's School (Nüzi xuexiao 女子学校), d. Li Mei-mi 李美弥, Taipei: Ziweixing Film.

Green, Green Grass of Home (Zai na hebang qingcao qing 在那河傍青草青), d. Hou Hsiao-hsien 候孝贤, Taipei: Dazhong.

Growing Up (Xiaobi de gushi 小毕的故事), d. Chen Kunhou 陈坤厚, Taipei: CMPC.

The Herdsman (Muma ren 牧马人), d. Xie Jin 谢晋, Shanghai: Shanghai Studio.

In Our Time (Gangyin de gushi 光阴的故事), d. Tao Te-chen 陶德辰, Edward Yang 杨德昌, Ko I-chen 柯一正, Chang Yi 张毅, Taipei: CMPC.

My Memory of Old Beijing (Chengnan jiushi 城南旧事), d. Wu Yigong 吴贻弓, Shanghai: Shanghai Studio.

Nomad (Liehuo qingchun 烈火青春), d. Patrick Tam 谭家明, Hong Kong: Century.

Six is Company (Qiaru caidie fei feifei 恰如彩蝶飞飞飞), d. Chen Kunhou 陈坤厚, Taipei: Dazhong.

1983

Ah Ying (Banbian ren 半边人), d. Allen Fong 方育平, Hong Kong: Phoenix.

The Boys from Fengkuei (Fenggui laide ren 风柜来的人), d. Hou Hsiao-hsien 侯孝贤, Taipei: Evergreen.

Girl Students' Dormitory (Nüdaxuesheng sushe 女大学生宿舍), d. Shi Shujun 史蜀君, Shanghai: Shanghai Studio.

The Sandwich Man (Erzi de da wanou 儿子的大玩偶), d. Hou Hsiao-hsien 侯孝贤, Wan Ren 万仁, Zeng Zhuangxiang 曾壮祥, Taipei: CMPC.

Sunset Street (Xizhao jie 夕照街), d. Wang Haowei 王好为, Beijing: Beijing Studio.

That Day on the Beach (Haitan shang de yitian 海滩上的一天), d. Edward Yang 杨德昌, Taipei: CMPC.

Zu: Warriors from the Magic Mountain (Xin shushan jianxia 新蜀山剑侠), d. Tsui Hark 徐克, Hong Kong: Golden Harvest.

1984

Border Town (Biancheng 边城), d. Ling Zifeng 凌子风, Beijing: Beijing Studio.

A Flower in the Rainy Night (Kanhai de rizi 看海的日子), d. Wang Tong 王童, Taipei: CMPC.

Girl in Red (Hongyi shaonü 红衣少女), d. Lu Xiaoya 陆小雅, Chengdu: Emei Studio.

The Girl Ming (Ming funiang 明姑娘), d. Dong Kena 董克娜, Beijing: Beijing Studio.

Homecoming (Sishui liunian 似水流年), d. Yim Ho 严浩, Hong Kong: Bluebird.

One and Eight (Yige he bage 一个和八个), d. Zhang Junzhao 张军钊, Nanning: Guangxi Studio.

A Summer at Grandpa's (Dongdong de jiaqi 冬冬的假期), d. Hou Hsiao-hsien 侯孝贤, Taipei: Wanbaolu.

Taipei Story (Qingmei zhuma 青梅竹马), d. Edward Yang 杨德昌, Taipei: CMPC.

Yamaha Fish Stall (Yamaha yudang 雅马哈鱼档), d. Zhang Liang 张良, Guangzhou: Pearl River Studio.

Yellow Earth (Huang tudi 黄土地), d. Chen Kaige 陈凯歌, Nanning: Guangxi Studio.

1985

Army Nurse (Nüer lou 女儿楼), d. Hu Mei 胡玫, Beijing: August First Studio.

A Girl from Hunan (Xiangnü xiaoxiao 湘女潇潇), d. Xie Fei 谢飞, Beijing: Youth Studio.

A Good Woman (Liangjia funü 良家妇女), d. Huang Jianzhong 黄健中, Beijing: Beijing Studio.

The Illegal Immigrant (Feifa yimin 非法移民), d. Mabel Cheung 张婉婷, Hong Kong: Shaw Brothers.

Juvenile Delinquents (Shaonian fan 少年犯), d. Zhang Liang 张良, Shenzhen: Shenzhen Studio.

Kuei-mei, A Woman (Wo zheyang guole yisheng 我这样过了一生), d. Zhang Yi 张毅, Taipei: CMPC.

Miami Vice, d. David Anspaugh, US: Michael Mann Productions.

My Name Ain't Suzie (Huajie shidai 花街时代), d. Angela Chan On Kei 陈安琪, Hong Kong: Shaw Brothers.

On the Hunting Ground (Liechang zhasa 猎场扎撒), d. Tian Zhuangzhuang 田壮壮, Hohhot: Inner Mongolian Studio.

Sacrifice of Youth (Qingchun ji 青春祭), d. Zhang Nuanxin 张暖忻, Beijing: Youth Studio.

Super Citizen (Chaoji shimin 超级市民), d. Wan Ren 万仁, Taipei: Wanbaolu.

Swan Song (Juexiang 绝响), d. Zhang Zeming 张泽鸣, Guangzhou: Pearl River Studio.

They Say the Moon is Fuller Here (Waiguo de yueliang yuanxie 外国的月亮圆些), d. Clara Law 罗卓瑶, London: National Film School.

A Time to Live, A Time to Die (Tongnian wangshi 童年往事), d. Hou Hsiao-hsien 侯孝贤, Taipei: CMPC.

Woman of Wrath (Shafu 杀夫), d. Zeng Zhuangxiang 曾壮祥, Taipei: Tomson.

Xiangsi Women's Hotel (Xiangsi nüzi kedian 相思女子客店), d. Dong Kena 董克娜, Beijing: Beijing Studio.

1986

Black Cannon Incident (Heipao shijian 黑炮事件), d. Huang Jianxin 黄建新, Xi'an: Xi'an Studio.

Dust in the Wind (Lianlian fengcheng 恋恋风尘), d. Hou Hsiao-hsien 侯孝贤, Taipei: CMPC.

Hibiscus Town (Furong zhen 芙蓉镇), d. Xie Jin 谢晋, Shanghai: Shanghai Studio.

Horse Thief (Daomazei 盗马贼), d. Tian Zhuangzhuang 田壮壮, Xi'an: Xi'an Studio.

Just Like Weather (Meiguo xin 美国心), d. Allen Fong 方育平, Hong Kong: Sil-Metropole.

Old Well (Lao jing 老井), d. Wu Tianming 吴天明, Xi'an: Xi'an Studio.

Passion (Zui ai 最爱), d. Sylvia Chang 张艾嘉, Hong Kong: D & B Films.

Peking Opera Blues (*Dao ma dan* 刀马旦), d. Tsui Hark 徐克, Hong Kong: Cinema City.

Questions for the Living (Yige sizhe dui shengzhe de fangwen 一个死者对生者的访问), d. Huang Jianzhong 黄健中, Beijing: Beijing Studio.

Tai-Pan, d. Daryl Duke, US: De Aurentiis Entertainment.

The Terrorizers (Kongbu fenzi 恐怖分子), d. Edward Yang 杨德昌, Taipei: CMPC.

The Vanished High School Girl (Shizong de nüzhongxue sheng 失踪的女中学生), d. Shi Shujun 史蜀君, Shanghai: Shanghai Studio.

1987

An Autumn's Tale (Qiutian de tonghua 秋天的童话), d. Mabel Cheung 张婉婷, Hong Kong: D & B Films.

The Game They Call Sex (Huangse gushi 黄色故事), d. Shau-Di Wang 王小棣, Sylvia Chang 张艾嘉, Jin Kuo-zhao 金国钊, Taipie: Tomson Films.

The Great Knight-Errant from the Yellow River (Huanghe daxia 黄河大侠), Zhang Xinyan 张鑫炎, Zhang Zi'en 张子恩, Xi'an: Xi'an Studio / Hong Kong: Zhongyuan.

Hey, Pals! (Hei, ge'ermen! 嘿，哥儿们！), d. Wang Fengkui 王凤奎, Changchun: Changchun Studio.

King of the Children (Haizi wang 孩子王), d. Chen Kaige 陈凯歌, Xian: Xian Studio.

The Last Emperor, d. Bernardo Bertolucci, UK: Recorded Picture, etc.

Red Sorghum (Hong gaoliang 红高粱), d. Zhang Yimou 张艺谋, Xi'an: Xi'an Studio.

Rock Kids (Yaogun qingnian 摇滚青年), d. Tian Zhuangzhuang 田壮壮, Beijing: Beijing Studio.

Rouge (Yanzhi kou 胭脂扣), d. Stanley Kwan 关锦鹏, Hong Kong: Golden Harvest.

Strawman (Daocao ren 稻草人), d. Wang Tong 王童, Taipei: CMPC.

Sunshine and Rain (Taiyangyu 太阳雨), d. Zhang Zeming 张泽鸣, Guangzhou: Pearl River Studio.

Twin Business (Er zi kaidian 二子开店), d. Wang Binglin 王秉林, Beijing: Youth Studio.

With Sugar (Gei kafei jia dian tang 给咖啡加点糖), d. Sun Zhou 孙周, Guangzhou: Pearl River Studio.

Woman Demon Human (Ren gui qing 人鬼情), d. Huang Shuqin 黄蜀芹, Shanghai: Shanghai Studio.

Women's Story (Nüren de gushi 女人的故事), d. Peng Xiaolian 彭小莲, Shanghai: Shanghai Studio.

Young Couples (Yuanyang lou 鸳鸯楼), d. Zheng Dongtian 郑洞天, Beijing: Youth Studio.

1988

As Tears Go By (Wangjiao kamen 旺角卡门), d. Wong Kar-wai 王家卫, Hong Kong: In-Gear Film.

Autumn Tempest (Luoshan feng 落山凤), d. Huang Yu-shan 黄玉珊, Taipei: CMPC.

The Case of Silver Snake (Yinshe mousha'an 银蛇谋杀案), d. Li Shaohong 李少红, Beijing: Beijing Studio.

Evening Bell (Wanzhong 晚钟), d. Wu Ziniu 吴子牛, Beijing: August First.

Gangs (Tongdang 童党), d. Lawrence Ah Mon 刘国昌, Hong Kong: Sil-Metropole.

Obsession (Fengkuang de daijia 疯狂的代价), d. Zhou Xiaowen 周晓文, Xi'an: Xi'an Studio.

The Other Half and the Other Half (Wo ai taikongren 我爱太空人), d. Clara Law 罗卓瑶, Hong Kong: Alan & Eric Films.

Samsara (Lunhui 轮回), d. Huang Jianxin 黄建新, Shanghai: Shanghai Studio.

The Troubleshooters (Wanzhu 顽主), d. Mi Jiashan 米家山, Chengdu: Emei Studio.

The Women of Yellow Earth Hill (Huangtupo de poyimen 黄土坡的婆姨们), d. Dong Kena 董克娜, Beijing: Beijing Studio.

1989

Ballad of the Yellow River (Huanghe yao 黄河谣), d. Teng Wenji 滕文骥, Xi'an: Xi'an Studio.

Banana Paradise (Xiangjiao tiantang 香蕉天堂), d. Wang Tong 王童, Taipei: CMPC.

A Better Tomorrow III (Yingxiong bense III 英雄本色 III), d. Tsui Hark 徐克, Hong Kong: Film Workshop.

City of Sadness (Beiqing chengshi 悲情城市), d. Hou Hsiao-hsien 候孝贤, Taipei: Era, 3H Films.

Eight Taels of Gold (Ba liang jin 八两金), d. Mabel Cheung 张婉婷, Hong Kong: Golden Harvest.

Ju Dou (Ju Dou 菊豆), d. Zhang Yimou 张艺谋, Japan: Tokuma Shoten.

The Last of the Aristocrats (Zuihou de guizu 最后的贵族), d. Xie Jin 谢晋, Shanghai: Shanghai Studio.

1990

Black Snow (Benmingnian 本命年), d. Xie Fei 谢飞, Beijing: Youth Studio.

Bloody Morning (Xuese qingchen 血色清晨), d. Li Shaohong 李少红, Beijing: Beijing Studio.

Bumming in Beijing (Liulang Beijing 流浪北京), d. Wu Wenguang 吴文光, Beijing, documentary.

Dancing Bull (Wuniu 舞牛), d. Allen Fong 方育平, Hong Kong: Dancing Bull Production.

Days of Being Wild (A Fei zhengchuan 阿飞正传), d. Wong Kar-wai 王家卫, Hong Kong: In-Gear Film.

Farewell China (Ai zai biexiang de jijie 爱在别乡的季节), d. Clara Law 罗卓瑶, Hong Kong: Youhe Film.

Founding Ceremony of the People's Republic (Kaiguo dadian 开国大典), d. Xiao Guiyun 肖桂云, Li Qiankuan 李前宽, Changchun: Changchun Studio.

Full Moon in New York (Renzai Niuyue 人在纽约), d. Stanley Kwan 关锦鹏, Hong Kong: Shiobu.

Good Morning, Beijing (Beijing, ni zao 北京，你早), d. Zhang Nuanxin 张暖忻, Beijing: Youth Studio.

Ju Dou (Ju Dou 菊豆), d. Zhang Yimou 张艺谋, Xi'an: Xi'an Studio.

Red Dust (Gungun hongchen 滚滚红尘), d. Yim Ho 严浩, Hong Kong: Tomson.

Song of the Exile (Ketu qiuhen 客途秋恨), d. Ann Hui 许鞍华, Hong Kong: Cos Group.

Sunless Days (Meiyou taiyang de rizi 没有太阳的日子), d. Shu Kei 舒琪, Hong Kong: Creative Workshop, documentary.

Swordsman (Xiaoao jianghu 笑傲江湖), d. King Hu 胡金铨, Hong Kong: Film Workshop.

1991

A Brighter Summer Day (Gulingjie shaonian sharen shijian 牯岭街少年杀人事件), d. Edward Yang 杨德昌, Taipei: CMPC, Yang Film Workshop.

Life on a String (Bianzou bianchang 边走边唱), d. Chen Kaige 陈凯歌, Germany: Serenity Productions.

Mama (Mama 妈妈), d. Zhang Yuan 张元, Xi'an: Xi'an Studio.

Raise the Red Lantern (Dahong denglong gaogao gua 大红灯笼高高挂), d. Zhang Yimou 张艺谋, Hong Kong: Era / Beijing: China Film Coproduction.

The Street Players (Gushu yiren 鼓书艺人), d. Tian Zhuangzhuang 田壮壮, Beijing: Beijing Studio.

Those Left Behind (Liushou nüshi 留守女士), d. Hu Xueyang 胡雪杨, Shanghai: Shanghai Studio.

Twin Bracelets (Shuangzhuo 双镯), d. Wang Yushan 黄玉珊, Hong Kong: Cosmopolitan Films.

1992

After Seperation (Da saba 大撒把), d. Xia Gang 夏钢, Beijing: Beijing Studio.

Autumn Moon (Qiuyue 秋月), d. Clara Law 罗卓瑶, Japan: Eizo Tanteisha.

Catholicism in Tibet (Tianzhu zai xizang 天主在西藏), d. Jiang Yue 蒋樾, Beijing, documentary.

Center Stage, a.k.a. *The Actress* (Ruan Lingyu 阮玲玉), d. Stanley Kwan 关锦鹏, Hong Kong: Golden Way.

Hill of No Return (Wuyan de shanqiu 无言的山丘), d. Wang Tong 王童, Taipei: CMPC.

The Holy Land for Ascetics (Qingpu 青朴), d. Wen Pulin 温普林, Tibet.

Mary from Beijing (Mengxing shifen 梦醒时分), d. Sylvia Chiang 张艾嘉, Hong Kong: Golden Harvest.

1992 New Dragon Gate Inn (Xin longmen kezhan 新龙门客栈), d. Raymond Lee 李惠民, Hong Kong: Golden Harvest.

No Regret about Youth (Qingchun wuhui 青春无悔), d. Zhou Xiaowen 周晓文, Xi'an: Xi'an Studio.

Pushing Hands (Tuishou 推手), d. Ang Lee 李安, Taipei: CMPC.

Rebels of the Neon God (Qingshaonian Nezha 青少年哪吒), d. Tsai Ming-liang 蔡明亮, Taipei: CMPC.

The Story of Qiu Ju (Qiu Ju da guansi 秋菊打官司), d. Zhang Yimou 张艺谋, Hong Kong: Sil-Metropole / Beijing: Youth Studio.

Swordsman II (Xiao'ao jianghu II – Dongfang bubai 笑傲江湖 II – 东方不败), d. Ching Siu-tung 程小东, Stanley Tong 唐季礼, Hong Kong: Film Workshop.

1993

Beijing Bastards (Beijing zazhong 北京杂种), d. Zhang Yuan 张元, Beijing: Beijing Bastards Film Team.

A Beijinger in New York (Beijingren zai Niuyue 北京人在纽约), d. Zheng Xiaolong 郑晓龙, Beijing, television series.

Big Tree County (Dashu xiang 大树乡), d. Hao Zhiqiang 郝智强, Beijing.

Blue Kite (Lan Fengzheng 蓝风筝), d. Tian Zhuangzhuang 田壮壮, Beijing: Beijing Studio.

The Days (Dongchun de rizi 冬春的日子), d. Wang Xiaoshuai 王小帅, Hong Kong: Shu Kei's Creative Workshop; Image Studio.

Eagle Shooting Heroes (Shediao yingxiong zhuan 射雕英雄传), d. Jeffrey Lau 刘镇伟, Hong Kong: Jet Tone.

Farewell My Concubine (Bawang bieji 霸王别姬), d. Chen Kaige 陈凯歌, Hong Kong: Tomson.

Flirting Scholar (Tang Bohu dian Qiuxiang 唐伯虎点秋香), d. Lik-Chi Lee 李力持, Hong Kong: Win's Movie Production.

Fong Sai Yuk (Fang Shiyu 方世玉), d. Corey Yuen 元奎, Hong Kong: Eastern Production.

For Fun (Zhao le 找乐), d. Ning Ying 宁瀛, Beijing: Beijing Studio, Van Ho Film & TV.

The Fugitive, Andrew Davis, US: Warner Brothers.

Heroic Trio (Dongfang sanxia 东方三侠), d. Johnnie To 杜琪峰, Hong Kong: China Entertainment.

1966, My Life in the Red Guards (1966, Wo de hongweibing shidai 1966，我的红卫兵时代), d. Wu Wenguang 吴文光, Beijing, documentary.

The Puppetmaster (Xi meng rensheng 戏梦人生), d. Hou Hsiao-hsien 候孝贤, Taipei: Era.

Red Beads (Xuanlian 悬恋), d. He Jianjun 何建军, Amsterdam: Fortissimo Films.

Sparkling Fox (Huohu 火狐), Wu Ziniu 吴子牛, Hong Kong: Senxin.

Swordsman III: The East is Red (Dongfang bubai – Fengyun zaiqi 东方不败 – 风云再起), d. Ching Siu-tung 程小东, Raymond Lee 李惠民, Hong Kong: Film Workshop.

Tibetan Opera Troupe in the Khams (Ganzi zangxi tuan 甘孜藏戏团), d. Fu Hongxing 傅红星, Beijing, documentary.

The Wedding Banquet (Xiyan 喜筵), d. Ang Lee 李安, Taipei: CMPC.

Weekend Lover (Zhoumo qingren 周末情人), d. Lou Ye 娄烨, Fuzhou: Fujian Studio.

Woman from the Lake of Scented Souls (Xianghun nü 香魂女), d. Xie Fei 谢飞, Tianjin: Tianjin Studio/Changchun: Changchun Studio.

A Woman Waiting for Her Period (Dengdai yueshi de nüren 等待月事的女人), d. Chien Wei-ssu 简伟斯, Taipei: Wei-Ssu Chien's Production, documentary.

1994

Ashes of Time (Dongxie xidu 东邪西毒), d. Wong Kar-wai 王家卫, Hong Kong: Jet Tone.

Chungking Express (Chongqing senlin 重庆森林), d. Wong Kar-wai 王家卫, Hong Kong: Jet Tone.

A Confucian Confusion (Duli shidai 独立时代), d. Edward Yang 杨德昌, Taipei: Atom.

The Day the Sun Turned Cold (Tianguo nizi 天国逆子), d. Yim Ho 严浩, Hong Kong: Pineast Pictures.

Dirt (Toufa luan le 头发乱了), d. Guan Hu 管虎, Hohhot: Inner Mongolia Studio.

Dou-san: A Borrowed Life (Duosang 多桑), d. Wu Nianzhen 吴念真, Taipei: Long Shong.

Eat Drink Man Woman (Yinshi nannü 饮食男女), d. Ang Lee 李安, Taipei: CMPC.

Ermo (Ermo 二嫫), d. Zhou Xiaowen 周晓文, Shanghai: Shanghai Studio.

He's a Woman She's a Man (Jinzhi yuye 金枝玉叶), d. Peter Chan 陈可辛, Hong Kong: UFO.

I Have Graduated (Wo biye le 我毕业了), d. Wang Guangli 王光利, producer Shi Jian 时间, Beijing, documentary.

In the Heat of the Sun (Yangguan canlan de rizi 阳光灿烂的日子), d. Jiang Wen 姜文, Hong Kong: Dragon Air Film/Beijing: China Film Coproduction, etc.

The Square (Guangchang 广场), d. Duan Jinchuan 段锦川, Zhang Yuan 张元, Beijing, documentary.

To Live (Huozhe 活着), d. Zhang Yimou 张艺谋, Hong Kong: Era/Shanghai: Shanghai Studio.

Vive l'Amour (Aiqing wansui 爱情万岁), d. Tsai Ming-liang 蔡明亮, Taipei: CMPC.

Who's the Woman Who's the Man (Jinzhi yuye II 金枝玉叶II), d. Peter Chan 陈可辛, Hong Kong: UFO.

1995

At Home in the World (Si hai wei jia 四海为家), d. Wu Wenguang 吴文光, Beijing, documentary.

The Cleverest Escape (Qiaoben miaotao 巧奔妙逃), d. Sun Min 孙敏, Chengdu: Emei Studio.

Fallen Angels (Duoluo tianshi 堕落天使), d. Wong Kar-wai 王家卫, Hong Kong: Jet Tone.

Frozen (Jidu hanleng 极度寒冷), d. Wang Xiaoshuai 王小帅, Hong Kong: Shu Kei's Creative Workshop.

Good Men, Good Women (Hao nan, hao nü 好男好女), d. Hou Hsiao-hsien 候孝贤, Taipei: 3H Films/Japan: Shochiku.

On the Beat (Minjing gushi 民警故事), d. Ning Ying 宁瀛, Beijing: Eurasia Communications, Beijing Studio.

The Other Bank (Bi'an 彼岸), d. Jiang Yue 蒋樾, Beijing, documentary.

Siao Yu (Shaonü Xiaoyu 少女小渔), d. Sylvia Chang 张艾嘉, Taipei: CMPC.

South Bakhor Street No. 16 (Bakuo nan jie 16 hao 八廓南街 16 号), d. Duan Jinchuan 段锦川, Tibet, documentary.

Temptress Moon (Fengyue 风月), d. Chen Kaige 陈凯歌, Hong Kong: Tomson.

1996

Buddha Bless America (Taiping tianguo 太平天国), d. Wu Nianzhen 吴念真, Taipei: Taiwan Film Center.

Drifting Life (Chunhua menglu 春花梦露), d. Lin Chengsheng 林正盛, Taipei: CMPC.

A Film About the Body (Shenti dianying 身体电影), d. Zero Chou 周美玲, Taipei: Firefly Image.

A Floating Life (Fusheng 浮生), d. Clara Law 罗卓瑶, Australia: Cineplex Odeon.

Goodbye South, Goodbye (Nanguo zaijian, nanguo 南国再见，南国), d. Hou Hsiao-hsien 候孝贤, Taipei: 3H Films.

Hu Du Men (Hudu men 虎度门), d. Shu Kei 舒琪, Hong Kong: Ko Chi-sum Productions.

Mahjong (Majiang 麻将), d. Edward Yang 杨德昌, Taipei: Atom Films.

Sons (Erzi 儿子), d. Zhang Yuan 张元, Beijing: Beijing Expression.

The Stunt Woman, a.k.a. *Ah Kam* (A Jin 阿金), d. Ann Hui 许鞍华, Hong Kong: Golden Harvest.

Yin +/− Yang: Gender in Chinese Cinema (Nansheng nüxiang: Zhongguo dianying zhi xingbie 男生女相: 中国电影之性别), d. Stanley Kwan 关锦鹏, UK: British Film Institute.

1997

Be There or Be Square (Bujian busan 不见不散), d. Feng Xiaogang 冯小刚, Beijing: Beijing Studio, Forbidden City.

Beautiful New World (Meili xin shijie 美丽新世界), d. Shi Runjiu 施润玖, Xi'an: Imar Film, Xi'an Studio.

The Dream Factory (Jiafang yifang 甲方乙方), d. Feng Xiaogang 冯小刚, Beijing: Beijing Studio.

Happy Together (Chunguang zhaxie 春光乍泄), d. Wong Kar-wai 王家卫, Hong Kong: Jet Tone.

HHH: Portrait of Hou Hsiao-hsien, d. Oliver Assayas, France: AMIP / Taipei: Arc Light Films.

Hold You Tight (Yu kuaile yu duoluo 愈快乐愈堕落), d. Stanley Kwan 关锦鹏, Hong Kong: Golden Harvest.

The Ice Storm, d. Ang Lee 李安, US: Fox Searchlight.

The Intimates (Zishu 自梳), d. Jacob Cheung 张之亮, Hong Kong: Golden Harvest.

Keep Cool (You hua haohao shuo 有话好好说), d. Zhang Yimou 张艺谋, Nanning: Guangxi Studio.

A Little Life Opera (Yisheng yitai xi 一生一台戏), d. Allen Fong 方育平, Hong Kong: Fujian Studio.

Murmur of Youth (Meili zai changge 美丽在唱歌), d. Lin Chengsheng 林正盛, Taipei: CMPC.

A Queer Story (Jilao sishi 基佬四十), d. Shu Kei 舒琪, Hong Kong: Long Shore Pictures.

The River (Heliu 河流), d. Tsai Ming-liang 蔡明亮, Taipei: Hoker Records.

Spicy Love Soup (Aiqing malatang 爱情麻辣烫), d. Zhang Yang 张扬, Xi'an: Imar Film, Xi'an Studio.

Still Love You After All These (Nianni ruxi 念你如昔), d. Stanley Kwan 关锦鹏, Hong Kong: Chinese Television Co.

Titanic, d. James Cameron, US: Paramount.

Xiao Wu (Xiao Wu 小武), d. Jia Zhangke 贾樟柯, Hong Kong: Hu Tong Communications.

Yin Yang (Yinyang 阴阳), d. Kang Jianning 康建宁, Yinchuan, documentary.

1998

Demolition and Relocation (Dingzi hu 钉子户), d. Zhang Yuan 张元, Japan: Hoso bunka Foundation, documentary.

Flowers of Shanghai (Haishanghua 海上花), d. Hou Xiaoxian 侯孝贤, Taipei: 3H Films / Japan: Shochiku.

Forever Fever (Gongfu wuwang 功夫舞王), d. Glen Goei 魏铭耀, Singapore: Chinarunn Pictures, Tiger Tiger Productions.

The Hole (Dong 洞), d. Tsai Ming-liang 蔡明亮, Taipei: Arc Light.

The Making of Steel (Zhangda chengren 长大成人), d. Lu Xuechang 路学长, Beijing: Beijing Studio.

Not One Less (Yige dou buneng shao 一个都不能少), d. Zhang Yimou 张艺谋, Xi'an: Xi'an Studio.

Peace All Year Round (Suisui ping an 岁岁平安), d. Qi Jian 戚健, Beijing: CCTV Movie Channel.

The Personals (Zhenghun qishi 征婚启事), d. Chen Guofu 陈国富, Taipei: CMPC, Zoom Hunt.

Portland Street Blues (Guhuozai qingyi pian zhi hongxing shisan mei 古惑仔情义篇之洪兴十三妹), d. Yip Wai Man 叶伟文, Hong Kong: Golden Harvest.

Restless, d. Jule Gilfillan, US: Celestial Pictures.

Sweet Degeneration (Fanglang 放浪), d. Lin Chengsheng 林正盛, Taipei: studio unknown.

1999

The Insider, d. Michael Mann, US: Touchstone, Disney.

Jiang Hu: Life on the Road (Jianghu 江湖), d. Wu Wenguang 吴文光, Beijing, documentary.

A Lingering Face (Feichang xiari 非常夏日), d. Lu Xuechang 路学长, Beijing: Beijing Studio, 1999.

Love in the Internet Age (Wanglu shidai de aiqing 网络时代的爱情), d. Jin Chen 金琛, Xi'an: Xi'an Studio.

Lunar Eclipse (Yueshi 月食), d. Wang Quan'an 王全安. Beijing: Beijing Studio.

Matrix, d. Andy Wachowski and Lana Wachowski, US: Warner Brothers.

My 1919 (Wo de 1919 我的 1919), d. Huang Jianzhong 黄健中, Beijing: Beijing Studio.

The National Anthem (Guoge 国歌), d. Wu Ziniu 吴子牛, Changsha: Xiaoxiang Studio.

Ordinary Heroes (Qianyan wanyu 千言万语), d. Ann Hui 许鞍华, Hong Kong: Class Limited.

Poetic Times (Shiyi de niandai 诗意的年代), d. Lü Yue 吕乐, Beijing: Forbidden City.

Ride with the Devil, d. Ang Lee 李安, US: Good Machine.

Seventeen Years (Guonian huijia 过年回家), d. Zhang Yuan 张元, Xi'an: Xi'an Studio, Keetman Limited.

Shower (Xizao 洗澡), d. Zhang Yang 张扬, Xi'an: Imar Film, Xi'an Studio.

Tempting Hearts (Xin dong 心动), d. Sylvia Chang 张艾嘉, Hong Kong: Media Asia.

A Tree in House (Mei shi touzhe le 没事偷着乐), d. Yang Yazhou 杨亚洲, Xi'an: Xi'an Studio.

2000

Betelnut Beauty (Ai ni di wo 爱你的我), d. Lin Chengsheng 林正盛, Taipei: Arc Light.

Bundled (Wo jiao Ahmingla 我叫阿铭啦), d. Singing Chen 陈芯宜, Taiwan: Xingyin.

Crazy English (Fengkuang yingyu 疯狂英语), d. Zhang Yuan 张元, Beijing: Keetman Limited, documentary.

Crouching Tiger, Hidden Dragon (Wohu canglong 卧虎藏龙), d. Ang Lee 李安, US: Columbia, Good Machine / Beijing: China Film Coproduction / Taipei: Zoom Hunt.

Devils on the Doorstop (Guizi laile 鬼子来了), d. Jiang Wen 姜文, Beijing: Huayi Brothers.

Diary: Snow, Nov. 21, 1998 (Riji: 1998, 11 yue 11 ri, xue 日记：1998, 11 月 11 日, 雪), d. Wu Wenguang 吴文光, Beijing, documentary.

Durian Durian (Liulian piaopiao 榴莲飘飘), d. Fruit Chan 陈果, Hong Kong: Golden Network / France: Canal +.

The Goddess of 1967 (Xunzhao 1967 de nüshen 寻找 1967 的女神), d. Clara Law 罗卓瑶, Australia: New South Wales Film & Television Office.

Grand Mansion Gate (Da zhaimen 大宅门), d. Guo Baochang 郭宝昌, television series.

Happy Times (Xingfu shiguang 幸福时光), d. Zhang Yimou 张艺谋, Nanning: Guangxi Studio.

I Love Beijing (Xiari nuanyangyang 夏日暖洋洋), d. Ning Ying 宁瀛, Beijing: Eurasia Communications, Happy Village.

In the Mood for Love (Huayang nianhua 花样年华), d. Wong Kar-wai 王家卫, Hong Kong: Jet Tone.

Life Show (Shenghuo xiu 生活秀), d. Huo Jianqi 霍建起, Beijing: Beijing Studio.

Nightingale, Not the Only Voice (Yeying bushi weiyi de gehou 夜莺不是唯一的歌喉), d. Tang Danhong 唐丹鸿, documentary.

Platform (Zhantai 站台), d. Jia Zhangke 贾樟柯, Japan: Tmark/Hong Kong: Hutong Communications/France: Artcam.

A Sigh (Yisheng tanxi 一声叹息), d. Feng Xiaogang 冯小刚, Beijing: Beijing Studio/Huayi Brothers.

Suzhou River (Suzhou he 苏州河), d. Lou Ye 娄烨, Shanghai: Dream Factory/Germany: Essential Film.

Unhappiness Does Not Stop At One (Bu kuaile buzhi yige 不快乐的不只一个), d. Wang Fen 王芬, documentary.

Yi Yi: A One and a Two (Yiyi 一一), d. Edward Yang 杨德昌, Taipei: Atom Films.

2001

Beijing Bicycle (Shiqi sui de danche 十七岁的单车), d. Wang Xiaoshuai 王小帅, Taipei: Arc Light/Beijing: Beijing Studio.

Beijing Rocks (Beijing le yu lu 北京乐与路), d. Mabel Cheung 张婉婷, Hong Kong: Media Asia.

Big Shot's Funeral (Dawan 大腕), d. Feng Xiaogang 冯小刚, Beijing: China Film Group.

Corner's (Si jiaoluo 私角落), d. Zero Chou 周美玲, Taipei: Zeho Illusion, documentary.

Dance with Farm Workers (He mingong tiaowu 和民工跳舞), d. Wu Wenguang 吴文光, Beijing.

Enter The Clowns (Choujiao dengchang 丑角登场), d. Cui Zi'en 崔子恩, Beijing: Cui Zi Studio.

Family Video (Jiating luxiang 家庭录像), d. Yang Tianyi 杨天乙, Beijing, documentary.

Fish and Elephant (Jinnian xiatian 今年夏天), d. Li Yu 李玉, Beijing: studio unknown.

Gege (Gege 哥哥), d. Yan Yan Mak 麦婉欣, Hong Kong: Lotus Film.

The Guasha Treatment (Guasha 刮痧), d. Zheng Xiaolong 郑晓龙, Beijing: Forbidden City.

In Public (Gonggong kongjian 公共空间), d. Jia Zhangke 贾樟柯, South Korea: SIDUS, documentary.

Innocent (Zhi'ai mosheng ren 只爱陌生人), d. Simon Chung 钟德胜, Hong Kong: Ying E Chi.

Lanyu (Lanyu 蓝宇), d. Stanley Kwan 关锦鹏，Hong Kong: Kwan's Creation Workshop.

Map of Sex and Love (Qingse ditu 情色地图), d. Evans Chan 陈耀成, Hong Kong: Ying E Chi.

Quitting (Zuotian 昨天), d. Zhang Yang 张扬, Xi'an: Imar Film, Xi'an Studio.

What Time Is It There? (Ni nabian jidian? 你那边几点？), d. Tsai Ming-liang 蔡明亮, Taipei: Arena Films, Homegreen Films.

Women Soup (Nütang 女汤), d. Emily Liu (Yi-Ming) 刘怡明, Taipei: Group Power Workshop.

Women's Private Parts (Nüren na huaer 女人那话儿), d. Barbara Wong 黄真真, Hong Kong: Dongfang.

2002

Blue Gate Crossing (Lanse damen 蓝色大门), d. Chih-Yen Yee 易智言, Taipei: Arc Light.

Bright Heart (Mingliang de xin 明亮的心), d. Hao Ran 颢然, Changchun: Changchun Studio.

Double Vision (Shuangtong 双瞳), d. Chen Guofu 陈国富, Taipei: Columbia Asia.

Empty Mirror (Kong jingzi 空镜子), d. Yang Yazhou 杨亚洲, Xi'an: Xi'an Studio.

Extras (Qunzhong yanyuan 群众演员), d. Zhu Chuanming 朱传明, Beijing, documentary.

Gone is the Person Who Held Me Dearest in the World (Shijie shang zui tengwo de ren qule 世界上最疼我的人去了), d. Ma Liwan 马俪文, Beijing: Hebang Film and Television.

Hero (Yingxiong 英雄), d. Zhang Yimou 张艺谋, Hong Kong: Edko Films/Beijing: New Picture, Huayi Brothers.

Hi, Frank (Hai, Fulanke 嗨，弗兰克), d. Huang Shuqin 黄蜀芹, Beijing: Beijing Zhengtian Media.

I Love You (Wo ai ni 我爱你), d. Zhang Yuan 张元, Xi'an: Xi'an Studio / Beijing: Beida Huayi.

Lai Man-Wa: Father of Hong Kong Cinema (Xianggang dianying zhi fu Li Minwei 香港电影之父——黎民伟), d. Cai Jiguang 蔡继光, Hong Kong: Dragon Ray Pictures, documentary.

Let's Love Hong Kong (Hao yu 好郁), d. Yau Ching 游静, Hong Kong: RTV.

Old Testament (Jiuyue 旧约), d. Cui Zi'en 崔子恩, Beijing: Cui Zi Studio.

Poles Extremity (Jiduan baodao 极端宝岛), d. Zero Chou 周美玲, Taipei: Zeho Illusion.

The Secret of My Success (Linqi da shetou 拎起大舌头), d. Duan Jinchuan 段锦川, Beijing, documentary.

Shanghai Women (Jiazhuang mei ganjue 假装没感觉), d. Peng Xiaolian 彭小莲, Shanghai: Shanghai Film Group.

Spring Subway (Kai wang chuntian de ditie 开往春天的地铁), d. Zhang Yibai 张一白, Beijing: Electric Orange Entertainment.

Sunrise (Richu 日出), d. Xie Fei 谢飞, television series.

Together with You (He ni zai yiqi 和你再一起), d. Chen Kaige 陈凯歌, Beijing: China Film Group, Century Hero, CCTV Movie Channel.

Voice of Waves (Nanian xiatian de langsheng 那年夏天的浪声), d. Lisa Chen 陈秀玉, Taipei: Long Stone Production.

2003

Autumn of Blue (Qiutian de landiao 秋天的蓝调), d. Lisa Chen 陈秀玉, Taiwan: Long Stone Production.

Ayaya Feeding Boys (A ya ya qu buru 哎呀呀，去哺乳), d. Cui Zi'en 崔子恩, Beijing: Cui Zi Studio.

Before the Flood (Yanmo 淹没), d. Li Yifan 李一凡, Yan Yu 鄢雨, documentary.

Blind Shaft (Mang shan 盲山), d. Li Yang 李扬, Hong Kong: Tang Splendor.

Cell Phone (Shouji 手机), d. Feng Xiaogang 冯小刚, Xi'an: Xi'an Film/Beijing: Huayi.

Crystal Boys (Niezi 孽子), d. Cao Ruiyuan 曹瑞原, Taipei: Taiwan Public Television.

Drifters (Erdi 二弟), d. Wang Xiaoshuai 王小帅, Hong Kong: Purple Light.

Good Morning, Beijing (Zao'an Beijing 早安北京, a.k.a. Sejie 色劫), d. Pan Jianlin 潘剑林, China: studio unknown.

Goodbye Dragon Inn (Busan 不散), d. Tsai Ming-liang 蔡明亮, Taiwan: Homegreen Films.

Houjie Township (Houjie 厚街), d. Zhou Hao 周浩, Ji Jianghong 吉江红, documentary.

Jade Green Station (Bise chezhan 碧色车站), d. Yu Jian 于坚, documentary.

Love Me, If You Can (Feiyue qinghai 飞跃情海), d. Alice Wang 王毓雅, Taipei: Core Image.

Night Scene (Yejing 夜景), d. Cui Zi'en 崔子恩, Beijing: Cui Zi Studio, documentary.

Taekwondo (Taiquan dao 跆拳道), d. Mai Lisi 麦丽丝, Beijing: China Film Group.

38 Degrees (Sanshiba du 三十八度), d. Liu Xin 刘新, Chengdu: Emei Studio.

West of the Tracks (Tiexi qu 铁西区), d. Wang Bing 王兵, documentary.

2004

Butterfly (Hudie 蝴蝶), d. Yan Yan Mak 麦婉欣, Hong Kong: Lotus Film.

The Concrete Revolution (Qian ru routi de chengshi 嵌入肉体的城市), d. Xiaolu Guo 郭小橹, UK: Orchid Films.

Crow in Winter (Hanya 寒鸦), d. Zhang Dali 张大力, studio unknown, documentary.

Dyke March (Nü tongzhi youxingri 女同志游行日), d. Shi Tou 石头, documentary.

Floating Dust (Xuanhua de chentu 喧哗的尘土), d. Huang Wenhai 黄文海, documentary.

Formula 17 (Shiqisui de tiankong 十七岁的天空), d. Chen Yin-jung 陈映蓉, Taipei: Three Dots Entertainment.

Gift of Life (Shengming 生命), d. Wu Yifeng 吴乙峰, Taipei: Full Shot Media, documentary.

House of Flying Daggers (Shimian maifu 十面埋伏), d. Zhang Yimou 张艺谋, Hong Kong: Edko Films / Beijing: New Picture, etc.

Jasmine Women (Moli huakai 茉莉花开), d. Hou Yong 侯咏, Beijing: Asian Union.

Kekexili: Mountain Patrol (Kekexili 可可西里), d. Lu Chuan 陆川, Xi'an: Xian Film / Beijing: Huayi.

Kungfu Hustle (Gongfu 功夫), d. Stephen Chow 周星驰, Hong Kong: Star Overseas.

Let It Be: The Last Rice Farmer (Wumi le 无米乐), d. Yan Lanquan 颜兰权, Zhuang Yizeng 庄益增, Taipei: Public Television, documentary.

A Letter from an Unknown Woman (Yifeng mosheng nüren de laixin 一封陌生女人的来信), d. Xu Jinglei 徐静蕾, Beijing: AUFM Media.

Letters to Ali (Gei Ali de xin 给阿里的信), d. Clara Law 罗卓瑶, Australia: Lunar Films, documentary.

Losing (Shisan 失散), d. Zuo Yixiao 左益虓, studio unknown.

Showdown (Tanpai 摊牌), d. Wang Jiabin 王加宾, Beijing: CCTV Movie Channel.

Splendid Float (Yan'guang sishe gewutuan 艳光四射歌舞团), d. Zero Chou 周美玲, Taipei: Zeho Illusion.

Star Appeal (Xingxing xiang xixi 星星相吸惜), d. Cui Zi'en 崔子恩, Beijing: Cui Zi Studio.

20, 30, 40, d. Sylvia Chang 张艾嘉, Hong Kong: Columbia Asia; Taipei: Tang Moon.

2046, d. Wong Kar-wai 王家卫, Hong Kong: Arte.

Viva Tonal: The Dance Age (Tiaowu shidai 跳舞时代), d. Jian Weisi 简伟斯, Guo Zhendi 郭珍弟, Taipei: Public Television, documentary.

The World (Shijie 世界), d. Jia Zhangke 贾樟柯, Shanghai: Shanghai Film Group / Beijing: Xstream.

A World Without Thieves (Tianxia wuzei 天下无贼), d. Feng Xiaogang 冯小刚, Beijing: Huayi Brother & Taihe, Forbidden City / Hong Kong: Media Asia.

2005

Brokeback Mountain, d. Ang Lee 李安, US: Focus Features, Good Machine, etc.

Curse of Lola (Zu zhou 诅咒), d. Li Hong 李虹, Shanghai: Shanghai Film Group.

Dam Street (Hong yan 红颜), d. Li Yu 李玉, Beijing: Laurel Films.

Electric Shadow (Dianying wangshi 电影往事), d. Xiao Jiang 小江, Beijing: AUFM Media.

50 Minutes of Women (Nüren wushi fenzhong 女人五十分钟), d. Shi Tou 石头, documentary.

Fishing Luck (Dengdai feiyu 等待飞鱼), d. Tseng Wen-chen 曾文珍, Taiwan: Ocean Deep Films.

Floating (Piao 飘), d. Huang Weikai 黄伟凯, documentary.

Fuck Cinema (Cao ta ma de dianying 操他妈的电影), d. Wu Wenguang 吴文光, Beijing, documentary.

Hurricane (Bao feng zhou yu 暴风骤雨), d. Duan Jinchuan 段锦川, documentary.

My Fair Son (Wo ruhuaxiyu de erzi 我如花似玉的儿子), d. Cui Zi'en 崔子恩, Beijing: Cui Zi Studio.

912 Rumors (912 chuanzhuo 912 传说), d. Zero Chou 周美玲, Wuna 吴静怡, Taipei: Zeho Illusion.

Oxhide (Niupi 牛皮), d. Liu Jiayin 刘伽茵, Beijing.

Peacock (Kongque 孔雀), d. Gu Changwei 顾长卫, Beijing: Asian Union.

The Promise (Wuji 无极), d. Chen Kaige 陈凯歌, Beijing: Huayi Brothers, 21st Century Shengkai, etc.

Senior Year (Gaosan 高三), d. Zhou Hao 周浩, documentary.

Shanghai Dreams (Qinghong 青红), d. Wang Xiaoshuai 王小帅, Beijing: Debo Film.

The Song of Yimeng (Yimeng xiaodiao 沂蒙小调), d. Zhang Xin 张鑫, Taiyuan: Shanxi Studio / Jinan: Shandong Province Broadcasting, etc.

Stolen Life (Shengsi jie 生死劫), d. Li Shaohong 李少红, Beijing: Rosat Film and TV.

The Strait Story (Nanfang jishi zhi fushi guanying 南方纪事之浮世光影), d. Huang Yu-shan 黄玉珊, Taipei: B & W Film.

Sunflower (Xiangrikui 向日葵), d. Zhang Yang 张扬, Beijing: China Film Group.

Visions of Darkness (Heian shijie 黑暗视界), d. Zero Chou 周美玲, Taipei: Zeho Illusion.

The Wayward Cloud (Tianbian yiduo yun 天边一朵云), d. Tsai Ming-liang 蔡明亮, Taipei: Arena Films, Homegreen Films.

Withering in a Blossom Season (Shaonian huacao huang 少年花草黄), d. Cui Zi'en 崔子恩, Beijing: Cui Zi Studio.

2006

After This Our Exile (Fuzi 父子), d. Patrick Tam 谭家明, Hong Kong: Focus Films.

The Banquet (Yeyan 夜宴), d. Feng Xiaogang 冯小刚, Beijing: Huayi Brothers / Hong Kong: Media Asia.

Crazy Racer (Fengkuang de saiche 疯狂的赛车), d. Ning Hao 宁浩, Beijing: China Film Group.

Crazy Stone (Fengkuang de shitou 疯狂的石头), d. Ning Hao 宁浩, Beijing: China Film Group, Warner Brothers-Hengdian.

Curse of the Golden Flower (Mancheng jindai huangjin jia 满城尽带黄金甲), d. Zhang Yimou 张艺谋, Beijing: New Picture / Hong Kong: Elite Group.

Dong (Dong 东), d. Jia Zhangke 贾樟柯, Beijing: Xstream, documentary.

Dream Walking (Mengyou 梦游), d. Huang Wenhai 黄文海, documentary.

Eternal Summer (Shengxia guangnian 盛夏光年), d. Lester Chen 陈正道, Taipei: Three Dots Entertainment.

Flags of Our Fathers, d. Clint Eastwood, US: Dreamworks, Warner Brothers.

High School Musical, d. Kenny Ortega, TV series.

I Don't Want To Sleep Alone (Hei yanjuan 黑眼圈), d. Tsai Ming-liang 蔡明亮, Taipei: Homegreen Films.

Island Etude (Lianxi qu 练习曲), d. Chen Huai'en 陈怀恩, Taipei: Zoom Hunt.

The Knot (Yunshui yao 云水谣), d. Yin Li 尹力, Beijing: Huaxia.

Little Red Flower (Kanshangqu hen mei 看上去很美), d. Zhang Yuan 张元, Beijing: Century Hero, Beijing Century Good Tidings, etc.

Lu Xiaofeng (Lu Xiaofeng chuanqi 陆小凤传奇), d. Yuan Yingming 袁英明, Deng Yancheng 邓衍成, Xue Chunwei 薛春炜, Beijing: CCTV Movie Channel/Shanghai: Springfilm.

Meishi Street (Meishi jie 煤市街), d. Ou Ning 欧宁, Beijing: Alternative Archive, documentary.

Mission: Impossible III, d. J. J. Abrams, US: Paramount.

Nana on the Run (Ming Ming 明明), d. Susie Au 区雪儿, Beijing: Concord Creation/Hong Kong: Fable Films.

Nostalgia (Xiangchou 乡愁), d. Shu Haolun 舒浩仑, Shanghai: Film Spirit, documentary.

The Painted Veil, d. John Curran, US: Stratus Film, etc.

Pediatric Department (Erke 儿科), d. Wang Hao 汪浩, studio unknown.

Persisting with Tears in Eyes (Hanlei huozhe 含泪活着), d. Zhang Liling 张丽玲, Japan, documentary.

The Postmodern Life of My Aunt (Yima de houxiandai shenghuo 姨妈的后现代生活), d. Ann Hui 许鞍华, Hong Kong: Class Limited, etc.

Red Snow (Hongse xue 红色雪), d. Peng Tao 彭韬, Beijing: New Youth Independent Film.

Sing Whenever I Want to (Xiangchang jiuchang 想唱就唱), d. Fang Junliang 方军亮, Beijing: CCTV Movie Channel.

Still Life (Sanxia haoren 三峡好人), d. Jia Zhangke 贾樟柯, Shanghai: Shanghai Film Group/Beijing: Xstream.

Summer Palace (Yihe yuan 颐和园), d. Lou Ye 娄烨, Beijing: Dream Factory/France: Centre National de la Cinematographie, etc.

The Third Eye (Xiao xinyan 小心眼), d. Carol Lai Miu-suet 黎妙雪, Hong Kong: Basic Pictures.

Tuya's Marriage (Tuya de hunshi 图雅的婚事), d. Wang Quan'an 王全安, Beijing: Huaxia.

2007

Assembly (Jijie hao 集结号), d. Feng Xiaogang 冯小刚, Beijing: Huayi Brothers/Hong Kong: Media Asia, etc.

Dark Matter, d. Shi-zheng Chen 陈士铮, US: Saltmill, Myriad Pictures.

Help Me Eros (Bangbang wo aisheng 帮帮我爱神), d. Lee Kang-sheng 李康生, Taipei: Homegreen Films.

Life is Beautiful (La vita è bella), d. Roberto Benigni, Italy: Cecchi Gori Group, Tiger Cinematografica.

Little Moth (Xuechan 血蝉), d. Peng Tao, 彭韬, Beijing: New Youth Independent Film.

Lost in Beijing (Pingguo 苹果), d. Li Yu 李玉, Beijing: Laurel Films.

Lust, Caution (Se · jie 色·戒), d. Ang Lee 李安, US: Focus Features/Hong Kong: Sil-Metropole, etc.

The Most Distant Course (Zui yaoyuan de juli 最遥远的距离), d. Lin Jing-Jie 林靖杰, Taipei: Qixia.

My Blueberry Nights (Lanmei zhiye 蓝莓之夜), d. Wong Kar-wai 王家卫, Hong Kong: Block 2 Pictures.

Naraka 19 (Di shijiuceng kongjian 第十九层空间), d. Carol Lai 黎妙雪, Hong Kong: Media Asia.

The Song of Chatien Mountain (Chatianshan zhi ge 插天山之歌), d. Huang Yu-shan 黄玉珊, Taipei: CPT Entertainment.

Spider Lilies (Ciqing 刺青), d. Zero Chou 周美玲, Taipei: The 3rd Vision Film.

Transformers II: Revenge of the Fallen, d. Michael Bay, US: Dreamworks, Paramount.

The Warlords (Toumingzhuang 投名状), d. Peter Chan 陈可辛, Hong Kong: Media Asia / Beijing: China Film Group, etc.

2008

Besieged City (Weicheng 围城), d. Lawrence Ah Mon 刘国昌, Hong Kong: Big Pictures.

Candy Rain (Hua chiliao nei nühai 花吃了那女孩), d. Chen Hung-i 陈宏一, Taipei: Red Society.

Cape No. 7 (Haijiao qihao 海角七号), d. Wei Te-sheng 魏德圣, Taiwan: Ars Film.

The Children of Huangshi, d. Roger Spottiswoode, Australia: Australian Film Finance Corp / US: Ming Productions, etc.

City Without Baseball (Wuye zhi cheng 无野之城), d. Lawrence Lau 刘国昌, Scud 云翔, Hong Kong: Golden Scene.

The Dark Knight, d. Christopher Nolan, US: Warner Brothers, etc.

Drifting Flowers (Piaolang qingchun 漂浪青春), d. Zero Chou 周美玲, Taipei: The Third Vision Films.

The Forbidden Kingdom, d. Rob Minkoff, US: Casey Silver Productions.

Forever Enthralled (Mei Lanfang 梅兰芳), d. Chen Kaige 陈凯歌, Beijing: China Film Group.

God Man Dog (Liulang shen gou ren 流浪神狗人), d. Singing Chen 陈芯宜, Taipei: Ocean Deep Films.

In Love We Trust (Zuoyou 左右), d. Wang Xiaoshuai 王小帅, Beijing: Debo Film, Stellar Megamedia.

Kungfu Panda, d. Mark Osborne, John Stevenson, US: Dreamworks, etc.

The Legend of Bruce Lee (Li Xiaolong chuanqi 李小龙传奇), d. Li Wenqi 李文岐, Beijing: China International TV.

Lost and Found (Wo jiao Liu Yuejin 我叫刘跃进), d. Ma Liwen 马俪文, Beijing: China Film Group, Chengtian Entertainment.

Miao Miao (Miaomiao 渺渺), d. Cheng Hsiao-tse 程孝泽, Hong Kong: Block 2 Pictures, Jet Tone.

The Mummy: Tomb of the Dragon Emperor, d. Rob Cohen, US: Universal.

Red Cliff (Chibi 赤壁), d. John Woo 吴宇森, Beijing: China Film Group / US: Lion Rock.

Soul of a Demon (Hudie 蝴蝶), d. Chang Tso-chi 张作骥, Taipei: CMC Entertainment.

24 City (Ershisi chengji 二十四城记), d. Jia Zhangke 贾樟柯, Shanghai: Shanghai Film Group.

Using (Long Ge 龙哥), d. Zhou Hao 周浩, documentary.

The Way We Are (Tianshuiwei de ri yu ye 天水围的日与夜), d. Ann Hui 许鞍华, Hong Kong: Class Limited.

We Went to Wonderland (Lengku xianjing 冷酷仙境), d. Xiaolu Guo 郭小橹, UK: Perspective Films.

2009

Avatar, d. James Cameron, US: Twentieth Century Fox, etc.

Bodyguards and Assassins (Shiyue weicheng 十月围城), d. Teddy Chan 陈德森, Hong Kong: Applause Entertainment.

Cannot Live Without You (Bu neng meiyou ni 不能没有你), d. Leon Dai 戴立忍, Taipei: Partyzoo Film.

City of Life and Death (Nanjing, Nanjing 南京南京), d. Lu Chuan 陆川, Beijing: Stellar Megamedia.

Condolences (Weiwen 慰问), d. Ying Liang 应亮, Shanghai: 90 Minuites Film Studio, short feature.

Cow (Douniu 斗牛), d. Guan Hu 管虎, Changchun: Changchun Studio.

District 9, d. Neill Blomkamp, US: TriStar Pictures, etc.

Face (Lian 脸), d. Tsai Ming-liang 蔡明亮, Taipei: Homegreen Films, etc.

The Founding of a Republic (Jianguo daye 建国大业), d. Han Sanping 韩三平, Huang Jianxin 黄建新, Beijing: China Film Group, Beijing Poly-bona Film / Hong Kong: Media Asia, etc.

Gasp (Qichuan xuxu 气喘吁吁), d. Zheng Zhong 郑重, Beijing: Enlight Pictures.

The Hangover, d. Todd Phillips, US: Warner Brothers, etc.

How Are You, Dad? (Ba, ni hao ma? 爸，你好吗？), d. Chang Tso-chi 张作骥, Taipei: Chang Tso-chi Studio.

Kids from Shanghai (Wo jianqiang de xiaochuan 我坚强的小船), d. Peng Xiaolian 彭小莲, Shanghai: Eastern Cultural Film & TV Group.

Looking for Jackie (Xunzhao Chenglong 寻找成龙), d. Fang Gangliang 方刚亮, Beijing: Beijing Studio.

The Message (Fengsheng 风声), d. Chen Guofu 陈国富, Beijing: Huayi Brothers.

New Beijing, New Marriage (Xinqianmen dajie 新前门大街), d. Fan Po Po, David Cheng, Beijing: China Queer Independent Film Group.

Night and Fog (Tianshuiwei de ye yu wu 天水围的夜与雾), d. Ann Hui 许鞍华, Hong Kong: Class Limited.

Oxhide II (Niu pi II 牛皮II), d. Liu Jiayin 刘伽茵, Beijing: sponsored by Hubert Bals Fund, Rotterdam.

Permanent Residence (Yongjiu juliu 永久居留), d. Scud 云翔, Hong Kong: Artwalker.

Pinoy Sunday (Taibei xingqitian 台北星期天), d. Wi Ding Ho 何蔚庭, Taipei: Changhe Films / Tokyo: NHK, etc.

Prince of Tears (Lei wanzi 泪王子), d. Yon Fan 杨凡, Hong Kong: Far Sun Film, etc.

Queer China, 'Comrade' China (Zhi tongzhi 志同志), d. Cui Zi'en 崔子恩, Beijing: Cui Zi Studio, documentary.

Red Cliff II (Chibi II 赤壁II), d. John Woo 吴宇森, Hong Kong: Media Asia.

She, A Chinese (Zhongguo gunian 中国姑娘), d. Xiaolu Guo 郭小橹, UK: UK Film Council.

Soundless Wind Chime (Wusheng fengling 无声风铃), d. Kit Hung 洪荣杰, Hong Kong: Keep In Touch.

Spring Fever (Chunfeng chenzui de wanshang 春风沉醉的晚上), d. Lou Ye 娄烨, Beijing: Dream Factory / France: Rosem Films.

Transformers II: Revenge of the Fallen, d. Michael Bay, US: Dreamworks, Paramount.

2012, d. Roland Emmerich, US: Columbia.

A Woman, a Gun and a Noodle Shop (Sanqiang paian jingqi 三抢拍案惊奇), d. Zhang Yimou 张艺谋, Beijing: New Picture.

Welcome To My Queer Bookstore (Huanying laidao wode tongzhi shudian 欢迎来到我的同志书店), d. Larry Tung, Taipei: Larry Tung, documentary short.

Yang Yang (Yangyang 阳阳), d. Cheng Yujie 郑有杰, Taipei: Zeus.

2010

Aftershock (Tangshan da dizhen 唐山大地震), d. Feng Xiaogang 冯小刚, Beijing: China Film Group, Huayi Brothers, etc.

Amphetamine (Anfeitaming 安非他命), d. Scud 云翔, Hong Kong: Artwalker.

Ip Man II (Ye Wen II 叶问II), d. Winston Yip 叶伟信, Zhengzhou: Henan Film & TV Production Group / Hong Kong: Mandarin Films, etc.

Thomas Mao (Xiao dongxi 小东西), d. Zhu Wen 朱文, Beijing: China Films Assist.

2011

The Grandmasters (Yidai zongshi 一代宗师), d. Wong Kar-wai 王家卫 (for release in 2011).

Seediq Bale (Saideke Balai 赛德克·巴莱), d. Wei Te-sheng 魏德圣, teaser in 2003; Part I *Flag of the Sun* (Taiyang qi 太阳旗), Part II *Rainbow* (Caihong 彩虹), Taipei: Ars Film.

Index

Note: This index excludes most critics, musicians, and painters as well as many titles for books, journals, plays, songs, and television works. Dates of birth and death are supplied for Chinese film personnel where available.